THE
2005
FRANCHISE
ANNUAL

- Since 1969-
"THE ORIGINAL" FRANCHISE
HANDBOOK AND DIRECTORY

PUBLISHED BY

INFO FRANCHISE NEWS, INC.

EDITOR/PUBLISHER: TED DIXON

EDITOR: LISA CARPENTER

INFO for International New Franchise Opportunities

12 CHURCH ST., P.O. BOX 755
ST. CATHARINES, ONTARIO
CANADA
L2R 6Y3
TELEPHONE: (905) 688-2665   FAX: (905) 688-7728

728 CENTER ST., P.O. BOX 826
LEWISTON, NEW YORK
U.S.A.
14092
TELEPHONE: (716) 754-4669

E-MAIL: infopress@infonews.com
Web Site:www.infonews.com

® INFO FRANCHISE NEWS INC.
a Division of INFO PRESS, INC.

LIBRARY OF CONGRESS CATALOG CARD NUMBER 76-17321
ISBN:0-9730132-3-0
ISSN: 0318-8752

COPYRIGHT © 2005 by INFO PRESS, INC.

TABLE OF CONTENTS

HANDBOOK

PUBLISHER'S INTRODUCTION

This is INFO'S 36th Edition of the *FRANCHISE ANNUAL DIRECTORY.* We stand alone as the major source of independent and reliable information about business format franchising. This edition includes **5,233** listings. There are 190 new listings. *All new listings are marked with *.*

There are: **3,436 American** listings, **1,276 Canadian** listings and **521 Overseas** listings.
(The most complete directory of franchisors in the world.)

Franchising remains a strong and ever growing major financial force throughout the world. **MAKE SURE THAT YOU WRITE TO MANY DIFFERENT COMPANIES AND COMPARE THE SYSTEMS THAT EACH OFFERS.** This is the purpose of this directory when used by the prospective franchisee. We want to provide basic information in order to help make general comparisons. However it is finally a personal choice. In order to make informed judgements, prospective franchisees must write to the franchisor and compare the offerings which they provide and then investigate, investigate, investigate.

Because every potential franchisee has different needs (some need financial assistance, some may not be able to relocate) the final choice of franchisor must be a personal decision. Anyone who claims to be able to make this decision for you will do more harm than good.

Beware of franchisor rating systems. These are usually compiled using arbitrary values fed into a computer. They seldom even reflect whether or not the franchisees are actually successful. Each prospective franchisee must make his/her own evaluation of possible franchsiors. **READ THE HANDBOOK SECTION CAREFULLY** and with your own common sense your chance of success as a franchisee will be greatly increased. Good luck.

Ted Dixon became involved with franchising in 1969 when he helped edit the first *Franchise Annual Directory*. He has been editor/publisher of the *Info Franchise Newsletter* and *The Franchise Annual Directory* since 1976.

Ted Dixon

Ted Dixon
Editor/Publisher

CATEGORICAL INDEX
AMERICAN LISTINGS

CANADIAN LISTINGS

OVERSEAS LISTINGS

FRANCHISING

Franchising is a method of distribution of goods and services. Some people refer to the franchise "industry". There really is no such thing. There is just this method of distribution, although franchisors have formed associations such as the **International Franchise Association.**

Essentially, franchising works due to such things as shared advertising costs and economies of scale attained through increased purchasing power. The franchisee purchases the right to run a business (the franchise fee) which the franchisor has shown to be successful. A franchisor must have a concept which is inherently franchiseable. This means that it must be possible to duplicate the business format in many different locations.

This is not possible if the pilot's success depends on its totally unique location, or a specific personality. Ultimately, a franchisee is hoping to purchase "risk reduction". The franchisor is providing the franchisee with the "know-how" to succeed. The franchisor benefits because he is using other people's money to expand his system.

There are no all-encompassing statistics available concerning the success rate of franchising. This does not preclude you from creating your own success by carefully studying the franchisor, the business, as well as your own financial position and personality. Diligent research in your own specific area raises the prospect of success even if broad-based statistics are not really available.

It is very important to establish clearly in your mind that it does not matter what any available statistics say either positively or negatively. Each prospective franchisee must do their own homework! You cannot rely on studies. (Even if there were reliable studies proving the success rate of franchising, you'd still have to do your homework to ensure that you personally succeeded.) You cannot rely on a franchisor being listed in a top 500 list. You cannot even rely on a franchisor's success in locations other than your own. You must know your own proposed location. You must understand the type of business you are entering. You must investigate the franchisor, closely question the franchisees, see if the economic niche in which the franchisor is operating is a secure one and finally ascertain if you could succeed at your location.

People always want to know what areas of the economy are "hot." For the last several years INFO has been saying that companies which offer time-saving services to the two-income family are good bets. We also still believe that because the baby-boomers are the largest, and increasingly the most wealthy segment of the population, they will largely influence the economy for the next forty years. Of course we can't guarantee success in any particular field, but, in order to get you thinking, here are some areas we like, most of which have related franchise opportunities:

Adult Learning And Business Skills Training,
Auto Care/Repair (Including Come To Your Office/Home),
Aquaculture (fish farming),
Bird Watching,
Children's Products And Services,
Clothiers That Custom Fit At Home/Office,
Computer Software, Games, Outdoor Computing,
Computer and Technology Training/Consulting,
Niche E-Commerce, Specialized Internet information,
Specialized Internet information services,
Web site design,
Custom Breweries,
Dentistry,
Educational Toy Stores,
Entertainment,
Financial Planning & Services,
Gardening (Do-it-yourself),
Golfing,
Gourmet meals for eat at home,
Healthy Mexican Food,
Health Services, (and self diagnostic products such as blood-pressure gauges and glucose meters, health care services such as spas, massage, therapy and herbal remedies),
Hiking,
House Renovation/Repair,
House Security,
Job Training/Retraining,
Lawn And Garden Care,
Longer Stay Hotel Rooms,
Maid Services,
Mobil Dry-Cleaning And Shoe Repair,
Optometry,
Outsourcing Business Services,
Paint-Your-Own Pottery Stores,
Personal Services/ Party Planners, Chefs, Concierges,
Personal Shoppers,
Pet Products/Services/Day Care,
Physical Therapy-Products,
Quick Service Restaurants- (special point of distribution units - smaller or seasonal- juice bars, wraps, soups - but also gourmet steaks and all-you-can-eat barbeque),
Take Home Food (Home-Style Cooking),
Recreation For The Aging Boomers,
Reselling Used Goods,
Roofing Repair,
Senior Services, Day Care, Home Health,
Funeral Arrangements
Specialized Living Facilities (Adult, Sports, Senior And Nursing Supported Life-styles),
Spiritual Fulfillment (Christian Bookstores etc.),
Temporary Employment Services (Particularly Specialized Staffing-Lawyers etc.),
Travel (Outdoor, Educational, Cruises customized services),
Vacation Home (Construction and Renovation),
Vitamins,

It's hard work investigating a franchise opportunity. Running a franchise can also be hard work. The good news is that you can do hard work. You probably have what it takes to succeed if you don't rush.

Franchising works, no matter what the studies say, either pro or con.

It is important to remember that we are in an age that is entirely brand driven. It is another important plus for franchising. People trust brands and recognize logos as indicating a company whose philosophy espouses such things as quality, cleanliness and service. Many people today do not remember what it was like just thirty years ago travelling with children. Unfamiliar restaurants made parents feel that making a decision to have lunch was like playing "Botulism Roulette". When you took your car into the local gas station to have your muffler repaired, you were often told to come back in two or three days.

It is estimated by the **International Franchise Association** *(Tel: (202) 628-8000)* that consumers spend some $800 billion each year at more than half a million franchised small businesses in the U.S.

In the words of **John Naisbitt**, author of *Megatrends* and *Megatrends 2000*:

"Franchising is the single most successful marketing concept ever."

It really is. But that doesn't mean if you attempt to create a franchise in a faulty part of the economy that you will succeed anyway!

There are many good reasons to think seriously about buying a franchise. It is the only type of job you can buy where your hard work will generate equity which you can sell after twenty years. But you must also work hard before you buy in order to see if there are going to be problems down the road.

Problems can arise when, for example, after the contract has expired, the franchisor wishes to take over the store. Company stores are often more profitable to the franchisor simply because head office receives all the profits and not simply a percentage of the monthly gross. Will the franchisor make it difficult for you to profit from your years of hard work?

Also, from the franchisee's point of view, it seems to be just human nature, four or five years into the contract, to start wondering why he or she needs the franchisor. You might start to feel that you know it all and begin to forget the initial fears of going into business alone.

It is up to the franchisor to continually reinforce his importance to the franchisee with new research and development, innovative advertising campaigns, supportive and educational newsletters, etc.

It is very important to beware of franchisor rating systems found in magazines, the top 500 etc. These have little basis in reality. Some of the top 500 franchisors are out of business the next year. The ratings are compiled using arbitrary values fed into a computer, so many points for number of franchisees, years in business etc. These simple-minded ratings may help sell magazines, but can be very misleading to a prospective franchisee. Just because a franchisor is in some supposed top 500, doesn't even mean its franchisees are making any money. No one has ever asked them. They are not part of the rating system.

While franchising has provided a successful means of marketing for many corporations, relationships between franchisors and franchisees are sometimes strained. One reason for this is that the franchisee typically owns only a limited-term license to operate a business according to the requirements of the franchisor's operating manual. An established franchisee may think that it has a right to continue to operate under the same terms, but a franchisee is only a party to a limited term contract. To the extent that franchisees are successful, the market values of their franchises are likely to increase. Thus, conflicts may arise between the franchisor and the franchisee at the time of contract renewal.

The last few years have been particularly interesting as twenty year contracts have come up for renewal.

A source of friction in some franchise relationships is that franchisors are developing alternative approaches to distributing their goods or services that bypass, and compete with, franchisees selling the same goods or services. For example, some food service companies now sell in grocery stores, from push carts, or at kiosks, the same products their franchisees sell only in the franchised outlet. Thus, while franchisors may increase market penetration and market share through the use of alternative distribution systems, franchisees may actually lose business. Mail order and telemarketing are also viewed as forms of encroachment, and of course, the internet.

As a result of concerns such as these, franchisee associations have emerged in the U.S.

The **American Franchisee Association** *(Tel: (312) 431-0545)* is one such organization. It is a broad-based affiliation of business format franchisees. It had an initial membership of more than 10,000 franchisees.

In the **United States** all franchisors must provide a disclosure document to the prospective franchisee before the contract is signed. This outlines the history of the company and its officers.

In **Canada**, **Alberta** and **Ontario** have disclosure requirements.

Bill 33, the *Arthur Wishart Act (Franchise Disclosure), 2000.* (the "Act"), was passed by the Ontario legislature on May 17, 2000. The Act received Royal Assent on June 8, 2000. S.O. 2000, Chap 3, and all provisions of the Act except those dealing with disclosure were proclaimed in force on July 1, 2000. The Regulation made under the Act setting forth the disclosure requirements was first published on October 31, 2000 and amended on November 23, 2000 and **came into force on January 31, 2001**, together with the provisions of the Act dealing with disclosure.

Because the world of franchising is not only growing but also changing rapidly, pre-sale disclosure of all material terms and conditions of the franchise agreement is more important than ever. Franchisees who understand their rights and obligations before they purchase their franchise are far less likely to experience strained relationships with their franchisors. The franchisor can also actually use a disclosure document as a marketing tool.

Ultimately, it is important to remember that by purchasing a franchise you are going to end up, not so much a franchisee, but a muffler shop owner, printer or tax consultant etc., who has entered the business by purchasing a franchise in the hopes of risk-reduction.

People always ask what's the best franchise? The only way to really ask this is "What's the best franchise for me?" The answer is a combination of four things.

1) What is the kind of business you would like to be in?
2) What types of businesses are succeeding these days, with every indication that they will continue to succeed?
3) Is someone offering a franchise in your area of interest, that you believe will help you to succeed, and that you can afford?
4) Can you work within the limits of a franchise system? Franchisors are not looking for real entrepreneurs, but more entrepreneurial sergeants who can fit into the system.

There is no magic in franchising. It works for good economic and social reasons. If you fully investigate the franchisor, there is every hope that you can make a choice that will significantly increase your chance of success in business.

The wise prospective franchisee should be looking for a franchisor who has been successfully doing business for several years and/or who can show that he will be doing a healthy business in the years to come. Franchising is essentially a "two-way street," with both parties entering into the franchise contract knowing that each has certain obligations to the other.

Real confidence can only be gained by your own thorough investigation of any franchisor. The franchise method is continually being adopted by small, growing, honest franchisors, one of whom might meet your needs, according to your business background, personality and financial resources.

It is important to COMPARE FRANCHISORS IF MORE THAN ONE HAS THE PRODUCT/SERVICE IN WHICH YOU ARE INTERESTED.

INVESTIGATING THE FRANCHISOR

The **Federal Trade Commission** requires franchisors in the U.S. to provide a disclosure statement based on either the **F.T.C. Franchise Rule** or the **Uniform Franchise Offering Circular (U.F.O.C.)** to the prospective franchisee at the appropriate time. (In **Canada**, only **Alberta** and **Ontario** require disclosure. In **Quebec** the disclosure requirements are part of the general provisions of the *Code Civil*, and accordingly there are no specific requirements regarding franchising.)

Briefly the Franchise Rule requires that a franchisor provide a prospective franchisee with a history of the company (the disclosure document) as well as a copy of the franchise agreement in time for them to be studied before the agreement is signed.

The U.F.O.C. requires franchisors to disclose more information than ever before in "plain English" with easy to read tables etc. The requirements mean that prospective franchisees will have a better idea of how many legal battles the franchisor has been involved in.

An earnings claim by the franchisor is any statement which tells you how much money you are going to earn. Under the F.T.C. Franchise Rule and the U.F.O.C., earnings claims can be made if they meet certain guidelines. Often franchisors prefer not to make any formal claims that they may later regret. This can result in "table napkin" outlines of profits that may be misleading.

A franchisor may call a franchise a success when the franchisee would claim he is barely staying in business. Or a franchisor may call a unit a success, even if it was closed and then re-sold. Obviously, the failed franchisee would not call it a success. The U.F.O.C. rules require the franchisor to include a clear outline of exactly what has happened to its franchisees.

Sometimes people think that because a franchisor has prepared a U.F.O.C. in compliance with Federal Trade Commission requirements, or in accordance with state registration regulations, that these documents amount to a stamp of approval by the government. This is false. Receiving a disclosure document should be just the starting point for the prospective franchisee. The first thing a prospective franchisee should do is contact present and past franchisees listed in the document.

When investigating the franchisor your aim should be to independently obtain information. You can obtain assistance in your investigation from many sources.

Be aware that different sources have differing points of view, franchisor associations vs franchisee associations, etc.

Important Sources

1) **Alberta Department of Municipal Affairs Director,** Industry Standards, Housing and Consumers Affairs Divisions, 18th Floor, Commerce Place, 10155, 102 Street, Edmonton, AB, T5J 4L4, Tel: (780) 427-8862, Fax: (780) 422-1419, E-Mail: comments@ma.gov.ab.on, Web Site: **www3.gov.ab.ca/ma**. (Alberta is the only Canadian province with disclosure legislation).
2) **The American Bar Association**, 750 North Lake Shore Dr., Chicago, IL, 60611, Tel: (312) 988-5794, Fax: (312) 988-5677, Web Site: **www.abanet.org**.
3) **The Ministry of Consumer and Commercial Relations** in your province.
4) **The Small Business Branch**, Ontario Ministry of Industry, Trade & Technology provides seminars entitled "Purchasing A Franchise" at different communities. Contact: 1-800-567-2345.
5) **American Franchisee Association** (AFA), 53 W. Jackson, Ste. 205, Chicago, IL, 60604. Tel: (312) 431-0545, Fax: (312) 431-1132, E-Mail: spkezios@franchisee.org, Web Site: **http://www.franchisee.org**.
6) **American Association of Franchisees & Dealers** (AAFD), P.O. Box 81887, San Diego, CA, 92138-1887. Tel: (800) 733-9858, Fax: (619) 209-3777, Web Site: **www.aafd.org**.
7) **Federal Trade Commission**, Division of Marketing Practices, Bureau of Consumer Protection, 600 Pennsylvania Ave., N.W., Washington, DC, 20580. Tel: (202) 326-2222, Web Site: **www.ftc.gov**.
8) **North American Securities Administrators Association** (NASAA), 10 G Street, N.E., Ste. 710, Washington, DC, 20002, Contact: Mr. Jeff Himstreet, Tel: (202) 737-0900, Fax: (202) 783-3571, E-Mail: info@nasaa.org, Web Site: **www.nasaa.org**.

Franchisor Associations

Argentine Franchise Association
Av. Libertador 222,7o-A Buenos Aires, Argentina, Tel: 54-11-4394-3318, Fax: 54-11-4326-5499, E-Mail: lsecades@cgmarcas.com,Web Site: **www.aafranchising.com**.

Asociacion de Franchising del Uruguay
Daniel Munoz 2240 CP. 11.200-Montevideo Uruguay, Tel: (598-2) 408-5189, Fax: (598-2) 408-5189, E-Mail: franqafu@adinet.com.uy, Web Site: **www.mtgroup-uy.com**.

Austrian Franchise Association
Bayerhamerstrasse 12, 1st Floor, Salzburg 5020, Austria, Tel: (43) 662-874-2360, Fax: (43) 662-874-2365, E-Mail: oefv@franchise.net, Web Site: **www.franchise.at**.

Belgian Franchise Federation
Boulevard de L'Humanite, 116/2 B-1070 Brussels, Belgium, Tel: (32-2) 523-9707, Fax: (32-2) 523-3510, E-Mail: info@bff.be, Web Site: **www.fbf-bff.be**.

Brazil Franchise Association
Avenida Brigadeiron Faria Lima, 1.739 Jardim Paulistano Sao Paulo Brasil CEP 01452-001, Tel: (55-11) 38-14-4200, Fax: (55-11) 3817-5986, Web Site: **www.abf.com.br**.

British Franchise Association
Thames View, Newton Road, Henley-on-the-Thames, Oxforshire, RG9 1HG, UNited Kingdom, Tel: (44) 1 491 578 050, Fax: (44) 1 491 573 517, E-Mail: mailroom@british-franchise.org, Web Site: **www.british-franchise.org.uk**.

Bulgarian Franchise Association
9000 Varna Ivan Vazov Str. 36, Tel: (00) 359-52-601043, Fax: (00) 359-52-601043, E-Mail: bulfa@infotel.bg.

Canadian Franchise Association
2585 Skymark Ave, Suite 300, Mississauga, ON, L4W 4L5, Tel: (905) 625-2896, Fax: (905) 625-9076, E-Mail: info@cfa.ca, Web Site: **www.cfa.ca**.

Chile Franchise Association
Rafel Canas 16 of. 1, Providencia, Santiago, Chile, Tel: (56-2) 236-3622, Fax: (56-2) 264-9134.

Colombia Franchise Association
Cra. 100 11-90 Torre Lili, of 606, , Cali, Columbia, Tel: (57-2) 339-2163, Fax: (57-2) 339-2166, E-Mail: jbarragan@telesat.com.co, Web Site: **www.centercourt.com/acolfran/**.

Czech Republic Franchise Association
Rytirska 18, 111 21 Prague 1-Czech Republic, Tel: (42-2) 2421-4703, E-Mail: caf@czech-franchise.cz, Web Site: **www.czech-franchise.cz**.

Danish Franchise Association
Lyngbyvej 20, DK-2100, Coppenhagen, Oe, Tel: (+45) 39-15-82-82, Fax: (+45) 39-15-80-10, E-Mail: info@dk-franchise.dk, Web Site: **www.dk-franchise.dk**.

Dominican Republic Franchise Association
Polibio Diaz #74, Apt. c-1 Edificio Alfonso, X Evaristo Morales, Santo Domingo, Dominican Republic, Tel: (809) 549-6383, Fax: (809) 563-1916.

Egyptian Franchise Association
1191 Corniche El Nil St., 15th Floor Cairo, Egypt, Tel: (20-2) 240-8937, Fax: (20-2) 240-8937.

Equador Franchise Association
P.O. Box 579 Quito Ecuador, Tel: (593-9) 310-555, Fax: (593-4) 280-078, E-Mail: vp@ecua.net.ec.

European Franchise Federation
179 Avenue Louise, B 1050 Brussels Belgium, Tel: (32-2) 520-1607, Fax: (32-2) 520-1735, E-Mail: eff-franchise@euronet.be, Web Site: **www.eff-franchise.com**.

Finnish Franchising Association
PL 868 08680 Lohja as Finland, Tel: (+358) 19-331-195, Fax: (+358) 19-331-075, Web Site: **www,franchising.fi**.

Franchise Association of Greece
24, Raidestou Str., 171 22 Nea Smyrni, Athens, Greece, Tel: (30) 1 324 32 71, Fax: (30) 1 322 93 29

Franchise Association of New Zealand
P.O. Box 23 364 Hunters Corner Papatoetoe, Auckland, New Zealand, Tel: (64-9) 3278-9012, Fax: (64-9) 278-9013, E-Mail: contact@franchise.org.nz, Web Site: **www.franchise.org.nz**.

FranchiseCouncil of Australia Ltd.
P.O. Box 1498N, Melbourne, Vic 3001, Australia, Tel: (61) 3-9650-1667, Fax: (61) 3-9659-1713.

Franchising Association of India
Elite House, 54-A, SIR M, Vasanji Road, Chakala, Andheri (East) Mumbai 400093, Tel: (+91) 22-5692-1258, Fax: (+91) 22-5692-1258, E-Mail: fai@vsnl.net.

French Franchise Association
60, rue La Boetie, Paris, 75008, France, Tel: (33-1) 53-75-22-25, Fax: (33-1) 53-75-22-20, E-Mail: info@franchise-fff.com, Web Site: **www.franchise-fff.com**.

German Franchise Association
Deutscher Franchise-Verband e.V. Luisenstr 41 10117, Berlin Germany, tel: (49-30) 27-89-020, fax: (49-30) 27-89-0215, E-Mail: info@dfv-franchise.de, Web Site: **www.dfv-franchise.de**.

Greek Franchise Association
Skoufou 10-105 57, Athens Greece, Tel: (+30) 210-32-34-620, Fax: (+30) 210-32-38-865, E-Mail: info@franchising.gr, Web Site: **www.franchising.gr**.

Hong Kong Franchise Association
22/F Unit A, United Centre, 95 Queensway, Hong Kong, Tel: (852) 2529-9229, Fax: (852) 2527-9843, E-Mail: hkfa@franchise.org.hk, Web Site: **www.franchise.orgf.hk**.

Hungarian Franchise Association
P.O. Box 446, Budapest H-1537, Hungary, Tel: (36-1) 212-4124, Fax: (36-1) 212-5712, E-Mail: franchise@franchise.hu, Web Site: **www.franchise.hu**.

Iceland Franchise Association
Borgartuni 35, 105 Reykjavik, Tel: 511-3000, Fax: 511-3001, E-Mail: franchise@franchise.is, Web Site: **www.franchise.is**.

Indonesia Franchise Association
A 19 Darmawanga X Kebayoran Baru, Jakarra, 12150, Indonesia, Tel: (62-21) 739-5577, Fax: (62-21) 723-4761.

International Franchise Association
1350 New York Ave., N.W., Ste. 900, Washington, DC, 20005, Tel: (202) 628-8000, Fax: (202) 628-0812, E-Mail: ifa@franchise.org, Web Site: **www.franchise.org**.

Irish Franchise Association
13 Frankfield Terrace Summerhill South Cork Dublin, Ireland,
Tel: (353-1) 21-27-08-59, Fax: (353-1) 21-27-0805.

Israel Franchise & Distribution Association
P.O. Box 3093, Herzeliya 46590, Israel, Tel/Fax: (972) 9-576-631.

Italian Franchise Association
Viale L. Majno, 42 20129 Milano, Italy, Tel: (02) 2900-37-79,
E-Mail: assofranchising@assofranchising.it, Web Site:
www.assofranchising.it.

Japan Franchise Association
2nd Akiyama Bldg, toranomon 3-6-2 Minato-Ku Tokyo 105-0001, Japan, Tel: (81-3) 03-5777-8704, Fax: (81-3) 03-5777-8711, E-Mail: jfa@msh.biglobe.ne.jp.

Korea (South) Franchise Association
Zipcode 143-202 Hyosan B/D 3F, 57-80 Gui-2Dong, Kwangjin-GU Seoul, Tel: (82-2) 855-6006, Fax: (82-2) 855-6788, Web
Site: **www.koreafranchise.co.kr**.

Latin America Franchise Federation
La Otra Banda #74/ Col. Tizapan San Angel, Mexico, 01090
D.F, Tel: (52-5) 616-0112/0434, Fax: (52-5) 550-4965.

Latvian Franchise Association
Lachplesha 81 Daugavpils LV-5403, Latvia, Tel: (+371) 54-26349, Fax: (+371) 54-27374, E-Mail: info@franch.lv, Web
Site: **www.franch.lv**.

Malaysian Franchise Association
Suite 1045, Level 10, Block A2/Leisure Complex 9, Jalan PJS
8/9-46150 Petaling Selangor Darul Ehsan, Malaysia, Tel: (60-3) 7877-1559, E-Mail: secrtmfa@tm.net.my, Web Site:
www.mfa.org.my.

Mexican Franchise Association (AMF)
Insurgentes Sur 1783, Ste. 303, Colonia Guadalupe Inn, Mexico,
DF 01020, Mexico, Tel: 525 661 0655, Fax: 525 663 2178.

Middle East Franchise & Distribution Association
P.O. Box 3093, Herziliya 46590, Israel, Tel/Fax: (972) 9 576 63

Netherlands Franchise Association
Boomberglaan 12, NL-1217 Hilversam, Netherlands, Tel: (31-35) 624-2300, Fax: (31-35) 624-9194, E-Mail: franchise@nfv.nl,
Web Site: **www.nfv.nl**.

New Zealand Franchise Association
P.O. Box 25650 St. Heloiers Auckland New Zealand, Tel: (64-9) 575-3804, Fax: (64-9) 575-3807, E-Mail: contact@franchise.
org.nz, Web Site: **www.franchise.org.nz**.

Nigerian International Franchise Association
5 Vori Close, Off Acme Road Ogba Industrial Estate Lagos
Nigeria, Tel: 497-4777, Fax: 496-0854, E-Mail: nifa@nigerian
franchise.org, Web Site: **www.nigerianfranchise.org**.

Norway Franchise Association
Drammensveien 30/Box 2900 Solli 0230 0510 Norway, Tel:
(47) 22-541-700, Fax: (47) 22-561-700, E-Mail: info@hsh-org.no, Web Site: **www.hsh-org.no**.

Peru Franchise Association
Gregoria Escobedo 398 Lima 11, Peru, Tel: (51-1) 562-1000,
Fax: (51-1) 562-1020.

Philippine Franchise Association
2/F Collins Bldg, 167 EDSA, Mandaluyong City, Philippines,
Tel: (63-2) 532-5663, Fax: (63-2) 532-5644, E-Mail: pfa@
nwave.net, Web Site: **www.philfranchise.com**.

Polish Franchise Association
ul. J.Kasprowicza 41 c 34520 Poronin Poland, Tel: (+48) 18-200-1010, Fax: (+48) 18-200-1012, E-Mail: info@franchise.pl. Web
Site: **www.franchise.com.pl**.

Portuguese Franchise Association
Rua Viriato 25 3 1050-234 Lisboa Portugal, Tel: (+351) 21-319-29-38, Fax: (+351) 21-319-29-39, E-Mail: apfranchise@
netcabo.pt, Web Site: **www.apfranchise.org**.

Romanian Franchise Association
86 Bd. Aviatorilor, Bucharest, Romania, Tel: 40 1 223 1989, Fax:
40 1 223 2307.

Russian Franchise Association
2-nd Proezd Perova Polya, 9, Moscow 111141, Russia, Tel: (7-095) 305-5777, Fax: (7-095) 305-5850, E-Mail: franch@matrix
.ru, Web Site: **www.a-z,ru/raf**.

Singapore International Franchise Association
5 International Business Park Singapore 609914, Tel: (65) 568-0802, Fax: (65) 568-0722, E-Mail: sifa@pacific.net.sg.

South African Franchise Association
Werksman Chambers 3rd Floor West Wing, 22 Girton Road
Parktown Johannesburg Guateng, South Africa, Tel: (+27-11)
484-1285, Fax: (+27-11) 484-1291, E-Mail: fasa@fasa.co.za,
Web Site: **www.fasa.co.za**.

Spainish Franchise Association
Avda, de, la F Erias S/N, P.O. Box 476, 46035 Valencia, Spain,
Tel: (+34) 96-386-11-23, Fax: (+34) 96-363-61-11, E-Mail:
aef@feriavalencia.com, Web Site: **www.franquiciadores.com**.

Swedish Franchise Association
Massansg, 18/Box 5243 40224, Goteborg, Sweden, Tel: (46-31)
836-943, Fax: (46-3) 811-072, E-Mail: karin@franchiseforeni
ngentelia.com, Web Site: **www.franchiseforeningen.a.se**.

Swiss Franchise Association
Lowenstrasse 11 Postfach CH-8023, Zurich, Switzerland, Tel:
(+41) 1-22-47-57, Fax: (+41) 1-225-47-77, Web Site: **www.fran
chiseverband.ch**.

Taiwanese Franchise Association
7F No. 197, Nan-King Road Section 4, Taipei Taiwan, Tel: (886)
2-2712-1250, Fax: (886) 2-2717-7997, E-Mail: stephenhsu@
kidcastle.com, Web Site: **www.tcfa.org.tw**.

Turkish Franchising Association (UFRAD)
Ergenekon cd., Panagalti Ishani, 89/15, Istanbul 80240, Turkey,
Tel: (90-212) 296-6628, Fax: (90-212) 224-5130.

Uruguayan Franchise Association
Daniel Munoz 2240, CP 11,200, Montevideo, Uruguay, Tel:
(598-2) 408-5189, E-Mail: milbea@adinet.com.uy.

Venezuela Chamber of Franchising
Oficentro Neur 3 - Altamira, Oficina N5, Caracas, Venezuela,
1060, Tel: (58-2) 261-0404, Fax: (58-2) 261-9620.

West African Franchise Association
66 Campbell Street, 2nd Floor Lagos Nigeria, Tel: (234-1) 263-21) 432-205, Fax: (381-21) 469-496.

6834, USA: (301) 927-7555, Fax: (301) 927-7398, E-Mail: demola@franchisewestafrica,org, Web Site: **www.franchise westafrica,org**.
Yugoslavian Franchise Association
Dr. Dorda Joanovica 6 21000 Novi Sad, Yugoslavia, Tel: (381-

21) 432-205, Fax: (381-21) 469-496.
Zimbabwian Franchise Association
Fidelity Life Tower, 98 Raleigh Street, P.O. Box 1934 Harare Zimbabwe, Tel: (263-4) 753-444, Fax: (263-4) 753-450.

THE FRANCHISOR

- ☐ Does the franchisor have the proper financial backing?
- ☐ Is the franchisor a subsidiary of another company? What are heir assets?
- ☐ Who is the parent company? Have they ever franchised other products or services?
- ☐ Is it a similar product?
- ☐ Would they be in competition with you?
- ☐ Was, or is, the other franchise operation successful?
- ☐ Can you see any of the franchisor's recently audited financialstatements?
- ☐ When do you get to see the contract, and disclosure document if there is one? Is there an earnings claim?
- ☐ Is it based on company run or franchisee run outlets?
- ☐ How long have each of the outlets used as a basis for the projection been in operation? Are they rural or urban?
- ☐ How long has the franchisor been in business? How long has he been offering franchises?
- ☐ What is the business experience of the franchise company's directors and officers?
- ☐ Does the franchisor provide post-opening training, if necessary, and other continuing assistance?
- ☐ Does the franchisor have a system for the inspection of the franchisees?
- ☐ Is he always available for on-the-spot counseling? Will he help recruit your personnel?
- ☐ Who pays for the grand opening discounts?
- ☐ Does the franchisor design store layouts and displays?
- ☐ Does the franchisor exercise good quality control?
- ☐ Is there computerized inventory control?
- ☐ Are there volume purchasing discounts?
- ☐ Are the administrative and bookkeeping procedures simple and well run?

- ☐ Have any of the franchisor's partners or company members ever gone bankrupt?
- ☐ Have any of them been invloved in litigation recently?
- ☐ Is it a public company? (If it is a public company you can obtain copies of their annual reports and also get copies of the detailed 10K reports.)
- ☐ When can you read the prospectus?
- ☐ Does the franchisor help you finance the purchase of the franchise?
- ☐ Does the franchisor have the kind of reputation and credit rating which would help you to obtain the financial backing needed to purchase the franchise?
- ☐ How many franchisees does the franchisor have? Can you contact them?
- ☐ Where will these be located?
- ☐ Does he have a good marketing plan?
- ☐ Does he provide a useful initial training program? Who pays for this?
- ☐ What is the advertising program? How much do you pay towards local advertising? National advertising?
- ☐ Do you have any say in the advertising format?
- ☐ Is the franchisor up-to-date in all his operations?
- ☐ Are his sales techniques modern?
- ☐ What innovations has the franchisor introduced since first starting?
- ☐ Does the franchisor provide a helpful and fully explanatory manual for the training of the staff and the operation of the franchise?
- ☐ Is the price of the franchise variable? If so, how?
- ☐ Can you purchase used equipment for a discount?

THE PRODUCT OR SERVICE

- ☐ What is the demand for the product/service?
- ☐ Would **you** buy the product or require the service?
- ☐ How long has it been on the market? Is the product/service seasonable?
- ☐ Is it a staple or a luxury?
- ☐ Will the franchisee depend on the tourist trade? To what extent?
- ☐ Is the product/service a fad?
- ☐ Is it marketable in your territory?
- ☐ Is the quality of the product/service acceptable?
- ☐ Are there federal or state/provincial requirements for the product/service?
- ☐ Are there product warranties or guarantees? Who backs them?
- ☐ Who makes the repairs? Who pays for the repairs?

- ☐ Is the price competitive with similar products or services on the market?
- ☐ Who controls the price?
- ☐ Can you purchase any of your stock from a source other than the franchisor or his designated suppliers?
- ☐ What percent of the population will be attracted to the product/service?
- ☐ Is its appeal limited to certain age groups?
- ☐ Is it properly packaged?
- ☐ Is it protected by trademark or copyright?
- ☐ Has the product been patented? Can it be easily copied?
- ☐ Is a well known person involved in selling the product? Is this celebrity involved financially?
- ☐ What would be the effect on the marketing of the product if the celebrity withdrew support?

THE FRANCHISEE

The following questions (and most of the previous ones) could be directed to franchisees who are already operating. get the franchisor to give you a likst of present franchisees and visit or phone them. You can also question franchisees in rival franchise systems!

- ☐ What was the total (not simply the downpayment) investment required by the franchisor?
- ☐ Where there hidden or unexpected costs?
- ☐ Has the merchandise, machinery and other equipment which the franchisor supplied been good quality?
- ☐ Is the franchisor prompt with his deliveries?
- ☐ How long was it before you hit the break-even point?
- ☐ How long before the franchise was able to support you? Were you trained? Was the training adequate?
- ☐ Were the projected sales of the franchise, which the franchisor supplied, accurate?
- ☐ Was the general profit projection accurate?

- ☐ Do you have a guaranteed (not right to) buy-back agreement in your contract on inventory and equipment?
- ☐ Have you ever had a serious disagreement with the franchisor?
- ☐ What about? Was it settled amicably?
- ☐ Do you know whether the franchisor has ever had to settle any problem through arbitration?
- ☐ Do you have to send a periodic report to the company?
- ☐ What does it include?
- ☐ Does the franchisor actively respond to the reports?
- ☐ Are you satisfied with the marketing, promotional and advertising assistance that you receive from the company?
- ☐ If you could change your contract, what would you change?
- ☐ Would you advise anyone to start a franchise with this franchisor?

THE TERRITORY

- ☐ Is it exclusive?
- ☐ What assurance do you have that it is exclusive?
- ☐ Can you choose the location or territory?
- ☐ Will the franchisor help you select a location?
- ☐ Has the franchisor conducted feasibility studies of the market potential in your proposed territory?
- ☐ Do you lease or buy the location?
- ☐ Are the equipment and fixtures specified?
- ☐ Can you buy or lease equipment and fixtures from someone other than the franchisor?
- ☐ Is the layout of the location specified?
- ☐ Can you change the layout?
- ☐ How near to you is the franchisor's next franchisee or company owned unit going to be? Can the franchisor tell you when this other new unit will be set up? (Will this hinder your development, i.e. competition, or will it help your development, i.e. more money in your area for advertising?)

- ☐ Is the territory well defined? Is it large enough? What are your expansion possibilities?
- ☐ What is the present population? What is the proposed population for five years from now?
- ☐ Are there any new highways planned?
- ☐ What is the industrial growth?
- ☐ What are the zoning laws? (Strict zoning laws in some areas may forbid opening a franchise at all.) Will these laws be changed?
- ☐ Are zoning licenses required?
- ☐ What is the average income level in the area?
- ☐ What is the competition in the area?
- ☐ How are other businesses doing in the area?
- ☐ What is the traffic count near your location? (both auto and pedestrian)
- ☐ What kind of insurance is available for the area? Is it expensive?

THE CONTRACT

There is usually a standard contract. However, do not hesitate to have your lawyer/attorney add any extra clauses which you feel are necessary. Do not be afraid to "haggle" a little. There has been a lot of talk about a David and Goliath situation existing between the franchisee and the franchisor. Whether this is the case or not in some instances, it is not the case with you as a prospective franchisee. When you sit down with your legal representative and the franchisor to draw up the contract there is no reason why you can't get up and walk away if you don't like the deal you are getting. However, it is important to understand that most franchisors will be adamant about keeping the standard contract for the sake of uniformity.

- ☐ Does the contract protect both parties?
- ☐ Are the nature, duration and extent of your training outlined in the contract?
- ☐ Is a franchise cost hidden in a minimum purchase of merchandise per year?
- ☐ Are there any additional fixed payments?
- ☐ Is the monthly royalty reasonable?
- ☐ Is there a monthly percentage of gross required for advertising?
- ☐ Does the franchisee have to pay a royalty when business is poor?

- [ ] What constitutes the "poor" business level?
- [ ] Is the sales quota at a minimum?
- [ ] What are the conditions for renewal of the contract?
- [ ] Does the franchisor agree to maintain a good reputation? (He could lose his trademark if he does not properly supervise the quality of the product/service).
- [ ] If a signed lease with the franchisor is involved, is it at a competitive price?
- [ ] Does your lease correspond in duration to the contract?
- [ ] Are there parallel renewal options for the contract and the lease?
- [ ] Does the contract cover in detail all the franchisor's verbal promises?
- [ ] Have you a right to the franchisor's latest innovations?
- [ ] Will the franchisor maintain any necessary Federal and State/Provincial registrations?
- [ ] Do you have the right to assign the franchise?

- [ ] Must the franchisor approve the new franchisee? Under what conditions?
- [ ] How can you terminate the franchise?
- [ ] When and how can the franchisor terminate your franchise?
- [ ] How will you be compensated for the "goodwill" which you have built up?
- [ ] What happens in the event of illness or death?
- [ ] What time have you to correct defaults?
- [ ] Is there an arbitration clause? Is there a mediation clause?
- [ ] If there is a legal dispute, must your attorneys journey to the franchisor's legal district?
- [ ] Must you promise not to enter into a business similar to the franchisor's for a period of time after you have separated from the franchisor (covenant not to compete)?
- [ ] Must you promise not to enter into any other business while you are a franchisee (full time and attention clause)?
- [ ] In what other business activities may you engage?

Get a Lawyer/Attorney. Get an Accountant. (And maybe even an Urban Economist.) Do you have a bank affiliation? No matter how much investigation you have done, you will need to consult a Lawyer and Accountant before investing. You probably will need to consult them during your investigation. And don't forget to consult your **Insurance Agent**. He may be aware of a few hidden costs about which you do not know. Investing in the cost of a lawyer and accountant is the best way to protect your final franchise investment. You need to invest in professional advice. **Do It.** There is no reliable alternative. But make sure your investigation has been a thorough one in order that you will be able to bring to your lawyer and accountant as much information as possible. It is only in this way that you can take full advantage of their services. You should know what you are investing in and you should have your own facts.

STATE REGULATIONS

The Following is a summary of the states which have legislation which directly concerns general business format franchising as well as pertinent government bodies to contact. (Auto, truck, beer, liquor and gasoline marketing legislation has been omitted.) For further details of state laws and other franchise legislation see "Franchising" by Glickman. Matthew Bender & Company. (1275 Broadway, Albany, NY, 12204-2694.)

ARKANSAS: Franchise Practices Act prevents termination of franchisee without good cause and governs renewal of franchise contract. Forbids fraud and deceit in sale of franchises.

CALIFORNIA: Franchise Investment Law requires registration and disclosure by franchisor. The modification of Existing Franchise amendment makes a material modification of an existing franchise the equivalent of a sale subject to the disclosure and registration provisions of the Franchise Investment Law. Another amendment, the Franchisee's Right to Join Trade Association, makes it a violation of the Act for a franchisor to restrict the right of franchisees to join a trade association or to prohibit free association among franchisees for any lawful purposes. The Seller Assisted Marketing Plan statute requires certain sellers of business opportunities to register with the Secretary of State (Legal Review) a disclosure statement and its salesmen before advertising or selling an opportunity and to give each purchase, at least forty-eight hours prior to the execution of any agreement or the receipt of consideration, a copy of the disclosure statement (franchises covered by the Franchise Investment Laware excluded). Franchise Relations Act covers termination and renewal of franchisee. It prevents termination without good cause and requires franchisor to give 180 days to franchisee if the franchisor does not intend to renew contracts and prohibits converting a non-renewed franchise to a company owned unit without compensating the franchisee. (Good Cause is defined as including but not limited to the failure of the franchisee to comply with any lawful requirements of the franchise agreement after being given notice and a reasonable opportunity, which in no event need be more than 30 days, to cure the failure). Contact: Department of Corporations, 320 West 4th Street, Los Angeles, CA, 90013. Tel: (213) 736-2741.

CONNECTICUT: Registration and disclosure by franchisor under Business Opportunity Investment Act. Franchising Fairness Law governs termination and non-renewal. Contact: Department of Banking, Securities Division, 260 Constitution Plaza, Hartford, CT, 06103, Tel: (860) 240-8230, Web Site: **www.state.ct.us**.

DELAWARE: Under Prohibited Trade Practices the Franchise Security Act prohibits unjust or bad faith termination of franchisee or refusal to renew a franchise.

DISTRICT OF COLUMBIA: Franchising Act establishes uniform standards for franchising agreements.

FLORIDA: Franchises and Distributorship Law forbids intentional misrepresentation in the sale of franchises and distributorships. Contact: Consumer Services Div. 235 Mayo Bldg, 407 South Calhoun St., Tallahassee, FL, 32399-0800. Tel: (850) 922-2966. Business Opportunity Act requires registration and disclosure by franchisor. Contact: Office of Attorney General. Dept. of Legal Affairs, Consumer Division, The Capitol, TL-01, Tallahassee, FL, 32399, Tel: (850) 487-1963, Fax: (850) 487-2564, Web Site: **www.myfloridalegal.com**.

GEORGIA: Business Opportunity statue aimed at preventing and fraudulent and deceptive practices in the sale of business opportunities. Governs disclosure and registration. Office of Consumer Affairs, 2 Martin Luther King Dr. S.E., Ste. 356, Atlanta, GA, 30334, Tel: (404) 651-8600, Fax: (404) 651-9018, Web Site: **www2.state.ga.us/GaOCA**. The Georgia Sale of Business Opportunities Act may include certain franchisors and sub-franchisors depending on whether the exemption under the law applies.

HAWAII: Franchise Investment Law outlines registration, disclosure, termination and renewal. Contact: Department of Commerce and Consumer Affairs, 1010 Richards Street, Honolulu, HI, 96813, Tel: (808) 586-2722, Web Site: **www.state.hi.us/dcca**.

ILLINOIS: The Franchise Disclosure Act regulates disclosure, registration, termination and non-renewal. Contact: Franchise Division, Attorney General's Office, 500 S. Second St., Springfield, IL, 62706. Tel: (217) 785-2771, Web Site: **www.ag.state.il.us**.

INDIANA: Franchise Disclosure Law. Deceptive Franchise Practices Act regulates the terms of franchise agreements and practices arising out of the relationship under the contracts. Contact: Securities Commissioner, 302 W. Washington St., Ste. E111, Indianapolis, IN, 46204. Tel: (317) 232-6681.

IOWA: Franchise Relationship Law and Business Opportunity Laws. Contact: Iowa Division of Insurance. Securities Division, 340 Maple Street, Des Moines, IA, 50319-0066, Tel: (515) 281-4441.

KENTUCKY: Business Opportunity Disclosure and Registration Act. The Capital Suite 118, 700 Capital Avenue, Frankfort, KY, 40601, Tel: (502) 564-2894, Fax: (502) 696-5300, Web Site: **www.law.state.ky.us**.

LOUISIANA: Business Opportunity Sellers and Agents Act.

MAINE: Business Opportunity Act outlines registration and disclosure requirements for sale of any business opportunity. Contact: Securities Division. Dept. of Professional & Financial Regulation. State House Station 121, Augusta, ME, 04333. Tel: (207) 624-8603, Fax: (207) 624-8690, Web Site: **www.state.me.us**.

MARYLAND: Franchise Registration and Disclosure Act. Contact: Office of Attorney General, Division of Securities, 200 St. Paul Pl., Baltimore, MD, 21202, Tel: (410) 576-7042, Fax: (410) 576-6532, E-Mail: securities@oag.state.md.us, Web Site: **www.oag.state.md.us**.

MICHIGAN: Franchise Investment Law. Contact: Attorney General Department, Consumer Protection Division, P.O. Box 30213, Lansing, MI, 48909. Tel: (517) 373-7117, Fax: (517) 335-1935, Web Site: **www.michigan.gov/ag**.

MINNESOTA: Department of Commerce, 85 7th Place East, Suite 500 St. Paul, MN, Tel: (651) 296-6328, Fax: (651) 284-4106, E-Mail: ann.hagestad@state.mn.us , Web Site: **www.commerce.state.mn.us**.

MISSOURI: Merchandising Practices Act.

NEBRASKA: Franchise Practices Act governs termination and renewal. Seller Assisted Marketing Plan Act governs seller-assisted marketing plans. Contact: Division of Securities, P.O. Box 95006, Lincoln, NE, 68509-5006. Tel: (402) 471-2171.

NEW HAMPSHIRE: Distributorship Disclosure Act governs registration and disclosure. Contact: Consumer Protection and Antitrust Bureau, 33 Capital St., Concord, NH, 03301, Tel: (603) 271-3658, Fax: (603) 271-2110, Web Site: **www.state.nh.us**.

NEW YORK: Franchise Sales Act. Contact: New York State, Department of Law, 120 Broadway, Room 23-122, New York, NY, 10271. Tel: (212) 416-8800. Also Rule 5-60 of the Rules of the City of New York, Vol. 3, Titles 6-8, enforced by Department of Consumer Affairs. Contact: Assistant Commissioner, Legal Affairs, 42 Broadway, New York, NY, 10004. Tel: (212) 487-4444, Web Site: **www.nyc.gov**.

NORTH CAROLINA: Business Opportunity Sales Law requires disclosure. Contact: Secretary of State, Securities Division, 300 N. Salsbury St., 1st. Floor, Raleigh, NC, 27603, Tel: (919) 733-3924.

NORTH DAKOTA: Franchise Investment Law governs registration, disclosure, termination and renewal. Contact: Office of Securities Commissioner, 5th Floor, 600 East Boulevard Ave., Bismarck, ND, 58505-0510, Tel: (701) 328-2910.

OHIO: Business Opportunity Law. Contact: Assistant Attorney General, Consumer Protection Division, State Office Tower, 25th Floor, 30 E. Broad St., Columbus, OH, 43215-3428, Tel: (614) 466-8831.

OKLAHOMA: Business Opportunity Sales Act.

OREGON: Franchise Law requires disclosures from franchisor. Contact: Department of Insurance and Finance, Div. of Finance and Corporate Securities, Securities Section, 21 Labour & Industries Building, 350 Winter St. N.E., Room 21, Salem, OR, 97310, Tel: (503) 378-4387.

PUERTO RICO: Dealer's Contracts Law covering termination and non-renewal of contract.

RHODE ISLAND: Franchise Investment Act requires full disclosure. Contact: State of Rhode Island, Department of Business Regulation, Securities Division, 233 Richmond St., Ste. 232, Providence Rhode Island, 02903-4232, Tel: (401) 222-3048.

SOUTH CAROLINA: Business Opportunity Sales Act covers disclosure. Contact: Attn: Jessica Smith, Secretary of State's Office, P.O. Box 11350, Columbia, SC, 29211, Tel: (803) 734-1951.

SOUTH DAKOTA: The South Dakota Franchise Law requires registration and disclosure. Contact: Franchise Administrator, Division of Securities, 118 W. Capitol, Pierre, SD, 57501-2000, Tel: (605) 773-4823.

TEXAS: Business Opportunity Disclosure Act requires disclosure and registration. (Franchisors who comply with F.T.C. requirements are exempt.)

UTAH: Business Opportunity Act requires a disclosure statement.

VIRGINIA: Retail Franchising Act covers termination, renewal, registration and disclosure. Contact: State Corporation Commission, Division of Securities and Retail Franchising, P.O. Box 1197 Richmond, Virginia 23218, Tel: (804) 371-9051, Fax: (804) 371-9911, E-Mail: SEC_Examination@scc.state.va.us, Web Site: **www.state.va.us**.

WASHINGTON: Franchise Investment Protection Act requires disclosure and registration. It also governs termination and renewal. Contact: Department of Financial Institutions Securities Division, P.O. Box 9033, Olympia, WA, 98507-9033, Tel: (360) 902-8760. Also: Business Opportunity Fraud Act covering disclosure and registration.

WISCONSIN: Franchise Investment Law requires registration and disclosure. Contact: Securities Commission, P.O. Box 1768, Madison, WI, 53701. Tel: (608) 266-3431. Also Dealership Practices Act covers termination and renewal.

ACCOUNTING AND TAX SERVICES

ABS SYSTEMS
Accounting Business Systems, Inc.
801 North Brand Blvd First Floor, Winter Springs, FL, 32708. - Tel: (407) 327-1530, Fax: (407) 327-1531. Complete accounting and tax franchise. Software, practice management systems, client acquisition, training and support. Established: 1987 - Franchising Since: 1991- No. of Units: Company Owned: 2 - Franchised: 35 - Franchise Fee: $9,500 - Royalty: $150/on fixed, no royalties - Total Inv: $10,000 (fee/training) - Financing: None.

ACCOUNTABLES
Accountables Franchising Corp.,
2200 Opitz Blvd., Ste. 345, Woodbridge, VA, 22191. - Tel: (703) 494-6215, (800) 830-0956, Fax: (703) 491-3502. Tax preparation, personal financial planning and small business bookkeeping. Established: 1979 - Franchising Since: 1996 - No. of Units: Company Owned: 2 - Franchised: 1 - Franchise Fee: $9,900 - Royalty: $100 weekly - Total Inv: $19,125-$22,300 - Financing: None.

ADVANTAGE PAYROLL SERVICES
Advantage Business Services
126 Merrow Road, P.O. Box 1330, Auburn, ME, 04211. Contact: Dave Meagher, Mktg. Manager -Tel: (877) 777-9567, Web Site: www.advantagepayroll.com. Payroll and payroll tax filing service for small businesses. Established: 1967 - Franchising Since: 1983 - No. of Units: Company Owned: 6 - Franchised: 31 - Total Inv: $150,000 plus, with working capital - Financing: $5,000.

AMERICOUNT BUSINESS CONSULTANTS, INC.
3800 Douglas Ave., Des Moines, IA, 50310. Contact: Leon Ebling, Pres. - Tel: (515) 274-4195, (800) 453-7179, Fax: (515) 274-6411, E-Mail: President@AmeriCount.Com, Web Site: www.americount.com. Accounting and business consulting for small to medium size business. Established: 1963 - Franchising Since: 1993 - No. of Units: Company Owned: 2 - Franchised: 1 - Franchise Fee: $25,000 plus $15,000 software license - Royalty: 5% of monthly billing on first $5,000, then graduate down to 1% - Total Inv: $25,000 fran. fee, $15,000 software license, $10,000 equip. - work. cap.

BECK, VILLATA & CO., P.A. CERTIFIED PUBLIC ACCOUNTANTS
6181 Miami Lakes Drive East, Miami, FL, 33014. Contact: Frank Beck, Partner - Tel: (305) 231-0911, Fax: (305) 231-8838. Senior partners are both extremely well versed and knowledgeable in franchise accounting and are available for consultations on issues relating to taxes, estate planning, new business setup, and financial statement preparation and projections as well as new business valuations and litigation support. We are a full service accounting office able to meet all your accounting needs. Established: 1990.

BLACK AMERICAN INCOME TAX SERVICE
American Tax and Financial Group
4650 S. Hampton #122, Dallas, TX, 75232. Contact: Calvin Brown, Founder & CEO - Tel: (214) 331-0796, (877) 224-8476, Fax: (214) 333-1411, E-Mail: baitgroup@aol.com, Web Site: www.baitgroup.com. Income tax preparation and electronic filing. We are the only national franchisor that uniquely caters to and targets the U.S. African-American population, which numbers approximately 40 million persons, and in our estimation, a $2 billion plus market segment. Established: 1997 - Franchising Since: 2003 - No. of Units: Company Owned: 1 - Franchise Fee: $20,000 - Royalty: 15% - Total Inv: $34,000-$44,000 - Financing: We provide financing of the the franchise fee for individuals that qualify.

BOOKKEEPING EXPRESS
10001 Derby Lane Suite 203, Westchester, IL, 60154. - Tel: (708) 615-1040. Own a home based bookkeeping and payroll processing business servicing all small businesses, contractors and professions. Established: 1985 - Licensing Since: 1987 - No. of Units: Licensed: 96 - Licensing fee: $7,500 - Total Inv: $7,500 - Financing: No.

CENTURY SMALL BUSINESS SOLUTIONS
2441 Honolulu Ave, Montrose, CA, 91020-1864. Contact: Triston Fisher, Franchise Coordinator - Tel: (949) 348-5100, (800) 323-9000, Web Site: www.centurysmallbiz.com. Century is an accounting, payroll, tax and business counseling franchise. Support and training in all aspects of the business. Established: 1935 - Franchising Since: 1965 - No. of Units: Company Owned: 8 - Franchised: 700 - Franchise Fee: $35,000 - Royalty: 8%, graduates downward on volume - Total Inv: $35,0000, franchise fee plus $15,000 working capital - Financing: Only outside sources.

ECONOTAX
Taxpro Inc.
P.O. Box 13829, Suite S-101, Jackson, MS, 39236. Contact: James T. Marsh, President - Tel: (800) 748-9106, Web Site: www.econotax.com. Provides the public professional tax services including tax preparation, electronic filing, refund loans, audit representation, and tax planning. Established: 1965 - Franchising Since: 1968 - No. of Units: Franchised: 54 - Franchise Fee: $10,000 - Royalty: 15% - Total Inv: $15,000 - Financing: Yes.

ELECTRONIC TAX FILERS
The St. Simons Corporation
P.O. Box 2077, Cary, NC, 27512-2077. Contact: Rachel Wishon - Tel: (919) 469-0651, (800) 945-9277, Fax: (919) 460-5935, E-Mail: rachelwishon@aol.com, Web Site: www.electronictaxfilers.com. We do no tax preparation! Instead, we provide a conveniently located site where taxpayers who want electronic filing services and refund loan products can bring their completed tax returns for e-filing direct to the IRS. Established: 1990 - Franchising Since: 1990 - No. of Units: Company Owned: 2 - Franchised: 42 - Franchise Fee: $9,000 - Royalty: 8% - Total Inv: $22,000 - Financing: Yes.

EXPRESSTAX
Express Tax Service, Inc.
3412 Kori Road, Jacksonville, FL, 32257. - Tel: (904) 262-0031, (888) 417-4461, Fax: (904) 262-2864, E-Mail: franchise@expresstax service.com, Web Site: www.expresstax service.com. Federal and state tax preparation and electronic filing. Established: 1997 - Franchising Since: 2002 - No. of Units: Company Owned: 1 - Franchised: 35 - Total Inv: $9,400-$16,050.

FIDUCIAL
Fiducial Franchises, Inc
10480 Little Patuxent Parkway, Third Floor, Columbia, MA, 21044. Contact: Howard Margolis - Tel: (410) 910-5860, (800) 323-9000, Fax: (410) 910-5903, E-Mail: franchise@fiducial.com, Web Site: www.fiducial.com. Franchisees provide small business owners and individuals with accounting and financial management, tax, financial, business counseling and payroll services. to enable you to provide these services, we provide you with our training programs, procedures, guidelines, software programs, processing centers, advertising materials, marketing and management support programs, and tax support services. Established: 1999 - Franchising Since: 2002 - No. of Units: Company Owned: 27 - Franchised: 554 - Franchise Fee: $25,000 - Royalty: 6%-3%-1.5% - Financing: None.

FREEDOM INSTANT - REFUND TAX SERVICE

1014 E. Charleston Ave, Las Vegas, NV, 89104. Contact: Allan Gonzales - Tel: (702) 316-1040, Fax: (702) 696-9446, E-Mail: freedom@instant-refund.com, Web Site: www.instant-refund.com. E-filing and tax preparation. Established: 2001 - Franchising Since: 2002 - No. of Units: Company Owned: 4 - Franchise Fee: $5,000 - Total Inv: $12,950-$20,200.

H & R BLOCK TAX SERVICES, INC.

4400 Main St., Kansas City, MO, 64111. Contact: Victoria Hall, V.P. Franchise Operations - Tel: (816) 932-8361, Web Site: www.h&rblock. com. Income tax return preparation and electronic filing. Established: 1955 - Franchising Since: 1956 - No. of Units: Company Owned: 5,215 worldwide - Franchised: 4,722 worldwide. At this time new territories not available. Several existing territories for sale by current franchisees.

JACKSON HEWITT TAX SERVICE

339 Jefferson Rd, Parsippany, NJ, 07054-3707. Contact: Marty Mazer, Dir. of Fran. Dev. - Tel: (757) 473-3300, Fax: (973) 496-1040. Computerized income tax preparation service. Established: 1960 - Franchising Since: 1986 - No. of Units: Company Owned: 88 - Franchised: 1,100 - Franchise Fee: $17,500 - Royalty: 12%, 6% adv. - Total Inv: $28,300-$38,600 - Financing: Yes.

LATINO INCOME TAX

American Tax and Financial Group

4650 S. Hampton #122, Dallas, TX, 75232. Contact: Calvin Dale Brown - Tel: (214) 331-0796, (877) 224-8476, Fax: (214) 333-1411, E-Mail: franchiseopp@americantaxandfinancialgroup.com, Web Site: www.americantaxandfinancialgroup.com. Income tax preparation and electronic filing. We are the only national franchisor that uniquely caters to and targets the U.S. African-American population, which numbers approximately 40 million persons, and in our estimation, a $2 billion plus market segment. Established: 1997 - Franchising Since: 2003 - No. of Units: Company Owned: 1 - Franchise Fee: $20,000 - Royalty: 15% - Total Inv: $34,000-$44,000 - Financing: We provide financing of the the franchise fee for individuals that qualify.

LEDGERPLUS

LedgerPlus, Inc

401 St. Francis St., Tallahassee, FL, 32301. Contact: John Harrison - Tel: (888) 643-1348, (850) 681-1941, Fax: (850) 561-1374, E-Mail: info@ledgerplus.com, Web Site: www.ledgerplus.com. International accounting franchise providing accounting, tax, payroll and consultation. Established: 1991 - Franchising Since: 1991 - No. of Units: Company Owned: 7 - Franchised: 154 - Franchise Fee: $16,000 - Royalty: 4-6% - Total Inv: $16,400-$32,000 - Financing: Yes.

LIBERTY TAX SERVICE

JTH Tax Inc

4575 Bonney Rd, Ste 1040, Virginia Beach, VA, 23462. Contact: Sue Wickham, Director of Franchise Development - Tel: (800) 790-3863, Fax: (757) 493-0169, E-Mail: sales@libtax.com, Web Site: www.libertytax.com. Liberty Tax Service is a retail income tax preparation firm serving the U.S. and Canada. Established: 1996 - Franchising Since: 1997 - No. of Units: Company Owned: 16 - Franchised: 900+ - Franchise Fee: $25,000 - Royalty: Varies - Total Inv: $38,050-$49,100 - Financing: To those who qualify.

NEXT DAY TAX CASH

2854 South Broadway, Englewood, CO, 80110. Contact: Carl Palmer, Sales Manager - Tel: (303) 761-8080, Fax: (303) 788-1416. Tax refund advances the next day. Electronic filing and tax preparation. Established: 1990 - Franchising Since: 1991 - No. of Units: Company Owned: 157 - Franchised: 3 - Franchise Fee: $3,000 - Royalty: $9/ loan - Total Inv: $5,000 including franchise fee - Financing: Yes.

PADGETT BUSINESS SERVICES

Padgett Business Services USA, Inc.

160 Hawthorne Park, Athens, GA, 30606. - Tel: (800) 723-4388, Fax: (800) 548-1040, Web Site: www.smallbizpros.com. Licensed individuals to operate their own accounting, income tax and business consulting practice. Four weeks of initial training, including in-area field support by home office are provided. Continuing support with yearly seminars. Established: 1966 - Franchising Since: 1975 - No. of Units: Franchised:

380 - Franchise Fee: $22,000 plus $12,500 training fee - Royalty: 4.5%-9% - Total Inv: Fee $34,500, work. cap. $20,000- $40,000 - Financing: Yes, $20,000.

PEOPLES INCOME TAX

Peoples, Inc

1801 Libbie Ave, #100, Richmond, VA, 23226. - Tel: (804) 204-1040, (800) 984-1040, Fax: (804) 213-4248, E-Mail:info@peoplestax.com, Web Site: www.peoplestax.com. Mass market income tax preparation service positioned for upwardly mobile individual and small business taxpayers; more personal and professional than traditional mass-market tax services. Established: 1987 - Franchising Since: 1998 - No. of Units: Company Owned: 16 - Franchise Fee: $15,000 - Royalty: 9% - Financing: Third party for start-up costs; Co. for franchise fee.

PEYRON TAX SERVICES

Peyron Associates, Inc.

3212 Preston St., Louisville, KY, 40213. Contact: Dan Peyron, Pres. - Tel: (502) 637-7483, Fax: (502) 637-7416. Tax return preparation in homes, malls, stores, storefronts. Also electronic filing and refund loans, tax newsletters and service booths in malls. "Our most successful operators are not accountants or tax preparers". Established: 1960 - Franchising Since: 1965 - No. of Units: Franchised: 500 - Franchise Fee: $3,000 - Royalty: 5% to Peyron - Financing: With 10% down.

PROFESSOR TAX OF NC, INC.

34 Maxwell St., Asheville, NC, 28801. Contact: Henry C. Baurley III, Pres. - Tel: (828) 254-0999, Fax: (828) 255-0990. Will provide unique marketing assistance, in person, at your office instead of our corporate office like most other franchisors require. This is a full tax and accounting year-round business with also your own in-house licensed schools. Established: 1981 - Franchising Since: 1994 - No. of Units: Company Owned: 1 - Franchised: 6 - Franchise Fee: $34,500 - Royalty: 12% - Total Inv: $34,500+$12,000 opening expenses - Financing: Help available.

TAX CENTERS OF AMERICA

Tax Centers Of America

1611 East Main, Russellville, AR, 72801. Contact: Gordon Thornsberry - Tel: (501) 968-4796, (800) 364-2012, Fax: (501) 968-8012, E-Mail: info@tcoa.net, Web Site: www.tcoa.net. Tax Centers of America specializes in income tax preparation and electronic tax filing. Offering unlimited earninng potential with a low investment provides one of the best business opportunities available. Visit our web site for more on this great investment opportunity! Established: 1993 - Franchising Since: 1995 - No. of Units: Franchised: 100 - Franchise Fee: $3,750 - Royalty: Varies - Total Inv: $7,700-$12,250 - Financing: No.

TAX MAN INC.

678 Massachusetts Ave., Room 202, Cambridge, MA, 02139. Contact: Mr. Garon, Exec. V.P. - Tel: (617) 868-1374, Fax: (617) 868-4265. Tax preparation. Available in New England only. Established: 1967 - No. of Units: 23 - Franchise Fee: $2,000 - Total Inv: $5,000.

TAX RECOVERY SYSTEMS *

1880 Office Club Pointe, Colorado Springs, CO, 80920. - Tel: (800) 714-3504, Fax: (719) 272-8065, Web Site: www.trsfranchisor.com. Companies and individuals provide us with their last years of tax returns to receive a second opinion. We provide this service with a No-Risk proposal. If there is no refund, there is absolutely No-Fee. It's a win-win because your clients either gain the peace of mind that they currently have a good tax payer or they receive a tax refund that averages $8,000. Established: 1995 - Franchising Since: 2003 - No. of Units: Franchised: 8000 - Franchise Fee: Varies - Capital requirements: $199-$125,000.

TAX REFUNDS NOW, INC

1803-A W. Palmetto Street, Florence, SC, 29501. Contact: Crystal Lewis - Tel: (843) 664-8797, (877) 747-7687, Fax: (843) 669-4570. Tax preparation. Established: 2001 - No. of Units: Company Owned: 1 - Franchised: 15 - Franchise Fee: Varies - Total Inv: $199-$125,000.

TAX SMART AMERICA

7520 El Cajon Blvd, #106, La Mesa, CA, 91941. - Tel: (619) 469-5800, Fax: (619) 465-7193, Web Site: www.taxsmartamerica.biz. We are a unique business model franchise opportunity for existing tax professionals. Establikshed: 1999 - Franchising Since: 2001 - No. of Units: Franchised: 16 - Franchise Fee: $25,000 - Royalty: 8% - Total Inv: $25,000 - Financing: Third party.

TRIPLE CHECK INCOME TAX SERVICE
Fiducial Triple Check
2441 Honolulu Ave, Montrose, CA, 91020. - Tel: (800) 525-2939, Web Site: www.fiducialtriplecheck.com. Franchisor offers full range of support services to build a quality tax and small business consulting/ accounting practice. Through Triple Check Financial Services, franchisees are able to add a separate profit center providing their clients with need-oriented, conservative financial planning. Established: 1968 - Franchising Since: 1977 - No. of Units: Company Owned: 1 - Franchised: 240 - Franchise Fee: None - Royalty: Varies - Total Inv: $5,700-$21,600 - Financing: Yes.

U & R TAX DEPOT
JTH Tax Inc.
4575 Bonney Rd, Virginia Beach, VA, 23462-3831. Contact: John Hewitt, President - Tel: (757) 340-7610, (800) 790-3863, Fax: (757) 340-7612, E-Mail: office@libtax.com, Web Site: www.libertytax.com. Fully computerized income tax preparation firm specializing in electronic filing. Established: 1972 - Franchising Since: 1986 - No. of Units: Company Owned: 8 - Franchised: 198 - Franchise Fee: $0, ($1,500 security deposit) - Royalty: Varies - Total Inv: $8,000-$10,000 - Financing: Some.

WASHINGTON TAX RESOLUTION, INC
400 Melrose Ave F., Ste. 507, Seattle, WA, 98102. Contact: Jason Harmon - Tel: (206) 329-2302, (800) 894-9304. Tax business. Established: 1989 - No. of Units: Company Owned: 2 - Franchised: 28.

ADVERTISING/DIRECT MAIL

ADVENTURES IN ADVERTISING
400 Crown Colony Dr., 2nd Floor, Quincy, MA, 02169. - Tel: (617) 472-9901, (800) 432-6332, Fax: (617) 472-9979, E-Mail: kurtc@advinadv.com, Web Site: www.advinadv.com. This franchise opportunity is specifically designed for salespeople, marketing and business professionals. If you enjoy working with corporate accounts and have experience in business-to-business sales, call today. Established: 1979 - Franchising Since: 1994 - No. of Units: Company Owned: 1 - Franchised: 95 - Franchise Fee: $27,500 - Royalty: 1%-6% of gross revenue - Total Inv: $40,000-$60,000 - Financing: Yes.

ADVERTISING ON THE MOVE
Mobil' Ambition
1900 NW 32nd St, Pompano Beach, FL, 33064. Contact: Robert Crist, Franchising - Tel: (954) 969-8558, Fax: (954) 969-8171. Advertising through vehicles. Established: 1994 - Franchising Since: 1995 - No. of Units: Company Owned: 1 - Franchised: 40 - Franchise Fee: $5,000-$10,000 - Financing: No.

ALTERNATIVE MEDIA GROUP
Box 1952, Grand Junction, CO, 81502. - Tel: (970) 242-6030. Provides advertising to businesses through cartoon maps and coupon books. Our trademarked products include Cartoon Cartographics and Calendars plus The Student Super-Saver. Established: 1982 - Licensing Since: 1990 - No. of Units: Company Owned: 2 - Licensed: 3 - License Fee: $4,995 - Royalty: 10.85% of gross sales - Total Inv: $5,000-$10,000 - Financing: Yes.

$AVE-A-BUCK
6348 Palmas Bay Circle, Port Orange, FL, 32127. Contact: M.V. Biro, Dir. - Tel: (904) 767-7523. Discount coupons advertising mailer (book and coupons) sales, production and mailing. Established: 1992 - Franchising Since: 1993 - No. of Units: Company Owned: 1 - Franchise Fee: $1,000 - Royalty: Min. $200 or 4% + 1% adv. - Total Inv: $8,000 - Financing: No.

BABIES 'N' BELLS INC
4489 Mira Vista Dr, Frisco, TX, 75034-7519. Contact: Dara Craft, CEO - Tel: (888) 418-BABY, Fax: (972) 418-5723, E-Mail: corp@babiesnbells.com, Web Site: www.babiesnbells.com. Invitation and announcement franchise which is home-based, yet we have kiosks in retail establishments such as Babies R Us, catalogs for mail order business and web site for internet marketing. Established: 1993 - Franchising: 1997 - No. of Units: Company Owned: 3 - Franchised: 82 - Franchise Fee: $9,000 - Royalty: 8% and 2% marketing fund fee - Total Inv: $25,000 - Financing: None.

BILLBOARD CONNECTION
P.O. Box 905, McDonough, GA, 30253. - Tel: (770) 472-7500, Fax: (678) 583-1605, E-Mail: don@billboardconnection.com, Web Site: www.BillboardConnection.com. We specialize in out-of-home media. We consult with clients and place their advertising on billboards, taxis, movie theaters, buses and more. Established: 1997 - Franchising Since: 2003 - Franchise Fee: $35,000.

BOULDER BLIMP COMPANY
505 Stacy Ct., #A, Lafayette, CO, 80026. Contact: April Bowersox - Tel: (303) 664-1122, Fax: (303) 664-1133, E-Mail: bbcinfo@ boulderblimp.com, Web Site: www.boulderblimp.com. We manufacture giant promotional inflatables, for all industries. We also do helium filled blimps, and point of purchase inflatables. Established: 1980.

BRIGHT BEGINNINGS
America Welcome Services, Inc.
26071 Merit Cir Ste 103, Laguna Hills, CA, 92653-7016. - Tel: (949) 752-2772, E-Mail: Melanie@BrightBeginnings.net, Web Site: www.brightbeginnings.net. Bright Beginnings is in the in-home welcoming service industry. An upscale advertising and community relations business combining neighbourly promotions and online targeted advertising. Established: 1986 - Franchising Since: 1989, New License 2000 - No. of Units: Company Owned: 15 - Franchised: 6 - Franchise Fee: $25,000 - Royalty: 3% - Total Inv: $45,000 (franchise fee $25,000, equipment, $5,000, training, $5,000, start up $7,500, misc. $2,500) - Financing: Yes.

BUSINESS PARTNER.COM
Business Partner Franchise Corp.
324 Main Street, Irwin, PA, 15642. Contact: Bruce D. Violette, President - Tel: (724) 863-7888, Fax: (724) 864-9673, E-Mail: bruce@business partner.com, Web Site: www.businesspartner.com. A one stop retail marketing center offering copies, shipping, printing, signs, specialty advertising, web design, video production all under one roof. Established: 1996 - Franchising Since: 2001 - No. of Units: Company Owned: 2 - Franchise Fee: $25,000 - Royalty: 5% - Total Inv: $108,000-$211,000.

BUTTON KING INC
2943 E Alexander Rd, Las Vegas, NV, 89030. Contact: Phillip Jarrett - Tel: (702) 643-6500, Fax: (702) 643-8900, E-Mail: jarrett@buttonking.com, Web Site: www.buttonking.com. Retail promotional product service with manufacturing capabilities for buttons, trade show displays, banners and full color digital printing and signs with support to sell promotional items to support customer base. Internet based leads and sales. Established: 1969 - Franchising Since: 2000 - No. of Units: Company Owned: 3 - Franchise Fee: $40,000 - Total Inv: $115,000-$130,000 - Financing: SBA financing assistance available.

CARTOON CARTOGRAPHICS & CALENDARS
Alternative Media Group
P.O. Box 1952, Grand Jct., CO, 81502. Contact: Kevin Van Gundy, Pres. - Tel: (970) 242-6030. America's highest quality cartoon promotional maps and calendars. Established: 1982 - Franchising Since: 1989 - No. of Units: Company Owned: 3 - Franchised: 3 - Franchise Fee: $4,995 - Royalty: 10% - Financing: Yes.

CHAPMAN PUBLISHING, INC.
222 Lakeview Ave., Ste. 160-116, West Palm Beach, FL, 33401. Contact: Lynda Wessel, President - Tel: (561) 845-6362. Full service public relations and advertising. Established: 1992.

COLORFAST MARKETING SYSTEMS INC.
9522 Topanga Cyn Blvd., Chatsworth, CA, 91311. Contact: Lynne Koenig, Sales Manager - Tel: (818) 407-1881, Fax: (818) 407-0267, E-Mail: colorf@colorfastmarketing.com. Manufacturers of photographic promotional material such as prepaid phone cards, business cards, keychains and postcards. Established: 1985 - Franchising Since: 1985

- No. of Units: Franchised: 1500 - Franchise Fee: $295 - Royalty: Pay to Colorfast wholesale - the rest is profit, up to 100% markup - Total Inv: $295 for distributor success kit - Financing: None.

CONNECT.AD
Connect.Ad, Inc.
1000 West McNab Rd., Ste. 236, Pompano Beach, FL, 33069. Contact: John Colodni, Dir. of Fran. Dev. - Tel: (561) 417-5535, Web Site: www.connectad.com. Connect.ad offers small and medium size businesses an affordable one-stop solution for having a presence on the Internet. As a Connect.ad partner, you assist with marketing the products and services of your local community. Established: 1995 - Franchising Since: 1996 - Franchise Fee: $9,500 plus - Royalty: 3%, 3% adv. - Total Inv: $30,000 (fran. fee, equip., etc.) - Financing: No.

CONSUMER NETWORK OF AMERICA
15965 Jeanette, Southfield, MI, 48075.Contact: Colleen McGaffey - Tel: (248) 557-2784. An innovative alternative advertising program for short term advertising for retailers. Extremely strong track record of performance. Unique franchise with no direct competition. A very profitable home-based business. Established: 1990 - Franchising Since: 1995 - No. of Units: Company Owned: 25 markets - Franchise Fee: $15,000 - Royalty: $10,000 per market.

COUPON TABLOID INTERNATIONAL INC.
5775 S.W. Jean Rd., #101, Lake Oswego, OR, 97035.Contact: Joanne Crane, V.P, Oper. - Tel: (503) 697-1968. Direct mail advertising. Established: 1986 - Franchising Since: 1994 - No. of Units: Franchised: 24 - Franchise Fee: $8,500 - Total Inv: $13,509-$20,185 - Financing: Franchise fee only.

COUPON-CASH SAVER
Coupon-Cash Saver Franchise Corp.
325 N. Milwaukee Ave Suite J, Wheeling, IL, 60090. - Tel: (847) 537-6420, Fax: (847) 537-6499, Web Site: www.couponcashsaver.com. Direct mail coupon advertising booklet. Established: 1984 - Franchising Since: 1990 - No. of Units: Company Owned: 5 - Franchised: 2 - Franchise Fee: $9,500 - Royalty: 6% - Total Inv: $22,600 - Financing: Yes.

DEI SALES TRAINING SYSTEMS *
888 7th Ave, 9th Floor, New York, NY, 10106 - Tel: (800) 224-2140, Fax: (212) 245-7897, Web Site: www.dei-sales.com. Our programs teach people how to gain more appointments, sell more efficiently, and manage more effectively. As a D.E.I. franchise owner, you'll sell some of the finest face-to-face, customized training workshops in the sales training industry. Established: 1979 - Franchising Since: 2003 - No. of Units: Franchised: 4 - Franchise Fee: $50,000.

DISCIPLE'S DIRECTORY
P.O. Box 100, Wilmington, MA, 01887. - Tel: (978) 657-7373, Fax: (978) 657-5411, Web Site: www.discoverymaps.com. Christian yellow pages and web site. Established: 1984 - Franchising Since: 1998 - No. of Units: Company Owned: 2 - Franchised: 5 - Franchise Fee: $7,500.

DISCOVERY MAP INTERNATIONAL
918 4th Street, Suite 200, Anacortes, WA, 98221. - Tel: (360) 588-0144, Fax: (360) 588-8344, Web Site: www.discoverymap.com. Advertising, sales and distribution of distinctive and functional "Birds Eye View" illustrated maps. Established: 1987 - Franchising Since: 1999 - No. of Units: Company Owned: 9 - Franchised: 5 - Franchise Fee: $15,000 - Total Inv: $36,000-$50,000.

EFFECTIVE MAILERS
Effective Direct Marketing Systems, Inc.
28510 Hayes Rd, Roseville, MI, 48066-2314. Contact: Jai Gupta, Pres. - Tel: (810) 777-3223, Fax: (810) 777-4141. Direct mail advertising business. We design, print, insert and mail coupons in envelopes. In technology, we are either at par or ahead of competitors. Clients advertising with us get one of the best responses. We train franchisees in coupon design, selling and all other aspects of the business. Established: 1982 - Franchising Since: 1993 - No. of Units: Company Owned: 1 - Franchised: 14 - Franchise Fee: $500 plus territory fee - Royalty: None - Total Inv: $25,000+ (fran. fee $500, territory $18,000, training and travel $3,000, initial supplies $1,100, plus misc.) - Financing: None.

EYECATCHERPLUS
23650 Woodward Ave Suite 201, Pleasant Ridge, MI, 48069. - Tel: (248) 546-7227, Fax: (248) 545-5943, Web Site: www.eyecatcherplus.com. EyeCatcherPlus is the forefront of the indoor/outdoor motion display advertising industry. The reason for our success is simple: EyeCatcherPlus is in the right place...at the right time. Our unique motion display advertising systems provide businesses with a results-producing way to promote their products and brand awareness for just pennies on the dollar. Established: 2000 - Franchising Since: 2000 - No. of Units: Franchised: 10 - Franchise Fee: $19,750 - Financing: No.

FELIX RUSLIN DIRECT RESPONSE, INC.
8308 S. Kedzie Ave., Chicago, IL, 60652. Contact: Steven Gilbertz, Pres. - Tel: (217) 356-7788, Fax: (217) 356-6876. Advertising and marketing agency specializing in direct response lead generation and franchise marketing materials, public relations, and direct mail for franchise support. Established: 1986.

FIESTA CARTOON MAPS
Fiesta Promotions
942 N. Orlando, Mesa, AZ, 85205-5152. Contact: Jack Eddy, Owners - Tel: (480) 396-8226, E-Mail: fiestamaps@aol.com, Web Site: www.fiestacartoonmaps.com. Advertising, maps and guides. Established: 1979 - Licensing Since: 1986 - No. of Units: Company Owned: 5 - Franchise Fee: $6,495 - Total Inv: $6,495 - Financing: No.

FISHMAN PUBLIC RELATIONS
1141 Lake Cook Rd., Ste. C-1, Deerfield, IL, 60015. - Tel: (847) 945-1300, Fax: (847) 945-3755, E-Mail: fishpr@aol.com. Publicity firm that basis its entire philosophy on providing customized public relations programs which creatively responds to all local, national and consumer publicity needs. Established: 1991.

GREETINGS
Greetings Inc.
P.O. Box 25623, Lexington, KY, 40524. Contact: Larry Kargel, Pres. - Tel: (606) 272-5624. Target market advertising. Produce a magazine to college and university students. Established: 1984 - Franchising Since: 1989 - No. of Units: Company Owned: 4 - Franchised: 5 - Franchise Fee: $15,000 - Royalty: 5% gross sales - Total Inv: $5,000 operating funds, $6,500 equip. - Financing: No.

HOMESTART
JG Creative Enterprises, Inc
P.O. Box 14185, Fuguay-Varina, NC, 27526. Contact: Anna Dunstan - Tel: (919) 567-9232. Direct mail targeting homebuyers in high population areas. Includes publication of magazine mailed monthly to all recent homebuyers. Established: 1997 - Franchising Since: 1999 - No. of Units: Company Owned: 2 - Franchise Fee: $9,700-$12,950 - Royalty: No royalty - service fees $200.00-$300.00 a month - Total Inv: Franchise fee + approx. $3,500 - Financing: No.

IMPACT DESIGNS
Impact Designs Inc.
675 Fairview Dr. Ste. 246, Carson City, NV, 89701. Contact: Michael Warner, President - Tel: (888) 203-5886, E-Mail: michael@impact designs.net, Web Site: www.impactdesigns.net. Consult with businesses that advertise in the phone companies yellow pages. Help them reduce their advertising costs by thousands of dollars a year while increeasing their profits. Receive half of the savings as your fee. Preset appointments. Established: 1990 - Franchising Since: 1994 - No. of Units: Company Owned: 2 - Franchised: 5 - Franchise Fee: $9,900 - Royalty: $5% of fees collected - Total Inv: $15,000-$9,900 training + $5,100 working capital - Financing: No.

INMAC PUBLISHING COMPANY
1765 Landess Ave., Ste. 27, Milpitas, CA, 95035. - Tel: (570) 351-1229, Fax: (510) 351-8649, E-Mail: omccog@sprintmail.com. Marketing and promotion business placemats, menus, fax blast coupons, and magazines for local businesses. Established: 1994 - Franchising Since: 1996 - No. of Units: Company Owned: 1 - Franchised: 2 - Franchise Fee: $995-$2995 - Royalty: 0 - Total Inv: Fee + training and support $300-$500 - Financing: No.

LOCAL MERCHANT DISPLAY CENTERS
Merchant Advertising Systems, Inc.
4115 Tiverton Rd., Randallstown, MD, 21133-2019. - Tel: (410) 655-3201, (800) 316-6461, Fax: (410) 655-0262. Unique display centers for custom-made local merchant signage and promotional literature, installed in major supermarket chains and shopping malls. Established: 1985 - Franchising Since: 1987 - No. of Units: Company Owned: 11 - Franchised: 2 - Franchise Fee: $13,500-$25,500 - Royalty: 0% (joint venture partnership alternative) - Total Inv: $17,000-$29,000 incl. start-up costs - Financing: Assistance with indirect financing.

MAIL MARKETING DIRECT
1827 N. Michigan Ave., Saginaw, MI, 48602. Contact: Dave Birnbaum, Dir. of Market Dev. - Tel: (517) 921-0000. Direct mail advertising coupon book. All artwork and layout, printing, assembly and mailing services are provided. Unique color format. Established: 1989 - Distributorships Since: 1990 - No. of Units: Company Owned: 1 - Distributorships: 41 - Franchise Fee: $495 - Royalty: None - Total Inv: Varies - Financing: No.

MFV EXPOSITIONS
210 Route 4 East, Suite 403, Paramus, NJ, 07652. Contact: Cheryl Burkhalter, Fran. Dev. - Tel: (201) 226-1130x171, Fax: (201) 226-1131, E-Mail: cburkhalter@mfvexpo.com, Web Site: www.franchise expo.com. We are the world's leading producer of franchise shows, producing approximately 50 expos throughout North America. We produce the International Franchise Expo, the IFE features over 300 franchise companies and visitors from over 80 countries. Established: 1980.

MILLENNIUM ENTERPRISE CO.
P.O. Box 1510, Wenatchee, WA, 98801. Contact: Gene Tougas - Tel: (509) 881-2117, (877) 806-4553, Fax: (504) 881-2117. Direct sales, distributor, mail order and networking. We help people build homebased businesses. Established: 2000 - Franchising Since: 2000 - No. of Units: Company Owned: 1 - Franchise Fee: $165. - Total Inv: $165.-$465.

MOBIL AMBITION U.S.A.
1900 NW 32nd Street, Pompano Beach, FL, 33064. Contact: Jack Jacquot, President - Tel: (954) 969-8558, Fax: (954) 969-8171, Web Site: www.adsonthemove.com. Moving advertising into the new century with our bright yellow vans scrolling 24 multiple advertising messages while it drives to the consumers. Also backlit for evening showings and special events. This new media is financially rewarding. Protected territory. Established: 1995 - Franchising Since: 1995 - No. of Units: Company Owned: 1 - Franchised: 14 - Franchise Fee: $35,000 - Royalty: $1,000 - Total Inv: $135,000 - Financing: No.

MOM & DAD / HOME & FOOD PUBLICATIONS, LLC
Assoc. of Direct Mail Publications
800 3rd St, Windsor, CO, 80550. Contact: Kristie Straube, Sales/Mkt Director - Tel: (970) 686-5805, (800) 611-6996, Fax: (800) 438-2150, E-Mail: kstraube@msn.com. Four color/gloss/high quality display ad direct mail magazine with editorial content. Franchisees sell ads to local businesses. Franchisor handles all production and distribution. Established: 1997 - Franchising Since: 1998 - No. of Units: Franchised: 4 - Franchise Fee: $5,000 - Total Inv: $7,700-$11,700.

MONEY MAILER
Money Mailer, Inc.
14271 Corporate Dr., Garden Grove, CA, 92843. Contact: Fran. Sales Dept - Tel: (714) 265-4100. Provide highly targeted advertising services to local and national businesses through a network of 500 franchisees. We have redefined state-of-the-art in design, production and distribution of direct mail. Comprehensive training and support are second to none. Established: 1979 - Franchising Since: 1980 - No. of Units: Franchised: 625 - Franchise Fee: $25,000-$50,000 - Royalty: Varies.

NATIONAL MAIL ORDER ASSOCIATION, L.L.C.
2807 Polk St. N.E., Minneapolis, MN, 55418-2954. - Tel: (612) 788-1673, Fax: (612) 788-1147, E-Mail: schulte@nmoa.org. Provides help to small and medium sized businesses in the use of direct mail and mail order marketing. Publishes Mail Order Digest and Washington Newsletter. Also operates "Mail Order Connection" for members to communicate worldwide. Internet www.nmoa.org, looking for international affiliates only. Established: 1972 - Total Inv: $10,000.

NATIONAL TELEPHONE MESSAGE
National Telephone Message Corp., Inc.
5975 W. Sunrise Blvd., Ste. 215, Sunrise, FL, 33313. Contact: Irwin Lubar, President - Tel: (954) 584-8191, (800) 789-4619, Fax: (954) 584-8348, (800) 532-6013. On-Hold telephone advertising gives every business a competitive edge. On-Hold messages tell callers about products, services, promotions etc. Our distributors market this unique product, NTMC does complete production. Established: 1990 - Distributor Program: 1997 - No. of Units: Company Owned: 1 - Distributor Fee: $7,998 - Royalty: None - Total Inv: $7,998 - Financing: None.

NEWMETHOD DIRECT
14 Inverness DR., East, C-108, Englewood, CO, 80112. Contact: James Orr - Tel: (303) 799-6090, (800) 824-3983, Fax: (303) 799-6087, E-Mail: jim@newmethodmarketing.com, Web Site: www.newmethod direct.com. We provide direct mail marketing materials and related marketing programs to real estate agents and other businesses desiring to market their products and services. Established: 1990 - Franchising Since: 2001 - No. of Units: Company Owned: 3 - Franchise Fee: $40,000 - Total Inv: $24,200-$49,850.

POINTS FOR PROFIT
Southwest Promotional Corporation
P.O. Box 2424, La Mesa, CA, 91943.Contact: Jerry Nesler, Pres. - Tel: (619) 588-0664, Fax: (619) 588-0664. Points for profit a proof of purchase advertising and marketing plan for broadcast stations to more easily sell their spot commercials to major and local advertisers. Station market exclusive. Ratings not a factor. Some stations 10th year. References. Established: 1970 - Franchising Since: 1975 - No. of Units: Franchised: 13 - Franchise Fee: 7.5% of gross sales - Total Inv: $750 down payment deducted from 7.5% sales.- Financing: No.

PRACTICAL PROMOTIONS
Practical Promotions, LLC
1205 Manley Loop, Dickson, TN, 37055. Contact: Terry Cahill, Gen Mgr. - Tel: (615) 441-3796, Fax: (615) 441-6859, Web Site: www.practicalpromotions.com. Manufacture Tornado Tube. Just plug it in! It turns itself from the size of a shoebox into a 1 1/2 tall "Beacon of Light" in two minutes flat! Home based rental of sales Biz. Established: 1992 - Franchise Fee: Zero inventory purchase only - Royalty: 0 - Total Inv: $495.00 - Financing: No.

PREMIUM SHOPPING GUIDE
Dolphin Publications of America, Inc.
1235 Sunset Grove Rd., Fallbrook, CA, 92028. Contact: Bob Neral, Nat'l Mkt. Dir. - Tel: (760) 723-2283, (800) 343-1056, Fax: (760) 728-3145. Direct mail coupon/display magazine. Franchisor does all production. Franchisee provides local marketing. Established: 1984 - Franchising Since: 1992 - No. of Units: Company Owned: 107 - Franchised: 41 - Franchise Fee: $8,900 - Total Inv: $8,900 + $500 startup (misc.) - Financing: Fran. fee only.

PROFIT-ON-HOLD
Ad-Comm International
3401 Ridgelake Dr., Ste. 108, Metairie, LA, 70002. Contact: Otto Mehrgut, Pres. - Tel: (504) 832-8000, (800) 564-hold, Fax: (504) 828-2141, E-Mail: otto@profit-on-hold-com, Web Site: www.profit-on-hold-com. On hold advertising. We create the script, install digital reproducing equip. and custom made informational messages while customers remain on hold. Established: 1991 - Franchising Since: 1993 - No. of Units: Company Owned: 4 - Franchised: 2 - Franchise Fee: $10,000 - Royalty: 3% adv. - Total Inv: $15,000 - Financing: No.

PRSTORE, LLC
PRS Franchise System
31402 Kline Cr.,Warrenville, IL, 60555. Contact: Daniel Gragen - Tel: (630) 393-9054, Fax: (630) 393-0220. Marketing and Ad agency. Established: 2001 - Franchising Since: 2002 - No. of Units: Company Owned: 1 - Franchised: 2 - Franchise Fee: $25,000-$40,000 - Financing: No.

PUMP RADIO NETWORK
Advance Information Systems Franchise Company, LLC
2820 Jefferson Ave, Midland, MI, 48640. Contact: Franchise Development - Tel: (517) 837-2460, (877) 682-5537, Fax: (517) 837-3597. Sell advertising space heard by customers at convenience stores and gas stations. The commercials are played over the patented fueling talker, which attaches to the fueling nozzle of a gas pump. Protected territories. Established: 1994 - Franchising Since: 1999- No. of Units: Company Owned: 4 - Franchised: 7 - Franchise Fee: $30,000 - Royalty: 10% - Total Inv: $75,000-$110,000 (including franchise fee and startup costs) - Financing: We will assist in presentations to lending companies.

RESORT MAPS
Resort Maps Franchise, Inc.
P.O. Box 726, Waitsfield, VT, 05673. Contact: Tom Gardner, Franchise Dir. - Tel: (802) 496-6277, (800) 788-5247, Fax: (802) 496-6278, E-Mail: tgardner@resortmaps.com, Web Site: www.resortmaps.com. A unique and creative alternative advertising media. Business and tourist information maps are published by our franchise owners. Established: 1978 - Franchising Since: 1993 - No. of Units: Company Owned: 12 - Franchised: 38 - Franchise Fee: $8,450 - Royalty: 10% of gross revenues - Total Inv: $12,050-$17,150 - Financing: No. Not franchising at this time.

SELF POWER
P.O. Box 268 - BOH, El Cajon, CA, 92022. Contact: Brian W. Fansher - Tel: (619) 441-7930. Discount advertising. Established: 1998 - No. of Units: Company Owned: 1 - Franchised: 1 - Total Inv: Capital requirements; $50-$200 - Financing: No.

SHOP TILL YOU DROP
All American Advertising
P.O. Box 123, Perrineville, NJ, 08535. Contact: Rick Latshaw - Tel: (888) 294-4354. Direct mail advertising. Established: 1995 - No. of Units: Company Owned: 1 - Franchised: 2 - Total Inv: Capital requirements; $1,650 - Financing: Yes.

SUPER COUPS
Mailcoups, Inc., The
180 Bodwell St., Avon, MA, 02322. Contact: Glen Liset,V.P. Sales, Marketing - Tel: (508) 580-4340, (800) 626-2620, Fax: (508) 588-3347, E-Mail: gliset@supercoups.com. Sell franchises in the co-operative direct mail industry. These franchises contact local business people to market their business to consumers in a 10,000 market profile. Established: 1982 - Franchising Since: 1983 - No. of Units: Company Owned: 4 - Franchised: 349 - Franchise Fee: $30,000 - Royalty: $148 per 10,000 home profile - Total Inv: Should have $20,000 in additional working cap. - Financing: No.

SUPER SAVER COUPONS
Community Publications of America, Inc.
80 Eighth Ave., New York, NY, 10011. Contact: Allan Horwitz, President - Tel: (212) 243-6800. Valuable money saving coupons mailed monthly to every household in zip code. No envelope to open 1/3 the price of other coupon mailers. Established: 1995 - Franchising Since: 1995 - No. of Units: Franchised: 4 - Franchise Fee: $5,000 - Royalty: None - Total Inv: Approx. $10,000 - Financing: Yes.

TALKING ADS
Talking Ads of America
P.O.Box 14804, Lenexa, KS, 66285-4804. Contact: Arvin Zwick, Pres./Founder - Tel: (913) 492-SAVE(7283), Fax: (913) 492-9552, E-Mail: arvinz@cysource.com. TA compliment newspaper, radio or TV ads, by allowing user to drastically reduce size and cost of their ads, etc., saving $100's to $1000's. Minimal investment, high profit margins, easy to operate and promote with staggering potential. Call about $10,000 worth of free advertising. Established: 1992 - Franchising Since: 1992 - No. of Units: Company Owned: 1 - Franchise Fee: None - Royalty: None - Total Inv: $477 plus $1,000 - $5,000 work. cap. - Financing: MC/V.

THE DISPLAY SOURCE, INC
1278 Glenneyre St, Laguna Beach, CA, 92651-3103. Contact: Paul Wartman, Executive V.P - Tel: (714) 557-7779, (800) 972-3022, E-Mail: tigermarkla@earthlink.net, Web Site: www.Displaysource.com.

Professional display/exhibit source for custom modular portable display systems, custom graphics, design services, shipping, installation, storage and promotional items. Established: 1988.

TIME & TEMPERATURE ADVERTISING
2040 Canyon Rd., Birmingham, AL, 35216-1904. Contact: Hal Harris, Jr., Owner - Tel: (205) 979-3000, Fax: (205) 979-3000. Provide local telephone number where the public may call to get the exact time and the current temperature. System sales and distributorship opportunities available in certain master territories. Established: 1989 - Franchising Since: 1991 - No. of Units: Company Owned: 3 - Franchised: 1 - Franchise Fee: $3,500-$15,000 - Royalty: $150 per month - Total Inv: Includes Time Pro2 equip. - Financing: No.

UNISON MARKETING COMMUNICATIONS
Unison Syndications
6312 S. Fiddler's Green Cir., 545 N., Englewood, CO, 80118. Contact: Leigh Umbarger - Tel: (303) 779-3004, Fax: (303) 779-3010. Healthcare marketing and advertising syndicated products. Established: 1983 - Franchising Since: 1990 - No. of Units: Company Owned: 1 - Franchised: 1 - Franchise Fee: $45,000-$75,000 - Royalty: 45% to franchisee, 55% to franchisor (franchisor supplies product) - Total Inv: F.F., $52,000-$90,500 start-up - Financing: Partial.

UNITED MARKETING SOLUTIONS, INC
7644 Dynatech Ct., Springfield, VA, 22153. Contact: Phil Trigg, Dir. of Fran. Dev. - Tel: (703) 644-0200, Fax: (703) 644-6550, E-Mail: info@unitedol.com, Web Site: www.unitedol.com. Offering our franchisees the most diversified array of proven products in the industry, United is a leader in providing direct mail, direct marketing and internet marketing solutions to the local market entrepreneur. Our franchise opportunity includes a low investment, the ability to work from home on a timetable you establish, comprehensive training and continous operations support. Established: 1981- Franchising Since: 1982 - No. of Units: Franchised: 49 - Franchise Fee: $31,500 - Royalty: None - Total Inv: Initial investment ranges from $26,845-$74,877 - Financing: Yes.

VALPAK
Val-Pak Direct Marketing Systems
8605 Largo Lakes Dr., Largo, FL, 33773. Contact: Richard Folsom, Director Franchise Sales - Tel: (800) 237-6266 x3548, Fax: (727) 392-0049, E-Mail: mary_dillard@valpak.com, Web Site: www.Valpak.com. North America's largest local co-op mailer, distributing over 12 billion coupons to over 400 million homes annually. A division of Cox Enterprises. Established: 1968 - Franchising Since: 1988 - No. of Units: Company Owned: 6 - Franchised: 200 - Franchise Fee: $15,000 - Royalty: None - Total Inv: Varies - Financing: No.

WAYNE R. IRWIN TRUST
Quickbuilders Association
4609 Meadowood Drive, Baytown, TX, 77521-2048. Contact: Wayne R. Irwin - Tel: (281) 424-7651, Fax: (281) 424-7676, E-Mail: wirwin7418@aol.com, Web Site: www.quickbuilders.com. Home based business that really works, presented in easy step by step instructions. Complete turnkey operation. Company does most of the work, no personal contact, phone or inventory. Established: 1999 - Franchising Since: 2000 - Total Inv: Below $300.00.

WHEELS AMERICA ADVERTISING
545 Charles St, Luzerne, PA, 18709. Contact: Susan Hanlon - Tel: (570) 283-5000, Fax: (570) 283-3245. Mobile advertising. Established: 1995 - Franchising Since: 2000 - No. of Units: Company Owned: 12 - Franchised: 12 - Franchise Fee: $25,000 - Financing: Yes.

YELLOW JACKET DIRECT MAIL ADVERTISING
Yellow Jacket Franchise Corporation
706 Cass Street, P.O. 357, Griswold, IA, 51535. Contact: Franchise Department - Tel: (800) 262-2440, Fax: (712) 778-4493. Cooperative direct mail advertising. Established: 1991 - Franchising Since: 1991 - No. of Units: Franchised: 13- Franchise Fee: $24,000 - Royalty: $15 per ad- Total Inv: $25,000: Fran. Fee + $6,000 cash flow - Financing: No.

AUTOMOBILE RENTAL & LEASING

A PLUS RENT A CAR® SYSTEM
P.O. Box 674, Johnson City, NY, 13790. Contact: Merv Short, V.P. - Tel: (800) 874-0360, Fax: (888) 874-0360, Web Site: www.aplusrentacar.com. New and used auto rentals, automated systems, training and ongoing support. Established: 1979 - Franchising Since: 1984 - No. of Units: Franchised: 389 - Franchise Fee: Varies - Total Inv: Varies - Financing: No.

AFFORDABLE CAR RENTAL
96 Freneau Ave., #2, Matawan, NJ, 07747. Contact: Charles Vitale, G.M. - Tel: (800) 631-2290, (732) 290-8300, Fax: (732) 290-8305. A program designed for new car dealers. Provide comprehensive training, quality insurance and management support for the rental of new and used cars. Established: 1981 - Licensing Since: 1981 - No. of Units: Franchised: 90 - Franchise Fee: $3,500-$6,000 - Mgt. Fee: $15-$10 per mo. per car - Financing: None.

AIR BROOK LIMOUSINE, INC.
P.O. Box 123, Rochelle Park, NJ, 07662. Contact: Jim Dziekunski, Fran. Dir. - Tel: (201) 843-6100, (800) 800-1990, Fax: (201) 587-8385. One of Metro New York's largest transportation companies. Sedans, vans, stretch limousines and buses. Established: 1968 - Franchising Since: 1971- No. of Units: Company Owned: 85 - Franchised: 90 - Franchise Fee: $7,500 - Royalty: 60%-40% - Total Inv: $7,500 fran. fee, $2,000 security deposit - Financing: Yes.

ALLSTAR RENT-A-CAR
Practical Rent-A-Car Systems, Inc.
4780 I 55 N Ste 300, Jackson, MS, 39211-5583. Contact: Ron Bavington, Pres. - Tel: (702) 798-5253, Fax: (702) 798-4739. Car rental business. Established: 1976 - Franchising Since: 1981 - No. of Units: Franchised: 130 - Franchise Fee: $2,500-$25,000 depending on population of territory - Royalty: $20 per car - Total Inv: $25,000-$125,000 - Financing: Yes.

BEARLY USED AUTO RENTAL
1100 SE 5th Ct., Ste. #72, Pompano Beach, FL, 33060. Contact: James Von Bampus - Tel: (954) 942-7743, Fax: (954) 783-6776. Used car rental. Established: 2002 - Franchising Since: 2002 - No. of Units: Company Owned: 2 - Franchised: 3 - Franchise Fee: $15,000.

BOX TROTTERS INTERNATIONAL
1108 Third Ave, Ste. 12, Conway, SC, 29526. Contact: Henry Cox - Tel: (843) 381-0596, (800) 269-8768, Fax: (843) 248-5499. Sale of truck rental services. Established: 1990 - No. of Units: Company Owned: 10 - Total Inv: $200 - Financing: Yes.

BUDGET RENT A CAR CORPORATION
4225 Naperville Rd., Lisle, IL, 60532-3662. Contact: Bill Weckstein, Dir. Fran. Dev.- Tel: (630) 955-1900 , Fax: (630) 955-7799. Car and truck rental. Established: 1958 - Franchising Since: 1960 - No. of Units: Company Owned: 558 - Franchised: 2,819 - Franchise Fee: $20,000 minimum (varies by population) - Royalty: 5% service fee, 2.5% franchise maintenance, $1.25 per car credit card fee - Total Inv: Varies by location - Financing: None.

DOLLAR RENT A CAR SYSTEMS, INC.
P.O. Box 33167, Tulsa, OK, 74153. - Tel: (918) 669-8563, (800) 951-4268, Fax: (918) 669-3006. Car and truck rental. Established: 1966 - Franchising Since: 1966 - No. of Units: Company Owned: 12 - Franchised: 500+ - Franchise Fee: $12,500 min. - Royalty: 8% of gross revenues. - Total Inv: Min. $75,000-$2,000,000 - Financing: Fleet leasing offered to qualified licensees.

EAGLERIDER FRANCHISES
EagleRider, Inc.
11860 S. La Cienega, Los Angeles, CA, 90250. - Tel: (310) 320-3456, Fax: (310) 320-6895, E-Mail: franchise@eaglerider.com, Web Site: www.eaglerider.com. Our expertise in the rental industry, connections in the worldwide travel industry, business relationship with Harley-Davidson, comprehensive insurance program, and worldwide brand recognition are just a few reasons why Entrepreneur Magazine ranked EagleRider, Inc. #309 in the Franchise 500 and $19 ranking in the "Top New Franchises" - January 2002. Established: 1992 - Franchising Since: 1999 - No. of Units: Company Owned: 5 - Franchised: 21 - Franchise Fee: $35,000 - Royalty: 10% of gross monthly rental revenue - Total Inv: $216,500-$674,000 - Financing: No.

EE-MART PREMIUM BATTERIES USA
Protec International
1832 Cedar Oak Rd, Placerville, CA, 95667. Contact: Trevor Simpson - Tel: (530) 622-8511, Fax: (530) 622-5945. 5 year battery warranties & reconditioning. Established: 1999 - No. of Units: Company Owned: 1 - Franchised: 4 - Total Inv: $30,000 - Financing: Yes.

PAYLESS CAR RENTAL SYSTEM, INC.
2350 34th St. North, St. Petersburg, FL, 33713. - Tel: (727) 321-6352, (800) 729-5255, Fax: (727) 323-6856, E-Mail: fran@PaylessCarRental. com, Web Site: www.PaylessCarRental.com. As Payless Car Rental System Inc., prepares to celebrate 30 years in the car rental industry, they continue to unveil advances in technology to benefit their franchisees. Established: 1971 - Franchising Since: 1971 - No. of Units: Franchised: 132- Franchise Fee: Varies by territory - Royalty: 5% + 3% adv. - Total Inv: Varies - Financing: Third party.

PRACTICAL RENT-A-CAR SYSTEMS, INC
Practical Rent-A-Car Systems, Inc.
4780 I- 55 N Ste 300, Jackson, MS, 39211. Contact: Marla Riebock, Manager Operations - Tel: (601) 713-4333, (800) 424-7722, Fax: (601) 713-4330, E-Mail: corp@practical-rentacar.com, Web Site: www.practical-rentacar.com. Car and truck rental operations dealing in airport, local, suburban and replacement rentals. Established: 1974 - Franchising Since: 1974 - No. of Units: Franchised: 85 - Franchise Fee: Varies by population of area - Royalty: Fixed by units - Total Inv: $25,000-$500,000 - Financing: Yes.

PRICE KING RENT-A-CAR
Price King Inc.
203 W. Mulberry, Ft. Collins, CO, 80517. Contact: Jerry Marshall, V.P./ Dir. of Marketing - Tel: (970) 490-2000, (800) 985-4647, Fax: (970) 490-1514, Web Site: www.pricekingrent-a-car.com. Rent-a-car designed as an additional profit center for new car and used car dealers. May be operated as a stand alone operation. Established: 1983 - Franchising Since: 1995 - No. of Units: Company Owned: 1 - Franchised: 23 - Franchise Fee: $3,900-$5,900 based on size of territory - Royalty: $20.00 per car/per month - Total Inv: Varies by size - Financing: No.

RACING LIMOS
Racing Limos, Inc
8242 Laurel Lakes Blvd, Naples, FL, 34119. Contact: Bryan Pease - Tel: (866) 746-LIMO (5466), Fax: (239) 304-4442, E-Mail: mail@racinglimos.com, Web Site: www.racinglimos.com. Limousines that look like stock cars! The Racing Limo can be chartered for: Concerts and Sporting Events, Nights Out On The Town, Graduation Parties, Unique Weddings, Trips To Local or Major Speedways, Children's Birthday Parties, Static Displays for Business Promotions and the Ability to Sell Local Sponsorships. Established: 2002 - Franchising Since: 2002 - No. of Units: Company Owned: 2 - Franchised: 5 - Franchise Fee: $7,500-$20,000 - Royalty: 7% - Total Inv: $75,000-$90,000 - Financing: Up to $50,000.

RENT A VETTE
Rent A Vette International
5021 Swenson Street, Las Vegas, NV, 89119. - Tel: (800) 372-1981. Automobile rentals, specializing in corvettes and other fine sports cars. We are unique, in-as-much as Rent A Vette is the only sports car rental franchise that specializes in corvettes. Established: 1981 - Franchising Since: 1992 - No. of Units: Company Owned: 2 - Franchised: 1 - Franchise Fee: $27,500 - Royalty: 3% 1st 12 mos, 5% thereafter - Total Inv: $325,000-$593,500 - Financing: Fran. fee only.

RENT N' DRIVE
2825 N. 48th St, Lincoln, NE, 68504. - Tel: (402) 441-4835, Fax: (402) 441-4836. Rent N' Drive provides an affordable alternative to high-priced new car rentals. Offering more flexible rental terms, increasing your customer base. Established: 1990 - Franchising Since: 1996 - No. of Units: Company Owned: 1 - Franchised: 1 - Franchise Fee: $20,000 - Royalty: 6%, 1% adv. - Total Inv: $95,750-$199,250 - Financing: Indirect.

RENT-A-WRECK OF AMERICA, INC.
Bundy American Corp.
10324 S. Dolfield Rd, Owings Mills, MD, 21117. - Tel: (800) 421-7253, Fax: (410) 581-1566, Web Site: www.rent-a-wreck.com. New and used auto resale, specializing in trucks, vans and cars, both new and used. Established: 1973 - Franchising Since: 1978 - No. of Units: Franchised: 629 - Franchise Fee: $5,000 and up depending on the size of territory - Royalty: $30.00 per car, 7% adv. per month - Total Inv: $25,000 and up - Financing: Up to 75%.

SENSIBLE CAR RENTALS,
Affordable Car Rental Affiliated Car Rental LC
96 Freneau Ave., Suite #2, Matawan, NJ, 07747. Contact: Michael Miller - Tel: (800) 367-5159, (732) 583-8500, Fax: (732) 290-8305, E-Mail: corporate@affiliatedcarrental.com, Web-Site: www.sensible carrental.com, affordablecarrental.com. Program provides training, insurance & ongoing support as the framwork for a perpetual franchise agreement. Established: 1981 - Franchising Since: 1981 - No. of Units: Franchised: 242 - Franchise Fee: Varies $6,000-$10,800 - Royalty: Varies - Total Inv: $46,400-$69,500 - Financing: Yes, third party.

THRIFTY CAR RENTAL
Thrifty Rent-A-Car System, Inc
5310 E 31 Street, Tulsa, OK, 74135. Contact: Vicki Karn, Coordinator - Tel: (918) 669-2219, (800) 532-3401, Fax: (918) 669-2061, E-Mail: franchisesales@thrifty.com, Web Site: www.thrifty.com. Thrifty is a franchised value-oriented car rental, truck rental and parking company that has a significant presence both in the airport and local markets. In the U.S., over 66% of its business is in the airport market, 34% in the local market. Established: 1950 - Franchising Since: 1962 - No. of Units: Company Owned: 3 - Franchised: 575 - Franchise Fee: $17,500 and up - Royalty: 3% admin., 2.5%-5% adv. - Total Inv: Varies - $150,00 min - Financing: Financing packages can be made available to qualified licensees.

U-SAVE AUTO RENTAL
U-Save Auto Rental of America Inc.
4870 1-55 North, Ste. 300, Jackson, MS, 39211. - Tel: (601) 713-4333, (800) 438-2300, Fax: (601) 713-4330, E-Mail: info@usave.net, Web Site: www.usave.net. Franchise for auto rental; rent cars, vans, light duty trucks to neighborhood customers, local businesses, and for replacement vehicles. Established: 1979 - Franchising Since: 1979 - No. of Units: Franchised: 500 - Franchise Fee: $20,000 - Royalty: $19-$29 per unit per month - Total Inv: Varies - Financing: Varies.

WHEELCHAIR GETAWAYS
Wheelchair Getaways, Inc.
P.O. Box 605,Versailles, KY, 40383. Contact: Richard Gatewood, President - Tel: (800) 536-5518, Fax: (859) 873-8039, E-Mail: corporate@wheelchairgetaways.com, Web Site: www.wheelchairget aways.com. Wheelchair/scooter accessible full size and mini van rentals available by the day, week, month or longer. Delivery and pickup are available. Established: 1988 - Franchising Since: 1989 - No. of Units: Owned: 1 - Franchised: 45 - Franchise Fee: $17,500 - Royalty: $550 year per vehicle year - Total Inv: $40,000-$108,000 - Financing: None.

AUTOMOTIVE: LUBRICATION & TUNEUP

ALL TUNE AND LUBE
ATL International, Inc.
8334 Veteran's Hwy., Millersville, MD, 21108. - Tel: (410) 987-1011, (800) 935-8863, Fax: (410) 987-9080, Web Site: www.alltuneand lube.com. One stop total car care, tune-ups, brakes, exhaust, and engine replacement. Established: 1985 - Franchising Since: 1986 - No. of Units: Franchised: 358 - Franchise Fee: $25,000 - Royalty: 7% - Total Inv: $124,900 - Financing: Yes.

AUTO-LAB DIAGNOSTIC & TUNE-UP CENTERS
Auto Lab Franchise Mgt. Corp.
1050 Columbia Ave W, Battle Creek, MI, 49015-3034. Contact: Daniel J. Kiefer, Pres. - Tel: (616) 966-0500, Fax: (616) 966-0520. Engine performance, electrical systems diagnostics and repair as well as general auto service. Established; 1983 - Franchising Since: 1989 - No. of Units:

Company Owned: 1 - Franchised: 20 - Franchise Fee: $19,500 - Royalty: 6%, 3% adv. - Total Inv: $45,000 operating, $75,000 equip. plus real estate - Financing: In-house and placement for outside.

EXPRESS OIL CHANGE
Express Oil Change, LLC
190 West Valley Ave., Birmingham, AL, 35209. Contact: R. Kent Feazell, V.P. Development - Tel: (205) 945-1771, (888) 945-1771, Fax: (205) 940-6025, E-Mail: kfeazell@expressoil.com, Web Site: www.expressoil.com. Fast oil change and minor automatic repair including transmission services, brakes, A/C amd other. Established: 1979 - Franchising Since: 1979 - No. of Units: Company Owned: 25 - Franchised: 124 - Franchise Fee: $27,500 - Royalty: 5% - Total Inv: $124,500-$200,000.

GREASE MONKEY
Grease Monkey International, Inc.
633 17th Street, Ste. 400, Denver, CO, 80202-5125. Contact: Michael Brunetti, V.P., Fran. Dev. - Tel: (303) 308-1660, (800) 364-0352, Fax: (303) 308-5908, Web Site: www.greasemonkeyintl.com. Grease Monkey is one of the largest vehicle preventive maintenance organizations not owned by a major oil company. It ranks fourth in size among all fast lube franchises. Grease Monkey provides a full range of automotive preventive maintenance services. Established: 1979 - Franchising Since: 1979 - No. of Units: Company Owned: 34 - Franchised: 160 - Franchise Fee: $28,000 - Royalty: 5% - Total Inv: Approx. $120,000-$220,000 for a single center - Financing: Third Party.

GUARANTEED TUNE UP
Guaranteed Tune Up, Inc.
6-L Dorado Drive, Morristown, NJ, 07960. Contact: William Okita, Pres. - Tel: (800) 543-5829. Although we specialize in automotive tune-ups, we also allow our franchisees to perform all automotive repairs, such as brakes, engine repairs, etc., thereby increasing sales volume and cash flow. Established: 1984 - Franchising Since: 1990 - No. of Units: Franchised: 6 - Franchise Fee: $15,000 - Royalty: 6% - Total Inv: $96,000 - Financing: Yes, thru third party.

INDY LUBE EXPRESS
Indy Lube
6515 E. 82nd St., Ste. 209, Indianapolis, IN, 46250. Contact: Jim Yates, Pres. - Tel: (317) 845-9444, Fax: (317) 577-3169. Upscale, modular, oil change center. Established: 1985 - Franchising Since: 1995 - No. of Units: Company Owned: 24- Franchised: 7 - Franchise Fee: $7,500 - Royalty: 4%, 3% adv. - Total Inv: $150,000.

JIFFY LUBE
Jiffy Lube International, Inc.
P.O. Box 2967, Houston, TX, 77252-2967. - Tel: (713) 546-4100, (800) 327-9532, Fax: (713) 546-8762. Largest quick lube system offering a preventative maintenance program for motor vehicles which includes oil changes, filter replacement, checking all fluid levels, that requires no appointment and can be completed in just minutes. Management background desired, retail experience preferred, geographical flexibility required. Established: 1990 - Franchising Since: 1990 - No. of Units: Company Owned: 589- Franchised: 660 - Franchise Fee: $35,000 - Royalty: 5% monthly gross first 3 yrs., 6% thereafter - Total Inv: $173,000-$194,000.

KING BEAR AUTO SERVICE CENTERS
King Bear Auto Service Centers, Inc
130-29 Merrick Blvd, Springfield Gardens, NY, 11434. - Tel: (718) 527-1252, (800) 311-5464, Fax: (718) 527-4985. Full service auto repair centers and used car sales facilities. King Bear handles virtually all types of auto services from state inspections (where applicable) oil change, tune up, under carriage (shocks, struts, brakes) diagnostic services and tire sales. Established: 1997 - Franchising Since: 1997 - No. of Units: Franchised: 34 - Franchise Fee: $29,500 - Royalty: 5% - Total Inv: $161,500-$275,600 - Financing: Various financing programs available.

LOCATIONLUBE INC
P.O. Box 700, E.Sandwich, MA, 02537. - Tel: (508) 888-5000, Fax: (508) 790-4700. Mobile oil change, vans and trailer. Turnkey business opportunity. Established: 1987 - Franchising Since: 1990 - No. of Units: Company Owned: 1 - Franchised: 225 - Franchise Fee: $1,000-$5,000 - Total Inv: $8,500-$34,000 - Financing: Yes with $2,000 down.

LUBE DEPOT
Precision Auto Care Inc.
1237 W. 4th St., OH, 44906. Contact: Gary Rambler, Nat'l. Fran. Dir. - Tel: (419) 529-5669, (800) 438-8863. A revolutionary modular single and 2 bay turnkey oil change re-locatable building. Lube Depot assists in financing and site selection. Provides training to franchise managers and employees, advertising and ongoing support. Lube Depot is ranked 28th in the 65 largest oil change companies. Established: 1995 - Franchising Since: 1995 - No. of Units: Company Owned: 1 - Franchised: 26 - Franchise Fee: $10,000 - Royalty: 5% - Total Inv: $128,700-$167,430 - Financing: Assistance.

LUBEPRO'S 10-MINUTE OIL CHANGE
LubePro's International, Inc.
1630 Colonial Pky., Inverness, IL, 60067. Contact: Franchise Director - Tel: (847) 776-2500, (800) 654-LUBE, Fax: (847) 776-2542. LubePro's has provided a complete 10-minute oil change and exclusive 21-point maintenance and safety program for over 25 years. Established: 1978 - Franchising Since: 1978 - No. of Units: Company Owned: 15 - Franchised: 24 - Franchise Fee: $25,000 - Royalty: 5% of sales - Total Inv: $220,000 initial investment, not including Land & Building - Financing: No.

MULTI-TUNE & TIRE
Multi Management Systems, Inc.
2457 Covington Pike, Memphis, TN, 38128. Contact: Glen Whiteman, Pres. - Tel: (901) 386-9600, Fax: (901) 386-9665. Auto tuneup and auto repair and tire sales. Established: 1986 - Franchising Since: 1986 - No. of Units: Company Owned: 3 - Franchise Fee: $17,500 - Royalty: 3% - Total Inv: $123,800-$168,000 - Financing: No.

OIL BUTLER
Oil Butler International, Corp.
1599 Rt. 22 West, Union, NJ, 07083. Contact: Pete Rosin - Tel: (908) 687-3283, Fax: (908) 687-7617, Web Site: www.oilbutler international.com. Mobile Oil Change & windshield repair service. High-Tech equipment, complete training & exclusive territory. Established: 1987 - Franchising Since: 1991 - No. of Units: Company Owned: 1 - Franchised: 153 - Franchise Fee: $6,000-$10,000 - Royalty: Yes - Financing: No.

OIL CAN HENRY'S QUICK LUBE CENTER
OCH International, Inc.
1200 N.W. Naito Parkway., Ste. 690, Portland, OR, 97209. - Tel: (503) 243-6311, (800) 765-6244, Fax: (503) 228-5227. Our famous 20 point full service oil-change for automobiles, vans, light trucks and motor homes, plus our famous Top-Up Guarantee. Established: 1972 - Franchising Since: 1988 - No. of Units: Company Owned: 1 - Franchised: 39 - Franchise Fee: $35,000 - Royalty: 5.5% - Total Inv: Business: $146,000-$182,900, w/land: $400,000-$650,000.

OILSTOP DRIVE-THRU OIL CHANGE
Oilstop, Inc/Ps1, Inc
6111 Redwood Dr., Rohnert Park, CA, 94928. Contact: Gary Woo - Tel: (707) 586-2047, Fax: (707) 586-2296, E-Mail: franchising@ oilstopinc.com, Web Site: www.oilstopinc.com. Convenient, attractively-designed, drive-through oil change centers that stress competency, courtesy, integrity, and service - the way it used to be. Oilstop realizes that its main product is not a lube, oil & filter service - it is guest relations. Oilstop's mission is to serve people with excellence, humbly, with a servant's heart. Established: 1978 - Franchising Since: 1999 - No. of Units: Company Owned: 12 - Franchised: 14 - Franchise Fee: $24,000-$35,000 - Royalty: 5% - Financing: No.

PRECISION AUTO CARE, INC.
748 Miller Drive S.E., Suite G-1, Leesburg, VA, 20175. - Tel: (703) 777-9095, (800) 438-8863, Fax: (703) 669-1539, E-Mail: franchising@precisionac.com, Web Site: www.precisionac.com. Precision Auto Care, Inc is the first and only nationally-recognized chain to combine automotive services (Precision Tune Auto Care) with car washes (Precision Auto Wash) and quick lubes (Precision Lube Express). Established: 1976 - Franchising Since: 1978 - No. of Units: Company Owned: 30 - Franchised: 479, 127 international - Franchise Fee: $12,500-$25,000 - Royalty: Varies depending on brand purchased - Total Inv: Varies depending on brand purchased - Financing: Yes.

PRECISION LUBE EXPRESS
Precision Auto Care
748 Miller Drive S.E., Leesburg, VA, 20175. Contact: Lisa Anderson, Sales & Marketing - Tel: (703) 777-9095 (x251), (800) 438-8863, Fax: (703) 779-0136, E-Mail: LISA.ANDERSON@PRECISIONAC.COM. Provides an oil change service that moves the customer through the process quickly, safely, conveniently and without hassle. Established: 1997 - Franchising Since: 1997 - No. of Units: Company Owned: 7 - Franchised: 9 - Franchise Fee: $12,500 - Royalty: 5% - Total Inv: Start-up costs (excluding franchise fee) $131,500-$253,450 - Financing: Yes.

Q LUBE
Q Lube, Inc., A Quaker State Company
1385 West 2200 South, Salt Lake City, UT, 84119. - Tel: (801) 975-4731. Oil change, lubrication and fluid maintenance. Established: 1977 - Franchising Since: 1978 - No. of Units: Company Owned: 386 - Franchised: 121 - Franchise Fee: $25,000 - Royalty: 4.5%, 6% adv. - Total Inv: $150,000-$450,000 - Financing: Yes.

SPEEDEE OIL CHANGE & TUNE-UP
P.O. Box 1350, Madisonville, LA, 70447. Contact: Kevin Bennett, Dir. of Fran. Dev. - Tel: (504) 845-1919, (800) 451-7461, Fax: (504) 845-1936. SpeeDee Oil Change and Tune-Up centers provide a full range of preventive and corrective maintenance services which includes oil and fluid change services, tune-up and engine maintenance services and complete brake services. Established: 1980 - Franchising Since: 1982 - No. of Units: Company Owned: 6 - Franchised: 138 - Franchise Fee: $30,000 - Royalty: 6%, 8% adv. - Total Inv: $186,000-$767,500 - Financing: No.

SPEEDY LUBE / QUIK MARTS
Southeast Companies
P.O. Box 1385, Waukesha, WI, 53187. Contact: John Theisen -Tel: (414) 524-7951, Fax: (414) 524-7950. 10 minute oil changes. Established: 1975 - Franchising Since: 1978 - No. of Units: Company Owned: 20 - Franchised: 14 - Franchise Fee: $20,000 - Royalty: 6%, 2% adv. - Total Inv: $125,000 land, $150,000 bldg., $25,000 equip. or leasing of entire facilities also available - Financing: Yes.

STAR LUBE
Texaco Refining & Marketing Inc.
1111 Bagby St., Houston, TX, 77002. Contact: Ken Barber, Mgr. Franchising - Tel: (713) 752-6706. Quick oil change (14 pt. service) drive thru - stay in your car - add on profit center to a Texaco gasoline location. Established: 1990 - Franchising Since: 1994 - No. of Units: Company Owned: 19 - Franchised: 14 - Franchise Fee: $10,000 - Royalty: 0 - Franchisee must purchase Texaco products - Total Inv: Building $100,000-$120,000, Equip. $20,000-$30,000 (Facility must be built on Texaco Gasoline site) - Financing: Yes, 80% 12 yr. amort.

TUNEX AUTOMOTIVE/DIAGNOSTIC SPECIALISTS
Tunex International, Inc.
556 E. 2100 South, Salt Lake City, UT, 84106. - Tel: (801) 486-8133, (800) 448-8639, Fax: (801) 484-4740, Web Site: www.tunex.com. Diagnostic services and repairs of engine related systems (i.e., ignition, carburetion, fuel injection, emission, computer controls, cooling, air conditioning). For maximum customer satisfaction, we analyze all systems for problems so that customers can make service and repair decisions. Established: 1974 - Franchising Since: 1975 - No. of Units: Company Owned: 3 - Franchised: 20 - Franchise Fee: $19,000 - Royalty: 5%, $750/mth. adv.- Total Inv: $65,000 cash $105,000-$120,000 - Financing: No.

VALVOLINE INSTANT OIL CHANGE
Valvoline Instant Oil Change
P.O. Box 14046, Lexington, KY, 40512. Contact: Josie Taylor - Tel: (800) 622-6846, Fax: (859) 357-7049, E-Mail: jjtaylor@ashland.com, Web Site: www.viocfranchise.com. VIOC operates 700 locations worldwide. The company is one of the nation's largest providers of "do-it-for-me" automotive fluid maintenance services. Each service center offers a complete selection of oil changes, preventive maintenance checks, free fluid top-offs and other services and products, presented in an environment with the highest emphasis on customer service. Established: 1986 - Franchising Since: 1989 - No. of Units: Company Owned: 360 - Franchised: 340 - Franchise Fee: $30,000 - Royalty: 6% - Total Inv: $650,000-$900,000 - Financing: Yes.

VICTORY LANE QUICK OIL CHANGE

405 Little Lake Drive, Ann Arbor, MI, 48103, Contact: Steve McCoy, Dir. of Franchise Sales - Tel: (734) 996-1196, Fax: (734) 996-4912, Web Site: www.victorylaneqoc.com. Ten minute quick oil change utilizing state of the art technology with an emphasis on speed, efficiency and customer participation. No previous experience or mechanical skill is necessary. Established: 1980 - Franchising Since: 1987 - No. of Units: Company Owned: 9 - Franchised: 40 - Franchise Fee: $20,000 - Royalty: 6% weekly gross sales - Total Inv: $60,000-$80,000 with leasing of equip. available - Financing: Franchisee to arrange own financing. Equipment leasing available. We will assist franchisee in arranging financing.

AUTOMOTIVE: MUFFLER SHOPS

LEAVERTON AUTO

827 So. 9th, St. Joseph, MO, 64501. Contact: Ronald J. Martin, Pres. - Tel: (816) 279-7483, Fax: (816) 279-8840. Automobile mufflers, brakes, shocks, alignment, quick lube. Franchising Since: 1992 - No. of Units: Company Owned: 2 - Franchise Fee: $25,000 - Royalty: 5% - Total Inv: $133,500-$203,000 includes fee.

MEINEKE DISCOUNT MUFFLER SHOPS

Meineke Discount Muffler Shops, Inc.
128 S. Tryon St., Ste. 900, Charlotte, NC, 28202. Contact: Administrative Assistant - Tel: (866) 957-2644, (800) 634-6353, Fax: (704) 372-4826, Web Site: www.meineke.com. Meineke Discount Muffler Shops offer fast, courteous service in the merchandising of automotive exhaust systems, shock absorbers, struts and brakes. Unique inventory control and group purchasing power enable Meineke dealers to adhere to a Discount Concept and deliver quality service. Established: 1972 - Franchising Since: 1972 - No. of Units: Company Owned: 1 - Franchised: 899 - Franchise Fee: $25,000 - Royalty: 7% + 10% adv. - Total Inv: $150,000 - Financing: Third party financing available to qualified individuals.

MIDAS

Midas International Corp.
1300 Ellington Heights Rd, Itasco, IL, 60143. - Tel: (800) 365-0007, (630) 438-3000, Fax: (630) 438-3700, Web Site: www.midasfran.com. Automotive aftermarket specialists in mufflers, shocks, struts, brakes and front end. Established: 1956 - Franchising Since: 1956 - No. of Units: Company Owned: 140 US; 238 Foreign - Franchised: 1,744 US; 382 Foreign - Franchise Fee: $20,000 - Royalty: 5%+5% adv. - Total Inv: $254,050-$357,500 - Financing: Third party.

USA MUFFLER AND BRAKES

USA Automotive Systems Inc.
4410 W 37th Ave Bldg F, Hobart, IN, 46342. Contact: James Petsas, V.P., Fran. Dev. - Tel: (219) 963-4129, Fax: (219) 963-7334, 1-800-ASK 4 USA. A business system that will operate as a retail automotive service center specializing in the sale, replacement and installation of motor vehicle exhaust systems, mufflers, brakes, shock absorbers, suspension including front end, emphasizing fast, friendly and convenient service 6 days a week, 9 hours a day. Established: 1987 - Franchising Since: 1989 - No. of Units: Company Owned: 8 - Franchised: 7 - Franchise Fee: $15,000 - Royalty: 5%, 6% adv., 1% warranty fund - Total Inv: $53,600-$596,250 - Financing: Assistance with loan package preparation for banks & SBA.

WEAR MASTER MUFFLER AND BRAKE CENTERS

Wear Master Company
235 Oakview Dr., Lapeer, MI, 48446. Contact: Brian E. Bedwell, Owner - Tel: (810) 664-4365, Fax: (810) 664-0694. Outlets specializing in the service of automobiles and light trucks for exhaust systems, brakes, shock absorbers and suspension systems in a clean, customer-oriented environment on a while-you-wait basis. (Wear Master® is a federally registered trademark). Established: 1972 - Franchising Since: 1992 - No. of Units: Company Owned: 4 - Franchised: 12 - Start Costs: $10,000 incl. security deposits, training, etc. - Royalty: 5% royalty/$1,100 a month adv. budget - Total Inv: $80,000-$150,000 incl. work. cap., inven., signage, start up exp.'s, equip., etc. - Financing: Not directly, except for a few locations company owned.

AUTOMOTIVE: PRODUCTS AND SERVICES

A. T. L. MOTOR MATE

ATL International
8334 Veterans Highway, Millersville, MD, 21108. Contact: Franchise Department - Tel: (410) 987-1011, (800) 935-8863, Fax: (410) 987-9080. Specializing in the installation of high quality remanufactured engines. Established: 1985 - Franchising Since: 1985 - No. of Units: Franchised: 150 - Franchise Fee: $25,000 - Royalty: 6% - Total Inv: $100,000 (inlcudes franchise fee) - Financing: Yes.

ABRA AUTO BODY & GLASS

6601 Shingle Creek Pkwy., Ste. 200, Brooklyn Center, MN, 55430. - Tel: (888) 872-2272. One of the finest automotive collision and glass franchises. Operating company and franchised auto body collision and autoglass replacement shops. Support with marketing, business management, equipment and material purchases. Investment opportunities for quality owners and managers. Established: 1984 - Franchising Since: 1987 - No. of Units: Company Owned: 18 - Franchised: 35 - Franchise Fee: $22,500 - Royalty: 5% of sales - Total Inv: $229,000-$287,500 (assuming building is leased) - Financing: None.

AERO-COLOURS

Aero-Colours, Inc.
10824 Nesbitt Ave., South, Bloomington, MN, 55437. Contact: Fran. Dev. - Tel: (800) 696-2376, Fax: (952) 942-0628. Aero-Colours® is a mobile air brush touch-up process serving the automotive industry. Vans are fully equipped mobile mixing labs that can custom match colors on-site. Established: 1985 - Franchising Since: 1993 - No. of Units: Company Owned: 10 - Franchised: 52 - Franchise Fee: $25,000 - Royalty: 7%-4% based on sales - Total Inv: $55,000.

AFTERMARKET APPEARANCE INDUSTRIES

Aftermarket Appearance Industries Inc.
P.O. Box 2124, Kenner, LA, 70063. Contact: Dir. of Franchise Relations - Tel: (504) 455-8025, (800) 678-5220, Fax: (504) 455-8025, E-Mail: altra@home.com, Web Site: www.altracolor.com. Mobile automotive paint touch-up and spot repair. Established: 1988 - Franchising Since: 1991 - No. of Units: Franchised: 82 - Franchise Fee: $9,950 - Royalty: $95 per week fixed - Total Inv: $25,200-$13,500 equip pkg; $9,950 franchise fee; $1,750 training - Financing: $13,500 equip. pkg is financiable O.A.L.

AIRBAG SERVICE

Airbag Technology International L.L.C.
9675 SE 36th Street., Suite 100, Mercer Island, WA, 98040. - Tel: (800) 224-7224, Fax: (206) 275-4112. Mobile automotive repair servicing airbags and airbag systems. Growing market and high tech support system. Established: 1992 - Franchising Since: 1995 - No. of Units: Company Owned: 1 - Franchised: 36 - Franchise Fee: $25,000 - Royalty: 8.5% of gross profit, 2% gross profit/adv. = 10.5% gross profit - Total Inv: $25,000 fran. fee - $40,000-$75,000 capital, equipment.

ALL NIGHT AUTO

Midnight Auto, Inc
3872 Rochester Rd, Troy, MI, 48083. Contact: Dennis Spencer, Vice President - Tel: (248) 619-9020, Fax: (248) 619-0596, Web Site: www.allnightautofranchise.com. Full service automotive repair. Open seven days, Monday-Thursday open 7am-midnight. Established: 1994 - Franchising Since: 1999 - No. of Units: Company Owned: 1 - Franchised: 1 - Franchise Fee: $25,000 - Royalty: 6%; 1.5% advertising - Total Inv: $80,000 minimum liquid - Financing: Variable.

ALL TUNE TRANSMISSION

ATL International, Inc.
8334 Veterans Highway, Millersville, MD, 21108. Contact: Franchise Development - Tel: (410) 987-1011, (800) 935-8863, Fax: (410) 987-9080. Specializing in transmission rebuilding and repair. Established: 1985 - Franchising Since: 1985 - No. of Units: Franchised: 100 - Franchise Fee: $25,000 - Royalty: 7% - Total Inv: $100,000 - Financing: Yes.

ALTA MERE WINDOW TINTING AND AUTO ALARMS
Alta Mere Industries, Inc
4444 W. 147th St., Midlothean, IL, 60445. - Tel: (800) 377-9247, Fax: (708) 389-9882, Web Site: www.altamere.com. Auto imaging specialists specializing in window tinting, auto alarms, car stereos, and after market accesories. Established: 1986 - Franchising Since: 1993 - No. of Units: Franchised: 34 - Franchise Fee: $27,500 - Royalty: 7% - Total Inv: $90,000 - Financing: Yes, third party.

APPEARANCE RECONDITIONING CO. INC.
P.O. Box 47127, Plymouth, MN, 55447-0127. Contact: D. Almen, Pres. - Tel: (800) 255-8537, Fax: (801)295-8214. Services to used car market - reconditioning interiors and vinyls, plastics, cloths and leathers. Established: 1977 - No. of Units: Franchised: 125 - Total Inv: $17,000 - Financing: Initial - no, additional units, yes.

ARMA COATINGS
Arma Quest
P.O. Box 21908, Eugene, OR, 97402. Contact: D. Pratt / C. Frkovich - Tel: (541) 688-3500, (800) 524-2762, Fax: (541) 688-0519. Spray-on bedliners and industrial coatings. Established: 1988 - Franchising Since: 1990 - No. of Units: Company Owned: 3 - Franchised: 100 - Total Inv: $45,000.

AT HOME TIRE SALES
At Home Tire Sales, Inc
3030 Segovia St, Coral Gables, FL, 33134. - Tel: (305) 635-1748. Mobile tire sales and installation selling all brands of tires. Established: 1989 - Franchising Since: 1992 - No. of Units: Company Owned: 1- Franchised: 3 - Franchise Fee: $45,000 plus equipment - Total Inv: $75,000 - Financing: No.

AUTO ONE
15965 Jeanette St., Southfield, MI, 48075. - Tel: (810) 227-2808. Auto appearance accessories including satellite radar tracking devices, cellular phones, specialize security systems and glass replacement. Established: 1984 - Franchising Since: 1988 - No. of Units: Franchised: 80 - Franchise Fee: $24,000 - Royalty: 5% w/cap - Total Inv: $70,000-$90,000 - Financing: Yes.

AUTO ONE GLASS & ACCESSORIES
Nu P.A.G.E. Inc.
2301 E. Michigan Ave., Ste. 203, Jackson, MI, 49202. Contact: Hank Weber, President - Tel: (517) 783-6442, (800) 922-8861, Fax: (517) 783-6782, E-Mail: autooneinc@aol.com, Web Site: www.autoone inc.com. Auto aftermarket franchise business specializing in windshield and auto glass replacement, auto alarms, cellular phones and pagers, detailing, appearance and protection and auto accessories including sunroofs. Established: 1984 - Franchising Since: 1984 - No. of Units: Company Owned: 1 - Franchised: 29 - Franchise Fee: $24,000 - Royalty: 5% of sales with cap. - Total Inv: $70,000-$94,000 - Financing: No.

AUTO PURCHASE CONSULTING
APC Franchise Development
9841 Airport Blvd., Ste. 1517, Los Angeles, CA, 90045. Contact: David Breslow, President - Tel: (888) 4321-CAR. A professional new car and truck buying, financing, leasing and consulting service for all 41 makes / 900 models featuring guaranteed lowest prices and interest rates. A low cost start-up, low over head and no inventory franchise. Free brochure. Established: 1984 - Franchising Since: 1997 - No. of Units: Company Owned: 1 - Franchised: 2 - Franchise Fee: $15,000 - Royalty: Greater of 8% of total income or $600 per month - Total Inv: $15,000 franchise fee, $22,000 equipment, $20,000 minimum working capital = $57,000 total - Financing: No. NOT FRANCHISING AT THIS TIME.

AUTOLIST CAR STORE INC.
Autolist Corporation
P.O. Box 1416, Gulf Breeze, FL, 32562-1416. Contact: Jimmy Griffin, CEO - Tel: (850) 934-7222, (800) 887-5478, Fax: (850) 934-7523. A used car sales and brokerage dealership franchise opportunity that specializes in selling and locating quality private owner vehicles. Each franchise also offers financing, warranties, and trade-ins. Established: 1988 - Franchising Since: 1988 - No. of Units: Franchised: 15 - Franchise Fee: $6,500 - Royalty: $350 flat - Total Inv: $100,000-$50,000 cash inv. - Financing: Yes.

AUTOPLUS™ WINDOW STICKERS
Tanner Communications
12750 Yacht Club Cir., Ft. Myers, FL, 33919. Contact: Larry Tanner - Tel: (239) 466-7641, (800) 825-4838, Fax: (239) 336-9561, Web Site: www.autoplusnet.com. The AutoPlus system produces new-car type window stickers for used car departments and independent dealers. Established: 1991 - No. of Units: 1 - Franchised: 150 - Franchise Fee: $495. - Total Inv: $495. min., distributorships from $3,495.

AX RACKS
Ax Rax Franchising, Inc.
2285 Austell Rd., Marietta, GA, 30008. Contact: Harvey Nix, Pres. - Tel: (770) 434-2277. Installation of CV axles, and rack and pinion steering units on automobiles. Established: 1996 - Franchising Since: 1996 - No. of Units: Company Owned: 1 - Franchise Fee: $25,000 - Royalty: $250 weekly - Total Inv: $60,000-$160,000 - Financing: Yes.

BIG BOYZ TOYS
13180 N. Cleveland Ave., #125, N. Fort Myers, FL, 33903. - Tel: (800) 347-9482, Fax: (941) 540-9770, Web Site: www.autotoysonline.com. Auto accessories/window tinting, graphics and alarms. Established: 1990 - Franchising Since: 1999 - No. of Units: Franchised: 21 - Franchise Fee: $17,000 - Royalty: 5% - Total Inv: $60,000.

BIG O TIRES
Big O Tires, Inc.
12650 E. Briarwood Ave., #2-D, Englewood, CO, 80112-6734 - Tel: (800) 622-2446, (303) 728-5500, Fax: (303) 728-5689. Fast growing franchisor of independent retail tire and under-car service centers in North America. Over 30 years of proven success, site selection assistance, comprehensive training, protected territory, on-going field support, and much more. Established: 1962 - Franchising Since: 1962 - No. of Units: Company Owned: 10 - Franchised: 445 - Franchise Fee: $25,000 - Royalty: 2% gross sales - Total Inv: $300,000 net worth, $100,000 cash - Financing: Equip. leasing.

BOOMER MCLOUD
In Stereo LLC
14 Industrial Park Pl., Middletown, CT, 06457. - Tel: (860) 632-4874, Fax: (860) 634-4877. Retail sales and installation of quality automotive audio equipment. Established: 1996 - Franchising Since: 1996 - No. of Units: Company Owned: 1 - Franchised: 32 - Franchise Fee: $7,500-$25,000 - Royalty: 5% of gross receipts subject to warehouse purchase credits - Total Inv: $36,000-$234,300 - Financing: Yes. NOT OFFERING FRANCHISES AT THIS TIME.

BRAKE CENTERS OF AMERICA
35 Old Battery Road, Bridgeport, CT, 06605. - Tel: (203) 336-1995, Fax: (203) 336-1995. Low cost, easy to run automotive brake specialty shop. Brake Centers of America offers it's customers a better job at about 1/2 the price of it's competitors. Established: 1989 - Franchising Since: 1995 - No. of Units: Company Owned: 8 - Franchise Fee: $12,000 - Royalty: 6% - Total Inv: $65,300 - Financing: None.

BRAKE MASTERS
Brake Masters Systems, Inc.
6179 E Broadway, Tucson, AZ, 85711. Contact: Dir. Fran. Dev. - Tel: (520) 512-0000, Fax: (520) 512-1000, Web Site: www.brakemasters.com. Brake and lubrication shops. Established: 1982 - Franchising Since: 1994 - No. of Units: Company Owned: 12 - Franchised: 18 - Franchise Fee: 17,500 - Royalty: 5% - Financing: Yes.

BRAKE SHOP, THE
P.O. Box 510, Fraser, MI, 48026-0510 - Tel: (800) 747-2113, (810) 415-2800. Automotive brake repair specialists. Established: 1987 - Franchising Since: 1989 - No. of Units: Company Owned: 16 - Franchised: 84 - Franchise Fee: $20,000 - Royalty: 8% - Total Inv: $48,000-$95,000 depends on location - Financing: Available to qualified candidates.

BULLHIDE LINER CORPORATION
2102 9th St, Greely, CO, 80631. - Tel: (970) 351-8603, Fax: (970) 351-8604. Bullhide Liner, as an add-on or stand-alone business, can be your entry into the fast growing truck/auto accessory market. Bullhide is spray-molded directly to the prepared pickup truckbed, forming a rubber-like, nonskid, liner. It protects truckbeds from damage due to rust, abrasion and chemical attack. Established: 1993 - Franchising

Since: 1994 - No. of Units: Company Owned: 1 - Franchised: 11 - Franchise Fee: None - Royalty: None - Total Inv: $60,000 incl. equip. - Financing: Yes.

BUMPER DOCTOR, THE
15560 N Frank Lloyd Wright Blvd #84 PMB 272, Scottsdale, AZ, 85260-2020. Contact: Scott Koblenz, CEO - Tel: (480) 314-1349, (800) 841-4425. Plastic auto bumper recycling and repair for body shops. A to-the-trade business with exceptionally low overhead and high profit margins. Established: 1987 - Franchising Since: 1994 - No. of Units: Company Owned: 1 - Franchised: 62 - Franchise Fee: $4,750 - Total Inv: $7,500 - Financing: No.

CAR TALKER, THE
Directcast Network Distribution, LLC
2820 Jefferson Ave, Midland, MI, 48640. Contact: Richard Zimmer - Tel: (877) 682-5537, Fax: (517) 837-3597. Sales and service of ads on cars and trucks. Established: 1998 - Franchising Since: 2000 - No. of Units: Company Owned: 2 - Franchised: 15 - Franchise Fee: $10,000 - Total Inv: $75,000-$100,000 - Financing: No. NOT FRANCHISING AT THIS TIME.

CAR WASH GUYS
5699 Kanan Rd., #130, Agoura Hills, CA, 91301. Contact: Lance Winslow - Tel: (888) WASH-GUY, Fax: (888) WASH-GAL, E-Mail: Lance@carwashguys.com, Web Site: www.carwashguys.com. Mobile car wash. Established: 1979 - Franchising Since: 1997 - No. of Units: Company Owned: 17 - Franchised: 90 - Franchise Fee: $20,000 - Royalty: $35 daily truck #1, $20 daily each additional truck - Total Inv: $55,000-$75,000 - Financing: Yes; $8,000 down finance the rest.

CAREFREE COATINGS BUSINESS OPPORTUNITES, L.L.C.
9620 Willow Lane, Mokena, IL, 60448. Contact: Director of Franchising - Tel: (888) 311-COAT, Fax: (708) 478-1575, Web Site: www.carefree coatings.com. Spray on bed-liners. Established: 1997 - Franchising Since: 1997 - No. of Units: Company Owned: 1 - Franchised: 2 - Franchise Fee: $15,000 - Royalty: 7.5% to franchisor, 1% nat'l adv. fund - Total Inv: $50,000 equipment + inventory - Financing: No.

CARSTAR AUTOMOTIVE, INC.
Carstar Franchise Systems, Inc
8400 W. 110th St., Ste. 200, Overland Park, KS, 66210. Contact: Development Manager - Tel: (800) 999-1949, Web Site: www.carstar.com. Collision repair specialist comprised of franchises and company-owned locations. Established: 1989 - Franchising Since: 1989 - No. of Units: Company Owned: 9 - Franchised: 188 in US/59 in Canada - Franchise Fee: Varies - Royalty: Percentage of gross revenue - Total Inv: Initial fee plus percentage of gross revenue - Financing: No.

CARTEX LIMITED - FABRION ® SYSTEM/CRIS-MAR ™ SYSTEM
Cartex Limited
42816 Mound Rd, Sterling Heights, MI, 48314. Contact: Lawrence Klukowski, President, CEO - Tel: (800) 421-7328, (586) 739-4330, Fax: (586) 739-4331, E-Mail: franchises@fabrion.net, Web Site: www.fabrion.net. Mobile service busines. Professional state of the art products exclusive to Fabrion and Cris-mar. We will train franchisee to repair fabric, vinyl, leather and plastic on late model vehicles. Training includes all equipment and materials necessary. Also provided is opening accounts in the field and on going support through corporate office. Established: 1988 - Franchising Since: 1988 - No. of Units: Franchised: 91 - Franchise Fee: $23,500 - Royalty: 7% of sales - Total Inv: $30,000 - Financing: Yes.

CAR-X AUTO SERVICE
CAR-X SERVICE SYSTEMS, INC.
8750 W. Bryn Mawr, Ste. 410, Chicago, IL, 60631. - Tel: (800) 359-2359, Web Site: www.carx.com. Retail automotive service centers that specialize in brakes, exhaust, road handling, steering systems, air conditioning and oil changes for all makes of cars and light trucks. Established: 1971 - Franchising Since: 1973 - No. of Units: Company Owned: 53 - Franchised: 132- Franchise Fee: $20,000 - Royalty: 5% of gross sales - Total Inv: $250,000-$310,000 for a 6- bay shop - Financing: Third party.

CASHMAX AUTO TITLE PAWN OF AMERICA INC.
2038 Watson Blvd., Warner Robins, GA, 31093. - Tel: (912) 923-0930, (800) 945-8789. Make small secured loans for short terms using automobile titles as collateral. Established: 1990 - Franchising Since: 1996 - No. of Units: Franchised: 1 - Franchise Fee: $25,000 - Royalty: 6% of total revenue plus 2% of total revenue for advertising - Total Inv: Cash $30,000, franchise fee $25,000 - Financing: No. Not offering franchises at this time.

CHIPSAWAY, INC
1536 Saw Mill Run Blvd., Pittsburgh, PA, 15210. Contact: Thomas Pikur - Tel: (800) 837-2447, Fax: (412) 885-3568, E-Mail: info@chipsaway.com, Web Site: www.chipsaway.com. Chipsaway provides everything required to enable anyone to earn $160 an hour by operating an in-house or mobile auto paint restoration business repairing stone chips, key scratches, and bumper scuffs. Established: 1988 - No. of Units: Company Owned: 1 - Franchised: 800 - Franchise Fee: $7,000 - Total Inv: $7,000-$14,000 - Financing: Third party financing and leasing.

CLUTCH DOCTORS BRAKE DOCTORS
Clutch Doctors International Limited
2701 N.W. Vaughn Street, Suite 438, Portland, OR, 97210. Contact: Bill Nootenboom - Tel: (503) 525-5808, (888) CLU-TCH8, Fax: (503) 525-5812, E-Mail: Bill@clutchdoctor.com, Web Site: www.clutchdoctor.com. Clutch Doctots Brake Doctors is the nation's leading clutch and brake repair franchise. We specialize in installing high performance and original equipment clutch and brake friction products. By specializing in the clutch and brake niche we dramatically reduce the equipment and inventory necessary to run a successful business. Established: 1995 - No. of Units: Company Owned: 6 - Franchised: 5 - Franchise Fee: $10,000-$20,000 - Total Inv: $56,000-$122,000 - Financing: No.

COLOR GLO INTERNATIONAL
CGI International, Inc
7111-7115 Ohms Lane, Minneapolis, MN, 55439. Contact: Scott Smith, Sales Director -Tel: (952) 835-1338,(800) 333-8523, Fax: (952) 835-1395, E-Mail: info@colorglo.com, Web Site: www.colorglo.com. Color Glo International is the worldwide leader in the repair, reconditioning and color restoration of leathers, plastics, vinyl's and cloths found in the automotive, marine, aviation, and commercial and residential furniture markets. Established: 1974 - Franchising Since: 1981 - No. of Units: Company Owned: 1 - Franchised: 150 - Franchise Fee: $30,000 - Royalty: 4% - Total Inv: Equipment Product and Training - Financing: Yes.

COLOR SEAL, INC
Color Seal, Inc
P.O. Box 2302, Brandon, FL, 33509-2302. - Tel: (813) 643-0320, (888) 801-0333, Fax: (813) 689-7522, E-Mail: colorsealusa1@aol.com, Web Site: www.colorsealusa.com. Professional Detailing with The Color Seal Wax No More System. A 2-step process, using orbital polishers we deoxidize cars, boats, planes, RV's and other painted surface. Again using orbital polishers we polish in our Teflon Color Seal Sealant, which provides a mirror gloss finish, which is warranted in writing for 1 or 5 years. Established: 1954 - Franchising Since: 2000 - Total Inv: $14,990 - Financing: No.

COLORS ON PARADE
Total Car Franchising Corporation, Inc.
642 Century Circle, Conway, SC, 29526. Contact: Isha Hemingway, General Manager Franchise Sales & Marketing - Tel: (843) 347-8818, (800) 929-3363, Fax: (843) 347-0349, E-Mail: hemingwayi@colors franchise.com, Web Site: www.colorsfranchise.com. Colors on Parade is an automotive after-market franchise providing on-site, same-day minor automotive paint, paintless dent removal and interior repair. Primarily servicing the needs of fleet operators such as: new and pre-owned car dealerships and rental companies. Established: 1988 - Franchising Since: 1991 - No. of Units: Company Owned: 12 - Franchised: 272 - Franchise Fee: $5,500-$15,500 - Royalty: Operator franchisee 30%; Area developer 7% - Total Inv: Operator estimated $50,000; Area developer $200,000-$550,000 - Financing: Third party financing for operating unit, equipment and supplies.

COLORWORKS
Colorworks Franchise Group
723 S Main St, Aberdeen, SD, 57401-6016. Contact: Rob Johnson, Pres. - Tel: (605) 225-9630, Fax: (605) 225-0966. The Colorworks Franchise Group sells franchised Colorworks stores; paint, body and equipment wholesale specialty outlets serving local market body shops. Established: 1987 - Franchising Since: 1994 - No. of Units: Franchised: 3 - Franchise Fee: $12,000 plus $3,000 pre-opening mktg. fee - Royalty: 2% plus 1% mktg. fund of gross revenue - Total Inv: $114,200-$195,000 incl. inven. - Financing: No.

CREATIVE COLORS INTERNATIONAL®
Creative Colors International, Inc.
5550 W. 175th St., Tinley Park, IL, 60477. Contact: Terri Sniegolsk Sr. Vice President. Tel: (708) 614-7786, Fax: (708) 614-9685, E-Mail: terri@creativecolorsintl.com, Web Site: www.creativecolorsintl.com. Mobile service business specializing in repair, dying, cleaning and restoration of leather, vinyl, cloth, velour, plastics and other upholstery surfaces. Established: 1980 - Franchising Since: 1991 - No. of Units: Company Owned: 2 - Franchised: 53 - Franchise Fee: $19,500-$27,500 - Royalty: 6% / 1% adv. - Total Inv: $$53,000-$69,000 - Financing: Yes.

CRYSTAL CLEAN PARTS WASHER SERVICE
Crystal Clean Services, LLC
3970 W. 10th St, Indianapolis, IN, 46222. Contact: Dir. of Franchising - Tel: (877) 227-4639, Fax: (317) 486-5087, Web Site: www.crystal-clean.com. A Crystal Clean Parts Washer Service franchise serves the environmental needs of automotive repair shops and industrial facilities by leasing and servicing parts washing machines and picking up small quantities of waste in containers. Established: 1989 - Franchising Since: 1998 - No. of Units: Company Owned: 21 - Franchised: 1 - Franchise Fee: $50,000 - Royalty: 8% + 0.75% national advertising fund - Total Inv: $200,000-$500,000 - Financing: No.

CUSTOM AUTO RESTORATION SYSTEMS
479 Interstate Ct #C, Sarasota, FL, 34240-8962. Contact: Bob Wyatt, Pres. - Tel: (941) 378-1193, Fax: (941) 378-3472, Web Site: www.autorestoration.com/cars/. Originator of mobile cosmetic reconditioning systems including paint restoration, vinyl and velour repair, glass repair, paintless dent repair and odor removal. Established: 1984 - Franchising Since: 1986 - No. of Units: Company Owned: 1 - Franchised: 1038 - Franchise Fee: $995-$6,195 - Royalty: None - Financing: Leasing program.

DEALER SPECIALTIES
Dealer Specialties Intl, Inc
4665 Emerald Way, Middletown, OK, 45044. Contact: George Nenni, Director of Operations - Tel: (513) 705-2000, (800) 647-8425, Fax: (513) 705-2002, E-Mail: info@getauto.com, Web Site: www.dealerspecialties.com. Dealer Specialties is a worldwide leader in providing automobile dealers with on-site preparation of descriptive used-vehicle window stickers which provide a listing of the vehicle's make, model and all options. This detailed data along with color digital photos is manually gathered by over 600 Dealer Specialties representatives in 46 states and uploaded daily to a network of internet partners. Established: 1989 - Franchising Since: 1995 - No. of Units: Franchised: 146- Franchise Fee: $2,500 - Royalty .66¢/sticker.

DENT DOCTOR
Dent Doctor, Inc.
P.O. Box 7680, Little Rock, AR, 72217. Contact: Tom Harris President - Tel: (501) 224-0500, (800) 946-3368, Fax: (501) 224-0507, E-Mail: info@dentdoctor.com, Web Site: www.dentdoctor.com. Den Doctor franchisees succeed in an ever growing market by offering same day repair of minor dents, door dings and hail damage without having to repaint the damaged panel. The exclusive Dent Doctor paint-FREE process makes body shop repairs for minor dents obsolete. No auto experience required. Established: 1986 - Franchising Since: 1990 - No. of Units: Company Owned: 3 - Franchised: 41 - Franchise Fee: $9,900-$19,900 - Royalty: 6% - Total Inv: $39,900-$79,000 - Financing: Third party.

DENT ZONE
925 L St, Lincoln, NE, 68508-2229. Contact: Jack L. Rediger, President - Tel: (402) 434-5620, (800) 865-2378. Dent Zone utilizes paintless dent removal (PDR) techniques to repair minor automotive dents and restore a car's body to its original condition. Established: 1993 - Franchising Since: 1997 - No. of Units: Company Owned: 1 - Franchised: 2 - Franchise Fee: $20,000 - Royalty: 8%, 1% adv. - Total Inv: $25,000-$50,000 - Financing: Indirect.

DENTPRO
DentPro Franchise Corp.
4075 Nelson Ave., Suite A, Concord, CA, 94520. - Tel: (800) 868-DENT, (925) 288-8900, Fax: (925) 288-8905, Web Site: www.dentpro.com. Our innovative, on site repair service is made possible by a fleet of specially equipped mobile units. Each truck is a complete repair shop on wheels, with the latest in metal sculpting tools and equipment. The DentPro technician can repair almost any ding or dent without the need for costly fillers, sanding or repainting. Established: 1991 - Franchising Since: 1993 - No. of Units: Company Owned: 1 - Franchised: 48 - Franchise Fee: $25,000+ - Royalty: 7% - Total Inv: $45,000+ - Financing: Yes.

DENTS PLUS
Automotive Dent Specialities
2960 Hartley Rd West, Jacksonville, FL, 32257-822. Contact: Jeffrey Block, V.P. - Tel: (904) 268-8700, Fax: (904) 268-8666. Mobile paintless dent repair service. Established: 1990 - Franchising Since: 1991 - No. of Units: Company Owned: 3 - Franchised: 10 - Franchise Fee: $15,000+ - Royalty: 0 - Total Inv: $40,000+ - Financing: No.

DETAIL PLUS CAR APPEARANCE CENTERS
Detail Plus Car Appearance Systems
P.O. Box 20755, Portland, OR, 97294. Contact: R. L. Abraham, Pres. - Tel: (800) 284-0123, (503) 251-2955, Fax: (503) 251-5975, E-Mail: dplus@worldnet.att.net, Web Site: www.detailplus.com. Manufacturer of auto detailing systems & related car care systems & automatic conveyorized car wash systems. Established: 1980 - Financing: Lease financing.

DING KING FRANCHISING
1280 Bison Ave, Ste. B-9, Newport Beach, CA, 92660. Contact: Todd Sudeck - Tel: (714) 775-9450, (800) 304-3464. Training of paintless dent removal. Established: 1993 - No. of Units: Company Owned: 35 - Franchise Fee: $25,000 - Financing: Yes.

DR. VINYL
Dr. Vinyl and Associates, Ltd.
821 Northwest Commerce Street, Lee's Summit, MO, 64086-9381. Contact: Tom Buckley, Pres. - Tel: (816) 525-6060, (800) 531-6600, Fax: (816) 525-6333, E-Mail: docvinyl@drvinly.com, Web Site: www.drvinyl.com. Vinyl, leather, windshield, hard plastic, and fabric repair, automotive paint touch-up, paintless dent removal, 24k gold plating, and a variety of auto aftermarket items, mobile, home-based. Established: 1972 - Franchising Since: 1981 - No. of Units: Franchised: 182 - Franchise Fee: $26,950 - Royalty: 7%+1% advertising - Total Inv: $30,000-$50,000 - Financing: Available.

ENDRUST AUTO APPEARANCE SPECIALISTS
Endrust International
1155 Greenbriar Dr., Bethel Park, PA, 15102. Contact: Gary B. Griser, V.P.- Tel: (412) 831-1255, Fax: (412) 833-3409. Complete auto appearance center. Established: 1969 - No. of Units: Franchised: 55 - Total Inv: $30,000 plus working cap. - Financing: Yes.

ESTRELLA INSURANCE
Estrella Insurance Franchising Corp.
3750 West Flagler Street, Miami, FL, 33134. - Tel: (305) 828-2444, (888) 511-7722. Car insurance agency/eight weeks training, operations manual, outstanding advertising, ongoing support and management evaluations. We seek owner/operator with moderate business experience who is eager to grow with a successful company. Established: 1980 - Franchising Since: 1997 - No. of Units: Company Owned: 35 - Franchised: 6 - Franchise Fee: $39,500 - Royalty: 3%-3.25% of sales - Total Inv: $79,500-$108,000 - Financing: We will assist in obtaining financing.

EVER-CLEAN CAR WASH
Dept. E.C., Block B, P.O. Box 24, Fayetteville, AR, 72702. Contact: Henry Nwauwa, Licensing Dir. - Tel: (501) 443-6791. Automatic and self service car wash centers featuring complete auto cleaning systems for cars and trucks, motorcycles, etc. Unique touchless and brushless

automatic car washing and drying. Established: 1996 - Franchising Since: 1997 - Franchise Fee: $15,000-$25,000 - Royalty: None - Total Inv: $150,000-$2,000,000 - Financing: Lease/Financing arch. design, equipment training and install assistance.

FABRION
Cartex Limited
42816 Mound Rd., Sterling Heights, MI, 48314. Contact: Larry Klukowski, Pres. - Tel: (586) 739-4330, (800) 421-7328, Fax: (586) 739-4331, E-Mail: crismar@aol.com, Web Site: www.Fabrion.net. Restoration and repair of cloth, velour, carpet, leather, vinyl and plastic on site in mobile pickups or vans. No experience necessary. Three weeks training on the job, at actual accounts with experienced personal trainers. Third week of training consists of assistance in opening accounts in the franchised territory. Established: 1980 - Franchising Since: 1988 - No. of Units: Company Owned: 1 - Franchised: 79- Franchise Fee: $23,500-$29,500-$36,500 - Royalty: 7% of gross sales - Total Inv: $34,450-$55,150 - Financing: Third party.

FAS-BREAK FRANCHISE CORPORATION
4014 E. Broadway Rd., #408, Phoenix, AZ, 85040. Contact: Kerry Soat, President - Tel: (602) 437-8282, (800) 777-5169, Fax: (602) 437-8848, Web Site: www.fas-break.com. Auto glass replacement centers with and/or windshield repair systems. Established: 1988 - Franchising Since: 1997 - No. of Units: Company Owned: 3 - Franchised: 100 - Franchise Fee: $8,000 auto glass center, $3,100 windshield repair - Royalty: $10 per windshield replacement/$25 month windshield repair system - Total Inv: Auto Glass Center: $18,450-$110,000, Windshield Repair Unit: $4,300-$31,000 - Financing: Yes.

FIXX-A-DENT
Fixx Enterprises Inc.
4959 N. Buford Hwy., Norcross, GA, 30071. - Tel: (770) 449-4878, Fax: (770) 448-8131. Automotive paintless dent removal service. Established: 1993 - Franchising Since: 1994 - No. of Units: Company Owned: 4 - Franchised: 1 - Franchise Fee: $40,000 - Royalty: 6% gross sales - Total Inv: $60,000-$70,000 - Financing: Yes.

FLEET
FleetEnterprises, Inc.
500 W 7th St #1720, Fort Worth, TX, 76102. - Tel: (817) 737-6390, (888) 243-5338, Web Site: www.fleetbaycorp.com. Fleetbay businesses are truck/bus paint and collision repair centers that specialize in fleet vehicles, such as trucks, buses, truck trailers, step vans, heavy equipment and similar vehicles. Established: 1992, Affiliate: 1996 - Franchising Since: 1996 - No. of Units: 1- Franchise Fee: $25,000 - Royalty: 3% - Total Inv: $25,500-$400,000 - Financing: Third party.

GAS TANK RENU-USA
3329 Auburn Street, Rockford, IL, 61101. Contact: Pres. - Tel: (815) 962-7998, Fax: (815) 962-4516. Auto aftermarket. Repair auto and marine fuel tanks. Lifetime warranty. No. of Units: Franchised: 30 - Franchise Fee: Depends on geographical population - Royalty: None - Total Inv: From $15,000-$55,000.

GLASS MECHANIX
4881 W. Hacienda Ave, #6, Las Vegas, NV, 89118. - Tel: (702) 932-1281, Fax: (702) 932-1287, E-Mail: Web Site: www.the-glass-mechanix.com. The Glass Mechanix specializes in repairing long cracks in windshields without replacing them. We also offer a scratch removal system and vinyl repair plus paint touch up. Established: 1981 - No. of Units: Company Owned: 6 - Franchised: 2475 - Franchise Fee: $2,497 - Financing: Yes.

GLASS TECHNOLOGY WINDSHIELD REPAIR
434 Turner Dr., Durango, CO, 81301. Contact: Kerry Wansterath, VP - Tel: (800) 441-4527 or (970) 247-9374, Fax: (970) 247-9375. Glass repair service for windshields, plate glass and scratch removal. Customers consisting of insurance companies, private car owners, commercial fleet accounts and retail store owners. Established: 1984 - No. of Units: Licensed: 3000 - Total Inv: $1500-$5000 equip. and supplies - Financing: No.

GREATFLORIDA INSURANCE
S.A.A.
955 S. Federal Hwy, Suite 102, Stuart, FL, 34994. Contact: Ike Peerbhai, Pres. - Tel: (772) 283-2933, Fax: (772) 283-2967, Web Site: www.greatflorida.com. Retail sales of auto insurance. Established: 1991 - Franchising Since: 1993 - No. of Units: Company Owned: 6 - Franchised: 31 - Franchise Fee: $5,000 - Royalty: 5% of gross income - Total Inv: $16,000 for office and $16,000 reserves - Financing: No.

GUARDIAN INTERLOCK SYSTEMS
13 West Park Square, Suite A, Marietta, GA, 30060. - Tel: (770) 499-0499, Fax: (770) 499-0533. The Guardian Interlock System connects a breath analyzer to a vehicle's electrical system. Once installed, the driver must pass a breath test before the vehicle will start. Courts use the system as an alternative sentencing for DWI offenders. Established: 1991 - Franchising Since: 1993 - No. of Units: Company Owned: 83 - Franchised: 7 - Franchise Fee: $8,500 and up - Total Inv: Fran. fee plus $3,500 equip. - Financing: Partial through third party, if qualified.

HONEST-1 AUTO CARE *
6767 West Tropicana Ave, Suite 223 Las Vegas, NV, 89103 - Tel: (702) 248-1077, Fax: (702) 248-1079, Web Site: www.honest1autocare.com. Auto care from: air conditioning, tune-ups, oil & lube to tires and rims. Established: 1992 - Franchising Since: 2003 - No. of Units: Company Owned: 12 - Franchise Fee: $25,000 - Total Inv: $106,650-$175,500.

HOUSE CALLS (TRAVELING AUTO REPAIR)
Tune Up Doctor, Inc., The
2508 Betty St., Orlando, FL, 32803. Contact: Stephen Villard, Owner - Tel: (407) 894-9717. Traveling auto repair. Established: 1989 - Franchising Since: 1995 - No. of Units: Company Owned: 1 - Franchise Fee: $15,000 - Royalty: 2% gross per month - Total Inv: $15,000 - Royalty: 2% gross per month - Total Inv: $25,000-$65,000 per area/city - Financing: Yes, to 100%.

HUBCAP MASTERS
Hubcap Masters International, Inc.
1838 Elmhill Pike.,Suite 116, Nashville, TN, 37210. - Tel: (888) 244-5558, (403) 244-5558, Fax: (403) 229-1513, E-Mail: info@hubcapmasters.net, Web Site: www.hubcapmasters.net. Hubcap Masters is the market of new and used hubcaps and wheels, as well as refurbishing and repairing them. The automotive industry servicing car rental agencies, new and used automobile dealerships, body shops, insurance companies and the general public. Operate in a boutique style retail strip mall located in the best part of town. Because of their computerized ordering and inventory system and industry contacts, they can save the wholesale and retail customer up to 75% of what they would typically spend for new hubcaps and wheels in a dealership. Established: 1991 - Franchising Since: 1994 - No. of Units: Company Owned: 1 - Franchised: 7 - Franchise Fee: $20,000 - Royalty: 7% - Total Inv: $75,000 - Financing: Third Party.

IT'S DENTS OR US
7801 W. 63rd. St., Overland Park, KS, 66202. - Tel: (913) 384-6787, Fax: (913) 384-6923. Paintless dent removal. Remove hail damage and everyday dents without harming factory paint or drilling excess holes. Established: 1992 - Franchising Since: 1992 - No. of Units: Company Owned: 1 - Franchise Fee: $18,000 - Royalty: $500 - Total Inv: $18,000-$25,000 - Financing: No.

J.D. BYRIDER SALES
J.D. Byrider Systems, Inc
12802 Hamilton Crossing Blvd, Carmel, IN, 46032. - Fax: (317) 249-3000, Fax: (317) 249-3001. J.D. Byrider is the nation's leader in the used-car sales and non-prime finance industry. We dominate the five to ten yr old used-car market with proven brand names operating systems, ongoing support and capital programs. Our market represents the largest and fastest growing segment of the auto retail industry. Established: 1989 - Franchising Since: 1989 - No. of Units: Company Owned: 9 - Franchised: 95 - Franchise Fee: $39,000 - Royalty: $1,750.00 per month nat'l adv fund - Total Inv: $350,000-$1807,000 - Financing: Yes.

LENTZ USA SERVICE CENTER
Lentz USA Franchise Corp.
1001 Riverview Dr., Kalamazoo, MI, 49048. Contact: Gary R. Thomas, Fran. Sales Dir. - Tel: (269) 342-2200, (800) 354-2131, Fax: (269) 342-9461, E-Mail: quietcar@lentzusa.com, Web Site: www.lentzusa.com. Specialty brake, muffler, chassis of and more auto repairs. Established: 1972 - Franchising Since: 1989 - No. of Units: Company Owned: 11 - Franchised: 15 - Franchise Fee: $20,000 - Royalty: 0-7% - Total Inv: $8,000 - Financing: Third party.

LINE-X
2400 So. Garnsey St, Santa Anna, CA, 92707. Contact: Scott Jewett - Tel: (800) 831-3232, Fax: (714) 850-8759, Web Site: www.linexcorp. com. Spray-On truck bed liners & industrial coatings. Established: 1993 - Franchising Since: 1999 - No. of Units: Franchised: 302 - Total Inv: $68,300-$147,000.

LOOK! NO-FAULT AUTO INSURANCE AGENCIES
35230 East Michigan Ave, Wayne, MI, 48184. Contact: President - Tel: (734) 467-5665, Fax: (734) 727-5665, E-Mail: lookinsurance@ ameritech.net. Non-standard auto insurance sales. Established: 1985 - Franchising Since: 1989 - No. of Units: Franchised: 42 - Franchise Fee: $5,000 (includes training) - Total Inv: $16,000 - Financing: Limited.

MAACO AUTO PAINTING & BODYWORKS
Maaco Enterprises, Inc.
381 Brooks Rd., King of Prussia, PA, 19406. - Tel: (866) 763-2579, (610) 265-6606, (800) 296-2226, E-Mail: franchise@maaco.com, Web Site: www.maaco.com. Production auto painting and bodyworks centers. No prior automotive experience necessary. Management and sales experience necessary. Four weeks training and on-going operational support. Established: 1972 - Franchising Since: 1972 - No. of Units: Franchised: 535 - Franchise Fee: $30,000 - Royalty: 8%-9% if late - Total Inv: $199,500-$60,000 cash - Financing: Third Party.

MATCO TOOLS
Danaher Corp.
4403 Allen Rd., Stow, OH, 44224. Contact: Franchise Sales Administrator - Tel: (330) 929-4949, (800) 368-6651, Fax: (330) 926-5320, Web Site: www.matcotools.com. Matco franchised distributors sell world class hand tools and test equipment to professional automotive technicians from mobile showrooms at their place of employment. Established: 1979 - Franchising Since: 1993- No. of Units: Franchised: 1300+ - Total Inv: $68,750 - Financing: $42,500.

MERLIN'S
Merlin's Franchising, Inc.
One North River Lane, Ste. 206, Geneva, IL, 60134. Contact: Mark Hameister, Dir. Franchise Dev. - Tel: (800) 652-9900, (630) 208-9900, Fax: (630) 208-8601, E-Mail: mhameister@merlins.com, Web Site: www.merlins.com. Merlin's is an upscale, automotive service franchise specializing in brakes, oil changes, exhaust, air conditioning, minor tune-ups, tires, suspension and related services. Established: 1975 - Franchising Since: 1975 - No. of Units: Company Owned: 66 - Franchised: 4 - Franchise Fee: $26,000-$30,000 - Royalty: 4.9%-6.9% - Total Inv: Fee $26-$30, Inv. $27,33,500, FF&E $85,000-$110,000, Inventory $27,000-$33,000, sufficient working capital to open business - Financing: Through third parties.

MERMAID CAR WASH
Mermaid Marketing, Inc.
526 Grand Canyon Dr., Madison, WI, 53719. Contact: Peter Aspinwall, Pres. - Tel: (608) 833-9273, Fax: (608) 833-9272. A business devoted to total service washing, cleaning, and waxing of cars, vans, pick-up trucks, RV's, motor homes and boats. Established: 1984 - Franchising Since: 1985 - No. of Units: Company Owned: 2 - Franchised: 4 - Franchise Fee: $50,000 - Royalty: 2% gross for 20 yrs.

MIGHTY AUTO PARTS
Mighty Distributing of America
650 Engineering Drive, Norcross, GA, 30092. Contact: Barry Teagle - Tel: (770) 448-3900, (800) 829-3900, Fax: (770) 446-8627, E-Mail: barry.teagle@mightyautoparts.com, Web Site: www.mightyauto parts.com. Wholesale distribution of original equipment-quality, MIGHTY-branded auto parts. Franchisees operate in exclusive territories, supplying automotive maintenance and repair facilities with undercar and underhood products, such as filters, belts, tune-up and brake parts. Established: 1963 - Franchising Since: 1970 - No. of Units: Company Owned: 5 - Franchised: 142 - Franchise Fee: 5% average fee: $18,000 - Total Inv: $137.000.

MILEX TUNE UP & BRAKE
Moran Industries, Inc
4444 W. 147th St., Midlothian, IL, 60445. - Tel: (708) 389-5922, (800) 581-8468, Fax: (240) 389-9882, Web Site: www.milextuneupbrake.com. Full service auto care specializing in tune ups, brakes and air conditioning. Established: 1967 - Franchising Since: 1967 - No. of Units: Franchised: 8 - Franchise Fee: $27,500 - Royalty: 7% - Total Inv: $144,000 - Financing: Yes, third party.

MINI-TANKERS USA
Mini-Tankers USA, Inc.
4739 University Way NE #1620, Seattle, WA, 98105-4495. - Tel: (877) 218-3003, (888) 4 REFUEL, Fax: (888) 682-2213. Mini-Tankers sells a mobile diesel fuelling service to on and off highway vehicles, fleets and single units. Established: 1996 - Franchising Since: 1997 - No. of Units: Company Owned: 2 - Franchised: 3 - Franchise Fee: $35,000 - Total Inv: $56,000 - Financing: Lease of tanker truck.

MIRACLE AUTO PAINTING & BODY REPAIR
3157 Corporate Place, Hayward, CA, 94545. Contact: Jim Jordan, Mktg. Dir. - Tel: (510) 887-2211, (877) mir-acle, Fax: (510) 887-3092, E-mail: jim@miracleautopainting.com, Web Site: www.miracleauto painting.com. Production auto painting and collision repair. Established: 1953 - Franchising Since: 1964 - No. of Units: Company Owned: 3 - Franchised: 25 - Franchise Fee: $35,000 - Royalty: 5% of gross - Total Inv: $7.5000 - Financing: Third party.

MISTER MOBILE ON SITE OIL CHANGE
Heddleson Enterprises Inc.
5592 61st Street North, St. Petersburg, FL, 33709. Contact: David Heddleson, President/Fran. - Tel: (727) 545-5823, Fax: (888) 545-5823. Franchisors will be operating home based business servicing commercial vehicles on-site. They will be trained on actual operating business, servicing subcompact cars to fifth wheel diesels. There is also technical and personal support. Established: 1990 - Franchising Since: 1996 - No. of Units: Company Owned: 1 - Franchised: 4 - Franchise Fee: $3,000 - Royalty: 4% - Total Inv: $3,500-$8,000 based on type of vehical/ equipment - Financing: Financing available based on personal credit.

MOBILE ACCESSORY STORE FRANCHISING
10620 Lawson River Ave, Fountain Valley, CA, 92708. Contact: Treanna Scholer - Tel: (714) 963-0700, (888) 806-7944, Fax: (714) 963-7799, E-Mail: tscholer@mobilaccessorystore.com, Web Site: www.mobileaccessorystore.com. Tire & wheel installation supplies and accessories. Established: 2000 - Franchising Since: 2001 - No. of Units: Franchised: 7 - Franchise Fee: $25,000.

MOBILE AUTO SYSTEMS
P.O. Box 2094, Dublin, CA, 94568. Contact: Lisa Trujillo, Accts. Mgr. - Tel: (925) 997-9197. Business manual and consultation services in the mobile automotive oil change and repair business. Established: 1989 - Franchising Since: 1989 - No. of Units: Company Owned: 1 - Royalty: None - Total Inv: $7,000-$47,000 - Financing: No.

MOBILE ELECTRONIC SPECIALIST
MES Enterprises, Inc
6137 Moonstone Ct, Lee Summit, MO, 64064. Contact: Ed Files - Tel: (866) 427-2346, Fax: (816) 373-3860. Sales and service of auto electronics. Established: 1996 - Franchising Since: 2000 - No. of Units: Company Owned: 3 - Franchised: 5 - Franchise Fee: $12,500 - Total Inv: $26,500-$45,000.

MOBILE TIRE GUYS *
P.O. Box 1644, Fuquay-Varnia, NC, 27526. - Tel: (919) 649-7679, Fax: (919) 557-7951. Mobile tire and sales service. Established: 1999 - Franchising Since: 2003 - Franchise fee: $30,000 - Royalty: 4% - Total Inv: $53,700-$76,000.

MOFA INCORPORATED

N. 1019 Spring Valley Dr, Hortonville, WI, 54944. Contact: Bert Broman - Tel: (920) 759-2047, (920) 757-1309. Mobile oil change service. Established: 1999 - Franchising Since: 2000 - No. of Units: Company Owned: 1 - Franchise Fee: $7,500 - Total Inv: $96,000-$115,000.

MOTORWORKS & DR. MOTORWORX REMANUFACTURED ENGINE INSTALLATION CENTERS.

Motorworks, Inc.

4210 Salem St., Philadelphia, PA, 19124. Contact: Dennis Prendergast - Tel: (800)327-9905, (215) 533-4456, Fax: (215) 533-8001, E-Mail:motorworks@motorworksinc.com, Web Site: www.motorworksinc.com. Automotive specialty shops specializing in remanufactured engines and installation for cars, trucks, vans, boats and RV'S. Established: 1987 - Franchising Since: 1987 - No. of Units: Company Owned: 2 - Franchised: 52- Franchise Fee: $23,500 - Royalty: 5% + 1% adv. - Total Inv: $55,200-$89,000 - Financing:Yes.

NOVUS WINDSHIELD REPAIR

10425 Hampshire Ave., South, Bloomington, MN, 55438. - Tel: (800) 944-6811, (952) 946-0447, Fax: (952) 9446-0481. Mobile, home-based windshield repair and replacement franchise. Factory training supplemented by sales and business management preparation. Established: 1972 - Franchising Since: 1985 - No. of Units: Company Owned: 18 - Franchised: 476 - Franchise Fee: $15,000 - Royalty: 6%, 2% adv.fund - Total Inv: $15,000 f.f., $3,000 equip/supplies - Financing: Yes.

ONE STOP UNDERCAR, INC.

2938 Daimler St, Santa Ana, CA, 92705. Contact: Fred Myers, Pres.- Tel: (949) 955-2600, Fax: (949) 833-1817. Distribution of automotive undercar parts to all types of automotive repair shops. Established: 1988 - Franchising Since: 1990 - No. of Units: Company Owned: 4 - Franchised: 10 - Franchise Fee: $40,000-$80,000 - Royalty: 5% of gross sales - Total Inv: $292,000-$460,000 - Financing: No.

OPTIKLEER WINDSHIELD REPAIR

NVS Corporation

271 Western Ave., Lynn, MA, 01904. Contact: Scott Macfarland - Tel: (781) 595-6224, (800) 695-6224, Fax: (781) 593-5773, E-Mail: nvs@glassfix.com, Web Site: www.glassfix.com. Mobile windshield repair (not replacement) & scratch removal products. Established: 1975- Franchising Since: 1997 - No. of Units: Franchsied: 1207 - Total Inv: $2,000 - Financing: No.

OWNER'S AUTO MART®

OAM National, L.L.C.

3100 West 12th Street, Ste. 108, Sioux Falls, SD, 57104. - Tel: (800) 308-9042, Fax: (605) 336-7375. A for-sale-by-owner vehicle display lot. Private vehicle sellers rent space on a weekly or monthly basis. Vehicles are well-presented to private buyers who enjoy a hassle-free shopping environment. A unique approach to the private market. Established: 1997 - Franchising Since: 1997 - No. of Units: Company Owned: 1 - Franchise Fee: Varies by size of lot: $4,500, $6,500, $8,500 - Royalty: 5% of gross revenue - Total Inv: Varies by size of lot: $11,200, $16,450, $22,600.

PICK-UPS PLUS INC.

4360 Ferguson Dr, Suite 120, Cincinnati, OH, 45245. Contact: Dir. of Fran. - Tel: (888) 249-7587, Web Site: www.pickupsplus.com. Pick-Ups Plus, is a franchise store geared to the owners of pick up trucks and sport utility vehicles (Explorers) at these stores we sell accessories for all pickups and sport utility vehicles. Established: 1992 - Franchising Since: 1996 - No. of Units: Company Owned: 1 - Franchised: 4 - Franchise Fee: $25,000 - Royalty: 6% - Total Inv: $125,000-$200,000 - Financing: Yes.

POLISHING SYSTEMS

Bri-Lee Enterprises

241 W. Grant Street, New Castle, PA, 16101. Contact: Sales Manager - Tel: (724) 658-2005, (800) 245-8118, Fax: (724) 658-6226. We put people in the car detailing business. Established: 1966 - Total Inv: Under $700.00.

POP-A-LOCK

The LSR Group, Inc

1018 Harding Street, #205, Lafayette, LA, 70503. - Tel: (337) 233-6211, Fax: (337) 6655, Web Site: www.pop-a-lock.com. Pop-A-Lock is the nations largest car door unlocking, locksmith and roadside assistance service. Established: 1991 - Franchising Since: 1994 - No. of Units: Franchised: 107 - Franchise Fee: $24,500 - Royalty: 6% - Total Inv: $23,400-$459,000 - Financing: None.

POWER WINDOW REPAIR EXPRESS INC

1801 W. Atlantic Ave, B3, Delray Beach, FL, 33444. Contact: Mark Roehrig - Tel: (561) 330-3710, Fax: (561) 330-3619, E-Mail: pwrexpress@aol.com, Web Site: www.pwrexpress.com. The most timely business in the world. As we are the only business of its kind filling a huge niche, Power Window Repair takes just 20 minutes per door with an average ticket of over $160. 200,000,000 vehicles out of warranty with 5 possible problems per door makes this a mutibillion dollar market! Established: 1996 - Franchising Since: 1999 - No. of Units: Company Owned: 1 - Franchised: 10 - Franchise Fee: $25,000 - Financing: Yes.

PRECISION AUTO WASH

Precision Auto Care, Inc

748 Miller Dr S.E., #G-1, Leesburg, VA, 20175. Contact: Franchise Sales - Tel: (703) 777-9095, ext 236, (800) 438-8863, Fax: (703) 779-0136, Web Site: www.precisionac.com. Touchless automatic wash and self service wash, can be open 7 days a week, 365 days a year. Day to day business management can be done from a home office computer. Advanced technology preferred by today's consumer. Established: 1997 - Franchising Since: 1997 - No. of Units: Company Owned: 36 - Franchised: 8 - Franchise Fee: $25,000 - Royalty: 7.5% - Total Inv: $22,000-$669,000 - Financing: Yes.

PROPAINT PLUS, INC.

1300 E 9th St #14th Fl, Cleveland, OH, 44114-1503 - Tel: (800) 72-PAINT (727-2468). Mobile system bringing a complete refurbishing service to the customer. Services include paint repair, velour, vinyl and leather repairs, paintless dent removal, windshield repair. System includes fully customized truck, all supplies and equipment, computer system, extensive marketing support program.Established: 1991 - Franchising Since: 1994 - No. of Units: Company Owned: 8 - Franchised: 4 - Franchise Fee: $20,000 - Royalty: 12% declining to 8% - Total Inv: $42,500 - Financing: Truck & equip. can be financed to qualified individuals. At this time not presently offering franchises.

RAMP SOLUTIONS, INC.

115 W. Canon Perdido, Santa Barbara, CA, 93101. - Tel: (805) 899-1503, (800) 969-7267, Fax: (805) 899-1505. Ramp Solutions offers nationwide distributorships for an innovative line of pick-up truck loading systems. Our newest product "The Rhino Ramp" is a steel ramp that attaches to the tailgate and handles 2000 lbs. Established: 1995 - Franchising Since: 1996 - Total Inv: $499 one time fee.

RENNSPORT

Rennsport Franchising Inc.

10390 Alpharetta St., Ste. 620, Roswell, GA, 30075. - Tel: (404) 992-9442, Fax: (404) 767-4442. Rennsport shops specialize in the repair, polishing and restoration of alloy wheels. Established: 1990 - Franchising Since: 1995 - No. of Units: Company Owned: 1 - Franchise Fee: $25,000 - Royalty: 6% service fee, 1% nat'l. adv. - Total Inv: $48,000-$146,500 - Financing: On equipment only. Not franchising at this time.

RYAN ENGINE EXCHANGE

Lakewood Engine Exchange d/b/a: Ryan Engine

2465 W. Evans Ave, Denver, CO, 80219. Contact: Johnny M. Wilson, President - Tel: (303) 232-0012, (800) 466-1664, Fax: (303) 205-0172, E-Mail: jwilson@ryanengineexchange.com, Web Site: www.ryanengineexchange.com. Specializes in the removal and replacement of remanufactured engines in autos, boats, RVs and commercial vechicles giving a 50,000 mile 5 year warranty. Established: 1989 - Franchising Since: 1999 - No. of Units: Company Owned: 1 - Franchised: 14 - Franchise Fee: $25,000 - Royalty: 5% - Total Inv: $100,000 - Financing: Leasing.

SAF-T AUTO CENTERS
R & R Enterprises, Inc.
121 No. Plains Industrial Rd., Wallingford, CT, 06492. Contact: Richard Bilodeau, Pres. - Tel: (203) 294-1094, (800) 382-7238, Fax: (203) 269-2532, Web Site: www.SAFTAUTO.COM. Auto repair shop offering steering, suspension, brakes, mufflers, lubrication and minor repairs. Established: 1978 - Franchising Since: 1985 - No. of Units: Franchised: 10 - Franchise Fee: $15,000 - Royalty: $500 per month - Total Inv: $65,000 - Financing: Third party assistance.

SELECT AUTO LEASING, INC.
Select Opportunity, Inc.
2942 N. 16th Street, Phoenix, AZ, 85016-7606. - Tel: (602) 279-3430, Fax: (602)279-6188. Buy and lease back program for automobiles. Established: 1994 - Franchising Since: 1994 - No. of Units: Company Owned: 3 - Franchised: 8 - Franchise Fee: $25,000 - Royalty: No - Total Inv: $200,000 - Financing: No. NOT FRANCHISING AT THIS TIME.

SNAP-ON-TOOLS COMPANY
2801 80th Street, Kenosha, WI, 53141-1410. Contact: Franchise Department - Tel: (800) 7756-3344, Fax: (262) 656-5088, Web Site: www.snapon.com. Distribution of professional mechanics tools using a mobile van tool showroom. Established: 1920 - Franchising Since: 1991 - No. of Independent Dealers: 392 - Franchises: 3,050 - Franchise Fee: $5,000 - Royalty: $50 per month - Total Inv: $121,67-$200,550 - Financing: Yes.

SPEEDY AUTO GLASS
965 Oliver Drive, Davis, CA, 95616. Contact: Dir. Fran. Sales - Tel: (530) 756-2000, Fax: (530) 756-8540. Replacement and repair of auto, residential and commercial glass, also, sliding glass doors, shower doors, mirrors and sunroofs. Established: 1946 - Franchising Since: 1982 (in Canada) - No. of Units: Company Owned 310 - Franchised: 212 - Franchise Fee: $30,000 for new, $10,000 for conversion - Total Inv: $25,000 for conversion, $140,000 for new - Financing: Assistance.

SPOT-NOT CAR WASHES
RACO Car Wash Systems, Inc.
P.O. Box 1269, Joplin, MO, 64802. Contact: Doug Myers, Exec. VP Franchising - Tel: (417) 781-6233, Fax: (417) 781-3906, Web Site: www.spot-not.com. Offering an automatic brushless washing system along with full featured self-service bays. Established: 1978 - Franchising Since: 1985 - No. of Units: Franchised: 37 - Franchise Fee: $25,000 - Royalty: 5%, 1% adv. - Total Inv: $622,000-$1,058,000 - Financing: No.

SPRAYGLO®AUTO REFINISHING & BODY REPAIR
Trinity Refinishers Inc
1959 Parker Ct., Ste.E, Stone Mountain, GA, 30087. Contact: H. Stuart Damron, President - Tel: (877) 286-7794, (678) 344-8065, Fax: (678) 344-7426. Sprayglo offers production auto painting and body repair at prices most anyone can afford, experience is not necessary, we look for great people skills and a strong work ethic. Established: 1986 - Franchising Since: 1994 - No. of Units: Franchised: 5 - Franchise Fees: $20,000-Royalty: 5% + 2% advertising - Total Inv: $88,500-$152,300 - Financing: No.

START YOUR ENGINES, INC
2201 Cantu Ct Ste. 118, Sarasota, FL, 34232-6254. Contact: Mike Hamilton - Tel: (941) 378-7001, (941) 724-4450, Fax: (941) 378-8497. Oil change and car wash center. Established: 1997 - Franchising Since: 1998 - No. of Units: Company Owned - 1 - Franchised - 1 - Franchise Fee: $25,000 - Royalty: Call for details - Total Inv: Call for details - Financing: No.

SUPERGLASS WINDSHIELD REPAIR
SuperGlass Windshield Repair, Inc.
6101 Chancellor Dr., #200, Orlando, FL, 32809. Contact: David A. Casey, Pres. - Tel: (407) 240-1920, (888) 771-2700, Fax: (407) 240-3266, E-Mail: sgwr@aol.com, Web Site: www.sgwr.com. Mobile windshield repair to commercial fleets, dealerships, rental companies and insurance industry. Complete two week training, national accounts, all equipment, one week in your exclusive territory for marketing support. Established: 1992 - Franchising Since: 1993 - No. of Units: Franchised: 217 - Franchise Fee: $5,000 - Royalty: 3% - Total Inv: $9,500 - Financing: 30% of total.

TECHNA GLASS FRANCHISE INC. *
460 W. 9000 South, Sandy, UT, 84070. Contact: Franchise Department - Tel: (801) 676-3390, Fax: (505) 564-3222, Web Site: www.techna glass.com. Windshield and glass repair. Established: 1991 - Franchising Since: 2004 - No. of Units: Company Owned: 8 - Franchise Fee: $30,000-$40,000 - Royalty: 6-9% - Total Inv: 234,900-$565,100 - Financing: No.

THE COLLISION SHOP, INC.
The Collision Shop Of America Inc.
2899 East Big Beaver Rd, #318, Troy, MI, 48083. - Tel: (800) 219-3113, Fax: (248) 634-8318, Web Site: www.collisionfranchise.com. Retail repair of newer vehicles which have been involved in an accident which 90% of the time are paid for by the major insurance companies. Established: 1992 - Franchising Since: 1992 - No. of Units: Company Owned: 1 - Franchised: 15 - Franchise Fee: $35,000 - Royalty: 6% of sales - Total Inv: $150,000-$175,000 - Financing: Will help with outside financing.

TILDEN CAR CARE CENTERS
Tilden Associates, Inc.
1325 Franklin Ave., Ste. 165, Garden City, NY, 11530. Contact: Jason Baskind, Director Franchise Development - Tel: (516) 746-7911, (800) 845-3367, Fax: (516) 746-1288, E-Mail: info@tildencarcare.com, Web Site: www.tildencarcare.com. We're not just brakes: The total car care center concept allows you to offer a full menu of automotive services for maximum customer procurement, rather than a limited niche market. You benefit from a system which was proven and perfected for 75 years before we began to offer franchises. Established: 1923 - Franchising Since: 1995 - No. of Units: Company Owned: 1 - Franchised: 60 - Franchise Fee: $25,000 - Royalty: 6% - Total Inv: $5,000-$7,000 - Financing: Assistance.

TIRE TIME RENTALS
Tire Time Rentals, Ltd
511 S. Gregg St, Big Spring, TX, 79720. Contact: Mike Hughes, Owner - Tel: (432) 263-8473. Rent to own tires and custom wheels. Established: 1994 - Franchising Since: 1995 - No. of Units: Franchised: 22 - Franchise Fee: $2,000-$20,000 - Royalty: 6% - Total Inv: $116,500 - Financing: No.

TIRE WAREHOUSE
Tire Warehouse Central, Inc.
492 Main St., Keene, NH, 03431. Contact: Franchise Development - Tel: (603) 352-4478, (800) 756-9876, Fax: (603) 358-6620, E-Mail: franchising@tirewarehouse.net, Web Site: www.tirewarehouse.net. Retail tire, automotive parts, wheels and accessories, sales and tire installation. Stores located in New England and New York. Affordable leasing available. Established: 1971 - Franchising Since: 1989 - No. of Units: Company Owned: 27 - Franchised: 24 - Franchise Fee: 0 - Royalty: 3% of sales after breakeven point is reached or 18 months - Total Inv: $100,000-$300,000 - Financing: No.

TOP VALUE CAR & TRUCK SERVICE CENTERS
International Top Vlaue Automotive, LLC
36887 Schoolcraft Rd., Livonia, MI, 48150. Contact: Richard E. Zimmer, Director of Franchise Dev. - Tel: (734) 462-3633, Ext 16, (800) 860-8258, ext. 16, Fax: (734)462-1088, Web Site: www.top-value.com. Full service repair center for cars and light trucks. One stop shopping for your repair customers including commercial and fleet accounts. Established: 1977 - Franchising Since: 1980 - No. of Units: Company Owned: 5 - Franchised: 32 - Franchise Fee: $15,000 - Royalty: Declines from 5% to 2% based upon gross sales - Total Inv: $104,500-$158,200 including working capital, inventory signage, start up expenses, equipment, etc - Financing: We will assist in presentations to lending companies.

TRUCK OPTIONS
On & Off Road Options
5865 University Blvd. W. Jacksonville, FL, 32216. Contact: Michael Balanky, Pres. - Tel: (904) 731-7548, Fax: (904) 731-3558, E-Mail: info@truckoptions.com, Web Site: www.truckoptions.com. Automotive aftermarket - sell and install aftermarket products for trucks, vans and sport utility vehicles. Established: 1987 - Franchising Since: 1995 - No. of Units: Company Owned: 2 - Franchise Fee: $20,000 - Royalty: 4% gross sales - Total Inv: $175,000-$280,000 - Financing: Conventional sources.

TUFFY AUTO SERVICE CENTERS
Tuffy Associates Corp.
1414 Baronial Plaza Dr., Toledo, OH, 43615. Contact: Jim Jacobs, Dir.of Franchising - Tel: (419) 865-6900, (800) 228-8339, Fax: (419) 865-7343, Web Site: www.tuffy.com. Up scale automotive repair franchise performing all repairs except transmissions and major engine work. Initial training and on going support in operations and advertising. Established: 1970 - Franchising Since: 1971 - No. of Units: Company Owned: 6 - Franchised: 233 - Franchise Fee: $25,000 - Royalty: 5%, 5% adv. - Total Inv: $156,500-$290,000 ($85,000 cash required) - Financing: Yes third party.

ULTIMATE LININGS USA INC
6630 Roxburgh Dr, Suite 175, Houston, TX, 77041. - Tel: (800) 989-9869, (713) 466-0302, Fax: (713) 937-0052, E-Mail: info@ultimate linings.com, Web Site: www.ultimatekinings.com. Spray-on polyurethane truck bed liners for pickup trucks, trailers. boats plus many other commercial applications. Established: 1989 - Business Opportunity: 1989 - No. of Units: Company Owned: 1 - Dealers: 160 - Total Inv: $28,000 - Financing: Yes.

VALU MUFFLER & BRAKE
4115 Main Street, Amherst, NY, 14226. Contact: Tom Shea - Tel: (716) 834-0575, (877) 536-0575, Fax: (716) 834-0575. Under car repair & exhaust systems. Established: 1997 - Franchising Since: 1999 - No. of Units: Company Owned: 2 - Franchise Fee: $12,500 - Total Inv: Capital requirements; $37,500-$97,700 - Financing: No.

VEHEX
3923 28th St SE, Grand Rapids, MI, 49512-1805. Contact: Mikel Muttery, President/CEO - Tel: (616) 975-2767, Fax: (616) 975-2768, Web Site: www.vehex.com. Commercial fleet maintenance and management facilities. Providing a full line of maintenance. Established: 1991 - Franchising Since: 1997 - No. of Units: Company Owned: 1 - Franchised: 3 - Franchise Fee: $25-$35,000 - Royalty: 7% - Total Inv: $75-$125,000 - Financing: Yes.

VORTEX SPRAYLINERS INC.
27161 Burbank St., Foothills Ranch, CA, 92610. Contact: Mike Powell, VP Marketing - Tel: (949) 770-2316, (866) 4 VORTEX, Fax: (949) 770-5101, E-Mail: info@vortexsprayliners.com, Web Site: www.vortexsprayliners.com. Worlds only truly portable spray on truck liner system. Spray a waterproof coating up to 1/4" thick and have it dry in seconds. Completely self contained, choice of colors. Established: 2000 - Franchising Since: 2000 - No. of Units: Company Owned: 2 - Franchised: 25 - Total Inv: $14,850 for equipment - Financing: Yes-Lease.

WATER DOCTORS INTERNATIONAL, INC.
2408 Madison Drive, Suite 201, N. Myrtle Beach, SC, 29582. - Tel: (843) 272-4597, (800) 441-5208, Fax: (843) 272-5969, Web Site: www.waterdoctors.com. Franchisor in the repair of automotive wind, water and dust leaks. Established: 1976 - Franchising Since: 1986 - No. of Units: Company Owned: 2 - Franchised: 92 - Franchise Fee: $37,500 - Royalty: 7% gross - Total Inv: $20,500 - Financing: $17,000 at 10% for 5 or 7 years.

WESTERN AUTO
Western Auto Supply Company
9680 Marion Rdg, Kansas City, MO, 64137-1284. - Tel: (816) 346-4573, (800) 274-6733, Fax: (816) 346-4188. Retail automotive supplies such as tires, parts, accessories and service supplemented as needed with big ticket home and leisure lines including bicycles, outdoor power equipment, major home appliances and consumer electronics. Established: 1909 - Franchising Since: 1935 - No. of Units: Company Owned: 612 - Franchised: 830 - Franchise Fee: None - Royalty: None - Total Inv: $125,000-$495,000 - Financing: None.

WINZER FRANCHISE COMPANY
Winzer Corp.
10560 Markison Rd., Dallas, TX, 75238. - Tel: (214) 341-2122, Fax: (800) 867-7714. Distribution of aftermarket repair supplies and fasteners to automotive and trucking dealerships, body shops and independent repair facilities. Established: 1978 - Franchising Since: 1991 - No. of Units: Company Owned: 35 - Franchised: 46 - Franchise Fee: $2,500-

$5,000, depending upon type - Royalty: 10%-16% of gross sales, depending upon volume - Financing: $5,000 (computer, merchandising, materials) - Financing: Yes.

YIPES STRIPES
T.D.A. Striping, Inc.
520 Court Street, Dover, DE, 19901. Contact: Diane Scinto, President - Tel: (302) 736-1735, (800) 947-3755, Fax: (302) 736-2693, Web Site: www.yipesstripes.com. Mobile painted pinstriping, graphics, and lettering. Exclusive territory, special insta-dry paint. Ongoing support and training. Wholesale directly to car dealerships or retail to the public. Established: 1977 - Franchising Since: 1988 - No. of Units: Company Owned: 1 - Franchised: 25 - Franchise Fee: $25,000 - Royalty: $500 minimum or 5% gross sales - Total Inv: $40,000-$75,000 - Financing: Yes.

ZIEBART TIDYCAR
Ziebart International Corp.
1290 E. Maple Rd., Troy, MI, 48083. Contact: Greg Longe, VP Fran. Dev. - Tel: (248) 588-4100, Fax: (248) 588-1444, E-Mail: info@ziebart.com, Web Site: www.ziebart.com. Car and truck detailing, accessory and protection retail stores. Established: 1959 - Franchising Since: 1962 - No. of Units: Company Owned: 20 - Franchised: 550 - Franchise Fee: $24,000 - Royalty: 5%-8% - Total Inv: $100,000-$161,000 - Financing: Yes.

AUTOMOTIVE: TRANSMISSION REPAIR

AAMCO TRANSMISSIONS
AAMCO Transmissions, Inc.
One Presidential Blvd., Bala Cynwyd, PA, 19004. - Tel: (800) 223-8887, (610) 292-8500, Fax: (610) 617-9532, E-Mail: franchise@aamco. com, Web Site: www.aamco.com. The world's largest chain of transmission specialist with over 700 centers throughout the United States and Canada. For over 35 years, AAMCO has set the standard for quality reliable service and customer satisfaction. From 1992 -1998, some store sales have increased 43%. Established: 1963 - Franchising Since: 1963 - No. of Units: Company Owned: 2 - Franchised: 712 - Franchise Fee: $30,000 - Royalty: 7% - Minimum Cash: $60,000 - Total Inv: $166,821-$175,911 - Financing: Third party financing available.

AMERICAN TRANSMISSIONS
American Transmission Inc
340 N Main St #207, Plymouth, MI, 48170-1237. Contact: John Folino, President/CEO - Tel: (734) 459-3104, Fax: (734) 459-1836. Franchise service centers provide service and repairs on automatic and standard transmissions; automobiles and trucks. Established: 1979 - Franchising Since: 1991 - No. of Units: Franchised: 6 - Franchise Fee: $25,000 - Royalty: 7% - Approx. Inv: $125,000 - Financing: Equipment leases available.

ATLAS TRANSMISSION
Moran Industries, Inc.
4444 West 147th St., Midlothian, IL, 60445. Contact: Virginia Smithson, Qualification Specialist - Tel: (800) 377-9247, (708) 389-5922, Fax: (240) 524-8894, E-Mail: vsmithsom@moranindustries.com, Web Site: www.moranindustries.com. Atlas Transmission operates transmission service centers in the state of Texas. We service wholesale, retail and fleet customers. Atlas specializes in foreign, domestic automotive and standard light trucks. Established: 1964 - Franchising Since: 1988 - No. of Units: Franchised: 18 - Franchise Fee: $27,500 - Royalty: 7% of weekly gross sales - Total Inv: $149,000 - Financing: Yes, third party.

COTTMAN TRANSMISSION CENTERS
Cottman Transmission Systems, Inc.
240 New York Dr., Ft. Washington, PA, 19034. - Tel: (800) 394-6116, (215) 643-5885, Fax: (215) 643-2519, Web Site: www.cottman.com. Transmission repair and care facilities servicing all types of transmissions whose company mission is to promote dynamic corporate and personal growth through honesty, integrity and professional service to our customers. Established: 1962 - Franchising Since: 1964 - No. of Units: Company Owned: 5 - Franchised: 202 - Franchise Fee: $31,000 - Royalty: 7.5% of gross sales/$550 per week adv. - Total Inv: $78,000-$106,000 - Financing: Yes, third party assistance.

DIAMOND QUALITY TRANSMISSION CENTERS OF (LOCATION)
Diamond Quality Transmission Centers of America, Inc.
P.O. Box 6147, Philadelphia, PA, 19115-6147. - Tel: (215) 742-8333. Automatic and standard auto and truck transmission service centers. Established: 1949 - Franchising Since: 1963 - No. of Units: Franchised: 6- Franchise Fee: $35,000 - Financing: With good credit available.

DR. NICK'S TRANSMISSIONS
Moran Industries, Inc.
4444 West 147th St., Midlothian, IL, 60445. - Tel: (800) 377-9247, (708) 389-5922, Fax: (708) 389-9882, Web Site: www.drnickstrans mission.com. Transmission repair and service centers. Established: 1978 - Franchising Since: 1978 - No. of Units: Franchised: 9 - Franchise Fee: $27,500 - Royalty: 7% of weekly gross sales - Total Inv: $149,000 - Financing: Yes, third party.

DURA-BUILT TRANSMISSIONS
Dura-Built Franchise System, Inc.
777 Campus Commons Rd. #200, Sacramento, CA, 95825. - Tel: (916) 441-6677, Fax: (916) 929-0448. Retail automotive transmission and related drive line service, repair and rebuilding. Established: 1971 - Franchising Since:1987 - No. of Units: Company Owned: 6 - Franchised: 15 - Franchise Fee: $20,000 - Royalty: 7% + 3% adv. - Total Inv: $45,000 fee, equip., deposits, work. cap. - Financing: No.

GOODEAL DISCOUNT TRANSMISSIONS
P.O. Box 50, National Park, NJ, 08063. Contact: John Mikulski, Pres. - Tel: (856) 456-2299, Fax: (856) 848-4660. Establishing center to rebuild and replace automobile and truck transmissions. Established: 1979 - Franchising Since: 1980 - No. of Units: Franchised: 30 - Franchise Fee: $19,500 - Royalty: $275 wkly - Total Inv: (inven., equip., signs) $17,000 + $32,500 + work cap. $20,000 - Financing: Will assist.

KENNEDY TRANSMISSION
Kennedy Franchising USA, Inc.
2225 Daniels St, Long Lake, MN, 55356-9276. Contact: Steve Hendrickson, Pres. - Tel: (952) 476-4338, Fax: (952) 476-1983. Service and repair of automatic and manual transmissions, clutches, transfer cases, differentials, and other driveline components. Established: 1962 - Franchising Since: 1976 - No. of Units: Company Owned: 2 - Franchised: 17 - Franchise Fee: $17,500 - Royalty: 6% - Total Inv: $83,500-$157,500 - Financing: None.

LEE MYLES TRANSMISSIONS
Lee Myles Assoc Corp.
140 Rte. 17 N., Paramus, NJ, 07652. - Tel: (201) 262-0555. Repair and replacement of automatic and standard transmissions, turnkey, existing and conversion sales available. Major expansion throughout U.S. Area developers agreements available. Established: 1947 - Franchising Since: 1964 - No. of Units: Franchised: 85 - Franchise Fee: $25,000 - Royalty: 7% gross sales - Total Inv: $97,000-$127,000 - Financing: No.

MR. MOTOR
Moran Industries, Inc
4444 W. 147th St., Midlothian, IL, 60445. Contact: Virginia Smithson, Qualification Specialist - Tel: (708) 389-5922, (800) 377-9247, Fax: (708) 389-9882, E-Mail: vsmithson@moranindustries.com, Web Site: www.moranindustries.com. Motor repair & replacement. Established: 1996 - Franchising Since: 1996 - No. of Units: Franchised: 1 - Franchise Fee: $27,500 - Royalty: 7% - Total Inv: $128,000 - Financing: Yes, third party.

MR. TRANSMISSION
Moran Industries, Inc.
4444 West 147th St., Midlothian, IL, 60445. - Tel: (800) 581-8468, (708) 389-9882, Fax: (708) 389-5922, Web Site: www.mrtrans mission.com. Transmission repair and service centers. Established: 1962 - Franchising Since: 1970 - No. of Units: Company Owned: 1 - Franchised: 106 - Franchise Fee: $27,500 - Royalty: 7% of weekly gross sales - Total Inv: $149,000 - Financing: Yes, third party.

MULTISTATE TRANSMISSION
Moran Industries, Inc.
4444 W. 147th St., Midlothian, IL, 60445. - Tel: (800) 581-8468, (708) 389-5922, Fax: (708) 389-9882, Web Site: www.multistatetrans mission.com. Transmission repair and service centers. Established: 1971 - Franchising Since: 1971 - No. of Units: Franchised: 31 - Franchise Fee: $27,500 - Royalty: 7% of weekly gross sales - Total Inv: $149,000 - Financing: Yes, third party.

SPEEDY TRANSMISSION CENTERS
Autotech Franchise Systems, Inc.
74 NE 4th Ave., Ste. #1, Del Ray Beach, FL, 33483. Contact: Dan Hinson - Tel: (561) 274-0445, (800) 331-0310, Fax: (561) 274-6456, E-Mail: speedytrans@mindspring.com, Web Site: www.speedytransmis sion.com. Repair and replacement of automatic and standard transmissions. Retail, commercial and fleet. Full training provided for sales and management. Technical service is provided. Established: 1974 - Franchising Since: 1974 - No. of Units: Franchised: 27 - Franchise Fee: $19,500 - Royalty: 7% - Total Inv: $75,000 - Financing: Yes.

TRANSMISSION USA
Moran Industries, Inc
4444 W 147th St, Midlothean, IL, 60445. Contact: Franchise Development - Tel: (708) 389-5922, Fax: (708) 389-9882, Web Site: www.moranindustries.com. Franchise of automotive aftermarket centers. Established: 1956 - Franchising Since: 1990 - No. of Units: Company Owned: 3 - Franchised: 200 - Franchise Fee: $25,000 - Financing: Yes.

BEVERAGES

BEVMAX THE WINE + LIQUOR SUPERSTORE
Bevmax International, Inc
17 Cedar St, Stamford, CT, 06902. - Tel: (203) 674-0705, Fax: (203) 316-0627. Retail superstores-wine + liquor products. Established: 1997 - Franchising Since: 1998 - No. of Units: Company Owned: 2 - Franchised: 4 - Franchise Fee: $35,000 - Total Inv: Call for details - Financing: No.

BORVIN BEVERAGE
Borvin Beverage Franchise Corp.
1022 King Street, Alexandria, VA, 22314. Contact: Don Mikovch, Pres. - Tel: (703) 683-9463, Fax: (703) 836-6654, E-Mail: contactinfo@ borvinbeverage.com, Web Site: www.borvinbeverage.com. Wine import and wholesale distribution. Established: 1991 - Franchising Since: 1991 - No. of Units: Company Owned: 1 - Franchised: 1 - Franchise Fee: $20,000 - Royalty: 5%, 2% adv. - Total Inv: $10,000 - Financing: Available.

CAFFINO *
3130 Crow Canyon Pl.,#120, San Ramon, CA, 94583. - Tel: (925) 543-2900, Fax: (925) 275-6868, Web Site: www.caffino.com. Double drive thru concept serving quality coffee and espresso drinks in 60 seconds. Established: 1993 - Franchising Since: 2002 - No. of Units: Company Owned: 6 - Franchised: 20 - Franchise Fee: $10,000 - Royalty: 5% - Total Inv: $212,900-$373,000.

CHEERWINE BOTTLERS
Carolina Beverage Corp.
P.O. Box 697, Salisbury, NC, 28145. Contact: Mark Ritchie, Pres. - Tel: (704) 637-5881, Fax: (704) 633-7491. Soft drink franchisor. Established: 1917 - Franchising Since: 1917 - No. of Units: Company Owned: 1 - Franchised: 29 - Approx. Inv: depends on market - Financing: None.

FAT TUESDAY
Fat T, Inc.
701 Metairie Rd., Metairie, LA, 70005. - Tel: (504) 831-9415, Fax: (800) 577-3456. Distinctive system relating to the operation of retail frozen beverage service business. Established: 1993 - Franchising Since: 1993 - No. of Units: Company Owned: 7 - Franchised: 2 - Franchise Fee: $25,000 - Royalty: 6%, 1% adv. - Total Inv: Ranges from $450,000-$850,000 - Financing: None.

FOREMOST LIQUOR STORES

4001 Devon, Chicago, IL, 60646. - Tel: (773) 545-3111, Fax: (773) 545-3330. Alcoholic beverages. Established: 1949 - Franchising Since: 1949 - No. of Units: Company Owned: 26 - Total Investment: $150,000 - Financing: Thru bank.

HAWAII'S JAVA KAI *
Java Kai Etcetera

2955 Aukele St Ste C, Lihue, HI, 96766. Contact: Brent, President - Tel: (858) 345-4158, (866) 528-2524, Fax: (808) 245-6503, E-Mail: info@javakai.com, Web Site: www.javakai.com. The best Hawaiian Kona coffee and other tasty Hawaii blends are fresh made and brought to you from Hawaii's own Java Kai. Java Kai brings the warmth, taste and Aloha Spirit to you, even if you're not in Kauaii. Established: 1997 - Franchising Since: 2000 - No. of Units: Company Owned: 1 - Franchised: 10 - Franchise Fee: $30,000 - Royalty: 6% - Total Inv: Min $180,000 - Financing: Third party.

JABOOKA JOOCE
TDW, LLC

2371 E. Lindsay Wood Lane, Sandy, UT, 84092. Contact: David Williams - Tel: (801) 453-0361, Fax: (801) 453-0364, Web Site: www.jabookajooce.com. Fresh juices, smoothies, soups and snacks. Established: 1999 - Franchising Since: 1999 - No. of Units: Company Owned: 2 - Franchised: 3 - Franchise Fee: $10,000 - Royalty: 5-7& - Total Inv: $80,400-$191,200 - Financing: No.

JO TO GO THE DRIVE THRU ESPRESSO BAR
Jo To Go America, Inc.

1263 Main Street, Green Bay, WI, 54302. Contact: Jon Lukens, Director of Marketing - Tel: (920) 884-6601, Fax: (920) 435-5444, E-Mail: jon1@jotogo.com, Web Site: www.jotogo.com. Premium drive-thru and walk-up/take-away gourmet coffee and espresso drinks, fresh bakery and smoothies. Established: 1998 - Franchising Since: 2001 - No. of Units: Company Owned: 4 - Franchised: 6 - Franchise Fee: $25,000 - Royalty: 7% - Total Inv: $82,500-$767,060 - Financing: No.

L'AMYX TEA BAR

4179 Piedmont Ave, Oakland, CA, 94611. Contact: Franchise Department - Tel: (510) 536-0791. Smoothie, coffee and tea franchise. Established: 2000 - Franchising Since: 2002 - No. of Units: Company Owned: 1 - Franchised: 1 - Franchise Fee: $30,000 - Total Inv: $180,000-$280,000 - Financing: No.

MAYAN JAMMA JUICE
The Taco Maker, Inc

4605 Harrison Blvd, Centennial Building, 3rd Floor, Ogden, UT, 84403. Contact: Bob Strong, Franchise Specialist - Tel: (801) 476-9780, (800) 207-5804, Fax: (801) 476-9788, E-Mail: franchise@tacomaker.com, Web Site: www.tacomaker.com. Mayon Jamma Juice is a fruit smoothie concept and works well for day part coverage. Established: 1978 - Franchising Since: 1978 - No. of Units: Company Owned: 3 - Franchised: 150 - Franchise Fee: $19,500-$29,000 - Royalty: 5% - Total Inv: $150,000-$300,000 - Financing: Third party.

MOCHA DELITES INC. *

3300 Northeast Expressway, Building 4, Suite J, Atlanta, GA, 30341. Contact: Tony Estrada - Tel: (770) 451-0901, (800) 539-9532, Fax: (770) 451-0902, E-Mail: franchisesales@mochadelites.com, Web Site: www.mochadelites.com. Mocha Delites serves customers delicious coffees made with traditional Arabica bean, and a wide variety of specialty coffee drinks, including our Caramel Praline Latte and naturally our popular drink, the Mocha Delite. Established: 2001 - Franchising Since: 2002 - No. of Units: Company Owned: 1 - Franchised: 34 - Franchise Fee: $22,500 - Royalty: 5% - Total Inv: $93,500-$388,500 - Financing: Yes.

NATURAL FRUIT CORP *

770 West 20th Street, Hialeak, FL, 33010. - Tel: (305) 887-7525, Fax: (305) 888-8208. Fruit bar serving drink's and smoothie's, mixes are nonalcoholic and made with only the finest ingredients. Established: 1986 - Franchising Since: 2003 - No. of Units: Franchised: 180 - Franchise Fee: $2,500 - Royalty: N/A - Total Inv: $35,000.

RED KANGAROO WINES

10625 N. Tatum Blvd, #142, Phoenix, AZ, 85028. - Tel: (480) 951-9486, Fax: (480) 991-5038. Retail wine store franchise. Established: 1997 - Franchising Since: 1999 - No. of Units: Company Owned: 1 - Franchise Fee: $25,000 - Total Inv: $75,000 - Financing: Yes.

SOUTH POLE SMOOTHIES *
South Pole Smoothies Franchise Systems, Inc.

2780 East Fowler Ave., #161, Tampa, FL, 33612. - Tel: (888) 495-7890, Fax: (813) 237-1517, E-Mail: info@southpolesmoothies.com, Web Site: www.southpolesmoothies.com. Dazzle customers with our fruit smoothies concoctions, such as Polar Punch, Glacial Grape or Island Hopper. Our smoothies include Penguin Coolada, a cool blend of coconut, pineapple and pineapple juice. Established: 1996 - Franchising Since: 2003 - No. of Units: Franchised: 2 - Franchise Fee: $10,000 - Royalty: 5% - Total Inv: $45,000-$55,000.

TAPIOCA EXPRESS INC *

1908 Central Ave, South El Monte, CA, 91733. - Tel: (626) 453-0777, (888) 887-1616, Fax: (626) 453-0778, E-Mail: franchise@tapiocaexpress.com, Web Site: www.tapiocaexpress.com. We use high quality ingredients, amintain a top notch team behind the counter and provide a friendly environment, all in the effort to bring the best Tapioca drinks. Serving over 150 different menu items: juice, tea, milk tea, coffee & snow bubbles all individually flavored. Established: 1999 - Franchising Since: 2000 - No. of Units: Company Owned: 3 - Franchised: 64 - Franchise Fee: $10,000 - Royalty: 0.045/cup - Total Inv: $69,600-$248,900 - Financing: Third party.

TEALUXE, A TEA BAR & CAFE *

9210 W. Harbor Isle Ct, Crystal River, FL, 34429. - Fax: (352) 795-9980, Web Site: www.tealuxe.com. Tea bar. Established: 1996 - Franchising Since: 2003 - No. of Units: Company Owned: 3 - Franchise Fee: $25,000 - Total Inv: $150,000-$250,000.

THE ENERJUICER *
GuyKo, LLC

2000 Rt. 38 Suite 1360, Chery Hill, NJ, 08002-2100. - Tel: (856) 665-3500, Fax: (856) 665—3507, E-Mail: theenerjuicer@aol.com, Web Site: www.theenerjuicer.com. The Enerjuicer is the only juice bar company, where you can choose between a selection of 16 different fresh fruit and vegetables to create your own fruit shake smoothie. Established: 1999 - Franchising Since: 2004 - No. of Units: Company Owned: 3 - Franchised: 1 - Franchise Fee: First 10 franchisees free, there after $20,000 - Royalty: 4.5% weekly gross - Total Inv: $33,750-$82,000.

THE GRAPE *

4300 Paces Ferry Rd., Ste 500A, Atlanta, GA, 30339. Contact: Martin Thallman - Tel: (678) 309-9463, Fax: (678) 309-1208, E-Mail: franchise@yourgrape.com, Web Site: www.yourgrape.com. Tap into an innovative opportunity that sets itself apart from other retail restaurant and wine bars. Established: 2000 - Franchising Since: 2004 - No. of Units: Company Owned: 1 - Franchise Fee: $50,000 - Total Inv: $450,000-$600,000.

ZUKA JUICE
Zuka Juice Franchise, Inc.

2468 Fort Union Blvd Ste 100, Salt Lake City, UT, 84121-3369 - Tel: (801) 265-8423, (888) 438-9852, Fax: (801) 265-3932, Web Site: www.zukajuice.com. Fresh squeezed juices and fruit and yogurt based smoothies or "ZUKA'S". Established: 1995 - Franchising Since: 1997 - No. of Units: Company Owned: 21 - Franchised: 45 - Franchise Fee: $20,000 - Royalty: 5%, 2% marketing - Total Inv: $177,500-$236,900 - Financing: No.

BUILDING PRODUCTS AND SERVICES

3 DAY KITCHEN & BATH INC

1872 Richard Rd, Sandy, UT, 84093. - Tel: (801) 636-2294, Web Site: www.3daykitchen.com. Kitchen & bathroom remodeling. Established: 1997 - Franchising Since: 2001 - No. of Units: Company Owned: 2 - Franchised: 4 - Franchise Fee: $25,000 - Royalty: $500. weekly - Total Inv: $85,500-$102,300 - Financing: No.

A-1 CONCRETE LEVELING INC.
1 Coscade Plaza., Ste 2100, Akron, OH, 44308. Contact: Jim Creed, President - Tel: (888) 675-3835, Fax: (330) 253-1261. Raise and level existing concrete slabs and foundations. Established: 1981 - Franchising Since: 1993 - No. of Units: Franchised: 20 - Franchise Fee: $20,000-$25,000 - Royalty: 6% - Total Inv: $65,000 - Financing: Yes.

A-SEAL
A-Seal Basement Waterproofing, Inc.
1341 Copley Road, Akron, OH, 44320. Contact: Robert Wakefield - Tel: (502) 244-1858, (800) 514-6359, E-Mail: info@a-seal.com, Web Site: www.a-seal.com. A-Seal is the culmination of nearly half-a-century of technology innovation in the waterproofing industry. State-of-the-art, patented waterproofing system and materials that have been evaluated for effectiveness and safety by the Building Officials & Code Administrators Evaluation Service (BOCA International) and Architectural Testing, Inc. Established: 2000 - Franchising Since: 2001 - No. of Units: Franchised: 6 - Franchise Fee: $60,000 - Royalty: 8% - Total Inv: $70,000-$105,000 - Financing: Yes.

ABC SEAMLESS, INC.
ABC Seamless, Inc.
3001 Fiechtner Drive, Fargo, ND, 58103. Contact: Deb Hendrickson - Tel: (701) 293-3107, (800) 732-6577, Web Site: www.abcseamless.com. Sale of Franchise of manufacturing, selling & installing seamless steel siding, seamless gutters, soffit and fascia on new & existing residential and commercial properties and multiple duellings. Established: 1973 - Franchising Since: 1978 - No. of Units: Company Owned: 9 - Franchised: 127 - Franchise Fee: $18,000 - Royalty: Varies 2-5% of gross receipts - Total Inv: $98,135-$212,500 - Financing: For equipment only.

AHRENS CHIMNEY TECH., INC.
2000 Industrial, Sioux Falls, SD, 57104. Contact: Monty Lutz, Sales Mgr. - Tel: (800) 843-4417, (605) 334-2827, Fax: (605) 335-1525. Chimney lining and restoration for residential and commercial masonry chimneys. Established: 1982 - Licensing Since: 1982 - No. of Units: Franchised: 177 - Total Inv: $10,000 - Financing: To qualified applicants.

AIRE SERV HEATING & AIR CONDITIONING
Aire Serv Corporation
1020 N. University Parks Dr., Waco, TX, 76707. Contact: Roger Goertz, President - Tel: (800) 583-2662, Fax: (254) 745-2546, Web Site: www.aireserv.com. America's Comfort Company - a heating, ventilating and air conditioning franchise creating top-of-the-mind consumer awareness and a national name for service excellence. Established: 1992 - Franchising Since: 1993 - No. of Units: Franchised: 60 - Franchise Fee: $17,500 min - Royalty: 4.5%-2.5% - Total Inv: $17,500 and up - Financing: Up to 70%.

AMBIC BUILDING INSPECTION CONSULTANTS
Building Inspection Consultants, Inc.
1200 Rt. 130, Robbinsville, NJ, 08691. Contact: David Goldstein, Pres. - Tel: (609) 448-3900, (800) 88-AMBIC, Fax: (609) 426-1230, Web Site: www.ambic.com. Inspections of residential, commercial and industrial buildings including environmental inspections (i.e., radon, lead, water, asbestos, septic), termite inspections and consulting services for prospective buyers and sellers and lenders. Established: 1987 - Franchising Since: 1988 - No. of Units: Franchised: 30 - Franchise Fee: $10,000 - Royalty: 6% on-going support, 3% adv. - Total Inv: $15,000-$26,500 incl. fran. fee. - Financing: For qualified individuals.

AMERICAN CONCRETE RAISING, INC
916 Westwood Ave, Addison, IL, 60101. - Tel: (630) 543-5775, Fax: (630) 543-5930. Concrete raising and restoration. Established: 1983 - Franchising Since: 1990 - No. of Units: Company Owned: 1 - Franchised: 2 - Franchise Fee: $15,000 - Royalty: 6% on gross sales - Total Inv: $45,000-$55,000 - Financing: No.

AMERICAN LEAK DETECTION
American Leak Detection
888 Research Dr., Palm Springs, CA, 92263. Contact: Sheila Bangs, Director, Fran. Sales - Tel: (760) 320-9991, (800) 755-6697, Fax: (760) 320-1288, E-Mail: sbangs@americanleakdetection.com, Web Site: www.americanleakdetection.com. Noninvasive detection of leaks hidden underground, in walls, slabs, swimming pools. Video inspection of sewers. Established: 1974 - Franchising Since: 1984 - No. of Units: Company Owned: 6 - Franchised: 233 - Franchise Fee: $57,500+ - Royalty: 6%-10% gross - Total Inv: $110,000 - Financing: Yes, o.a.c.

AMERICAN ROOF-BRITE
4492 Acworth Ind. Drive, #102, Acworth, GA, 30101. Contact: Sales Director - Tel: (770) 966-1080, (800) 476-9271, Fax: (770) 975-4647. Removal and prevention of ugly roof stains. This is a world wide problem for ashphalt, fiberglass shingles, wood, slate and other roofing products. Residential and commercial. Established: 1990 - Franchising Since: 1990 - No. of Units: Franchised: 100 - Franchise Fee: $7,995 - Royalty: 10% product fee - Financing: Yes.

AMERICAN WOOD-BRITE
American Roof-Brite Inc.
4492 Acworth Ind. Drive.,#102, Acworth, GA, 30101. Contact: Sales Dir. - Tel: (770) 966-1080, (800) 476-9271, Fax: (770) 975-4647. Clean ugly stained wood roofing shingles. High demand business, little or no competition in wood shingle restoration preservation. Established: 1997 - Franchising Since: 1997 - No. of Units: Company Owned: 1 - Franchise Fee: $9,995 - Royalty: None - Total Inv: Includes products, training, marketing, tools and equipment - Financing: None.

AMERISPEC HOME INSPECTION SERVICE, INC.
ServiceMaster
889 Ridge Lake Blvd., MS C3-1842, Memphis, TN, 38120. Contact: Franchise Department - Tel: (800) 426-2270, (901) 820-8509, Fax: (901) 820-8520, E-Mail: sales@amerispec.net, Web Site: www.amerispec.net. Number one home inspection company in North America. Exclusive locations, superior technical training in state of the art facility, company sponsored internet support system, and functional in-field data collection + report generation system. Established: 1987 - Franchising Since: 1988 - No. of Units: Franchised: 320 - Franchise Fee: $18,900-$26,900 - Royalty: 7%, 3% adv. - Total Inv: $18,910-$59,900 - Financing: Yes, 80% @ prime + 3 points variable.

AMERITECK PAINTING
Paint Masters, Inc.
2226 E Thistle Ridge Cir, Highlands Ranch, CO, 80126-2638. - Tel: (303) 471-2456, (800) 278-1861, Fax: (303) 741-9710. Full service painting business. Residential interior and exterior painting commercial interior and exterior painting. Computer software package to assist in estimating. Established: 1997 - Franchising Since: 1998 - No. of Units: Franchised: 3 - Franchise Fee: $12,500 - Royalty: $1,000 per month, $200 advertising - Total Inv: Equipment $11,000-$13,000, Working Capital, $3,00-$5,000, Start up cost $4,000-$9,000 - Financing: Yes on equipment.

ARTISTIC STONE PRODUCTS, INC
9290 Matt Hwy, Ballground, GA, 30107. Contact: Todd Hamby, President - Tel: (770) 888-8278, (888) 852-4845, Fax: (770) 888-8658, Web Site: www.artisticstoneproducts.com. The manufacture and sales of the Artistic Stone, manufactured light weight stone products. Established: 1994 - Franchising Since: 1998 - No. of Units: Company Owned: 1 - Franchise Fee: $3,500 annually - Total Inv: Approx. $56,000 - Financing: No.

BABY GATE ™
Pool Fence Manufacturer, Inc
132 D. Tomahawk Dr., Indian Harbour Beach, FL, 32937. - Tel: (407) 777-6977, (800) 293-BABY, Fax: (407) 777-3815, Web Site: www.babygate.net. Baby Gate™ provides the highest quality pool fence. Baby Gate™ protects the most precious god given gift, our children. Established: 1998 - Franchising Since: 1998 - No. of Units: Company Owned: 1 - Franchise Fee: $10,000.

BATH FITTER®
Bath Fitter® Franchising Inc.
27 Berard Dr., #2701, South Burlington, VT, 05403-5810. Contact: Linda Brakel, V.P. Franchise Operations - Tel: (802) 860-2919, (800) 892-2847, Fax: (802) 862-7976, E-Mail: infobath@bathfitter.com, Web Site: www.bathfitter.com. Since 1994, Bath Fitter has been installing custom-molded acrylic bathtub liners, shower bases and one-piece, seamless wall surrounds over existing fixtures in just a few hours in countless residential and commercial properties. We provide full training, specialized tools, marketing and technical manuals and on-going support through regular visits to your location. We award

exclusive territories with enormous residential and commercial market potential to qualified franchise owners. Established: 1984 - Franchising Since: 1992 - No. of Units: Company Owned: 15 - Franchised: 94 - Franchise Fee: $24,500 - Royalty: 0% - Total Inv: $60,000-$100,000 - Financing: No.

BATHCREST
Bathcrest, Inc.
5195 W. 4700 S., Salt Lake City, UT, 84119. Contact: Lloyd Peterson, V.P. Franchise Sales - Tel: (801) 957-1400, (800) 826-6790, Fax: (801)955-6499, E-Mail: info@bathcrest.com, Web Site: www.bathcrest.com. Multiple revenue sources with high-profit potential. Our "same day bathroom renovation" specialty saves homeowners $1000s, time and remodeling hassles, while providing you with a stable income. Low investment, low overhead. Established: 1979 - Franchising Since: 1985 - No. of Units: Company Owned: 1 - Franchised: 162 - Franchise Fee: $4,500 - Royalty: None - Total Inv: $24,500 - Financing: Yes; 100% of franchise fee.

BENJAMIN FRANKLIN PLUMBING
3120 S. Know It All Ln, Rogersville, MO, 65742. - Tel: (417) 753-4046, Fax: (417) 753-3685, Web Site: www.benfranklinplumbing.com. Plumbing services which can be home based. Established: 2000 - Franchising Since: 2001 - No. of Units: Franchised: 15 - Franchise Fee: $5,000 - Royalty: 3-5% - Total Inv: $46,500-$371,500 - Financing: No.

BLINDS, SHADES & SHUTTERS
269 Market Place Blvd, #342, Cartersville, GA, 30121. Contact: Al Asano - Tel: (770) 975-1688, Fax: (770) 529-9018, E-Mail: info@clean-money.com, Web Site: www.clean-money.com. We clean, repair, sell & install blinds, shades & shutters. Established: 1977 - Franchising Since: 1980 - No. of Units: Franchised: 120 - Franchise Fee: $9,990 - Financing: 40%.

BORDER MAGIC
1503 Country Rd., 2700 N., Rantoul, IL, 61866. Contact: Franchise Department - Tel: (217) 892-2954, fax: (217) 893-3739, Web Site: www.bordermagic.com. Seamless concrete landscape edging that has the look and feel of real brick. Established: 1984 - Franchising Since: 2002 - No. of Units: Franchised: 57 - Royalty: 4% - Total Inv: $326,500.

BUILD YOUR OWN AMERICAN HOME
BYOAH
604 N. Central Expwy, Allen, TX, 75013. - Tel: (972) 359-8686, (800) 720-3070, Fax: (801) 848-4363, Web Site: www.buildyourown americanhome.com. BYOAH is a full service, home-building consulting company. The homeowner/builder makes all the decisions concerning the design, construction, subcontractor selections, interior decor and finishing of their dream home. Established: 1974 - Franchising Since: 2003 - No. of Units: Franchised: 5 - Franchise Fee: $25,000 - Royalty: 10%.

CALIFORNIA CLOSET COMPANY
1000 4th Street, Ste. 800, San Rafael, CA, 94901-3121. Contact: David Lamb - Tel: (800) 241-3222, Fax: (415) 256-8501, Web Site: www.calclosets.com. Custom designed and installed storage systems for both residential and commercial applications. Closet and garage systems, office systems and more. Established: 1978 - Franchising Since: 1982 - No. of Units: Franchised: 151- Franchise Fee: $39,500 - Royalty: 6% - Total Inv: $103,000-$283,500 - Financing: Third party.

CASE HANDYMAN SERVICES
Case Handyman Services, LLC
4701 Sangmore Rd., Ste. P. 40, Bethesda, MD, 20816. Contact: V.P. Franchise Development - Tel: (301) 229-9380, (800) 426-9434, Fax: (301) 229-2089, Web Site: www.casehandyman.com. Quality, professional craftsmanship for all home repairs and improvements, providing a one-stop solution for today's busy consumers. Our Case Handyman Repair Specialists have expertise in all areas of home repair, a minimum 10 years experience and must pass a security background check. All franchisees are supported by custom designed computer software, and top notch sales and marketing support to keep their business efficient and professional. Established: 1961 - Franchising Since: 1998 - No. of Units: Company Owned: 2 - Franchised: 45 - Franchise Fee: $40,000 - Royalty: 6% - Total Inv: $45,000-$60,000 - Financing: Not at this time.

CASTART BY NATURESCAPES
1041 East Miles St., Tucson, AZ, 85719. Contact: VP Franchising - Tel: (520) 623-8858, (800) 871-8838, Fax: (520) 670-0062, Web Site: www.castartinc.com. Enjoy the natural look and feel of rock waterfalls, streams, ponds, pools and spas with Castart rock and water features. Our exclusive building blocks create consistently great installations. You can see our work in the massive rock waterfalls and pools at the newly renovated Desert Inn, Las Vegas and in finer restaurants, apartments, office buildings and homes. Established: 1995 - Franchising Since: 1997 - No. of Units: Company Owned: 1 - Franchised: 6 - Franchise Fee: $12,800 - Royalty: $125.00-$600 monthly based on territory size - Total Inv: Without franchise fee $13,600-$62,100 - Financing: SBA.

CLASSIC HANDYMAN COMPANY
C.H. Franchising, Inc.
306 46th Avenue North, Nashville, TN, 37209. - Tel: (615) 298-3668, (888) 578-3668, Fax: (615) 298-6623, E-Mail: clhndymn@bellsouth.net. Small to medium home repairs and improvements to the upper income residential community where client convenience and top service is in high demand. Established: 1996 - Franchising Since: 2002 - No. of Units: Company Owned: 1 - Franchised: 2 - Franchise Fee: $25,000-$50,000 - Total Inv: $70,000-$150,000.

CLASSY CLOSETS ETC.
1235 S. Akimel Lane ., #5063, Chandler, AZ, 85226-5170. Contact: Morris Christensen, Fran. Dir. - Tel: (480) 967-2200, (800) 992-2448 ext. 114, Fax: (602) 438-2304. Manufacture and install custom closets and storage units. Established: 1983 - Franchising Since: 1989 - No. of Units: Dealerships: 30 - Dealership Training Fee: $2,500 - Total Inv: $9,500 without equip. - Financing: No.

CLOSET FACTORY, THE
Closet Factory Franchise Corp., The
12800 Broadway, Los Angeles, CA, 90066. Contact: David Louy, V.P. & Fran. Dir. - Tel: (310) 715-1000, Fax: (310) 516-8065, E-Mail: info@closetfactory.com, Web Site: www.closetfactory.com. Design, build and install custom closet and storage systems. Established: 1983 - Franchising Since: 1986 - No. of Units: Company Owned: 1 - Franchised: 114 and in 7 countries - Franchise Fee: $28,500-$39,500 - Royalty: 5 3/4% gross receipts - Total Inv: $99,500-$185,000 - Financing: Third party, SBA.

CLOSET + STORAGE CONCEPTS
424 Commerce Lane., Ste 1, W. Berlin, NJ, 08091. Contact: Bob Lewis, President - Tel: (856) 767-5700, (888) THE-CLOSET, Fax: (856) 768-8698, Web Site: www.closetandstorageconcepts.com. Closet + Storage Concepts designs, manufactures and installs a variety of custom closet, laundry room, home office and storage units. Established: 1987 - Franchising Since: 2000 - No. of Units: Company Owned: 1 - Franchised: 1 - Franchise Fee: $40,000 - Total Inv: $125,000 - Financing: Third party.

CLOSETS TO GO
Closets To Go, Inc.
9540 SW Tigard St, Tigard, OR, 97223. Contact: Jeff Turner, Fran. Dir. - Tel: (503) 639-5089, Fax: (503) 639-7068. A non-manufacturing company that customizes closets and other storage areas for the home and office. Concept allows for the concentration of sales and services by having all products in stock. Established: 1985 - Franchising Since: 1987 - No. of Units: Company Owned: 1 - Franchised: 5 - Franchise Fee: $3,300-$17,000 - Royalty: 5%, 2% adv. fund - Total Inv: $32,30-$118,900 - Financing: Yes, indirectly.

CLOSETTEC
Closettec Franchise Corp.
55 Carnegie Row, Norwood, MA, 02062. Contact: David Rogers, Pres. - Tel: (781) 769-9997, (800) 365-2021, Fax: (781) 769-9996, Web Site: www.closettec.com. Building of custom closet systems. Established: 1985 - Franchising Since: 1986 - No. of Units: Franchised: 34 - Franchise Fee: $30,000 - Royalty: 5.5% - Total Inv: $128,000-$230,000.

COLOR CROWN CORPORATION
928 Sligh Ave, Sefner, FL, 33584-3142. Contact: Director of Development - Tel: (813) 655-4880, (800) 282-1599, Fax: (813) 655-8830, E-Mail: info@stardek.com, Web Site: www.stardek.com. In 1972, Color Crown Corporation manufacturer of StarDek decorative

concrete products, applied their first decorative driveway coating. With over 1100 installers in the U.S. and 4 operating in other countries, we continue to be the leader in the industry. Stardek coatings are easily applied & are oil, rust & mildew resistant. Stardek not only repairs & protects old damaged concrete it also adds aesthetic value. Established: 1972.

COMPREHENSIVE PAINTING
Comprehensive Franchising Systems, Inc.
4705 Chromium Dr., Colorado Springs, CO, 80918. Contact: Michael Cranford, Pres. - Tel: (719) 599-8983, Fax: (719) 599-0471. A residential home painting business which offers customers painting, staining, wallpapering and wood restoration services, which enables franchisees to take advantage of the experience, proven track record and unlimited income potential of an efficiently designed franchise system. Established: 1986 - Franchising Since: 1992 - No. of Units: Company Owned: 1- Franchised: 2 - Franchise Fee: $6,500 - Royalty: 0.06% - Total Inv: $11,500-$30,000 - Financing: Yes.

CONCRETE TECHNOLOGY, INC
1255 Starkey Road, Largo, FL, 33771. Contact: VP Sales & Marketing - Tel: (727) 535-4651, (800) 447-6573. Installation of acrylic concrete coating that restores, beautifies and protects all cement surfaces. Established: 1991 - Franchising Since: 1991 - No. of Units: Franchised: 856 - Franchise Fee: $10,000 secured by inventory - Total Inv: $10,000 - Financing: No.

CORNWELL QUALITY TOOLS COMPANY
667 Seville Road, Wadworth, OH, 44281. - Tel: (330) 336-3506, (800) 321-8356, Fax: (330) 336-3337, E-Mail: info@cornwelltools.com, Web Site: www:cornwelltools.com. Franchised mobile tool company who manufactures hardline tools and offers complete line of professional hand tools distributed by mobile tool trucks. Established: 1919 - Franchising Since: 1996 - No. of Units: Franchised: 153 - Total Inv: $24,075-$145,075 - Financing: Internal financing to those who qualify.

CRACK TEAM, THE
11694 Lackland Rd, St. Louis, MO, 63146. - Tel: (314) 426-0900, Fax: (314) 426-0915, Web Site: www.thecrackteam.com. The Crack Team franchisees waterproof foundation wall cracks for customers. Established: 1985 - Franchising Since: 2000 - No. of Units: Company Owned: 6 - Franchised: 4 - Franchise Fee: $15,000 - Royalty: 6% - Total Inv: $38,600-$69,100 - Financing: No.

CRITERIUM ENGINEERS
Coast To Coast Engineering Services, Inc.
22 Monument SQ Ste 600, Portland, ME, 04101-4096. Contact: Dir. of Operations - Tel: (207) 828-1969, Fax: (207) 775-4405. Consulting engineering, specializing in existing buildings, including inspection, due diligence, evaluation, maintenance planning, insurance investigation, feasibility studies, plan of repair, environmental assessment, and related services. Established: 1957 - Franchising Since: 1958 - No. of Units: Franchised: 67 - Franchise Fee: $21,500 - Royalty: 6%, 1% communications fee - Financing: Yes.

DELBE HOME SERVICES
Delbe Home Systems, LLC
5185 MacArthur Blvd., N.W #115, Washington, DC, 20016. Contact: Howard Margolis - Tel: (202) 237-0187, (800)75D-ELBE, Fax: (202) 237-0348, E-Mail: hjm@delbefranchise.com, Web Site: www.delbefranchise.com. DHS is a membership based service, which assists homeowners (members) in solving their home's maintenance, repair and improvement needs. Franchisees provides his/her members with licensed & insured contractors. No repair experience necessary. Established: 1996 - Franchising Since: 2001 - No. of Units: Franchised: 1 - Franchise Fee: $18,500-$40,000 - Royalty: 3% - Total Inv: $25,300-$61,900 - Financing: Third party.

DIAMOND SEAL
Diamond Seal, Inc.
4001 South, 700 East., Suite 500, Salt Lake City, UT, 84107. Contact: Doug Turnquist, President & CEO - Tel: (801) 975-9988, (800) 599-9401, Fax: (801) 975-9989, Web Site: www.diamondseal.com. World leader in the development and distribution of hydrophobic coatings for glass and glass glazed products. Diamond Seal beautifies and protects windows, shower doors, ceramic tile, and granite surfaces from the damaging effects of water, acid rain, and pollutants. Established: 1994 - Franchising Since: 1997 - No. of Units: Franchised: 14 - Franchise Fee: $7,500-$100,000 - Royalty: 6% of gross revenues - Total Inv: $14,250-$155,700 - Financing: Yes.

DONAHUE CONSTRUCTION CORP.
3701 N. 32nd Street, Phoenix, AZ, 85018. - Tel: (602) 957-6427, (800) 400-3983, Fax: (602) 957-6573. Donahue construction is a general contractor specializing in restaurant and retail construction. Established: 1994.

DREAMMAKER BATH & KITCHEN
Worldwide Refinishing Systems, Inc.
1020 N. University Parks Dr, Waco, TX, 76707. Contact: Karen Cagle, Vice President of Franchising - Tel: (254) 745-2477, (800) 583-9099, Fax: (254) 745-2588, E-Mail: dreamMaker@dwyergroup.com, Web Site: www.dreammaker-remodel.com. A total remodeling business which includes both complete renovation and remodeling alternatives that provide the customer with a full range of options. A complete business system with training, marketing and technical support. Established: 1975 - Franchising Since: 1988 - No. of Units: Franchised: 120 - Franchise Fee: $27,000 depending on size of territory and current business - Royalty: Starts at 6% and drops incrementally down to 3% based on revenues - Total Inv: $35,000-$75,000 - Financing: Several methods available.

DRY-B-L-O
Dry-B-L-O International Inc
310 Tribble Gap Rd., Ste. B, Cumming, GA, 30040. Contact: Grant Moore, Director of Franchising - Tel: (770) 781-4754, (800) 437-9256, Fax: (770) 886-7408. Home improvements. Established: 1996 - Franchising Since: 2000 - No. of Units: Company Owned: 1 - Franchised: 9 - Franchise Fee: $25,000.

DRY-CO BASEMENT WATERPROOFING
P.O. Box 6633, Portsmouth, NH, 03802. Contact: Doug Erickson, President - Tel: (207) 748-1271, Fax: (207)748-1271, E-Mail: franchise@drycowaterproofing.com, Web Site: www.drycowaterproofing.com. Home-based business, offering high profit margins and low overhead with the ability to generate six figure incomes. Established: 1987 - Franchising Since: 1990 - No. of Units: Company Owned: 1 - Franchised: 1 - Franchise Fee: $30,000 - Total Inv: $35,000-$40,000.

DUPONT FLOORING SYSTEMS
DuPont Flooring Systems Franchise Company
125 Town Park Commons, Kennesaw, GA, 30144. Contact: Rone Rose/ Tim Pierse, President/ V.P. Operations - Tel: (770) 420-7800, Fax: (770) 420-7838. Commercial flooring dealers in DuPont Flooring Systems, best practices including installation, maintenace, reclamation and recycling, indoor air quality. Established: 1997 - Franchising Since: 1998 - No. of Units: Company Owned: 50 - Franchised: 18 - Financing: Yes.

DURA-OAK CABINET REFACING PRODUCTS
Kitchen By D.J. Mills, Inc
863 Texas Avenue, Shreveport, LA, 71101. Contact: D.J. Mills - Tel: (318) 227-9610, (800) 228-7702, Fax: (318) 424-8252, E-Mail: djmills@dura-oak.com, Web Site: www.dura-oak.com. Full line of wood, vinyl and parts to install refacing. 3.5 hrs on How to Install Refacing + 3 hrs on How to Install Solid Surface Counter Top videos. Mannuals, trade shows, track selling, newspaper ads, radio ads and TV commercials. Established: 1974 - Franchising Since: 1974 - No. of Units: Company Owned: 1 - Franchised: 66 - Franchise Fee: $10,000 - Financing: Yes.

ENERGY WISE INC.
2145 Dutton Avenue, Sebastopol, CA, 95472. Contact: Michael Gross, President - Tel: (707) 824-8775, Fax:(707) 824-6967, Web Site: www.energywiseinc.com. Providing annual major appliance maintenance, products and services for home safety and efficiency. Established: 1990 - Franchising Since: 1996 No. of Units: Company Owned: ? - Franchised: 3 - Franchise Fee: $12,500 - Royalty: 5% of gross sales - Total Inv: $29,500-$47,500 - Financing: Possible.

ENGRAVE-A-CRETE®, INC.
1390 - G Commerce Blvd., Sarasota, FL, 34243. - Tel: (941) 355-2114, (800) 884-2114, Fax: (941) 351-2171, Web Site: www.engrave-a-crete.com. Patented equipment and system, transforms existing dull gray concrete into brick, tile or cobblestone, system changes the color of the concrete than machine grooves pattern into surface. Established: 1991- Business Opp: 110 - Total Inv: $7,900-$19,900 - Financing: Lease to own.

ENVIROBATE
3301 East 26th Street, Minneapolis, MN, 55406-1725. - Tel: (612) 729-1080, Fax: (612) 729-1021, E-Mail: contact@envirbatemetro.com, Web Site: www.envirobate.com. National environmental services franchise. Superb training program. Established: 1989 - Franchising Since: 1991 - No. of Units: Franchised: 8 - Franchise Fee: $25,000 - Royalty: 6% - Total Inv: $90,000 - Financing: SBA and other.

ENVIROFREE INSPECTIONS
CEI Lead Consultants
4763 Old U.S. 23, Ste. A, Brighton, MI, 48114. Contact: Franchise Development - Tel: (810) 220-3097, (800) 220-0013. Environmental home inspection including lead in paint, radon, water qualtity, asbestos, well and septic, fuel oil tanks and enviromental assessments. Established: 1989 - Franchising Since: 1997 - No. of Units: Company Owned: 1 - Franchised: 5 - Franchise Fee: $15,000 - Royalty: $100 per week - Total Inv: $15,000 fee, $11,000 equipment + deposit and advertising - Financing: Yes.

ESSENTIALS PROTECTIVE COATINGS
Essentials Franchise Corporation
5209 Capitals Blvd, Raleigh, NC, 27616-2925. - Tel: (919) 785-3015, (888) 372-8827, Fax: (919) 785-3319. The EPC business is focused on the sale and application of a technologically advanced protective coating. EPC is ready to provide a new solution to the new home building and remodeling industry in coating inside fixtures for protection during the construction/remodeling process. Established: 1996 - Franchising Since: 1997 - No. of Units: Franchised: 16 - Franchise Fee: $25,000 - Royalty: 8% - Financing: No.

EVER-DRY WATERPROOFING
Ohio State Waterproofing
365 E. Highland Rd., Macedonia, OH, 44056. Contact: Jack Jones, V.P. - Tel: (330) 467-1055, Fax: (330) 468-3231. Basement waterproofing and foundation repair. Patented system. Established: 1977 - Franchising Since: 1984 - No. of Units: Company Owned: 2 - Franchised: 16 - Franchise Fee: $18,000-$60,000 - Royalty: 6% - Total Inv: $60,000-$100,000 - Financing: To qualified applicants.

FEATHER RIVER WOOD & GLASS CO, INC
2345 Forest Ave, Chico, CA, 95928. - Tel: (530) 895-0762, (800) 395-3667, Fax: (530) 895-9207, Web Site: www.frwginc.com. Offering the finest handmade custom doors and entryways. Each franchise store also offers complete millwork packages, designer art glass, custom bars, room dividers and fireplace mantels. Established: 1971 - Franchising Since: 1998 - No. of Units: Company Owned: 1 - Franchised: 2 - Franchise Fee: $37,000 - Royalty: 6% - Total Inv: $150,000-$190,000 including build-out, display fee and working capital - Financing: No.

FIBRE TECH, INC.
2323 34th Way North, Largo, FL, 33771. Contact: Hugh Lynch, V.P. of Sales - Tel: (727) 585-5829, (800) 393-7283. Resurfacing of swimming pools, spas, fountains, water attractions, storage tanks. Established: 1987 - Franchising Since: 1988 - No. of Units: Company Owned: 1 - Franchised: 41 - Franchise Fee: $5,500 (includes materials to start) - Royalty: None-must buy resin from us - Financing: No.

FORESIGHT ENGINEERING, INC.
17 Cook Ave., Box 621, Madison, NJ, 07940. - Tel: (973) 377-0600, Fax: (973) 377-6445. Home and building inspection, radon testing, environmental testing, radon mitigation. Established: 1984 - Franchising Since: 1987 - No. of Units: Company Owned: 1 - Franchised: 6 - Franchise Fee: $15,000 - Royalty: 7% + 2% adv. - Total Inv: No other investment required - Financing: Yes.

FOUR SEASONS SUNROOMS
Four Seasons Marketing Corp.
5005 Veterans Memorial Hwy., Holbrook, NY, 11741. Contact: Tony Russo, VP Business Development - Tel: (631) 563-4000, (800) 521-0179, Fax: (631) 563-4010, E-Mail: tonyr@four-seasons-sunrooms.com, Web Site: www.four-seasons-sunrooms.com. Offer and sell the world's finest line of sunrooms, conservatories and patio rooms. Established: 1975 - Franchising Since: 1984 - No. of Units: Company Owned: 3 - Franchised: 234 - Franchise Fee: $7,500, $10,000, $15,000 - Total Inv: $13,250-$82,500 - Financing: No.

GUTTER SHIELD, THE
American Roof-Brite, Inc
4492 Acworth Industrial Drive., #102, Acworth, GA, 30101. Contact: Ray Johnson, President - Tel: (770) 966-1080, (800) 476-9271, E-Mail: shield@aok.org, Web Site: www.oak.org. Aluminum gutter shield, protection from clogged drains. Established: 1973 - Franchising Since: 1980 - No. of Units: Franchised: 80 - Franchise Fee: $1,995 - Royalty: None - Financing: No.

H. JACK'S PLUMBING & HOME COMFORT CO.
H. Jack Langer, Inc.
1523 Cascade St., Erie, PA, 16502. Contact: Bill Krause, Dir. of Sales - Tel: (814) 836-0286, (888) 454-8462, Fax: (814) 459-7484. Full service plumbing, drain cleaning and HVAC franchisor for conversion or start-up franchises. Established: 1997 - Franchising Since: 1997 - No. of Units: Company Owned: 12 - Franchise Fee: $7,500 and up - Royalty: 3%-6% - Total Inv: $36,565-$90,400 - Financing: No.

HANDYMAN CONNECTION
Mamar, Inc.
10250 Alliance Rd., Ste. 100, Cincinnati, OH, 45242. Contact: Fred Harms, Vice President - Tel: (513) 771-3003, (800) 466-5530, Fax: (513) 771-6439, Web Site: www.handymanconnection.com. Small to medium sized home repairs and remodeling at discounted price. Established: 1990 - Franchising Since: 1993 - No. of Units: Company Owned: 5- Franchised: 119 - Franchise Fee: $30,000 and up - Royalty: 5% - Total Inv: $75,000 and up - Financing: Franchise Fee.

HANDYMAN MATTERS FRANCHISE, INC
Handyman Matters, Inc
12136 W. Bayaud Ave Suite 105, Lakewood, CO, 80228. Contact: Andy Bell - Tel: (303) 984-0177, (303) 942-5993, E-Mail: franchiseinfo@handymanmatters.com, Web Site: www.handymanmatters.com. We repair, maintain carpenrty, plumbing, painting, roofing, flooring and other tasks for residential and commercial properties. Established: 1998 - Franchising Since: 2000 - No. of Units: Company Owned: 3 - Franchised: 10 - Franchise Fee: $25,000 - Financing: SBA approved.

HANDYMAN NETWORK *
1165 San Antonio Dr, #G, Long Beach, CA, 90807. - Tel: (877) 942-6396, Fax: (562) 984-4370, Web Site: www.handyman-network.com. We are a fully insured and licensed general contractor. We focus on small to medium sized home improvements. We can build, install, repair and improve just about everything around your house. Established: 2000 - Franchising Since: 2002 - No. of Units: Company Owned: 1 - Franchised: 16 - Franchise Fee: $29,500 - Royalty: 6% - Total Inv: $71,400-$96,400 - Financing: Third party.

HERITAGE LOG HOMES, INC.
P.O. Box 8080, Sevierville, TN, 37864. - Tel: (877) 655-1588, Fax: (865) 429-4434. Manufacturers of pre-cut, do-it-yourself log home kits for residential and commercial use. Established: 1974 - Franchising Since: 1974 - No. of Units: Company Owned: 1 - Franchised: 30+ - Franchise Fee: Purchase of model home - $10,000 average kit price - Total Inv: $50,000-$100,000 in model and commercial high traffic setting - Financing: None.

HONKA LOG HOMES
Honka Homes USA, Inc
35715 US Highway 40 ST. D-303, Evergreen, CO, 80439. Contact: Pekka Laine, President - Tel: (303) 679-0568, (877) US HONKA, Fax: (303) 679-0641, E-Mail: info@honka.com, Web Site: www.honka.com. Log homes sales and design manufacturing. Established: 1958 -

Franchising Since: 1999 - No. of Units: Franchised: 2 - Franchise Fee: $50,000 - Royalty: 2.5% - Total Inv: $500,000-$1,000,000 - Financing: Yes.

HORIZON, USA, INC.

2701 Lisenby Ave., Panama City, FL, 32405. - Tel: (850) 285-1994, (800) 476-3246, Fax: (850) 769-1122. Sunrooms and windows. Established: 1979 - Franchising Since: 1998 - No. of Units: Franchised: 7 - Franchise Fee: $50,000 - Royalty: 9%, 1% adv - Total Inv: $70,000-$20,000 start up - Financing: Yes.

HOUSE DOCTORS HANDYMAN SERVICE
H.D. Franchising Systems, LLC

575 Chamber Dr., Milford, OH, 445150. Contact: Franchise Department - Tel: (513) 469-2443, (800) 319-3359, Fax: (513) 469-2226, E-Mail: info@housedoctors.com, Web Site: www.housedoctors.com. Handyman service specializing in minor home repairs. Established: 1994 - Franchising Since: 1995 - No. of Units: Franchised: 235 - Franchise Fee: $13,900-$31,900 - Royalty: 6% - Total Inv: $19,450-$45,550 - Financing: Yes.

HOUSE MENDERS

1561 N. Grandview Ln, Provo, UT, 84604. Contact: Gerald J. Nebeker - Tel: (801) 796-9540, Fax: (801) 796-9561, E-Mail: housemender@email.msn.com, Web Site: www.HouseMenders.com. Our focus is on remodeling & repair of residential & commercial buildings. Established: 1997 - Franchising Since: 2000 - No. of Units: Company Owned: 1 - Franchise Fee: $10,000-$55,000 - Total Inv: $72,200-$157,550 - Financing: Will finance upto 50% of the franchise fee.

HYDRO PHYSICS PIPE INSPECTION CORP.

1855 West Union Ave., Unit N, Englewood, CO, 80110. Contact: Thomas (T.J.) Suiter, President/CEO - Tel: (303) 781-2474, (800) 781-3164, Fax: (303) 781-0477, E-Mail: hydrophys@aol.com. We specialize in inspecting underground pipeline systems. We photograph the lines and find problem areas for repair. Established: 1991 - Franchising Since: 1997 - No. of Units: Company Owned: 1 - Franchised: 6 - Franchise Fee: $19,500 - Royalty: 7.5%, 2% nat'l. adv. - Total Inv: $99,500 - Third party.

INSULATED DRY-ROOF SYSTEM
IDRS, Inc.

152 S.E. 5th Ave., Hillsboro, OR, 97123. Contact: Nat'l. Fran. Dir. - Tel: (503) 693-1619, Fax: (503) 693-1993. Sell and install vinyl roofing, some with shingle imprint on it: for mobile and manufactured homes, low slope residential and commercial. Lifetime warranty, no experience necessary. Established: 1986 - Franchising Since: 1989 - No. of Units: Franchised: 30 - Franchise Fee: $25,000-$50,000 (based on territory) - Royalty: 3% of gross sales - Total Inv: $50,000-$100,000, open. cap. - Financing: Some.

INSURANCE REPAIR CORPORATION OF AMERICA
(IRCOA)

3936 S.Semorah Blvd #1405, P.O Box 560427, Orlando, FL, 32822. - Tel: (407) 737-1220, Fax: (407) 851-8930, E-Mail: Ron@ircoa.com, Web Site: www.ircoa.com. Insurance repair contracting to existing national accounts. Background in construction not necessary. Our franchisees manage jobs, they do not need to sell, estimate or market work. Established:1997 - Franchising Since: 1997 - No. of Units: Company Owned: 3 - Franchised: 1 - Franchise Fee: $10,000 minimum-fee based on population - Royalty: 5% - Financing: Yes.

K & N MOBILE DISTRIBUTION SYSTEM®
K & N Electric Franchising, Inc

4909 Rondo Drive, Fort Worth, TX, 76160. - Tel: (817) 626-2885. Sales of electric parts and hardware. Established: 1972 - No. of Units: Company Owned: 10 - Franchised: 23 - Franchise Fee: $23,500 - Total Inv: $22,400-$82,300 - Financing: Yes.

KITCHEN SOLVERS
Kitchen Solvers, Inc

401 Jay St., La Crosse, WI, 54601. - Tel: (608) 791-5518, (800) 845-6779, Fax: (608) 784-2917, Web Site: www.kitchensolvers.com. Home based kitchen & bath remodeling franchise, specializing in cabinet refacing, new cabinets, solid surface countertops and acrylic bath & shower liners. Low franchise investment. Established: 1982 - Franchising

Since: 1984 - No. of Units: Company Owned: 1 - Franchised: 128 - Franchise Fee: $25,000-$29,500 - Royalty: 4-6% - Total Inv: $40,300-$73,00 - Financing: Yes.

KITCHEN TUNE-UP
KTU Worldwide, Inc

813 Circle Dr, Aberdeen, SD, 57401. Contact: Craig Green, Franchise Director - Tel: (605) 225-4049, (800) 333-6385, (605) 225-1371, Fax: (605) 225-1371, E-Mail: ktu@kitchentuneup.com, Web Site: www.kitchentuneup.com. KTU offers residential & commercial remodeling services. 1-day wood restoration, cabinet refacing, custom cabinets, acrylic tub lining systems, cabinet accressories & no-sand wood floor restoration. Established: 1986 - Franchising Since: 1988 - No. of Units: Franchised: 310+ - Franchise Fee: $25,000 - Royalty: 4.5%-7% - Total Inv: $40,000-$50,000 - Financing: Third party.

KITCHENPRO

10451 Mill Run Cir., Ste. 400, Owings Mills, MD, 21117. Contact: Franchise Coordinator - Tel: (410) 356-8889, Fax: (410) 356-8804. Kitchen and bath design showrooms. Established: 1993 - Franchising Since: 1993 - Franchise Fee: $25,000 - Total Inv: $136,000-$252,000 incl. fran. fee - Financing: None.

LIBERTY SEAMLESS GUTTERS
Liberty Seamless Enterprises

102 E. Railroad Ave., Knoxville, PA, 16928. Contact: Kurt Heisey, President - Tel: (814) 326-4121, (800) 806-7109, Fax: (814) 326-4123. Install seamless main gutters and downspouts out of a cube van. Established:1994 - Franchising Since: 1997 - No. of Units: Company Owned: 4 - Franchised: 2 - Franchise Fee: $15,000 - Royalty: $1,000 per month - Total Inv: $28,500-$72, 850 - Financing: No.

LINC CORPORATION,THE

4 North Shore Center, Pittsburgh, PA, 15212. Contact: Franchise Dept. V.P. - Tel: (412) 359-2123, Fax: (412) 321-3809. Maintenance of mechanical systems in non-residential buildings. Established: 1978 - Franchising Since: 1979 - No. of Units: Franchised: 92 - Franchise Fee: $30,000 - Total Inv: $50,000 - Royalty: Graduated scale 4.5% (high) to 1% (low) based on gross revenues.

LUXURY BATH SYSTEMS

1958 Brandon Ct, Glendale Heights, IL, 60139. - Tel: (630) 295-9084, Fax: (630) 295-9418, E-Mail: luxurybath@aol.com, Web Site: www.luxurybath.com. One day bathroom remodelling, using acrylic bathtub liners and acrylic wall surrounds. Established: 1989 - Franchising Since: 1990 - No. of Units: Franchised: 66 - Franchise Fee: $16,000 - Royalty: None - Total Inv: $50,000-$100,000 must open retail showroom.

MAGNUM PIERING

13230 Ferguson Lane, Bridgeton, MO, 63044. Contact: Mark G. Murphy, Pres. - Tel: (314) 291-7437. Company stabilizes and corrects building settlement utilizing patented products and processes. System can be used on residential and commercial structures. Established: 1985 - Franchising Since: 1985 - No. of Units: Franchised: 7 - Franchise Fee: $20,000 - Royalty: 6% gross receipts - Total Inv: $75,000-$105,000 excl. fran. fee - Financing: None.

MAINTENANCE MADE SIMPLE
ServiceMate Corporation

9820 E. Dreyfus Ave, Scottsdale, AZ, 85260. Contact: Jim Butler, Dir. of Business Development - Tel: (602) 618-7748, (866) 778-6283, E-Mail:info@m2simple.com, Web Site: www.m2simple.com. Maintenance Made Simple offers Handyman an Home Repair Franchise Opportunities. We have taken the traitional industry and brought it into the 21st century with a new concept, our advanced marketing an sales, an innovative technology. Established: 2003 - Franchising Since: 2003 - Franchise Fee: $30,000 - Royalty: 7% - Total Inv: $35,300-$64,800 - Financing: No.

MARBLELIFE

805 W North Carrier Pkwy., Ste. 220, Grand Prairie, TX, 75050. Contact: Kimberly Colclaure, Marketing Director - Tel: (972) 623-0500, (800) 627-4569, Fax: (972) 623-0220, E-Mail: marbilelife@marblelife.com, Web Site: www.marblelife.com. Specializing in the restoration, preservation, and maintenance services for natural stones and other surfaces. Established: 1989 - Franchising Since: 1989 - No.

of Units: Company Owned: 1 - Franchised: 48 - Franchise Fee: $10,000-$75,000 - Royalty: 6%, 2% adv. - Total Inv: $56,000-$140,000 - Financing: Yes for qualified applicants.

METAL MAINTENANCE SERVICES
Metal Maintenance Services Intl.
P.O. Box 953307, Lake Mary, FL, 32795-3307. Contact: Gene Dignoti Sr., CEO - Tel: (407) 321-3995, ext.14,(800) 959-0466, ext.14, Fax:(407) 324-1619, E-Mail: gfdsr@metalmaintenance.com, Web Site: www.metalmaintenance.com. Metal Maintenance Services mobile operations specializes in restoring and preserving a wide range of architectural metal surfaces from elevator doors to sculptures. Established: 1996 - Franchising Since: 1998 - No. of Units: Franchised: 6 - Franchise Fee: $11,900-$35,700 - Royalty: 4% - Total Inv: $20,400-$48,900 - Financing: No.

MICHAEL HOLIGAN HOMES
Michael Holigan Franchise Systems, Ltd
13760 Noel Road, 5th Floor, Dallas, TX, 75240. Contact: J. David Young, President - Tel: (972) 701-8485, (800) 444-5690, Fax: (972) 701-8582, Web Site: www.Yournewhouse.com. Franchisor, residential home builders. Established: 1999 - Franchising Since: 1999 - No. of Units: Company Owned: 1 - Franchised: 21 - Franchise Fee: $50,000 - Royalty: 3% of total contract sales price, 1/2 of 1% of total contract sales price for marketing and advertising, completion construction fund: 1/2 0f 1% of total contract sales price - Total Inv: Conversion of existing home builders - Financing: Third party.

MIRACLE METHOD SURFACE RESTORATION
Miracle Method Surface Restoration
4239 N.Nevada Ave #115, Colorado Springs, CO, 80907. Contact: Paul Leonard - Tel: (719) 594-9196, (800) 444-8827, Fax: (719) 594-9282, E-Mail: sales@miraclemethod.com, Web Site: www.miracle method.com. Miracle Method provides promising business opportunities in the surface restoration industry for the motivated business person. Operate as a single operator from your home, or grow into a multi-truck operation with several technicians and a proper office and showroom. Established: 1979 - Franchising Since: 1979 - No. of Units: Company Owned: 1 - Franchised: 80 - Franchise Fee: $18,000 - Royalty: 5% - Total Inv: $20,000 - Financing: Yes.

MR. APPLIANCE
1010 N. University Parks Dr., Waco, TX, 76707. - Tel: (800) 290-1422, Fax: (254) 745-5098, E-Mail: mowens@mrappliance.com, Web Site: www.dwyergroup.com. 24-hour appliance repair. Established: 1996 - Franchising Since: 1996 - No. of Units: Franchised: 23 - Franchise Fee: $15,900 - Royalty: 6%-3% - Total Inv: $22,435-$26,015 - Financing: Yes on equip. purchased.

MR. ELECTRIC
1010 N. University Parks Dr., Waco, TX, 76707. - Tel: (800) 253-9151, Fax: (254) 745-5068. Web Site: www.mrelectric.com. Electrical service and repair franchise for residential and light commercial customers. Locations in 26 states, the United Kingdom, New Zealand, Saudi Arabia and Canada. Established: 1994 - Franchising Since: 1995 - No. of Units: Franchised: 60 - Franchise Fee: $15,000 - Royalty: 6%-3% - Total Inv: $25,000-$150,000 depending on size of territory - Financing: Yes.

MR. HANDYMAN
Service Brands International
3948 Ranchero Dr, Ann Arbor, MI, 48108. - Tel: (734) 822-6535, Fax: (734) 822-6888, E-Mail: info@mrhandyman.com, Web Site: www.mrhandyman.com. Mr. Handyman is a leader in a high-demand service that caters to 100 million U.S. homeowners and commercial customer's needing property repairs. Established: 2000 - Franchising Since: 2000 - No. of Units: Franchised: 120 - Franchise Fee: $9,500 - Total Inv: $47,000 - Financing: Yes.

MR. ROOTER CORP.
1010 N. University Parks Dr., Waco, TX, 76707. Contact: Franchise Department - Tel: (800) 298-6855, Fax: (254) 745-5098. Full service plumbing and sewer and drain. Established: 1968 - Franchising Since: 1972 - No. of Units: Franchised: 260 - Franchise Fee: $17,500 per 100,000 population - Royalty: 6% to 3% on gross rev. - Total Inv: $25,000-$100,000 plus depending on area - Financing: To qualified parties.

N-HANCE *
1530 N. 1000 West, Logan, UT, 84321. - Tel: (435) 755-0099, Fax: (435) 755-0021, Web Site: www.nhancefranchise.com. Wood floor & cabinet renewal system. Established: 2001 - Franchising Since: 2003 - No. of Units: Franchised: 3 - Franchise Fee: Varies - Royalty: $220-$660/Mo. - Total Inv: $22,500-$37,500.

NEWCOMERS OF AMERICA HOME INSPECTION SERVICE, INC.
7734 Prairie Rd, Eagle River, WI, 54521-9660. Contact: Dir. of Fran. Sales - Tel: (414) 549-8070, Fax: (414) 549-8065. Home inspection at time of buying a home. Established: 1988 - Franchising Since: 1994 - No. of Units: Company Owned: 13 - Franchised: 70 - Franchise Fee: $16,275 - Royalty: 7% of revenue, 1.5% nat'l. adv. - Financing: On more than one unit. Not franchising at this time.

OLDE WORLD TILE MANUFACTURING
Olde World Enterprises, Inc
1517 Moccasin Creek Rd., P.O. Box 531, Murphy, NC, 28906. Contact: John McKenzie Panagos, President - Tel: (828) 837-0357, Fax: (828) 837-1458, E-Mail: Info@Oldeworld.com, Web Site: www.OldeWorld Tile.com. Learn to manufacture and market hand-made, custom floor tile for under $500. Complete Training Package and 8 FREE Bonuses have you making tile in a week! LIFETIME tech, marketing and moral support included, and no franchise fees or royalties to pay. Established: 1991 - Franchising Since: 1994 - No. of Units: Company Owned: 1 - Franchised: 50 - Total Inv: $477 Training/Start-up Supplies and another $500 or less in raw materials - Financing: No, but you receive a $477 credit once 500 sf of molds are purchased. Like getting your training FREE!

ONE HOUR AIR CONDITIONING *
2 N. Tamiami Trail, #506, Sarasota, FL, 43236. Contact: Franchise Department - Tel: (800) 746-0458, Fax: (941) 552-5130, Web Site: www.onehourair.com. Residential HVAC replacement & services. Established: 1999 - Franchising Since: 2003 - No. of Units: Company Owned: 7 - Franchised: 87 - Franchise Fee: $15,000 - Royalty: 4% - Total Inv: $46,000-$400,000.

ONLY THE FINEST
P.O. Box 43, Holland, OH, 43528. Contact: Danny L. Noe, President - Tel: (419) 867-1133, (888) 867-1133, Fax: (419) 867-7781. Custom manufacture of counter tops, vanity tops, tub decks, shower surrounds. Established: 1990 - Franchising Since: 1997 - No. of Units: Franchised: 3 - Franchise Fee: Under $10,000 - Royalty: 5% of gross sales with $850.00 CAP - Total Inv: Approx. $30,000 (tools $13,000, fee: under $10,000, operating capital $7,000) - Financing: Possible SBA funds.

PAINTNET INCORPORATED
P.O. Box 18274, Rochester, NY, 14618-0274. Contact: President - Tel: (716) 458-5320, (800) 505-6210, Fax: (716) 458-1803, Web Site: www.paintnetinc.com. Franchisees will receive training and on going support for marketing, sales, estimating, systems applications and procedures. Franchisees will offer to the commercial and industrial clients painting and wallcovering services. Established: 1996 - Franchising Since: 1998 - Franchise Fee: $15,000 - Royalty: Min. of $1,000 a month or 5% of the gross - Total Inv: $31,585-$46,350 including franchise fee - Financing: No.

PAUL W. DAVIS SYSTEMS, INC.
1 Independent Dr, Suite 2300, Jacksonville, FL, 32202-5039. - Tel: (800) 722-1818, Fax: (904) 737-4204, Web Site: www.pdrestoration.com. Computerized insurance restoration service working with major insurance companies. Established: 1966 - Franchising Since: 1970 - No. of Units: Franchised: 250 - Franchise Fee: $48,500 - Royalty: 3.5% - Total Inv: $102,400-$150,200 - Financing: Yes.

PERMA CERAM
Perma Ceram Enterprises, Inc.
65 Smithtown Blvd., Smithtown, NY, 11787. Contact: Joseph Tumolo, Pres. - Tel: (631) 724-1205, (800) 645-5039, Fax: (631) 724-9626. Bathroom fixture resurfacing in private homes, hotels, motels, apartment houses, hospitals, etc., with our own PORCELAINCOTE. Wherever there is a bathroom there is a need for our service. Established: 1975 - Franchising Since: 1976 - No. of Units: Company Owned: 1 - Franchised: 186 - Total Inv: $24,500.

PERMA* CRETE RESURFACING SURFACES

501 Metroplex Dr. Ste 115, Nashville, TN, 37211. Contact: Mr. Greg Hill, Senior Vice President - Tel: (615) 331-9200, (800) 607-3762, Fax: (615) 834-1335. A PERMA*CRETE surface is a three-part, acrylic polymer cementatious resurfacing system of over 6000 psi compressive strength that provides an architectural, load-bearing surface. It's sealed and non-porous, resists chemicals and freezing. Established: 1990 - Total Inv: Product purchase $5,000 min - Financing: No.

PERMA-GLAZE INC.

1638 S. Research Loop Rd., Ste. 160, Tucson, AZ, 85710. Contact: Dale Young, President - Tel: (520) 722-9718, (800) 332-7397, Fax: (520) 296-4393, E-Mail: permaglaze@permaglaze.com, Web Site: www.permaglaze.com. Multi-surface restoration of bathtubs, sinks, countertops, appliances and much more. Established: 1978 - Franchising Since: 1981 No. of Units: Company Owned: 2 - Franchised: 162 - Franchise Fee: Starting at $21,500 - Royalty: No royalty fee - Total Inv: $19,500 + $3,000 start-up - Financing: No.

PERMA-JACK CO.

9066 Watson Rd., St. Louis, MO, 63126. - Tel: (314) 843-1957. Stabilizing building foundations with steel piers driven to rockor equal load bearing strata, fast, with no expensive excavation. Established: 1974 - Franchising Since: 1975 - No. of Units: Franchised: 38 - Franchise Fee: 0 - Royalty: 5% - Total Inv: $24,200-$68,300 - Financing: No.

PILLAR TO POST PROFESSIONAL HOME INSPECTION

Pillar To Post Inc

13902 N. Dale Mabry Hwy., Ste. 300, Tampa, FL, 33618. Contact: Director of Franchising - Tel: (877) 963-3129, Web Site: www.pillartopost.com. Provide training, marketing, and on-going support in the home inspection business. Established: 1994- Franchising Since: 1994 - No. of Units: Franchised: 173 - Franchise Fee: $13,900-$23,900 - Royalty: 7% gross - Total Inv: $17,000-$34,000 - Financing: Yes.

PIRTEK

Pirtek USA

501 Haverty Court, Rockledge, FL, 32955. Contact: Morgan Arundel, President - Tel: (407) 504-4422, (888) 7-PIRTEK, Fax: (407) 504-4433, E-Mail: pirtekusa@pirtekusa.com, Web Site: www.pirtekusa.com. Pirtek offers a business format franchise proven successful since 1980 in 9 countries. We provide mobile hose repair service to all industries. Established: 1997 - Franchising Since: 1997 - No. of Units: Company Owned: 1 - Franchised: 2 - Franchise Fee: $35,000 - Royalty: 4% license, 1 1/2% marketing - Total Inv: $300,000 - Financing: Third party.

POSIGRIP

Acousti-Clean Inc

331 S. River Dr., Ste.1, Tempe, AZ, 85281. Contact: Greg Ohlinger, Dir of Bus. Devel. - Tel: (480) 804-0517,(800) 847-9605, Fax: (480) 804-0547. When product applied to floors, tubs, pool decks, showers etc, it will make surface nonslip when wet. Established: 1996 - No. of Units: Company Owned: 1 - Franchised: 125 - Total Inv: $6,995-$9,995 - Financing: No.

POTTY DOCTOR PLUMBING SERVICE

Potty Doctor Franchise Systems

P.O. Box 1426, Lake Worth, FL, 33460. Contact: Mr. Guthrie Pres. - Tel: (561) 582-0571. Residential plumbing service. Service agreements, faucet and sink repair and replacement, water filtration and conservation. Established: 1992 - Franchising Since: 1993 - No. of Units: Company Owned: 1 - Franchised: 1 - Franchise Fee: $15,000-$30,000 - Royalty: 6% of gross sales, 2% adv. - Total Inv: Depends on applicant - Financing: None.

PRECISION CONCRETE CUTTING

3191 N. Canyon Rd, Provo, UT, 84604. Contact: Aaron Ollivier, Director of Marketing and Sales - Tel: (801) 373-4060, (800) 833-7770, Fax: (801) 373-6088, E-Mail: info@pccconcrete.com, Web Site: www.pccfranchise.com. We specialize in removing trip hazards from the sidewalk in compliance with the Americans with Disablties Act. We use a unique saw-cutting method to remove the hazard providing a much smoother finished product than grinders or scarifiers. Established:

1992 - No. of Units: Company Owned: 1 - Franchised: 6 - Franchise Fee: $95,000 - Total Inv: $100,000 - Financing: Yes, circumstances may vary.

PROFESSIONAL HOUSE DOCTORS

Professional House Doctors, Inc.

1406 E. 14th St., Des Moines, IA, 50316. Contact: Dane J. Shearer, Pres. - Tel: (515) 265-6667, Fax: (515) 278-2070. Environmental and building science specialists. Established: 1982 - Franchising Since: 1991 - No. of Units: Company Owned: 1 - Franchised: 3 - Franchise Fee: $9,800 - Royalty: 6%+ 2% adv. co-op - Total Inv: $15,000 - Financing: Yes.

PROHOME OF (NAME OF CITY)

ProHome Incorporated

7701 E. Kellogg, Ste. 890, Wichita, KS, 67207. Contact: Jack Salmans, Pres. - Tel: (316) 687-6776, (800) 899-2451, Fax: (316) 687-0455. Provides warranty callback service for home builders and new home buyers. Established: 1983 - Franchising Since: 1993 - No. of Units: Company Owned: 2 - Franchised: 10 - Franchise Fee: $40,000 - Royalty: 7% gross sales - Total Inv: $80,000-$100,000 - Financing: Yes.

PTR BATHTUB RESTORATION

SPR International

4492 Acworth Industrial Drive., Ste. 102, Acworth, GA, 30101. Contact: Ray Johnson, Sales Dir. - Tel: (770) 966-1331, Fax: (770) 975-4647, E-Mail: aokray@hotmail.com, Web Site: www.aok.org. Restoration of old bathtubs, no spraying, no odours and no dust. Ready to use the same day. In demand for hotels, apartments, nursing homes and private homes world wide. Established: 1989 - Franchising Since: 1989 - No. of Units: Franchised: 55 - Franchise Fee: $7,995 - Royalty: 10% product fee, for product used - Total Inv: $7,995 - Financing: Yes.

PULL-OUT SHELF COMPANY, INC.

5600 E Rio Verde Vista Dr., Tucson, AZ, 85750-1969. Contact: E.B. Kessler, President - Tel: (520) 299-2402, Fax: (520) 299-5751, Web Site: www.pulloutshelfusa.com. Manufacturer of pull-out shelves that can be retro-fitted into kitchen and bathroom cabinets. Unique patented system. Exclusive territories available. Established: 1993 - Franchising Since: 1993 - No. of Units: Company Owned: 1 - Franchised and Dealers: 24 - Franchise Fee: Dealers only at present time $2000 - Royalty: N/A - Total Inv: $3,500 - Financing: No.

QUARZTEX & SURE-TREP

Trend Coating, Inc

1850 Porter Lake Dr Ste 107, Sarasota, FL, 34240-7806. Contact: Anthony Goslin, President & CEO. - Tel: (941)923-6292,(800) 632-2063, Fax: (941)342-4323. During the past 52 years we have built a reputation for providing our customers with the best quality products, services and most reasonable prices.Quartex® is a non-skid acrylic coating system modified with epoxy, sio2 and pomex. Our special formula of these elements creates an extremely hard and durable, yet flexible, weatherproof coating system designed to combine safety and design aesthetics. QUARZTEX™ has virtually unlimited uses in both residential and commercial. Established: 1946 - Franchising Since: 1997 - No. of Units: Company Owned: 2 - Franchised: 5 - Franchise Fee: $5,000-$40,000 - Royalty: None - Total Inv: $8,895 - Financing: Negotiable.

RE-BATH

Re-Bath Corporation

1055 S. Country Club Dr., Mesa, AZ, 85210-4613. - Tel: (800) 426-4573, (480) 844-1575, Fax: (480) 833-7199, E-Mail: newfranchise@re-bath.com, Web Site: www.re-bath.com. We specialize in one-day bathroom remodeling with acrylic bathtub liners, wall surround systems and shower base liners. Easy sale and quick installation. No inventory required. Established: 1979 - Franchising Since: 1991 - No. of Units: Company Owned: 1 - Franchised: 107 - Franchise Fee: $20,000-$40,000 - Royalty: $25 per unit - Total Inv: $49,900-$129,000 - Financing: No.

REJUVINAIR®

4852 Pimlico Dr, Tallahassee, FL, 32308. Contact: Richard - Tel: (850) 894-2203, (888) STE-AM99, Fax: (850) 893-7604, E-Mail: rejuvinair@netally.com, Web Site: www.rejuvinair.com. Air conditioners which are environmentally safe, 305-degree steam uses no acids or chemicals! Clean air, huge energy savings, lower replacement and repair costs. Established: 1997 - Franchising Since: 1999 - No. of Units: Company Owned: 4 - Franchise Fee: $10,000-$50,000 - Total Inv: $95,900-$162,900.

RESIDENTIAL BUILDING INSPECTORS

701 Fairway Dr., Clayton, NC, 27520. - Tel: (919) 553-3959. Home inspection service. Established: 1986 - Franchising Since: 1989 - No. of Units: Franchised: 8 - Franchise Fee: $6,875 - Royalty: 10% - Total Inv: $1,500-$4,000 start-up + fran. fee.

ROCKY MOUNTAIN LOG HOMES

Montana Sundown, Inc.
1883 Hwy. 93 S., Hamilton, MT, 59840. Contact: Mark Moreland, V.P. Sales. - Tel: (406) 363-5680, Fax: (406) 363-2109. Log home manufacturer seeking distributors for home packages, provide 30+ standard plans and support for custom home packages. Established: 1974 - Licensing Since: 1974 - No. of Units: Company Owned: 2 - Licensed: 90 - Franchise Fee: $500-$3,000 - Total Inv: $75,000.

ROLL-A-WAY INC.

10601 Oak St., N.E., St. Petersburg, FL, 33716. Contact: V.P. Fran. & Bus.Dev. - Tel: (888) 765-5292, Fax: (727) 579-9410, E-Mail: info@roll-a-way.com, Web Site: www.roll-a-way.com. Manufacturer of security and storm shutters. Established: 1955 - Franchising Since: 1994 - No. of Units: Company Owned: 3 - Franchised: 51 - Franchise Fee: $19,000-$43,000 determined by population - Royalty: None - Total Inv: $80,000 including fee - Financing: No.

ROOF AMERICA PLUS INC.

530 E. Lexington Ave., Ste. 175, Elkhart, IN, 46516. Contact: Kurt Hostetler, Pres. - Tel: (800) 291-9817, (219) 522-4453, Fax: (219) 522-2672. Home based franchisees tap into the $3.8 billion re-roofing market and provide the homeowner with a unique alternative to re-roofing their house. This proprietary system seals and waterproofs the roof providing years of protection against the elements. Full training and ongoing field support included. Established: 1995 - Franchising Since: 1996 - Franchise Fee: $25,000 - Royalty: 4% on gross sales - Total Inv: $60,000-$80,000 (includes franchise fee), inv. working cap. mktg promotions, etc. - Financing: No.

ROOF CHAMPION, INC.

Roof Champion
8022 N. Ridgeway, Skokie, IL, 60076. - Tel: (847) 673-7663, Fax: (847) 673-7611. Franchise roof applicators and deck cleaning process to apply a new elastomeric. 100% acrylic roof coating to existing roofs extending the roof life for 10 years. Also supplying retail outlets with product. Established: 1996 - Franchising Since: 1997 - No. of Units: Company Owned: 1 - Franchised: 2 - Franchise Fee: $25,000-$35,000 - Royalty: Percent of product sold - Total Inv: Franchise Fee $25,000-$35,000+ start up costs $10,000 - Financing: No.

ROOF PATCH MASTERS, LLC

310 Polo Pony, Austin, TX, 78683. Contact: Tim Adams - Tel: (512) 635-6483, Web Site: www.roofpatchmasters.com. Roof Patch Masters franchisees repair and maintain commercial and residential roofs and provide other roof related services. Established: 1965 - Franchising Since: 2001 - No. of Units: Company Owned: 1 - Franchised: 2 - Franchise Fee: $7,500 - Total Inv: Capital requirements; $4,750 - Financing: No.

ROOTER-MAN

268 Rangeway Rd, North Billerica, MA, 01862. - Tel: (800) 700-8062, Fax: (978) 663-0061, Web Site: www.rooterman.com. Rooter-Man is a successful and proven systems built around the exclusive use of our US registered service marks in your local area. With your license you will have access to the management skills and know how of professionals who have had years of experience in the sewer and drain cleaning industry. Established: 1970 - Franchising Since: 1981 - No. of Units: Franchised: 62 - Franchise Fee: $3,980 - Royalty: Varies - Total Inv: $46,800-$137,600.

ROTO-ROOTER CORP.

300 Ashworth Rd., West Des Moines, IA, 50265. Contact: Paul E. Barkman, Dir. of Int'l. Dev. - Tel: (515) 223-1343, Fax: (515) 223-6109. We are seeking serious, financially capable individuals or entities for master license opportunities in plumbing repair, sewer-drain service and related service product opportunities worldwide. Roto-Rooter offers training, advertising, support and over 60 years of industry experience to qualified principals. Established: 1934 - Licensing Since: 1935 - No. of Units: Company Owned: 84 - Licensed: 566 - License Fee: Varies - Royalty: Per agreement - Total Inv: Varies by country - Financing: No.

SCHUMACHER GARAGE DOOR

P.O. Box 891780, Temecula, CA, 92589. Contact: Larry Schumacher, President - Tel: (909) 676-1902,(800) 671-0977, Fax: (909) 678-9880. Repair of garage door systems, home based, home service business, loan investment, mobile van, complete training. Established: 1987 - Franchising Since: 1997 - No. of Units: Company Owned: 1 - Franchise Fee: $15,000 - Royalty: 5%-0% adv. - Total Inv: $30,000-$60,000 - Financing: No.

SERVICE WORLD

Service Centers Internationall, Inc.
1801 Central, Suite H, Hot Springs, AK, 71903. Contact: Franchise Director - Tel: (901) 368-3361, Fax: (901) 368-1144. Provide a single place to call at any time to get help with electrical work, house painting, landscaping, remodelling, and repair needs that you may have. Established: 1995 - Franchising Since: 1997 - No. of Units: Franchised: 4 - Franchise Fee: $24,500 - Royalty: 7.5% , 1% adv - Total Inv: $33,900-$52,150 - Financing: No.

SHINGLE CARE SYSTEMS INC

102 Drennen Rd., Ste A-4, Orlando, FL, 32806. Contact: Randy Rucker - Tel: (407) 246-7237, (800) 578-5981, Fax: (407) 447-3680, E-Mail: mail@shinglecare.com, Web Site: www.shingleacre.com. We provide roof cleaning and preventative maintenance. Established: 1999 - No. of Units: Company Owned: 1 - Franchised: 19 - Total Inv: Capital requuirements; $2,500-$10,000 - Financing: Equipment leasing and financing packages available.

SOFT TOUCH INTERIORS

Soft Touch International
801 North Brand Blvd First Floor, Glendale, CA, 91203. - Tel: (818) 265-9700, Fax: (818) 265-9707. Soft Touch offers property owners a way to restyle their homes by using the high tech instant remodeling Soft Touch system. Our franchisees bring computer imaging, morphing capabilities to the client allowing them to see the home improvements they want before their job is even started. Established: 1993 - Franchising Since: 1996 - No. of Units: Company Owned: 1 - Franchised: 1 - Franchise Fee: $18,000 - Royalty: 6% - Total Inv: $25,000-$30,000 - Financing: Yes.

SPEED FAB-CRETE CORP.

P.O. Box 15580, Fort Worth, TX, 76119. Contact; David Bloxom, Pres. - Tel: (817) 478-1137, Fax: (817) 561-2544, Web Site: www.speedfab-crete.com. Design-build general contractor specializing with a plant manufactured, precast concrete wall panel building system since 1962. Established: 1962 - Licensing Since: 1962 - License Fee: $50,000 - Royalty: 1% gross sales monthly - Total Inv: Varies depending on size and direction of plant operations - Financing: No.

SPR COUNTER TOP & TUB REPAIR SERVICE

SPR International Inc.
4492 Acworth Industrial Drive #102, Acworth, GA, 30101. Contact: Sales Director - Tel: (770) 966-1331, (800) 476-9271, Fax: (770) 975-4647, Web Site: www.aok.org. Repair of bathtubs and countertops, porcelain, fiberglass, acrylic, marble, formica chips, cracks and burns, needed in new construction, apartments, hotels and homes being re-sold. Established: 1973 - Franchising Since: 1974 - No. of Units: Franchised: 10 - Franchise Fee: $7,995.00 - Royalty: 10% - Total Inv: Includes tools, training and products - Financing: Yes.

SPR MARBLE REPAIR

SPR International Inc.
4492 Acworth Ind. Dr. # 102, Acworth, GA, 30101. Contact: Larry Stevens, President - Tel: (770) 966-1331, Fax: (770) 975-4647, E-Mail: marble@aok.org, Web Site: www.aok.org. Repair and restoration of marble statues, tables, lamps, fireplace hearths. Sealing of marble surface to prevent staining. Commercial and residential. Established: 1974 - Franchising Since: 1974 - No. of Units: Company Owned: 1 - Franchised: 3 - Franchise Fee: $7,995 - Royalty: 10% product fee for products - Financing: Yes.

SPR TILE RESTORATION
SPR International
4492 Acworth Industrial Dr., #102, Acworth, GA, 30101. Contact: Ray Johnson, Sales Dir. - Tel: (770) 966-1331, (800) 476-9271, Fax: (770) 975-4647, E-Mail: aokray@hotmail.com, Web Site: www.aok.org. Restoration of ceramic tile, walls and floors. Make old tile look like new. New grout colors, repair holes and cracks. Established: 1973 - Franchising Since: 1980 - No. of Units: Franchised: 30 - Franchise Fee: $7,995 - Royalty: 10% - chemicals - Financing: Yes.

STARDEK *
928 Sligh Ave, Seffner, FL, 33584. Contact: Lisa Simmons - Tel: (813) 655-4880, (800) 282-1599, Fax: (813) 655-8830, E-Mail: info@stardek.com, Web Site: www.stardek.com. Making concrete beautiful from driveway's, walkways, to pool decks and more. Established: 1972 - Franchising Since: 1972 - Franchise Fee: 0 - Total Inv: $350.-$5,000.

SUPERIOR WALLS OF AMERICA
937 East Earl Rd, New Holland, PA, 17557. - Tel: (717) 351-9255, (800) 452-9255, Fax: (717) 351-9263, Web Site: www.superior walls.com. Franchisor offering opportunity to manufacture, sell and install precast insulated concrete studded walls for basement foundation and above ground. Wall system is waterproof and is delivered to the job site ready to finish. Installed time is less than 4 hours for most jobs. Established: 1981 - Franchising Since: 1986 - No. of Units: Franchised: 20 - Franchise Fee: $30,000 - Royalty: 4% of gross sales - Total Inv: $300,000-$400,000 - Financing: Third party.

SURFACE DOCTOR RESURFACING
4239 N. Nevada #115, Colorado Springs, CO, 80907. Contact: Paul Leonard, Vice President - Tel: (719) 594-9091, (800) 735-5055, Fax: (719) 594-9282, E-Mail: sales@surfacedoctor.com, Web Site: www.surfacedoctor.com. Resurfacing of tubs, tile, counters and cabinets. Save up to 70% of replacement costs. Established: 1996 - Franchising since: 1996 - No. of Units: Franchised: 51 - Franchise Fee: $16,500 - Royalty: 5% of gross revenue - Total Inv: $24,50-$50,000 - Financing: Yes.

SURFACE SPECIALISTS
Surface Specialists Systems, Inc.
621-B Stallings Rd, Matthews, NC, 28105. Contact: Amy Irali, Mktg/Sales Dir. - Tel: (704) 821-3380, (866) 239-8707, Fax: (704) 821-2097, E-Mail: amy@surfacespecialists.com, Web Site: www.surface specialists.com. With 8 distinct profit centers to choose from focused on bath tub and kitchen repair and refinishing and over 20 years of experience in the industry. Find out why we are the repair and refinishing experts. Established: 1981 - Franchising Since: 1982 - No. of Units: Franchised: 39 - Franchise Fee: $19,500 - Royalty: 5% - Total Inv: $25,300-$34,900 - Financing: Yes.

SYSTEMS PAVING
Systems Paving Franchising, Inc.
1600 Dove Street., #250, Newport Beach, CA, 92660. Contact: Larry Green, President - Tel: (949) 263-8300, (800) 801-7283, Fax: (949) 263-0452, E-Mail: contact@systempaving.com, Web Site: www.systempaving.com. Sales and imarketing of interlocking paving stones. Home improvement company that replaces asphalt/concrete driveways, patios, walkways, pool decks with interlocking paving stones. Established: 1992 - Franchising Since: 2001 - No. of Units: Company Owned: 4 - Franchised: 4 - Franchise Fee: $39,750 - Royalty: 6% plus 2% co-op advertising - Total Inv: $100,000.

THE GUTTER GUYS *
2547 Fire Rd Ste E5, Egg Harbor Twp, NJ, 08234. Contact: Charles Johnson - Tel: (800) 8GU-TTER, (609) 646-4888, Fax: (609) 646-7283. Franchise sells seamless gutters manufactured at the job site, repairs and cleans gutters and sell Guttergard protection system. Established: 1988 - Franchising Since: 2000 - No. of Units: Company Owned: 4 - Franchised: 10 - Franchise Fee: $15,000 - Total Inv: $90,000.

THE SCREEN MACHINE
Wayne's Screen Machine, Inc
19636 8th St. E., Sonoma, CA, 95476. Contact: Wayne Wirick. Sr, Pres. - Tel: (707) 996-5551, Fax: (707) 996-0139, E-Mail: screens@ screen_machine.com. Mobile unit to homes or business for window and door screens. Established: 1986 - Franchising Since: 1988 - No. of Units: Company Owned: 1 - Franchised: 23 - Franchise Fee: $25,000 - Royalty: 5% - Total Inv: $62,500 - Financing: No.

U.S. ROOTER SERVICE
U.S. Rooter Corp.
17025 Batesville Pike, North Little Rock, AR, 72120-1701. - Tel: (501) 835-8020, Fax: (501) 835-3107. Franchise the use of our name, trademark and patented sewer and drain cleaning equipment. Established: 1965 - Franchising Since: 1968 - No. of Units: Franchised: 10 - Franchise Fee: min. $10,000 - Royalty: Flat fee based on population/tele book coverage - Total Inv: Approx. $30,000, depending on what kind of vehicle franchisee would purchase + supplies, fran. fee etc. - Financing: No.

UBUILDIT CORPORATION
UBuildIt Corporation
12006 98th Ave, NE, Suite 200, Kirkland, WA, 98034. Contact: Kathe Noyes - Tel: (425) 821-6200 x2, (800) 992-4357 x2, Fax: (425) 821-6876, E-Mail: franchiseinfo@ubuildit.com, Web Site: www.ubuildit.com. The UBuildIt system offers customers who are building or remodeling the benefits of a builder with the flexibility and cost savings of doing-it-themselves. The owner is teamed with an experienced construction professional who brings the subcontractors, project management tools, ongoing expertise and site visit support. A savvy entrepreneur will appreciate the huge untapped multi-billion dollar market with little competition and high margins, builders will benefit from reduced liability, increased cash flow, and the competitive edge. Established: 1988 - Franchising Since: 1998 - No. of Units: Franchised: 80 - Franchise Fee: $25,000 - Royalty: 5%-8%- Total Inv: $50,000-$125,000 - Financing: Yes third party.

UNITED ENERGY
P.O. Box 416, Fenton, MO, 63026-0416. - Tel: (636) 305-8400, (800) 467-8887. Energy management through lighting and controls. Established: 1992 - Franchising Since: 1995 - No. of Units: Company Owned: 1 - Franchised: 6 - Franchise Fee: $36,000 - Royalty: Sliding scale based on gross profit - Financing: No.

UNITED STATES SEAMLESS, INC.
2001 1st Ave. N., Fargo, ND, 58102. - Tel: (701) 241-8888, Fax: (701) 241-9999. Unites States Seamless is a nationwide franchisor of seamless steel siding offering protected franchise territories for the sale and installation of seamless steel siding, gutters and vinyl replacement. Established: 1992 - Franchising Since: 1992 - No. of Units: Company Owned: 9 - Franchised: 67 - Franchise Fee: $8,500 - Royalty: Based on number of machines owned - Total Inv: $52,000-$94,000 - Financing: Yes.

US STRUCTURES, INC
Archadeck
2112 W. Laburnum Ave., Ste. 100, Richmond, VA, 23227. - Tel: (804) 353-6999, (800) 789-DECK, Fax: (804) 358-1878, E-Mail: petew@ussi.net, Web Site: www.archadeck.com. For entrepreneurs with sales and or management skills. Archadeck specializes in custom exterior structures such as decks, porches, gazebos, and more. Not your ordinary opportunity. Established: 1980 - Franchising Since: 1984 - No. of Units: Franchised: 55 - Royalty: 7.5% declining - Total Inv: $35,000-$75,000 - Financing: Yes.

WILDERNESS LOG HOMES, INC.
N. 5821 County Rd. S., Plymouth, WI, 53073. Contact: Jan Koepsell, Mktg. Dir. - Tel: (920) 893-8416, Fax: (920) 892-2414. Manufacturer of log home kits. Established: 1972 - Franchising Since: 1973 - No. of Units: Company Owned: 1 - Dealers: 110 - Dealership Fee: $10,000 - Total Inv: $125,000 - Royalty: Commission.

WISE WINDOWS AND DOORS
G.F.V. Inc
9275 Rolston Rd., Arvada, CO, 80002. Contact: Dave Thomas, President - Tel: (303) 421-2464, Fax: (303) 412-3047. Same day,same night (usually within 3 hours) replacement of broken sealed glass window units, 8yrs experience. Special process makes us unique eliminating plywood board ups after accident or break-in, professional training and no experience necessary, also includes in home window sales for retrofit

windows. Established: 1993 - No. of Units: Company Owned: 1 - Franchise Fee: $20,000 - Royalty: 5% of gross sales - Total Inv: $62,750-$71,500 - Financing: No. NOT FRANCHISING AT THIS TIME.

XTERIOR EXPERTS *
9521 Camelot St., Pickerington, OH, 43147. Contact: Michael Pirwitz, President - Tel: (614) 860-1985, Fax: (614) 575-9801. We provide a unique opportunity in the exterior home improvement industry. We are the only franchisor to offer vinyl/wood decks, fences and sunrooms in a complete package. Excellent profit potential. Established: 1999 - Franchising Since: 2002 - No. of Units: Company Owned: 1 - Franchise Fee: 412,000-$14,000 - Royalty: 5% - Total Inv: $30,000-$45,000 - Financing: No.

YOU BUY/WE INSTALL
POP Sons Inc.
295 Stebbings Ct., Ste. #1, Bradley, IL, 60915. - Tel: (815) 932-9733, (800) 331-6815, Fax: (815) 932-7792. Small home repairs. Offering prompt service, quality workmanship, fully guaranteed. Established: 1994 - Franchising Since:1996 - No. of Units: Company Owned: 2 - Franchise Fee: $15,000 - Royalty: 6% monthly - Total Inv: $25,000: $15,000 franchise fee, $10,000 working capital - Financing: Yes.

BURGLAR & FIRE PREVENTION

CITIZENS AGAINST CRIME
Division of Training Experience Intl.
2001 North Collins Rd., Ste. 107, Richardson, TX, 75080. - Tel: (972) 578-2287, (800) 466-1010, Fax: (972) 509-0054. National safety corporation providing crime prevention seminars for business and organizations. Safety products are sold in conjunction with the seminar. Established: 1980 - Franchising Since: 1986 - No. of Units: Company Owned: 1 - Franchised: 40 - Franchise Fee: $22,500 - Royalty: Not at this time - Total Inv: $30,000-$100,000 - Financing: Yes.

DYNAMARK SECURITY CENTERS, INC.
P.O. Box 2068, Hagerstown, MD, 21742-2068. - Tel: (800) 342-4243. Residential/light commercial security systems. Established: 1975 - Franchising Since: 1984 - No. of Units: Franchised: 132 - Franchise Fee: $15,000 - Royalty: $100 - Total Inv: $42,000-$46,000 - Financing: Yes.

FIRE DEFENSE INTERNATIONAL, INC.
6120-10 Powers Ave, Box 144, Jacksonville, FL, 32217. - Tel: (904) 731-1833. Guaranteed sales: Sales and service of fire extinguishers, restaurant hood systems, first aid and municipal supplies. Established: 1973 - Franchising Since:1987 - No. of Units: Company Owned: 42 - Franchised: 24 - Franchise Fee: $22,500 - Royalty: 10% weekly - Total Inv: $23,000 - Financing: Yes, up to $10,000 for qualified applicants.

MACE SECURITY CENTER
Mace Security Centers, Inc.
662 South Fulton Street, Denver, CO, 80231. Contact: Howard Edecman, President - Tel: (303)363-7968, (800) 836-8220, Fax: (303)367-9962. Retailer of personal protection, safety and security products including home, auto and child protection communication, spy technology. Established: 1965 - Franchising Since: 1998 - No. of Units: Company Owned: 1 - Franchised: 2 - Franchise Fee: $20,000 - Royalty: 4% - Total Inv: Kiosk $44,500-$75,000, Store $92,700-$152,500 - Financing: Yes.

SECURITY PLUS
P.O Box 10003, Yakima, WA, 98909-1003. Contact: Jack Baugher, President - Tel: (509) 575-1797,(800) 735-1797, Fax: (509) 575-1875. Sale of home, car, personal alarms, pepper spray, stun guns and more. Established: 1990.

SECURITY WORLD INTERNATIONAL®
Winner Holdings
3403 NW 55th St., Bldg. 10, Ft. Lauderdale, FL, 33309. Contact: Richard J. Dayton, VP, Franchise Deptartment - Tel: (954) 846-2400, (888) 238-3116, Fax: (954) 846-9686, E-Mail: franchising@security world.com, Web Site: www.securityworld.com. Personal, home, auto, child security devices and cellular phone retailer, 3 weeks training at corporate headquarters in South Florida. State-of-the-art mall based

specialty retailer. Established: 1994 - Franchising Since: 1998 - No. of Units: Franchised: 14 - Franchise Fee: $35,000 - Total Inv: $236,000 - Financing: No.

SIGNATURE ALERT SECURITY *
746 E. Winchester St., #G10, Salt Lake City, UT, 84107. Contact: Franchise Department - Tel: (801) 743-0101, (800) 957-1030, Fax: (801) 743-0808, Web Site: www.signaturealert.com. Install Honeywell equipment which is the highest quality, most user friendly, equipment on the market today. Established: 1999 - Franchising Since: 2003 - No. of Units: Company Owned: 3 - Franchised: 10 - Franchise Fee: $19,000 - Royalty: 10% - Total Inv: $21,000-$41,000.

SONITROL
Sonitrol Corporation
211 North Union St., #350, Alexandria, VA, 22314. Contact: Frank Minni Fran. Dev. Mgr. - Tel: (703) 684-6606, Fax: (703) 684-6613. Sale, installation, monitoring and service of electronic security services. Established: 1960 - Franchising Since: 1963 - No. of Units: Company Owned: 15 - Franchised: 165 - Franchise Fee: $20,000-$50,000 - Royalty: 2.5% gross - Total Inv: $200,000-$800,000 - Financing: No.

BUSINESS PRODUCTS AND SERVICES

1ST CHOICE MORTGAGE LOAN & FINANCE
Harbor Fin. Mtg. Corp (First City)
2855 Mangum St., #502, Houston, TX, 77092. - Tel: (713) 263-9343, (800) 492-0062, Fax: (713) 263-8869. Originate and process residential, commercial property loans and morgages for purchase, refinance, equity cash out, combination loans, all credit grades ,forecloser buyout, all states. Established: 1975 - No. of Units: Company Owned: 150 - Franchise Fee: % of cash loan on split - Total Inv: Reserve money to start and promote - Financing: Equity loans on property of parties.

24SEVEN *
1601 Cloverfield Blvd, South Tower, Suite 2097, Santa Monica, CA, 90404. - Tel: (310) 460-3668, Fax: (310) 460-3667, E-Mail: info@24 seven.com, Web Site: www.24seven.com. Convenience retailing brand that uses vending machines to serve customers 24 hours a day seven days a week. Established: 1997 - Franchising Since: 2002 - No. of Units: Franchised: 35 - Franchise Fee: $150,000 - Financing: Third party.

ACCTCORP INTERNATIONAL
1307 NE 78th Street #2, Vancouver, WA, 98665. Contact: Dir. of Fran. - Tel: (800) 844-4024. Third party collection of delinquent accounts. Established: 1994 - Franchising Since: 1995 - No. of Units: Company Owned: 3 - Franchised: 22 - Franchise Fee: $10,000 -$25,000 - Royalty: 8%, 1% adv. - Total Inv: $13,000-$35,000 - Financing: Yes.

ACCURATE SOLUTIONS
Accurate Solutions Franchising, Inc.
2000 E Randol Mill Rd Ste 608, Arlington, TX, 76011-8208 - Tel: (214) 637-7797, (800) 213-5505, Fax: (214) 637-7793, E-Mail: fisher@ asicertified.com, Web Site: www.asicertified.com. A high margin niche business to business franchise supplying on-site "total calibration" services to quality conscious industries, utilizing a unique and exclusive system, including the ASI Certified computer program. Full training is provided. Established: 1995 - Franchising Since: 1998 - No. of Units; Company Owned: 2 - Franchised: 24, Franchise Fee: $35,000 - Royalty: 9% - Total Inv: Fee $35,000, Equipment $20,000, Grand Opening $5,000, Travel $4,000 - Financing: Limited.

ACTION INTERNATIONAL
Action International
5670 Wynn Rd., Las Vegas, NV, 89118. Contact: Richard Bernstein, US Sales Manager - Tel: (702) 795-3188, (888) 483-2828, Fax: (702) 795-3183, E-Mail: actionusa@actioninternational.com, Web Site: www.action-international.com. As the world's largest business coaching company, we are looking for successful, passionate, results oriented people who can be dedicatred to helping others succeed in businesses

and in life. Established: 1993 - Franchising Since: 1997 - No. of Units: Franchised: 575 - Franchise Fee: $65,000-$90,000 - Royalty: $1,500 per month fixed - Total Inv: $100,000 - Financing: Third party.

ADVISOR ONE
Broker One Securities Corp.
1097-C Irongate Lane, Columbus, OH, 43213. Contact: Raymond A. Strohl, Pres. - Tel: (614) 864-1440. Advising and consulting on investments. Stockbroker and commodities broker, loan broker, credit cards, shared offices suites, financial plans for individuals, couples, and small businesses. Established: 1983 - Franchising Since: 1986 - No. of Units: Company Owned: 1 - Franchised: 8 - Franchise Fee: Varies, but small - Total Inv: Varies, but small - Financing: No.

ALLEGRA PRINT & IMAGING
Allegra Network LLC
21680 Haggerty Rd, Suite 105S, Northville, MI, 48167. Contact: Meredithz Zielinski, Development Program Manager - Tel: (248) 614-3700, (888) 258-2730, E-Mail: meredithz@allegranetwork.com, Web Site: www.allegranetwork.com. Allegra Network links nearly 500 locations in the U.S, Canada, Poland and Japan. The company ranked 54th among Entrepreneur Magazine's Annual Franchsie 500 anmd was named the 20th fastest growing franchise. Allegra Print & Imaging, offers full-service print and graphic communications services including full-color printing, graphic design, digital color copying, high speed copying and online file transfer. Established: 1976 - Franchising Since: 1977 - No. of Units: Franchised: 490 - Franchise Fee: $25,000 - Royalty: 6%-3.6% - Total Inv: $256,000-$358,500 - Financing: Third party.

ALLIANCE COST CONTAINMENT
Alliance Cost Containment LLC
9921 Fringe Tree Court, Louisville, KY, 40241. Contact: Doug Arbuckle, President - Tel: (502) 429-5011, (800) 872-3709, Fax: (502) 327-9380, E-Mail: darbuck@costcontain.com, Web Site: www.costcontain.com. Business to business expense reduction. Established: 1992 - Franchising Since: 1996 - No. of Units: Company Owned: 2 - Franchised: 28 - Franchise Fee: $29,900 - Royalty: 9% - Total Inv: $29,900-$34,900 - Financing: No.

ALPHA NET
P.O. Box 706, Ridgewood, NJ, 07451. - Tel: (888) 993-1113. Alphanumeric and number paging equipment and services. Full turn key operations available, call today and start your business tomorrow. Established: 1952 - Franchising Since: 1985 - No. of Units: Company Owned: 1 - Franchised: 1585- Franchise Fee: $495.00 - Royalty: Percentage based on discount - Total Inv: $495.00-$100,000 - Financing: Yes.

ALTERNATIVE BOARD TAB®, THE
IHTAB
225 E. 16th Ave., #1200, Denver, CO, 80203. - Tel: (303) 839-1200, (800) 7219-7718, Web Site: www.TABboards.com. The Alternative Board TAB® provides a business consulting system that includes forming and facilitating monthly meetings for CEOs, presidents, and owners of small and mid-sized businesses, as well as providing private business consultation. Established: 1990 - Franchising Since: 1996 - No. of Units: Company Owned: 38 - Franchised: 44 - Franchise Fee: $39,900 - Royalty: 20-10-8-6% (sliding scale) - Total Inv: $25,400-$58,250 - Financing: Yes.

AMALISA SERVICES
Dept. AS, Ste. A, P.O.Box 24, Fayetteville, AR, 72702. Contact: Henry Nwauwa, Liz Ama, Pres., Sales Manager - Tel: (501) 443-9785, Fax: (501) 443-4024. Dealership in sales and leasing of office/business equipment and supplies, printed products and advertising specialties. Licensed and protected territories are available. Established: 1977 - Franchising Since: 1990 - No. of Units: Company Owned: 2 - Franchise Fee: $25-$500 - Total Inv: $25-$9,900 - Financing: Yes.

AMERICAN LENDERS SERVICE CO.
P.O. Drawer 7238, Odessa, TX, 79760-7238. Contact: Jim Golden, Pres. - Tel: (432) 332-0361, Fax: (432) 332-1065, Web Site: www.americanlenders.com. A vehicle and collateral recovery business. Established: 1979 - Franchising Since: 1979 - No. of Units: Company Owned: 2 - Franchised: 125 - Franchise Fee: Varies - Royalty: 5% of gross billings - Total Inv: $50,000 - Financing: Yes.

AMERICAN UNITED CAPITAL
3915 Mission Ave., Ste. 7414, Oceanside, CA, 92054. Contact: Richard Johnson, Manager - Tel: (760) 599-3502. Provides financing for new and existing small businesses. Established: 1989 - No. of Units: Company Owned: 1.

ASSET ONE
Broker One Securities Corp.
1097-C Irongate Lane, Columbus, OH, 43213. Contact: Raymond A. Strohl, Pres. - Tel: (614) 864-1440. Financial and investment planning service. Advice given on budgeting, plans to reduce taxes, and advice given on various investment. Advice given on sources of real estate and business loans and financing and equipment leasing. Asset One affiliates are stockbrokers and commodity brokers. Established: 1989 - Franchising Since: 1989 - No. of Units: Company Owned: 1 - Franchised: 6 - Franchise Fee: Varies - Royalty: Varies, but small - Total Inv: Varies but small - Financing: Not needed.

ATHERTON CAPITAL INCORPORATED
Atherton Capital Incorporated
1001 Bayhill Dr., Ste. 155, San Bruno, CA, 94066. Contact: Marketing Coordinator - Tel: (800) 277-4232, (650) 827-7800, Fax: (650) 827-7950, E-Mail: info@atherton.net, Web Site: www.atherton.net. Long-term fixed rate, non-recourse financing to existing approved franchisees for: rcfinancing existing debt, equipment, development and construction of additional units, and real estate purchases available to owners/operators of quick service and casual dining restaurants, gas station and convenience stores and automotive after market retail outlets. Established: 1989.

BARTERCARD USA, INC
2216 N. Main Street, Santa Ana, CA, 92706-2704. - Tel: (714) 876-2444, Fax: (714) 876-2440, E-Mail: franchise@bartercardusa.com, Web Site: www.bartercardusa.com. Bartercard is a business to business global barter trading system. It assits its members in increasing their sales, cash flow and profit. Established: 1991 - Franchising Since: 1991 - No. of Units: Company Owned: 1 - Franchise Fee: $40,000 - Total Inv: $85,000-$110,000.

BISON ADVERTISING, INC *
6385 Old Sandy Oak Road, Eden Prairie, MN, 55344. Contact: Kimberly M. Ellis, President - Tel: (952) 345-8480, (800) 641-7291, Fax: (952) 345-8490, E-Mail: inquires@bison.com, Web Site: www.bison.com. Bison, the franchise network, features the best franchised and business opportunities for entrepreneurs and investors. Established: 1995.

BUSINESS BROKERS HAWAII (MAUI, KAUAI, AND HAWAII ISLANDS)
Business Brokers Hawaii, Inc
3230 Pikai Way, Wailea, HI, 96753-7702. Contact: Milton Docktor, Founder-President - Tel: (808) 879-8833, (866) 239-1567, Fax: (808) 879-5966, E-Mail: mdr@business-brokers.com, Web Site: www.business-brokers.com. Our Big Island (of Hawaii) Joint Venturee is an accomplished CPA, while the Kauai Joint Venture's President is a very accomplished businesswomen. We are well established on the three outer islands and are poised to enter Oahu, containing America's 11th largest city, Honolulu. There we will install a few domestic joint ventures and one international Business Intermediary to servce Europe, another for the Orient, and a third for South America. Established: 1984 - Franchising Since: 2002 - No. of Units: Company Owned: 1 - Franchised: 2 - Franchise Fee: Zero - Sixty Day Training Fee - $75,000 - Royalty: 0 - Total Inv: Approx $5,000 - Financing: Yes 1/3rd.

BUSINESS CONSULTANTS OF AMERICA
Horizons of America, Inc.
222 Munson Rd., Wolcott, CT, 06716-2708. - Tel: (203) 879-4675, Fax: (203) 879-4178. Franchised offices for business brokerage and consulting. Established: 1951 - Franchising Since: 1973 - No. of Units: 7 - Franchise Fee: $15,000 - Royalty: 5% - Total Inv: $25,000-$30,000 incl. fran fee - Financing: Assistance.

BUSINESS INFORMATION INTERNATIONAL
955 Captiva Dr, Hollywood, FL, 33019-5046. - Tel: (901) 336-8400, Fax: (901) 578-5577, Web Site: www.biiinfo.com. A unique information age concept providing powerful direct marketing information to help companies build their new and existing customer business. These "sales

leads" are delivered in the form of mailing/telemarketing/fax lists and databases on diskette to business-to-business and business-to-residential direct marketers. Established: 1994 - Franchise Fee: $6,250-$75,000 - Total Inv: $19,450-$131,450. NOT FRANCHISING AT THIS TIME.

BUSINESS PRODUCTS EXPRESS, INC

1350 E. Reynolds Ave., #104, Irvine, CA, 92614. Contact: Anthony Lauberth - Tel: (800) 908-3334, Fax: (800) 908-3336. Commercial office supply sales. Established: 1996 - Franchising Since: 2000 - No. of Units: Company Owned: 5 - Franchised: 11 - Franchise Fee: $25,000 - Total Inv: $50,000.

CAREER BLAZER RESUME SERVICES
Career Blazers

590 Fifth Ave., 7th Fl., New York, NY, 10036. Contact: Exec. V.P. - Tel: (800) 284-3232-US only, (212) 719-3232, Fax: (212) 921-1827. Our product/service is consistently utilized by all levels of the working population. Write, format and produce resumes using proven formulas. Provide career services such as cover letter preparation, direct mail and occupational testing. Affiliated with Career Blazers Personnel Services. Established: 1949 - Franchising Since: 1992 - No. of Units: Company Owned: 1 - Franchised: 2 - Franchise Fee: $12,000 - Royalty: 8% of net receipts - Total Inv: $4,750-$14,750 capital required.

CHECKCARE SYSTEMS, INC.
Checkcare Enterprises

8900 Greeneway Commons Place Suite 200, Louisville, KY, 40220-4070. Contact: Bill Brandon, Senior President - Tel: (502) 719-0295, Web Site: checkcare.com. Check guarantee/verification service. Established: 1982 - Franchising Since: 1984 - No. of Units: Franchised: 78 - Franchise Fee: $12,500-$45,000 - Royalty: 5% on gross revenues - Total Inv: $110,000-$169,000 (includes franchise fee, computer hardware and software) - Financing: Yes.

You Can't Manage Without Us.

CITY WIDE MAINTENANCE
City Wide Franchise Company, Inc.

8460 Nieman Rd, Lenexa, KS, 66214. Contact: Jeff Oddo & Adam Stiles - Tel: (913) 888-5700, (866) 887-4029, Fax: (913) 888-5151, E-Mail: astiles@gocitywide.com, Web Site: www.citywidefranchise.com. We are a business to business facility maintenance company that is able to provide over 20 different services through a proven, unique, sales, marketing and management business model that utilizes a network of independent services providers to perform the various services. We have been perfecting this model for over 40 years and it's proven to be highly successful. Established: 1959 - Franchising Since: 2001 - No. of Units: Company Owned: 1 - Franchised: 5 - Franchise Fee: $100,000 - Royalty: 5% - Total Inv: $150,000-$200,000 - Financing: Yes.

COMMISSION EXPRESS
Commission Express National, Inc

8306 Professional Hill Dr., Fairfax, VA, 22031. Contact: John L. Stedman, President - Tel: (703) 560-5500, (888) 560-5501, Fax: (703) 560-5502, E-Mail: manager@commissionexpress.com, Web Site: www.commissionexpress.com. Purchasing real estate commissions (accounts receivable) from real estate agents and brokers at a discount, using a well regarded financial service called factoring. Established: 1994 - Franchising Since: 1996 - No. of Units: Company Owned: 1 - Franchised: 39 - Franchise Fee: $15,000-$50,000 - Royalty: Up to 9%; 1% advertsing fee - Total Inv: $88,00-$182,000 - Financing: Some.

COMMWORLD
Communications World International, Inc.

7388 S. Revere Pkwy., Ste. 1000, Englewood, CO, 80112-3998. Contact: Mark Bennett, Dir., Fran. Dev. - Tel: (303) 721-8200, Fax: (303) 721-8299. Franchisor of interconnect communications companies offering equipment, training and support. Established: 1979 - Franchising Since: 1983 - No. of Units: Company Owned: 4 - Franchised: 60 - Franchise Fee: $7,500-$12,500 - Royalty: 4%-18% - Financing: Limited.

CONFIDENTIAL BUSINESS CONNECTION
Confidential Business Connection, LLC

4155 E. Jewell Ave., Ste. 1010, Denver, CO, 80222. Contact: Chris W. Sales, President - Tel: (303) 759-2334, Fax: (303) 584-0793. Confidential "Clearinghouse" brokerage services, matching business/franchise buyers and sellers through the use of a unique system utilizing confidential profiles and proprietary matching software. Franchisee provides a unique alternative to traditional brokerage market. Established: 1996 - Franchising Since: 1997 - No. of Units: Franchised: 1 - Franchise Fee: $15,500 + varies based on territory - Royalty; 6%, 2% adv. - Total Inv: $36,500-$75,000 excluding franchise fee - Financing: None.

COPY CLUB
Copy Club, Inc.

12715 Telge Road, Cypress, TX, 77429. Contact: Exec. Dir. Franchise Sales - Tel: (281) 256-4100, Fax: (281) 373-4450, Web Site: www.copyclub.com. High visibility, high traffic digital imaging and copying and business/communications center open 24 hours a day. Dynamic retail environment. Also offering self-service copying and computer rentals. 5 weeks of classroom training, 2 weeks in store training. Established: 1992 - Franchising Since: 1994 - No. of Units: Franchised: 14 - Franchise Fee: $30,000 - Royalty: 7% - Minimum Cash Required: $100,000 - Financing: Assistance, yes.

CRESTCOM INTERNATIONAL, LTD.
Crestcom International Ltd

6900 E. Belleview Ave., Greenwood Village, CO, 80111. Contact: Mr. Kelly Krause, Dir. of International Mktg. - Tel: (303) 267-8200, (888) CRESTCOM, Fax: (303) 267-8207, E-Mail: franchiseinfo@crestcom.com, Web Site: www.crestcom.com. Crestcom is rated the #1 management/sales training franchiseby the most recent rankings of Entrepreneur, Income Opportunities and Success magazines. Crestcom's video-based, live-facilitated instruction is used by thousands of leading organizations in 50 countries/20+languages. Established: 1987 - Franchising Since: 1992 - No. of Units: Franchised: 130 - Franchise Fee: $35,000-$52,500 - Royalty: 1.5% - Total Inv: $44,355-$73,160 - Financing: Yes.

DATABAR INC.

2908 Meridian East, Ste. 201, Edgewood, WA, 98371. - Tel: (253) 770-7338, Fax: (253) 770-1637. Business office products distribution. Established: 1986 - Franchising Since: 1990 - No. of Units: Company Owned: 4 - Franchised: 7 - Franchise Fee: $15,000 - Financing: Yes.

DIRECT OPINIONS™
Direct Opinions Franchising, Inc.

23600 Mercantile Rd., Beachwood, OH, 44122. Contact: Simon L. Cohen, Director of Franchising - Tel: (216) 831-7979, (800) 229-7978, Fax: (216) 464-0621, E-Mail: marketing@directopinions.com, Web Site: www.directopinions.com. Outbound telemarketing services, including customer satisfaction surveys, market surveys, lead generation and database updates. Established: 1983 - Franchising Since: 1992 - No. of Units: Company Owned: 1 - Franchised: 2 - Franchise Fee: $10,000 min, $1,000 per 1 million population - Royalty: 6% of 1st $100,000 gross revenue; 4% thereafter - Total Inv: $22,750-$39,500 with min $10,000 franchise fee - Financing: Partial financing for franchise fee in excess of $20,000. NOT FRANCHISING AT THIS TIME.

DISCOUNT IMAGING
Discounting Imaging Franchise Corp.

305B Wood Street, West Monroe, LA, 71291. Contact: Brad Hargrove, National Sales Manager - Tel: (800) 579-8258, Web Site: www.difcorp.com. Designed to be a home or office based business, Discount Imaging is a business-to-business franchise specializing in imaging supply items such as laser printer toner cartridges & ink jet cartridges This constant demand item results in repeat sales to a business clientele. Discount Imaging franchisees are part of a recession proof industry in which every business is a potential client. Program features proprietary product line, purchasing power, & other support services. Established: 1995 - Franchising Since: 1998 - No. of Units: Company Owned: 1 - Franchised: 6 - Franchise Fee: $25,000 - Royalty: Sliding scale 6% down to 3% based on volume - Total Inv: $50,000-$75,000 - Financing: No.

DUN & BRADSTREET RMS FRANCHISE CORP.
Dun & Bradstreet
One Diamond Hill Road, Murray Hill, NJ, 07974. - Tel: (801) 635-6171, (908) 665-5331, Fax: (908) 665-5062. Franchise will solicit clients for Dun & Bradstreet's commercial debt collection and receivable management services (but the franchisee will not perform any of these services). Established: 1995 - Franchising Since: 1995 - No. of Units: Company Owned: 18 - Franchised: 3 - Franchise Fee: $25,000 plus 10% of gross earnings in previous years $36,000-$46,000 - Royalty: 35% commission for sale of D&B services - Total Inv: $50,000 - Financing: No.

E. K. WILLIAMS & CO.
Century Business Solutions
1077 West 17th St, Santa Anna, CA, 92706. Contact: Mike Hawkins, VP - Tel: (800) 992-0706, (714) 558-0591, Fax: (714) 558-1691. A business management service specializing in maximizing small business profits through a network of franchised offices. Provides accounting, tax, business counseling, payroll, training, H.R. services and financial services. Established: 1935 - Franchising Since: 1947 - No. of Units: Franchised: 160 - Franchise Fee: $35,000 - Royalty: 8%-2% - Total Inv: $40,000-$45,000 - Financing: Yes.

EMPIRE BUSINESS BROKERS, USA, INC.
4040 Clinton St, Buffalo, NY, 14224. Contact: Nick Gugliuzza, President - Tel: (716) 674-2015, Fax: (603) 308-0577, E-Mail: nick@empirebbcom, Web Site: www.empirebb.com. Sell existing businesses and business opportunities to the public. Established: 1981 - Franchising Since: 1989 - No. of Units: Company Owned: 1 - Franchised: 66 - Franchise Fee: $15,900 - Royalty: $150/mo - Total Inv: $15,000 - Financing: No.

"Your success is our only business"

ENTREPRENEUR'S SOURCE, THE
TES Franchising LLC
900 Main Street South, Bldg. #2, Southbury, CT, 06488. - Tel: (203) 264-2006, (800) 289-0086, Fax: (203) 264-3516, E-Mail: info@theesource.com, Web Site: www.franchisesearch.com. The premier international source for information about the wide range of self-employment options. Provides an education and coaching process that offers objective guidance for entrepreneurs. Using informal interviews and profiling tools, The Entrepreneur's Source helps clients zero-in on the options that are in harmony with their lifestyle and income goals. Established: 1984 - Franchising Since: 1997 - No. of Units: Franchised: 260 total units in 40 states and 2 in Canada - Franchise Fee: $45,000 - Royalty: None - Total Inv: $75,000 - Financing: None.

EWM, INC.
4760 Route 9, South, Howell, NJ, 07731. - Tel: (888) 972-0585, Fax: (732) 905-8606. Provides franchisees with tools necessary to effectively and efficiently operate a residential property management company complete with an accredited training program and multi-volume operations manual. Established: 1986 - Franchising Since: 1997 - No. of Units: Company Owned: 2 - Franchise Fee: $20,000 - Royalty: 5% of Gross revenues - Total Inv: $20,000 fee; $25,000 start up costs inclusive of first 3 months operations, office source etc. - Financing: Third Party.

• • • • • • • • • • • • • • • • • • •
• Check out Latest Press Releases: •
• *www.infonews.com* •
• • • • • • • • • • • • • • • • • • •

EXPENSE REDUCTION CONSULTING
Expense Reduction Two, Inc.
10616 Scripps Summit Ct., Ste. 250, San Diego, CA, 92131 - Tel: (877) 872-3721, Fax: (858) 795-7401. Firm assists companies in reducing business expenses by helping them purchase more effectively. Contingency based. Turnkey package. Established: 1993 - Franchising Since: 1998 - No. of Units: Company Owned: 5 - Franchised: 2 - Franchise Fee: $8,000 - Royalty: 10% - Total Inv: $8,000 - Financing: Yes.

FACTUAL DATA
Factual Data Corp.
5200 Hahns Peak Dr., Loveland, CO, 80538. Contact: J. Donnan Pres. - Tel: (800) 929-3400, Fax: (800) 929-3297. Services the mortgage and rental industry by furnishing accurate and timely residential mortgage and rental reliance credit reports. Established: 1985 - Franchising Since: 1987 - No. of Units: Company Owned:11 - Franchised:10 - Franchise Fee: $120,000 - Total Inv: $120,000 fran. fee, $30,000 cap. - Royalty: Sliding scale to 11%- Financing: Yes.

FAX-9
Fax-9 Holding Corp.
1235 Lake Plaza Dr., #127, Colorado Springs, CO, 80906. Contact; Sales Dept. or Rene Boutin, Pres. - Tel: (800) 727-3299, Fax: (719) 579-0952. An international network of public fax stations. Fax-9 will assist in securing an existing retail store (contracts signed with large national chains) which will operate the fax service for a small percentage of the fax revenues. This concept eliminates virtually all monthly overhead. Established: 1988 - Franchising Since: 1988 - No. of Units: Company Owned: 63 - Franchised: 491 - Franchise Fee: $3,500 - Royalty: $25 a month - Total Inv: $3,500 - Financing: No.

FINDERBINDER™ & SOURCE BOOK™ DIRECTORIES
California Publicom, Inc.
5173 Waring Rd #S, San Diego, CA, 92120. Contact: Kathy Zwolinski - Tel: (619) 582-8500, (800) 255- 2575, Fax: (619) 582-3396, E-Mail: kzwolinski@yahoo.com,, Web Site: www.finderbinder.com. These newsmedia and local clubs & association directories are add-on profit centers for existing consulting firms and P.R. agencies. They are practional franchises. Established: 1975 - Franchising Since: 1978 - No. of Units: Company Owned: 1 - Franchised: 20 - Franchise Fee: $1,000 - Royalty: 5%-10% - Total Inv: $15,000 - Financing: No.

FIRST PIC INC.
32 Norfolk Ave, Weymouth, MA, 02188. Contact: David Blanchard, President - Tel: (781) 340-0404. Corporate mail service. Established: 1994 - Franchising Since: 1994 - No. of Units: Company Owned: 4 - Franchised: 1 - Franchise Fee: $25,000 - Royalty: 6%, 2% for billing - Total Inv: $25,000 + $15,000 (vans, office expense etc.) - Financing: No. NOT FRANCHISING AT THIS TIME.

FKA AM MARKETING
Business Images Distributing
57 Elberon Ave. Pittsfield, MA, 01201-2840. Contact: Tom Reynolds, Owner - Tel: (413) 442-9966. Full color photo business cards and post cards. Established: 1990 - Franchising Since: 1990 - No. of Units: Company Owned: 1 - Franchised: 974 - Franchise Fee: $500 - Financing: No.

FRANCHISE OPPORTUNITY NETWORK
National Association of Home Based Businesses, Inc
10451 Mill Run Circle, Suite 400, Owings Mills, MD, 21117. - Tel: (410) 363-3698, Fax: (410) 356-1672, Web Site: www.usahomebusines. com. The Franchise Opportunity Network was established by the National Association of Home Based Businesses, (NAHBB) to locate and promote high quality franchises that can be managed from home. The network publishes a directory and maintains a website. The NAHBB also certifies franchise marketers and brokers who consult new and existing franchises. Established: 1998.

FRANKLIN TRAFFIC SERVICE, INC.
5251 Shawnee Rd., P.O. Box 100, Sanborn, NY, 14132. Contact: Mgr. Franc. Sales - Tel: (716) 731-3131, Fax: (716) 731-2705. Hands on traffic managers to small and medium sized businesses. Franchisee sells both traffic management and freight bill payment/audit and associated

traffic services in exclusive territory. Established: 1969 - Franchising Since: 1984 - No. of Units: 1 - Franchise Fee: $25,000 - Royalty: Varies - Total Inv: Varies depending on location - Financing: To qualified applicants.

FREEFONE
Freefone Development Corp
1001 West Loop South #603, Houston, TX, 77027. Contact: Patrick Palmer, President - Tel: (713) 355-1886, (888) 355-1886. Free local telephone calls, service supportors by the sale of advertising inside the enclusure. Established: 1996 - Franchising Since: 1998 - No. of Units: Company Owned: 2 - Franchised: 29 - Franchise fee: $4995 - Royalty: $25 per booth per month - Total Inv: Franchise fee $4995 one booth $3000 = $7995 - Financing: Yes.

FULL CIRCLE IMAGE
6256 34th Ave. N.W., Rochester, MN, 55901. Contact: Charles Renson, President - Tel: (507) 280-0136, (800) 584-7244, Fax: (507) 280-4425, E-Mail: fullinfo@fullcircleimage.com, Web Site: www.fullcircle image.com. Full Circle Image is a direct sales franchise specializing in remanufactured laser toner, ink jet and printer ribbon cartridges. Tap into the $15 billion industry of imaging products used in every business, every day. Help reduce waste through recycling while presenting your customers with guaranteed product with guaranteed savings of 20%-50% over retail. Established: 1991 - Franchising Since: 1997 - No. of Units: Company Owned: 2 - Franchised: 24 - Franchise Fee: $20,000 - Royalty: 5%, 3% advertising - Total Inv: $21,000 - Financing: No.

GENERAL BUSINESS SERVICES, INC.
Century Small Business Solutions
2441 Honolulu Ave, Montrose, CA, 91020-1864. Contact: Karen Cagle, VP - Tel: (800) 323-9000, Fax: (818) 249-5344. Business counseling, financial management and tax related products and services. Established: 1962 - Franchising Since: 1962 - No. of Units: 500+ - Franchise Fee: $35,000 plus 6 months current living expenses - Royalty: 8%-2% - Total Inv: $40,000-$65,000 - Financing: No.

GOFAX PUBLIC PHONE/FAX STATIONS
Continental Telefax
4101 S.W. 73rd Ave., Miami, FL, 33155. Contact: Ralph F. Geronimo, Pres. - Tel: (954) 704-4920, Fax: (954) 704-7850. Package of six Gofax credit card phone/fax stations as a business opportunity. Investor secures own locations or a locater is recommended. Investor receives a check monthly, marketing support and more. Established: 1988 - Franchising Since: 1990 - Total Inv: $29,500 - Financing: Yes.

GOLD MINE, INC., THE
11110 W Oakland Park Blvd #337, Sunrise, FL, 33351-6808. Contact; Warren Scott, Owner - Tel: (954) 748-0066, (800) 877-0066, Fax: (954) 748-9543, Web Site: www.warrensgoldmine.com. Manufacturing gold plating supplies, machines and chemicals. Established: 1994 - Franchising Since: 1994 - No. of Units: Company Owned: 1 - Franchised: 500 - Franchise Fee: $1,600.00 - Royalty: None - Total Inv: $0 - Financing: Yes.

GROWTH COACH
10700 Montgomery Rd., Ste. 300, Cincinnati, OH, 45242. Contact: Daniel Murphy, President - Tel: (888) 292-7992, Fax: (513) 563-2691, Web Site: www.thegrowthcoach.com. Business coaching, with emphasis on stratgic process for buisness owners and self-employed. Established: 2002 - Franchising Since: 2003 - No. of Units: Franchised: 15 - Franchise Fee: $17,900 - Royalty: 6% - Total Inv: $22,500-$34,900.

HOMEBIZ GLOBAL CENTER
NAHBB Franchise Development Company, Inc
10451 Mill Run Circle, Suite 400, Owings Mills, MD, 21117. Contact: Franchise Department - Tel: (410) 581-1373, Fax: (410) 356-1672. Executive conference and meeting room facility, with on-site services including, telephone answering, video conferencing, faxing, copy/print, mailing services, internet marketing, exporting and importing agency services, and more than 25 additional programs and services. Centers are considered international business and trade incubators for small and home based businesses. Established: 1998 - No. of Units: Company Owned: 1 - Franchise Fee: $38,000 - Royalty: 6% - Total Inv: $150,000-$200,000 - Financing: No.

HOMEMART LOANS & REAL ESTATE
Inmac Corp
1765 Landess Ave #27, Milpitas, CA, 95035. Contact: Larue McKenzie - Tel: (510) 351-1229, (888) 298-9928, Fax: (510) 351-8649. Start your own mortgage co, purchase and refinance, debt consolidation in your local area. Low start-up, sound opportunity. Established: 1998 - Franchising Since: 1998 - No. of Units: Company Owned: 1 - Franchise Fee: $395 - Royalty: 10% - Total Inv: Ongoing support & processing 10% manual + training $395.00 - Financing: No.

HQ NETWORK SYSTEMS
HQ Network Systems, Inc.
15950 Dallas Pkwy #400, Dallas, TX, 75248-6628. - Tel: (972) 361-8000, (800) 480-2020, Fax: (972) 392-0793. Provider of offices, administrative services and telecommunications in a shared, overhead environment. Established: 1977 - Franchising Since: 1979 - No. of Units: Franchised: 164 - Franchise Fee: $30,000-$200,000 - Royalty: 2.35% - Total Inv: $352,000-$1,500,000 - Financing: No.

HR FIRST CONTACT *
12750 Merit Dr., Ste. 1215, Dallas, TX, 75251. - Tel: (972) 404-4479, Fax: (972) 404-4415, Web Site: www.hrfirstcontact.com. HR First Contact provides pre-employment screening services, including drug testing, criminal and credit records research, attitude and knowledge testing, identification badging and employment and education verifications. Established: 2001 - Franchising Since: 2002 - No. of Units: Company Owned: 3 - Franchised: 1 - Franchise Fee: $35,000 - Royalty: 6% - Total Inv: $89,100-$206,400.

IMPRESSIONS ON HOLD INTERNATIONAL
4880 S. Lewis, Ste. 200, Tulsa, OK, 74105. Contact: John Miller, Fran. Relations - Tel: (800) 580-4653, (918) 744-0988, Fax: (918) 746-7936. Custom write and produce "on-hold" advertising for business phone systems. Franchise owner markets and sells our product on their local level, and corporate produces the work and administrates. Established: 1991 - Franchising Since: 1994 - No. of Units: Franchised: 73 - Franchise Fee: $49,000 - Royalty: 5% on gross sales (4% royalty, 1% adv.) - Financing: No.

INFOLINK SCAN CENTER
Infolink Technologies, Inc
821 North 300 West, Pleasant Grove, UT, 84062. - Tel: (801) 796-8665, (800) 523-SCAN, Fax: (801) 796-9315. Service bureau to scan paper documents for storage on cd-rom. Established: 1988 - Franchising Since: 1993 - No. of Units: Company Owned: 3 - Franchised: 13 - Total Inv: $50,000 - Financing: USA, International.

INTERFORM GRAPHICS
1264 West 50 Siuth, P.O. 577, Centerville, UT, 84014. - Tel: (801) 292-7971, (800) 488-7961, Fax: (801) 292-7990, Web Site: www.interformgraphics.com. Providing business with business printing needs. No printing equipment required to operate this franchise. Established: 1996 - Franchising Since: 1997 - No. of Units: Franchised: 12 - Franchise Fee: Based on population - Royalty: 5% of gross sales - Total Inv: $14,000-$200,000 - Financing: No.

INTERNATIONAL MERGERS & ACQUISITIONS
International Mergers & Acquisitions, Inc
4300 N. Miller Rd., Ste. 230, Scottsdale, AZ, 85251. Contact: Neil D. Lewis, Pres. - Tel: (480) 990-3899, Fax: (480) 990-7480, E-Mail: nlewis@ima-world.com, Web Site: www.ima-world.com. IMA is a international affiliation of entrepreneurs engaged in the profession of serving merger and acquisition minded companies in the areas of consulting, financing, divestitures, mergers and acquisitions. Established: 1969 - Franchising Since: 1977 - No. of Units: Franchised: 30 - Franchise Fee: $15,000 - Royalty: $500/Quarter - Total Inv: $15,000 - Financing: No.

INVISIBLE AUDIT INCORPORATED
P.O. Box 272, 32 Everett St, Southbridge, MA, 01550-0272. Contact; Stacey Richer, Marketing Director - Tel: (508) 764-8400, Fax: (508) 764-5310. Selling licenses to future independent contractors to become mystery shoppers. Established: 1995 - Franchising Since: 1996 - No. of Units: Company Owned: 1 - Franchised: 30 - Franchise Fee: $219.95 - Total Inv: $500.00 - Financing: None.

JAY ROBERTS & ASSOCIATES, INC.

608 Mack Street, Joliet, IL, 60435. Contact: John S. Meers, Pres. - Tel: (815) 726-9359, Fax: (815) 726-9359. Financial consultants and brokers specializing in government business loans, commercial business and real estate loan and turnaround consulting. Established: 1965 - Franchising Since: 1982 - No. of Units: Company Owned: 2 - Franchised: 31 - Franchise Fee: $5,000 - Financing: No.

JET BLACK INTERNATIONAL

Jet Black Seal Coating & Repair
25 West Cliff Rd., #103, Burnsville, MN, 55337-1690. Contact: Franchise Department - Tel: (952) 890-8343, (888) 538-2525, Fax: (952) 890-7022, Web Site: www.jet-black.com. Asphalt sealcoating, hot rubber crack filling, oil spot treatment, grass edging, patch work and paint stripping. Established: 1988 - Franchising Since: 1992 - No. of Units: Company Owned: 1 - Franchised: 34 - Franchise Fee: $9,500 - Royalty: 8% - Total Inv: $23,500 (includes franchise fee) - Financing: Yes.

KEEP IN TOUCH STUFF

The ABC Group, Inc.
120 McGaw Drive, Edison, NJ, 08837. Contact; Director of franchising - Tel: (732) 346-4451 ext. 331, (877) kitstuff, Fax: (732) 417-0326, Web Site: www.kitstuff.com. Wireless communication business specializing in the sale of cellular phones and pagers. With the excellent reputation established with the cellular carriers you now can take part in what we believe to be the most exciting franchise opportunity. Established: 1996 - Franchising Since: 1999 - No. of Units: Company Owned: 37 - Franchise Fee: $25,000 - Total Inv: $80,700-$171,000 - Financing: Yes.

KNOWLEDGE DEVELOPMENT CENTERS

Knowledge Development Centers, Inc.
445 Hutchinson Ave., Ste. 120, Columbus, OH, 43235. - Tel: (614) 888-2444, Fax: (614) 888-0411. Rentable training facility franchise. We provide state-of-the-art facilities fully equipped with hardware, software, production and sound equipment. We are utilized by companies such as Oracle, Sybase, Microsoft, Powersoft to host technical classes. Established: 1993 - Franchising Since: 1994 - No. of Units: Company Owned: 1 - Franchised: 2 - Franchise Fee: $25,000 - Royalty: 5%, 1% nat'l. adv. fund - Total Inv: $230,000-$360,000 - Financing: Limited.

MAIL BOXES ETC.

6060 Cornerstone Court. W., San Diego, CA, 92121-3795. Contact: Franchise Department - Tel: (877) 623-7253, (858) 597-8513, Fax: (858) 546-7493, Web Site: www.mbe.com. MBE provides convenient and value-added business services to general consumers, corporate "road warriors" and the small-office/home-office (SOHO) market. Established: 1980 - Franchising Since: 1980 - No. of Units: Franchised: 4,385 - Franchise Fee: $29,950 - Royalty: 5% - Total Inv: $140,993-$217,051 - Financing: Up to $50,000.

MONEY BROKER ONE

Broker One Securities Corp.
1097-C Irongate Lane, Columbus, OH, 43213. Contact: Raymond A. Strohl, Pres. - Tel: (614) 864-1440. Offering loans and financing to individuals, businesses and churches for almost any worthwhile project. Offer real estate loans and business loans, and equipment leasing. There is no upper limit on the size of the loans. Also act as a business broker, re: sales of businesses. Established: 1983 - Franchising Since: 1989 - No. of Units: Company Owned: 1 - Franchised: 5 - Franchise Fee: Varies, but small - Royalty: None - Total Inv: Varies, but small - Financing: Not needed.

NATIONAL TENANT NETWORK

National Tenant Network, Inc.
P.O. Box 1664, Lake Oswego, OR, 97034. Contact: Ed Byczynski, Pres. - Tel: (800) 228-0989, Fax: (800) 340-1116. Tenant screening including residential and commercial tenant performance reporting involving credit analysis and fraud detection as well as local tenant performance. Nationally network services. Established: 1980 - Franchising Since: 1987 - No. of Units: Company Owned: 3 - Franchised: 20 - Franchise Fee: $30,000 - Royalty: 10% - Total Inv: $60,000 ($3,500 mkt. study/ $30,000 inv. in operation, $30,000 franchise fee) - Financing: Varies.

OFFICE ONE

1097-C Irongate Lane, Columbus, OH, 43213. Contact: Raymond A. Strohl, Pres. - Tel: (614) 864-1440. Subletting office space to professional people, sales reps, and small businesses. Also, the furnishing of various office services. Established: 1989 - Franchising Since: 1989 - No. of Units: Company Owned: 1 - Franchised: 3 - Franchise Fee: Varies greatly - Royalty: Varies greatly - Total Inv: Varies greatly - Financing: No.

ONE DAY RESUME

540 S. Mendenhall Rd., Ste. 4, Memphis, TN, 38117-4200. Contact: Fran. Dir. - Tel: (901) 685-1950. Highly efficient and effective resume preparation service with unique and very successful system. Established: 1990 - Franchising Since: 1993 - No. of Units: Company Owned: 1- Franchised: 26 - Franchise Fee: $10,000 - Royalty: 5%, 1% adv. - Total Inv: $25,000 - Financing: Yes partial.

PAYZ, INC.

4102 42 Ave S., Minneapolis, MN, 55406. Contact: John Rogers, Mgr. Fran. Dev. - Tel: (800) 999-6633, (612) 729-8361. Payroll service for smaller businesses. Also automates 401 k and section 125 reports and compliance to enable employers of all sizes to reduce employee's taxes. Can be operated part time from home. Established: 1996 - Franchising Since: 1996 - No. of Units: Company Owned: 1 - Franchise Fee: $100 - Royalty: 5-10% advertising ($200/per month minimum) - Total Inv: Computer printers, phone, fax, unique advertising program gets customers. etc., $4,000.

POWER BROKER SYSTEMS

HMO Membership Health Plans, Inc
320 Nautilus St, La Jolla, CA, 92037-5965. - Tel: (619) 459-7020, (800) 336-9222. Turnkey HMO health and life insurance marketing. Established: 1984 - Franchising Since: 1994 - No. of Units: Company Owned: 1 - Franchised: 120 - Franchise Fee: $2,500-$50,000 (capital requirement $4,000-$50,000 depending on territory, number of agents and marketing) - Financing: Yes.

PRECISION DOOR SERVICE INC.

571 Haverty Ct., #W, Rockledge, FL, 32955. - Tel: (888) 833-3494, (321) 433-3494, Fax: (321) 433-3062, Web Site: www.preceision door.net. Garage door repair and installation service. Established: 1997 - Franchising Since: 1999 - No. of Units: Company Owned: 5 - Franchised: 55 - Franchise Fee: $125,000-$200,000 - Royalty: $1000-$2,500 weekly - Total Inv: $73,548-$1037,564.

PRIORITY MANAGEMENT SYSTEMS, INC.

P.O. Box 4007, Blaine, WA, 98231-4007. Contact: John White, V.P., Fran. Dev. - Tel: (604) 214-7772, (800) 221-9031, Fax: (604) 214-7773, E-Mail: whitej@prioritymanagement.com, Web Site: www.priority management.com. Management training and skills development for individuals and organizations to increase productivity and maintain a balanced lifestlyle. Established: 1981 - Franchising Since: 1984 - No. of Units: Company Owned: 3 - Franchised: 162 worldwide - Franchise Fee: $29,500 - Royalty: 9%, 1% adv. - Total Inv: $29,500+$8,500-$22,500 operating capital - Financing: No.

PROFIT-TELL *

Profit-Tell International, Inc.
15 Spinning Wheel Rd., #114, Hinsdale, IL, 60521. Contact: Michael Johnson, Director of Franchise Development - Tel: (888) 366-4653, (630) 655-3700, Fax: (630) 655-4542, E-Mail: mjohnson@profit-tell.com, Web Site: www.profit-tell.com. Franchises build a consulting practice that provides advertising & marketing solutions to all types of businesses. Low investment, home-based, immediate cash flow and short-selling cycle. Established: 1993 - Franchising Since: 2002 - No. of Units: Company Owned: 1 - Franchised: 11 - Franchise Fee: $22,500 - Royalty: 0 - Total Inv: $30,000 - Financing: Third party.

PROFORMA

PFG Ventures
8800 E. Pleasant Valley Rd., Cleveland, OH, 44131. Contact: Fran. Dev. Dept. - Tel: (216) 520-8400, (800) 825-1525, Fax: (216) 520-8474, Web Site: www.connectwithproforma.com. Sale of printed and promotional products to business. Established: 1978 - Franchising

Since: 1985 - No. of Units: Franchised: 270 - Franchise Fee: $14,500 - Royalty: 9% + 1% adv. - Total Inv: $9,500 initial franchise fee, up to $28,350 business startup expenditures - Financing: No.

PROMENTUM®
Promentum, LLC
22 E. Lahon St, Park Ridge, IL, 60068-2746. Contact; Gerry Waller, Managing Member - Tel: (847) 384-1900, (888) 552-7761, Fax: (847) 825-1701, E-Mail: probiz1@aol.com, Web Site: www.promentum.com. The Promentum® franchise is a performance consulting business that helps companies increase productivity by providing training, process improvment services, executive development and more. Established: 1998 - Franchising Since: 1999 - No. of Units: Company Owned: 1 - Franchised: 1 - Franchise Fee: $27,000 - Royalty: 10% - Total Inv: Approx $70,000-$110,000 - Financing: Third party. NOT FRANCHIISNG AT THIS TIME.

PROVENTURE
Proventure Business Group, Inc.
P.O. Box 338, Needham Heights, MA, 02494. Contact: William J. Tedoldi, Pres. - Tel: (781) 444-8278, Fax: (781) 444-0565, E-Mail: proventure@aol.com. All-inclusive New England based brokerage, consulting and management company for going businesses (up to $50 million). Also offered is a moderately priced consulting service for new franchise start-ups. Established: 1979 - Franchising Since: 1981 - No. of Units: Company Owned: 4 - Franchised: 5 - Franchise Fee: $10,000 - Royalty: 6% - Total Inv: $35,000 - Financing: No.

QPOINT HOME MORTGAGE LOANS
Qpoint International, Inc.
10900 NE 4th St., Ste. 1040, Bellevue, WA, 98004. Contact: Business Development Manager - Tel: (425) 462-6590, (800) 780-6575, Fax: (425) 462-4691, E-Mail: franchise@qpoint.com, Web Site: www.qpoint.com. Turn-key residential mortgage office. Benefits include corporate intranets, marketing materials, training, access to mortgage products, benefits. Established: 1993 - Franchising Since: 1994 - No. of Units: Company Owned: 2 - Franchised: 13 - Franchise Fee: $2,000-$10,000 - Royalty: $200 per closed loan/$30 ad fund/$2 Qpoint Foundation - Financing: No.

RENAISSANCE EXECUTIVE FORUMS
Renaissance Executive Forums, Inc.
7855 Ivanhoe Ave., Ste. 300, La Jolla, CA, 92037-4509. Contact: Franchise Department - Tel: (858) 551-6600, Fax: (858) 551-8777, E-Mail: moreinfo@executiveforums.com, Web Site: www.executive forums.com. Build and facilitate advisory boards for the top executive of businesses (CEO'S, Presidents and Owners exclusively). Established: 1993 - Franchising Since: 1994 - No. of Units: Franchised: 28 - Franchise Fee: $19,500 - Royalty: 20% - Total Inv: $44,515-$71,175 - Financing: No.

SAVEITNOW! BUSINESS PURCHASING SOLUTIONS
SaveItNow! Franchising Systems LLC
9100 Keystone Crossing, Suite 750, Indianapolis, IN, 46240. Contact: Danielle Davis - Tel: (317) 208-4800, (800) 755-7283, Fax: (888) 886-7367, E-Mail: ddavis@saveitnow.com, Web Site: www.saveitnow.com. We provide web based purchasing solutions and discounted prices to reduce buisness operating costs. Products include: Office products; furniture; janitorial supplies; IT supplies and printing. Established: 1986 - Franchising Since: 2002 - No. of Units: Franchised: 10 - Franchise Fee: $27,500 - Royalty: 6% - Total Inv: $53,000.

SERVICE INTELLIGENCE
5400 Laurel Springs Pkwy, Suite 602, Suwanee, GA, 30024. Contact: Franchise Sales Manager - Tel: (678) 513-4776, Fax: (678) 513-4869, Web Site: www.serviceintelligence.com. We offer franchises for the establishment and operation of a business which is designed to help other companies increase sales and overall performance by improving customer services, customer relationships and rising their level of customer satisfaction and customer loyalty. We design to enhance each client's reputation for providing services primarily to "Fortune 500" and other large corporations and organizations. Established: 1998 - Franchising Since: 1999 - No. of Units: Company Owned: 3 - Franchise Fee: $30,000 - Royalty: 6% of gross sales (option of 1% rebate based on sales) - Total Inv: $200,000 - Financing: No.

SHANE'S OFFICE SUPPLY
Shane's Franchise Group, Inc
2717 Curtiss Street, Downers Grove, IL, 60515. Contact: Tom Apicella, Jr. - Tel: (630) 437-5212, (800) 258-6055, Fax: (630) 435-3970, E-Mail: tom@eshanes.com, Web Site: www.eshanes.com. Commercial vendor for office supplies & office furniture. Established: 1989 - Franchising Since: 2003 - No. of Units: Company Owned: 1 - Franchise Fee: $26,000 - Royalty: 2%-6% - Total Inv: $76,000-$137,000 - Financing: No.

SHRED-IT
7617 Somerset Blvd., Paramount, CA, 90723. Contact: Fran. Development - Tel: (562) 529-2200, Fax: (562) 529-8895. Shred-it is the world's largest paper shredding and recycling business serving fortune 100 companies, hospitals, banks, financial institutions, government, large and small business. A mobile franchise operation business to business. Established: 1989 - Franchising Since: 1993 - No. of Units: Company Owned: 12 - Franchised: 33 - Franchise Fee: $45,000 - Royalty: 5% royalty, 1.5% ad fund - Total Inv: $500,000 net worth, $150,000 cash - Financing: Yes.

SIGNAL GRAPHICS
SAMPA Corp.
852 Broadway Ste. 300, Denver, CO, 80203. Contact: Dan Stone, Sales Director - Tel: (800) 852-6336, (303) 779-6789, Fax: (303)779-8445, E-Mail: info@signalgraphics.com, Web Site: www.signalgraphics.com. Full service graphic communication center including multi-color printing, high speed copying, desk top publishing and digital services. Established: 1974 - Franchising Since: 1982 - No. of Units: Company Owned: 3 - Franchised: 39 - Franchise Fee: $25,000 - Royalty: 5% (royalty rebate program available) - Total Inv: $142,000-$178,000 ($45,000 minimum cash) - Financing: Yes through third party sources.

STAR TACK WIRELESS SERVICES
Dagger International
1416 W Tennessee St #A, Tallahasee, FL, 32304-3403. - Tel: (305) 233-3411 x+3, (888) 906-9800, Fax: (305) 233-3411. Seeking dealers to sell fixed and portable satellite phones for land-sea and air. Dealers will also earn residential income for satellite air time used worldwide. Established: 1997 - Total Inv: Phone hardware $5,000-$25,000 - Financing: No.

STEN-TEL TRANSCRIPTIONS, INC
One Monarch Place., Suite 1800, 1414 Main Street, Springfield, MA, 01144. - Tel: (413) 732-8100, (888) 783-6835, Fax: (413) 739-4226. Sten-Tel franchises provide automated transcription service of important documents for the medical, legal, insurance, law enforcement and corporate communities. We provide telephone and internet based service to clients who need their dictation of reports transcribed same day or next. Established: 1990 - Franchising Since: 1996 - No. of Units: Company Owned: 1 - Franchised: 40 - Franchise Fee: $2500.00 - Royalty: 6% - Total Inv: $44,995 - Financing: Lease option provided.

STRATEGIC BUSINESS SYSTEMS, INC.
P.O. Box 137, Star Prairie, WI, 54026-0137. Contact: Richard Danielson, CEO - Tel: (715) 248-3289, (800) 522-8204, Fax: (715) 248-3659, Web Site: www.netcontact.com. Founded to provide small businesses with effective, yet affordable, computer management systems for franchises. It's first product, AUTOnet, is designed for the car care industry. Established: 1985.

STRATIS BUSINESS CENTERS
1925 Vaughn Rd, Suite 105, Kennsaw, GA, 30144. - Tel: (888) 778-7284, Fax: (843) 357-8599, E-Mail: info@stratisnet.com, Web Site: www.stratisnet.com. We provide fully staffed & equipped offices, conference rooms, telecomminucations & business support services. Established: 1996 - Franchising Since: 1997 - No. of Units: Company Owned: 2 - Franchised: 33 - Franchise Fee: $29,500 - Total Inv: $79,000-$195,000 - Financing: Third Party.

SUNBELT BUSINESS BROKERS
474 Wando Park Blvd #204, Mount Pleasant, SC, 29464. - Tel: (800) 771-7866, Fax: (843) 284-2419. We offer business brokerage and mergers and acquisition franchises. Sunbelt offers name recognition, quality training programs and hands on assistants. We take no percentage fees. All services are covered by our low semi-annual fee. Established:

1978 - Franchising Since: 1993 - No. of Units: Company Owned: 1 - Franchised: 180 - Franchise Fee: $5,000 or $10,000 - Royalty: $1,500 or $3,000 every 6 mo. - Total Inv: $50,000 - Financing: None.

TELEPHONE DOCTOR
3312 Piedmont Rd., Ste. 315, Atlanta, GA, 30305. - Tel: (404) 816-7550, Fax: (404) 816-7095. Telephone Doctor provides customer service for companies in all businesses. Established: 1983 - Franchising Since: 2002 - No. of Units: Company Owned: 1 - Franchise Fee: $20,000 - Total Inv: $106,000-$132,000 - Financing: Third party assistance.

TRADEBANK INTERNATIONAL FRANCHISING CORP.
Tradebank International
4220 Pleasantdale Rd., Atlanta, GA, 30340. - Tel: (770) 446-7600, (800) 899-1111, Fax: (770) 446-7600. International Barter Exchange. We coordinate barter transactions between thousands of businesses in the US and Canada. Established: 1987 - Franchising Since: 1995 - No. of Units: Company Owned: 4 - Franchised: 16 - Franchise Fee: $30,000 - Royalty: Franchisee is paid up to 70% of all fees collected from client base - Total Inv: $45,000-$50,000, $30,000 fran. fee, $15,000-$20,000 start-up - Financing: Up to 50%.

TURBO LEADERSHIP SYSTEM *
36280 NE Wilsonville, Newberg, OR, 97132. Contact: Larry Dennis - Tel: (503) 625-2699, Fax: (503) 625-2699. Leadership, customer service and management training. Established: 1985 - Franchising Since: 2000 - No. of Units: Franchised: 2 - Franchise Fee: $29,000 - Financing: No.

TYPING TIGERS
P.O. Box 8, San Marcos, TX, 78667. Contact: Manager - Tel: (830) 629-1400. Typesetting and desk top publishing for the small business user. Established: 1987 - Licensed Since: 1988 - No. of Units: Company Owned: 1- Royalty: $300 monthly.

VOCAM
Vocam USA LLC
855 E Golf Rd #2145, Arlington Heights, IL, 60005. - Tel: (847) 734-3000, (888) 388-6226, Fax: (847) 734-7159, Web Site: www.vocam.com. Vocam produces and distributes training programs for staff training for osha compliace. Established: 1996 - Franchising Since: 1998 - No. of Units: Company Owned: 3 - Franchised: 22 - Franchise Fee: $15,000-$60,000 - Royalty: 50% of retail, stock on consignment - Total Inv: $30,000-$105,000 - Financing: No.

VR BUSINESS BROKERS
Brinkley King Acavisitions, Inc
2601 E. Oakland Park Blvd., Suite 205, Ft. Lauderdale, FL, 33308. Contact: Gelnn Haddad - Tel: (800) 377-8722, Fax: (954) 565-6855, E-Mail: ghaddad@vrbusinessbrokers.com, Web Site: www.vrbusiness brokers.com. International and local business brokerage. Established: 1979 - Franchising Since: 1979 - No. of Units: Franchised: 81 - Franchise Fee: $12,000 - Royalty: 6% plus $250. monthly service fee, $150. monthly advertising fee - Total Inv: $50,000 approximately - Financing: No.

WARREN'S GLASS REPAIR, INC
1110 Oakland Park, Blcd, #337, Sunrise, FL, 33351. Contact: Warren, Owner - Tel: (954) 748-0066, (800) 877-0066, Fax: (954) 748-9543, E-Mail: warrenscott@computer.com, Web Site: www.warrensgold mine.com. Gold plating supplies, chemicals and machines. Established: 1994 - Franchising Since: 1994 - No. of Units: Company Owned: 1 - Franchised: 500 - Franchise Fee: $1,600.00 - Financing: Yes.

WE THE PEOPLE
We The People Forms And Services Centers USA, Inc.
1501 State Street, Santa Barbara, CA, 93101. - Tel: (805) 962-4100, Fax: (805) 962-9602. Established: 1985 - Franchising Since: 1996 - No. of Units: Company Owned: 1 - Franchised: 32 - Franchise Fee: $89,500 - Royalty: None - Total Inv: $114,500 (inlcudes franchise fee & $25,000 working capital) - Financing: None.

WESTERN APPRAISERS
West App. Inc.
2075 Winchester Blvd., Ste. 103, Campbell, CA, 95008-3432. Contact: Lou Celentano, Pres. - Tel: (408) 374-3551. Appraising and evaluating of damage to automobiles, equipment, farm machinery and recreational

vehicles. Established: 1960 - Franchising Since: 1975 - Royalty: 7% of gross income - Total Inv: $20,200-$32,000.

WORLDWIDE BUSINESS BROKERS
Worldwide Business Brokers, Inc
100 Pinewood Road, Suite 221, Virginia Beach, VA, 23451. Contact: Alan Guinn, International Managing Director - Tel: (757) 425-1077, Fax: (509) 275-1077, E-Mail: info@WorldwideBusinessBrokers.com, Web Site: www.WorldwideBusinessBrokers.com. A network of offices specializing in matching business owners that wish to sell their businesses with qualified buyers liking for businesses to buy. Exactly like Century 21 Real Estate except that our focus is the transfer of businesses rather than real estate. Established: 2001 - Franchising Since: 2002 - No. of Units: Company Owned: 1 - Franchised: 1 - Franchise Fee: $10,000 - Royalty: 7.5% - Total Inv: $20,000-$42,000 - Financing: No.

YOUR OFFICE USA INC.
6135 Park South Drive, Suite 510, Charlotte, NC, 28210. Contact: Dir. Unit Franchise Sales - Tel: (704) 945-7111, (888) 400-5139, Fax: (704) 945-7101. Full service business center with full or part-time executive suites and business address, conference rooms and admin. support to the home based business, corporate reps and people starting a new business. Established: 1989 - Franchising Since: 1989 - No. of Units: Company Owned: 1 - Franchised: 120+ - Franchise Fee: $38,000 - Royalty: 6% - Total Inv: $135,000-$340,000 - Financing: Yes, SBA and equipment programs.

ZIP2 CORPORATION
444 Castro St., Suite 101, Mountain View, CA, 94014. Contact: Keith Lorizio, National Sales - Tel: (650) 429-4400, Fax: (650) 429-4500, Web Site: www.zip2.com. Zip2 Corp., is the leading provider of online city guides to media companies in the local content space. Established: 1995.

CARPET, DRAPERY AND UPHOLSTERY CLEANING

A-PRO SERVICES
A-Pro Services Inc.
P.O. Box 132, Newfield, NJ, 08344. Contact: Charles A. Simpson, Pres. - Tel: (609) 641-8080. Full carpet service: carpet and upholstery dyeing and cleaning, mobile floor covering sales and installations, water restoration, deodorization, carpet repair etc. Established: 1987 - Franchising Since: 1992 - No. of Units: Company Owned: 1 - Franchised: 6 - Franchise Fee: $7,000 - Royalty: $200/mo. - Total Inv: $10,700 - Financing: 0% interest on fran. fee, equipment leasing available.

CAPITAL CARPET CLEANING
Capital Sales Corp.
1306 Coral Park Lane, Vero Beach, FL, 32963-4058. Contact: Robert Campbell, Pres. - Tel: (561) 234-3707, Fax: (561) 234-9216. Ultra high powered carpet and upholstery cleaning company. Established: 1983 - Franchising Since: 1990 - No. of Units: Company Owned: 5 - Franchised: 9 - Franchise Fee: $5,000 - Total Inv: Van $20,000, equipment $15,000 - Financing: Yes.

CARPET ONE CLEANING
4301 Earthcity Expressway, Earth City, MO, 63045. Contact: Franchise Development Cord - Tel: (314) 506-0000, (800) 466-6984, Fax: (314) 291-6674, Web Site: www.carpetone.com. Carpet cleaning, upholstery cleaning and water damage restoration. Established: 1997 - Franchising Since: 1997 - No. of Units: Company Owned: 1 - Franchised: 26 - Franchise Fee: Based on market population - Royalty: sliding scale starting at 6% - Total Inv: franchise fee plus chemical and equipment package - Financing: Yes.

CARPETMATE
Justek, Inc.
P.O. Box 445, 1563 Sumneytown Pike, Kulpsville, PA, 19443-0445. - Tel: (215) 368-6155, (800) 832-4070, Fax: (215) 361-1452. Unique Dry Carpet Cleaning Franchise with a strong and proven marketing program. We teach our franchisees how to get customers affordably. Nobody goes out of business because they have too many customers. We teach our

franchisees how to fish so they can feed themselves. We Guarantee your success! Established: 1995 - Franchising Since: 1996 - No. of Units: Company Owned: 1 - Franchised: 6 - Franchise Fee: $8,550 - Royalty: Flat fee based on population, averages $100 per month - Total Inv: $8,550 franchise fee plus $3,950 equipment and computer = $12,500 - Financing: Yes, $5,000 down, finance balance interest fee for 48 months.

CHEM-DRY® CARPET, DRAPERY AND UPHOLSTERY CLEANING
Harris Research Inc
1530 North 1000 West, Logan, UT, 84321. Contact: Nat'l. Fran. Dir. - Tel: (800) 243-6379, Fax: (435) 755-8490, E-Mail: charlie@chem dry.com, Web Site: www.chemdry.com. Number one rated franchise in the service industry. Chem-Dry offers a unique, patented process which utilizes a non-toxic cleaning solution in conjunction with carbonation. We specialize in the hard-to-clean stains such as red dye, gum, grease, oil, indelible ink, pet stains and odors, etc. Established: 1977 - Franchising Since: 1978 - No. of Units: Franchised: 3,871 - Franchise Fee: $19,950 - Royalty: $197.50/month, flat fee - Total Inv: $6,950 down - $19,950 total - Financing: $13,000 financed over 56 months at 5% simple interest.

COIT SERVICES, INC
897 Hinckley Rd., Burlingame, CA, 94010. Contact: Craig Ratkovich, Dir. of Franchise Development - Tel: (650) 697-5471 ext 122, (888) 882-2648 ext 122, Fax: (650) 697-6117, E-Mail: craig@coit.com, Web Site: www.coit.com. Granting large exclusive territories, Coit provides a huge opportunity in the specialty cleaning areas offering many profit centers such as carpet, upholstery, drapery, area rugs and duct cleaning. Established: 1950 - Franchising Since: 1963 - No. of Units: Company Owned: 13 divisions - Franchised: 57 approx. - Franchise Fee: $20,000 + - Royalty: 6%-2% - Total Inv: $40,000-$105,000 - Financing: Third party.

DURACLEAN INTERNATIONAL, INC.
220 W Campus Dr #A, Arlington Heights, IL, 60004-1498. Contact: Mike Higgins, Vice President-Global Expansion - Tel: (800) 251-7070, Fax: (847) 704-7101, E-Mail: franchise@duraclean.com. Multi-revenue services including: carpet cleaning, upholstery and drapery cleaning, ceiling and wall cleaning, fire and water restoration, janitorial services, floor cleaning, ventilation duct cleaning, pressure washing and ultrasonic cleaning, can deliver continuous growth. Established: 1930 - Franchising Since: 1945 - No. of Units: Company Owned: 1 - Franchised: 347 - Franchise Fee: $10,000 - Royalty: 6-8% - Total Inv: $32,000 plus working cap. - Financing: Yes.

FIBER SEAL
Fiber Seal, Inc.
5565 Red Bird Center DR, #150, Dallas, TX, 75237. Contact: Kurt Falbey, Fran. Dir. - Tel: (214) 333-9400, Fax: (214) 333-9435. A service business providing treatment and cleaning of fabric, upholstery and carpet, using unique techniques. Regional franchises available. Established: 1971 - Franchising Since: 1994 - No. of Units: Company Owned: 1 - License sold: 69 - License Fee: $15,000-$20,000 - Royalty: 5% - Total Inv: $11,600-$28,500 - Financing: Yes.

HEAVEN'S BEST CARPET & UPHOLSTERY CLEANING
M-Co., Inc.
P.O. Box 607, 247 N. 1st E, Rexburg, ID, 83440. Contact: Cody Howard, Owner - Tel: (208) 359-1106, (800) 359-2095, Fax: (208) 359-1236, E-Mail: mcoinc@heavensbest.com, Web Site: www.heavensbest.com. Fastest growing carpet & upholstery cleaning company for 3 years in a row. Customers love our low moisture process. Established: 1983 - Franchising Since: 1983 - No. of Units: Franchised: 650 - Franchise Fee: $2,900 - Royalty: $80/mo. - Total Inv: $15,900 - Financing: Yes.

JOY CARPET DRY CLEANING
Joy Franchising Inc.
3209 Premier Drive #115, Plano, TX, 75075. Contact: Franchise Director - Tel: (901) 368-3361, Fax: (901) 368-1144. Special dry cleaning of carpets, upholstery, vents, restoration after fires and floods. Established: 1983 - Franchising Since: 1997 - No. of Units: Company Owned: 1 - Franchised: 1 - Franchise Fee: $20,000 - Royalty: 5%, 1% adv - Total Inv: $43,950-$93,000 - Financing: Yes.

KAMEHAMEKA CARPET CLEANERS
American Enterprises Inc.
P.O. Box 4366, Kailua - Kona, HI, 96745. Contact: Ray Dille, Pres. - Tel: (808) 325-1431. We discovered a new chemical and rinse system which makes all other carpet cleaning systems obsolete. Simple to use efficient, absolutely restores carpet to like new condition, leaving no residue, passes all EPA standards testing. Established: 1985 - Franchising Since: 1996 - No. of Units: Company Owned: 1 - Franchise Fee: $14,500 - Royalty: 3-5% - Total Inv: $20,000-$25,000 we set you up in your location or territory completely all equipment and supplies.

KWIK DRY CARPET & UPHOLSTERY CLEANING
Kwik Dry International Inc.
13553 Golden Eagle Cir., Plainfield, IL, 60544. - Tel: (815) 436-0333. A unique, user friendly, "dry extraction" system of cleaning both carpet and upholstery in homes and businesses. Package includes all equipment, supplies, training and marketing (which includes $1,000 initial marketing). Established: 1967 - Franchising Since: 1995 - No. of Units: Franchised: 17 in 5 states - Franchise Fee: $11,750 - Royalty: $175 per month - Total Inv: $11,750.00.

LANGENWALTER CARPET DYEING
Langenwalter Industries Inc.
1111 S. Richfield Rd., Placentia, CA, 92870. - Tel: (714) 528-7610, (800) 422-4370, Fax: (714) 528-7620, Web Site: www.landdye.com. Complete carpet correction services. To include bleach spots, pet rust, punch fading and other discolorations. Established: 1975 - Franchising Since: 1980 - No. of Units: Company Owned: 4 - Franchised: 165 - Franchise Fee: $18,000 - Royalty: $300/mnth - Total Inv: $ 60,000 - Financing: No.

LASER CHEM ADVANCED CARPET & UPHOLSTERY DRY CLEANING
Laser Chem International Corp.
7022 South 400 West, Midvale, UT, 84047. - Tel: (801) 569-9500, (800) 272-2741, Fax: (801) 569-8400. Professional carpet and upholstery cleaning using the famous Laser Chem Advanced Dry Cleaning System. Deep cleaning that dries in minutes and leaves no residue. Established: 1993 - Franchising Since: 1993 - No. of Units: Company Owned: 1 - Franchised: 14 - Franchise Fee: $300 plus equipment & supplies - Total Inv: $2,300 - Financing: No.

MAXCARE PROFESSIONAL CLEANING SYSTEMS
The Maxim Group, Inc.
210 Town Park Dr., Kennesaw, GA, 30144. Contact: Director of Franchise Sales - Tel: (678) 355-4000, (800) 331-1744, Web Site: www.maxcarecleaning.com. Carpet, upholstery, wood, tile, hard surfaces cleaning systems. Established: 1997 - Franchising since; 1997 - No. of Units: Company Owned: 1 - Franchised: 61 - Franchise Fee: $12,500 and up - Royalty: 6% decreasing to 4% with volume - Total Inv: Varies by market - Financing: Yes.

MEDICLEAN
Restorx, Inc.
1135 Braddock Ave., Braddock, PA, 15104. - Tel: (412) 351-8686. Carpet cleaning and sanitizing system. Established: 1993 - Franchising Since: 1995 - No. of Units: Company Owned: 1 - Franchise Fee: $5,000 - Royalty: Flat Fee $50-$250 per week - Total Inv: Fran fee, $10,000 vehicle/equip., $5,000 work. cap. - Financing: Partial.

MODERNISTIC CLEANING SERVICES
Koppang Franchise Development
1460 Rankin St, Troy, MI, 48083. Contact: Vic Koppang - Tel: (800) 609-1000, Web Site: www.koppang.com. We offer a full service carpet and upholstery cleaning company. We specialize in cleaning carpet, upholstery, ceiling tiles and repairing flood damage and water restoration. Established: 1972 - Franchising Since: 1999 - No. of Units: Franchised: 4 - Franchise Fee: $30,000 - Total Inv: $65,000.

PERFECTIONIST, THE
The Perfectionist Cleaninng Services, Inc
2040 E. Bell Rd Ste. 170, Phoenix, AZ, 85022. Contact: Tim Lee - Tel: (866) 493-1233, Fax: (602) 569-0166, E-Mail: timless@earthlink.net, Web Site: www.theperfectionist.net. Residential cleaning; carpet, tile

etc. Established: 1995 - Franchising Since: 2001 - No. of Units: Company Owned: 1 - Franchise Fee: $13,500 - Total Inv: Capital requirements; $2,500-$20,000 - Financing: Yes.

PROFESSIONAL CARPET SYSTEMS
Professional Carpet Systems, Inc
4211 Atlantic Ave, Raleigh, NC, 27604. Contact: Fritz Thompson, President, CO-CEO - Tel: (800) 925-5055, (919) 875-8871, Fax: (919) 895-9855, E-Mail: info@procarpetsys.com, Web Site: www.procarpetsys.com. Incredible opportunity to do it all. Repair, restore, rejuvendate & replace carpet and other hard surfaces. Start with 1,2 or 3 of our 13 services and ad others as you grow. Established: 1978 - Franchising Since: 1982 - No. of Units: Franchised: 62 - Franchise Fee: $14,995 - Royalty: 3%-6% - Total Inv: $19,500-$52,500 - Financing: Yes.

PUROCLEAN
PuroSystems, Inc
5350 N.W. 35th Ave, Ft. Lauderdale, FL, 33309. Contact: Chrystal Shacklock - Tel: (800) 247-9047, (954) 777-2431, Fax: (800) 995-8527, E-Mail: cvanderwyde@puroclean.com, Web Site: www.puroclean.com. Puroclean is a franchise that truly provides the organization, experience, and support for attaining the entrepreneurial formula for success. Our dynamic turnkey opportunity in the high-growth restoration and cleaning industry is known as the system to rely on by many insurance companies nation wide. Puroclean delivers a proven operating business, on-going support, extensive training programs and a track record of success. Established: 1986 - Franchising Since: 1990 - No. of Units: Franchised: 89 - Franchise Fee: $25,000 - Royalty: 8%-10% - Total Inv: $79,250-$122,200 - Financing: Assistance available.

RAINBOW INTERNATIONAL CARPET
1010 N. University Parks Dr., Waco, TX, 76707. - Tel: (800) 583-9100, Fax: (254) 745-2592, Web Site: www.rainbowintl.com. Carpet cleaning, dyeing, repair, reinstallation, upholstery, drapery and ceiling cleaning, deodorization services, water and smoke restoration services for residential and commercial buildings. Established: 1980 - Franchising Since: 1981 - No. of Units: Franchised: 417 - Franchise Fee: $19,000 - Royalty: 7%, 2% adv. - Total Inv: $28,950-$86,000 - Financing: Yes, for 1/2 of franchise fee only.

SEARS CARPET & UPHOLSTERY CARE
Sears, Roebuck & Company
8101 N. High Street, Ste. 260, Columbus, OH, 43235. - Tel: (800) 586-1603. Carpet, upholstery and tile cleaners. Established: 1996 - No. of Units: Company Owned: 8 - Franchised: 131 - Franchise Fee: $5,040-$94,500 - Total Inv: $68,390-$282,300 (including franchise fee, equip/truck & start-up cost) - Financing: Yes.

SERVICEMASTER CLEAN
83 Ridge Lake Blvd, Memphis, TN, 38120. Contact: Dinah Coopwood, Franchise Lead Manager - Tel: (901) 684-7500, (800) 255-9687, Fax: (901) 684-7580, E-Mail: brwilliams@smclean.com, Web Site: www.ownafranchise.com. Professional carpet/upholstery cleaning, janitorial and disaster restoration franchise with over 50 years experience. Established: 1947 - Franchising Since: 1952 - No. of Units: Franchised: 4544 - Franchise Fee: $16,900-$31,500 - Royalty: 7-10% - Total Inv: $25,000-$90,000 - Financing: Yes up to 80% of franchise fee/products & equipment.

STANLEY STEEMER INTERNATIONAL INC.
5500 Stanley Steemer Parkway, Dublin, OH, 43016. Contact: Philip Ryser, Executive Vice President - Tel: (614) 764-2007, (800) 848-7496, Fax: (614) 764-1506. Carpet and upholstery cleaning. Established: 1947 - Franchising Since: 1972 - No. of Units: Company Owned: 37 - Franchised: 257 - Franchise Fee: General rule: $20,000 per 100,000 population - Royalty: 7% - Total Inv: Approx. $77,050-$336,075 - Financing: We offer two plans under which to finance initial franchise fee, truck and equipment financing is also available.

STEAM BROTHERS PROFESSIONAL CLEANING & RESTORATION SERVICE
Steam Brothers, Inc.
2124 East Sweet Ave, Bismarek, ND, 58504. - Tel: (800) 767-5064, Fax: (701) 222-1372. Residential and commercial carpet, upholstery, drapery / blind, wall and ceiling; furnace air duct cleaning; water smoke

and fire restoration. Established: 1977 - Franchising Since: 1983 - No. of Units: Franchised: 22 - Franchise Fee: $16,000 - Royalty: 5%-6.5% - Total Inv: $22,000-$53,500 - Financing: Leasing.

STEAM-MASTERS
413 Litchfield Drive, Windsor Locks, CT, 06096. Contact: Donald Michaud, President - Tel: (860) 623-9274, (800) 448-5871. Carpet/upholstery cleaning, utilizing truck mounted equipment only. Established: 1988 - Franchising Since: 1996 - No. of Units: Company Owned: 1 - Franchised: 1 - Franchise Fee: $15,000 - Royalty: Monthly yes - Total Inv: $25,000 including all equipment - Financing: No.

STEAMATIC
Steamatic, Inc.
303 Arthur St., Fort Worth , TX, 76107-2352. Contact: Chris Clark, VP - Tel: (817) 332-1576, Fax: (817) 332-5349, E-Mail: cclark@steamatic.com. Indoor air control, air duct cleaning, fire and water restoration, odor control, corrosion control, carpet, furniture and drapery cleaning and wood restoration. Established: 1948 - Franchising Since: 1967 - No. of Units: Company Owned: 9 - Franchised: 264 - Franchise Fee: $12,000-$18,000 - Royalty: 8% down to 5% - Total Inv: Fran. fee + equip. pkg. $34,000 + oper. cap. $15,000-$45,000 - Financing: Yes, of the $34,000 equip. pkg. will finance up to 100% from 1-5 yrs.

SYLVAN CHEMICAL CO., INC.
201 Lukken Industrial Dr., West, LaOrange, GA, 30240. - Tel: (706) 880-3377, Fax: (706) 880-3279, Web Site: www.millicare.com. Millicare Enviromental Services franchisees provide environmentally friendly carpet maintenance and refurbishment services and also upholstery cleaning to large commercial customers. Established: 1984 - Franchising Since: 1996 - No. of Units: Franchised: 73 - Franchise Fee: $18,000 - Royalty: 6%, 2% Promo Fee - Total Inv: $60,000-$160,000 - Financing: No.

THRIFTY CLEAN INC *
Easy Clean Franchising Inc
765 East Greg St., Ste. 104, Sparks, NV, 89431.- Tel: (775) 971-3904, (877) 4THRIFTY, Fax: (775) 971-3922, E-Mail: info@thriftyclean.com, Web Site: www.thriftyclean.com. Thrifty Clean manufactures reliable, user-friendly carpet cleaning rental equipment and cleaning products. Established: 2000 - Franchising Since: 2003 - No. of Units: Company Owned: 3 - Franchised: 2 - Franchise Fee: $15,000 - Total Inv: $34,000 - Financing: No.

TRI-COLOR FRANCHISE SYSTEMS
603 West Main St., Glasgow, KY, 42141. - Tel: (270) 651-7879, (800) 452-9065, Fax: (270) 651-6048, E-Mail: randy@tri-color.com, Web Site: www.tri-color.com. Offers total carpet care and restoration services. Includes carpet cleaning, dyeing and repairs plus complete water damage restoration all services marketed to commercial and residential customers. Established: 1984 - Franchising Since: 1997 - No. of Units: Company Owned: 8 - Franchised: 3 - Franchise Fee: $17,500 - Total Inv: $17,500-$65,000 (includes equipment package, franchise fee) - Financing: Yes.

CHILDREN'S PRODUCTS AND SERVICES

3D MEMORIES *
3D Franchising, LLS
64 Seagull Circle, Colorado Springs, CO, 80921. Contact: David Taylor, Director, Sales & Marketing - Tel: (719) 481-5710, Fax: (719) 481-0665, E-Mail: sales@handmolds.com, Web Site: www.handmolds.com. Using a proprietary molding and casting process, 3D Memories keepsakes memorialize life's most important moments, capturing time and preserving memories. Births, weddings, and special accomplishments are just the beginning of the endless possibilities. Established: 2001 - Franchising Since: 2004 - No. of Units: Company Owned: 2 - Franchised: 1 - Franchise Fee: $4,900-$9,900 - Royalty: 5% royalty, 2% ad fee - Total Inv: $6,150-$15,350 - Financing: No.

A CHOICE NANNY
ACN Franchise Systems, Inc.
5110 Ridgefield Rd. Ste. 403, Bethesda, MD, 20816. - Fax: (703) 685-0175. Nanny referral business. Franchise fee includes computer system, 1-2 weeks training for 2 people, advertising materials and brochures,

start-up, public relations, sample legal contracts and paperwork. Established: 1983 - Franchising Since: 1988 - No. of Units: Company Owned: 2 - Franchised: 14 - Franchise Fee: $24,900 - Royalty: 7.5% - 10% gross sales - Total Inv: $36,000-$46,000 (incl. fran. fee) - Financing: Yes, thru qualified lenders.

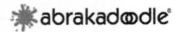

ABRAKADOODLE ART EDUCATION *
1800 Robert Fulton Drive, Suite 250, Reston, VA, 22192. Contact: Rosemarie Hartnett, Vice President of Franchise Development - Tel: (703) 871-7356, Fax: (703) 766-3606, E-Mail: info@abrakadoodle.com, Web Site: www.abrakadoodle.com. Abrakadoodle brings remarkable, educationally sound, imaginative art education programs to children ages 20 months to 12 years old. This home-managed business offers classes at host educational sites, such as schools (private and public), park programs, community centers, day care centers and others. Established: 2002 - Franchising Since: 2004 - No. of Units: Company Owned: 4 - Franchised: 1 - Franchise Fee: $28,900 - Royalty: 8-6% support fee, 1% advertising fee - Total Inv: $36,975-$44,650 - Financing: Third party.

ADVENTURE CUTS INC. *
4028-K Cox Rd, Glen Allen, VA, 23060. - Tel: (804) 527-2887, Fax: (804) 562-1580, Web Site: www.adventurecuts.com. A new way for kids to get a haircut and have fun all at the same time. Established: 2002 - Franchising Since: 2004 - No. of Units: Company Owned: 2 - Franchise Fee: $15,000 - Royalty: 5% - Total Inv: $75,000-$110,000 - Financing: No.

BABY NEWS STORES
Baby News
6909 Las Positas RD # A, Livermore, CA, 94551. Contact: Roger O'Callaghan, Pres. - Tel: (925) 245-1370, Fax: (925) 245-1376, E-Mail: info@stanforddistributing.com, Web Site: www.babynewsstores.com. Complete children's shoes. Established: 1949 - Franchising Since: 1961 - No. of Units: Company Owned: 1 - Franchised: 54 - Franchise Fee: $15,000 - Royalty: 1% - Total Inv: $200,000 - Financing: No.

BABY POWER
P.O. 526, Annandale, NJ, 08801. - Tel: (800) 365-4847, Fax: (908) 713-6567, Web Site: www.babypower.com. Parent and child play program. Established: 1979 - Franchising Since: 1997 - No. of Units: Company Owned: 1 - Franchised: 5 - Franchise Fee: $15,000 - Royalty: 5%.

BABY-TENDA CORP.
123 S. Belmont, Kansas City, MO, 64123. Contact; David Garnett, Gen. Mgr. - Tel: (816) 231-2300. Direct sale of safety equipment for babies. Person should enjoy speaking to expectant couples. Established: 1937 - Franchising Since: 1962 - No. of Units: Company Owned: 8 - Franchised: 56 - Total Inv: $6,800 - Financing: Yes.

BUILDING BLOCKS TOY STORES
Building Blocks Franchise Corp.
6209 Deeside Dr, Dublin, OH, 43017. - Tel: (614) 336-9238, (888) 654-TOYS [8697]. Toy stores offering a wide assortment of educational and specialty toys from around the world. Stores are colorful, inter-active and community involved. Established: 1997 - Franchising Since: 1997 - No. of Units: Company Owned: 1 - Franchised: 3 - Franchise Fee: $25,000 - Royalty: 3% 1st year, 4% 2nd year, 5% 3rd and continuing years - Total Inv: $180,000-$290,000.

CHILD CARE CHOICES
Child Care Choices, Inc
P.O. Box 4, Spring City, PA, 19475. Contact: Julann Alessi, VP. - Tel: (610) 792-3044, (877) SIT-4YOU, Fax: (610) 792-3709, E-Mail: jalessi @chilcarechoicesinc.com, Web Site: www.childcarechoices inc.com. Child Care Choices is a revolutionary new childcare referral network. With locations across the U.S. CCC offers uniquely affordable childcare screening and matching services to families in need of quality childcare. Established: 1998 - Franchising Since: 1999 - No. of Units: Company Owned: 5 - Franchised: 10 - Franchise Fee: $19,000 - Royalty: 6%; plus 2% advertising - Financing: Yes.

CHILDREN'S LIGHTHOUSE
101 South Jennings, Suite 209, FT. Worth, TX, 76104-1112. Contact: Mike Brown, President - Tel: (817) 338-1332, (888) 338-4466, Fax: (817) 338-2716, Web Site: www.childrenslighthouse.com. Childcare. Established: 1997 - Franchising Since: 1999 - No. of Units: Company Owned: 8 - Franchised: 3 - Franchise Fee: $45,000 - Total Inv: $1,500,000-$1,700,000 (land, building franchise fee and equipment) - Financing: Good SBA product.

CHILDREN'S ORCHARD
Children's Orchard, Inc.
2100 South Main Street, Ste. B, Ann Arbor, MI, 48103. Contact: Lisa Morgan - Tel: (734) 994-9199, (800) 999-5437, Fax: (734) 994-9323, E-Mail: FranchiseHeadquarters@childorch.com, Web Site: www.childrens orchard.com. Upscale boutiques selling new and gently used children's clothing, toys, furniture, equipment, and accessories. Established: 1980 - Franchising Since: 1985 - No. of Units: Company Owned: 1 - Franchised: 85 - Franchise Fee: $19,500 - Royalty: 5% - Total Inv: $69,450-$144,950 - Financing: Third party, but will assist on obtaining financing with business plan, loan proposal, etc.

CHIP THE CHILD I.D. PROGRAM OF AMERICA
The Child I.D. Program, Inc
15300 Devonshire Street, Suite 4, Mission Hills, CA, 91345. Contact: Marc Bakerman, President - Tel: (818) 894-4784, (866) 244-7462, Fax: (818) 894-4782, E-Mail: franchise@4childid.com, Web Site: www.4childid.com. CHIP is a Child Identification & School Safety Event; A home-based business providing parents, children and schools with photo identification cards, educational lesson plans and campus security. Established: 2001 - Franchising Since: 2002 - No. of Units: Franchised: 102 - Franchise Fee: $27,900 - Total Inv: $27,900-$43,500.

COMPUCHILD
CompuChild
602 Main St, Suite 2, Rochester, IN, 46975. Contact: Rob & Theresa Shafer - Tel: (574) 223-5437, (800) 619-KIDS(5437), Fax: (574) 8223-4422, E-Mail: compuchild@tcol.net, Web Site: www.compuchild.com. CompuChild is the nation's leader in preschool computer education. Together with nearly 100 independently owned franchise territories located throughout the U.S, Bermuda and Puerto Rico. CompuChild is dedicated to preparing preschoolers for the academic challenges of tomorrow through computer education today. Established: 1994 - Franchising Since: 1995 - No. of Units: Company Owned: 1 - Franchised: 90 - Franchise Fee: $12,500 - Royalty: $150.00 Monthly - Total Inv: $12,500-$15,000 - Financing: No.

COMPUTERTOTS & COMPUTER EXPLORERS
ECW Corp.
12715 Telge Rd, Cypress, TX, 77429. Contact: Cyndee Perkins - Tel: (888) 638-8722, Fax: (281) 256-4178, Web Site: www.computertots.com. Computertots is a worldwide network of computer education services. Programs are offered through learning centers and outreach programs at private and public educational facilities. The company is actively seeking international candidates who have financial and experiential ability to take the award-winning COMPUTERTOTS program and expand services in their respective countries. Established: 1984 - Franchising Since: 1988 - No. of Units: Company Owned: 2 - Franchised: 92 - Franchise Fee: $15,000-$25,000 - Royalty: 8%, 1% ad fund - Total Inv: $37,675-$43,800 - Financing: No.

CREATIVE PLAYTHINGS
Creative Playthings Franchising, Corp.
33 Lorning Dr, Framingham, MA, 01702. Contact: Kevin Sutter - Tel: (800) 444-0901, Fax: (508) 872-3120, E-Mail: ksutter@creativeplay things.com, Web Site: www.creativeplay things.com. We offer the finest products for backyard fun. Established: 1951 - Franchising Since: 2002 - No. of Units: Company Owned: 19 - Franchised: 2 - Franchise Fee: $25,000 - Capital Requirements: $75,000.

CREATIVE WORLD SCHOOL FRANCHISING CO., INC

Creative World, Inc,
13315 Orange Grove Drive, Tampa, FL, 33618. Contact: Duane McCabe - Tel: (813) 968-9154, (800) 362-5940, Fax: (813) 264-7266. Childcare franchise. Established: 1970 - Franchising Since: 2000 - No. of Units: Company Owned: 22 - Franchised: 2 - Franchise Fee: $48,000 - Total Inv: Capital requirements; $150,000-$180,000 - Financing: No.

DANCERCISE KIDS®

International Education Resources Corp.
P.O. Box 219, Anoka, MN, 55303-0219. Contact: Franchise Operations Director - Tel: (952) 920-9880, (800) 613-8231, Fax: (952) 925-1141, E-Mail: franchiseinfo@dancercise.com, Web Site: www.dancercise.com. Educational, mobile dance program for children. Established: 1987 - Franchising Since: 1999 - No. of Units: Company Owned: 9 - Franchised: 1 - Franchise Fee: $9,500 - Royalty: 10% monthly gross sales - Total Inv: $16,800-$23,300 - Financing: No.

DANCING BEARS DANCE CLASSES FOR KIDS

Dancing Bears Dance Company
28005 N. Smyth Dr., Ste. 158, Velencia, CA, 91354. Contact: Monica Geisz-Benitez - Tel: (866) 26B-EARS, (661) 263-8905, Fax: (661) 263-8905, E-Mail: monica@dancingbearsclasses.com, Web Site: www.DancingBearsClasses.com. Mobile dance classes for kids. Established: 1999 - Franchising Since: 2002 - No. of Units: Company Owned: 6 - Total Inv: $13,500 - Financing: No.

DAYCAMPS OF AMERICA INC.

Empire Business Brokers
527 Meadow Dr, Williamsville, NY, 14224-1517. - Tel: (716) 677-5229. Children's day camps. Established: 1973 - Franchising Since: 1995 - No. of Units: Company Owned: 1 - Franchised: 10 - Franchise Fee: $4,900 - Royalty: $100/month - Total Inv: $7,000-$12,000 - Financing: No.

DINOSAUR-US FAMILY ENTERTAINMENT CENTER

P.O. Box 1937, Glendora, CA, 91740. - Tel: (626) 852-0920, Fax: (626) 852-0930. Dinosaur shaped pizzas. Established: 1993 - Franchising Since: 1999 - No. of Units: Company Owned: 1 - Franchised: 1 - Franchise Fee: $50,000 - Total Inv: Small units $150,000-$175,000 - Financing: No.

DISCOVERY EXPRESS

Children's Discovery Center
3905 Talmadge Road, Toledo, OH, 43606. - Tel: (419) 292-2600, (800) 277-1717, Fax: (419) 472-6344. Unique child care system. Established: 1982 - Franchising Since: 1997 - No. of Units: Company Owned: 5 - Franchise Fee: $40,000 - Financing: No.

DISCOVERY POINT CHILD DEVELOPMENT CENTERS.

Discovery Point Franchising, Inc
1140A Old Peachtree Rd, Duluth, GA, 30097-5121. Contact: Clifford M. Clark, Pres. - Tel: (770) 622-2112, Fax: (770) 622-2388, Web Site: www.discoverypoint.com. Child care centers for children ages 6 weeks to 12 years. Established: 1988 - Franchising Since: 1990 - No. of Units: Franchised: 24 - Franchise Fee: $25,000 - Royalty: Approx. 4.% - Total Inv: Min $150,000 - Financing: Yes.

DRAMA KIDS INTERNATIONAL

Drama Kids International, Inc
3225-B Corporate Court, Ellicott City, MD, 21042, Contact: Doug Howard, Director of Franchise Development - Tel: (410) 480-2015, Fax: (410) 480-2026, Web Site: www.dramakids.com. Drama Kids & its international affiliate, Helen O'Grady Drama Academy, is the largest after-school drama program in the world with over 25,000 children currently enrolled. Our award winning drama curriculum uses a wide variety of fun and creative drama activities that are new each week, all designed to help our Drama Kids act confidently and speak clearly. Advancing class activities and special yearend productions are conducted for children ages 5-8, 9-12, and 13-17. Drama experience NOT required, but a love of children is. Established: 1979 - Franchising Since: 1989 - No. of Units: Company Owned: 2 - Franchised: 96 - Franchise Fee: $25,000 - Royalty: 10% - Total Inv: $40,000 - Financing: No.

EDUCATE "R" KIDS

IMG Franchise Learning Centers, Inc
P.O. Box 401050, Redford, MI, 48240-9050. - Tel: (313) 963-8555, (888) 598-KIDS, Fax: (313) 964-1106. Child care learning centers for ages 6 weeks to 12 years old. Established: 1994 - Franchising Since: 1998 - No. of Units: Company Owned: 2 - Franchised: 2 - Franchise Fee: $30,000, capital requirement $100,000-$270,000 - Financing: No.

ENCOURAGYM *

9800 Greentree Dr, Carmel, IN, 46032. - Tel: (317) 334-1966, Fax: (317) 334-1966, Web Site: www.encouragym.com. Using our acclaimed lessons and business systems we will teach you how to start your own EncouraGYM franchise for babies, toddlers and preschoolers at a fraction of the cost of a traditional franchise. Established: 2001 - Franchising Since: 2004 - Franchise Fee: $9,500 - Royalty: 7% - Total Inv: $87,500-$150,500.

EXPLORATIONS

Explorations Entertainament Group, Inc.
2500 N Military TRL Ste 225, Boca Raton, FL, 33431-6342. - Tel: (561) 998-3435, Fax: (561) 998-4635. Children's fitness and entertainment centers featuring proprietary play structures, licensed characters, full-view restaurant, arcade, classes and programs and merchandise. Established: 1995 - Licensing Since: 1995 - No. of Units: Company Owned: 2 - Licensed: 3 - Franchise Fee: $30,000 - Total Inv: $350,000-$550,000 - Financing: No.

FASTRACKIDS INTERNATIONAL LTD

FasTracKids International Ltd.
6900 East Belleview Avenue, Greenwood Village, CO, 80111. Contact: Mr. Kevin Kraus - Tel: (303) 224-0200, (888) 576-6888, Fax: (303) 224-0222, E-Mail: info@fastrackids.com, Web Site: www.fastrac kids.com. Fastrackids is a remarkable new educational system designed to enrich the knowledge of young children. FasTracKids utilizes state-of-the-art technology to develop a child's creativity, leadership, speaking and communication skills in a stimulating, participatory learning environment. Established: 1998 - Franchising Since: 1998 - No. of Units: Franchised: 140 - Franchise Fee: $5,000-$15,000 - Royalty: 1.5% - Total Inv: $10,755-$39,600 - Financing: Yes.

FOURTH R YOUTH PROGRAM, THE

The Fourth R. Inc.
1715 Market St., Ste. 103, Kirkland, WA, 98033. Contact: Robert McCauley, Marketing - Tel: (425) 828-0336, (800) 821-8653, Fax: (425) 828-0192, E-Mail: bob@fourthr.com, Web Site: www.fourthr.com. The Fourth R Youth Program franchise is primarily a home-based operation with a low initial investment. Franchise partners offer on-site computer training courses to children under 18 years of age and to teachers at local schools and community centers. Courses are offered during scool (intracurricular) or after school (extracurricular). Camps and courses for teachers are popular during the summer. Established: 1991 - Franchising Since: 2002 - No. of Units: Franchised: 25 - Franchise Fee: $16,000 - Royalty: 6% sales - Total Inv: From $28,000 - Financing: No.

FRENCH TOAST

Lollytgos Ltd.
100 W. 33rd St., Ste. 1012, New York, NY, 10001-2900. Contact: V.P. Licensing - Tel: (212) 594-4740, Fax: (212) 594-3030. Children's apparel/footwear and accessories. Established: 1955 - Franchising Since: 1990 - No. of Units: 12 Licensed Accessory Mfrs. - Franchise Fee: Negotiable - Royalty: 6% - Total Inv: $250,000 - Financing: None.

FUN BUS *

32 Timothy Lane, Tinton Falls, NJ, 07724. - Tel: (732) 578-1287, Fax: (732) 389-7824, Web Site: www.funbuses.com. A dual air conditioned and heated bus that is guaranteed to bring the fun to you! The Fun Bus is a full sized school bus whose seats have been removed and walls and floor carpeted and padded. Fitness classes take place right on the bus and it never moves, we can park wherever; a driveway, a parking lot, school, or any safe spot on the street. Established: 2000 - Franchising Since: 2003 - No. of Units: Franchised: 5 - Franchise Fee: $25,000 - Royalty: 7% - Total Inv: $48,000-$71,000 - Financing: No.

FUN TIME LIVE, INC.
Fun Time Live
3820 Premier Ave., Memphis, TN, 38118. Contact: Fran. Dir. - Tel: (901) 368-3361, Fax: (901) 368-3724. Provide supervised recreation and entertainment for children ages 9-14. Training and support provided. Established: 1995 - No. of Units: Company Owned: 1 - Franchised: 16 - Franchise Fee: $11,000 - Royalty: 5%, adv. 3% - Total Inv: $47,450-$162,500 - Financing: No.

FUTUREKIDS®
1000 N Studebaker Rd #1, Long Beach, CA, 90815-4976. - Tel: (562) 296-1111 Fax: (562) 296-1110, E-Mail: kandrew@futurekids.com, Web Site: www.futurekids.com. One of the fastest growing franchise systems in the world, we specialize in technology education for children and adults, and technology training for teachers at both public and private schools. Established: 1983 - Franchising Since: 1989 - No. of Units: Franchised: 700+ - Franchise Fee: $35,000 - Royalty: 10% - Total Inv: $70,000-$100,000 (includes $35,000 franchise fee) - Financing: Third party.

GODDARD SCHOOL, THE
1016 9th Ave, Ste. 210, King Of Prussia, PA, 19406. - Tel: (800)272-4901, Fax: (610) 265-8867. High quality pre-school offering day-care hours. All teachers have 4 year degrees in early childhood or elementary education. Established: 1986 - Franchising Since: 1988 - No. of Units: Company Owned: 12 - Franchised: 98 - Franchise Fee: $50,000 - Royalty: 7% - Total Inv: $275,000 - Financing: Assistance available.

GYM DANDY FOR TOTS
1445 Pine Brook Ct., Yorktown Heights, NY, 10598-4938. Contact: Bob Arenholz, V.P. - Tel: (800) 831-6283-US only, (914) 381-6059. Parent-toddler play and party program. Established: 1983 - Franchising Since: 1990 - No. of Units: Company Owned: 1 - Franchised: 9 - Franchise Fee: $22,000 - Royalty: 6%, 2% adv. - Total Inv: $44,000.

GYM N' AROUND
Kelly's Gymnastics Inc.
715-A Seminole Dr., West Columbia, SC, 29169. Contact: Kelly Coyle, Pres. - Tel: (803) 892-6984, Fax: (803) 892-5631. Childrens entertainment mobile business caters to childrens gymnastics, fitness and partys. Established: 1987 - Franchising Since: 1994 - No. of Units: Company Owned: 3 - Franchised: 3 - Franchise Fee: $8,500-$10,000 - Royalty: 8% - Financing: None.

GYM ROMPERS
Gym Rompers Franchise, Inc.
1140 City Park Ave, New Orleans, LA, 70119 - Tel: (504) 482-5460. Children's music/movement/learning program. Established: 1984 - Franchising Since: 1993 - No. of Units: Company Owned: 2 - Franchised: 1 - Franchise Fee: $10,000 - Royalty: 5% gross - Total Inv: $13,000 equip. - Financing: None.

GYMBOREE PLAY & MUSIC
Gymboree Play Programs, Inc.
700 Airport Blvd., Ste. 200, Burlingame, CA, 94019. Contact: Franchise Development Department - Tel: (800) 520-PLAY, Fax: (650) 696-7452, E-Mail: play_franchise@gymboree.com, Web Site: www.gymboree.com. Our unique curriculum has created strong customer loyalty to our age appropriate programs offered in Play, Music and Art venues. Our brand image and full support in all avenues of operating the franchise offers a strong foundation for our franchisees to develop appropriate markets. Established: 1976 - Franchising Since 1976 - No. of Units: Company Owned: 9 - Franchised: 516 - Franchise Fee: $45,000 - Royalty: 6% - Total Inv: $141,000-$287,000 - Financing: No.

GYMNASTICS IN MOTION/KANGAROO KIDS, INC.
5728 Maplecrest Rd., Ft. Wayne, IN, 46815-3879. Contact: Mary McGaharan, Pres. - Tel: (219) 485-2524. Classes in gymnastics for kids (18 months and up) and adults, including bars, beams, vaulting, tumbling, mini and full sized trampolines. Established: 1981 - Franchising Since: 1983 - No. of Units: 2 - Franchise Fee: $2,000 - Royalty: 10% gross - Total Inv: $10,000 - Financing: No.

GYMSTERS®, INC.
6135 E. Danbury Rd, Scottsdale, AZ, 85254-6447. - Tel: (480) 315-0351, Fax: (480) 315-0311. The fitness program that comes to children at private schools, daycare centers, etc.; specialize in providing physical education instruction for children from two through twelve. Established: 1980 - Franchising Since: 1988 - No. of Units: Company Owned: 1 - Franchised: 7 - Franchise Fee: $12,000 - Royalty: 7%, 3% adv. - Total Inv: $19,000-$24,500 - Financing: No.

HEAD OVER HEELS
Head Over Heels Franchise System, Inc.
2106 Cahaba Rd., Birmingham, AL, 35223. Contact: Dir. of Fran. Sales - Tel: (205) 879-6305, (800) 850-3547, Fax: (205) 877-8372. Head Over Heels is a creative gymnastics program for children ages three and up. Head Over Heels works to develop strength, balance, flexibility and overall body coordination in each child. Established: 1990 - Franchising Since: 1993 - No. of Units: Company Owned: 2 - Franchised: 8 - Franchise Fee: $12,500 - Royalty: 8% gross revenues - Total Inv: $19,000-$30,000 - Financing: No.

HIGH TOUCH - HIGH TECH
High Touch Investment Corp.
12352 Wiles Rd, Coral Springs, FL, 33076. Contact: Daniel Shaw, President - Tel: (954) 755-2900, (800) 444-4968, Fax: (954) 755-1242. Hands-on science experiences for children serving schools as an in-school field trip. Also science birthday parties for children. Established: 1990 - Franchising Since: 1994 - No. of Units: Company Owned: 2 - Franchised: 18 - Franchise Fee: $35,000 - Royalty: 7% - Total Inv: $50,000+$8,000-$10,000 in start-up costs - Financing: Yes.

HOOHOBBERS
Hoohobers Store Development, Ltd
2847 W. 47th Place, Chicago, IL, 60632. Contact: Robert Tischler, President - Tel: (773) 890-1466, (800) 533-1505, Fax: (773) 890-1467, Web Site: www.hoohobbers.com. A full, exclusive line of patented, award winning child portable furniture, soft goods and apparel for newborns to age 6. Established: 1981 - Franchising Since: 1998 - No. of Units: Company Owned: 2 - Franchised: 1 - Franchise Fee: $25,000 - Royalty: 5%, 3% advertising - Total Inv: $148,000-$250,000 includes - franchise fee, inventory, leasehold, capital, insurance, fixtures and furniture - Financing: No.

IDENT-A-KID PROGRAM
Ident-A-Kid Services of America, Inc
2810 Scherer Dr., Ste. 100, St. Petersburg, FL, 33716. - Tel: (727) 577-4646, (800) 890-1000, Fax: (727) 576-8258, E-Mail: orders@ident-a-kid.com, Web Site: www.ident-a-kid.com. Home-based business that provides child ID cards to parents through schools. Established: 1986 - Franchising Since: 1987 - No. of Units: Franchised: 200 - Franchise Fee: $29,500 - Royalty: None - Total Inv: $29,500 - Financing: None.

IMAGINE THAT!!!
P.O. Box 493, New Vernon, NJ, 07976. - Tel: (973) 267-2907, (800) 820-1145, Fax: (973) 455-1917. A hands on children's museum with over 50 area of exhibits. 7 different avenues of producing revenue, field trips, general admission, birthday parties, cafe, retail gift shops, drop off service and advertising programs. Established: 1993 - Franchising Since: 1995 - No. of Units: Company Owned: 1 - Franchised: 2 - Franchise Fee: $25,000 - Royalty: 6% of gross receipts - Total Inv: $485,000-$550,000 - Financing: None.

J.W. TUMBLES®, A CHILDREN'S GYM
J.W. Tumbles Licensing Corp.
12750 Carmel Country Rd., #102, San Diego, CA, 92130. Contact: Jeffrey Woods, President - Tel: (858) 481-5576, Web Site: www.jwtumbles.com. Children's Gym, instructional facility for children 4 months - 9 years. Mobile programs, birthday parties, kids night out, camp programs, instruction in basic gymnastics, tumbling and sports preparation skills. Established: 1985 - Franchising Since: 1993 - No. of Units: Company Owned: 1- Franchised: 7 - Franchise Fee: $30,000 - Royalty: None license fee $3600-$500 monthly - Total Inv: $98,500-$140,000 includes franchise fee and equipment - Financing: No.

JACADI
Jacfran Corp.
70 West Red Oak Lane, White Plains, NY, 10604. Contact: Peggy Waldo - Tel: (914) 697-7684, Fax: (914) 697-7679, E-Mail: jacadi@juno.com, Web Site: www.jacadiusa.com. An upscale children's wear retail company whose collections include clothing, shoes, accessories, furniture and nursery items in newborn through size 12 for boys and girls. Established: 1978 (USA) - Franchising Since: 1992 (USA) - No. of Units: Company Owned: 6 - Franchised: 25 - Franchise Fee: $20,000 - Royalty: 4% plus 1% nat. adv. - Total Inv: $183,000-$313,000 - Financing: No.

JUMPBUNCH
302 Annapolis St, Annapolis, MD, 21401. Contact: Franchise Department - Tel: (866) 826-5645, Web Site: www.jumpbunch.com. Sports & fitness for young children. Established: 1997 - Franchising Since: 2002 - No. of Units: Company Owned: 1 - Franchise Fee: $5,000-$15,000 - Total Inv: $10,000-$38,000 - Financing: No.

KANGAKAB INC.
8501 Maple Ave, Pennsauken, NJ, 08109-3337. Contact: Tracey Wilson, President - Tel: (609) 424-5437. Transportation service for kids. Established: 1992 - Franchising Since: 1993 - No. of Units: Company Owned: 1 - Franchised: 7 - Franchise Fee: $18,500 - Royalty: 5% after 6 months - Total Inv: $34,000 - Financing: No.

KID KINGDOM
15965 Jeanette St., Southfield, MI, 48075. - Tel: (248) 557-2784, Fax: (248) 557-7931. Family physical fitness and fun indoor play park in a safe, clean, climate-controlled supervised environment that stimulates children's imagination and challenges them physically. Kid Kingdom is a place where parents and their children can have hours of fun together. Safe and imaginative play is a concept that will never grow old. Established: 1993 - Franchising Since: 1994 - No. of Units: Company Owned: 1 - Franchise Fee: $30,000 - Royalty: 5% - Total Inv: $400,000-$650,000 - Financing: Yes.

KID TO KID
Kid to Kid Franchise System, Inc.
452 E. 500 S., Salt Lake City, UT, 84111. Contact: Scott Sloan - Tel: (888) 543-2543, (801) 359-0071, Fax: (801) 359-3207, E-Mail: scott@kidtokid.com, Web Site: www.kidtokid.com. Kid to Kid is an upscale children's resale store based on the premise that "kids grow faster than paychecks". Parents buy and sell better quality used children's clothing, toys, equipment, and accessories. Established: 1992 - Franchising Since: 1994 - No. of Units: Company Owned: 5 - Franchised: 40 - Franchise Fee: $25,000 - Royalty: 5% - Total Inv: $99,149-$142,849 - Financing: Third Party.

KIDDIE ACADEMY CHILD CARE LEARNING CENTERS
Kiddie Academy International, Inc.
108 Wheel Rd., Ste. 200, Bel Air, MD, 21015. Contact: Director of Franchise Admissions - Tel: (410) 515-0788, (800) 554-3343, Fax: (410) 569-2729, Web Site: www.kiddieacademy.com. Kiddie Academy is actively seeking franchise partners who will share in their focus on quality, excellence and service. Partnering with quality franchise owners is central to their branding and expansion plans. Once identified, franchise partners receive comprehensive training and expert on-going support. The franchise program is well organized with hands-on assistance for site-selection, construction management, staff recruitment and trainign, marketing and curriculum. A true turnkey opportunity, allowing you to focus on running a successful business. Established: 1981 - Franchising Since: 1992 - No. of Units: Company Owned: 12 - Franchised: 85 - Franchise Fee: $50,000 - Royalty: 7.5% - Total Inv: $194,800-$492,000 - Financing: Yes.

KIDS KARS *
Kids Kars Franchising LLC
800 N. Rainbow Blvd, Suite 208, Las Vegas, NV, 89107. - Tel: (702) 948-7605, Fax: (310) 388-6029, Web Site: www.kidskars.com. Unique mini-car business. Mobile business can be set up any where there are kids. Customized trailer is transported where ever there is kids. Five little gasoline cars, inflatable air barrier, blower and signage. Established: 2002 - Franchising Since: 2004 - No. of Units: Company Owned: 1 - Franchise Fee: $1,500-$3,000 - Financing: Third party.

KIDSTAGE
P.O. Box 1072, Appleton, WI, 54912. - Tel: (877) 415-5115, Fax: (920) 993-1193, E-Mail: kidstage@yahoo.com, Web Site: www.kidstage franchise.com. KidStage is an after school drama program which involves acting classes, theatre activities and performance opportunities for kids of all ages. Established: 1997 - Franchising Since: 2003 - No. of Units: Company Owned: 2 - Franchise Fee: $8,500 - Royalty: 6% - Total Inv: $8,500-$18,500 - Financing: No.

KIDZART®
1327 Dime Box Circle, New Braunfels, TX, 78130. Contact: Shell Herman, CEO/Director - Tel: (830) 626-1959, (800) 379-8302, Fax: (830) 626-1959, E-Mail: info@kidzart.com, Web Site: www.kidzart.com. KidzArt® is an awesome and unique drawing-based art education program for students of all ages from preschool to senior citizens. Based on fifteen years of experience and development of our programs, KidzArt is offering it's educational classes in public, private and charter schools, preschools, parks and recreation centers, YMCA's, assisted living centers (SeniorzArt), as well as in many other venues. KidzArt is meeting the demand for high quality drawing/art programs. We are seeking high energy creative individuals with great communication, business, and marketing/sales and management skills who have a passion for enriching the lives of others through art, while making a difference in their communities. Established: 1997 - Franchising Since: 2002 - No. of Units: Franchised: 40 - Franchise Fee: $28,500 - Royalty: 7% monthly, 2% advertising fund- Financing: Third party.

KINDERDANCE®
Kinderdance International, Inc.
268 North Babcock St., Melbourne, FL, 32935. Contact: Jerry Perch - Tel: (321) 242-0590, (800) 554-2334, Fax: (321) 254-3388, E-Mail: leads@kinderdance.com, Web Site: www.kinderdance.com. Kinderdance® franchisees teach developmental dance and gymnastics programs in childcare facilities to children 2 to 8 years old. Franchisees work out of their homes, a true low investment, low overhead business opportunity. Established: 1979 - Franchising Since: 1985 - No. of Units: Company Owned: 1 - Franchised: 80 - Franchise Fee: $10,000-$21,000 - Royalty: 6%-15% - Total Inv: $9,350-$25,600 - Financing: Yes.

KUMON MATH & READING CENTERS
Kumon North America, Inc.
300 Frank W Burr Blvd. 5th Floor, Teaneck, NJ, 07666. Contact: Mark Mele - V.P. Franchising - Tel: (201) 928-0444, (866) 633-0740, Fax: (201) 928-0044, E-Mail: Franchise@kumon.com, Web Site: www.kumon.com. Kumon is the world's largest provider of supplemental math and reading programs. Our neighborhood learning centers serve children of all ages and abilities, from pre-school through high school. The Kumon after-school programs help children achieve better math and reading skills, stronger concentration, and improve improve self-confidence. Kumon has a national training facility located in Chicago, IL, and company offices worldwide to provide training, support and on-site consultation to franchisees. Established: 1958 - Franchising Since: 1980 - No. of Units: Company Owned: 22 - Franchised: 1389 - Franchise Fee: $1000. - Royalty: $30-$33.75 - Total Inv: $9,250-$29,265 - Financing: No.

LEARNING EXPERIENCE, THE *
10 Sylvan Wy., #110, Parsippany, NJ, 07054. - Tel: (888) 865-7775, Web Site: www.thelearningexperience.net. Child care services. Established: 1979 - Franchising Since: 2003 - No. of Units: Company Owned: 5 - Franchise Fee: $50,000 - Royalty: 3-6% - Total Inv: $275,000.

LEGACY ACADEMY

4536 Nelson Brogdon Blvd #A, Buford, GA, 30518. Contact: Frank Turner - Tel: (800) 298-4046. Educational services for children. Established: 1997 - Franchising Since: 2001 - No. of Units: Company Owned: 1 - Franchised: 10 - Franchise Fee: $30,000 - Total Inv: Capital requirments; $125,000 min - Financing: Yes.

LICENSED KIDS CAN SEW INSTRUCTIONS
Kids Can Sew

10300 W. Charleston Blvd, #130144, Las Vegas, NV, 89135. Contact: Carolyn Curtis, Director of Sales - Tel: (435) 634-6237, (800) 543-7739, Fax: (866) 242-5091, E-Mail: sales@kidscansew.com, Web Site: www.kidscansew.com. Home or store based business teaching kids, teens and adults to sew. No prior sewing experience necessary. Training seminars, coaching, sewing machines and equipment available. Established: 1986 - No. of Units: Company Owned: 1 - Franchised: 200+ - Franchise Fee: Starting at $7,000 - Royalty: $250 per year - Total Inv: $7,000 - Financing: Yes.

LITTLE GYM, THE
Little Gym International, Inc., The

8970 East Raintree Drive #200, Scottsdale, AZ, 85260. Contact: Franchise Development Manager - Tel: (888) 228-2878, Fax: (480) 948-2765. The Little Gym fitness centers for children age 4 months to 12 years, offers a unique integrated approach to child development that not only teaches basic motor skills, gymnastics, sports skill development and karate, but also helps build positive self-esteem and a love for physical exercise. Established: 1976 - Franchising Since: 1992 - No. of Units: Company Owned: 5 - Franchised: 278 - Franchise Fee: $49,500 - Royalty: 8% - 1% mktg. fund - Total Inv: $105,000 min - $145,000, incl $20,000 equipment - Financing: No.

LITTLE PRINCESS TEA PARTIES
Little Princess Franchise Development Corp.

7249 Ridgedale Dr, Warrenton, VA, 20186 - Tel: (703) 724-0689, (800) 489-OTEA, Fax: (703) 754-1334. Children's birthday parties + more. Established: 1997 - Franchising Since: 1998 - No. of Units: Company Owned: 1 - Franchised: 1 - Franchise Fee: $7,500 - Total Inv: $18,500 - Financing: No.

LITTLE SCIENTISTS®
Little Scientists Franchise Corp.

14 Selden, Woodbridge, CT, 06525. - Tel: (800) FACT-FUN!, (203) 389-9801, Fax: (203) 397-2165. Hands-on science education products and services for young children ages 3 - 3rd grade. Established: 1995 - Franchising Since: 1996 - No. of Units: Company Owned: 1 - Franchised: 4 - Franchise Fee: $20,000 - Royalty: 6% gross, 1% advertising - Total Inv: $20,000.

MCGRUFF SAFE KIDS TOTAL IDENTIFICATION SYSTEMS *

15500 Wayzata Blvd #812, Wayzata, MN, 55391. Contact: Neil Arfmann - Tel: (952) 473-7322, (800) 228-3344, Fax: (952) 473-7123, E-Mail: info@mcgruff-safe-kids.com, Web Site: www.mcgruff-safe-kids.com. Computerized children's identification system. Established: 2001 - Franchising Since: 2002 - No. of Units: Franchised: 38 - Franchise Fee: $30,000 - Total Inv: $33,000-$37,000 - Financing: Yes.

MONDAY MORNING MOMS®
Monday Morning America, Inc.

276 White Oak Ridge Rd., Bridgewater, NJ, 08807. - Tel: (800) 335-4MOM, Fax: (908) 526-3156. Family day care management service, recruiting family day care providers into a privately managed network, comprehensively servicing the family day care providers, and marketing the network to parents and employers in need of quality child care. Established: 1981 - Franchising Since: 1991- No. of Units: Franchised: 7 - Franchise Fee: $9,000 - Royalty: 6% first 18 months, 5% 2nd 18 months, 4% thereafter - Total Inv: $14,000-$28,000 - Financing: No.

MUSIC EXPERIENCE, THE
PJM Associates

P.O. Box 3, Flourtown, PA, 19031. Contact: Peter Moses - Tel: (215) 233-5795, (800) 350-9504. Children's music and song program. Established: 1990 - No. of Units: Company Owned: 28 - Franchised: 30 - Total Inv: Cappital requirements; $500-$6,000 - Financing: No.

MY GYM CHILDREN'S FITNESS CENTER
My Gym Enterprises

15300 Ventura Blvd. #423, Sherman Oaks, CA, 91403. - Tel: (818) 907-6966, (800) 469-4967, Fax: (818) 907-0735, Web Site: www.my-gym.com. My Gym helps youngsters 3 months to 9 years develop physically, creatively & emotionally. Structured age appropriate weekly classes incorporate music, dance, relays, games, specials rides, gymnastics, sports and original activities. We provide wonderful birthday parties as well. Established: 1983 - Franchising Since: 1994 - No. of Units: Company Owned: 4 - Franchised: 92 - Franchise Fee: $39,000 - Royalty: 6% - Total Inv: $130,000-$170,000 - Financing: Assistance for qualified applicants.

ONCE UPON A CHILD®
Winmark Corporation

4200 Dahlberg Dr. Suite 100, Minneapolis, MN, 55422. Contact: Franchise Department - Tel: (763) 520-8490, (800) 453-7750, Fax: (763) 520-8501, Web Site: www.ouac.com. Once Upon A Child stores buy and sell quality used and new brand name children's apparel, toys, furniture, equipment and more. Established: 1984 - Franchising Since: 1993 - No. of Units: Company Owned: 1 - Franchised: 230 - Franchise Fee: $20,000 - Royalty: 5% of gross sales - Total Inv: $124,543-$194,389.

OTHER MOTHER

18425 N. Division Rd, Colbert, WA, 99005. Contact: Franchise Department - Tel: (403) 556-6563, Fax: (509) 467-5147, Web Site: www.othermothers.com. Top quality previously-owned and new children's and maternity clothes, baby furniture and toys. Established: 1979 - Franchising Since: 1995 - No. of Units: Company Owned: 6 - Franchised: 4 - Franchise Fee: $15,000 - Royalty: 3% - Total Inv: $55,000-$79,000.

PARTIES TO GO
F.L. Price & Associates

5128 Salinas Court, Holly Springs, NC, 27540. Contact: Frank Price - Tel: (919) 567-3873, Fax: (919) 567-3873. Mobile home parties and company picinics. Established: 1997 - No. of Units: Franchised: 3 - Franchise Fee: $20,000-$25,000 - Financing: Yes.

PEE WEE WORKOUT
Cardiac Carr Co.

34976 Aspenwood Ln., Willoughby, OH, 44094. - Tel & Fax: (440) 946-7888, Web Site: www.peeweeworkout.com. Aerobic fitness program for children. Established: 1986 - Franchising Since: 1987 - No. of Units: Company Owned: 1 - Franchised: 36 - Franchise Fee: $2,000 - Royalty: 10% - Total Inv: $2,000 - Financing: No.

PERSONALIZED CHILDREN'S BOOKS
Best Personalized Books, Inc.

4201 Airborn Drive, Addison, TX, 75248. Contact: New Accounts Department - Tel: (800) 275-7770, (972) 250-1000, Fax: (972) 930-1010, E-Mail: www.bestpersonalizedbooks.com. Personalized children's books at home or on location in just 3 minutes. Low start-up, no experience necessary. Distributors receive a license to produce this patented product. License includes software and technical and marketing support. Also customize invitations, name certificates, stationery, clocks, business cards and holiday letters. Established: 1991 - Franchising Since: 1991 - No. of Units: Franchised: 3,500 - Franchise Fee: $795 - Royalty: No - Total Inv: $795 - Financing: None.

PIGTAILS & CREWCUTS *

1100 Old Ellis Rd., #600, Roswell, GA, 30076. - Tel: (770) 752-6800, Fax: (770) 752-8880, Web Site: www.pigtailsandcrewcuts.com. Upscale children's hair boutique where both parents and children can feel comfortable and welcome. Established: 2002 - Franchising Since: 2004 - No. of Units: Franchised: 2 - Franchise Fee: $25,000 - Royalty: 5% - Total Inv: $76,800-$139,500 - Financing: Third party.

PITTERPATS

960 Primavera Lane, Nipomo, CA, 93444. - Tel: (805) 929-1303, Web Site: www.pitterpats.com. Children's hand and feet impressions in porcelain clay. Unlike the products that offer plaster of paris impressions, mail order, over baked or air dried; pitterpats is a forever memory! The

finished product is beautifully glazed in porcelain. Established: 1991 - Franchising Since: 1998 - No. of Units: Company Owned: 1 - Franchised: 7 - Franchise Fee: None - Total Inv: $200.-$2,000.

PLAYBERRY LLC *
9101 Monroe Rd, Suite 155, Charlotte, NC, 28270. - Tel: (704) 708-6020, Fax: (704) 708-6022, Web Site: www.playberryforkids.com. Indoor children's entertainment center. Established: 1999 - Franchising Since: 2002 - No. of Units: Company Owned: 1 - Franchise Fee: $30,000 - Royalty: 6% - Total Inv: $589,000.

PLAYTIME PIANO INSTRUCTION
Playtime Piano Corps, L.L.C.
P.O. Box 600, Randallstown, MD, 21117. Contact: Scott McGowan - Tel: (410) 654-9042, (877) 823-6664 code 6227, Fax: (410) 654-9042, E-Mail: playtimepiano@comcast.net, Web Site: www.playtime piano.com. Playtime Piano Instruction is a educational & financially sound in-home music lesson service being franchised in the U.S. We provide primarily piano/keyboard lessons (but may offer other instuments by request) for both children & adults. A music background is NOT required! Franchisees hire instructors, schedule lessons & bill customers. Established: 1997 - Franchising Since: 2002 - No. of Units: Company Owned: 1 - Franchised: 1 - Franchise Fee: $27,500-$35,000 - Royalty: 8% graduated - Total Inv: $30,000 - Financing: N/A.

PRE-FIT FRANCHISES
Pre-Fit, Inc.
10926 So. Western Ave., Chicago, IL, 60643. Contact: Fran. Dir. - Tel: (773) 233-7771, Fax: (773) 233-7121, Web Site: www.prefit.com. A mobile preschool fitness program of sports, exercise, and health. Franchisees are trained to market schools and conduct on-site physical education classes for children two through six years of age. Franchisees also receive uniforms and start-up equipment. Established: 1987 - Franchising Since: 1992 - No. of Units: Franchised: 52 - Franchise Fee: $8,500 = mobile fitness program - Royalty: 10% - 8%% adv. - Total Inv: $10,155-$11,250 including franchise fee.

PRECIOUS PLACES
Precious Places, Ltd.
8629 Cross Chase Crt., Fairfax Station, VA, 22039-3352. Contact: V.P. Mktg. & Fran. - Tel: (800) 937-6880, (703) 690-0854. Shop-at-home service for decorating children's rooms. Established: 1989 - Franchising Since: 1993 - No. of Units: Company Owned: 1 - Franchised: 3 - Franchise Fee: $9,000 - Royalty: 7% - Total Inv: $2,720-$8,800 + fran. fee - Financing: No.

PUMP IT UP
5820 Stoneridge Mall Rd, Ste. 300, Pleasanton, CA, 94508. Contact: Michael Martin - Tel: (925) 397-1300, (866) 325-9663, Fax: (925) 730-0175, E-Mail: mmartin@piuparty.com, Web Site: www.pumpitup party.com. Non-stop action has made interactive inflatables a high-grow industry, transforming a hot trend into a recreational staple for kids of all ages. Now, Pumpit Up, is taking the inflatable rental industry in an exciting new direction. We offer parents an indoor facility with interactive inflatables a private party experience/facility and everything to host a great celebration. We take care of the party! Established: 2000 - Franchising Since: 2001 - No. of Units: Company Owned: 1 - Franchised: 190 - Franchise Fee: $35,000 - Royalty: 6% - Total Inv: Call - Financing: No.

RAINBOW STATION
Prism, Inc
3307 Church Road, Ste. 205, Richmond, VA, 23233. Contact: Earl Johnson - Tel: (804) 747-5900, (888) 747-1552, Fax: (804) 747-8016, E-Mail: rej@rainbowstation.org, Web Site: www.rainbowstation.org. Preschool amd afterschool recreation programs, with mildly ill care, nationally accredites. Established: 1989 - Franchising Since: 1999 - No. of Units: Company Owned: 6 - Franchised: 4 - Franchise Fee: $30,000 - Royalty: 6% - Total Inv: $3,000,000+ - Financing: Third party.

RAINBOW YEARS PRESCHOOL CENTER
Rainbow Years Franchises & Consulting, LLC
106 Windeler Rd., P.O. Box 273, Howell, NJ, 07731. Contact: Bidget Voorand - Tel: (732) 740-7612, Fax: (732) 780-2298, E-Mail: franchiseinfo@rainbowyears.com, Web Site: www.rainbowyears.com. We provide quality childcare & preschool classes from infancy to

kindergarten as well as before and after school care for elementary children to age 12. Established: 1986 - Franchising Since: 2002 - No. of Units: Company Owned: 2 - Franchise Fee: $20,000-$25,000.

READING FRIENDS
5228 Pwershing, Fort Worth, TX, 76107. Contact: Nancy Spencer, CEO - Tel: (817) 738-6662, Fax: (817) 732-2079, E-Mail: nancyspencer@ readingfriends.org, Web Site: www.readingfriends.org. Preschool that provides an academically based, structured curriculum for children ages 2-5. Established: 1980 - Franchising Since: 2002 - No. of Units: Company Owned: 1 - Franchised: 1 - Franchise Fee: $35,000 - Total Inv: $120,000-$304,500.

SAFE KIDS CARD, INC.
17100 B-Bear Valley Rd #238, Victorville, CA, 92392. Contact: Joe Veeser, Sales Manager - Tel: (909) 496-9982, Fax: (760) 249-5751, E-Mail: joeveeser@safekidscard.com, Web Site: www.safekidscard.com. Most Advanced Child, Adult, & Pet CD ROM all digital Identification Card. We are a fast growing home-based business with unlimited potential. Established: 2002 - Franchising Since: 2003 - No. of Units: Franchised: 15 - Franchise Fee: $11,900 - Royalty: Flat $75 per month and supply orders - Total Inv: $18,900 - Financing: Assistance.

SAFE NOT SORRY
Proteam, Inc.
421 W. Union Ave, Bound Brook, NJ, 08805. Contact: John Granito, Dir. Fran. Sales - Tel: (888) 469-3900, (732) 469-7874, Web Site: www.safenotsorry.com. Home safety with emphasis on child proofing, senior well-being, home care and pet control. Technical and marketing training. Liability insurance, exclusive and protected territories. perfect for all ages, male and female. Established: 1988 - Franchising Since: 1997 - Franchised: 21 - Franchise Fee: $10,000-$20,000 - Royalty: 8% - Total Inv: $21,250-$49,000 - Financing: Yes.

SAFE & SOUND
530 S. Henderson Road., Suite D, King of Prussia, PA, 19406. Contact: Ron Sommers, Dir. of Franchise Dev. - Tel: (610) 265-5155, Fax: (610) 265-5149, E-Mail: rsommers@123safe.com, Web Site: www.123safe.com. America's leading child safety company providing parental education and safety solutions for homes and businesses. Established: 1993 - Fanchising Since: 1998 - No. of Units: Company Owned: 1 - Franchised: 9 - Franchise Fee: $19,500 - Royalty: 5%, 2% advertising fee - Total Inv: $30,700-$43,100 - Financing: Assistance with business plan, SBA, third party financing.

SAFE-CARD ID SERVICES
4801 E. Independence Blvd., Ste. 705, Charlotte, NC, 28212. Contact: Greg Stephens, President - Tel: (704) 535-5200, Fax: 704) 535-0703, Web Site: www.safecardid.com. Emotionally satisfying, financially rewarding home based business providing continuous security with patented products for today's child. Work at schools, day cares, and community events. Complete turn key operation. Established: 1989 - Franchising Since: 1996 - No. of Units: Company Owned: 1 - Franchise Fee: $16,500 - Royalty: $195.00 per month 1st year - Total Inv: $23,000-$16,500 franchise fee, $6,500 recommended for start up costs license fee, professional fees and misc.

SANDY DECK PARTIES
148 Veterans Drive, Northdale, NJ, 07647. Contact: William Winters - Tel: (201) 569-1350, E-Mail: williamjwinters@hotmail.com, Web Site: www.sandydeckparties.com. We create fun filled creative parties for children, we supply everything for a fun and exciting child's party from a Carnival theme, Plastercraft, Karaoke, Sand Art, Jewelry Beading, Tea Party, Hair, Nails & Makeup, Cheerleading & Stuff-A-Pet. We also supply the invitations, food, party favors, supplies, and even the clean up. All the client has to do or supply is a camera. Established: 1985 - Franchising Since: 2003 - No. of Units: Company Owned: 3 - Franchise Fee: $20,000 - Total Inv: $65,000-$87,700.

SENTRYKIDS
Sentry Technology Inc
P.O. Box 1022, Bensalem, PA, 19020. Contact: Chris Brown - Tel: (888) 926-KIDS, Fax: (610) 380-1125. Portable fingerprint scanning system. Established: 1995 - No. of Units: Franchised: 37 - Financing: Yes.

SNIP-ITS *

1085 Worchester Rd, Natick, MA, 01760. - Tel: (877) SNIP-ITS, Fax: (508) 651-7052, Web Site: www.snipits.com. From start to finish, and beyond, a haircut at Snip-its is truly an adventure. The most amazing place for a kid to get a haircut! Established: 1995 - Franchising Since: 2003 - No. of Units: Company Owned: 5 - Franchised: 1 - Franchise Fee: $20,000 - Total Inv: $120,000-$220,000.

STRETCH-N-GROW

Stretch-N-Grow International Inc.

3501 Seltzer Dr., Plano, TX, 75023. - Tel: (972) 519-1635, (800) 348-0166, Fax: (972) 612-5819, E-Mail: sngintl@usa.net, Web Site: stretch-n-grow.com. A fun fitness program for pre-schooler's marketed to childcare centers. Home based, all classes done on premises of pre-schools, day care etc. Established: 1992 - Franchising Since: 1992 - No. of Units: Franchised: 85 - Franchise Fee: $7,600-$12,600 - Royalty: $100 per month flat - Total Inv: An additional $200-$400 - Financing: No.

TENNISKIDS

1894 Summercloud Drive, Thousand Oaks, CA, 91362. - Web Site: www.tenniskids.net. You: are athletic, want to set your own hours and positively impact the lives of kids. We: are a former world ranked tennis professional and proven marketing specialist who will train you and provide continual on-going support as you gain success running your own fun business from your home. Established: 1991 - Franchising Since: 1994 - No. of Units: Company Owned: 11 - Franchised: 13 - Franchise Fee: $10,000 - Royalty: 6%, 2% marketing fund - Total Inv: $10,000 - Financing: No.

THE WHOLE CHILD LEARNING CO.

921 Belvin St, San Marcos, TX, 78666. - Tel: (512) 396-2740, Fax: (512) 392-7820, Web Site: www.wholechild.com. Children's enrichment programs. Established: 1996 - Franchising Since: 2000 - No. of Units: Company Owned: 5 - Franchised: 5 - Franchise Fee: $15,000 - Royalty: 5% - Total Inv: $15,000-$16,500.

THE YELLOW BALLOON

12130 Ventura Blvd, Studio City, CA, 91604. - Tel: (514) 486-4149, Fax: (514) 486-0887, Web Site: www.theyellowballoon.com. The Yellow Balloon caters to kids, featuring mini-cares and toy boxes, and offering young customers balloons, cookies and popcorn, To commemorate a baby's first haircut, parents are given a framed photo, certificate and a lock of hair. Also serving adults. Established: 1983 - Franchising Since: 2000 - No. of Units: Company Owned: 1 - Franchised: 1 - Franchise Fee: $25,000 - Royalty: 4% - Total Inv: $55,000-$103,500.

TUTOR TIME CHILD CARE LEARNING CENTERS

Tutor Time Franchise Learning Centers, Inc

621 N.W. 53rd St, Suite 115, Boca Raton, FL, 33487. Contact: Dennis G. Fuller, Sr. V.P/Franchise Development - Tel: (800) 275-1235 ext 203, Fax: (561) 237-3403, E-Mail: dfuller@tutortime.com, Web Site: www.tutortime.com. Child care franchise. Tutor Time's beautiful state of the art facilities offer a tremendous curriculum developed for the appropriate ages of our children along with providing a safe and secure enviroment. Tutor Time is where children learn to feel good about themselves. Established: 1979 - Franchising Since: 1990 - No. of Units: Company Owned: 68 - Franchised: 170 - Franchise Fee: $50,000 - Royalty: 6% plus 1.25% national adv. - Total Inv: $190,000-$250,000 (leased site) - Financing: Available through third party sources.

UPPY, INC

Uppy Franchising Intl, L.L.C.

601 W. Golf Rd., Ste 108, Mt. Prospect, IL, 60056. Contact: Neal Katz - Tel: (847) 981-8779, (800) 958-8779. Playground safety surface material, training and support provided. Established: 1995 - Franchising Since: 1996 - Franchise Fee: Varies - Total Inv: Varies.

USA BABY

Baby's Room USA, Inc

857 N. Larch Ave, Elmhurst, IL, 60126. Contact: James Courtney, Sr.Mngr. Fran. Dev. - Tel: (630) 832-9880, (800) 323-4108, Fax: (630) 832-0139, Web Site: www.usababy.com. USA Baby is America's leading specialty retailer of infant and juvenile furniture and accessories. Franchisees receive market evaluation, site selection, store design, financing, opening, advertising, merchandising and on-going operational support. Established: 1975 - Franchising Since: 1986 - No. of Units: Franchised: 62 - Franchise Fee: $42,500 - Royalty: 3% - Total Inv: $450,000-$650,000 - Financing: Third party.

VICTORIAN WINDOW INC, THE

12510 Summit Street, Kansasw City, MO, 64145. Contact: Patty Cambiano - Tel: (816) 943-1046. Children's victorian dress-up parties. Established: 1991 - No. of Units: Franchised: 3 - Franchise Fee: $750 - Financing: No.

WEBBY DANCE COMPANY

7275C Dixie Hwy, Fairfield, OH, 45069. Contact: Helen Marshall - Tel: (513) 942-0100, (888) 243-2623, Fax: (513) 942-0707, Web Site: www.webbydancecompany.com. Webby Dance Company is a turn-key operation providing you with training and support. Our creative dance program is offered on-site at daycare centers and private schools. Established: 1995 - Franchising Since: 1999 - No. of Units: Company Owned: 2 - Franchised: 2 - Franchise Fee: $15,000 - Total Inv: $33,900-$53,900 - Financing: No.

WONDERS OF WISDOM CHILDREN'S CENTERS

WOW Development Corp.

3114 Golansky Blvd., Ste. 201, Prince William, VA, 22192-4200. Contact: Domini Anderson, Dir. of Fran. Sales - Tel: (703) 670-9344, (800) 424-0550, Fax: (703) 670-2851. Early learning centers featuring the SMILE Plus multiple intelligences curriculum and in-house training for staff resulting in a national credential in early childhood. Established:1989 - Franchising Since:1989 - No. of Units: Company Owned: 2 - Franchised: 4 - Franchise Fee: $25,000 - Royalty: 6% - Total Inv: $112,925-$215,300 incl. fran. fee and leased facility - Financing: No.

WOODPLAY

Family Industries

2101 Harrod St, Raleigh, NC, 27604. Contact: Neal DePersia, Franchise Department - Tel: (919) 875-4499, (800) 966-3752, Fax: (919) 875-4256, Web Site: www.woodplay.com. Woodplay is a lucrative, personally fulfilling, + family oriented career focussed on the sale of quality redwood residential playground equipment and other children's play products. Established: 1975 - Franchising Since:1999 - No. of Units: Company Owned: 1 - Franchised: 3 - Franchise Fee: $25,000 - Total Inv: $150,000 (including fran. fee) - Financing: No.

YELLO DYNO CHILD PROTECTION PROGRAMS SAFE-T-CHILD, INC.

203 Barsana Avenue, Austin, TX, 78737. Contact: Dennis Wagner, V.P. - Tel: (512) 288-2882, Ext. 201, Fax: (512) 288-2898, E-Mail: dennis@yellodyno.com, Web Site: www.yellodyno.com. Entertainment driven child protection educational programs. Established: 1986 - Franchising Since: 1992 - No. of Units: Company Owned: 1 - Franchised: 47 - Franchise Fee: $20.000 - Royalty: 6% - Total Inv: $30.000 - Financing: No.

YOUNG REMBRANDTS FRANCHISE INC.

Young Rembrandts, Inc.

23 N. Union Street, Elgin, IL, 60123. Contact: Kim Swanson, Director of Franchise Operations - Tel: (847) 742-6966, (866) 300-6010, Fax: (847) 742-7197, E-Mail: yr@youngrembrandts.com, Web Site: www.youngrembrandts.com. Young Rembrandts is a franchise offering a well organized, high quality program that teaches a valuable drawing curriculum to children. This Elgin, Illinois based company began in 1988 and over the next 13 years, Bette Fetter, the founder, fine tuned the Young Rembrandts teaching methods, techniques and subject matter for children. Established: 1988 - Franchising Since: 2000 - No. of Units: Company Owned: 1 - Franchised: 39 - Franchise Fee: $31,500 - Royalty: 10% on 1st $75,000 gross revenues, 8% on gross revenues in excess of $75,000 per year, minimum $250 per month - Total Inv: $39,500-$48,800 - Financing: No.

CLEANING PRODUCTS AND SERVICES

A-ALL-PRO ULTRASONIC BLIND CLEANING
Hessonic Ultrasonic Co.
30682 Cinnamon Teal, Canyon Lake, CA, 92587. Contact: James R. Hesson - Tel: (909) 244-0372, (800) 552-0372, Fax: (909) 244-9454, E-Mail: hessonic@aol.com, Web Site: www.hessonic.com. Ultrasonic Blind Cleaners, aqueous degreasers, fire restoration tanks, injection mold cleaning, golf club; special ultrasonic cleaning systems. Established: 1987 - No. of Units: Company Owned: 4 - Royalty: Up to 10%.

ACOUSTIC CLEAN INTERNATIONAL
Tangible research & Development Corp
2901 Wayzata Blvd., Minneapolis, MN, 55405. Contact: Gordon Hamilton, Pres. - Tel: (612) 374-1105, Fax: (612) 374-4840. One of the oldest, largest, and most reputable firms in the ceiling cleaning industry, giant mist, low pressure tank system with a 20 year unmatched history of perfection in cleaning all types of soiling on walls and ceilings. Low overhead, high margin of profit: Over 400 dealers worldwide have been trained. Established: 1978 - No. of Units: Company Owned: 1 - Franchised: Offering licenses in the U.S. - Total Inv: $5,900+, International from $9900 USD. - Financing: Available.

AEROWEST SERVICES, INC
West Sanitation Services, Inc.
3882 Del Amo Blvd, Torrence, CA, 90503. Contact: Den Elder, Manager, U.S. Operations, Sales & Service - Tel: (310) 793-4242, (888) 663-6726, Fax: (310) 793-4250, E-Mail: info@westsanitation.com, Web Site: www.westsanitation.com. Restroom deodorization service performed every 28 days. Established: 19884 - Franchising Since: 1982 - No. of Units: Company Owned: 3 - Franchised: 60 - Franchise Fee: $4,000 - Royalty: 35% (8% royalty, 4% adv., 23% administrative fee) - Total Inv: $4,000.

AIRE-MASTER
Aire-Master of America, Inc.
P.O. Box 2310/1821 N. Hwy CC, Nixa, MO, 65714. Contact: Jim Roudenis, Franchise Director - Tel: (417) 725-2691, (800) 525-0957, Fax: (417) 725-5737, E-Mail: fran1@airemaster.com, Web Site: www.airemaster.com. Unique system of odor control and restroom fixture cleaning. Unlike the majority of 'air-fresheners' on the market, Aire-Master deodorizers and deodorant products actually eliminate odors by oxidation. You don't need prior experience to qualify for an Aire-Master franchise. Established: 1958 - Franchising Since: 1976 - No. of Units: Company Owned: 5 - Franchised: 58 - Franchise Fee: $22,000 - Royalty: 5% - Total Inv: $30,000-$80,000 - Financing: Registered on SBA Franchise Registry.

AMERICA'S WASH-N-STOR
America's Family Business Franchise Company
201 Barton Springs Rd, Austin, TX, 78704. Contact: Franchise Department - Tel: (512) 457-1337, Fax: (512) 457-1335. Coin laundry, car wash and self storage. Established: 1985 - Franchising Since: 1998 - No. of Units: Company Owned: 2 - Franchised: 1 - Franchise Fee: $12,500 - Total Inv: $130,000.

AMERICAN AIR CARE, INC.
4751 Lydell Rd., Cheverly, MD, 20781. - Tel: (301) 772-2000, Fax: (301) 722-8446. Professional commercial and residential air duct cleaning. Established: 1961 - Franchising Since: 1990 - No. of Units: Company Owned: 1 - Franchised: 2 - Franchise Fee: $25,500 - Royalty: 7%-10% - Total Inv: $108,000-$180,000 - Financing: Third party financing to qualified individuals.

AMERICAN RESTORATION SERVICES
American Exterior Cleaning Corp.
2061 Monongahela Ave., Pittsburgh, PA, 15218. Contact: Russell K. Case, Pres. - Tel: (412) 466-8303. An international company specializing in exterior and interior cleaning systems. These systems, which use exclusive spray-on/rinse-off formulas, are clean, fast, and environmentally safe. Established: 1970 - Franchising Since: 1976 - No. of Units: Company Owned: 1 - Franchised: 255 in 26 states in 5 countries - Franchise Fee: $12,500 - Royalty: $1,500 renewal fee, $300 advertising fee - Total Inv: $22,500 (includes fran. fee) - Financing: Partial financing available through leasing company.

AMERICARE SANITATION & SUPPLY, INC.
225 W. Laura Dr., Addison, IL, 60101-5013. - Tel: (630) 458-1990, (800) 745-6191. Restroom sanitation, resale supplies for restrooms. Established: 1990 - Franchising Since: 1993 - No. of Units: Company Owned: 11 - Franchised: 4 - Franchise Fee: $9,500 - Royalty: 30% - Total Inv: $9,500-$23,500 - Financing: Possibly.

ANAGO CLEANING SYSTEMS
Anago Franchising
1515 University Dr., Ste. 203, Coral Springs, FL, 33071. - Tel: (954) 754-0193, (800) 213-5857, Fax: (954) 656-1014, Web Site: www.anago usa.com. Anago Cleaning Systems, Inc. is attaining incredible growth in our Master Franchise Program. Using a proven concept and applying innovative technology to our "Marketing and Support Programs". As a Master Franchise Owner, you will be building a network of sub-franchisees within a defined U.S. metropliten area. This unique and rare opportunity allows you to develop a Top-Notch Marketing organization supported by a talented team of cleaning industry veterans. Established: 1989 - Franchising Since: 1991 - No. of Units: Master Franchises: 18 Master - 400 Units - Franchise Fee: $50,000-$450,000 - Royalty: 5% - Total Inv: $150,000-$495,000 - Financing: Yes-long term.

AT YOUR SERVICE CLEANING
At Your Service Cleaning, Inc.
516 W. 8th Ave., Denver, CO, 80204. Contact: Cynthia McKay, President/Ceo - Tel: (720) 932-7373, (866) 9-AYS-INC, Fax: (303) 623-0559, Web Site: www.ayscleaning.com. Complete setup, training and referrals for residential and commercial cleaning service. Established: 1995 - Franchising Since: 1999 - No. of Units: Company Owned: 1 - Franchise Fee: $3,500 - Total Inv: $3,500 - Financing: Yes.

BEARCOM BUILDING SERVICES
BearCom Building Services, Inc.
7022 S. 400 West, Midvale, UT, 84047. Contact: Joseph Jenkins - Tel: (801) 569-9500, (866) GET-BEAR, Fax: (801) 569-8400, E-Mail: joseph@bearcomservices.com, Web Site: www.bearcomservices.com. Janitorial cleaning franchise using specialize system of cleaning and communication. Established: 1993 - Franchising Since: 1994 - No. of Units: Company Owned: 1 - Franchised: 61 - Franchise Fee: $9,995 + - Royalty: 8% - Total Inv: $12,787+ - Financing: Yes.

BONUS BUILDING CARE
4950 Keller Care Rd., Ste 190, Addison, TX, 75001-6205. Contact: Margaret Masterson, President - Tel: (972) 931-1100, (800) 931-1102, Fax: (972) 789-9399, E-Mail: bonusinc@aol.com, Web Site: www.bonusbuildingcare.com. World's best low investment opportunity in commercial cleaning, offering managed growth in a recession resistant business which is based on long term monthly contracts. You will receive a complete business package backed by veterans of the cleaning industry. You are offered customers, training, insurance, financing, clerical and procedural assistance as well as opportunities for expansion. Total investment which can be partially financed by Bonus is $7,335 to $10,559. Master franchises available. Established: 1997 - Franchising Since: 1997 - No. of Units: Company Owned: 4 - Franchised: 215 - Franchise Fee: $6,500 - Royalty: 10% -Total Inv: Approx. $10,000 - Financing: Guaranteed in-house.

BRITE SITE
4616 W. Fullerton, Chicago, IL, 60639-1816. Contact: Andreas Vassilos, Pres. - Tel: (773) 772-7300, Fax: (773) 772-7631. Providing cleaning services to retailers in defined territories. Established: 1971 - Franchising Since: 1992 - No. of Units: Company Owned: 2 - Franchised: 7 - Franchise Fee: $2,500-$25,000 - Royalty: 10% - Total Inv: $5,000-$25,000 - Financing: Yes.

BUCKETS & BOWS MAID SERVICE
Buckets & Bows Franchising Inc.
3700 Forums Dr., Ste. 111, Flower Mound, TX, 75028. Contact: Deborah Sardone, President - Tel: (972) 539-9270, (888) 258-5540. Residential and commercial maid service. Established: 1981 - Franchising Since: 1998 - No. of Units: Company Owned: 2 - Franchised: 2 - Franchise Fee: $12,500 - Royalty: 5% - Total Inv: $12,500 franchise fee plus $5,000-$20,000 start-up costs - Financing: None.

BUILDING SERVICES OF AMERICA INC
11900 W. 87th St. Ste.135, Lenexa, KS, 66215. - Tel: (913) 599-6200, Fax: (913) 599-4441. Selling of office cleaning franchises and providing on going support to such. Established: 1992 - Franchising: 1990 - No. of Units: Company Owned: 1 - Franchised: 33 - Franchise Fee: $7,495-$13,495 - Royalty: 8% - Total Inv: $7,495-$13,495 - Financing: Yes.

BUILDING STARS, INC
11489 Page Service Dr, St. Louis, MO, 63146. - Tel: (314) 991-3356, Fax: (314) 991-3198, Web Site: www.buildingstars.com. Commercial cleaning. Established: 1999 - Franchising Since: 2001 - No. of Units: Company Owned: Franchised: 115 - Franchise Fee: $995-$3,990 - Royalty: 10% - Total Inv: $1,900-$42,200 - Financing: No.

CEILING CLEAN
D.P.L. Enterprises, Inc.
3868 East Post Rd., Las Vegas, NV, 89120. Contact: Richard Papaleo, Pres. - Tel: (702) 454-5515, Fax: (702) 454-5225. Manufacture and distribute acoustic ceiling cleaning equipment and chemicals. Established: 1978 - Franchising Since: 1978 - No. of Units: Company Owned: 1 - Dealers: 305 - Total Inv: $12,500 - Financing: Yes.

CEILING DOCTOR
Ceiling Doctor Inc.
P.O Box 794007, Dallas, TX, 75379-4007. - Tel: (972) 250-3311. Specialty cleaning of commercial buildings. The role as the franchisee is that of a manager and a supervisor with employees doing the actual cleaning. Established: 1984 - Franchising Since: 1986 - No. of Units: Company Owned: 1 - Franchised: 150 - Franchise Fee: $12,500 - Royalty: 8% - Total Inv: $25,000 - Financing: No.

CEILTECH CEILING CLEANING
7411 East 6th Ave, Ste. 205, Scottsdale, AZ, 85251. - Tel: (480) 946-3527, Fax: (480) 946-2388. Manufacturer of acoustical ceiling and wall cleaning equipment featuring an exclusive nontoxic, nonflammable detergent based solution and complete marketing program. Established: 1986 - Licensing Since: 1987 - No. of Units: Company Owned: 1 - Licensed: 1,541 - Total Inv: $6,995-$8,995 - Financing: Leasing to qualified applicants, visa, amex, mc, discover.

CHEMSTATION
ChemStation International
3400 Encrete Lane, Dayton, OH, 45439. Contact: John D. Shofer, Dir. of Operations - Tel: (800) 554-8265, Fax: (937) 294-5360, E-Mail: customerservice@chemstation.com, Web Site: www.chemstation.com. ChemStation manufactures industrial cleaners at each franchise location. The chemicals are supplied to the customer in refillable containers. Established: 1980 - Franchising Since: 1981 - No. of Units: Company Owned: 6 - Franchised: 34 - Franchise Fee: $45,000 - Royalty: 4% gross sales - Total Inv: $600,000, $200,000 - hard costs, $400,000 working capital - Financing: Limited.

CLASSY MAIDS
Classy Maids USA, Inc.
P O Box 8552, Madison, WI, 53708. Contact: William Olday, Vice Pres. - Tel: (800) 445-5238, (608) 242-8943. Multi-service franchise. Low investment. Flat rate royalties. No advertising fees. Simple to learn and operate. Average customer spends $2,500/year. Cash business. Established: 1980 - Franchising Since: 1985 - No. of Units: Franchised: 6 - Franchise Fee: $5,900 + - Royalty: From $100/mo. - Total Inv: Less than $8,000 - Financing: Yes - Up to $3,000.

CLEAN & HAPPY WINDOWS
10019 Des Moines Memorial Dr, Seattle, WA, 98168. Contact: Franchise Department - Tel: (806) 762-7617, Fax: (206) 762-7637, Web Site: www.cleanhappy.com. Window cleaning, gutter cleaning, pressure washing system. No franchise fee for the first 10 people who sign up!

Established: 1990 - Franchising Since: 1999 - No. of Units: Company Owned: 1 - Franchise Fee: 0 - Royalty: 7% - Total Inv: $1,000-$3,000 - Financing: No.

CLEANING AUTHORITY, THE
6994 Columbia Gateway Drive, Columbia, MD, 21046. - Tel: (410) 740-1900, (800) 504-6221, Web Site: www.thecleaningauthority.com. Residential cleaning service. Established: 1978 - Franchising Since: 1996 - No. of Units: Company Owned: 1 - Franchised: 85 - Franchise Fee: $9,000-$16,800 - Royalty: 7-6-5% depending on gross revenue - Total Inv: $70,000-$80,000 - Financing: No.

CLEANING IDEAS INC.
Davis Franchise Group Inc.
1023 Morales Street, San Antonio, TX, 78207. Contact: President - Tel: (210) 227-9161, Fax: (210) 227-4949, Web Site: www.cleaning ideas.com. Janitorial supplies to homeowner and businesses. Established: 1972 - Franchising Since: 1986 - No. of Units: Franchised: 14 - Franchise Fee: $5,000 - Total Inv: Inventory $10,000, fixtures sign $5,000, misc. $5,000 - Financing: No.

CLEANING SUPPLIER
6544 South State St, Murray, UT, 84017. - Tel: (801) 270-8300, Fax: (801) 270-8500. Sell janitorial products and vacuums. Established: 1994 - No. of Units: Company Owned: 1 - Franchised: 1 - Franchise Fee: $25,000.

CLEANNET USA
9861 Broken Land Pkwy., Ste. 208, Columbia, MD, 21046. - Tel: (410) 720-6444, Fax: (410) 720-5307. Commercial office cleaning and other commercial facilities - full service. Established: 1987 - Franchising Since: 1988 - No. of Units: Franchised: 1834 - Franchise Fee: $2,950-$32,000 - Royalty: 3% - Total Inv: $3,500-$37,500 - Financing: Yes @ 9%.

CLEN TECH ACOUSTIC CLEAN
Tangible Research and Development Corp.
2901 Wayzata Blvd., Minneapolis, MN, 55405. Contact: Gordon Hamilton, President/Owner - Tel: (612) 374-5852, (800) 328-4650, Fax: (612) 374-4840, E-Mail: trda@usinternet.com. Atomized mist cleaning of acoustical ceilings, vinyl and stucco walls and ceilings using specialized equipment and propriotory cleaning solutions with advanced chemical technology. Established: 1977 - Franchising Since: 1985 - No. of Units: Company Owned: 1 - Franchise Fee: Included in start up costs - foreign countries only - Royalty: None - Total Inv: $9,900-$27,900 - Financing: None.

COTTAGECARE
CottageCare, Inc
6323 West 110th St., Overland Park, KS, 66211. Contact: M. Paul - Tel: (800) 718-8100, Fax: (913) 469-0822, E-Mail: mpaul@cottagecare.com, Web Site: www.cottagecare.com. House cleaning franchise. Established: 1988 - Franchising Since: 1989 - No. of Units: Company Owned: 2 - Franchised: 53 - Franchise Fee: $17,000 - Royalty: 5.5% - Total Inv: $69,500 - Financing: No.

COUSTIC-GLO INTERNATIONAL
CGI International Inc.
7111-7115 Ohms Lane, Minneapolis, MN, 55439. Contact: Scott Smith, Mktg. - Tel: (952) 835-1338, (800) 333-8523, Fax: (952) 835-1395, E-mail: info@cousticglo.com, Web Site: www.cousticglo.com. Ceiling and wall cleaning and restoration. Established: 1979 - Franchising Since: 1982 - No. of Units: Company Owned: 1 - Franchised: 100 - Franchise Fee: $12,000 - Royalty: 5% - Total Inv: Training & Services - Financing: Yes.

COVERALL CLEANING CONCEPTS
Coverall North America, Inc.
500 West Cypress Creek, Ste. 580, Ft. Lauderdale, FL, 33309. Contact: Jack Caughey - Tel: (954) 351-1110, (800) 537-3371, Fax: (954) 492-5044, E-Mail: info@coverall.com, Web Site: www.coverall.com. Coverall Cleaning Concepts is one of the nation's leading commercial cleaning franchise companies with more than 6,000 Franchise Owners servicing over 32,000 customers worldwide. Established: 1985 - Franchising Since: 1985 - No. of Units: Company Owned: 26 - Franchised: 4500 - Franchise Fee: $6,000-$32,200+ - Royalty: 5% monthly based on gross sales - Total Inv: $7,738-$76,190 - Financing: Options available.

CUSTOM MAID, INC.
Cam Systems Inc.
14500 W. 8 Mile Rd., Ste. 301, Oak Park, MI, 48237. Contact: Shenell C. Toliver, Off. Mgr. - Tel: (248) 967-4002, Fax: (248) 967-4038. Maid service for both domestic and commercial applications in the marketplace. A proven, time-tested system dedicated to the old fashioned tradition of quality maid service. An extensive training and support program with computerized or manual operations and management system. Established: 1982 - Franchising Since: 1987 - No. of Units: Company Owned: 1 - Franchised: 1 - Franchise Fee: $12,500 - Royalty: 8%, 1%-3% adv. - Total Inv: $28,000 - Financing: Limited.

DECKARE
Deckare Services, Inc
1501 Raff Rd. SW., Canton, OH, 44710. Contact: Joe McClellan, Vice President - Tel: (330) 478-3665, (800) 4-DECKARE, Fax: (330) 478-0311, E-Mail: Deckare1@aol.com, Web Site: www.deckare.com. Cleaning and protecting all natural exterior wood (decks, fences, docks, gazebos, houses), complete maintenance service, commercial and residential. Established: 1995 - Franchising Since: 1997 - No. of Units: Franchised: 37 - Franchise Fee: $14,500 - Royalty: 5% gross sales - Total Inv: $25,000, franchise fee and equipment - Financing: No.

DELTA JANITORIAL SYSTEMS, INC.
2701 West Airport Frwy., #118, Irving, TX, 75062. - Tel: (972) 256-6475, Fax: (972) 256-4194. Janitorial broker. Established: 1975 - Franchising Since: 1981 - No. of Units: Franchised: 120 - Franchise Fee: $3,000 - Royalty: 6% admin., 4% royalty - Total Inv: $3,000 fran., $4,000 contracts, $500 supplies - Financing: Yes.

DIAMOND HOME CLEANING SERVICES, INC.
4887 E. LaPalma Ave., Ste. 708, Anaheim, CA, 92807. Contact: Tom Devlin, President - Tel: (714) 701-9771, (800) 393-MAID (6243), Fax: (714) 693-8106, E-Mail: mtgi@maintenanceinc.com, Web Site: www.diamondhomecleaning.com. America's economy is booming...and so is the demand for home cleaning services. Diamond Home Cleaning is the only active maid service franchisor headquartered on the West Coast thereby enabling the company to more effectively support its franchise partners. Established: 1993 - Franchising Since: 1997 - No. of Units: Company Owned:7 - Franchised: 23 - Franchise Fee: $15,000 - Royalty: Sliding scale 4%, 4.5%, 5%, 6% - Total Inv: $29,000-$61,200 - Financing: No.

DRAIN TECH, INC.
540 Robeson St., Reading, PA, 19601. Contact: Eugene Tobolski, Pres. - Tel: (610) 372-8541. Plumbing contractor, sewer and drain cleaning, also general plumbing, repair and installation. Established: 1990 - Franchising Since: 1990 - No. of Units: Company Owned: 1 - Franchised: 2 - Franchise Fee: $15,000-$25,000 - Royalty: Varies 3%-6% depending on program chosen - Total Inv: $10,000-$25,000 - Financing: Yes.

DUCTBUSTERS
Buster Enterprises, Inc
29160 U.S. Hwy, 19N, Clearwater, FL, 33761-2400. Contact: Franchise Department - Tel: (727) 787-7087, (800) 786-3828, E-Mail: info@ductbusters.com, Web Site: www.ductbusters.com. Duct cleaning and HVAC system cleaning. Established: 1985 - Franchising Since: 1992 - No. of Units: Franchised: 22 - Franchise Fee: $7,500-$30,000 - Royalty: 5.5%-7%.

E.P.I.C. SYSTEMS™, INC.
EPIC Systems, Inc
402 E. Maryland St., Evansville, IN, 47711. Contact: Jeffrey Schaper John - Tel: (812) 428-7750, (800) 230-3742, Fax: (812) 428-4162, E-Mail: jrs@speedex.net. Unit franchises available and master franchises and territories also available. Established: 1994 - Franchising Since: 1994 - No. of Units: Franchised: 8 - Franchise Fee: $6,500 - Royalty: Varies between 10%-4% - Total Inv: $12,500 - Financing: Yes.

ENVIRONMENTAL BIOTECH, INC.
1701 Biotech Way, Sarasota, FL, 34243. Contact: Global Development Dept. - Tel: (941) 358-9112, (800) 314-6263, Fax: (941) 359-9744, E-Mail: info@environmentalbiotech.com, Web Site: www.environ mentalbiotech.com. EBI provides preventative drain line maintenance and odor management services to industrial and commercial clients, utilizing biologically based systems for waste eradication. We are drain and odor experts. Established: 1991 - Franchising Since: 1991 - No. of Units: Company Owned: 1 - Franchised: 63 - Franchise Fee: $35,000 - Royalty: 5% - Total Inv: $79,700-$91,600 - Financing: No.

FISH WINDOW CLEANING
Fish Window Cleaning Services, Inc.
200 Enchanted Pkwy, Manchester, MO, 63021. - Tel: (636) 530-7334, Fax: (636) 530-7856, Web Site: www.fishwindowcleaning.com. Ground work window cleaning for residential and commercial route work. Computerized routing and scheduling with proven account bidding process. Established: 1978 - Franchising Since: 1998 - No. of Units: Company Owned: 1 - Franchised: 60 - Franchise Fee: $19,500 - Royalty: 8% - Total Inv: $33,000-$84,000 - Financing: Yes, 50% of the franchise fee for 36 months.

FOR DESIGNERS, LLC
Nex Systems, Inc
235 Frank West Circle, Stockton, CA, 95206. Contact: Keith Bewley, President - Tel: (209) 982-0600, Fax: (209) 982-0624, E-Mail: info@nexsystems, Web Site: www.nexsystems.com. Dry organic, natural extraction carpet cleaning process. Our recently patented process eliminates wet carpets, traffic lanes, reoccurring spots, harsh chemicals. We train at your location and constant field support. Established: 1990 - Franchising Since: 1998 - No. of Units: Company Owned: 3 - Franchised: 4 - Franchise Fee: $18,950 - Royalty: 5% - Total Inv: 5 days training at your location, equipment, signage, 3 months chemical supply $20,000-$25,000 - Financing: No.

GROUT WIZARD
1056 El Captain Dr, Danville, CA, 94526. - Tel: (925) 866-5000, Fax: (925) 552-6358. Grout cleaning and restoration. Established: 1997 - Franchising Since: 2001 - No. of Units: Company Owned: 1 - Franchised: 10 - Franchise Fee: $12,500 - Royalty: Varies - Total Inv: $15,000-$24,000 - Financing: No.

HOME CLEANING CENTERS OF AMERICA
HOME CLEANING CENTERS OF AMERICA
10851 Mastin Blvd, Suite 130, Overland Park, KS, 66210. Contact: Mike Calhoon, Pres. - Tel: (913) 327-5227,(800) 767-1118, Fax: (913) 327-5272, E-Mail: mcalhoon@homecleaningcenters.com, Web Site: www.homecleaningcenters.com. Large franchise zones specializing in house, office, carpet & window cleaning! Established: 1984 - Franchising Since: 1984 - No. of Units: Franchised: 39 - Franchise Fee: $9,500 - Royalty: 3%-5% - Total Inv: $25,000-$30,000 - Financing: No.

HYDRO-CHEM SYSTEMS, INC. (EST. 1971)
5550 Clay Ave., S.W., Grand Rapids, MI, 49548. - Tel: (616) 531-6420, Fax: (616) 531-8692. Chemical sales and delivery as well as pressure washer sales and service. Specializing in truck fleet wash chemicals and equipment as well as industrial degreasers and floor cleaners. Also large selection of cleaning accessories, equipment accessories, and specialty cleaners. Comprehensive training at HCS and in franchise territory. Exclusive area or territory. Territories located in Michigan and Ohio. Franchise Fee: $20,000 - Royalty: 5% – Total Inv: $36,000-$79,000, depends on vehicle, equip., and tools already owned by franchisee - Financing: Negotiable.

ICLEAN

Iclean Corporate
2030 Main Street, Ste. 1300, Irvine, CA, 92614. Contact: Franchise Sales - Tel: (949) 260-4788, (877) 898-9500, Fax: (949) 260-4799, Web Site: www.iclean.com. Commercial/office cleaning. Established: 1996 - Franchising Since: 1996 - No. of Units: Franchised: 84 - Franchise Fee: $3,750+ - Royalty: 3% - Total Inv: $3,805+ - Financing: Franchise Fee, additional business.

JAN-PRO

Jan-Pro Cleaning Systems
383 Strand Industrial Dr, Little River, SC, 29566. Contact: Franchise Division - Tel: (843) 399-9895, (800) 668-1001, Fax: (843) 399-9890. A commercial cleaning franchise business. Established: 1991 - No. of Units: Franchised: 515 - Franchise Fee: $2,800 ($900 down, $1850 financed over 3 years) - Royalty: 8% - Total Inv: $2,800 and up - Financing: Varies over a 36 month period.

JANI-KING INTERNATIONAL, INC.

16885 Dallas Parkway, Addison, TX, 75001. Contact: Jerry L. Crawford, President Jani-King International - Tel: (972) 991-0900, (800) JANIKING, Fax: (972) 239-7706, E-Mail: info@janiking, Web Site: www.janiking.com. World's largest commercial cleaning franchisor with more than 30 years of experience. Federally registered trademark #139797. Most programs include a specified amount of initial business, depending on the area and plan purchased. Professional training and continuous support while franchisees provide commercial cleaning services on a long-term contract basis. The program has proven itself many times over and produces 100's of successful business people every year. Established: 1969 - Franchising Since: 1974 - No. of Units: Company Owned: 32 - Franchised: 9,000+ - Franchise Fee: $5,500-$15,750 and up - Royalty: 10% on gross unit franchise - Total Inv: $8,200-$33,550 and up - Financing: No. Master and associate franchises are also available.

JANTIZE

Jantize America Inc.
15449 Middlebelt, Livonia, MI, 48154. Contact: Jerry Grabowski, Franchisor - Tel: (734) 421-4733, (800) 968-9182, Fax: (734) 421-4936, E-Mail: franchise@jantize.com, Web Site: www.jantize.com. Commercial office cleaning business. Master franchises available. Established: 1986 - Franchising Since: 1986 - No. of Units: Company Owned: 2 - Franchised: 24 - Franchise Fee: $3,500-$8,500 - Royalty: 6-9% royalty - Total Inv: $9,800-$16,800 - Financing: Yes.

KIWI CARPET CLEANING

Tiki Inc.
3230 Commander, Carrolton, TX, 75006. - Tel: (972) 818-6984. No Mom & Pop operation. Residential carpet and upholstery cleaning with 30 employees. Absentee ownership possible. Established: 1989 - Franchising Since: 1994 - No. of Units: Company Owned: 1 - Franchised: 8 - Franchise Fee: $25,000 - Royalty: 5% - Financing: Yes.

MAGNA-DRY USA LLC

P.O. Box 440848, Aurdra, CO, 80044-0848. Contact: Johnny M. Wilson, President - Tel: (303) 338-0848, (800) 275-9000, Fax: (303) 338-0803, E-Mail: magnadry@aol.com, Web Site: www.stain busters.com. Enviromentally safe cleaning of commercial and residential carpets, drapes, fibers and leather within drying time of less than thirty minutes. Established: 1987 - Franchising Since: 1997 - No. of Units: Franchised: 4 - Franchise Fee: $25.000 - Royalty: 10% - Total Inv: $56,000 - Financing: Yes.

MAID BRIGADE SERVICES

Maid Brigade Systems , Inc.
4 Concourse Parkway, Ste. 200, Atlanta, GA, 30328. Contact: Dir Fran. Recruitment - Tel: (770) 551-9630, (800) 722-6243, Fax: (770) 391-9092, Web Site: www.maidbrigade.com. Maid Brigade personalizes homecleaning services. Our three new large major and regional market franchises offer the best value. We provide unparalleled support, business development and the latest technology. Established: 1979 - Franchising Since: 1980 - No. of Units: Company Owned: 5 - Franchised: 255 - Franchise Fee: From $18,500 - Royalty: 3%-7% - Total Inv: From $45,000 - Financing: Yes.

MAID SERVICES OF AMERICA

475 E. Main St., Ste. 151, Cartersville, GA, 30121. Contact: Tammy Spivey - Tel: (770) 387-2455, (800) 289-8642, Fax: (770) 382-0501, E-Mail: maidmoney@aol.com, Web Site: www.maidservices ofamerica.com. You can't push the broom and the business at the same time. We are not showing you how to clean homes. We are teaching you how to operate a business in a industry that has demostrated continious growth since 1980. Low overhead, high profits, and no territorial restrictions. Established: 1977 - Franchising Since: 1981 - No. of Units: Company Owned: 1 - Franchised: 229 - Franchise Fee: $4,495 - Royalty: 0 - Total Inv: $4,495 - Financing: 50% down / 0% interest.

MAID TO PERFECTION

1101 Opal Ct., 2nd Fl, Hagerstown, MD, 21093. Contact: Todd Cearfoss, Franchise Sales Director - Tel: (301) 790-7900, (800) 648-6243, Fax: (301) 790-3949, E-Mail: maidsvc@aol.com, Web Site: www.maidto perfectioncorp.com. Maid to Perfection provides customized cleaning designed for today's sophisticated customer, making service easy to sell. A residential and commercial business. Proven record of offering choices and diversification to franchisees, which leads to higher profits. Established: 1980 - Franchising Since: 1990 - No. of Units: Company Owned: 1 - Franchised: 243 - Franchise Fee: $9,995 - Royalty: 7% - Total Inv: $36,278-$43,573 - Financing: Yes - Entire investment if qualified, and all expansion territories.

MAIDPRO

180 Canal Street, Boston, MA, 02114. Contact: Chuck Lynch, Franchise Coordinator - Tel: (617) 742-8787, (888) MaidPro, Fax: (617) 720-0700, E-Mail: info@maidpro.com, Web Site: www.maidpro.com. Professional residential cleaning service. Established: 1991 - Franchising Since: 1997 - No. of Units: Company Owned: 1 - Franchised: 24 - Franchise Fee: $7,900 - Royalty: 3%-6% - Total Inv: $25,300-$46,600 - Financing: Third party.

MAIDS ETC *

4907 Hollenden Drive, Suite 208, Raleigh, NC, 27616. Contact: LaVerne Artis - Tel: (919) 834-8215, (866) 578-6243, Fax: (919) 834-7630, E-Mail: franchise@maidsetc.com, Web Site: www.maidsetc.com. It's time to clean up with Maids Etc. and create your own future in the residential and commercial cleaning industries, which are experiencing explosive growth. We are the "Full Service People" offering full-service residential and commercial Bulls's-Eye Cleaning Systems. Established: 1995 - Franchising Since: 2003 - No. of Units: Company Owned: 1 - Franchised: 4 - Franchise Fee: $9,995 - Royalty: 5-7% - Total Inv: $36,000-$56,000 - Financing: Yes.

MAIDS, THE

Maids International, The
4820 Dodge St., Omaha, NE, 68132. Contact: Mike Fagen, E.V.P. Sales - Tel: (402) 558-5555, (800) 843-6243, Fax: (402) 558-4112, Web Site: www.maids.com. Residential cleaning service. Established: 1979 - Franchising Since: 1980 - No. of Units: Company Owned: 53 - Franchised: 403 - Franchise Fee: $17,500-$61,000 - Royalty: 3.3%-7%, adv. 1% - Total Inv: $56,300-$89,700, $163,800-$255,100 - Financing: Yes.

MAIDS TO ORDER® "THE PERSONAL TOUCH PEOPLE®"

Maids to Order International Inc
919 East Cherry Street, Suite B, Canal Fullon, OH, 44614. Contact: Todd Petty, Franchise Sales Manager - Tel: (330) 854-3576, (800) 701-maid, Fax: (330) 854-9382, E-Mail: maidsorder@aol.com, Web Site: www.maidstoorder.com. We offer a unique, turn key franchise opportunity in the fastest growing inustry in the US. We send one maid, the same maid each and every time we clean a customer's home or office. We give our franchisees the largest territories in franchising, by entire county, not by zip codes. Established: 1988 - Franchising Since: 1992 - No. of Units: Franchised: 53 - Franchise Fee: $12,000 and up depending upon population - Royalty: 3% first year, 5% thereafter - Total Inv: $30,000-$55,000 - Financing: Up to 50% of franchise fee.

MAINTAIN CLEANING SYSTEMS
Maintain Systems, Inc.
P.O Box 867, Milford, OH, 45150-0867. Contact: Fran. Dir. - Tel: (513) 576-6622. Commercial cleaning services with ongoing support. Established: 1993 - Franchising Since: 1993 - No. of Units: Franchised: 32 - Franchise Fee: $7,000 - Royalty: 5% - Total Inv: $7,500 - Financing: Yes.

MARBLE RENEWAL
SVI Inc. DBA Marble Renewal
6807 W. 12th Street, Little Rock, AR, 72204. Contact; Gary Perritt, CEO/Founder - Tel: (501) 663-2080, (800) 664-7866, Web Site: www.marblerenewal.com. Marble, granite and other natural stone and restoration and maintenance. Exclusive chemicals and processes. International network of trained professionals. Established: 1988 - Franchising Since: 1988 - No. of Units: Franchised: 24 - Franchise Fee: $17,500-$50,000 - Royalty: 5%-8% of gross revenues - Total Inv: $50,000-$250,000. NOT FRANCHISING AT THIS TIME.

MASTER STROKE
1 Alfred Rd, South Easton, MA, 02375-1546. Contact: Alex Kulpa, Owner - Tel: (508) 532-8485. Residential window cleaning. Established: 1986 - Franchising Since: 1987 - No. of Units: Company Owned: 1 - Franchised: 15 - Franchise Fee: $5,000 - Royalty: 6% - Total Inv: $7,500 - Financing: Yes.

MEND-A-BATH INTERNATIONAL
8501 Benjamin Street, Chalmette, LA, 70043. - Tel: (504) 276-8318, Fax: (504) 276-8318, Web Site: www.mendabathusa.com. Sanitary ware refinishing, tile and tub resurfacing. Established: 1976 - Franchising Since: 1981 - No. of Units: Company Owned: 6 - Franchised: In 53 countries - Franchise Fee: $35,000 - Royalty: 4% of gross sales - Financing: Yes.

MERRY MAIDS
P.O. Box 751017, Memphis, TN, 38175-1017. Contact: Franchise Sales Manager - Tel: (800) 637-7962, Fax: (901) 597-8140, Web Site: www.merrymaids.com. Provides a comprehensive initial training program at its headquarters and continuous follow-up assistance through Merry Maids support staff of 51 + full-time employees, 31 regional coordinators, regional meetings and workshops, a national convention, newsletters and a modern bulletin board. Established: 1979 - Franchising Since: 1980 - No. of Units: Company Owned: 172 - Franchised: 1409 - Franchise Fee: $16,000-$24,000 - Royalty: 7% - Total Inv: $32,500-$49,500 - Financing: Available.

MINI MAID
Mini Maid Services Co., Inc., The
2727 Canton Rd., Ste 550, Marietta, GA, 30066. Contact: Leone Ackerly, Owner/President - Tel: (770) 794-9938, Fax: (770) 794-1877. Team residential cleaning business. Established: 1973 - Franchising Since: 1976 - No. of Units: Franchised: 87 - Franchise Fee: $12,500 - Royalty: 6% 1st $100, 5% next $100, 4% next $100 and 3% next $100 - Total Inv: $19,000-$25,000 - Financing: No.

MINT CONDITION
Mint Condition Franchising, Inc.
1061 521 Corporate Center Drive, Suite 170, Fort Mill, SC, 29715. Contact: Patrick Wood, V.P. - Tel: (803) 548-6121, Fax: (803) 548-4578, E-Mail: info@mintconditioninc.com, Web Site: www.mint condition.biz. A Mint Condition franchise gives you access to a proven and successful business, providing commercial cleaning services for business customers. Established: 1996 - Franchising Since: 1996 - No. of Units: Company Owned: 1 - Franchised: 64 - Franchise Fee: $500.- $10,000 - Total Inv: $5,314-$36,532.

MOLLY MAID
Molly Maid Inc.
3948 Ranchero Drive, Ann Arbor, MI, 48108. Contact: Jenn Osness - Tel: (734) 822-6800, (800) 665-5962, Fax: (734) 822-6888, E-Mail: info@mollymaid.com, Web Site: www.mollymaid.com. Residential cleaning services. Established: 1979 - Franchising Since: 1984 - No. of Units: Company Owned: 1 - Franchised: 540 - Franchise Fee: $9,900 - Total Inv: $87,900-$107,900 - Financing: Third party.

MR. SUDS
Mr. Suds Franchise System
205 English Town Industrial Park, Harrison, NJ, 07726. Contact: Walter J. Harizeupa Jr., President - Tel: (732) 786-9114, (800) 307-7837, Fax: (732) 521-4656. Carpet, upholstery, window and floor cleaning to both residential and commercial customers. Complete training and support. Established: 1991 - Franchising Since: 1998 - No. of Units: Company Owned: 1 - Franchise Fee: $5,995.00 (includes startup chemicals, equipment, training) - Royalty: $150 per month - Total Inv: $10,000-$15,000 - Financing: Visa, Mastercard.

NATIONAL HYGIENE/LIEN OF ...(YOUR HOMETOWN OR AREA)
National Hygiene Franchise Corp.
225 W. Laura Dr., Ste A, Addison, IL, 60101-5017. Contact: Fran. Sales Dir. - Tel: (847) 487-9400, (800) 888-8407. Commercial restroom sanitation and air freshening services. Offering "Service" and "Master" franchise opportunities nation-wide. "We've been in more bathrooms than anyone in America." We do all billing and collecting. Established: 1964/1929 - Franchising Since: 1968/1940 - No. of Units: Company Owned: 6 - Franchised: 27 - Franchise Fee: Service: $9,500 - Master: $50,000 - Royalty: Varies...different for service vs. master - Total Inv: $15,000 ave. - service/$65,500 ave. - master - Financing: Yes.

NATIONAL MAINTENANCE CONTRACTORS
National Maintenance Franchise Corp.
1801-130th Ave., N.E., Bellevue, WA, 98005. Contact: Lyle Graddon, Pres. - Tel: (800) 347-7844, Fax: (425) 883-4785. Janitorial franchise business actively looking for master and unit franchisees in major metropolitan markets. Established: 1970 - Franchising Since: 1973 - No. of Units: Company Owned: 2 - Franchised: 300 - Franchise Fee: $2,000-$5,000 unit, $50,000-$100,000 master - Royalty: 20% unit, 3%-4% master - Financing: Yes.

NAUT-A-CARE
Naut-A-Care Marine Services, Inc
2507 W. Coast Hwy., Ste. 204, Newport Beach, CA, 92663-4755. Contact: Don Drysdale, C.E.O - Tel: (949) 631-5823, Fax: (949) 631-2502, Web Site: www.naut-a-care.com. Providing bilge steam cleaning and oil changing services to marine vessels from custom service craft. Established: 1998 - Franchising Since: 1999 - No. of Units: Company Owned: 1 - Franchised: 2 - Franchise Fee: $25,000 - Royalty: $500 flat fee per month - Total Inv: $164,900-$205,550 (includes custom service craft) - Financing: Yes, 1/2 of initail franchise fee. NOT FRANCHISING AT THIS TIME.

NUTECH CLEANING SYSTEMS
P.O. Box 793, Bountiful, UT, 84011-0793. Contact: Martin Ehman, Franchise Development - Tel: (801) 298-3196. Multiple cleaning franchise. Full training and support provided. Established: 1996 - Franchising Since: 1996 - No. of Units: Franchised: 2 - Franchise Fee: $9,995 - Total Inv: $13,500-$16,500 - Financing: Yes.

OCTOCLEAN
OctoClean Franchising Systems
1760 Chicago Ave., Ste. J-15, Riverside, CA, 92507. Contact: Charles Stowe - Tel: (909) 683-5859, Fax: (909) 779-0270. Commercial janitorial cleaning. Established: 1983 - Franchising Since: 2001 - No. of Units: Company Owned: 1 - Franchised: 21 - Royalty: 5% - Total Inv: Capital requirements; $8,000-$57,500 - Financing: Yes.

OFFICE PRIDE
Faith Franchising Company, Inc
170 N. Jackson St, Franklin, IN, 46131. Contact: Mark Wages - Tel: (888) 641-2310. Commercial cleaning services. Established: 1992 - Franchising Since: 1996 - No. of Units: Company Owned: 3 - Franchised: 25 - Franchise Fee: $7,000 - Total Inv: $30,000 - Financing: Yes.

OMEX - OFFICE MAINTENANCE EXPERTS
OMEX International, Inc.
3905 Hartzdale Dr. Ste. 506, Camp Hill, PA, 17011. Contact: Franchise Rep. - Tel: (800) 827-6639, (717) 737-7311, Fax: (717) 737-9271, E-Mail: info@omexcorp.com, Web-Site: www.omexcorp.com. Commercial contract cleaning services to first class office facilities including Fortune 500 companies, large office buildings, banks and

medical clinics. Established: 1979 - Franchising Since: 1994 - No. of Units: Company Owned: 1 - Franchised: 11 - Franchise Fee: $15,000-$25,000 - Royalty: 4% - Total Inv: $40,400 -$70,600 - Financing: None.

OTHER WOMAN, THE
9136 NE Glisan, Portland, OR, 97220. Contact: Cindy Wells - Tel: (503) 252-4336, (800) 846-6052, Fax: (503) 252-9259, Web Site: www.theotherwoman.com. The Other Woman is a professional cleaning service. We provide continued support, including computer software, business forms, printed brochures and private label cleaning supplies. Established: 1988 - Franchising Since: 1998 - No. of Units: Company Owned: 7 - Franchised: 7 - Franchise Fee: $15,000.

PAUL'S PROFESSIONAL WINDOW WASHING *
P.O. Box 284, Montrose, CA, 91021. - Tel: (818) 249-7917, Fax: (818) 249-7806, E-Mail: paulsprowindow@aol.com, Web Site: www.paulsprowindow.com. Paul's Professional Window Washing does more than wash windows. Our services include interior and exterior cleaning, fall and spring maintenance, and screen and door services. Established: 1981 - Franchising Since: 2004 - Franchise Fee: $17,500 - Royalty: 6%.

RACS INTERNATIONAL INC.
Racs International
10333 N. Meridian Suite 170, Indianapolis, IN, 46290. Contact: Chuck Morrison, Pres. - Tel: (317) 844-8152, (800) 949-7227, Fax: (317) 844-2270, E-Mail: racsint@earthlink.net, Web Site: www.racsclean.com. Commercial cleaning franchise. Established: 1990 - Franchising Since: 1991 - No. of Units: Company Owned: 24 - Franchised: 10 - Franchise Fee: $3,500-$31,500 - Royalty: 5% - Total Inv: $1,400-$11,600 - Financing: Yes.

RECEIL IT CEILING RESTORATION
ReCeil It International, Inc.
175 B Liberty Street, Copiague, NY, 11726-1207. Contact: Alex Annibell, Director of Franchise Development - Tel: (631) 842-0099, (800) CEILING, Fax: (631) 980-7668, E-Mail: alex@receilit.com, Web Site: www.receilit.com. Your ReCeil It franchise is a home based business opportunity which provides professional ceiling cleaning and restoration services to commercial and industrial accounts. Established: 1992 - Franchising Since: 2002 - No. of Units: Company Owned: 1 - Franchise Fee: $35,000 - Royalty: 7% of gross sales - Total Inv: $38,900 - Financing: None.

REMODELING CONTRACTING & CLEANING SERVICE, INC.
13845 West 107th Street, Lenexa, KS, 66215. - Tel: (913) 327-8700, (800) 289-1389, Fax: (913) 327-8701. Fire, water and storm structural/cleaning restoration - residential and commercial. Established: 1974 - Franchising Since: 1991 - No. of Units: Franchised: 8 - Franchise Fee: $20,000 - Royalty: 5% - Total Inv: $50,000-$90,000 - Financing: Yes.

RESTORX, INC.
1135 Braddock Ave., Braddock, PA, 15104. Contact: Cliff Zlotnik, Franchise Dev - Tel: (412) 351-8686, Fax: (412) 351-1394. Restoration of fire and water damaged property. Established: 1982 - Franchising Since: 1982 - No. of Units: Company Owned: 1- Franchised: 40 - Franchise Fee: $5,000-$20,000 - Royalty: Flat fee $150-$275 weekly - Total Inv: Fran. fee, $25,000 vehicle/equip., $15,000 work. cap. - Financing: Partial.

SCRUBWAY INC.
P.O. Box 2468, Southeastern, PA, 19399-2468. Contact: Chuck Lomagro, V.P. - Tel: (800) 355-3000, (610) 278-9000, Fax: (610) 275-7360. Franchisees provide restroom hygiene services to retail and commercial properties in an exclusive territory. Complete on-going support accounting and supply package included, training and equipment also included. Established: 1994 - Franchising Since: 1994 - No. of Units: Company Owned: 1 - Franchised: 5 - Franchise Fee: $10,000-$30,000 - Royalty: 6% - Total Inv: $35,000-$40,000 - Financing: Yes.

SERV U-1ST
Serv U-1, Inc.
2706 NE Sandy Blvd, Portland, OR, 97232-2344. - Tel: (503) 244-7628. Janitorial maintenance business serving commercial and industrial clients. Low investment with ongoing training in financial control,

procuring clients, production and management. Regional may provide accounts. Established: 1988 - Franchising: 1988 - No. of Units: Franchised: 11 - Franchise Fee: $3,300 - Royalty: 12% of 1st, $3,000 gross/m, 3% of total gross/m. - Total Inv. Varies - Financing: Yes.

SERVICE ONE JANITORIAL
5104 N. Orange Blossom Tr., Ste. 114, Orlando, FL, 32810. Contact: Steve Rathel, Owner - Tel: (407) 293-7645, (800) 522-7111, Fax: (407) 299-4306, E-Mail: service_onex12@aol.com. Janitorial contract cleaning. Established: 1985 - Franchising Since: 1985 - No. of Units: Company Owned: 6 - Franchised: 173 - Franchise Fee: $9,750-$18,500 - Royalty: Sliding scale - Financing: Yes - 100%.

SERVICE TEAM OF PROFESSIONALS
S.T.O.P., Inc
P.O. Box 1493, Platte City, MO, 64079-1493. Contact: Brian Clark, Consultant - Tel: (800) 452-TEAM, (816) 858-2800, Fax: (816) 858-2901, Web Site: www.stopinc.net. In-depth management marketing, operational and technical support in the cleaning and restoration industry, (primarily insurance work). Initial training and 4 conventions/year. Established: 1971 - Franchising Since: 1996 - No. of Units: Franchised: 34 - Franchise Fee: $31,400 - Royalty: 5% to 8% depending on initial fee paid or finance - Total Inv: $10,000-$100,000 - Financing: Yes, up to 90% A.O.C.

SERVICE-TECH CLEANING
Service-Tech Corporation
7589 First Pl, Cleveland, OH, 44146-6711. Contact: Alan Sutton, Pres. - Tel: (800) 992-9302, (440) 735-1433. Offering extensive line of services which include: air duct cleaning, kitchen exhaust, pressure washing and vacuum cleaning, plus more, to hospitals, restaurants, schools, homes and industrial and commercial customers. Established: 1960 - Franchising Since: 1988 - No. of Units: Company Owned: 5 - Franchised: 3 - Franchise Fee: $19,000 - Royalty: 4%-6% plus 1% adv. - Total Inv: $49,000 ($19,000 fran. fee, $30,000 equip., training etc.) - Financing: None.

SERVPRO
Servpro Industries, Inc.
575 Airport Blvd., Gallatin, TN, 37066. Contact: Director Franchise Expansion - Tel: (800) 826-9586, (615) 451-0200. Fax: (615) 451-1602, E-Mail: jvaughn@servpronet.com, Web Site: www.servpro.com. Premier cleaning and restoration company. Servpro's niche is the insurance restoration market, which accounts for a large portion of Servpro's overall volume. Established: 1967 - Franchising Since: 1969 - No. of Units: Franchised: 1250 - Franchise Fee: $78,000 (includes license & products & equipment) - Royalty: 3%-10% depending on volume and work provided - Total Inv: $95,450-$139,400 - Financing: Some financing provided by franchiser with approved credit.

SHINE-A-BLIND
P.O. Box 165, St. Clair, MI, 48079. Contact: Dan Griffin, Pres. - Tel: (810) 329-8600, Fax: (810) 329-8604. Manufacture and distribute ultrasonic mini-blind cleaning equipment. International network of 315 members. Established: 1988 - Franchising since: 1988 - No. of Units: Company Owned: 2 - Franchised: 300+ - Franchise Fee: $1,000 - Royalty: $100 per month - Total Inv: $15,000 - Financing: Yes.

SLATS BLIND CLEANING
Porter Gulch Business Dev.
3119 Porter Gulch Rd, Aptos, CA, 95003. - Tel: (831) 423-6464, (800) 667-5287, Fax: (831) 476-2480, Web Site: www.slats.com. Ultrasonic cleaning and repair of blinds and shades. Shop based or home based service to residential and commercial market. Established: 1990 - Franchising Since: 1996 - No. of Units: Company Owned: 2 - Franchised: 3 - Franchise Fee: $17,500 - Royalty: 5% - Total Inv: $39,000-$64,500 - Financing: Yes.

SPARKLE WASH
Sparkle International Inc.
26851 Richmond Rd., Cleveland, OH, 44146. Contact: Hans Pete Funk, Vice Chairman - Tel: (800) 321-0770, (216) 464-4212, Fax: (216) 464-8869. Safe, on-site cleaning and restoration of buildings, homes, truck fleets, wood patio and decks. Established: 1965 - Franchising Since:

1967 - No. of Units: Company Owned: 1 - Franchised: 173 - Franchise Fee: Min. $15,000 - Royalty: 3%-5% - Financing: Third party for equipment and vehicle.

SPARKLING MAID
Sparkling Maid, Inc.
7936 E. Arapahoe Ct., Ste. 2400, Englewood, CO, 80112. Contact: Eileen T. Martin, Pres. - Tel: (303) 770-6059, Fax: (720) 482-7924, E-Mail: etmnj@earthlink.net. Housecleaning service, buyers pay for own phone lines, office equipment, liability insurance, workmans compensation, bonding insurance, advertising. Established: 1979 - Franchising Since: 1983 - No. of Units: Franchised: 1 - Franchise Fee: $10,000 - Royalty: $200/mo. - Total Inv: $8,000 training for 30 hours, $2,000 start up and equipment - Financing: Yes with 25% down & 36 months to pay with 7% interest.

SQUEEGEE PRO
Squeegee Pro Franchising, Inc
23251 Peralta Dr., #U, Laguan Hills, CA, 92653. Contact: Greg S. Harline - Tel: (949) 470-0296, (877) GO2-SPWC, Web Site: www.squeegeepro.com. Squeegee Pro is a full-service window, pressure and blind cleaning company that caters to residential and small commercial markets. Established: 1997 - Franchising Since: 2000 - No. of Units: Company Owned: 1 - Franchise Fee: $10,000 - Total Inv: $18,000-$30,000 plus franchise fee.

SUPER CLEAN YACHT SERVICE
Super Clean Yacht Service Franchising, Inc
910 West Coast Highway, Newport Beach, CA, 92660-5645. Contact: Lisa Barreth, President - Tel: (949) 646-2990, Fax: (949) 646-9311, E-Mail: info@supercleanyachtservice.com, Web Site: www.supercleanyachtservice.com. Super Clean Yacht Service franchise owners provide wash-down, waxing, varnishing, detailing, interior cleaning and teak oiling services to pleasure boats and yatchs in designated harbors or marinas. Our franchise owners don't clean boats, they own and manage boat-cleaning businesses, using trained crews, harbor-friendly Super Clean proprietary soaps and cleaning products. Established: 1998 - Franchising Since: 2000 - No. of Units: Company Owned: 1 - Franchised: 3 - Franchise Fee: $7,500-$25,000 - Royalty: $500. per month flat fee - Total Inv: $12,400-$51,100 - Financing: Yes.

SWISHER HYGIENE
Swisher Hygiene Franchise Corp.
6849 Fairview Rd., Charlotte, NC, 28210. Contact: Mery Thompson, Franchise Sales Admin. - Tel: (704) 364-7707 , (800) 444-4138 , Fax: (704) 364-1117, E-Mail: mthompson@swisheronline.com, Web Site: www.swisheronline.com. Franchisees operating within a protected territory, offering hygiene services and products along with commercial pest control service to all types of commercial and industrial outlets; ie, restaurants, retail outlets, industrial buildings, etc. Established: 1983 - Franchising Since: 1990 - No. of Units: Company Owned: 2 - Franchised: 119 - Franchise Fee: $35,000-$75,000 - Royalty: 6% - Total Inv: $60,000-$140,00 - Financing: Yes, for qualified candidates.

TEAM CLEAN, INC.
4725 N, 43rd Ave., Ste. 6, Phoenix, AZ, 85031. - Tel: (877) 832-6256, Fax: (623) 435-5800. Janitorial services. Established: 1997 - Franchising Since: 2002 - No. of Units: Company Owned: 1 - Franchise Fee: $3,500-$26,000 - Total Inv: Varies - Financing: Yes.

TEAM-WORKS BUILDING SERVICES
TeamWorks Building Services Franchise Corp.
412 Rt. 130 North, Cinnaminson, NJ, 08077-5236. Contact: Steve Izzi, President - Tel: (856) 596-4196, Fax: (609) 829-2055. Commercial cleaning services. Established: 1990 - Franchising Since: 1993 - No. of Units: Franchised: 40 - Franchise Fee: Variable - Total Inv: Variable - Financing: Yes.

TOWN AND COUNTRY OFFICE & CARPET CARE SYSTEMS
2570 San Ramon Valley Blvd., Ste. A102, San Ramon, CA, 94583. - Tel: (925) 867-3850, Fax: (925) 867-2756. Janitorial and carpet care. Established: 1971 - Franchising Since: 1986 - No. of Units: Franchised: 86 - Franchise Fee: $1,500 - Royalty: $75 per month - Total Inv: $2,900-$10,000 - Financing: Yes.

VALUE LINE MAINTENANCE SYS.
Western Maintenance Co.
P.O. Box 6450, Great Falls, MT, 59406. Contact: Jerry McAllister, General Mgr. - Tel: (406) 761-4471, (800) 824-4838, Fax: (406) 761-4486. Flexible cleaning programs for supermarkets and other large retail outlets. Established: 1959 - No. of Units: 32 - Franchise Fee: $30,000 - Royalty: 10% - Total Inv: $50,800 - Financing: Yes.

VANGUARD CLEANING SYSTEMS
655 Mariners Island Blvd., Ste. 303, San Mateo, CA, 94404. - Tel: (800) 564-6422, Fax: (650) 372-1513, Web Site: www.vanguardcleaning.com. Commercial cleaning franchise. Both master and unit franchises available. Established: 1984 - Franchising Since: 1984 - No. of Units: Company Owned: 2 - Franchised: 180 - Franchise Fee: $6,800-$20,300 for unit franchises - Royalty: 5% - Total Inv: $7,075-$21,200 for unit franchises - Financing: Yes.

WACKY BEAR FACTORY EXPRESS *
6795 W. Park Ave., Houma, LA, 70360. - Tel: (985) 872-5798, Fax: (985) 872-1357, E-Mail: franchising@wackybear.com, Web Site: www.wackybear.com. An interactive teddy bear experience that lets you stuff, dress and name your beary own special pal. Established: 2000 - Franchising Since: 2004 - No. of Units: Company Owned: 3 - Franchise Fee: $30,000 - Royalty: 4% - Total Inv: $150,000-$187,500 - Financing: No.

WASH ON WHEELS
2988 Windward Dr NW, Kennesaw, GA, 30152-4665. Contact: Jim Good, Pres. - Tel: (407) 298-4218. WOW is a general purpose mobile wash cleaning service addressing all surface dirt: indoor and/or outdoor directed at the residential, commercial and industrial marketplace. The chemicals, training, customized software and continuing franchise development program support growth and success. Established: 1964 - Franchising Since: 1986 - No. of Units: Franchised: 142 - Franchise Fee: $7,500 - Royalty: $80/mo. - Total Inv: $14,500-$60,000 - Financing: Yes.

WELCOME HOME ENTERPRISES INC.
3866 Trade Center Dr., Ann Arbor, MI, 48108. - Tel: (734) 973-8937. Reliable and personalized residential cleaning service tailored to our customer needs. Established: 1993 - Franchising Since: 1997 - No. of Units: Company Owned: 1 - Franchised: 1 - Franchise Fee: $3,000-$15,000 - Royalty: 3%, 1% convention fee - Total Inv: $3,000-$25,000 - Financing: Yes.

WEST SANTITATION SERVICES, INC
West Sanitation Services, Inc.
3882 Del Amo Blvd., Ste. 602, Torrance, CA, 90503. Contact: Ben Elder, Manager, U.S. Operations - Tel: (310) 793-4242, (888) 663-6726, Fax: (310) 793-4250, E-Mail: info@westsanitation.com, Web Site: www.westsanitation.com. Restroom deodorization service performed every 28 days. Established: 1884 - Franchising Since: 1982 - No. of Units: Company Owned: 3 - Franchised: 60 - Franchise Fee: $4,000 - Royalty: 35% (8% royalty, 4% adv., 23% administration fee) - Total Inv: $4,000 - Financing: On existing routes.

WINCH ENTERPRISES
PMB 249, 227 BellevueWay N.E., Bellevue, WA, 98004. Contact: Brian Winch, Owner - Tel: (403) 236-7551, Fax: (403) 246-0582. Earn big money cleaning up litter from commercial properties. Simple operation from home or office, work full or part time. Established: 1981 - No. of Units: Company Owned: 1 - Total Inv: $29.95 for how-to-guide. Financing: No.

WINCO WINDOW CLEANING & MAINTENANCE
Muchville Arcade
Colonial Terrace #27, Knoxville, IA, 50138. Contact: David Wolerr, Owner - Tel: (515) 828-7794. "Guide to business professional window cleaning" $80 guaranteed "Operations Manual" Janitorial: gutter-chimney-pest control. Logo consultation and support. Established: 1977 - Franchising Since: 1989 - Franchise Fee: $3,900 limited - Royalty: None - Financing: No.

WINDOW BRIGADE *
Window Brigade, Inc.
4907 Hollenden Drive, Suite 208, Raleigh, NC, 27616. Contact: LaVerne Artis - Tel: (919) 834-8215, (866) 578-6243, Fax: (919) 834-7630, E-Mail: franchise@windowbrigade.com, Web Site: www.windowbrigade. com. It's time to clean up with Window Brigade and create your own future in the residential and commercial cleaning industries, which are experiencing explosive growth. We are the "Full Service People" offering full-service residential and commercial window, blind, gutter and pressure wash Bulls's-Eye Cleaning Systems. Established: 2000 - Franchising Since: 2003 - No. of Units: Company Owned: 1 - Franchised: 4 - Franchise Fee: $6,000+ - Royalty: 5-7% - Total Inv: $12,000-$56,000 - Financing: Yes.

WINDOW BUTLER
W.B. Franchising Systems, Inc.
6355 East Kemper Road, Ste. 250, Cincinnati, OH, 45241. Contact: Franchise Development - Tel: (513) 489-4000, (800) 808-6470, Fax: (513) 469-2226, Web Site: www.windowbutler.com. Home services are in demand! A Window Butler franchise provides busy homeowners with window and gutter cleaning and deck maintenance. Established: 1997 - Franchising Since: 1997 - No. of Units: Franchised: 16 - Franchise Fee: $9,900-$18,900 - Royalty: 6%, 3% advertising - Total Inv: $15,000-$40,000 - Financing: Up to 50% of franchise fee.

WINDOW GANG
Window Gang Ventures Corp
405 Arendell St, Morehead City, NC, 28557. Contact: Tim McCullen, President - Tel: (252) 726-1463, (800) 849-2308, Fax: (252) 726-2837, E-Mail: t.m@windowgang.com, Web Site: www.windowgang.com. Window and pressure cleaning, residential & commercial. Established: 1986 - Franchising Since: 1996 - No. of Units: Company Owned: 1 - Franchised: 114 - Franchise Fee: $5,000-$75,000 - Royalty: 6% - Financing: Yes.

WINDOW GENIE
For Franchising, LLC
350 Gest St, Cincinnati, OH, 45203. Contact: Richard Nonelle, President - Tel: (513) 412-7762, (800) 700-0022, Fax: (513) 412-7760, E-Mail: info@windowgenie.com, Web Site: www.windowgenie.com. Residential and commercial service company. Home-based and mobile franchise with 3 major service categories; window cleaning, window tinting and pressure washing. A very buildable white collar opportunity in a mom-and-pop industry. Established: 1993 - Franchising Since: 1998 - No. of Units: Franchised: 45 - Franchise Fee: $19,500 - Royalty: 6%; 1% marketing fund - Total Inv: $19,500 fee; $10,000 start-up package, $20,000 advertising - Financing: None.

WOOD RE NEW
Wood Re New
220 S. Dysart, Springfield, MO, 65802. Contact: Stan Krempges - Tel: (417) 833-3303, (888) 244-3303, Fax: (417) 833-5479, E-Mail: stan@woodrenew.com, Web Site: www.woodrenew.com. Cleaning and preserving decks, docks, fences, cedar & redwood siding. Established: 1993 - Franchising Since: 2001 - No. of Units: Company Owned: 1 - Franchised: 10 - Franchise Fee: $20,000 - Royalty: 4% - Total Inv: $40,000-$50,000 - Financing: No.

COMPUTER/ELECTRONICS/INTERNET SERVICES

A WORLDWIDE MARKETING GROUP
16406 Millstream Lane, Cerritos, CA, 90703. - Tel: (800) 695-2293, Fax: (413) 502-9503. Internet advertising consultant. Established: 2000 - Franchising Since: 2001 - No. of Units: Company Owned: 1 - Franchised: 1 - Franchise Fee: $500. - Total Inv: $2,000.

ADCIRCUIT.COM
444 Ravenna Boulevard, Seattle, WA, 98115. Contact: John Lindauer - Fax: (206) 985-3844. Telemarket local internet sites. Established: 1999 - Franchising Since: 2000 - No. of Units: Company Owned: 1532 - Franchised: 1600.

AL & ED'S AUTOSOUND *
6855 Hayvenhurst Ave, Van Nuys, CA, 91406. - Tel: (818) 908-5700, Fax: (818) 908-5701, E-Mail: gary@al-eds.com, Web Site: www.al-eds.com. Mobile electronic sales & installation. Established: 1954 - Franchising Since: 1986 - No. of Units: Company Owned: 21 - Franchised: 14 - Franchise Fee: $25,000 - Royalty: 7% - Total Inv: $160,300-$560,200.

ALTERNATIVE VIRTUAL MALL
P.O. Box 562, Mystic Islands, NJ, 08087. - Tel: (609) 294-2120, Fax: (609) 294-2120. A virtual mall for the Internet. Franchise fee includes everything to get started, the web page design, products, service provider, support, etc. The Internet is hot and you can get involved instantly. Established: 1993 - Franchising Since: 1995 - No. of Units: Company Owned: 1 - Franchised: 3 - Franchise Fee: $2,000 - Royalty: Profit sharing on products - Total Inv: $2,000 + $200 monthly for service provider - Financing: Yes. NOT FRANCHISING AT THIS TIME.

BOOMERANG GAMEWARE
4986 Park Avenue, Memphis, TN, 38118. Contact; Franchise Director - Tel: (901) 368-3333. Sale, exchange and rental of video games, computer discs, laser discs and computer porgrams. Established: 1991 - Franchising Since: 1995 - No. of Units: Company Owned: 2 - Franchised: 21 - Franchise Fee: $20,000 - Royalty: Share, 1% adv - Total Inv: $89,000-$125,000 - Financing: Outsourcing.

CABOODLE CARTRIDGE *
3233F De La Cruz Blvd, Santa Clara, CA, 95054 - Tel: (408) 988-0064, Fax: (408) 988-0074, Web Site: www.cacartridge.com. Caboodle Cartridge is offering a franchise program that will allow you to setup your own store. You will be able to offer a very broad range of remanufactured cartridges for inkjet printers, laser printers, copiers and faxes. Established: 2003 - Franchising Since: 2004 - No. of Units: Company Owned: 2 - Franchised: 1 - Franchise Fee: $20,000 - Royalty: 5% - Total Inv: $60,000-$115,000.

CD WAREHOUSE
CD Warehouse, Inc
1204 Sovereign Row, Oklahoma City, OK, 73112. Contact: Vicky Sugg, Franchise Sales Manager - Tel: (405) 949-2422, (800) 641-9394, Fax: (405) 949-2566, E-Mail: mail@cdwarehouse.com, Web Site: cdwarehouse.com, or, www.cdwi.com. CD Warehouse, Inc is a rapidly growing chain of music stores. Our primary focus is on buying, selling and trading of pre-owned CD'S. Our stores also sell top 100 new CD'S, DVD, CD Rom Games and other music related items. Established: 1992 - Franchising Since: 1992 - No. of Units: Company Owned: 73 - Franchised: 255 - Franchise Fee: $20,000 for initial franchise, $15,000 for others - Royalty: 5% of gross sales - Total Inv: $125,000-$169,300 - Financing: Yes.

COMPUTER BUILDERS WAREHOUSE
CBW Enterprises
1993 Tobsal Court, Warren, MI, 48091. Contact: Franchise Development - Tel: (586) 756-2600, Fax: (586) 756-8715, Web Site: www.computerfranchise.com. Leading technology into the new millennium for less! Custom build computers in our state of the art manufacturing facility, we provide turnkey operation unparalleled inventory control system, CBW stores are high profit centers. Established: 1990 - Franchising Since: 1999 - No. of Units: Company Owned: 3 - Franchised: 4 - Franchise Fee: $35,000 - Royalty: 1.5% for full CBW, 2% for CBW express store - Total Inv: As low as $190 for CBW express store - Financing: Yes, through SBA.

COMPUTER DOCTOR
Computer Doctor Franchise Systems, Inc.
29529 W 9 Mile Road, Farmington Hills, MI, 48336. - Tel: (248) 426-7500, Fax: (248) 427-8175. Computer Doctor retail stores buy, trade-in, resell, used computer parts and systems, sell new computer parts, systems, printers, and components, sell computer supplies, cables, and adapters, combined with mobile on-site or in-store computer and printer repair services and upgrades. A multiple profit center in one franchise with unlimited market potential. Established: 1992 - Franchising Since: 1996 - No. of Units: Franchised: 67 in 14 states - Franchise Fee: $20,000 - Royalty: 3% - Total Inv: $117,900-$170,700 - Financing: None.

COMPUTER MAINTENANCE SERVICE

P.O. Box 335, San Marcos, TX, 78667. Contact: Floyd MacKenzie, G.M. - Tel: (830) 629-1400. Repair, maintenance and service of the personal computer market and peripherals. Established: 1987 - Franchising Since: 1988 - No. of Units: 1 - Royalty: $300 monthly - Total Inv: $10,000 + tools - Financing: No.

COMPUTER RENAISSANCE

Grow Biz International

124 South Florida Ave, Lakeland, FL, 33801. - Tel: (863) 669-1155, Fax: (863) 709-0790. Retail computer stores that buy, sell and trade used and new computer equipment. Established: 1988 - Franchising Since: 1993 - No. of Units: Company Owned: 5 - Franchised: 38 - Franchise Fee: $25,000 - Royalty: 3% - Total Inv: $128,700-$193,500 - Financing: SBA financing available, up to two-thirds of capital.

COMPUTER TECHS/AXIOM CONSULTING

43678 Lotus Dr., Canton, MI, 48188. - Tel: (734) 523-2705. Computer maintenance, repairs, sales of new and refurbished computer equipment systems integration, software services, consulting and help desk services. Programming, web sites, year 2000 issues. Established: 1997 - Franchising Since: 1997 - No. of Units: Company Owned: 1 - Franchise Fee: $8,000 - Royalty: 7% - Total Inv: $15,000-$45,000 - Financing: Yes.

CONCERTO NETWORKS *

501 W. Broadway Ste. 800, San Diego, CA, 92101 - Tel: (858) 366-0122, Fax: (858) 366-0124, E-Mail: info@concertonetworks.com, Web Site: www.concertonetworks.com. Provides quality information technology/computer and network services to small office's and home offices. Established: 2002 - Franchising Since: 2003 - No. of Units: Franchised: 2 - Franchise Fee: $15,750 - Royalty: 14% - Total Inv: $36,500-$49,900.

CYBER EXCHANGE COMPUTER SOFTWARE

1068 N Camden LN, South Elgin, IL 60177-2849. - Tel: (630) 443-0397, (800) 520-7311, Fax: (630) 443-0398, Web Site: www.cyberexchange.com. Individual consumers and businesses have a unique opportunity to buy, sell and trade new and used computers, peripherals, games, productivity and a wide range of entertaiment software at any one of 64 stores in 25 different states. Our exclusive database accurately tracks over 70,000 pieces of software for our franchisees. Established: 1993 - Franchising Since: 1994 - No. of Units: Company Owned: 2 - Franchised: 64 - Franchise Fee: $15,000 - Royalty: 5% used software, 4% new SW, 3% used hardware, 1.5% new hardware - Total Inv: $89,500-$140,000 - Financing: No.

DATA DOCTORS

2090 E. University, #101, Tempe, AZ, 85281. - Tel: (480) 921-2444, Fax: (480) 921-2975, E-Mail: franchises@datadoctors.com, Web Site: www.datadoctors.com. Computer sales & services including web services. Established: 1988 - Franchising Since: 2002 - No. of Units: Company Owned: 4 - Franchised: 39 - Franchise Fee: $35,000 - Royalty: 5% - Total Inv: $75,400-$105,200 - Financing: Third party.

EXECUTRAIN CORPORATION

2500 Northwinds Pkwy, #600, Alpharetta, GA, 30044. Contact: Dawn Weiss, Int. Regional Mgr. - Tel: (770) 667-7700, (800) 843-6984, Fax: (770) 664-2006, E-Mail: DAWNW@executrain.com, Web Site: www.executrain.com. Computer training on business related software. Courses available encompass standard desktop courses for end-users, and technical courses for more advanced users. Established: 1984 - Franchising Since: 1986 - No. of Units: Company Owned: 25 - Franchised: 73 US, 59 Outside US - Franchise Fee: $30,000 U.S., $50,000 Master outside US, $35,000 for unit outside US - Royalty: 6%-9% of monthly gross sales - Total Inv: $250,000 - Financing: No.

EXPETEC TECHNOLOGY SERVICES

Computer Doctor International, Inc.

12 2nd Ave SW, Aberdeen, SD, 57401. Contact: Lisa Hinz - Tel: (605) 225-4122, (888) 297-2292, Fax: (605) 225-5176, E-Mail: sales@expetec.biz, Web Site: www.expetec.biz. Expetec franchisees provide mobile, on-site, high-level technolgy services to business and consumer customers. You will have the latest testing and diagnostic equipment available. This equipment, coupled with an advanced mobile business management over every other service provider. Additionally,

our national network of franchisees is truly a team committed to quality service. Established: 1992 - Franchising Since: 1996 - No. of Units: Franchised: 45 - Franchise Fee: $20,000 - Royalty: Min. $50/wk then scale - Total Inv: $57,200-$88,200 - Financing: Fill-In house.

FIRST INTERNET ALLIANCE

First Internet Franchise Corp.

1060 Calle Cordillera, Suite 101, San Clemente, CA, 92673. Contact: VP Franchise Licensing - Tel: (949) 369-5900, (800) 617-4227, Fax: (949) 369-5909, E-Mail:info@fia.net. Fast growing nationwide franchisor of internet services businesses. Twelve different revenue streams, 5 day training, hardware and software, recognized leader in explosive industry, excellent territories, proven programs. Established: 1995 - Franchising Since: 1996 - No. of Units: Franchised: 17 - Franchise Fee: $10,000 - Royalty: $1/month/customer - Total Inv: $23,900 - Franchising: Yes.

FRANCHISE.COM

P.O. Box 230928, Encinitas, CA, 92023. Contact: Gene S. Fisher, Exec. Vice-President - Tel: (760) 943-0080, (866) 325-0012, Fax: (760) 436-5387, E-Mail: info@franchise.com, Web Site: www.franchise.com. Internet advertising web site to generate leads for franchisors. Established: 1991.

FRIENDLY COMPUTER

Friendly Computers

3145 N. Rainbow Blvd, Las Vegas, NV, 89108. Contact: Vicki Pooling - Tel: (702) 656-2780, (800) 656-3115, Fax: (702) 656-9487, E-Mail: vicki@friendly2u.com, Web Site: www.friendlymobilecomputers.com. On site mobile computer repair, upgrades and sales of new computers! 10 years experience in the business, low upfront investment, high profit margins! Established: 1992 - Franchising Since: 2000 - No. of Units: Company Owned: 3 - Franchised: 16 - Franchise Fee: $9,500-$25,000 - Royalty: 3% first year; 4% second year; 5% cap years 3-10 - Total Inv: $15,000-$150,000 - Financing: No.

GEEKS ON CALL

Geeks on Call America

814 Kempsville Rd, $106, Norfolk, VA, 23502. - Tel: (757) 466-3448, (888) 667-4577, Fax: (757) 466-3457, E-Mail: info@geeksoncall.com, Web Site: www.geeksoncall.com. On-site computer solutions. Established: 1999 - Franchising Since: 2001 - No. of Units: Company Owned: 1 - Franchised: 2 - Franchise Fee: $20,000 - Royalty: 8.5% - Total Inv: $32,000-$57,000 - Financing: Yes.

GREAT AMERICAN INTERNET CORPORATION (GAIC)

8380 Miramar Mall, #234, San Diego, CA, 92121. Contact: Joel Pollock - Tel: (888) 563-4242, Web Site: www.GAICHQ.com. GAIC handles every aspect of the day to day operations of your adult superstore - including 24 hour credit card processing, accounts receivables, customer service, site maintenance and hosting, shipping/handleing, product selection, merchandise warehousing, and all licensing requirements. Established: 1998 - No. of Units: Company Owned: 2 - Franchised: 200 - Franchise Fee: $495.00.

I.M.B.C.

Interactive Media Broadcasting Company

25820 Southfield Rd., Ste. 201, Southfield, MI, 48075. Contact: Franchise Dept. - Tel: (248) 559-1415, Fax: (248) 557-7931. Franchise network of broadcasting associates. Provides interactive audio entertainment through the internet. Established: 1996 - Franchising Since: 1997 - No. of Units: Company Owned: 1 - Franchised: 1 - Franchise Fee: $62,000 - Royalty: $5,000 per month - Total Inv: $100,000 - Financing: Limited.

IC SOLUTIONS, INC.

9800 Centre Parkway, Ste.800, Houston, TX, 77036-8223. - Tel: (713) 773-1200, Fax: (713) 773-1411. Internet web service and telecommunications business. Business to business marketing. Focus on effective web site design and marketing applications. No computer experience required. Established: 1997 - Franchising Since: 1997 - No. of Units: Company Owned: 1 - Franchised: 10 - Franchise Fee: $7,500-$25,000 - Royalty: 6%, no adv. - Total Inv: $30,000-$45,000 - Financing: No. At the present time not offering franchises.

INACOM CORP.
Valmont Industries, Inc.
150 Hembree Park Dr, Roswell, GA, 30076-3873. Contact: Franchise Director - Tel: (402) 894-2198. Sale of IBM and Compaq personal computers, peripherals, software, training and classes. Established: 1981 - Franchising Since: 1982 - No. of Units: Company Owned: 51 - Franchised: 75 - Franchise Fee: $20,000 - Total Inv: $150,000-$250,000 - Royalty: 8%.

INTEGRITY ONLINE INTERNATIONAL
P.O Box 12467, Jackson, MS, 39236-2467. - Tel: (503) 649-3001 (800) 585-6603. Franchising opportunities to set up and run filtered internet service. Established: 1996 - Franchising Since: 1997 - No. of Units: Franchised: 70 - Franchise Fee: $15,000-$35,000 - Royalty: 7% of gross revenue, 3% advertising fee - Total Inv: $56,000-$250,000 - Financing: No.

KLICKKRAZY
The Super Sites
1325 S. Kihei Rd., #218, Kihei, HI, 96753. Contact: Greg Koestering - Tel: (808) 891-1269, (877) 891-1269, Fax: (808) 874-4964. Custom web building. Established: 1997 - Franchising Since: 2000 - No. of Units: Company Owned: 1 - Franchise Fee: $26,000 - Total Inv: $45,000 - Financing: Yes.

LAPTOP TRAINING SOLUTIONS
DAT, Inc.
8690 Aero Dr., Ste. 101, San Diego, CA, 92123. Contact: Franchise Department - Tel: (858) 616-6922, Fax: (858) 616-6401. Computer training. Established: 1998 - Franchising Since: 1999 - No. of Units: Comnpany Owned: 2 - Franchised: 5 - Franchise Fee: $55,000 - Total Inv: $75,000-$100,000 - Financing: Yes.

LASERQUIPT
Laserquipt International ltd.
4870 12th Ave E., Shakopee, MN, 55379. Contact: Franchising Dept. - Fax: (952) 496-3200. Independent service organization that provides service and supplies for laser printer users. In addition, we sell, rent and lease laser printers. Established; 1989 - Franchising Since: 1995 - No. of Units: Company Owned: 1 - Franchised: 2 - Franchise Fee: $35,000 - Royalty: 10% - Total Inv: $35,000 fran. fee, $20,000 inven., $40,000 capital - Financing: None.

MUSIC VENDING INC.
P.O. Box 816759, Hollywood, FL, 33081-0759. Contact: V.P., Fran. - Tel: (800) 585-3269. Automated video jukebox that vends CDs, cassettes, concert tickets, and phone cards. Established: 1993 - Franchising Since: 1995 - No. of Units: Franchised: 2 - Franchise Fee: $26,000 - Royalty: $1,000 per mo. or $50 per machine - Total Inv: $377,000 - Financing: No. NOT FRANCHISING AT THIS TIME.

MYCITY.COM
169 E. Flagler St., 2nd Floor, Miami, FL, 33131. Contact; Chuck Woolweaver, VP Franchising Development - Tel: (305) 531-7139 (800) 4MY- CITY   Fax: (305) 531-7139, Web Site: www.mycity.com/ www.mywebkit.com. Online city guides for every city in the U.S. Established: 1996 - Franchising Since: 2000 - No. of Units: Company Owned: 2 - Franchised: 2 - Franchise Fee: $27,500 - Royalty: None - Total Inv: $40,000, franchise fee - $27,500 + $12,500 training and misc - Financing: No.

NETSPACE
2801 N.E. 208th Terrace, 2nd Floor, Miami, FL, 33180. - Tel: (305) 931-4000, Fax: (305) 931-7772. Work with companies to increase their sales, lower their costs and improve customer servcice by using the internet. Established: 1997 - Franchising Since: 2001 - No. of Units: Franchised: 10 - Franchise Fee: $35,000.

NEXTWAVE COMPUTERS *
1825 Tamiami Trail Unit B-3, Port Charlotte, FL, 33948. - Tel: (877) 734-+5800, Fax: (941) 764-0094, E-Mail: info@nextwavecomputer.com, Web Site: www.nextwavecomputers.com. Computer hardware services and repair. Established: 1999 - Franchising Since: 2003 - No. of Units: Company Owned: 1 - Franchise Fee: $25,000 - Royalty: 5% - Total Inv: $76,000-$125,000 - Financing: No.

NOVA E-COMMERCE COUNTIES, INC
Nova Media, Inc
1724 N. State, Big Rapids, MI, 49307. - Tel: (231) 796-4637, E-Mail: trund@nov.com, Web Site: www.nov.com. Units of counties across the USA starting with the established ones in Michigan, shall be offered for e-commerce use on the internet. Established: 1981 - Franchising Since: 1999 - No. of Units: Company Owned: 1 - Franchised: 1 - Franchise Fee: $5,000 down - Royalty: Depends on population - Total Inv: $50,000 - Financing: $45,000.

NOVA MEDIA MULTI MEDIA INTERNET SHOP™
Nova Media Inc.
1724 N. State, Big Rapids, MI, 49307-9073. Contact: Mktg. Mgr. - Tel: (231) 796-4637, E-Mail: Trund@nov.com, Web Site: www.nov.com. Multi media presentation development and design that combines audio, including music and voice, graphics, photo and other images on internet for printers, resume counselors, employment agencies and placement companies plus recording studios. Established: 1981 - No. of Units: Company Owned: 1 - Franchised: 1 - Dealership Fee: $20,000 - Royalty: 5% - Total Inv: $75,000-$300,000 incl. equip. & work. cap. - Financing: Yes, plus leasing.

NOVA REALTY, INC
1724 N. State, Big Rapids, MI, 49307. Contact: Arne Rundquist, Sales - Tel: (231) 796-4637, Fax: (231) 592-9802, Web Site: www.nov.com. Listing service of owner representation listing service independent of normal channels in Michigan just on the internet. Established: 1981 - Franchising Since: 1999 - No. of Units: Company Owned: 1 - Franchised: 1 - Franchise Fee: $5,000 - Royalty: Dependent on situation - Total Inv: $50,000 - Financing: Varies.

PC PARAMEDIC COMPUTER REPAIR
7056 Beracassa Way, #208, Boca Raton, FL, 33433. - Tel: (561)750-7879, (888)PC1-2345, Fax: (561) 750-9872. Providing emergency computer repair service, either on-site or in-house. Fully turn-key package including training, authorizations and national accounts. Established: 1989 - Franchising Since: 1995 - No. of Units: Company Owned: 2 - Franchise Fee: Call for details - Financing: Yes.

PCHUT.COM
PCHut.com, Inc
4619 Emerald St #B, Boise, ID, 83706-2051. Contact: Rod Russell - Tel: (205) 580-2574, Fax: (208) 580-2001. Retailing technology products. Established: 1997 - Franchising Since: 1998 - No. of Units: Company Owned: 5 - Franchise Fee: $4,000-$185,000 - Total Inv: $15,000-$500,000 - Financing: Yes.

PLANET CASH
Planet Cash LLC
1861 Craig Rd, St. Louis, MO, 63146. Contact; John Clark, Franchise Sales Manager - Tel: (214) 205-2227, (888) 887-9595, Fax: (314) 205-0300, E-Mail: franchise@planetcash.biz, Web Site: www.planetcash.biz. The franchise offered is for the retail operation of business providing high-quality Internet access service along with related services to the general public. Depending on the type of service for which a customer contracts, you may elect to offer a rebate as a marketing incentive, although you are not required to do so, our customers tend to favor our "high spped cash rebate program". Established: 2001 - Franchising Since: 2002 - No. of Units: Company Owned: 12 - Franchise Fee: $30,000 - Royalty: 8% + 1% marketing - Total Inv: $151,800-$214,100 - Financing: No.

POWERPLAYUSA
PowerPlayUSA, LLC
108A S. Catalina Ave, Redondo Beach, CA, 90277. Contact: Chris P. Cladis, CEO - Tel: (310) 406-0256, Fax: (310) 406-0497, E-Mail: chris@powerplayusa.com, Web Site: www.powerplayusa.com. All-inclusive, plug-a-play PC Gaming systems with complete Control Module, Point of Sale, Accounting, various payment schemes etc. The first such PC Gaming business. Worldwide coverage. Established: 2002 - Franchising Since: 2002 - No. of Units: Company Owned: 3 - Franchised: 3 - Franchise Fee: $28,500 - Royalty: 2.5% - Total Inv: $125,000 - Financing: Yes.

PRODUCTIVITY POINT INTERNATIONAL
Global Training Network
15 Salt Creek Ln., Suite 421, Hinsdale, IL, 60521. Contact: Ralph Loberger - Tel: (800) 848-0980, Fax: (630) 920-0986. Computer training and related services. Established: 1982 - Franchising Since: 1990 - No. of Units: Company Owned: 1 - Franchised: 111 - Franchise Fee: $30,000, $300,000-$400,000 capital requirement - Financing: Yes.

QUIK INTERNET
Quik International
170 E. 17th St., Suite 101, Costa Mesa, CA, 92627. Contact: Murray Mead, CEO - Tel: (949) 548-2171, (800) 784-5266, Fax: (949) 548-0569, E-Mail: murray@quik.com, Web Site: www.quik.com. The only internet franchise offering local sales and service that is worldwide. Franchisees sell access, web sites, all internet services and offer free customer training. Established: 1996 - Franchising Since: 1996 - No. of Units: Franchised: 240 - Franchise Fee: $35,000 - Royalty: 10% - Total Inv: $55,000 - Financing: No.

RADIO SHACK
300 West 3rd St., Suite 1600, Ft. Worth, TX, 76102. - Tel: (817) 415-3381, Fax: (817) 415-3809. Retail consumer electronics. Established: 1922 - No. of Units: Company Owned: 4,835 - Franchised: 2,246.

RESCUECOM
2560 Burnet Ave., Syracuse, NY, 13208. - Tel: (800) RES-CUE7, (800) 737-2837, Fax: (315) 433-5228, Web Site: www.rescuecom.com. Computer sales. Established: 1997 - Franchising Since: 1998 - No. of Units: Company Owned: 3 - Franchised: 1 - Franchise Fee: $1,490-$18,800 - Royalty: 18% - Total Inv: $43,000-$61,000 - Financing: Yes.

REZCITY.COM
Rezconnect Technologies, Inc.
560 Sylvan Ave, Englewood Cliffs, NY, 07632. Contact: Michael Brent - Tel: (201) 567-8500, (800) 609-9000, Fax: (201) 567-3265, E-Mail: mbrent@rexcity.com, Web Site: www.rezcity.biz. Your city and 50,000 others offering on-line local city guides and on-line travel stores featuring rexconnect... Reserve, Confirm & Schedule appointments on-line. Established: 1982 - Franchising Since: 2002 - No. of Units: Company Owned: 1 - Franchise Fee: $1000 for 25,000 pop - Total Inv: $3,000-$7,000.

ROUND 2 COMPUTERS
801 S. Greenville Ave., #117, Allen, TX, 75002. - Tel: (972) 359-6633, Fax: (972) 727-1615. Used hardware and software on consignment. Established: 1987 - Franchising Since: 2002 - No. of Units: Company Owned: 1 - Franchise Fee: $23,000 - Financing: No.

SCREENZ COMPUTING CENTERS *
2717 N. Clark St., Chicago, IL, 60614. - Tel: (773) 296-0300, Fax: (773) 296-0971, Web Site: www.screenz.com. Screenz is a successful chain of neighborhood computing and print centers. We specialize in making out-of-home office computing and internet access simple. Our customers have access to state-of-the-art hardware and software to help them accomplish any computer-related project they wish. Established: 1996 - Franchising Since: 2004 - No. of Units: Company Owned: 3 - Franchise Fee: $30,000 - Royalty: 6% - Total Inv: $229,000-$473,480.

SIMPLY LAPTOPS AND NERDS ON DEMAND
World Vision Franchising Corp.
4830 N. 16th St, Phoenix, AZ, 85016. Contact: Franchise Department - Tel: (888) 547-NERD, Fax: (602) 287-8991, Web Site: www.simplylaptops.com, or www.nerdsondemand.com. Broad market potential with simply laptops specializing in selling, buying + trading new, pre-owned + refurbished laptops + accessories. Nerds On Demand is three profit centers, (1) in-store express PC computer repair + upgrades, (2) poduct reseller, (3) mobile repair service. Established: 1996 - Franchising Since: 1998 - No. of Units: 1 - Franchise Fee: $29,500 - Total Inv: Capital $134,050 - initial $184,000 - Financing: Financing guidance with lending sources.

SISNA FRANCHISE COMPANY
265 E. 100 South Ste. 255, Salt Lake City, UT, 84111. - Tel: (877) 472-1916, Web Site: www.sisna.com. Wholesale and retail internet services. Established: 1993 - Franchising Since: 1996 - No. of Units: Company Owned: 1 - Franchised: 35 - Franchise Fee: $10,000-$25,000 - Financing: No.

SOFTWARE CITY
26 Franklin St, Tenafly, NJ, 07670-2000. - Tel: (201) 569-8900. Offers computers, software and peripherals to business accounts, school systems and government agencies. Established: 1980 - Franchising Since: 1982 - No. of Units: Franchised: 20 - Franchise Fee: $500.00 - Royalty: 1.5% of gross sales on orders processed by franchisee, and 25% of gross profits on each order secured by franchisee processed through Software City's web site - Total Inv: $10,500-$59,500.

TECHNO NERDS, INC
710 West Colonial Dr., Suite 205, Orlando, FL, 32804. - Tel: (877) 99N-ERDS, (407) 650-9292, Fax: (407) 650-0042. Computer, network & web sales and services. Established: 1997 - No. of Units: Company owned: 1 - Franchise Fee: $25,000.

THE BEST IN YOUR TOWN.COM
2293 E. Quiet Canyon Dr, Tucsan, AZ, 85718. George Kimble - Tel: (520) 877-3867, (716) 398-0099, Fax: (520) 877-3867. Local internet advertising franchise. Established: 1999 - No. of Units: Company Owned: 3 - Franchise Fee: $7,500-$22,500 - Total Inv: $50,000.

US ONLINE
US OnLine Franchise Corp.
1202 Laurel Oak Rd., Voorhees, NJ, 08043-4318. Contact: Pete Capriotti, V.P. - Tel: (609) 778-8383, (800) 570-8765, Fax: (609) 231-8898, E-Mail: franchiseinfo@uscom.com, Web Site: www.uscom.com. US OnLine offers an exciting internet franchise opportunity with web site design, hosting web site marketing, network design, software development and internet training. Established: 1995 - No. of Units: Company Owned: 27 - Franchised: 13 - Franchise Fee: $20,000-$60,000 - Royalty: Profit sharing - Total Inv: $65,000-$325,000 - Financing: Yes.

VIDEO SURVEILLANCE SYSTEMS
Cecon Inc
P.O. Box 463, Lilburn, GA, 30048. Contact: David Boels - Tel: (770) 717-8286, (800) 937-9974, Fax: (770) 717-5684. Sales/installation video security systems. Established: 1998 - Franchising Since: 2000 - No. of Units: Company Owned: 1 - Franchise Fee: $35,000 - Total Inv: $130,000.

ZAIO.COM
93 Center Pointe Drive, St. Charles, MO, 63304. Contact: Dennis Fuller, Regional V.P. - Tel: (636) 447-4429, (877) 233-9563, Fax: (636) 498-0923, E-Mail: franchise@zaio.com, Web Site: www.zaio.com. Internet based provider of digital photographs to the real estate, banking and insurance industries. Established: 1999 - Franchising Since: 2000 - No. of Units: Franchised: 1 - Franchise Fee: $15,000 - Total In: $30,000 - Financing: Third party financing available.

ZLAND.COM
ZLand, Inc
27081 Aliso Creek Rd., Aliso Viejo, CA, 92656-3399. Contact: Stephanie Dela Torre, Dir. Franchise Leasing - Tel: (949) 544-4000, (800) 337-2342, Fax: (949) 544-4001, E-Mail: franchise@zland.com, Web Site: www.zland.com. Z Land develops and markets a suite of internet-enabled business solutions for small and mid-sized businesses. Our products help clients operate their business more efficiently, save money, and transact more business. Established: 1995 - Franchising Since: 1998 - No. of Units: Company Owned: 5 - Franchised: 35 - Franchise Fee: $30,000 - Total Inv: $150,000.

• Check out our On-Line Listings: •
www.infonews.com

CONSUMER BUYING SERVICES

UCC TOTALHOME
UCC TotalHome, Inc
8450 Broadway, Merrillville, IN, 46410. Contact: Director of Franchise Development - Tel: (219) 736-1100, (800) 827-6400, Fax: (219) 755-6208, E-Mail: dbowen@ucctotalhome.com, Web Site: www.ucctotalhome.com/franchising. UCC TotalHome enables members to avoid traditional store markups and purchase from an unprecedented selection of quality merchandise direct from more than 700 brand name manufacturers and their authorized suppliers. Franchisees enroll members through our time-tested marketing system and service these members with support from moree than 190 professionals at the Corporate Support Center. Established: 1971 - Franchising Since: 1972 - No. of Units: Company Owned: 9 - Franchised: 79 - Franchise Fee: $55,000 - Royalty: 22% - Total Inv: $105,000-$237,000 - Financing: Up to $40,000.

UNIWAY MANAGEMENT CORP.
5182-A Old Dixie Hwy, Forest Park, GA, 30297. Contact: Robert C. Hardy, Pres./CEO - Tel: (404) 363-6200, Fax: (404)363-8848. Buying service - Uniway members have access to over 600 major manufacturers, furniture, appliances, carpet and other merchandise for in and around the home. Members may order merchandise through Uniway at Uniway's cost. Established: 1972 - No. of Units: Company Owned: 1 - Franchised: 13 - Franchise Fee: $25,000-$50,000 - Royalty: 8%-11% on membership gross sales - Total Inv: $75,000-$100,000 - Financing: N/A.

DATING SERVICES

CALCULATED COUPLES
4839 E. Greenway Rd., #183, Scottsdale, AZ, 85254. Contact: David E. Gorman, President - Tel: (800)44-MATCH, Web Site: www.cupid help.com. Singles matchmaking party business. Part time okay. All cash business. Established: 1983 - Licensing Since: 1987 - No. of Units: Company Owned: 6 - Licensed: 9 - License Fee: $495 - Royalty: None - Total Inv: $495 - Financing: No.

IT'S JUST LUNCH FRANCHISE LLC
919 Fourth Ave, Suite 2500, San Diego, CA, 92101. Contact: Irene LaCota - Tel: (619) 234-7200, Fax: (619) 234-8500, Web Site: www.itsjustlunch.com. Dating service for busy professionals. We set singles up on lunch dates, minimizing the stress of the first date. Established: 1992 - Franchising Since: 2000 - No. of Units: Company Owned: 5 - Franchised: 30 - Franchise Fee: $25,000 - Royalty: 9% - Total Inv: $77,000+ - Financing: No.

LUNCH COUPLES OF AMERICA
51 Morton St, Needham, MA, 02194. Contact: Mary Ann Siersdale, President - Tel: (781) 455-7164. Dating service for single people. Established: 1983 - Franchising Since: 1985 - No. of Units: Company Owned: 1 - Franchised: 4 - Franchise Fee: $12,900 - Total Inv: $16,000 - Financing: No.

SINGLE SEARCH GLOBAL
13176 N. Dale Mabry Ste. 305, Tampa, FL, 33618. Contact: Lisa Bentsen - Tel: (813) 264-1705, (800) 779-8362, Fax: (603) 754-5271, E-Mail: singles@singlesearch.com, Web Site: www.singlesearch.com. Matchmaking and Dating Service for singles seeking compatibility in relationships. Exclusive territories available worldwide beginning at $1,500 US. Financing available. Established: 1988 - Franchising Since: 1994 - No. of Units: Company Owned: 125 - Franchised: 245 - Franchise Fee: $40 per month - Royalty: None - Total Inv: $1,500-$5,500 US - Financing: Yes.

DISTRIBUTORS

ADHESIVE ENGINEERING & SUPPLY
AE & S, Inc.
P.O. Box 2449-11 New Zealand Rd., Seabrook, NH, 03874. - Tel: (603) 474-3070, (800) 888-GLUE, Fax: (603) 474-2750. Industrial distribution of product assembly adhesives, application and curing equipment. Established: 1987 - Franchising Since: 1994 - No. of Units: Company Owned: 1 - Franchised: 2 - Franchise Fee: $30,000 - Royalty: 6% on adhesives and equipment - Total Inv: $35,000-$100,000 depending on inventory and location - Financing: None.

AGI SOFTWARE
Amerasia Group, Inc.
P.O. Box 53114, Indianapolis, IN, 46253. Contact; Ben Yanto Jr., Pres. - Tel: (317) 299-8827. Specializing in shareware and public domain programs for IBM, Apple, Commodore and Mac computers. The economy software store. Established: 1987 - Distributing Since: 1989 - No. of Units: Company Owned: 2 - Distributed: 6 - Franchise Fee: $500 - Royalty: None - Total Inv: $2,000 + fran. fee - Financing: $500 down, $2,500 payable in 10 months.

AIRFLO
Hankins Marketing Corp
P.O. Box 1681, Salisbury, NC, 28145-1681. - Tel: (704) 637-3589, Fax:(704) 639-0379. According to the American Medical Association 'aching feet is America's # 1 medical complaint". The airflo insole is a breakthrough in foot comfort because it allows air to enter the insole when the foot is lifted and gradually releases as you step down, airflo master distributors place airflo in retail stores and store chains and earn $57.60 royalty on each order plus $51.00 retail profit on each dozen. The MD start-up package is only $65.00. Established: 1988 - No. of Distributors: 11,000 - Franchise Fee: $65.00 - Royalty: $57.60 on each order - Total Inv: $65.00 - Financing: No.

ALL STAR CARTS & VEHICLES
1565 Fifth Industrial Court, Bayshore, NY, 11706. Contact: Robert Kronrad, Vice President - Tel: (631) 666-5252, Fax: (631) 666-1319. Manufacturing of modular food & merchandising kiosks, vending trailers, trucks and carts. Established: 1971 - Offering Distributorships Since: 1971 - No. of Units: Company Owned: 80 - Distributors: 500 - Total Inv: Starting at $1,495 - Financing: On trucks only.

ALOE SHOPPE
Nature's Choice
1645 South East Third Court, Deerfield Beach, FL, 33441. Contact: Larry Frates - Tel: (954) 571-7001, (800) 322-2563, Fax: (954) 571-7009, (305) 418-7431, Web Site: www.natureschoicealoe.com. Carts and kiosks, retail store and wholesale routes. Established: 1982 - Offering Distributorships Since: 1982 - No. of Units: Company Owned: 1 - Total Inv: $5,000-$10,000 - Financing: No.

AMAVEND VENDING SYSTEMS
Dept. Av., Ste. A, P.O. Box 24, Fayetteville, AR, 72702. Contact: Henry K.U.A. Nwauwa, Pres. - Tel: (501) 443-6791, Fax: (501) 443-4024. Vending and amusement machines. Business opportunity and distributorships for individuals and companies. Guaranteed financing with our secured lease program. Publisher of the guides to coin-operated businesses. Established: 1987 - Franchising Since: 1989 - No. of Units: Company Owned: 2 - Franchise Fee: None - Royalty: 0% for independent units, 5% for licensed units - Total Inv: $6,000 (min.) - Financing: Yes, guaranteed financing (secured lease), regular leasing program available.

AMERVEND CORPORATION
4101 S.W. 73 Avenue, Miami, FL, 33155. - Tel: (305) 264-6060, (800) 780-9274, Fax: (305) 264-0850. Vendor and distributor of commercial laundry equipment. Central and South America and the Caribbean can profit from our expertise in having built over 1,000 coin laundry and dry cleaning stores. Smart Card technology too. Established:1959 - Distributing Since: 1959.

AMI PIZZA WHOLESALE

176 Thompson Ln Ste 210, Nashville, TN, 37211-2468. Contact: Don Hunt, CEO - Tel: (615) 259-2629, Fax: (615) 259-2873. A wholesale pizza distributorship that provides a fresh dough pizza program. Established: Started in pizza wholesale business in 1962.

AQUAPURA CORPORATION, THE

24 Desiree Dr., Greenwich, CT, 06830. Contact: James Iorio, Pres. - Tel: (203) 661-6064. Manufacture and sell home water purifiers direct to the consumer and commercial end users through independent distributors. Established: 1976 - Offering Distributorships Since: 1979 - No. of Distributors: 18 - Inv: $4,500.

ASUKA CORPORATION

7800 River Rd. N. Bergen, NJ, 07047. Contact: Roy Kanda, Pres. - Tel: (201) 861-5450. Direct importer of pearl oysters from its own factory in Japan. Distribute throughout the USA and other countries. Pearl home parties, fairs, jewelry stores, etc. are main outlets. Established: 1979 - Offering Distributorships Since: 1979 - Total Inv: $2,500-$3,000 - Financing: No.

ATLANTIC MOWER PARTS & SUPPLIES, INC.

13421 S.W. 14th Place, Ft. Lauderdale, FL, 33325. Contact: Robert J. Bettelli, Pres. - Tel: (954) 474-4942, Fax: (954) 475-0414, E-Mail: www.ampsone@bellsouth.net. Whole sale outdoor power equipment parts. Established: 1978 - Franchising Since: 1988 - No. of Units: Franchised: 10 - Franchise Fee: $15,900 - Royalty: 5% - Total Inv: $50,000 - Financing: None.

AUTHENTIC LOG HOMES CORP.

P.O. Box 1288, Laramie, WY, 82073. Contact: James O. Davis, President - Tel: (307) 742-3786, Fax: (307)742-8536. We manufacture log home kits. Reseal, restore, and repair, existing log homes. Established: 1973.

AVANTI VENDING MACHINES

1698 Market St #123, Redding, CA, 96001-1021. Contact: Phil Scrima, Pres. - Tel: (800) 541-7943, (916) 244-8070. Sell full line vending machines. (Also, small machines,counter tops, etc.) Snacks, soft drink, hot bev., cold food etc. Established: 1974 - Financing: Yes.

BLACK MAGIC CHIMNEY SWEEPS, INT'L.

Haldorn & Mann, Inc./Black Magic Supply
21 New Street, Cambridge, MA, 02138. - Tel: (617) 876-4456. Training and equipment to get started in the business of chimney sweeping and flue technology. Established: 1978 - Total Inv: $2,500 - Financing: No.

BOSCO JEWELERS INC.

6344 Linn Ave., N.E., Albuquerque, NM, 87108. Contact: Warren, Cindy or Antoinette - Tel: (800) 545-6262, Fax: (505)265-4003. Jewelry wholesale, Southwestern contemporary gold and silver sales booklets provided and displays are available. Fast order processing through our toll free 800 number. Established: 1979 - Distributing Since: 1979 - No. of Units: Company Owned: 1 - Distributorships: 2,900 - Total Inv: $375 starting inventory recommended - Financing: Visa/MC.

BUTLER LEARNING SYSTEMS

Butler Associates Inc.
1325 W. Dorothy Lane, Dayton, OH, 45409. Contact: Bob Butler, President - Tel: (937) 298-7462, Fax: (937) 298-5022, E-Mail: butler@butler-learning.com, Web Site: www.butler-learning.com. Audio visual training program for supervisors, managers, all workers and sales professionals. Sell programs and/or hold seminars for all organizations. Established: 1959 - Distributing Since: 1975 - No. of Units: Company Owned: 1 - Distributed: 55 - Fee: Inventory - under $500 - Royalty: 10% - Approx. Inv: $10,000 for working cap. - Financing: No.

CALIDO CHILE TRADERS

Calido Chile Traders Systems Inc.
5360 Merriam Dr., Merriam, KS, 66203. Contact: John Shannon, Pres. - Tel: (913) 384-0019, (800) 783-4857, Fax: (913) 432-5880. Southwestern-style retail store which carries salsas, spices, and cookware. We now offer trademark licensing which is renewable every year. Established: 1993 - Franchising Since: 1994 - No. of Units: Company Owned: 4 - Franchised: 32 - Franchise Fee: $25,000 - Royalty: 5% - Total Inv: $125,850-$225,000 - Financing: Assistance in preparation for financing.

CANDLEFUN

3850 Wind Drift Dr E Apt 20, Indianapolis, IN, 46254-3229. - Tel: (317) 299-2050. Candle carving equipment and training. Established: 1999 - Franchising Since: 2000 - Total Inv: $4,000.

CARL'S SEASONING

Carl's Seasoning
P.O. Box 51, Eagleville, TN, 37060. Contact: Franchise Director - Tel: (615) 274-2277, Fax: (615) 274-2899. Distributor of food seasoning. Established: 1990 - No. of Units: Company Owned: 1 - Distributors: 16 - Franchise Fee: Inventory only - Royalty: None - Total Inv: $5,000-$8,000 - Financing: No.

CARS ON LINE

WebKrafters
P.O. Box 537, Menomonee Falls, WI, 53052. Contact: Larry Kolb, President - Tel: (414) 628-0883, Fax: (414) 628-2195. Classic auto site on the Internet. Established: 1993.

CHEM-MARK INTERNATIONAL

635 E. Chapman Ave., P.O. Box 1126, Orange, CA, 92666. Contact: Darol Carlson, Pres. - Tel: (714) 633-8560. Food service equipment. Low energy dishwashing machine, bar glass brushes, swing-mark valves, chemicals, air cleaners. Established: 1959 - Distributing Since: 1964 - No. of Units: Company Owned: 1 - Distributorships: 83 - Total Inv: Under $10,000 - Royalty: 25 cents per month per Swing-mark valve - Financing: No.

CHISHOLM TRAIL BUILDERS

P.O. Box 335, San Marcos, TX, 78667. Contact: Floyd MacKenzie, Treasurer - Tel: (830) 629-1400, Fax: (512) 353-5333. Country and rustic homes, preformed and partially factory built modular homes. Established: 1986 - Distributing Since: 1987 - No. of Units: Company Owned: 1- Royalty: $300 month fixed fee -Total Inv: Approx. $20,000 cost of home - Financing: No.

CLOSET CLASSICS

Windquest Companies, Inc
3311 Windquest Dr., Holland, MI, 49424. Contact: Adam Breit, Nat'l. Sales Mgr. - Tel: (800) 562-4257, (616) 399-3311, Fax: (616) 399-8784, E-Mail: adamb@windquestco.com, Web Site: www.windquestco.com. Dealer based business. Sell and install custom closet systems, wall beds, home office and storage utilization products using components supplied by Closet Classics. Premium quality, construction and service. Established: 1984 - Offering Dealerships Since: 1986 - No. of Units: Company Owned: 155 - Total Inv: $10,000-$15,000 - Financing: Yes.

COLOR-PRO

Tech Systems Inc.
36 Tuttle Dr, Acton, MA, 01720-2830. Contact: Ronald Stoll, V.P., Mktg. - Tel: (617) 561-0400, (800) 447-6646, Fax: (770) 399-5329. These full color printing systems produce sublimation transfers for T-shirts, caps, jackets, bumper stickers, pennants, metal, plastic, wood, leather, and most other materials. This opportunity puts you in a 3 billion dollar industry for ad specialities, premium incentives, imprinted sportswear, awards/trophy, non-profit organizations, signage, and custom gift items. Training in Los Angeles, Boston and Chicago. Established: 1987 - Distributing Since: 1988 - No. of Units: Company Owned: 12 - Distributed: 622 - Royalty: None - Total Inv: $3,550 cash on lease with option to buy equipment - Financing: Yes.

COLOR/MATCH

AAA Dye and Chemicals Co.
1872 Del Amo Blvd., Ste. C, Torrance, CA, 90501. Contact: Don David, Mktg. Dir. - Tel: (310) 618-1165, (800) 228-3240, Fax: (310) 618-1727. Carpet dyeing, restoration of original color or new color conversions. Training with manual, on-site and video. Support after training with technical assistance, marketing and co-op advertising. Established: 1979 - Offering Distributorships Since: 1984 - Total Inv: $1,000-$25,000 - Financing: Yes.

COMPLETESEAL FABRIC PROTECTION

P.O. Box 700149, San Antonio, TX, 78270. Contact: Chris Amundsen, Pres. - Tel: (210) 545-3376, E-Mail: compseal@texas.net, Web Site: www.completeseal.com. Completeseal textile protection fluid guards against permanent staining from most water born and oil based solutions.

Also guards against mildewing, sun fading, flame spread, and reduces smoke density. CompleteSeal protective seal last for at least two years and is maintained in an alternative less damaging cleaning methods. Established: 1977. CompleteSeal is a business opportunity.

CREDIT PLUS CARD
American Security Financial Corp.
4132 Shoreline Dr., Ste. J, Earth City, MO, 63045. Contact: John Weigel, Pres - Tel: (314) 344-1111, Web Site: www.creditplus card.com. Provide consumers with Credit Plus card which includes an initial $2,500-$5000 credit line, $2000 merchandise check, everyone is approved, no credit rejects. Dealers earn $100 per card issued. Established: 1977 - Offering Since: 1977 - No. of Units: 851 - Total Inv: $495 - Financing: Yes.

CURBMATE CORP.
111 E. 5600 S., #222, Salt Lake City, UT, 84107. - Tel: (801) 262-7509, Fax: (801) 269-1268. Produces continuous concrete landscape edging for lawns and flower beds. Excellent cash flow business. No experience necessary. Established: 1983 - Distributing Since: 1983 - No. of Units: Distributed: 700 - Fee: $5,495 for the curbmate machine - Financing: Leasing.

CUTLERY SPECIALTIES
22 Morris Lane, Great Neck, NY, 11024-1707. Contact: Dennis Blaine, Owner - Tel: (516) 829-5899, Fax: (516) 773-8076, E-Mail: Dennis13@aol.com, Web Site: www.restorationproduct.com. U.S Agent/ Distributor of "Renaissance-wax/polish" and other highend restoration products used by museums, galleries, professionals and collectors worldwide! Established: 1993.

D.J. GILL ASSOCIATES, INC.
P.O. Box 591, 1595 Imperial Way, Unit 114, Thorofare, NJ, 08086-0591. Contact: Don Gill, Pres - Tel: (856) 384-0440, Fax: (856) 384-0044, E-Mail: sales@gillassociates.com, Web Site: www.thevendor schoice.com. Sales and distribution of all types of vending machines. Coin-operated including snack, soda, gum, candy, toy machines, etc. Established: 1981 - Franchising Since: 1986 - No. of Units: Company Owned: 3 - Franchised: 15,000+ - Franchise Fee: None - Royalty: None - Total Inv: $500.00-$50,000 - Financing: Yes.

DELCO CLEANING SYSTEMS
Rahsco Manufacturing Co, Inc.
2513 Warfield, Ft. Worth, TX, 76106. Contact: Robert Hinderliter, Pres - Tel: (800) 433-2113, (817) 625-4213, Fax: (817) 625-2059. Mobile power wash operation. Clean cars, trucks, heavy equipment, exterior building restoration, kitchen vent hoods, airplanes and more. Video tape training, seminars, and schools. Established: 1973 - Total Inv: $1,000-$15,000 - Financing: No.

DISABLED DEALER MAGAZINE
Disabled Dealer Ent., Inc.
426 Island Cay Way, Apollo Beach, FL, 33572-2658. - Tel: (813) 645-0138, (800) 555-4036, E-Mail: disdeal@aol.com. Buy-Sell-Trade publication for people with disabilities. New and used medical equipment, wheelchair accessible vans, homes, scooters, wheelchairs, articles and events. Established: 1995 - Franchising Since: 1997 - No. of Units: Company Owned: 1 - Franchised: 4 - Franchise Fee: $15,000-$20,000 (joint venture fee) Royalty: Approx. 5% of gross sales - Total Inv: $20,000-$25,000 - Financing: Possible.

DURASTILL OF (LOCATION)
86 Reservoir Park Dr, Rockland, MA, 02370. - Tel: (781) 878-5577, Fax: (781) 878-2224. Premier manufacturer of drinking water purification systems. DURASTILL distillers boil the water and kill Cryptosporidium plus virtually all other water borne parasites, and also removes such undesirable contaminants as lead, copper cadmium, and nitrates. Durastill distillers are recognized world wide. Established:1969 - Offering Distributorships Since:1979 -Total Inv: $5,000 or less - Financing: None.

DYNAMIC DEVELOPMENT ASSOCIATES
381 Bridle Lane, P.O. Box 18, Media, PA, 19063. Contact: Bill Eggert, President - Tel: (610) 565-3860, Fax: (610) 565-5557. We equip and train new franchisees to be independent consultants and trainers. You can train and consult with all types and sizes of organizations. There are no geographic or financial restrictions. Established: 1969 - Franchising Since: 1969 - Total Inv: Less than $1000.

EASI
Energy Automation System, INC.
145 Anderson Lane, Hendersonville, TN, 37075. Contact: Debra Brown Director - Tel: (615) 847-8509, Fax: (615) 847-3885, E-Mail: eesp@easipro.com, Web Site: www.energysavingbusiness.com. EASI provides energy savings systems to industrial/commercial clients worldwide. Two business opportunities are available: Become an Affiliate and enjoy all the profits; Become a Sales Profressional at a significant commission. Established: 1978 - Distributing Since: 1986 - No. of Units: Distributed: 400 - Fee: $29,875-$39,875 - Financing: No.

ELEPHANT HOUSE INC
Elephant House Inc
3007 Longhorn Blvd., Suite 101, Austin, TX, 78758-7632. Contact: National Sales Director - Tel: (512) 339-3004, (800) 729-2273, Fax: (512) 339-7990, Web Site: www.elephanthouse.com. Home based franchise operating in your own protected territory supplying retail outlets with greeting cards. Established: 1995 - Franchising Since: 1995 - No. of Units: Company Owned: 1 - Franchised: 47 - Franchise Fee: $26,500 - Royalty: None - Total Inv: $25,000 - Financing: No.

END-A-FLAT TIRE SAFETY SEALANT
Endrust International
1155 Greenbriar Dr., Bethel Park, PA, 15102-2615. Contact: Gary B. Griser, V.P. - Tel: (412) 831-1255, Fax: (412) 833-3409. Sales of tire safety sealant. Established: 1980 - No. of Units: Franchised: 10 - Total Inv: $10,000 - Financing: Yes.

ESPRESSO ITALIA MARKETING
1301 N. Congress Ave., Ste. 410, Boynton Beach, FL, 33426. - Tel: (800) 565-6447, Fax: (561) 742-0905, Web Site: www.e-zespresso.com. Espresso Italia has been providing entrepreneurs the turn key solutions for sucess in this billion dollar coffee industry. From the finest machines and coffees from all over the world. Established: 2000 - Franchise Fee: $16,000.

FORD GUM & MACHINE COMPANY
18 Newton Ave., Akron, NY, 14001. Contact: George Stege, Pres. - Tel: (716) 542-4561, Fax: (716) 542-4610. Bulk vending operators. Company provides product and equipment. Machines sponsored by local charities. Established: 1934 - Offering Distributorships Since: 1939 - No. of Distributors: 187.

GLOBAL SECURITY PRODUCTS
662 S. Fulton St, Denver, CO, 80231. Contact; Sherri Kononov, V.P. - Tel: (303) 341-7276, (800) 824-7110, Fax: (303) 367-9962. Manufacturer and distributor of personal protection products including mace brand self defense sprays, stun guns, personal alarms, child protection products, pepper spray and cutlery. Established: 1980 .

GOLD MEDAL PRODUCTS
10700 Medallion Dr., Cincinnati, OH, 45241. - Tel: (513) 769-7676. Gold Medal is a full line concession manufacturer and distributor with dealers throughout the world. The products produced include popcorn machines, cotton candy machines, nacho equipment, snokone and shave ice equipment, hot dog cookers, pizza/pretzel equipment and much more. Established: 1931 - No. of Units: Company Owned: 8.

GOLDSTOCKS SPORTING GOODS
98 Freemans Bridge Rd., Scotia, NY, 12302-3507. Contact: H. Goldstock or Mike Kausch, Pres. - Tel: (518) 382-2030, Fax: (518) 382-2030. Distributorship for sports equipment to schools, teams, leagues, etc. No inventory necessary. Established: 1980 - Offering Distributorships Since: 1980 - No. of Distributors: 255 - Approx. Inv: $4,000 - Financing: No.

HAPPY & HEALTHY PRODUCTS INC.
1600 S. Dixie Hwy., #200, Boca Raton, FL, 33442. Contact: Susan Scotts - Tel: (800) 764-6114, Fax: (561) 368-5267, E-Mail: franchiseinfo @fruitfull.com, Web Site: www.fruitfull.com. A fun, flexible, full or part-time franchise that you can run from home and is available in three

levels of investment. Established: 1991 - Franchising Since: 1993 - No. of Units: Franchised: 90 - Franchise Fee: $20,500 or $24,000 depending upon level of investment - Total Inv: $34,562-$54,843 - Financing: No.

HERMAN'S WORLD OF SPORTS *
1055 Stewart Ave., #4, Bethpage, NY, 11714. - Tel: (516) 470-9000, Fax: (516) 470-9004, Web Site: www.hermansdirect.com. As a franchise owner in your community, you'll be able to uniform the little league team, outfit the leagues in your town, equip the local highschool, supply the local company with logo'd golf shirt and balls for that special golf event, or dress up the employees of your favorite restaurant. It's up to you, because as a franchise owner you can do it all. Established: 2000 - Franchising Since: 2003 - No. of Units: Franchised: 12 - Franchise Fee: $25,000 - Royalty: 6% - Total Inv: $75,000 - Financing: Third party.

HUB COMMUNICATIONS LTD.
36 Tuttle Dr, Acton, MA, 01720-2830. Contact: Ron Stoll, V.P. - Tel: (800) 447-6646, (617) 561-0400, Fax: (617) 569-2164. Coin operated public telephones. Smart phones, durable, and call back 800 service. Earn $ every time someone makes a call! Established: 1978 - Franchising Since: 1984 - No. of Units: Company Owned: 37 - Franchised: 11,000 phones - Franchise Fee: None - Total Inv: $1,700+ - Financing: Lease, if qualified. NOT FRANCHISING AT THIS TIME.

HUEBSCH COMMERCIAL LAUNDRY
Alliance Laundry Systems
Shepard St., P.O. Box 990, Ripon, WI, 54971-0990. - Tel: (920) 748-3121, (800) 553-5120, Fax: (920) 748-3121, E-Mail: sales@alliancels.com, Web Site: www.huebsch.com. Huebsch paves the way to enter the coin laundry business. We can assist you with site location, store layout & design, equipment and finance. Established: 1908 - Total Inv: Varies by location - Financing: Yes.

INKY DEW, LLC
7297 University Ave., La Mesa, CA, 91941-5927. Contact: Eileen Cummings, Pres. - Tel: (619) 465-9339, Fax: (619) 469-9371, Web Site: www.inkydew.com. Turn-key operation packages sold to re-ink and reload computer, cash register and calculator ribbons. Also, refill inkjet cartridges. Established: 1988 - Licensing Since: 1988 - No. of Units: Company Owned: 1 - Licensed: 60+ worldwide - Total Inv: $2,000 entry level or $10,000 comprehensive pkg. - Financing: Visa, MC, Discover.

INNOVATIVE MOVING SYSTEMS, INC.
P.O. Box 700169, Oostburg, WI, 53070. Contact: Elmer Hazen, Sales Mgr. - Tel: (920) 564-6272, (800) 619-0625, Fax: (920) 564-2322. Manufacture and distribute material handling equipment. Main product is the Lectro Truck, a battery powered stair climbing hand truck for powering loads up or down stairs, from trucks, docks, semis, etc. Established: 1973 - No. of Units: Distributors: 8 - Dealers: 144 - Total Inv: $5,000 for inv. and training.

INTERNATIONAL ENTERTAINMENT SYSTEMS (IES)
United Ventures, Inc.
4501 N. Route 12, Richmond, IL, 60071. Contact: A.H. Shambaugh, Sales Mgr. - Tel: (815) 675-2277. Manufacturer of large screen television systems, lecterns, screen stands, tv wall mounts and projector stands - supplier of motion picture equipment and film rental as an entertainment system. Established: 1971 - Franchising Since: 1972 - No. of Units: Company Owned: 1 - Dealers: 142 - Total Inv: $10,000 representative equipment inventory - Financing: Yes, both dealer and dealer's customer.

JET, INC.
750 Alpha Dr., Cleveland, OH, 44143. Contact: Sales Dept. - Tel: (440) 461-2000, Fax: (440) 442-9008. Manufacturer of home and commercial waste water treatment systems, pressure dosing systems, JET-CHLOR Tablet Chlorinators, JET-CHLOR, CHLOR-AWAY, BIO JET-7 and Air Seal Diffusers. Established: 1955 - Offering Distributorships Since: 1957 - Royalty: Varies with product - Total Inv: $10,000 for waste water treatment systems. None for other products - Financing: No.

KAMELEON INTERNATIONAL INC.
16018 SW Parker Road, Lake Oswego, OR, 97035. - Tel: (503) 699-8200, Fax: (503) 635-6383. Vending systems. Established: 1994 - Franchising Since: 1994 - No. of Units: Company Owned: 6 - Franchised: 14 - Franchise Fee: $250-$5,000 - Royalty: 3% - Total Inv: $10,000-$30,000 - Financing: No.

KEMPER INTERNATIONAL INC.
K.I.S.S. Corp.
20438 N.E. 15th Court, Miami, FL, 33179. Contact: Dennis Lamb or Bob Kemper, President/VP - Tel: (305) 653-3333, (305) 653-2940, E-Mail: antimic@aol.com. Safety - slip resistance on tubs and tile, flame retardant. Established: 1968 - Dealerships Since: 1992 - No. of Units: Company Owned: 1 - Dealerships: 10 - Total Inv: Depends on size desired - Financing: Yes.

KENSINGTON CANDLE COMPANY
P.O. Box 529, Bohemia, NY, 11716. - Tel: (631) 244-7293, (877) 463-1797, Fax: (631) 218-8149. High quality scented candles and other scented products as well as coordinating accessories. Established: 1998 - Franchising Since: 1999 - No. of Units: Company Owned: 1 - Franchised: 25 - Franchise Fee: Varies - Total Varies: Varies - Financing: None.

KUSTOM CARDS INT'L INC
1018 E Willow Grove Ae, Wyndmoor, PA, 19038-7938. Contact: Larry Callan, President - Tel: (215) 233-1678, (800) 207-1678, Fax: (215) 233-2245. Distributors selling our digital magnets and business cards. Established: 1985 - Franchising Since: 1985 - No. of Units: Company Owned: 1 - Franchised: 1250 - Franchise Fee: $350.00-$175.00 (special offers).

LEE'S FAMOUS RECIPE RESTAURANT
Winners International
6045 Barfield Road, Atlanta, GA, 30328. Contact: Julie Reed, Franchise Assistant - Tel: (404) 459-5800, Fax: (404) 459-5797, Web Site: www.winners-international.com. Winners International is a multi-category, multi-brand, international growth company focused on the quick, convenient distribution of food. QSR-chicken. Established: 1966 - Franchising Since: 1966 - No.of Units: Company Owned: 18 - Franchised: 159 - Franchise Fee: $20,000 - Royalty: 4%, 2% national art fees - Total Inv: $410,000-$1,146,300 - Financing: Through outside lenders.

LIL' ORBITS MINI DONUTS
Lil' Orbits Inc.
2850 Vicksburg Lane North, Minneapolis, MN, 55447. - Tel: (763) 559-7505, (800) 228-8305, Fax: (763) 559-7545, E-Mail: contact@lilorbits.com, Web Site: www.donutsgalore.com. Automatic donut machine and accessory turnkey packages with supplies, high profit, fast selling food item - mini donuts. Established: 1974 - Franchising Since: 1974 - No. of Units: Franchised: 15,000 - Total Inv: $5,000 - Financing: Leasing program available.

LOSURDO'S RESTAURANT
Losurdo's Foods, Inc.
20 Owens Rd., Hackensack, NJ, 07601. Contact: Mike Losurdo, Sr., Pres./C.E.O. - Tel: (201) 343-6680, Fax: (201) 343-8078. Italian family restaurant. Established: 1959 - No. of Units: Distributorships: 3.

MAC TOOLS, INC.
4635 Hilton Corporate Dr., Columbus, OH, 43232-4151. - Tel: (614) 755-7000, Fax: (614) 755-7186. Carrying complete inventory of over 8000 items, sockets, wrenches, chisels, screwdrivers, tool boxes, pneumatic tools and specialty items selling directly to mechanics and light industry. Established: 1938 - Offering Distributorships Since: 1938 - No. of Units: 1,600 - Approx. Inv: $30,000 plus initial investment for tool truck, business supplies and back up capital - Financing: On initial inventory for qualified applicants.

MARKETING SERVICES BY VECTRA, INC.
3990 Business Park Drive, Columbus, OH, 43204-5008. - Tel: (614) 351-6868, Fax: (614) 351-4569, Web Site: www.vetra.com. Print and distribute marketing materials for franchise organizations. Provide point of purchase printing, couponing, direct mail, warehousing and fulfilment services worldwide. Established: 1982.

MAXUM SELF DEFENCE
Hankins Marketing Corp
128 N Merritt Ave, Salisbury, NC, 28145. - Tel: (704) 637-3589, Fax: (704) 639-0379. The Maxum Self Defense weapon is especially designed for civilian use. Maxum master distributors can multiply their earning power by hundreds of individuals, retail stores and store chains

and earn $30.00 per dozen on each order plus $106.00 per dozen retail profit. The marketing kit features color brochures, product displays and sales manual. Established: 1994 - No. of Units: Distributors: 2,200 - Distributor start-up: $25.00 - Royalty: $30.00 per dozen plus $106.00 per dozen retail - Total Inv: $25.00.

MEGA POWER DISTRIBUTORS
Mega Power, Inc, Intl
330 Scarlet Blvd, Oldsmar, FL, 34677. Contact; Mark Heywood - Tel: (813) 855-6664, (800) 749-6433, Fax: (813) 855-9441, E-Mail: mheywood@megapowerinc.com, Web Site: www.megapowerinc.com. Distributor of automotive & industrial additives, lubricant & fluid exchange equipment. Established: 1984 - Franchising Since: 1984 - No. of Units: Company Owned: 1 - Franchised: 39 - Franchise Fee: None - Royalty: None - Total Inv: Min $10,000 - Financing: No.

MONEY STRETCHERS
Media Marketing
6799 Parma Park, Cleveland, OH, 44130. Contact: Joan Gallagher, Pres. - Tel: (440) 842-9080, Fax: (440) 842-9080. Full color direct mail advertising business opportunity. Established: 1981 - Offering Distributorships Since: 1982 - No. of Units: Company Owned: 1 - Distributorships: 18 - Total Inv: $495 - Financing: Not available.

MOTOR KOTE, INC.
1386 E. Clinton Trail, Charlotte, MI, 48813. Contact: Dr. David Persell, Pres. - Tel: (517) 543-3552, Fax: (517) 543-3178, E-Mail: motorkote @voyager.net, Web Site: www.motorkote.com. Manufactures and distributes MotorKote 100 engine wear protector. Four times more concentrated than the brand leaders. Available in 1 car to 55 gallon drum sizes sold worldwide. Test machines available. Established: 1991 - Total Inv: Minimum cash requirement - Financing: No.

MOUNTAIN MAN NUT & FRUIT CO.
P.O. Box l60, l0338 S. Progress Way, Parker, CO, 80134. Contat: David Conner, Pres. - Tel: (303) 841-4041, Fax: (303) 841-4100, Web Site: www.mountainmannut.com. Distribution of nuts, dried fruits, chocolates, and trail mixes. Established: 1977 - Distributing Since: 1978 - No. of Units: Company Owned: 4 - Distributors: 275 - Fee: $3,500 - Total Inv: $6,000 - Financing: Not necessary.

MOUNTAIN MARKETING
P.O. Box 210, Cottageville, WV, 25239. Contact: Glen A. Durst, Owner - Tel: (304) 372-2902, Fax: (304) 372-2902. Network marketing business allows you to build a lucrative monthly income from home, part-time or full-time. No ceiling on income. No employees necessary. No territorial restrictions. Minimal overhead. No experience necessary. Free professional consultation. Income is residual. Established: 1981 - Total Inv: Business can usually be launched for less than $150 - Financing: Not necessary.

MR. CHECKOUT
Mr. Checkout Distributors, Inc.
1650 S.W. 22nd Ave., Boca Raton, FL, 33486. Contact: Bob Goldstein, Pres. - Tel: (800) 367-0076, Fax: (561) 367-0021. Wholesale route distributors of general merchandise and health and beauty aids (GM/HBA) to convenience stores and marts. Established: 1989 - No. of Distributors: 125 - Fee: $17,900 - Royalty: None - Total Inv: $25,000 complete - Financing: None.

MUSCLE PRODUCTS CORP.
I.A.A.D.
126 Snee Dr., Jefferson Hills, PA, 15025. - Tel: (412) 655-9098. High-tech lubricants for auto, industrial, transportation, fire arms and marine use. Lubricants are a blend of petrochemical products containing no synthetics, such as teflon, silicone, graphite or moly. Established: 1979 - No. of Units: Company Owned: 79 in 36 states in 6 countries - Total Inv: $2,000-$6,000 regional territories secured by product and sales items - Financing: No.

NATIONAL ASSOCIATION OF BUSINESS LEADERS (NABL)
4132 Shoreline Dr., Ste. J, St. Louis, MO, 63045. Contact; John Weigel, President - Tel: (314) 344-0920, Fax: (314) 298-9110, E-Mail: nabl@nabl.com, Web Site: www.nabl.com. Take calls requesting membership information for our small business association. Established:

1986 - Franchising Since: 1994 - No. of Units: Company Owned: 1 - Franchised: 45 - Franchise Fee: $495 - Total Inv: $495 plus advertising - Financing: Yes.

NATIONAL PROTECTIVE ASSOCIATION
The Synergetics Group
25707 W Long Lake Rd, Ford, WA, 99013-9509. - Tel: (509) 624-0392, Fax: (509) 624-0392. Wholesale distribution of self-defense sprays, personal alarms, wireless entry alarms and security decals. Exclusive distributor of "The Equalizer" line of pepper defense sprays, Fed. Trademark #1,884,838. Established: 1990 - Independent Dealerships Since: 1991 - No. of Units: Company Owned: 1 - Distributors: 2,500 - Total Inv: Inventory Only - Financing: No.

NEIGHBORHOOD DIAPER DELIVERY
ZFC, Inc
2201 Long Prairie Rd., Ste. 107-123, Flower Mound, TX, 75022. Contact: Raymond Zinar - Tel: (972) 355-8400, (888) 326-1419, Fax: (972) 874-0751. Disposable diaper delivery service. Established: 1997 - No. of Units: Franchised: 1 - Franchise Fee: Distributor = $50,000-$75,000; Dealer = $1,500-$3,000 - Financing: No.

NESS STUDIOS
Dept FN
83 Scarcliffe Dr., Malverne, NY, 11565. Contact: Howard Ness, Owner/Dir. - Tel: (516) 593-2410. Hand-painted oil portraits on canvas from any photo. We ask for agents to sell our work. Anyone can sell our paintings and make big profits. Established: 1967 - Distributing Since: 1967 - Franchise Fee: $5 for agent kit - Royalty: 40% commissions - Financing: $5 for dealer/distributor/agent kit.

PARKWAY MACHINE CORP.
2301 York Rd., Timonium, MD, 21093-0277. Contact: Steve Kovens , Oper. Mgr. - Tel: (410) 252-1020, Fax: (410) 252-7137. Manufacture and sale of bulk vending machines and merchandise. Established: 1944 - Total Inv: $1,000 - Financing: Yes.

PATTY-CAKES® INTERNATIONAL INC.
1726 West Third St., Montgomery, AL, 36106. Contact: Jimmy Hill Vice President - Tel: (334) 272-2826, Fax: (334) 264-9062. To create a lasting keepsake, we make the actual impression of your child's hand and foot and cast it in unbreakable bronze. Established: 1956 - Franchising Since: 1989 - No. of Units: Franchised: 58 - Biz. ops Units: 5 - Total Inv: $5500 approx - Financing: No.

PHOTO ADVERTISING INDUSTRIES INC.
262 S. Coconut Lane, Miami Beach, FL, 33139. Contact: Rick Dronsky, Pres. - Tel: (305) 673-3686. Turn-key photography kits, focused on the selling of photo-key ring (photographs in key rings) to customers of restaurants, clubs, etc. while they are dining. Established: 1981 - Licensing Since: 1985 - No. of Units: Company Owned: 6 - Licensed: 9 - License Fee: $3,500 - Total Inv: $3,500 - Financing: No.

PRO-LITE, INC.
3505 Cadillac Ave., Bldg. D, Costa Mesa, CA, 92626-1430. Contact; Wayne Lin, Sales Mgr. - Tel: (714) 668-9988, Fax: (714) 668-9980. New invented outdoor L.E.D. (Low Energy Maintenance) electronic information displays, single color and multicolor. Established: 1986 - Distributing Since: 1986 - No. of Units: Distributed: 350 - Fee: $10,000 - Total Inv: $10,000 - Financing: Yes.

PROMISE TECHNOLOGIES
Promise Technologies, Inc.
157 N. Woodland Ave, Avon Park, FL, 33825. Contact: Fran. Dir. - Tel: (901) 453-0660, Fax: (901) 453-7454. Distribution of unique shower enclosures to dealers, hotels and distributors. Established: 1992 - No. of Units: Company Owned: 1 - Franchised: 8 - Franchise Fee: $10,000 - Royalty: 1% adv - Total Inv: $15,000 - Financing: No.

PUBLISHERS ONLINE MEDIA
Hoelscher Marketing Group
1145 N 2nd St, El Cajon, CA, 92021-5024. - Tel: (619) 588-2155, Fax: (619) 588-9103, Web Site: www.rvhfreegate.com. Business opportunity for independant agents who sell web sites or place advertising on the internet. Established: 1996 - Bus.Opportunity Since: 1997 - Distributors: 27 - Distributor Fee: $99.00 one time fee - Royalty: 50% on all sales - Total Inv: $99.00 plus marketing cost - Financing: No.

R & S INDUSTRIES CORP.

8255 Brentwood Industrial Dr., St. Louis, MO, 63144-2814. Contact; Ronald B. Schwartz, Pres. - Tel: (314) 781-5400, Fax: (314) 781-5169. Manufacture Miracle Polishing Cloth and sell it at wholesale to independent distributors. Established: 1965 - Franchising Since: 1965 - Total Inv: Free sample - Financing: No.

RIGHTLOOK.COM

7616 Miramar Rd., #5300, San Diego, CA, 92126. Contact: Stephen Powers - Tel: (858) 271-4271, (800) 883-3446, Fax: (858) 271-4303, E-Mail: sales@rightlook.com, Web Site: www.rightlook.com. Rightlook.com is a manufacturer and distributor of auto reconditioning equipment and supplies. Established: 1998 - Franchising Since: 1999 - No. of Units: Company Owned: 1.

ROJOS POPCORN CO.
RoJo's U.S.A., Inc.

140 Longmeadow Dr., Burlington, WI, 53105. Contact: Jim Bortmess, Pres. - Tel: (262) 763-9434, Fax: (262) 763-9435. Wholesale popcorn to retail outlets. Established: 1982 - Offering Distributorships Since: 1983 - No. of Units: Company Owned: 1 - Franchised: 20 - Total Inv: $7,000-$20,000 - Financing: No.

ROMANCO PUBLISHERS
Nutrition World

2842 Ridge Rd., P.O. Box 324, Lansing, IL, 60438-0324. Contact: Secretary - Tel: (708) 474-0493, Fax: (708) 474-0798. Advanced anti oxidant business, buy wholesale, sell distributionships, free bottle one life anti oxidant one pays only $5 s.h. Established: 1988 - Franchising Since: 1988 - No. of Units: Company Owned: 1 - Franchised: 1000 - Total Inv: Less than $1,000 - Financing: None.

RX SURGICAL SERVICES

525 Lisbon Ave., Rio Rancho, NM, 87124. Contact: Ozzie Martin, Owner - Tel: (505) 892-9520. Sharpening and repair of surgical instruments on hospital site via mobile truck. Established: 1983 - Franchising Since: 1983 - No. of Units: Company Owned: 2 - Franchised: 6 - Total Inv: $100,000.

SAS TAX PAC DISTRIBUTORS
SAS Enterprises

24831 Alicia #E298, Laguna Hills, CA, 92653. Contact: Davest Adams, Sales Mgr. - Tel: (949) 855-9389, Fax: (949) 855-4914. Financial business managers small to med corp tax trustees, defined ben. adms. Key Man Ins. Established: 1981 - Offering Distributorships Since: 1981 - No. of Units: 5 - Royalty: 75% - Total Inv: $10,000 - Financing: Yes.

SELECTIVE BOOKS INC.

Box 984, Okdsman, FL, 34677. - Tel: (813) 855-5791. Mail order book selling. We publish manuals, books and trade directories which are sold by mail order dealers in US and abroad. Up to 1,000% profit to registered dealers. Established: 1969 - No. of Units: Company Owned: 1 - Independent Dealers: 1000 - Registered dealer fee: $129.95 - Total Inv: Varies - Financing: None.

SMALL BUSINESS CLUB

P.O. Box 2440, Midland, MI, 48641-2440. Contact: Mktg. Dir. - Tel: (517) 496-2551, Fax: (800) 934-1571. For a small yearly fee, members receive the clubs monthly newsletter as well as services for: logo preparation, typesetting, media and list selection, ad preparation, military marketing service, mailing list service, database dev. and main., wholesale printing, publicity releases prepared, and a number of other services for the small business person. Established: 1990 - Franchising Since: 1990 - No. of Units: Company Owned: 1 - Franchised: 275 - Franchise Fee: below $100 - Royalty: None - Total Inv: below $100 - Financing: Visa/MC.

SMOKEETER ELECTRONIC AIR CLEANERS & INDOOR AIR QUALITY SYSTEMS
United Air Specialists, Inc.

4440 Creek Rd., Cincinnati, OH, 45242. Contact: Julie Rentz, Media Assistant - Tel: (513) 891-0400, (800) 551-5401, Fax: (513) 891-4882, E-Mail: uas@uasinc.com, Web Site: www.uasinc.com. For 30 years, United Air Specialists has provided solutions to air quality problems by designing, engineering, manufacturing and installing air cleaning systems. In addition to strong performance guarantees, UAS backs its products through ISO 9001 certification. Established: 1966 - Offering Distributorships Since: 1967 - No. of Distributors: 53 -Total Inv: $30,000.

SOLID/FLUE CHIMNEY SYSTEMS, INC.

4937 Starr St., S.E., Grand Rapids, MI, 49546-6350. Contact: Doug La Fleur, Pres. - Tel: (616) 940-8809, (616) 940-0921. Chimney lining and restoration. Established: 1980 - Offering Dealerships Since: 1989 - No. of Dealerships: 25 - Fee: $9,800 - Total Inv: $40,000.

SUPER CARD
Card One Incorporated

1097-C Irongate Lane, Columbus, OH, 43213. - Tel: (614) 864-1440. Distributorships for secured credit cards, and smart cards. We pay distributors $20 to $25 for each card issued. Established: 1994 - Distributing Since: 1996 - No. of Units: Company Owned: 1 - Distributorships: 34 - Distributor Fee: $145 - Royalty: $20-$25 for each card issued - Total Inv: $145 - Financing: Not needed.

TEAM DISTRIBUTORS
The Crack Team

10765 Indian Head Ind, Blvd, St. Louis, MO, 63132. Contact: Bob Kodner, President - Tel: (314) 426-0900, (800) fix-crax, Fax: (314) 426-0915. Team distributors, a division of the crack team, sells its pre-packaged epoxy injection crack repair kits and support materials for those interested in entering the foundation crack repair business. Established: 1997 - Total Inv: $2500 - Financing: No.

TOF DISTRIBUTING LLC

2346 Charles St, Dallas, TX, 75228. Contact: George Burke, President - Tel: (214) 319-8600, (877) 486-5673. Diet supplement that is guaranteed better than Metabolife or your money back - at half the price. Established: 1999 - Franchising Since: 1999 - No. of Units: Company Owned: 1 - Total Inv: $420.00.

TOM'S FOOD, INC.

900 8th St., Columbus, GA, 31902. Contact: Dir. Fran. Dev. - Tel: (706) 323-2721, Fax: (800) 803-2628, (706) 323-8231. Snack foods under Tom's brand name. Distribution in 46 states. Established: 1925 - Franchising Since: 1985 - No. of Units: Company Owned: 20 - Franchised: 439 - Franchise Fee: Varies with size (min. $7,500 for single route) - Total Inv: Varies with size of business - Financing: Yes, for qualified applicants.

ULTRA BOND, INC.

2458 I-70 Business Loop, #B1, Grand Junction, CO, 81501. Contact: Richard Campfield, Pres. - Tel: (800) 347-2820, Fax: (970) 256-1786. Specializing in windshield repair, stone damage and long cracks. The original patented long crack repair inventor and the edgeguard crack proof, coating for windshields. Established: 1989 - No. of Units: Company Owned: 1 - Distributed: 500 - Fee: $1,950 - Total Inv: $3,450 - Financing: No.

UNCO INDUSTRIES, INC.

7802 Old Spring St., Racine, WI, 53406. - Tel: (800) 728-2415, Fax: (262) 886-2296. Manufacturer of nightcrawlers and organic fertilizers. Established: 1980 - No. of Units: Company Owned: 1 - Dealership Fee: $3,490 - Total Inv: Depends on level of production - Financing: Partial.

VENDOR$ CHOICE® INTERNATIONAL, INC, THE

P.O. Box 591, 1595 Imperial Way, Unit 114, Thorofare, NJ, 08086-0591. Contact: Lory Gill, V.P. - Tel: (856) 384-0440, Fax: (856) 384-0044, Web site: www.thevendorschoice.com. Set up and design of all types of vending routes and machines wholesale to the public. Established: 1981 - Franchising Since: 1988 - No. of Units: Company Owned: 3 - Franchised: 15,000+ - Franchise Fee: None - Royalty: None - Total Inv: $495-$100,000 - Financing: Yes.

VENDX MARKETING INC.
Vendx

3808 E. 109th North, Idaho Falls, ID, 83401. Contact: Byard Cox, Sales - Tel: (208) 529-8363. Vending machine business. Established: 1976 - No. of Units: Company Owned: 100+ - Total Inv: $4,400.

VITAMIN POWER
Vitamin Power Incorporated
39 St. Mary's Place, Freeport, NY, 11520. Contact: Bob Edwards, Dir. of Marketing - Tel: (516) 378-0900, Fax: (516) 378-0919. Producers of over 350 health and fitness nutritional products including body-building, dieting, skin-care and functionalized nutritional purposes. Effective sales support material available. Established: 1975 - No. of Independent Distributors: 10,000.

WASCOMAT
461 Doughty Blvd., Inwood, NY, 11096. Contact: Franchise Department - Tel: (516) 371-4400, Fax: (516) 371-4204. Coin operated laundry centers. Total Inv: Variable.

WIMBERLEY HOMES
P.O. Box 736, Wimberley, TX, 78676. Contact: Floyd MacKenzie, Treasurer - Tel: (800) 660-0945, Fax: (512) 847-9292. Construction of homes under $50,000. Modular and pre-constructed at factory. Established: 1987 - Licensed Since: 1988 - No. of Units: 1 - Royalty: $300/mthly. - Total Inv: Cost of home - Financing: No.

WORLD CASH PROVIDERS, INC.
3621 W. Beechwood Ave., Fresno, CA, 93711. Contact: Paul Ferroggiaro, Exec. VP Sales & Marketing - Tel: (559) 261-2258, (888) 257-2274, Fax: (559) 261-2970, Web Site: www.wcpinc.net. Cash ticket machine. A cashless ATM which is placed at no cost to the merchant. Established: 1996.

WORM WAREHOUSE
Flynn Rd., Burke, NY, 12917. Conrad Kruger, Owner - Tel: (518) 483-7687, (800) 535-2248, Fax: (518)483-8390. Live bait packaging and distribution. Includes worms, night crawlers, fish, crayfish and insects. Established: 1970 - Distributing Since: 1991 - No. of Units: Company Owned: 2 - Total Inv: $5,000 - Financing: No.

YAMAHA MOTOR CORP., USA
6555 Katella Ave., Cypress, CA, 90630. Contact: Dealership Dept. - Tel: (714) 761-7300, Fax: (714) 229-7974. Distributor Yamaha motorized products. Established: 1966 - Offering Distributorships Since: 1966 - Approx. Inv: $30,000-$100,000 - Financing: Inventory.

YELLOWSTONE LOG HOMES
280 N. Yellowstone Hwy., Rigby, ID, 83442. Contact: Lynn Youngstrom, Owner - Tel: (208) 745-8108, Fax: (208) 745-8525, E-Mail: www.yellowstoneloghomes.com. Manufactures logs for homes. Machined to a uniform size. Established: 1962 - No. of Units: 1 - Total Inv: $4,000 - Financing: No. Offering Dealerships.

EMPLOYMENT & PERSONNEL

A-1 EMPLOYMENT SERVICES
P.O. Box 9430, Elizabeth, NJ, 07202-0430. - Tel: (908) 351-9111, Fax: (908) 351-0108. Two franchises are available: Apoxiforce is a temporary employment service; Plusmates is a permanent employment service. Involving recruitment and placement of professional and clerical personnel. Franchising available only in the states of NJ, NY, PA & CT. Established: 1960 - Franchising Since: 1962 - No. of Units: Company Owned: 6 - Franchise Fee: $15,000 - Royalty: 6-7%- assist in payroll funding, billing & collection - Total Inv: $25,000-$30,000 - Financing: Can be made available.

ACCOUNTANTS INC. SERVICES
111 Anza Blvd., Ste. 400, Burlingame, CA, 94010. - Tel: (650) 579-1111, Web Site: www.accountantsinc.com. Temporary/permanent placement of finance professionals. Established: 1986 - Franchising Since: 1994 - No. of Units: Company Owned: 23 - Franchised: 16 - Franchise Fee: $30,000 - Royalty: 10% (sliding scale) of revenue - Total Inv: $144,400-$193,700 working capital.

ACE PERSONNEL
Ace Personnel Franchise Corp.
6400 Glennwood Ste. 309, Overland Park, KS, 66202. - Tel: (913) 362-0090, (800) 700-0005, Fax: (913) 362-9076. Staffing services for the temporary employment market. Established: 1989 - Franchising

Since: 1996 - No. of Units: Company Owned: 4 - Franchised: 2 - Franchise Fee: $5,000-$15,000 - Royalty: 6% of gross billings - Total Inv: $83,450-$134,600 - Financing: No.

AHEAD HUMAN RESOURCES - STAFFING
AHEAD Human Resources, Inc.
2207 Heather Lane, Louisville, KY, 40218. Contact: Rick Mabrey - Tel: (877) 485-5858, (502) 485-1000, Fax: (502) 485-0801, E-Mail: franchise@aheadhr.com, Web Site: www.aheadhr.com. Temp. staffing/ pro. placement and recruiting. Established: 1995 - Franchising Since: 2000 - No. of Units: Company Owned: 2 - Franchised: 9 - Franchise Fee: $15,500-$19,500 - Total Inv: $120,950 - Financing: No.

ATC HEALTH CARE SERVICES
Staff Builders, Inc.
1983 Marcus Ave., Lake Success, NY, 11042. - Tel: (516) 327-3379, Fax: (516) 7358-3678. Provide supplemental staffing to all areas of the health care industry: hospitals, nursing homes, rehab centers, sub-acute and outpatient facilities, doctors groups, labs, insurance companies and industries. Utilizing nursing, allied and therapy professionals, medical admin and technical personnel. Established: 1982 - Franchising Since: 1995 - No. of Units: Company Owned: 2 - Franchised: 34 - Franchise Fee: $19,500 - Royalty: Varies - Total Inv: $77,000-$100,000 - Financing: For qualified candidates.

ATS PERSONNEL
ATS Services, Inc.
9700 Phillips Hwy #101, Jacksonville, FL, 32256-1320. - Tel: (904) 645-9505, Fax: (904) 224-1410. Temporary and permanent employment services specializing in clerical, accounting, data processing and technical staffing. Established: 1978 - Franchising Since: 1991 - No. of Units: Company Owned: 7 - Franchised: 11 - Franchise Fee: $12,500 - Royalty: Sliding from 6.9% - Total Inv: $75,000-$110,000 - Financing: Fianance Payroll.

ATWORK PERSONNEL SERVICES, INC.
Atwork Franchise, Inc.
1470 Main Street, P.O. Box 989, White Pine, TN, 37890. - Tel: (800) 233-6846, Fax: (865) 674-8780. Employment services, selling temporary help, staff leasing, professional placement services. Established: 1990 - Franchising Since: 1992 - No. of Units: Franchised: 35 - Franchise Fee: $11,500, training $2,500 - Royalty: 7.1% volume discount scale - Total Inv: $25,00-$50,000 - Financing: Funding of payroll.

BELCAN
10200 Anderson Way, Cincinnati, OH, 45242. - Tel: (513) 891-0972, (800) 423-5226, Fax: (513) 985-7421. Temporary clerical/technical personnel. Established: 1958 - Franchisng Since: 1998 - No. of Units: Company Owned: 20 - Franchised: 2 - Franchise Fee: $30,000 - Total Inv: $89,000-$124,250 (fran. fee included) - Financing: No.

BURNETT PERSONNEL SERVICES
Burnett Companies Consolidated
9800 Richmond St., Ste. 800, Houston, TX, 77042. - Tel: (713) 977-4777, Fax: (713) 977-7533. Personnel business. Permanent and temporary help service. Established: 1974 - Franchising Since: 1990 - No. of Units: Company Owned: 11 - Franchised: 1 - Franchise Fee: $15,000 - Total Inv: $15,000 - Financing: Yes.

CAREER BLAZERS STAFFING SERVICES
590 Fifth Ave., 7th Fl., New York, NY, 10036. Contact: Exec. V.P. - Tel: (800) 284-3232-US only, (212) 730-1575, Fax: (212) 921-1827.Full service employment organization specializing in permanent and temporary personnel. Focus is on administrative support through middle management. Established: 1949 - Franchising Since: 1987 - No. of Units: Company Owned: 4 - Franchised/Licensed: 8 - Franchise Fee: $15,000-$18,000 - Royalty: Varies with gross billings - Total Inv: $90,000-$120,000 capital required - Financing: Full financing of temporary payroll includes all mandatory payroll expenses, accounts receivable, credit and collections support.

CAREERS U.S.A., INC.
6501 Congress Ave. Suite 200, Boca Raton, FL, 33487. Contact: Gregory R. Hielsberg, Dir. of Franchising Dev. - Tel: (561) 995-7000, (888) CAREERS, Fax: (561) 995-7001, E-Mail: hq@careersusa.com, Web Site: www.careersusa.com. Careers USA provides temporary,

temp to hire, and permanent personnel to businesses and corporations in your market area. Careers USA's propiatery computer software program computes the franchisees temporary payroll, taxes and insurances. You, the franchisee, can download and analyze your sales, margins, rates, cash flow, and other data that is critical to the success of your business. Careers USA finances 100% of your temporary payroll and accounts receivable. Established: 1981 - Franchising Since: 1987 - No. of Units: Company Owned: 18 - Franchised: 5 - Franchise Fee: $14,500 - Royalty: Permanent Placement: 7% - Temporary Placement: Varies wirh gross margin - Total Inv: $ 69,415-$130,155 - Financing: No.

CHECKMATE
Checkmate Systems, Inc.
P.O. Box 32034, Charleston, SC, 29417. Contact: V.P. Mktg. - Tel: (843) 763-9393, Fax: (843) 571-1851. Employee leasing. Established: 1992 - Franchising Since: 1993 - No. of Units: Franchised: 15 - Franchise Fee: $19,500 - Royalty: 7.5% of gross fees received - Total Inv: $40,400-$51,000 - Financing: None.

CONSULTIS INC.
1615 S. Federal Hwy, Boca Raton, FL, 33432. Contact: Barbara Fleming, President/CEO - Tel: (561) 362-9104, (800) 275-2667, Fax: (561) 367-9802, E-Mail: opportunity@consultis.com, Web Site: www.consultis. com. National temp staffing service, specializing in tech. support in the data processing industry. Established: 1984 - Franchising Since: 1990 - No. of Units: Company Owned: 9 - Franchised: 31 - Franchise Fee: $30,000 - Royalty: 7% of gross sales - Total Inv: $175,000-$205,000 - Financing: No.

DUNHILL PROFESSIONAL SEARCH (PERM PLACEMENT OUTLETS)/DUNHILL STAFFING SYSTEMS (TEMP OUTLETS)
Dunhill Staffing Systems, Inc.
150 Motor Pkwy., Hauppauge, NY, 11788. Contact: Robert R. Stidham Jr., President, Franchise Division - Tel: (631) 952-3000, (800)386-7823, Fax: (631) 952-3500, E-Mail: franop@dunhillstaff.com, Web Site: www.dunhillstaff.com. Dunhill offers Professional Search and Temporary Staffing franchises. Our franchisees specialize in permanent, temporary anbd contract staffing placements in every segment of business. Established: 1952 - Franchising Since: 1961 - No. of Units: Company Owned: 26 - Franchised: 116 - Franchise Fee: $17,000 (Temp), $55,000 (Prof. Search) - Royalty: 7% Professional Search; Temporary Staffing: Varies - Total Inv: $85,000-$140,000 - Financing: Yes.

EXECUSERVE
P.O. Box 1006, Mathewa, VA, 23109. Contact: Tom Eley - Tel: (804) 725-5480, Fax: (804) 725-5238, Web Site: www.execuserveusa.com. We are an executive placement franchise using advanced interview asistance software to aid companies. Established: 1989 - Franchising Since: 2000 - No. of Units: Company Owned: 1 - Franchise Fee: $22,500 - Total Inv: $40,500 - Financing: No.

EXPRESS PERSONNEL SERVICES
Express Services, Inc.
8516 NW Expressway, Oklahoma City, OK, 73162. Contact: VP Franchising - Tel: (405) 840-5000, (800) 652-6400, Fax: (405) 717-5665, E-Mail: franchising@expresspersonnel.com, Web Site: www.expresspersonnel.com. Express franchise combines Express Personnel Services which includes recruiting and placing temporary employees, and recruiting and placing full-time employees and Express Professional Staffing which includes recruiting and placing contract staffing employees and professional search into one franchise. Established: 1983 - Franchising Since: 1985 - No. of Units: Company Owned: 2 - Franchised: 404 - Franchise Fee: $17,500-$20,500 - Royalty: Stanard split 60/40; 8% of placement fees - Total Inv: $120,000-$160,000 - Financing: 100% payroll financing.

F-O-R-T-U-N-E PERSONNEL CONSULTANTS
F-O-R-T-U-N-E Franchise Corporation
1140 Avenue of the Americas, New York, NY, 10036. Contact: Dir. Of Franchise Development - Tel: (212) 302-1141, (800) 886-7839, Fax: (212) 302-2422, Web Site: www.fpcweb.com. As one of the largest and most successful Executive Recruiting firms in the world, F-O-R-T-U-N-E Personnel Consultants has set a distinguished standard of leadership and integrity in the executive placement industry. F-O-R-T-U-N-E franchise owners enjoy all of today's technologies, including our

nationwide computerized exchange program, along with good old-fashioned service. Intensive training and unparalleled support by industry experienced training consists of two weeks at national headquarters focusing on management, operations, sales, technology and industry specific topics with an additional week of training at franchise office. Sound continued support and ongoing training includes 800 consulting line, on-site training, regularly scheduled training seminars, annual national conference and franchise Board of Advisors. Established: 1959 - Franchising Since: 1973 - No. of Units: Company Owned: 1 - Franchised: 98 - Franchise Fee: $40,000 - Royalty: 7% and 1% adv. - Total Inv: $32,364 -$67,540 - Financing: Up to 50% of fran. fee.

FRIEND OF THE FAMILY
Merlin Services Corp.
3964 Atlanta Rd SE, Smyrna, GA, 30080. Contact: Franchise Department, - Tel: (770) 725-2748. Booking agency for child care, elder care and other staff. Established: 1984 - Franchising Since: 1990 - No. of Units: Company Owned: 2 - Licensed: 5 - License Fee: $14,500 - Total Inv: $30,000-$40,000 - Financing: No.

HANDI-MAN, PRO-TEM
JBS, Inc
214 N. Main St., #202, Natick, MA, 01760-1131. - Tel: (508) 650-0026, Fax: (508) 650-0035. Industrial or clerical staffing service. Established: 1970 - Franchising Since: 1975 - No. of Units: Franchised: 15 - Franchise Fee: $25,000 - Financing: Yes.

HEALTH FORCE, INC.
Career Employment Services
P.O Box 26565, New York, NY, 10087-6565. Contact: Dir. of Fran. Dev. - Tel: (516) 496-2300, Fax: (516) 677-6023. Temporary nursing service which specializes in home care and staffing. Payroll funding, fully computerized, become involved in one of the fastest growing industries. Established: 1975 - Franchising Since: 1982 - No. of Units: Company Owned: 25 - Franchised: 48 - Franchise Fee: $19,500 - Royalty: Sliding scale - Total Inv: $100,000-$125,000 - Financing: Payroll funding accounts receivable.

HEALTHCARE RECRUITERS INT'L / DALLAS
4100 Spring Valley Rd., Ste. 800, Dallas, TX, 75244. Contact: Jim Wimberly, President/Owner - Tel: (214) 420-9370, Fax: (972) 687-0039. Recruiting medical sales, sales management and marketing personnel throughout the U.S. and Canada, utilizing our exclusive registered client candidate referral system. Established: 1983 - Franchising Since: 1985 - No. of Units: 35 - Franchise Fee: 20%-30% of base.

HOPE CAREER CENTERS
Helping Others Pursue Education
2735 S. Newton St., Denver, CO, 80236. - Tel: (303) 934-1018, Fax: (303) 934-1112, Web Site: www.busop1.com. Hope offers a business of helping others providing education and financial help including scholarships, funding assistance, career planning, college planning, corporate reimbursement programs for displaced workers, undergraduates, veterans, college bound students, disadvantaged citizens, and people wanting career change for home entrepreneurs. Established: 1985 - Franchising Since: 1989 - No. of Units: Company Owned: 1 - Franchised: 1200 plus - Franchise Fee: $599.00 - Royalty: None - Total Inv: $699.00 - Financing: Yes.

JASNEEK STAFFING
8590 Georgetown Rd, Indianapolis, IN, 46268. - Tel: (866) 527-6335, Fax: (317) 872-4563. We fill temporary and permament positions for hospitals, medical offices an long term care facilities. Established: 1996 - Franchising Since: 2000 - No. of Units: Company Owned: 3 - Franchised: 6 - Franchise Fee: 17,000 - Royalty: 5.5% - Total Inv: $54,000-$186,000 - Financing: Third party.

LABOR FINDERS
Labor Finders International, Inc.
3910 RCA Blvd., #1001, Palm Beach Gardens, FL, 33410. Contact: Robert R. Gallagher, VP Franchise Development - Tel: (561) 627-6507, (800) 864-7749, Fax: (561) 627-6556, E-Mail: robert.gallagher @laborfinders.com, Web Site: www.laborfinders.com. Industrial staffing services serving construction, manufacturing, distribution, landscaping

and commercial businesses. Established: 1975 - Franchising Since: 1975- No. of Units: Company Owned: 13 - Franchised: 187 - Franchise Fee: $10,000 - Royalty: 2.5% of Labor costs - Financing: Some.

LABOR FORCE STAFFING SERVICES
Labor Force Franchising, Inc.
5225 Katy Freeway, Ste. 600, Houston, TX, 77007. Contact: President - Tel: (713) 802-1284, Fax: (713) 802-9633, Web Site: www.labor force.com. Provider of temporary staffing services. Established: 1970 - Franchising Since: 1992 - No. of Units: Company Owned: 12 - Franchised: 26 - Franchise Fee: $10,000 - Royalty: Declining from 4.5% of sales to 3% - Total Inv: $50,000-$100,000 startup costs, plus fee - Financing: Accounts receivable factoring.

LAWCORPS® LEGAL STAFFING SERVICE
LawCorps® Franchise Corp.
1819 L. St, NW, Washington, DC, 20036. - Tel: (202)785-5996, (800) 437-8809, Fax: (202) 785-1118, E-Mail: info@lawcorps.com, Web Site: www.lawcorps.com. Temporary legal staffing: Attorneys, Law Clerks and Paralegals. Established: 1988 - Franchising Since: 1995 - No. of Units: Company Owned: 4 - Franchised: 3 - Franchise Fee: $25,000 - Royalty: 8% - Total Inv: $84,200-$108,500 - Financing: No.

LINK STAFFING SERVICES
Link Staffing Services
1800 Bering Dr., Ste. 800, Houston, TX, 77057. Contact: Don Lawrence, V.P. Franchise Development - Tel: (713) 784-4400, (800) 848-5465, Fax: (713) 784-4454, E-Mail: franchise@linkstaffing.com, Web Site: www.linkstaffing.com. Link Staffing Services provides a wide variety of flexible staffing and productivity solutions to business and industry. Our clients tell us that our comprehensive screening processes consistently deliver higher-quality workers. Established: 1980 - Franchising Since: 1994 - No. of Units: Company Owned: 8 - Franchised: 33 - Franchise Fee: $17,000 - Royalty: Varies - Total Inv: $85,500-$156,000 - Financing: 100% of the temporary employee payroll.

LLOYD STAFFING
lloyd Personnel Systems, Inc
445 Broadhollow Rd, Melville, NY, 11747. - Tel: (631) 777-7600, (888) 292-6678, Fax: (631) 777-7626, E-Mail: franchise@lloydstaffing.com, Web Site: www.lloydstaffing.com. A full service, multi staffing company. Lloyd assists its client's companies with a broad range of hiring and training services such as temporary, direct hire and consulting. Established: 1971 - Franchising Since: 1988 - No. of Units: Company Owned: 7 - Franchised: 8 - Franchise Fee: $20,000 - Royalty: 60/40 on temporary & 7% on direct hire - Total Inv: $93,500-$155,300 - Financing: No.

M.A. GROUP, INC
4466 N. Milwaukee Ave, Chicago, IL, 60630. Contact: Bob Shea, President - Tel: (773) 736-7188, Fax: (773) 736-7111. Provides trained temporary labor to the moving industry. The M.A. Group offer complete invoicing and payroll services allowing franchisees to focus on successful staffing. Established: 1995 - Franchising Since: 1999 - No. of Units: Company Owned: 1 - Franchise Fee: $20,000 - Royalty: 6% of gross revenue - Total Inv: $16,200-$18,200 - Financing: No.

MANAGEMENT RECRUITERS / SALES CONSULTANTS
Management Recruiters International, Inc.
200 Public Sq., 31st floor, Cleveland, OH, 44114. Contact: V.P. Fran. Mktg. - Tel: (216) 696-1127, Fax: (216) 696-6612. Complete range of recruitment and staffing services permanent executive, mid-management, professional, marketing, sales management, and sales placement; interim professional and sales force outsourcing; video conferencing, permanent and temporary office support personnel; compatibility assessment and international search with coverage on all continents through strategic alliances with leading search firms. Established: 1957 - Franchising

Since: 1965 - No. of Units: Company Owned: 47 - Franchised: 703 - Franchise Fee: $65,000 U.S. - Royalty: U.S. 7% 5% adv - Total Inv:U.S. $90,000-$120,000 - Financing: Will assist in obtaining loans from non-affiliated third party lenders.

MEDOFFICE BILLING CENTERS
MedOffice Systems, Inc
7676 Hazard Center Dr, 5th Floor, San Diego, CA, 92108. - Tel: (800) 400-9558, Fax: (800) 503-9461, E-Mail: info@medofficeinc.com, Web Site: www.medofficeinc.com. As a MedOffice Billing Center you operate a medical/dental billing office which serves health care providers in filing insurance claims. You also perform other billing functions and provide doctors with consulting services on software, insurance issues and office help. Established: 1993 - Franchising Since: 1997 - No. of Units: Company Owned: 1 - Franchised: 17 - Franchise Fee: $9,900 - Royalty: No royalties $395.00 annual support, $50.00 monthly for national advertising - Total Inv: $12,400-$22,900 - Financing: Yes.

NAT'L RESTAURANT SEARCH, INC.
555 Sun Valley Drive, Suite J1, Roswell, GA, 30076. Contact: John W. Chitvanni, Pres. - Tel: (770) 650-1800, Fax: (770) 650-1801. Executive search for key executives and presidents. Handle search assignments in the areas of operations, franchise sales and development, real estate and construction, marketing, finance and human resources. Established: 1981.

NETWORK PROFESSIONALS INC.
Network Professionals Inc
125 Hivue Lane, Pittsburgh, PA, 15237. Contact: Eve Peterson, President - Tel: (412) 761-8583, (800) 929-Lead, Fax: (412) 761-8584, E-Mail: NPI@npinet.com, Web Site: www.npinet.com. NPI is an organization that establishes networking groups across the country. The group members are professionals and business owners that want to increase their business through referrals. This is a license opportunity that is very unique. Requires no employees, can start part-time, home office okay, no inventory, and the administrative work is handled by the corporate office so the owner simply focuses on growing their business! Established: 1991 - Franchising Since: 1995 - No. of Units: Company Owned: 4 - Franchised: 96 - Franchise Fee: $29,995 - Royalty: 30-35% of membership dues - Total Inv: $35,000 - Financing: No.

NORRELL TEMPORARY SERVICES
Norrell Corporation
3535 Piedmont Rd., N.E., Atlanta, GA, 30305. Contact: Franchise Development Manager - Tel: (404) 240-3000, (800) 765-6342, Fax: (404) 240-3084, E-Mail: Eballance@norrell.com, Web Site: www.norrell.com. National Franchise offering distinctive, high quality services, ranging from traditional temporary staffing, to supporting clients with customized staffing solutions, through managed staffing and outsourcing. Our services include office automation, light industrial, and call center staffing. Established: 1969 - Franchising Since: 1969 - No. of Units: Company Owned: 161 - Franchised: 114 - Royalty: Varies - Total Inv: $79,530-$179,600 - Financing: None.

OFFICESTARS
7030 Pointe Inverness Way, Suite 250, Fort Wayne, IN, 46804. Contact: John Shank - Tel: (260) 432-3800, Fax: (260) 432-6237, E-Mail: john.shank@officestars.com, Web Site: www.officestars.com. Professional office and clerical staffing company utilizing state-of-the-art technology. Established: 1993 - Franchising Since: 2002 - No. of Units: Company Owned: 1 - Franchise Fee: $17,500 - Royalty: 35% of gross margin - Total Inv: $76,350-$155,200.

OUTSOURCE FRANCHISING INC.
Outsource International
1144 East Newport Center Dr., Deerfield Beach, FL, 33442. Contact: Franchise Department - Tel: (954) 418-6200 (800) 696-0856, Fax: (954) 418-4405, Web Site: www.outsourceint.com. Temporary help and employee leasing. Established: 1974 - Franchising Since: 1988 - No. of Units: Company Owned: 104 - Franchised: 48 - Franchise Fee: $22,000 - Financing: On working capital for payroll needs.

PRIDESTAFF
6780 N. West Avenue, Ste. 103, Fresno, CA, 93711-1393. - Tel: (559) 432-7780, Fax: (559) 432-4371. A human resource service company offering temporary staffing franchises specializing in office clerical and

light industrial services. Established: 1978 - Franchising Since: 1996 - No. of Units: Company Owned: 11 - Franchised: 8 - Franchise Fee: 0 - Royalty: 65/35 split of GM$ in favor of franchisee - Total Inv: $50,000-$70,000 - Financing: Yes - Pridestaff offers furnishings and equipment leasing.

PROFESSIONAL DYNAMETRIC PROGRAMS/PDP, INC.

750 E. Hwy 24, Bldg. 1, Woodland Park, CO, 80863. Contact: Jim Farmer, Executive VP - Tel: (719) 687-6074, (719) 687-8587, Fax: (719) 687-8587. A business to business franchise. Interface with corporate decision makers and CEO's. Sell, train, consult and service large and small businesses in comprehensive management programs for: hiring, motivating, stress managing and evaluating performances. Established: 1978 - Franchising Since: 1980 - No. of Units: Franchised: 28 - Franchise Fee: $29,500 - Royalty: 10% - Total Inv: $5,000-$10,000 work cap. + fran. fee - Financing: $15,000 down, 1 yr. zero interest note on balance.

PROFILES - SECURITY & PERSONNEL RISK ASSESSMENTS
Profiles
P.O. Box 880461, San Diego, CA, 92168. - Tel: (619) 280-3486. Accurate assessments about an applicant's or employee's past and their potential capabilities. Attitudes, security risk, alcohol or drug abuse, psychological adjustment, theft investigations. Evaluations of clerks, vehicle drivers, supervisors, managers, and executives. No one can match our price or provide employers with as many methods for answering this very important question - Asset or Liability? Make money by providing this valuable answer. Established: 1982 - Franchising Since: 1986 - No. of Units: Company Owned: 1 - Franchised: 10 - Royalty: $3.50 per test - Total Inv: $1,500-$15,000 - Financing: Varies.

REGIONAL NETWORK OF PERSONNEL CONSULTANTS, THE
Murphy Management Corporation
211 W. 22nd St., Ste. 221, Oak Brook, IL, 60521. Contact: Wm Murphy, Pres. - Tel: (630) 571-1088, Fax: (630) 575-5650. Local area network of existing private employment agencies/search/recruiting firms sharing job orders, job order information and placements. Established: 1984 - Franchising Since: 1985 - No. of Units: Company Owned: 3 - Franchised: 8 - Total Inv: $5,000 plus additional $5,000 for computer equipment - Financing: None.

REMEDY TEMP, INC.
Remedy Intelligent Staffing
101 Enterprise, Aliso Viejo, CA, 92656. - Tel: (800) 736-3392, Fax: (800) 291-2060. A national full service staffing franchise committed to providing quality personnel in the following fields: office automation, clerical, accounting, legal and light industrial. Established: 1965 - Franchising Since: 1987 - No. of Units: Company Owned: 85 - Franchised: 114 - Franchise Fee: $17,000 - Royalty: Varies with performance - Total Inv: $60,000 pre-opening, $45,000-$90,000 working cap. - Financing: Thru SBA.

RESOURCES IN FOOD & FOOD TEAM
Food Services Franchise Corp
112 South Handley Rd., Ste. 105, St. Louis, MO, 63105. Contact: Wm. F. Timmons, President - Tel: (314) 727-0002, Fax: (314) 727-5590. Food service temporary employment. Established: 1989 - Franchising Since: 1996 - No. of Units: Company Owned: 10 - Franchised: 7 - Franchise Fee: $40,000 one time fee - Royalty: 8% of management placement fees, 2% of temp. billings - Total Inv: $50,000-$60,000 + franchise fee - Financing: None.

ROTH YOUNG PERSONNEL SERVICES, INC.
Winston Franchise Corp.
535 Fifth Ave., New York, NY, 10017. Contact: William Beck, Pres. - Tel: (212) 557-8181, Fax: (210) 972-3364. Franchise sales of executive recruiting. Established: 1962 - Franchising Since: 1964 - No. of Units: Company Owned: 18 - Franchised: 18 - Franchise Fee: $35,000 up-front cash - Royalty: 3%-8% - Total Inv: $50,000 - Financing: No.

RUSSOLI TEMPS
Grey Fox Ltd.
2137 Walbert Ave., Allentown, PA, 18104. Contact: Fran. Dir. - Tel: (610) 432-3699, Fax: (610) 770-1773. Provide temporary employees to companies in the following fields: clerical, light industrial, accounting, home companion care, data processing and technical. Established: 1978 - Franchising Since: 1986 - No. of Units: Company Owned: 1 - Franchised: 10 - Franchise Fee: $14,000 - Royalty: 5%-$700,000 billings, 4.5% $700,000 - $1,000,000, 4% over $1,000,000 - Total Inv: $66,600 incl. $43,000 work. cap. & fran. fee - Financing: Payroll funding available.

SANFORD ROSE ASSOCIATES
SRA International, Inc.
3737 Embassy Pkwy., Suite 200, Akron, OH, 44333-8369. Contact: George Snider, President - Tel: (800) 731-7724, E-Mail: sraintl@aol.com, Web Site: www.franchisesra.com. SRA International, Inc. operates the Sanford Rose Associates Executive Search System, a franchise network of highly motivated men and women who have left their jobs in corporate America for the challenges and rewards of private business ownership. As top-flight recruiters of professional, managerial and executive talent, they continue to make full use of their corporate skills while gaining the opportunity for personal and financial independence. Established: 1959 - Franchising Since: 1970 - No. of Units: Franchised: 53 - Franchise Fee: $40,000 - Royalty: 7%-3% - Total Inv: $52,000-$83,000 - Financing: Yes.

SMARTPEOPLE
SmartPeople, Inc
17555 Collins Ave Apt# 2903, Miami, FL, 33160-2890. Contact: Mark Zilbert - Tel: (800) 484-2609 ext 6187. Job placement service. Established: 1994 - Franchising Since: 1995 - No. of Units: Company Owned: 1 - Franchised: 1 - Franchise Fee: $12,500 + - Total Inv: $60,000-$90,000 - Financing: Yes.

SNELLING PERSONNEL SERVICES
Snelling and Snelling, Inc.
12801 N. Central Expy., Ste. 700, Dallas, TX, 75243. - Tel: (800) 766-5556, (972) 776-1288, Fax: (972) 239-6365, Web Site: www.snelling.com. Full staffing service offering temporary temp-to-hire career placement. Established: 1951 - Franchising Since: 1955 - No. of Units: Company Owned: 33 - Franchised: 275 - Franchise Fee: $20,000 - Royalty: 7.5% career, 4.5% temporary - Total Inv: $76,000-$135,000 - Financing: Third party.

SPHERION
2050 Spectrum Blvd., Ft. Lauderdale, FL, 33309. Contact: Franchise Licence Division - Tel: (800) 840-6568, (954) 938-7600, Fax: (954) 938-7770, Web Site: www.spherion.com. One of the largest providers of nurses and para-professionals in home health care as well as hospitals and nursing homes. Established: 1946 - Franchising Since: 1956 - No. of Units: Company Owned: 98 - Franchised: 290 - Franchise Fee: $5,000 - Royalty: 5% to 8% of sales - Total Inv: $125,000, start-up & operating expenses - Financing: Payroll funding and invoicing by franchisor.

TALENT TREE
Talent Tree
9703 Richmond Ave., Houston, TX, 77042. - Tel: (713) 789-1818, (800) 999-1515, Fax: (713) 974-6507, E-Mail: franchise@talenttree.com, Web Site: www.talenttree.com. Offering a full-service staffing franchise opportunity for the placement of clerical, light industrial, professional, and technical support staff with client companies. Established: 1976 - Franchising Since: 1990 - No. of Units: Company Owned: 156, Franchised: 24 - Franchise Fee: $20,000 - Royalty: Scaled based on GM$ - Total Inv: $75,000-$150,000 - Financing: Third party.

TECHSTAFF
Techstaff, Inc.
21180 W. Capitol Drive, Pewaukee, WI, 53072. Contact: Thomas Montgomery, Sales Director - Tel: (262) 373-1390, Fax: (262) 781-2607, E-Mail: tom@techstaff.com, Web Site: www.techstaff.com. Contract staffing and direct recruiting in technical engineering and its profession. Established: 1985 - Franchising Since: 1987 - No. of Units: Company Owned: 3 - Franchised: 8 - Franchise Fee: $25,000 - Royalty: 6.9%-5.9%-4.9% - Total Inv: $125,000 - Financing: Accountant receivable.

THOMAS INTERNATIONAL

8401 North Central Expressway, Suite 20, LB-5, Dallas, TX, 75225. Contact: Thomas Hendrickson, CEO - Tel: (800) 528-5153, Fax: (972) 739-7441. A program giving franchisors the opportunity to place the right person in the position where personality, motivation and goals can be integrated right into the job. Established: 1972.

TIME TEMPORARY SERVICES
Time Services, Inc.

6422 Lima Rd., Fort Wayne, IN, 46818. Contact: Thomas C. Ward, COO - Tel: (219) 489-2020, Fax: (219) 489-1466. Clerical, industrial, technical temporary help. Plant staff, staffing services. Established: 1981 - Franchising Since: 1984 - No. of Units: Company Owned: 10 - Franchised: 4 - Franchise Fee: Negotiable - Royalty: Franchisee 60%, franchisor 40% - Total Inv: $80,000+ - Financing: Negotiable.

TODAYS STAFFING

18111 Preston Rd., Ste. 700, Dallas, TX, 75252. Contact: Janis Domino, Franchise Development - Tel: (800) 822-7868, (214) 754-0700, Fax: (214) 754-0711. Provides temporary help services to large and small companies. Emphasis is on providing skilled clerical personnel whose skills have been tested and references thoroughly checked. Established: 1982 - Franchising Since: 1983 - No. of Units: Company Owned: 75 - Franchised: 29 - Franchise Fee: Varies - Royalty: Varies - Total Inv: $90,000-$145,000 - Financing: Funds 100% of temp. employees' payroll and accounts receivables. Also, 50% of local advertising on pre-approved programs.

TRC STAFFING SERVICES, INC.

100 Ashford Ctr. N. #500, Atlanta, GA, 30338. Contact: Brad Smith, V.P. Fran. - Tel: (770) 392-1411, (800) 488-8008, Fax: (770) 393-2472. Provides a full service temporary help franchise program. Skill classifications filled by TRC are clerical, secretarial, word and data processing, accounting, computer related activities and light industrial. Established: 1980 - Franchising Since: 1984 - No. of Units: Company Owned: 27 - Franchised: 31 - Royalty: Varies - Total Inv: $75,000-$125,000 - Financing: Yes.

UNIFORCE STAFFING SERVICES

415 Crossways Park Drive, Woodbury, NY, 11797. Contact: John Fanning, CEO - Tel: (516) 437-3300, Fax: (516) 437-3392. Uniforce Temporary Services grants exclusive licenses to operate offices which provide temporary personnel with a large variety of skills to employers in business, industry, and government. Also, provide personnel in general/automated office, MIS, marketing, records management, hospitality, legal, technical and light industrial categories. Established: 1961 - Franchising Since: 1964 - No. of Units: Company Owned: 78 - Franchised: 9 - Franchise Fee: $15,000 - Royalty: 45% - Total Inv: $15,000, plus $75,000-$100,000 - Financing: N/A.

USA EMPLOYMENT
USA Employment Inc

5533 Central Ave, St. Petersburg, FL, 33710. Contact: Colleen Rounds, President - Tel: (727) 343-3044, (800) 801-5627, Fax: (727) 343-2953, E-Mail: aaausa@cftnet.com, Web Site: www.aaa-usaemployment.com. Permanent employment agencies affiliated with AAA employment. Total training and continuous support, 30 day in house training. Established: 1957 - Franchising Since: 1999 - No.of Units: Franchised: 21- Franchise Fee: $15,000 - Royalty: 10% of gross sales - Total Inv: $5,000 down - $5,000 working capital - Financing: Yes balance of fee.

V.I.P. COMPANION-CARE, INC.

P.O. Box 630, Skaneateles, NY, 13152-0630. Contact: Arnold Benson, Pres. - Tel: (315) 422-4222, Fax: (315) 685-3888. A professional service providing care and companionship to the elderly in their own home as an alternative to institutionalization. Established: 1984 - Franchising Since: 1988 - No. of Units: Company Owned: 1 - Franchised: 1 - Franchise Fee: $25,000 - Royalty: 7%, 1/2% adv.- Total Inv: $125,000-$175,000 - Financing: Affiliated with financing company.

WESTSTAFF

301 Lennon Lane, Walnut Creek, CA, 94598. - Tel: (925) 930-5300, (800) USA-TEMP, Fax: (925) 256-1515. Full-service international staffing service. Western grants exclusive territories, comprehensive training, complete temporary payroll, A/R financing, state of the art integrated payroll, billing, accounting, search and retrieval system, credit - collections expertise. Established: 1948 - Franchising Since: 1957 - No. of Units: Company Owned: 300 (incl. 28 medical) - Franchised: 100 (incl. 27 medical) - Franchise Fee: $10,000+ varies with pop. - Royalty: 8% service fee - Total Inv: $50,000-$100,000 - Financing: Franchise fee financing for staffing industry professionals.

ENTERTAINMENT

AFTER THE GOLD RUSH, INC.
Entertainment Concepts, Ltd.

6464 Greenbriar Dr., Englewood, CO, 80111. Contact: Rob or Dennis Muck, Mktg. Dir. - Tel: (303) 740-7331. Quality entertainment centers offering a modern versatile entertainment format. Established: 1972 - Licensing Since: 1978 - No. of Units: 5 - Total Inv: Varies with location and size of facility.

AMACADE AMUSEMENT & ENTERTAINMENT CENTERS

Ste. A, Block AA-1, P.O. Box 24, Fayetteville, AR, 72702. Contact: Licensing Dir. - Tel: (501) 443-6791, Fax: (501) 443-4024. Licensed game rooms, arcades, family entertainment centers, sports games centers and game parks, featuring various games, amusement rides, etc. stand-alone, mobile and co-branded units, turnkey investment. Established: 1988 - Franchising Since: 1990 - No. of Units: Company Owned: 2 - Franchise Fee: $5,000-$50,000 - Royalty: None - Total Inv: $60,000-$20,000,000 - Financing: Limited equipment lease financing. Design and training provided.

AMERICAN DARTERS ASSOCIATION, INC.

1000 Lake St. Louis Blvd., Ste. 310, Lake St. Louis, MO, 63367. Contact: Glenn Remick, Pres. - Tel: (636) 625-8621ext. 7048, (888) 327-8752, Fax: (636) 625-2975. Sell Anheuser-Busch Bud Light Dart League sponsored franchises. Established: 1991 - Franchising Since: 1991 - No. of Units: Franchised: 75 - Franchise Fee: Entry level $1,000 - Financing: No.

AMERICAN MOBILE SOUND
AMS Franchise Corp.

600 Ward Dr. Ste. A-1, Santa Barbara, CA, 93111. - Tel: (805) 681-8132, (800) 788-9007, Fax: (918) 427-4989. Professional mobile disc jockey service, providing MC's and amplified music for any occasion. Established: 1991 - Franchising Since: 1994 - No. of Units: Franchised: 28 - Franchise Fee: $6,000-$15,000 - Royalty: 7% - Total Inv: $10,510 - Financing: Yes.

BLUE NOTE INTERNATIONAL

131 West 3rd St., New York, NY, 10012. - Tel: (212) 475-0049, Fax: (212) 529-1038. Internationally renown jazz club, restaurant and café. Established: 1981 - Licensing Since: 1987 - No. of Units: Company Owned: 1 - Licensed: 5 - Management Service Fee: $100,000 plus Licensing Fee: $200,000 - Royalty: 10% - Total Inv: $2,000,000-$2,500,000 - Financing: No.

COMPLETE MUSIC

7877 L St., #3, Omaha, NE, 68127-1808. Contact: G. E. Maas, Pres. - Tel: (402) 339-0001, (800) 843-3866, Fax: (402) 339-1285. Disc jockey entertainment, providing dance music for over 1,000,000 people each year. The uniqueness of this business allows owners to use their skills in management to hire and book their own Complete Music trained D.J.'s for all types of special events. Established: 1972 - Franchising Since: 1981 - No. of Units: Company Owned: 1 - Franchised: 143 - Franchise Fee: $15,500 - Royalty: 6%-8% - Total Inv: $15,500-$35,500 - Financing: Yes.

DINE-OUT MEAL CLUBS OF AMERICA
Big Sky Press, Inc.

5805 Helena Dr., Missoula, MT, 59803. Contact: Pete Addeo, Owner/ President - Tel: (406) 251-5189, (800) 636-8266, Fax: (406) 251-4683. Publish and sell your own Dine Out Meal Club menu book. Memebrship good for "buy 1, get 1 meal free" at hundreds of restaurants. Menu book shows entire menus of all member restaurants. No coupons. Unique home based franchise with little or no overhead. Begin earning income within 6-8 Weeks. Established: 1992 - Franchising Since: 1997 - No. of

Units: Company Owned: 4 - Franchise Fee: $15,000 - Royalty: 5% gross income paid monthly - Total Inv: Initial startup fees for flyers, brochures, dpps, etc $4-$6,000 - Financing: No.

DOCTORDISC CD SWAP SHOPS
Doctor Disc Franchising, LLC
2351 E. Morris Blvd., Morristown, TN, 37813. Contact: Joe Moore, Jeff Moore, Greg Moore - Tel: (423) 581-1004, Fax: (423) 581-1004. Buy-Trade-Sell cassettes, CDs, movies, video games, sell posters, stickers, shirts and related items. A fun/clean business dealing in items people normally have no used market for. New CDs and cassettes the day released. Established: 1993 - Franchising Since: 1997 - No. of Units: Company Owned: 2 - Franchise Fee: $18,500 - Royalty: 5% first $4,000/wk, 4% $4000 + (minimum $200/wk) - Total Inv: $60,550-$175,550 - Financing: No.

EXACTMATCH
P.O. Box 15461, Chesapeake, VA, 23328. Contact: J.R. Fisher - Tel: (801) 409-8604, (800) 300-3091, Fax: (801) 409-8604. Home based matching service. Established: 1996 - Franchising Since: 2000 - No. of Units: Company Owned: 5 - Franchise Fee: $1,495 - Total Inv: $1,495-$2,550 - Financing: N/A.

FRED ASTAIRE FRANCHISED DANCE STUDIO
Fred Astaire Dance Studios, Inc
7900 Glades Road, Suite 630, Boca Raton, FL, 33431. Contact: Linda Milo, Franchise Manager - Tel: (561) 218-3237, (800) 278-2473, Fax: (561) 218-3299, E-Mail: dancefads@aol.com, Web Site: www.fred astaire.com. Adult ballroom dance instruction. Established: 1947 - Franchising Since: 1952 - No. of Units: Franchised:108 - Franchise Fee: $15,000 - Royalty: 8% - Total Inv: $138,000-$357,000 - Financing: Third party.

FUN SERVICES
Play-By-Play Toy's & Novelties
P.O. Box 18267, San Antonio, TX, 78218. - Tel: (210) 829-4666, Fax: (210) 824-6565, E-Mail: loperk@pbpus.com. Corporate picnics, Santa secret shops, fun fairs and holiday gift shops. Established: 1970 - Franchising Since: 1970 - No. of Units: Franchised: 50 - Franchise Fee: $75.00-$200.00 - Royalty: None.

GAMEWYZE
GameWyze, Lt.
3825 Spring Creek Pkwy, Suite 201, Plano, TX, 75023. Contact: Amy O'Brien, Director of Communications - Tel: (877) GET-WYZE, Fax: (972) 335-8801, E-Mail: franchise@gamewyze.com, Web Site: www.gamewyze.com. GameWyze offers a community hub for competitive and recreational computer/console-based entertainment with access to cutting-edge computers and consoles with the latest video games, tournaments, Internet access, and so much more. Established: 2001 - No. of Units: Company Owned: 1 - Franchised: 1.

INDOOR GRAND PRIX INTERNATIONAL
Indoor Grand Prix
9616 Santa Fe Circle, Irving, TX, 75063. - Tel: (972) 506-0834, Fax: (972) 869-3926. A family entertainment center featuring indoor competitve go kart racing for adults, featuring a computerized timing system. Corporate and childrens party rooms, and a Captain Nickel's redemption arcade. Established: 1994 - Franchising Since: 1997 - No. of Units: Company Owned: 2 - Franchise Fee: $29,500-$39,500 - Royalty: 2%-7% depending on sales volume - Total Inv: $202,792-$610,000 - Financing: No.

IT'S ABOUT GAMES
Grow Biz International, Inc
4200 Dahlberg Dr., Minneapolis, MN, 55422. Contact: Brad Tait, President - Tel: (612) 520-8500, (800) 645-7299, Fax: (612) 520-8623, Web Site: www.growbiz.com. Retail store that buys and sells new and used video games and accessories. Established: 1997 - Franchising Since: 1997 - No. of Units: Company Owned: 45 - Franchised: 4 - Franchise Fee: $20,000 - Royalty: 4% of gross sales - Toatal Inv: $165,000 (US) approximately - Financing: No.

MARTY WOLF GAME CO.
2120 S. Highland Dr., Ste. G, Las Vegas, NV, 89102. - Tel: (702) 385-2963, Fax: (702)3 85-6963, Web Site: www.casinodealerhomestudy.com. Casino party rental business - Casino equipment rental and/or turnkey "Las Vegas Nite" parties for fundraisers, theme parties. Start up package vary from - one blackjack table kit to 100 participant party. Established: 1970 - Total Inv: $170.00 - Financing: Possible.

MUZAK LIMITED PARTNERSHIP
Muzak
5550 77 Center Dr Ste 380, Charlotte, NC, 28217-0703. Contact: Jack D. Craig, V.P. Aff.Sales & Dev. - Tel: (800) 331-3340, (206) 633-3000, Fax: (704) 926-3694. Muzak is a provider of business music and is heard by an estimated 80 million people each day in the U.S. and 11foreign countries. The company has evolved into a high-tech, broad-based multimedia company, delivering music, videos, advertisements, data and information to businesses around the world via satellite, private radio signal and through on-site tape systems. Established: 1934 - Franchising Since: 1934 - No. of Units: Company Owned: 34 - Franchised: 138 - Franchise Fee: Varies by market - Royalty: % of gross billing or fee per subscriber - Total Inv: Min. $250,000 (start-up) - Financing: No.

PARTY PERSONNEL FRANCHISE SYSTEMS *
11720 Hadley, Overland Park, KS, 66210 - Tel: (913) 451-0218, Fax: (913) 451-8941, Web Site: www.partypersonnelkc.com. Party Personnel provides staff based on your specific needs. Whether it's skilled bartenders for a convention or waiters for a reception. Established: 1993 - Franchising Since: 2003 - No. of Units: Company Owned: 1 - Franchise Fee: $15,000 - Royalty: 3% - Total Inv: $22,500-$40,000 - Financing: No.

RIPLEY'S BELIEVE IT OR NOT!
Ripley Entertainment, Inc
5728 Major Blvd., Ste. 700, Orlando, FL, 32819. Contact: Exec. VP of Attractions - Tel: (407) 345-8010, Fax: (407) 345-0801, E-Mail: deska @ripleys.com, Web Site: www.ripleys.com. Walk through attractions featuring the strange, unusual and the unbelievable. Established: 1962 - Franchising Since: 1990 - No. of Units: Company Owned: 6 - Franchised: 20 - Franchise Fee: $50,000 U.S. - Royalty: 15% of gross admissions - Total Inv: Varies with size of museum and market - Financing: None.

SINGING MACHINE COMPANY INC., THE
6601 Lyons Rd Bldg A7, Coconut Creek, FL, 33073. Contact: Gene Settler, Pres. - Tel: (954) 596-1000, Fax: (954) 596-2000. Recording booths, portable and stationary - Karaoke hardware and software products. Established: 1982 - Franchising Since: 1985 - No. of Units: Company Owned: 2 - Franchised: 38 - Franchise Fee: Depends on location - Total Inv: $10,000-$12,000 - Financing: Yes.

SOME DUDE'S PLAYGROUND
Some Dude's Enterprises, Inc
1052 W. Hillfield Rd, Layton, UT, 84041. Contact: Lane Bird - Tel: (801) 479-3479, (801) 725-1593, Fax: (801) 479-3638. Complete family entertainment center. Established: 1999 - Franchising Since: 2002 - No. of Units: Company Owned: 3 - Franchise Fee: $25,000 - Financing: No.

SOUNDSTATION ENTERTAINMENT SERVICES
21515 Chagrin Rd., Cleveland, OH, 44122-5307. Contact: Mark Cheplowitz, President - Tel: (216) 561-5700, (216) 644-9900, Fax: (216) 561-3600. Entertainment production company. Training and support provided. Established: 1982 - No. of Units: Company Owned: 1 - Franchise Fee: $25,000 - Total Inv: $45,000.

STAR VIDEO GROUP
13710 - E. Rice Place, Aurora, CO, 80015. Contact: Paul Sanders, VP - Tel: (720) 870-9651, (800) 567-7710, Fax: (720) 870-9653, Web Site: www.starvideogroup.com. Specializing in neighborhood video rental stores. Turnkey, set-up, on-going support, steady rotation of product. Best selection of movies, games, DVD, music, apparel and more. Established: 1990 - Franchising Since: 1994 - No. of Units: Company Owned: 6 - Franchised: 72 - Franchise Fee: $10,000 - Royalty: 8% - Total Inv: $180,000-$250,000 - Financing: Yes.

THE RIGHT ONE
PAFCO International Inc
160 Old Derby St., Suite 339, Hingham, MA, 02043. Contact: Paul A. Falzone, CEO - Tel: (781) 749-2360, (800) 818-3283, Fax: (781) 749-2390, E-Mail: carole@therightone.com, Web Site: www.theright one.com. Personal introduction service for single people looking for a relationship. Established: 1990 - Franchising Since: 1999 - No. of Units: Company Owned: 9 - Franchised: 6 - Franchise Fee: $50,000-$80,000 - Total Inv: $98,400-$184,900 - Financing: Some in-house.

VIDEO DATA SERVICES
26 Chatham Woods, Pittsford, NY, 14534. Contact: Stuart J. Dizah, Pres - Tel: (716) 381-9240,(800) 772-4667, Fax: (716) 381-9277, E-Mail: vdsvideo@aol.com, Web Site: www.vdsvideo.com. Video production, duplication, editing and film to tape transfer. Established: 1981 - Franchising Since: 1989 - No. of Units: Company Owned: 1 - Franchised: 236 - Franchise Fee: $22.500 - Royalty: Flat $750 per year - Total Inv: $10,000 equipment, $12,500 franchise fee - Financing: No.

WEST COAST VIDEO
West Coast Entertainment Corp
9998 Global Rd #2nd Flr, Philadelphia, PA, 19115-1006. - Tel: (215) 497-5835, (800) 433-5171, Fax: (215) 968-5164, E-Mail: Dweiss@ moviebuff.com, Web Site: www.Westcoastvideo.com. Video rentals and sales, also accessories. Established: 1985 - Franchising Since: 1985 - Franchise Fee: $25,000.00 Individual $8,5000. developmental - Royalty: 5%, 2% national marketing fund - Total Inv: $250,000.

WORLD CHAMPIONSHIP ARMWRESTLING *
P.O. Box 882, Ames, IA, 50010. Contact: Don Myers, Operations Manager - Tel: (515) 232-5023, (866) 232-5023, Fax: (515) 232-5036, E-Mail: info@realitysportsent.com, Web Site: www.worldchampionarm wrestling.com. Franchisees promote and run arm wrestling tournaments santioned by World Championship Armwrestling, using a state of the art machine called the Enforcer. Established: 2002 - Franchising Since: 2003 - No. of Units: Company Owned: 1 - Franchised: 2 - Franchise Fee: $50,000 - Royalty: $50-$100 per event - Financing: Yes.

FINANCIAL SERVICES

ACE AMERICA'S CASH EXPRESS
ACE Cash Express, Inc.
1231 Greenway Dr. Ste. 800, Irving, TX, 75038. Contact: Franchise Development - Tel: (972) 550-5000, (800) 713-3338, Fax: (972) 582-1409, Web Site: www.acecashexpress.com. ACE is a 30 year old publicity traded company (NASAQ:AACE) operating and franchising over 750 money centers across 28 states. ACE offers customers a number of financial services including check cashing, short-term loans, money orders, wire transfers, pre-paid phone service, bill payments and other related services. Established: 1968 - Franchising Since: 1996 - No. of Units: Company Owned: 600 - Franchised: 100 - Franchise Fee: $30,000 std. / $15,000 kiosk - Royalty: 5% - Total Inv: $130,000-$187,000 (standard), $79,200-$97,000 (kiosk) - Financing: Yes, third party.

ACFN
ACFN Franchised Inc.
96 North Third Street Suite 680, San Jose, CA, 95112. Contact: Avi Blankroth, VP Franchise Development - Tel: (888) 794-2236, Fax: (888) 708-8600, E-Mail: franchising@acfn.info, Web Site: www.acfnfranchise.com. ACFN-the ATM Franchise business. Develop and operate your own private network of ATM machines in hotels amnd other travel & entertainment based businesses. Established: 1986 - Franchising Since: 2003 - No. of Units: Company Owned: 151 - Franchised: 4 - Franchise Fee: $29,000 - Royalty: 0% - Total Inv: Each new location added to network, Triton 9700 ATM $5,995, shipping $200, sales tax, average cash needed to operate ATM $7,000 - Financing: Yes.

```
• • • • • • • • • • • • • • • • •
•                                 •
•      Have you seen the          •
•   Info Franchise Newsletter?    •
•                                 •
• • • • • • • • • • • • • • • • •
```

ATM BANKING SERVICES
Merchant Advertising Systems, Inc
4115 Tiverton Rd, Randallstown, MD, 21133. Contact: Don Goldvarg, President - Tel: (410) 655-3201, (800) 316-6461, Fax: (410) 655-0262. On-site location, ATM banking services. Established: 1985 - Franchising Since: 1987 - No. of Units: Company Owned: 6 - Franchise Fee: $9,500-$18,750 - Total Inv: $9,500 min, (plus $1,750 expenses).

BANKS, BENTLEY & CROSS, INC.
1601 Dove Street., Suite 185, Newport Beach, CA, 92660. Contact: Bud Bergeron - Tel: (949) 786-9111, Fax: (949) 660-0839, E-Mail: klbergeron@earthlink.net. Professional debt management and debt negotiation. Established: 1985 - Franchising Since: 1990 - Franchise Fee: $995.00.

CASH PLUS
Cash Plus,Inc.
3002 Dow Ave., #120, Tustin, CA, 92780-7247. Contact: Craig Bade - Tel: (714) 731-2274, (888) 707-2274, Fax: (714) 731-2099, E-Mail: gbade@cashplusinc.com, Web Site: www.cashpluslusinc.com. Check cashing, payday advancement, money orders, wire transfers, debit cards, mail box rentals, foreign currency exchange, etc. Established: 1984 - Franchising Since: 1988 - No. of Units: Compay Owned: 3- Franchised: 75 - Franchise Fee: $30,000 - Royalty: 6% - Total Inv: $141,000-$212,000 - Financing: Third party.

CHECK MART
Convenience Money Centers, Inc
608 Garrison St Ste L, Lakewood, CO, 80215-5881. Contact: Ron Higmire, Pres. - Tel: (303) 892-7171. Check cashing and related services. Established: 1983 - Licensor Since: 1985 - No. of Units: Company Owned: 7 - Licensed: 9 - Fee: $7,500 - Royalty: 5%- Total Inv: $7,500 fran. fee, $20,000 buildout, 6 mo. oper. exp., $40,000 line of credit - Financing: Yes.

CHECK PATROL
P.O. Box 10143, Bozeman, MT, 59719-0143. Contact: Raul Luciani, Pres. - Tel: (406) 586-7744, Fax: (406) 586-0017. Return check recovery. Recovery of returned checks for merchants issued by customers. A return fee is charged to the check writer. Established: 1985 - Franchising Since: 1991 - No. of Units: Franchised: 8 - Franchise Fee: $15,000 - Royalty: 6% on gross receipts from fees charged for check recovery - Total Inv: $15,000 fran. fee, $7,000 equip. & supply - Financing: Yes.

COMMERCIAL UNION ATM DIVISION
3127 E. Otero Blvd, Littleton, CO, 80112. Contact: Richard Godwin - Tel: (866) 423-5009, Fax: (866) 423-5009. Sell and service ATM. Established: 2000 - Franchising Since: 2001 - No. of Units: Company Owned: 3 - Franchised: 3 - Franchise Fee: $30,000 - Total Inv: $100,000 - Financing: Yes.

EDSA GROUP, THE
Edsa Group, Inc, The
1 Oak Square, 8280 YMCA Plaza Dr., #4, Baton Rouge, LA, 70810-0918. - Tel: (225) 291-0343, (800) 942-2777, Fax: (225) 291-0419. Franchisor of financial education programs. Our affiliates contract with corporations to train their employees regarding money management issues including retirement planning, tax planning, budgeting, insurance planning, and company benefits. Established: 1993- Franchising Since: 1994 - No. of Units: Franchised: 34 - Franchise Fee: $6,950 - Royalty: 10% of minimum suggested educational fee for each program - Total Inv: $6,950 managing executive franchise, $3,450 financial education consultant franchise, plus $500 travel expense to training session - Financing: No.

FAST BUCKS CHECK CASHING SERVICE
3615 N 44th #1, Lincoln, NE, 68504. - Tel: (402) 464-3949. Fast Bucks Check Cashing has proven to be a highly attractive alternative to traditional banking. Provides customers with check cashing, western union wires, payroll advancing, notary services, money orders, cashier's checks and other related services. Established: 1994 - Franchising Since: 1995 - No. of Units: Company Owned: 2 - Franchised: 7 - Franchise Fee: $20,000 - Royalty: 5%, 2% adv. - Total Inv: $48,000-$95,000 - Financing: Indirect.

HEAVENLY GOLD CARD™
Nova Media Inc
1724 N. State, Big Rapids, MI, 49307-9073. Contact: Manager Sales - Tel: (231) 796-4637, E-Mail: trund@nov.com. Bank card or credit card for fundraising for non-profits, churches. The smart card can be programmed for goodwill sales, special events or any reason for donations as well as use on the Internet. Established: 1981 - Franchising Since: 1998 - No. of Units: Company Owned: 1 - Franchised: 1 - Franchise Fee: $75,000-$300,000 - Royalty: Flexible based on zip code population - Total Inv: $400,000-$600,000 - Financing: Yes.

INVESTEAM FINANCIAL, INC.
7289 Garden Road, Ste. 205, West Palm Beach, FL, 33404. Contact: Lawrence Cinquemani, President - Tel: (561) 842-9333, (800) 638-2544, Fax: (561) 842-2442, E-Mail: atm@investeam.com, Web Site: www.investeam.com. ATM Sales business: privately owned ATM's sold on a fully managed turnkey basis. Established: 1996 - Franchising Since: 1996 - No. of Units: Company Owned: 5 - Franchised: 200+ - Franchise Fee: $18,990 total cost - Total Inv: $18,990 per ATM - Financing: Nationally - Malls, Airports, Colleges, Etc.

MERCHANT ADVERTISING SYSTEMS, INC.
415 Tiverton Road, Randallstown, MD, 21133. Contact: Don Goldwarg, President - Tel: (410) 655-3201, (800) 992-1615, Fax: (410) 655-0262. ATM, Bank card services, complete turn key operation, on how to find, select, sell, install and market, ATM's profitably in any given metropolitan area. (Full training and materials available). Established: 1997 - Franchising Since: 1999 - No. of Units: Company Owned: 31 - Franchise Fee: $9,500-$18,500 (contigent on population base) - Royalty: Nil - Total Inv: Franchise Fee plus $1,750 expenses - Financing: Yes.

MONEY MASTERS
Debt Doctors Franchising
2472 Glick St., Lafayette, IN, 47905. Contact: Norm Neiburger, Pres. - Tel: (765) 477-7377, Fax: (765) 477-7377. We offer training in professional credit counselling and debt management, helping indebted consumers get out of debt without borrowing. Our clients stay with our program longer than anyone else in the industry. Established: 1966 - Franchising Since: 1993 - No. of Units: Company Owned: 3 - Franchised: 1 - Franchise Fee: $10,000 - Royalty: 7.5% of fees - Total Inv: Fran. fee plus $5,000 start-up adv. & office furn. - Financing: No.

MONEYWORX FRANCHISING, INC.
25400 U.S. Hwy. 19 N., Ste. 240, Clearwater, FL, 33763. - Tel: (727) 793-9201, Fax: (727) 793-9203. Equipment leasing & financial services. Established: 2002 - Franchising Since: 2002 - No. of Units: Franchised: 4 - Franchise Fee: $25,000-$100,000 - Financing: Yes.

NIX CHECK CASHING
Thomas Nix Distributor, Inc
17019 Kingsview Ave, Carson, CA, 90746. - Tel: (310) 538-2242, (800) 325-1718, Fax: (310) 538-0131. Check cashing and financial service center. Established: 1966 - Franchising Since: 1993 - No. of Units: Company Owned: 70 - Franchised: 18 - Franchise Fee: $19,995 - Financing: Yes.

PAID, INC
4 Brussels St, Worchester, MA, 01610. - Tel: (719) 534-0292, Web Site: www.paiding.com. This business franchise provides you with the ability to offer affordable, convenient, and secure financial services that help businesses meet the challenges of tomorrow, by improving and maximizing their cash flow. You as a franchisee will realize residual income on every transaction. Electronic automation of business cash flow is the future... PAID, Inc. makes that future a reality! Established: 1998 - Franchising Since: 1999 - No. of Units: Company Owned: 1 - Franchised: 17 - Franchise Fee: $24,500 - Royalty: N/A - Total Inv: $24,500 - Financing: N/A.

QUICK CASH
IMI Ink
2344 Fieldstone Drive, Conyers, GA, 30013. - Tel: (770) 860-8999, Fax: (770) 860-0712. We put in the lucrative and profitable check cashing business. Turn key operation, all equipment, computers and training included. Demographic studies are free. $3,000 will get you in. Established: 1986 - Franchising Since: 1996 - No. of Units: Company

Owned: 25 - Franchised 45 - Franchise Fee: None - Royalty: 5% of other services & products - Total Inv: $65,000-$95,000 - Financing: 100% financing available.

UNITED CHECK CASHING
United Check Cashing Co. Inc.
400 Market St., Ste. 1030, Philadelphia, PA, 19106. - Tel: (800) 626-0787, Fax: (215) 238-9056. Convience store of financial services. Check cashing, money orders, Western Union, ATMS, payday loans, authorized bill payment and many more. Established: 1977 - Franchising Since: 1992 - No. of Units: Company Owned: 3 - Franchised: 92 - Franchise Fee: $27,500 - Royalty: .2% of check cashing and debit card vol, 5% gross receipts - Total Inv: $156,000 - Financing: Yes, third party.

VALCOR ARBITRATIN SERVICES, LTD.
3753 Howard Hughes Parkway, Ste. 200, Las Vegas, NV, 89109. - Tel: (702) 892-3779. Business debt mediation and financial consulting capital acquisition, arbitration, negotiation and affiliate training. Established: 1960 - Franchising: 1994 - No. of Units: Franchised: 400 worldwide - Franchise Fee: $11,900 - Royalty: None - Total Inv: $11,900 - Financing: Yes.

X-BANKERS CHECK CASHING
X-Bankers Express, Inc.
113 Pinepoint Drive, Bridgeport, CT, 06606-1951. Contact: Robert Swift, Pres. - Tel: (203) 374-1377. Check cashing and financial services. Franchising Since: 1982 - No. of Units: Franchised: 13 - Franchise Fee: $14,500 - Royalty: 3% of gross revenues - Total Inv: $71,500-$83,000 - Financing: Yes, part of franchise fee.

FITNESS CENTERS

ANYTIME FITNESS INC
P.O. Box 18213, W. St. Paul, MN, 55118. Contact: Jeff Klinger - Tel: (800) 704-5004, (651) 554-0144, Fax: (651) 554-0311, E-Mail: info@anytimefitness.com, Web Site: www.anytimefitness.com. A 24 hour access for members. Established: 2002 - Franchising Since: 2002 - No. of Units: Franchised: 2 - Franchise Fee: $1,900.

BUTTERFLY LIFE *
2404 San Ramon Valley Blvd, Suite 200, San Ramon, CA, 94583. - Tel: (800) 288-8373, Fax: (925) 743-8820, Web Site: www.butterfly.com. Women's fitness franchise promoting weight loss and healthy living. Established: 2003 - Franchising Since: 2003 - No. of Units: Company Owned: 1 - Franchised: 4 - Franchise Fee: $29,500 - Royalty: $600 on going - Total Inv: $59,500.

COM*PLEX SKIN FITNESS CLINICS COLO. SKIN CARE CLINIC, INC.
393 S. Harlan, Villa 2, Ste. 200, Lakewood, CO, 80226. Contact: Jan Trujillo, Pres. - Tel: (303) 937-7777, Fax: (303) 937-7779. All phases of skin care, with training at Colorado School of Paramedical Esthetics. Specializing in cystic acne, acne vultgari, without any drugs. Established: 1972 - Franchising Since: 1995 - No. of Units: Company Owned: 1 - Franchise Fee: $25,000 - Royalty: $136,000-$290,000 - Financing: Yes.

CONTOURS EXPRESS
Contours Express, Inc
156 Imperial Way, Nicholasville, KY, 40356. Contact: Daren Carter, President - Tel: (859) 885-6441, (877) 227-2282, Fax: (859) 885-8397, E-Mail: sales@contoursexpress.com, Web Site: www.Contours Express.com. Ladies only fitness and weight loss studio. Clubs offer members a 29 minute workout combining strength training with aerobic exercise. Proven systems allow successful clubs in town of 7,000 or larger. Start up assistance and ongoing support provided. No prior business or fitness experience necessary! Established: 1998 - Franchising Since: 1998 - No. of Units: Company Owned: 8- Franchised: 20 - Franchise Fee: $9,995 - Royalty: $395.00 per month - Total Inv: $31,200-$45,700 - Financing: No.

CROSSTRAINING CLUB , THE
11954 Roe Ave, Overland Park, KS, 66209. Contact: Erin Merritt, Owner - Tel: (913) 469-8850, Fax: (949) 481-7410. The Crosstraining Club does personal fitness training in a small group setting in order to

make it more affordable for our clients. A CTC trainer will give you organized cardiora scular and weight training work outs, personal instruction and motivation through the most efficient effective, enjoyable work out programs available. Established: 1993 - Franchisng Since: 1997 - No. of Units: Company Owned: 2 - Franchised: 3 - Franchise Fee: $10,000.00 - Royalty: 5% of gross - Total Inv: $75,000.00-$95,000.00 - Financing: N/A.

CURVES FOR WOMEN
Curves International, Inc.
400 Schroeder, Waco, TX, 76710. - Tel: (254) 399-9285, (800) 848-1096, Fax: (254) 399-9731. 30 minute fitness and weight loss centers for women. Established: 1995 - Franchising Since: 1995 - No. of Units: Franchised: 600 - Franchise Fee: $19,900 - Royalty: $395 monthly - Total Inv: $19,900 included equipment - Financing: Yes.

FITNESS FOR LIFE FRANCHISE *
399 Perry Street #300, Castle Rock, CO, 80104. - Tel: (303) 663-0880, (877) 663-0880, Fax: (303) 663-1617, E-Mail: info@fitnesstogether.com, Web Site: www.fitnesstogetherfranchise.com. Fitness Together is the World's largest personal training organization. Established: 1984 - Franchising Since: 1996 - No. of Units: Company Owned: 1 - Franchised: 73 - Franchise Fee: $29,000 - Royalty: 5% - Total Inv: $130,000-$175,000.

GOLD'S GYM FRANCHISING INC.
358 Hampton Dr., Venice, CA, 90291. Contact: Paul M. Grymkowski, President/ International Director - Tel: (310) 392-3005, (800)457-5375, Fax: (310) 392-4680, Web Site: www.goldsgym.com. Gym and fitness centers. Established: 1960 - Franchising Since: 1980 - No. of Units: Company Owned: 1 - Franchised: 530 - Franchise Fee: $12,000 initial fee; $6,000 annual renewal - Total Inv: $434,000-$1,750,000 includes buildout costs, equipment, opening expenses, add'l funds est. for first three months of operations - Financing: No.

HEALTH CLUBS OF AMERICA
500 E. Broward Blvd., Suite 1650, Ft. Lauderdale, FL, 33394. Contact: Charles Cavuoto, President - Tel: (954) 527-5373, (800) 833-5239, Fax: (954) 527-5436. Specializing in aerobics and weight training - full training and support provided. Established: 1983 - No. of Units: Company Owned: 13 - Franchised: 80 - Franchise Fee: $50,000 - Financing: Yes.

IM=X XERCISE STUDIO *
566 7th Ave, Suite 701, New York, NY, 10018. - Tel: (866) IMX-7763, Fax: (212) 997-7356, E-Mail: franchise@xercizestudio.com, Web Site: www.xercizestudio.com. The IM=X Xercise Studio is a turn-key business. Whether you are an instructor, personal trainer, business owner or fitness enthusiast, you can own one or several successful IM=X pilates studios! Established: 1994 - Franchising Since: 2003 - No. of Units: Company Owned: 1 - Franchise Fee: $6,000.

INTRIVAH HEALTH AND WELLNESS *
Intrivah Inc.
2012 8th Avenue, Altoona, PA, 16602. Contact: Michael McConnell, Vice President - Tel: (814) 937-9868, (800) 941-9251, Fax: (814) 941-8260, E-Mail: info@intrivah.com, Web Site: www.intravah.com. Intrivah is a innovative, cutting-edge fitness and nutrition center with superb methodologies, an outstanding business system, and a dynamic franchise opportunity. Consultants develop personalized wellness programs for people of all fitness levels in a safe, non-intimidating environment. Established: 2002 - Franchising Since: 2004 - No. of Units: Company Owned: 1 - Franchise Fee: $30,000 - Royalty: 5% of Gross Sales - Total Inv: $133,750-$224,750 - Financing: Through indirect sources.

JAZZERCISE FRANCHISEE
Jazzercise, Inc.
2460 Impala Drive, Carlsbad, CA, 92008. Contact: Director Franchise Programs/Services - Tel: (760) 476-1750, (800) FIT-IS-IT, Fax: (760) 602-7180, E-Mail: jazzinc@jazzercise.com. Web Site: www.jazzercise.com. International dance-fitness program. Established: 1979 - Franchising Since: 1982- No. of Units: Company Owned: 2 - Franchised: 5126- Franchise Fee: $325 foreign; $650 U.S. - Royalty: 20% of gross - Total Inv: Ranges between $1,475-$5,100.

LADIES WORKOUT EXPRESS
602 Bombay Lane, Roswell, GA, 30076. Contact: Sean Nealy, Franchise Development - Tel: (770) 360-1540. Ladies only fitness franchised. Full training provided. Established: 1993 - Franchising Since: 1996 - No. of Units: Company Owned: 5 - Franchised: 85 - Franchise Fee: $15,000 - Total Inv: $25,000 - Financing: Yes.

LADY OF AMERICA
Health Clubs of America
500 E. Broward Blvd. Suite 1650, Ft. Lauderdale, FL, 33394. Contact: Charles Cavuoto, Intl. Franchise Dir.- Tel: (800) 833-5239, (954) 527-5373, Fax: (954) 527-5436, E-Mail: charles@ladyofamerica.com, Web Site: www.ladyofamerica.com. Lady of America fitness centers specializing in aerobics. Full service with equipment and cardiovascular machinery. Established: 1986 - Franchising Since: 1996 - No. of Units: Franchised: 250 - Franchise Fee: $12,500 - Royalty: 10% - Total Inv: $26,000-$288,000 - Financing: Yes.

LADY OF AMERICA FITNESS CENTERS
2400 E. Commercial Blvd., #808, Ft. Lauderdale, FL, 33308. Contact: Franchise Department - Tel: (800) 833-5239, Fax: (954) 527-5436. Fitness facilities with weight training, cardio vascular equipment, aerobics and dietary control. Established: 1984 - Franchising Since: 1984 - No. of Units: Company Owned: 5 - Franchised: 250 - Franchise Fee: $12,500 - Royalty: 10% - Total Inv: $25,000-$60,000 - Financing: Yes.

NATIONAL ATHLETIC-CLUB
709 Johnnie Dodds Blvd, Mt. Pleasant, SC, 29464. Contact: Michael Mason, President - Tel: (843) 849-3000, (888) 826-2582, E-Mail: mrmason@aol.com, Web Site: www.nationalathleticclub.com. Co-ed fitness facilities. Large scale locations with pools and juice bars. Specializing in marketing to the 40+ demographic. Established: 1982 - Franchising Since: 1998 - No. of Units: Company Owned: 3 - Franchise Fee: $25,000 - Royalty: $1,500 monthly - Total Inv: $489,000-$855,000 - Financing: Third party.

SCHUMAN'S SPEED CENTER *
49 Finnigan Ave., Suite Q3, Saddle Brook, NJ, 07663. Contact: Contact: David Schuman, Owner - Tel: (201) 587-0965, (888) SCH-UMAN, Fax: (201) 221-7605, E-Mail: dschumanspeed.com, Web Site: www.schumanspeed.com. Schuman's Speed Center has quickly emerged as the nation's most respected name in the world of speed, quickness, and agility training for sports. Our franchise is different most because we feel it is imperative that we support and stay involved to help make you successful. We provide you with every facet available to enable you to succeed. Established: 2003 - Franchising Since: 2004 - No. of Units: Company Owned: 12 - Franchise Fee: $25,000 - Royalty: 80% to franchisee, 20% to franchisor - Total Inv: $50,000 - Financing: Yes.

SUPERSLOW ZONE LLC, THE *
285 W. Central Pkwy., #1726, Altamonte Springs, FL, 32714. - Tel: (407) 937-0050. Strength training facilities. Established: 2004 - Franchising Since: 2004 - No. of Units: Company Owned: 1 - Franchise Fee: $20,000-$25,000 - Royalty: Varies - Total Inv: $98,700-$186,500 - Financing: No.

WOMEN'S 17 MINUTE WORKOUT
Women's 17 Minute Workout, Inc
4790 Douglas Cir., N.W., Canton, OH, 44718. Contact: Director of Franchise Sales - Tel: (330) 305-1717, (888) 832-1717, Fax: (330) 497-6453, E-Mail: wo17minute@aol.com, Web Site: www.womens17 minuteworkout.com. Exclusive sales, marketing and service system of women only fitness clubs. Featuring a progressive and aerobic fitness program designed to help women rapidly increase their lean, shapely, calorie - consuming muscle while decreasing their excess body fat. System features certified trainers, fat-reducing nutritional programs and tanning. Complete training and ongoing support provided. Established: 1996 - Franchising Since: 1998 - No. of Units: Company Owned: 5 - Franchised: 2 - Franchise Fee: $34,900 - Royalty: 6% + 1% adv. - Total Inv: $177,000-$295,322 (includes franchise fee and working capital) - Financing: Yes - franchise fee/equipment.

WOMEN'S WORKOUT WORLD
16015 South Harlem Ave., Tinley Park, IL, 60477-1631. Contact: Shari Whitley, CEO - Tel: (708) 429-7766. Offering a unique exercise program for women at an affordable price. The program offers state-of-

the-art exercise equipment, weight loss and continuous exercise classes within a modern health club setting. Established: 1969 - Franchising Since: 1986 - No. of Units: Company Owned: 15 - Franchised: 12 - Franchise Fee: $35,000 - Royalty: 10% - Total Inv: $150,000-$225,000 - Financing: None.

Mike Uretz
Chief Executive Officer

**World Gym
Internattional, Inc.**

3223 Washington Boulevard
Marina del Rey, CA 90292
(310) 827-7705
(800) 544-7441 *Toll Free*
(310) 827-6355 *Fax*
www.worldgym.com

WORLD GYM
World Gym International
3223 Washington Blvd, Marina del Rey, CA, 90292. Contact: Mike Uretz/ Karin Michael, CEO & Execu. Asst. - Tel: (310) 827-7705, (800) 544-7441, Fax: (310) 827-6355, E-Mail: info@worldgym.com, Web Site: www.worldgym.com. One of the largest co-ed franchises in the fitness business. Located in 39 states and 31 countries. Established: 1976 - Franchising Since: 1985 - No. of Units: Company Owned: 1 - Franchised: 500 - Franchise Fee: $13,000 - Royalty: $7,000 per year - Total Inv: $300,000 - Financing: Yes.

FLORIST SHOPS

1-800-FLOWERS
Conroy's Inc.
1600 Stewart Ave, Westbury, NY, 11590. Contact: Director of Franchise Development - Tel: (800) 557-4770, (516) 237-6000, Fax: (516) 237-6097, Web Site: www.1800flowers.com. Full service florists and mass merchandisers of cut flowers. The stores are approximately 2,500 sq. ft. and located on high exposure signalized intersections or highly visible shopping centers. Four week training program in either Southern CA or New York. Franchisor coordinates initial set-up and grand opening, 1-800- Flowers coordinates national and regional advertising programs. Established: 1962 - Franchising Since: 1974 - No. of Units: Company Owned: 32 - Franchised: 101 - Franchise Fee: $28,500 - Royalty: 6% - Total Inv: $203,200-$298,500- Financing: From third parties.

ALLEN'S FLOWERS & PLANTS
Allen's Flowers, Inc.
18500 Sherman Way, Reseda, CA, 91335. Contact: Nace Goldman, V.P. - Tel: (818) 996-2603, Fax: (818) 996-7927. High volume and visibility retail flower shops located in high density corners,with an emphasis on cash and carry trade. Turn-key operation. Established: 1978 - Franchising Since: 1980 - No. of Units: Company Owned: 2 - Franchised: 5 - Franchise Fee: $50,000 - Royalty: 6%-10%- Total Inv: $125,000 depending on location - Financing: Yes.

BUNING THE FLORIST
3860 W. Commercial Blvd., Ft. Lauderdale, FL, 33309. - Tel: (954) 731-1776, Fax: (954) 627-1180. Florist. Established: 1956 - Franchising Since: 1972 - No. of Units: Company Owned: 25 - Franchised: 4 - Franchise Fee: $15,000 - Royalty: $300/mo 1st yr., 3.6% 2nd yr. - Total Inv: $45,000 - Financing: No.

DIAL A ROSE
629 Holly Dr, Palm Beach Gardens, FL, 33410. Contact: Gina Galiano - Tel: (561) 622-1843, Fax: (561) 622-1843, Web Site: www.dial arose.com. Dial A Rose is a speedy rose delivery service. Established: 1985 - Franchising Since: 1997 - No. of Units: Company Owned: 1 - Franchise Fee: N/A - Royalty: $50. per month - Total Inv: $27,000.

FLOWERAMA
Flowerama of America, Inc.
3165 West Airline Hwy., Waterloo, IA, 50703. Contact: Chuck Nygrey, V.P - Tel: (800) 728-6004, (319) 291-6004, Fax: (319) 291-8676, E-Mail: info@flowerama.com, Web Site: www.flowerama.com. Retail floral center. Sale of fresh flowers and floral arrangements, green and blooming plants, gift items, balloons, baskets, and other product. Established: 1967 - Franchising Since: 1971 - No. of Units: Company Owned: 11 - Franchised: 90 - Franchise Fee: $35,000 - Royalty: 6% discounts to 5% - Total Inv: Varies, depending on ownership of real estate - Financing: Yes.

KABLOOM *
200 Wildwood Ave, Woburn, MA, 01801. - Tel: (781) 935-6500, Fax: (781) 935-9410, Web Site: www.kabloom.com. KaBloom locations carry as many as 250 varieties of fresh-cut flowers, all bought directly from growers. Established: 1998 - Franchising Since: 2001 - No. of Units: Copmpany Owned: 11 - Franchised: 56 - Franchise Fee: $30,000 - Royalty: 4.5%-5.5% - Total Inv: $169,000-$266,000.

ROSES ONLY FRANCHISE INC.
457 Main St., #374, Farmingdale, NY, 11735-3510. Contact: Carl Hanson, Exec. VP - Tel: (212) 869-7673, (800) 92-ROSES, Fax: (212) 869-7710. Floral Franchise selling only roses in 7 different stem lengths. Farm direct in 50 different varieties. Established: 1989 - Franchising Since: 1996 - No. of Units: Company Owned: 4 - Franchised: 2 - Franchise Fee: $15,000 - Royalty: 5% of gross sales - Total Inv: $50,000-$75,000.

SILK PLANT PLUS
1045 W. Brandon Blvd., Brandon, FL, 33511.- Tel: (813)684-7414,(888) sendsilk, Fax: (813) 651-3326. Silk Plants Plus is a fast growing, professionally run, silk flowers, plants and home accessory speciality store, with a proven sales and marketing technique. Offering comprehensive training and assistance to franchises. Established: 1989 - Franchising Since: 1997 - No. of Units: Franchised: 3 - Franchise Fee: $15,000 - Royalty: 2%-5% - Total Inv: $67,500 - Financing: Third party.

FOOD: BAKED GOODS/DONUTS/PASTRY

ALL AMERICAN FOOD GROUP
1 University Plaza Dr Ste 209, Hackensack, NJ, 07601-6206. Contact: Michael Vizziello, Director of Franchise - Tel: (908) 757-3022, (800) 922-4350, Fax: (908) 757-8857, Web Site: www.thebagelpage.com. Bagel Franchise. Established: 1994 - Franchising Since: 1996 - No. of Units: Company Owned: 5 - franchised: 35 - Franchise Fee: $25,000 - Royalty: 5% - Total Inv: $50,000-$100,000 - Financing: Yes, Third party.

ALL MY MUFFINS
AMM Licensing Inc.
P.O. Box 852, Hillside, IL, 60162. Contact: Paul Bernstein, V.P. - Tel: (630) 415-0324. Gourmet muffins, soups, salads. Over 250 different types of muffins baked from scratch in each store. Established: 1984 - Franchising Since: 1985 - No. of Units: Franchised: 3 - Franchise Fee: $20,000 - Royalty: 6%, 2% adv. - Total Inv: $99,000-$175,000 - Financing: No.

ARABICA COFFEEHOUSE
Restaurant Developers Corp.
5755 Granger Rd, Suite 200, Independance, OH, 44131. Contact: Franchise Sales Consultant - Tel: (216) 398-110, (800) 837-9599, Fax: (216) 398-0707. Neighborhood gathering place featuring special coffee drinks, gourmet coffee's, fresh in store baked muffins and pastries. Easy to manage, simple to operate. Established: 1976 - Franchising Since: 1995 - No. of Units: Franchised: 26 - Franchise Fee: $22,500 - Royalty: 5.5%/1.5% adv. - Total Inv: $125,000-$363,000 - Financing: Third party.

ATLANTA BREAD CO.
1200 A. Wilson Way SE #A-100, Smyrna, GA, 30082-7207. Contact: John Byron, VP Franchising - Tel: (770) 432-0933, (800) 398-3728, Fax: (770) 444-9082, Web Site: www.atlantabread.com. Bakery cafe: bakery has 20 different breads, 20 muffins, 20 bagels, 10 danish and

many specialty cakes and desserts. Deli serves soups, salads, sandwiches, pillo pies etc. Established: 1993 - Franchising Since: 1995 - No. of Units: Company Owned: 1 - Franchised: 83 - Franchise Fee: $40,000, 1st - $30,000, 2nd - Royalty: 5% - Total Inv: Approx. $490,000-$650,000 - Financing: Yes third party.

AU BON PAIN
19 Fid Kennedy Ave., Boston, MA, 02210. Contact: Mr. Shaich, C.E.O. - Tel: (617) 423-2100, Fax: (617) 423-7879. Bakery/cafe. Offering franchises in multiple units only. Established: 1981 - No. of Units: Company Owned: 115 - Franchised: 30.

AUNTIE ANNE'S HAND-ROLLED SOFT PRETZELS
Auntie Anne's Inc.
160-A Route 41, P.O. Box 529, Gap, PA, 17527. Contact: Terry Wisdo, VP. of Fran. - Tel: (717) 442-4766, Fax: (717) 442-4139. Unique soft pretzel shops, selling a variety of specialty flavored pretzels, assorted dips and fresh-squeezed lemonade and Dutch Ice, a refreshing iced beverage. Product is made fresh and in full view of the customer. Established: 1988 - Franchising Since: 1989 - No. of Units: Company Owned: 15 - Franchised: 500 - Franchise Fee: $30,000 - Royalty: 6%, 1% adv. fund - Total Inv: $156,000-$252,000 - Financing: No.

B.C.C. ENTERPRISE, INC.
157 Barnwood Drive, Edgewood, KY, 41017. Contact: Mark D. Hannahan, President - Tel: (606) 331-7600, Fax: (606) 331-7604, E-Mail: bluechip@fuse.net, Web Site: www.bluechipcookies.com. Blue Chip Cookies is a gourmet cookie company that specializes in fresh, baked from scratch cookies, muffins and brownies. Training and support provided. Established: 1984 - No. of Units: Company Owned: 15 - Franchised: 15 - Franchise Fee: $19,500 - Total Inv: $150,000.

BAGEL BARN FRANCHISE CORPORATION
11850 S.W. 94 Street, Miami, FL, 33186. Contact: Marc Davis, President - Tel: (305) 373-7445, Fax: (305) 373-1528. Bagel/deli, catering, delivery, fresh fruit smoothies, gourmet wraps, edy's yogurt and ice-cream and gourmet coffees. Established: 1993 - Franchising Since: 1997 - No. of Units: Company Owned: 1 - Franchised: 1 - Franchise Fee: $25,000 - Royalty: 6% - Total Inv: $125,000-$155,000 - Financing: Through Merrill Lynch.

BAGEL PATCH
Marketing Resources Group
71-58 Austin St, Forest Hills, NY, 11375. Contact: Bill Mertzer, Franchise Sales Director - Tel: (718) 261-8882. Retail bagel store and cafe. Features fresh baked bagels baked on premises all day, sells bagels by the dozen. Serves breakfast, lunch, snacks, soups, sandwiches, salads, cakes, cookies and homemade chees spreads. Informal catering for homes and offices. Party platters. Eat in or carry out. Established: 1980 - Franchising Since: 1994 - No. of Units: 1 - Franchised: 9 - Franchise Fee: $15,000 - Royalty: 4%, 2% adevertising - Total Inv: $120,000-$146,000 including F.F. - Financing: Franchisor will give assistance.

BAGELS ARE FOREVER!
Centrix Group, The
2947 University Ave P.O. Box 5547, Madison, WI, 53705. - Tel: (608) 231-2427, Fax: (608) 231-1249. Retail bagel shops. Turn-key package for inexperienced persons. Eat-in/take-out. May add muffins, deli meats, soups, sandwiches etc. Recommend that bagels be made from scratch, on premises. May use the name "Bagels are Forever" or choose any other name. Established: 1994 - Franchise Fee: Included in package price - Royalty: None - Total Inv: $95,000-$145,000 - Financing: About one-half total cost, from third party sources.

BAGELZ FRANCHISING CORPORATION
95 Oak Street, Glastonburg, CT, 06033. Contact: Wesley Becher, President - Tel: (860) 657-4400, (800) 270-7900, Fax: (860) 657-2345. Bagelz - The Bagel Bakery offers bagels, gourmet coffee, soup, salads, sandwiches and desserts. Bagelz has low franchise fee and start-up costs with initial and ongoing support and training. Established: 1990 - Franchising Since: 1994 - No. of Units: Company Owned: 4 - Franchised: 22 - Franchise Fee: $10,000 - Royalty: 8% franchise company, 2.5% adv. fund - Financing: No. Not offering franchising at this time.

BEANER'S GOURMET COFFEE
Global Orange Development LLC
206 E. Grand River, Lansing, MI, 48906. Contact: Michael McFall, Franchise Development - Tel: (517) 482-8145, (877) 423-2637, Fax: (517) 482-8625. Italian style espresso bar with lunch menu and breakfast items available like bagels and pastry's. Extraordinary effort has been put into the development of the logo and operating philosophy. We are distinct visually and operationally. Established: 1995 - Franchising Since: 1998 - No. of Units: Company Owned: 2 - Franchised: 2 - Franchise Fee: $20,000 - Royalty: 5% of gross and 1-3% for advertising fund - Total Inv: $65,000-$82,000 liquid.

BENNY'S BAGELS
Benny's Bagels Franchising, Inc.
2636 Walnut Hill Lane Ste. 110, Dallas, TX, 75229-5616. - Tel: (214) 351-2600. Fresh bagel bakery, with specialty cream cheeses, gourmet coffees, and sandwiches. Established: 1994 - Franchising Since: 1996 - No. of Units: Company Owned: 3 - Franchised: 10 - Franchise Fee: $20,000 - Royalty: 5%, 1% adv. - Total Inv: $160,000-$225,000 - Financing: No.

BEST BAGELS IN TOWN
480-19 Patchogue, Holbrook, NY, 11741. Contact: Jay Squatriglia, Pres. - Tel: (631) 472-4104, Fax: (631) 472-4105. Retail bagel bakery restaurant. Established: 1988 - Franchising Since: 1988 - No. of Units: Company Owned: 2 - Franchised: 19 - Franchise Fee: $15,000 - Royalty: 4% gross sales - Total Inv: $135,000-$190,000 excl. fran. fee - Financing: Assistance.

BETWEEN ROUNDS BAGEL DELI & BAKERY
Between Rounds Franchise Corp.
19A John Fitch Blvd., South Windsor, CT, 06074. - Tel: (860) 291-0323, Fax: (860) 289-2732. Bagel/deli/bakery. Sit down, take out and catering. Established: 1990 - Franchising Since: 1992 - No. of Units: Company Owned: 4 - Franchised: 3 - Franchise Fee: $18,000 - Royalty: 4% - Total Inv: $161,000-$208,000 - Financing: No.

BIG APPLE BAGELS
BAB, Inc.
8501 W. Higgins Rd., Ste. 320, Chicago, IL, 60631. Contact: Anthony Cervini, Director of Development - Tel: (773) 380-6100, (800) 251-6101, Fax: (773) 380-6183, E-Mail: bab@babcorp.com, Web Site: www.babcorp.com. Bakery-cafe featuring three brands, fresh-from-scratch Big Apple Bagels, My Favorite Muffin and freshly roasted Brewsters specialty coffee. Our product offering covers many day parts with a delicious assortment of made-to-order gourmet sandwiches, salads, espresso beverages, and fruit smoothies. Established: 1992 - Franchising Since: 1993 - No. of Units: Company Owned: 4 - Franchised: 172 - Franchise Fee: $25,000 - Royalty: 5%; 1% marketing fund - Total Inv: $174,800-$349,500 - Financing: No.

BIG CITY BAGELS
1010 University Ave, Uptown Center in Hillcrest, San Diego, CA, 92103. - Tel: (619) 574-7878, Fax: (6149) 574-7733, E-Mail: mkgilbert @aol.com, Web Site: www.bigcitybagels.com. Bagel bakery café featuring fresh baked authentic N.Y. style bagels, fresh varietal cream cheeses, salads, soups, sandwiches and gourmet coffees. Established: 1992 - Franchising Since: 1993 - No. of Units: Company Owned: 3 - Franchised: 14 - Franchise Fee: $30,000 - Royalty: 4% - Total Inv: $250,000-$300,000 - Financing: Through outside sources.

BIG SKY BREAD COMPANY
188 N Brookwood Ave, Hamilton, OH, 45013-1212. Contact: Harold Tieger, Co-Chairman - Tel: (800) 536-5050, Fax: (513) 651-2709. Whole grain retail bread bakery featuring breads, cookies, muffins, rolls and gourmet coffee. Established: 1990 - Franchising Since: 1992 - No. of Units: Company Owned: 12 - Franchised: 22 - Franchise Fee: $25,000 - Royalty: 5% - Total Inv: $500,000 - Financing: No.

BLACKJACK BAGELS AND COHENS KOSHER
232 Summit Ave., New Milford, NJ, 07646. - Tel: (201) 986-0559. Bagel bakery, bakery, deli appetizing with sit down eating area. Five locations pending in the PA and NY area. Established: 1994 - Franchising Since: 1994 - No. of Units: Company Owned: 4 - Franchised: 1 - Franchise Fee: No franchise fee - Royalty: 2% - Total Inv: $160,000 - Financing: Yes.

BLUE CHIP COOKIES
Blue Chip Franchises Corp.
157 Barnwood Drive, Eaglewood, KY, 41017. Contact: Mark D. Hannahan, President - Tel: (606) 331-7600, Fax: (606) 331-7604. Retail gourmet cookies, brownies, muffins, cinnamon rolls and a complete line of complimentary beverages. Only freshly baked, on premise production. Established: 1983 - Franchising Since: 1985 - No. of Units: Company Owned: 20 - Franchised: 15 - Franchise Fee: $19,500 - Royalty: 6% - Total Inv: $150,000-$180,000 - Financing: No.

BREADSMITH
Breadsmith Franchising, Inc.
409 East Silver Spring Dr., Whitefish Bay, WI, 53217. - Tel: (414) 962-1965, Fax: (414) 962-5888, Web Site: www.breadsmith.com. Hand made hearth baked artison breads and bakery products. Established: 1993 - Franchising Since: 1994 - No. of Units: Company Owned: 1 - Franchised: 38 - Franchise Fee: $30,000 - Royalty: Year 1, 7%; year 2, 6%; year 3, 5% - Total Inv: $217,000-$415,000 - Financing: Assistance.

BREADSOUL CAFE
Breadsoul Franchise, Inc.
118 East 60, New York, NY, 10022. Contact: Dori Evans, Pres. - Tel: (212) 832-7495. Specializes in coffee, cappuccino, imported bread dough baked in stores, gourmet sandwiches and pastries. Take-out, upscale country decor. Established: 1990 - Franchising Since: 1993 - No. of Units: Company Owned: 4 - Franchised: 1 - Franchise Fee: $10,000 - Royalty: $200-$300/wk., no percentage - Total Inv: $75,000-$138,000 - Financing: Not at this time.

BREADSTICK BAKER, THE
The Breadstick Baker Inc
947 Paoli Pike, West Chester, PA, 19382. Contact: Carmen Amodel - Tel: (800) 871-2970. Breadstick baker, located in food courts. Established: 1995 - Franchising Since: 1996 - No. of Units: Company Owned: 1 - Franchise Fee: $22,000 - Total Inv: $87,800-$94,000 incl. franchise fee.

CENTRAL BAKERY PORTUGUESE MUFFIN CAFE
Central Bakery Development Corp.
711 Pleasant St., Fall River, MA, 02723. - Tel: (508) 675-7620, Fax: (508) 677-4523. High quality retail and wholesale bakery selling all natural gourmet portuguese muffins ("Bolos Levedose"). Third generation secret family recipe. Training provided. Established: 1975 - Franchising Since: 1996 - No. of Units: Company Owned: 1 - Franchise Fee: $22,000 - Royalty: 4% of gross sales - Total Inv: $65,832-$72,110 excluding fran. fee - Financing: No.

CHESAPEAKE BAGEL BAKERY
1636 Connecticut Ave NW, Washington, DC, 20009-1043. Contact: Dan Rowe, Dir. Fran. Dev. - Tel: (202) 483-2068. Full - scratch bagel bakery restaurant café/coffee house. Oldest and largest chain in the country. Established: 1981 - Franchising Since: 1984 - No. of Units: Company Owned: 8 - Franchised: 135 - Franchise Fee: $22,500 - Royalty: 4% - Total Inv: $300,000 - Financing: Third party.

CINDY'S CINNAMON ROLLS
P.O. Box 1480, Fallbrook, CA, 92088-1480. Contact: Tom Harris, Pres. - Tel: (760) 723-1121, (800) HOT-ROLL, Fax: (760) 723-4143. Specialty bakery - major malls only - bake from scratch all day. Established: 1985 - Franchising Since: 1986 - No. of Units: Franchised: 35 - Franchise Fee: $25,000 - Royalty: 5% - Total Inv: $62,000-$102,000 - excluding franchise fee - Financing: No.

CINNAMONSTER
CinnaMonster Franchise Group
7346 S. Alton Way, #10-A, Englewood, CO, 80112. - Tel: (303) 770-5075, Fax: (303) 770-5083. Unique upscale bakery. Established: 1991 - Franchising Since: 1992 - No. of Units: Company Owned: 5 - Franchised: 27 - Franchise Fee: $20,000 - Total Inv: Call for details - Financing: No.

COFFEE BEANERY
3429 Pierson Place, Flushing, MI, 48433. Contact: Stacy - Tel: (810) 733-1020, (888) 385-2326, Fax: (810) 733-1536, Web Site: www.coffeebeanery.com. Specialty coffee products in a warm and inviting atmosphere. Established: 1976 - Franchising Since: 1985 - No. of Units: Company Owned: 5 - Franchised: 170 - Franchise Fee: $27,500 - Royalty: 6% - Total Inv: $250,000-$350,000 - Financing: Assistance.

COOKIE BOUQUET/COOKIES BY DESIGN
MGW Group, Inc.
1865 Summit Ave., Ste. 605, Plano, TX, 75074-8147. Contact: David Patterson, V.P. - Tel: (972) 398-9536, (800) 945-2665, Fax: (972) 398-9542, E-Mail: frandevelopment@mgwmail.com, Web Site: www.cookiesbydesign.com. Gift bakery, specializing in hand-decorated cookie arrangements and gourmet cookies, decorated for special events, holidays, centerpieces etc. A wonderfully delicious alternative to flowers or balloons. Established: 1983 - Franchising Since: 1987 - No. of Units: Company Owned: 1 - Franchised: 219 - Franchise Fee: $20,000 - Royalty: 6% - Total Inv: $80,000-$145,000 - Financing: No.

COOKIE MUG, THE
Cookie Mug Inc., The
5526 Peach Street, Erie, PA, 16509. - Tel: (800) 455-0440, (814) 866-6847, Fax: (814) 864-0357. Gourmet cookie bouquet delivery service. Established: 1989 - Franchising Since: 1993 - No. of Units: Company Owned: 1 - Franchised: 1 - Franchise Fee: $10,000 - Royalty: 5%, 0% adv. - Total Inv: $52,800 - (incl. fran. fee) - Financing: None at present.

COOKIES IN BLOOM
Cookies In Bloom, Inc.
12700 Hillcrest Rd #251, Dallas, TX, 75230. Contact: Franchise Department - Tel: (800) 222-3104, Fax: (972) 490-8646. Cookie gift shops, specializing in hand decorated cookie arrangements. Our delicious sugar short-bread cookies come in well over 200 shapes and our baskets and other vases are continually being rotated with new styles and motifs. Established: 1988 - Franchising Since: 1992 - No. of Units: Franchised: 14 - Franchise Fee: $12,500 - Royalty: 5% + 2% adv. - Total Inv: $53,000-$107,000 - Financing: None.

CRESCENT CITY BEIGNETS
Crescent City Beignets, Inc.
3272 Westheimer Road, Suite 1, Houston, TX, 77098. Contact: Stacey Gallagher - Tel: (703) 549-5332, (800) 230-6133, Fax: (703) 549-0740, E-Mail: staceyg@fransmart.com, Web Site: www.crescentcity beignets.com. Crescent City is an original New Orleans cafe/coffee house true to those found on the French Quarter. Our menu offers guests authentic beignets, cafe au lait, Cerole dishes, and Po's Boys along with other selections consistent with the traditions of New Orleans. Established: 1997 - Franchising Since: 2000 - No. of Units: Company Owned: 1 - Franchised: 17 open, over 100 sold - Franchise Fee: $25,000 - Royalty: 5% - Total Inv: $330,750-$448,000 - Financing: Third party.

DAILY'S BAKERY & CAFE
Daily's Franchise Corporation
1415 N. 5th St., Milwaukee, WI, 53212. Contact: Bruce Gendelman, President - Tel: (414) 964-6555, (800) 722-8657. European style bakery and cafe. Established: 1994 - Franchising Since: 1996 - No. of Units: Company Owned: 3 - Franchised: 3 - Franchise Fee: $22,500 - Total Inv: $175,000-$400,000 - Financing: Yes.

DAYLIGHT DONUTS
Daylight Corporation
P.O. Box 580818, Tulsa, OK, 74158-0818. - Tel: (800) 331-2245. Full line donut and pastry retail shops. Established: 1954 - Franchising Since: 1954 - No. of Units: Company Owned: 2 - Franchised: 135 - Total Inv: $25,000 equip., $3,000 inventory, $10,000 approx. remodel - Financing: 70% of equip.

DONUT CONNECTION
Donut Connection Cooperative Corp.
P.O. Box 15405, Pittsburgh, PA, 15237. Contact: James R. Morton, General Manager - Tel: (412) 367-4885, Fax: (412) 367-4885, Web Site: www.donutconnection.com. 160 unit purchasing co-op, no franchise fee, no on-going royalty. Established: 1994 - Franchising Since: 1994 - No. of Units: Franchised: 160 - Training Fee: $10,000 - Financing: No.

DONUT INN
Donut Inn, Inc.
17525 Ventura Blvd Ste 200, Encino, CA, 91316-5107. Contact: Art Pfefferman, Pres. - Tel: (818) 888-2220. Upscale donut, pastry, muffin and bagel shoppes. Registered in 37 states and overseas. Training and manuals provided. Established: 1975 - No. of Units: Company Owned: 1 - Franchised: 27 - Capital Required: $100,000-$150,000 - Royalty: 5.95%, 3% adv. - Total Inv: $145,000-$175,000.

DUNKIN
Daylight Corporation
P.O. Box 580818, Tulsa, OK, 74158-0818. Contact: Jim Perrymore, Sales Mgr. - Tel: (918) 438-0800, Fax: (918) 438-0804. Full line donut and pastry retail shops. Established: 1954 - Franchising Since: 1954 - No. of Units: Company Owned: 2 - Franchised: 135 - Total Inv: $25,000 equip., $3,000 inventory, $10,000 approx. remodel - Financing: 70% of equip.

DUNKIN' DONUTS/BASKIN ROBBINS/TOGOS
14 Pacella Park Drive, Randolph, MA, 02368. Contact: Franchise Department - Tel: (800) 777-9983. Franchised coffee and donut shops featuring drive-in and walk-in units. Retail selling of more than 55 varieties of donuts along with coffee and soft drinks. Established: 1950 - Franchising Since: 1955 - No. of Units: Company Owned: 2 - Franchised: 2,900 - Franchise Fee: $40,000 producing unit, $10,000 satellite - Royalty: 4.9% royalty fees, 5% adv. - Total Inv: Total cost for real estate dev., equip., signs, fran. fee. Shop ranges from $130,000-$600,000 depending on area of country & type of real estate dev. - Financing: No.

EAST COAST BAGEL
P.O. Box 1456, Agoura, CA, 91376-1456. Contact: Franchise Dept. - Tel: (310) 449-4460. Bagel cafe's. Established: 1990 - Franchising Since: 1993 - No. of Units: Company Owned: 30 - Franchised: 5 - Franchise Fee: $25,000 - Royalty: 5% - Total Inv: $200,000-$300,000 - Financing: No.

FLYING SAUCERS GOURMET COFFEE & TEA
Flying Saucers, Inc
1004 Pemble Rd, Leesburg, FL, 34748. Contact: Paul Hanson - Fax: (419) 828-3647, E-Mail: sales@flyingsaucers.com, Web Site: www.flyingsaucers.com. Themed gourmet coffee & sci-fi merchandise. Established: 1994 - Franchising Since: 1995 - No. of Units: Company Owned: 2 - Franchised: 18 - Franchise Fee: $10,000 - Royalty: 5% - Financing: Yes.

GLORIA JEAN'S COFFEES
Gloria Jeans Gourmet Coffees Corp.
28 Executive Park, Ste. 200, Irvine, CA, 92614-4741. Contact: David Jenkins - Tel: (949) 260-1600, Fax: (949) 260-1610, E-Mail: djenkins@gloriajeans.com. Americas largest retail gourmet coffees, teas, and accessories. Each store offers up to 64 varieties of our exclusive coffee. Established: 1979 - Franchising Since: 1986 - No. of Units: Company Owned: 34 - Franchised: 243 - Franchise Fee: $30,000 - Royalty: 6%, 2% adv - Total Inv: $128,000-$389,500 - Financing: Yes.

GOLDBERGS NY BAGEL, DELI & SOUP
All American Food Group
1 David LN Apt 8H, Yonkers, NY, 10701-1120. Contact: Michael Vizziello, Director of Franchising & Licensing - Tel: (800) 922-4350, Fax: (908) 757-8857, E-Mail: aafg@aol.com, Web Site: www.thebagelpage.com. Bagel and deli concept featuring Goldbergs bagels and deli or our kosher bagels with a meatless menu a full array of gourmet coffee and espresso based drinks. Established: 1993 - Franchising Since: 1995 - No. of Units: Company Owned: 7 - Franchised: 35 - Franchise Fee: Traditional $25,000 - Non-traditional: $12,500 - Royalty: 5%. 1% adv. - Financing: Yes, third party.

GREAT AMERICAN BAGEL, THE
Great American Bagel, Inc., The
519 N. Cass Ave., Westmont, IL, 60559. - Tel: (630) 963-3393, (888) BAGEL-ME, Fax: (630) 963-7799, E-Mail: greatambgl@aol.com, Web Site: www.greatamericanbagel.com. Featuring bagels baked-from-scratch daily, homemade cream cheeses, savory soups, gourmet coffees, distinctive catering trays and more! Established: 1987 - Franchising Since: 1994 - No. of Units: Company Owned: 6 - Franchised: 41 - Franchise Fee: $20,000 - Royalty: 4% of gross sales - Total Inv: $200,000-$300,000 - Financing: Indirect.

GREAT AMERICAN COOKIE COMPANY, INC
Mrs. Fields Famous Brands
2855 E. Cottonwood Pkwy., Suite 400, Salt Lake City, UT, 84121. Contact: Franchise Development - Tel: (801) 736-5600, Fax: (801) 736-5936. "Share the fun of cookies". Established cookie concept with a great old family recipe, attractive retail price points, unique cookie cake program available in combination store formats for traditional and non-traditional venues. Established: 1977 - Franchising Since: 1978 - Franchise Fee: $25,000 - Royalty: 7% - Total Inv: $120,000-$625,000 - Financing: None.

GREAT HARVEST BREAD CO.
Great Harvest Franchising, Inc.
28 S. Montana St., Dillon, MT, 59725. Contact: Dawn M. Eisenzimer, Director of New Franchise Development - Tel: (406) 683-6842, (800) 442-0424, Fax: (406) 683-5537, E-Mail: dawne@greatharvest.com, Web Site: www.greatharvest.com. Great Harvest is a nationwide franchise of whole wheat neighborhood bread companies. We are dedicated to finding the people in the world who share our core values, our love for life, and our passion to run a great business. Those values are summed up in our brief but heartfelt mission statement: Be loose and have fun, bake phenomenal bread, run fast to help customers, create strong exciting bakeries, and give generously to others. Established: 1976 - Franchising Since: 1978 - No. of Units: Franchised: 208 - Franchise Fee: $30,000 - Royalty: 7-6-5% - Total Inv: $220,000 - Financing: SBA preferred.

GRETEL'S PRETZELS
Restaurant Systems International
1000 South Ave., Staten Island, NY, 10314. Contact: VP, Franchise Development - Tel: (718) 494-8888, (800) 205-6050, Fax: (718) 494-8776, E-Mail: treats@restsys.com, Web Site: www.restsys.com. Fresh baked hand-rolled pretzels and shakes. Established: 1995 - Franchising Since: 1981 - No. of Units: Company Owned: 1 - Franchised: 11 - Franchise Fee: $20,000 - Royalty: 5% royalty, 1% advertising fund - Financing: Yes.

HONEY DEW DONUTS
Honey Dew Associates, Inc.
35 Braintree Hill Park Ste. 203, Braintree, MA, 02184. Contact: Richard Bowen, Pres. - Tel: (800) 946-6393, Fax: (781) 849-3111. A coffee and bake shop. Established: 1973 - No. of Units: Company Owned: 1 - Franchised: 124.

HOUSE OF BREAD
858 Higuera St, San Luis Obispo, CA, 93401. Contact: Sheila McCann, President - Tel: (805) 542-0257, (800) 545-5146, Fax: (805) 542-0257, E-Mail: franchise@houseofbread.com, Web Site: www.houseof bread.com. Retail micro bakery offering healthy, great tasting breads and other products in an open production facility. Customers experience the grinding of freshly milled flour and the aroma of baking bread. Established: 1996 - Franchising Since: 1998 - No. of Units: Company Owned: 2 - Franchised: 2 - Franchise Fee: $28,000 - Royalty: 6% - Total Inv: $75,000-$204,000 - Financing: No.

HOUSE OF COFFEE INC.
10 Bridge Ave., Red Bank, NJ, 07701. Contact: Hunter Brown, Dir. Franc. - Tel: (732) 741-6333, Fax: (732) 741-3015. Coffee house/café. Coffee franchise that roasts it's own coffee, serving coffee and pastries in a coffee house atmosphere. Established: 1988 - Franchising Since: 1989 - No. of Units: Company Owned: 2 - Franchised: 3 - Franchise Fee: $20,000 - Royalty: 5% - Total Inv: Franc. Fee + $60,000 constr., $50,000 equip. - Financing: Assistance.

IKE'S DELI & BAKERY INC.
3000 Sunrise Blvd., Ste. 6, Rancho Cordova, CA, 95670. - Tel: (916) 635-9808, Fax: (916) 635-5073. Bakery and deli. Established: 1985 - Franchising Since: 1993 - No. of Units: Company Owned: 1 - Franchised: 1 - Franchise Fee: $10,000 - Royalty: $500-$5,000, 3% thereafter - Total Inv: $60,000 - Financing: None.

INCREDIBLE CHOCOLATE CHIP COOKIE COMPANY
I.C.C.C.
640 Lower Poplar St., P.O Box 6375, Macon, GA, 31208. Contact: Franchise Department - Tel: (912) 742-8455, Fax: (478) 746-1881. Fast Food - ice cream/yogurt/cookies. Established:1980 - No. of Units: Company Owned: 10 - Franchised: 2.

JAVA'S BREWIN
Java's Brewin Development Inc
95 Boston Rd, Billerica, MA, 01862. Contact: Cristos Greyoris, President - Tel: (781) 944-1757, Fax: (617) 944-7202. Gourmet coffee house and bakery. Established:1997 - Franchising since: 1997 - No. of Units: Company Owned: 1 - Franchise Fee: $17,500 - Royalty: 5% gross sales - Total Inv: $36,600-$53,350 excl f. fee and RE - Incl equip, marketing, inventory and grand opening - Financing: No.

JOLLY PIRATE ENTERPRISES
3923 E. Broad St., Columbus, OH, 43213. Contact: Nick Soulas, President - Tel: (614) 235-4501, Fax: (614) 235-4533. Donut and coffee shop open 24 hours catering to the general public featuring fresh hand cut donuts and complimentary beverages. Established: 1961 - Franchising Since: 1970 - No. of Units: Company Owned: 6 - Franchised: 18 - Royalty: 4%, adv. 3% - Total Inv: $300,000.

KRISPY KREME DOUGHNUT CORP.
P.O. Box 83, Winston-Salem, NC, 27102. Contact: Scott Livengood, Pres. - Tel: (336) 725-2981, Fax: (336) 733-3791. Established: 1937 - No. of Units: Company Owned: 75 - Franchised: 75.

LAMAR'S DONUTS
LaMar's Franchising, Inc.
385 Inverness Dr., S. Ste. 440, Englewood, CO, 80112. - Tel: (800) 533-7489, (303) 792-9200, Fax: (303) 790-0708, Web Site: www.lamars.com. A rapidly growing chain of retail donut shops, founded in Kansas City, specializing in handmade donuts since 1933. Franchising Since: 1993 - No. of Units: Company Owned: 1 - Franchised: 21 in 4 states - Franchise Fee: $28,500 - Royalty: 5% of gross sales, 1% adv. fund - Total Inv: $150,000-$175,000 - Financing: No.

LE CROISSANT SHOP
Blue Mill Enterprises Corp.
227 West 40th St., New York, NY, 10018. Contact: Arnaud Thieffry Dir. of Franchising - Tel: (212) 719-5940, Fax: (212) 944-0269, E-Mail: LCS@lecroissantsho.com, Web Site: www.lecroissantshop.com. French café bakery, serving freshly baked goods, specialty coffees, sandwiches, soups and salads in an upscale atmosphere. Established: 1981 - Franchising Since: 1984 - No. of Units: Company Owned: 3 - Franchised: 17 - Franchise Fee: $22,500 - Royalty: 5% - Total Inv: $200,000-$550,000 - Financing: None.

LOX OF BAGELS
11801 Prestwick Rd, Potomac, MD, 20854. Contact: Ted Taylor, V.P. - Tel: (800) 879-6927, Web Site: www.bagelfranchise.com. Since 1986, we have built our reputation on marketing great tasting bagels, cream cheeses, deli sandwiches, bagel chips and gourmet coffees in Southern California. We also show you how to make pizzas and various breads. In fact, our bagel chips are sold nationally in food stores in over 40 states under our trademark "King David's Bagel Chips". Established: 1986 - Franchising Since: 1995 - No. of Units: Company Owned: 3 - Franchised: 8 - Franchise Fee: $24,500 - Royalty: No - Total Inv: $145,000-$195,000.

MILL, THE
800 P Street, Lincoln, NE, 68508. - Tel: (800) 301-9504. Full service gourmet coffee house and gift shop featuring the finest coffees and teas and a variety of unique gifts. Established: 1979 - Franchising Since: 1993 - No. of Units: Company Owned: 1 - Franchise Fee: $20,000 - Royalty: 6% - Total Inv: $80,000-$225,000 - Financing: No.

MOXIE JAVA
Moxie Java International
199 E. 52nd., Boise, ID, 83714. Contact: Fran. Dir. - Tel: (800) 659-6963, (208) 322-1166, Fax: (208) 322-6226. Sell licenses for Moxie Java Systems which consist of carts, kiosks and cafés that serve exceptional espresso beverages. Established: 1989 - Franchising Since: 1991 - No.

of Units: Company Owned: 4 - Licensed: 25 - Licensing Fee: $10,000 - Royalty: None - Total Inv: $150,000 - Financing: No, but have ongoing relations with local bank.

MRS. FIELDS COOKIES
Mrs. Fields Famous Brands
2855 E. Cottonwood Pkwy, Ste. 400, Salt Lake City, UT, 84121. Contact: Franchise Dept. - Tel: (801) 736-5600, Fax: (801) 736-5936, Web Site: www.mrsfields.com. Premier cookie business with uncompromising quality, 94% brand recognition, easy to operate, flexible designs and combination store options that operate in traditional and non-traditional venues. Established: 1977 - Franchising Since: 1990 - No. of Units: Company Owned: 130 - Franchised: 192 - Franchise Fee: $25,000 - Royalty: 6%, 1% adv. - Total Inv: $172,000-$240,000 - Financing: None.

MUFFIN TIN, THE
AMT Inc.
P.O .Box 202, Helena St., Alden, MI, 49612. Contact: Jane Van Etten, Pres. - Tel: (231) 331-6808. Specialty bakery: muffins, cookies, scones, coffee/teas. Established: 1987 - Franchising Since: 1994 - No. of Units: Company Owned: 2 - Franchise Fee: $20,000 - Royalty: 10%, 10% adv. - Total Inv: $50,000-$80,000 - Financing: None.

MY FAVORITE MUFFIN, BREWSTER'S COFFEES
BAB Holdings, Inc.
500 Lake Cook Rd #475, Deerfield, IL, 60015. Contact: Tony Cervini - Tel: (800) 251-6101, Fax: (847) 405-8140, E-Mail: tcervini@babcorp.com, Web Site: www.babcorp.com. Specialty bagel café featuring fresh-from-scratch proprietary bagels, cream cheeses, muffins and gourmet coffees. This tri-brand concept provides our franchisees with three of the hottest trends in food retailing today. Established: 1992 - Franchising Since: 1993 - No. of Units: Company Owned: 9 - Franchised: 220 - Franchise Fee: $25,000 - Royalty: 5% - Total Inv: $250,000-$330,000 - Financing: No.

MY MOTHER'S DELICACIES™ CAFE
My Mother's Delicacies, Inc.
501 South Washington Ave., Scranton, PA, 18505. Contact: Dev./Pres. - Tel: (717) 343-5266, Fax: (717) 961-8861. Upscale European specialty bakery/coffee bar. Established: 1988 - Franchising Since: 1991- No. of Units: Company Owned: 1 National Distributor = Parent Co. - Franchise Fee: $15,000-$25,000.00 - Royalty: 6% - Total Inv: $94,000-$185,100 - Financing: No.

NESTLE TOLL HOUSE CAFE BY CHIP
Crest Foods, Inc
1900 Preston Rd., Ste. 267-314, Plano, TX, 75093. Contact: Andrea Towers - Tel: (214) 495-9533 x924, Fax: (214) 853-5347. Cookies, baked goods, ice cream and more. Established: 1998 - Franchising Since: 2000 - No. of Units: Franchised: 21 - Franchise Fee: $25,000 - Total Inv: $150,000 - Financing: No.

NEW YORK BAGEL CAFE & DELI
New York Bagel Enterprises Inc.
P.O. Box 1267, Stillwater, OK, 74076. - Tel: (316) 267-7373, Fax: (316) 267-8154. Bagel cafe and deli. Established: 1986 - Franchising Since: 1993 - No. of Units: Company Owned: 29 - Franchised: 45 - Franchised Fee: $21,000 Baking Facility, $12,000 Satellite Shop - Royalty: 4% gross, .5% national ad fund - Total Inv: $250,000 bakery, $125,000 satellite - Financing: No.

P.J.'S COFFEE & TEA
P.J.'s USA, Inc.
1100 Poydras St #1150, New Orleans, LA, 70163. Contact: Bryan O'Rourke, President - Tel: (504) 582-2264, Fax: (504) 582-2265. Serving quality coffees, teas, pastries and sandwiches in a relaxing atmosphere. Established: 1978 - Franchising Since: 1988 - No. of Units: Company Owned: 6 - Franchised: 20 - Franchise Fee: $20,000 - Royalty: 5% of gross, 1% marketing fee - Total Inv: Approx. $100,000-$200,000 - Financing: Assistance with lenders.

PARADISE BAKERY & CAFÉ
Paradise Bakery & Café, Inc.
500 West Main St, Aspen, CO, 81611. Contact: Dan Patterson, CEO / Pres - Tel: (970) 920-1444, Fax: (970) 920-9918. Retail bakery and café serving freshly baked products plus freshly prepared light meals including soups, salads, and sandwiches. Established: 1976 - Franchising Since: 1986 - No. of Units: Company Owned: 23 - Franchised: 13 - Franchise Fee: $35,000 - Royalty: 5% - Total Inv: $350,000-$650,000 - Financing: No.

PENNSYLVANIA PRETZEL COMPANY
295 Greenwich St., New York City, NY, 10007. - Tel: (212) 587-5938, Fax: (212) 964-5530. Soft-handrolled pretzels, gourmet gelato, sorb, fruit ices and espresso bar. Established: 1993 - Franchising Since: 1994 - No. of Units: Company Owned: 3 - Franchised: 5 - Franchise Fee: $20,000 - Royalty: 6% - Total Inv: $120,000 - Financing: Yes.

PEPPERIDGE FARM, INC.
P.O. Box 06856, Norwalk, CT, 06856. - Tel: (203) 846-7000. Direct store delivery of bakery (bread, rolls, dry stuffing mix), biscuits and snack crackers to retail stores. Established: 1937 - Franchising Since: 1941 - No. of Units: 2,000 - Approx. Inv: Varies - Financing: Yes.

PRETZEL MILL
6006 Greenbelt Rd., Suite 335, Greenbelt, MD, 20070. - Tel: (301) 459-4190, (800)880-6194,. Highest quality, freshly baked, hand rolled soft pretzels and specialty pretzels. Also offers superior dips and beverages. Extensive training and support programs. Established: 1994 -Franchising Since: 1996 - No. of Units: Company Owned: 1 - Franchised: 3 - Franchise Fee: $20,000 - Royalty: 5%, 1% adv. fee on gross sales - Total Inv: $125,000-$206,000 excluding franchise fee - Financing: Under certain circumstances.

PRETZEL TIME
Mrs. Fields Famous Brands
2855 E. Cottonwood Pkwy., #400, Salt Lake City, UT, 84121. Contact: Franchise Development - Tel: (801) 3736-5600, Fax: (801) 736-5936. "Freshness with a twist" retail pretzel stores offering a healthy snack alternative that is freshly mixed, rolled and baked. Unique combination store options are available for traditional and non-traditional venues. Established: 1991 - Franchising Since: 1992 - No. of Units: Company Owned: 86 - Franchised: 143 - Franchise Fee: $25,000 - Royalty: 7%, 1% nat'l adv. - Total Inv: $117,000-$236,000 - Financing: None.

PRETZEL TWISTER
Mister Twister Pretzels, Inc.
2706 South Horseshoe Dr. Ste. 112, Naples, FL, 34104. - Tel: (941) 643-2075, Fax: (239) 591-3971. Gourmet hand-rolled soft pretzels and frozen blended fruitshakes. Established: 1992 - Franchising Since: 1993 - No. of Units: Franchised: 33 - Franchise Fee: $12,500 - Royalty: 5% + .25% to 2% adv. - Total Inv: $82,700-$140,200 - Financing: Yes.

PRETZELMAKER
Mrs. Fields Famous Brands
2855 E. Cottonwood Pkwy., Suite 400, Salt Lake City, UT, 84121-7050. Contact: Franchise Development - Tel: (801) 736-5600, (800) 348-6311, Fax: (801) 736-5936, Web Site: www.pretzelmaker.com. The "Worlds Best Soft Pretzels" hand rolled and served hot with high consumer acceptance, precision portion control and available in combination store configurations. May be operated in both traditional and non-traditional venues. Established: 1991 - Franchising Since: 1992 - No. of Units: Company Owned: 4 - Franchised: 154 - Franchise Fee: $20,000 - Royalty: 5% gross sales, 1.5% adv. - Total Inv: $95,000-$208,000 - Financing: No.

PRETZELS PLUS
Pretzels Plus, Inc.
639 Frederick St., Hanover, PA, 17331. Contact: Alan Harbaugh, Dir. of Fran. - Tel: (717) 633-7927, (800) 559-7927, Fax: (717) 633-5078, E-Mail: harb@pretzelsplus.com, Web Site: www.pretzelsplus.com Hand rolled soft pretzels, smoothies and sandwiches. Established: 1991 - Franchising Since: 1991 - No. of Units: Franchised: 27 - Franchise Fee: $12,000 - Royalty: 4% - Total Inv: $25,000 - Financing: No.

SCKAKOLAD CHOCOLATE FACTORY
480 N. Orlando Ave., #131, Winter Park, FL, 32789. Contact: Edgar Schaked - Tel: (407) 677-4114, Fax: (407) 677-4118. Hand made fine chocolate made on premises. Established: 1995 - Franchising Since: 1999 - No. of Units: Company Owned: 2 - Franchised: 4 - Franchise Fee: $22,500 - Financing: No.

SOUTH BEACH CAFE
South Beach Cafe Int'l Franchise Corp.
P.O Box 50368, Sarasota, FL, 34232-0303. Contact: Pamela Burnham, President - Tel: (941)377-7225, Fax: (941) 377-1836. Full range of premium estate grown coffees, fresh fruit smoothies and veggie drinks. A wide variety of bagels and spreads, croissants, soups, salads and other fresh pastries and baked goods. Established: 1997 - Franchising Since: 1997 - No. of Units: Company Owned: 5 - Franchise Fee: $18,500 - Royalty: 4% - Total Inv: $142,500-$375,000 - Financing: No.

SOUTHERN MAID DONUT SHOP
3615 Cavalier Dr., Garland, TX, 750427599. Contact: D. Franklin, Lon Hargrove, V.P., Pres. - Tel: (972) 272-6425, Fax: (972) 276-3549, E-Mail: info@southernmaiddonuts.com, Web Site: www.southernmaid donuts.com. Manufacturer of donut mixes. Established: 1937 - Franchising Since: 1939 - No. of Units: 85 - Franchise Fee: $5,000 - Total Inv: $50,000.

STONE HEARTH BREADS U.S.A.
Stone Hearth Equip. Co.
12301 Coller Highway, Tipton, WI, 49287. Contact: Vincent D. Cassone Pres. - Tel: (517) 431-2593, Fax: (517) 431-3408. Traditional breads bakery, producing authentic hearth breads and rolls for retail stores and restaurant suppliers. Established: 1995 - Franchising Since: 1999 - No. of Units: Company Owned: 1 - Franchise Fee: $20,000 - Royalty: 4% on volume, 2% adv. - Total Inv: $155,000 all equipment $20,000 F.F.

T.J. CINNAMONS BAKERY
Triarc Restaurant Group
1000 Corporate Drive, Ft. Lauderdale, FL, 33334. Contact: Franchise Department - Tel: (954) 351-5373, Fax: (954) 351-5192. An upscale gourmet bakery concept featuring our warm, gooey original Gourmet Cinnamon Roll®. The T.J. Cinnamons dual brand Classic Bakeries are located within the confines of an Arby's® Restaurant. Established: 1996 - Franchising Since: 1996 - No. of Units: Franchised: 344 - Franchise Fee: $5,000 - Royalty: 4% gross monthly - Total Inv: $32,600-$47,200 - Financing: No.

TIM HORTONS
T.H.D. Donut (Delaware), Inc.
4150 Tuller Rd., Unit 236, Dublin, OH, 43017. Contact: Manager of Franchise Development - Tel: (614) 791-4202. Retail, offering premium coffee and a wide variety of fresh baked goods. Established: 1964 - Franchising Since: 1965 - No. of Units: Company Owned: 125 - Franchised: 1630 - Franchise Fee: $35,000 U.S - Royalty: 4.5% - Total Inv: $300,000-$734,900 U.S - Financing: Through financing institutions.

TOMMIE'S DONUTS
1576 S. 500 W #200, Woods Cross, UT, 84087. - Tel: (801) 397-1595, Web Site: www.tommies.com. Hot, fresh, glazed donuts. Franchising Since: 2002 - No. of Units: Franchised: 1- - Franchise Fee: $20,000 - Total Inv: $197,000-$460,500.

WETZEL'S PRETZELS
65 N. Raymond Ave, Ste. 310, Pasadena, CA, 91103. - Tel: (626) 626) 432-6900, Fax: (626) 432-6904. Gourmet hand rolled pretzel bakeries featuring fresh squeezed lemonade. Established: 1994 - Franchising Since: 1996 - No. of Units: Company Owned: 5 - Franchised: 37 - Franchise Fee: $20,000 - Royalty: 6% - Total Inv: $120,000-$150,000 - Financing: Yes.

WINCHELL'S EXPRESS
Winchell's Donut Houses, LLP
2223 Wellington Ave #300, Santa Ana, CA, 92701-3101. - Tel: (714) 565-1800, (800) 347-9347, Fax: (714) 565-1801. Baked prefried, frozen donuts, muffins, bagels and bagel sandwiches in 100 sq feet . Designed for convenience stores, food courts, airports, etc. Established: 1948 - Franchising Since: 1989 - No. of Units: Company Owned: 200 -

Franchised: 100 - Franchise Fee: $7,500 - Royalty: 7% royalty, 3% advertising - Total Inv: Equipment $18,000-$22,000 - Financing: Third party.

FOOD: CANDY/POPCORN/SNACKS

AMERICANDY
USA Candy Inc.
3618 St. Germaine Ct, Louisville, KY, 40207. Contact: Omar Tatum, Pres./Founder - Tel: (502) 583-1776, Fax: (502) 583-1776, E-Mail: americandy@aol.com, Web Site: www.americandy.com. A tour of America thru candy while buying the favorite candies from all 50 states. Established: 1990 - Franchising Since: 1992 - No. of Units: Company Owned: 1 - Franchise Fee: $25,000 - Royalty: 6% - Total Inv: $135,000 - Financing: Third party.

BOARDWALK PEANUT SHOPPE, THE
Boardwalk Franchise Corp.
28 West Washington, Pleasantville, NJ, 08232. Contact: Leo Yeager, III, Pres. - Tel: (609) 272-1511, Fax: (609) 407-0937. Retail nut and candy shop. Established: 1971 - Franchising Since: 1988 - No. of Units: Company Owned: 3 - Franchised: 4 - Franchise Fee: $12,000 - Royalty: 5% - Total Inv: $45,500-$90,000 depending on leasehold - Financing: No.

BOURBON STREET CANDY CO.
Ste. 287, 266 N. Elmwood Ave., Buffalo, NY, 14222. Contact: Blaine McGrath, President - Tel: (905) 894-4819, (888) 568-BSCC, Fax: (905) 894-3072. Bulk candy selection, homemade fudge made on premises, gift lines, custom made or pre-made. Established: 1990 - Franchising Since: 1991 - No. of Units: Company Owned: 3 - Franchised: 28 - Franchise Fee: $25,000 - Royalty: 5% - Total Inv: $69,000-$201,000.

CANDY BOUQUET
Candy Bouquet International, Inc.
423 East Third Street, Little Rock, AR, 72201. - Tel: (501) 375-9990, (877) CANDY-01, Fax: (501) 375-9990, E-Mail: yumyum@candy bouquet.com, Web Site: www.candybouquet.com. Candy Bouquet arrangements are designer food gifts that incorporate candies, world-class chocolates and accessories into floral-like bouquets that retail for $20.00-$250.00. Franchises from $3,500. Full training in product creation, plus marketing and corporate support. Over 360 franchise territories awarded in 46 states and 19 countries. Established: 1989 - Franchising Since: 1993 - No. of Units: Company Owned: 1 - Franchised: 360 - Franchise Fee: $3,500-$41,000 - Royalty: 0% - Total Inv: $7,500-$41,000 - Financing: No.

CATERINA'S
Caterina's Franchise Company, Inc.
P.O. Box 5587, San Clemente, CA, 92674-5587. Contact: Franchise Sales - Tel: (949) 498-8871,(800) 765-4311, Fax: (714) 770-3084. Upscale candy, chocolates, gifts, espresso, ice cream, yogurt. Established: 1990 - Franchising Since: 1993 - No. of Units: Franchised: 4 - Franchise Fee: $19,000 - Royalty: 5% - Total Inv: $148,238-$254,460 - Financing: No.

FUDGE CO., THE
103 Belvedere Ave., Charlevoix, MI, 49720. Contact: R.L. Hoffman, Pres. - Tel: (231) 547-9941, Fax: (231) 547-4612. Retail fudge store. An important part of the operation is cooking in large copper kettles and creaming (forming) done on large marble slabs. Only natural ingredients are used and combined with the showmanship of making fudge provides a unique, enjoyable and profitable retail operation. Each store requires 400-600 sq. ft. Company provides all equipment. Franchisee leases or purchases its own building, with guidance from Fudge Co. Established: 1977 - Franchising Since: 1978 - No. of Units: Company Owned: 1 - Franchised: 6 - Franchise Fee: $12,500-$15,000 - Royalty: 3% - Total Inv: $35,000-$45,000 - Financing: No.

FUZZIWIG'S CANDY FACTORY INC.
Fuzziwig's Candy Factory Inc.
10 Town Plaza, Durango, CO, 81301. Contact: Kayo Folsom or Kim Cox, President - Tel: (970) 247-2700, (877) 247-2700, Fax: (970) 247-2735, E-Mail: info@fuzzuwigscandyfactory.com, Web Site: www.fuzziwigscandyfactory.com. Fuzziwig's Candy Factory is a self serve candy store cleaverly designed to look like a fun wimsical: unusual candies. Established: 1995 - Franchising Since: 1995 - No. of Units: Company Owned: 20 - Franchised: 52 - Franchise Fee: $30,000 - Royalty: 6% - Total Inv: $183,300-$298,050 - Financing: No.

KILWIN'S CHOCOLATES AND ICE CREAM
Kilwin's Chocolates Franchise
355 N. Division Rd., Petoskey, MI, 49770. Contact: Leanna Hart, Franchise Licensing - Tel: (231) 347-3800, (810) 326-4146, Fax: (231) 347-6951, E-Mail: lhartsales@aol.com, Web Site: www.kilwins.com. Full-line confectionary shoppes featuring, quality hand made chocolates, fudge, and kilwin's own premium ice cream. Established: 1947 - Franchising Since: 1981 - No. of Units: Company Owned: 4 - Franchised: 36 - Franchise Fee: $25,000 - Royalty: 5% gross - Total Inv: $288,670-$599,000 - Financing: No.

KRON CHOCOLATIERS
Consolidated Brands
5 Bond Street, Great Neck, NY, 11021. - Tel: (516) 829-5550, Fax: (516) 829-9322. Chocolates and gift baskets. Established: 1932 - Franchising Since: 1980 - No. of Units: Company Owned: 3 - Franchised: 8 - Franchise Fee: $25,000 - Royalty: 4% - Total Inv: $100,000+ - Financing: No.

MAISON DU POPCORN
188 Washington Street, Norwich, CT, 06360. Contact: William Abate - Tel: (203) 886-0360. Gourmet popcorn, hot pretzels and snow cones - full training and support provided. Established: 1986 - Franchising since: 1987 - No. of Units: Franchised: 12 - Franchise Fee: $20,000 - Total Inv: $50,000 - Financing: Yes.

MR. BULKY TREATS & GIFTS
Sweet Ideas Limited Partnership
1311 Maplelawn Dr., Troy, MI, 48084-5301. Contact: Melissa Williams, Fran. Dept. - Tel: (248) 649-6900. Upscale retail centers located in major malls coast to coast. Offering self service merchandise centers featuring a dazzling array of quality mouthwatering domestic and international candies and snacks sold by the ounce or pound. Stores also merchandise a wide selection of gifts and treats, over 1,000 individually selected items from around the world. Established: 1984 - Franchising Since: 1984 - No. of Units: Company Owned: 85 - Franchised: 57 - Franchise Fee: $30,000, annual franchise fee $10,000 - Royalty: 2% monthly - Total Inv: $206,000-$275,000 - Financing: No.

OLD FASHIONED EGG CREAM CO. INC.
Original Egg Cream Co.
3350 NW Boca Raton Blvd Ste A28, Boca Raton, FL, 33431-6653. - Tel: (561) 417-6800, Fax: (561) 417-6888. An idea based on fond memories of enjoying a frosty egg cream with a pretzel rod. Also serve bakery confections. One is the Charlotte Russe and another is the Old Fashioned Cookie On A Stick, along with our Old Fashioned Gourmet Fountain Sodas. All served from a beautiful self-contained mobile wood and brass cart. Well received at malls, business centers, sports complexes and other locations where people meet. Established: 1994 - Franchising Since: 1995 - No. of Units: Company Owned: 2 - Franchised: 2 - Franchise Fee: $10,000-$15,000 - Royalty: 5% (10% at stadiums) - Total Inv: $10,000-$15,000 + $20,000-$25,000 (other invest. & open. costs) - Financing: None.

PERFECT PRETZEL, THE
Perfect Pretzel, Inc.
4 Garden Rd., Little Silver, NJ, 07739. Contact: Ronald S. Hari, Dir. of Fran. - Tel: (908) 741-7347. Fresh baked pretzels hand rolled with 10 different flavors. Established: 1992 - Franchising Since: 1992 - No. of Units: Company Owned: 2 - Franchised: 1 - Franchise Fee: $6,000 - Royalty: 5% of gross - Total Inv: $65,000: $30,000 construction, $10,000 equip., $6,000 fee, $19,000 lease - Financing: Will assist.

POP N' GO
Pop N go, Inc.
12429 East Putnam Street, Whitter, CA, 90602.Contact: Franchise Director - Tel: (901) 368-3361, Fax: (901) 368-1144. Unique popcorn machines for lease installation in theaters, lounges, bars, malls. Established: 1996 - Franchising Since: 1997 - No. of Units: Company Owned: 1 - Franchised: 60 - Franchise Fee: $10,000 - Royalty: 5%, Adv. 1% - Total Inv: $13,710-$65,700 - Financing: Leasing (machine).

SWEET CITY EXPRESS
Sweet City Supply, Inc
5908 Thurston Ave, Virginia Beach, VA, 23455. - Tel: (757) 456-0800, (800) 793-3824, Fax: (757) 456-9980, Web Site: www.sweetcity.com. Self serve bulk candy, gift, and novelty item kiosks. Small stores, owner operated. Established: 1995 - Franchising Since: 1999 - No. of Units: Company Owned: 2 - Franchised: 2 - Franchise Fee: $5,995-$11,995 - Royalty: .5%-125,000, 2% -$125,000 2 wk; 3%-$200,000 - Total Inv: $31,000-$49,000 - Financing: Yes.

SWEETS FROM HEAVEN/CANDY HQTRS
Sweets From Heaven U.S.A., LP
1830 Forbes Ave., Pittsburgh, PA, 15219. Contact: Mark R. Lando, Pres.- Tel: (412) 434-6711, Fax: (412) 434-6718, E-Mail: sfheaven@aol.com, Web Site: www.sweetsfromheaven.com. Self serve bulk candy with large selection of imported and unique bulk and non-bulk items. Also featuring candy related gift items, nuts, dried fruits, popcorn and ice cream. Established: 1996 - Franchising Since: 1996 - No. of Units: Company Owned: 16 - Franchised: 45 - Franchise Fee: $30,000 - Royalty: 6% - Total Inv: $125,000-$225,000 - Financing: Lease program for equipment.

TROPIK SUN FRUIT & NUT
Diversifoods, Inc.
14052 Petronella Dr, Suite 102, Libertyville, IL, 60048. Contact: Barbara Nellaris - Tel: (847) 968-4415, Fax: (847) 968-5535, E-Mail: tropikhdqr @aol.com, Web Site: www.tropiksun.com. Candy, nuts, homemade carmelcorn, "Fun Munchies", smoothies. Franchisor will provide turn-key mall location. Established: 1980 - Franchising Since: 1981 - No. of Units: Company Owned: 2 - Franchised: 64 - Franchise Fee: $20,000 - Royalty: 6% - Total Inv: $99,000-$198,000 - Financing: Yes, third party for qualified applicants.

"WE MUST BE...NUTS!!! DISTRIBUTORS OF
Kish and Molnar Enterprises, Inc.
P.O. Box 813, Clarcona, FL, 32710. Contact: Glenn C. Kish, President, - Tel: (407) 672-3609, (800) 689-NUTS (6887), Fax: (407) 290-5458, E-Mail: nuttycoon6@aol.com, Web Site: www.kish-distributors.com. Cinnamon roasted nut business. Learn to roast all types of nuts in the olde world style. Smell the aroma of success & be in business for yourself, but not by yourself. We have training, consulting, start-up supplies & cart renderings. Established: 1993 - Franchising Since: 1993 - No. of Units: Company Owned: 100+ - Distributorship Fee: $12,500 - Royalty: None - Total Inv: $12,500 - Financing: No.

YE OLDE KETTLE COOKER™
Concessions Manufacturing Ltd. Co
34320 South 620 Rd, Grove, OK, 74344. - Tel: (918) 786-5100, (888) POPCORN, Fax: (918) 786-2498, E-Mail: harts@galstar.com, Web Site: www.aimsintl.org/cmn.htm. 1800's rustic kettle popcorn and pork rind cooker. Gross up to $400.00 pr/hr at mere 10% food cost. Established: 1995 - Franchising Since: 1999 - No. of Units: Company Owned: 3 - Franchised: 72 - Total Inv: $25,000.00 - Financing: Yes.

FOOD: CONVENIENCE STORES

6 TWELVE CONVENIENT MART
P.O. Box 86009, Gaithersburg, MD, 20886-6009. Contact: Aris Mardirossian, Pres./CEO - Tel: (301) 840-8559. Convenience stores. Established: 1984 - Franchising Since: 1985 - No. of Units: Company Owned: 10 - Franchised: 29 - Franchise Fee: $30,000 - Royalty: 5%, 2% adv. - Total Inv: $300,000 - Financing: Yes.

7-ELEVEN, INC.
2711 N. Haskell Ave., Dallas, TX, 75204. Contact: Jeanne Lynch - Tel: (800) 255-0711, (800) 255-0711, Fax: (214) 841-6776, E-Mail: 7-11 .com, Web Site: www.7-11.com. 7-Eleven is focused on meeting the needs of convenience-oriented customers by providing a broad selection of fresh, high-quality products and services at everyday fair prices, speedy transactions and a clean, and friendly shopping environment. Established: 1927 - Franchising Since: 1964 - No. of Units: Company Owned: 2547 - Franchised: 21,887 - Franchise Fee: Varies by store - Total Inv: Varies by store - Financing: No.

A & M FOOD STORES, INC.
450, S. Old Dixie Hwy, #8, Jupiter, FL, 33458. - Tel: (561) 747-4384, Fax: (561) 747-5850. Convenience stores franchise having 60 stores, located in South Florida. Established: 1980 - Franchising Since: 1981 - No. of Units: Company Owned: 60 - Franchise Fee: $40,000 max. - Royalty: $900 per month or 3% of gross revenue - Total Inv: $50,000 per store - Financing: No.

ALWAYS OPEN FRANCHISING CORP.
PO Box 1485, Melrose Park, IL, 60161-1485. Contact: Dir. of Fran. - Tel: (630) 663-9882, (888) Always Open, Fax: (219) 365-4185, Web Site: www.alwaysopenfranchising.com. Convenience store franchise with gasoline and branded fast food. Established: 1987 - Franchising Since: 1992 - No. of Units: Company Owned: 2 - Franchised: 10 - Licensed: 5 - Franchise Fee: $10,000 - Royalty: 4% merchandise and blended fast food sales, 25% concession - Total Inv: Approx. $75,551-$131,088 - Financing: No.

COGO'S / COGO'S EXPRESS COGO'S CO
2589 Boyce Plaza Road, Pittsburgh, PA, 15241-3981. Contact: Joseph Donas, Vice President - Tel: (412) 257-1550, Fax: (412) 257-9174. Gasoline and convenience operation. Established: 1962 - Franchising Since: 1999 - No. of Units: Company Owned: 53 - Franchise Fee: $25,000-$1,300,000 (start-up) - Total Inv: $40,000-$1,400,000.

CONVENIENT FOOD MART
Convenient Food Mart Inc.
467 N. State St., Painsville, OH, 44077. Contact: Barb Mahoney, Fran. Dir. - Tel: (440) 639-6515, (800) 860-4844, Fax: (440) 639-6526, E-Mail: convenientfoodmart@compserve.com, Web Site: www.convenient foodmart.com. Small grocery, gasoline and pharmacy outlets. Established: 1958 - Franchising Since: 1958 - No. of Units: Company Owned: 4 - Franchised: 321 - Franchise Fee: $18,000 - Royalty: 5% - Total Inv: $150,000-$300,000 - Financing: Yes.

ELLIOTTS' OFF BROADWAY DELI, INC.
404 Royal Glen Ct., Oak Brook, IL, 60523. Contact: Franchise Dir./Pres. - Fax: (630) 279-4681. Offering pizza, breakfast and desserts, sandwiches, soups, bagels, lunch and dinner with daily specials. Basically self-serve. Established: 1988 - Franchising Since: 1988 - No. of Units: Company Owned: 1 - Franchised: 12 - Franchise Fee: $12,500 - Royalty: 4%, 1% adv. - Total Inv: $50,000-$100,000 - Financing: No.

EXPRESS MART
Petr-All Petroleum Corp.
6567 Kinne Rd., P.O. Box 46, DeWitt, NY, 13214. Contact: Robbin Jeran - Tel: (315) 446-0125, Fax: (315) 446-1355, Web Site: www.expressmart.com. Your future-Express Mart, intensely focused, fiercely competitive & highly customer driven. Sophisticated stores w/ a daily pulse on customer service, product mix, image, shrink, advertising, inventory control, store appearance, presentation, & atmosphere. Your Business! Established: 1975 - Franchising Since: 1987 - No. of Units: Company Owned: 49 - Franchised: 17- Franchise Fee: $15,000 - Royalty: 4%, 1% adv. - Financing: Third party assistance.

HEAVENLY HAM
Paradise Foods, Inc.
1100 Old Ellis Rd., Ste. 100, Roswell, GA, 30076-4814. Contact: Franchise Dept. - Tel: (770) 752-1999, (800) 899-2228, Fax: (770) 752-4653. Retail stores selling honey-spiced glazed, spiral sliced, fully baked, whole and half hams, plus smoked turkey, barbecued ribs, bacon, and other food related items. Established: 1984 - Franchising Since: 1984 - No. of Units: Company Owned: 2 - Franchised: 150 - Franchise Fee: $30,000 - Royalty: 5%, 1% adv. - Total Inv: $91,300-$216,120 inc. franc. fee - Financing: No.

JACKPOT FOOD MART
Jackpot Convenience Stores, Inc.
P.O. Box 24447, Seattle, WA, 98124. Contact: Steve Gray, Fran. Mgr. - Tel: (206) 286-6436, Fax: (206) 286-4496. Jackpot Convenience Stores, Inc. has active franchises in Washington, Oregon, California, Nevada and Idaho. JCSI provides franchisees with a wide array of services, including training and marketing programs. Established: 1990 - Franchising Since: 1990 - No. of Units: Company Owned: 2 - Franchised: 99 - Franchise Fee: $5,000 - Royalty: .5%, advertising fee 1% - Total Inv: $65,300-$165,300 - Financing: No. (some exceptions).

JOEY PAGODAS ORIENTAL EXPRESS
Orion Food Systems
2930 W Maple, Sioux Falls, SD, 57101. Contact: National Director of Development - Tel: (800) 648-6227, (605) 336-6961, Fax: (605) 336-0141, Web Site: www.orionfoodsys.com. Quick service format, developing in convenience stores and foodcourts. Established: 1984 - Franchising Since: 1985 - No. of Units: Company Owned: 4 - Franchised: 18 - Franchise Fee: $4,950 - Total Inv: $25,000 + - Financing: Third Party.

JOHNNY QUIK FOOD STORES, INC.
5816 E. Shields Ave., #102, Fresno, CA, 93727-7820. Contact: Ernie Beal, V.P. - Tel: (559) 291-7136, Fax: (559) 291-1656. Convenience stores with gas and fast food program. Established: 1985 - Licensing Since: 1985 - No. of Units: Franchised: 22 - Franchise Fee: $35,000 - Royalty: 2 1/2%/mth -1/4 of 1% goes to advertising - Total Inv: $35,000 franc. fee, $250,000 equip. - Financing: Some for equipment.

JR. FOOD MART
J.F.M., Inc.
2680 Insurance Center, Jackson, MS, 39216. Contact: Dan Davis, V.P. of Fran. Operations - Tel: (601) 987-0100, Fax: (601) 987-0111. Convenience food marts - multiple profit centers. Self serve gasoline, convenience grocery and branded fast service restaurant. Established: 1920 - Franchising Since: 1920 - Franchise Fee: $20,000 single unit and $35,000 non-exclusive territory - Royalty: 2% single unit and 1.5% territory - Total Inv: Single unit: $75,000 and assets of $100,000+, Territory: $150,000 and assets of $250,000+ - Financing: Assistance available.

MAC'S CONVENIENT STORE
Alimentation Couche-Tard, Inc
315 Commons Mall, Columbus, IN, 47201. Contact: Tim Beech, Dir. of Franchising - Tel: (330) 342-6758, (800) 844-8661, Fax: (330) 342-6804, E-Mail: tbeech@macsstores.com, Web Site: www.couche-tard.qc.ca. 2,400 to 3,000 square foot convenience food stores. Established: 1980 - Franchising Since: 1985 - No. of Units: Company Owned: 1800 - Franchised: 100 - Franchise Fee: $17,500 - Royalty: 14% - Total Inv: $25,000-$60,000 - Financing: None.

OKY-DOKY FOODS
TFM, Co.
1250 Iowa St., Dubuque, IA, 52001. Contact: J. F. Thompson, Pres. - Tel: (319) 556-8050. Convenience stores. Established: 1916 - Franchising Since: 1970 - No. of Units: Company Owned: 6 - Franchised: 6 - Franchise Fee: None - Royalty: 1.5% - Total Inv: $25,000 inventory - Financing: Lease equipment.

QUIK STOP MARKETS, INC
Quik Stop Markets, Inc.
4567 Enterprise St., Fremont, CA, 94538. Contact: William L. Rankin, Dir. of Franchising/Real Estate - Tel: (510) 657-8500, Fax: (510) 657-1544. 24-hour convenience market with self-serve gasoline located in Northern California. Established: 1965 - Franchising Since: 1965- No. of Units: Franchised: 113 - Franchise Fee: $25,000-$70,000 - Royalty: Min. of 15% to max. of 17% of net sales - Total Inv: $55,000-$100,000 - Financing: Yes.

STUCKEY'S
Stuckey's Corporation
4601 Willard Ave., Chevy Chase, MD, 20815-4641. Contact: Walter S. Tellegen, CEO - Franchising - Tel: (301) 913-9800, ext. 23, Fax: (301) 913-5424. The sale of candy, gifts, fast food items as well as gasoline. Established: 1933 - No. of Units: Franchised: 140 - Franchise Fee: $5,000 - Royalty: $275 per month with a 5% annual increase - Total Inv: $9,000-$15,000.

SUGAR CREEK STORES LLC
760 Brooks Ave., Rochester, NY, 14619. - Tel: (716) 436-5360, (716) 328-0787. Convenience stores with self serve fuel operations. Established: 1982 - Franchising Since: 1989 - No. of Units: Company Owned: 102 - Franchised: 5 - Franchise Fee: $15,000 - Royalty: 4.5%, 1 adv. - Total Inv: $297,140-$475,280 - Financing: No.

TEDESCHI FOOD SHOPS / LI'L PEACH CONV. STORES
TFS Franchise Corporation
14 Howard Street, Rockland, MA, 02370. Contact: Administrative/Training Specialist - Tel: (781) 878-8210, (800) TEDESCHI, Fax: (781) 878-0476, Web Site: www.shoptfs.com. Convenience store - full line of grocery items, HBA, dairy, lottery, some stores have full deli section and some have beer and wine. Established: 1972 - Franchising Since: 1972 - No. of Units: Company Owned: 54 - Franchised: 78 - Franchise Fee: $10,000-$30,000 - Royalty: 10%-20% of net sales, 25% lottery - Total Inv: $43,500-$78,500 - Financing: Yes.

TOTALLY LOW CARB STORES INC. *
5209 S, Sixth Street, Las Vegas, NV, 89101. - Tel: (800) 631-2272, Fax: (702) 736-8621, Web Site: www.tlcstores.com. Low carb grocery store. Established: 2003 - Franchising Since: 2003 - No. of Units: Franchised: 1 - Franchise Fee: $19,500 - Royalty: 3% - Total Inv: $30,000-$225,000 - Financing: No.

UNCLE SAM'S CONVENIENT STORE
CSF, Inc.
300 East Hwy. 107, Elsa, TX, 78543-0870. Contact: Jackie L. Thomas, Executive V.P. - Tel: (956) 262-7273, (888) 786-7373, Fax: (956) 262-7290, Web Site: www.unclesamscstore.com. A full scale convenience store and motor fuel franchise. Established: 1970 - Franchising Since: 1997 - No. of Units; Company Owned: 52 - Franchise Fee: $25,000 - Royalty: 5% of gross sales excluding fuel and lotto sales - Total Inv: $800,000 - Financing: Yes.

WHITE HEN PANTRY, INC.
3003 Butterfield Road, Oakbrook, IL, 60523. Contact: Tony Abbattista - Tel: (800) PANTRY-1, (630) 366-3100, Fax: (630) 366-3447, E-Mail: tony.abbattista@whitehen.com, Web Site: www.whitehen.com. For nearly 40 years White Hen Pantry has served as the premier convenience store chain in metropolitan Chicago and greater Boston. Renowned for its quality, cleanliness and customer service, White Hen Pantry's 285 stores, predominantly franchisee-operated, serve more than a quarter million customers each day with a full line of distinctive products including national brand, fresh-sliced deli items, custom-made sandwiches, salads, soup, coffee and more. From traditional suburban and city profiles to office-worker and rural settings, White Hen's expertise in delivering first-rate quality products and outstanding service is the hallmark of the brand. There are 285 White Hen stores in Illinois, northern Indiana, Massachusetts and New Hampshire. White Hen currently ranks in the top 50 convenience store chains nationally. Established: 1965 - Franchising Since: 1965 - No. of Units: Company Owned: 8 - Franchised: 217 - Franchise Fee: $10,000-$25,000 - Royalty: 7% plus base fee - Total Inv: Between $51,800-$66,800 - Financing: Yes. At this time we are only franchising in Massachusetts and Illinois.

• • • • • • • • • • • • • • • • • • •
• Check out Latest Press Releases: •
• *www.infonews.com* •
• • • • • • • • • • • • • • • • • • •

FOOD: ICE CREAM AND YOGURT

2 SCOOPS CAFE
2 Scoops Cafe Franchise Development Corp.
4651 36th St., Suite 600, Orlando, FL, 32811. Contact: Mary Ann Kilgallon - Tel: (407) 381-0378, (866) 2 SCOOPS, Fax: (407) 996-1214, E-Mail: info@2scoopscafe.com, Web Site: www.2scoopscafe.com. Old fashion good time Ice Cream Parlor/Cafe. Established: 2002 - Franchising Since: 2002 - No. of Units: Company Owned: 1 - Franchised: 3 - Franchise Fee: $24,000 - Royalty: 5% - Total Inv: $70,000-$92,200 - Financing: No.

ABBOTT'S FROZEN CUSTARD, INC.
4791 Lake Ave., Rochester, NY, 14612. - Tel: (585) 865-7400. Abbott's Frozen Custard is an ice cream business offering to sell the franchisee the right to operate one or more retail frozen custard (and related products) stands where the public may purchase frozen custard, frozen yogurt, sherbert, soft drinks, and other desserts and related food products. Established: 1903 - Franchising Since: 1954 - No. of Units: Company Owned: 6 - Franchised: 18 - Franchise Fee: $24,500 - Royalty: 5.5%, 2% adv. - Total Inv: $60,000 equip., $24,500 fee, $25,000 leasehold improv. & signs - Financing: No.

ALL AMERICAN FROZEN YOGURT AND ICE CREAM SHOPS
All American Frozen Yogurt Co., Inc., The
812 SW Washington St., Ste. 1110, Portland, OR, 97205-3215. - Tel: (503) 224-6199, Fax: (503) 224-5042. Frozen yogurt and ice cream shops located in the regional enclosed shopping malls. Established: 1986 - Franchising Since: 1988 - No. of Units: Company Owned: 2 - Franchised: 18 - Franchise Fee: $13,200-$20,000 - Royalty: 5% adv. - 1% - Total Inv: $78,150-$158,400 - Financing: Assistance only.

ALOHA ICE CREAM SHOPS
Aloha Ice Cream Shops, Inc.
3680 North Abbey Street, Fresno, CA, 93726. - Tel: (909) 699-4027, (800) 928-7283, Fax: (909) 694-0195. Aloha Ice Cream Shops offer Hawaii/tropical theme stores featuring premium quality ice cream, yogurt snacks, shaved ice, limited baked goods, fruit smoothies and iced coffees. Established: 1995 - Franchising Since: 1996 - No. of Units: Company Owned: 1 - Franchised: 3 - Franchise Fee: $25,000 - Royalty: 10% operations, 2% marketing - Total Inv: $60,000-$130,000 ($50,000 liquid) - Financing: Yes.

AUSTRALIAN HOMEMADE *
180 Varick Street Ste. 1202, New York, NY, 10014. - Tel: (212) 209-1190, Fax: (212) 209-1188. Premium ice cream and cholocate coffee. Established: 1989 - Franchising Since: 2000 - No. of Units: Company Owned: 10 - Franchised: 54 - Franchise Fee: $25,000.

BAHAMA BUCK'S ORIGINAL SHAVED ICE COMPANY
Bahama Buck's Franchise Corporation
465 E. Chilton Dr., Ste. 5, Chandler, AZ, 85225. - Tel: (480) 894-4408, Fax: (480) 894-4409. Serve gourmet Hawaiian shaved ice, tropical drinks, and fresh squeezed 100% natural lemonades and limeades in a fun tropical atmosphere. Established: 1989 - Franchising Since: 1993 - No. of Units: Company Owned: 3 - Franchised: 6 - Franchise Fee: $15,000 - Royalty: 5% of gross sales - Total Inv: $60,000-$145,000 - Financing: No.

BASKIN-ROBBINS '31' ICE CREAM AND YOGURT
14 Pacella Park Dr., Randolph, MA, 02368. Contact: Fran. Dept. - Tel: (800) 777-9983, Web Site: www.baskinrobbins.com. Ice cream stores. Established: 1948 - Franchising Since: 1948 - No. of Units: Company Owned: 29 - Franchised: 3,557 - Franchise Fee: $30,000 - Total Inv: $142,500-$187,500 - Financing: Yes.

BEN & JERRY'S
Ben & Jerry's Franchising, Inc.
30 Community Dr., South Burlington, VT, 05403. Contact: Greta Barker, Franchise Sales Specialist - Tel: (802) 846-1500, Fax: (802) 846-1538, E-Mail: franchiseinfo@benjerry.com, Web Site: www.benjerry.com. When you step into a Ben & Jerry's scoop shop, you're in for a whole lot more than a treat, you're in for the wholly extraordinary Ben & Jerry's ice cream experience we call "joy for the belly & soul". Established: 1978 - Franchising Since: 1981 - No. of Units: Company Owned: 14 - Franchised: 300 - Franchise Fee: $5,000-$30,000 - Royalty: 2% royalty, 2% Local marketing, 2% National marketing fund - Financing: Third party.

BOBA HAWAIIAN
3505D Cadillac Ave, Costa Mesa, CA, 92626. Contact: Andy Kaoh - Tel: (714) 404-2883, Fax: (714) 668-9999. Topioca drinks in all tropical flavors, ice cream, yogurt and pastries. Established: 1998 - Franchising Since: 2001 - No. of Units: Company Owned: 1 - Franchised: 2 - Franchise Fee: $15,000 - Royalty: 3% - Total Inv: $600,000 - Financing: None.

BRIDGEMAN'S, THE ORIGINAL ICE CREAM RESTAURANTS, BRIDGEMAN'S DIPPING STATIONS, BRIDGEMAN'S SODA FOUNTAINS
Bridgeman's Restaurants, Inc.
5700 Smetana Dr., #110, Minnetonka, MN, 55343. Contact: Steve Lampi, Pres. - Tel: (800) 297-5050, (952) 931-3099, Fax: (952) 931-3199. Bridgeman's franchises are available in 4 forms: 1) Full service, family style restaurant featuring our famous ice cream specialty treats and American style cuisine. 2) Dip Shoppe, good in food court setting, offering ice cream treats along with a limited sandwich menu. 3) Soda Fountain, ice cream treats in other retail areas. 4) Dip Station, ice cream for cones. Established: 1936 - Franchising Since: 1967 - No. of Units: Company Owned: 5 - Franchised: 27 - Franchise Fee: $750 for rural dip stations to $25,000 for urban restaurants - Royalty: 2% on gross sales, 2% adv. - Total Inv: Minimum $7,000-$350,000 for full restaurant - Financing: None.

BRUSTER'S OLD-FASHIONED ICE CREAM & YOGURT
730 Mulberry Street, Bridgewater, PA, 15009. Contact: Dave Guido, President - Tel: (724) 774-4250, Fax: (724) 774-0666, Web Site: www.brustersicecream.com. Bruster's features fresh, delicious homemade ice cream, and it's made fresh daily on site. We use only the best ingredients - whole nuts, cherries, etc and serve our products on homemade waffle cones. Our main goals are quality product and quality service. Established: 1989 - Franchising Since: 1993 - No. of Units: Company Owned: 3 - Franchised: 34 - Franchise Fee: $30,000 - Royalty: 5% of net sales - Total Inv: $500,000-$750,000 - Financing: No.

CARVEL ICE CREAM BAKERY
Carvel Corp.
200 Glenridge Point Pkwy, #200, Atlanta, GA, 30342. - Tel: (800) 227-8353, Fax: (404) 255-4978. Positioned to provide high quality, custom ice cream desserts and novelties professionally prepared from scratch, on premises. In addition to full-service retail outlets, branch unit opportunities include kiosks, mini-stores and vending carts, as well as participation in a Branded Freezer Program in supermarkets and convenience stores. Established: 1934 - Franchising Since: 1947 - No. of Units: Company Owned: 5 - Franchised: 420 - Franchise Fee: $10,000 - Royalty: $1.57/gallon, min. 8,000 gallons = $11,280 - Total Inv: $175,000-$205,000 - Financing: Third party.

CHICAGO TASTEE-FREEZ CORPORATION
5627 W. Dempster Street, Morton Grove, IL, 60053. - Tel: (773) 334-3300, Fax: (847) 498-2295. Ice cream/fast food. Established: 1955 - Franchising Since: 1955 - No. of Units: Franchised: 20 - Franchise Fee: $7,500-$25,000 - Royalty: 6%, 1% adv. - Total Inv: Varies, size and type of operation $75,000,000-$150,000,000 - Financing: No direct financing.

COLE'S CONCRETE FACTORY
Custard Factory Inc.
744-F Spirit of St. Louis Blvd, Chesterfield, MO, 63005. Contact: Brian Krieger - Tel: (800) 323-6786, Web Site: www.colesconcretefactory.com. Our team is experienced and equipped to deliver a proven system for providing the best frozen custard in a fun atmosphere. Franchising Since: 2003 - No. of Units: Company Owned: 1 - Franchised: 1 - Franchise Fee: $25,000 - Total Inv: $50,000-$250,000.

CULVER'S FROZEN CUSTARD
Culver Franchising Systems, Inc.
540 Water St, Prairie Du Sac, WI, 53578. - Tel: (608) 644-2130, Fax: (608) 643-7982. Fast service specialty restaurant featuring butterburgers and frozen custard. Established: 1984 - Franchising Since: 1988 - No. of Units: Company Owned: 3 - Franchised: 79 - Franchise Fee: $42,500 - Royalty: 4%, 2% adv - Total Inv: $900,000-$1,900,000- Financing: No.

DIAMOND
Petrucci's Franchising, Inc.
1958 kirkbride Cir, Yardley, PA, 19067-7221. Contact: Franchise Sales - Tel: (215) 860-4848, (888) 738-7822, Fax: (215) 860-6123. 47+ flavors of soft serve ice cream and frozen yogurt, Italian water ice, ice cream cakes and pies. Various concepts - cones, shakes,sundaes, frozen novelties, funnel cakes, soft pretzels, Belgian waffles. Established: 1983 - Franchising Since: 1995 - No. of Units: Franchised: 97 - Franchise Fee: $20,000 - Royalty: 5% gross sales - Total Inv: $94,800-$133,800 - Financing: Third party.

DIPPIN DOTS *
5101 Charter Oak Dr, Paducah, KY, 42001. - Tel: (270) 575-6990, Fax: (270) 575-6997, Web Site: wwwdippindots.com. Dippin Dots offers single unit franchises for retail ice cream stores, festivals and fairs. Established: 1988 - Franchising Since: 2000 - No. of Units: Company Owned: 1 - Franchised: 535 - Franchise Fee: $12,500.

EMACK & BOLIO'S ICE CREAM FOR THE CONNOISSEUR
Gone Troppo, Inc.
P.O. Box 703, Brookline Village, MA, 02447. Contact: Bob Rook, Pres. - Tel: (617) 739-7995, Fax: (617) 232-1102, E-Mail: enbic@aol.com, Web Site: www.emackbolios.com. Super premium ice creams, yogurt, smoothies, espresso drinks in a fun funny atmosphere. Established: 1975 - Franchising Since: 1977 - No. of Units: Company Owned: 3 - Franchised: 31 - Total Inv: $95,000 - Financing: No.

EVERYTHING YOGURT EXPRESS
Restaurant Systems International, Inc
1000 South Avenue, Staten Island, NY, 10314. Contact: VP, Franchise Development - Tel: (718) 494-8888, (800) 205-6050, Fax: (718) 494-8776, E-Mail: treats@restsys.com, Web Site: www.restsys.com. Frozen yogurt sundaes and shakes. Established: 1976 - Franchising Since: 1981 - No. of Units: Franchised: 16 - Franchise Fee: $15,000 - Royalty: 5% royalty, 1% advertising fund - Financing: Yes.

FROOTS *
Froots Franchising Companies
3325 Hollywood Blvd Ste. 303, Hollywood, FL, 33021. Contact: Cristine Cavallo - Tel: (954) 650-3288, (877) 376-6871, Fax: (954) 964-9830, E-Mail: franchises@frootssmoothies.com, Web Site: www.frootssmoothies.com. Casual dining, tropical setting, smoothie, salads & wraps. Established: 2001 - Franchising Since: 2004 - No. of Units: Company Owned: 4 - Franchised: 4 - Franchise Fee: $25,000 - Royalty: 5% - Total Inv: $75,000-$225,000 - Financing: No.

FROZEN FUSION FRUIT SMOOTHIES
Native Planet Foods
8900 E Chaparral Rd #1000, Scottsdale, AZ, 85250-2600. Contact: Franchise Department - Tel: (480) 948-5604, (800) 240-1507, Fax: (480) 948-6203, Web Site: www.frozenfusion.com. Healthy high energy food considered a meal in a cup and a meal replacement. Established: 1996 - Franchising Since: 1997 - No. of Units: Company Owned: 6 - Franchised: 18 - Franchise Fee: $25,000 - Royalty: 5%, 3% advertising - Total Inv: $150,000-$200,000 - Financing: Third party.

GELATO AMARE
11504 Hyde Place, Raleigh, NC, 27614. Contact: John Franklin, Pres. - Tel: (919) 847-4435. Retail stores serving homemade super premium Italian style low fat ice cream, no fat yogurt-smoothies, espresso, cappuccino, pastries, light salads and sandwiches. Established: 1983 - Franchising Since:1986- No. of Units: Company Owned: 1 - Franchised: 2 - Franchise Fee: $18,900 1st store, $7,000 each addit'l store - Royalty: 5% of sales - Total Inv: $175,000-$225,000 - Financing: Will assist.

HAAGEN-DAZS
Haagen-Dazs Shoppe Company, Inc., The
200 South 6th Street MS 28J2, Minneapolis, MN, 55402-1464. - Tel: (612) 330-4873, Fax: (612) 330-7074. Ice cream and frozen dessert shop. Established: 1961 - Franchising Since: 1978 - No. of Units: Company Owned: 3 - Franchised: 235 - Franchise Fee: $20,000 - Royalty: $1.16/gallon - Total Inv: $200,000 - Financing: No.

HEIDI'S FROZEN YOGURT SHOPPE
Heidi's Frozen Yogurt Shoppes, Inc.
4175 Veterans Hwy., Ronkonkoma, NY, 11779. - Tel: (516) 585-0900, Fax: (516) 737-9792. Frozen Yogurt Shoppes. Established: 1983-Franchising Since: 1984 - No. of Units: Company Owned: 4 - Franchised: 63 - Franchise Fee: $25,000 - Royalty: 4% - Total Inv: $175,000 - Financing: No.

HELEN HUTCHLEYS
Helen Hutchleys Inc.
P.O. Box 80995, Stn. C, Canton, OH, 44708-0995. - Tel: (330) 477-4515, Fax: (330) 477-5908. Ice cream and candy stores. Hand dipped old fashioned ice cream with a complete line of homestyle gourmet chocolates and hundreds of other candies. Established: 1963 - Franchising Since: 1965 - No. of Units: Franchised: 7 - Franchise Fee: $10,000 - Royalty: 4% - Total Inv: $76,000-$175,000 - Financing: No.

HOGI YOGI SANDWICHES AND FROZEN YOGURT
Hogi Yogi Franchising Corporation
4833 North Edgewood Dr., Provo, UT, 84604-5606. - Tel: (801) 222-9004, Fax: (801) 222-0977. Unique combination of fresh, custom-made sandwiches and custom-blended frozen yogurt under one roof. Complete initial training and thorough continual support provided. Firm commitment to the success of each individual franchisee. Established: 1989 - Franchising Since: 1992 - No. of Units: Company Owned: 2 - Franchised: 81 - Franchise Fee: $15,000 - Royalty: 6% of net sales plus 2% of net sales for adv. - Total Inv: $90,000-$160,000+ including fran. fee - Financing: Total investment required.

ICE CREAM CHURN
4175 Veteran's Hwy, Rononkoma, NY, 11779. - Tel: (800) 423-2763. Old fashioned ice cream and yogurt. Full training and support provided. Established: 1973 - Franchising since: 1978 - No. of Units: Franchised: 470 - Franchise Fee: $5,000 - Total Inv: $15,000-$45,000 (add on concept-fran fee-$25,000 mall kiosk) - Financing: Yes.

ICE CREAM & YOGURT CLUB, THE
Ice Cream Club, Inc., The
1580 High Ridge Rd., Boynton Beach, FL, 33426. Contact: Richard Draper, Pres. - Tel: (800) 535-7711, Fax: (561) 731-0311. Retail ice cream and yogurt shops. Better income areas and upscale locations sought. Premium products and attractive decor. Established: 1982 - Franchising Since: 1984 - No. of Units: Company Owned: 3 - Franchised: 14 - Franchise Fee: $20,000 - Total Inv: $87,000 incl. fran. fee - Financing: Equip. lease programs - Franchising in Southeast Florida locations only.

ICE HUT, THE
P.O. Box 633, Navesink, NJ, 07752-0633. - Tel: (888) 4-ICE HUT. Italian ice and ice cream in spring/summer then stores convert to the Soup hut for fall/winter. Established: 1994 - Franchising Since: 1997 - No. of Units: Company Owned: 1 - Franchised: 4 - Franchise Fee: $15,000 - Royalty: 6.5% - Total Inv: $72,000-$132,000 - Financing: Qualified franchisees can get equipment financing.

JULIE ANN'S FROZEN CUSTARD
Julie Ann's Corporation
4314-E. Crystal Lake, McHenry, IL, 60050. Contact: Peter Wisniewski, Pres., CEO - Tel: (815) 459-9193, Fax: (815) 459-9195, Web Site: www.julieanns.com. Americas finest frozen custard dessert products and fast food products. Established: 1985 - Franchising Since: 1995 - No. of Units: Company Owned: 1 - Franchised: 4 - Franchise Fee: $25,000-$35,000 - Royalty: 4%-4.5% - Total Inv: $138,000-$351,500 (Leased locations) - Financing: No.

KOHR BROS. FROZEN CUSTARD
Kohr Bros. Franchise Systems, Inc
2115 Berkmar Dr., Charlottesville, VA, 22901. Contact: Exec. Dir.Fran. - Tel: (434) 975-1500, Fax: (434) 975-1505, Web Site: www.kohr bros.com. Kohr Bros® is the original frozen custard since 1919. Our stores which are bright and easily maintained, offer a simple and unique frozen concept. Established: 1919 - Franchising Since: 1994 - No. of Units: Company Owned: 11 - Franchised: 27 - Franchise Fee: $27,500 - Royalty: 5% - Total Inv: $145,900-$277,500 - Financing: Third party.

LARRY'S ICE CREAM & YOGURT PARLOURS
4175 Veterans Memorial Hwy Ste 303, Ronkonkoma, NY, 11779-7639. Contact: Gayle Longmore, Director Franchise Sales - Tel: (972) 788-4788, (800) 269-4374. Ice cream and yogurt our specialty. Full training and support provided. Established: 1982 - Franchised: 30 - Franchise Fee: $15,000 - Total Inv: $125,000-$225,000 - Financing: Yes.

LIC'S LLOYD'S ICE CREAM, INC.
11 N.W. 5th St., Evansville, IN, 47708-1601. Contact: Franchise Department - Tel: (812) 424-3066, Fax: (812) 424-3055. Ice cream, yogurt, and sandwiches. Regional - IN, IL, KY, TN. Established: 1950 - Franchising Since: 1988 - No. of Units: Company Owned: 9 - Franchised: 2 - Franchise Fee: $10,000 - Royalty: 4% - Total Inv: $100,000-$125,000 - Financing: No.

LITTLE SCOOPS *
135 E. Erie Street,Blauvelt, NY, 10913. - Tel: (845) 365-4500, Fax: (845) 365-4501, Web Site: www.littlescoops.com. 1950s style ice cream parlor specializing in children's parties. Established: 2002 - Franchising Since: 2003 - No. of Units: Company Owned: 1 - Franchise Fee: $20,000 - Royalty: 5% - Total Inv: $87,000-$152,000 - Financing: No.

LOARD'S ICE CREAM & CANDIES
2000 Wayne Ave., San Leandro, CA, 94577. Contact: Russell B. Falyards, Pres. - Tel: (510) 633-1330. Fast food/ice cream restaurant. Established: 1950 - No. of Units: Company Owned: 9 - Franchised: 13.

LOVE'S YOGURT
Love's Group
3703 W. Lake Ave., Ste. 202, Glenview, IL, 60025-1266. Contact: Franchise Department - Tel: (773) 525-5300, Fax: (773) 525-2805. Offers a unique soft-serve frozen yogurt and salad bar concept. The emphasis is toward fresh, healthy, quality foods with salads prepared daily, sandwiches, soups, chili, baked potatoes with toppings, and unique wraps. Personalized service is our specialty. Established: 1987 - Franchising Since: 1988 - No. of Units: Company Owned: 3 - Franchised: 4 - Franchise Fee: $20,000 - Royalty: 4%, 2% adv. - Total Inv: $160,000-$200,000 - Financing: No, indirect assistance.

MAGGIEMOO'S ICE CREAM & TREATERY
Maggie Moo's International, LLC
10025 Governor Warfield Pkwy, Suite 301, Columbia, MD, 21044. - Tel: (410) 740-2100, Fax: (410) 740-1500, Web Site: www.maggie moos.com. Unique and exciting retail shops featuring homemade, super-premium ice-cream, non-fat ice cream. sorbet, smoothies, homemade fudge, custom made cakes and pies, plus a line of specialty merchandise. Established: 1996 - Franchising since: 1997 - No. of Units: Company Owned: 2 - Franchised: 21 - Franchise Fee: $23,000 - Royalty: 5%, 2% advertising - Total Inv: $148,000-$228,000 - Financing: No.

MARBLE SLAB CREAMERY
Marble Slab Creamery, Inc.
3100 S. Gessner, Ste. 305, Houston, TX, 77063. Contact: VP of Fran. Dev. - Tel: (713) 780-3601, Fax: (713) 780-0264. Retail ice cream stores featuring super-premium ice cream, daily baked cones, fresh frozen yogurt, pies, cakes, homemade cookies and brownies. Ice cream is custom designed for customer on frozen marble slabs and made daily in the store. Established: 1983 - Franchising Since: 1984 - No. of Units: Company Owned: 1 - Franchised: 132 - Franchise Fee: $28,000 - Royalty: 6% - Total Inv: $165,975-$247,975 - Financing: No.

MAUI WOWI SMOOTHIES
5601 S. Broadway Ste. 20, Littleton, CO, 80121. - Tel: (303) 781-7800, (888) 862-8555, Fax: (303) 781-2438, Web Site: www.mauiwowi.com. Mobile smoothie carts. Established: 1982 - Franchising Since: 1997 - No. of Units: Company Owned: 3 - Franchised: 52 - Franchise Fee: $20,000 - Total Inv: $42,000-$54,000 - Financing: No.

MISTER SOFTEE, INC
901 East Clements Bridge Rd, Runnemede, NJ, 08078. Contact: James Conway Jr - Tel: (856) 939-4103, Fax: (856) 939-0490. Soft ice cream on wheels. Established: 1956 - Franchising Since: 1958 - No. of Units: Company Owned: 2 - Franchised: 552 - Franchise Fee: $5,000 - Total Inv: Min $25,000 cash - Financing: Yes.

MORRONE'S ITALIAN ICES & HOME TREATS
Ice American Corp.
P.O Box 1322, Havertown, PA, 19083-5922. Contact: Dennis Mason, Fran. Dev. Dir. - Tel: (610) 446-2784, Fax: (610) 446-8381. Italian water ice, soft ice cream and snack outlet. Established: 1925 - Franchising Since: 1996 - No. of Units: Company Owned: 2 - Franchised: 5 - Franchise Fee: $15,000 - Royalty: 5% of gross sales - Total Inv: $68,900-$123,800 - Financing: Will assist in obtaining financing.

NATURALLY YOGURT & SPEEDSTER'S CAFE'S NY CORP.
P.O. Box 511, San Ramon, CA, 94583-0511. Contact: Franchise Department - Tel: (510) 743-9234. A quality, fresh frozen yogurt operation. Clean high-tech graphics in a unique presentation offering a wide range of toppings, sundaes, shakes, smoothies, and other specialty items. Speedster's offers fresh salads, homemade soups, baked potatoes, and a complete yogurt presentation. Established: 1983 - Franchising Since: 1984 - No. of Units: Franchised: 3 - Franchise Fee: $20,000 - Royalty: 0-5% - Total Inv: $155,000-$225,000 - Financing: No.

NEW ORLEANS SNOWBALLS ®
New Orleans Snowballs, Inc
214 Woodhaven Trail, Boone, NC, 26607. Contact: Monty Joynes, Pres. - Tel: (828) 264-0037, E-Mail: drmonty@helicon.net. Snow-like shaved ice and fresh-made syrups made into snowballs and snowshakes. Famous for snowballs with cream. Also hot beverage products for year round operation. Established: 1985 - Licensing Since: 1986 - No. of Units: Company Owned: 2 - Licensed: 150 - Fee: $5,295 (includes 2 days training and ice shaving equip.) - Total Inv: equip., initial supplies, training - Financing: No.

PERKITS YOGURT SHOPS
P.O. Box 2862, Cleveland, TN, 37320. Contact: Franchise Department - Tel: (423) 559-7900. Frozen yogurt shops. Established: 1985 - Franchising Since: 1986 - No. of Units: Company Owned: 1 - Franchised: 31 - Franchise Fee: $5,000 - Royalty: 1% - Total Inv: $20,000-$30,000.

PETRUCCI'S ICE CREAM CO. / MICK'S ITALIAN ICE'S
Petrucci's Franchising, Inc.
1958 Kirkbride Cir, Yardley, PA, 19067-7221. Contact: Mick Perrotta, President - Tel: (215) 860-4848, (888) 738-7822, Fax: (215) 860-6123, E-Mail: mpmogul@aol.com, Web Site: www.petruccis.com. 50 flavors of frozen yogurt, homemade Italian ice, premium handdipped Ice cream, sundaes, shakes, mega blend®, old fashioned creamsicle, cakes and frozen novelties. Established: 1983 - Franchising Since: 1996 - No. of Units: Company Owned: 1 - Franchised: 24 - Franchise Fee: $20,000 - Royalty: 5% gross sales - Total Inv: $139,900-$229,900 - Financing: Third party.

PIRATE PAT'S HAWAIIAN SHAVE ICE
Pirate Pat World Wide
P.O. Box 12791, Pensacola, FL, 32591-2791. Contact: Stacy Page, Franchising Marketing Director - Tel: (866) 99-PIRATE, (850) 995-3237, E-Mail: piratepat@yahoo.com. We sell the planet's best Hawaiian shave ice. If we didn't mean it, we wouldn't say it. Established: 2000 - Franchising Since: 2002 - No. of Units: Company Owned: 3 - Franchised: 2 - Franchise Fee: $20,000 - Royalty: 6% - Total Inv: $45,000-$63,000 - Financing: None.

RITA'S ICES CONES SHAKES & OTHER COOL STUFF
Rita's Water Ice Franchise Corp.
1525 Ford Road, Bensalem, PA, 19020. Contact: Steven Beagelman, V.P. of Franchising - Tel: (215) 633-9899, (800) 677-7482, Fax: (215) 633-9922, E-Mail: sales@rirascorp.com, Web Site: www.ritasice.com. Rita's is the largest and fasyesy growing Water Ice Chain in the country. Rita's operates in 9 states with 260 franchised locations. Our product line offers 21 Italian Ice Flavors, 4 Cream Ice Flavours, which is a creamier version of Italian Ice. We also offer Gelati's, which is a layered concoction of custard and your favorite Rita's Italian Ice Flavour. A Misto Shake is a creamy, cool combination of your favorite custarrd and Italian Ice blended together. Our custard comes in chocolate, vanilla or twist. Established: 1984 - Franchising Since: 1989 - No. of Units: Company Owned: 1 - Franchised: 260 - Franchise Fee: $25,000 - Royalty: 6.5%, 2.5% adv. - Total Inv: $135,650-$242,000 - Financing: Third party.

RITTER'S FROZEN CUSTARD
RFC Franchising, Inc.
5222 S. East Street, Bldg. B-1, Indianapolis, IN, 46227. Contact: Director of Franchising - Tel: (317) 786-3000, Web Site: wwww.ritters frozencustard.com. Requires co. designed shoppe as free standing building, walk-up window service, frozen custard with related frozen sundaes, etc. Established: 1990 - Franchising Since: 1995 - No. of Units: Company Owned: 2 - Franchised: 45 - Franchise Fee: $25,000 - Royalty: 5% - Total Inv: Average total $600,000 - Financing: No.

ROBIN ROSE ICE CREAM & CHOCOLATE
Robin Rose America, Inc.
4050 Via Dolce #339, Marina DEl Rey, CA, 90292-5256. Contact: Robin Rose, Pres. - Tel: (310) 392-4921, Fax: (310) 821-6666. Retail sales of gourmet ice cream, chocolate, non-fat yogurt, beverages, with possibly baked goods. Established: 1981 - Licensing Since: 1985 - No. of Units: Company Owned: 3 - Licensed: 3 - Total Inv: Store build-out + equip, ranges from $50,000-$95,000 - Financing: No.

SCOOPERS ICE CREAM
Scoopers Ice Cream Inc.
22 Woodrow Ave., Youngstown, OH, 44512. Contact: Norman Hughes, Pres. - Tel: (330) 758-3857. Retail old fashioned ice cream stores. Made fresh daily. Established: 1980 - Franchising Since: 1991 - No. of Units: Company Owned: 2 - Franchised: 6 - Franchise Fee: $15,000 - Royalty: 5% - Total Inv: $50,000: $35,000 equip. + fran. fee - Financing: No.

SHAKE'S FROZEN CUSTARD
Shake's Frozen Custard, Inc
244 W. Dickson St, Fayetteville, AR, 72701. Contact: Jim Buckner - Tel: (501) 587-9115, Fax: (501) 587-0780, E-Mail: info@shakesfrozen custard.com, Web Site: www.shakesfrozencustard.com. Shake's Frozen Custard is where friends gather, couples fall in love, and people of all ages come to enjoy the vibrant nostalgic atmosphere of the 40's and 50's. Featuring an extensive menu consisting of our one-of-a-kind, delicious frozen custard and a wide variety of innovative concepts, Shake's is a rapidly growing franchise system. With intensive training and continous support, we will always ensure your business is operating to its maximum potential. Established: 1991 - Franchising Since: 1999 - No. of Units: Company Owned: 3 - Franchised: 25 - Franchise Fee: $30,000 - Royalty: 5% - Total Inv: $500-$250,000 - Financing: Third party.

SHOW PLACE ICE CREAM PARLOURS
202 Centre St., Beach Haven, NJ, 08008. Contact: Fran. Dev. - Tel: (800) 835-2567, (609) 492-2639, Fax: (609) 492-4469. A unique blend of family entertainment and premium ice cream. Customers perform for the desserts and each seating culminates in a Broadway Revue by The Show Place Singing Waiters. Ranked top ten ice cream parlour for families in America by Child Magazine and received "Vacationers Choice Award" for Best Ice Cream Shop. Seasonal/year round locations available, full support package. Established: 1975 - Franchising Since: 1995 - No. of Units: Franchised: 1 - Franchise Fee: $20,000 - Royalty: 5% gross - Total Inv: $190,000+ - Financing: No.

SNO SHACK SHAVED ICE
360 Whitney Avenue, Salt Lake City, UT, 84115. Contact: Cheryl Lewis, CEO - Tel: (801) 466-1771, Fax: (801) 466-1790, E-Mail: sales@snoshack, Web Site: www.snoshack.com. Manufacturer & distributor of all shaved ice/snow cone flavors, supplies, Real Snow Cube and Block Shavers. Concession Trailers, Carts, Kiosks, Sno Shack trailers for all uses. Full line of concessions & equipment for Shaved Ice. Established: 1978 - Franchising Since: 1998 - No. of Units: Company Owned: 12 - Franchised: 830 - Franchise Fee: Use of Trademark and Sno Shack name/Real Snow - Total Inv: Start up from $2,700-$17,900 depending on needs - Financing: Online financing available.

SOUTH BEACH SMOOTHIE
7222 Red Rd., South Miami, FL, 33143. Contact: Andrew Bellinson, Pres. - Tel: (305) 666-2153, Fax: (305) 661-5546. Smoothie juice bar comfortable dine in take out experience. Wide variety of healthy snacks and some supplements. Established: 1992 - No. of Units: Company Owned: 3 - Franchise Fee: $10,000 - Royalty: 5%, 1% adv - Total Inv: $60,000-$150,000 variable buildout - Financing: No.

SWENSON'S ICE CREAM
Cool Brands International
4175 Veteran's Hwy, Ronkonkoma, NY, 11779. Contact: Joe Arancio, VP Franchise Development - Tel: (800) 423-2763. Swenson's is a premium ice cream and food concept and can be franchised alone or co-franchised with I Can't Believe It's Yogurt or Swirl Frozen Yogurt at no additional franchise fee. Established: 1948 - No. of Units: Company Owned: 2 - Franchised: 60 - Franchise Fee: $10,000-$25,000 - Total Inv: $125,000-$250,000 - Financing: No.

TASTEE-FREEZ
Tastee-Freez International
48380 Van Dyke Ave., Utica, MI, 48317-3270. Contact: Fran. Dept. - Tel: (586) 739-5520, Fax: (586)739-8351. Fast food/soft serve ice cream. Established: 1950 - Franchising Since: 1950 - No. of Units: Franchised: 250 - Franchise Fee: $15,000 - Royalty: 4% & 1% - Total Inv: Estimated: low $30,000, high $550,000 - Financing: No.

TCBY/TCBY TREATS
TCBY International
2855 E. Cottonwood Pkwy, Ste. 400, Salt Lake City, UT, 84121. - Tel: (801) 736-5600, Fax: (801) 736-5936, Web Site: www.tcby.com. Yogurt, ice cream, coffee and pastry retail stores in an clean attractive environment. Established: 1981 - Franchising Since: 1983 - No. of Units: Company Owned: 100 - Franchised: 2,900 - Franchise Fee: $25,000 - Royalty: 0% - Total Inv: $100,000 - Financing: No.

TOPSY'S POPCORN & ICE CREAM SHOPPE
221 W. 74 Terrace, Kansas City, MO, 64114. - Tel: (816) 523-5555, Fax: (816) 523-4747. Shoppes retail quality gourmet popcorn, ice cream and related confection food items. No. of Units: Company Owned: 5 - Franchised: 8 - Franchise Fee: $20,000 - Royalty: 5% + 3% adv. - Total Inv: $100,000-$130,000 - Financing: Yes, through local lenders.

TREAT STREET
Restaurant Systems International, Inc
1110 South Avenue, Staten Island, NY, 10314. Contact: Larry Feierstein - Tel: (718) 494-8888, Fax: (718) 494-8776. Treat Street is "Fun Foods for the Kid in All of Us", featuring frozen yogurt, frostie & smoothie drinks, and hand-rolled pretzels. Established: 1976- Franchising Since: 1998 - No. of Units: Company Owned: 1 - Franchised: 34 - Franchise Fee: $22,000 - Royalty: 6% - Total Inv: $114,200-$300,500 - Financing: No.

UNCLE LOUIE G-HOMEMADE GOURMET ITALIAN ICES & ICE CREAM *
Uncle Louie G, Inc
1235A McDonald Avenue, Brooklyn, NY, 11230. Contact: Raymond S. Payne, Chielf Executive Officer - Tel: (718) 677-9551, Fax: (718) 677-9686, E-Mail: ray@unclelouieg.com, Web Site: www.unclelouieg.com. Uncle Louie G, Inc. is a premiere manufacturer of Italian Ices, Ice Cream and Chocolates. Our products are made with the best ingredients available in the marketplace. We aim to provide premium products coupled with exceptional service. Established: 1999 - Franchising Since: 2000 - No. of Units: Company Owned: 5 - Franchised: 65 - Franchise Fee: $30,000 - Royalty: 4% - Total Inv: $125,000-$225,000 - Financing: Third party.

YOGURTERIA
Yogurteria Franchise Corp.
1325 Franklin Ave, Ste. 165, Garden City, NY, 11530. Contact: Dominic Maggiore - Tel: (516) 773-9191. Eatery featuring yogurt. Established: 1987 - Franchising Since: 1993 - No. of Units: Franchised: 7 - Franchise Fee: $15,000 - Total Inv: $150,000 - Financing: Yes.

ZACK'S FAMOUS FROZEN YOGURT, INC.
254 Eaton Road, Mocksville, NC, 27028. Contact: Sherri England, V.P. - Tel: (336) 774-3767, Fax: (336) 724-1221. A chain of up-scale, leading edge fun food outlets with frozen yogurt as the primary menu item. Established: 1977 - Franchising Since: 1978 - No. of Units: Franchised: 31.

FOOD: RESTAURANTS

1 POTATO 2, INC.
P.O. Box 29325, Brooklyn Center, MN, 55429-0325. Contact: Connie Martin, Marketing Mgr. - Tel: (612) 537-3833. Fast food restaurant chain with a unique menu concept featuring baked potato entrees with a variety of toppings, and fresh cut fries. Established: 1977 - Franchising Since: 1984 - No. of Units: Company Owned: 5 - Franchised: 36 - Franchise Fee: $20,000 - Royalty: 4.5% - Total Inv: $95,000-$160,000 - Financing: Negotiable.

5 & DINER
5 & Diner Franchise Corp
1140 E Greenway Ste. 1, Mesa, AZ, 85203. Contact: Ken Higginbotham - Tel: (480) 962-7104, Fax: (480) 962-0159, Web Site: www.5and diner.com. Food-Fun-Fifties. A fifties diner & concept with delicious burgers, fries, milk shakes and blue plate specials - Breakfast, Lunch, Diner served in a setting of juke boxes, flashy chrome, checkerboard trim and servers who quickly become family friends. Established: 1987 - Franchising Since: 1995 - No. of Units: Company Owned: 1 - Franchised: 18 - Franchise Fee: $35,000 - Royalty: 5% of sales - Total Inv: $6,000 - Financing: No.

A & W RESTAURANTS
A & W Restaurants, Inc.
1441 Gardiner Lane, Louisville, KY, 40213. Contact: Fran. Sales Dept. - Tel: (800) 545-8360. Quick service restaurant featuring world famous A&W Root Beer and floats, hamburgers, hot dogs, coney dogs, grilled chicken sandwiches, french fries and onion rings. Various configurations for food courts and in-lines in malls to free-standing building. Conversions also considered. Established: 1919 - Franchising Since: 1925 - No. of Units: Company Owned: 174 - Franchised: 700 - Franchise Fee: $20,000 - Royalty: 4% gross sales monthly - Total Inv: $150,000-$600,000 - Financing: No direct financial assistance.

ABERDEEN BARNS
A.B. Franchise Corp.
2018 Holiday Dr., Charlottesville, VA, 22901. Contact: Terry Spathos, Pres. - Tel: (804) 296-9906. Dinnerhouse - American. Established: 1965 - No. of Units: Company Owned: 2 - Franchised: 2.

AJ TEXAS HOTS
AJ Texas Hots Fast Food Franchise
824 Foote Ave., Jamestown, NY, 14701. Contact: Samuel G. Colera, Pres. - Tel: (716) 484-9646. Fast food specializing in a unique Texas Hot (hot dog), and burgers. Also fish, chicken, ham and cheese sandwiches, fries and onion rings. Drive Thru - 1st in Chauto City. Established: 1968 - Franchising Since: 1994 - No. of Units: Company Owned: 1 - Franchised: Working on 2 - Franchise Fee: $25,000 - Royalty: $300 per mo. 1st yr., $400 per mo. 2nd yr, $500 per mo. after - Total Inv: $100,000 - Financing: None.

AL'S CHICAGO #1 ITALIAN BEEF
Chicago Franchise Systems, Inc
1079 West Taylor Street, Chicago, IL, 60607. Contact: V.P. Franchise Development - Tel: (630) 858-9121. Al's Chicago #1 Italian beef sandwich originated on a small curbside stand on Lafun & Harrison in 1938. Al's grew to its present location at 1079 W. Taylor St, in Chicago. Al's #1 Italian beef has won several awards for their "Famous Italian Beef Fries". Established: 1938 - Franchising Since: 2000 - Franchise Fee: $20,000 - Royalty: 5%, 2% advertising - Total Inv: $20,000 F.F (included in start up cost), $137,000-$252,000 no start up costs. - Financing: No.

ALAMO STEAKHOUSE & GRILL
Elephant & Castle International Inc
13300 Old Blanco Rd., Ste. 323, San Antonio, TX, 78216. Contact: David Evans - Tel: (210) 764-1911, Fax: (210) 764-1922. Steakhouse & bar. Established: 1977 - Franchising Since: 1997 - No. of Units: Company Owned: 2 - Franchised: 6 - Franchise Fee: $35,000 - Total Inv: $800,000 - Financing: No.

AMECI PIZZA AND PASTA INC.
6603 B Independence Ave., Canoga Park, CA, 91303. - Tel: (818) 712-0792, Fax: (818)712-0110, Web Site: www.amecipizza.com. Selling quality food at inexpensive prices. More than just pizza, Italian fast food. Take-out, delivery, pick-up. Established: 1984 - Franchising Since: 1986 - No. of Units: Company Owned: 3 - Franchised: 45 - Franchise Fee: $25,000 - Royalty: 4% weekly - Total Inv: $185,000 - Financing: None.

AMERICAN HERO, THE
A.G. Hero Int.
7031 Cahill Rd., Edina, MN, 55439. - Tel: (612) 943-8148, Fax: (612) 943-8149. Healthy upscale sandwich shop serving sandwiches, yogurt and baked goods. The American Hero is the "Fresh Rescue From Fast Food". Established: 1990 - Franchising Since: 1993 - No. of Units: Company Owned: 2 - Franchised: 1 - Franchise Fee: $9,900 - Royalty: Continuing fee 5%, adv. 3% - Total Inv: $70,000-$125,000.

ANDERSON'S FROZEN CUSTARD & ROAST BEEF
6075 Main Street, Willaimsville, NY, 14221. Contact: Kirk Wildermuth - Tel: (716) 633-2302, Fax: (716) 633-2671. Anderson's Frozen Custard and Roast Beef is a favorite of Western New York. Roast Beef on Kimmelwek, made to order fast casual dining. Frozen custard, ice cream, leamon ice, and many other fabulous desert products. Established: 1946 - Franchising Since: 1996 - No. of Units: Company Owned: 3 - Franchised: 8 - Franchise Fee: $150,000.

ANDREW SMASH
Smash International, Inc
P.O. Box 12233, Eugene, OR, 97440. Contact: Carl Jeffers - Tel: (541) 465-9088, Fax: (541) 349-0391. Meatless burger + smoothie restaurant. Established: 1995 - Franchising Since: 1998 - No. of Units: Company Owned: 1 - Franchise Fee: $27,500 - Total Inv: Phone for details - Financing: No.

ANGILO'S PIZZA
911 Church Street, Cincinnati, OH, 45215. Contact: Steven Jones, V.P. Dir. Franc. - Tel: (513) 821-6292. Fast food - pizza. Established: 1959 - No. of Units: Franchised: 36.

ANNTONY'S CARIBBEAN CAFE
P.O. Box 3030, Charlotte, NC, 28217. Contact; John L. Holding - Tel: (704) 339-0303, Fax:(704) 339-0353. Caribbean cafe. Established: 1995 - Franchising Since: 1995 - No. of Units: Company Owned: 1 - Franchise Fee: $16,000 (capital requirements $70,000-$190,000) - Financing: No.

ANTONELLO'S
Mangiamo Franchise Corp.
15965 Jeanette St., Southfield, MI, 48075. Contact: Franchise Dir. - Tel: (248) 557-2784. Authentic Italian dining, with a unique spice advice "Spice-ometer™". Antonello's has over 40 years in the Italian food industry, making Antonello's the obvious choice for delicious variations on a familiar theme. Established: 1957 - Franchising Since: 1997 - No. of Units: Company Owned: 1 - Franchise Fee: $20,000 - Royalty: 5% - Total Inv: $146,600-$236,000 - Financing: Yes, third party. NOT FRANCHISING AT THIS TIME.

APPLEBEE'S NEIGHBORHOOD GRILL & BAR/RIO BRAVO CANTINA
Applebee's International, Inc.
4551 W. 107th St., #100, Overland Park, KS, 66207. Contact: Franchise Director - Tel: (913) 967-4000, Fax: (913) 967-4135. Developer, operator and franchisor of restaurants under the trademark Applebee's Neighborhood Grill & Bar and Rio Bravo Mexican Cantinas. Established:

1983 - Franchising Since: 1983 - No. of Units: Company Owned: 166 - Franchised: 708 - Franchise Fee: Applebee's $35,000 in USA, $40,000 int'l. - Royalty: Applebee's 4% of each calendar month's gross sales, 5% international - Total Inv: Applebee's $1.7-$3.1 million - Financing: No.

ARBY'S, INC.
Triarc Restaurant Group
1000 Corporate Drive, Ft. Lauderdale, FL, 33334. Contact: Coordinator, Business Development - Tel: (954) 351-5200, (800) 592-6245, Fax: (954) 351-5222, E-Mail: roshins@arbys.com, Web Site: www.arbys.com. Arby's offers Cut Above menu options including a complete line of roast beef and chicken sandwiches, chicken fingers, a light sandwich menu, salads and three fry varieties. Development opportunities available. An experienced brand with over 3,100 locations. Established: 1964 - Franchising Since: 1965 - No. of Units: Franchised: 3,123 - Franchise Fee: 1st unit $37,500, 2nd & subsequent units $25,000 - Royalty: 4% of total gross sales - Total Inv: Estimated initial investment ranges $212,900-$2,253,200 depending on standard costs and whether leased or purchased property - Financing: No.

ARCTIC CIRCLE RESTAURANTS, INC.
Arctic Circle Restaurants, Inc
411 W. 7200 S., Ste. 200., P.O. Box 339, Midvale, UT, 84047. Contact: George D. Morgan, Exec. Vice President - Tel: (801) 561-3620, Fax: (801) 561-9646. Arctic Circle Restaurants feature a variety of 25 different handmade milk shakes which include fruit. Their food variety is just as unique, featuring hamburgers, chicken fingers, chicken sandwiches, taco salads, specialty drinks and more. All this in a fast-food environment. Established: 1953 - Franchising Since: 1956 - No. of Units: Company Owned: 27 - Franchised: 59 - Franchise Fee: $20,000 - Royalty: 3% of sales - Total Inv: $575,000-$1,071,500 - Financing: No.

ARIZONA PIZZA COMPANY
370 SE 15th Ave., Pompano Beach, FL, 33060. Contact: Linda Biciocchi - Tel: (954) 942-9424, Fax: (954) 783-5177. Pizza and pasta set in a casual restaurant/bar. Established: 2002 - Franchising Since: 2003 - No. of Units: Company Owned: 3 - Franchised: 1 - Franchise Fee: $25,000 - Royalty: $225/Mo. - Total Inv: $36,000-$62,000 - Financing: No.

ARNI'S INC.
Arni's Franchising Inc.
2415 N. 18th St., Lafayette, IN, 47904. Contact: Bradley Cohen, Dir. of Fran. Srvcs. - Tel: (765) 742-7455, Fax: (765) 742-6123. Family style restaurant specializing in pizza, salads, sandwiches, some pasta. Operations consist of dine in and carry out. Some have bars. Unique decors. Established: 1965 - Franchising Since: 1991 - No. of Units: Company Owned: 8 - Franchised: 8 - Franchise Fee: $7,500-$20,000 - Royalty: 4%.

ARTHUR TREACHER'S FISH & CHIPS
Arthur Treacher's, Inc.
5 Dakota Dr #302, Lake Success, NY, 11042. Contact: Michael Proulx, Dir. Fran. Dev. - Tel: (516) 358-0600, Fax: (516) 358-5076. Fast food seafood restaurant chain serving English style fish and chips, chicken, shrimp, clams, hushpuppies, coleslaw and beverages. Established: 1969 - Franchising Since: 1970 - No. of Units: Company Owned: 30 - Franchised: 130 - Franchise Fee: $19,500 - Royalty: 5% - Total Inv: $197,000-$379,000 - Financing: No.

ATLANTIC CITY SUB SHOPS
AC Subs Inc
124 Warf Rd, Egg Harbour TWP, NJ, 08234. Contact: Santo J. Formica, V.P. Owner - Tel: (609) 926-4560, Fax: (609) 645-3636. Full service restuarant, sub sandwiches, salads and deserts. Eat in, take out or delivery. Established: 1986 - Franchising Since: 1986 - No. of Units: Company Owned: 2 - Franchised: 3 - Franchise Fee: $15,000 - Royalty: 5% + 2% Advertising - Total Inv: $185,000-$275,000 - Financing: No.

AUNT SARAH'S PANCAKE HOUSE
Aunt Sarah's Franchises Inc.
P.O. Box 9504, Richmond, VA, 23228. - Tel: (804) 264-9189, Fax: (804) 266-1255. Family style restaurants. Established: 1964 - Franchising Since: 1968 - No. of Units: Company Owned: 14 - Franchised: 3 - Franchise Fee: $25,000 - Royalty: 4% - Financing: No.

AURELIO'S PIZZA, INC.
18162 Harwood Ave., Homewood, IL, 60430. Contact: Mr. Aurelio, Pres. - Tel: (708) 798-8050, Fax: (708) 798-6692. Pizzerias, limited menu, pasta, salads, sandwiches, dessert. Dine-in, carry-out and delivery. Established: 1959 - Franchising Since: 1978 - No. of Units: Company Owned: 4 - Franchised: 24 - Franchise Fee: $20,000 - Royalty: 3% - Total Inv: $100,000-$2,200,000 (location and services offered).

BACK YARD BURGERS
Back Yard Burgers, Inc.
1657 N Shelby Oaks Dr., #105, Memphis, TN, 38134-7436. Contact: Dir. of Fran. Sales - Tel: (901) 367-0888 ext. 1203, Fax: (901) 367-0999. 1/3 lb. charbroiled hamburgers, chicken, sandwiches and other food of gourmet quality like customer would cook in their own Back Yard. A unique concept, well placed for success in the nineties and the century ahead. Established: 1987 - Franchising Since: 1988 - No. of Units: Company Owned: 35 - Franchised: 50 - Franchise Fee: $25,000 - Royalty: 4% of wkly. sales, 2% local adv., 1% nat'l adv. - Total Inv: $350,000-$832,000 - Financing: No.

BAD BOB'S BARBEQUE RESTAURANT *
2005 St. John Ave, Dyersburg, TN, 38024. Contact: Bobby Grooms - Tel: (731) 286-5256, E-Mail: badbobsllc@scscorp.net, Web Site: www.badbobs.net. Bring the greatest tasting Memphis style BBQ of Badbob's BBQ & Grill to your favorite location and invest in a Badbob's franchise. Established: 1997 - Franchising Since: 2002 - No. of Units: Franchised: 6 - Franchise Fee: $10,000-$15,000 - Royalty: 4%.

BAGEL BREAK FRANCHISING
1615 Old Hunters Trace, Marietta, GA, 30062. - Tel: (770) 565-8710, (800) 551-2245, Fax: (770) 973-9375. Retail bagel restaurant. Established: 1994 - Franchising Since: 1994 - No. of Units: Franchised: 3 - Franchise Fee: $25,000 - Royalty: 4% - Total Inv: $100,000-$350,000 - Financing: No.

BAGEL HOUSE & DELI
Bagel Franchise Enterprises, Inc.
1100 Hooksett Road., Unit 109, Hooksett, NH, 03106. Contact: George Orfander, Exec. VP - Tel: (603) 644-8200. High quality, fast service breakfast and lunch place which serves fresh bagels, gourmet coffee and made to order deli sandwiches. Professional training and continuous support. Exclusive territory. Established: 1994 - Franchising Since: 1996 - No. of Units: Company Owned: 2 - Franchised: 1 - Franchise Fee: $17,500 - Royalty: 4% on gross sales - Total Inv: $56,300-$79,500 excluding fran. fee - Financing: No.

BAGELSMITH RESTAURANTS & FOOD STORES
Bagelsmith Franchising Company, Inc.
37 Van Syckel Rd., Hampton, NJ, 08827. Contact: Wayne Smith, Pres. - Tel: (908) 730-8600. What makes us special is, of course, our Bagelsmith Bagel. But we are also famous for our delicatessen, featuring only high quality products. Whether in our restaurants or in our convenience food stores, we provide our customers with high quality products and friendly knowledgeable service, in a clean, pleasant, family-oriented environment. Established: 1979 - Franchising Since: 1982 - No. of Units: Company Owned: 2 - Franchised: 18 - Franchise Fee: $25,000 - Royalty: Under 500,000 - 1%; $500,000-$599,999 - 1.5%; $600,000-$699,999 - 2%; $700,000-$999,999 - 3%; Over $1,000,000 - 2% - Total Inv: $185,000-$225,000 - Financing: No.

BAJA SOL TORTILLA GRILL *
7173 Oak Pointe Curve, Bloomington, MN, 55438. - Tel: (612) 280-1467, Fax: (952) 944-2001, Web Site: www.bajasol.com. Serving taco's, burritos, fajitas and quesadillas, all made with fresh ingredients. Established: 1995 - Franchising Since: 1999 - No. of Units: Company Owned: 5 - Franchised: 4 - Franchise Fee: $25,000 - Royalty: 4.5% - Total Inv: $166,000-$400,000.

BALDINO'S GIANT JERSEY SUBS, INC.
760 Elaine St., Hinesville, GA, 31313. Contact: William Baer, Pres. - Tel: (912) 368-2822, Fax: (912) 369-3923. Freshest Subs in Town - Sandwich chain with a variety of hot and cold subs, sliced fresh as ordered. Also in store baking, and grilled steak subs. Multi production lines for faster service. Established: 1975 - Franchising Since: 1985 - No. of Units: Company Owned: 6 - Franchised: 15 - Franchise Fee:

BAR-B-CUTIE DRIVE-IN *

5221 Nolensville Road, Nashville, TN, 37211. Contact: Brett McFarland - Tel: (615) 834-6556, Fax: (615) 834-0003, E-Mail: franchise@bar-b-cutie.com, Web Site: www.bar-b-cutie.com. Hickory-smoked southern charm! The best Bar-B-Que you've ever had the pleasure of tasting! This restaurant has specialized in hickory pit Bar-B-Que for nearly 60 years and has perfected the art of southern cuisine. Established: 1950 - Franchising Since: 2003 - No. of Units: Company Owned: 3 - Franchise Fee: $30,000 - Royalty: 5% - Total Inv: $260,000-$418,000.

BASIL'S FRANCHISING, INC.

5601 Manatee Ave., Bradenton, FL, 34209. - Tel: (941) 795-0848. Chicken and ribs fast food restaurant. Established: 1987 - Franchising Since: 1997 - No. of Units: Company Owned: 2 - Franchised: 1 - Franchise Fee: $20,000-$25,000 - Royalty: 5%, 1% adv. - Total Inv: $190,000-$250,000 - Financing: No.

BASSETT'S ORIGINAL TURKEY RESTAURANTS
Bassett Management Co.

20000 Horizon Way Ste 170, Mount Laurel, NJ, 08054-4320. Contact: Steve Beagleman, VP Fran. Sales - Tel: (215) 830-1362, (800) 282-TURK, Fax: (215) 675-9690. Quick service restaurant featuring fresh roasted turkey sandwiches and platters. Established: 1983 - Franchising Since: 1989 - No. of Units: Company Owned: 3 - Franchised: 6 - Franchise Fee: $25,000 - Royalty: 5% - Total Inv: $200,000-$300,000 - Financing: Yes, third party.

BATES BURGERS, INC.

9930 Riverview #923, Lakeland, MI, 48143. Contact: Gary Bates, Owner - Tel: (248) 349-3033. Sit down and carry-out "Bag of Burgers". High volume slider type hamburger business with proven record of high quality and success. Established: 1985 - Franchising Since: 1994 - No. of Units: Company Owned: 3 - Franchise Fee: $10,000 - Royalty: 6% of gross sales - Total Inv: $20,000-$150,000 - Financing: Possible financing available.

BEAR ROCK CAFE *

1225 Crescent Green Dr, Cary, NC, 27511. Contact: Chris Cheek - Tel: (919) 859-6610, Fax: (919) 859-0170, E-Mail: info@bearrockfoods.com, Web Site: www.bearrockfoods.com. Comfort food served in a comfortable setting, delicious sandwiches made with the freshest ingredients. Established: 1997 - Franchising Since: 1998 - No. of Units: Company Owned: 4 - Franchised: 14 - Franchise Fee: $35,000 - Royalty: 4% of gross sales - Total Inv: $449,500-$593,000.

BEEF O'BRADY'S FAMILY SPORTS PUB
Family Sports Concepts, Inc

5510 W. LaSalle St., Ste. 200, Tampa, FL, 33607. Contact: Franchise Department - Tel: (813) 226-2333, (800) 728-8878, Fax: (813) 226-0030, Web Site: www.beefobradys.com. Family style sports pub-restaurant. Established: 1985 - Franchising Since: 1997 - No. of Units: Company Owned: 1 - Franchised: 81 - Franchise Fee: $25,000 - Royalty: 3.5% - Total Inv: $325,000 - Financing: Yes SBA, needs $70,000 cash.

BEEFSTEAK CHARLIE'S
Bombay Palace Restaurants, Inc.

236 W. 48th St., New York, NY, 10036-1424. Contact: Marketing Dept. - Tel: (212) 563-7440, Fax: (212) 629-0942. Full service family restaurants serving steaks, BBQ ribs, chicken and seafood. Also featuring unlimited shrimp and salad bar with beer, wine, soda or sangria with your meal. Established: 1978 - Franchising Since: 1985 - No. of Units: Company Owned: 8 - Franchised: 8 - Franchise Fee: $25,000 - Royalty: 5% - Total Inv: $250,000+ - Financing: No. NOT FRANCHISING AT THIS TIME.

BENIHANA OF TOKYO
Benihana, Inc.

8685 N. W. 53rd Terrace, Miami, FL, 33166. Contact: Michael W. Kata, Rep. - Tel: (305) 593-0770, (800) 327-3369, Fax: (305) 592-6371, E-Mail: tvrabel@benihana.com, Web Site: www.benihana.com. Benihana is an award winning Japanese steakhouse chain featuring teppanyaki cooking. Each guest's meal is prepared right before their eyes by an entertaining chef who introduces all ingredients before he masterfully cooks. Established: 1963 - Franchising Since: 1970 - No. of Units: Company Owned: 40 - Franchised: 22 - Franchise Fee: $50,000 per unit - Royalty: 6%, .5% adv. - Total Inv: $1,200,000-$1,800,000 - Financing: No.

BENNETT'S BAR-B-QUE, INC.

6551 S. Revere Pky. #285, Englewood, CO, 80111. Contact: Bennett Shotwell, Owner - Tel: (303) 792-3088, Fax: (303) 792-5801, Web Site: www.bennettsbbq.com. Family restaurant serving barbeque beef, pork, chicken and pork ribs, 4 steaks, fish and grilled chicken. Established: 1984 - Franchising Since: 1986 - No. of Units: Company Owned: 4 - Franchised: 6 - Franchise Fee: $35,000 - Royalty: 3.5% - Financing: No.

BENNIGAN'S GRILL & TAVERN
Bennigan's Grill & Tavern

6500 International Parkway, Plano, TX, 75093. Contact: Lynette McKee, Vice President, Franchise Development - Tel: (407) 333-3533, (800) 543-9670, Fax: (407) 333-1380, E-Mail: lmckee@metrogroup.com, Web Site: www.bennigans.com. Bennigan's is an Irish Pub theme, casual dining restaurant serving a wide assortment of moderately priced foods, as well as alcoholic beverages in a warm, friendly atmosphere. Established: 1976 - Franchising Since: 1995 - No. of Units: Company Owned: 181 - Franchised: 127 - Franchise Fee: $65,000 - Royalty: 4% - Total Inv: $1,181,300-$2,208,750 - Financing: Third party.

BERRYHILL BAJA GRILL *

5603 Willersway, Houston, TX, 77056. - Tel: (713) 446-4466, Fax: (713) 621-0854, Web Site: www.berryhillbajagrill.com. Restaurant chain featuring unique baja-style cuisine. Established: 1991 - Franchising Since: 2000 - No. of Units: Company Owned: 2 - Franchised: 6 - Franchise Fee: $25,500-$30,000 - Royalty: 5% - Total Inv: $257,500-$527,500.

BIG BOB'S BARBEQUE RESTAURANT *

2005 St. John Ave, Dyersburg, TN, 38024. Contact: Bobby Grooms - Tel: (731) 286-5256, E-Mail: badbobsllc@scscorp.net, Web Site: www.badbobs.net. Bring the greatest tasting Memphis style BBQ of Badbob's BBQ & Grill to your favorite location and invest in a BadBob's franchise. Established: 1997 - Franchising Since: 2002 - No. of Units: Company Franchised: 6 - Franchise Fee: $10,000-$15,000 - Royalty: 4%.

BIG BOY FAMILY RESTAURANTS
Elias Brothers Restaurants, Inc.

4199 Marcy Dr., Warren, MI, 48091. Contact: Dave Knitter, Franchise Department - Tel: (586) 759-6000., E-Mail: dknitter@bigboy.com, Web Site: www.bigboy.com. Full service family restaurant and bakery featuring a breakfast bar and soup, salad and fruit bar. Established: 1936 - Franchising Since: 1952 - No. of Units: Company Owned: 82 - Franchised: 423 - Franchise Fee: $40,000 - Total Inv: $500,000 - Financing: No, however will assit in locating lenders.

BIG CITY BURRITO *
Big City Holdings, Inc.

51 Cherry Hills Farm Drive, Englewood, CO, 80113. Contact: George Lee - Tel: (303) 781-4022, Fax: (303) 789-1823, E-Mail: leeco@ecentral.com. Fast, fresh Mexican restaurant. Established: 1984 - Franchising Since: 2003 - No. of Units: Company Owned: 1 - Franchised: 4 - Franchise Fee: $25,000 - Royalty: 6% - Total Inv: $150,000-$200,000.

BIG ORANGE OF FLORIDA

P.O. Box 448, Stapleton, AL, 36578. - Tel: (334) 960-1118, Fax: (334) 960-1118. Kiosk constructed like a orange selling fresh squeezed oranges, pre - prepared sandwiches and fresh fruit from Florida shipped direct to customer. Free standing unit. Established: 1972 - Franchising Since: 1972 - No. of Units: Company Owned: 5 - Franchised: 4 - Franchise Fee: $1,000 - Royalty: $200.00 month for 15 years then ends - Total Inv: $10,000 for unit plus $5,000 equipment - Open any where U.S.A. and overseas.

BIG TOWN HERO
Hero Systems Inc.
912 Southwest Third Ave, Portland, OR, 97204. Contact: Rick Olson, Director of Franchise Development - Tel: (503) 228-4376, Fax: (503) 228-8778, E-Mail: rick@bth.com, Web Site: www.bigtownhero.com. Sub sandwiches, soups and salads in a cafe atmosphere. Strong emphasis on bread made from scratch every day allowing multiple flavors. Marketing push on corprate catering. Established: 1982 - Franchising Since: 1990 - No. of Units: Franchised: 42 - Franchise Fee: $14,500 - Royalty: 6% of gross sales weekly - Total Inv: $55,000-$120,000 - Financing: Third party.

BILL'S SANDWICH SHOPS
2425 Wilmington Rd., New Castle, PA, 16105. - Tel: (412) 654-7573. Fast food restaurants with 55-85 seats specializing in hot dogs with special hot chili sauce, subs, steak sandwiches, gyros, and french fries. Established: 1973 - No. of Units: Company Owned: 3 - Franchise Fee: $10,000 - Royalty: 3% of gross sales, 3% adv. - Total Inv: $60,000 equip., $70,000 improv. (May vary) - Financing: No.

BJ'S KOUNTRY KITCHEN
4539 N Brawley Ave Ste 105, Fresno, CA, 93722-3950. - Tel: (559) 275-1981, Fax: (559) 275-8786. Family restaurant. Established: 1981 - No. of Units: Company Owned: 1 - Franchised: 9.

BLACKJACK PIZZA
Blackjack Pizza Franchising Inc.
9088 Marshall Ct., Westminster, CO, 80031. - Tel: (303) 426-1921, Fax: (303) 428-0174, Web Site: www.blackjackpizza.com. Quick good tasting pizza. Established: 1983 - Franchising Since: 1988 - No. of Units: Company Owned: 2 - Franchised: 42 - Franchise Fee: $10,000 - Royalty: 4% - Total Inv: $140,800-$300,000.

BLIMPIE INTERNATIONAL, INC.
180 Interstate North Pkwy., Ste. 500, Atlanta, GA, 30339. Contact: Nat. Fran. Dev. Dir. - Tel: (770) 984-2707, Fax: (770) 952-3558, Web Site: www.blimpie.com. Fast food, subs and salads, non-cooking food. Established: 1964 - Franchising Since: 1971 - No. of Units: Franchised: 1700 - Franchise Fee: $18,000/$10,000 - Royalty: 6%, 4% adv. - Total Inv: $90,000-$120,000 - Financing: Thru third party sources.

BLUEBERRY HILL
401 Newport Center Dr. Ste. A103, Newport Beach, CA, 92660. Contact: Trevor Scheftz, Franchise Development - Tel: (714) 644-2705, Fax: (714) 760-9525. Upscale hamburgers, salads, fries - eat in, take-out. Training and support provided. Established: 1985 - Franchising since: 1995 - No. of Units: Company Owned: 13 - Franchised: 2 - Franchise Fee: $25,000 - Total Inv: $150,000-$395,000 - Financing: No.

BOARDWALK FRIES, INC.
8980 Route 108, Suite J, Ellicott City, MD, 21045. Contact: David DiFerdinando, President - Tel: (410) 715-0500, Fax: (410) 715-0711, E-Mail: brandedbwf@aol.com, Web Site: wwwboardwalkfries.com. Fast food specializing in fresh cut gourmet french fries, wide menu range available, primarily in food courts in major malls. Established: 1981 - Franchising Since: 1983 - No of Units: Company Owned: 4 Franchised: 43 - Franchise Fee: $3,000-$25,000 - Royalty: 5-7% - Total Inv: $130,000 - Financing: No.

BOBBY RUBINO'S BBQ EXPRESS
Bobby Rubino's Ribs on the Run, Inc.
1990 E. Sunrise Blvd., Ft. Lauderdale, FL, 33304. Contact: Kay Ferrara, Dir of Fran. Oper. - Tel: (954) 763-9871, Fax: (954) 467-1192. Delivery, take-out with dine-in counter service restaurant offering primarily BBQ ribs, chicken, salads, and sandwiches. Established: 1998 - Franchising Since: 1998 - No. of Units: Franchised: 2- Franchise Fee: $25,000 - Royalty: 4% - Total Inv: $200,000-$275,000 - Financing: None.

BOBBY RUBINO'S PLACE FOR RIBS
Bobby Rubino's USA, Inc.
1990 E. Sunrise Blvd., Ft. Lauderdale, FL, 33304. Contact: Kay Ferrara, Dir. Of Oper. - Tel: (954) 763-9871, Fax: (954) 467-1192. Casual, full service restaurant offering barbecued ribs and chicken, steaks, seafood, salads and more in an inviting, comfortable atmosphere. Full service.

Established: 1978 - Franchising Since: 1982 - No. of Units: Franchised: 6 - Franchise Fee: $50,000 - Royalty: 4% - Total Inv: $430,000-$650,000 - Financing: None.

BOJANGLES'FAMOUS CHICKEN N' BISCUITS
Bojangles' Restaurants, Inc.
9432 Southern Pine Blvd, Charlotte, NC, 28273. - Tel: (704) 527-2675, (800) 366-9921, Fax: (704) 523-6803, Web Site: www.bojangles.com. Our mission is to secure the best chicken & bisciuts, one customer at a time. Our menu consists of freshly prepared items. We operate for breakfast, lunch and dinner in traditional full-size units and co-branded locations. Established: 1977 - Franchising Since: 1979 - No. of Units: Company Owned: 149 - Franchised: 135 - Franchise Fee: $20,000, full size unit; $12,000 Co-branded - Royalty: 4%, 1% marketing production = 5% - Financing: No.

BOSTON BEANERY RESTAURANT & TAVERN
Boston Beanery Restaurants, Inc.
2931 University Ave., Ste. B, Morgantown, WV, 26505-4658. Contact: Steven Jones, V.P. Admin. - Tel: (304) 598-8828, Fax: (304) 598-7201. American casual theme restaurants specializing in sandwiches and dinners. Value oriented, large portions, unique menu, plus full bar with 1890's Boston theme. Flexible sites, low investments, full training and design services are featured. Established: 1983 - Franchising Since: 1988 - No. of Units: Company Owned: 2 - Franchised: 4 - Franchise Fee: $20,000 - Royalty: 4% gross sales - Total Inv: Equip + fix ($250,000-$375,000), inven.($8,500-$17,500), work cap. & pre-paid exps.($20,000-$35,000) - Financing: None.

BOX LUNCH, INC.
Sandwich Specialists, Inc.
50 Briar Lane, Wellfleet, MA, 02667. Contact: Owen MacNutt, Pres. - Tel: (508) 349-3509. We franchise Rollwich sandwich shops to the broad lunch market. Rollwiches are rolled pita sandwiches of a very high quality. Established: 1977 - Franchising Since: 1986 - No. of Units: Company Owned: 1 - Franchised: 14 - Franchise Fee: $15,000 - Royalty: 4.5%, 3% adv. - Total Inv: $75,000-$206,000 - Financing: No.

BOZ INC.
901 California, Dolton, IL, 60419. Contact: Robert Hart - Tel: (708) 717-3870, Fax: (708) 841-4770. Limited menu-hot dogs, polish & beef. Established: 1969 - Franchising Since: 1973 - No. of Units: Company Owned: 2 - Franchised: 14 - Royalty: 3 of gross sales - Financing: No.

BREADEAUX PIZZA
Breadeaux Pisa, Inc.
1010 West Saint Maartens, P.O. 6158, St. Joseph, MO, 64506. Contact: Matthew Gilliland - Tel: (816) 364-1088, (800) 835-6534, Fax: (816) 364-3739, E-mail: matt@breadeauxpizza.com, Web Site: www.bread eauxpizza.com. Pizza restaurants. (delivery)-(dine-in), Assistance in location, floor plan, accounting and marketing. Training at corp H.Q. and in the field. Award winning pizza plus subs, pasta, and salads. Established: 1985 - Franchising Since: 1985 - No. of Units: Company Owned: 3 - Franchised: 92 - Franchise Fee: $15,000 - Royalty: 5% - ad fund 3% - Total Inv: $58,000-$313,000 - Financing: Third party.

BROADWAY
Broadway Pizza
1818 Wooddale Dr. Ste. 202, Woodbury, MN, 55125. Contact: President - Tel: (651) 731-0800, Fax: (651) 731-9609. Family restaurant specializing in pizza. Established: 1953 - Franchising Since: 1982 - No. of Units: Company Owned: 2 - Franchised: 14 - Franchise Fee: $15,000-$25,000 - Royalty: 4% - Total Inv: $200,000-$450,000 - Financing: No.

BROASTER COMPANY, THE
2855 Cranston Rd, Beloit, WI, 53511. Contact: Richard Schrank - Tel: (608) 365-0193, (800) 365-8278, Fax: (608) 363-7957. Licensed genuine broaster chicken concept. Established: 1954 - No. of Units: Company Owned: 1 - Franchised: 200.

BROWN BAGGERS
925 L St, Lincoln, NE, 68508-2229. - Tel: (402) 434-5620, (800) 865-2378, Fax: (402) 434-5624. Brown Baggers offers a healthy alternative to "fast food" establishments in addition to the clean and relaxed atmosphere inside our restaurants. We also offer catering services and deliver to business customers. Established: 1988 - Franchising Since:

1993 - No. of Units: Company Owned: 2 - Franchised: 1 - Franchise Fee: $20,000 - Royalty: 6%, 1% adv. - Total Inv: $74,775-$142,700 - Financing: Indirect. NOT OFFERING FRANCHISES AT THIS TIME..

BRU-GO'S TAKE-N-BAKE PIZZA
26590 Hwy 88, Pioneer, CA, 95666-9584. Contact: Rick Goss - Tel: (800) 560-3434, Fax: (209) 295-2229, Web Site: www.takenbakepizza .com. No dine-in or delivery, no adverising costs, no grill not even a oven. Established: 1991 - Franchising Since: 2002 - No. of Units: Company Owned: 2 - Franchise Fee: $19,500 - Royalty: 5% sliding scale - Total Inv: $70,450-$128,750.

BUCK'S PIZZA
P.O. Box 405, DuBois, PA, 15801. Contact: Dir. of Fran. Sales - Tel: (814) 371-3076, Fax: (814) 371-4214. Retail carry-out / delivery pizza shop. Menu items include pizza, baked hoagies, strombolis. $95,000 total startup. Established: 1994 - Franchising Since: 1994 - No. of Units: Franchised: 38 - Franchise Fee: $10,000 - Royalty: 3% of gross sales - Total Inv: $95,000: $10,000 fran. fee, $6,000 unit dev., $60,000 equip., $19,000 work. cap, remodeling, inventory, deposits - Financing: Assist franchisee with business plan.

BUDDY'S BAR-B-Q, INC.
5806 Kingston Pike, Knoxville, TN, 37919. Contact: V.P. Fran. - Tel: (865) 558-9253, Fax: (865) 588-7211. Upscale fast food barbeque. Dine or drive thru. All meats are smoked on site at each location. Established: 1972 - Franchising Since: 1992 - No. of Units: Company Owned: 9 - Franchised: 6 - Franchise Fee: $30,000 - Royalty: 4% + .25% adv. - Total Inv: $486,500-$992,500 - Financing: No. NOT FRANCHISING AT THIS TIME.

BUFFALO WILD WINGS GRILL & BAR
Buffalo Wild Wings International, Inc
1600 Utica Ave South, Suite 700, Minneapolis, MN, 55416. Contact: Bill McClintock, V.P Franchise Dev - Tel: (513) 723-1886, Fax: (513) 723-0465, E-Mail: franchiseinfo@buffalowildwings.com, Web Site: www.buffalowildwings.com. Sports themed, family friendly restaurant. Wings, burgers, full alcohol and trivia. Established: 1982 - Franchising Since: 1991 - No. of Units: Company Owned: 62 - Franchised: 125 - Franchise Fee: $37,500 - Royalty: 5% - Total Inv: $800,000.

BUFFALO WINGS & RINGS
Wings & Rings, Inc.
900 Adams Xing #B, Cincinnati, OH, 45202-1698. - Tel: (716) 853-1791, Fax: (716) 853-2011. Family-style restaurants with table service, beer and wine or liquor service, casual, fun atmosphere, reasonably priced. Established: 1988 - Franchising Since: 1989 - No. of Units: Company Owned: 3 - Franchised: 24 - Franchise Fee: $25,000 - Royalty: 4% royalty, paid monthly of gross sales minus sales tax - Total Inv: $206,500-$384,500, varies by geographic location - Financing: No.

BUFFALO'S CAFE
Buffalo's Franchise Concepts Inc.
707 Whitlock Ave., SW, Bldg. H, Ste. 13, Marietta, GA, 30064-3033. Contact: Kevin Culkin, Dir. of Fran. - Tel: (770) 420-1800, (800) 45 WINGS (94647), Fax: (770) 420-1811.Casual, old west style neighbourhood restaurant. A limited menu specializing in Buffalo style chicken wings and all fresh food concept. Established: 1985 - Franchising Since: 1990 - No. of Units: Company Owned: 6 - Franchised: 36 - Franchise Fee: $35,000 - Royalty: 5% of gross sales - Total Inv: $450,000 - Financing: SBA approved franchisor.

BULLETS
Bullets Corp. of America
9201 Forest Hill Ave #109, Richmond, VA, 23235. - Tel: (804) 330-0837, Fax: (804) 330-5405. Restaurant chain that serves flame broiled hamburgers and chicken, Oscar Meyer hot dogs, barbecue, french fries, shakes, cinnamon bun and Eskimo Pie ice cream from a variety of outlets, drive thrus, sit downs, c-stores and kiosks. Established: 1990 - Franchising Since: 1993 - No. of Units: Company Owned: 8 - Franchised: 46 - Franchise Fee: $18,000-$20,000 - Royalty: 6%, 1% nat'l adv. - Total Inv: $100,000-$200,000 - Financing: No.

BULLWINKLE'S RESTAURANT AND THE FAMILY FUN CENTERS
Bullwinkles International
18300 Von Karman, #900, Irvine, CA, 92612. - Tel: (949) 261-0404, Fax: (949) 261-1414, Web Site: www.bullwinkiles.com. The only family entertainment concept to combine great food with indoor and outdoor fun center attractions. Established: 1959 - Franchising Since: 1992 - No. of Units: Company Owned: 7 - Franchised: 2 - Franchise Fee: $25,000-$75,000 - Royalty: 4% - Total Inv: $400,000-$5,300,000 - Financing: No.

BUMPERS DRIVE-IN
1554 West Peace St, Canton, MS, 39046. Contact: VP Operations - Tel: (601) 859-2005. Fast food drive-in providing quality hamburgers, chicken, hot dogs, ice cream, and even potatoe pearls. Established: 1985 - Franchising Since: 19685 - No. of Units: Company Owned: 25 - Franchised: 5 - Franchise Fee: $15,000 - Royalty: 4% - Total Inv: $435,000-$735,000.

BURGER KING CORPORATION
5505 Blue Lagoon Drive, Miami, FL, 33126. Contact: Mike Alonso, Mgr. US Fran. Dev. - Tel: (305)378-3000. Highly recognized, worldwide brand with over 8,292 points of distribution. New, lower cost facility design and flexible ownership guidelines continue to make Burger King an attractive franchise investment. Established: 1954 - Franchising Since: 1961 - No. of Units: Company Owned: 794 - Franchised: 7,826 - Franchise Fee: $50,000 - Royalty: 4.5% mthly. gross sales - Total Inv: $235,500-$2,376,000 (excl. real estate) - Financing: Yes.

BURRITO VILLE *
1111 Marcus Ave., #M27, Lake Success, NY, 11042. Contact: Franchise Department - Tel: (516) 918-3300, Fax: (516) 918-3301, Web Site: www.trufoods.com. Serving tacos, quesdillas, nacjos to wraps. Established: 1992 - Franchising Since: 2004 - No. of Units: Company Owned: 12 - Franchise Fee: $30,000 - Royalty: 5% - Total Inv: $151,500-$644,400.

CABOTO'S
Caboto's Associated Food Services Inc
389 North Industrial, Suite #8, St. George, UT, 84770. Contact: Herbert Davis, Chief Executive Officer - Tel: (435) 757-3407, E-Mail: info@cabotos.com, Web Site: www.cabotos.com. Mobile unit selling delicious food & drink. Established: 1998 - Franchising Since: 2001 - No. of Units: Company Owned: 6 - Franchise Fee: $15,000 - Royalty: 0 - Total Inv: $20,000-$85,000.

CAFÉ LA FRANCE
72 Pine St, Providence, RI, 02903-2836. - Tel: (401) 453-2233, (800) 791-CAFE, Fax: (401) 453-0319. European cafe featuring morning and lunch menu. Easy hours (Monday-Friday), catering to working professionals. Established: 1989 - Franchising Since: 1993 - No. of Units: Company Owned: 10 - Franchised: 7 - Franchise Fee: $15,000 - Royalty: 5% - Total Inv: $95,000-$125,000 - Financing: No.

CAFÉ ON MAIN
1621 Washington St., Blair, NE, 68008. - Tel: (800) 301-9504. Restaurant specializing in sophisticated homemade, garden-style fare in a warm, bistro-style atmosphere. Established: 1986 - Franchising Since: 1993 - No. of Units: Franchised: 1 - Franchise Fee: $19,500 - Royalty: 5% - Total Inv: $67,750 - Financing: No.

CAFÉ SANTA FE™ SOUTHWEST RESTAURANTS
CSF Franchise Group, LLC
4410 Knox Rd, College Park, MD, 207401. - Tel: (301) 779-1345, Fax: (301) 779-4522. Serving America's best Southwest style food and spirits in a relaxing, fun atmosphere. Established: 1982 - Franchising Since: 1997 - No. of Units: Company Owned: 1 - Franchised: 5 - Franchise Fee: $35,000 - Royalty: 4.5%, 1% marketing - Total Inv: $280,000-$590,000 - Financing: No.

CAFFE APPASSIONATO
Caffe Appassionato Franchise Company Inc.
4001 21 St. Ave., West, Seattle, WA, 98199. Contact: Franchise Marketing Director - Tel: (206) 281-8040, Fax: (206) 282-5218. Upscale retail coffee houses featuring specialty coffee beverages, light pasta and food offerings, and general related retail merchandise. Established: 1989 -

Franchising Since: 1991 - No. of Units: Company Owned: 11 - Franchised: 6 - Franchise Fee: $25,000 - Royalty: 4.5% on gross sales, 1% advertising - Total Inv: $150,000-$240,000 total turnkey - Financing: Not directly from company but third party institutions including SBA due provide financing.

CAFFE CLASSICO
2500 Annalisa Dr, Concord, CA, 94520-1219. Contact: Tom Heffernan, Dir. of Dev. - Tel: (415) 621-7998. European style cafe, featuring high quality coffees, sandwiches, salads, espresso and award winning gelato (Italian Ice Cream). Established: 1976 - Franchising Since: 1982 - No. of Units: Company Owned: 1- Franchised: 30 - Franchise Fee: $25,000 - Royalty: 5% - Total Inv: $131,000-$220,000 includes franc. fee - Financing: Available.

CAFFEE TAZZA
Coffee Group, The
P.O. Box 6120, NewPort Beach, CA, 92658-6120. - Tel: (714) 434-6191, (888) 223-3824, Fax: (714) 434-0997. Specialty coffee outlet developer and franchisor - exclusive mall locations. Established: 1995 - Franchising Since: 1996 - No. of Units: Company Owned: 1 - Franchised: 1 - Franchise Fee: $25,000 - Royalty: 6% plus 1% adv. - Total Inv: $125,000-$250,000 - Financing: Thru SBA.

CAJUN CAFE
The Original Ragin Cajun Co.
100 Farmington Drive, Lafayette, LA, 70503. Contact: Franchise Director - Tel: (901) 368-3361. Gourmet cajun entrees with entertainment and full service bar and catering options. Established: 1993 - Franchising Since: 1998 - No. of Units: Company Owned: 1 - Franchised: 1 - Franchise Fee: $25,000 - Royalty: 4%, 1% adv - Total Inv: $172,800-$320,000 - Financing: Leasing and financing available.

CAMILLE'S SIDEWALK CAFE
Camille's Franchise System, Inc
8801 S. Yale, Suite 400, Tulsa, OK, 74137. Contact: Stacey Gallaher - Tel: (703) 549-5332, (800) 230-7004, Fax: (703) 549-0740, E-Mail: staceyg@fransmart.com, Web Site: www.camillescafe.com. Camille's Sidewalk Cafe is an upscale coastal-influenced cafe serving breakfast, lunch and diner with unlimited catering potential. Camille's is a tantalizing alternative to the tiresome choices of most quick-serve food. Camille's Sidewalk Cafe's popularity is based on its ability to provide a fresh quality sandwich, panini or wrap with distinctive flavors at a reasonable priced in a relaxed, comfortable atmosphere. Established: 1996 - Franchising Since: 1999 - No. of Units: Company Owned: 1 - Franchised: 50 open, 500+ sold - Franchise Fee: $25,000 - Royalty: 5% - Total Inv: $210,000-$470,000 - Financing: Third party.

CAP'N TACO
California Restaurant Systems Inc.
16099 Brookpark Rd., Brook Park, OH, 44142. Contact: Dir. Fran. Sales - Tel: (216) 676-9830. Mexican Quick services with beer and margaritas and a tongue-in-cheek fighter pilot theme/ an in house customer club called "The Cap'N Taco Flying Squadron", the "Top Gun" in Mexfood. Established: 1976 - Franchising Since: 1986 - No. of Units: Company Owned: 2 - Franchised: 1 - Franchise Fee: $15,000 - Royalty: 5%, 2% combined adv., 1% indiv. adv. - Total Inv: $80,000-$100,000, $30,000 equipment - Financing: Yes.

CAPT'N NEMO'S
Capt'n Nemo's Franchise Systems, Inc.
7367 N. Clark St., Chicago, IL, 60626. Contact: Steve Ragusi, Exec. V.P. - Tel: (773) 973-0570, Fax: (773) 973-9950. Restaurant operation which specializes in homemade soups and quality submarine sandwiches served quickly. A unique system which is simple to operate and easy to control. Established: 1971 - Franchising Since: 1988 - No. of Units: Company Owned: 2 - Franchised: 1 - Franchise Fee: $14,000 - Royalty: 5% + 2% to co-op nat'l adv. - Total Inv: $99,960 - Financing: Assistance provided.

CAPTAIN D'S SEAFOOD
Captain D's, Inc
1717 Elm Hill Pike, Ste. A-1, Nashville, TN, 37210. - Tel: (615) 391-5461, Fax: (615) 231-2309, E-Mail: franchise_info@captainds.com, Web Site: www.captainds.com. Quick casual seafood and chicken. Dine-in, drive-thru or take out. Established: 1969 - Franchising Since:

1969 - No. of Units: Company Owned: 334 - Franchised: 230 - Franchise Fee: $20,000 - Royalty: 3.5% - Total Inv: $291,750-$587,000 non-traditional; $571,750-$656,500 end cap; $863,000-$1,036,000 38-68 seat unit; $1,148,000-$1,585,000 trdaitional 82-118 seat unit - Financing: No.

CAPTAIN TONY'S PIZZA & PASTA EMPORIUM
Captain Tony's Pizza, Inc
2607 South Woodland Blvd., PMB 300, Deland, FL, 32702. Contact: Michael J. Martella, Pres. - Tel: (386) 736-9855, Fax: (386) 736-7237. Take-out, delivery and dine in pizza, pasta, wings and deli made subs. Established: 1972 - Franchising Since: 1987 - No. of Units: Franchised: 9 - Franchise Fee: $10,000-$20,000 - Royalty: 4.5% - Total Inv: $80,000-$150,000 for take out - Financing: Third party.

CARBONE & SONS
680 E. Seventh St., St. Paul, MN, 55106. Contact: Dir. Fran. Dev. - Tel: (651) 771-5553, Fax: (651) 771-3320. Family pizza restaurants. Established: 1953 - Franchising Since: 1963 - No. of Units: Company Owned: 3 - Franchised: 16 - Franchise Fee: $10,000 - Royalty: 4% + 1% adv. - Total Inv: $175,000-$450,000 - Financing: No.

CARL'S JR. RESTAURANTS
Carl Karcher Enterprises, Inc.
3916 State Street Garden Suite, Santa Barbara, CA, 93105. Contact: Craig Hopkins, Director Franchise Development & Sales - Tel: (877) 799-7827, Fax: (714) 780-6320. Quick service restaurants featuring charbroiled hamburgers and chicken sandwiches. Established: 1941 - Franchising Since: 1984 - No. of Units: Company Owned: 390 - Franchised: 236 - Franchise Fee: $35,000 - Royalty: 4% - Total Inv: $1,011,500-$1,787,500: fran. fee, equip., signs, work. cap., training, start-up supplies - Financing: No.

CASA MIA RESTAURANTS
716 Plum St. SE, Olympia, WA, 98501. Contact: Robert Knudson, President - Tel: (360) 352-0440, Fax: (360)753-8526. Family style Italian restaurant and pizzeria. Established: 1952 - Franchising Since: 1989 - No. of Units: Company Owned: 3 - Franchised: 4 - Franchise Fee: $18,500 - Royalty: 5% - Total Inv: $43,000-$150,000 - Financing: No.

CASA OLE RESTAURANT & CANTINAS
1135 Edgebrook Dr., Houston, TX, 77034-1803. Contact: Director of Franchising - Tel: (713) 943-7574, Fax: (713) 943-9554. Dinnerhouse - Mexican. Established: 1973 - No. of Units: Company Owned: 19 - Franchised: 17.

CENTRAL PARK
Central Park USA, Inc.
300 High St., Chattanooga, TN, 37403. Contact: Franchise Department - Tel: (423) 855-0991. Double drive through hamburgers. Established: 1982 - Franchising Since: 1986 - No. of Units: Company Owned: 22 - Franchised: 56 - Franchise Fee: $20,000 - Royalty: 4% - Total Inv: $300,000-$350,000 - Financing: No.

CHARLEY'S GRILLED SUBS
Gosh Enterprises, Inc.
2500 Farmers Dr., Ste. 140, Columbus, OH, 43235-5706. Contact: V.P. of Development - Tel: (614) 923-4700, (800) 437-8325, Fax: (614) 923-4701, Web Site: www.cgsubs.com. Chraley's Steakery is a quick service restaurant specializing if "Fresh Grilled" Philadelphia style steak & chicken subs, fresh gourmet fries, and fresh lemonade & salads. Established: 1986 - Franchising Since: 1991 - No. of Units: Company Owned: 8 - Franchised: 189 - Franchise Fee: $19,500 - Royalty: 5% - Total Inv: $124,500-$294,500 - Financing: Third Party.

CHARLIE WILLIAMS' PINCREST
Charlie's Franchising, Inc.
1 Pinecrest Lodge Rd., Athens, GA, 30605. - Tel: (706) 353-2606, (800) 551-4267, Fax: (706) 543-1009. Fast service catfish, barbecue, and seafood reataurant. Established: 1929 - Franchising Since: 1997 - No. of Units: Franchised: 5 - Franchise Fee: $25,000 - Royalty: 5% monthly - Total Inv: $265,775-$777, 202 - Financing: No.

CHARLIE'S CHICKEN
Charlie's Chicken of America, Inc.
3325 West Olkmulgee, Muskogee, OK, 74403. Contact: Jim Harris, Fran. Dir. - Tel: (918) 687-8741, (888) 844-CHIC, Fax: (918) 687-0375. Restaurant business offering unique chicken preparation and related items with pick up and drive through. Training and support provided. Established: 1978 (incorporated 1993) - No. of Units: Company Owned: 2 - Franchised: 30 - Franchise Fee: $25,000 - Royalty: 3%, adv. 1% - Total Inv: $311,000-$804,000 - Financing: No.

CHARO CHICKEN
Charo Chicken Systems, Inc
1077 Pacific Coast Hwy., Suite 182, Seal Beach, CA, 90740. Contact: VP Franchising - Tel: (714) 960-2348, Fax: (714) 374-1889, Web Site: www.charochicken.com. Char-broiled chicken with a Mexican flavor, dine-in, takeout and delivery. Established: 1984 - Franchising Since: 1999 - No. of Units: Company Owned: 4 - Franchised: 11 - Franchise Fee: $25,000 - Royalty: 5% royalty, 2% + 2% advertising fee - Total Inv: $349,000-$389,000 - Financing: SBA approved.

CHECKERS DRIVE-IN RESTAURANTS, INC.
Checkers Drive-In Restaurants, Inc
4300 West Cypress St., #600, Tampa, FL, 33607. Contact: V.P. Franchise Sales & Dev. - Tel: (727) 519-2000, (800) 275-3628, Fax: (727) 519-2218, E-Mail: Fransales@checkers.com, Web Site: www.checkers.com. Double drive-thru restaurant offering lightening fast service, great burgers, fries and colas with a 1950's ratro look. Established: 1986 - Franchising Since: 1988 - No. of Units: Company Owned: 224 - Franchised: 650 - Franchise Fee: $20,000 - Royalty: 4% - Financing: None.

CHEDDAR'S CASUAL CAFE *
616 Six Flags Drive, Arlington, TX, 76011. Contact: Douglas Rogers, President - Tel: (817) 640-4344, Fax: (817) 633-4452, E-Mail: cheddarsins@aol.com, Web Site: www.cheddarscasualcafe.com. Full service traditional menu restaurant with great prices and value. Established: 1978 - Franchising Since: 1984 - No. of Units: Company Owned: 18 - Franchised: 24 - Franchise Fee: $30,000 - Royalty: 3% - Total Inv: $1.5-1.9 MM - Financing: No.

CHEEBURGER CHEEBURGER
Cheeburger Cheeburger Restaurants Inc.
15951 McGregor, Ft. Myers, FL, 33908. - Tel: (941) 437-1611, (800) 487-6211, Fax: (941) 437-1512. Full service restaurant specializing in high quality burgers, shakes, fries and related products. Established: 1986 - Franchising Since: 1990 - No. of Units: Company Owned: 1 - Franchised: 5 - Franchise Fee: $17,500 - Royalty: 4.5% gross sales - Total Inv: $175,000-$225,000 - Financing: No.

CHEESE VILLA
ISCO, Ltd.
414 Walnut #508, Cincinnati, OH, 45202-3903. Contact: Carl Perin, Pres. - Tel: (513) 579-0023. Limited menu non-cooking restaurants located in downtown high density, high traffic office buildings and commercial locations. Established: 1975 - Franchising Since: 1975 - No. of Units: Company Owned: 3 - Franchised: 8 - Franchise Fee: $12,500 - Royalty: 5% of gross sales - Total Inv: $150,000-$250,000 depending upon locations - Financing: No. NOT FRANCHISING AT THIS TIME.

CHESTER'S INT'L LLC *
2750 Gunter Park Dr, West, Montgomery, AL, 36109. - Tel: (800) 288-1555, (334) 272-3528, Web Site: www.chesterinternational.com. Quick service chiken restaurant. Established: 1952 - Franchising Since: 2004 - No. of Units: Company Owned: 1 - Franchise Fee: $5,000-$15,000 - Total Inv: $60,000-$400,000.

CHICAGO'S PIZZA
Chicago's Pizza Franchises
1111 N. Broadway, Greenfield, IN, 46140. - Tel: (317) 467-1877. Pizza, sandwiches, inside dining/carry out/drive-thru. Established: 1979 - Franchising Since: 1980 - No. of Units: Franchised: 12 - Franchise Fee: $10,000 - Royalty: 4%, 2% adv. - Total Inv: $75,000-$350,000 - Financing: None.

CHICKEN CHARLIES
P.O. Box 4451, Northbrook, IL, 60062. - Tel: (847) 559-9090, Fax: (847) 559-9095. Upscale fast food grilled chicken, grilled chicken sandwiches, salads. Established: 1989 - Franchising Since: 1994 - No. of Units: Company Owned: 2 - Franchised: 1 - Franchise Fee: $17,500 - Royalty: 5% of gross sales - Total Inv: $200,000-$225,000 build-out and capital.

CHICKEN CONNECTION FRANCHISE CORP
International Restaurant Management Group
4104 Aurora St, Coral Gables, FL, 33146-1416. Contact: Franchise Department - Tel: (888) 662-1668. Variety of chicken menu items. Established: 1997 - Franchising Since: 1998 - No. of Units: Company Owned: 7 - Franchised: 1 - Franchise Fee: $30,000 - Financing: No.

CHICO'S
Chico's International, Inc.
41715 Enterprise Circle North #201, Temecula, CA, 92590. Contact: Daniel J. Rush, Pres. - Tel: (909) 296-0170, (800) 772-4426. "Fresh Mex At Its Best". Fast but fine dining in a unique transferring atmosphere. Fastest growing chain development in Southern California at 120 restaurants in the next 15 years. Established: 1988 - Franchising Since: 1993 - No. of Units: Franchised: 31 - Franchise Fee: $25,000-$250,000 - Royalty: 5% - Total Inv: $200,000-$350,000 - Financing: Yes.

CHIX THE CHICKEN STATION
Orion Food Systems
2930 W. Maple, Sioux Falls, SD, 57101. Contact: Director of Development - Tel: (800) 648-6227, (605) 336-6961, Fax: (605) 336-0141, Web Site: www.orionfoodsys.com. Quick service format, developing in convenience stores and foodcourts. Established: 1984 - Franchising Since: 1985 - No. of Units: Company Owned: 2 - Franchised: 175 - Franchise Fee: $4,950 - Total Inv: $25,000 + - Financing: Third Party.

CHOICE PICKS FOOD COURTS
Choice Hotels Inaternational
10750 Columbia Pike, Silver Spring, MD, 20901-4494. - Tel: (301) 592-5000, (800) 424-6423, Web Site: www.choicehotels.com. Choice picks food court combines national brand names like Pizzeria Uno, Nathan's Famous, Healthy Choice and others, with an advanced modular food service system that greatly reduces staffing and operational requirements. Established: 1995 - Franchising Since: 1995 - No. of Units: Franchised: 30 - Franchise Fee: $20,000 - Royalty: 6% - Total Inv: $150,000-$250,000 - Financing: Third party financing and leasing.

CHOWDERHEAD'S SEAFOOD RESTAURANT
How Many Chowderhead's...Inc.
430 E. Bridge St, Westbrook, ME, 04092. Contact: Franchise Department - Tel: (207) 854-5052, (888) 883-8330, Fax: (207) 854-5052. An eat in and take out, quick serve seafood restaurant specializing in custom prepared seafood, available fried, broiled and grilled. Award winning seafood chowder, homemade onion rings and more. Established: 1990 - Franchising Since: 1997 - No. of Units: Company Owned: 1 - Franchised: 4 - Franchise Fee: $11,500 - Royalty: 6% - Total Inv: $55,000-$95,000 including fran. fee - Financing: No.

CHUBBY'S DINER
Chubby's Food Service, Inc.
23799 Monterey Salinas Hwy, Ste. 36, Salinas, CA, 93908-9331. Contact: V.P. Fran. Sales - Tel: (800) 892-2749, Fax: (916) 863-6778. A 1950's style restaurant. Established: 1990 - Franchising Since: 1991 - No. of Units: Franchised: 56 - Franchise Fee: $12,000 + $1,000 adv. fee - Royalty: 6% of net sales wkly. - Total Inv: Varies - Financing: No.

CHURCHS CHICKEN
980 Hammond Dr Suite #1100, NE, Atlanta, GA, 30328. Contact: Franchise Mktng - Tel: (800) 848-8248, (770) 350-3881, Fax: (770) 512-3922. World's second-largest quick service chicken company. Features southern fried chicken, mash potatoes, corn, biscuits, and other side items. Established: 1952 - Franchising Since: 1964 - No. of Units: Company Owned: 593 - Franchised: 604 - Franchise Fee: $10,000 dev. fee; $15,000 fran. fee - Royalty: .5% gross revenue - Total Inv: Traditional $214,800-$290,600; Alternative $147,300-$270,600 - Financing: N/A.

CICI'S PIZZA
CiCi Enterprises, Inc.
1080 W Bethel Rd, Coppell, TX, 75019. Contact: Angie Zimmermann - Tel: (972) 745-4200, Fax: (972) 745-4204, E-Mail: finformation @cicispizza.com, Web Site: www.cicispizza.com. Founded in 1985, CiCi's Pizza has been fueled by its commitment to serving high quality food at phenomenally low prices. CiCi's offers 16 kinds of fresh, hot, delicious pizza, pasta, salad and desserts in a $3.99 all-you-can-eat buffet format (price may vary by location). There are currently over 450 CiCi's Pizza buffet restaurants in 21 states, and growing rapidly. For maore information, visit our web site at www.cicispizza.com. Established: 1985 - Franchising Since: 1988 - No. of Units: Company Owned: 24 - Franchised: 430 - Franchise Fee: $25,000-$30,000 - Royalty: .04% - Total Inv: $400,900-$606,900 - Financing: No.

CINEMA GRILL
Cinema & Grill Systems
P.O. Box 28467, Atlanta, GA, 30328. Contact: John Duffy, VP - Tel: (404) 250-9536, Fax: (404) 256-1569, E-Mail: cinegrill@aol.com, Web Site: www.cinemagrill.com. Cinema Grill (great movies, spirit and food). The ultimate experience in movie theatre plus restaurant experience. Established: 1995 - Franchising Since: 1995 - No. of Units: Company Owned: 1 - Franchised: 19 - Franchise Fee: $30,000 - Royalty: 3% - Total Inv: $500,000-$600,000 - Financing: Assistance.

CINNAMON STREET BAKERY & COFFEE COMPANY
Orion Food Systems
2930 W Maple, Sioux Falls, SD, 57101. Contact: Director of Development - Tel: (800) 648-6227, (605) 336-6961, Fax: (605) 336-0141, Web Site: www.orionfoodsys.com. Quick service format, developing in convenience stores and foodcourts. Established: 1984 - Franchising Since: 1985 - No. of Units: Company Owned: 3 - Franchised: 237 - Franchise Fee: $4,950 - Total Inv: $25,000 + - Financing: Third Party.

CITY WOK *
City Wok, LLC
2220 St. George Lane, Chico, CA, 95926. Contact: Stacey Gallagher - Tel: (703) 549-5332, (800) 563-8592, Fax: (703) 549-0740, E-Mail: staceyg@fransmart.com, Web Site: www.citywok.com. City Wok offers fresh, health consciously prepared, authentic gourmet Chinese Cuisine at affordable prices. Our progessional chef's fire-up their woks in contemporary exhibition kitchens to prepare food that is served with care, the way you want it. Established: 1990 - Franchising Since: 2004 - No. of Units: Company Owned: 4 - Franchise Fee: $30,000 - Royalty: 5% - Total Inv: $243,350-$568,500 - Financing: No.

CJ'S STEAKLOFT
CJ'S Steakloft Franchise Corp.
369 W Main Street, Northboro, MA, 01532. Contact: Carolyn Johnson, President - Tel: (888) 785-5638. Full service American steakhouse and bar. Full training provided. Established: 1986 - Franchising Since: 1995 - No. of Units: Company Owned: 1 - Franchise Fee: $30,000 - Total Inv: $178,000-$218,000 (includes franchise fee).

CLARKE'S CHARCOAL BROILER
Clarke's Franchising, Inc.
680-A Rancho Shopping Ctr., Los Altos, CA, 94024-4942. Contact: James P. Blach, Pres. - Tel: (650) 917-1709, Fax: (650) 917-8295. Specializing in 1/3 lb. Clarkesburgers done over charcoal B-B-Q style, using fresh meat, along with other great items such as B-B-Q baby back ribs (pork). Great milk shakes made with real ice cream, thick and flavorful, including our peanut butter shake, with beer and wine for those that like it. Just a great place. Established: 1944 - Franchising Since: 1993 - No. of Units: Company Owned: 1 - Franchised: 6 - Franchise Fee: $27,000 - Royalty: 6%/wk. - Total Inv: $130,000-$180,000 depending on size - Financing: SBA & other.

CLUCK-U-CHICKEN
Cluck-U-Chicken, Inc.
P.O. Box Q, College Park, MD, 20741-3015. Postal only. Retail food service, chicken, chicken wing specialty. Established: 1985 - Franchising Since: 1991 - No. of Units: Franchised: 20 - Franchise Fee: $20,000 - Royalty: 4% of weekly sales - Total Inv: $150,000-$230,000 - Financing: Through SBA.

CO-BRANDS, INC
245 S. 84th St., Suite 200, Lincoln, NE, 68521. - Tel: (402) 484-7100, (800) 301-9504, Fax: (402) 484-7811. A 5 concept express food. Established: 1997 - Franchising Since: 1997 - No. of Units: Franchised: 3 - Franchise Fee: $5,000-$7,500 - Total Inv: $20,000-$88,500 - Financing: No.

COCK OF THE WALK
Keelboat Concepts, Inc.
P.O. Box 2324, Daphne, AL, 36526-2324. Contact: Mike Rickels, Owner/Pres. - Tel: (334) 626-2322, Fax: (334) 626-2322. Specialty catfish family restaurant. Established: 1977 - Franchising Since: 1980 - No. of Units: Franchised: 11 - Franchise Fee: $25,000 - Royalty: 3-4% - Total Inv: $850,000 - Financing: No.

COCO'S/CARROWS
CFC Franchising Company
3355 Michelson Dr., Ste. 350, Irvine, CA, 92612. Contact: Jerry Greco, Development Franchise Manager - Tel: (949) 251-5700, (888) 352-5900, Fax: (949) 251-5231. Upscale family-style restaurant serving breakfast, lunch and dinner. Both concepts one positioned in the main stream of popular priced family restaurants. Established: 1979 - Franchising Since: 1996 - No. of Units: Company Owned: 300 - Franchised: 35 - Franchise Fee: $35,000 - Royalty: 4% of sales - Total Inv: $1,100,000-$1,300,000, on build to suits - Financing: No.

COLD CUT KRUISE
25820 Southfield Road, Southfield, MI, 48075. Contact: Geoffrey Stebbins - Tel: (248) 559-1415, Fax: (248) 557-7931. Drive through sandwich shop, using radio control ordering, thus reducing turn around time and the number of employees needed. Established: 1990 - Franchising Since: 1998 - No. of Units: Company Owned: 1 - Franchise Fee: $25,000 - Royalty: 5% - Total Inv: $120,000-$150,000 - Financing: Yes.

COLONEL MUZZY'S TEXAS BBQ
Muzzy's Franchising Inc.
6505 Halsey Ct, Austin, TX, 78739. Contact: John Muzzy - Tel: (512) 288-3977, (877) 468-9220, Fax: (512) 288-5012, E-Mail: jmuzzy@austin.rr.com, Web Site: www.colmuzzybbq.com. Looking for something different? "Authentic Texas BBQ" prepared by the REAL Colonel. Locations include food courts and strip malls. Brisket, pork, ribs, sausage and chicken plates and sandwiches. Training and continued support. Established: 1989 - Franchising Since: 2000 - No. of Units: Company Owned: 1 - Franchised: 6 - Franchise Fee: $20,000 - Royalty: 5% - Total Inv: $175,000-$400,000.

COLTER'S BAR-B-Q- RESTAURANTS
5910 N. Central Expy, #1355, Dallas, TX, 75206. Contact: VP Fran. - Tel: (972) 724-4488, (888) COLTERS. Authentic Texas barbecue, hickory smoked for 18 hours. Served in a self-service format with a western decor. Products include beef bisque, smoked turkey, rib, ham and great side dishes too. Established: 1985 - Franchising Since: 1995 - No. of Units: Company Owned: 5 - Franchised: 8 - Franchise Fee: 30,000 - Royalty: 4%, mktg fee .5%, adv. 3% - Total Inv: $730,000-$1,030,000 without land - Financing: No.

COLUMBIA STEAK EXPRESS
Penn Brothers Enterprises
261 Midland Dr., Lexington, KY, 40508. - Tel: (606) 231-0008, Fax: (606) 231-0012. Steak house restaurants. Established: 1948 - Franchising Since: 1982 - No. of Units: Company Owned: 5 - Franchised: 3 - Franchise Fee: $20,000 plus training, time and travel - Royalty: 4% - Total Inv: Varies - Financing: No.

CONGRESS ROTISSERIE
49 Cherry St., East Hartford, CT, 06108-3922. - Tel: (860) 549-2211. Made-to-order specialty sandwiches, healthful rotisserie chicken, a variety of homemade soups, salads, hot vegetables and freshly baked breads and pastries. Proprietary dressings including honey mustard and balsamic vinaigrette also are customer favorites. Established: 1986 - Franchising Since: 1992 - No. of Units: Company Owned: 5 - Franchised: 8 - Franchise Fee: $20,000 satellite store, $25,000 full production facility - Royalty: 6% gross receipts - Total Inv: $150,000-$225,000 excluding leasehold improv. & fran. fee - Financing: No.

COPELAND'S OF NEW ORLEANS, INC.
A1 Copeland Investments
1405 Airline DR, P.O. 277, Metairie, LA, 70001. Contact: Ashley Akers - Tel: (504) 830-1000, Fax: (504) 830-1038. Casual Cajun dining. Established: 1984 - Franchising Since: 1994 - No. of Units: Company Owned: 10 - Franchised: 3 - Franchise Fee: $100,000 - Royalty: 3.5% - Total Inv: $1,800,000 - Financing: No.

CORKY'S RIBS + BBQ
1862 Highway 45 By-Pass, 2nd Fl, Jackson, TN, 38305. Contact: Lonne Lard, President / CEO - Tel: (901) 664-3066. Full service casual dining BBQ restaurant and catering operation with drive thru. Established: 1984 - Franchising Since: 1991 - No. of Units: Company Owned: 3 - Franchised: 11 - Total Inv: $500,000-$600,000 plus real estate.

CORN DOG 7
Corn Dog 7, Inc.
Hwy 161, Corn Dog Lane, P.O. Box 907, Hughes Springs, TX, 75656. Contact; Mike Wellborn, V.P. - Tel: (903) 639-3575, Fax: (903) 639-3647. Retail sales of fast food in shopping malls. Specializing in corn dogs, and fresh lemonade. Established: 1978 - Franchising Since: 1982 - No. of Units: Company Owned: 31 - Franchised: 50 - Franchise Fee: $5,000 - Royalty: 5% of net sales - Total Inv: $50,000 lease. improve.; $30,000 equip.; $5,000 fran. fee - Financing: No.

CORN DOG FACTORY *
12 S. Main Street., Ste. 206, Layton, UT, 84041. - Tel: (801) 546-9909. Serving corn dogs, fries and chicago dogs. Established: 1974 - Franchising Since: 2001 - No. of Units: Franchised: 5 - Franchise Fee: $20,000.

COTTAGE INN PIZZA
4390 Concourse Blvd, Ann Arbor, MI, 48103. - Tel: (734) 663-2470, Fax: (734) 747-7177. Pizza delivery company. Established: 1948 - Franchising Since: 1982 - No. of Units: Company Owned: 8 - Franchised: 12 - Franchise Fee: $15,000 - Royalty: 5%, 1% adv. - Total Inv: $85,000-$130,000 - Financing: No.

COUCH'S BAR B CUE
Couch's Inc.
3820 Premier Ave., Memphis, TN, 38118. Contact: Franchise Director - Tel: (901) 368-3361. Full service restaurant specializing in barbecue pork, beef, chicken with a large capacity seating. Established: 1969 - Franchising Since: 1986 - No. of Units: Company Owned: 2 - Franchised: 2 - Franchise Fee: $20,000 - Royalty: 5%, 1% adv. - Total Inv: $280,000 - Financing: No.

COUNTRY KITCHEN RESTAURANT
Kitchen Investment Group, Inc
801 Deming Way, Madison, WI, 53717-1918. Contact: Charles M. Myers, President - Tel: (608) 274-5030, (608) 274-9999. Family restaurant - full service. Established: 1939 - Franchising Since: 1957 - No. of Units: Company Owned: 35 - Franchised: 230 - Franchise Fee: Initial fee $35,000 - Royalty: 4% continuing - 1% adv. production - Total Inv: Bldg $800.000 approx, Equipment $300.000.

COUSINS SUBS
Cousins Subs Systems, Inc.
N83 W13400 Leon Rd., Menomonee Falls, WI, 53051. - Tel: (262) 253-7700, (800) 238-9736, Fax: (262) 253-7710, E-Mail: betterfranchise@cousinssubs.com, Web Site: www.cousinssubs.com. 30 years of commitment to excellence is rolled into the Cousins Subs distinctive quick service, volume oriented. "Eastern Style" submarine sandwich concept. Exceptional freshly baked bread & quality ingredients highlight our hot & cold subs, which may be enjoyed with our delicious soups & garden fresh salads. Soft drinks, bottled water, coffee & chips accompany our menu items and "just out of the over" cookies & brownies put the finishing touch on the Cousins experience. Established: 1972 - Franchising Since: 1985 - No. of Units: Company Owned: 40 - Franchised: 130 - Franchise Fee: $20,000 - Royalty: 6%-$750,000, 5% next $250,000, 4% over $1,000,000 - Total Inv: $159,300-$268,600 - Financing: Third party, SBA/bank relationship.

COYOTE CANYON
2908 N. Plum St, Hutchinson, KS, 67502. Contact: Terry Harsted, V.P. Operations - Tel: (620) 669-9372, Fax: (620) 669-0531, Web Site: www.stockadecompaines.com. All you can eat eat steak buffet, featuring a self-service salad bar,a hot food buffet, a desert bar and a display bakery at one affordable price. Established: 1984 - Franchising Since: 1984 - No. of Units: Company Owned: 1 - Franchised: 6 - Franchise Fee: $20,000 - Royalty: 3% - Total Inv: $1.2,000-$2.2,000.

COZZOLI'S PIZZA
Cozzoli's Pizza Systems, Inc.
Bay Pt. Twr., #1040, 4770 Biscayne Blvd., Miami, FL, 33137. Contact: John Cozzoli, Vice Pres. - Tel: (305) 576-1922, Fax: (305) 576-8831. Fast food pizza. Established: 1953 - No. of Units: Company Owned: 26 - Franchised: 65.

CRACKED CRAB
751 Price Street, Pismo Beach, CA, 93449. Contact: Mike Lee - Tel: (805) 773-0740, Fax: (805) 773-1048, E-Mail: mike@crackedcrab.com, Web Site: www.crackedcrab.com. We serve the finest seafood available in a casual and fun atmosphere. Established: 1999 - Franchising Since: 2002 - No. of Units: Company Owned: 2 - Franchise Fee: $35,000 - Financing: Third party.

CREATIVE CROISSANTS
St. Clair Development Corp.
6335 Ferris SQ #GH, San Diego, CA, 92121-3249. Contact: Pres. - Tel: (619) 587-7300. Bakery and café featuring soups, salads, and sandwiches. Established: 1981 - Franchising Since: 1988 - No. of Units: Company Owned: 3 - Franchised: 37 - Franchise Fee: $17,500 - Royalty: 4.5%, 2% mktg/adv. - Total Inv: $95,000-$125,000 - Financing: No.

D'ANGELO SANDWICH SHOPS
D'Angelo's Sandwich Shops, Inc.
600 Providence Hwy, Dedham, MA, 02026. Contact: Dir. of Franchising - Tel: (888) 374-2830, Fax: (781) 326-6819, Web Site: www.dangelos.com. Upscale sandwich shop featuring subs, pitas, salads and soup. Menu includes grilled items and D'Angelo D'Lite sandwiches for adults and kids. Established: 1967 - Franchising Since: 1988 - No. of Units: Company Owned: 156 - Franchised: 55 - Franchise Fee: $20,000 - Royalty: 6% - Total Inv: $205,944-$348,280.

DAIRY BELLE FREEZE DEVELOPMENT CO., INC.
P.O Box 360830, Milpitas, CA, 95036-0830. - Tel: (408) 433-9337, Fax: (408) 433-9395. Fast food franchisor. Established: 1957 - No. of Units: Franchised: 14 - Franchise Fee: $12,500 - Royalty: 4.5%, 2.% adv. - Total Inv: $130,000-$253,001 - Financing: None, but could assist.

DAIRY QUEEN
Interstate Dairy Queen Corp.
4601 Willard Ave., Chevy Chase, MD, 20815. Contact: Walt Tellegen, Pres. - Tel: (952) 830-0200. Specialists in co-branding with fuel centers. Fast food/treat franchisor on interstate highways. Established: 1977 - Franchising Since: 1977 - No. of Units: Franchised: 165 - Franchise Fee: $25,000 - Royalty: 4% or 7% - Total Inv: Varies with building - Financing: No.

DAIRY QUEEN®, KARMELKORN SHOPPES, ORANGE JULIUS
IDQ Companies
7505 Metro Blvd., Minneapolis, MN, 55439-0286. Contact: Development Department - Tel: (612) 830-0200, (800) 285-8515, Fax: (612) 830-0450, Web Site: www.dairyqueen.com. Dairy Queen® stores offer a variety of quick service food and treat items including hamburgers, hot dogs, cones, sundaes, the "Blizzard"® flavor treat, frozen cakes and more! With more than 5800 stores world-wide. Established: 1940 - Franchising Since: 1940 - No. of Units: Company Owned: 50 - Franchised: 5807 - Franchise Fee: $20,000- $35,000 - Royalty: 4%-6% varies with program - Total Inv: $147,240-$585,140 (excluding real estate and improvement costs) - Financing: No.

DAMON'S, RIBS, PRIME RIB & MORE
Damon's International,Inc.
4645 Executive Dr., Columbus, OH, 43220. Contact: Ed Williams, V.P. of Dev. - Tel: (614) 442-7900, Fax: (614) 442-7787, E-Mail: franchise @damons.com, Web Site: www.damons.com. A casual theme full service restaurant specializing in BBQ ribs and prime rib together with the signature item onion loaf. The Clubhouse is known for its sports theme dining room with the same great menu. Established: 1979 -

Franchising Since: 1982 - No. of Units: Company Owned: 23 - Franchised: 112 - Franchise Fee: $30,000 - Royalty: 4% - Total Inv: $1,210,500-$1,796,000 - Financing: No.

DEB'S WINGS-N-SUBS, INC.
Deb's Enterprises Inc.
3002 Four Season's Dr., Effingham, IL, 62401. Contact: Rick Wittenberg, Pres. - Tel: (217) 536-9464, Fax: (217) 868-5116. Family style fast food operation specializing in 7 different flavours of buffalo style wings, submarine sandwiches and oven baked subs. Unique counter ordering combined with table service able to provide 5-8 minute service from order to food delivery. Established: 1995 - Franchising Since: 1996 - No. of Units: Company Owned: 1 - Franchise Fee: $10,000-$25,000 - Royalty: 6% of Gross Sales - Financing: N/A,

DEL TACO
Del Taco, Inc.
25521 Commercentre Dr, Lake Forest, CA, 92630. - Tel: (949) 462-7422, Fax: (949) 462-7444. Quick-service Mexican/American restaurant chain. Established: 1964 - Franchising Since: 1967 - No. of Units: Company Owned: 214 - Franchised: 101 - Franchise Fee: $25,000 - Royalty: 5% - Total Inv: Varies - Financing: Yes.

DENNY'S
Denny's, Inc.
203 E. Main St., Spartanburg, SC, 29319. Contact: Beth Cauthan, Franchise Admin - Tel: (864) 597-7317, (800) 304-0222, Fax: (864) 597-7708, Web Site: www.dennys.com. One of America's largest full-service restaurant chain, serving nearly one million customers a day and is one of America's most recognized names in family dining. Denny's is well known for it's around-the-clock breakfast entrees, including its famous original Grand Slam breakfasts, and value meals for breakfast and lunch. Full-service restaurant chain where most restaurants are open 24 hours a day, 7 days a week. Established: 1953 - Franchising Since: 1963 - No. of Units: Company Owned: 577 - Franchised: 1108 - Franchise Fee: $40,000 - Royalty: 4% + 3% adv.- Total Inv: $941,000-$1,772,000 - Financing: No.

DESERT MOON FRESH MEXICAN GRILL
Desert Moon
612 Corporate Way, Suite 1M, Valley Cottage, NY, 10989. Contact: Jeff Percey, Director of Franchise Developments - Tel: (877) 564-6362, E-Mail: jeffp@fransmart.com, Web Site: www.desertmooncafe.com. Desert Moon is one of the most attractive franchise opportunities available, positioned in the fast casual, fresh-Mexican segment and built on a proven management team, superior unit economics and the highest quality food available. Desert Moon provides a fast-casual solution to consumers who want great tasting, high quality, and all natural food along with speed, value and convenience. Established: 1992 - Franchising Since: 1999 - No. of Units: Company Owned: 5 - Franchised: 9 - Franchise Fee: $25,000 - Royalty: 5% - Total Inv: $186,500-$356,400 - Financing: Third party.

DESI'S
434 Hazel St, Wilkes-Barre, PA, 18702. Contact: Frank Desiderio, Owner - Tel: (570) 674-9084, (800) 694-3374. Delivery, dine-in, take-out pizza, subs, wings, and other delicious food items. Established: 1989 - Franchising Since: 1995 - No. of Units: Company Owned: 3 - Franchise Fee: $15,000 - Royalty: 5% - Total Inv: Prototype A $100,000, Prototype B $175,000 - Financing: No.

DIAL & DINE
69 Prospect Ave, West Hartford, CT, 06106. Contact: Franchise Department - Tel: (860) 231-8888, Fax: (860) 231-8795. Restaurant marketing and delivery service. Established: 1992 - Franchising Since: 1995 - No. of Units: Company Owned: 2 - Franchised: 1 - Franchise Fee: $15,000 - Financing: No.

DIAMOND DAVE'S TACO CO.
Diamond Dave's Taco Co., Inc.
201 S. Clinton St. #281, Iowa City, IA, 52240-4011. Contact: Stanley J. White, Pres. - Tel: (319) 337-7690. Mexican/American restaurant featuring full service dining with a bar. Established: 1979 - Franchising Since: 1981 - No. of Units: Company Owned: 4 - Franchised: 31 - Franchise Fee: $15,000 - Royalty: 4%+1% adv. - Total Inv: $122,200-$250,000 - Financing: None.

DIFFERENT TWIST PRETZEL, THE
6052 Route 8, Bakerstown, PA, 15007. Contact: August P. Maggio, Pres./Owner - Tel: (724) 443-8010, Fax: (724) 443-7287. Hand made fresh sweet soft pretzel. Established: 1992 - Licensing Since: 1992 - No. of Units: Licensed: 15 in 6 states - Franchise Fee: $5,000 - Total Inv: $40,000-$100,000.

DINO'S PIZZA
Triad Development Inc.
P.O. Box 97244, Raleigh, NC, 27624-7244. - Tel: (919) 676-1080, Fax: (919) 687-1081. Delivery, take-out cafe. Full training and support provided. Established: 1992 - Franchising Since: 1992 - No, of Units: Company Owned: 1 - Franchised: 28 - Franchise Fee: $10,000 - Total Inv: $30,000-$50,000 - Financing: Yes.

DOG N SUDS® DRIVE-IN RESTAURANTS
Dogs N Suds® Restaurants, Inc.
4945 Fairway Drive, Plainfield, IN, 46168. Contact: Richard T. Morath, President - Tel: (317) 718-0772, (800) DOG-N-SUDS, Fax: (317) 718-0773. Drive-in restaurant featuring root beer and coney dogs - training and support provided. Established: 1992 - Franchising Since: 1996 - No. of Units: Company Owned: 4 - Franchised: 9 - Franchise Fee: $25,000/$15,000 - Total Inv: $100,000-$300,000 - Financing: No.

DOGOUT, THE
P.O. Box 2038, Pismo Beach, CA, 93448. Contact: Brock Matheson - Tel: (800) 794-0117, E-Mail: info@theddogout.com, Web Site: www.thedogout.com. A quick service restaurant featuring sausage, hot dogs, old-fashion french fries and other related products. Established: 2002 - Franchising Since: 2002 - No. of Units: Company Owned: 2 - Franchised: 13 - Franchise Fee: $25,000 - Total Inv: $204,000-$474,000 - Financing: Third party.

DOLLY'S PIZZA
Dolly's Pizza Franchising, Inc.
1097 B Union Lake Rd., White Lake, MI, 48386. Contact: John Davidson, Director of Franchising - Tel: (248) 360-6440, Fax: (248) 360-7020, Web Site: www.dollyspizza.com. Pizza carry out/delivery and dine in. Menu includes pizza, subs, salads, breadsticks, and chicken dinners. Established: 1966 - Franchising Since: 1993 - No. of Units: Company Owned: 3 - Franchised: 25 - Franchise Fee: $12,500 - Royalty: 4% - Total Inv: Equipment $50,000 , buildout $60,000, misc $30,000 - Financing: We work closely with many third party sources.

DOMINIC'S OF NEW YORK
Foodnet Franchising, Inc
4949 - B Cox Road, Glen Allen, VA, 23060. Contact; Nick DiMarino, Director of Development - Tel: (804) 273-0600, (888) DOM-OF-NY, Fax: (804) 273-0152, E-Mail: comments@domofny.com. Fast food / Italin sausage, philly cheese steaks, grilled chicken sandwiches, portobella mushroom sandwiches and hot dogs, all available with famous grilled onions and sweet peppers. Established: 1994 - Franchising Since: 1997 - No. of Units: Company Owned: 38 - Franchised: 9 - Franchise Fee: $10,000 - Royalty: 2.5%, require 3% of sales local advertising - Financing: SBA backed loans, leasing companies, etc, all third party.

DOMINO'S PIZZA
Domino's Pizza, Inc
30 Frank Lloyd Wright Dr., Ann Arbor, MI, 48105. Contact: Paul Skinner, Dir. of Dev. - Tel: (734) 930-3030. Pizza delivery. Established: 1960 - Franchising Since: 1967 - No. of Units: Company Owned: 1,200 - Franchised: 4,400 - Franchise Fee: $10,000 - Royalty: 5.5% of net sales - Total Inv: $150,000: $100,000 equip./leaseholds; $50,000 fees/work. cap. - Financing: No.

DONATOS PIZZA, INC.
1 Easton Oval, Suite 200, Columbus, OH, 43219. Contact: Franchise Dept. - Tel: (614) 416-7700, Fax: (614) 416-7702. Retail outlet specializing in the sale of pizza and other products and featuring carry-out dine-in and delivery services. Established: 1963 - Franchising Since: 1991 - No. of Units: Company Owned: 84 - Franchised: 46 - Franchise Fee: $35,000 - Royalty: 4% of net sales - Total Inv: $350,000-$750,000: $180,000 equip., $75,000 leasehold, $50,000 work cap. - Financing: None.

EAST OF CHICAGO PIZZA COMPANY
318 West Walton., P.O. 388, Willard, OH, 44890. Contact: Dir. of Dev. - Tel: (419) 935-3033. Dine-in, take out franchise- we have pan pizza, thin crust pizza, crispy crust pizza, apple pizza, peanut butter and jelly pizza, a wide selection of subs. Established: 1990 - Franchising Since: 1991 - No. of Units: Company Owned: 6 - Franchised: 100 - Franchise Fee: $16,000 - Royalty: 5% of gross sales, 2% of sales mkt. fee - Total Inv: Dine-in - $182,700-$289,700/carry out $147,900-$235,600 - Financing: No.

EATZA PIZZA
4800 N. Scottsdale Rd, #1600, Scottsdale, AZ, 85251. Contact: Chris Utterback - Tel: (480) 941-5200, Fax: (480) 941-5202, Web Site: www.eatzapizza.com. All you can eat pizza, pasta, salad and desert family style buffet. Established: 1999 - Franchising Since: 1999 - No. of Units: Company Owned: 5 - Franchised: 16 - Franchise Fee: $25,000 - Royalty: 5% - Total Inv: $266,500.

EDDIE PEPPER'S TREAT MEXICAN RESTAURANT
Orion Food Systems
2930 W Maple, Sioux Falls, SD, 57101. Contact: Director of Development - Tel: (800) 648-6227, (605) 336-6961, Fax: (605) 336-0141, Web Site: www.orionfoodsys.com. Quick service format, developing in convenience stores and foodcourts. Established: 1984 - Franchising Since: 1985 - No. of Units: Company Owned: 4 - Franchised: 107 - Franchise Fee: $4,950 - Total Inv: $25,000+ - Financing: Third Party.

EL CHICO
El Chico Restaurants, Inc.
12200 Stemmons Freeway, Ste. 100, Dallas, TX, 75234. - Tel: (972) 241-5500, Web Site: www.elchico.com. Full-service, family Mexican restaurants. Established: 1940 - Franchising Since: 1969 - No. of Units: Company Owned: 56 - Franchised: 29 - Franchise Fee: $35,000 - Royalty: 4% + 1% marketing fee - Total Inv: $1,000,000 - Financing: No.

EL POLLO LOCO
Denny's Inc.
333 Michelson Drive., Suite 550, Irvine, CA, 92612. Contact: Julie Weeks, Director of Franchising - Tel: (949) 399-2000, Fax: (949) 399-2025, E-Mail: jweeks@elpolloloco.com, Web Site: www.elpollo loco.com. Fast food serving chicken. Established: 1980 - No. of Units: Company Owned: 125 - Franchised: 125.

EL TACO RESTAURANTS
7870 E. Florence, Downey, CA, 90240. Contact: J. Toogood, Pres. - Tel: (562) 692-5400. Mexican fast food. Established: 1958 - Franchising Since: 1978 - No. of Units: Company Owned: 3 - Franchised: 27 - Franchise Fee: $75,000 - Royalty: 5% - Total Inv: $150,000.

EL TORITO, EL TORITO GRILL, EL TORITO EXPRESS, SOUTHWEST GRILL
El Torito Franchising Company
4001 Via Oro Ave, Long Beach, CA, 90810. Contact; Dir. International Franchise - Tel: (310) 513-7527, (800) 735-3501 x 527, Fax: (310) 522-9810, E-Mail: jmmushkin@aol.com, Web Site: www.eltorito.com. The original Mexican dinnerhouse, responsible for introducing fajitas, blended and hand-shaken margaritas and other innovations to America, now available for franchising in Canada, Europe, Australia, New Zealand and developed Asian and Latin American countries. Established: 1954 - Franchising Since: 1988 - No. of Units: Company Owned: 95 - Franchised: 12 - Franchise Fee: Negotiable - Royalty: Negotiable - Financing: No.

ELIAS BROTHERS RESTAURANTS
Big Boy Restaurant & Bakery
4199 Marcy, Warren, MI, 48091. Contact; Dir. of Corp. Dev - Tel: (810) 755-8113. Full - service family restaurant with breakfast buffet, soup, salad and fruit bar, in-store bakery and gift shop. Established: 1938 - Franchising Since: 1952 - No. of Units: Company Owned: 100 - Franchised: 600 - Franchise Fee: $40,000 - Royalty: 4% + 3% - Total Inv: $850,000-$1,700,000 - Financing: Will assist locating lenders.

ELMER'S BREAKFAST-LUNCH-DINNER
Elmer's Restaurants, Inc.
11802 S.E. Stark, Portland, OR, 97216. Contact: Jerry Scott, Vice President - Tel: (503) 252-1485, (800) 325-5188, Fax: (503) 252-6706, Web Site: www.elmers-restaurants.com. Elmer's is a full-service family dining restaurant company. Founded in 1960, Elmer's is known for exceptional guest service and full franchise support. Established: 1960 - Franchising Since: 1974 - No. of Units: Company Owned: 10 - Franchised: 23 - Franchise Fee: $40,000 - Royalty: 4% royalty; 2% regional marketing - Total Inv: $400,000-$1.3 million, depending on type of development - Financing: Company coordinates with outside lenders.

EMBERS AMERICA RESTAURANTS
Embers America, LLC
1664 University Ave, St. Paul, MN, 55104. Contact: Greg Poling, Dir. of Mkt Dev - Tel: (651) 645-6473, (888) 805-3448, Fax: (651) 645-6866, E-Mail: gpoling@embersamerica.com, Web Site: www.embers america.com. Full service family style restaurants. Established: 1956 - Franchising Since: 1998 - No. of Units: Company Owned: 1 - Franchised: 59 - Franchise Fee: $15,000-$25,000 - Total Inv: TBA - Financing: N/A.

EMPRESS CHILI
Empress Food Products, Inc.
10592 Taconic Terr., Cincinnati, OH, 45215. Contact: J. Kiradjieff, Pres. - Tel: (513) 771-1441. Making or processing of chili, for super markets and our franchise stores. These are put in containers and 5 gal. pails. Established: 1959 - Franchising Since: 1960 - No. of Units: 100% franchised - Franchise Fee: $6,000 - Total Inv: $60,000-$80,000 - Financing: Yes.

ENTREES ON TRAYS
3 Lombardy Terrace, Ft. Worth, TX, 76132-1011. Contact: Don Shipe, Founder-Owner - Tel: (817) 737-5584. Dinner delivery service serving the finer restaurants of Ft. Worth with chef uniformed drivers. Operated from home. Now one of the oldest dinner delivery services in America. Established: 1986 - Business Opp. Since: 1990 - No. of Units: Company Owned: 1 - Lic. Agree: 4 - License Fee: $8,750 incl. all equip. except radios - Royalty: 0 - Total Inv: Approx. $11,000 incl. radios - Financing: None.

ERBERT & GERBERT'S SUBS & CLUBS
E&G Franchise Systems, Inc.
205 East Grand Avenue, Eau Claire, WI, 54701. Contact: Kevin Schippers, Pres. - Tel: (715) 833-1375, (800) 283-5241, Fax: (715) 833-8523, E-Mail: info@erbertandgerberts.com, Web Site: www.erbertand gerberts.com. Erbert & Gerbert's Subs & Clubs restaurants offer delicious sub & club sandwiches that are unequalled in quality, freshness and consistency. Delivery service and late night hours make us unique to the sandwich industry. Established: 1988 - Franchising Since: 1992 - No. of Units: Company Owned: 1 - Franchised: 25 - Franchise Fee: $25,00 - Royalty: 6% - Total Inv: $194,000-$356,000 - Financing: No.

ERIK'S DELICAFE FRANCHISES INC.
365 Coral St., Santa Cruz, CA, 95060. Contact: Pam Gruen, Franc. Dir. - Tel: (831) 458-1818, Fax: (831) 458-9797. Limited service restaurant. Soups, salads and sandwiches. Western theme oriented setting. (No preservatives). Established: 1973 - Franchising Since: 1986 - No. of Units: Company Owned: 10 - Franchised: 13 - Franchise Fee - $20,000 - Royalty: 5% - Total Inv: $126,000-$157,000 - Financing: No.

EXTREME PIZZA
OOC Inc
1052 Folsom St, San Francisco, CA, 94103. Contact: Jimmy Ryan - Tel: (415) 703-8122, (866) 695-5595, Fax: (415) 503-1633. Gourmet pizza, subs and salads. Established: 1994 - Franchising Since: 2000 - No. of Units: Company Owned: 4 - Franchised: 2 - Franchise Fee: $25,000 - Financing: No.

FAJITA WILLIE'S CAFE & CANTINA
Frijoles Restaurants, Inc.
1131 Jones Road West Suite G, Houston, TX, 77065. - Tel: (281) 807-5200, Fax: (281) 807-0666. Fajita Willie's operates and controls a comprehensive restaurant system for the retailing of a menu of uniform and quality food products in a fast, efficient, clean and comfortable

atmosphere. Established: 1985 - Franchising Since: 1987 - No. of Units: Company Owned: 1 - Franchised: 1 - Franchise Fee: $25,000 - Royalty: 4% - Total Inv: $300,000-$350,000 - Financing: None.

FAMILY RESTAURANTS
P.O. Box 19561, Irvine, CA, 92623-9561. Contact: Marilyn Dunn, Pres. - Tel: (949) 863-6400, Fax: (949) 724-9914. Dinnerhouse. Established: 1954 - No. of Units: Company Owned: 183 - Franchised: 4.

FAMOUS SAM'S
Famous Sam's Inc.
1930 South Alma School Rd., Suite C-105, Mesa, AZ, 85210. Contact: David Peters - Tel: (480) 756-9800, Fax: (480) 756-9884, E-Mail: corp@famoussams.net, Web Site: www.famoussams.com. Restaurant sports bar that offers overstuffed sandwiches, burgers and full bar. Established: 1963 - Franchising Since: 1989 - No. of Units: Franchised: 31 - Franchise Fee: $30,000 for single unit - Royalty: 5% - Total Inv: $583,500-$1,150,000 - Financing: Assist with third party.

FAMOUS UNCLE AL'S
3045 Shore Dr., Virgina Beach, VA, 23451. Contact: Al Stein, President - Tel: (757) 481-2718. Hot dogs, fries, hamburgers, NY hot sausage, cheesecake, sandwiches. Established: 1985 - Franchising Since: 1997 - No. of Units: Company Owned: 2 - Franchised: 4 - Franchise Fee: $58,000 - Royalty 2% up to 5% - Total Inv. $52,000 + $6,000 franchise fee - Financing: None.

FARMER BOYS
Farmer Boys Food Inc.
3452 University, Riverside, CA, 92501. Contact: Bill Foss - Tel: (909) 275-9900, (888) 930-FARM, Fax: (909) 275-9930, E-Mail: bfoss@farmerboys.com, Web Site: www.farmerboys.com. Quality food served quickly in a warm environment. Established: 1981 - Franchising Since: 1997 - No. of Units: Company Owned: 10 - Franchised: 11 - Franchise Fee: $35,000 - Royalty: 5% - Total Inv: $400,00-$600,000 - Financing: No.

FASTA PASTA
Fasta Pasta Franchising. Corp.
955 East Javelina Ave, Ste. 114, Mesa, AZ, 85204. Contact: Robert Palmer/Sharon Snyder - Tel: (480) 503-3363, (800) 711-4036, Fax: (480) 503-1850, E-Mail: info@fastapasta.com, Web Site: www.fastapasta.com. Fasta Pasta is a quick casual restaurant serving quality "Fresh Made" pasta. "Gourmet pastas at home-cooked prices." Established: 1998 - Franchising Since: 2001 - No. of Units: Company Owned: 1 - Franchise Fee: $20,000 - Royalty: 4% - Total Inv: $200,000-$300,000 - Financing: Yes, third party available to qualified applicants.

FAT BOYS' BAR-B-Q
Fat Boys' Bar-B-Q Franchise Systems, Inc.
1940 10th Ave Ste B, Vero Beach, FL, 32960. Contact: L. A. McLain, President - Tel: (561) 794-1080, Fax: (561) 794-9590. Bar-B-Q restaurant with full service 167 seat, with take-out and catering services. Established: 1958 - Franchising Since: 1970 - No. of Units: Franchised: 16 - Franchise Fee: $25,000 - Royalty: 3% of gross sales - Total Inv: Variable.

FATBURGER
Fatburger North America, Inc.
1218 3rd Steet Promenade, Santa Monica, CA, 90401. - Tel: (310) 319-1850, Fax: (310) 319-1863. Quick service restaurant. Established: 1952 - Franchising Since: 1982- No. of Units: Company Owned: 23 - Franchised: 27 - Franchise Fee: $40,000 - Royalty: 6%; 2% - Total Inv: $380,000-$748,000 - Financing: SBA, third party.

FAZOLI'S RESTAURANTS
Seed Restaurant Group, Inc
2470 Palumbo Drive, Lexington, KY, 40509. - Tel: (606) 268-1668, Fax: (606) 268-2263, E-Mail: franchise@fazolis.com, Web Site: www.fazolis.com. Fazoli's "quick casual" Italian concept combines the convenience and price of fast food with the food quality and atmosphere associated with casual dining. Established: 1990 - Franchising Since: 1991 - No. of Units: Company Owned: 172 - Franchised: 138 - Franchise Fee: $20,000 - Total Inv: $60,000-$120,000 start-up cash; $400,000-$905,000 total investment plus land - Financing: No.

FIGARO'S PIZZA
Figaro's Italian Pizza Inc.
1500 Liberty St., S.E., #160, Salem, OR, 97302. Contact: Steve Nilsby - Tel: (503) 371-9318, Fax: (503) 363-5364, E-Mail:figaros@figaros.com, Web site: www.figaros.com. Take-and-bake and baked fresh pizza, lasagna and calzone's. Established: 1981 - Franchising Since: 1986 - No. of Units: Franchised: 96 - Franchise Fee: $7,500-$20,000 - Royalty: 5% - Total Inv: $103,500-$319,000 - Financing: Yes.

FIREGRILL
America's Steak Experts, Inc.
56 Inverness Dr., E, Ste. 111, Englewood, CO, 80112-5100. - Tel: (303) 293-0200, (800) 937-2830, Fax: (303) 293-0299. The Firegrill restaurant is a casual dining steakhouse, accenting the innovative and delicious food is the unique Southwestern 'Dine Under The Stars' decor. Established: 1992 - Franchising Since: 1993 - No. of Units: Franchised: 3 - Franchise Fee: $25,000 - Royalty: 4%, 1.5% adv. - Total Inv: $801,500-$1,057,000 with ground lease - Financing: No.

FIRKIN PUBS *
Firkin Pubs, LLC
132 King Street, Alexandria, VA, 23214. Contact: Stacey Gallagher - Tel: (703) 549-5332, (877) 347-5464, Fax: (703) 549-0740, E-Mail: staceyg@fransmart.com, Web Site: www.firkinpubs.com. Since 1987, Firkin Pubs has been offering patrons a one-of-a-kind English, neighborhood pub experience. Our superior, yet affordable, menu-complete with a variety of beverages and pub fares - has quickly built a stable of regulars in each our 43 unique pub locations. Every Firkin's a litlte different and one's just right for you... Established: 1987 - Franchising Since: 2003- No. of Units: Comnpany Owned: 1 - Franchised: 43 open, 40+ sold - Franchsie Fee: $25,000 - Royalty: 5% - Total Inv: $220,000-$509,500 - Financing: Third party.

FIVE GUYS BURGERS & FRIES *
4403 Kirchner Ct., 3202, Alexandria, VA, 22304. - Tel: (703) 751-6844, Fax: (703) 751-5021, Web Site: www.fiveguys.com. The best burger & fries in any town. Established: 1986 - Franchising Since: 2002 - No. of Units: Company Owned: 5 - Franchised: 7 - Franchise Fee: $25,000 - Royalty: 6% - Total Inv: $152,600-$360,300.

FLAMERS CHARBROILED HAMBURGERS
FCI Food Group
500 S. 3rd Street, Jacksonville Beach, FL, 32250. Contact: Dir. of Franchise Development - Tel: (904) 241-3737, Fax: (904) 241-1301, E-Mail: flamersgrill@usa.net, Web Site: www.flamersgrill.com. Gourmet hamburgers and chicken sandwiches cooked over an open flame grill, fast food. Established: 1987 - Franchising Since: 1987 - No. of Units: Company Owned: 9 - Franchised: 84 - Franchise Fee: $25,000 - Royalty: 5%, 1% adv. - Total Inv: $175,000-$225,000 - Financing: Yes, third party.

FLUKY'S
5225 West Touhy Ave., Ste. 103, Skokie, IL, 60077-3266. Contact: Jack Drexler, Fran. Dept. - Tel: (847) 329-1409, Fax: (847) 329-1454, Web Site: wwwflukys.com. Top quality hot dog establishment. Established: 1928 - Franchising Since: 1980 - No. of Units: Company Owned: 3 - Franchised: 2 - Franchise Fee: $25,000 - Royalty: 5% - Total Inv: $324,500 incl. leasehold improvements - Financing: No.

FMS MANAGEMENT SYSTEMS, INC.
2655 N.E. 189th St., North Miami Beach, FL, 33180. Contact: Carlos Diaz, V.P. Finance and Admin. - Tel: (305) 931-5454, Fax: (305) 933-3300. International House of Pancakes franchising in the state of Florida. Established: 1963 - Franchising Since: 1963 - No. of Units: Company Owned: 50 - Franchised: 40 - Franchise Fee: Varies upon location - Royalty: Varies upon location - Total Inv: Varies upon location - Financing: Assistance.

FONTANO'S SUBS
Fontano's Subs Franchise System Inc.
1058 W. Polk St., Chicago, IL, 60607. Contact: Fontano Family, Owners - Tel: (312) 421-4474, Fax: (312) 421-1424. Deli/sub sandwiches. Family style store. Established: 1935 - Franchising Since: 1995 - No. of Units: Company Owned: 2 - Franchised: 3 - Franchise Fee: $12,500 stores 1-5, $15,000 stores 6-10 - Royalty: 5%, 2% adv. - Total Inv: $90,000-$150,000 - Financing: No.

FOOD CART SYSTEMS, INC

601 Cleveland Street, Suite 330, Clearwater, FL, 33755. Contact: Jack Fleck, V.P. of Sales & Marketing - Tel: (727) 449-8700, (888) 718-7600, Fax: (727) 449-1881, E-Mail: franchising@foodcartsystems.com, Web Site: www.foodcartsystems.com. Food Cart Systems, Inc. operates under the registered trade name HOT Stop. The franchise program provides the assets and training necessary to operate Cart Systems at amusement and water parks. Qualified franchisees are provided with contracts for locations. Established: 1997 - Franchising Since: 2002 - No. of Units: Company Owned: 8 - Franchise Fee: $25,000 per cart - Royalty: 6%-8% - Total Inv: Varies by location - Financing: Yes.

FOODEE'S PIZZA FOODEE'S INC.

26 South Main Street, # 84, Concord, NH, 03301. Contact: Franchise Licensing - Tel: (603) 435-6500. International and specialty pizzas, using old bread recipes for crusts and international pastas. Winner "Best Pizza In New England" by WBZ Radio Boston, MA. Established: 1985 - Franchising Since: 1987 - No. of Units: Franchised: 15 - Franchise Fee: $15,000 full size store, $6,000 Foodee's Jr. - Royalty: 5% for full size, 5%-6% depending on sales for Foodee's Jr. - Total Inv: Full Size: $173,400-$460,500 - Foodee Jr.: $56,500-$120,250 - Financing: None.

FOSTERS FREEZE/FOSTERS FREEZE JR.

Fosters Freeze International, Inc.
8300 Utica Ave STE 157, Rancho Cucamonga, CA, 91730-3880. Contact: Franchise Department - Tel: (805) 781-6100, Fax: (805) 781-6106. Fosters Freeze Int'l is the franchisor of Fosters Freeze. Fast food chain offers a full fountain with limited menu and designed to go into strip shopping centers, and some free standing, smaller drive-thru restaurant models. Established: 1946 - Franchising Since: 1946 - No. of Units: Company Owned: 1 - Franchised: 163 - Franchise Fee: $40,000 Fosters Freeze - $25,000 Fosters Freeze Jr. - Royalty: 4% gross sales - Total Inv: Approx. $160,000 - Financing: Assistance in the location of financing available through corp. office.

FOUR STAR PIZZA

P.O.Box W, 139 Ealy Road, Claysville, PA, 15323. - Tel: (724) 484-9235, (800) 628-3398, Fax: (724) 484-9267. Free home delivery of fresh made (nothing is frozen!) pizza, subs and other products. Focus is on product and profit! Established: 1981 - Franchising Since: 1985 - No. of Units: Company Owned: 6 - Franchised: 30 - Franchise Fee: $2,000 - Royalty: 5% sales - Total Inv: $50,000.

FOX'S PIZZA DEN

Fox's Pizza Den Inc.
3243 Old Frankstown Rd., Pittsburgh, PA, 15239. Contact: Jim Fox, President/Owner - Tel: (800) 899-3697, Web Site: www.foxspizza.com. Fox's Pizza is a take-out/delivery or dine-in (if desired) pizza & sandwich operation with almost 30 years of successful franchising experience. Royalty is only $200 per month with no advertising fee. A low initial investment, combined with the low royalty, enables owners to become profitable much more quickly. We make owning a franchise more accessible to people of average means while also seeking multi-unit operators for aggressive expansion. Established: 1971 - Franchising Since: 1974 - No. of Units: Company Owned: 1 - Franchised: 220 - Franchise Fee: $8,000 - Royalty: $200 monthly - Total Inv: $75,000 - Financing: Assistance Available.

FRANK & STEIN DOGS & DRAFTS

Caldwell Enterprises, Inc.
1630 Braeborn Dr., Ste. A, Salem, VA, 24153. Contact: C. Gregory Caldwell, Pres. - Tel: (540) 389-8435, Fax: (540) 389-1780. Fast food restaurant; selling gourmet style hot dogs and sausages as well as full menu options selling hamburgers and other items, featuring draft beer through on-counter brass beer towers. Units in major retail shopping centers and airport food courts. Established: 1985 - Franchising Since: 1986 - No. of Units: Company Owned: 3 - Franchised: 32 - Franchise Fee: $20,000 - Royalty: 4% of sales, 1% adv. - Total Inv: $20,000 fee, $50,000 equip., $90,000 constr. - Financing: Equip. leasing pkgs.

FRANKFURTER RESTAURANTS, THE

Frankfurter USA, Inc., The
226 S. Orcas St., Seattle, WA, 98108. Contact: Stan Moffett, Pres. - Tel: (206) 763-9669, Fax: (206) 763-2783. Retail specialty food service. Featuring uniquely seasoned old world sausages on a french roll, fresh squeezed lemonade and fresh baked cookies. Franchising Since: 1990 - No. of Units: Company Owned: 12 - Franchise Fee: $15,000 - Royalty: 5% sales - Financing: No.

FRANKIE'S FAMILY RESTAURANTS

Frankie's Franchise Systems Inc.
643 Lakewood Rd., Waterbury, CT, 06704. Contact: Jerry Daddona, Office Mgr. - Tel: (203) 756-2935, Fax: (203) 757-5361. Restaurants. Established: 1938 - Franchising Since: 1978 - No. of Units: Company Owned: 4 - Franchised: 3 - Franchise Fee: $28,000 - Royalty: 3% - Total Inv: $80,000 - Financing: N/A.

FRESH CITY *

145 Rosemary Street Suite C, Needham, MA, 02494. - Tel: (781) 453-0200, Fax: (781) 453-8686, Web Site: www.freshcity.com. We are meccas for customers seeking alternatives to fast food. Are well-trained team members turn out Cookin' Wraps, Salad Wraps, Salad Bowls, Sandwiches, Asian Noodles, Fresh Fruit Smoothies, Espresso Drinks, Cafe Chillers, Fresh Baked Goods, and more. Established: 1997 - Franchising Since: 2003 - No. of Units: Company Owned: 5 - Franchise Fee: $35,000 - Royalty: 5% - Total Inv: $696,000.

FRIDAY'S FRONT ROW SPORTS GRILL

Carlson Restaurants Worldwide
7540 LBJ Fwy., Ste. 100, Dallas, TX, 75251. Contact: Wallace Doolin, Pres. & CEO - Tel: (972) 450-5775. Casual theme, full service restaurants. Initial Fee: $150,000 - Royalty: 4% gross food plus 5% non-food sales - Adv./Mktg. Fee: Capped at 4% gross sales - Outside U.S.- Franchise Fee: $150,000 - Consulting Fee: $250,000 - Royalty Fee: 4% gross sales plus 5% merchandise sales.

FRISCH'S RESTAURANTS, INC.

Elias Brothers
2800 Gilbert Ave., Cincinnati, OH, 45206. Contact: David R. Kuklman, Fran. Dev. - Tel: (513) 559-5304. Family restaurant with drive-thru. Full training and support provided. Established: 1947 - Franchising Since: 1953 - No. of Units: Company Owned: 103 - Franchised: 39 - Franchise Fee: $30,000 - Total Inv: $100,000-$150,000 liquid.

FRULLATI CAFE & BAKERY

Frullati Franchise Systems, Inc.
7730 East Greenway Rd #104, Scottsdale, AZ, 85260. - Tel: (480) 443-0200, Fax: (480) 443-1972. Experience a fresh break from the ordinary...food court locations in shopping malls featuring a healthful, lite-fare menu of salads, sandwiches, soups, fresh baked goods and our signature line of "fruit smoothies". Established: 1985 - Franchising Since: 1994 - No. of Units: Company Owned: 35 - Franchised: 48 - Franchise Fee: $20,000 - Royalty: 6% - Total Inv: $150,000-$250,000 - Financing: Yes sources.

FUDDRUCKERS

66 Cherry Hill Dr., Suite 200, Beverly, MA, 01915-1054. Contact: Craig Nelson, Sr. V.P. Dev. - Tel: (978) 9921-9020. Upscale hamburger casual family restaurant featuring 1/2 and 1/3 lb. burgers, chicken, fish and hot dog sandwiches and salads. On premise butcher shop and bakery to insure freshness. Full produce bar to do your own thing. Established: 1980 - Franchising Since: 1983 - No. of Units: Company Owned: 116 - Franchised: 85 - Franchise Fee: $50,000 - Royalty: 5% mthly. sales - Financing: No.

GARFIELD'S RESTAURANT & PUB

Eaterie's, Inc
1220 South Santa Fe Ave, Edmond, OK, 73003.Contact: Laurence Bader, VP-Franchising - Tel: (405) 705-5077, Fax: (405) 705-5005, E-Mail: laurenceb@eats-inc.com, Web Site: www.garfields.net. A friendly casual dining restaurant with full bar serving an American menu of convenience, quality and price/value. Established: 1984 - Franchising Since: 1987 - No. of Units: Company Owned: 48 - Franchised: 10 - Franchise Fee: $30,000 - Royalty: 4% remitted monthly - Total Inv: $1,185,000-$1,955,000 - Financing: Yes.

GENGHIS GRILL

JPS Enterprises, Inc
2625 Main Street, Dallas, TX, 75226-1411. Contact: Ashley Campos, Director of Franchise Relations - Tel: (214) 742-5426, Fax: (214) 742-4329, E-Mail: franchise@genghisgrill.com, Web Site: www.geng

hisgrill.com. Full service casual restaurant where you build your own bowl of stir-fry. Select any our fresh ingredients: fresh meats, veggies, sauces and spices. Established: 1998 - Franchising Since: 2002 - No. of Units: Company Owned: 4 - Franchised: 31 - Franchise Fee: $30,000 - Total Inv: $305,000-$680,000.

GEORGE WEBB RESTAURANTS
George Webb Corporation
N7 W22081 Johnson Drive, Waukesha, WI, 53186. - Tel: (262) 970-0084, Fax: (262) 970-7123, E-Mail: jaliota@georgewebb.com. 24hr neighborhood restaurant catering to all your needs. Full training and support povided. Established: 1948 - Franchising Since: 1953 - No. of Units: Company Owned: 9 - Franchised: 33 - Franchise Fee: $19,500 - Total Inv: $234,000-$346,000 - Financing: No.

GEPPETTO'S PIZZA & RIBS
3314 Warren Rd., Cleveland, OH, 44111. Contact: Michael O'Malley, Pres. - Tel: (216) 251-1335. Delivery or take-out of pizza and ribs. Established: 1979 - Franchising Since: 1986 - No. of Units: Company Owned: 2 - Franchised: 1 - Franchise Fee: $15,000 - Royalty: 5% + 1% adv. - Total Inv: $110,000 - Financing: No.

GET-EM-N-GO
5324 Plainfield NE, Grand Rapids, MI, 49525. Contact: Glenn MacDonald, COO - Tel: (616) 364-0446, Fax: (616) 364-0499. Quick service, drive thru only, offering combo's, kid's meals, low prices, - professional training and continous support - leasing on equipment available. Established: 1986 - Franchising Since: 1999 - No. of Units: Company Owned: 5 - Franchise Fee: $15,000 - Royalty: 4% monthly - Total Inv: $375,000-$575,000 - Financing: No.

GIFF'S SUB SHOP
Giff's Sub Shop Franchise System Inc.
494 Kelly Street, Destin, FL, 32548. - Tel: (850) 863-9011. Submarine sandwiches, specializing in steak subs. Each sub is custom made. Established: 1977 - Franchising Since: 1985 - No. of Units: Company Owned: 1 - Franchised: 6 - Franchise Fee: $10,500 - Royalty: 4%, 2% adv. - Total Inv: $25,000-$30,000 depending on renovation required - Financing: None.

GIGGLEBEES
Galaxy Enterprises, Inc.
519 S. Minnesota Ave., Sioux Falls, SD, 57104. Contact: Fran. Dev. - Tel: (605) 331-4242, Fax: (605) 334-4514. Children's pizza restaurant with remote controlled robots delivering the food to the tables. There is also an adjacent game center with rides and redemption. Established: 1985 - Franchising Since: 1993 - No. of Units: Company Owned: 1 - Franchised: 1 - Franchise Fee: $25,000 - Royalty: 4.5% on gross sales - Total Inv: $273,900-$370,600 not incl. real estate - Financing: No.

GIOVANNI'S PIZZA
Giovanni's Pizza Inc.
715 Greenup Ave., Ashland, KY, 41101. Contact: Fran. Supervisor - Tel: (800) 955-9055, (606) 325-9743. Pickup, delivery and full service pizza restaurants serving pizza, pasta, salads and sandwiches. Locations: OH, KY, WV, VA, NC, TN. Established: 1964 - Franchising Since: 1969 - No. of Units: Franchised: 100 - Franchise Fee: $5,000 - Royalty: 3% - Total Inv: Equip. $30,000-$80,000 - Financing: No.

GODFATHER'S PIZZA
Godfather's Pizza, Inc.
9140 W. Dodge Rd., #300, Omaha, NE, 68114. Contact: Bruce C Cannon, Senior Vice President - Tel: (402) 391-1452, Fax: (402) 255-2685, E-Mail: franchise@godfathers.com, Web Site: www.godfathers.com. Pizza restaurant chain featuring dine-in, carry-out and delivery. Established: 1973 - Franchising Since: 1974 - No. of Units: Company Owned: 127 - Franchised: 482 - Franchise Fee: $7,500-$20,000 - Royalty: 3% service + 2% royalty - Total Inv: $72,000-$291,000 - Financing: No.

GOLD COAST DOGS
Gold Coast Dogs Franchise Systems, Inc.
401 N. Michigan Ave., Ste. 2600, Chicago, IL, 60611. - Tel: (312) 836-1896, (800) 922-5060, Fax: (312) 644-4423. Upscale fast food. Hot dogs, hamburgers, chicken, tuna, turkey, fresh cut fries. Established:

1985 - Franchising Since: 1994 - No. of Units: Company Owned: 4 - Franchised: 11 - Franchise Fee: $17,500 - Royalty: 4.5% - Total Inv: $125,000-$200,000 - Financing: No.

GOLDCUP ALEHOUSE BREWERY & RESTAURANT
1563 Solano Ave., #405, Berkeley, CA, 94707. Contact: Jerry Roberts - Tel: (415) 999-4301. Restaurant. Established: 2000 - Franchising Since: 2000 - No. of Units: Franchised: 1 - Franchise Fee: $50,000 - Financing: Yes.

GOLDEN CHICK
Golden Franchising Corporation
1801 Royal Ln Ste 607, Dallas, TX, 75229. Contact: Franchise Coordinator - Tel: (972) 831-0911, Fax: (972) 831-0401,Web Site: www.goldenchick.com. Fast food chicken retail. Established: 1967 - Franchising Since: 1972 - No. of Units: Company Owned: 5 - Franchised: 65 - Franchise Fee: $15,000 - Royalty: 4% - Financing: No.

GOLDEN CHICKEN FRANCHISES
3810 West National Ave., Milwaukee, WI, 53215. Contact: Marliss Bloom, Pres. - Tel: (414) 384-3160. Fast food specializing in chicken, pizza and seafood. Both carryout and home delivery. Established: 1959 - No. of Units: Company Owned: 6 - Franchised: 6 - Franchise Fee: Varies - Total Inv: $30,000 - Financing: No.

GOLDEN CORRAL STEAKS, BUFFET & BAKERY
Golden Corral Corp.
P.O. Box 29502, Raleigh, NC, 27626. - Tel: (919) 8781-9310, (800) 284-5673, Fax: (919) 881- 5252. Family style steak house featuring steaks, chicken and seafood entrees, golden choice buffet (salad bar and hot items) in-store bakery, dessert bar. Established: 1973 - Franchising Since: 1986 - No. of Units: Company Owned: 148 - Franchised: 298 - Franchise Fee: $40,000 - Royalty: 4% gross sales mtly. - Total Inv: $1,800,000-$2,300,000 - Financing: No.

GORIN'S HOMEMADE CAFE & GRILL
Gorin's Homemade, Inc.
4 Executive Park E., Ste. 315, Atlanta, GA, 30329. - Tel: 404) 248-9900, (800) 489-7277, Fax: (404) 248-0180, Web Site: www.gorins.com. Sandwich chain specializing in gourmet deli sandwiches and famous "Melt" sandwiches such as Almond Chicken melt, reuben, turkey and bacon and signature ice-cream. Established: 1981 - Franchising Since: 1983 - No. of Units: Company Owned: 1 - Franchised: 31 - Franchise Fee: $17,000 - Royalty: 5% + .5-2.5adv. - Total Inv: Approx. $190,000-$250,000 - Financing: No.

GRANDY'S RESTAURANT
Grandy's Inc.
997 Grandy's Lane, Lewisville, TX, 75077. Contact: Brian Gilbert, VP Development - Tel: (972) 317-8086, (877) 457-8145, Fax: (972) 317-8174, E-Mail: bgilbert@grandys.com, Web Site: www.grandys.com. Grandy's is a chain of more than 100 locations in 15 states. Grandy's is a "Home-Style" in a hurry concept that serves country style breakfasts, fried chicken, grilled chicken fresh baked biscuits, dinner rolls and homestyle vegetables. Established: 1973 - Franchising Since: 1977 - No. of Units: Company Owned: 8 - Franchised: 102 - Franchise Fee: $30,000 - Royalty: 5% - Total Inv: $1.1 million-$$1.3 million.

GRANNY FEELGOOD'S NATURAL FOOD
25 West Flagler Street, Miami, FL, 33130. Contact: Irving Fields, Pres. - Tel: (305) 377-9600, Fax: (305) 377-9675. Restaurant featuring natural food products. Established: 1969 - Franchising Since: 1984 - No. of Units: Company Owned: 3 - Franchised: 1 - Franchise Fee: $15,000 - Royalty: 5% gross - Total Inv: $150,000 - Financing: No. Not franchising at this time.

GREAT STEAK & POTATO COMPANY, THE
Nicar Franchising, Inc.
7730 E. greenway Dr., Ste. 104, Scottsdale, AZ, 85260. - Tel: (480) 443-0200, Fax: (480) 443-1972, Web Site: www.thegreatsteak.com. Upscale, quick service restaurant specializing in regional shopping malls and mixed-use projects. Specializing in America's premier cheeseteak, grilled to order sandwiches, fresh cut fries, baked potatoes and salads. Established: 1982 - Franchising Since: 1984 - No. of Units: Company Owned: 20 - Franchised: 220 - Franchise Fee: $20,000 - Royalty: 5% of net sales - Total Inv: $160,000-$250,000 - Financing: No.

GREAT WRAPS!

Gyro Wrap, Inc.
57 Executive Park South, Ste. 440, Atlanta, GA, 30329. Contact: Mark Kaplan, Chairman - Tel: (404) 248-9900, (888) GT-WRAPS, Fax: (404) 248-0180, E-Mail: franchise@gretwraps.net, Web Site: www.great wraps.net. The original and #1 wrap sandwich franchise, featuring a full line of pita wraps, tortilla wraps and smoothies. Exciting new food catagory, with lots of growth potential. Established: 1978 - Franchising Since: 1983 - No. of Units: Company Owned: 1 - Franchised: 42 - Franchise Fee: $17,500 - Royalty: 5%, 2% adv. - Total Inv: $175,000-$260,000 - Financing: No.

GREEK'S PIZZERIA / PIZZA FORUM

1600 University Ave., Muncie, IN, 47303. Contact; Chris Karamesines, Founder & Owner - Tel: (765) 284-5655, (800) 453-6786. Casual dining with the availability of a unique 'Patented' amusement concept. Specialties are Neapolitan and Gourmet style pizzas, pastas, wraps, sandwiches, fresh baked bread, salads, imported and domestic beers and wines. Established: 1969 - Franchising Since: 1978 - No. of Units: Company Owned: 34 - Franchised: 32 - Franchise Fee: $6,500 - Royalty: 7% wkly. gross sales - Total Inv: Limited dining $88,500, full dining $425,500 - Financing: Consultation offered.

GREEN MILL

Mill Restaurant, Inc.
4105 Lexington Ave N., Suite 240, Arden Hills, MN, 55126. - Tel: (651) 690-1946, Fax: (651) 766-8477. Casual dining restaurant and bar, featuring award-winning pizzas and a wide variety of entrees, sandwiches, salads and appetizers. 7500 square foot restaurant average over 2 million annually. Established: 1975 - Franchising: 1991 - No. of Units: Franchised: 17 - Franchise Fee: $30,000 - Royallty: 4%, 1-2% adv. - Total Inv: $709,500-$926,000 not including bldg/land - Financing: Assistance.

GREENLEAF'S GRILLE

Restaurant Systems International, Inc
1000 South Ave, Staten Island, NY, 10314. Contact: Franchise Development Department - Tel: (718) 494-8888, (800) 205-6050, Fax: (718) 494-8776, E-Mail: treats@restsys.com, Web Site: www.restsys.com. Greenleaf's Grille is "Fast Food Served Fast", featuring made-to-order grilled sandwiches, salads, wraps, and gourmet sandwiches served in an open kitchen setting. Established: 1976 - Franchising Since: 1998 - No. of Units: Company Owned: 1 - Franchised: 19 - Franchise Fee: $25,000 - Royalty: 5% - Total Inv: $190,200-$399,500 - Financing: No.

GRINDERS ABOVE & BEYOND RESTAURANTS

Grinders & Such, Inc.
805 E. Lincolnway, Minerva, OH, 44657. Contact: Dennis Hosterman, V.P. Operations - Tel: (330) 868-6100 ext. 863, Fax: (330) 868-3001, Web Site: www.grinders.net. Full service family restaurant featuring gourmet sandwiches, homemade soups and desserts in a casual dining theme designed by Morris Nathanson Group. Established: 1976 - Franchising Since: 1982 in Ohio only - No. of Units: Company Owned: 3 - Franchised: 6 - Franchise Fee: $30,000 - Royalty: 4% + 1.5% adv. - Total Inv: $700,000 - Financing: No

GROUCHO'S DELI

Groucho's Franchise Systems LLC
611 Harden St, Columbia, SC, 29205. - Tel: (803) 799-5708, Fax: (803) 799-2297, E-Mail: bmicah@aol.com, Web Site: www.grouchos.com. Groucho's Deli is famous for serving giant high quality subs and salads with Famous Formula 45 sauce since 1941. Our unique sub style and famous recipes for sandwich and salad dressings were thought up during our founder's childhood in a Philadelphia orphanage in the early 1900's. Established: 1941 - Franchising Since: 1999 - No. of Units: Company Owned: 1 - Franchised: 6 - Franchise Fee: $15,000 - Royalty: 4% - Total Inv: $60,000-$100,000.

GROUND ROUND RESTAURANTS

American Hospitallity Concepts, Inc
703 Granite St., P.O. 859078, Braintree, MA, 02184-9078. - Tel: (781) 380-3132, Fax: (781) 380-3233. Full service family restaurant, casual theme, variety of menu offerings. Alcoholic beverages available. Established: 1969 - Franchising Since: 1970 - No. of Units: Company Owned: 98 - Franchised: 45 - Franchise Fee: $40,000 - Royalty: 3.5%, 2.5% mktg. - Total Inv: Conversions $300,000-$600,000; Ground Up $1,200,000 - Financing: No. Not franchising at this time.

GUIDO'S PREMIUM PIZZA

1396 S. Lapeer, Oxford, MI, 48371. Contact: Shawn McGuire, Owner/Operator - Tel: (248) 969-2111, Fax: (248)969-2009, Web Site: www.guidopizza.com. Specializing in home delivered premium pizza, fresh salads, giant subs, zesty bread sticks, pasta, carry out and dine in. "Exceptional Quality and Value! Be a part of our growing franchise!". "Federally Registered Trademark". Established: 1993 - Franchising Since: 1995 - No. of Units: Company Owned: 1 - Franchised: 3 - Franchise Fee: $8,000 - Royalty: 0-6 month- none, 7-12 months 3%, 12+ 4% - Total Inv: $55,000-$93,000 - Financing: No.

GUMBY'S PIZZA INTERNATIONAL

7731 Newberry Rd., Suite A-3, Gainsville, FL, 32606. Contact: Joe O'Brien - Tel: (850) 980-6399. Quality Pizza, Pokey Stix and Pepperoni Rolls. Established: 1995 - No. of Units: Company Owned: 20 - Franchise Fee: $10,000 - Royalty: 3% - Total Inv: $82,000 - Financing: No.

HAMBURGER MARY'S®

Hanburger Mary's® Int'l, LLc
P.O. Box 456, Corona Del Mar, CA, 92625. Contact: Stan Sax, President - Tel: (949) 729-8000, (888) 834-MARY, Fax: (949) 675-9979, E-Mail: hamburgermary@cox.net, Web Site: www.hamburgermarys.net. Largest and only national restaurant franchise targeting the GLBT market and general public! 12 locations across USA with sit-down ad full-service bars. Established: 1972 - Franchising Since: 1998 - No. of Units: Company Owned: 1 - Franchised: 11 - Franchise Fee: $50,000 - Royalty: 5% - Total Inv: Varies - Financing: SBA or local banks.

HAPPI HOUSE

Happi House Franchising Corp.
2901 Moorepark Ave., #255, San Jose, CA, 95128. - Tel: (408) 244-0665, Fax: (408) 244-9262. Japanese fast food. Established: 1975 - Franchising Since: 1990 - No. of Units: Company Owned: 6 - Franchise Fee: $25,000 - Royalty: 4% 1st yr., 5% every other yr. - Total Inv: $192,000-$235,000 incl. franc. fee - Financing: No.

HAPPY JOE'S PIZZA & ICE CREAM PARLORS, INC.

2705 Happy Joe Drive, Bettendorf, IA, 52722. Contact: VP of Sales & Marketing - Tel: (563) 332-8811, Fax: (563) 332-5822, E-Mail: info@happyjoes.com, Web Site: www.happyjoes.com. Restuarant featuring pizza, pasta and ice-cream. Established: 1972 - Franchising Since: 1973 - No. of Units: Company Owned: 12 - Franchised: 57 - Franchise Fee: Full size $5,000-$20,000, Delco facility (Delivery and carry out with limited seating) $3,750-$15,000, COE facility (limited on-premises dining - no delivery service) $1,875-$7,500, Express franchise $1,000-$1,750 - Royalty: 4.5% - Total Inv: $24,000-$1,019,000 - Financing: Possible.

HARD TIMES CAFE

American Chili Management Company
515 King Street, Suite 440, Alexandria, VA, 22314. Contact: Dan Rowe, CEO - Tel: (703) 683-8545, (888) 482-4454, Fax: (703) 683-7966. A western-themed, 1930's depression-era chili parlour specializing in Texas, Cincinnati and vegetarian chili, fresh appitizers, sandwiches and salads. Also serves beer and wine. Established: 1980 - Franchising Since: 1987 - No. of Units: Company Owned: 3 - Franchised : 5 - Franchise Fee: $30,000 - Royalty: 5% .

HARDEE'S FOOD SYSTEMS, INC.

3916 State Street, Garden Suite, Santa Barbara, CA, 93105. Contact: Senior VP of Franchsing - Tel: (805) 898-4204, Fax: (805) 898-4206. Hardee's is America's third largest fast food hamburger chain, with about 4000 restaurants. Established: 1960 - Franchising Since: 1961 - No. of Units: Company Owned: 892 - Franchised: 2359 - Franchise Fee: $15,000 - Royalty: 3.5% yrs 1-5, 4% yrs 6-20 - Total Inv: $699,000-$1,740,000 - Financing: Hardee's will assist in securing financing.

HARTZ CHICKEN, INC

14451 Cornerstone Village Dr., Ste. 250, Houston, TX, 77014. Contact: Rex Washburn, Pres./CEO - Tel: (281) 583-0020, Fax: (281) 580-3752. Retail fast food chicken restaurant. Established: 1972 - Franchising Since: 1975 - No. of Units: Company Owned: 1 - Franchised: 47 - Royalty: 4% + 4% adv. fee - Approx. Inv: $170,000-$700,000.

HEALTHY BITES GRILL
Health Express USA

1761 W. Hillsboro Blvd, Suite 203, Deerfield Beach, FL, 33442. Contact: Raymond Nevin - Tel: (954) 570-5900, (800) 575-4144, Fax: (954) 570-5917, Web Site: www.hexas.com. Healthy fast casual restaurant featuring "The food you crave-without the guilt". Lean burgers + air baked fries, salads, sandwiches + wraps. Drive-thru, dine-in + carry out. Free standing, in-line, conversions. Established: 2001 - Franchising Since: 2003 - No. of Units: Company Owned: 1 - Franchised: 2 - Franchise Fee: $30,000 - Royalty: 4% - Total Inv: $228,000-$600,000 - Financing: No.

HOOTERS OF AMERICA, INC.

1815 The Exchange, Atlanta, GA, 30339. Contact: VP Fran. Operations - Tel: (770) 951-2040, Fax: (770) 980-2452. Casual, full-service dining. Limited menu featuring chicken wings, seafood, hamburgers and sandwiches, beer and wine. Established: 1983 - Franchising Since: 1988 - No. of Units: Company Owned: 60 approx. - Franchised: 140 approx. - Franchise Fee: $75,000 - Royalty: 6% gross sales, 1% nat'l adv. - Total Inv: $500,000 - Financing: No.

HOT DOG CHARLIE ENTERPRISES

626 2nd Ave., Troy, NY, 12182. Contact: Chuck Fentekes, Pres. - Tel: (518) 235-2485, E-Mail: hotdog1922@aol.com. Specialize in mini hot dogs, fish fries on hot dog roll and Italian sausage torpedo. Established: 1922 - Franchising Since: 1987 - No. of Units: Company Owned: 4 - Franchised: 1 - Franchise Fee: $8,000 - Royalty: 5% - Total Inv: $75,000-$125,000 - Financing: No.

HOT DOG ON A STICK, FRANCHISE, INC.

5601 Palmer Way, Carlsbad, CA, 92008-7242. - Tel: (760) 930-0456, (800) 321-8400, Fax: (760) 930-0420, Web Site: www.hotdogona stick.com. Concession, food courts urban malls, of hot dogs (corn dogs) and lemonade. Established: 1946 - Franchising Since: 1997 - No. of Units: Company Owned: 100 - Franchised: 4 - Franchise Fee: $30,000 - Royalty: 2% net sales, 1st three years, 4% net sales after that - Total Inv: Franchise fee plus construction costs of $186,500-$281,000 - Financing: No.

HOT STOP
Food Cart Systems, Inc

533 Cleveland Street, Clearwater, FL, 33755. Contact: Paul F. Gibson, President - Tel: (727) 449-8700 (888) 718-7600 Fax: (727) 449-1881 E-Mail: franchising@foodcartsystems.com, Web Site: www.foodcart systems.com. Established: 1997 - Franchising Since: 1997 - No. of Units: Company Owned: 2 - Franchised: 3 - Franchise Fee: $15,000 - Royalty: Fixed $975.00/mo. or 5% of gross sales $1 - $100,000, 7% of gross sales $100,001-$200,000, 5% of gross sales $200,001 + - Financing: Yes.

HOT STUFF PIZZA
Orion Food Systems

2930 W Maple, Sioux Falls, SD, 57101. Contact: Director of Development - Tel: (800) 648-6227, (605) 336-6961, Fax: (605) 336-0141, Web Site: www.orionfoodsys.com. Quick service format, developing in convenience stores and foodcourts. Established: 1984 - Franchising Since: 1985 - No. of Units: Company Owned: 14 - Franchised: 1100 - Franchise Fee: $4,950 - Total Inv: $25,000 + - Financing: Third party.

HOT'N NOW HAMBURGERS

4205 Charlar #3, Holt, MI, 48842. Contact: Dir. Franchise Sales - Tel: (517) 694-4240, Fax: (517) 694-6370. Fast Food drive-thru only, restaurant chain. Established: 1983 - Franchising Since: 1984 - No. of Units: Company Owned: 32 - Franchised: 30 - Franchise Fee: $22,000 - Royalty: 4% royalty, .5% advertising - Total Inv: $400,000-1MM - Financing: No.

HOULIHAN'S RESTAURANTS
Houlihan's Restaurant Group

P.O. Box 16000, Kansas City, MO, 64112. - Tel: (816) 756-2200, Fax: (816) 751-8285. Houlihan's are full service, casual dining restaurants specializing in the sale of high quality, moderately priced food and alcohol in an upscale environment. Established: 1972 - Franchising Since: 1994 - No. of Units: Company Owned: 61 - Franchised: 52 - Franchise Fee: $35,000 development fee, $10,000 per unit - Royalty: 4% gross, .5% marketing fund - Total Inv: $1,800,000-$2,200,000 - Financing: Yes, third party vendors.

HOVAN GOURMET SANDWICH SHOPPE
Hovan Franchising Corp.

P.O. Box 80505, Atlanta, GA, 30366-0505. Contact: Director of Franchising - Tel: (770) 393-2675, (770) 452-7770, Fax: (770) 986-8956. A unique sandwich shop located in enclosed malls featuring a rolled sandwich made with Lavash Bread (American style). We also sell soups, salads, condiments and drinks. No cooking involved. Established: 1983 - Franchising Since: 1994 - No. of Units: Company Owned: 6 - Franchised: 5 - Franchise Fee: $20,000 - Royalty: 5% of gross sales - Total Inv: $90,000-$125,000 - Financing: No.

HOWARD JOHNSON'S RESTAURANTS
Franchise Associates Inc.

541 Main St., Ste. 320, So. Weymouth, MA, 02190-1845. Contact: Mr G. Catter, CEO - Tel: (781) 337-7940, Fax: (781) 337-1777. National restaurants with expanded menus ranging from snack items to full course dinners popularly priced. Take-out service is also available. Most locations serve alcoholic beverages and many have salad bars. Restaurants are usually open 16 hours a day. Established: 1986 - Franchising Since: 1986 - No. of Units: Company Owned: 9 - Franchised: 45 - Franchise Fee: $10,000 - Royalty: 2% gross food and beverage.

HUBB'S
Pubb's Worldwide, Inc.

1231 Florida Ave S, Rockledge, FL, 32955-2423. Contact: David Ungar, Consultant - Tel: (321) 639-5080, Fax: (321) 639-8050, E-Mail: davehubbs@aol.com, Web Site: www.hubbspub.com. Restaurant ("The Home of Colossal Sandwiches") specializing in imported beers from around the world. Each unit has 39 taps for draft beer and over 200 bottled brands. "Hubbs...where you always meet a friend". Established: 1982 - Franchising Since: 1992 - No. of Units: Franchised: 1 (1 under const.) - Franchise Fee: $25,000 - Royalty: 2% first year, 3% second year, 4% thereafter - Total Inv: $250,000-$450,000 - Financing: Yes.

HUDDLE HOUSE
Huddle House, Inc.

2969 East Ponce de Leon Avenue, Decatur, GA, 30030. Contact: Franchise Development Administrator - Tel: (404) 377-5700, (800) 868-5700, Fax: (404) 377-0497, E-Mail: franchise@huddlehouse.com, Web Site: www.huddlehouse.com. Everyone knows a house is a great investment! Huddle House is a 24 hr. full service restaurant serving breakfast, lunch & dinner anytime. Established: 1964 - Franchising Since: 1966 - No. of Units: Company Owned: 25 - Franchised: 380+ - Franchise Fee: $20,000 - Royalty: 4% 1% Adv - Total Inv: $300,000-$750,000 - Financing: No.

HUDSON'S GRILL
Hudson's Grill of America, Inc.

16970 Dallas Pkwy., Ste. 402, Dallas, TX, 75248-1928. Contact: David Osborn, President - Tel: (972) 931-9237, Fax: (972) 931-1326. Casual dining, serving lunch and dinner full-service restaurants and bar. Theme restaurant with a late 50's and early 60's rock'n'roll motif with authentic Hudson's automobile as highlight. Established: 1985 - Franchising Since: 1988 - No. of Units: Company Owned: 2 - Franchised: 16 - Franchise Fee: $25,000 - Royalty: 4% sales, 1% adv. - Total Inv: $250,000 net worth, $125,000 liquid. - Financing: No.

HUHOT MONGOLIAN GRILL *

777 Vintage Rd, Missoula, MT, 59803. - Tel: (406) 251-4303, Fax: (406) 251-4575, Web Site: www.huhot.com. Fast casual Asian food. Bright decor and a unique architectural and artistic experience bring families, couples and business clientele back for more. Established: 1999 - Franchising Since: 2001 - No. of Units: Company Owned: 1 - Franchised: 4 - Franchise Fee: $30,000 - Royalty: 5% - Total Inv: $327,000-$622,000.

HUNGRY HOWIE'S PIZZA & SUBS

30300 Stephenson Hwy., Ste. 200, Madison Heights, MI, 48071. Contact: Bob Cuffaro - Tel: (248) 414-3300, Fax: (248) 414-3301, E-Mail: franinfo@hungryhowies.com, Web Site: www.hungryhowies.com. Flavored crust pizza, carry out, delivery, menu offers eight varieties of the original crust pizza, salads and subs. Established: 1973 - Franchising Since: 1982 - No. of Units: Franchised: 425 - Franchise Fee: $15,000 - Royalty: 5% - Total Inv: $85,000-$125,000 - Financing: Franchisee secures own.

ICEBERG DRIVE INN
Iceberg Drive Inn, Inc

894 East 3900 South, Salt Lake City, UT, 84107. Contact: Jay Woolley, VP Franchise Development - Tel: (801) 747-3423, (800) 897-5681, Fax: (801) 747-3422, E-Mail: franchise@icebergdriveinn.com, Web Site: www.icebergdriveinn.com. Iceberg Drive Inn, Inc is the franchisor and operator of the Iceberg Drive Inn quick serve restaurants that specialize in quality hand made ice treats, old-fashioned hamburgers, french fries amd hand breaded onion rings. Established: 1960 - Franchising Since: 2000 - No. of Units: Franchised: 11 - Franchise Fee: $25,000 - Royalty: 6%, ad fee 2% - Total Inv: $132,000-$556,000 - Financing: Have preferred sources.

INDIGO JOE'S SPORTS PUB & RESTAURANT *

132 N. El Camino Real, Ste. 384, Encinitas, CA, 92024. Contact:Troy Taylor - Tel: (888) 303-5637, Fax: (760) 633-3563. Neighborhood sports bar and restaurant. Established: 1994 - Franchising Since: 2003 - No. of Units: Company Owned: 1 - Franchised: 1 - Franchise Fee: $25,000.

INTERNATIONAL HOUSE OF PANCAKES RESTAURANTS
IHOP, Inc.

450 N Brand Blvd #7th Flr, Glendale, CA 91203-2346. Contact: Anna Ulvan, V.P. Fran. - Tel: (818) 240-6055, Fax: (818) 637-4730. Full service family restaurants featuring breakfast, lunch and dinner. Established: 1958 - Franchising Since: 1960 - No. of Units: Company Owned: 61 - Franchised: 429 - Franchise Fee: $50,000-$600,000 - Royalty: 4.5% - Total Inv: Varies - Financing: No.

ITALIAN PLACE, THE
Gledhill Enterprises

1086 South State Street, Orem, UT, 84097. Contact: Robert Gledhill, Pres. - Tel: (801) 224-6317. Sandwiches, pizzas. Established: 1971 - No. of Units: Company Owned: 1 - Franchised: 3 - Franchise Fee: $25,000-$40,000 - Total Inv: $80,000-$120,000 per unit.

ITALO'S PIZZA SHOP, INC.

3560 Middlebranch Rd., N.E., Canton, OH, 44705. - Tel: (330) 455-6428. Carry-out, dine in pizza, pasta, subs and chicken, delivery optional. Established: 1966 - Franchising Since: 1975 - No. of Units: Company Owned: 3 - Franchised: 11 - Franchise Fee: $12,000 - Royalty: 5% gross - Total Inv: $75,000-$150,000 - Financing: None.

IZZY'S PIZZA RESTAURANTS
Covalt Enterprises, Inc.

P.O. Box 1689, Albany, OR, 97321. Contact: Franchise Dept. - Tel: (541) 926-8693, Fax: (541) 928-8127. Restaurants serving pizza, chicken, sandwiches, hot buffet and salad bar. Established: 1970 - Franchising Since: 1983 - No. of Units: Company Owned: 12 - Franchised 12 - Franchise Fee: $35,000 - Royalty: 4% - Total Inv: $100,000+ - Financing: No.

JAKE'S OVER THE TOP
The Taco Maker, Inc

4605 Harrison Blvd, Centennial Building 3rd Floor, Ogden, UT, 84403. Contact: Bob Strong, Franchise Specialist - Tel: (801) 476-9780, (800) 207-5804, Fax: (801) 476-9788, E-Mail: franchise@tacomaker.com, Web Site: www.tacomaker.com. Jake's Over The Top is a '50's-style concept serving over-the-top shakes, hamburgers, and fries. Established: 1978 - No. of Units: Company Owned: 3 - Franchised: 150 - Franchise Fee: $19,000-$29,000 - Royalty: 5% - Total Inv: $150,000-$300,000 - Financing: Third party.

JAKE'S PIZZA
Jake's Pizza Enterprises

27W101 Geneva Rd, Winfield, IL, 60190. - Tel: (630) 752-111, Fax: (630) 752-0606. Specialize in the sale of premium thin crust, pan and stuffed pizza. Eat in, pick up and delivery service is provided. Established: 1961- Franchising Since: 1965 - No. of Units: Franchised: 27 - Franchise Fee: $15,000 - Royalty: 5% - Total Inv: $118,000 - Financing: No.

JASON'S DELI
Deli Management, Inc

2400 Broadway, Beaumont, TX, 77702. Contact: Michael Neal, Director of Franchising - Tel: (409) 838-1976, Fax: (409) 838-1906, E-Mail: lunch@jasonsdeli.com, Web Site: www.jasonsdeli.com. Deli restaurant serving sandwiches, fresh salads and potatoes. Also an extensive selection of party trays and business catering ideas. Established: 1976 - Franchising Since: 1988 - No. of Units: Company Owned: 49 - Franchised: 23 - Total Inv: $575,000-$650,000.

JAVA CENTRALE
Paradise Holdings Inc.

1610 Arden Wy #145, Sacramento, CA, 95815. - Tel: (916) 568-2310. Nationwide franchisor of European-style gourmet coffee cafés and kiosks. Fresh brewed and specialty coffee beverages, hot and iced together with deli-style sandwiches, salads and soups, pastries and desserts. Established: 1992 - Franchising Since: 1992 - No. of Units: Company Owned: 5 - Franchised: 33 - Franchise Fee: $35,000 - Royalty: 6% - Total Inv: $175,000-$350,000 - Financing: Third party assistance.

JERRY'S SUBS AND PIZZA
Jerry's Systems, Inc.

15942 Shady Grove Rd., Gaithersburg, MD, 20877. Contact: Dir. Fran. Dev. - Tel: (301) 921-8777, Fax: (301) 948-3508. This mid-Atlantic based franchise, famous for overstuffed sub sandwiches and New York-style pizza, offers self service dining in upscale, high volume, high traffic locations. Established: 1954 - Franchising Since: 1981 - No. of Units: Company Owned: 3 - Franchised: 100 - Franchise Fee: $25,000 - Royalty: 5% + 3% adv. - Total Inv: $150,000-$225,000 - Financing: Qualifies for SBA financing.

JERSEY MIKE'S SUBMARINES
Jersey Mike's Franchise Systems Inc.

2251 Landmark Pl., Manasquan, NJ, 08736. - Tel: (800) 321-7676, Fax: (732) 223-0777, E-Mail: info@jerseymikes.com, Web Site: www.jerseymikes.com. Submarine, sandwich franchise featuring subs made to order in the authentic, northeast deli-style fashion. Established: 1956 - Franchising Since: 1986- No. of Units: Company Owned: 5 - Franchised: 235 - Franchise Fee: $18,500 - Royalty: 5% -Total Inv: $170,000-$221,000 - Financing: Outside sources.

JETS PIZZA

37177 Mound Rd., Sterling Hts., MI, 48310. Contact: Eugene Jetts Jr., President - Tel: (810) 268-5870. Carry-out pizzeria and delivery pizza, subs, salads. Established: 1978 - Franchising Since: 1993 - No. of Units: Company Owned: 7 - Franchised: 40- Franchise Fee: $15,000 - Royalty: 8% first year, 9% second year, 10% 3rd year of food cost - Total Inv: $170,000 - Financing: No.

JIMBOY'S TACOS

1485 Response Rd., #110, Sacramento, CA, 95815. Contact: Don D'Rapisura, V.P. - Tel: (916) 564-8226, (800) JIMBOYS, (800) 546-2697. Mexican food. Established: 1954 - Franchising Since: 1965 - No. of Units: 25 - Franchise Fee: $18,000 - Royalty: 3.5%+3% adv. - Total Inv: $150,000-$185,000 - Financing: No.

JIMMY JOHN'S GOURMET SANDWICH SHOPS

600 Tollgate Road, Ste. B, Elgin, IL, 60123. - Tel: (847) 888-7206, (800) 546-6904, Fax: (847) 888-7070, Web Site: www.wwz.JimmyJohn's.com. Gourmet sandwich shops specializing in subs and clubs. Established: 1983 - Franchising Since: 1993 - No. of Units: Company Owned: 8 - Franchised: 65 - Franchise Fee: $25,000 - Royalty: 6%+2% adv. - Total Inv: $178,000.

JIMMY'S PIZZA
Jimmy's Pizza Inc.
2015 1st Street SW., Ste. 119, Willmar, MN, 56201. Contact: Dir. of Franchising - Tel: (320) 235-7844, Fax: (320) 235-7837. Pizza franchise business. Eat in, pick up, delivery. Established; 1986 - Franchising Since: 1995 - No. of Units: Company Owned: 2 - Franchised: 31 - Franchise Fee: $15,000 - Royalty: 2.5%, .5% production fee - Total Inv: $50,000-$120,000 - Financing:Yes.

JODY MARONI'S SAUSAGE KINGDOM
5441 West 104th Street, Los Angeles, CA, 90045. Contact: Franchise Department - Tel: (310) 348-1500, (800) 628-8364, Fax: (310) 348-1510, E-Mail: rich@jodymaroni.com, Web Site: www.jodymaroni.com. Fast food concept made famous on Venice Beach serving family recipe grilled sausage sandwiches, all-beef hot dogs, hand-cut fries and fresh squeezed lemonade. Established: 1979 - Franchising Since: 1998 - No. of Units: Company Owned: 2 - Franchised: 23 - Total Inv: $105,000-$500,000.

JOHNNY'S "NEW YORK STYLE" PIZZA
Johnny's Pizza Franchise Systems, Inc.
834 Virginia Ave., Hapeville, GA, 30354. Contact: Scott Allen, Fran. Dev. - Tel: (404) 766-3727, Fax: (404)766-0260. Neighborhood pizzeria serving pizza, subs, etc. - Full training and support provided. Established: 1978 Fanchising Since: 1995 - No. of Units: company Owned: 3 - Franchised: 8 - Franchise Fee: $18,000 - Total Inv: $50,000-$125,000 - Financing: No.

JON SMITH SUBS
Jon Smith Enterprises, Inc.
6021 Duckweed Rd., Lake Worth, FL, 33467-5811. - Tel: (561) 791-9028. A high-quality alternative to the sub shop concept. Prepares all products in own kitchens and specializes in marinated sirloin steak subs. Committed to serving the absolutely highest quality subs. Established: 1988 - Franchising Since: 1992 - No. of Units: Company Owned: 7 - Franchised: 4 - Franchise Fee: $12,000 - Royalty - 6%, 3% reg. adv., 1% local adv. - Total Inv: $89,000-$128,000 - Financing: Available for purchase of company stores only.

JRECK SUBS, INC.
P.O. Box 6, Watertown, NY, 13601. Contact: Peter Whitmore, Pres/ Fran. Dir. - Tel: (315) 782-0760. Fast food establishment serving submarine sandwiches and beverages. Established: 1969 - Franchising Since: 1974 - No. of Units: Franchised: 54 - Franchise Fee: $10,000 - Royalty: 6% - Total Inv: $49,800-$254,000 - Financing: No.

JUICE CABANA
222 N. Spepulveda Blvd., Ste. 2000, El Segundo, CA, 90245. Contact: Franchise Sales - Tel: (310) 364-5245, (877) JUICE99, Fax: (570) 824-5273, E-Mail: info@juicecabana.com, Web Site: www.juicecabana.com. Retail juice and smoothie bars offering healthy alternative to fast food, fresh fruits, juices, yogurts, and CaBana cultivators are blended to make various smoothies. Bagels and trail mixes are also offered. Established: 1996 - Franchising Since: 1999 - No. of Units: Company Owned: 7 - Franchise Fee: $22,000 for individual brands or $30,000 for co-brands - Royalty: 5% weekly gross sales or 8% for co-brands - Total Inv: $97,400-$151,000, $170,000-$205,000 co-brands - Financing: Third Party.

JUICE KITCHEN
1050 17th St., Ste B195, Denver, CO, 80265. - Tel: (303) 573-7060, Fax: (303) 573-7055. Fruit smoothies, juices, snacks and more. Established: 1999 - Franchising Since: 2000 - No. of Units: Company Owned: 16 - Franchise Fee: $20,000 - Total Inv: $138,600-$216,000.

JUICE STOP FRANCHISING
1050 17th St #B-195, Denver, CO, 80265-1050. - Tel: (303) 573-7060, Fax: (303) 768-0404, Web Site: www.juicestop.com. Fresh fruit smoothies and healthy snacks. Established: 1993 - Franchising Since: 1996 - No. of Units: Company Owned: 18 - Franchised: 90 - Franchise Fee: $25,000 - Royalty: 5%, 1% national ad fund - Total Inv: $150,000-$200,000 - Financing: Assistance available for qualified candidates.

JUICY LUCY'S DRIVE-THRU
FMI Franchise Corp
5029 NW 106th Way, Coral Springs, FL, 33076-2713. Contact: Anthony Foster, President of Operations - Tel: (941) 939-4686. Double drive-thru restaurant with emphasis on quality products. Fresh pattied hamburgers, hand cut chicken breasts, pork loins, and BBQ pork prepared from scratch. Breakfast menu consists of various fresh egg sandwiches made to order. Established: 1988 - Franchising Since: 1990 - No. of Units: Company Owned: 6 - Franchised: 7 - Franchise Fee: $25,000 - Royalty: 5% wkly gross - Total Inv: $325,000-$375,000 plus land - Financing: No. NOT FRANCHISING AT THIS TIME.

K-BOB'S STEAKHOUSE
K-Bob's Capital Resource Group, Ltd.
3700 Rio Grande Blvd NW Ste 6, Albuquerque, NM, 87107-2876. Contact: Franchise Dept. - Tel: (505) 341-2504. Steakhouse chain catering to small communities with an emphasis on affordable, yet quality food - "A good steak at an honest price®". Established: 1966 - Franchising Since: 1975 - No. of Units: Company Owned: 8 - Franchised: 27 - Franchise Fee: $25,000 - Royalty: 3% - Total Inv: Land/bldg. - $750,000, equip. $200,000 - Financing: No.

KATY'S PLACE
Katy's Place Restaurants Corporation
915 Hilby Ave., Ste. 26, Seaside, CA, 93955. - Tel: (831) 899-1006, Fax: (831) 899-5907. Restaurant serving breakfast and lunch. Established: 1989 - Franchising Since: 2001 - No. of Units: Company Owned: 1 - Franchise Fee: $50,000.

KENNY ROGERS ROASTERS
Roasters Corp.
1400 Old Country Rd Suite 400, Westbury, NY, 11590. - Tel: (516) 338-8500, Fax: (516) 338-7220. Restaurant. Established: 1991 - Franchising Since: 1991 - No. of Units: Company Owned: 29 - Franchised: 203 - Franchise Fee: $29,500 - Royalty: 4.5% - Total Inv: $347,500 for building, equipment and sign costs; $8,000 opening inven., $10,000 security deposit, $20,000 misc. expenses, $5,000 grand opening, plus fran. fee, legal or accounting costs.

KETTLE RESTAURANTS, INC.
P.O BOX 495909, Garland, TX, 75049-5909. Contact: Dir. of Fran. - Tel: (800) 929-2391. Full menu restaurant, open 24 hours daily. Established: 1968 - Franchising Since: 1973 - No. of Units: Company Owned: 93 - Franchised: 93 - Royalty: 5% - Total Inv: $20,000 - Total Inv: $84,000 - Financing: No.

KFC
KFC Corporation
1441 Gardiner Lane, Louisville, KY, 40213. - Tel: (416) 664-5202. Quick service chicken restaurants. Established: 1952 - Franchising Since: 1952 - No. of Units: Company Owned: 3,192 - Franchised: 6,239, 50 states and 76 countries - Franchise Fee: $25,000 - Royalty: 4% - Total Inv: $950,000-$1,400,000.

KOJO OF JAPAN
Kojo Inc.
4204 Meridian St, Suite 103, Bellingham, WA, 98226. Contact: Shigeru Takano, Owner - Tel: (360)671-4290, Fax: (360)671-4538. Japanese Teppan-Yaki fast food mainly in mall food court. Established: 1979 - No. of Units: Company Owned: 10.

KRIEGER'S SPORTS BAR & GRILL
Krieger's Franchising Inc.
744-F Spirit of St. Louis Blvd, Chesterfield, MO, 63005. Contact: Al Genovese - Tel: (636) 530-1395, Fax: (636) 530-6890, E-Mail: algeno@sbcglobal.net, Web Site: www.kriegerspub.com. Voted #1 sports bar in St. Louis, #1 place to take your kids and #1 bar and grill, from corner to corner, every Krieger's is covered with sport pictures, articles and unique trinkets. Designed as an Irish/Sports bar. Also voted Best Burgers, Bets Wings, Best Fries, best casual lunch and Best Pub. Established: 1991 - Franchising Since: 2002 - No. of Units: Company Owned: 6 - Franchised: 16 - Franchise Fee: $30,000 - Royalty: 5% - Total Inv: $400,000-$2,000,000 - Financing: No.

KRYSTAL
Krystal Company, The
One Union Square, Chattanooga, TN, 37402. Contact: Franchise Department - Tel: (800) 458-5912, Fax: (423) 757-1588, E-Mail: jprice@krystalco.com, Web Site: www.krystal.com. The Krystal Company is a unique brand with over 71 years of success in the quick serve industry. We occupy a true niche in the burger business. We will continue our aggressive growth throughout the Southeast through franchising, and the use of exclusive multi unit development agreements. We require at least a three-unit development agreement with a minimum cash liquidity of $600,000 and a net worth of 1.2 million. Krystal-fresh, hot, small and square. Established: 1932 - Franchising Since: 1990 - No. of Units: Company Owned: 246 - Franchised: 185 - Franchise Fee: $32,500 - Royalty: 4.5% - Total Inv: $425,000-$575,000 - Financing: Assistance with approved lenders.

LA CASITA RESTAURANTS
2006 Madison, Memphis, TN, 38104. - Tel: (901) 726-1873. Full service Mexican restaurant. No. of Units: Company Owned: 2. NOT FRANCHISING AT THIS TIME.

LA PIZZA LOCA
Crazy Pizza Inc.
7920 Orangethorpe Ave., Buena Park, CA, 90620. Contact: Fran. Dev. - Tel: (714) 670-0934, Fax: (714) 670-7849. Hispanic pizza delivery company. Unique Latin flavored pizzas. Fast, free delivery. Targeted to the rapidly growing Hispanic market in southwestern U.S. Established: 1986 - Franchising Since: 1991 - No. of Units: Company Owned: 32 - Franchised: 20 - Franchise Fee: $10,000 - Royalty: 5% of net total sales - Total Inv: $125,000 - Financing: None.

LA SALSA FRESH MEXICAN GRILL
La Salsa Holding Co.
3916 State Street, #200, Santa Barbara, CA, 93105. Contact: V.P. Fran. Dev. - Tel: (800) 527-2572, Fax: (805) 563-3844. Fresh Mexican grill QSR's serving tacos al carbon, gourmet burritos and fresh salsas. Established: 1979 - Franchising Since: 1989 - No. of Units: Company Owned: 25 - Franchised: 25 - Franchise Fee: $29,500 per unit - Royalty: 5%, 1% nat'l. mktg. fund - Total Inv: Minimum 3 units @ $29,500 + $200,000 build-out per unit - Financing: No.

LA SENORITA MEXICAN RESTAURANTS
La Senorita Franchise
1026 Hannah, Traverse City, MI, 49686. Contact: Kenneth Kleinrichert, Owner - Tel: (231) 947-8889, Fax: (231) 947-8137. Mexican food and beverages. Family-style casual dining. Established: 1980 - Franchising Since: 1992 - No. of Units: Company Owned: 5 - Franchised: 4 - Franchise Fee: $20,000 - Royalty: 5%, 3% adv. - Total Inv: Varies $300,000-$1,500,000.

LAMPPOST PIZZA
Lamppost Franchise Corporation
3002 Dow Ave.,#320, Tustin, CA, 92780. - Tel: (714) 731-6171, Fax: (714) 731-0951. Family restaurant with emphasis on sports include satellite antenna and wide screen t.v.'s. Established: 1976 - Franchising Since: 1981 - No. of Units: Company Owned: 5 - Franchised: 47 - Franchise Fee: $20,000 - Royalty: 4%, 1.5% adv. - Total Inv: $275,000 - fran. fee, equip., fixtures, leasehold improv. - Financing: No.

LARASA'S, INC.
233 Boudinot St., Cincinnati, OH, 45238. Contact: Franchise Director - Tel: (513) 347-5660, Fax: (513) 347-4660. Full service Italian style family restaurant. Full training and support provided. Established: 1954 - Franchising Since: 1955 - No. of Units: Franchised: 40 - Total Inv: $50,000 - Financing: Yes.

LARRY'S GIANT SUBS
8616 Baymeadows Rd., Jacksonville, FL, 32256. Contact: Larry Raikes, President - Tel: (904) 739-9069, (800) 358-6870, Fax: (904) 739-1218, Web Site: www.bigone@larryssubs.com. Submarine sandwich franchise. Established: 1982 - Franchising Since: 1986 - No. of Units: Company Owned: 2 - Franchised: 70 - Franchise Fee: $17,000 - Royalty: 6%, 2% adv. - Total Inv: $125,000.

LEDO PIZZA
Ledo Pizza Systems, Inc.
2568 A Riva Rd Ste 202, Annapolis, MD, 21401. Contact: Dir. of Marketing & System Dev - Tel: (410)721-6887, Fax: (410) 266-6888, Web Site: www.ledopizza. Franchise pizza and sub shops in MO, DC, VA and PA. Established: 1955 - Franchising Since: 1989 - No. of Units: Franchised: 51 - Franchise Fee: $20,000 - Royalty: 5%, 2% adv. fund - Total Inv: $119,000-$419,000 - Financing: No.

LENNY AND VINNYS' NEW YORK PIZZERIA AND BAKERY
3102 W Waters Ave #201, Tampa, FL, 33614-2875. Contact: Doug Anderson, VP Franchising - Tel: (813) 882-4336, (888) YOV-INNY, Fax: (813) 885-1486. Full service dine in - take-out and delivery. Full training and support provided. Established: 1991 - Franchising since: 1996 - No. of Units: Company Owned: 13 - Franchised: 3 - Franchise Fee: $17,500 - Total Inv: $185,000-$287,500 - Financing: Yes.

LI'KE LI'KE HAWAIIAN BBQ GRILL
Li'ke Li'ke Hawaiian BBQ Grill, Inc.
1313 Post Avenue, Torrance, CA, 90501. Contact: Bobby Chang, Franchise Development & Operations - Tel: (310) 781-3023, Fax: (310) 781-1914, E-Mail: bobbyc@likelikebbq.com, Web Site: www.likelike bbq.com. We deliver great food, great service, and great value. All served up Hawaiian style in a contemporary island setting. Established: 2002 - Franchising Since: 2002 - No. of Units: Company Owned: 2 - Franchise Fee: $25,000 - Royalty: 4% - Total Inv: $300,000-$350,000.

LINDA'S ROTISSERIE & KITCHEN
Linda's Diversified Holdings, Inc.
11 Commerce Dr., Crawford, NJ, 07016. Contact: Peter Weissbrod - Tel: (908) 272-4006. Quick service restaurant and take-out. Established: 1991 - Franchising Since: 1994 - No. of Units: Company Owned: 2 - Franchised: 6 - Franchise Fee: $25,000 - Total Inv: $250,000-$100,00 cash - Financing: No.

LINDY-GERTIE'S
8437 Park Ave., Burr Ridge, IL, 60527. Contact: Joseph Yesutis, President - Tel: (630) 323-8003, Fax: (630) 323-5449, Web Site: www.lindyschili.com. Lindy-Gertie restaurants sell Lindy's chili, the oldest chili parlor in Chicago. Established: 1986 - Franchising Since: 1987 - No. of Units: Franchised: 9 - Franchise Fee: $9,500 - Royalty: 6%.

LITTLE CAESARS' PIZZA
2211 Woodward Ave., Detroit, MI, 48201. - Tel: (313) 983-6000 , Fax: (313) 983-6193, Web Site: www.littlecaesars.com. Carryout and delivery of pizza. Established: 1959 - Franchising Since: 1962 - No. of Units: Franchised: N/A - Franchise Fee: $20,000 - Royalty: 5% - Total Inv: $120,000-$150,000- Financing: Yes.

LITTLE KING DELI & SUBS
Little King, Inc.
11811 "I" Street, Omaha, NE, 68137. Contact: Bob Wertheim - Tel: (402) 330-8019, (800) 788-9478, Fax: (402) 330-3221, Web Site: www.littleking.us. We serve fresh sliced herb & deli style sandwiches along with soup, salad & fresh baked desserts. They are all made with fresh baked breads. Established: 1968 - Franchising Since: 1978 - No. of Units: Franchised: 25 - Franchise Fee: $18,000.00 - Royalty: 6% - Total Inv: $135,000-$195,000 - Financing: Third party.

LIZIO'S SPAGHETTI VENDORS
Spaghetti Vendors Franchise System Inc.
402 E Greenway Pkwy Ste. 2, Phoenix, AZ, 85022-2351. Contact: Emanuel Lizio Pres. - Tel: (480) 951-3499. A fresh pasta and sauce restaurant with a large selection of salads. Established: 1987 - Franchising Since: 1991 - No. of Units: Company Owned: 1 - Franchised: 5 - Franchise Fee: $17,500 - Royalty: 5% gross sales - Total Inv: $120,000-$150,000 - Financing: No.

LOGAN'S ROADHOUSE
CBRL Group Inc.
P.O. Box 787, Lebanon, TN, 37088-0787. - Tel: (615) 444-5533. Full service casual theme restaurants. Established: 1991 - Franchising Since: 1996 - No. of Units: Company Owned: 15 - Franchised: 2 - Franchise Fee: $30,000 - Royalty: 3% gross sales, 1-3% advertising - Total Inv: Building $800,000, fran. fee and equip. $450,000 + land cost.

LONG JOHN SILVER'S SEAFOOD SHOPPES

950 Breckenridge Lane, #300, Louisville, KY, 40207. Contact: Dir. Fran. Sales - Tel: (502) 896-5900. Quick service fish and seafood restaurants with a variety of fish, shrimp, chicken and salad meals served in a warm, friendly environment. Established: 1969 - Franchising Since: 1970 - No. of Units: Company Owned: 1,004 - Franchised: 481 - Franchise Fee: $20,000 - Royalty: 4% - Total Inv: $300,000 in liquid assets required for qualification - Financing: No.

LONGBRANCH STEAKHOUSE & SALOON

Longbranch Steakhouse & Saloon, Inc.

105 Deercreek Rd., Ste. M-204, Deerfield Beach, FL, 33442. Contact: Bill Manseau, Fran. Director - Tel: (954) 360-9927, (800) 416-5582, Fax: (954) 421-2145. Western style family steakhouse. Full training and support provided. Established: 1991 - Franchising Since: 1992 - No. of Units: Company Owned: 2 - Franchised: 20 - Franchise Fee: $50,000 - Total Inv: $500,00-$700,000 (for leased locations). Financing: No.

MACAYO MEXICAN RESTAURANTS

3117 N. 16th St., Phoenix, AZ, 85016-7609. - Tel: (602) 264-1831. Full service Mexican restaurants with lounges. Established: 1945 - Franchising Since: 1987 - No. of Units: Company Owned: 12 - Franchise Fee: $45,000 - Royalty: 4% - Total Inv: $600,000-$1,800,000 - Financing: None.

MAGIC WOK

N.S. & T.

2060 W. Laskey Rd., Toledo, OH, 43613. Contact: Sutas Pipatjarasgit, Pres. - Tel: (419) 471-0696, Fax: (419) 471-0405. Chinese fast food. Established: 1983 - Franchising Since: 1991 - No. of Units: Company Owned: 6 - Franchised: 20 - Franchise Fee: $12,500 - Royalty: 5% - Total Inv: $94,900-$149,500 - Financing: No.

MAJOR MAGIC'S ALL STAR PIZZA REVUE INC.

22601 Stevenson, Clinton Township, MI, 48035. - Tel: (810) 792-6933. Pizza entertainment restaurants seating 750 persons and averaging l6,000 sq. ft. with animated robot shows. Established: 198l - Franchising Since: 1982 - No. of Units: Company Owned: 6 - Franchised: 1 - Franchise Fee: $25,000 - Royalty: 6.5% - Total Inv: $850,000 - Financing: No.

MAMMA ILARDO'S PIZZERIA

Mamma Ilardo's Corp.

3600 Clipper Mill Rd., #260, Baltimore, MD, 21211. Contact: John A. Filipiak, V.P. Oper. & Dev. - Tel: (410) 662-1930, Fax: (410) 662-1936, E-Mail: pizza@mammailardos.com, Web Site: www.mamailardos.com. Pizza by the slice chian offering pizzeria and express pizza restaurant formats. Menu includes NY-style and signature pan pizza as well as pasta, salads, calzones and breakfast pizza. Established: 1976 - Franchising Since: 1984 - No. of Units: Company Owned: 3 - Franchised: 55 - Franchise Fee: Pizzeria: $25,000, Express: $ 4,000 - Royalty: Pizzeria: 5%, Express: 8% - Total Inv: $175,000-$320,000 - Financing: Indirect.

MANCHU WOK

S.C. Food Services (USA) Inc.

816 S. Military Trail - Bldg #6, Deerfield Beach, FL, 33442. Contact: Franchise Sales Manager - Tel: (954) 481-9555, (800) 423-4009, Fax: (954) 481-9670. Oriental quick service restaurant chain operating primarily in mall food courts of regional malls. Established: 1981 - Franchising Since: 1981 - No. of Units: Company Owned: 15-Can, 43-US - Franchised:60-Can, 1 US - Franchise Fee: $20,000 - Royalty: 7%, 1% adv. - Total Inv: $262,000-$306,500 equipment =$77,000, leasehold =$122,500-$157,500 - Financing: Yes.

MANHATTAN BAGEL CO.

Manhattan Bagel Co., Inc.

246 Industrial Way W., Eatontown, NJ, 07724. Contact: Dan Levy, Dir Of Franchising - Tel: (732) 544-0155, (800) 258-4082, Fax: (732) 544-1315. Franchisor of bagel bakery and deli. Established: 1987 - Franchising Since: 1988 - No. of Units: Company Owned: 19 - Franchised: 200 (sold & operating) - Franchise Fee: $30,000 - Royalty: 5% - Total Inv: $210,000 ($30,000 fran. fee, $80,000 const., $80,000 equip., $20,000 misc.) - Financing: 2 sources, Stephens & SBA.

MANNY & OLGA'S PIZZA

Manny & Olga's Pizza System, Inc

13707 NorthGate Dr, Silver Spring, MD, 20906. Contact: Bobby Athanasakis, President - Tel: (301) 588-2500, (866) 520-OLGA, Fax: (301) 924-1151, E-Mail: mannyandolgas@webtv.net, Web Site: www.mannyandolgas.com. Pizza delivery offering a expanded menu of subs, salads, pasta, wings & Greek specialities. Established: 1983 - Franchising Since: 1998 - No. of Units: Company Owned: 4 - Franchised: 1 - Franchise Fee: $25,000 - Royalty: 5% weekly - Total Inv: $120,000-$220,000 - Financing: Third party.

MARCO'S PIZZA

Marco's Inc.

5252Monroe St., Toledo, OH, 43623. Contact: Eric F. Schmitt, Dir. of Fran. Sales - Tel: (419) 885-7000, (800) 262-7267, Fax: (419) 885-5215. Offer premium quality pizza and hot submarine sandwiches, cheesebread and salads for carryout and delivery. Their emphasis on high quality, excellent service and tremendous value has enabled Marco's Pizza to become the leading pizza company in their major markets. Seeking experienced food service operators. Established: 1978 - Franchising Since: 1979 - No. of Units: Company Owned: 38 - Franchised: 92 - Franchise Fee: $8,000-$12,000 - Royalty: 3%-4.5% - Total Inv: $115,000-$170,000 - Financing: Third party.

MARIO'S PIZZA

DSUSA

2901 S Highland Dr Ste 14-C, Las Vegas, NV, 89109-1055. Contact: Connie D'Amico, Director - Tel: (888)291-4957, E-Mail: carlcarlsson @yahoo.com, Web Site: www.franchisebusinessusa.com. Mario's first store was established in 1959 in Arlington, VA. It's system is now being offered as an international franchise. Established: 1959 - Franchising Since: 1998 - No. of Units: Company Owned: 1 - Franchise Fee: $25,000 single unit, $50,000 Area developer - Royalty: 5% of gross - Total Inv: $75,000 for all equipment or less - Financing: No.

MARK PI'S EXPRESS

Asian Concepts, Inc

3126 Valleyview Dr, Columbas, OH, 43204. - Tel: (800) 280-2778, Web Site: www.MarkPi.com. Chinese fast food. Established: 1997 - Franchising Since: 1997 - No. of Units: Franchised: 45 - Franchise Fee: $15,000 - Royalty: 4% - Total Inv: $100,000-$500,000 - Financing: No.

MARY'S PIZZA SHACK

793 Broadway, Sonoma, CA, 95476. - Tel: (707) 938-3602, Fax: (707) 938-5976. Full service pizza and Italian restaurant, serving lunch and dinner in a casual atmosphere. Established: 1959 - Franchising Since: 1990 - No. of Units: Company Owned: 9 - Franchised: 3 - Franchise Fee: $30,000 - Royalty: 5%, 3% adv. - Total Inv: $150,000 leasehold imp., $170,000 fran. fee and equip, $46,000 soft cost, $50,000 work. cap. - Financing: No.

MASH HOAGIES/MASH SUBS & SALADS

Mash Hoagies Inc.

3164 Lake Washington Rd., Melbourne, FL, 32934. Contact: Alan Lee, Pres. - Tel: (407) 242-2066. Sub/sandwich/salad franchise. Established: 1982 - Franchising Since: 1982 - No. of Units: Franchised: 17 - Franchise Fee: $7,500 - Royalty: 3%, 2% adv. - Total Inv: $50,000 - Financing: Fran. fee may be financed, equipment leasing available.

MAUI TACOS

Maui Tacos International, Inc

1775 The Exchange, Suite 540, Atlanta, GA, 30339. Contact: Norman Willden, Vice President - Tel: (770) 226-8226, (888) 628-4822, Fax: (770) 541-2300. Fast, casual Mexican, featuring gourmet burritos, tacos, taco salads and smoothies. Established: 1993 - Franchising Since: 1998 - No. of Units: Company Owned: 7 - Franchise Fee: $20,000 - Royalty: 6% - Total Inv: $150,000-$260,000 - Financing: Third party.

MAURICE'S GOURMET BARBEQUE/PIGGIE PARK RESTAURANTS

Piggie Park Enterprises, Inc.

P.O. Box 6847, West Columbia, SC, 29171. Contact: Franchise Dept. - Tel: (803) 791-5887, Fax: (803) 791-8707. Specialize in gourmet barbeque with a mustard base barbeque sauce. Considered a mini dinner house with an in-house corporate test kitchen, which delivers barbequed items and hamburgers with a fast food style. Offer financial stability with 50 years plus experience in the barbeque business. Established: 1951 - Franchising Since: 1991 - No. of Units: Company Owned: 7 - Franchised: 1 - Franchise Fee: Initial fee $33,500: ($5,000 dev. & $28,500 fran. fee) - Royalty: 5%, 2% adv., 1% company opt. adv. fee - Total Inv: Facility bldg. & equip. $325,000 & land costs - Financing: None.

MAVERICK FAMILY STEAK HOUSE
1104 West Reynolds, Springfield, IL, 62702. Contact: Russ Ruby, Pres. - Tel: (217) 787-4660, Fax: (217) 787-9869. Semi-cafeteria style steak house. Established: 1983 - No. of Units: 4 - Approx. Inv: $100,000-$150,000 - Financing: None.

MAX'S DELI & RESTAURANT
Deli Corporation of America, Inc.
210 Skokie Valley Rd, Highland Park, IL, 60035-4464. - Tel: (440) 356-2977. Delicatessen/restaurant. Established: 1989 - Franchising Since: 1994 - No. of Units: Company Owned: 2 - Franchised: 1 - Franchise Fee: $20,000.

MAZZIO'S PIZZA
Mazzio's Corporation
4441 S. 72nd E. Ave., Tulsa, OK, 74145-4692. Contact: Mark Long, Mgr. of Brand Dev./Licensing - Tel: (918) 663-8880, (800) 827-1910, Fax: (918) 641-1236, Web Site: www.mazzios.com. Upscale Italian restaurant featuring 3 types of pizza along with excellent pasta, calzone rings, sandwiches and salad. There is an emphasis on an attractive decor and surroundings along with a distinctive exterior. Delivery is available from an existing dine-in unit. Established: 1961 - Franchising Since: 1966 - No. of Units: Company Owned: 105 - Franchised: 145 - Franchise Fee: $25,000 - Royalty: 3%, adv. 1% - Total Inv: $309,000-$606,000 with out real estate $684,000-$976,000 with real estate - Financing: Third party.

MCALISTER'S DELI
McAlister's Corp.
731 South Pear Orchard Road, Suite 51, Ridgeland, MS, 39157. Contact: Michael Kutcher, Manager of Franchise Sales - Tel: (601) 952-1100, (888) 855-3354, Fax: (601) 952-1138, E-Mail: franchising@mcalistersdeli.com, Web Site: www.mcalistersdeli.com. Upscale, fast casual Southern-style deli restaurant featuring hot and cold deli sandwiches, baked potatoes, salads, soups, deserts, iced tea and other food and beverage products. Established: 1989 - Franchising Since: 1994 - No. of Units: Company Owned: 23 - Franchised: 94 - Franchise Fee: $30,000 - Royalty: 5% of gross sales - Total Inv: $329,500-$1,424,000 - Financing: Third party sources.

MCDONALD'S
McDonald's Corp.
2915 Jorie Blvd., Oak Brook, IL, 60523. Contact: Franchising Dept. - Tel: (888) 800-7257. McDonald's is the world's leading food service retailer in the global consumer marketplace, with over 23,000 restaurants in 110 countries. Eighty-six percent of the McDonald's restaurant businesses in the U.S. are locally owned and operated by independent entrepreneurs. Established: 1955 - Franchising Since: 1955 - No. of Units: Company Owned: 5262 - Franchised: 18,361- Franchise Fee: $45,000 - Royalty: 4% - Total Inv: $413,100-$672,200 - Financing: No.

MCGREGORS MARKET
Orion Food Systems
2930 W Maple, Sioux Falls, SD, 57101. Contact: Director of Development - Tel: (800) 648-6227, Fax: (605) 336-0141, Web Site: www.orionfoodsys.com. Broad menu of high quality offerings for breakfast, lunch and dinner. Designed plus opening in specialty locations. Established: 1984 - Franchising Since: 1986 - Franchise Fee: $4,950 - Total Inv: $25,000-$140,000 per brand - Financing: Third party.

MD PLUCKERS WING FACTORY & GRILL
MD Pluckers Franchising L.P.
2222 Rio Granfe D-108, Austin, TX, 78705. - Tel: (512) 236-9112, (877) 206-WING, (512) 236-9113. Chicken wings, hamburgers, cheesburgers and more. Established: 1995 - Franchising Since: 2000 - No. of Units: Company Owned: 1 - Franchise Fee: $25,000 - Royalty: 4-5% - Total Inv: $150,000-$500,000.

ME-N-ED'S PIZZERIAS
Pizza World Supreme
5701 N. West Ave., Fresno, CA, 93711. - Tel: (559) 432-0399, Fax: (559) 432-0398, Web Site: www.pwspizza@aol.com. Featuring pizzas made with vine ripened tomatoes, fresh dough, and 5 California cheeses. Original thin or California style thick crust with up to 24 toppings. Established: 1958 - Franchising: 1998 - No. of Units: Company Owned: 52 - Franchised: 6 - Franchise Fee: $25,000 - Total Inv: $150,000 - Financing: Will provide referral to several national lending and financing sources.

MEAN GENE'S BURGERS
Orion Food Systems
2930 W Maple, Sioux Falls, SD, 57101. Contact: Director of Development - Tel: (800) 648-6227, (605) 336-6961, Fax: (605) 336-0141, Web Site: www.orionfoodsys.com. Quick service format, developing in convenience stores and foodcourts. Established: 1984 - Franchising Since: 1985 - No. of Units: Company Owned: 3 - Franchised: 29 - Franchise Fee: $4,950 - Total Inv: $25,000 + - Financing: Third Party.

MELLOW MUSHROOM
Home Grown Industries
265 Ponce de Leon Place, Decatur, GA, 30030. Contact: Fran. Dir. - Tel: (404) 370-0008. Pizza and sandwich restaurant. Established: 1974 - Franchising Since: 1987 - No. of Units: Company Owned: 1 - Franchised: 12 - Franchise Fee: $25,000 - Royalty: 5%, 1% adv. - Total Inv: $75,000-$85,000.

MELTING POT RESTAURANT, THE
Melting Pot Restaurants, Inc., The
8810 Twin Lakes Blvd, Columbus, OH, 43204. - Tel: (813) 881-0055, Fax: (813) 889-9361. Casual upscale dinner restaurant featuring full service fondue dining. Established: 1975 - Franchising Since: 1984 - No. of Units: Company Owned: 3 - Franchised: 47 - Franchise Fee: $35,000 - Royalty: 4.5% on gross - Total Inv: $162,000-$280,000 - Financing: No.

METROMEDIA FAMILY STEAKHOUSES-PONDEROSA & BONANZA
Metromedia Family Steakhouses, Inc.
6500 International Parkway, Ste. 1000, Plano, TX, 75093. Contact: Larry Stein, Dir. of Fran. Dev. - Tel: (972) 588-5887 (800) 543-9670, Fax: (972) 588-5806, E-Mail: franchise@metrogroup.com, Web Site: www.metromediarestaurants.com. A mid-priced family restaurant specializing in quality food served in a bright, fun atmosphere. The menu features a variety of great-tasting steaks, chicken, and seafood entrees, along with the all-you-can-eat buffet. Established: 1965 - Franchising Since: 1965 - No. of Units: Company Owned: 162 - Franchised: 401 - Franchise Fee: $40,000 per unit - Royalty: 4% - Total Inv: $1,045,200-$2,177,500 - Financing: No.

MIAMI SUBS
Miami Subs Corporation
6300 N.W. 31st. Ave., Ft. Lauderdale, FL, 33309. Contact: Donald L. Perlyn, President - Tel: (954) 973-0000, Fax: (954) 973-7616. Quick service restaurant concept featuring fresh food cooked-to-order, providing a diverse menu with exceptional quality and moderately priced items designed to encourage frequent visits. Our lively, bright, distinctive decors create both a daytime and evening appeal. Established: 1983 - Franchising Since: 1986 - No. of Units: Company Owned: 29 - Franchised: 132 - Franchise Fee: $25,000 - Royalty: 4%, 1% adv. - Total Inv: $275,000 ($175,000 equip. & $100,000 constr. cost) - Financing: Offer equip - Financing to qualified franchisees through an independent company.

MICKEY FINN'S SPORTS CAFE
Castle Rose, Inc
P.O. Box 12430, Omaha, NE, 68112-0430. Contact: Franchise Department - Tel: (402) 341-2424. Neighborhood sports bar and grill. Established: 1989 - Franchising Since: 1989 - No. of Units: Company Owned: 1 - Franchised: 6 - Franchise Fee: $17,500 - Total Inv: $17,500 - Financing: No.

MIKE ANDERSON'S SEAFOOD RESTAURANTS
Mike Anderson's Seafood Restaurant Consulting, Inc.
215 Bourbon St., New Orleans, LA, 70130-2204. Contact: Richard Williams, Co-Owner - Tel: (504) 524-3884. Casual, family priced seafood restaurant specializing in high quality, fresh Louisiana seafood. High volume establishment with attention to detail. Maintain excellent reputation with customers. Established: 1975 - Franchising Since: 1986 - No. of Units: Company Owned: 4 - Franchised: 1 - Franchise Fee: $75,000 - Royalty: 2%-4% - Financing: No.

MILWAUKEE GRILL
2601 Morse St, Janesville, WI, 3545. Contact: Mark Otis - Tel: (608) 754-1919, (608) 754-1919, Fax: (608) 754-7581. Specializing in chicken and beef. Established: 1989 - Franchising Since: 2001 - No. of Units: Company Owned: 1 - Franchise Fee: $30,000 - Royalty: 4.5% - Total Inv: $270,750-$454,330.

MINUTE MAN
Minute Man of America
P.O. Box 828, Little Rock, AR, 72203. Contact: James L. Hansen, Owner - Tel: (501) 666-8271. Charbroiled hamburgers and Mexican food. Established: 1949 - Franchising Since: 1965 - No. of Units: Franchised: 2 - Franchise Fee: $7,500 - Royalty: 3% sales - Total Inv: $75,000.

MISTER BAR-B-QUE
Smokey P Inc.
1134 Grove Dr., Rockledge, FL, 32955. Contact: Cleatrice Price, President - Tel: (321) 639-0038, (888) 766-5399, Fax: (321) 639-4318, E-Mail: smokeyp@digital.net, Web Site: www.digital.net/~mr.bbq. Dine in -Take out and catering services. Specializing in open-pit cooked barbecue, other meat dishes and southern style fresh/frozen vegetables. Requires minimum facility of 1,600 square feet, unless otherwise approved. Established: 1988 - Franchising Since: 1997 - No. of Units: Company Owned: 1 - Franchise Fee: $15,000 - Royalty: 6% - Total Inv: $161,000 - Financing: May help arrange.

MOBILE CHEF
Augies, Inc.
1900 W. County Rd. C., St. Paul, MN, 55113. Contact: Ray Augustine, Pres. - Tel: (651) 633-5308, Fax: (651) 633-5308. Industrial catering lunch trucks. Established: 1957 - Franchising Since: 1977 - No. of Units: Company Owned: 3 - Franchised: 55 - Approx. Inv: $20,000.

MOE'S ITALIAN SANDWICHES
Moestogo Corp.
2915 Peachtree Rd, Atlanta, GA, 30305. - Tel: (603) 431-0005, (800) 588-6637, Fax: (603) 431-5845, E-Mail: sdeloid@moesitalainsand wiches.com, Web Site: www.moesitalians andwiches.com. Quick service sandwich shops featuring Italian style sandwiches, wraps and soups. No grills or on site baking. Expanding in New England. Established: 1959 - Franchising Since: 1993 - No. of Units: Franchised: 14 - Franchise Fee: $10,000-$12,500 - Royalty: 5%, 1% adv. - Total Inv: $50,000-$119,000 - Financing: No.

MOE'S SOUTHWEST GRILL
2915 Peachtree Rd, Atlanta, GA, 30305. Tel: (404) 844-8335, Web Site: www.moes.com. Established: 2001 - Franchising Since: 2002 - No. of Units: Franchised: 40 - Franchise Fee: $20,000-$60,000 - Royalty: 5% - Total Inv: $244,000-$626,000.

MOM'S BAKE AT HOME PIZZA
Mom's Pizza, Inc
4457-59 Main St., Philadelphia, PA, 19127. Contact: Martin Bair, V.P. - Tel: (215) 482-1044, (800) 311-MOMS, Fax: (215) 482-0402, E-Mail: bakehome@aol.com. Franchise bake at home pizza stores. Established: 1961 - Franchising Since: 1981 - No. of Units: Franchised: 14 - Franchise Fee: $15,000 - Financing: No.

MORGAN'S FOREST
Morgan's Forest Inc.
18196 Deep Passage Lane, Fort Myers Beach, FL, 33931. Contact: Mike McGuigan, Owner - Tel: (941) 466-5830, Fax: (941) 466-5830, E-Mail: morgansfor@aol.com, Web Site: www.morgansforest.com. Tropical theme restaurant with special effects lighting, ground fog, moving animals and animal sounds. Specializing in fresh seafood with a South American flare. Established: 1996 - Franchising Since: 1998 - No. of Units: Company Owned: 1 - Franchise Fee: $25,000 - Royalty: 5% - Total Inv: $175,000-$800,000 - Financing: No.

MR. GATTI'S, INC.
P.O. Box 1522, 444 Sidney Baker South, Kerrville, TX, 78028. - Contact: Director of Franchise - Tel: (830) 792-5700, Fax: (830) 257-2003. Pizza restaurants with salads, submarine sandwiches, pasta. Established: 1969 - No. of Units: Company Owned: 109 - Franchised: 174 - Franchise Fee: $20,000 - Total Inv: $315,000-$500,000 - Financing: None.

MR. GOODBURGERS *
5173 Warning Rd, Suite 35, San Diego, CA, 92120-4373. - Tel: (619) 287-4373, E-Mail: sales@mrgoodburgers.com, Web Site: www.mrgood burgers.com. Our meatless burger is made with soy, which contains no cholestrol, are high in fibre and have only 5 grams of saturated fat. Established: 2003 - Franchising Since: 2003 - No. of Units: Company Owned: 1 - Franchise Fee: $25,000 - Royalty: 7% - Total Inv: $225,000.

MR. GOODCENTS SUBS & PASTAS
Mr. Goodcents Franchise Systems, Inc.
8997 Commerce Drive, DeSota, KS, 66018. Contact: Margot A. Bubien - Tel: (913) 583-8400, (800) 648-2368, Fax: (913) 583-3500, E-Mail: frandev@mrgoodcents.com, Web Site: www.mrgoodcents.com. Mr. Goodcents Subs & Pastas giant sub sandwiches share the spotlight with pasta entrees. In addition to dine in and take out, customer options include delivery and catering. More than 50 menu items satisfy health conscious customers with 17 varieties of subs, hot pasta dishes, protein rich salads and delicious soups. Fresh baked bread and cookies baked daily in the restaurants and meats and cheeses are sliced fresh to order for each customer. Established: 1989 - Franchising Since: 1990 - No. of Units: Company Owned: 3 - Franchised: 120 - Franchise Fee: $12,500 - Royalty: 5% - Total Inv: $71,850-$182,250 - Financing: Third party.

MR. HERO
Restaurant Developers Corp.
5755 Granger Rd., 2nd Floor, Independence, OH, 44131-1410. Contact: Franchise Sales Consultants - Tel: (216) 398-1101, (800) 837-9599, Fax: (216) 398-0707, Web Site: www.mrhero.com. Adult oriented foods featuring proprietary menu items only you can offer. Established: 1969 - Franchising Since: 1976 - No. of Units: Company Owned:18 - Franchised: 96 - Franchise Fee: $18,000 - Royalty: 5.5% - Total Inv: $111,100-$305,000 - Financing: Third party.

MR. JIMS PIZZA
Mr. Jim Pizza Inc.
4276 Kellway Circle, Addison, TX, 75001. - Tel: (972) 267-5467, (800) 583-5960, Fax: (972) 267-5463. Pizza delivery and takeout - Low upfront costs. Established: 1975 - Franchising Since: 1981 - No. of Units: Franchised: 65 - Franchise Fee: $10,000 - Royalty: 5% - Total Inv: $80,000 - Financing: No.

MR. PITA
Pita Franchise Corp.
48238 Lake Valley Dr, Shelby Township, MI, 40317-2123. Contact: Frank Lombardo, Pres., Founder - Tel: (810) 247-7254. Fast food, dine-in, carry-out, delivery and catering of fresh rolled variety of pita sandwiches, soups and salads. Established: 1993 - Franchising Since: 1995 - No. of Units: Company Owned: 4 - Franchised: 18 - Franchise Fee: $12,500 - Royalty: 3% 1st 5 years, 5% thereafter - Total Inv: $140,000-$200,000 - Financing: No.

MR. SUBB
Mr. Subb Franchise
601 Columbia St., Cohoes, NY, 12047. Contact: William F. Pompa, Pres. - Tel: (518) 783-0276, ext. 23, (800) 267-7822, ext. 23, Fax: (518) 783-0294, Web Site: www.mrsubb.com. Submarine sandwich shop featuring subs, salads, soups, snacks and breakfast. Established: 1978 - Franchising Since: 1994 - No. of Units: Company Owned: 20 - Franchised: 15 - Franchise Fee: $15,000 - Royalty: 6%, 2% adv. - Total Inv: Equipment - $55,000, construction - $50,000, working capital - $30,000 - Financing: No.

MRS. WINNER'S CHICKEN & BISCUITS

5995 Barfield Rd, Atlanta, GA, 30328. Contact: Franchise Department - Tel: (404) 256-4900. Quick-service restaurant. Established: 1977 - Franchising Since: 1989 - No. of Units: Company Owned: 111 - Franchised: 44 - Franchise Fee: $20,000 - Royalty: 4-5% - Total Inv: $755,000.

MY FRIEND'S PLACE
MFP Franchise Systems, Inc.

106 Hammond Dr., Atlanta, GA, 30328. - Tel: (404) 843-2803, Fax: (404) 843-0371. Retail restaurant specializing in quality sandwiches, salads, soups, and homemade desserts. Established: 1980 - Franchising Since: 1990 - No. of Units: Company Owned: 2 - Franchised: 10 - Franchise Fee: $17,500 - Royalty: Flat fee, wkly, mos. 1-12: $150 per. wk, mos. 13-60: $200 per wk., etc. - Total Inv: $95,000-$175,000 - Financing: No.

NACHO NANA'S
Nacho Nana's Worldwide, Inc.

1220 S. Alma School Rd #101, Mesa, AZ, 85210. - Tel: (602) 644-1340. Up-scale quick service Mexican Restaurant Concept. Units aver. 2,000 sq. ft., 45-60 seats. Using only quality ingredients, no ground beef, cholesterol free oil's, salsa made fresh daily and salsa bar with warm tortilla chips and other condiments. Unique decor and good price/value sets our concept apart. Established: 1993 - Franchising Since: 1993 - No. of Units: Franchised: 14 - Franchise Fee: $25,000 - Royalty: 6% - Total Inv: $176,000-$199,950 turn-key - Financing: Minimum cash needed $50,000.

NANCY'S PIZZERIA
Chicago Franchise Systems, Inc.

8200 W. 185th St., #J, Tinley Park, IL, 60477. Contact; VP Franchise Dev. - Tel: (708) 444-4411, (800) 626-2977, Fax: (708) 444-4422. Nancy's Pizzeria invented stuffed pizza in 1974 in Chicago, within a year Chicago Magazine and it's readers chose Nancy's as "THE BEST PIZZA IN CHICAGO". We now serve stuffed pizza, thin pizza, pastas, sandwiches, appetizers and salads. Established: 1974 - Franchising Since: 1995 - No. of Units: Franchised: 66 - Franchise Fee: $20,000 - Royalty: 5% - Total Inv: $190,000-$250,000 - Financing: No.

NATHAN'S
Nathan's Famous, Inc.

1400 Old Country Rd., Westbury, NY, 11590. Contact: Carl Paley, Sr. V.P. Franchising - Tel: (516) 338-8500, (800) NATHANS, Fax: (516) 338-7220. Fast food restaurants, kiosks, and modulars, featuring all beef Nathan's hot dogs, fresh cut fries, and a large variety of additional menu items. Established: 1916 - Franchising Since: 1989 - No. of Units: Company Owned: 25 - Franchised: 202 - Franchise Fee: $30,000 / $15,000 cart, kiosk, modular - Royalty: 4.5% - Total Inv: Modulars, Kiosks - $25,000-$70,000, full service $200,000-$400,000.

NATURE'S TABLE
Nature's Table Systems, Inc.

920 Main St., Ste. 209, Kansas City, MO, 64105-2008. - Tel: (816) 452-2898. Healthy and sensible food restaurant for the enclosed regional mall food courts. Established: 1977 - Franchising Since: 1987 - No. of Units: Company Owned: 6 - Franchised: 18 - Franchise Fee: $25,000 - Royalty: 5% - Total Inv: $101,800-$185,500 - Financing: None.

NEIGHBORHOOD STREATS
Street Eats Limited

2626 West Lake Street, Minneapolis, MN, 55416. Contact: Richard Ambrose - Tel: (612) 928-1375, Fax: (612) 928-1360, Web Site: www.streeteats.net or www.streats.net. Neighborhood Streats is a self-contained, mobile fast food franchise serving nationally recognized brands. Streats franchises are located on site at major retail outlets and other high foot-traffic venues. Established: 2001 - Franchising Since: 2001 - No. of Units Company Owned: 4 - Franchise Fee: $2,500-$10,000 - Royalty: 6% - Total Inv: $26,800-$140,050 - Financing: None.

NELSONS SERVICE SYSTEM
T.G. Corp.

2420 Hickory Road, Mishawaka, IN, 46545. Contact: Todd Gongiwer, President - Tel: (219) 257-7522. Corporate catering, fund raising, special event operations based upon a unique high volume, low overhead cooking process. Established: 1968 - Franchising Since: 1995 - No. of Units: Company Owned: 1 - Franchised: 2 - Franchise Fee: $4,000-$50,000 - Royalty: 3% 1st 500,000, 1% everything exceeding 500,000 - Total Inv: $16,500-$126,500 - Financing: Yes.

NEW WORLD COFFEE
New World Coffee & Bagels

246 Industrial Way, Eatontown, NJ, 07724-3206. - Tel: (732) 544-0155, Fax: (732) 544-1315. High productivity specialty coffee and baked on premise bagel/bakery. 2 concepts in 1. Above average square foot sales. Established: 1992 - Franchising Since: 1997 - No. of Units: Company Owned: 40 - Franchise Fee: $25,000 - Royalty: 5% - Total Inv: Turn-key $250,000 plus - Financing: Yes.

NEW YORK BURRITO-GOURMET WRAPS
NYB Foods, Inc

300 International Pkwy, Suite 100, Heathrow, FL, 32746. - Tel: (866) 990-3200, Web Site: www.newyorkburrito.com. Casual/upscale quick serve restaurant serving multi cultural gourmet wraps and burritos. Established: 1995 - Franchising Since: 1996 - No. of Units: Franchised: 102+ - Franchise Fee: $15,000 - Royalty: 7% - Total Inv: $75,000-$140,000 - Financing: Third party to qualified applicants.

NEW YORK NY FRESH DELI
New York Subs Franchising Corp.

100 West Hoover Ave, Suite 12-14, Mesa, AZ, 85210. Contact: Robert Palmer, President - Tel: (480) 632-9884, (800) 285-7310, Fax: (480) 503-1850, E-Mail: rpalmer@newyorksubs.com, Web Site: www.nynyfreshdeli.com. Fresh deli speciality sandwich concept featuring hot and cold fresh made to order sandwiches and salads. Established: 2001 - Franchising Since: 2002 - No. of Units: Company Owned: 1 - Franchised: 27 - Franchise Fee: $15,000 - Royalty: 6% of net sales - Total Inv: $$168,000-$283,000 - Financing: Some third party available.

NICK-N-WILLY'S WORLD FAMOUS TAKE-N-BAKE-PIZZA *

9777 S. Yasemite St, #230, Lone Tree, CO, 80124. Contact: Barry Stolbof - Tel: (303) 706-9090, (888) 642-6945, Fax: (303) 706-0330, E-Mail: barry@nicknwillyspizza.com, Web Site: www.nicknwillys.com. Take N Bake Pizza, Established: 1988 - Franchising Since: 1992 - No. of Units: Company Owned: 3 - Franchise Fee: $25,000 - Royalty: 6% - Total Inv: $159,400-$248,250 - Financing: Third Party.

NOBLE ROMAN'S PIZZA EXPRESS
Noble Roman Inc.

One Virginia Ave., Ste. 800, Indianapolis, IN, 46204. - Tel: (317) 634-3377, Fax: (317) 685-2294, E-Mail: amancino@earthlink.net. Simple to run kiosk style concept (200sq. feet). Fresh made pizza and breadsticks. Highest quality product made in kiosk setup. Can be run by 1 person. Projected food cost of 25%, labor 20% - Established: 1972 - Franchising Since: 1982 - No. of Units: Company Owned: 48 - Franchised: 57 - Franchise Fee: $3,500 - Royalty: 7% - Total Inv: $15,000-$45,000 - Financing: Yes.

NU MAGIC PIZZA

312 S. Cedros Ave, #315, Solana Beach, CA, 92075. - Tel: (858) 259-6322, Fax: (858) 259-6328. Fresh high quality food. Established: 1973 - Franchise Fee: $7,500 - Royalty: 4.5% gross sales - Total Inv: $84,000-$170,500.

NU-VENTURES INC.

1324 W Milham Ave, Portage, MI, 49024-1209. Contact: Samuel Mancino Jr, President - Tel: (616) 327-6800, (888) 432-8379, Fax: (616) 226-4466. Italian Eatery, casual dining, counter service. Established: 1993 - Franchising Since: 1993 - No. of Units: Franchised: 23 - Franchise Fee: $25,000 - Royalty: 5% - Total Inv: $139,700-$215,200 - Financing: Will help find financing.

NUMERO UNO
Numero Uno Franchise Corp. Gelet Enterprises, Inc.

3550 Wilshire Blvd #1725, Los Angeles , CA, 90010-2401. - Tel: (213) 252-9991, Fax: (213) 252-9995, E-Mail: numagicpizza.com. Full-service Italian restaurant with emphasis on deep dish pizza, thin crust pizza, pastas, salads, sandwiches, variety of wines, beers and desserts.

Established: 1973 - Franchising Since: 1975 - No. of Units: Company Owned: 7 - Franchised: 54 - Franchise Fee: $25,000 - Royalty: 10% incl. adv. - Total Inv: $175,000-$250,000 - Financing: No.

NYPD PIZZA *
1701 Park Center Dr, Orlando, FL, 32835. Contact: Susan McDaniel - Tel: (407) 253-9972, (866) 256-9550, E-Mail: franchise@nypdpizza.net, Web Site: www.nypdpizza.net. NYPD restaurants offer the highest quality pizza products and Italian restaurant menu items made of all the freshest ingredients. All of our pizzas are hand tossed, made with our own unique pizza dough, high quality 100% cheese, and our specially spiced tomato sauce, finished with fresh toppings, and baked in a brick oven. Established: 1987 - Franchising Since: 2004 - No. of Units: Company Owned: 5 - Franchise Fee: $25,000-$35,000 - Total Inv: $222,000-$336,000.

O. T. HODGE CHILI PARLORS
Eirten's Parlors, Inc.
1622 South Jefferson, St. Louis, MO, 63104. Contact: John Eirten, Owner - Tel: (314) 772-1215, Fax: (314) 772-1215. Fast food sit down diner motif featuring chili. Established: 1904 - Franchising Since: 1985 - No. of Units: Company Owned: 1 - Franchised: 3 - Royalty: 5% - Total Inv: $100,000-$200,000 - Financing: No.

OBEE'S SOUP-SALAD-SUBS
1777 Tamiami Trail Suite 206, Port Charlotte, FL, 33948. Contact: Jim Patrick, President - Tel: (941) 625-0773, (866) 623-3462, Fax: (941) 625-1501, E-Mail: office@obees.com, Web Site: www.obees.com. World's greatest fresh food restaurant. Our subs are made from the highest quality meats, cheeses and condiments available. The vegatables that go into our subs are sliced daily. Established: 1995 - Franchising Since: 2000 - No. of Units: Company Owned: 1 - Franchised: 65 - Franchise Fee: $15,000 - Royalty: 6%+1% advertising - Total Inv: $85,000-$100,000 - Financing: Yes, SBA with 25% down.

OFF THE GRILL
Off The Grill Franchising, Inc
7110 Crossroads Blvd., Suite 500, Brentwood, TN, 37027. Contact: Alan Thompson- Tel: (615) 370-0700, (877) 684-2100, Fax: (615) 371-1405, E-Mail: info@offthegrill.com, Web Site: www.offthegrill.com. We are a fast casual restaurant with an upscale product, offered through quick serve dine in, fast take-out and free delivery. Established: 1998 - Franchising Since: 1999 - No. of Units: Company Owned: 3 - Franchised: 17 - Franchise Fee: $25,000 - Royalty: 4%, 2% ad - Total Inv: $275,000 - Financing: SBA leasing companies.

OLD SAN FRANCISCO STEAKHOUSE
9809 McCullough, San Antonio, TX, 78216. - Tel: (210) 341-3189, Fax: (210) 341-3585. 30 year old high volume steakhouse chain. Set in the 1890's, Barbery coast featuring family entertainment of the "girl on the red velvet swing", Dueling grand pianos, certified angus beef and 12lb blocks of swiss cheese on every table. Established: 1968 - Franchising Since: 1994 - No. of Units: Company Owned: 4 - Franchised: 7 - Franchise Fee: $50,000 - Royalty: 4% F.B. - 10% retail - Total Inv: Varies depending on unit size.

OREAN THE HEALTH EXPRESS
817 N. Lake Ave., Pasadena, CA, 91104-4561. Contact: Orean Thomas, Pres. - Tel: (626) 794-0861, Fax: (626) 794-0861. The first fast food vegetarian restaurant. Established: 1984 - Franchising Since: 1990 - No. of Units: Company Owned: 1 - Franchise Fee: $25,000 - Royalty: 6% - Financing: None. NOT FRANCHISING AT THIS TIME.

ORIGINAL CHICAGO HOAGIE HUT, THE
The Original Chicago Hoagie Hut, Inc.
2807 Grand Ave., Waukegan, IL, 60085. - Tel: (888) 5HO-AGIE, Fax: (847) 249-3190. Restaurant specializing in hoagies. Full training and support provided. Established: 1966 - Franchising Since: 1998 - No. of Units: Company Owned: 3 - Franchised: 1 - Franchise Fee: $20,000 - Total Inv: $160,000 - Financing: No.

ORIGINAL GINO'S EAST OF CHICAGO, THE
Bravo Restaurants, Inc.
205 W. Wacker, Ste. 1800, Chicago, IL, 60606. Contact: William Bronner, VP Franchising - Tel: (312) 346-5455, (800) 944-3393, Fax: (312) 345-8522. Authentic Chicago-style pizza - training and support

provided. Established: 1966 - Franchising since: 1992 - No. of Units: Company Owned: 4 - Franchised: 3 - Franchise Fee: $35,000 - Total Inv: $400,000-$800,000 - Financing: No.

ORIGINAL HAMBURGER STAND
Galardi Group, Inc.
4440 Von Karman Ave., Ste. 222, Newport Beach, CA, 92660. - Tel: (714) 752-5800, (800) 426-0036. Fast food restaurant. Full training and support provided. Established: 1982 - Franchising Since: 1985 - No. of Units: Franchised: 23 - Franchise Fee: $20,000 - Royalty: 5% - Total Inv.: $250,000-$800,000 - Financing: Yes.

ORIGINAL PANCAKE HOUSE, THE
8601 S.W. 24th Ave., Portland, OR, 97219. Contact: Ann Liss, Franchise Dept. - Tel: (503) 246-9007. Family Restaurant. Established: 1953 - No. of Units: Company Owned: 1 - Franchised: 80.

ORIGINAL PASTA COMPANY, THE
Watermarc Food Mgt. Com
1111 Wilcrest Green, #350, Houston, TX, 77042. - Tel: (713) 783-0500, Fax: (713) 783-4608. High quality- contemporary Italian cuisine. Variety of specialty pastas and gourmet pizza. Casual family atmosphere and moderately priced. Established: 1993 - Franchising Since: 1997 - No. of Units: Company Owned: 17 - Franchise Fee: $35,000 - Royalty: 4% of gross sales - Total Inv: Range - $420,000-$750,000 - Financing: No.

ORIGINAL PITA SUB SHOP
4063 17 Mile Rd., Sterling Hts., MI, 48310. Contact: Mr. Mazen, Owner - Tel: (810) 264-5480, Fax: (810) 264-7067. Sub shop, sales of subs, salads, soups, soft drinks. Established: 1986 - Franchising Since: 1990 - No. of Units: Company Owned: 1 - Franchised: 1 - Franchise Fee: $15,000 - Royalty: 4% of gross sales - Total Inv: $80,000 - Financing: No.

ORIGINAL RAGIN CAJUN CO.
Original Ragin Cajun
100 Farmington Dr., Lafayette, LA, 70503. Contact: Fran. Dir. - Tel: (901) 368-3361, Fax: (901) 368-3724. Specialty cajun food with many original cajun entrees and entertainment. Training and support provided. Established: 1996 - No. of Units: Company Owned: 1 - Franchised: 1 - Franchise Fee: $25,000 - Royalty: 5%, adv. 1% - Total Inv: $250,000-$450,000 - Financing: Available.

ORIGINAL TACO CABANA MEXICAN PATIO CAFE, THE
Taco Cabana, Inc.
8918 Tesoro Dr., Ste. 200, San Antonio, TX, 78217. Contact: James Eliasberg, Sr. V.P. & General Counsel - Tel: (210) 804-0990, Fax: (210) 804-2135. 24 hour retail Mexican fast food, patio dining with drive-through service. Established: 1978 - Franchising Since: 1987 - No. of Units: Company Owned: 36 - Franchised: 16 - Franchise Fee: $50,000 per store; 3 store min. - Royalty: 4% of gross - Total Inv: $800,000-$1,200,000 - Financing: None by franchisor.

OTTOMANELLI'S CAFE FRANCHISING CORP.
1549 York Ave., New York, NY, 10028. Contact: Nicolo Ottomanelli, Chairman - Tel: (212) 772-8423, Fax: (212) 772-8436. Italian/American cafe, featuring pasta, pizza, burger and ribs. Catering to families and others who appreciate good quality food at a moderate price. Established: 1988 - Franchising Since: 1989 - No. of Units: Company Owned: 4 - Franchised: 14 - Franchise Fee: $19,540 - Royalty: 3.5%, 1% adv. - Total Inv: $150,000-$475,000.

PADOWS HAMS & DELI.
Padow's Deli Inc.
4925 W. Broad St., Ste. 407, Richmond, VA, 23230. - Tel: (804) 358-4267. Deli sandwiches, boxed lunches, party platters, corporate catering. 2 types of franchises. Both include the above, but Hams & Deli includes mail order hams, peanuts and gifts. Established: 1994 - Franchising Since: 1995 - No. of Units: Company Owned: 3 - Franchised: 5 - Franchise Fee: $15,000 Deli Shop, $25,000 Hams & Deli - Royalty: 4% of net sales - Total Inv: $110,000-$150,000 Deli Shop, $240,000-$350,000 Hams & Deli format - Financing: No.

PANCAKE COTTAGE FAMILY RESTAURANTS
Captains Cottage Franchise, Inc.
P.O. Box 1909, Massapequa, NY, 11758. Contact: Chris Levano, V.P. Fran. Dev. - Tel: (516) 271-0221. Full service family restaurant - full training and support provided. Established: 1964 - Franchising Since: 1967 - No. of Units: Franchised: 22 - Franchise Fee: $35,000 - Total Inv. $75,000+ - Financing: No.

PANCHERO'S MEXICAN GRILL
Panchero's Franchise Corporation
P.O. Box 1786, Iowa City, IA, 52244-1786. Contact: Franchise Rep. - Tel: (888) 639-2378, Fax: (319) 358-6435. Made-to-order, authentic Mexican food prepared in an exciting and fun-to-watch display cooking area. Established: 1992 - Franchising Since: 1995 - No. of Units: Company Owned: 8 - Franchised: 1 - Franchise Fee: $15,000-$25,000 - Royalty: 5% - Total Inv: $100,000-$350,000 - Financing: No.

PANERA BREAD
Saint Louis Bread Company Inc.
7930 Big Bend Blvd., St. Louis, MO, 63119-2711. Contact: Franchise Department - Tel: (314) 918-7779 Ext 6312, (800) 301-5566, Fax: (314) 918-7773, E-Mail: paul_evans@aubonpain.com, Web Site: www.panerabread.com. The heart of our business is bread. Our more than 25 varieties of sourdough-based breads and bagels are complemented by traditional French and other European breads. Our menu was developed to enhance this bread tradition and includes made-to-order sandwiches, soups, salads, coffee and espresso drinks along with croissants, muffins and cookies. Established: 1987 - Franchising Since: 1993 - No. of Units: Company Owned: 78 - Franchised: 72 - Franchise Fee: $35,000 - Royalty: 5% gross - Total Inv: $550,000-$800,000 - Financing: No.

PAPA JOHN'S PIZZA
Papa John's International, Inc.
P.O. Box 99900, Louisville, KY, 40269-9990. - Tel: (888) 777-7272. Pizza delivery and carry-out. Established: 1985 - Franchising Since: 1986 - No. of Units: Company Owned: 169 - Franchised: 560 - Franchise Fee: $20,000 - Royalty: 4% - Total Inv: $120,000-$170,000 - Financing: None.

PAPA MURPHY'S PIZZA
8000 NE Parkway Dr., #350, Vancouver, WA, 98662. - Tel: (360) 260-7272, (800) 257-7272, Fax: (360) 260-0500, Web Site: www.papamurphys.com. Fresh, high quality pizza made to order, that the customer bakes at home. Established: 1981 - Franchising Since: 1982 - No. of Units: Company Owned: 10 - Franchised: 652 - Franchise Fee: $25,000 - Royalty: 5% - Total Inv: $148,800-$199,500 including franchise fee - Financing: No.

PAPA ROMANO'S
24387 Halsted Rd, Farmington Hills, MI, 48335. Contact: Daniel J. Morelli V.P. - Tel: (248) 888-7272, (800) 4-A-PAPAS, Fax: (248) 888-0033. Delivery/carryout pizzeria. (Some units offer dine-in). Established: 1970 - Franchising Since: 1986 - No. of Units: Company Owned: 6 - Franchised: 78 - Franchise Fee: $20,000 - Royalty: 6% of sales - Total Inv: $155,000: $5,000 adv., $70,000 equip., $20,000 fran. fee, $60,000 buildout - Financing: Yes.

PAPA'S PIZZA TO-GO
Papas Pizza To-Go, Inc
4465 Commerce Dr., Ste. 101, Buford, GA, 30518. Contact: Kathy Underwood, Director of Franchise Sales - Tel: (770) 614-6676, Fax: (770) 614-9095, E-Mail: papa2go@bellsouth.net, Web Site: www.papaspizzatogo.com. Pizza restaurant selling pizza, subs, salads, wings, pasta, quesadillas, wraps, chicken fingers. Many stores have an all you can eat lunch buffet. Some stores are twice as big and have an "ALL DAY, EVERYDAY PIZZA BUFFET". Established: 1986 - Franchising Since: 1986 - No. of Units: Company Owned: 13 - Franchised: 74 - Franchise Fee: $9,500-$12,500 - Royalty: 5% - Total Inv: $135,000-$300,000 - Financing: Third party.

Check out our On-Line listings:
www.infonews.com

PAPACHINO'S RISTORANTE & PIZZA RESTAURANTS
Papachino's Franchise Corp., Inc.
2650 Via De La Valle, Del Mar, CA, 92014-1909. Contact: Stephen Slamon, V.P. - Tel: (858) 481-7171, Fax: (848) 794-0414. Full service Italian restaurant offering full menu of fine Italian food including pizza, pasta, sandwiches, veal, chicken and beverages. Established: 1977 - Franchising Since: 1988 - No. of Units: Company Owned: 2 - Franchised: 3 - Franchise Fee: $25,000 - Royalty: 2% - Total Inv: $100,000-$350,000 - Financing: No.

PAPPARDELLE'S PIZZA & PASTA EATERY
Pappardelle's Franchising, Inc.
554 Stewart Ave, Bethpage, NY, 11714. Contact: Vincent DiMartino, CEO - Tel: (516) 433-2463, (888) 3 EATERY, Fax: (516) 433-2467, E-Mail: pappar3@aol.com, Web Site: www.pappardelle's. Authentic family style Italian pizza and pasta quick service restaurants. Concept features 20 gourmet style pizzas, fast free delivery and design your own pizza. Established: 1986 - Franchising Since: 1997 - No. of Units: Franchised: 3 - Franchise Fee: $19,900 - Royalty: 5% - Total Inv: $1150,000-$350,000 - Financing: Yes, third party S.B.A.

PASQUALE'S PIZZA & PASTA
5330 Stadium Trace Pkwy #325, Birmingham, AL, 35244-4538. Contact: Millard L. Deason, Pres. - Tel: (205) 664-1839, (800) 239-1839. Pizza, pasta and sandwiches. Established: 1952 - Franchising Since: 1952 - No. of Units: Franchised: 34 - Franchise Fee: $5,000 - Royalty: 5% - Total Inv: $126,500-$180,000 - Financing: Limited financing available.

PASTA TO GO
15965 Jeanette St., Southfield, MI, 48075. Contact: Colleen McGaffey - Tel: (248) 557-2784. Take out, delivery and sit down. Pasta to go is a fast food pasta chain for people on the go who still want good healthy Italian food. Established: 1987 - Franchising Since: 1992 - No. of Units: Company Owned: 1 - Franchised: 20 - Franchise Fee: $20,000 - Royalty: 5% - Total Inv: $62,000-$120,000 - Financing: Yes, third party available to qualified applicants.

PAUL REVERE'S PIZZA
Paul Revere's Pizza Int'l., Ltd.
1570 42nd Street NE, Cedar Rapids, IA, 52402. Contact: Larry Schuster, Pres. - Tel: (319) 395-9113, (800) 995-9437, Fax: (319) 395-9115, E-Mail: larrys@paulrevesespizza.com, Web Site: www.paulreverespizza.com. Pizza deliver. Established: 1975 - Franchising Since: 1982 - No. of Units: Franchised: 26 - Franchise Fee: $15,000 - Royalty: 4% sales/2% advertising - Total Inv: $75,000-$150,000 - Financing: None.

PEGGY LAWTON KITCHENS, INC.
P.O. Box 33, East Walpole, MA, 02032-0033. Contact: William Wolf, V.P./G.M. - Tel: (800) 843-7325 - US only. Eastern seaboard areas licensed for development. Route selling portion packaged snacks to other businesses. Sales repeat weekly. High quality line. Established: 1949 - Licensing Since: 1979 - No. of Licensees: 3 - Approx. Inv: $60,000 - License Fee: Flat $3,000 yr.

PENGUIN POINT
Penguin Point Franchise Systems, Inc.
2691 U.S. 30 E., P.O. Box 975, Warsaw, IN, 46581. Contact: W.E. Stouder Jr., Pres. - Tel: (219) 267-3107, Fax: (219) 267-3154. Quick serve, drive thru, chicken burgers, specialty sandwiches, catering. Established: 1961 - Franchising Since: 1995 - No. of Units: Company Owned: 15 - Franchise Fee: $15,000 - Royalty: 4% continuing service fee, 1% adv. - Total Inv: $435,000-$605,000 - Financing: None.

PENN STATION EAST COAST SUBS
Penn Station, Inc.
8276 Beechmont Ave., Cincinnati, OH, 45255. Contact: Mark Partusch, Dir. of Sales - Tel: (513) 474-5957, Fax: (513) 474-7116. Retail sale of Philadelphia style cheesesteaks, East Coast style sub sandwiches, fresh cut fries and fresh squeezed lemonade. Established: 1985 - Franchising Since: 1988 - No. of Units: Company Owned: 3 - Franchised: 68 - Franchise Fee: $22,500 - Royalty: 4%-8% - Total Inv: $210,000-$275,000 - Financing: No.

PEPE'S MEXICAN RESTAURANTS
PePe's, Incorporated
1325 W. 15th St., Chicago, IL, 60608. Contact: Edwin Ptak, Fran. Dir. - Tel: (312) 733-2500, Fax: (312) 733-2564, E-Mail: info@pepes.com, Web Site: www.pepes.com. Full service family Mexican restaurant. Carry available at each location. Established: 1967 - Franchising Since: 1967 - No. of Units: Franchised: 54 - Franchise Fee: $15,000 - Royalty: 4% (4% adv. fee) - Total Inv: $150,000-$300,000 - Financing: No.

PERFETTO PIZZA & PASTA
Perfetto Pizza & Pasta, Inc
P.O. Box 2062 Delray Beach, FL, 33447-2062. Contact: Robert A. Spuck, President - Tel: (954) 396-4991, (800) 839-4931, Fax: (954) 396-4993, E-Mail: perfettopp@aol.com. Trendy restaurant serving pizzas, pastas, salads and subs, offering dine-up, take-out, and delivery services. Established: 1999 - Franchising Since: 1999 - No. of Units: Franchised: 1 - Franchise Fee: $25,000 - Royalty: 6%; 3% adv. - Total Inv: $150,000-$200,000 - Financing: Third party.

PERKINS RESTAURANT & BAKERY
The Restaurant Company
6075 Poplar Ave., Ste. 800, Memphis, TN, 38119. Contact: Robert J. Winters, Vice President, Franchise Development & Relations - Tel: (800) 877-7375, (901) 766-6400, Fax: (901) 766-6482, E-Mail: franchise@perkinsrestaurants.com, Web Site: www.perkins restaurants.com. Perkins is a mid-scale restaurant chain serving abundant portions of delicious food and featuring signature items for breakfast, lunch, dinner as well as bakery products, while guaranteeing great service in a comfortable, friendly atmosphere. Established: 1958 - Franchising Since: 1958 - No. of Units: Company Owned: 154 - Franchised: 333 - Franchise Fee: $40,000 - Royalty: 4% of sales - Total Inv: $1,700,000-$2,500,000 with 20% equity - Financing: No.

PETER PIPER PIZZA
Peter Piper Inc.
14635 N. Kierland Blvd, #160, Scottsdale, AZ, 85254. Contact: Dir. Fran. - Tel: (800) 899-3425, Fax: (480) 609-6413. Safe, casual, family fun pizza restaurants serving quality products at value pricing. Families, parties and groups enjoy our prizes, games, rides and videos. We always treat kids special. Established: 1972 - Franchising Since: 1976 - No. of Units: Company Owned: 60 - Franchised: 75 - Franchise Fee: $25,000 domestic - Royalty: 5% - Total Inv: $700,000 - Financing: Referrals to sources.

PETRO'S CHILI & CHIPS
Scandavian Shop & More, Inc.
5614 Kingston Pike, 2nd Floor, Knoxville, TN, 37919. Contact: Dir. of Franchising - Tel: (423) 588-1076, (800) PETROFY, Fax: (423) 588-0916, E-Mail: petros@petros.com. World's Fair originated chili concept. Ideal for food court setting. Chili, chili-related products, frozen yogurt and salads. Established: 1985 - Franchising Since: 1992 - No. of Units: Company Owned: 6 - Franchised: 9 - Franchise Fee: $15,000 - Royalty: 5% - Total Inv: $181,500-$453,500 - Financing: No.

PHILLY CONNECTION
Philly Franchising Co., The
120 Interstate N. Parkway E., #112, Atlanta, GA, 30339. Contact: John Pollock, SR VP - Tel: (800) 886-8826, (770) 952-6152, Fax: (770) 952-3168, E-Mail: phillyconnection@mindspring.com, Web Site: www.phillyconnection.com. Quick-service restaurant chain specializing in the Philly Cheese steak sandwich. Also serving a complete line of hot and cold haogies, salads and fries. Established: 1984 - Franchising Since: 1987 - No. of Units: Franchised: 135 - Franchise Fee: $20,000 - Royalty: 6% - Total Inv: $20,000 - Financing: Third party.

PHILLY'S FRANCHISING, LLC *
1954 Opitz Blvd, Woodbridge, VA, 22191. Contact: Chris Roth, Chief Wing Commander - Tel: (703) 490-3428, Fax: (703) 490-3427, E-Mail: info@buffalophillys.com, Web Site: www.buffalophillys.com. A fast casual concept serving Buffalo style chicken wings and Philadelphia cheesesteaks. Dine-in, carry-out, 25-50 seats, TV's and counter service. Established: 2000 - Franchising Since: 2004 - No. of Units: Company Owned: 1 - Franchise Fee: $18,000 - Royalty: 4% - Total Inv: $200,000-$315,000 - Financing: No.

PICASSO'S PIZZA EXPRESS
2714 Sheridan Dr., Buffalo, NY, 14150. Contact: Fran. Dir. - Tel: (716) 833-5633. Offering pizza, wings, salads, and sandwiches. Also take-out and delivery. Established: 1990 - Franchising Since: 1991 - No. of Units: Company Owned: 17 - Franchised: 1 - Franchise Fee: $15,000 - Royalty: 5%, 2% adv.

PICCADILLY CIRCUS PIZZA
Land Mark Products, Inc.
1007 Okobaji Ave, Box 188, Milford, IA, 51351. Contact: Jerry Ryker, Gen. Mgr. - Tel: (800) 338-4340, (712) 338-2771, Fax: (712) 338-2263. Fast food pizza, carry out and delivery, convenience store format, non-traditional format. Established: 1977 - Franchising Since: 1977 - No. of Units: Franchised: 650 - Total Inv: Convenience and non- traditional $22,000-$30,000, carry out, delivery $30,000-$150,000 - Financing: Yes.

PICCOLO'S PIZZA
405 N I St #B, Madera, CA, 93637-3029. Contact: Stephen L. Frazier, Pres. - Tel: (559) 661-1800. Take n bake pizza. Established: 1983 - Franchising Since: 1985 - No. of Units: Company Owned: 2 - Franchised: 10 - Franchise Fee: $9,500 - Royalty: 4% first five years, 3% after that - Total Inv: $65,000-$95,000 - Financing: No.

PICKERMAN'S SOUP & SANDWICH SHOP
Pickerman's Development Company, Inc
2301 Clay Street, Cedar Falls, IA, 50613. Contact: Administrative Assistant - Tel: (319) 266-7141, (800) 273-2172, Fax: (319) 277-1201, Web Site: www.pickermans.com. High end soup and sandwich shop. Established: 1974 - Franchising Since: 1998 - No. of Units: Franchised: 10 - Franchise Fee: $10,000 - Royalty: 4% - Total Inv: $105,000-$115,000 - Financing: No.

PIETRO'S PIZZA PARLORS
317 E. Kettleman Ln., Lodi, CA, 95240. Contact: Jim Murdaca, Pres. - Tel: (209) 368-0613, Fax: (209) 368-3801. Restaurant. Established: 1958 - Franchising Since: 1971 - No. of Units: Company Owned: 2 - Franchised: 9 - Approx. Inv: $200,000 - Financing: No.

PIGGASO'S BARBEQUE *
P.O. Box 8261, Seneca, SC, 29678. - Tel: (864) 888-8216, Fax: (864) 885-1133. BBQ restaurant. Established: 1959 - Franchising Since: 2001 - No. of Units: Company Owned: 2 - Franchised: 2 - Franchise Fee: $18,000.

PIZZA COLORE
Pizza Colore Franchising, Inc.
P.O. Box 446, Princeton, NJ, 08542-0446. Contact: Venanzio A. Momo, President - Tel: (609) 924-0777, Fax: (609) 924-4074. European style specialty pizzeria cafe. Pizza in three colors, red, white, green pesto sauce. Pizza, pasta, panini, calzones, salads, desserts and coffee. Established: 1992 - Franchising Since: 1992 - No. of Units: Company Owned: 1 - Franchised: 10 - Franchise Fee: $15,000 - Royalty: 5% - Total Inv: $153,000-$258,000 - Financing: No.

PIZZA DEPOT
Pizza Depot Inc.
3722 Wheatsheaf Rd., Huntington Valley, PA, 19006. Contact: Fred Malitas, Pres. - Tel: (215) 947-8716. Pizzas, subs and steaks. Established: 1985 - Franchising Since: 1986 - No. of Units: Company Owned: 4 - Franchised: 4 - Franchise Fee: $7,500 - Royalty: 4% - Total Inv: $140,000-$190,000 - Financing: No.

PIZZA FACTORY, INC
We Toss'em, They're Awesome Pizza Factory
49430 Road 426, P.O. Box 989, Oakhurst, CA, 93644. Contact: Ron Willey, V.P. - Tel: (559) 683-3377, Fax: (559) 683-6879. Family style restaurant serving pizza, pasta, and sandwiches. Handmade dough tossed the old fashioned way. Established: 1979 - Franchising Since: 1984 - No. of Units: Company Owned: 3 - Franchised: 93 - Franchise Fee: $5,000-$20,000 - Royalty: 5% - Total Inv: $129,200-$300,000 - Financing: Assistance with financing.

PIZZA HUT, INC.
14841 North Dallas Prkwy, Dallas, TX, 75240. Contact: VP Fran. - Tel: (972) 338-7700, Fax: (972) 338-7188. Pizza restaurants. Established: 1958.

PIZZA INN
Pizza Inn, Inc.
3551 Plano Pkwy, The Colony, TX, 75056. Contact: Franchise Sales Dept.- Tel: (800) 284-3466, E-Mail: fran_opps@pizzainn.com, Web Site: www.pizzainn.com. Pizza Inn, with over 35 years of franchise experience and more than 500 franchises worldwide, is seeking franchisees for single locations, mulitple locations and master agreements for specific areas in the United States and around the world. Established: 1961 - Franchising Since: 1963 - No. of Units: Company Owned: 3 - Franchised: 500 - Franchise Fee: $3,500-$20,000 - Royalty: 4% & 5% - Total Inv: $400,00-$600,000 - Financing: No.

PIZZA JOE'S
Pizza Joe's, Inc.
2105 Commerce Rd, P.O. Box 7928, New Castle, PA, 16107-7928. Contact: Joe Seminara, Pres. - Tel: (724) 658-1716, Fax: (724) 658-6063. Fast food - pizza. Established: l98l - No. of Units: Company Owned: 5 - Franchised: l7 - Franchise Fee: $10,000 - Total Inv: $90,000-$150,000.

PIZZA MAN
El Centro Foods, Inc.
6930-1/2 Tujunga Ave., North Hollywood, CA, 91605. Contact: Robert Ohanian, Pres. - Tel: (818) 766-4395, Fax: (818) 766-1496, E-Mail: pizzaman@thepizzaman.com. Established: 1971- Franchising Since: 1978 - No. of Units: Company Owned: 3 - Franchised: 62 - Franchise Fee: $25,000 - Royalty: 4% - Total Inv: $110,000 - Financing: Yes, up to 40% of O.A.C.

PIZZA OUTLET
Pizza Outlet, L.P
2101 Greentree Road, Suite A-202, Pittsburgh, PA, 15220. Contact: Dir. of Franchise Marketing - Tel: (412) 279-9100, (866) 279-9100, Fax: (412) 279-9781, Web Site: www.pizzaoutlet.com. High quality pizza & subs for take out or delivery. Established: 1988 - Franchising Since: 1988 - No. of Units: Company Owned: 39 - Franchised: 68 - Franchise Fee: $15,000 - Royalty: 4% of sales - Total Inv: $95,000-$185,000 - Financing: No.

PIZZA PATRON *
1228 Northwest Hwy, Garland, TX, 75041. - Tel: (972) 613-8000, Fax: (972) 613-8014, Web Site: www.pizzapatron.com. Pizza Patron is a unique and highly focused pizza concept which is leading the industry by locating exclusively in Hispanic communities. Established: 1986 - Franchising Since: 2003 - No. of Units: Company Owned: 4 - Franchise Fee: $20,000 - Royalty: 5% - Total Inv: $122,800-$176,050 - Financing: Third party.

PIZZA PIE-ER FRANCHISE ENTERPRISES
374 Wickender St., Providence, RI, 02903. Contact: Bahman Jalili, Pres. - Tel: (401) 351-3663, Fax: (401) 351-3663. Pizza franchise. Established: 1993 - No. of Units: Company Owned: 1 - Franchise Fee: $20,000 - Royalty: 5% - Total Inv: $75,000.

PIZZA PIPELINE, THE
418 W. Sharp, Spokane, WA, 99201. Contact: Gene J. Boik, V.P. - Tel: (509) 326-1977, Fax: (509) 326-3017. A delivery and carry out pizza business offering 25 different items and assorted sauces along with salads, Tricky Stix®, sub sandwiches and chicken wings. Established: 1988 - Franchising Since: 1990 - No. of Units: Company Owned: 5 - Franchised: 5 - Franchise Fee: $5,000 - Royalty: 3% of gross corporate fee, 1% of gross nat'l. adv. - Total Inv: $120,000-$250,000 - Financing: None.

PIZZA PIT
Pizza Pit Investment Enterprises, Inc.
433 Grand Canyon Dr., Ste. 204, Madison, WI, 53719. Contact: Kerry Cook, V.P. - Tel: (608) 221-6777, Fax: (608) 321-6771. Free home delivery and carry-out of handcrafted pizzas and specialty sandwiches. Units are also adaptable to inside seating with prepared salads and pizza by the slice. Also, catering and food court. Established: 1969 - Franchising Since: 1982 - No. of Units: Company Owned: 9 - Franchised: 36 - Franchise Fee: $16,000-$17,500 - Total Inv: $109,000-$237,000 - Royalty: 5.5%, 1% adv. - Financing: None.

PIZZA PRO, INC.
P.O. Box 1285, Cabot, AR, 72023-1285. - Tel: (800) 777-7554, Fax: (501) 605-1204. Pizza franchises including free standing, convenience store, video store and supermarket operations. Established: 1985 - Franchising Since: 1992 - No. of Units: Company Owned: 14 - Franchised: 162 - Franchise Fee: $2,000 - Royalty: 5% of gross less sales tax - Total Inv: Approx. $18,000-$65,000 - Financing: In approved areas.

PIZZA RANCH
1121Main, Box 823, Hull, IA, 51239. Contact: Lawrence M. Vander Esch, Co-Founder - Tel: (712) 439-1150, (800) 321-3401, Fax: (712) 439-1125, Web Site: www.pizzaranch.com. Pizza, chicken, salad bar, buffet and sandwiches. Established: 1981 - Franchising Since: 1984 - No. of Units: Company Owned: 8 - Franchised: 82 - Franchise Fee: $10,000 - Royalty: 4% - Total Inv: $50,000-$100,000 equip., $2,000-$4,000 inven., $5,000 misc., $3,000-$5,000 signs, $5,000-$10,000 working cap. - Financing: Not directly, but will assist in arranging.

PIZZA SCHMIZZA *
1055 N.E. 25th, #B, Hillsboro, OR, 97124. Contact: Rick Glenn - Tel: (503) 640-2328, Fax: (503) 726-0797, E-Mail: rickglenn@schmizza.com, Web Site: www.schmizza. We make our hand-tossed pizza dough fresh each and everyday. If you are a high-energy individual that is motivated to serve others and who will help maintain the quality and personality of Pizza Schimma then please contact us. Established: 1993 - Franchising Since: 2002 - No. of Units: Company Owned: 8 - Franchised: 16 - Franchise Fee: $15,000 - Royalty: 5% - Total Inv: $181.400-$244,900.

PIZZA, U.S.A.
Pizza USA Franchise Corp.
1761 W. Hillsboro Blvd., Ste. 401, Deerfield Beach, FL, 33442-1502. Contact: Ray Nevin, Pres. - Tel: (954)428-5660, Fax: (954) 428-5560. Sale of Italian specialty items including pizza, calzone, pasta, salad. Specialize in mall food courts. Also offer "Express" and "Cafe" formats. Established: 1982 - Franchising Since: 1994 - No. of Units: Company Owned: 11 - Franchised: 10 - Franchise Fee: $25,000 - Royalty: 5%, .25% admin. fee, 2.5% adv. - Total Inv: Varies $170,000-$250,000 - Financing: No.

PIZZA WORLD / GOURMET PIZZA
Pizza World International Franchise Corp
P.O Box 50368, Sarasota, FL, 34232-0303. Contact: Eric Wortham, President - Tel: (941) 378-4845, Fax: (941) 377-1836. Delivery and carryout of gourmet and traditional pizza, calzones, subs and salads , all made with fresh wholesome ingredients. Established: 1997 - Franchising Since: 1997 - No. of Units: Company Owned: 2 - Franchised: 20 - Franchise Fee: $18,500 - Royalty: 4% - Total Inv: $142,500-$350,000 - Financing: No.

PIZZAS BY MARCHELLONI
Italian Express Franchise Corp.
1520 N Rock Dr #6, Joliet, IL, 60435-3153. Contact: Alan Mirkiani, Dir. Oper. - Tel: (815) 722-6200, Fax: (815) 722-6274. Pizza delivery, carry-out or dine-in. Strong local restaurant marketing. Featuring pan pizza, thin pizza, garlic bread and soft drinks. Established: 1986 - Franchising Since: 1989 - No. of Units: Company Owned: 1 - Franchised: 47 - Franchise Fee: $18,500 - Royalty: 5% + 2% adv. - Total Inv: $35,000-$192,000 - Financing: None.

PIZZAS OF EIGHT
Pizzas of Eight, Inc.
11800 Borman Drive, St. Louis, MO, 63146. Contact: Chuck McMillen, Managing Partner - Tel: (314) 432-8290, (800) 422-2901, Fax: (314) 432-0266. Presents complete, turnkey pizza system. Programs are small, simple to use and prepare a delicious, hot oven baked pizza in minutes. Packages include full equipment, marketing materials, training, private labeled ingredients, service and support. Established: 1993 - Franchising Since: 1993 - No. of Units: Franchised: 160 - Franchise Fee: No franchise fee - Royalty: Branded program - Total Inv: $20,000 - Financing: Yes.

PIZZERIA UNO.
UNO Restaurants Corp.
100 Charles Park Rd., West Roxbury, MA, 02132. Contact: Randy Clifton - Tel: (617) 218-5325, Fax: (617) 218-5376, E-Mail: randy.clifton @unos.com, Web Site: www.unos.com. 190+ unit chain with both

demestic and internationl locations we are the creators of chicago style deep dish pizzas, Uno's is the only casual dinning concept that offers america's favorite food as our signature product. Established: 1978 - Franchising Since: 1979 - No. of Units: Company Owned: 120 - Franchised: 78.

PLANET SMOOTHIE
1100 Poyadras St., 1150, New Orleans, LA, 70163. - Tel: (504) 582-2241, Fax: (504) 582-2265, Web Site: www.planetsmoothie.com. Retail outlet that sells smoothies, Round-A-Bout wrap sandwiches and vitamins/supplements. Established: 1995 - Franchising: 1998 - No. of Units: Company Owned: 6 - Franchised Since: 100 - Franchise Fee: $20,000 - Royalty: 5% - Total Inv: $70,000-$130,000 - Financing: Yes.

PLUS 1 PIZZA
R.D.F. Developments, Inc.
1354 Clark Street, P.O. Box 516, Cambridge, OH, 43725-0516. Contact: Robert Fettes, Sr., Pres. - Tel: (740) 439-1333, Fax: (740) 439-9898. Carry-out and delivery pizza business selling pizzas 2 for 1. Established: l977 - Franchising Since: l988 - No. of Units: Company Owned: 11 - Franchised: 3 - Franchise Fee: $20,000 - Royalty: 5%, 2% adv. fee - Total Inv: $34,900-$89,900 - Financing: Assistance with lenders and bank presentation.

POFOLKS
PoFolks Express
508 Harmon Ave, Panama City, FL 32401. - Tel: (850) 763-0501, Fax: (850) 872-0072. A full-service restaurant serving home-style meals in large portions, priced moderately, in a rustic country setting. Beverages (non-alcoholic) are served in mason jars, country music plays in the background, and the extensive menu is written in traditional country idioms. Established: 1975 - Franchising Since: 1978 - No. of Units: Franchised: 30 - Franchise Fee: $20,000 - Royalty: 3% - Total Inv: $150,000-$900,000 - Financing: No.

POLLO TROPICAL
Pollo Tropical, Inc.
7300 N. Kendall Dr., 8th Floor, Miami, FL, 33156. - Tel: (305) 670-POYO (7696), Fax: (305) 670-6403. Quick service flame grilled chicken with Caribbean and traditional side dishes served in a festive and inviting atmosphere. Established: 1988 - Franchising Since: 1993 - No. of Units: Company Owned: 35 - Franchised: 5 - Franchise Fee: $40,000 - Royalty: 4% - Total Inv: $700,000-$800,000 - Financing: No.

PONDEROSA STEAKHOUSES
Metromedia Family Steakhouses
6500 International Parkway, Suite 1000, Plano, TX, 75093-8226. Contact: Larry Stein, Dir. of Fran. Dev. - Tel: (972) 588-5887, (800) 543-9670, Fax: (972) 404-5806. Ponderosa is an affordable priced steakhouse with over 509 restaurants in the U.S. and overseas. Grand Buffet food bar and 3-day part service. New construction or conversion opportunities available in most areas. Established: 1966 - Franchising Since: 1966- No. of Units: Company Owned: 162 - Franchised: 347 - Franchise Fee: $40,000 per unit - Royalty: 4% - Total Inv: $1,045,200-$2,177,500 - Financing: No.

POPEYES CHICKEN & BISCUITS
AFC Enterprises
5555 Glenridge Connector, #300, Atlanta, GA, 30342. Contact: Tad Phelps, Dir. of New Bus. Dev. - Tel: (404) 459-4486, (800) 639-3780, Fax: (404) 459-4523. World's second largest quick service chicken company featuring buttermilk biscuits, seafood specialties, onion rings, battered french fries and more. Established: 1972 - Franchising Since: 1976 - No. of Units: Company Owned: 96 - Franchised: 1620 - Franchise Fee: $30,000 - Royalty: 5%, 3% ad fund - Total Inv: $450,000-$650,000 not including real estate - Financing: N/A.

PORT OF SUBS
Port of Subs, Inc.
5365 Mae Anne Ave., #A-29, Reno, NV, 89523. Contact: John Larsen, Pres. - Tel: (800) 245-0245. Up-scale fresh-sliced submarine sandwiches served on custom rolls baked on premises, salads, party platters, breakfast sandwiches and pastries. Established: 1975 - Franchising Since: 1986 - No. of Units: Company Owned: 11- Franchised: 105 - Franchise Fee: $16,000 - Royalty: 5.5% of net sales - Total Inv: $137,000-$205,000 - Financing: No.

POTATO SACK, THE
Potato Sack Franchise Corp.
201 Monroeville Mall, Monroeville, PA, 15146. - Tel: (800) 828-3770, (412) 373-0850, Fax: (412) 373-4497. Regional mall food court operation specializing in baked potatoes, fresh cut french fries and potato skins with a wide variety of gourmet toppings. Established: 1980 - Franchising Since: 1992 - No. of Units: Company Owned: 2 - Franchised: 4 - Franchise Fee: $20,000 - Royalty: 5% - Total Inv: $150,000-$225,000 - Financing: None.

POTATOES PLUS
Potatoes Plus Corp.
4701 N Billen Ave, Oklahoma City, OK, 73112-8312. Contact: Shirley Grace - Tel: (405) 478-7653, Fax: (405) 478-7331. We are a unique new franchise opportunity specializing in baked potatoes with a variety of toppings Our carefully crafted menu was designed to provide virtually unlimited variety, offering sandwiches and soups. Established: 1988 - Franchising Since: 1998 - No. of Units: Franchised: 1 - Franchise Fee: $20,000 - Total Inv: $95,000-$189,000 - Financing: No.

POTTS' HOT DOGS INC.
16305 San Carlos Blvd., Ft. Myers, FL, 33908. Contact: Michael A Potts, Pres. - Tel: (941) 466-7747, E-Mail: potts@wevutc.com, Web Site: www.wevctv.com/potts. Hot dogs shops and hot dogs - wings, burgers, etc. breakfast, lunch, dinner. Established: 1971- Franchising Since: 1986 - No. of Units: Company Owned: 4 - Franchised: 3 - Franchise Fee: $15,000 - Royalty: 4% gross sales - Total Inv: Hot Dog Shops $30,000, Restaurants $70,000 - Financing: No.

POWER SMOOTHIE
Power Smoothie, Inc.
160 S. University Dr., Ste. B, Plantation, FL, 33324. Contact: Adam Mandel - Tel: (954) 370-3913, Fax: (954) 370-3902, Web Site: www.powersmoothie.com. Fruit smoothie, healthy gourmet sandwiches and low fat snacks served in a fast and energetic atmosphere. Established: 1991 - Franchising Since: 1997 - No. of Units: Franchised: 20 - Franchise Fee: $10,000 - Total Inv: $84,400-$143,900 - Financing: Third Party.

PUDGIES FAMOUS CHICKEN
5 Dakota Drive, Lake Success, NY, 11042. Contact; Steven R. Gardner, Director Franchise Devel. - Tel: (516) 358-0600, (800) PUDGIES, Fax: (516) 358-5076. Fast food, premium skinless chicken concept utilizing our proprietary breading. 70% delivery and takeout. Established: 1981 - Franchising Since: 1981 - No. of Units: Company Owned: 12- Franchise Fee: $30,000 - Royalty: 5%, 3% advertising - Financing: Through referral.

QDOBA MEXICAN GRILL *
4865 Ward Rd., #500, Wheat Ridge, CO, 80033. - Tel: (720) 898-2300, Fax: (720) 898-2396, Web Site: www.qdoba.com. Fast casual Mexican restaurant serving: Burritos, Tacos, Nachos & Quesadillas. Established: 1995 - Franchising Since: 1997 - No. of Units: Company Owned: 31 - Franchised: 70 - Franchise Fee: $25,000 - Royalty: 5% - Total Inv: $300,000-$450,000 - Financing: No.

QUIZNO'S SUBS
Quizno's Corp.
1475 Lawrence St, #400, Denver, CO, 80202. Contact: Scott Adams, Dan Demolli, Area Dev. Mgr., Dev. Director - Tel: (720) 359-3300, (800) 335-4782, Fax: (720) 359-3399, Web Site: www.quiznos.com. Denver, Co. based Quizno's Subs has over 850 Quizno's restaurants open worldwide. Quizno's is a franchise based company selling over baked subs, salads, soups and deserts. Established: 1981 - Franchising Since: 1981 - No. of Units: Company Owned: 24 - Franchised: 840+ - Franchise Fee: $25,000 - Royalty: 7% - Total Inv: $170,036-$225,163, $200,000 incl. FF (turn key) - Financing: Yes, third party.

R.J. BOAR'S BBQ RESTAURANTS
R.J. Boar's Franchising Corp
3127 Brady St. Suite #3, Davenport, IA, 52803. Contact: Director of Franchise Sales - Tel: (319) 322-2627, Fax: (319) 322-1947, Web Site: www.rjboars.com. Award winning restaurant specializing in hickory smoked BBQ. We offer a concept of guest focused management, a formula involving a broad and varied menu, and the documented support you would expect from a professional organization. Established: 1993

- Franchising Since: 1998 - No. of Units: Company Owned: 4 - Franchised: 1 - Franchise Fee: $35,000 - Royalty: 4% of net sales paid weekly - Total Inv: $378,000-$909,000 - Financing: No.

R.J. GATOR'S HOMETOWN GRILL & BAR
R.J. Gator's Inc.
609 N. Hepburn Ave. #103, Jupiter, FL, 33458. Contact: Andrew Howard, Vice President Franchise - Tel: (561) 575-0326, (800) 438-4286, Fax: (561) 575-9220, E-Mail: andyh@rjgators.com, Web Site: www.rjgators.com. R.J. Gators is a trip to the Florida Everglades where friends and family go to experience consistent great times, every time. Serving up great tasting Florida food with an emphasis on fresh seafood and tropical drinks in an upbeat casual, comfortable atmosphere of the Everglades. Established: 1986 - Franchising Since: 1991 - No. of Units: Company Owned: 7 - Franchised: 7 - Franchise Fee: $350,000 - Royalty: 4% - Total Inv: $625,000-$1.4 million without land - Financing: Third party contacts.

RALLY'S HAMBURGERS, INC
14255 49th St N. Building 1, Clearwater, FL, 33762. - Tel: (888) 913-9135. Double drive-thru hamburger (fast food) limited menu with outside patio area. Established: 1985 - Franchising Since: 1986 - No. of Units: Company Owned: 229 - Franchised: 253- Franchise Fee: $20,000 per store - Royalty: 4% sales, 4% adv. - Total Inv: $550,000 for build., equip. & site prep. costs - Financing: None.

RAMS HORN RESTAURANTS INC.
24225 W. Nine Mile, Ste. 214, Southfield, MI, 48034. - Tel: (248) 350-3430, Fax: (248) 350-1024. Family restaurants. Established: 1967 - No. of Units: Company Owned: 8 - Franchised: 16.

RANCH *1
Ranch 1 Group. Inc.
567 7th Ave 3rd Floor, New York, NY, 10018. - Tel: (212) 354-6666, Fax: (212) 730-4444. Fresh grilled chicken sandwiches and other chicken specialties. Established: 1990 - Franchising Since: 1993 - No. of Units: Company Owned: 16 - Franchised: 15 - Franchise Fee: $40,000 - Royalty: 5% - Total Inv: $350,000 - Financing: Assistance.

RED HOT & BLUE
1701 Claredon Blvd., #105, Arlington, VA, 22209. Contact: Bob Friedman, Pres. - Tel: (703) 276-8833, Fax: (703) 528-4789, Web Site: www.redhotandblue.com. Casual - theme BAR-B-QUE restaurant featuring hickory-smoked Memphis-style BBQ . Established: 1988 - Franchising Since: 1990 - No. of Units: Company Owned: 6 - Franchised: 32- Franchise Fee: $35,000 - Royalty: 5% - Total Inv: $397,750 - Financing: No.

RED ROBIN BURGER & SPIRITS EMPORIUM
Red Robin International, Inc.
5575 DTC Parkway Ste. 110, Englewood, CO, 80111. - Tel: (972) 331-2519, Fax: (972) 331-2558. Full service, casual dining restaurants offering high quality, moderately priced food and alcoholic beverages in an attractive, informal setting that is decorated to entertain. Established: 1969 - Franchising Since: 1979 - No. of Units: Company Owned: 47 - Franchised: 79 - Franchise Fee: $35,000 per restaurant - Royalty: 4%, .5% adv. - Total Inv: $1,000,000-$3,500,000 - Financing: Outside financing available.

RED'S BACKWOODS BBQ
The BBQ Co., Inc
2255 Glades Rd., Suite 110-E, Boca Raton, FL, 33431. Contact: Director of Franchise Dev. - Tel: (561) 998-2250, (888) 311-7337, Fax: (561) 998-2249, Web Site: www.redsbbq.com. Red's Backwoods BBQ is a full service "fast casual" neighborhood restaurant specializing in barbeque pork, St. Louis style ribs, beef and chicken served along with our six award winning BBQ sauces. Restaurants are typically 2,000 - 2,700 Sq.f with 50-100 seats in neighborhood shopping crenters and offer takeout, catering & delivery. Established: 1996 - Franchising Since: 1997 - No. of Units: Company Owned: 6 - Franchised: 10 - Franchise Fee: $25,000 initial - Royalty: 5% of sales - ongoing - Total Inv: $334,400-$486,100 - Financing: N/A.

RENZIOS
Renzios Inc
4690 S. Yosemite, Greenwood Village, CO, 80111-1227. Contact: Tom Rentizios - Tel: (303) 267-0300, (800) 892-3441, Fax: (303) 267-0088. Greek fast food restaurant. Established: 1978 - Franchising Since: 1993 - No. of Units: Company Owned: 9 - Franchised: 9 - Franchise Fee: $22,000.

RIB CITY GRILL
2122 Second Street, Ft. Myers, FL, 33901. Contact: Lynn Brewer - Tel: (239) 561-2591, Fax: (239) 332-7232. Fast growing franchise opportunity. Great family style restaurant with comfortable surroundings and friendly trained staff. Established: 1989 - Franchising Since: 1990 - No. of Units: Company Owned: 12 - Franchise Fee: $40,000 - Royalty: 4% - Financing: No.

RIB CRIB CORP.
4271 W. Albany, Broken Arrow, OK, 74012. - Tel: (918) 728-6458, Web Site: www.ribcrib.com. A full service casual dining barbeque concept. The first concept to deliver the great taste of barbeque that people love using an entertaining, value and service oriented casual dining system. Established: 1992 - Franchising Since: 2001 - No. of Units: Company Owned: 18 - Franchised: 2 - Franchise Fee: $25,000 - Royalty: 4% - Total Inv: $400,000-$700,000.

RICKY'S ALL DAY GRILL
1710 Chuckanut Cres Drive, Bellingham, WA, 98226. Contact: Ron Hildebrand, President & CEO - Tel: (800) 774-2599, (360) 738-2207, Fax: (360) 647-4594, E-Mail: ron@rickys-restaurants.com. New millennium diner limited editions available 1800-2600sq ft. Established: 1965 - Franchising Since: 1987 - No. of Units: Company Owned: 5 - Franchised: 39 - Franchise Fee: $25,000-$45,000 - Royalty: 4.5% + 2% ad - Total Inv: $250,000-$475,000.

RISING STAR GRILL
Metromedia Rest Group
12404 Park Central Drive, Dallas, TX, 75251. Contact: Kenneth L. Myres - Tel: (214) 404-5860, (800) 543-9670. Texas theme style restaurant, casual dining - full training and support provided. Established: 1995 - Franchising Since: 1995 - No. of Units: Franchised: 1 - Franchise Fee: $40,000 - Total Inv: $500,000 liquid - Financing: Yes.

ROCCO RACCOON'S INDOOR PLAYGROUNDS, INC.
8 Alabamma Place, Lockport, NY, 14094. Contact: Mr. Varlis, Franchise Dept. - Tel: (716) 434-7553, Fax: (716) 810-0571, E-Mail: KRoccoRaccoon@aol.com, Web Site: www.RoccoRaccoons.com. We specialize in opening family fun play centers with indoor supervised play areas, with a full menu (including) pizza, gift shops, skill testing games and animated characters. Established: 1994 - Franchising Since: 1994 - No. of Units: Company Owned: 2 - Franchised: 2 - Franchise Fee: $40,000 - Royalty: 3% of gross annual sales - Total Inv: $250,000-$500,000 - Financing: Bank/SBL.

ROCK ROCOCO PIZZA & PASTA
Rococo Franchise Corporation
105 E. Wisconsin Ave. Suite 101, Oconomowoc, WI, 53066. - Tel: (262) 569-5580, (800) 888-ROCKY (7625). Quick service, quality pizza and pasta restaurants. Strip center locations in Wisconsin. Established: 1974 - Franchising Since: 1996 - No. of Units: Company Owned: 13 - Franchised: 18 - Franchise Fee: $17,500 - Royalty: 5% - Total Inv: $198,500-$333,000 - Financing: No.

ROCKIN' BAJA LOBSTER *
Rockin' Baja Lobster, LLC
132 King Street, Alexandria, VA, 22314. Contact: Stacey Gallagher - Tel: (703) 349-5332, (877) 762-2252, Fax: (703) 349-0740, E-Mail: staceyg@fransmart.com, Web Site: www.rockinbaja.com. Known for their 'party in a bucket' Rockin' Baja Lobster offers authentic Baja-style seafood buckets brimming with shrimp, lobsters, and chicken. With 6 locations already open, this popular Cantina & grill is never short on amazing food choices, a wide range of cocktails and beer selections and a rockin' good time. Established: 1985 - Franchising Since: 2004 - No. of Units: Company Owned: 6 - Franchised: 10 - Franchise Fee: $30,000 - Royalty: 5% - Total Inv: $232,850-$654,500 - Financing: Third party.

ROLLERZ *
Kahala Corp
7730 E. Greenway Rd Ste. 104 Scottsdale, AZ, 85260. - Tel: 480) 443-0200, Fax: (480) 443-1972. Gourmet sandwiches, salads and soups. Established: 1999 - Franchising Since: 2000 - No. of Units: Company Owned: 1 - Franchised: 80 - Franchise Fee: $30,000.

RON'S PIZZA DELIVERY/RON'S PIZZA HOUSE/A & R PIZZA
P.O. Box 251, Danielsville, GA, 30633. Contact: Franchise Department - Tel: (706) 549-0800. Family restaurant. Established: 1961 - No. of Units: Company Owned: 4 - Franchised: 6.

RONZIO PIZZA
Pizzeria Management Systems
194 Waterman Street, Providence, RI, 02906. - Tel: (401) 751-4470, Fax: (401) 231-4720. Pizza and subs featuring delivery and takeout. Established: 1986 - Franchising: 1989 - No. of Units: Franchised: 17 - Franchise Fee: $10,000 - Total Inv: $85,000-$121,000 - Financing: No.

ROSATI'S PIZZA
Rossati's Franchise Systems, Inc.
33 W. Higgins Rd. Ste. 1010, S. Barrington, IL, 60010. Contact: Ron Stockman, President - Tel: (847) 836-0400, (800) 210-1322. Carry-out / delivery Chicago style pizza. Established: 1964 - Franchising Since: 1988 - No. of Units: Franchised: 36 - Franchise Fee: $15,000 - Total Inv: $110,00-$170,000 - Financing: No.

ROTELLI PIZZA & PASTA
501 E. Atlantic Ave, Delray Beach, FL, 33483. Contact: Robert A. Spuck, President - Tel: (561) 272-4807, (888) BE THE BOSS, Fax: (561) 272-8495, Web Site: www.rotellipp.com. Rotelli Pizza & Pasta is a fast-casual Italian theme restaurant that serves superior yet affordable cuisine, prepared fresh to order, and artistically presented in an upscale environment. Our restaurants are designed to occupy approximately 1500-1800 sqaure feet and offer consumers a choice of dine-in, take-out, or delivery services. Rotelli's offices and training center's are located in Delray Beach, Florida. Established: 1999 - Franchising Since: 1999 - No. of Units: Franchised: 4 - Franchise Fee: $29,000 - Royalty: 6% royalty + 3% advertising - Total Inv: Approx $300,000 including franchise fee + working capital - Financing: Assistance in finding third party finance.

ROUND TABLE PIZZA
Round Table Franchise Corp.
2175 N. California, Ste. 400, Walnut Creek, CA, 94596. - Tel: (800) 866-5866. Family style pizza restaurant that provides the public with quality pizza and related food products. Established: 1959 - Franchising Since: 1962 - No. of Units: Franchised: 560- Franchise Fee: $25,000 - Royalty: 8%-4% fran. fee and 4% adv. fee - Total Inv: $300,000-$100,000 cash and $200,000 equity - Financing: We offer third party lending to qualified franchisees.

ROYAL WAFFLE KING
P.O. 1025, Alpharetta, GA, 30009. Contact: Franchise Department - Tel: (770) 442-3800, Fax: (770) 475-0763. 24 hour full service restaurant. Established: 1986 - No. of Units: Company Owned: 1 - Franchised: 21 - Franchise Fee: $20,000 - Royalty: 4% - Total Inv: $430,000 - Financing: No.

RUBIO'S BAJA GRILL
Rubio's Restaurant
1902 Wright Place, #300, Carlsbad, CA, 92008. Contact: John Ramsay - Tel: (760) 929-8226, Fax: (760) 929-8203. Casual Mexican restaurant. Established: 1983 - Franchising Since: 2000 - No. of Units: Company Owned: 102 - Franchise Fee: $35,000 - Total Inv: $382,300-$559,300.

RUBY'S DINER
Ruby's Restaurant Group
660 Newport Center Drive Suite 850, Newport Beach, CA, 92660. Contact: Franchise Department - Tel: (949) 644-7829, Fax: (949) 644-4625. Full serve restaurant. Established: 1982 - Franchising Since: 1988 - No. of Units: Company Owned: 10 - Franchised: 5 - Franchise Fee: $40,000 - Royalty: 5%, 1% adv., 2% self directed adv. - Total Inv: $300,000-$800,000 depending on location - Financing: None.

RUNZA DRIVE INN RESTAURANTS
P.O. Box 6042, Lincoln, NE, 68506. - Tel: (402) 423-2394, Fax: (402) 423-5726. Fast food restaurant featuring unique Runza sandwiches, and homemade onion rings. Our food is top quality. Franchising Since: 1979 - No. of Units: Company Owned: 20 - Franchised: 35 - Franchise Fee: $22,000 - Royalty: 5%, 1.5% - Total Inv: $150,000-$675,000.

RYAN'S FAMILY STEAK HOUSE
405 Lancaster Ave., P.O. Box 100, Greer, SC, 29652. Contact: Randy Hart, Fran. Dir. - Tel: (864) 879-1000, Fax: (864) 877-0974. Family restaurant. Established: 1977 - No. of Units: Company Owned: 104 - Franchised: 28.

SALADWORKS INC
Eight Tower Bridge, 16 Washington St, #225, Conshohocken, PA, 19428. - Tel: (610) 825-3080, Fax: (610) 825-3280. Quick casual dining or carry-out. Established: 1986 - No. of Units: Franchised: 25 - Franchise Fee: $35,000 - Total Inv: $213,800-$272,200 - Financing: No.

SALSARITA'S FRESH CANTINA*
7301 Carmel Executive Park Dr #101-A, Charlotte, NC, 28226. - Tel: (704) 540-9447, Fax: (704) 540-9448, Web Site: www.salsaritas.com. Fresh Mex-Style cantina featuring Tacos, Burritos, Nachos, Salads & Quesadillas. Established: 1999 - Franchising Since: 2000 - No. of Units: Franchised: 6 - Franchise Fee: $20,000 - Royalty: 5-6% - Total Inv: $179,800-$299,500 - Financing: No.

SALUBRE-PIZZA, SUBSATION'S SANDWICHES
Bull's Eye Brands
2337 Perimeter Park Dr Ste 200, Chamblee, GA, 30341-1313. - Tel: (770) 457-7611, (800) 310-9640. Restaurants franchised to non-traditional locations, primarily convenience stores. Salubre is a pizza shop and subsations is a sub sandwich shop. Established: 1996 - Franchising Since: 1996 - No. of Units: Franchised: 40 - Royalty: Upcharge on food products - Total Inv: $47,000, cabinetry, equipment, signage - Financing: Third party leasing.

SALVATORE SCALLOPINI
Scallopini Ventures
1650 East 12 Mile Rd, Madison Heights, MI, 48071. - Tel: (248) 542-3281, Fax: (248) 542-7660. Full-service restaurant with liquor, and authentic Italian fare. Specialize in homemade pasta. Carry-out from menu available. Also catering service. Established: 1983 - Franchising Since: 1988 - No. of Units: Company Owned: 5 - Franchised: 6 - Franchise fee: $25,000 - Royalty: 4% - Total Inv: $275,000-$525,000 - Financing: No. NOT FRANCHISING AT THIS TIME.

SAM'S HOT DOGS
Sam's Hot Dogs, Inc.
P.O. Box 539, Waynesboro, VA, 22980. Contact: Frank Lucente, Pres. - Tel: (800) 337-6260. Fast food restaurant. Established: 1988 - Franchising Since: 1990 - No. of Units: Franchised: 24 - Franchise Fee: $4,000 - Royalty: 4% gross sales - Total Inv: $18,000-$35,000.

SAM'S ITALIAN FOODS
268 Main St., Lewiston, ME, 04240. - Tel: (207) 782-2550, Fax: (207) 782-3827. Dinnerhouse - Fast food. Established: 1969 - No. of Units: Company Owned: 5 - Franchised: 10.

SAMMI'S DELI
Sammi's Deli Inc.
114 Wilton Hill Rd., Columbia, SC, 29212. - Tel: (803) 256-7763, Fax: (803) 771-7958. Fast food with fast free delivery. Established: 1983 - Franchising Since: 1995 - No. of Units: Company Owned: 1 - Franchised: 1 - Franchise Fee: $9,500 - Royalty: 6% or $400 whichever is higher - Total Inv: $50,000-$60,000 - Financing: No.

SAMUEL MANCINO'S ITALIAN EATERY
Nu-Ventures Inc.
1324 W Milham Ave, Portage, MI, 49024-1209. Contact: Samuel Mancino, Jr. or Chris Schneider - Tel: (616) 327-6800, (888) 432-8379, Fax: (616) 226-4466. Casual Italian dining. Established: 1994 - No. of Units: Franchised: 25 - Franchise Fee: $40,000 - Royalty: 5% - Total Inv: $150,000-$240,000 - Financing: No.

SAMURAI SAM'S TERIYAKI GRILL

SP Franchising, Inc.
7730 E. Greenway Rd, Suite 104, Scottsdale, AZ, 85260. - Tel: (480) 443-0200, Web Site: www.samurisams.net. Fast food franchise of Japanese food. Established: 1994 - Franchising Since: 1997 - No. of Units: Company Owned: 2 - Franchised: 42 - Franchise Fee: $20,000 - Royalty: 5% - Total Inv: $120,00-$170,000.

SAN FRANCISCO OVEN

SFO Franchise Development, LTD
9150 South Hills Blvd, Suite 225, Cleveland, OH, 44147. Contact: Stacey Gallagher - Tel: (703) 549-5332, (800) 230-7202, Fax: (703) 549-0740, E-Mail: staceyg@fransmart.com, Web Site: www.sanfrancisc oven.com.. From the sidewalk cafes of North Beach to the wine gardens of the Napa Valley, San Francisco Oven brings the culinary traditions of the bay area to the doorsteps of every American neighborhood. Driven by CIA graduate, executive chef & co-founder, Eddie Cerino, San Francisco Oven's menu is centered around a brick oven, and offers guests premium pizzas, sandwiches, entrees and salads. Established: 2001 - Franchising Since: 2003 - No. of Units: Company Owned: 1 - Franchised: 1 - Franchise Fee: $25,000 - Royalty: 5% - Total Inv: $225,500-$480,000 - Financing: Third party.

SANDELLA'S CAFÉ

9 Brookside Place, West Redding, CT, 06896. Contact: V.P. of Franchise Development - Tel: (203) 544-9984, (888) 544-9984, Fax: (203) 544-7749, Web Site: www.sandellas.com. Positioned in the explosive sophisticated sandwich market. Fresh distinctive food at affordable prices. Established: 1995 - Franchising Since: 1998 - No. of Units: Company Owned: 2 - Franchised: 14 - Franchise Fee: $20,000 - Royalty: 6% of gross revenues - Total Inv: $150,000-$250,000 - Financing: Registered with the S.B.A.

SANDY'S ASSOCIATES, INC.

1503 N. Boeke Rd, Evansville, IN, 47711. - Tel: (812) 477-5569, Fax: (812) 474-1653. Fast food restaurants. Established: 1963 - No. of Units: Franchised: 16.

SBARRO

Sbarro, Inc.
401 Broadhollow Rd, Melville, NY, 11747. Contact: Jerry Sbarro, President-Global Franchise - Tel: (631) 715-4145, (800) 955-7227, Fax: (631) 715-4197, E-Mail: jerrysbarro@sbarro.com, Web Site: www.sbarro.com. Sbarro Inc, is the industry leader in quick casual Italian dinning offering an array different size and style units. Established: 1954 - Franchising Since: 1979 - No. of Units: Company Owned: 540 - Franchised: 360 - Franchise Fee: $15,000-$35,000 - Royalty: 76% - Total Inv: $90,000-$330,000 - Financing: All markets.

SCHLOTZSKY'S DELI RESTAURANT

Schlotzsky's Inc.
203 Colorado St., Ste. 600, Austin, TX, 78701. Contact: Sr. Franchse Licensing Mgr - Tel: (512) 236-3800, Fax: (512) 236-3650. Bakery/deli/restaurant. Deli sandwiches served on Schlotzsky's unique proprietary bread, sourdough crust pizzas, soups, salads, desserts, gourmet coffees, and specialty breakfast items. Established: 1971 - Franchising Since: 1977 - No. of Units: Company Owned: 10 - Franchised: 712 - Franchise Fee: $30,000 - Royalty: 6%, 1% nat'l mktg, 3% regional mktg - Total Inv: $400,000-$1,500,000 - Financing: Yes.

SCHOOP'S HAMBURGERS

Schoop's Hamburgers, Inc.
215 Ridge Rd., Munster, IN, 46321. Contact: Mark Schoop, Pres. - Tel: (219) 836-6233. Fast food/hamburgers. Established: 1948 - No. of Units: Franchised: 21. NOT FRANCHISING AT THIS TIME.

SCOOBIES DRIVE-IN RESTAURANT, INC

2014 Drew Street, Clearwater, FL, 34619. - Tel: (727) 467-0331, (800) 739-5000, Fax: (727) 466-6333. Fast food restaurants specializing in hot dogs. Established: 1996 - Franchising Since: 1997 - No. of Units: Company Owned: 1 - Franchise Fee: $19,000 - Royalty: 4% - Total Inv: $300,000-$500,000 - Financing: Yes.

SEATTLE SUTTON'S HEALTHY EATING

611 E. Steveson Rd, Ottawa, IL, 61350. Contact: Seattle Sutton, Founder/Owner - Tel: (815) 433-4494, (888) 442-3438, Fax: (815) 795-3493, E-Mail: corp@sshe.com, Web Site: www.sshe.com. Freshly prepared healthy eating meals. Every breakfast, lunch and diner. Established: 1989 - Franchising Since: 2001 - Franchise Fee: $35,000 - Royalty: 5% - Total Inv: $800,000 - Financing: No.

SHAKEY'S PIZZA RESTAURANTS

Shakey's, Inc.
350 S. Figueroa St, Suite 501, Los Angeles, CA, 90071. - Tel: (213) 995-3500, Fax: (213) 995-3501, E-Mail: franchiseopportunities@sha keys.com, Web Site: www.shakeys.com. Family pizza restaurant featuring pizza, salad bar, chicken, mojo-potatoes, and pasta. Also offer expanded lunch display. Established: 1954 - Franchising Since: 1958 - No. of Units: Company Owned: 20 - Franchised: 371 - Franchise Fee: $25,000 - Royalty: 4.5%, 2% nat'l adv. fund - Total Inv: $350,000-$500,000 - Financing: By local sources or equip. leasing comp.

SHOOTERS ON THE WATER

Shooters International, Inc.
3061 N.E. 32nd Ave., Fort Lauderdale, FL, 33308. Contact: V.P.Fran. Dev. - Tel: (954) 566-3044, Fax: (954) 566-2953. Upscale waterfront cafe and bar. Both indoor and patio dining, boat docking. Established: 1982 - Franchising Since: 1985 - No. of Units: Company Owned: 1 - Franchised: 5 - Franchise Fee: $75,000 - Royalty: 4% gross - Total Inv: $1,500,000-$1,620,000 - Financing: No. NOT FRANCHISING AT THIS TIME.

SHRIMP BUSTERS

3820 Premier Ave, Memphis, TN, 38118. - Tel: (901) 368-3333, Fax: (901) 368-1144. Fast food restaurant. Established: 2000 - Franchising Since: 2001 - No. of Units: Company Owned: 1 - Franchise Fee: $66,000.

SICILY'S, THE PIZZA PLACE, INC./SICILY'S PIZZA JR.

2109 South Burnside, Ste. D, Gonzales, LA, 70737. Contact: Eric North, Pres. - Tel: (504) 647-5847, (800) 660-6962. Quality pizza, lasagna and sandwiches, salad bar, beer, served in an upscale dining atmosphere. Table service. Established: 1975 - Franchising Since: 1984 - No. of Units: Company Owned: 3 - Franchised: 9 - Franchise Fee: $10,000 - Royalty: 4% - Total Inv: Approx. $125,000 for full service.

SILVER MINE SUBS

925 E. Harmony Rd., Ste. 500, Fort Collins, CO, 80525. Contact: Keith Dudek - Tel: (970) 266-2600, Fax: (970) 267-3538. Offering hot and cold subs. Established: 1996 - Franchising Since: 2002 - No. of Units: Company Owned: 6 - Franchise Fee: $20,000-$62,500 - Royalty: 6% - Total Inv: $168,500-$291,000 - Financing: No.

SIMPLE SIMON'S PIZZA

J&H Foods
6650 S. Lewis, Tulsa, OK, 74136. Contact: Fran. Dir. - Tel: (918) 496-1272, (800) 271-6375, Fax: (918) 493-6516. A full service and non-traditional pizza company that specializes in small, rural and niche markets. Emphasis is on quality and a great price - value relationship for customers. Established: 1985 - Franchising Since: 1987 - No. of Units: Company Owned: 120 - Franchised: 42 - Franchise Fee: $15,000 first and $10,000 subsequent - Royalty: 3%, 1% adv. - Total Inv: $80,000-$120,000 - Financing: No.

SIRLOIN STOCKADE FAMILY RESTAURANTS

Sirloin Stockade International, Inc.
2908 North Plum, Hutchinson, KS, 67502. - Tel: (620) 669-9372, Fax: (620) 669-0531. Featuring a selection of top quality steaks, chicken and fish; self-service salad, hot food buffet, and display bakery, at affordable prices. Restaurants seat 300-400 guests; approx. 10,000 sq. ft. bldg; requires 1.5+ acres of land. Established: 1984 - Franchising Since: 1984 - No. of Units: Company Owned: 5 - Franchised: 66 - Franchise Fee: $5,000 in USA - Royalty: 3% in USA + .33% mktg. fund - Total Inv: $1,200,000-$2,260,000 - Financing: None.

SIZZLER
Sizzler Restaurants International, Inc.
15301 Ventura Blvd, Garden Office Building Bldg B #300, Shermon Oaks, CA, 91403. - Tel: (818) 662-9900, Fax: (818) 662-9870. Specializing in steaks, seafood and salads. Established: 1954 - No. of Units: Company Owned: 265 - Franchised: 430. Unfortunately Sizzler is not expanding at this time. But will assist in the resale of existing franchises.

SKYLINE CHILI
Skyline Chili, Inc.
4180 Thunderbird Lane, Fairfield, OH, 45014. - Tel: (513) 874-1188, (800) 443-4317, Fax: (513) 874-3591, Web Site: www.skylinechili.com. Quick service, casual dining restaurants located in Ohio, Indiana, Kentucky and Florida, serving limited menu of Cincinnati style chili, coneys, burritos, baked potatoes and salads. Established: 1949 - Franchising Since: 1961- No. of Units: Company Owned: 35 - Franchised: 66 - Franchise Fee: $15,000 - Royalty: 4%, 3% adv. - Total Inv: $150,000 F & E, $350,000-$400,000 bldg and site dev. plus land - Financing: No.

SMASH HIT SUBS
Orion Food Systems
2930 W. Maple, P.O. Box 780, Sioux Falls, SD, 57101. Contact: Director of Development - Tel: (605) 336-0141 Fax: (605) 330-7504. Quick service format, developing in convenience stores and foodcourts. Established: 1984 - Franchising Since: 1985 - No. of Units: Company Owned: 8 - Franchised: 417 - Franchise Fee: $4,950 - Total Inv: $25,000+ - Financing: Third Party.

SMOKEY PIG BAR B CUE
Smokey Pig Barbecue, Inc.
1617 11th Avenue, Columbus, GA, 31901. Contact: Franchise Director - Tel: (901) 368-3361, Fax: (901) 368-1144. Old fashioned slow-cooked and smoked barbecue-beef, pork, chicken and turkey. Established: 1953 - Franchising Since: 1996 - No. of Units: Company Owned: 2 - Franchised: 1 - Franchise Fee: $20,000 - Royalty: 6%, Adv. 1% - Total Inv: $72,000-$127,000 - Financing: No.

SNAPPY TOMATO PIZZA
Snappy Tomato Pizza
7230 Turfway Rd, Florence, KY, 41042. Contact: Bret Witte - Tel: (859) 525-4680, (888) 463-SNAP, Fax: (859) 525-4686, E-Mail: snappy@snappytomato.com, Web Site: www.snappytomato.com. We specialize in providing top quality pizzas, veggies, salads & snappetizers w/efficient friendly service. Our committment to quality is eveident through our made fresh daily dough, blend of fresh cheeses, our unique homemade pizza sauce recipe, fresh veggies + high grade meat toppings. Established: 1978 - Franchising Since: 1982 - No. of Units: Company Owned: 2 - Franchised: 50 - Franchise Fee: $15,000 - Royalty: 5% of net sales, 2.5% of net sales for regional advertising - Total Inv: $60,000-$200,000.

SOBIK'S SUBS
Jreck Subs Group, Inc
300 International Pkwy, Ste. 100, Heathrow, FL, 32746. - Tel: (407) 333-8998, Fax: (407) 333-8852. Specilaizing in pizza and subs. Established: 1969 - Franchising Since: 1972 - No. of Units: Company Owned: 1 - Franchised: 29 - Franchise Fee: $12,500 - Royalty: 5% - Total Inv: $125,000 - Financing: Yes.

SODA FOUNTAIN, THE
The Soda Fountain, Inc.
1805 Oriole Road, Gatlinburg, TN, 37738. Contact: Franchise Director - Tel: (901) 368-3361, Fax: (901) 368-1144. Old fashioned soda fountain and sandwich store with nostalgic items for sale also. Established: 1992 - Franchising Since: 1997 - No. of Units: Company Owned: 2 - Franchised: 2 - Franchise Fee: $15,000 - Royalty: 5%, 1% adv - Total Inv: $71,817-$100,517 - Financing: Yes.

SONIC DRIVE-IN
Sonic Industries Inc.
101 Park Ave., Oklahoma City, OK, 73102. Contact: Dave Vernon, Dir. Fran. Sales - Tel: (405) 280-7654, (800) 569-6656, Web Site: www.sonic drivein.com. Drive-in restaurants, fast food. Established: 1953 - No. of Units: Company Owned: 312 - Franchised: 1,665 - Franchise Fee: $30,000 - Total Inv: Varied.

SONNY'S REAL PIT BAR-B-QUE, INC.
Sonny's Franchise Co.
2605 Maitland Center Pky #C, Maitland, FL, 32751. Contact: Jenny Wolfe, Fran. Administrator - Tel: (407) 660-8888, Fax: (407) 660-9050. Sonny's Real Pit Bar BQ offers franchises for full service barbeque restaurants. Family dining with a salad bar, childrens menu, variety of lunch specials and diet plates. Take-out and catering service also available. Established: 1969 - No. of Units: Company Owned: 8 - Franchised: 88 - Franchise Fee: $20,000 - Royalty: 3.0%, 1% adv. - Financing: No.

SOUPY'S HOMEMADE SOUPS AND DELI SANDWICHES
Soupy's, Inc.
3019 Breckinridge Lane, Louisville, KY, 40220. Contact: Houston D. Jones, JR, Dir. of Franchise & Development - Tel: (502) 228-7799, (502) 419-7799, Fax: (502) 228-4908. Soupy's homemade soups and sandwiches was born in 1995 from recipes of Mama Lesch, John Lesch's mother and Dan Bowlings mother in law. Mama Lesch had a constant stream of requests for hot, thick, delicious soups, which delighted her. She put the soups in Dan's deli, Soupy's was born. Established: 1995 - Franchising Since: 1997 - No. of Units; Company Owned: 1 - Franchised: 4 - Franchise Fee: $15,000 - Royalty: 4%, 11/2% adv. - Total Inv: $85,000-$195,000 depending on location/ ff&e $60,000-$75,0000 - Financing: Assistance is available.

SOUTH PHILLY STEAKS & FRIES
Restaurant Systems International
1000 South Ave., Staten Island, NY, 10314. Contact: Franchise Development Department - Tel: (718) 494-8888, (800) 205-6050, Fax: (718) 494-8776, E-Mail: treats@restsys.com, Web Site: www.rest sys.com. South Philly Steaks & Fries is "For Meat and Potato Lovers", featuring steak sandwiches, subs and french fries. Established: 1976 - Franchising Since: 1986 - No. of Units: Franchised: 14 - Franchise Fee: $25,000 - Royalty: 5% - Total Inv: $105,300-$235,200 - Financing: No.

SPACE ALIENS*
1304 East Century Ave, Bismark, ND, 58503. - Tel: (701) 223-6220, Fax: (701) 223-2252, Web Site: www.spacealiens.cc. Serving Bar-B-Que ribs, giant stuffed baked potatoes, seasoned martian munchies all served under a 30 foot high domed ceiling that displays a view of outer space. Established: 1997 - Franchising Since: 2003 - No. of Units: Company Owned: 2 - Franchised: 1 - Franchise Fee: $10,000.

SPAD'S PIZZA, INC.
P.O. Box 50, Pinckney, MI, 48169-0050. Contact: Dir. of Mktg - Tel: (734) 878-1595. Pizza by the slice drive-thru only. The concept was developed by Frank R. Spadafore in 1991 to capture the untapped niche of pizza by the slice drive-thru market. Established: 1991 - Franchising Since: 1992 - No. of Units: Company Owned: 1 - Franchised: 14 - Franchise Fee: $15,000 - Royalty: 4% of gross sales - Total Inv: $225,000-$250,000 not including land - Financing: None at the present time.

SPAGHETTI JACK'S FAST ITALIAN
1938 N. Woodlawn St., Ste. 301, Wichita, KS, 67208. Contact: Louis Stoico, Jr., Chairman/President - Tel: (316) 529-4455, (800) 454-2199, Fax: (316) 636-2871, Web Site: www.stoico.com. Valued-priced, high-quality, healthful alternative to typical fast food. Fast Italian concept features lasagna, spaghetti, baked subs, salads, fettuccine alfredo, fresh-baked garlic bread and pizza. Established: 1991 - Franchising Since: 1993 - No. of Units: Company Owned: 11 - Franchised: 5 - Franchise Fee: $25,000 - Royalty: 5%, 1% adv. - Total Inv: $350,000-$750,000 - Financing: No. Not franchising at this time.

SPICY PICKLE SUB SHOP *

90 Madison Street, #700, Denver, CO, 80206. Contact: Franchise Department - Tel: (303) 297-1902, Fax: (303) 297-1903, Web Site: www.spicypickle.com. Serving panini, salads, subs & soups. Established: 1999 - Franchising Since: 2003 - No. of Units: Company Owned: 3 - Franchised: 4 - Franchise Fee: $25,000 - Royalty: 5% - Total Inv: $274,500-$332,500 - Financing: No.

SPOON'S FRESH BURGERS/ICE CREAM

415 Hawthorne Lane, Charlotte, NC, 28204. Contact: Jerry Bardin, Owner - Tel: (704) 376-0974. Specializing in homemade ice cream, fresh meat burgers, hot dogs and deli sandwiches. Established: 1929 - Franchising Since: 1982 - No. of Units: Company Owned: 6 - Franchised: 3 - Franchise Fee: $20,000 - Royalty: 2% - Total Inv: $70,000.

STEAK AND ALE RESTAURANTS
Metromedia Restaurant Group

6500 International Pkwy #1000, Plano, TX, 75093. Contact: Franchise Development - Tel: (972) 588-5000, (800) 543-9670, Fax: (972) 588-5806, E-Mail: franchise@metrogroup.com, Web Site: www.metromedia restaurants.com. Steak and Ale is a upscale restaurant that features a variety of distinctive tastes such as prime rib, steaks and fresh salad bar served in a casually elegant atmosphere. Established: 1966 - Franchising Since: 1999 - No. of Units: Company Owned:112 - Franchised: 1 - Franchise Fee: $50,000.00 per unit - Royalty: 4% of gross sales - Total Inv: $1,009,300-$2,173,750 - Financing: None provided.

STEAK AROUND
Steak Around, Inc.

4370 King St, Alexandria, VA, 22302-1508. - Tel: (703) 379-2300, (800) 28-STEAK, Fax: (703) 516-4901, Web Site: www.steak around.com. Steak restaurant. Established: 1993 - Franchising Since: 1995 - No. of Units: Company Owned: 4 - Franchised: 6 - Franchise Fee: $25,000 - Royalty: 4% - Total Inv: $175,000-$200,000 - Financing: None.

STEAK & EGGER

583 W. 26th St., Cicero, IL, 60804. Contact: Terrance Carr, Pres. - Tel: (708) 652-5522. Fast food. Established: 1965 - No. of Units: Company Owned: 1 - Franchised: 6.

STEAK ESCAPE, THE
Escape Enterprises Inc.

222 Neilston St., Columbus, OH, 43215-2636. Contact: Franchise Development - Tel: (614) 224-0300, Fax: (614) 224-6460, Web Site: www.steakescape.com. Quick-service made to order, genuine Philadelphia style cheesesteaks, freshly cut french fries, freshly squeezed lemonade, smashed potators ™, grilled salads served with a friendly, interactive manner. Established: 1982 - Franchising Since: 1983 - No. of Units: Company Owned: 12 - Franchised: 150 - Franchise Fee: $20,000 - Royalty: 6%, .5% mktg. - Total Inv: $190,200-$1,267,000 - Financing: Third party financing from FMAC.

STEAK & HOAGIE SHOP, THE
T & P Hoagie Systems, Inc.

2620 N. Sharon Amity Rd., Charlotte, NC, 28205. - Tel: (704) 568-7352. Fast food steak and deli sandwich shops. Established: 1979 - Franchising Since: 1987 - No. of Units: Company Owned: 3 - Franchised: 15 - Franchise Fee: $8,500 - Royalty: 4%, 3% adv. - Total Inv: $50,000-$70,000 - Financing: 30% of total inv.

STEAK 'N SHAKE
Steak N Shake, Inc.

500 Century Building, 36 South Pennsylvania St, Indianapolis, IN, 46204. Contact: Franchise Development - Tel: (317) 633-4100, Fax: (317) 633-4100. Unique restaurant concept serving quick-seared steak-burgers, thin french fries, genuine chili and hand dipped milk shakes. Steak N Shake offers full waitress service with food served on china as well as drive thru and take out service, in a casual environment reminiscent of the 50's. Established: 1934 - Franchising Since: 1939 - No. of Units: Company Owned: 187 - Franchised: 53 - Franchise Fee: $30,000 per location - Royalty: 4%, 5% adv. - Total Inv: $1,125,000-$2,360,000 - Financing: No.

STEAK-OUT CHARBROILED DELIVERY
Steak-Out Franchising, Inc.

6801 Governors Lake Pkwy #100, Norcross, GA, 30071. Contact: Joe McCord, Vice President - Tel: (678) 533-6000, (877) 878-3257, Fax: (678) 291-0222, E-Mail: jmccord@steakout.com, Web Site: www.steakout.com. Steak-Out satisfies the need of busy consumers that choose not to cook. Steak-Out specializes in the home and office delivery of charbroiled steaks, chicken and burgers - other menu items include freshly made chef salads and specialty desserts. Established: 1986 - Franchising Since: 1987 - No. of Units: Company Owned: 4 - Franchised: 64 - Franchise Fee: $25,000 - Royalty: 5% - Total Inv: $221,400-$342,200 - Financing: Third party, SBA approved.

STEAKS TO GO
Steaks To Go Franchise Inc.

6558 Roswell Rd. Suite 6-G, Atlanta, GA, 30328. Contact: Daniel O'Konta, C.O.O. - Tel: (770) 492-0400, (404) 236 0845, Fax: (770) 492-0404. Home and office delivery of cooked steaks, chicken and sandwiches. Established: 1990 - Franchising Since: 1995 - No. of Units: Company Owned: 1 - Franchised: 6 - Franchise Fee: $19,500 - Royalty: 3% - Total Inv: $90,000-$130,000 - Financing: Only in Atlanta, GA area.

STEWART'S RESTAURANTS
Stewart's Restaurants, Inc.

114 W. Atlantic Ave., Clementon, NJ, 08021. Contact: Michael W. Fessler - Tel: (609) 346-1300. 50's style drive-in, car hop service - full training and support provided. Established: 1924 - No. of Units: Franchised: 63.

STRAW HAT PIZZA
Straw Hat Cooperative Corporation

18 Crow Canyon CT STE 150, San Ramon, CA, 94583-1669. Contact: Joshua V. Richman, Pres./C.E.O. - Tel: (925) 837-3400, Web Site: www.strawhatpizza.com. Eat-in, take-out, or delivery of pizza, salads, sandwiches, spaghetti, beer, wine and soft drinks. Also gourmet pizzas, kids meals, cartoons and old-time movies. Group parties, birthdays, sports sponsorships, school programs and community fundraisers. Established: 1969 - Franchising Since: 1970 - No. of Units: Franchised: 60 - Franchise Fee: $10,000 - Royalty: Administrative 2%; Mktg. .75% - Total Inv: $50,000-$500,000 - Financing: No.

STRINGS ITALIAN CAFE
Strings Franchises Inc.

11344 Coloma Rd. #545, Gold River, CA, 95670. Contact: Albert DeCaprio, Pres. - Tel: (916) 635-6465, Fax: (916) 631-9775. Full service, casual restaurant. Menu focus on variety of pasta entrees, pizza, salads, desserts, espresso. Central kitchen/commissary provides most of product requirements. Established: 1987 - Franchising Since: 1989 - No. of Units: Company Owned: 3 - Franchised: 17 - Franchise Fee: $37,500 - Royalty: 5% - Total Inv: $265,000-$350,000 - Financing: No.

STUFT PIZZA
Stuft Pizza Franchise Corp.

50855 Washington Street, #210, Laquinta, CA, 92253. Contact: Jack Bertram, Pres. - Tel: (760) 777-1948, Fax: (760) 777-1660, E-Mail: jbertstuft@aol.com, Web Site: www.stuftpizza.com. Food court to full service. Currently developing Quick Serve concept using six different cooking methods to serve in five minutes, in about 2000 square feet, with other quick serve food. Can incorporate microbrews. Established: 1976 - Franchising Since: 1986 - No. of Units: Company Owned: 1 - Franchised: 22 - Franchise Fee: $30,000 - Royalty: 4% - Total Inv: $400,000 - Financing: No.

SUB STATION II
Sub Station II, Inc.

425 North Main St., Sumter, SC, 29150. Contact: V.P. Fran. - Tel: (803) 773-4711, Fax: (803) 775-2220. Sandwich shops offering a variety of over 25 submarine sandwiches, developing an efficient method of preparing each sandwich to the customer's specifications. Emphasis on high quality food and cleanliness. Established: 1975 - Franchising Since: 1976 - No. of Units: Company Owned: 1 - Franchised: 91 - Franchise Fee: $10,500 - Royalty: 4% - Total Inv: $75,000-$100,000 - Financing: Indirect.

SUBWAY
Doctor's Associates, Inc.
325 Bic Dr., Milford, CT, 06460. Contact: Fran. Sales Dept. - Tel: (800) 888-4848, (203) 877-4281, Fax: (203) 876-6688, E-Mail: franchise @subway.com, Web Site: www.subway.com. Subway is a submarine and salads franchise, operating in all 50 states and 65 countries. Subway offers quality products, simple operation (no cooking involved), low initial investment, minimal space requirements, and co-branding options. Established: 1965 - Franchising Since: 1974 - Franchised: 13,365 - Franchise Fee: $10,000 - Royalty: 8% + 3.5% adv. - Total Inv: $61,700-$170,700 - Financing: Equipment leasing to qualified candidates.

SUBZONE, INC
700 Pratt Ave, Huntsville, AL, 35801. - Tel: (256) 551-1072, Fax: (256) 551-0173, Web Site: www.subzoneinc.com. Specilaizing in subs. Established: 1988 - Franchising Since: 1993 - No. of Units: Company Owned: 1 - Franchised: 12 - Franchise Fee: $15,000 - Total Inv: $100,000-$200,000 - Financing: No.

SUGAR DADDY'S DINER
290 Underwood Road, Fletcher, NC, 28732. Contact: Jeanie Tyler Guice - Tel: (828) 654-9393, Fax: (828) 654-9466. 1950's setting diner. Established: 1998 - Franchising Since: 2002 - No. of Units: Company Owned: 1 - Franchise Fee: $50,000.

SUKI HANA FRANCHISE CORP.
International Restaurant Management Group
4104 Aurora St, Coral Gables, FL, 33146. Contact: David Dinkel - Tel: (305) 476-1611, Fax: (305) 476-9622. Japanese style food, located primarily in malls, Established: 1989 - Franchising Since: 1998 - No. of Units: Company Owned: 17 - Franchised: 2 - Franchise Fee: $30,000 - Total Inv: $230,500-$496,000.

SUNSHINE CAFE RESTAURANTS
SunQuest Systems, Inc.
7112 Zionsville Rd., Indianapolis, IN, 46268. Contact: James L. Frederick, CEO - Tel: (317) 299-3391, (800) 808-4774, Fax: (317) 299-3390. Full service casual dining restaurant offering a complete menu of freshly prepared items in breakfast, lunch and dinner segments. Units accommodate 120 to 150 guests. Established: 1986 - Franchising Since: 1986 - No. of Units: Company Owned: 1 - Franchised: 13 - Franchise Fee: $25,000 - Royalty: 3% monthly royalty, 3% advertising royalty - Total Inv: $100,000 (conversion) to $1.1 million new development - Financing: No.

T.G.I. FRIDAY'S
Carlson Restaurnats Worldwide
4201 marsh Lane, Carrollton, TX, 75007. Contact: Franchise Department - Tel: (972) 662-5400. Casual theme, full service restaurants. Established: 1965 - Franchising Since: 1970 - No. of Units: Company Owned: 253 - Franchised: 156 - Franchise Fee: $75,000 for 1st restaurant, $65,000 for 2nd and $50,000 for remaining restaurants - Royalty: 4% - Total Inv: $3,000,000 net worth, $1,000,000 liquid cash - Financing: No.

TACO BELL CORP.
17901 Von Karman, Irvine, CA, 92614. Contact: Fran. Dept. - Tel: (949) 863-4500, (949) 863-2270. Mexican style fast food restaurants. Established: 1962 - Franchising Since: 1964 - No. of Units: Company Owned: 1,232 - Franchised: 1,035 - Franchise Fee: $35,000 - Royalty: 5.5% weekly - Total Inv: $750,000 average costs including land, bldg. & equip. - Financing: Through outside approved financing companies.

TACO CASA
Taco Casa International, Ltd.
1002 North Pleasantburg Dr, Greenville, SC, 29607. - Tel: (864) 232-1021. Fast food Mexican restaurants. Established: 1963 - Franchising Since: 1976 - No. of Units: Company Owned: 1 - Franchised: 20 - Franchise Fee: $15,000 - Royalty: 4% - Financing: No.

TACO GRANDE
P.O. Box 279, Kechi, KS, 67067-0279. Contact: John Wylie, Pres. - Tel: (316) 744-0200. Limited-menu Mexican restaurant featuring drive-thru service. Recipes are authentic Mexican recipes. Successful operation for over 37 years. Offer excellent products, training and a cost efficient and labor-saving building design. Established: 1960 - Franchising Since: 1966 - No. of Units: Company Owned: 8 - Franchised: 4 - Franchise Fee: $20,000 - Royalty: 3% - Total Inv: $250,000-$450,000 - Financing: No.

TACO HUT
Taco Hut America Inc.
2014 S Rangeline, Joplin, MO, 64804. Contact: Gloria Gray, Pres. - Tel: (417) 781-4781, Fax: (417) 781-4782. Mexican food cooked fresh on each location. 28 years in business. Three franchisees in Kansas. Family owned. We operate four restaurants in Missouri, lease two others. We don't fry anything. We steam or braise food. Established: 1972 - Franchising Since: 1989 - No. of Units: Company Owned: 4 - Franchised: 3 - Franchise Fee: $15,000 - Royalty: 3% gross sales less sales tax - Total Inv: $250,000 net worth $300,000 investment plus $75,000 for expenses - Financing: No.

TACO JOHN'S RESTAURANTS
Taco John's International, Inc.
808 W. 20th St, Cheyenne, WY, 82001. Contact: Jim DeBolt - Tel: (307) 635-0101, (800) 854-0819, Fax: (307) 772-0369, E-Mail: ownone@ tacojohns.com, Web Site: www.tacojohns.com. Taco John's Restaurants offer generous portions of high quality, authentic, freshly prepared-to-order Mexican food for a fair price. Established: 1969 - Franchising Since: 1969 - No. of Units: Company Owned: 6 - Franchised: 410 - Franchise Fee: $15,000-$22,500 - Royalty: 4% - Total Inv: $505,000-$814,500 - Financing: No.

TACO LOCO
Taco Concepts, Inc.
349-B West Tremont Ave., Charlotte, NC, 28203. - Tel: (704) 375-9450. Mexican restaurant. Established: 1984 - Franchising Since: 1991 - No. of Units: Franchised: 3 - Franchise Fee: $15,000 - Royalty: 4% of net sales, 3% adv. - Total Inv: Equip. $33,000, leasehold $35,000-$40,000, misc. $5,000-$7,000 - Financing: Yes.

TACO MAYO
Taco Mayo Franchise Systems, Inc.
10405 Greenbriar Pl., Oklahoma City, OK, 73159. Contact: Debbie Jackson, Franchise Qualification Specialist - Tel: (405) 691-8226, Fax: (405) 691-2572, Web Site: www.tacomayo.com. Quick service restaurant featuring Tex-Mex favorites like tacos, burritos, nachos and salads. Established: 1978 - Franchising Since: 1980 - No. of Units: Company Owned: 34 - Franchised: 70 - Franchise Fee: $15,000 - Royalty: 4% - Total Inv: $100,000 (liquid), $250,000 (net worth) - Financing: No.

TACO PALACE
Taco Palace National Franchise, LLC.
P.O. Box 87, Monett, MO, 65708. Contact: Matt Deves - Tel: (573) 216-1739, (417) 235-6595, Fax: (573) 374-8226, E-Mail: larry@taco palace.com, Web Site: www.tacopalace.com. Affordable franchise, exciting expansion store opportunity offers no royalty fees for life! Unique money savings concept. Established: 1985 - Franchising Since: 1997 - No. of Units: Company Owned: 2 - Franchised: 13 - Franchise Fee: $15,000 - Royalty: None - Total Inv: Varies - Financing: No.

TACO TICO, INC.
260 N. Rock Rd., #220, Wichita, KS, 67206-2240. - Tel: (316) 681-0220. Mexican style fast food. Established: 1967 - Franchising Since: 1968 - No. of Units: Company Owned: 72 - Franchised: 42 - Franchise Fee: $10,000 - Royalty: 4% gross - Total Inv: $120,000 - Financing: No.

TACO TIME
Taco Time International, Inc.
7730 East Greenway Rd, #104, Scottsdale, AZ, 85260. - Tel: (480) 443-0200. Taco Time is a dynamic leader in the Mexican fast food business. Outstanding food products feature quality fresh ingredients, and exciting menu items. Established: 1959 - Franchising Since: 1960 - No. of Units: Company Owned: 5 - Franchised: 300 - Franchise Fee: $25,000 - Royalty: 5% - Financing: No.

TACO TREAT
Taco Treat Inc.
1316 Central Ave.,Great Falls, MT, 59401. Contact: Jack Deck, V.P. - Tel: (406) 727-7582, Fax: (406)727-7583. Fast food (Mexican). Established: 1960 - Franchising Since: 1980 - No. of Units: Company Owned: 4 - Franchised: 3 - Franchise Fee: $10,000-$15,000 - Royalty: 3%, no adv. fee - Financing: Open.

TACONE
Tacone Franchise Director
4801 Wilshire Blvd Ste 280, Los Angeles, CA,90010-3813. Contact: Franchise Development - Tel: (323) 634-9430, Web Site: www.tacone.com. Quick service restaurant featuring soups, sandwiches, salads and smoothies. High volume fast service concept. Only the freshest ingredients go into our products. Full training and ongoing support provided. Established: 1994 - Franchising Since: 1999 - No. of Units: Company Owned: 9 - Franchised: 5 - Franchise Fee: $25,000 - Royalty: 6%, 2% adv. - Total Inv: $175,000-$300,000 - Financing: Yes, third party.

TACONE WRAPS
4223 Glencoe Ave. C 200, Marina Del Ray, CA, 90290. Contact: Michael Conti - Tel: (310) 574-8177, (877) 4TA-CONE, Fax: (310) 574-8179. Restaurant featuring wrapped sandwiches. Full training and support provided. Established: 1995 - Franchising Since: 1998 - No. of Units: Company Owned: 9 - Franchise Fee: $25,000 - Total Inv: $178,000 - Financing: Yes.

TANNER'S
RTOSF, Inc
911 N.W. Loop 281., Suite 111, Longview, TX, 75604. Contact: Curtis Swanson, President - Tel: (903) 295-6800, (800) 259-2675, Fax: (903) 295-6805, E-Mail: curtiss@rteams.com, Web Site: www.rteams.com. A full service family casual diner, specializing in rotesserie chicken and bbq ribs. We do serve alcohol which is between 2% and 4% of gross sales. Established: 1985 - Franchising Since: 2000 - No. of Units: Company Owned: 7 - Franchised: 1 - Franchise Fee: $30,000 - Royalty: 5% of gross royalty, 2% of gross advertising - Total Inv: $334,000-$472,000 - Financing: No - have lease company referals.

TAXIS RESTAURANTS INTERNATIONAL
1840 San Miguel Drive, Suite 206, Walnut Creek, CA, 94596. Contact: Jeffrey Neustadt, President - Tel: (925) 939-5021, (877) 448-8294, Fax: (925) 937-7227, Web Site: www.taxishamburgers.com. Taxis Hamburgers is a chain of fast casual restaurants offering a varied menu of hamburgers, salads, soups, sandwiches, shakes and a Top-Your-Own baked potato bar. Restaurants feature a lively atmosphere. Established: 1991 - Franchising Since: 2000 - No. of Units: Company Owned: 5 - Franchised: 5 - Franchise Fee: $25,000 - Royalty: 4.5% of sales - Total Inv: $395,000-$450,000.

THE LOOP PIZZA GILL
One San Jose Place Suite #1, Jacksonville, FL, 32257. Contact: Mark Starbuck - Tel: (904) 268-2609, Fax: (904) 268-5809, E-Mail: mstarbuck@looppizzagrill.com, Web Site: www.looppizzagrill.com. The Loop is a unique restaurant combining convenience, no-nonsense service. The decor is funky and upbeat, relaxed and casual. Perfect for family meals, business lunch or just a snack. Serving award winning Chicgao style and California pizzas, burgers, sandwiches and gourmet salads. Established: 1981 - No. of Units: Franchised: 19 - Franchise Fee: $30,000 - Royalty: 4% of gross receipts weekly - Total Inv: $289,700-$524,000.

THE TACO MAKER
The Taco Maker, Inc
4605 Harrison Blvd, Centennial Building, 3rd Foloor, Ogden, UT, 84403. Contact: Bob Strong, Franchise Specialist - Tel: (801) 476-9780, (800) 207-5804, Fax: (801) 476-9788, E-Mail: franchise@tacomaker.com, Web Site: www.tacomaker.com. Fresh Mexican fast food. Established: 1978 - Franchising Since: 1978 - No. of Units: Company Owned: 3 - Franchised: 150- Franchise Fee: $19,000-$29,000 - Royalty: 5% - Total Inv: $150,000-$300,000 - Financing: Third party.

THIS IS IT! BBQ & SEAFOOD
Jesus & Butch
4405 Mall Blvd Ste. 320, Union City, GA, 30291. Contact: Shelley Anthony, President - Tel: (770) 964-1668, Fax: (770) 964-8539. Fast food (BBQ and Seafood). Established: 1982 - Franchising Since: 1991 - No. of Units: Company Owned: 3 - Franchised: 3 - Franchise Fee: $12,500 - Royalty: Not available - Total Inv: Not available - Financing: Corporate.

THUNDERCLOUD SUBS
ThunderCloud Licensing, Inc.
1102 W. 6th St., Austin, TX, 78703. Contact: David E. Cohen, Fran. Dir. - Tel: (512) 479-8805, (800) 256-7895, Fax: (512) 479-8806, Web Site: www.thundercloud.com. Prepares fresh submarine sandwiches, salads, soups, and other complimentary items. A unique atmosphere different from other fast food restaurants. Occupies 800 sq. ft. to 1,500 sq. ft. in a retail strip center or free-standing site. Full seating, limited seating, drive-thru, or drive-thru only. Established: 1975 - Franchising Since: 1989 - No. of Units: Company Owned: 10 - Franchised: 19 - Franchise Fee: $10,000 - Royalty: 4% gross sales - Total Inv: $52,500-$126,000 - Financing: No.

TIAJUANA TAXIE TUNE UP DOCTOR, INC., THE
2508 Betty St., Orlando, FL, 32803. Contact: Stephen Villard, Owner - Tel: (407) 894-9717. Drive-thru/delivery of a variety of ethnic foods - Mexican, Italian, Chinese and American. Established: 1989 - Franchising Since: 1995 - No. of Units: Company Owned: 1 - Franchise Fee: $15,000 - Royalty: 2% gross monthly - Total Inv: $25,000-$65,000 per store - Financing: Some financing available. NOT FRANCHISING AT THIS TIME.

TIPPY'S TACO HOUSE
Locklier Co., Inc.
5025 Falcon Hollow Rd., McKinney, TX, 75070. Contact: W.L. Locklier, Owner - Tel: (972) 547-0888, Fax: (972) 547-0888. True "Tex Mex" Mexican food take-out/drive-thru and eat in. Established: 1958 - Franchising Since: 1968 - No. of Units: Franchised: 15 - Franchise Fee: $10,000 - Royalty: 3% - Total Inv: $100,000 - Financing: None.

TOARMINA'S PIZZA
673 Barbara, Westland, MI, 48185. Contact: Lou Toarmina, President - Tel: (313) 729-9067. Pizza carry-out and delivery. Established: 1987 - Franchising Since: 1992 - No. of Units: Franchised: 19 - Franchise Fee: $5,000 - Royalty: 3% - Total Inv: $50,000 - Financing: No.

TOGO'S EATERY
M.T.C. Management, Inc.
14 pacella Park Drive, Randolph, MA, 02368. - Tel: (800) 777-9983. A high quality, fast service, specialty sandwich restaurant. Established: 1972 - Franchising Since: 1977- No. of Units: Company Owned: 16 - Franchised: 175 - Franchise Fee: $12,500-$40,000 - Royalty: 5% of sales - Total Inv: $180,000-$200,000 - Financing: No.

TOM & JERRY'S BURGERS & BEER
Tom & Jerry's, Inc.
401 N. 10th St., McAllen, TX, 78501-4509. Contact: Jerry L. Pace, Pres. - Tel: (956) 630-5223. Restaurant and bar with casual dining featuring burgers, fajitas, chicken and hot dogs which are all charbroiled. Established: 1976 - No. of Units: Company Owned: 4 - Franchise Fee: $25,000 - Royalty: 5%.

TOMATO STREET
Tomato Street LLC
520 West Main Street, Spokane, WA, 99201. - Tel: (509) 747-3048, (800) 772-5280. Family style Italian restaurant serving made from scratch fresh Italian food in an existing and entertaining and fun atmosphere. We specialize in converting your dining concept into a solid performer. Established: 1992 - Franchising Since: 1996 - No. of Units: Company Owned: 2 - Franchise Fee: $45,000 - Royalty 4.5%, .5% adv. - Total Inv: Depends on available building and remodeling costs.

TONY MARONI'S FAMOUS GOURMET PIZZA
TMFS, INC.
222 112th Ave. N.E., Ste. L-105, Bellevue, WA, 98004. - Tel: (425) 453-5500, (800) 884-4534. Gourmet delivery and take out pizza to upper income neighbourhoods in a protected territory. Established: 1987 -

Franchising Since: 1996 - No. of Units: Company Owned: 4 - Franchised: 17 - Franchise Fee: $20,000 - Royalty: 5%, 1% mktg. - Total Inv: $150,000 average including work cap. - Financing: Access to funds. NOT FRANCHISING AT THIS TIME.

TONY ROMA'S, A PLACE FOR RIBS
Roma Corporation
9304 Forest Ln., Ste. 200, Dallas, TX, 75243-8953. Contact: V.P. of Dev. - Tel: (214) 343-7800, Fax: (214) 343-2680. Dinnerhouse specializing in BBQ ribs and chicken along with famous onion ring loaf. A special niche in the industry with great price/value relationship, high quality food products and full service bar. Also offering take-out and delivery. Established: 1972 - Franchising Since: 1979 - No. of Units: Company Owned: 57 - Franchised: 165 - Franchise Fee: $50,000 - Royalty: 4%+.5% adv. - Total Inv: $1,000,000 - Financing: No.

TOWN PUMP FOOD STORES, INC.
600 S. Main, Butte, MT, 59701. - Tel: (406) 782-9121. Family restaurant, fast food. No. of Units: Company Owned: 30 - Franchised: 30.

TUBBY'S GRILLED SUBMARINES
Tubby's Sub Shops, Inc.
35807 Moravian, Clinton Twp, MI, 48035. Contact: Jennifer Ciampa - Tel: (586) 792-2369, (800) 752-0644, Fax: (586) 792-4250, E-Mail: info@tubby.com, Web Site: www.tubby.com. Deli-style and grilled to perfection submarine sandwiches along with soups, healthy salads, various side items, including fries and freshly baked desserts. Established: 1968 - Franchising Since: 1978 - No. of Units: Company Owned: 1 - Franchised: 95 - Franchise Fee: $12,500-$15,000 - Royalty: 6% + 4% advertising - Total Inv: $100,000-$250,000 - Financing: Third party only.

TUDOR'S BISCUIT WORLD
P.O. Box 3603, Charleston, WV, 25336. Contact: Dir. of Franchising - Tel: (304) 343-4026, Fax: (304) 727-1400. Fast food breakfast, country lunch and dinner. Established: 1980 - No. of Units: Company Owned: 7 - Franchised: 48 - Franchise Fee: $10,000 - Royalty: 4%, 3% adv. - Total Inv: Varies - Financing: No.

TUMBLEWEED SOUTHWEST MESQUITE GRILL & BAR
Tumbleweed, Inc
2301 River Road, #200, Louisville, KY, 40206. - Tel: (502) 893-0323. South West family restaurant. Established: 1975 - Franchising Since: 1980 - No. of Units: Company Owned: 28 - Franchised: 20 - Franchise Fee: $35,000 - Royalty: 3%-5% varies - Total Inv: Land $200,000-$500,000, Bldg, $400,000-$6000,000, Equip $190,000-$260,000 - Financing: No.

U.S BISTRO
CBFG, Inc
1630 Braeburn Dr., Ste. A, Salem, VA, 24152. Contact: Gregory Caldwell - Tel: (540) 389-8435, Fax: (540) 389-1780. Gourmet wraps, soups, sandwiches and salads. Established: 1999 - Franchising Since: 1999 - No. of Units: Company Owned: 4 - Franchised: 9 - Franchise Fee: $20,000.

UNCLE TONY'S PIZZA & PASTA RESTAURANTS
Uncle Tony's International, Inc.
27 Airport Plaza, 1800 Post Road, Warwick, RI, 02886. Contact: Edward A. Carosi, Pres. - Tel: (401) 738-1321, Fax: (401) 732-1936. Family style Italian restaurant featuring pizza and pasta, beer and wine. Established: 1970 - Franchising Since: 1976 - No. of Units: Company Owned: 3 - Franchised: 7 - Franchise Fee: $35,000 - Royalty: 4%, 3% adv. - Total Inv: $500,000-$600,000 - Financing: Will assist.

UNO CHICAGO BAR & GRILL PIZZARIA
Uno Corporation
100 Charles Park Rd., Boston, MA, 02132. Contact: Barry Hillerstrom, Director Franchise Services - Tel: (617) 218-5272, (877) 855-8667, Fax: (877) 855-8667, E-Mail: bhillerstrom@unos.com, Web Site: www.unos.com. Casual theme grill and bar featuring great steaks, pastas, salads, sandwiches, seafood and our signature deep dish pizza. Established: 1943 - Franchising Since: 1979 - No. of Units: Company Owned: 123 - Franchised: 85 - Franchise Fee: $35,000 per location, $5,000 development fee - Royalty: 5% of gross - Financing: No.

UPPER KRUST
6149 Far Hills, Dayton, OH, 45459. Contact: Douglas Goudy, V.P. Dir. Fran. Dev. - Tel: (937) 435-9464, Fax: (937) 435-9131. Fast food - sandwich. Established: 1970 - No. of Units: Company Owned: 3 - Franchised: 1.

VALENTINO'S OF AMERICA, INC
P.O. Box 6206, Lincoln, NE, 68506. Contact: Duane L. Thomas, Pres. - Tel: (402) 434-9350, Fax: (402) 434-9860, Web Site: www.valentinos.com. Italian restaurant known best for it's grand Italian buffett. Established: 1957 - Franchising Since: 1976 - No. of Units: Company Owned: 21 - Franchised: 28 - Franchise Fee: $15,000-$25,000 - Royalty: 3% - Total Inv: $249,000-$954,000 - Financing: No.

VILLA PIZZA
Villa Enterprises Management
17 Elm St., Morristown, NJ, 07960. Contact: Adam Torine, Dir. of Bus Dev & Marketing - Tel: (973) 285-4800, Fax: (973) 285-5252, E-Mail: develoopment@villapizza.com, Web Site: www.villapizza.com. Quick service pizza and Italian restaurant chain, primarily located in regional malls and outlet centers either in food court or in-line locations. We use only the freshest cheeses, seasonings, homemade sauces and other ingredients. Our large, tantalizing food display offers customers a wide variety of homemade dishes. Established: 1964 - Franchising Since: 1995 - No. of Units: Company Owned: 130 - Franchised: 70 - Franchise Fee: $25,000 - Royalty: 5% - Total Inv: $190,000-$400,000 - Financing: Third party.

VILLAGE INN RESTAURANTS
VICORP Restaurants, Inc.
400 W. 48th Ave., Denver, CO, 80216. Contact: Maxine Crogle, Qualifications Spec. - Tel: (303) 296-2121, (800) 800-3644, Fax: (303) 672-2212, Web Site: www.vicorpinc.com. Mid-scale family restaurants serving all day. Established: 1958 - Franchising Since: 1961 - No. of Units: Company Owned: 109 - Franchised: 115 - Franchise Fee: $40,000 - Royalty: 4% - Total Inv: $597,000-$2,681,000 - Financing: No.

VIVA BURRITO COMPANY
Viva Burrito Development Corp.
1008 E. 6th St.,Tucson, AZ, 85719. Contact: Richard Beuzekom, Franchise Development - Tel: (520) 882-8713, Fax: (520) 620-6466. Mexican fast food restaurant. Full training and support provided. Established: 1996 - Franchising Since: 1998 - No. of Units: Company Owned: 13 - Franchised: 3 - Franchise Fee: $17,500 - Total Inv: $90,000 - Financing: Yes.

WALL STREET DELI
Wall Street Deli, Inc.
One Independence Plaza, Ste. 100, Birmingham, AL, 35209. Contact: VP - Franchising - Tel: (205) 870-0020, (888) 351-2514, Fax: (205) 868-0860. Wall Street Deli is a quick service delicatessen style restaurant offering specialty sandwiches, soups, salads and other quality food products. We have locations in major markets across the US and are seeking quality people interested in sharing in our growth in the US and Canada. A net worth of $250,000 with $150,000 in liquid assets is required. Established: 1967 - Franchising Since: 1997 - No. of Units: Company Owned: 115 - Franchised: 12 - Franchise Fee: $25,000 - Royalty: 5% - Total Inv: $65,000-$570,000 exclusive of site - Financing: Will refer to financial sources.

WARD'S FOOD SYSTEMS, INC.
7 Professional Parkway, Hattiesburg, MS, 39402. Contact: Kenneth R. Hrdlica, Pres. - Tel: (601) 268-9273, Fax: (601) 268-9283, E-Mail: wfsinc@netdoor.com, Web Site: www.wardsrestaurants.com. Fast food restaurant chain featuring chili-burgers, chili-dogs, and frosted mugs of homemade rootbeer. Menu is complimented by full breakfast line and a variety of sandwiches, fries and beverages. Established: 1985 - Franchising Since: 1985 - No. of Units: Company Owned: 1 - Franchised: 19 - Franchise Fee: $20,000 - Royalty: 4-5% - Total Inv: $250,000-$400,000 - Financing: None.

WE LOVE SUSHI
Sushi Trend Co, Inc
4460 Arville St Ste 5, Las Vegas, NV, 89103-3817. Contact: Eddie Okita, President - Tel: (702) 364-0384, (888) 447-8744, Fax: (702) 364-0451. Sushi take out. Established: 1997 - Franchising Since: 1997 - No.

of Units: Company Owned: 1 - Franchise Fee: $150,000-$200,000 (start-up cash) - Total Inv: $300,000-$600,000 - ($50,000-$100,000 equipment) - Financing: Third party.

WE'RE ROLLING PRETZEL COMPANY
WRPC, Inc
2500 West State Street, Alliance, OH, 44601. Contact: Kevin Krabill, President - Tel: (330) 823-0575, (888) 549-7655, Fax: (330) 821-8908, E-Mail: kkrabill@wererolling.com, Web Site: www.wererolling.com. A homemade soft pretzel concept with simplke operations, a quality product and ongoing support systems which will work in a variety of settings. Established: 1996 - Franchising Since: 2000 - No. of Units: Company Owned: 2 - Franchised: 26 - Franchise Fee: $15,000 - Royalty: 5%; 1% ad - Total Inv: $90,000-$125,00 - Financing: Third party.

WENDY'S RESTAURANTS
Wendy's International, Inc.
4288 W. Dublin Granville Rd., Dublin, OH, 43017. - Tel: (614) 764-8434, Web Site: www.wendy's.com. Operates quick service, primary hamburgers, restaurant. Established: 1969 - Franchising Since: 1972 - No. of Units: Company Owned: 1319 - Franchised: 3583 - Franchise Fee: $25,000 application fee $5,000- Royalty: 4%, 4% adv. - Total Inv: $885 ($1,000,000, equip. $250,000) - Financing: Approved financial sources by third parties.

WESTERN SIZZLIN
Western Sizzlin, Corp.
P.O. Box 12167, Roanoke, VA, 24023-2167. - Tel: (800) 24-STEAK, (540) 345-3195, Fax: (877) 329-6300. A full line of steak, chicken and seafood entre's as well as an extensive food bar featuring protein items, vegetables and bakery in unison with an expanded salad bar. Established: 1962 - Franchising Since: 1976 - No. of Units: Company Owned: 26 - Franchised: 244 - Franchise Fee: $20,000 plus $10,000 training and assistance with your new store opening - Royalty: 2%-3% of gross sales and marketing development fee of $190 per month - Total Inv: $811,000-$2,300,000 - Financing: No.

WESTERN STEER FAMILY RESTAURANTS
WSMP, Inc.
WSMP Dr., P.O. Box 399, Claremont, NC, 28610. Contact: Kenneth L. Moser, V.P. Fran. - Tel: (828) 459-7626, Fax: (828) 459-3114. Economy family steakhouse with full steak menu, some chicken, full salad and hot food bar. Established: 1967 - Franchising Since: 1970 - No. of Units: Company Owned: 31 - Franchised: 105 - Franchise Fee: $25,000 - Royalty: 3% gross sales - Total Inv: $800,000-$1,200,000 - Financing: No.

WG GRINDERS
W.G. Grinders Franchise Inc.
220 W Bridge St Ste 200., Dublin, OH, 43017-1178. Contact: Constance S. Bellisari, CEO - Tel: (614) 766-2313, Fax: (614) 766-4030, E-Mail: grinders@wggrinders.com, Web Site: www.wggrinders.com. W.G. Grinders is a one-of-a-kind deli restaurant featuring over 20 varieties of oven baked gourmet sandwiches loaded with the freshest meats, cheeses and vegetables, as well as an assortment of homemade soups, salads and desserts. Established: 1989 - Franchising Since: 1996 - No. of Units: Company Owned: 7 - Franchised: 9 - Franchise Fee: $15,000-$22,500 - Royalty: 4.5% license fee, 2% advertising - Total Inv: $225,000-$300,000 - Financing: No.

WHATABURGER
Whataburger, Inc.
One Whataburger Way, Corpus Christi, TX, 78411. Contact: Wayne Powell, Dir. Fran. Services - Tel: (361) 878-0650, Fax: (361) 878-0473. Fast food restaurant, high quality made to order hamburgers and breakfast. Most units opened 24 hrs. Established: 1950 - Franchising Since: 1953 - No. of Units: Company Owned: 278 - Franchised: 166 - Franchise Fee: $15,000 - Royalty: 5% gross monthly sales - Total Inv: $500,000-$800,000 - Financing: No.

WIENERSCHNITZEL
Galardi Group Franchise, Inc.
4440 Von Karman Ave, Ste. 222, Newport Beach, CA, 92660. Contact: Mr. Frank Coyle, Fran. Sales Dir. - Tel: (800) 764-9353, ext. 609, (949) 752-5800, Fax: (949) 851-2618, Web Site: www.wienerschnitzel.com. Largest hot dog fast food chain with over 325 locations throughtout California, the Southwest and the Pacific Northwest. Wienerschnitzel features a full line of hot dogs, burgers, french fries our award winning chili and pepsi soft drinks. Established: 1961 - Franchising Since: 1965 - No. of Units: Franchised: 344 - Franchise Fee: $25,000 - Royalty: 5% service fee, 1% Nat'l adv, 3-5% Local adv - Total Inv: $136,100-$1,044,800,000 - Financing: Assistance through SBA.

WIFE SAVER
P.O. Box 14515, Augusta, GA, 30919. Contact: Chris Cunningham, Pres. - Tel: (706) 733-8390. Fast food delivery. Established: 1965 - Franchising Since: 1965 - No. of Units: Company Owned: 3 - Franchised: 6 - Approx. Inv: $375,000 - Financing: No.

WILLY T'S *
P.O. Box 1179, Eufaula, AL, 36072. - Tel: (334) 687-7533, Fax: (334) 687-7575, Web Site: www.willyts.com. Serving chicken fingers, wings and hamburgers. Established: 1994 - Franchising Since: 2000 - No. of Units: Company Owned: 2 - Franchised: 3 - Franchise Fee: $20,000 - Royalty: 5% - Total Inv: $197,100-$394,500.

WINDMILL GOURMET FAST FOODS
Windmill Franchise Corporation
200 Ocean Avenue, Long Branch,NJ, 07740. Contact: Rona Levine Levy, CEO - Tel: (732) 870-8282, (800) 874-8282, Fax: (732) 870-9613. Restaurant franchise specializing in gourmet fast foods. Established: 1963 - Franchising Since: 1991 - No. of Units: Company Owned: 4 - Franchised: 10 - Franchise Fee: $25,000.00 - Royalty: 5% - Total Inv: Approx $200,000 - Fiancing: SBA approved.

WING WAGON
Wing-It of Watertown, Inc.
71 Public Square, Watertown, NY, 13601. Contact: Charles G. Wert Pres. - Tel: (315) 788-4580, Fax: (315) 788-4580. Fast food specializing in Buffalo style chicken wings with 7 different sauces. Also pizza and various side dishes. Established: 1982 - Franchising Since: 1989 - No. of Units: Company Owned: 1 - Franchised: 2 - Franchise Fee: $10,000 - Royalty: $100/week for 6 mths, $150 thereafter (flat rate) - Total Inv: $65,000-$95,000 - Financing: No.

WING ZONE
1720 Peachtree St, #940, Atlanta, GA, 30309. Contact:Nat'l Franchise Sales - Tel: (404) 875-5045, Fax: (404) 875-6631, E-Mail: info @wingzone.com, Web Site: www.wingzone.com. Take out and delivery of 25 flavors of jumbo fresh chicken wings, specializing in sandwiches, salads, and appetizers. Established: 1991 - Franchising Since: 1999 - No. of Units: Company Owned: 7 - Franchised: 20 - Franchise Fee: $25,000 - Royalty: 5% - Total Inv: $130,000-$190,000 - Financing: Third party available.

WINGER'S DINER
Winger's Franchising, Inc
404 East 4500 South, #A12, Salt Lake City, UT, 84107. Contact: Eric Slaymaker, President - Tel: (801)261-3700, Fax: (801)261-1615, Web Site: www.wingersdiner.com. Small scale restaurant/diner that specializes in buffalo wings, ribs, sandwiches, salads, fajitas, and more. Established: 1993 - Franchising Since: 1997 - No. of Units: Company Owned: 16 - Franchised: 12 - Franchise Fee: $30,000 - Royalty: 4% plus .5% joint marketing fee - Total Inv: $325,000 (not including real estate).

WINGS TO GO
Wings To Go, Inc.
846 Ritchie Highway Suite 1B, Severna Park, MD, 21165. - Tel: (800) 552-WING. Eat-in and carry-out restaurant specializing in high quality authentic Buffalo style chicken wings. Established: 1985 - Franchising Since: 1989 - No. of Units: Company Owned: 2 - Franchised: 45 - Franchise Fee: $16,000 - Royalty: 4% gross, 2% adv. - Total Inv: $50,000-$85,000 - Financing: No.

WINGSTOP®
Wingstop Restaurants, Inc.
1234 Northwest Highway, Garland, TX, 75041. Contact: Bruce Evans - Tel: (972) 686-6500, Fax: (972) 686-6502, E-Mail: info@wingstop.com, Web Site: www.wingstop.com. Wingstop provides quality products with superior customer services at an exceptional value everyday. We have developed a menu that is attractive to the vast majority of consumers, through the development of our proprietary sauces. Established: 1994

- Franchising Since: 1997- No. of Units: Company Owned: 1 - Franchised: 33 - Franchise Fee: $20,000 - Royalty: 5% - Total Inv: $181,500-$229,500 - Financing: Third party.

WOODY'S BAR-B-Q
Woody's Bar-B-Q Franchise Sales, Inc.
6960 Bonnevillw Rd, Jacksonville, FL, 32216-4042. Contact: V.P. Fran. Dev. - Tel: (904) 296-6940 x 12, Fax: (904) 296-6943. Casual-full service Bar B.Q. Established: 1980 - Franchising Since: 1989 - No. of Units: Company Owned: 4 - Franchised: 28 - Franchise Fee: $30,000 - Royalty: 4%,1% adv. - Total Inv: $372,500-$495,000 - Financing: No.

WORLD LINKS
8665 Wilshire Blvd., #309, Beverly Hills, CA, 90211. Contact: Will Knox, CEO - Tel: (310) 652-7786, (888) 652-1183, Fax: (310) 652-7663, E-Mail: worldlinks@aol.com, Web Site: www.world-links.com. Small space retailer specializing in gourmet sausages/hot dogs and oven baked fries. Established: 1992 - Franchising Since: 1996 - No. of Units: Company Owned: 1 - Franchised: 10 - Franchise Fee: $15,000 - Royalty: 5% of gross sales - Total Inv: $5,000-$200,000 - Financing: Yes.

WORLDLY WRAPS
221 Sequoia Rd #222, Louisville, KY, 40207. Contact: Anna Barley, President - Tel: (510) 839-5462, Fax: (510) 839-2104, E-Mail: franinfo@worldlywraps.com, Web Site: www.worldlywraps.com. 17 different wraps, also serving smoothies and health drinks. Established: 1994 - Franchising Since: 1995 - No. of Units: Company Owned: 6 - Franchised: 24 - Franchise Fee: $19,500 - Royalty: 7% - Total Inv: $200,000-$280,000.

YAYA'S FLAME BROILED CHICKEN
C.S.C. Inc.
521 S. Dort, Flint, MI, 48503. Contact: John Chinonis, Pres. - Tel: (800) 754-1242, (810) 239-9330, Fax: (810) 235-5210. Dine in and take out flame broiled chicken marinated in YAYA's marinate mix. Established: 1985 - Franchising Since: 1988 - No. of Units: Company Owned: 7 - Franchised: 15 - Franchise Fee: $15,000 - Royalty: 4% - Total Inv: $208,000-$311,000 - Financing: No.

YEUNG'S LOTUS EXPRESS FRANCHISE CORP
4104 Aurora St, Coral Gables, FL, 33146-1416. Contact: David Dinkel - Tel: (305) 476-1611, Fax: (305) 476-9622. Specializing in Chinese food, primarily located in malls. Established: 1987 - Franchising Since: 1998 - No. of Units: Company Owned: 20 - Franchised: 10 - Franchise Fee: $30,000.

YOGURT & SUCH CAFÉ
Yogurt & Such Franchise Systems, Inc.
1504 Old Country Rd Ste 126, Westbury, NY, 11590-5178. Contact: Al Spennato, President / CEO - Tel: (516) 827-0200, (800) YOG-SUCH. Quick service contemporary café serving frozen desserts, smoothies, sandwiches, salads, and baked goods with a healthful flair. Established: 1982 - Franchising Since: 1989 - No. of Units: Company Owned: 4 - Franchised: 11 - Franchise Fee: $25,000 - Royalty: 4% - Total Inv: $187,000-$267,500 - Financing: Third party assistance.

YUKON STEAKHOUSE
Trammell Crow Corp.
22 Enterprise Pkwy., Ste. 150, Rampton, VA, 23666-5844. Contact: Charlie Mc Cotter, CEO - Tel: (757) 425-0771, Fax: (757) 651-4454. Mid price steakhouse business. Established: 1993 - Franchising Since: 1995 - No. of Units: Company Owned: 1 - Franchised: 3 - Franchise Fee: $35,000 - Royalty: 4% - Total Inv: $750,000 - Financing: Not at this time.

ZEPPE'S PIZZERIA
JTC Management, Inc.
25780 Miles Rd Unit A, Bedford Heights, OH, 44146. - Tel; (216) 360-9100, Fax: (216) 360-9888. Zeppe's specializes in pizza, pasta, subs, salads, and wings. Zeppe's offers 10 different types of pizza from traditional to gourmet; 17 different subs; 6 different salads, 9 types of pasta dinners, plus Zeppe's famous wings with 6 flavors of sauce to choose from. Established: 1987 - Franchising Since: 1990 - No. of Units: Company Owned: 12 - Franchised: 19 - Franchise Fee: $15,000 - Royalty: 5% - Total Inv: Approx. $150,000 - Financing: Upon review of financials.

ZERO'S SUBS
Zero's Mr Submarine, Inc.
2106 Pacific Avenue, Virginia Beach, VA, 23451. Contact: Rachael Schmidt-Davanzo, VP of Franchising - Tel: (757) 425-5745, (800) 588-0782, Fax: (757) 422-9157, E-Mail: zero's@zeros.com, Web Site: www.zeros.com. Quick service restaurant specializing in hot oven-baked submarine sandwiches, pizza, philly-style grilled subs, salads and desserts. Established: 1969 - Franchising Since: 1991 - No. of Units: Company Owned: 0 - Franchised: 58 - Franchise Fee: $15,000 - Royalty: 6%, 2% adv. - Total Inv: $114,000-$160,000 - Financing: Indirect.

ZOUP! *
Fresh Soup Co.
23231 Woodward Ave, Ferndale, MI, 48220. Contact: Franchise Department - Tel: (248) 434-4123, Fax: (248) 399-6505, Web Site: www.zoup.com. Serving soups, salads, sandwiches, smoothies and more. Established: 1998 - Franchising Since: 2004 - No. of Units: Company Owned: 5 - Franchised: 6 - Franchise Fee: $25,000 - Royalty: 5% - Total Inv: $225,500-$397,000 - Financing: No.

ZPIZZA
450 Newport Center Dr Suite 630, Newport Beach, CA, 92660. Contact: Chris Bright, President - Tel: (949) 719-3800, Fax: (949) 719-4053, Web Site: www.zpizza.com. Gourmet pizza, pasta, and salads in a up-scale California style. Established: 1986 - Franchising Since: 1997 - No. of Units: Company Owned: 12 - Franchised: 10 - Franchise Fee: $25,000 - Royalty: 5% - Total Inv: $150,000.

ZUZU HANDMADE MEXICAN FOOD RESTAURANTS
ZuZu Franchising Corp.
2651 N. Harwood #100, Dallas, TX, 75201. - Tel: (800) 824-8830, (214) 521-4456, Fax: (214) 922-8226. Authentic, handmade Mexican food, served in a quick, casual atmosphere. Established: 1989 - Franchising Since: 1992 - No. of Units: Company Owned: 5 - Franchised: 41 - Franchise Fee: $25,000 - Royalty: 4.5%, 4% adv. - Total Inv: $160,000-$280,000 - Financing: No, but will assist in obtaining outside financing.

ZYNG ASIAN GRILL *
Zyng International, LLC
132 King Street, Alexandria, VA, 22314. Contact: Stacey Gallagher - Tel: (703) 549-5332, (800) 272-6094, Fax: (703) 549-0740, E-Mail: staceyg@fransmart.com, Web Site: www.zynginternational.com. ZYNG Asian Grill combines the best, most popular Asian dishes from China, Japan, Thailand, Vietnam, Singapore and Korea. Serving an amazing selection of delicious appetizers, entrees, soups, salads, desserts, beer, wine, sake, and teas. Zyng meets the needs of any palate. Established: 1998 - Franchising Since: 1999 - No. of Units: Company Owned: 1 - Franchised: 17 - Franchise Fee: $25,000 - Royalty: 5% - Total Inv: $211,000-$630,000 - Financing: Yes, third party.

FOOD: SPECIALTY SHOPS

BAKER BROS AMERICAN DELI
BB Franchising Inc
5500 Greenville Ave, Suite 1102, Dallas, TX, 75206. Contact: Dale Ross - Tel: (214) 696-8780, Fax: (214) 696-8809, Web Site: www.bakerbrosdeli.com. Up scale deli with sandwiches, soups, salads, potatoes and pizza. Fast casual concept. Established: 1998 - Franchising Since: 2000 - No. of Units: Company Owned: 4 - Franchised: 1 - Franchise Fee: $30,000 - Royalty: 4%-5% - Total Inv: $400,000-$600,000 - Financing: No.

BON APPETIT INTERNATIONAL GOURMET FOODS, INC.
1409 S 900 E, Salt Lake City, UT, 84105. Contact: Mick Chandler, Pres. - Tel: (801) 463-9917, (888) 278-3663, Web Site: bonappetit-int.com. In home gourmet food sales. Franchises available in Northwest only at this time. Our systematic approach on getting and keeping customers is second to none. Established: 1978 - Franchising Since: 1994 - No. of Units: Franchised: 4 - Franchise Fee: $25,000 - Royalty: 6% on gross sales - Total Inv: $25,000 - Financing: 25% plus van.

CAFE ALA CARTE
Cafe Ala Carte Corporation
589 Slippery Rock Road, Ft. Lauderdale, FL, 33327. Contact: Bonnie Fimiano - Tel: (877) 925-2227, Fax: (954) 349-3100, E-Mail: alacart@aol.com, Web Site: www.cafealacarte.com. Cafe Ala Carte franchises are mobile specialty coffee carts that feature high quality coffee products provided primarily at social and business group functions. Established: 1996 - Franchising Since: 2000 - No. of Units: Company Owned: 6 - Franchised: 7 - Franchise Fee: $10,000 - Total Inv: $55,000 - Financing: Yes.

CHILI CHOMPERS
Chili Champers, Inc.
927A Main Street, Stone Mountain, GA, 30006. Contact: David Barnett - Tel: (770) 465-7111, (888) 575-7111. Spicy foods specialty store. Full training and support provided. Established: 1994 - Franchising Since: 1997 - No. of Units: Company Owned: 4 - Franchised: 5 - Franchise Fee: $25,000 - Total Inv: $75,000-$100,000 (including Fran Fee, inventory, all opening expenses) - Financing: No.

CHOCOLATE CHOCOLATE CHOCOLATE COMPANY
*
112 N. Kirkwood Rd, St. Louis, MO, 63122. - Tel: (314) 832-2639, Fax: (314) 832-2299, Web Site: www.chocolatechocolate.com. Freshly made chocolate covered strawberries, hand crafted truffle, yum yum chocolates and much much more. Established: 1981 - Franchising Since: 2003 - No. of Units: Francised: 8 - Franchise Fee: $20,000 - Royalty: 5% - Total Inv: $185,000.

CLUB SANDWICH
Club Sandwich Franchising, Inc.
107 Cherry St., New Canaan, CT, 06840. Contact: Diane DeVito, Ex. V.P. - Tel: (203) 966-4053, Fax: (203) 966-4053. Gourmet sandwich shop. Established: 1986 - Franchising Since: 1990 - No. of Units: Franchised: 1 - Franchise Fee: $25,000 - Royalty: 5% wkly, 1% adv. - Total Inv: $130,000, $60,000 equip, $25,000 imp, fran fee.

COFFEE CAVERN
Coffee Cavern Inc.
P.O. Box 6280, Moraga, CA, 94570. Contact: Steve Selover, President - Tel: (925) 376-1109, (800) LATTE-2-U, Fax: (925) 376-6542, E-Mail: coffeecavern@coffeecavern.com, Web Site: www.coffeecavern.com. Gourmet coffee house with a unique tropical cavern decor. Established: 1994 - Franchising Since: 1997 - No. of Units: Company Owned: 3 - Franchised: 2 - Franchise Fee: $20,000 - Royalty: 5%, marketing advertising =1% - Total Inv: $198,100-$322,600 - Financing: No.

COFFEE EXPRESS™
4 Union Plaza, #9, Bangor, ME, 04401. - Tel: (207) 947-5101, Fax: (207) 990-1477. European-style cafe, with double drive thru. Established: 1993 - Franchising Since: 1995 - No. of Units: Company Owned: 4 - Franchised: 4 - Franchise Fee: $20,000 - Total Inv: $255,000 - Financing: Yes.

CORPORATE CAFE
Corporate Cafe Franchise, Inc.
One Corporate Drive, Andover, MA, 01810. Contact: Mark Copomaccio/ Raymond Nardone, Franchise Development - Tel: (800) 562-9665. Corporate cafeterias. Established: 1992 - No, of Units: Company Owned: 2 - Franchise Fee: $15,000 - Total Inv: $32,050-$41,000 (includes fran fee) - Financing: No.

DOC CHEY'S NOODLE HOUSE *
1409 N. Highland Ave., #M, Atlanta, GA, 30306. - Tel: (404) 541-1077, Fax: (404) 541-1079, E-Mail: franchise@doccheys.com, Web Site: www.doccheys.com. We serve fresh prepared tasty Pan Asian dishes. Established: 1997 - Franchising Since: 2004 - No. of Units: Company Owned: 3 - Franchise Fee: $21,000 - Royalty: 6% - Total Inv: $287,500-$462,000 - Financing: No.

E Z PANTRY INC
P.O. Box 1342, Medford, NJ, 08055. Contact: Marketing Director - Tel: (609) 767-0555, Fax: (609) 654-2728. We are a grocery shopping and delivery service. Customers order food by the phone and the internet, we bring it to their home. Established: 1991 - Franchising Since: 1998 - No. of Units: Company Owned: 1 - Franchised: 1 - Franchise Fee: $32,500 - Royalty: $0 for year #1 - 1% gross there after - Total Inv: (excluding franchise fee) $13,700-$25,760 including working capital - Financing: Third party, in-house.

EDIBLE ARRANGEMENTS
1920 Dixwell Ave, Suite 200, Hamden, CT, 06512. Contact: Zahida Shamoon - Tel: (888) 727-7258, (203) 907-0070, Fax: (203) 230-0792, Web Site: www.ediblearrangements.com. Sculpted fruit arrangement for any occasion. Our delicious designs are made with the freshest of fruit without any additives or preservatives. Established: 1999 - Franchising Since: 2001 - No. of Units: Company Owned: 2 - Franchised: 2 - Total Inv: $75,000-$125,000.

EDWARDO'S NATURAL PIZZA RESTAURANTS
Mid-Continent Restaurants, Inc.
205 W. Wacker, Ste. 1400, Chicago, IL, 60606. Contact: Director of Franchising - Tel: (312) 346-5455, (800) 944-3393, Fax: (312) 346-2115. Chicago-style stuffed pizza and more. Full training and support provided. Established: 1978 - Franchising Since: 1979 - No. of Units: Company Owned: 17 - Franchised: 11 - Franchise Fee: $25,000 - Total Inv: $270,000-$550,000 - Financing: No.

FILTERFRESH
378 University Ave., Westwood, MA, 02090. Contact: Glenn Cooper, VP of Fran. Dev. - Tel: (617) 461-8734. Hi-tech office coffee service using patented coffee/computer and gourmet coffee. Established: 1987 - Franchising Since: 1987 - No. of Units: Company Owned: 7 - Franchised: 41 - Franchise Fee: $24,500 - Royalty: 5%, 2% adv - Total Inv: Full franchise $200,000 work. cap., $250,000 financing - Financing: Yes joint venture franchise $50,000-$100,000. NOT FRANCHISING AT THIS TIME.

FIRE GLAZED HAM BY THE SWISS COLONY
Swiss Colony Stores Inc.
1112 Seventh Ave., Monroe, WI, 53566. Contact: Gene Curran, VP - Tel: (608) 324-6000, Fax: (608) 242-1001. Specializing in spiral sliced honey glazed ham and turkey, Swiss Colony products and a unique upscale cafe all in one retail store. Established: 1963 - Franchising Since: 1993 - No. of Units: Company Owned: 2 - Franchised: 17 - Franchise Fee: $20,000 - Royalty: 4% of gross sales - Total Inv: $150,000 - Financing: No.

FISH COVE FRANCHISING
1802 Teall Ave, Syeacuse, NY, 13206. Contact: Joseph Falcone, President - Tel: (315) 463-6990, Fax: (315) 463-1038. Fresh and frozen seafoods, prepared and unprepared. Established: 1949 - Franchising Since: 1996 - No. of Units: Company Owned: 3 - Franchise Fee: $17,500 - Royalty: 4% - Total Inv: $70,000-$90,000.

HERE'S THE SCOOP
HTSF, Inc
27 S. Main St, Manville, NJ, 08835. Contact: Doug Klein, President - Tel: (908) 429-2105, (800) 564-8014, Fax: (908) 429-0799, E-Mail: info@heresthescoop.com, Web Site: www.heresthescoop.com. Retail and wholesale of frozen deserts. Italian ices, cakes, pies and novelties all made on the premises with our award winning formulas and recipes. Established: 1994 - Franchising Since: 1998 - No. of Units: Company Owned: 1 - Franchised: 1 - Franchise Fee: $20,000 - Royalty: 4% - Total Inv: $85,000-$175,000 - Financing: Equipment leasing if qualified.

HONEYBAKED HAM CO & CAFE, THE
5445 Triangle Pkwy, #400, Norcross, GA, 30092. - Tel: (800) 968-7424, Fax: (678) 966-3133, Web Site: www.honeybakedonline.com. We offer sweetly glazed hams, turkey breast, cheesecake, pies and more. Established: 1957 - Franchising Since: 1998 - No. of Units: Company Owned: 308 - Franchised: 39 - Franchise Fee: $30,000 - Royalty: 5-6% - Total Inv: $249,600-$390,400.

INCREDIBLY-EDIBLE-DELITES
1 Summit Ave, Broomall, PA, 19008-2517. Contact: Dir of Fran. Sales - Tel: (610) 353-8844, Fax: (610) 359-9188, E-Mail: ied@fruit flowers.com, Web Site: www.fruitflowers.com. Create floral fruit bouquets from fresh cut fruit. Established: 1984 - Franchising Since: 1993 - No. of Units: Company Owned: 1 - Franchised: 6 - Franchise Fee: $25,000 - Royalty: 4.5% merchandise + delivery, 1-2% advertising - Total Inv: $75,000-$145,000 - Financing: No.

IT'S A GRIND COFFEE HOUSE
6272 E. Pacific Coast Hwy., Ste.E, Long Beach, CA, 90803. - Tel: (562) 594-5600, (866) 424-5282, Fax: (562) 594-4100. Coffee house franchise. Established: 1995 - Franchising Since: 2000 - No. of Units: Company Owned: 5 - Franchised: 34 - Franchise Fee: $30,000 - Total Inv: $137,800-$244,100 - Financing: Yes.

JAVA DAVE'S COFFEE
Tuba Coffee Service
6239 E. 15th St, Tulsa, OK, 74112. Contact: Mike Blair, Nat'l Franchise Sales Mgr - Tel: (918) 836-5570, (800) 725-7315, Fax: (918) 835-4348, Web Site: www.javadavescoffee.com. The Java Dave's Coffee House concept is a unique blend of a drink bar for specialty gourmet products including smoothies and a full retail coffee market. Java Dave's works with franchisees to mazimize each unit's full potential. Established: 1981 - Franchising Since: 1993 - No. of Units: Company Owned: 2 - Franchised: 13 - Franchise Fee: $17,500 - Royalty: 3% - Total Inv: $150,000-$175,000 - Financing: Limited.

JAVA HUT & PHOTO EXPRESSO
148 Bamboo Lane, Fallbrook, CA, 92028. - Tel: (760) 728-2255. Drive-thru coffee and film kiosk. Established: 1994 - Franchising Since: 1999 - No. of Units: Company Owned: 1 - Franchise Fee: $10,000 - Royalty: .03% - Total Inv: $20,000-$50,000 - Financing: No.

JERKY HUT
Jerky Hut International, Inc.
P.O. Box 308, Hubbard, OR, 97032-0308. - Tel: (800) 537-5975, Fax: (503) 981-7692. Business to business route sales - retail sales of Jerky Hut products, fairs, shows and events, wholesale route and fund raising, mail order. Established: 1991 - Franchising Since: 1991 - No. of Units: Company Owned: 1 - Franchised: 8 - Franchise Fee: $15,000 - Royalty: 5% gross sales, 1% adv. - Total Inv: Fran. fee plus $28,000 van, $7,000 equip., $5,000-$10,000 work. cap., $5,000-$10,000 start up inventory - Financing: Yes, 50% of franchise fee O.A.C.

JUICE CONNECTION®, INC
2323 North Tustin Avenue, Suite C-123, Santa Ana, CA, 92705. Contact: Sue Claus, President - Tel: (760) 630-3991, E-Mail: info@juiceconnection.com. Juice/smoothie bar. Established: 1995 - Franchising Since: 1995 - No. of Units: Company Owned: 3 - Franchised: 2 - Franchise Fee: $20,000 - Royalty: 5% gross sales - Total Inv: Build out $80,000-$130,000 - Financing: Conventional.

JUICE WORKS
Juice Works Development, Inc.
10005 Colonel Glenn Rd, Little Rock, AR, 72204-8135. - Tel: (800) 449-JUICE (5842), Fax: (602) 998-0129. A Juice Works Store operated by you would sell a line of food and beverages targeted toward health conscious consumers, frozen yogurt, based fruit smoothies and fresh and natural juice drinks made from fruits and vegetables constitute the primary menu. Established: 1986 - Franchising Since: 1986 - No. of Units: Company Owned: 2 - Franchised: 30 - Franchise Fee: $20,000 Traditional, $5,000 Non-Traditional - Royalty: 4%, 3% adv. fee - Total Inv: $200,000-$250,000 - Financing: Third party financing available to qualified parties.

JUICE WORLD
6766 Pinehaven Rd, Oakland, CA, 94611-1014. Contact: Michael Fullam, Pres. - Tel: (805) 481-9596. Healthy fast food alternative juice and smoothie bar. Established: 1995 - Franchising Since: 1995 - No. of Units: Company Owned: 3 - Franchised: 4 - Franchise Fee: $20,000 - Royalty: 6%, 2% - Total Inv: $114,000-$210,000 - Financing: No.

KELLY'S COFFEE & FUDGE FACTORY
Kelly's Enterprises, Inc.
P.O. Box 21538, Bakerfield, CA, 93390. - Tel: (866) GO-COFFEE, Fax: (661) 664-4785. Franchisor of gourmet coffee houses, with fresh baked products and fresh homemade fudge. Menu includes light sandwiches, salads to frozen blended drinks and desserts. National expansion presently occuring. Established: 1983 - Franchising Since: 1983 - No. of Units: Franchised: 35 - Franchise Fee: $30,000 - Royalty: 6% of adjusted gross. - Total Inv: $100,000 (express store) to $170,000 (full store) - Financing: Yes.

L.A. SMOOTHIE HEALTHMART AND CAFE
L.A. Smoothie Franchises, Inc.
4141 Veterans Hwy, Ste 336, Metairie, LA, 70002. Contact: Albert Gardes C.O.O. - Tel: (504) 486-0036, Fax: (504) 455-5891. Via total health concept stores and carts, sells fresh fruit vitamin/supplement boosted smoothies, healthy line of soups, salads, sandwiches plus vitamins, suppliments and activewear. Established: 1991 - Franchising Since: 1992 - No. of Units: Franchised: 17 in USA, 1 International - Franchise Fee: $20,000 per store or $9,000 per cart - Royalty: 5% - Total Inv: $100,000-store/$29,900-cart - Financing: Third party lenders.

LA PALETERA
La Paletera Franchise Systems, Inc.
3000 Weslayan Dr, St. 108, Houston, TX, 77027. Contact: C.K. Hudson, CEO - Tel: (713) 621-6200, (866) 621-6200, Fax: (713) 621-8200, E-Mail: seaboard07@aol.com, Web Site: www.lapaletera.com. Healthy 100% natural fruit concept selling fruit cups and bars, fruit trays, natural fruit smoothie's, ice cream and other treats. Established: 1997 - Franchising Since: 2003 - No. of Units: Company Owned: 3 - Franchised: 27 - Franchise Fee: $28,000 - Royalty: 5% - Total Inv: $110,000-$160,000 - Financing: Third party available.

NEW YORK BUTCHER SHOPPE
1256 Ben Sawyer Blvd Suite F, Mt. Pleasant, SC, 29464. - Tel: (843) 388-0080, Fax: (843) 388-0079, Web Site: www.nybutcher.com. Gourmet food store. Established: 1999 - Franchising Since: 2003 - No. of Units: Company Owned: 1 - Franchise Fee: $25,000 - Royalty: $6% - Total Inv: $173.500-$237,500 - Financing: No.

PEABERRY *
1299 E. 58th Avenue, Denver, CO, 80216. - Tel: (303) 292-9324, Fax: (303) 292-5179, Web Site: www.peaberrycoffee.com. Selection of locally roasted beans (over 40 varieties), the Peaberry profile system enable's our customers to identify and select coffee best suited for their taste, for both drip coffee served at the stores and beans to take home. Established: 1990 - Franchising Since: 2003 - No. of Units: Company Owned: 21 - Franchised: 9 - Franchise Fee: $35,000 - Total Inv: $197,000-$479,000.

QUIKAVA
Chock Full O' Nuts
100 Foxborough Blvd., Ste. 220, Foxborough, MA, 02035. Contact: Gerry Pelissier, V.P. - Tel: (508) 698-2223, Fax: (508) 698-2224, (800) 381-6303, Web Site: www.quikava.com. We have combined two of the hottest trends in food service today, gourmet coffees and drive-thru convenience. We serve over 30 gourmet/specialty coffees and fresh baked goods, from a free standing modular double drive-thru 600 sq. ft. bldg. This wholly-owned subsidiary of the Chock Full O' Nuts Corp., a 60 year old coffee roaster listed on the NYSE, is seeking experienced business principals to become single or multi-unit Quikava franchise operators throughout the U.S. Established: 1990 - Franchising Since: 1994 - No. of Units: Company Owned: 6 - Franchised: 43 - Franchise Fee: $20,000 - Royalty: 5% of gross yr. - Financing: No.

ROBEKS *
1230 E. Rosecrans Ave., #250, Manhattan Beach, CA, 90266. - Tel: (310) 727-0500, Fax: (310) 727-0502, Web Site: www.robeks.com. Serving healthy foods including fruit smoothies. Established: 1996 - Franchising Since: 2001 - No. of Units: Franchised: 51 - Franchise Fee: $25,000 - Royalty: 7% - Total In v: $190,800-$324,600.

ROBIN HOOD EXPRESS
2105 South Lake Drive, Texarkana, TX, 75501. Contact: Franchise Department - Tel: (903) 792-1978, (800) 616-4663. Quality frozen food with home delivery service. Established: 1993 - Franchising Since: 1999 - No. of Units: Company Owned: 6 - Franchise Fee: $5,000 - Total Inv: $85,000-$100,000 - Financing: No.

ROCKTONIC JUICE & COFFEE
11448 Deerfield Dr., #2 PMB 201, Truckee, CA, 96161. Contact: Franchise Department - Tel: (530) 550-9919, Fax: (530) 579-3209, Web Site: www.rocktonic.com. Urban juice and coffee, providing the highest quality ingredients and recipes. Established: 2002 - Franchising Since: 2003 - No. of Units: Company Owned: 2 - Franchise Fee: $24,000 - Royalty: 5% - Total Inv: $175,000-$350,000.

ROLI BOLI

109 Main Street, Sayreville, NJ, 08872. Contact: Anthony Felicetta, President - Tel: (732) 257-8100, Fax: (732) 257-3255. Specialty sandwich in a french bread dough stuffed with a selection of 24 ingredients. Established: 1987 - Franchising Since: 1987 - No. of Units: Company Owned: 3 - Franchised: 11 - Franchise Fee: $20,000 - Royalty: 5% - Total Inv: $130,000-$195,000.

ROLY POLY FRANCHISE SYSTEMS LLC *

13245 Atlantic Ave., #4-399, Jacksonville, FL, 32225. - Fax: (305) 295-9371, Web Site: www.rolypolyusa.com. Fresh original rolled sandwiches made with sundried tomotoes, fresh sliced avocados, red pepper and mango chutnet to name a few. Established: 1992 - Franchising Since: 1997 - No. of Units: Franchised: 171 - Franchise Fee: $20,000 - Royalty: 4-6% - Total Inv: $77,500-$126,400.

ROYAL APPLES, INC.

11156 Fruit Ridge Ave NW, Sparta, MI, 49345-9728. Contact: Tim Klein, Pres. - Tel: (616) 887-1782. Franchise of nutritional fruit vending machines. Established: 1992 - Franchising Since: 1995 - No. of Units: Company Owned: 6 - Franchised: 125 - Franchise Fee: None - Royalty: 5% or 4 1/2¢/vend - Total Inv: $5,995 cost of machine, 12 minimum - Financing: Third party lease, equipment only. NOT FRANCHISING AT THIS TIME.

SEEKERS COFFEE HOUSE & CAFE *

13365 Smith Road, Middleburg Heights, OH, 44130. Contact: Franchise Department - Tel: (440) 884-4888, Fax: (440) 888-8332, Web Site: www.seekerscoffeehouse.com. Sole national venue for Christian entertainment. SEEKERS attracts local, national and international Christian artists, musicians and bands. With a very strong emphasis on community, SEEKERS offers a wholesome environment for all ages, terrific coffees, tasty foods, catering, great music and so much more. A Godly place be! Established: 2001 - Franchising Since: 2002 - No. of Units: Company Owned: 1 - Franchised: 2 - Franchise Fee: $15,000 - Royalty: 5% - Total Inv: $189,000-$369,000.

SWISS COLONY SEASONALS

Swiss Colony Stores Inc.
1112 Seventh Ave., Monroe, WI, 53566. Contact: Gene Curran, V.P. - Tel: (608) 324-6000, Fax: (608) 242-1000. Holiday locations featuring Swiss Colony gifts and specialty foods, located in shopping malls around the country. Established: 1963 - Franchising Since: 1963 - No. of Units: Company Owned: 8 - Franchised: 110 - Franchise Fee: $500 per location per year - Royalty: 4% of gross sales - Total Inv: $20,000-$60,000 - Financing: No.

TINDER BOX

Tinder Box International, Inc.
3 Bala Plaza E., Ste. 102, Bala Cynwyd, PA, 19004. Contact: Franchise Department - Tel: (800) 846-3372, (610) 668-4220, Fax: (610) 668-4266, Web Site: www.tinderbox.com. Tinder Box Int'l is the largest and oldest franchisor of premium cigar assessories and gift stores in the USA; featuring elegant retail stores which include private smoking club rooms or smoking lounges. Established: 1928 - Franchising Since: 1965 - No. of Units: Company Owned: 4 - Franchised: 128 - Franchise Fee: $30,000 for the first license, $15,000 thru after - Royalty: 4% of gross, stores in regional malls, 5% of gross, in all other locations - Total Inv: Build out $75,000-$150,000. inventory $75,000-$100,000 - Financing: Third part financing available.

TOTAL JUICE+

1125 E. Glendale Ave, Phoenix, AZ, 85020. - Tel: (800) 49J-UICE. Juice and smoothie bar, using fresh juices and health additives. Established: 1994 - Franchising Since: 1995 - No. of Units: Company Owned: 1 - Franchised: 6 - Franchise Fee: $20,000 - Total Inv: $120,000-$160,000 - Financing: Third party.

TROPICAL SMOOTHIE CAFE

Tropical Smoothie Franchise Development, Inc
1190 Eglin Pkwy, Shalimar, FL, 32579. - Tel: (850) 609-6022, (888) 292-2522, Fax: (850) 604-6023, Web Site: www.tropicalsmoothie.com. Tropical Smoothie serves only the highest quality products to create the ultimate refreshing nutritional beverage. We offer over 35 flavors of smoothies with great recipes to create the perfect smoothie for everyone, we offer gourmet wraps, sandwiches, tortizzas, specialty coffee's, juices

and various suppliments. Established: 1993 - Franchising Since: 1997 - No. of Units: Company Owned: 48 - Franchised: 125 - Franchise Fee: $15,000 - Royalty: 6%, 2% local adv, 1% national adv - Total Inv: $70,000-$120,000 - Financing: No.

WOODY'S HOT DOGS AND WOODY'S CHICAGO STYLE

Woody's Hot Doga Hawaii, Inc
P.O. Box 600, Makita, HI, 96792. Contact: Coe D. Meyer, President - Tel: (808) 696-5483, (807) Go Woody, Fax: (808) 696-5481, Web Site: www.woodyshotdogs.com. Mobile and fixed fast food concessions working on a "Chicago style" sausage format. Established: 1990 - Franchising Since: 1992 - No. of Units: Company Owned: 2 - Franchised: 48 - Franchise Fee: $45,000 - Royalty: 6% gross - Total Inv: $50,000-$55,000 - Financing: Yes.

FOOD: SUPERMARKETS

DAIRY MART & BIGFOOT

Mac's Convenience Stores LLC
2204 Enterprise Parkway East, Twinsburg, OH, 44087. Contact: Tim Beech, Director of Franchise Operations - Tel: (330) 963-6100, Fax: (330) 963-6128, E-Mail: t_beech@macsstores.com. Basic convenience store that typically offers cigarettes, pop, beer, snacks, lottery, atm and grocery items. Established: 1939 - No. of Units: Company Owned: 500 - Franchised: 78 - Franchise Fee: $17,500 - Royalty: 14%; Dairy Mart maintains equipment, pays rent & utilities - Total Inv: $52,300-$106,000 - Financing: No.

FOOD-N-FUEL

Food-N-Fuel, Inc.
4366 Round Lake Rd. W., Arden Hills, MN, 55112. - Tel: (763) 633-7863. Retail grocery and gasoline. Established: 1978 - Franchising Since: 1979 - No. of Units: Company Owned: 27 - Franchised: 79 - Franchise Fee: $10,000 - Royalty: 3.5% of sales, no fee on gas sales - Total Inv: $350,000-$600,000.

PIGGLY WIGGLY

Piggly Wiggly Corporation
1991 Corporate Ave., Memphis, TN, 38132. Contact: Larry Wright, President - Tel: (901) 395-8215. Retail supermarkets. Established: 1916 - Franchising Since: 1919 - No. of Units: Franchised: 811 - Total Inv: Varies.

FORMAL WEAR RENTAL

CLASSIC TUXEDO

Classic Tuxedo Franchising, Inc
P.O. Box 4384, NH, 03802-4384. Contact: Dir. of Franchising - Tel: (603) 431-5900, Web Site: www.classictuxedo.com. Upscale tuxedo rental business, located in malls and shopping centers. Top name designer labels for rental and retail sales. Full training and support, turn-key business with very high margins. Established: 1990 - Franchising Since: 1999 - No. of Units: Company Owned: 7 - Franchised: 6 - Franchise Fee: $15,000 - Royalty: Flat fee of $193.00 per week ($10,000/yr) - Total Inv: $71,000-$125,000 includes operation capital and franchise fee - Financing: Yes third party.

GINGISS FORMALWEAR CENTERS

Gingiss International, Inc.
2101 Executive Dr., Addison, IL, 60101. Contact: Tom Ryan, V.P. Franchise Development - Tel: (630) 620-9050, (800) 621-7125, Fax: (630) 620-8840, E-Mail: gingiss@gingiss.com, Web Site: www.gingiss.com. National leader in the formal wear industry. Rental and sales of mens and boys formal wear and related accessories. Established: 1936 - Franchising Since: 1968 - No. of Units: Company Owned: 59 - Franchised: 189 - Franchise Fee: $15,000 - Royalty: 6% - Total Inv: $65,000 inven., $25,000-$110,000 constr., $8,000 equip. - Financing: Yes.

FRANCHISE CONSULTANTS AND FRANCHISE SERVICES

AAA FRANCHISE FINDERS
Franchise Foundations
Napa Valley Office - 1818 School Street, Calistoga, CA, 94515. Contact: Franchise Counselor - Tel: (707) 942-4444, (800) 942-4402, Fax: (707) 942-0444, E-Mail: FranFnds@ix.netcom.com, Web Site: www.webpage.com/franchise. In-depth research and reporting on desired franchise companies, including education about interviewing procedures, franchise relationships and developing your own Personal Franchise Profile. Based on 20 years experience in evaluating over 500 franchises. Established: 1980 - No. of Units: Company Owned: 1.

ABBEY FRANCHISE CONSULTING
508 E. Howe Rd., Tallmadge, OH, 44278. Contact: David Drylie, President - Tel: (330) 633-7888, (800)459-8364. Services for prospective Franchise Buyers and Franchisors including: Unbiased information on hundreds of Franchisors, Profile Matching, Franchisee Canvassing, Competitive Market Surveys, Training and our special PRN service where our franchise experienced staff satisfies your specific needs. Established: 1995 - No. of Units: Company Owned: 1.

ABX - ASSOCIATES BUSINESS XCHANGE
First Main Capital Corporation
16000 Dallas Parkway Ste 375, Dallas, TX, 75248. Contact: Don McIver BCB, FCBI, CBI, President - Tel: (214) 545-5776, Fax: (214) 545-5777, E-Mail: dmciver@abxbuyabiz.com, Web Site: www.abxbuyabiz.com. Franchise, Brokers, Business Opportunity Brokers, Real Estate Brokers, Business Price Evaluations, Business Consultanting. Nationwide Brokerage. Members of the International Business Brokers Association and The Texas Association of Business Brokers. Established: 1969.

ADVANCED FRANCHISING WORLDWIDE
7100 E. Lincoln Dr., Ste. B-123, Scottsdale, AZ, 85253-4434. Contact: Chris Wright, Diane Wright, Pres., Vice Pres. - Tel: (800)288-3054, (480) 443-0432, E-Mail: info@afww.com, Web Site: www.afww.com. Business expansion assistance through franchising, branchising, dealerships, distributorships, agents and more. Marketing of new business concept. Hands on development of prototype for pre-expansion entrepreneurs. Emphasis on creative, affordable solutions. Offices worldwide. Established: 1979.

ADVANCED TECHNOLOGY CONSULTING, LLC
8431 B. Washington St., NE, Alburquerque, NM, 87113. Contact: Gary D. Frech, Principal - Tel: (505) 823-6400, Web Site: www.atc-1.com. Technology consulting, planning and project management services specific to quick serve restaurant headquarters and store level management. Authorized distributor of DP Software Services, Inc., Restaurant Operations Management Software (ROMS). Providing ROMS service bureau alternatives to individual stores with total management solutions for the multiple store franchisees.

ALLAN COHEN & ASSOC., INC.
P.O. Box 1722, Hallandale, FL, 33008-1722. Contact: Allan Cohen, Pres. - Tel: (305) 215-3668, Fax: (954) 454-7216. Marketing and management consultants to retailers, hotels, restaurants, distributors and manufacturers of consumer goods and services in Canada and the U.S. Established: 1967.

AMERICAN ASSOCIATION OF FRANCHISEES & DEALERS
P.O. Box 81887, San Diego, CA, 92138-1887. Contact: Robert Purvin Jr., Fran Dev - Tel: (619) 209-3775, (800) 733-9858, Fax: (619) 209-3777. Services and benefits for franchisees, etc. Established: 1992.

THE AMERICAN FRANCHISEE ASSOCIATION

AMERICAN FRANCHISEE ASSOCIATION (AFA)
53 W. Jackson Blvd., Ste. 1157, Chicago, IL, 60604. Contact: Larry Beck - Tel: (312) 431-0545, Fax: (312) 431-1469, E-Mail: larrybeck@franchisee.org. National trade association representing the interests of franchisees. Represents 15,000 members who own over 30,000 outlets in 66 industries. Assists in the formation of independent franchisee associations. Provides telephone consultation to prospective and current franchisees. Makes available legal white papers on-line regarding a variety of topics of interest to prospective and current franchisees. Provides on-line listing of franchisee attorneys. Established: 1993.

AMERIDIAL INC., FRANCHISE SERVICES
4535 Strausser St. N.W., N. Canton, OH, 44720. Contact; Steve Trifelos, Sales & Mktg. Mgr.- Tel: (800) 445-7128, Fax: (330) 497-5500. For Franchisors: We provide lead generation telemarketing service as a value added service passed on to franchisees. For Franchisee: We ensure immediate start-up business activity through lead generation telemarketing. Long and proven track record. Ten phoning centers with 1000 telemarketers.

ANDREX CONSULTING SERVICES
10-21 Clintonville St, Whitestone, NY, 11357. Contact: Ed Possumato, Pres. - Tel: (718) 746-9465, Web Site: www.andrexconsulting.com. Consulting services: All areas, UFOC updates, franchise agreement revisions, business plans, start up and turnaround situations. Established: 1989.

AON RISK SERVICES & CONSULTING
8300 Norman Center Dr #400, Bloomington, MN, 55437-1027. Contact: Jim Walters, A.V.P. - Tel: (800) 541-2539, (800) 444-3017, (952) 656-8000, Fax: (952) 656-8001. Providing and administering sponsored national insurance programs for franchisors with over 100 units. Programs include property, casualty, workers compensation, auto, group health, accident and life insurance. Established: 1963.

ARTHUR ANDERSEN LLP
33 W. Monroe St., Ste. 2720, Chicago, IL, 60603-5385. Contact: Leonard N. Swartz, Managing Dir/Franchise Services - Tel: (312) 580-0033, Fax: (312) 507-6748. An international professional services firm with over 340 offices in 79 countries providing service in the areas of franchise consulting, auditing, tax and financial planning, appraisals and valuation, info systems, management consulting, small business advisory services and litigation support. Established: 1913.

ASGAT AGENCY, INC.
15965 Jeanette, Southfield, MI, 48075. Contact: Geoffrey Stebbins, Dir. of Special Projects - Tel: (248) 559-1415, (800) 745-1415. Full consultation services to develop companies into franchises including feasibility studies, UFOC documentation, brochures and strategic marketing plans. Asgat Agency also provides sales and marketing support and expertise to established franchisors, general business consulting and assists in acquiring venture capital financing. Established: 1973.

ASSOCIATION CONSULTANTS
1922 East Augusta Ave., Phoenix, AZ, 85020-4424. - Tel: (715) 686-2633. Franchisee and Franchise Association Consultant, expert witness, professional speaker on franchising subjects including franchisor bankruptcy from franchisee point of view.

B. MUNLIN CONSULTING SERVICES
800 Second Avenue, 8th Floor, New York, NY, 10017. - Tel: (212) 972-1821, Fax: (212) 972-1715, E-Mail: bjmunlin@msn.com. Assist in the development of business plans, identification of financing for start-up costs, machinery and equipment, leasehold improvements and working capital. Established: 1996.

BABCOCK & SCHMID, LOUIS & PARTNERS
P.O. Box 808, Bath, OH, 44210-0808. - Tel: (330) 659-3161, Fax: (330) 659-3502. Provide corporate identification design, package design, prototype facility design and product design. Clients include Goodyear, Pizza Hut, Sherwin Williams, Midas International, Ponderosa, KFC, Stouffers, T.J. Cinnamons & Bob Evans Farms.

BENCHMARK GROUP
121 West Walnut St., Rogers, AR, 72756. Contact: Jim Parks, Dir. of Mktg. - Tel: (479) 636-5004, Fax: (479) 636-9687, E-Mail: jim@bgark.com, Web Site: www.bgark.com. Architectural/Engineering firm offering building design services to companies with on-going building programs. Established: 1978.

BERMAN, AARON M.
Aaron M. Berman CPA
29350 Southfield Rd., Ste. 127, Southfield, MI, 48076.Contact: Aaron Berman, CPA - Tel: (248) 443-2410. Consulting and accounting services to franchisors and franchisees including audit and tax services. Established: 1982.

BERNARD J. HERBERT & ASSOCIATES
275 Dartmoor Circle, Atlanta, GA, 30328. Contact; H.B. Rust, Pres./ Owner - Tel: (770) 393-2437. Franchise consulting, development and marketing service. 37 years of diversified experience in franchising. Established: 1961.

BRAVA CAPITAL
2851 E La Palma Ave, Anaheim , CA, 92806-2404. Contact; Ginny Young, Pres. - Tel: (714) 771-8400, (800) 920-8870. We specialize in franchise financing to both start-up franchisees and multi-unit operators nationwide.

BROWN, TODD & HEYBURN PLLC
400 W. Market., Suite 3200, Louisville, KY, 40202. Contact: Robert Y. Gwin, Partner - Tel: (502) 589-5400, Web Site: www.bth-pllc.com. Law firm representing franchising clients, franchisees and franchise purchasing, trademark protection, and general corporate matters and taxation. Established: 1972.

BUSINESS AMERICA
Business America Associates, Inc.
2120 Greentree Rd., Pittsburgh, PA, 15220-1406. Contact: Thomas Atkins, Pres. - Tel: (412) 276-7701. Complete line of business and franchise brokerage. Confidential handling of businesses and buyers. Commissions earned on sales of businesses or acceptance of licensee on franchises. Established: 1984 - Franchising Since: 1985 - No. of Units: Franchised: 4 - Franchise Fee: $4,995 - Royalty: None - Total Inv: $10,000 equip., $4,995 fran. fee, $5,000 misc.- Financing: No.

CAPODICE & ASSOCIATES
1243 S. Tamiami Trail, Sarasota, FL, 34239. Contact: Peter Capodice, President - Tel: (941) 906-1990, Fax: (941) 906-1991, E-Mail: Picap123@aol.com, Web Site: www.capodice.com. The nation's preeminent retained executive search firm has set a new standard for the industry. By integrating one of the leading competency-based assessment tools into the search & selection process, Capodice & Associates expertly evaluates and predicts candidate behavioral patterns. This facilitates "fit and chemistry" decisions for client organizations. Established: 1995.

CASH CONNECTION
11902 S.E. Stark St., Portland, OR, 97216. - Tel: (503) 255-2274, Fax: (503) 255-4387. Franchisor Consultant.

CATON DESIGN
6489 Camden Ave Ste 206, San Jose, CA, 95120-2851. Contact: Jeannie Caton, President - Tel: (408) 280-1101. Marketing, printing and creative services. We provide a wide range of solutions & growth oportunities for your business. Established: 1990.

CHUNOWITZ, TEITELBAUM & BAERSON, LTD., CERTIFIED PUBLIC ACCOUNTANTS
401 Huehl Rd.,Northbrook, IL, 60062. Contact: Martin Magida, Partner - Tel: (847) 498-9620, Fax: (847) 498-6130, E-Mail: msm@ctbltd.com. Personal and timely service throughout the country and the Virgin Islands. Over twenty-six years of franchise accounting, tax planning, cash flow analysis, appraisals and valuations, personal financial planning and litigation support. Established: 1973.

COMPANY CORPORATION, THE
2711 Centerville Rd Ste. 400, Wilmington, DE, 19808-1645. Contact: Dir. of Mktg. - Tel: (302) 636-5440. Provider of incorporation services in all 50 states, without legal fees. Specialize in Delaware corporations, but can incorporate in any state, for as little as $45 plus state filing fees. Established: 1972.

COMPREHENSIVE FRANCHISING, INC.
FPI
2465 Ridgecrest Ave., Orange Park, FL, 32065. Contact: Franchise Department - Tel: (904) 272-6567, Fax: (904) 272-6750. Import and export of master and regional, foreign and domestic franchises worldwide, global introductions, full service international documentation packaging, recruits candidates to purchase regional and master territories in all markets. Complete monitoring, profit and control for overseas expansion. Established: 1988.

CONCEPTUAL EDGE, THE
P.O. Box 54043, Irvine, CA, 92619-4043. Contact: John Collins, Pres. - Tel: (949) 552-1732, E-Mail: info@conceptualedge.com, Web Site: www.conceptualedge.com. Franchise development and consulting firm. Concept, structure, operations and marketing assistance. Feasibility studies, strategic planning, financial projections, legal documentation, operations manuals, problem solving, marketing and sales materials. Sales Videos and Web Sites. Established in 1980.

CONNEX INTERNATIONAL, INC.
40 Old Ridgebury Rd., #317, Danbury, CT, 06810-5119. - Tel: (800) 426-6639, (203) 731-5400, Fax: (203) 731-5425. Connex International is a communications management company supplying audio teleconferencing services to franchise corporations, as well as the International Franchise Association. Connex provides bridging capabilities to link multiple domestic and international locations by telephone for conference calls. Additionally, Connex provides consulting services on audio conferencing, product launch, growth management and international expansion. Established: 1982.

CONSULTANTS AMERICA CORP.
Consultants America Corp.
3820 Premier Ave., Memphis, TN, 38118. Contact: Franchise Director - Tel: (901) 368-3333, Fax: (901) 368-1144. Specialize in developing new franchises and restructuring and servicing established franchises. Established: 1976 - Franchising Since: 1976 - No. of Units: Company Owned: 4 - Franchised: 108 - Franchise Fee: $1,000 - Royalty: $100/mnth. Total Inv: $2,000 - Financing: Yes.

CONSULTANTS, THE
Franchise Consultants, Inc.
Oliver's Corner, P.O. Box 403, Essex, CT, 06426-0403. Contact: Theron Kearney, President - Tel: (941) 498-7802. Complete franchise development services including legal documentation, operations manuals and promotional packages. Site locating and equipment financing. Franchise sales and franchisor consulting. Twenty plus yrs. experience. Now interviewing individuals with franchise or sales experience to open affiliate offices in select areas of U.S. No. of Units: Company Owned: 4.

CREATIVE SALES SOLUTIONS/CSS FRANCHISING
177 Main Street, Ft. Lee, NJ, 07024. Contact: Gary Occhiogrosso, Franchise Development - Tel: (201) 585-4753. Franchise sales, advertising and marketing. Established: 1991.

DAMAS & ASSOCIATES
6810 S. Cedar St., Ste. 2B, Lansing, MI, 48911. Contact: Raymond J. Damas, Pres. - Tel: (517) 694-0910 or (800) 443-2627, Fax: (517) 694-1377. For over 12 yrs we have been investigating and evaluating franchises which persons are considering purchasing, and have been developing successful businesses into franchises. Includes feasibility studies, business plans, trademark protection, operating and training manuals, marketing materials, and franchise marketing. Established: 1979.

DEAN CONSULTANTS
17300 17th St., Ste. J-PMB 204, Tustin, CA, 92780. Contact: Paul Wilmoth, Pres. - Tel: (714) 546-6773, (800) 732-5537, Fax: (714) 546-6769. Consulting to new and existing franchise business. Established: 1986.

DELOITTE & TOUCHE
1633 Broadway, New York, NY, 10019. Contact: Frank Quix . - Tel: (212) 436-3059, Fax: (212) 653-5132, E-Mail: fquix@deloitte.nl, Web Site: www.deloitte.com. Consultants and business advisors with significant experience in franchising, licensing and international expansion through involvement in franchise trade organizations and consulting with many franchise clients throughout the world. We pride ourselves on developing innovative and cost-effective planning strategies for franchise companies.

DELOITTE & TOUCHE LLP
1200 Two Ruan Center, 601 Locust St., Des Moines, IA, 50309. Contact: John L. Allbery, Dir. of Fran. Consult.Practice - Tel: (515) 288-1200, Fax: (515) 288-7801. Independent CPA's and business advisors with significant experience in the franchise industry through involvement in franchise trade organizations and consulting with many international franchise clients. Work with start-up franchise organizations and other established companies evaluating franchising as an alternative operational and growth strategy. Develop innovative and cost-effective planning strategies for franchise industry companies.

DEUTSCH GROUP, THE
1140 Highland Ave., Ste. 200, Manhattan Beach, CA, 90266-5325. Contact: Barry J. Deutsch, Pres. - Tel: (562) 596-5544. The Deutsch Group offers all of the franchise development services required to franchise a business, including feasibility studies and analysis, strategic planning, direction, all legal documentation, sales kits, development of operational marketing and training manuals, business plan development and going public. Established: 1970.

DEVELOPMENTAL RESOURCES GROUP, INC.
499 Clover Mill Rd., Exton, PA, 19341. Contact: Steven Cucenotti, Franchise Development - Tel: (610) 363-0977. Business consulting to expanding companies. Established: 1989.

DOCUCORP
1246 Limestone Ave, Loveland, CO, 80537-5098. Contact; Donald W. Ettinger, Pres. - Full franchise development programs, operations consultant, specialized training for start- up franchisors. NO NEW CLIENTS AT THIS TIME.

E.J. KRAUSE & ASSOCIATES INC.
6550 Rock Spring Dr., #500, Bethesda, MD, 20817. Contact: Dir.of Fran. - Tel: (301) 493-5500, Fax: (301) 493-5705. E.J. Krause is a major organizor of exhibitions worldwide. The company organizes the International Franchise Expo in Buenos Aires, Argentina, as well as expos in Brazil and Italy. Established: 1984.

ELDORADO BANK
24012 Calle De La Plata Ste. 150, Laguna Hills, CA, 92653-3644. - Tel: (949) 699-4344, E-Mail: btompkins@eldoradobank.com. Specializes in financing (SBA loans) for new expanding franchises from 7-25 yrs. - $75,000 and up. Ninety percent real estate loans for acquisition and / or construction of owner-occupied commercial buildings. Established: 1972.

ENTREPRENEUR'S SOURCE, THE
TES Franchising LLC
900 Main Street South, Bldg. #2, Southbury, CT, 06488. - Tel: (203) 264-2006, (800) 289-0086, Fax: (203) 264-3516, E-Mail: info@theesource.com, Web Site: www.franchisesearch.com. The premier international source for information about the wide range of self-employment options. Provides an education and coaching process that offers objective guidance for entrepreneurs. Using informal interviews and profiling tools, The Entrepreneur's Source helps clients zero-in on the options that are in harmony with their lifestyle and income goals. Established: 1984 - Franchising Since: 1997 - No. of Units: Franchised: 260 total units in 40 states and 2 in Canada - Franchise Fee: $45,000 - Royalty: None - Total Inv: $75,000 - Financing: None.

EQUITY PROPERTIES
600 Haverford Rd., Ste. 204, Haverford, PA, 19041. - Tel: (610) 645-7700, ext. 107, Fax: (610) 645-5454. Develops market development strategies, performs total site selection, and negotiates leases / purchases on behalf of franchising companies. Established: 1995.

ERNST & YOUNG
1221 McKinney St. #2400, Houston, TX, 77010-2007. Contact: Pam Cobb, Associate Adm. for Gulf Coast - Tel: (713) 750-1500, Fax: (713)750-1501. Consists of 450 offices worldwide. Provides finance, accounting and tax assistance to help franchisors deal with business problems of growing up. Established: 1903.

EUGENE O. GETCHELL, CFE
Eugene O. Getchell, Inc
711 Kirkland Drive, Lexington, KY, 40502. Contact: Gene Getchell, President - Tel: (606) 277-4860. Counseling small or new start-up franchises for future growth. Franchise litigation-consultant and expertwitness. Established: 1992.

EVERYTHING FRANCHISING, INC.
2132 Charlotte Amalie Court, P.O. Box 512809, Punta Gorda, FL, 33951. Contact: Theron V. Kearney, Exec. V.P. - Tel: (941) 639-1922, Fax: (941) 833-4365, E-Mail: TheronK@aol.com, Web Site: www.everythingfranchising.com. Specializing in franchise development programs and consulting providing a full range of services including: feasibility studies, developing franchise agreements, preparing franchise documents, creating franchise brochures, writing operations manuals design report forms, systems and controls, financing, web site design, building franchise support programs. Established: 1974 - No. of Units: Company Owned: 2.

EXPERTS IN FRANCHISING
E.I. Franchising, Inc.
222 Lakeview Ave., #160-255, West Palm Beach, FL, 33401. - Tel: (800) 655-0343, Fax: (305) 517-9752, E-Mail: frandocs@aol.com, Web Site: www.frandocs.com. Franchise development and sales. Established: 1990.

F.C.I.A.
Franchise Consultants International Association
5147 South Angela Rd., Memphis, TN, 38117. Contact: W.C. Richey, President - Tel: (901) 368-3333, Fax: (901) 368-1144, E-Mail: franmark@msn.com. An organization of professional consultants who specialize in sales, advertising, development, seminars, training, education, supply supervision, support and management involved with the franchise industry. Established: 1986 - Members: 2800+ - Membership Fee: $315 (12 months).

FAI

P.O. Box 200248, Denver, CO, 80220-0248. Contact: Gary Franklin, CEO - Tel: (303) 388-8486, (800) 739-0761, Fax: (303) 355-4213. Franchise recruiters and franchise consultants. The employer will be guided to the right applicant and the franchisee to the right franchise. Established: 1996.

FELTENSTEIN NEIGHBORHOOD MARKETING INSTITUTE

44 Coconut Row, #T-5, Palm Beach, FL, 33480-4005. Contact: Tom Feltenstein, Senior Principal - Tel: (561) 655-9207, Fax: (561) 832-7502. Assisting start up and existing franchisors with their franchising program, corporate marketing, franchise marketing plans, sales and compliances, human resources and training, trade area marketing programs. Established: 1989.

FINANCING BUSINESS PLANS

Devitt Consulting Group Ltd.
1400 E. Olive St., Milwaukee, WI, 53211-1828. Contact: Michael Devitt, President - Tel: (414) 962-4414, Fax: (414) 962-4415. Pre-packaged franchise business plans. Established: 1982.

FRANCHISE 2000 CORPORATION

P.O. Box 4384, Portsmouth, NH, 03802. Contact: Robert Tortoriello, President - Tel: (603) 431-5900, Fax: (603) 431-5900, E-Mail: franchise @franchise2000.com. Full service management consulting firm specializing in franchising, licensing and product distribution. Expertise in program development, marketing legal compliance and continuing support. Established: 1982 - No. of Units: Company Owned: 2.

FRANCHISE ARCHITECTS, THE

2275 Half Day Road, Suite 350, Bannock Burn, IL, 60015. Contact: Craig S. Slavin, Chairman - Tel: (847) 808-0870, Fax: (847) 821-2610. Established: 1979. Franchise consulting firm specializing in the design of custom expansion programs. Our proprietary Franchise Architecture process is well tested and the basis for the expansion programs for hundreds of worldwide companies in over 40 industries and 4 continents. Development program includes all operations, marketing, advertising, sales, financial, organizational structure, human resource, staffing and compliance issues and franchise sales and marketing assistance. Also the creators of the Franchise Success System and the original Franchise Match and the Franchise Navigator, on America On-Line.

FRANCHISE ASSOCIATES, THE

541 Main St., South Weymouth, MA, 02190. Contact: Franchise Dir./ Pres. - Tel: (781) 337-7940. Franchisor/Franchisee Consultant.

FRANCHISE AXIS

Franchise Profiles International
2465 Ridgecrest Ave., Orange Park, FL, 32065. Contact: Connie B. D'Imperio, Pres. - Tel: (904) 272-6567, (800) 321-6567. Marketing and research service for franchisors that recruits and screens potential candidates for master franchise areas. Established: 1988.

FRANCHISE BUSINESS INTERNATIONAL

5310 Zelzah, #305, Encino, CA, 91316. - Tel: (818) 705-3222, (800) 468-5008, Fax: (310) 453-7778. Franchise consultant - structure franchise companies in USA, Europe, Canada, Asia and South America. Established: 1954.- Franchising Consulting Since: 1954.

FRANCHISE BUSINESS SYSTEMS INC.

4200 Dahlberg Dr., Minneapolis, MN, 55422. - Tel: (612) 520-8500. Consulting firm with emphasis on sales and managing of franchises. Established: 1986.

FRANCHISE CENTRAL, INC.

14983 Gentle Breeze Way, Surprise, AZ, 85374. Contact: Alan S. Hoffman, Pres. - Tel: (623) 328-9038, (888) 325-9860, Fax: (623) 328-9037, E-Mail: ALH713@cox.net. Franchise consulting specializing in the marketing, sales and operational support, with franchisors in food service, retail and service throughout North America. Established: 1995.

FRANCHISE CENTRE™ (FRANCHISE NETWORK OF COLORADO)

6888 S. Clinton Street, #207, Greenwood Village, CO, 801112. Contact: M. Stacy Swift, Franchise Consultant - Tel: (303) 715-0397, Fax: (303) 715-0405, E-Mail: colorado@frannet.com, Web Site: www.frannet.com. Providing education and assistance to clients interested in purchasing a franchise. Member of franchise network, USA, representing over 65 different franchise companies. Full franchise development and consulting services also. Established: 1970.

FRANCHISE CONSORTIUM INTERNATIONAL

245 S. 84th, Ste. 200, Lincoln, NE, 68510. - Tel: (402) 484-7100, Fax: (402) 484-7811. Full service franchise developer. Established: 1990.

FRANCHISE DEVELOPERS

925 L St, Lincoln, NE, 68508-2229. Contact: Jack L. Rediger, Pres. - Tel: (402) 434-5620, (800) 865-2378. If your existing business is worthy of franchising, it's worth a call to Franchise Developers. Complete franchise development services including, in-house legal, marketing, sales and support, experience with superior customer service. Excellent references. Established: 1994.

FRANCHISE DEVELOPMENT INTERNATIONAL, (DBA)

370 S.E. 15th Ave., Pompano Beach, FL, 33060-7624. - Tel: (954) 942-9424, Fax: (954) 783-5177. Franchise/marketing consulting firm specializing in small successful businesses looking to expand through franchising. Principals are a group of qualified professionals in the areas of law, marketing, operations, finance, advertising, purchasing, and real estate. Established: 1991.

FRANCHISE DEVELOPMENTS, INC.

4730 Centre Avenue, Pittsburgh, PA, 15213. Contact: Kenneth Franklin, Pres. - Tel: (412) 687-8484, (800) 576-5115, Fax: (412) 687-0541, E-Mail: franchise-dev@earthlink.net, Web Site: www.franchise-dev.com. Specializing in designing and implementing a total franchise development program. Package includes strategic and financial planning, systems and infrastructure design, operations manual, training outline and programs, franchisee support programs, franchise sales recruitment program, marketing plan and sales brochures and ads, legal documents, and ongoing franchise consulting. Established: 1970.

FRANCHISE DISPUTE RESOLUTIONS

4900 Falls Of Neuse Rd., Ste. 212, Raleigh, NC, 27609-5477. Contact: Richard Farrell, Senior Attorney - Tel: (919) 872-0300. Cost effective and efficient resolution of franchisor-franchisee disputes thru mediation or arbitration by neutral attorneys with long-term experience in the industry representing both franchisors and franchisees. Established: 1993.

FRANCHISE FOUNDATIONS

Napa Valley Office - 1818 School Street, Calistoga, CA, 94515. Contact: Dir. of Operations - Tel: (707) 942-4444, (800) 942-4402, Fax: (707) 942-0444, E-Mail: FranFnds@ix.netcom.com, Web Site: www.webpage.com/franchise. Franchise development and expansion including feasibility studies, business plans, UFOC's, operational documentation, training and field support programs developed under the direction of a nationally recognized franchise expert, author, attorney and instructor. Established: 1980 - No. of Units: Company Owned: 1.

FRANCHISE GROUP, THE

108 Wilmot Road, Ste. 110, Deerfield, IL, 60015. - Tel: (847) 236-1000, Fax: (847) 267-3401. Specializing in providing franchise program development, consulting and implementation services to emerging and established franchisors. Services include: feasibility studies, financing arrangements, management systems and procedures review, franchise offering analysis/review, marketing, operations manual preparation, legal documentation and general management consulting. Established: 1987.

FRANCHISE GROWTH PARTNERS

4400 PGA Blvd., Ste. 700, Palm Beach Gardens, FL, 33418. - Tel: (561) 624-0506, Fax: (561) 775-3890. Holding company building franchise related companies through merger, acquisition, strategic alliance and equity investment. Established: 1997.

FRANCHISE LIBRARY

Franchise Library & Marketing Company
P.O. Box 83-2062, Del Raye Beach, FL, 33483. Contact: Robert Spuck, Pres. - Tel: (561) 483-9699, (800) 839-4931. The Franchise Library is the only national resource network for buyers and sellers of both new and existing franchises. As the "Multiple Listing Service" of franchising, the organization boasts an extensive databank including potential franchisees, franchisors, and sellers of established franchises. More than 30 experienced consultants are available throughout the US and Canada to provide a wide range of personalized services. No fees for buyers. Established: 1992 - No. of Units: Company Owned: 1 - Consultants: 30.

FRANCHISE MASTERS INTERNATIONAL, INC

8301 Golden Valley Road #230, Minneapolis, MN, 55427. - Tel: (612) 541-1385, (800) 328-4158, Fax: (612) 542-2246. Franchise development company. Consulting-law firm-advertising agency - operations manuals - training programs - strategy planning (franchise/other bus. expansion techniques). Established: 1981.

FRANCHISE NETWORK INTERNATIONAL (DBA)

Trans Pacific Investment Corp.
P.O. Box 11359, Honolulu, HI, 96826-0359. - Tel: (808) 738-9533, Fax: (808) 973-0235. Sale of U.S. franchising companies and operating franchises to Asian investors, consultant to M & A Depts. of foreign banks on U.S. franchise acquisition and intermediary services for international franchise licensing agreement. Established: 1986.

FRANCHISE PROFILES

FPI
2465 Ridgecrest Ave., Orange Park, FL, 32065. - Tel: (904) 272-6567 or (800) 321-6567. Educational and investigative service for franchisors and franchisees. Complete franchise documentation. Established: 1975.

FRANCHISE RECRUITERS LTD. ™

Franchise Recruiters Ltd. ™
3500 Innsbruck, Lincolnshire Country Club, Village of Crete, IL, 60417. Contact: Jerry Wilkerson, Former President IFA - Tel: (708) 757-5595, (800) 334-6257, Fax: (708) 758-8222, E-Mail: franchise@att.net, Web Site: www.franchiserecruiters.com. Twenty-six years of franchising experience. An international executive search corporation dedicated exclusively to franchising. Unconditional one-year guarantee. Excellent client references. Placement of professional in sales, operations, executive, marketing, training, finance, legal and international development. Contigency search only. Franchise Recruiters Ltd. is a strategic partner with the iFranchise Group. Established: 1984 - No. of Locations: 2.

FRANCHISE RELATIONSHIP CONSULTING

Johnson Franchise Consulting, Inc.
2330 South 75th Street, Lincoln, NB, 68506, Contact: Jeff Johnson. - Tel: (402) 489-5205, Fax: (402) 489-5205, E-Mail: jeff@johnsonfran consult.com, Web Site: www.johnsonfranconsult.com. Franchise Relationship Consulting: We work with franchisors and franchisees associations to minimize conflict and maximize opportunities through proactive intervention. Established: 2003.

FRANCHISE SALES CENTER

1423 Knights Bridge Turn, Crofton, MD, 21114-2641. Contact: George M. Palmer, Dir. - Tel: (240) 602-7132, Fax: (301) 931-1366. The center works in a franchise sales capacity only. Directed toward the Mid-Atlantic states, the center represents a select group of franchisors looking to establish themselves in the Washington, DC/Baltimore markets. Established: 1982.

FRANCHISE SEARCH, INC.

48 Burb Street, Suite. 101, Nyack, NY, 10960. Contact: Doug T. Kushell, Pres. - Tel: (845) 727-4103, Fax: (845) 727-3918, E-Mail: info@franchise-search.com, Web Site: www.franchise-search.com. Franchise Search, Inc., franchising's premier recruiting firm, is the world's leading source for experienced franchise professionals in all disciplines. Our search process is custom made to match the hiring needs of any size franchisor, resulting in a win-win scenario for both companies and candidates alike. Established: 1983.

FRANCHISE SERVICES ASSOCIATES

23 Walker Brook Dr, Reading, MA, 01867. Contact: Suzanne Cummings - Tel: (800) 982-9636, Fax: (781) 334-2186. Full service franchise consulting firm.

FRANCHISE STORES INTERNATIONAL

Franchise Stores
3820 Premier Ave., Memphis, TN, 38118. Contact: Franchise Director - Tel: (901) 368-3361, Fax: (901) 368-1144. Marketing of franchises license distributorships, services and products exclusively listed by global systems. Established: 1976 - Franchising Since: 1996 - No. of Units: Company Owned: 7 - Franchised: 101 - Franchise Fee: $2,500 - Royalty: 3%, 1% adv - Total Inv: $7,500 - Financing: No.

FRANCHISE SYSTEMS

4638 Secret River, Port Orange, FL, 32129. - Tel: (386) 322-8899. Franchise development, consulting, sales training. Established: 1963.

FRANCHISE VALUATIONS LIMITED

404 Park Avenue South, 16th Floor, New York, NY, 10016. Contact: Bruce S. Schaeffer, Pres. - Tel: (212) 689-0400. Franchise valuations and appraisals for lending, litigation and succession planning. Established: 1995.

FRANCHISEBUYERSAGENT

Franchise One, Inc
9463 Hwy 377 South - Suite 111, Fort Worth, TX, 76126. Contact: Michael Childs , President - Tel: (817) 249-2126, (800) 288-6247, E-Mail: mjc@franchise-one.com, Web Site: www.franchisebuyers agent.com. We offer exclusive franchise consulting services for franchise buyers including the 350-Page Franchise Buyer's Guide & Workbook that can show anyone how to find, analyze and buy the right franchise. Established: 1992.

FRANCHISEHELP INC.

101 Executive Blvd. Second Floor, Elmsford, NY, 10523. Contact: Mary E. Tomzack, Pres. - Tel: (914) 347-6735, (800) 401-1446, Fax: (914) 347-4063. Franchisehelp supplies information to prospective and current franchisees, franchisors, investors and suppliers to franchises worldwide. Services also includes assistance to businesses that want to become franchises and the sale of current Uniform Franchise Offering Circulars (UFOC'S). Established: 1995.

FRANCHISING BUSINESS CONCEPTS, LTD.

6253 N. Fair Oaks Pl., Boise, ID, 83703. Contact: Bob Schmellick, Owner - Tel: (208) 853-0126, Fax: (208) 853-0127, E-Mail: fbcltd@ aol.com. Consultant to franchisors - Develop, sell and market a successful franchise program. Established: 1985.

FRANCHISING WORKS

P.O. Box 100, Dousman, WI, 53118. - Tel: (262) 965-2212. System development for franchisors.

FRANCHISINTERNATIONAL, INC.

4730 Centre Ave., Pittsburgh, PA, 15213, Contact: Ken Franklin, President - Tel: (412) 687-2760, Fax: (412) 687-0541, E-Mail: fdi@sgi.net. Franchise consultants and brokers worldwide with special focus on the Caribbean and Latin American market - Brazil, Chile, Argentina, Peru, Colombia and Mexico. Established: 1991.

FRANCHOICE INC.

FranChoice Inc.
10125 Crosstown Circle, Suite 105, Eden Prairie, MN, 55344. - Tel: (952) 942-5561, Fax: (952) 942-5793, E-Mail: info@franchoice.com, Web Site: www.franchisechoices.com. FranChoice provides consumers with free guidance and advice to help them select a franchise opportunity that matches their individual interests and financial qualifications. Established: 2000.

FRANCORP, INC.

20200 Governors Dr., Olympia Fields, IL, 60461. Contact: Christiane Cabot, President - Tel: (708) 481-2900, (800) 372-6244, Fax: (708) 481-5885, E-Mail: info@francorp.com, Web Site: www.francorp.com.

Francorp is a consulting and development firm. Francorp has consulted thousands of companies on the feasibility of franchised growth and assisted franchisors in producing better results from their existing programs. With offices in 9 countries, Francorp is uniquely positioned to assist clients with both domestic and international growth. Established: 1976 - No. of Units: Company Owned: 1 - Franchised: 9.

FRANDATA
Frandata Corp.
1655 North Fort Myer Dr., Suite 410, Arlington, VA, 22209. Contact: Erik Schonher, Director of Marketing - Tel: (202) 659-8640, (800) 793-8640, E-Mail: info@frandata.com, Web Site: www.frandata.com. Information specialist to the franchise community, providing research, consulting, mailing lists, and UFOC retrival services and 4 web sites: FranchisePlanet.com, the first B2B marketplace exchange designed solely for the franchise community. FranchiseDocs.com, the first third-party web site to provide electronic storage for, and delivery services of, franchise disclosure documents. FranchiseResearch.com, an online provider of franchise disclosure documents, industry research reports and franchise mailing lists for the franchisor and vendor community. www.FranchiseRegistry.com, the only web site approved by the government to provide an online application and review process of franchise systems for expedited loan processing by the US Small Business Administration. Founded 1989.

FRANDOCS
81904 Overseas Hwy, West Palm Beach, FL, 334032. Contact: Corporate Headquarters, Franchise Development - Tel: (305) 517-9751, (800) 655-0343, E-Mail: frandocs@aol.com, Web Site: www.frandocs.com. Franchise Development Operations Manuals Franchise Consulting. Established: 1980.

FRANNET OF COLORADO
The Franchise Centre
6888 S. Clinton Street #207, Greenwood Village, CO, 80112. Contact: M. Stacy Swift - Tel: (303) 715-0397, (888) 925-3887, Fax: (303) 715-0405, E-Mail: frannetco@aol.com, Web Site: www.frannetco.com. Franchise broker/consultant representing 65+ franchises. member of franchise network (Frannet) with over 60 offices in the U.S. and Canada. Established: 1980.

FRANNET OF MINNESOTA
Plymouth Valley, Inc.
5775 Wayzata Blvd., Ste. 700, Minneapolis, MN, 55416. Contact: Chris Bostrom, President - Tel: (952) 525-2291. Franchise marketing and development consultants who work with over 60 franchise companies. We offer a wide choice of franchise concepts so people are better able to find the one that fits their personal goals and finances. There is no cost or obligation, our fee is paid by the franchise company. Our clients can learn about many different industries, all from a local franchise processional. Established: 1997.

FRANSTAFF, INC.
73 S. Palm Avenue, Ste. 219, Sarasota, FL, 34236. Contact: James Dement, Pres. - Tel: (941) 952-9555, (800) 413-9756, Fax: (941) 952-9520, E-Mail: mail@franstaff.com, Web Site: www.franstaff.com. Franstaff is considered the largest and most effective executive search firm in franchising today, and the only recruiting firm staffed with "hands-on" franchising professionals. A consistently dependable source for uniquely qualified management, sales, and support staff, and comparative compensation advice. Offering the most competitive fees and replacement guarantees in the industry. Established: 1993.

FRANWAY INTERNATIONAL
Business Opportunities of America, Inc.
PO Box 31685, Tucson, AZ, 85751-1685. Contact: R.A. Beuzekom, Pres. - Tel: (520) 751-8709, Fax: (520) 886-4459. An international franchise marketing and consulting company. Established: 1975.

GARY R. DUVALL
Dorsey & Whitney LLP
1420 5th Avenue, Seattle, WA, 98101. Contact: Gary R. Duvall, Shareholder - Tel: (206) 903-8700, (800) 566-1718 #8700, Fax: (206) 903-8820, E-Mail: duvall.gray@dorsey.com, Web Site: www.dorsey.com. Full Legal Support for International Franchising. U.S. and International Franchise Agreements, Disclosure Documents, Registrations, Dispute Resolution, and Structuring. International Trademark Protection and Maintenance. Established: 1977.

GIVENS & WILLIAMS INSURANCE SERVICES
3975 Fair Ridge Dr., #110, Fairfax, VA, 22033. Contact: Tom S. Field. Jr., Vice President - Tel: (703) 352-2222, (800) 320-9006, Fax: (703) 352-0867, E-Mail: tfield@bbandt.com, Web Site: www.bbundt.com. We specialize in the development and management of franchisor sponsored insurance programs. Custom designed, comprehensive and competitively priced. Web based applications. Established: 1928.

GLOBAL X CHANGE
3820 Premier Ave, Memphis, TN, 38118. Contact: Franchise Director - Tel: (901) 368-3333. An international corporation that helps franchisors to immediately find regional franchises through GX members and financing to fit their growth plans. Established: 1997 - Franchising Since: 1997 - No. of Units: Company Owned: 6 - Franchised: 108 - Franchise Fee: $1,000 - Royalty: $100 - Total Inv: $2,000 - Financing: Yes.

HADELER WHITE PUBLIC RELATIONS/ THE HAYES GROUP
3 Lincoln Ctr., 5430 LBJ Fwy. Ste. 1100, Dallas, TX, 75240. - Tel: (972) 776-8020. Firm is engaged in the development, marketing and promotions of franchised businesses nationally and internationally. Established: 1986. Offices in Dallas, TX and New York, NY.

HOSPITALITY SOLUTIONS LLC *
3 Golden Corner Way, Randolph, NJ, 07869. Contact: Steve Belmonte - Tel: (973) 598-0839, Fax: (973) 927-4082, E-Mail: stevenbelmonte@aol.com, Web Site: www.stevenbelmonte.com. We negotiate franchise agreements for all and any type of franchise. We also negotiate termination/liquidated damages, litagation support, expert witness - training sessions. Established: 2001.

HYLANT
Hylant Group, Inc
1505 Jefferson Avenue, P.O. Box 1687, Toledo, OH, 43603. Contact: Jeannie Y. Hylant, VP - Tel: (419) 259-2721, (800) 249-5268, Fax: (419) 255-7557, E-Mail: jeannie.hylant@hylant.com, Web Site: www.hylant.com. Insurance products for franchisors and franchises - including: employment franchisees, liability business insurance, health insurance, professional employer organization (PEO) services, franchisor liability. Established: 1935 - No. of Units: Locations: 8.

IFRANCHISE GROUP
1820 Ridge Road, Suite 300, Homewood, IL, 60430. Contact: Laurie Ludes, Senior Consultant - Tel: (708) 957-2300, Fax: (708) 957-2395, Web Site: www.ifranchise.net. The iFranchise Group is a coalition of the nation's top professionals in strategic planning, franchise law, operations documentation, franchisee training, franchise marketing and sales, and executive recruiting for franchisors. Whether you are an experienced franchisor refining or improving an established company or looking to expand through franchising for the first time, the iFranchise Group can provide the real world guidance and hands-on assistance needed to reach your full growth potential.

IMAGE COMMUNICATIONS INCORPORATED
15 Union Street, Lawrence, MA, 01840. Contact: Carrie Lavoie, President - Tel: (978) 681-7700, Fax: (978) 681-7797. Serving clients nationwide. Every aspect of launching a new concept/updating an old one. Specialists in graphic design, total identity systems, including logos and trademarks, creative merchandising, design of franchised units, store signage, packaging, labels, photography. All go-to-market elements for a franchisor's sales efforts, presentations, brochures, closing materials, mailing pieces, advertising creation, etc. Established: 1991.

IMPERIAL PREMIUM FINANCE/SUNAMERICA
Sunamerica
P.O. Box 517, Edison, NJ, 08818-0517. - Tel: (732) 577-0909, (800) 388-6727, #414, Fax: (212) 480-3398. Financial services with emphasis on insurance premium financing for franchise owners and operators - franchisees. Established: 1972.

IMTEC (INTERNATIONAL MANAGEMENT TECHNOLOGY CORPORATION)
78 Fox Hill Rd, Stamford, CT, 06903-2219. Contact: Joseph A. Lev, Pres. - Tel: (203) 964-9619, Fax: (203) 356-1557, E-Mail: IMTEC@compuserve.com. Arrange tie-ups between U.S. companies and companies in the Far East etc. International management consulting firm. Established: 1982.

INFORMATION SERVICES INC.
2811 NE 46th St., Lighthouse Pt., FL, 33064. - Tel: (954) 942-0242, Fax: (954) 783-2570. Sell franchise and business opportunities. Established: 1982.

INSIGNIA FRANCHISE REAL ESTATE SERVICES
130 Newport Center Dr., Ste. 130, Newport Beach, CA, 92660. - Tel: (714) 644-3420, Fax: (714) 644-1088. Site selection service and consulting. Established: 1985.

INTEL MARKETING ASSOCIATES, INC.
227 Bellevue Way NE, Ste. #178, Bellevue, WA, 98004. Contact: C. Jeffers, President - Tel: (213) 891-3907, Fax: (425) 867-0909. Franchise consulting firm specializing in franchise package structuring and franchise sales. Guest speaking at franchise conventions. Franchise Sales Evaluation. Established: 1989.

INTERNATIONAL BOARD OF DIRECTORS
4206 Spyglass Hills Dr, Katy, TX, 77450-5231. Contact: Craig S. Rice, Pres. - Tel: (281) 398-4588, (800) 851-8371. IBD is a full service consulting firm specializing in facilitating entry or expansion of U.S. and Canadian franchises into Mexico. Established: 1985.

INTERNATIONAL FRANCHISE ASSOCIATION
1350 New York Ave., N.W., Ste.900, Washington, DC, 20005-4009. Contact: Don DeBolt, President - Tel: (202) 628-8000, Fax: (202) 628-0812, Web Site: www.franchise.org.

INTERNATIONAL FRANCHISE DEVELOPMENT
3659 Green Rd., Ste. 100, Beachwood, OH, 44122-5715. - Tel: (216) 831-2610, Fax: (216)831-3533. Franchise development with a focus on marketing. Our team can handle all aspects of franchising including legal documents, brochures and manuals. We are a member of Frannet Place, www.frannet.com, Franchise Matchmakers. Established: 1990.

IRV H. KAUFMAN & ASSOCIATES
401 Milford Rd., Deerfield, IL, 60015-4352. - Tel: (847) 945-0145. Sales, marketing, management consulting specializing in franchise development. Sales broker development. Established: 1964 - Franchising Since: 1964 - Financing: Yes.

J.A.M.S./ ENDISPUTE
1920 Maid Street., Suite 300, Irvine, CA, 92714. - Tel: (949) 224-1810, (800) 400-3773, Fax: (949) 862-9241. Alternate dispute resolution services. Established: 1981.

KANALY TRUST COMPANY
4550 Post Oak Place Drive, Houston, TX, 77027. Contact: E. Deane Kanaly, Chairman & C.E.O - Tel: (713) 626-9483, Fax: (713) 629-8118. Exclusive private trust company with national and international clientele, is the acknowledged leader in providing custom sophisticated financial services on a fees only basis. Offers Master Retirement Plans to franchisors and franchisees.

KEMP STRATEGIES
2800 Farview Lane, Minneapolis, MN, 55356. Contact: Linda Kemp, Owner - Tel: (612) 476-0232, Fax: (612) 476-6096. Specializes in developing training strategies for rapidly growing franchisees and franchisors. Works with franchisors to design and develop new training, re-design their current training programs, as well as focus on needs of seasoned franchisees. Established: 1989.

KOACH ENTERPRISES, INC.
5529 N. 18th St., Arlington, VA, 22205. Contact: Joseph L. Koach, C.E.O. - Tel: (703) 241-8361, Fax: (703) 241-8623. Franchise Developer/ Franchise Consultant. Former president of the International Franchise Association. Established: 1981.

KUSHELL ASSOCIATES, INC.
Franchise Advisors Worldwide
235 Fearrington Post, Pittsboro Chapel Hill, NC, 27312. Contact: Bob Kushell, Pres. - Tel: (919) 542-3500, Fax: (919) 542-1156. Our consulting group advises multinational, entrepreneurial and minority owned companies on how to develop franchise systems. We assist established franchisors to "grow" their franchise system and maintain harmonious and healthy franchise relationships with their existing franchise units. We have offices in New York, South America and the Middle East. Extensive experience as an expert witness representing both franchisor & franchisee. Established: 1984.

LADAS & PARRY
26 West 61st Street, New York, NY, 10023. Contact: Ian Jay Kaufman, Partner - Tel: (212) 708-1800, Fax: (212) 246-8959. International intellectual property, licensing and franchising lawyers. Offices also located in Chicago and Los Angeles.

LAMY GROUP, LTD., THE
650 Poydras St., Ste. 2245, New Orleans, LA, 70130. Contact: Kenneth S. Lamy, President - Tel: (504) 525-9914, (800) 999-LAMY, Fax: (504) 525-9915. Management consulting firm comprised of CPA's and MBA's specializing in retail sales, compliance, royalty payments and specialty examinations for franchisors throughout North America. Established: 1989 - Franchising Since: 1989 - No. of Units: Company Owned: l.

LARUE MARKETING CONSULTANTS
P.O. Box 11223, Pompano Beach, FL, 33061. - Tel: (954) 784-6816, Fax: (954) 784-6817. Counsel and service to established and prospective franchisors. Feasibility studies. Marketing strategies and plans. Concept development and refinement. Marketing analysis and research. Evaluation of alternative channels of distribution. Sales/marketing theme development. Marketing communication plans and programs. Merchandising strategies. Competitive analysis. Area potential forecasts. Training programs. In-the-field monitoring of program execution. Materials for closing of sales to franchisees. Complete identity program, graphic design, public relations, advertising. Established: 1968.

LEE GARVIN, CCIM, CRE, GRI.
111 Carey Dr., Noblesville, IN, 46060. Contact: Lee Garvin, Pres. - Tel: (317) 773-7855, Fax: (317) 773-7869, E-Mail: leeganin@aol.com. Commercial real estate site selection, and consulting service. Complete demographic reports, feasibility studies, aerials and other pertinent data. Established: 1964.

LEON GOTTLIEB USA/INTL FRANCHISE/ RESTAURANT CONSULTANTS
Leon Gottlieb & Associates
4601 Sendero Pl., Tarzana, CA, 91356-4821. - Tel: (818) 757-1131, Fax: (818) 757-1131. Consultant, expert witness arbitrator. Established: 1980.

LESOURD ASSOCIATES INC.
3143 W. Laurelhurst Dr. ME, Seattle, WA, 98105. Contact: Chris LeSound, President - Tel: (206) 523-8037, Fax: (206) 523-0340. Assistance in preparing your restaurant organization for expansion or franchising. Expert witness services, strategic repositioning, concept development and operational analysis, restaurant valuations.

LOANSFORBUSINESS.COM
P.O. Box 540, Lake Orion, MI, 48361. Contact: Larry Rogers, President - Tel: (248) 693-9383, (888) 539-9093, Fax: (248) 693-9093, E-Mail: lrogers@loansforbusiness.com, Web Site: www.LoansForBuisness.com. Commercial loans available for franchise start-ups, acquisitions and expansions. Extremely competitive rates and terms. Financing available for all 48 contiguous states. Established: 1998.

LUCE SMITH & SCOTT INC.
6880 W. Snowville Rd, Suite 220, Cleaveland, OH, 64064. - Tel: (440) 746-1700, Fax: (440) 746-1130. Utilizing the buying power of franchisees, at no cost to the franchisor, we negotiate with top insurance carriers to establish competitive insurance programs for franchisees. Specialists in group property, liability, auto and workers compensation insurance. Established: 1925.

M&I BUSINESS DEVELOPMENTS
7510 Brous Ave, Philadelphia, PA, 19152-3906. Contact: Stephen J. Izzi, Pres. - Tel: (800) 557-7562, Fax: (215) 953-8314. Franchise development & sales. Established: 1990.

MADDIN HAUSER WARTELL ROTH HELLER PESSES, PC
Third Floor Essex Centre, 28400 Northwestern Highway, Southfield, MI, 48034-8004. - Tel: (248) 355-5200, Fax: (248) 354-1422. Law firm with experience in drafting and registering franchise documents, negotiations with franchisees and franchisors on behalf of franchisees.

MANAGEMENT 2000
Gappa & Kirkham, Inc.
11757 Katy Fwy Ste 1300, Houston, TX, 77079-1725. Contact: Bob Gappa, Pres. - Tel: (713) 952-3177, Fax: (713) 952-3830. Products and services include: Complete program for "start-up" companies; How to "Close More Franchise Sales"; How to get your franchisees to use business plans; Convention speeches; Strategic planning; Customer acquisition/retention strategies; Strategies to build average unit volumes; How to improve the effectiveness of your field consultants; Customer services strategies; Prospect profiling; Franchisee attitude survey; Improving the effectiveness of your area developers, and more. Established: 1981.

MANAGEMENT ACTION PROGRAMS
4747 N 7th St., Ste. 302, Phoenix, AZ, 85014-3656. - Tel: (602) 279-7700, Fax: (602) 279-6990, E-Mail: mpac@compuserve.com. Consultants specializing in developing and managing franchise companies. Maximize return on investment through better operations and successful franchisees. Achieve high growth without losing control of quality. Established: 1960 - No. of Units: Company Owned: 12.

MANUFACTURING MANAGEMENT ASSOCIATES L.C.
2625 Butterfield Rd, Ste. 212E, Oak Brook, IL, 60523. Contact: Roger E. Dykstra, Pres. - Tel: (630) 575-8700, (800) 574-0307, Fax: (630) 574-0309, E-Mail: DYKSTRA@consult-mma.com, Web Site: www.consult-mma.com. Help clients solve their business problems. We provide information and apply technology. We do manufacturing information systems. Engineering and technology. We do manufacturing systems. Engineering and technology development. Business Performance improvement and total quality namangement. We have project managers with hands on installation experience in all major manufacturing and distribution software packages. Established: 1982 - Franchising Since: 1990 - No. of Units: Franchised: 8 - Franchise Fee: $8,000 per owner, Royalty: 6% - Total Inv: Under $25,000 - Financing: No.

MARK W. CARNES & ASSOCIATES INC.
5770 Hopkins Rd., Richmond, VA, 23234-6614. - Tel: (804) 271-7522. Mark W. Carnes & Assoc. is a cause-related wholesale benefits supplier to franchise systems & franchise associations. Individual and packaged benefits range from insurance to long distance. Established: 1988.

MARKET POTENTIAL MAPPING
P.O. Box 1602, Lake Junaluska, NC, 28745-1602. Contact: Thomas Tveidt, Fran Dev - Tel: (888) 627-2770, Fax: (828) 627-1525. Location strategy/site selection. Training and support provided. Established: 1997.

MARKETING CONSULTANTS OF AMERICA 'MCA'
Consultants of America Professional Corp.
3820 Premier Ave., Memphis, TN, 38118. Contact: B. Richey - Tel: (901) 368-3333, Fax: (901) 368-1144. Franchisor consulting, managing, financing, logistics, structuring and re-structuring, documentation, registration, manuals, site location, sales, training, advertising and sales material preparation. Established: 1976 - No. of Units: Company Owned: 1 - Franchised: 54 - Franchise Fee: $1,000-$400,000 - Royalty: None - Total Inv: $25,000-$500,000 - Financing: Yes.

MARKETING RESOURCES GROUP
71-58 Austin St., Forest Hills, NY, 11375. Contact: Franchise Marketing Dept.- Tel: (718) 261-8882. Franchise sales. Complete comprehensive franchise development services. Franchise marketing. Franchise consulting. Assisting companies to become franchisors. Franchisor strategic planning services. Advertising, promotion and public relations programs developed and services implemented.

MCGROW CONSULTING
30 North Street, Hingham, MA, 02043. Contact: Jack McBirney, Pres. - Tel: (800) 358-8011, Fax: (781) 740-2287, E-Mail: mcgrow@mcgrow.com, Web Site: www.mcgrow.com. Full range of services assisting companies to become franchisors. This firm has many success stories and is recognized as one of the leading franchise consulting firms in the U.S. Established: 1981.

MCKENNA ASSOCIATES, CORP THE FRANCHISE REAL ESTATE INSTITUTE
52 Crestview Road, Milton, MA, 02186. Contact: Jim McKenna, Pres. - Tel: (617) 333-4967, Fax: (617) 364-8244. Complete consulting services to franchisor, concept evaluation, documents, recruitment, market planning, manuals, site selection models, franchisee relations, organizational development, strategic planning. Development training programs & seminars. Established: 1994 - Franchising Since: 1977.

MICHAEL H. SEID & ASSOCIATES, LLC
Michael H. Seid & Assoc.
94 Mohegan Drive, W. Hartford, CT, 06117. Contact: Michael Seid, Managing Director - Tel: (860) 523-4257, Fax: (860) 523-4530, E-Mail: michaelseid@msn.com, Web Site: www.msaworldwide.com. MSA provides domestic and international franchise advisory services to franchisors and companies seeking to establish franchise and licensing systems. Our services include tatical strategies, franchise system design and development, domestic and international expansion. Established: 1985.

MID-ATLANTIC FRANCHISE ASSOCIATES
5520 High Tor Hill, Columbia, MD, 21045. Contact: Valerie Maione, President - Tel: (410) 964-1884, Fax: (410) 964-2233, E-Mail: vmaione@comcast.net. Operations manuals, pre-opening guides and training manuals, annual updates. Established: 1992.

MOORE BUSINESS FORMS & SYSTEMS DIVISION
275 N. Field Dr., Lake Forest, IL, 60045. - Tel: (847) 615-6000. Multinational organization providing business information management solutions designed to enhance the efficiency and profitability of franchise operation. Established: 1885.

MUTUAL OF OMAHA COMPANIES
Mutual of Omaha Plaza, Omaha, NE, 68175. Contact: Paul Jensen, Nat'l Account Mgr. - Tel: (402) 351-2078, (800) 624-5554, Fax: (402) 351-5829, E-Mail: paul.jensen@mutualofomaha.com, Web Site: www.mutualofomaha.com. The Mutual of Omaha Companies offer franchisees enhanced benefits and reduced premium insurance plans (medical, disability, life, business overhead expenses, etc...) through the American Association of Franchisees and Dealers and thousands of Mutual of Omaha representation nationwide. Established: 1906.

NATIONAL COOPERATIVE BANK
1401 Eye St. NW, #700, Washington, DC, 20005-2204. - Tel: (202) 336-7641, (800) 266-7562, Fax: (800) 622-1329. Provides commercial, leasing and development banking services to franchise co-operatives, as well as consultation on employee stock ownership plans (ESOP) and the formation of cooperatives within the franchising system. Established: 1980 - Financing: For co-operatives.

NATIONAL FRANCHISE ASSOCIATES, INC.
240 Lake View Ct, Lavonia, GA, 30553. Contact: Cindi Iacono, Vice President - Tel: (770) 945-0660, Fax: (706) 338-1603, E-Mail: nfa@nationalfranchise.com, Web Site: www.nationalfranchise.com. Full service consulting and developmental firm with expertise in Franchise

Agreements and UFOCs, advertising and public relations campaigns, operations manuals, franchise sales programs and on-going franchise consulting. Established: 1981 - No. of Offices: 1.

NATIONAL FRANCHISE CONSULTANTS
N.F.C., Inc.
290 Glenshore Dr., Cullowhee, NC, 28732-8748. Contact: Steve Ruttenberg, Pres.- Tel: (828) 743-1000, (800) 444-4199, Fax: (828) 743-1799. Full service franchise development and marketing firm. Assists companies with the most cost effective method of franchise expansion. Established: 1987 - No. of Offices: 3.

NATIONAL FRANCHISE SALES
1520 Brookhollow Dr Ste 45, Santa Ana, CA, 92705-5422. Contact: Michael Ingram, Vice President - Tel: (714) 434-9400, (888) 982-4446, Fax: (714) 434-9401, E-Mail: mi@nationalfranchisesales.com, Web Site: www.nationalfranchisesales.com. Specializing in the resale of franchised businesses and small chains. Established: 1978.   .

NATIONWIDE FRANCHISE MARKETING SERVICES
18715 Gibbons Dr, Dallas, TX, 75287-4045. Contact: Marvin J. Migdol, Owner - Tel: (972) 733-9942, Fax: (972) 335-6581, E-Mail: mmigdol@ careington.com. Full service franchise evaluation and development. Feasibility studies, marketing, training, video presentations, public relations, legal coordination. Serves franchisors, franchisees and prospective franchisees. Extensive fund-raising experience; buisness and marketing plands. Established: 1971.

NEXUS - CONSULTANTS TO MANAGEMENT
501 Woodlake Dr., Santa Rosa, CA, 95405-9203. - Tel: (415) 897-4400, Fax: (415) 898-2252. Strategic management consulting serving more than 100 large (NYSE) and small ($5-milion x sales x $50-million) clients since 1962 from board room to factory floor. We consult to owners, boards, and CEOs nationally from California about high change rates, start-up, rapid growth, diversification, turnaround, exit. We help clients develop efficient, productive managers using executive advising, coaching, mentoring.

NICHOL & COMPANY, LTD.
Betsy Nichol & Company, Ltd.
245 Fifth Ave., 6th Floor, New York, NY, 10016. Contact: Betsy Nichol, Pres. - Tel: (212) 889-6401, Fax: (212) 532-4062. Public relations and advertising agency, specializing in meeting the needs of franchised companies. Established: 1981.

PACIFIC FUNDING GROUP, INC.
Pacific Funding Group
36 Lancaster Ct, Alamo, CA, 94507-1750. - Tel: (800) 454-1711, (925) 484-1711. Specializing in franchise financing pacific funding group offers franchisees innovative programs for start ups expansions, remodels, resales, and equipment upgrades. Established: 1986.

PALTNIUM 2000 FRANCHISING, INC.
5251 NW 80th Ter, Parkland, FL, 33067-1137. Contact: Bill Landman, Pres. - Tel: (305) 875-9442, Fax: (954) 340-3218. Full service firm specializing in franchise sales, development, location, site selection and lease negotiation. Established: 1990.

PATTER MARKETING SERVICES
International Marketing Systems, Inc.
2929 E. Commercial Blvd., #205, Fort Lauderdale, FL, 33308. Contact: Patrick Terhune, Chairman/CEO - Tel: (954) 351-0663, Fax: (954) 351-0665. Consultants in the restaurant industry. Established: 1989.

PEAK BUSINESS INVESTMENTS
1901 E. University #200, Mesa, AZ, 85201. Contact: Brandan Veater - Tel: (430) 344-2777, (888) 300-3611, Fax: (480) 344-2777, E-Mail: info@pbihome.com, Web Site: www.pbihome.com. As you have found out searching for a franchise is not as easy as it sounds. First of all there are so many different franchises out there, where do you start? Plus there is a lot of misleading advertising and when it comes down to it a lot of franchisors aren't always honest. Duhh!! At Peak Business Investments we are constantly searching for market leading franchise opportunities. We have a wide range of opportunities in several diferent industries. What type of franchise arrangement are you looking for? Do you want a single franchise or are you looking at area development or master franchising? If you are tired of spinning your wheels see what we can do for you. We are the next generation of franchise consulting. Visit our web site at www.pbihome.com or give us a call at 1-888-300-3611.

PENNANT RESOURCES
1481 W 12600 S., Riverton, UT, 84065. Contact: Tyler England, Fran Dev. - Tel: (801) 523-8098. Restaurant market reports and site selection.

PERFORMANCE GROUP LTD.
P.O. Box 437, Barrington, IL, 60011. Contact: Jim Burns, Pres.- Tel: (847) 526-9298. Consulting services and contract management for both new and seasoned franchisors. Specialists in franchise program development, marketing and retail location acquisition. Established: 1979.

PLUMER & ASSOCIATES, INC.
4094 Stonecypher Rd., Suwanee, GA, 30024. - Tel: (770) 945-9182. Franchise brochures, ad, video and kits.

PMC CAPITAL INC.
18111 Preston Rd #600, Dallas, TX, 75252. Contact: Director of Marketing - Tel: (972) 349-3253, (800) 486-3223, Fax: (972) 349-3265, Web Site: www.pmccapital.com. PMC Capital, Inc. is a direct lender offering multiple loan programs including SBA and conventional loans. We are a preferred lender in many SBA districts nationwide. PMC can finance start-ups, renovations, acquisitions and new construction we offer low fixed and floating rates. Established: 1979 - Financing: Nationwide Direct Lender.

PRO-TECT
Pro-Tect Franchising, Inc.
660 Whiteplains Rd., TerryTown, NY, 10591. Contact: Mark Mitchell, President/CEO - Tel: (914) 366-0800, (800) 261-1218. Lead testing and consulting services for home and businesses. Established: 1994 - Franchising Since: 1994 - No. of Units: Franchised: 20 - Franchise Fee: $15,000 - Royalty: 5%, 2.5% nat'l adv. - Total Inv: Low $88,600-$181,000 High - Financing: Van and equipment financing available. NOT FRANCHISING AT THIS TIME.

R.C. KNOX AND COMPANY, INC.
1 Goodwin Sq., Hartford, CT, 06103-4305. Contact: Mike O'Hara, Fran. Insurance Mgr. - Tel: (860) 524-7600, Fax: (860) 240-1586. Provides all forms of insurance services to companies who are franchisors. Programs take advantage of the group buying power of many businesses and pass the savings on to the franchise owners. Established: 1893.

RAGER AND ASSOCIATES
1957 Howell Mill Rd. N.W., Atlanta, GA, 30318. - Tel: (404) 355-7364, Fax: (404) 355-7364. Franchise consultants providing assistance for the development, financing and marketing of a franchise expansion effort. Established: 1979.

RETAIL TECHNOLOGIES INTERNATIONAL
4800 Manzanita Ave., Ste. 1, Carmichael, CA, 95608. - Tel: (800) 233-0793, (916) 483-1656, Fax: (916) 481-6903. Developer of Retail Pro®, the world leader in PC based point-of-sale inventory control software for retail industry. We have the solution to standardizing franchise operations. Established: 1986.

RETAILINK
555 17th Street, Ste. 3300, Denver, CO, 80202. Contact: Ken Purvis, Pres. - Tel: (303) 298-9323, (888) 866-8069. Retailink is a franchise consulting company providing complete franchise development services with offices in both the United States and Canada as well as international strategic alliances. Established: 1994.

RG PARTNERS, INC.
1100 Prosperity Farms Rd. #301, Palm Beach Gardens, FL, 33410. - Tel: (561) 748-0302. A full service Real Estate Firm specializing in site selection and consulting. Specific services include demographic analysis, market studies, lease negotiations, construction management, operational management.

ROBERT AMES FRANCHISE SERVICES ASSOCIATES
23 Walkers Brook Drive, Reading, MA, 01867. - Tel: (781) 942-9220, (800) 982-9636, Fax: (781) 334-2186, E-Mail: franchiseservices@shore.net, Web Site: www.shore.net/~franserv. Franchise and business development, consulting and marketing service. Established: 1985.

ROBERT J. BAER MARKETING
64 Niuiki Cir., Honolulu, HI, 96821-2318. Contact: Robert J. Baer, Pres. - Tel: (808) 373-8877, Fax: (808) 373-8877. Active consulting firm whose dedicated purposes are to consult on marketing practices with special emphasis on franchising. Robert Baer also taught a course on franchising at the Hawaii Pacific University. Also, the founder of TeleCheck Services and Certified Franchise Exec. Established: 1985 - Franchising Since: 1967.

S. MORANTZ, INC
9984 Gantry Road, Philadelphia, PA, 19115. Contact: Stan Morantz, President - Tel: (800) 695-4522, (215) 969-0266, Fax: (215) 969-0566, E-Mail: stanm@morantz.com, Web Site: www.morantz.com. Offering unique business opportunities in screen printing t-shirts, hats, bags and more. Ultrasonic cleaning of window blinds. Established: 1935 - Total Inv: $5,000-$25,000 - Financing: Yes.

SANDERSON & ASSOCIATES
450 Rice Lane, Millsap, TX, 76066. Contact: Rhonda Sanderson, Pres. - Tel: (940) 682-4509, Fax: (940) 682-4592. Currently the premier company in franchise publicity with emphasis on highest quality media placements and personal service. Established: 1985.

SANWA BUSINESS CREDIT CORPORATION
One South Wacker Drive, Chicago, IL, 60606. Contact: Perry Danos, VP - Tel: (312) 782-8080. A subsidiary of Sanwa Bank Ltd., one of the world's 5 largest banks. Over 25 yrs. experience in finance programs and provides full service financing for franchisees and franchisors.

SEABOARD FRANCHISE SERVICES COMPANY
3000 Weslayan Dr., Ste. 108, Houston, TX, 77027. Contact: Keith Hudson - Tel: (713) 621-6200, (866) 621-6200, Fax: (713) 621-8200, E-mail: mail@seaboardfranchise.com, Web Site: www.seaboardfranchise.com. Full franchise franchise firm specializing in all aspects of launching new franchises. Established: 1992.

SELLER DIRECT, INC.
1954 First St. #161, Highland Park, IL, 60035. Contact: Ronald Schwechter, Partner - Tel: (847) 266-0082, Fax: (312) 853-1366. Brokerage support of franchise resales. Established: 1998.

SIBLEY INTERNATIONAL CORP.
2121 K Street NW Suite 210, Washington, DC, 20037. - Tel: (202) 833-9588, Fax: (202) 775-9416. Specialists in developing the small business sector in emerging economics through franchising and other market channels. Operate in both private and public sector. Unparalleled experience in the developing markets of the world. Established: 1990.

SIEGEL FINANCIAL GROUP
1 Bala Plaza, Ste. 516, Bala Cynwyd, PA, 19004. - Tel: (610) 668-9780, Fax: (610) 668-3041, E-Mail: info@siegelcapital.com, Web Site: www.siegelcapital.com. We do loan expediting for business acquisition, business expansion & business loan refinancing. 4 step process the 1st being prequalification. Established: 1983.

SINGER, LEWAK, GREENBAUM, & GOLDSTEIN
10960 Wilshire Blvd., Ste. 1100, Los Angeles, CA, 90024. Contact: Fran. Dept. - Tel: (310) 477-3924, Fax: (310) 478-6070. CPA's and management consultants to franchises. Established: 1959.

SOL ABRAMS P.R./MARKETING CONSULTANTS & PRACTIONERS
331 Webster Dr., New Milford, NJ, 07646. Contact: Sol Abrams, Founder/Chairman - Tel: (201) 262-4111, Fax: (201) 262-7669. Marketing, PR, Consulting counsel. Established: 1943.

SOUTHERN FINANCE & INSURANCE
983 Valdosta Hwy., Homerville, GA, 31634. Contact: Brett Blitch/Elaine Day, Fran Dev - Tel: (912) 487-2071, Fax: (912) 487-3276. Assist in finding funds for equipment. Established: 1997.

SPECTRUM COMMERCIAL GROUP, INC.
3600 W. Commercial Blvd., Ste. 216, Ft. Lauderdale, FL, 33309. Contact: Anita Levin, Franchise Development - Tel: (954) 777-5151, Fax: (954) 777-5118. Site selection, lease/purchase negotiation. Established: 1991.

STRATEGIC CREATIVE SERVICES
7 Summitt Ave., Bronxville, NY, 10708. Contact: Peter M. Johnson, Pres. - Tel: (914) 771-9260, Fax: (914) 771-9260. Providing franchisors with advertising without wasting money on an advertising agency. Established: 1990.

STREAMLINED INFORMATION SYSTEMS
1708 East 5550 South Suite 23, Ogden, UT, 84403. Contact: Marketing Dept. - Tel: (800) 521-2999-US only, (801) 476-9077, Fax: (801) 476-9585. Software provider of Retail POS Systems for general retail, gift shops, electronics, trading card, sporting goods, and apparel. The system tracks serialized inventory, multiple stocking levels, sales history and rate of return. Searches by UPC code and generates purchase orders. Established: 1981.

THE MARSHALL GROUP FRANCHISE SEARCH CORP.
316 Mid Valley Center., Ste. 226, Carmel, CA, 93923. Contact: Lois Vana Marshall, President - Tel: (831) 620-1144, Fax: (831) 620-0984, E-Mail: lois@the-marshall-group.com. Executive search services to franchise systems exclusively. 33 years of service global in scope. Attractive fee and guarantee. Ask for references. Established: 1969.

THE VIKING GROUP
100 West Boston St, #6, Chandler, AZ, 85225. - Tel: (480) 659-3840, Fax: (480) 659-3842. Consulting firm serving franchisors and franchisees. Established: 1978.

THIRTEEN-ONE, INC.
2221 Westcreek Ln. 15F, Houston, TX, 77027. Contact: Andrew H. Cohen, Pres. - Tel: (713) 622-7209, Beeper: (713) 833-1388. Franchise consulting and sales. Also assists prospective franchisees in evaluating franchises. Experienced in re-sales and start up as well as established franchises. Established: 1980.

TORRENCE ENTERPRISES (BROKER)
1307 National Ave., Rockford, IL, 61103-7141. - Tel: (815) 961-0456, Fax: (815) 961-0457. Business Brokers - assist in franchising opportunities as well as real estate.

TOWNSEND, O'LEARY
18061 Fitch, Irvine, CA, 92614-6018. Contact: Steve O'Leary, Chairman - Tel: (714) 957-1314, Fax: (949) 823-9155. 19 yrs experience in franchise, advertising and marketing specialized in working with all levels of franchise companies to produce motivational image advertising and effective franchise sales material and field services presentations and organizational consultations.

TPMC REALTY SERVICES GROUP
2741 Beltline, Ste. 106, Carrollton, TX, 75006.Contact: Ken Bendolin, Vice President - Tel: (214) 416-5225, Fax: (214) 416-7919. Site selection and lease negotiation. Established: 1987.

US CREDIT SERVICES, LTD.
3100 Ridgelake Dr., Ste. 200, Metairie, LA, 70001. Contact: Roxanne Melerine, Fran. Dev. - Tel: (800) 543-5493. Credit and financial investigation.

VAN BORTEL AUTO MARKETING CONSULTING
696 Mosley Rd., Fairport, NY, 14450. - Tel: (716) 453-2235. New car franchise consultant. Established: 1946.

VENTURE MARKETING ASSOC.
800 Palisade Ave., #907, Fort Lee, NJ, 07024-4111. Contact: S. Altshuler, Pres. - Tel: (800) 342-7311, E-Mail: venturemkt@aol.com. Provides a wide range of services to franchisors including preliminary planning, franchise agreements, disclosures, manuals, internal controls, lead generation programs, program revitalization, program evaluation. Established: 1976.

VENTURE RESOURCES, INC.
800 W. 47th St. Ste. 420, Kansas City, MO, 64112. Contact: Larry K. Childers, Fran Dev - Tel: (816) 531-8898, Fax: (816) 531-8898. Franchise and leasing consultant.

WLH & ASSOCIATES
5622 Dumfries Ct. West, Dublin, OH, 43017. Contact: William Hart, Fran Dev - Tel: (614) 764-1644, Fax: (614) 761-8995. Consulting in franchise sales and marketing. Established: 1984.

WOMEN IN FRANCHISING,INC. (WIF)
53 W. Jackson Blvd., Ste. 1157, Chicago, IL, 60604. Contact: Larry Beck - Tel: (312) 431-1467, Fax: (312) 431-1469, E-Mail: larrybeck@womeninfranchising.com, Web Site: www.womeninfranchising.com. Provides telephone and face-to-face franchise consulting services to women and minorities interested in becoming either franchisees or franchisors. Compiles data on the number of women and minorities in franchising. Periodically conducts national seminars to educate consumers on the advantages to owning a franchise and the pitfalls to avoid. Offers, "Buying a Franchise: How to Make the Right Choice" and "Growing a Business-The Franchise Option" white papers on-line. Provides on-line listings of franchisee attorneys. Established: 1987.

WORLD FRANCHISE CONSULTANTS
25820 Southfield Rd., Ste. 201, Southfield, MI, 48075-1828. Contact: Geoffrey Stebbins, President - Tel: (248) 559-1415. Screens refers, consults, searches, and researches for people looking to get into business and helps them choose the most appropriate business opportunity for their individual needs and goals. W.F.C. provides assistance in evaluating and helping a prospective franchisee do due diligence on franchisors, reviews UFOC, investigates and negotiates with the franchisor, helps prepare business plans, and assists in finance sources. World Franchise

Consultants provides full consultation services including feasibility studies, UFOC documentation, brochures and strategic-marketing plans. Established: 1973.

WORLD TRADE NETWORK
580 Lincoln Park Blvd. Ste. 255, Dayton, OH, 45429. Contact: Mike Wenzler, Pres. & CEO - Tel: (937) 298-3383, Fax: (937) 298-2550, E-Mail: wtnet@infinet.com. Established: 1993 - Franchising Since: 1993 - No. of Units: Franchised: 40 - Franchise Fee: $12,000 - Royalty: 7% - Total Inv: $85,000-$135,000 - Financing: Partial initial fee only.

WRITERS' BLOC, THE
621 Seaview Ln, Costa Mesa, CA, 92626-3148. - Tel: (800) 600-3862. Full-service documentation specialists offering the following to franchisors: Turnkey operations manual packages, training guides, custom forms, brochures and information kits, and more. Combining more than a decade of writing experience with first-hand knowledge of running a retail store and restaurant, The Writers' Bloc provides customized documentation that is detailed, reader-friendly, and visually appealing. Established: 1984.

YOPP & SWEENEY, PLC
414 Union Street, Suite 1100, Nashville, TN, 37219. Contact: Michael T. Folks - Tel: (615) 313-3300, Fax: (615) 313-3310, E-Mail: mfolks@tys.com. Full service commercial law firm with substantial experience in franchise development and litigation, trademarks, business finance, real estate development, and alternative dispute resolution. Established: 1994.

ZORING INTERNATIONAL INC.
555 17th St. Ste. 3300, Denver, CO, 80202. Contact: Bob Orban, V.P. - Tel: (303) 292-4595. Sell master franchises in foreign countries. Established: 1997.

FRANCHISE CONSULTANTS - FINANCIAL

ATLAS MORTGAGE
207 Norwood Gardens, Johnstown, PA, 15905. Contact: D. Sharp, Assistant V.P. -Tel: (215) 552-8857, (800) 796-2351, Fax: (209) 796-7832, E-Mail: varied@usa.net. Provides mortgage to property buyers with lesser credit and at better rates than others. Marketers give self-closing brochure to sellers. Company handles everything! No license - no experience neccessary. Earn $1200 + per sale & recruit others too! Established: 1993 - Franchising Since: 1996 - No. of Units: Company Owned: 2 - Franchised: 206 - Total Inv: $300.00.

BOTTOM LINE CONSULTANTS
1500 Cedarbluff Dr., Richmond, VA, 23233. Contact: Richard L. Russakoff, Pres. - Tel: (804) 741-5771, Fax: (804) 740-3383. Franchise consulting, speaking and training. Complete customized programs for franchisors/franchisees on increasing profitability of others, complete re-sale programs, mediation, speeches and seminars to train, inspire and innovate.

CAPITALFIRST FUNDING
LDR Enterprises, Inc.
P.O. Box 540, Lake Orion, MI, 48361.Contact: Larry Rogers, President - Tel: (248) 396-4141, (888) 539-9390, Fax: (248) 693-9093, E-Mail: info@loansforbusiness.com, Web Site: www.loansforbusiness.com. Offers commercial financing for franchises and many types of businesses. Loan programs available for start ups, acquisitions, expansions, and multi-unit locations. Nationwide funding available. Established: 1998.

CAPITAL CAPITOL CORP.
4013 Hwy. 620 N., Austin, TX, 78734. - Tel: (512) 266-2822, Fax: (512) 266-2976. Training offered as a mortgage loan officer and/or as a private funds note broker. Company subsidizes part of the cost in order to keep it low. Company will also do processing and funding of transaction. Franchise Fee: $495 - Total Inv: $495 - Financing: None.

CAPTEC FINANCIAL GROUP, INC.
24 Frank Lloyd Wright, Lobby L 4th Flr., P.O. Box 544, Ann Arbor, MI, 48106-0544. Contact: Reid Sherard, Senior V.P. Sales & Mktg. - Tel: (734) 994-5505, Fax: (734) 994-1376. Nationwide supplier of capital to

franchisors and franchisees. Service provided through creative leasing programs and mortgage financing designed to assist in the easy rapid expansion of operations.

FIRST UNION SMALL BUSINESS CAPITAL

11601 Wilshire Blvd. Ste. 500, Los Angeles, CA, 90025. - Tel: (916) 617-1300, Fax: (916) 617-1090. Lender of SBA guaranteed, long term business loans, loans for working capital, equipment and real estate. Established: 1967.

HOLMAN FINANCIAL GROUP LTD

4747 Lincoln Highway, Suite 300, Matteson, IL, 60443. Contact: Guy Holman, President - Tel: (708) 481-3024, Fax: (708) 481-3699, Web Site: www.holmanfinancial.com. We provide commercial loans for franchise acquisitions, refinancing and expansion, equipment leasing and construction. Established: 1997.

INTERFACE FINANCIAL GROUP, THE
Interface Financial Corp.

4521 PGA Boulevard, Suite 211, Palm Beach Gardens, FL, 33418. Contact: David T. Banfield, President - Tel: (905) 475-5701, (800) 387-0860, Fax: (905) 475-8688, E-Mail: ifg@interfacefinancial.com, Web Site: www.interfacefinancial.com. Provides short term working capital to growing businesses by purchasing invoices (Accounts Receivable) for cash at a discount. Established: 1970 - Franchising Since: 1990 - No. of Units: Franchised: 30 Canada, 18 USA - Franchise Fee: $25,000 - Royalty: 8% of gross income or .8% of sales. Total Inv: $25,000 fee + $5,000 equipment + working capital - Financing: Franchise fee only.

LEXINGTON CAPITAL SERVICES CORP.

19 Westh 34th Street, Romm 810, New York, NY, 10001-3006. - Tel: (212) 279-0772, (212) 268-0724, Fax: (212) 279-0160. We arrange financing for both franchisee and franchisor. We will also arrange financing for both companies that are in business and start-up operations. Established: 1993.

MERIDIAN FINANCIAL CORP.

1200 Harger Road, Suite 319, Oak Brook, IL, 60523. - Tel: (630) 572-2000, Fax: (630) 572-0028, Web Site: www.medidianfc.com. Customized financing for franchisees of regional and national restaurant chains. Established: 1993 - Financing: Yes.

MERRILL LYNCH BUSINESS FINANCIAL SERVICES

222 Brfoadway 17th Floor, New York, NY, 10038. - Tel: (312) 269-4452. Service provider of finance to franchisees. Equipment financing, lines of credit and real estate (in most states) at favorable terms and rates.

NATIONAL FINANCIAL COMPANY

4722 Ridge Top Rd., Mariposa, CA, 95338. Contact: Leonard Vander Bie, CEO - Tel: (209) 966-3456. Clients seeking business capital will utilize over 15,000 viable sources of capital that have been computerized for clients. Also makes compensating balance deposits in your clients banks to give the banks incentive to do business with clients. Established: 1957 - Franchising Since: 1957 - No. of Units: Company Owned: 1 - Franchised: 640 - Franchise Fee $18,000 - Total Inv: $18,000 plus $4,500 start up cap. - Financing: No.

WEST COAST COMMERCIAL CREDIT
USA Gateway Franchise Credit Products

P.O. Box 19241, San Diego, CA, 92159. Contact: Gary D. Anderson, Fran Dev. - Tel: (800) 804-7901, Fax: (619) 463-0734. Full service franchise financing. Established: 1987.

WORLD ACCESS INTERNATIONAL, INC.

4312 Main St. Ste. 414, Philadelphia , PA, 19127. Contact: Samuel Freedman, Partner - Tel: (215) 483-4707. Credit cards to franchisors/franchisees.

FRANCHISE CONSULTANTS - LEGAL

AAA FRANCHISE LEGAL HELP HOTLINE
FRANCHISE FOUNDATIONS

Napa Valley Office - 1818 School Street, Calistoga, CA, 94515. Contact: Dir. of Operations - Tel: (707) 942-4444, (800) 942-4402, E-Mail: FranFnds@ix.netcom.com, Web Site: www.webpage.com/franchise. A free referral service for questions or assistance with franchise-related matters including UFOC review, franchise relationship problems, contractual disputes and other issues. The Hotline includes franchise attorneys throughout the U.S. and franchise expert witnesses. Established: 1997 - No. of Units: Company Owned: 1.

ABRAHAM PRESSMAN & BAUER, P.C.

1818 Market St., 35th Floor, Philadelphia, PA, 19103. - Tel: (215) 569-9796, Fax: (215) 569-4372. Franchise Attorney.

ACCURATE LEGAL OPINIONS
Franchise Foundations

1818 School Street, Calistoga, CA, 94515. - Tel: (707) 942-4444. Law firm that specializes in providing expert opinions, including testimony in arbitration and litigation matters, on all aspects of franchisor-franchisee relationships as well as custom and practice in the franchise industry. Established: 1980 - No. of Units: Company Owned: 7.

ALCANTAR, BETH ANNE, ESQ.
Anthony J. Madonia & Associates, Ltd.

150 N. Wacker Dr., Ste. 900, Chicago, IL, 60606. Contact: Beth Anne Alcantar, Attorney - Tel: (312) 578-9300, (888) 391-9300, Fax: (312) 578-9303, E-Mail: betha@madonia.com, Web Site: www.madonia.com. Attorney assisting franchisors with their disclosure, transactional, and litigation needs.

ALSCHULER GROSSMAN STEIN & KAHAN, LLP

2049 Century Park E #39th Fl, Los Angeles, CA,, 90067-3213. Contact: Susan Grueneberg, Partner - Tel: (310) 277-1226, Fax: (310) 552-6077, E-Mail: agrueneberg@agsk.com, Web Site: www.agsk.com. Alschuler Grossman Stein & Kahan, LLP is a full - service Los Angeles, California law firm with extensive experience in franchising law, intellectual property and high technology law. Its clients range from Fortune 500 companies to emerging businesses. Established: 1952.

ANGIULI, POZNANSKY, KATKIN, GENTILE & SERAFINO, LLP

60 Bay Street 8th Floor, Staten Island,NY, 10301. Contact: Gary C. Angiuli Partner - Tel: (718) 816-0005, Fax: (718) 727-5835. Attorneys for franchisors and franchisees, business law, comercial real estate and commercial leasing. Established: 1984.

ANNE L. KLEINDIENST
Jennings, Strouss & Salmon, P.L.C.

2 N. Central Ave., Ste. 1600, Phoenix, AZ, 85004. - Tel: (602) 262-5950, Fax: (602) 253-3255. Attorney engaged in practice of franchise law.

ARMSTRONG, TEASDALE LLP

2345 Grand Blvd., Ste. 2000, Kansas City, MO, 64108-2625. Contact: Edward R. Spalty, Partner - Tel: (816) 221-3420, (800) 243-5070, Fax: (816) 221-0786, E-Mail: espalty@armstrongteasdale.com, Web Site: www.armstrongteasdale.com. Armstrong Teasdale regularly represents regional, national and international franchise and distribution system clients in both litigation and business contexts in a wide variety of industries. Established: 1883.

ARNOLD COHEN, ESQ.
2424 N. Federal Highway, Ste. 314, Boca Raton FL, 33431. Contact: Arnold Cohen, Attorney - Tel: (561) 750-6706, Fax: (561) 750-7143, E-Mail: acohenboca@aol.com. Law office also located at 7600 Jericho Turnpike,Suite 308, Woodbury, New York, 11797. - Tel: (516) 741-7771, Fax: (516) 921-1777.

BAKER, DONELSON, BREARMAN & CALDWELL
165 Madison Ave, 20th Fl, First Tenn Bank Building, Memphis, TN, 38103. Contact: Grady M. Garrison - Tel: (901) 526-2000, Fax: (901) 577-2303. Law firm.

BAKER & MCKENZIE
4500 Trammell Crow Center, 2001 Ross Ave, Dallas,TX, 75252. Contact: Anita Nesser, Attorney - Tel: (214) 978-3086, Fax: (214) 978-3099. Worldwide search and clearance of trademarks for use and registration; worldwide trademark protection and prosecution. Established: 1949.

BARBARA I. BERSCHLER, ATTORNEY
1115 Massachusetts N.W., Washington, DC, 20005. Contact: Barbara Berschler, Attorney - Tel: (202)638-0606, Fax: (202) 638-3332. Legal services for small business owners including franchise review, business set up, lease negotiations. Established: 1986.

BARBIER & BARBIER
319 Lincoln Ave., Grosse Pointe Woods, MI, 48230. - Tel: (313) 567-7000, Fax: (313) 567-6473. Law Firm. Established: 1967.

BARTKO, ZANKEL, TARRANT & MILLER
900 Front St., Ste. 300, San Francisco, CA, 94111. Contact: Charles G. Miller, C. Griffith Towle, Darryl A. Hart, Attorneys - Tel: (415) 956-1900, Fax: (415) 956-1152, E-Mail: CMILLER@bztm.com, or CTOWLE@bztm.com, or DHART@bztm.com. Law firm which specializes in domestic and international franchise and distribution law and franchise litigation.

BAUCH, REVA S.
1414 Barry Ave., Chicago, IL, 60657. Contact: Reva S. Bauch - Tel: (312) 248-6630. Legal and consulting services. Established: 1985.

BECKETT LAW FIRM
P.O. Box 13185, Kansas City, MO, 64199-3425. - Tel: (816) 471-7500, Fax: (816) 471-2978. Deal with franchising.

BELLAVIA & KASSELL, P.C.
200 Old Country Road, Mineola, NY, 11501. Contact: Leonard A. Bellavia, Esq., Attorney - Tel: (516) 873-1900, Fax: (516) 873-9032. Full service franchise attorneys.

BLUMENFELD, KAPLAN & SANDWEISS, P.C.
168 North Meramec Ave, St. Louis, MO, 63105. Contact: Leonard Vines, Principle - Tel: (314) 863-0800, Fax: (314) 863-9388, E-Mail: ldv@bks-law.com, Web Site: www.bks-law.com. Legal representation of franchisors and franchisees.

BRIGGS AND MORGAN, PA
80 So. 8th St., 2400 IDS Center, Minneapolis, MN, 55402. Contact: Andrew C. Selden, Attorney - Tel: (612) 334-8485, Fax: (612) 334-8650, E-Mail: seland@briggs.com, Web Site: www.briggs.com. Law Firm. Established: 1883.

BRUCE S. SCHAEFFER, ESQ.
404 Park Ave. S., 16th Flr., New York, NY, 10016. - Tel: (212) 689-0400, Fax: (212) 689-3315. Legal, financial and tax counseling for the franchise community. Established: 1975.

BUCHANAN INGERSOLL, P.C.
301 Grant St., 20 th Floor, Pittsburgh, PA, 15219-1410. Contact: R. Pressman, Co-Chairman of Franchising - Tel: (412) 562-8800, Fax: (412) 562-1041. The Franchising Group is part of a full service law firm, dedicated to high quality, innovative, cost effective legal services. Has assisted both national and regional franchisors and franchisees.

BUCHANAN INGERSOLL PROFESSIONAL CORPORATION
One Oxford Centre, 301 Grant Street 20th Floor, Pittsburgh, PA, 15219-1410 - Tel: (412) 562-8800, Fax: (412) 562-1041. Offices also located at: 1701 'K' Street N.W., Suite 750 Washington, DC 20006. Contact Andrew P. Loewinger, Shareholder - Tel: (202) 223-9018. Represents franchisors in litigation and regulatory matters. Established: 1973.

BUCKINGHAM, DOOLITTLE & BURROUGHS
1375 East 9th Street, Cleveland, OH, 44114-1724. Contact: Thos. R. Brule, Esq. - Tel: (800) 686-2825, Fax:(216) 621-5440. Franchise Attorney. Established: 1913.

BUCKINGHAM, DOOLITTLE & BURROUGHS, LLP
4518 Fulton Dr. NW, Canton, OH, 44735. Contact: Robert Newbold - Tel: (330) 491-5258, (800) 686-2825, Fax: (330) 492-9625, E-Mail: rnewbold@bdblaw.com, Web Site: www.bdblaw.com. We provide a full range of legal services.

BUNDY & MORRILL, INC., P.S.
12351 Lake City Way N.E., Ste. 202, Seattle, WA, 98125-5437. Contact: Howard E. Bundy - Tel: (206) 367-4640, Fax: (206) 367-5507, E-Mail: bundy@bundymorrill.com, Web Site: www.bundymorrill.com. Complete franchise legal-services for franchisors, franchisees & prospectrive franchisees. Established: 198.

C. DOUGLAS WELTY P.C.
2101 Wilson Blvd #950, Arlington, VA, 22201-3082. - Tel: (703) 276-0114, Fax: (703) 522-9107. Legal services relating to franchising registration and disclosure, franchisor/franchisee relations, protection of proprietary marks and information, marketing and advertising, contract enforcement and administration, dispute resolution, multi-unit and three-tiered franchising, and international franchising. Participated in revision of UFOC Guidelines as member of NASAA Franchise Advisory Committee.

CARTER & TANI
402 E. Roosevelt Rd., Ste. 206, Wheaton, IL, 60187. Contact: Doris Adkins Carter or Christine Tani, Partners - Tel: (630) 668-2135, Fax: (630) 668-9009, E-Mail: cartertani@cartertani.com, Web Site: www.cartertani.com. Experienced attorneys concentrating in franchise law, representing start-ups and established franchisors and franchisees. Established: 1977.

CATES & HAN
19800 MacArthur Blvd., Ste. 300, Irvine, CA, 92612. Contact: James W. Han - Tel: (888) 276-2976, Fax: (949) 459-7772. Complete range of services to franchisees including purchases and sales of businesses, formation of corporations, limited liability companies, and partnerships, estate planning, tax counsel, dispute resolution and litigation. Established: 1990.

CHANDLER, FRANKLIN & O'BRYAN
2564 Ivy Road, Charlottesville, VA, 22903. - Tel: (804) 971-7273, (800) 572-2099. Franchise litigation services. Established: 1982.

CHARLES ROWE ROWE & ALLEN
550 West "C" Street, Ste. 800, San Diego, CA, 92101-3573. Contact: Charles Rowe, Attorney - Tel: (619) 233-1900, Fax: (619) 238-1616. Franchise attorney.

CHERNOW & ASSOCIATES, PC *
610 Harper Avenue, Jenkintown, PA, 19046. Contact: Harris Chernow, Esquire - Tel: (215) 572-8000, Fax: (215) 572-8191, E-Mail: hchernow@chernowlaw.com, Web Site: www.chernowlaw.com. A national franchise practice providing comprehensive, practical, solution-oriented franchise, distribution and business representation representing leaders in franchising and retail distribution, including single and multi-unit franchise owners, area developers, master franchisees, franchisee association, franchisors, distributors and buisness owners desiring to expand through franchising and distribution systems. The firm provides its franchise clients with general business, real estate/leasing, employment, financial services, day-to-day colunseling and dispute resolution services, including mediation and arbitration matters. Attorneys in Pennsylvania, New Jersey and Maryland.

CHESTER E. BACHELLER, ESQ.
Holland & Knight LLT
P.O. Box 1288, Tampa, FL, 33601-1288. Contact: Chester E. Bacheller, Attorney - Tel: (813) 227-6437, Fax: (813) 227-6550, E-Mail: cbachell@hklaw.com. Legal representation of franchisors and franchisees. Established: 1985 - Franchising Since: 1985.

COATES & DAVENPORT
5206 Markel Rd., P.O. Box 11787, Richmond, VA, 23230. Contact: James Wilson, Attorney - Tel: (804) 285-7000, Fax: (804) 285-2849. Law firm representing franchisors and franchisees. We have assisted franchisors in drafting the UFOC and taking the UFOC through the registration process. We are also experienced in counseling potential franchisees through selection and purchase. Established: 1974.

COFFMAN, GODARD & NASH
604 Main Street, P.O. Box 1147, Zanesville, OH,, 43702-1147. Contact: Randy Godard, Lawyer - Tel: (614) 454-1010. Full service franchise attorney.

COHEN GETTINGS DUNHAM & DAVIS, PC
2200 Wilson Blvd., Ste. 800, Arlington, VA, 22201. Contact: R. Scott Caulkins, Principal - Tel: (703) 525-2260, Fax: (703) 525-2489, E-Mail: scaulkins@cohengettings.com. The law firm provides a broad range of legal services for franchisors and franchisees, including drafting franchise agreements and disclosure documents, franchise registrations, franchise litigation and counseling prospective franchisees. Established: 1972.

CORBALLY GARTLAND & RAPPLEYEA
35 Market St., Poughkeepsie, NY, 12601. Contact: Vincent DeBiase, Partner - Tel: (914) 454-1111, Fax: (914) 471-4593. Broad array of legal services for franchisees. Established: 1876.

CORPORATE INFORMATION SYSTEMS INC.
Pascal & Carter Process Service Inc.
700 13th St. N.W., Ste 950, Washington, DC, 20005. Contact: R.D. Carter Jr., Fran. Dev. - Tel: (202) 434-8948. Business plan incorporation preparation. Established: 1995.

CROWE & DUNLEVY
321 S. Boston, 500 Kennedy Bldg., Tulsa, OK, 74103-3313. Contact: Kathy Taylor, Shareholder/Director - Tel: (918) 592-9800, Fax: (918) 592-9801. Attorney specializing in franchise and distribution law, securities, corporate and international law. Formerly vice president and general counsel of Thrifty Car Rental and Dollar Rent A Car. Year Firm Organized: 1981 - Practicing: 1984.

DADY & GARNER, P.A.
4000 IDS Center, 80 S. Eighth St., Minneapolis, MN, 55402. Contact: J. Michael Dady, W. Michael Garner, Attorneys - Tel: (612) 359-9000, Fax: (612) 359-3507. A seven member firm of trial lawyers representing franchisees, dealers and distributors in business threatening disputes throughout the United States. Established: 1994.

DAVEY LAW CORPORATION
650 Town Center Dr 6th Floor, Costa Masa, CA, 92626-1989. Contact: Gerard P. Davey, Pres. - Tel: (714) 434-9100, Fax: (714) 434-9111. Law practice specializing in franchise law matters. Established: 1974 - Franchising Since: 1977.

DAVID E. HOLMES
1411 Marsh St. Ste. 206, San Luis Obispo, CA, 93401-2953. Contact: David Holmes, Attorney - Tel: (805) 547-0697, Fax: (805) 547-0716, E-Mail: holmesfranchiselaw@fix.net, Web Site: www.holmesfranchise law.com. Domestic and international franchise law, concentrating on the structuring and development of new and established franchise systems, drafting of documents for registration and legal compliance and international expansion. Formerly Associate General Counsel, International House of Pancakes and Vice-President and Counsel, Century 21. Established: 1975.

DOEPKEN KEEVICAN & WEISS
58th Floor USX Tower, 600 Grant Street, Pittsburgh, PA, 15219. Contact: Jeffrey Letwin, Partner - Tel: (412) 355-2600. Law firm. Established: 1989.

DOUGHERTY & ASSOCIATES
60 Howe Rd., Cohasset, MA, 02025. Contact: John Dougherty, Attorney - Tel: (781) 383-7041, Fax: (781) 383-7051. Franchise, real estate and commercial law representing franchisors and franchisees. Established: 1986.

DOWNEY BRAND SEYMOUR & ROHWER
555 Capital Mall, 10th Floor, Sacramento, CA, 95814. Contact: Franchise Department - Tel: (916) 441-0131, Fax: (916) 441-0121. Law firm specializing in franchise law, representing both franchisors and franchisees. Established: 1926.

DUNN, CARNEY, ALLEN, HIGGINS & TONGUE
851 S.W. 6th Ave., Ste. 1500, Portland, OR, 97204. Contact: Jay Fountain, Partner - Tel: (503) 224-6440, Fax: (503) 224-7324, E-Mail: jmf@dunn-carney.com. Law firm specializing in business, corporate, franchising, general practice. Established: 1925.

DYKEMA, GOSSETT PLPP
1577 Woodward N. St 530, Bloomfield, MI, 48304-2820. - Tel: (313) 568-6866, Fax: (248) 203-0763. Law firm representing many franchisors from the Great Lake Region.

EDWARD M. DOLSON
Swanson, Midgley Law Firm
2420 Pershing Rd., Suite 406, Kansas City, MO, 64108. Contact: Edward M. Dolson, Partner - Tel: (816) 842-6100, Fax: (816) 842-0013. Law firm. Franchising Since: 1971.

FAIRWORLD INVESTMENT, INC.
7531 Leesburg Pike, Ste. 201, Falls Church, VA, 22043. Contact: Alan B. Lee/James Jo - Tel: (703) 821-6808, Fax: (703) 356-3670. Franchising consultation. Established: 1988.

FARRELL FRITZ, P.C.
EAB Plaza, West Tower, 14th Floor, Uniondale, NY, 11556. Contact: Harold L. Kestenbaum, Counsel - Tel: (516) 745-0099, Fax: (516) 745-0293, E-Mail: hkestenbaum@farrellfritz.com, Web Site: www.franchis eatty.com. We are a law firm that represnts new and existing franchisors, located anywhere. Harold Kestenbaum has been representing franchisors for more than 27 years. Established: 1997.

FEINER WOLFSON LLC - ATTORNEYS AT LAW
100 Constitution Plaza, Ste. 600, Hartford, CT, 06103. Contact: Robert Feiner, Attorney - Tel: (860) 713-8900, Fax: (860) 713-8905. Law firm practicing principally in the areas of business law, including franchise law, corporations, limited liability companies, business and tax litigation,

and employment law. The firm currently represents only franchisees, but one of its members has in the past represented franchisors. Established: 1998.

FELDMAN, WALDMAN & KLINE
332 Pine St Ste 200, San Francisco, CA, 94104-3214. Contact: Kenneth Jones, Chairman Fran. Practice Group - Tel: (415) 951-8900-Ken Jones, (415) 981-1300, Fax: (415) 951-8901. A full service law firm experienced in franchise law, including disclosure and registration matters, preparation of franchise related agreements, intellectual property protection, franchise litigation and dispute resolution and business planning. Established: 1958.

FITZGERALD ABBOTT & BEARDSLEY *
1221 Broadway, 21st Floor, Oakland, CA, 94612. Contact: Mary Beth Trice, Special Counsel - Tel: (510) 451-3300, Fax: (510) 451-1527, E-Mail: mtrice@fablaw.com, Web Site: www.fablaw.com. Full service law firm in San Franchisco Bay Area representing franchisors, subfranchisors and franchisees in regulatory, transactional, trademark and litigation matters. Established: 1883.

FOSTER PEPPER & SHEFELMAN PLLC
1111 3rd Ave., Ste. 3400, Seattle, WA, 98101. Contact: Franchise Department - Tel: (206) 447-4400. Emphasis on commercial matters. Legal counsel available for franchisors and franchisees. Established: 1921.

FOX, ROTHSCHILD, O'BRIEN & FRANKEL
2000 Market Street, 10th Floor, Philadelphia, PA, 19103. - Tel: (215) 299-2090, Fax: (215) 299-2150, E-Mail: areich@frof.com. Law firm providing legal services to franchisors and franchisees. Established: 1907.

FRANCHISE BUYERS ADVISORY SERVICE
51 Morton St., Needham, MA, 02194. Contact: David Siersdale, President - Tel: (617) 455-8526. Advisory service to prospective franchisees. Established: 1976.

FRANCHISE LAW TEAM
30021 Tomas, Ste. 260, Rancho Santa Margarita, CA, 92688. - Tel: (949) 459-7474, (888) 276-2976, Fax: (949) 459-7772, E-Mail: franmail @franchiselawteam.com, Web Site: www.franchiselaw team.com. Law firm specializing in domestic and international franchise and distribution law. Established: 1985 - In Practice Since: 1975.

FRANCHISEE LEGALINE™
American Association of Franchisees & Dealers
P.O. Box 81887, San Diego, CA, 92138-1887. Contact: Debra Vylene Green, Member Services - Tel: (800) 733-9858, Fax: (619) 209-3777. Discounted legal reviews of franchise opportunities. Established: 1992.

FRANKIE FOOK-LUN LEUNG, ATTORNEY AT LAW
Lewis D'Amato Brisbois & Bisgaard
221 No. Figueroa St., Ste. 1200, Los Angeles, CA, 90012. - Tel: (213) 680-5119, Fax: (213) 250-7900. Advise American franchisors to expand business overseas. Established: 1970 - No. of Units: Company Owned: 7.

FRANLAW: EDWARDS, LISS & MURRAY
1301 West 22nd Street, Suite 709, Oak Brook, IL, 60523. Contact: Michael Liss, Franchise Attorney - Tel: (630) 571-5626, (888) FRAN-LAW, Fax: (630) 571-1882, E-Mail: mliss@FRANLAW.com, Web Site: FRANLAW.com. Complete franchise legal services. Extensive background representing franchisees, distributors, and franchisors in all transactions, litigation and arbitration matters since 1980. Represents franchisee associations. Negotiates franchise contracts initially and upon renewal. Expertise in selling businesses, leasing, financing, incorporating and estate planning. Expert witness. National practice. Established: 1980.

FRIEDMAN, ROSENWASSER & GOLDBAUM
The Plaza, Ste. 801, 5355 Town Center Rd., Boca Raton, FL, 33486. Contact: Ronald N. Rosenwasser, Partner- Tel: (561) 395-5511, Fax: (561) 395-2648, Web Site: www.franchiselaw.com. All aspects of franchising/licensing and distribution law, including development of domestic and international programs, review and preparation of disclosure statements and agreements, state and federal agency negotiations, business

structuring and financing, wide ranging transactional expertise and litigation services. Services include trademark protection, lease negotiations, acquisitions and sales, joint ventures, computer law, and general commerical representation. Founding member and former chairman of Florida Bar's Franchise Law Committee. AV rating (highest) from Martindale-Hubbell International Legal Directory. Established: 1986.

GOLDSTEIN & LOOTS PC
1700 K Street NW, #801, Washington, DC, 20006. Contact: James M. Loots, Partner - Tel: (202) 223-1983, Fax: (202) 223-2002, E-Mail: info@goldlootslaw.com, Web Site: www.goldlootslaw.com. Providing comprehensive legal services for franchisees, including incorporation, franchise review & negotiation, lease negotiation and dispute resolution. Established: 1992.

GRAHAM & DUNN
1420 5th Ave., 33rd Floor, Seattle, WA, 98101-2390. Contact: Gary R. Duvall, Shareholder - Tel: (206) 340-9663, (800) 458-1075, Fax: (206) 340-9599, E-Mail: gduvall@grahamdunn.com. Full service law firm providing franchisors and franchisees all necessary legal services, including registrations and disclosure compliance, dispute resolution, intellectual property protection, and legal compliance audits. Established 1890 - Franchising Since: 1977.

GREENSPAN & GREENSPAN ATTORNEYS AT LAW
34 S. Broadway, 6th floor, White Plains, NY, 10601. - Tel: (914) 946-2500, (800) 553-6009. Full service law firm.

GREGORY J. ELLIS & ASSOCIATES
999 North Plaza Dr #777, Schaumburg, IL, 60173-6022. Contact: Gregory J. Ellis, Attorney - Tel: (847) 413-0999, Fax: (847) 413-0959, Web Site: www.franchiselawfirm.com, E-Mail: GregEllisEsq@aol.com. Law firm concentrating in franchise law and related litigation providing full range of legal services to franchisors.

GROCOCK LOFTIS & ABRAMSON
205 East Central Blvd. Suite 601, Orlando, FL, 32801. Contact: J.Bennett Grocock, Sr. Partner - Tel: (407) 422-0300. Law firm specializing in franchise offerings and registrations. Established: 1990.

GUNSTER, YOAKLEY, VALDES-FAULI & STEWART P.A.
500 E. Broward Blvd., Ste. 1400, Ft. Lauderdale, FL, 33394. Contact: Michael G. Platner, Chairman/Fran. Practice Group - Tel: (954) 462-2000, Fax: (954) 523-1722. Franchise Practice Group consists of experienced attorneys from diverse technical backgrounds, all relating to franchising and the distribution of products and services. The firm is a full service law firm with over 115+ lawyers in South Florida. Established: 1924.

GUST ROSENFELD PLC
201 N. Central Ave., Ste. 3300, Phoenix, AZ, 85073. Contact: John L. Hay, Judith M. Bailey, Charles W. Workin, Lawyer - Tel: (602) 257-7468, Fax: (602) 254-4878. Law firm specializing in franchise law matters. Established: 1921 - Advising Franchisors Since: 1976.

HARNISCH & HOHAUSER, PC
30700 Telegraph Road., Suite 3475, Bingham Farms, MI, 48025-4527. Contact: Alan C.Harnisch, President - Tel: (248) 644-8600. Represents business entities, emphasizing civil litigation with considerable expertise in franchise matters for over 20 years, particularly in franchisor/franchisee disputes. Represents major franchisors and enjoys strong lasting relationships with its major business clients. Established: 1980.

HAROLD BROWN & ASSOCIATES
84 State St Ste 11, Boston, MA, 02109-2202. - Tel: (617) 720-4200, Fax: (617) 720-0240. Harold Brown has represented both franchisors and groups of franchisees. He is a founding member of the ABA Forum Committee on Franchising and has served on its council for six years.

HAROLD L. KESTENBAUM, P.C.
Farrel Fritz, PC.
EAB Plaza-West Tower 14th Floor, Uniondale, NY, 11556. Contact: Harold L. Kestenbaum, Counsel - Tel: (516) 745-0099, Fax: (516) 745-0293, E-Mail: hKesten@farrellfritz.com, Web Site: www.franchiseatty.

com. Full service law firm specializing in representing start-up and established franchisors, both domestically and internationally. Established: 1977.

HOGAN & HARTSON, LLP
555 Thirteenth Street, N.W., Washington, DC, 20004. Contact: John F. Dienelt, Partner - Tel: (202) 637-5655, Fax: (202) 637-5910, E-Mail: jfdienelt@hhlaw.com, Web Site: www.hhlaw.com. Legal services. Established: 1904.

HURT SINISI & PAPADAKIS
1050 Crown Pointe Pkwy., Ste. 310, Atlanta, GA, 30338. - Tel: (770)913-9999, Fax: (770)671-8513. International law firm with offices in U.S., Greece and Italy. Established: 1992 - No. of Offices: 6.

ICE MILLER DONADIO & RYAN
One American Square, Box 82001, Indianapolis, IN, 46282-0002. - Tel: (317) 236-2100. Full service law firm with numerous specialty practice groups including business, litigation, real estate, bankruptcy, securities and is thus able to offer franchise clients quality legal service in all areas. Established: 1910.

IN SITE FRANCHISE CONSULTANTS
In Site Realty, Inc.
2400 E. Commercial Blvd., Ste 808, Ft. Lauderdale, FL, 33308. Contact: Bill Landman, Partner - Tel: (954) 875-9442. Represent the franchise buyer. Established: 1989.

JAMES B. SHEETS, ATTORNEY AT LAW
1 Summit Ave., Ste. 304, Fort Worth, TX, 76102. Contact: James B. Sheets, Attorney - Tel: (817) 335-6040, Fax: (817) 335-2503. Legal services.

JENKENS & GILCHRIST
1445 Ross Ave., Ste. 3200, Dallas, TX, 75202-2799. - Tel: (214) 855-4500, Fax: (214) 855-4300. Jenkens & Gilchrist is a full service law firm with over 450 attorneys providing legal services to clients throughout the world. The firm's Franchise and Distribution Law Practice Group is one of the largest in the country, representing companies offering goods and services through franchise and other distribution arrangements, nationally and internationally.

JERRY COLE EXPERT WITNESS ON FRANCHISE MATTERS
Jerry Cole Franchise Consultant
28686 Charreadas, Laguna Niguel, CA, 92677-4562. Tel: (310) 472-0212, Fax: (310) 472-0212. Franchise Consultant, expert witness on franchise matters, experienced expert witness. Highly qualified at any level, franchisor sub franchisor, franchisee. Business format or conversion franchise, 23 years experience of top level franchise experience. Founder and president of two large national franchise programs.

JOHN F. FLEMING
31900 Utica Rd., Ste. 202, Fraser, MI, 48026. Contact: John Fleming, Attorney - Tel: (810) 415-2809. Attorney providing legal advice to franchisors and franchisees.

JOSEPH J. WALCZAK, P.C.
14744 Sprucecreek Ln., Orland Park, IL, 60462-7211. Contact: Joseph Walczak, Attorney - Tel: (708) 349-6908, Fax: (708) 349-2438. Franchising and trademark law practicing in Chicago and Northern Illinois area. Established: 1988 - Franchising Since: 1988.

KANOUSE & WALKER, P.A.
One Boca Place, Suite 324 Atrilium, Boca Raton, FL, 33431. Contact: Keith J. Kanouse, President - Tel: (561) 451-8090, Fax: (561) 451-8089, E-Mail: Keith@Kanouse.com, Web Site: www.Kanouse.com. Represents franchisees in purchase of a franchise including franchise agreement negotiation, business entity formation and lease negotiation. Established: 1990.

KATTEN MUCHIN & ZAVIS
1025 Thomas Jefferson St., N.W. East Lobby, Ste. 700, Washington, DC, 20007. - Tel: (202) 625-3500, Fax: (202) 298-7570. Law firm specializing in franchise litigation.

KENNETH F. DARROW, PA
9400 S. Dadelard Blvd. PH5, Miami, FL, 33156-2994. Contact: Kenneth F. Darrow, Principal - Tel: (305) 670-8200, Fax: (305) 670-2048. Law firm providing all aspects of representation to franchisors and franchisees. Over 20 years of experience in the franchise field. In practice 30 years.

KENNETH P. ROBERTS
Kenneth P. Roberts, A Law Corp.
6355 Topanga Canyon Blvd., Ste. 403, Woodland Hills, CA, 91367-2102. Contact: Kenneth P. Roberts, Attorney - Tel: (818) 888-3553, Fax: (818) 888-2686. Franchisor litigation, registration and legal services to franchisees and franchisors. Established:1977.

KILPATRICK STOCKTON LLP
1100 Peachtree St., Ste. 2800, Atlanta, GA, 30309-4530. Contact: Rupert M. Barkoff, Partner - Tel: (404) 815-6500, Fax: (404) 815-6555, E-Mail: RBARKOFF@KILSTOCK.COM. Attorneys- 475 lawyers in 11 offices- Specialize in franchise structuring; preparation of franchise agreements and disclosure documents; franchise relationships; counselling; and franchise litigation. Established: 1874.

KRASS & MONROE CHARTERED
1650 W. 82nd St., Ste.1100, Minneapolis, MN, 55431-1447. Contact: Dennis L. Monroe, Partner - Tel: (952) 885-5999, Fax: (952) 885-5969. Franchise law and financial services.

KRASSENSTEIN & ASSOCIATES PROFESSIONAL CORP.
7500 Brooktree Dr., Wexford, PA, 15090. Contact: Jonathan T. Krassenstein, Attorney - Tel: (724) 935-6227, Fax: (724) 935-0742, E-Mail: jtk@krasslaw.com, Web Site: www.Krasslaw.com. High quality, cost-effective legal services, representing franchisors and franchisees on a national and local basis, contract drafting and negotiation, commercial litigation, franchise and business opportunity and evaluation, registration and compliance. Established: 1987.

LARKIN HOFFMAN DALY & LINDGREN, LTD.
7900 Xerxes Avenue South, 1500 Wells Fargo Plaza, Minneapolis, MN, 55431. Contact: Charles S. Modell, Chair, Franchise Practice Group - Tel: (952) 835-3800, Fax: (952) 896-3333, E-Mail: APERRIN@larkinhoffman.com, Web Site: www.larkinhoffman.com. Larkin Hoffmanh assists franchisors in very aspect of franchising, from consultation on the benefits and disadvantages of franchising, preparation and registration of franchise documents, to counseling franchisors on franchise relationship issues. We represent mature multinational franchisors, as well as regional and start-up franchisors. Established: 1958.

LAW OFFICE OF DON M. DRYSDALE
3501 Jamboree Rd Ste 6000, Newport Beach, CA, 92660-2960. Contact: Don M. Drysdale, Owner - Tel: (949) 856-3205, Fax: (949) 7856-3245, E-Mail: dmd@donmdrysdale.com, Web Site: www.donmdrysdale.com. Law firm concentrating on franchise documentation and domestic and international franchise regulatory compliance. We also form California corporations and limited companies for our franchise clients and file California and federal trademark applications. Most of the services are provided on a flat fee basis. Our firm's mission is to provide the highest quality legal services to our clients, in a timely manner and for a reasonable fee. Effective representation and client satisfaction are our primary goals. Established: 1987.

LAW OFFICE OF RONALD PETER ROMAN
8306 Mills Dr., Ste 699, Miami, FL, 33183. - Tel & Fax: (305) 279-5180. Law office specializing in franchise and trademark law.

LAW OFFICES OF STEVEN D. WIENER
337 Eashington Boulevard, Suite 2200, Marina del Rey, CA, 90292-4400. Contact: Steve Wiener, Attorney - Tel: (310) 827-4400, Fax: (310) 827-4005, E-Mail: steveW@WienerLawOffices.com. Litigation, arbitration and dispute resolution primarily on behalf of franchisors. Established: 1998.

LAW OFFICES OF VAN ELMORE

600 17th St., Suite 2800 South, Denver, CO, 80202-5402. Contact: Van Elmore, Principal - Tel: (303) 659-7342, Fax: (303) 659-1051, E-Mail: vel6@qwest.net. Domestic and International franchising legal services; Intellectual Property; Arbitration and Mediation; Russian Language Capability. Established: 1992.

LAWRENCE KRIEGER, ATTORNEY AT LAW

The Wilder Bldg., One East Main St., Ste. 400, Rochester, NY,14614. Contact: Lawrence Krieger, Attorney - Tel: (716) 325-2640, (800) 719-3260, Fax: (716) 325-1946. Attorneys for franchisees, review and negotiations of franchise agreements, real estate law, full service general practice for small to medium businesses in upstate New York. Established: 1991.

LEGAL SOLUTIONS GROUP, L.L.P., THE

1629 Fifth Ave., San Rafael, CA, 94901-1828. - Tel: (415) 460-0100, Fax: (415) 460-1099. Law firm specializing in franchise advice, arbitration and litigation. Established: 1996 - No. of Units: Company Owned: 1.

LEWIS & KOLTON, PLLC

1150 18th St., NW, Ste. 875, Washington, DC, 20036-3816. Contact: Warren L. Lewis, Member - Tel: (202) 331-1416, (800) 333-2540, Fax: (202) 331-7904, E-Mail: info@lewisandkolton.com, Web Site: www.lewisandkolton.com. Lewis & Kolton is a law firm that represents established and start-up franchisors, subfranchisors, licensors, licensees and other organizations with counseling and litigation needs in the franchise, licensing, trademark, copyright, unfair competition and antitrust fields.

LOCKE LIDDELL & SAPP LLP

2200 Ross Ave., Ste. 2200, Dallas, TX, 75201-6776. Contact: Kevin Twining, Partner - Tel: (214) 740-8688, Fax: (214) 740-8800, E-Mail: ktwining@lockeliddell.com. Established: 1893.

LOPATKA AND ASSOCIATES

1824 West Stewart Ave., Park Ridge, IL, 60068. - Tel: (847) 692-9585, Fax: (847) 692-6809. Provides legal services and site selection services to franchisors and franchisees.

MACKALL, CROUNSE & MOORE, PLC

1400 AT&T Tower, 901 Marquette Ave., Minneapolis, MN, 55402-2859. Contact: G. Thomas MacIntosh II, Attorney At Law - Tel: (612) 305-1400, Fax: (612) 305-1414. Mackall, Crounse & Moore, PLC represents international and domestic franchisors, master franchisors, manufacturers and distributors throughout the free world in (i) planning, structuring and restructuring franchise, distribution and dealer business concepts and programs; (ii) complying with franchise, distribution, business opportunity and related business laws and regulations; (iii) franchise and dealer litigation; (iv) private placements and public offerings; (v) real estate development, licensing and financing; (vi) mergers and acquisitions; (vii) tax and business planning; (viii) executive compensation and employment law; (ix) registration and protection of patents, service marks, trademarks and copyrights, and (x) software protection and computer law. Established: 1918.

MARKS & ASSOCIATES, ATTORNEYS-AT-LAW

63 Riverside Ave, Red Bank, NJ, 07701-1007. - Tel: (732) 747-7100, Fax: (732) 219-0625. Representation of all franchise matters with an emphasis on franchisee rights.

MASTERSON, BRAUNFELD & MILNER, LLP

Suite 702, One Montgomery Plaza, Norristown, PA, 19401. Contact: Kenneth P. Milner, Esquire - Tel: (610) 277-1700, Fax: (610) 277-9979, E-Mail: kmilner@masterbraun.com. Providing legal services to franchisors and franchisees of all types and sizes. Established: 1980.

MAY, SIMPSON & STROTE

100 W. Long Lake Road, P.O. Box 1134, Bloomfield, MI, 48303-1134. Contact: John A. Forrest, Partner - Tel: (248) 646-9500, Fax: (248) 646-4648. Legal assistance to franchisors in all matters. Established: 1961.

MCGUIRE, WOODS, BATTLE & BOOTHE

1750 Tyson Blvd., Ste. 1800, McLean, VA, 22102. - Tel: (703) 712-5000, Fax: (703) 712-5050, Web Site: www.mrrbb.com. Counsels franchisees and franchisors through franchise agreement negotiations, establish appropriate business entities, and assist with tax, real estate, employment and general corporate matters. Preparation of offering circulars and franchise agreements and dispute resolution. Established: 1982.

MERCHANT, GOULD, SMITH, EDELL, WELTER & SCHMIDT, P.A.

3100 Norwest Center, 90 South 7th Street, Minneapolis, MN, 55402. Contact: John L. Beard, Partner, Chair of Trademark Section - Tel: (612) 371-5236, Fax: (612) 371-5220, E-Mail: jbeard@merchant-gould.com. Specializes in intellectual property law, including trademark, patents, copyright and unfair competition matter, as well as, licensing, trade secrets and domain name disputes.

MILNER, KENNETH P. ESQUIRE

McTighe, Weiss, O'Rourke & MIlner, P.C.
11 East Airy St., P.O. Box 510, Norristown, PA, 19404. Contact: Kenneth P. Milner, Attorney at Law - Tel: (610) 275-8800, Fax: (610) 272-5325, E-Mail: kmilner@montcolawyer.com. Legal Representation of franchisors and franchisees.

MITCHELL J. KASSOFF, FRANCHISE ATTORNEY

Two Foster Court, South Orange, NJ, 07079-1002. Contact: Mitchell Kassoff, Owner - Tel: (973) 762-1776, E-Mail: franatty@concentric.net, Web Site: www.concentric.net/~Franatty. Nationwide representation of franchisors and franchisees since 1983.

MOHR, JOHN R.

7545 Winding Wy., Tipp City, OH, 45371-9240. Contact: John R. Mohr - Tel: (937) 824-2808. Franchise Attorney.

MURTAUGH, MILLER, MEYER & NELSON

2603 Main Street, 9th Floor, Irvine, CA, 92614. - Tel: (949) 794-4000, Fax: (949) 794-4099. Legal services to franchisors and franchisees. Established: 1975.

NELSON, BARRY E.

4010 Executive Park Drive, Ste. 100, Cincinnati, OH, 45241. Contact: Barry E. Nelson - Attorney - Tel: (513) 563-2345, Fax: (513) 563-2691. Franchise consulting and legal services. Established: 1984.

NEWBOLD & ASSOCIATES

4518 Fulton Dr NW, Canton, OH, 44718-2332. Contact: Rob Newbold, President - Tel: (330) 497-9119, (800) 637-8362, Fax: (330) 497-9123. Franchise legal services and support. Established: 1994.

NIXON, PEABODY LLP

437 Madison Avenue, New York, NY, 10022. Contact: Robert Calihan/H. Hughes, Partner - Tel: (212) 940-3000, Fax: (212) 940-3111, E-Mail: rcalihan@nhdd.com, Web Site: www.nhdd.com. The firm's franchise industry team provides comprehensive legal services to franchisors and large franchisees throughout the world. Nixon Hargrave represents franchisors and franchisees in litigation in state and federal courts and counsels them on a broad range of issues, including franchise agreements, disclosure obligations, terminations and renewals, intellectual property, antitrust, relationship statutes, premises liability, franchisee associations, dual branding, bankruptcy, real estate, tax, and labor and employee benefits. Established: 1875.

PARKER, POE, ADAMS & BERSTEIN L.L.P.

2500 Charlotte Plaza, Charlotte, NC, 28244. Contact: Paul S. Donohue, Partner - Tel: (704) 372-9000, Fax: (704) 334-4706, E-Mail: psd@parkerpoe.com, Web Site: www.parkerpoe.com. Law firm. Offices in: Columbia SC, Raleigh NC, Spartanburg SC, Frankfort Germany.

PAUL, HASTINGS, JANOFSKY & WALKER

600 Peachtree St. N.E., Ste. 2400, Atlanta, GA, 30308-2222. Contact: Richard M. Asbill, Partner - Tel: (404) 815-2400, Fax: (404) 815-2424. Full service, eight-office firm specializing in domestic/international franchising, distribution, trade regulation, international trade, real estate, securities, venture capital, employment law, tax and litigation.

PEAR SPERLING EGGAN & MUSKOVITZ, P.C.

24 Frank Lloyd Wright Drive, Ann Arbor, MI, 48105. - Tel: (734) 665-4441, Fax: (734) 665-8788. Complete legal administration services for franchisors including disclosure/registration, negotiation and litigation management. Established: 1969.

BETER HOPPENFELD & BARRINGTON CHEMICA
16 School Street, Rye, NY, 10580-2952. - Tel: (914) 698-3440, Fax: (914) 698-0368. Law firm involved in franchising and distribution. Extensive experience in domestic and international franchising as well as issues relating to direct sales, infomercials, seminar sales, licensing and technology issues. Established: 1989.

PHILLIPS, NIZER, BENJAMIN, KRIM & BALLON
666 Fifth Ave. 28th Floor, New York, NY, 10103-0084. Contact: Jonathan R. Tillem, Partner - Tel: (212) 977-9700, Fax: (212) 262-5152. Full service law firm with special depts., in franchising, corporate, labor, litigation, entertainment, trust and estate specialties. Established: 1927.

PILLSBURY, MADISON & SUTRO
725 S. Figueroa St., Los Angeles, CA, 90017. Contact: Blase P. Dillingham, Partner- Tel: (213) 488-7100, Fax: (213) 488-7101. Full service law firm including all aspects of state and federal franchise disclosure, registration and enforcement law, preparation of franchise-related agreements, trademark and service mark protection and related litigation, securities, taxation, environmental and anti-trust laws.

PIPER RUDNICK GRAY CARY US LLP
1775 Wiehle Avenue, Suite 400, Reston, VA, 20190-5159. Contact: Bret H. Lowell, Partner - Tel: (703) 773-4242, (703) 773-4000, Fax: (703) 773-5053, E-Mail: info@dlapiper.com, Web Site: www.dlapiper. com. DLA Piper Rudnick Gray Cary US LLP has more than 2,700 lawyers in 49 offices in 18 cities nationwide. Our Franchise and Distribution practice is ranked the world leader. It has been one of the national and international leaders in franchise and distribution law since modern franchising began, helping to shape the franchising industry from its conception. We are proud to represent hundreds of franchisors and other enterprises that distribute products and services throughout the world. Our clients represent most of the 75 business sectors that have adopted franchising as a method of distribution, and a broad spectrum of size and experience, from entrepreneurs and start-up companies that are establishing new programs to the largest franchisors, manufacturers and distributors.

PIPER RUDNICK GRAY CARY US LLP
1200 Nineteenth Street, NW, Washington, DC, 20036-2412. Contact: Philip Zeidman, Partner - Tel: (202) 861-6676, Fax: (202) 223-2085, E-Mail: info@dlapiper, Web Site: www.dlapiper. DLA Piper Rudnick Gray Cary US LLP has more than 2,700 lawyers in 49 offices in 18 cities nationwide. Our Franchise and Distribution practice is ranked the world leader. It has been one of the national and international leaders in franchise and distribution law since modern franchising began, helping to shape the franchising industry from its conception. We are proud to represent hundreds of franchisors and other enterprises that distribute products and services throughout the world. Our clients represent most of the 75 business sectors that have adopted franchising as a method of distribution, and a broad spectrum of size and experience, from entrepreneurs and start-up companies that are establishing new programs to the largest franchisors, manufacturers and distributors.

PIPER RUDNICK GRAY CARY US LLP
101 E. Kennedy Boulevard, Suite 2000, Tampa, FL, 33602. Contact: David A. Beyer, Partner - Tel: (813) 222-5911, (813) 229-2111, Fax: (813) 229-1447, E-Mail: info@dlapiper.com, Web Site: www.dlapiper. com. DLA Piper Rudnick Gray Cary US LLP has more than 2,700 lawyers in 49 offices in 18 cities nationwide. Our Franchise and Distribution practice is ranked the world leader. It has been one of the national and international leaders in franchise and distribution law since modern franchising began, helping to shape the franchising industry from its conception. We are proud to represent hundreds of franchisors and other enterprises that distribute products and services throughout the world. Our clients represent most of the 75 business sectors that have adopted franchising as a method of distribution, and a broad spectrum of size and experience, from entrepreneurs and start-up companies that are establishing new programs to the largest franchisors, manufacturers and distributors.

PIPER RUDNICK GRAY CARY US LLP
1717 Main Street, Suite 4600, Dallas, TX, 75201-4605. Contact: Ann Hurwitz - Tel: (214) 743-4521, (214) 743-4500, Fax: (214) 743-4545, E-Mail: info@dlapiper.com, Web Site: www.dlapiper.com. DLA Piper Rudnick Gray Cary LLP has more than 2,700 lawyers in 49 offices in 18

cities nationwide. Our Franchise and Distribution practice is ranked the world leader. It has been one of the national and international leaders in franchise and distribution law since modern franchising began, helping to shape the franchising industry from its conception. We are proud to represent hundreds of franchisors and other enterprises that distribute products and services throughout the world. Our clients represent most of the 75 business sectors that have adopted franchising as a method of distribution, and a broad spectrum of size and experience, from entrepreneurs and start-up companies that are establishing new programs to the largest franchisors, manufacturers and distributors.

PIPER RUDNICK GRAY CARY US LLP

203 N. Lasalle Street, Suite 1900, Chicago, IL, 60601-1293. Contact: Dennis E. Wieczorek, Partner - Tel: (312) 368-4087, (312) 368-4000, Fax: (312) 236-7516, E-Mail: info@dlapiper.com, Web Site: www.dlapiper.com. DLA Piper Rudnick Gray Cary US LLP has more than 2,700 lawyers in 49 offices in 18 cities nationwide. Our Franchise and Distribution practice is ranked the world leader. It has been one of the national and international leaders in franchise and distribution law since modern franchising began, helping to shape the franchising industry from its conception. We are proud to represent hundreds of franchisors and other enterprises that distribute products and services throughout the world. Our clients represent most of the 75 business sectors that have adopted franchising as a method of distribution, and a broad spectrum of size and experience, from entrepreneurs and start-up companies that are establishing new programs to the largest franchisors, manufacturers and distributors.

PITEGOFF LAW OFFICE *

10 Banks Street, Suite 540, White Plains, NY, 10606. Contact: Tom Pitegoff, Attorney at Law - Tel: (914) 681-0100, Fax: (914) 682-7501, E-Mail: pitegoff@pitlaw.com, Web Site: www.pitlaw.com. Internationally recognized franchise law practice, representing franchiors and franchisees in drafting and reviewing franchise documents, regulatory compliance, business transactions, trademarks, real estate and litigation.

PLUNKETT & COONEY

505 North Woodward, Ste. 3000, Bloomfield Hills, MI, 48304. Contact: Sally Lee Foley, Attorney - Tel: 9248) 901-4043, Fax: (248) 901-4040, Web Site: www.plunkettlaw.com. Franchise Lawyers.

REED, SMITH, SHAW & MCCLAY

1301 K. Street, N.W. Ste. 1100, East Tower, Washington, DC, 20005. - Tel: (202) 414-9200, Fax: (202) 414-9299. Represents franchising companies, in regard to anti-trust, contractual, litigation, registration and disclosure and termination issues. Offices: Pittsburgh, Philadelphia, Harrisburg (PA) and McLean, Virginia. Established: before 1900.

RICHARD A. SOLOMON, LAW FIRM

11502 Overbrook, Houston, TX, 77077. Contact: Richard Solomon, Attorney - Tel: (281) 584-0519, Fax: (281) 597-8250, E-Mail: RSolomon@franchiseremedies.com, Web Site: www.franchiseremedies.com. Law firm specializing in franchising, licensing, analysis of crisis situations, litigation and counselling. Established: 1972.

ROBERT L. PURVIN JR. ESQ.

P.O. Box 81887, San Diego, CA, 92138-1887. Contact: Robert L. Purvon, Attorney - Tel: (619) 235-2556, Fax: (619) 235-2565. Specialized legal services. Established: 1973.

ROGER J. MCLAUGHLIN, ESQ

1305 Campus Pky., #202, Neptune, NJ, 07753. - Tel: (732) 919-1155, Fax: (732) 919-1881, E-Mail: counsel@mclaughlinbennet.com, Web Site: www.,claughlinbennet.com. Deals in franchise law.

RONALD AXELROD ATTORNEY

30 Corporate Woods. Ste. 280, Rochester, NY, 14623. Contact: Ronald J. Axelrod, Attorney - Tel: (716) 272-7820. Counsel to several national franchisors, represented nemerous francisees, assistance with strategic planning.

SCHMELTZER, APTAKER & SHEPARD, P.C.

2600 Virginia Ave., N.W., Suite 1000, washington, DC, 20037. Contact: Robert L. Zisk, Shareholder - Tel: (202) 333-8800, Fax: (202) 625-3311, Web Site: www.saspc.com. The firm provides counsel to franchisors in litigation and business matters relating to franchisees, employees and

regulatory bodies. Our specialty is litigation relating to enforcement of standards, underreporting of sales, and trademark infringement.

SCHNADER, HARRISON, SEGAL & LEWIS

140 Broadway, New York, NY, 10005-1101. Contact: Franchise Attorney - Tel: (212) 973-8022, Fax: (212) 972-8798. Law firm specializing in franchise and distribution matters. represents franchisors and franchisees in all aspects of franchising. Established: 1935.

SEIDLER & MCERLEAN

161 N. Clark St., Ste. 2650, Chicago, IL, 60601. Contact: Marc P. Seidler, Partner - Tel: 9312) 516-0700, Fax: (312) 516-0709. Law firm engaged in commercial litigation practice specializing in franchise, dealer, distriborship and trade regulation litigation, arbitration and mediation

SEVERSON & WERSON

1 Embaracadero Ctr., Ste. 2600, San Francisco, CA, 94111. Contact: Jeffrey C. Selman, Attorney - Tel: (415) 398-0700, Fax: (415) 956-0439. Law firm involved in entirecycle of buisness life with group specializing in the franchise area. Counsel franchisors in areas of capital information, intellectual property, registration and compliance, operations, asset purchase and sales, workouts, bankruptcy and trial work and other forms of dispute resolutions. established: 1945.

SHULMAN, ROGERS, GANDAL, PORDY & ECKER, P.A.

11921 Rockville Pike, Ste. 300, Rockville, MD, 20852. - Tel: (301) 230-5216, Fax: (301) 230-2891, E-Mail: roshoway@srgpe.com, Web Site: www.srgpe.com. Full service law firm. Established: 1972.

SILVER FREEDMAN & TAFF

1700 Wisconsin Ave N.W., Washington, DC, 20007. - Tel: (202) 337-5502. Legal and strategic planning services for early stage and growing franchisors. Established: 1970.

SIMMONS & LOOTS, P.C.

Franchise Law Group

900 17th St NW., Ste. 900, Washington, DC, 20006-2512. Contact: James Loots, Mng. Attorney - Tel: (202) 326-8604, Fax: (202) 223-2002. Attorneys experienced nationally and internationally in advising franchisees in negotiating franchise purchase and sale and dispute resolution. Established: 1982.

SMITH, MCCULLOUGH, P.C.

4643 S. Ulster Street, Ste. 900, Denver, CO, 80237. - Tel: (303) 221-6000, Fax: (303) 221-6001. Law firm providing transactional and litigation services for both developing and established franchisors. Practice areas include franchising and distribution, securities, real estate, intellectual property, trademark protection and international distribution. Established: 1996.

SMITH & UNDERWOOD & PERKINS

5420 LBJ Fwy, 2 Lincoln Ctr. Ste 600, Dallas, TX, 75240. Contact: William J. Underwood Jr. - Tel: (972) 661-5114, Fax: (972) 661-5691. Full service law firm, provides legal counsel to franchisors and franchisees. Established: 1980.

SNELL & WILMER

Snell & Wilmer L.L.P.

400 East Van Buren, Phoenix, AZ, 85004-0001. - Tel: (602) 382-6000, Fax: (602) 382-6007. Full service law firm. Established: 1938.

SOLISH JORDAN ARBITER & WEINER

12100 Wilshire Blvd., 15th Fl. Los Angeles, CA, 90025. Contact: Franchise Attorney - Tel: (310) 826-2255, Fax: (310) 820-8859. Attorneys at Law. Established: 1978.

SONNENSCHEIN, NATH & ROSENTHAL

800 Sears Tower, Chicago, IL, 60606. - Tel: (312) 876-8000, Fax: (312) 876-7934. Law firm.

STEPHEN FEIDELMAN, ATTORNEY

1940 Harrison St., Ste. 300, Hollywood, FL, 33020-6605. Contact: Stephen Feidelman, Attorney - Tel: (954) 927-2889, Fax: (954) 922-4400.

STEVEN A. CHASE - ATTORNEY AT LAW
10260 S.W. Greenburg Rd., Ste. 400, Portland, OR, 97223. Contact: Steven A. Chase, Attorney - Tel: (503) 293-3594, Fax: (503) 293-8499. Specialized legal services.

STEVEN S. RAAB LAW OFFICE
P.O. Box 471, Ardmore, PA, 19003. - Tel: (610) 446-6994, Fax: (610) 446-4514. Franchise legal services, including UFOC review and contract negotiations. Established: 1979.

STRASBURGER & PRICE, L.L.P.
901 Main Street, Ste. 4300, Dallas, TX, 75202. Contact: John M. Vernon, Partner - Tel: (214) 651-4300, Fax: (214) 651-4330, E-Mail: vernonj@strasburger.com, Web Site: info@strasburger.com. The firm's Franchise and Distribution Law Practice Group specializes in the comprehensive representation of business using franchising, licensing, dealership or direct selling arrangements for the distribution of goods and services in a broad range of business areas, both domestically and internationally, involving transactions, regulatory compliance, intellectual property, litigation, arbitration and administrative proceedings. Established: 1939.

TANNENBAUM HELPERN SYRACUSE HIRSCHTRIT, LLP
900 3Rd Ave Fl 13, New York, NY, 10022. Contact: Joel A. Klorreich, Partner - Tel: (212) 508-6747, Fax: (212) 371-6797. A full service commercial law firm specializing in franchising and distribution, litigation and arbitration, securities, merger and acquistions, real estate, leasing, employment, and labor law.

THE FRANCHISE CONSULTING GROUP
Edward Kushell
1888 Century Park East Suite #1900, Los Angeles, CA, 90067. Contact: Edward Kushell, President - Tel: (310)552-2901, Fax: (310) 284-3290. Franchise consultants. Established: 1978.

THELEN, REID & PRIEST L.L.P.
101 Second Street, Suite 1800, San Francisco, CA, 94105. Contact: R. Jonas, R.L. Meyer, Partners - Tel: (415) 371-1211, Fax: (415) 371-1211. Law firm with specialties in franchising, antitrust, other distribution systems.

THOMAS, BALLENGER, VOGELMAN & TURNER, P.C.
124 S. Royal St., Alexandria, VA, 22314. Contact: John M. Ballenger, Attorney - Tel: (703) 836-3400, Fax: (703) 836-3549. Law firm engaged in practice of franchise law (among other fields of law). Established: 1982 - Franchise Law Since: 1985 - No. of Units: Company Owned: 1 - Fee: $150@ hr.

THOMAS D. FRIEMUTH
1919 S. 40th St. Ste. 202, Lincoln, NE, 68506. Contact: Thomas Friemuth, Attorney - Tel: (402) 434-5623. Full legal service for franchisors. Established: 1990.

THOMPSON & KNIGHT, P.C.
1700 Pacific Ave., Ste. 3300, Dallas, TX, 75201. Contact: Gayle Cannon, Attorney - Tel: (214) 969-1700, Fax: (214) 969-1751, E-Mail: cannong@tklaw.com. Broad range legal services to franchisors and franchisees. Emphasizing contracts and disclosure statement drafting for start up franchisors, contract analysis/negotiations for prospective franchisees, and litigation relating to franchise and distribution law.

VLOCK & ASSOCIATES
230 Park Ave., Ste. 2525, New York, NY, 10169. - Tel: (212) 557-0020. Law firm.

VORYS SATER SEYMOUR & PEASE
52 East Gay St., P.O. Box 1008, Columbus, OH, 43216-1008. Contact: Stephen R. Buchenroth, Partner - Tel: (614) 464-6400. Full service law firm with an active franchise and distribution law practice. Established: 1909.

WESTON, PATRICK, WILLARD & REDDING
84 State Street, Boston, MA, 02109. Contact: L. Seth Stadfeld, Member - Tel: (617) 742-9310, Fax: (617) 742-5734, Web Site: www.franchise-counsel.com. Legal counsel to the franchise community. Established: 1897.

WILLIAMS MULLEN
8270 Greensboro Drive, Suite 700, McLean, VA, 22102. Contact: Warren Lewis, Partner - Tel: (703) 760-5228, (888) 783-8181 ext 1228, Fax: (703) 748-0244, E-Mail: wlewis@williamsmullen.com, Web Site: www.williamsmullen.com. Law firm with offices in Virginia, Washington DC, Michigan and London. The firm's clients include start-up franchisors, established franchisors, subfranchisors, area developers and franchisees. Established: 1909.

WITMER, KARP, WARNER & THUOTTE LLP
22 Batterymarch Street, Boston, MA, 02109. Contact: Eric H. Karp, Partner - Tel: (617) 248-0550, Fax: (617) 248-0607, E-Mail: ekarp@wkwtlaw.com. Eric H. Karp is a partner in the Boston law firm of Witmer, Karp, Warner & Thoutte LLP where he specializes in franchise law, representing national franchisee associations and franchisees throughout the country in a wide variety of franchise issues including sales, purchases, relocations, remodels, transfers, defaults and terminations and lease issues. Mr. Karp is a Director of the American Franchisee Association (AFA), served as Chair of the AFA Model Responsible Franchise Practices Act Committee, was the principal author of the Model Act and served as the Program Chair of the 1999 AFA Franchisee Legal Symposium.

ZARCO & PARDO P.A.
Nations Bank Tower, 100 S.E. 2nd Street, Ste. 2700, Miami, FL, 33131. Contact: Robert Zarco, Attorney-Partner - Tel (305) 374-5418, Fax: (305) 374-5428. The law firm has and is currently representing distributors, major corporations, and financial institutions in matters involving litigation over franchisee/franchisor relationships, contract disputes, business fraud, commercial torts, encroachment issues, trademark disputes, as well as other types of commercial/civil litigation in both the federal and state courts. Established: 1992.

FUNDRAISING

JOE CORBIS® PIZZA KIT FUND-RAISING PROGRAM
325 Meadowlands Blvd #314, Washington, PA, 15301-8904. Contact: Joseph Violi, Adm Assistant - Tel: (410) 525-8331, (800) 587-7677, Fax: (412) 851-1730, E-Mail: joecorbi.com, Web Site: www.joecorbi.com. Specializing in the sale of fund raising pizza kits, breads and other fund items, as well as related goods and services which are marked to chairitable municipal, civic and other organizations. Established: 1984 - Franchising Since: 1999 - No. of Units: Company Owned: 6 - Franchised: 1 - Franchise Fee: $25,000-$50,000 - Total Inv: $50,400-$105,500 - Financing: No.

MAGIS FUND RAISING SPECIALISTS, INC.
845 Heathermoor Lane, Perrysburg, OH, 43551. - Tel: (419) 874-4459, Fax: (419) 874-4459. $100 million plus raised for non-profits through capital, annual and endowment campaigns. Leadership training. Fund raising audits, money back guarantee. Try it for 24 months! Established: 1991 - Franchising Since: 1991 - No. of Units: Company Owned: 2 - Franchised: 4 - Franchise Fee: $7,500 - Royalty: 8%, 2% adv. - Total Inv: $25,000 - Financing: Yes.

RED WHEEL FUNDRAISING
Reineke's Inc.
722 Walnut Street, Ste. 1102, Kansas City, MO, 64106. - Tel: (816) 221-2699, (800) 269-0667. Fundraising items for non-profit organizations. Established: 1984 - Franchising Since: 1988 - No. of Units: Franchised: 18 - Franchise Fee: $10,000 - Financing: Yes.

Check out Latest Press Releases:
www.infonews.com

FURNITURE REFINISHING AND REPAIR

BIX FURNITURE STRIPPING
6 Clark Cir., P.O. Box 309, Bethel, CT, 06801. Contact: Rick White, Sales Mgr. - Tel: (203) 743-3263, Fax: (203) 743-7028. Furniture stripping and refinishing service. Utilizes Flo-on and Immersion stripping systems featuring built-in ventilation. Removing compounds are non-flammable, non-caustic and do not discolor wood. Established: 1958 - Offering Licenses Since: 1963 - No. of Units: Licensed: 200 of 600 shops serviced - Approx. Inv: $6,000-$15,000 - Financing: None.

DIP 'N STRIP, INC.
2141 S. Platte River Dr., Denver, CO, 80223. Contact: E. Roger Schuyler, Pres. - Tel: (303) 935-1112. Furniture stripping, providing the household community, antique dealers, furniture refinishers, industrial and commercial accounts in the removal of finishes from wood and metal. Established: 1970 - Franchising Since: 1972 - No. of Units: Company Owned: 1 - Franchised: 250 - Franchise Fee: None - Royalty: 6% of which 3% returned for co-op advertising - Total Inv: $12,500 - Financing: None.

EXPRESSIONS CUSTOM FURNITURE
1040 N. Tustin Ave., Anaheim, CA, 92807-1724. Contact: Paul S. Wartman, Fran Dev. - Tel: (714) 577-8407. Custom upholstery furniture. Established: 1978 - Franchising Since: 1979 - No. of Units: Company Owned: 3 - Franchised: 58 - Franchise Fee: $30,000- Total Inv: $300,000.

FURNITURE MEDIC
Furniture Medic
3839 Forest Hill-Irene Rd, Memphis, TN, 38125. Contact: Dinah Coopwood, Franchise Lead Manager - Tel: (901) 820-8600, (800) 255-9687, Fax: (901) 820-8660, E-Mail: brwilliams@smclean.com, Web Site: www.furnituremedicfranchise.com. On-site furniture refinishing and repair services for residential and commercial customers. Number one in the industry with over 10 years experience. Established: 1992 - Franchising Since: 1993 - No. of Units: Franchised: 610 - Franchise Fee: $22,000 - Royalty: 7% - Total Inv: $22,000 Franchise fee/$13,000 Products & equipment - Financing: Yes up to 80% of total investment.

GUARDSMAN WOODPRO
Lilly Industries Inc
4999 36th St. SE, Grand Rapids, MI, 49512. Contact: Franchise Department - Tel: (800) 496-6377, Fax: (616) 2285-7882. Mobile furniture repair and refinishing. Established: 1865 - Franchising Since: 1994- No. of Units: Franchised: 120+ - Franchise Fee: $7,000 - Royalty: 8%-6% - Total Inv: $25,000 cash - Financing: Third party.

MINUTEMAN FURNITURE RESTORATION
P.O. Box 8, Waterloo, WI, 53594-0008. - Tel: (800) 773-1776. Provides a complete range of equipment, supplies, and products for the furniture restoration and wood furnishing industry. Complete turn-key business packages available. Established: 1970 - Total Inv: $2,000-$15,000 - Financing: Yes.

PROFUSION SYSTEMS
PFS Franchising, Corp.
3212 Pinewood Dr, Arlington, TX, 76010-5305. Contact: Bob Engel, President - Tel: (303) 373-9600, (800) 777-3873, Fax: (303) 373-5830, E-Mail: bengel@profusionsystems.com, Web Site: www.profusion systems.com. Company markets maintenance and restoration services including repair, coloring, replacement, and cleaning services to commercial customers, including restaurants, hotels, offices, institutions, transportation, insurance restoration, furniture stores, health care facilities, fitness and leisure and residential. Established: 1984 - Franchising Since: 1984 - No. of Units: Company Owned: 1 - Franchised: 44 - Franchise Fee: $25,000 - Royalty: 6%, 1% adv. - Total Inv: $35,000-$100,000 - Financing: Yes direct and indirect. NOT FRANCHISING AT THIS TIME.

GREETING SERVICES

A SOUTHERN GREETING
ASG LLC
920 Mt. Gilead Rd, Building C-1, P.O. Box 1713, Murrells Inlet, SC, 29576. Contact: Scott Feagin - Tel: (843) 357-1416, (888) 250-1851, Fax: (843) 357-2858. Welcoming service. Established: 1995 - Franchising Since: 1999 - No. of Units: Company Owned: 2 - Franchised: 5 - Fanchise Fee: $8,500-$415,000 - Total Inv: $39,000-$92,000.

AMERICAN SINGING TELEGRAMS
390 W. Sahara Ave., Las Vegas, NV, 89102-5011. Contact: Marty Shadin, Pres. - Tel: (702) 671-0117, Fax: (702) 671-0121. The business is sold as a kit containing costumes, songs and supplies and act - descriptions, enabling one to start out of the home or add on to an existing business. Over 200 telegram act combinations for every occasion, birthdays, anniversaries, etc. Established: 1978 - Offering Opportunities Since: 1987 - Total Inv: $4,000.

CARDSENDERS®
Susan Lane Enterprises, Inc
145 Plaza Drive, Suite 207 PMB 573, Vallejo, CA, 94591-3703. Contact: Susan Lane - Tel: (707) 648-1467, (800) 843-6055, Fax: (707) 552-5434, E-Mail: susan@cardsenders.com, Web Site: www.cardsenders.com. Fulfill your dreams with your own highly profitable card sending business! In today's world, business people instinctively know the importance of the personal touch. cardSenders licensees help businesses provide the personal touch in a cost-effective way. Established: 1985 - Franchising Since: 1991 - No. of License Fee: $6,900; Group Training Class $1,000; Individual Training Class $2,000 - Concultant fee: $995. - Total Inv: Varies.

CARDSMART RETAIL CORPORATION
Paramount Cards, Inc.
400 Pine St, Pawtucket, RI, 02860-1833. Contact: Frank Feely - Tel: (401) 723-3068, Fax: (401) 726-2384, E-Mail: agrilk@cardsmart. com, Web Site: www.cardsmart.com. Upscale card and gift shop selling high quality nationally branded greeting cards and gift wrap at 50% off. Established: 1996 - Franchising Since: 2001 - No. of Units: Company Owned: 5 - Franchised: 1 - Total Inv: $150,000-$197,000.

GARDENING GREETINGS
189A Paradise Cir, Woodland Park, CO, 80863. Contact: Sally Silgy - Tel: (719) 686-1472, Fax: (719) 1473. Greeting card business. Established: 1997 - Franchising Since: 2001 - No. of Units: Company Owned: 1 - Franchise Fee: $800. - Financing: No.

GREETING CARD DEPOT, INC.
P.O. Box 5732, Ft. Lauderdale, FL, 33310-5732. Contact: Tim Boyer, Dir. of Marketing - Tel: (954) 956-7500, (888)740-3456, Fax: (954) 956-7666, Web Site: www.greetingcarddepot.com. An established local route of greeting card displays. No selling required, simply service the route, restocking, displays and collecting monies for cards sold for you, also supply fund raisers of every description with greeting cards as the product sold by the fund raisers. Established: 1986 - Franchising Since: 1998 - No. of Units: Company Owned: 2 - Franchised: 240 - Franchise Fee: None - Royalty: None - Total Inv: $9850 and up (inventory, supplied, and equipment) - Finanicng: No. NOT FRANCHISING AT THIS TIME.

PAPYRUS
Papyrus Franchise Corp.
500 Chadbourne Rd, Box 6030, Fairfield, CA, 94533. Contact: Kathleen A. Low, Dir. of Fran. Dev. - Tel: (800) 872-7978, (707) 428-0200, Fax: (707) 425-8066, Web Site: www.papyrusonline.com. A Papyrus store offers the finest in greeting cards, paper accessories, gifts and custom printed and engraved invitations, announcements and stationery. An exciting alternative to the traditional card store. Established: 1973 - Franchising Since: 1988 - No. of Units: Company Owned: 65 - Franchised: 66 - Franchise Fee: $29,500 - Royalty: 6% - Total Inv: $270,500-$465,500 - Financing: No.

STORK NEWS OF.........
Stork News Of America
1305 Hope Mills Rd., Ste. A, Fayetteville, NC, 28304. - Tel: (800) 633-6395, Fax: (910) 426-2473, E-Mail: jayjy@storknews.com. New born announcement service. Large stork in the front yard of new parents, grandparents plus many assorted announcement retail gifts for pre/post-birth celebration. Established: 1983 - Franchising Since: 1985 - No. of Units: Company Owned: 1 - Franchised: 173 - Franchise Fee: $8,000-$10,000 - Royalty: $400-$800 Based on territory - Total Inv: $8,000-$15,000 - Financing: Limited.

TABLE FOR EIGHT
Synchrony Ltd.
60 Thackeray Rd., Wellesley, MA, 02481. Contact: Johanna Noyes, President - Tel: (781) 239-3370. A social introduction service, which arranges dinners for eight. College educated professionals (4 men and 4 women). Established: 1986 - Franchising Since: 1998 - No. of Units: Company Owned: 1 - Franchise Fee: $25,000-$50,000 - Royalty: 10% gross monthly - Total Inv: $40,000-$75,000 - Financing: No.

THRIFTY MUGS
Thrifty Impressions
853 W. Bryan Rd, Pocatello, ID, 83201. Contact: John Savage - Tel: (208) 238-7573, Web Site: www.thrifty2.com. Personalization & photo imprinting on a wide range of products: cofee mugs. T-shirts, mouse pads, hats, hand puppets, puzzels, plaques, trophies, ties, aprons, computer portraits, rubber stamps, banners, temporary tattoo creation's etc. Established: 1984 - Franchising Since: 1999 - No. of Units: Company Owned: 1 - Franchised: 93 - Franchise Fee: $18.00-$10,000.

WELCOME HOST
Welcome Host of America, Inc.
13953 Perkins Rd., Baton Rouge, LA, 70810-3438. Contact: Fran. Dir. - Tel: (225) 769-3000, (800) 962-5431, Fax: (225) 751-9039. Direct mail welcoming service aimed at new residents and movers, parents of new babies, newlyweds. Established: 1987 - Franchising Since: 1992 - No. of Units: Company Owned: 3 - Franchised: 3 - Franchise Fee: $6,000-$8,000 - Royalty: 6% - Total Inv: $8,000-$12,000 incl. fran. fee - Financing: On franchise fee only.

HAIRSTYLING & COSMETICS

ACCENT HAIR SALON
Hair Salon Management Systems, Inc.
3200 Shiloh Springs Rd., Ste. 202, Dayton, OH, 45426-2299. Contact: Mary L. Tingle, Pres. & COO. - Tel: (937) 854-7535. The choice for total black hair care, featuring convenient walk-in service, prompt service, attractive mall location, affordable prices and a full range of black hair care products. A carefully-planned salon system designed with today's black woman in mind. Established: 1981 - Franchising Since: 1987 - No. of Units: Company Owned: 2 - Franchised: 6 - Franchise Fee: $20,000 - Royalty: 5% Franchise - Total Inv: $100,000-$200,000 ($30,000-$40,000 cash invest. $20,000 fran. fee) - Financing: None available.

ALOETTE COSMETICS, INC.
4900 Highland Parkway, Smyrna, GA, 30082. - Tel: (800) 256-3883, Fax: (678) 444-2564. Direct sales of skin care products and cosmetics by the companies marketing system at home shows. Established: 1978 - Franchising Since: 1978 - No. of Units: 47 USA, 32 Canada, 3 U.K., 1 Australia - Franchise Fee: $20,000 - Royalty: 5%.

AMERICUTS FAMILY BARBER SHOPS
41 Durant Ave, Ste. 103, Bethel, CT, 06801. - Tel: (800) 718-2887. Family fun barber shops. Established: 1989 - Franchising Since: 1995 - No. of Units: Company Owned: 1 - Franchised: 1 - Franchise Fee: $19,500.

AROMA TERRA
P.O. Box 83027, Phoenix, AZ, 85701-3027. - Tel: (602) 371-4676, Fax: (602) 371-4672. Offering natural, cruelty-free American made body care, aromatherapy and perfumes. Choose from over 300 fragrances. Can custom-scent our lotions, oils, soaps, haircare, and massage products. Established: 1995 - No. of Units: Company Owned: 1- Total Inv: $2,000-$25,000 - Financing: No.

ATIR NATURAL NAIL CARE *
1303 Jamestown Rd., #101, Williamsburg, VA, 23185. Contact: Franchise Department - Tel: (757) 258-0696, Fax: (757) 258-8999, Web Site: www.atirnaturalnailclinic.com. Total hand and nail care program. Established: 2004 - Franchising Since: 2004 - No. of Units: Company Owned: 1 - Franchise Fee: $25,000 - Royalty: 4% - Total Inv: $108,000-$211,000.

BEAUTY BRANDS SALON - SPA - SUPERSTORE
Beauty Brands Franchising
4600 Madison, Ste. 400, Kansas City, MO, 64112. Contact: Steve Eckman, VP of Corp. Devel. & Franchising - Tel: (816) 531-2266, Fax: (816) 531-7122, E-Mail: franchising@beautybrands.com. A full service salon/spa with an extensive line of retail products. Established: 1995 - Franchising Since: 1999 - No. of Units: Company Owned: 17 - Franchise Fee: $5,000-$40,000 - Royalty: 4% - Total Inv: $594,500-$936,000 per store - Financing: No.

BEAUTYFIRST
4727 S. Emporia, Wichita, KS, 67216. - Tel: (316) 529-1430, Fax: (316) 529-0920, Web Site: www.beautyfirst.com. Beauty stores, salons and spa's. Established: 1983 - Franchising Since: 1992 - No. of Units: Company Owned: 10 - Franchised: 72 - Franchise Fee: $10,000 - Royalty: 4% sales, 1% national marketing - Total Inv: $150,000-$250,000 - Financing: Assistance.

BERNAR'S SALON & DAY SPA
100 Springdale Rd, Cherry Hill, NJ, 08003. Contact: Joe Serpente - Tel: (856) 489-9704, (856) 795-1707, Fax: (856) 354-0073, Web Site: www.bernardssalon.com. We're a full service salon that is open every day. Featuring the latest in cuts and colors, perms, skin an body spa services, manicures and pedicures, massage, make-up and MediSpa services. Established: 1992 - Franchising Since: 2001 - No. of Units: Company Owned: 1 - Franchise Fee: $35,000 - Royalty: 3% - Total Inv: $520,000-$638,500 - Financing: No.

BOCA BEAUTY FRANCHISE INC.
8221 Glades Rd, Boca Raton, FL, 33434. - Tel: (800) 916-2622. Full service beauty salon operating on a club basis. Established: 1990 - Franchising Since: 1991 - No. of Units: Company Owned: 2 - Franchised: 8 - Franchise Fee: $25,000 - Royalty: 5%, 1% mktg. - Total Inv: $75,000-$100,000 incl. fee - Financing: Yes.

BODY SHOP, THE
Buth-Na-Bodhaige
5036 One World Way, Wake Forest, NC, 27587. Contact: Franchise Department - Tel: (919) 554-4900, Fax: (919) 554-4361. Not actively seeking franchisees at this time in the United States, but accepting letters of intent. We are offering internationally. Established: 1988 - Franchising Since: 1990.

BUCA'S HAIR SALON
Buca's Hair International
26812 Cherry Hills Blvd., Ste. 240, Sun City, CA, 92586. Contact: Jerry Roberts - Tel: (909) 699-4027, Fax: (909) 694-0195. Walk in hair cuts. All haircuts are $10.00. Established: 1995 - Franchising Since: 1997 - No. of Units: 1 - Franchise Fee: $20,500 - Total Inv: $75,000-$150,000 - Financing: Yes.

CARTOON CUTS
Cartoon Cuts Franchising, Inc.
5501 Backlick Rd., Suite 118, Springfield, VA, 22151. Contact: Linda Bufano - Tel: (703) 354-3801, (800) 701-2887, Fax: (703) 354-4431, E-Mail: lbufano@cartooncuts.biz, Web Site: www.cartooncuts.com. Cartoon Cuts, hair salons designed for children of all ages, is part of a nearly recession proof $30 billion industry. The company has 21 stores in operation and twelve years of proven success. Established: 1991 - Franchising Since: 2001 - No. of Units: Company Owned: 21 - Franchise Fee: $25,000 - Royalty: 5% - Total Inv: $96,000-$221,000 - Financing: No.

COCOZZO - GROOMING FOR DISCERNING GENTLEMEN

384 Broadway, Saratogo Springs, NY, 12866. Contact: Patricia Cocozzo, CEO - Tel: (518) 581-1958, Fax: (518) 581-2941. Full service men's hair salon. Established: 1998 - Franchising Since: 2000 - No. of Units: Company Owned: 1 - Franchise Fee: $25,000 - Financing: No.

COST CUTTERS FAMILY HAIR CARE
The Barbers a Division of Regis Corp

7201 Metro Blvd, Edina, MN, 55439. - Tel: (952) 947-7777, Fax: (952) 947-7300, Web Site: www.costcutters.com. Cost Cutters franchises provide value priced, quality hair services and products for the family, with each service being offered at a separate price. Established: 1963 - Franchising Since: Parent company since 1982 - No. of Units: Company Owned: 175 - Franchised: 675 - Franchise Fee: $12,500$22,500 - Royalty: 6% - Total Inv: $69,000-$148,000 - Financing: Third party.

EXCLUSIVES BEAUTY BAR, THE *

347 W. Berry Street #700, Fort Wayne, IN, 46802. - Tel: (260) 437-5405, Fax: (260) 426-1152, E-Mail: franchiseinfo@theexclusives beautybar.com, Web Site: www.theexclusivesbeautybar.com. Patent pending process for offering customized personal care products can be established in your salon, spa or women's boutique. Established: 2002 - Franchising Since: 2003 - No. of Units: Company Owned: 1 - Franchise Fee: $15,000 - Royalty: 9% - Total Inv: $29,500-$109,000.

FANTASTIC SAMS®
FS Concepts, Inc

1400 N. Kellogg Dr., #E, Anaheim, CA, 92807. Contact: Terry Cooper, S.R. V.P. Franchise Licensing - Tel: (800) 441-6588, Fax: (714) 779-3422, E-Mail: franchise@fantasticsams.com, Web Site: www.fantastic sams.com. World's largest full-service hair care franchise with over 1350 salons in 5 countries. No appointment salon's offer quality cuts, perm and color. On-going support provided through local/national training, national advertising, marketing, PR and recruiting/retention programs. Fixed royalty fees, individual, multi and master licenses available. No haircare experience required. Established: 1974 - Franchising Since: 1976 - No. of Units: Company Owned: 3 - Franchised: 1356 - Franchise Fee: $25,000 - Royalty: $216.46/wk - Total Inv: $75,000-$165,000 - Financing: We have various sources.

FIRST CHOICE HAIRCUTTER, INC

10014 North Dale Mabry, Suite 101, Tampa, FL, 33618. Contact: Allen Castleman, Franchise Sales Rep - Tel: (813) 964-9779, (877) 964-2111, Fax: (813) 961-2395, Web Site: www.firstchoice.com. We're a cutting-edge chain of price-value family haircare salons with over 300 locations across Canada and the States. Since 1980, we've built a strong base of customer loyalty. You don't have to have any hair experience or become a stylist to own a single unit, multiple salons or even a territory. We will provide you with all the tools and training you'll need to effectively manage your business. At First Choice Haircutters our philosophy is simple: your sucess is our success. Established: 1980 - Franchising Since: 1982 - No. of Units: Company Owned: 124 - Franchised: 187 - Franchise Fee: $10,000-$25,000 - Royalty: 5%-7% - Total Inv: $70,000-$80,000 - Financing: Third party.

GOUBAUD
Fern Laboratories, Inc.

280 Smith St., Farmingdale, NY, 11735. Contact: Emil Backstrom, Pres. - Tel: (631) 420-8000, Fax: (631) 420-8003. Skin care and cosmetics. Established: 1946 - Franchising Since: 1946 - No. of Units: Company Owned: 1 - Franchised: 25 - Royalty: Products sold at discount - Financing: No.

GREAT CLIPS
Great Clips, Inc.

7700 France Ave South Suite 425, Minneapolis, MN, 55435. Contact: Development Department - Tel: (952) 746-6414, (800) 999-5959, Fax: (952) 844-3443, E-Mail: franchise@greatclips.com, Web Site: www.greatclipsfranchise.com. The largest single salon brand in the $50 billion-a-year haircare industry and is also one of the fastest growing franchise companies in the United States. Established: 1982 - Franchising Since: 1983 - No. of Units: Franchised: 2200 - Franchise Fee: $25,000 - Royalty: 6% - Total Inv: $96,550-$182,050 - Financing: Yes.

GREAT CUTS
Landa Corporation

3030 Bridgeway Ste 231, Sausalito, CA, 94965-2810. Contact: Franchise Dept. - Tel: (415) 331-9144. Company provides haircutting services and retail hair care products to men, women and children. Established: 1983 - Franchising Since: 1985 - No. of Units: Company Owned: 8 - Franchised: 5 - Franchise Fee: $16,500 - Royalty: 10% continuing service fee + 5% adv. fund - Total Inv: Approx. $120,000 - Financing: No, but will offer assistance in this area.

GREAT EXPECTATIONS PRECISION HAIRCUTTERS
CutCo Industries, Inc.

125 S. Service Rd., P.O. Box 265, Jericho, NY, 11753. Contact: Don Vonliebermann, Pres. - Tel: (516) 677-0320, (800) 992-0139. Full service hair care salon serving 18 to 50 year old image and fashion conscious clientele. Salons offer contemporary hair care services including precision haircutting, perms and coloring. Franchise package offers a modern, attractively designed salon, operational support, advertising material training, grand opening and on-going assistance. Established: 1955 - Franchising Since: 1961 - No. of Units: Company Owned: 28 - Franchised: 157 - Franchise Fee: $20,000 - Royalty: 6% - Total Inv: $83,000-$176,500 - Financing: To qualified applicants.

HAIR REPLACEMENT SYSTEMS / HRS
Hair Associates, Inc.

400 S. Dixie Hwy., Hallandale, FL, 33009. Contact: Fran. Oper. - Tel: (800) 327-7971, (954) 457-5559, Fax: (954) 457-0054. Sales and service of non-surgical men's and women's hair replacement procedures. Established: 1969 - Franchising Since: 1980 - No. of Units: Franchised: 33 - Franchise Fee: $9,500 plus $1,000 for each 100,000 of population - Royalty: Fixed rate based population - Total Inv: $60,000 for small areas to $150,000 for large - Financing: No.

HAIRCRAFTERS
CutCo Industries, Inc.

48 S Service Rd., Ste 100, Melville, NY, 11747-2335. Contact: Ron Orne, Pres. - Tel: (952) 947-7314, (310) 979-8055, Fax: (952) 947-7300. Full service hair care salon serving the entire family. Franchise package offers a modern, attractively designed salon, operational support, advertising material, training, grand opening and on-going assistance. Established: 1955 - Franchising Since: 1961 - No. of Units: Company Owned: 20 - Franchised: 295 - Franchise Fee: $20,000 - Royalty: 6% - Total Inv: $73,000-$131,500 - Financing: To qualified applicants.

HAIRLINES FRANCHISE SYSTEMS, INC.

656 E. Golf Road., Arlington Heights, IL, 60005. Contact: Paul V. Finamore, Pres. - Tel: (847) 593-7900, Fax: (847) 593-7955. Manufacture, sales and service of hair replacements, hair additions and hair pieces. Established: 1989 - Franchising Since: 1992 - No. of Units: Company Owned: 4 - Franchised: 1 - Franchise Fee: $35,000 - Royalty: 8% - Total Inv: $35,000 fran. fee plus $70,000 for furniture, fixtures, supplies and working capital = $105,000 est. total - Financing: No, however, the SBA has approved our franchise agreement.

HCX SALONS INT'L

4850 W. Prospect Rd, Ft. Lauderdale, FL, 33309. Contact: Franchise Department - Tel: (954) 315-4900, Fax: (954) 486-5623, Web Site: www.hcx.com. Hair color & products. Established: 2000 - Franchising Since: 2001 - No. of Units: Company Owned: 1 - Franchised: 44 - Franchise Fee: $15,000 - Royalty: 6% - Total Inv: $199,000-$295,000.

HEADCUTTERS, INC

1325 Franklin Ave, Ste. 165, Garden City, NY, 11530. Contact: Jason Baskin - Tel: (516) 746-7911, Fax: (516) 746-1288. All ages budget haircuts. Established: 1996 - No. of Units: Company Owned: 4 - Franchised: 1 - Franchise Fee: $12,500 - Total Inv: Capital requirement; $50,000 - Financing: Yes.

HOUSE OF DELARA FRAGRANCES

1810 West 47th Street, Cleveland, OH, 44102. Contact: Fay M. Harris - Tel: (216) 651-5803, Fax: (216) 651-5831, E-Mail: info@houseofdelara.com, Web Site: www.houseofdelara.com. Manufacturer of over 50 men's and women's designer alternative fragrances. High quality, long lasting perfumes. Estabvlished: 1987 - Franchising Since: 1987 - No. of Units: Company Owned: 100 - Total Inv: Under $100.

JENNIFER MAXX
Jennifer Maxx USA, Inc
1133 Broadway, New York, NY, 10011. Contact: Jennifer Berton - Tel: (212) 645-9212, Fax: (212) 756-0800, Web Site: www.jennmaxx.com. A cutting edge studio for hair removal and skin care that provides hair customers with the most advanced technologies. Established: 1994 - Franchising Since: 2000 - No. of Units: Company Owned: 3 - Franchise Fee: $5,000 - Total Inv: $95,000-$120,000.

JON RIC SALON & DAY SPAS
Jon Ric International
5272 N.W. 89th Drive, Coral Springs, FL, 33067. Contact: Franchise Department - Tel: (954) 341-5853, Fax: (413) 403-8386, Web Site: www.jonric.com. Upscale full-service hair salon and day spas. No prior hair care or day spa experience needed. Established: 1983 - Franchise Fee: $15,000 - Royalty: $100.00-$200.00 flat weekly fee - Total Inv: $140,000-$265,000.

KEY WEST ALOE, INC.
Key West Aloe, Inc.
524 Front Street, Key West, FL, 33040. Contact: Kathy Rentz, Dir. of Sales & Mktg - Tel: (305) 294-5592, (800) 445-2563, Fax: (305) 294-0832. Manufacturer of Aloe- based skincare, suncare, bath and body, hair care, cosmetics and fragrance. Established: 1970 - Franchising Since : 1970 - No. of Units: Company Owned: 6 - Franchised: 15 - Franchise Fee: $7,500 - Royalty: None - Total Inv:$25,000 - Financing: No.

KIDS SUPER SALON
Kids Super Salon Franchise, Inc.
7408 W. Commercial Blvd, Lauderhill, FL, 33319. Contact: Carlos M. Fluxa, President - Tel: (800) 405-9466, (954) 355-2589, Fax: (954) 746-5119. Children's specialty hair salon's. Franchisor provides a comprehensive operations and management training program designed to train individuals with no haircare industry experience. Franchisor offers a turn key package. Initial investment is $75,000-$88,000, including franchise fee. Established: 1994 - Franchising Since: 1998 - No. of Units: Company Owned: 1 - Franchised: 1 - Franchise Fee: $15,000 - Royalty: $600/mo -Advertising Fee: $150/mo. - Financing: No.

LEMON TREE A UNISEX HAIRCUTTING ESTABLISHMENT, THE
Joan M. Cables La Femmina Beauty Salons, Inc.
One Division Ave, Levittown, NY, 11756. Contact: John L. Wagner, V.P. - Tel: (516) 735-2828, (800) 345-9156, Fax: (516) 735-1851, Web Site: www.lemontree.com. Lemon Tree meets the hair care needs of all people, servicing the entire family at low affordable prices, name brand quality products and hours from early morning to late evening, seven days a per week. Established: 1974 - Franchising Since: 1976 - No. of Units: Franchised: 64 - Franchise Fee: $15,000 - Royalty: 6% - Total Inv: $42,000-$70,000 - Financing: Yes; 1/2 franchise fee, 1/2 equipment fee.

LORD'S AND LADY'S HAIR SALONS
450 Belgrade Ave., W. Roxbury, MA, 02132. Contact: Michael M. Barsamian, Pres. - Tel: (617) 323-4714, Fax: (617) 323-4059. Hair styling full service for men and women. Established: 1972 - Franchising Since: 1979 - No. of Units: Company Owned: 16 - Franchised: 12 - Franchise Fee: $25,000 - Royalty: 6% - Total Inv: $125,000-$175,000 - Financing: No.

LUCKY HEART COSMETICS, INC
138 Huling Ave, Memphis, TN, 38103. Contact: Gary Young or Chandra Miller - Tel: (901) 526-7658, Fax: (901) 526-7660. Manufacturer & sales of personal care products. Established: 1935 - No. of Units: Franchised: 3500 - Franchise Fee: $20.00 - Financing: No.

MARSHA SCOTT'S HAIR LOSS CLINIC FOR WOMEN
30 Grassy Plain Street, Bethel, CT, 06801. Contact: Marsha Scott - Tel: (203) 792-1800, (800) 625-4214, Fax: (203) 743-6793, Web Site: www.HLCFW.com. Marsha Scott's Hair Lss Clinic for Women specializes in high quality, safe, non-surgical hair replacement techniques. Established: 1987 - Franchising Since: 2000 - No. of Units: Company Owned: 1 - Franchise Fee: $30,000 - Royalty: 5% - Total Inv: $80,000-$150,000.

MERLE NORMAN COSMETIC STUDIO
Merle Norman Cosmetics, Inc
9130 Bellanca Ave., Los Angeles, CA, 90045. - Tel: (310) 641-3000, (800) 421-6648, Fax: (310) 337-2370, E-Mail: mpham@merlenorman.com, Web Site: www.merlenorman.com. Retail sale of Merle Norman cosmetic skiin care and color products. Established: 1931 - Franchising Since: 1988 - No. of Units: Company Owned: 11 - Franchised: 1883 - Franchise Fee: None - Royalty: None - Total Inv: $33,099-$153,069 - Financing: Initial inventory of cosmetic products.

N TIME FAMILY SALONS *
P.O. Box 604, Daphine, AL, 36526 - Tel: (251) 634-5173, Fax: (251) 633-0772, Web Site: www.ntimefamilysalons.com. Professional, contemporary look with top selling products, colors and samples with extended hours. Established: 2001 - Franchising Since: 2003 - No. of Units: Franchised: 2 - Franchise Fee: $5,000 - Royalty: 5% - Total Inv: $26,200-$43,500 - Financing: No.

NATURAL SWISS SKIN CARE
20 Cove Rd, #3, Stonington, CT, 06378. Contact: Sarah St. Amour - Tel: (860) 536-2604, (877) 718-0164. Natural skin care, cosmetics and nutrition. Established: 1980 - No of Units: Franchised: 3500 - Franchise Fee: $29.-$1,000 - Financing: No.

NU-KUTZ
Nu-Kutz
3900 Washington Street, Gurnee, IL, 60031. Contact: Jane Yde, Owner - Tel: (847) 625-2730, Web Site: www.nu-kutz.com. Hair salon and retail sales. Established: 1994 - Franchising Since: 1995 - No. Units: Company Owned: 2 - Franchise Fee: $12,500 - Royalty: 5% - Total Inv: $50,000 - Financing: No. NOT FRANCHISING AT THIS TIME.

PAMPERED NAILS PLUS
216 West Erwin, Tyler, TX, 75702. Contact: Louann Hooten, Owner - Tel: (877) 592-0717. Nail salon. Established: 1998 - Franchising Since: 2000 - No. of Units: Company Owned: 1 - Franchised: 1 - Franchise Fee: $30,000-$40,000 - Total Inv: $50,000.

PERFUME PIZAZZ
Perfume Pizazz, Franchise Systems Inc.
18810-C East 39th Street, Independence, MO, 64055. - Tel: (816) 795-7901, (888) 258-2458, Fax: (816) 795-7913, Web Site: www.perfume pizazz.com. Bring department store fragrances to the customer at discount prices, offering a wide variety of European fragrances that people have seen only when travelling abroad. Established: 1989 - Franchising Since: 1998 - No. of Units: Company Owned: 4 - Franchise Fee: $25,000 - Royalty: 5.5% - Total Inv: $250,000-$322,175 (total inventory, signage, equipment, working capital, start up expenses, etc) - Financing: Not at this time.

PRO-CUTS
7201 Metro Blvd, Edina, MN, 55439. - Tel: (888) 888-7008, Fax: (952) 947-7301, E-Mail: franchsieleads@regiscorp.com, Web Site: www.pro-cuts.com. Professional haircuts for the whole family at affordable prices. Established: 1982 - Franchising Since: 1983 - No. of Units: Company Owned: 24 - Franchised: 181 - Franchise Fee: $6,000-$23,000 - Royalty: 4%-6% - Total Inv: $115,000-$125,000 - Financing: Third party.

SNIP N' CLIP HAIRCUT SHOPS
SNC Franchise Corp.
11427 Strang Line Rd, Lenexa, KS, 66215. - Tel: (800) 622-6804, Fax: (913) 345-1554, Web Site: www.snipnclip.net. Family haircut shops in 19 states in strip centers, budget priced, no appointment, open 7 days and nights. Established: 1976 - Franchising Since: 1986 - No. of Units: Company Owned: 47 - Franchised: 44 - Franchise Fee: $15,000 - Royalty: 5% - Total Inv: $51,750 ($10,000 fran. fee - turnkey, 8 chair shop $41,750) - Financing: Yes, leasing program.

SPORT CLIPS
Sport Clips, Inc.
110 Briarwood, Georgetown, TX, 78628. Contact: Judy Mills, Franchise Development - Tel: (512) 869-1201, (800) 872-4247, Fax: (512) 868-3591, E-Mail: judith@sportclips.com, Web Site: www.sportclips.com. The most exciting and unique concept in hair care today! Sports-themed haircutting stores targeting men and boys, a 125,000,000 "niche market" that is virtually ignored by private salons and other chains. Not a "Me

too" concept-lots of unique selling points. Big-screen TV's, first-class "locker room" look and feel. Retail sale of hair care products and sports memorabilia. Established: 1993 - Franchising Since: 1995 - No. of Units: Company Owned: 10 - Franchised: 101 - Franchise Fee: $39,500 - Royalty: 6% payable weekly - Total Inv: $150,000-$250,000 - Financing: Available from franchisor recommended parties.

SUPERCUTS®
7201 Metro Boulevard, Minneapolis, MN, 55439. - Tel: (888) 888-7008, Fax: (952) 947-7301, Web Site: www.supercuts.com. Top quality affordable hair care salons, with the highest brand name awareness in the hair care industry. Supercuts offers an extraodrinary growth opportunity in key Canadian markets. Full training and support provided. Franchising only available in Canada. Established: 1972 - No. of Units: Franchised: 1200 - Total Inv: $90,000-$120,000.

SYD SIMONS COSMETICS, INC.
6601 West North Ave, Oak Park, IL, 60302. Contact: Jerry Weitzel, Pres. - Tel: (708) 660-0266, (877) 943-2333, Fax: (708) 660-0994. Makeup and skin care products and related services and accessories. Established: 1936 - Licensing Since: 1974 - No. of Units: Company Owned: 1 - Licensed: 6 - Approx. Inv: $40,000-$60,000 plus $15,000-$25,000 working capital - Financing: No, Licensor will assist in obtaining local financing.

TOP OF THE LINE FRAGRANCES
T.O.L. Franchise Group, Inc.
515 Bath Ave., Long Branch, NJ, 07740. Contact: Steven Ciaverelli, VP - Tel: (732) 229-0014, (800) 929-3083, Web Site: www.tolfranchise.com. Nationally advertised designer brand fragrances sold at discount in retail malls, strip centers, and large outlet centers. Established: 1987 - Franchising Since: 1987 - No. of Units: Franchised: 4 - Franchise Fee: $20,000 - Royalty: 5% of gross sales - Total Inv: $150,000 - Financing: SBA.

TRADE SECRET
Regis Corporation
7201 Metro Blvd., Minneapolis, MN, 55439. - Tel: (612) 947-7777, Fax: (612) 947-7500. Mall-based retail concept specializing in "salon-only" hair care products. Trade Secret presents an exciting retail product environment to shoppers, while operating a compact, yet full service salon. Established: 1982 - Franchising Since: 1988 - No. of Units: Company Owned: 104 - Franchised: 68 - Franchise Fee: $27,500 - Royalty: 6.5% - discounted for timely payment - Total Inv: $117,000-$197,000 incl. fran. fee - Financing: No.

VOLPE NAILS, INC.
P.O. Box 19979, Sarasota, FL, 34276-2979. Contact: Gary Donson, V.P. - Tel: (941) 917-0963, Fax: (941) 906-8044. Sale of nail care franchises. Specializing in sculptured acrylic nails, natural nail care and quality nail care products. Currently offering business opportunities. Established: 1980 - Franchising Since: 1989 - No. of Units: Company Owned: 1 - Franchised: 53 - Franchise Fee: $5,000-$15,000 - Royalty: No royalty or adv. - Total Inv: $14,000-$103,000 (fran. fee, equip and inven. $6,500-$41,300 & work. cap. $3,800-$50,000) - Financing: No.

HEALTH AIDS AND SERVICES

ADAPTIVE MEDICAL EQUIPMENT CO
2427 Wallace Ave, Spartanburg, SC, 29302. Contact: Greg Tucker - Tel: (864) 597-0061, Fax: (864) 597-0069, E-Mail: FundingSources @aol.com. Provider of medical equipment. Established: 1994 - Franchising Since: 2001 - No. of Units: Company Owned: 1 - Franchised: 2 - Franchise Fee: $5,000-$25,000 - Total Inv: Capital requirements; $5,000-$50,000.

ADARA HEALTHCARE STAFFING *
291 Maple Hollow Rd, Duncansville, PA, 16635. - Tel: (814) 69391415, Fax: (814) 693-9880, Web Site: www.health-care-staffing.com. Provide quality healthcare to local hospitals and long care facilities. Established: 1998 - Franchising Since: 2003 - No. of Units: Company Owned: 27 - Franchise Fee: $20,000 - Financing: No.

AGELESS PLACEMENTS, INC
8031 66th St, No. Suite 4, Pinellas Park, FL, 33781. Contact: Paula Kay - Tel: (727) 547-4337, Fax: (727) 549-4049, E-Mail: paulak412@aol.com. Non-medical home care agency that recruits active retirees to assist seniors in their homes with daily living. Established: 1992 - Franchising Since: 1999 - No. of Units: Company Owned: 1 - Franchised: 32 - Franchise Fee: $2,000 - Royalty: N/A - Financing: Yes, $500. down payment with balance in paid in12 months.

AIRSOPURE
Airsopure International Group, Inc
15400 Knoll Trail, Ste. 200, Dallas, TX, 75248. Contact: V.P. Franchise Dev - Tel: (972) 960-9400, ext. 119 , (800) 752-3322, ext. 119, Fax: (972) 960-9488, Web Site: www.airsopure.com. Incredibly low cost, turnkey franchise opportunity. Airsopure products have long been the "caddillac" of the air purification industry and we are offering franchises to professional sales people for direct marketing to the consumer. Franchise fee includes intial inventory. Established: 1994 - Franchising Since: 1997 - No. of Units: Company Owned: 4 - Franchised: 24 - Franchise Fee: $15,000 - Royalty: None - Total Inv: $16,000-$25,000 - Financing: No.

AMERICAN CRITICAL CARE SERVICES
221 Ruthers Rd, Suite 103, Richmond, VA, 23235. Contact: Franchise Department - Tel: (804) 320-1113, (800) 245-4011, Fax: (804) 330-9460, Web Site: www.accs-agape.com. Temporary staffing agency of RN's, LPN's and CNA's, plus therapies for facility staffing and home health. Established: 1986 - Franchising Since: 1999 - No. of Units: Company Owned: 2 - Franchise Fee: $30,000 - Royalty: 7% of gross receipts - Total Inv: $100,000-$200,000 - Financing: No.

AMERICAN NURSING CARE
300 Techne Center Dr., Ste. C, Milford, OH, 45150-2786. Contact: Tom Karpinski, Pres. - Tel: (513) 576-0262, Fax: (513) 576-0381. Temporary staffing and private duty nursing. Franchising Since: 1982 - No. of Units: 6 - Approx. Inv: $30,000-$40,000.

AMERICAN PHYSICAL REHABILITATION NETWORK APRN, INC.
4747 Holland-Sylvania Rd, Sylvania, OH, 43560. Contact: Harvey Bowes, C.F.O. - Tel: (419) 824-3434 , (800) 331-3058, Fax: (419) 824-3435. A total system for management and operation of free-standing physical therapy clinics. Established: 1957 - Franchising Since: 1987 - No. of Units: Franchised: 6 - Franchise Fee: $25,000 - Royalty: 7% + 1% adv. - Total Inv: $232,632 - Financing: No, will assist with feasibility and may consider partnership.

AMERICARE/DENTAL CENTERS, U.S.A.
6232 N 7th St Ste 105, Phoenix, AZ, 85014-1850. - Tel: (602) 548-9178, Fax: (602) 548-9472. Dental office development administration and management/accounting services available for dental offices. Established: 1978 - Franchising Since: 1983 - No. of Units: Franchised: 5 - Franchise Fee: $25,000 - Royalty: 7% adv + 3% use of name, 5% management - Total Inv: Up to $250,000 - Financing: Yes (100% financing available) 100% operator owned.

AMIGO MOBILITY CENTER
Mobility Center, Inc.
6693 Dixie Hwy., Bridgeport, MI, 48722. Contact: Dave Crispin, CEO - Tel: (989) 777-8184. Sales and service of mobility products to the huge health care and senior markets, anyone who has trouble walking, 3 & 4 wheeled scooters, wheelchairs, lifts, ramps and many other products. We sell-rent-lease-service. Established: 1968 - Franchising Since: 1984 - No. of Units: Company Owned: 4 - Franchised: 22 - Franchise Fee: $20,000+ - Royalty: 5% decreasing to 2%, 1% adv. - Total Inv: $75,000-$135,000 - Financing: No.

ANNE PENMAN LASER THERAPY *
6690 Roswell Rd, Suite 350, Atlanta, GA, 30328. Contact: Franchise Department - Tel: (404) 256-2609, Fax: (404) 256-2234, Web Site: www.annepenmanlasertherapy.com. Exciting franchise opportunity using state-of-the-art, innovative low-level lasers for smoking reduction and cessation. Established: 2003 - Franchising Since: 2004 - No. of Units: Company Owned: 1 - Franchised: 16 - Franchise Fee: $20,000 - Royalty: 10% - Total Inv: $30,000-$70,000.

ARISTOCARE *

1200 N, El Dorado Pl, Suite A-130, Tucson, AZ, 85715. - Tel: (866) 731-2273, Fax: (520) 529-0862, Web Site: www.aristocarefranchise.net. Provide private home healthcare. Established: 1999 - Franchising Since: 2003 - No. of Units: Company Owned: 3 - Franchise Fee: $36,000 - Royalty: 6% - Total Inv: $180,000.

ARROW PHARMACY & NUTRITION CENTER
Arrow Corporation

312 Farmington Avenue, Farmington, CT, 06032. Contact: Michael Marusa, Director of Business Development - Tel: (860) 676-1222, (800) 203-2776, Fax: (860) 676-1499. Professional retail pharmacies with a vision to be the nationally recognized leader in the development and implementation of pharmacy care practice sites that combine pharmaceutical and nutrition care. Established: 1969 - Franchising Since: 1990 - No. of Units: Company Owned: 71 - Franchised: 25 - Franchise Fee: Initial fee ranges from $7,500 to $15,000 - Royalty: 6% of gross receipts - Total Inv: $140,000-$250,000 for new pharmacy $30,000-$112,000 for a conversion pharmacy - Financing: Yes.

ATWORK HELPINGHANDS SERVICES *

3215 John Sevier Hwy, Knoxville, TN, 37920. - Tel: (800) 383-0804, Fax: (865) 573-1171, Web Site: www.atworkfranchise.com. Network of service providers supplying a variety of non-medical in-home care and or service perssonal to individuals who desire assistance. Established: 1990 - Franchising Since: 2003 - No. of Units: Franchised: 8 - Franchise Fee: $11,500 - Royalty: 6% - Total Inv: $59,500-$105,000.

BASIC NEEDS HOME COMPANION SERVICES
Basic Needs Enterprises, Inc.

440 Chelsea Woods Dr., P.O. Box 12672, Lexington, KY, 40583. Contact: Phyllis W. Berry, Pres. - Tel: (606) 269-7611, (800) 269-8461. A home-based specialized, non-medical home care service for the elderly or homebound. Established: 1992 - No. of Units: Company Owned: 1 - Franchise Fee: $5,000 - Royalty: 4% total gross sales, but no less than $250 per week - Total Inv: $10,000-$16,000, including fran. fee - Financing: No.

BEE HIVE HOMES

1406 E 1st St Ste 114, Meridian, ID, 83642-1798. Contact: Vance Fager, President - Tel: (208) 884-8004, (800) 884-6269, Fax: (208) 884-8879. Senior Assisted living homes, 24 hour a day personal care for the elderly. Established: 1986 - Franchising Since: 1994 - No. of Units: Company Owned: 10 - Franchised: 80 - Franchise Fee: $27,500 - Royalty: Percentage of gross rent - Financing: Assistance with preferred sources.

BENEFICIAL HEALTH & BEAUTY, INC.
Beneficial International

1780 W. 500 So., Salt Lake City, UT, 84104. Contact: Linda T. Nelson, Ph.D. Pres. - Tel: (801) 973-7778, Fax: (801) 973-8836. Urban health and beauty spas using products unsurpassed for quality and effectiveness. Total health and beauty care at local outlets. Established: 1981 - Franchising Since: 1990 - No. of Units: Franchised: 28 - Franchise Fee: $15,000 - Royalty: 3%, 4% adv. - Total Inv: F.F., $14,500 product & equip., lease space costs - Financing: No.

BETTER BACK STORE FRANCHISES
Thomas Blantz Enterprises

P.O. Box 36366, Denver, CO, 80236-0366. - Tel: (303) 721-1369, (800) 501-BACK, Fax: (303) 721-1091, Web Site: www.betterback.com. Retail stores selling products for back care. Training and support provided by franchisor. Also retail specialty store carrying over 1,000 healthful items for home, work, travel and leisure. Established: 1981 - Franchising Since: 1992 - No. of Units: Company Owned: 1 - Franchised: 15 - Franchise Fee: $22,000 - Royalty: 4%, 1% nat'l adv. fund - Total Inv: $136,000-$229,000 - Financing: SBA approved.

BODYWORK FRANCHISE INC.
LifePath, Center For Therapeutic Massage

7820 N. University, #110, Peoria, IL, 61614. - Tel: (309) 693-7284, (888) 2 LifePath, Fax: (309) 693-6234, E-Mail: rwasher@flink.com. Center for Therapeutic Massage and other complementary health care options. Selling self-help books, tapes, nutritional supplements. Offering workshops, yoga, etc. for increasing well-being. Established: 1990 - Franchising Since: 1997 - Franchise Fee: $15,000, $10,000 for LifePath School of Massage graduates, decreasing by $5,000 for additional units - Royalty: 4% of gross sales - Total Inv: $22,550-$47,900 - Financing: SBA.

BRIDGE TO INDEPENDENCE
Bridge To Independence Franchise Service

1200 E. Davis Ste. 115MB217, Mesquite, TX, 75181. Contact: Colleen Day - Tel: (866) 998-CARE. We offer two programs in one franchise servicing both independent seniors and those in need of assistance by providing light housekeeping, bathing, grooming, meal planning, monitoring medications, companionship and other services. Established: 1998 - Franchising Since: 2001 - No. of Units: Company Owned: 1 - Franchise Fee: $17,500 - Total Inv: $26,000.

CARBWATCHERS *

1133 Broadway Ste. 232, New York, NY, 10010. - Tel: (866) 999-5326, Fax: (212) 851-8198, E-Mail: info@carbwatchers.com, Web Site: www.carbwatchers.com. Offers low carb weight loss programs designed for each person. Established: 2002 - Franchising Since: 2003 - No. of Units: Company Owned: 2 - Franchised: 1 - Franchise Fee: $20,000 - Total Inv: $25,500-$50,000 - Financing: No.

CAREINGTON INTERNATIONAL

13155 Noel Rd., 15th floor, Dallas, TX, 75240. - Tel: (800) 290-0523, Fax: (972) 661-0427. Provides health benefits for franchisors. Main specialty is dental care. We also have vision, prescription and other health care available. Client companies include Subway (nationwide), Krystal, Deck The Walls and Morrison's. Established: 1979.

CAROL BLOCK
Carol Block Ltd.

1403 S. Belden, McHenry, IL, 60050. Contact: Neal Rohr, Fran. Dev.- Tel: (815) 344-0488. Permanent hair removal, full training and support provided. Established: 1937 - Franchising Since: 1986 - No. of Units: Company Owned: 13 - Franchised: 4 - Total Inv: $10,000.

CENTER SANCTUM, THE
The Center Sanctum Ltd.

3620 Court Dr., Zanesville, OH, 43701. Contact: Dir. of Franchise - Tel: (740) 455-9440, (888) 374-6398. Retail weight and life management centers offering medically supervised plans and exclusive sanctum line of natural supplements. Extensive training, manuals and support. Established: 1996 - Franchising Since: 1997 - No. of Units; Company Owned: 2 - Franchised: 8 - Franchise Fee: $25,000 - Royalty: 6% - Financing: No.

CHALL-AIDE MEDICAL PRODUCTS

Rt. 15 - P.O. Box 965, Sparta, NJ, 07871. - Tel: (973) 383-0700. Offering the market the right product at the right time. Medical kits and products as well. Established: 1975.

COLE VISION CORP
Cole Vision Corp

1925 Enterprise Pkwy, Twinsburg, OH, 44087. Contact: Franchise Department - Tel: (330) 486-3000, Fax: (330) 486-3596. Provide complete optical services with retail sales of optical products. Many locations with one hour service and also has own manufacturing lab. Established: 1949 - Franchising Since: 1983 - No. of Units: Company Owned: 130 - Franchised: 80 - Franchise Fee: $15,000 - Royalty: 8.5% plus adv. fee of 7% - Total Inv: $60,000-$500,000 - Financing: Yes.

COMFORCARE SENIOR SERVICES
Comforcare Healthcare Holdings, Inc

42505 Woodward Ave, 250, Bloomfield Hills, MI, 48304. - Tel: (800) 886-4044, Fax: (248) 745-9763, E-Mail: home@ComForcare.com, Web Site: www.ComForcare.com. Provides the most extensive non-medical home health care services. Established: 1996 - Franchising Since: 2000 - No. of Units: Company Owned: 1 - Franchise Fee: $12,500 - Total Inv: $29,900.

COMP-U-MED SYSTEMS, INC.

5777 West Century Blvd, Los Angeles, CA, 90045. - Tel: (310) 258-5000, Fax: (310) 645-5880. Medical equipment leasing. Established: 1973 - Franchising Since: 1978 - No. of Units: - Franchised: 1,211 - Total Inv: $7,000-$36,000.

CORPORATE BODY FRANCHISE , THE
100 South Bis Cayne Blvd, Miami, FL, 33131. Contact: Ronald Schwab - Tel: (954) 942-9424, (305) 357-0059, Fax: (954) 783-5177. Alternative medicine. Established: 1995 - Franchising Since: 2001 - No. of Units: Company Owned: 1 - Franchise Fee: $15,000 - Total Inv: $159,999 - Financing: No.

CPR SERVICES
CPR Services, Inc
22 Stoneybrook Drive, Ashland, MA, 01721. Contact: Steven H. Greenberg, Sales Manager - Tel: (508) 881-8010, (800) 357-0091, Fax: (508) 881-4718, E-Mail: info@cpr-services.com, Web Site: www.cpr-services.com. Health education and training specializing in CPR and first aid instuction. Established: 1984 - Franchising Since: 2001 - No. of Units: Company Owned: 1 - Franchised: 1 - Franchise Fee: $7,500 - Total Inv: $7,500 - Financing: No.

DENTAL STORE, THE
Dental Store, Ltd. The
1061 South Roselle Rd., Schaumburg, IL, 60193-3900. Contact: Dr. Neil H. Shulkin, Pres. - Tel: (847)301-0400. A license (exclusive, territorial) for the use of 'The Dental Store' registered trademarks in the operation of pre-existing dental offices. Established: 1986 - Licensing Since: 1992 - No. of Units: Company Owned: 1 - Franchise Fee: $2,500 - Royalty: 1.5% - Total Inv: License fee only - Financing: One year financing available.

DENTIST'S CHOICE, THE
Dentist's Choice Inc., The
34700 Coast Hwy., #200, Capistrano Beach, CA, 92624. - Tel: (949) 443-2070, (800) 757-1333, Fax: (949) 443-2074. Repair of dental handpieces. Established: 1992 - Franchising Since: 1994 - No. of Units: Company Owned: 1 - Franchised: 82 - Franchise Fee: $15,000 - Royalty: 5% of monthly gross - Total Inv: $15,000 - Fran. fee + $5,950 (tools, parts, inventory, training) - Financing: No.

DERMACULTURE CLINIC
P.O Box 3576, Newport Beach, CA, 92659-8576. Contact: Dir. of Sales & Marketing - Tel: (949) 673-7171, Fax: (949) 673-8407. Skin care franchises. Offering a unique skin treatment procures. The product line includes cleaners, toners, moisturizers, etc. Established: 1937 - Franchising Since: 1939 - No. of Units: 30. Not franchising at this time.

DIET CENTERS
Health Management Group
395 Springside Dr., Akron, OH, 44333-2496. Contact: Dir. of Franchise Dev. - Tel: (330) 665-5861, (800) 656-3294, Fax: (330) 666-2197. Weight Loss and related products. Established: 1973 - Franchising Since: 1975 - No. of Units: Franchised: 325 - Franchise Fee: $4,900 - Royalty: 8% -4% - Total Inv: $15,740-$32,000 - Financing: No.

DIRECT LINK
4338 Glendale Milford Rd, Cincinnati, OH, 45242-3706. Contact: Franchise Department - Tel: (800) 413-4899, Fax: (513) 563-2691. Emergency medical monitoring system. Direct link allows the elderly to remain in the comfort of their home while "never being alone". Established: 1998 - Franchising Since: 1999 - Franchise Fee: $11,900 - $23,900 - Royalty: 6% - Total Inv: Capital required $7,550-$15,650 - Financing: Up to 50% of franchise fee.

DISCOUNT SPORT NUTRITION FRANCHISING
Discount Sport Nutrition, LLC
1525 N. Stemmons Freeway Ste. 200, Carrollton, TX, 75006. - Tel: (972) 245-1798, (877) 9SP-ORT3, Fax: (214) 292-8619. Nutritional sport supplements retail store. Established: 1996 - Franchising Since: 2000 - No. of Units: Company Owned: 1 - Franchised: 2 - Franchise Fee: $25,000 - Total Inv: $87,795-$170,295 - Financing: No.

ECHOSOURCE.COM
3400 Peachtree Rd, #147, Atlanta, GA, 30326. - Tel: (404) 231-0369, (800) 823-3246, Fax: (404) 231-3503, Web Site: www.echosource.com. Vitamins, minerals and herbs. Established: 1999 - Franchising Since: 2000 - No. of Units: Company Owned: 1 - Franchise Fee: $10,000 - Total Inv: $20,000.

EDUCATIONAL MARKETING GROUP
10091 Streeter Rd., Ste. 7, Auburn, CA, 95602-8512. Contact: Bill Mann, President - Tel: (530) 268-2727, (800) 943-3163, Fax: (530) 268-2793. Medical/dental billing, work at home on your computer processing insurance claims and market medical/dental software to doctors. Established: 1995 - Franchising Since: 1995 - No. of Units: Company Owned: 2 - Franchised: 400 - Total Inv: $5,000-$9,000 - Financing: Yes.

ELDIRECT HOMECARE
21 West Mountain St., Ste. 120, Fayetteville, AR, 72701. Contact: Leigh Davis - Tel: (479) 443-7173, E-Mail: eldirecthomecare@yahoo.com, Web Site: www.eldirecthomecare.com. ELDirect Homecare offers a complete package of support services, including training, operations manuals, strategic planning and more. Established: 1996 - Franchising Since: 2002 - No. of Units: Company Owned: 1 - Franchised: 1 - Franchise Fee: $15,000 - Financing: No.

ELEVATORS ETC
EMR Accessibility Inc
6802 Ringgold Rd, Chattanooga, TN, 37412. - Tel: (423) 267-lift, (800) 451-8336, Fax: (423) 265-7477, Web Site: www.elevatorsetc.com. Sale, service and repair (lulu) elevators, reidential elevators, stairlifts, wheelchair lift and dumbwaiters. Established: 1987 - Franchising Since: 1998 - No. of Units: Company Owned: 3 - Franchise Fee: $28,500 - Royalty: 5% + 1% for marketing and advertising - Total Inv: $45,000-$100,000 - Financing: No.

EMSAR
Equipment Management Services & Repair
1032 W. Main St., Wilmington, OH, 45177. - Tel: (937) 383-1052. Servicing medical equipment. Established: 1993 - Franchising Since: 1993 - No. of Units: Franchised: 32 - Franchise Fee: $20,000 - Royalty: 15% - Financing: No.

ETERNAL LIFE HEALTH
Eternal Life Health
P.O. Box 30090, Houston, TX, 77249. Contact: Robert Nicholson, President - Tel: (713) 683-8700, Fax: (713) 683-8796, E-Mail: jac53@prodigy.net, Web Site: www.Eternallifehealth.com. Private label vitamins, herbs, dietary supplements. Established: 1995 - Franchising Since: 2001 - No. of Units: Company Owned: 1 - Total Inv: Varies - Financing: No.

EUROPEAN TREATMENT CENTERS, USA
5206 N. Scottsdale Road, Scottsdale, AZ, 85253. - Tel: (480) 970-0300, (800) 970-0498, Fax: (480) 970-0595. Our nonsurgical body contouring and facial rejuvenation is noninvasive and provides noticeable results fast! These techniques along with our cosmetic line can help you succeed in the fast growing personal care industry. Established: 1998 - Franchising Since: 1998 - No. of Units: Company Owned: 2 - Franchise Fee: $35,000 - Royalty: 7.5% of gross monthly receipts - Total Inv: $150,000-$300,000 .

FABULOS FACES, LLC
3473 Cortina Cir, Colorado Springs, CO, 80918-1801. - Tel: (719) 598-6515, Fax: (719) 495-8280. A unique program of isometric facial exercise that improves muscle shape and tone to reduce the appearance of aging. Established: 1992 - Franchising Since: 1994 - No. of Units: Company Owned: 2 - Franchised: 2 - Franchise Fee: $14,995 - Royalty: Product purchase only - approx. 8-10% of sales - Total Inv: $20,000-$25,000.

FETAL FOTOS *
5217 S. State, #200, Murray, UT, 84107. - Tel: (801) 277-6121, Fax: (801) 277-1474, Web Site: www.fetalfotosusa.com. High-quality prenatal ultrasound services. Established: 1994 - Franchising Since: 2002 - No. of Units: Company Owned: 3 - Franchised: 19 - Franchise Fee: $35,000-$50,000 - Royalty: 6% - Total Inv: $61,500-$130,000.

FIRSTAT NURSING SERVICES
Firstat of America, Inc
801 Village Blvd., #304, West Palm Beach, FL, 33409. Tel: (561) 684-9000, Fax: (905) 684-9008. Critical care nursing in homes + facilities. Training and support provided. Established: 1989 - Franchising Since: 1990 - No. of Units: Company Owned: 2 - Franchised: 37 - Franchise Fee: $30,000 - Total Inv: $200,000 - Financing: No.

GIGI'S HAIR GALLERY
690 Carlsbad Village Dr., Ste. 2034, Carlsbad, CA, 92008. Contact: Christina Mangin - Tel: (877) 346-3340, Fax: (760) 720-5293. Hair pieces & hair accessories. Established: 1999 - Franchising Since: 2001 - No. of Units: Company Owned: 6 - Franchised: 71 - Franchise Fee: $10,000 - Financing: No.

GREAT AMERICAN BACK RUB STORE
Great American Back Rub Inc.
P.O. Box 1134, Dunedin, FL, 34697-1134. Contact: Ricardo Coia, President - Tel: (813) 532-4818, (800) 210-6163, Fax: (813) 532-4737. Massage and stress relief outlet. Fully clothed massages and sale of stress relief products. Established: 1992 - Franchising Since: 1994 - No. of Units: Company Owned: 2 - Franchised: 80 - Franchise Fee: $20,000 - Royalty: 6% of gross sales, 3% marketing fund - Total Inv: $118,000-$180,000.

GRISWOLD SPECIAL CARE
717 Bethleham Pike, #300, Erdenheim, PA, 19038. - Tel: (215) 402-0200, Fax: (215) 402-0202. Non-medical care. Established: 1982 - No. of Units: Company Owned: 4 - Franchise Fee: $9,000 - Total Inv: $10,000.

HANDPIECE EXPRESS
1020 Railrood Avenue #A-1, Novato, CA, 94945. Contact: Glenn Williams - Tel: (415) 892-1282, (800) 895-7111, Fax: (415) 892-1212, E-Mail: handpieceexpress@cs.com, Web Site: www.handpiece express.com. Unique home based business serving dental professionals. Proven business model of success. Complete startup package including training, tools, videos and manuals. Ongoing support including technical and marketing assistance, marketing materials, etc. Established: 1994 - Franchising Since: 2000 - No. of Units: Company Owned: 1 - Franchised: 14 - Franchise Fee: $23,500 - Royalty: $100 per month - Total Inv: $32,500 - Financing: No.

HAYES HANDPIECE COMPANY
Hayes Handpiece Franchises Inc.
5375 Avenida Encinas Ste C, Charsbad, CA, 92008-4362. Contact: Joe Hayes, President - Tel: (760) 602-0521, (800) 228-0521, Fax: (760) 602-0505, E-Mail: Joe-Hayes@HayesHandpiece.com, Web Site: www.hayeshandpiece.com. Dental handpiece repair, home based. Established: 1989 - Franchising Since: 1995 - No. of Units: Company Owned: 7 - Franchised: 47 - Franchise Fee: $17,000 - Royalty: 3.5% to 5% - Total Inv: $23,000 - Financing: None.

HEALTH MART
McKesson Corporation
2124 Research Rave, Dallas, TX , 75006. Contact: John Kogut, Pres. - Tel: (334) 712-1054, Fax: (334) 712-1054. Full-line, community-based drug stores. Established: 1980 - Franchising Since: 1982 - No. of Units: 650 - Total Inv: Varies - Financing: No.

HEALTHCARE DATA MANAGEMENT, INC.
HDM - Healthcare Data Management, Inc
303 W Lancaster Ave, Wayne, PA, 19087-3938. - Tel: 610) 341-8608, (800) 859-5119, Fax: (610) 989-0658, Web Site: www.healthaudit.com. HDM provides an auditing service to recover overcharges on medical bills. Training for this home-based business also includes business systems and full year support. $8500.00 investment. Established: 1992 - Total Inv: $8500 with trainig $7500 without training - Financing: Yes.

HEALTHY BACK
The Healthy Back Store Franchise Company
P.O. Box 1296, Newington, VA, 22122-1296. - Tel: (703) 339-1300 ext 32, Fax: (703) 339-0671, Web Site: www.healthyback.com. The Healthy Back Store is a retail store which specializes in selling ergonomically designed products such as beds, pillows, footrests, office chairs and more. Established: 1993 - Franchising Since: 1999 - No. of Units: Company Owned: 10 - Franchised: 12 - Franchise Fee: $25,000 - Total Inv: Liquid cash $100,000 net worth $650,000.

HEALTHY HOME INSPECTORS®
1406 E. 14th St, Des Moines, IA, 50316-2406. Contact: Dane J. Shearer, Pres. - Tel: (515) 265-6667, (800) 288-7437, Fax: (515) 278-2070. Environmental testing and consulting service. Established: 1998 -

Franchising Since: 1998 - No.of Units: Company Owned: 1 - Franchise Fee: $9800.00 - Royalty: 6%+2% adv co-op - Total Inv: $15,000 - Financing: Yes.

HERBAL PATH-A NATURAL PHARMACY, THE
Herbal Path Franchising Corp.
P.O. Box 4384, Portsmouth, NH, 03802-4384. Contact: Dir. of Franchising - Tel: (603) 431-5900, Fax: (603) 431-5900, E-Mail: franchise@franchise2000.com, Web Site: www.herbalpath.com. A natural pharmacy with a registered pharmacist on staff, specializing in home pathic, naturopathic, herbal, nutritional, alternative healthcare. Unique retail store. Need not be a P.PH to own. Established: 1996 - Franchising Since: 1999 - No. of Units: Company Owned: 1 - Franchised: 4 - Franchise Fee: $20,000 - Royalty: 5% of gross, 4%-6% to advertising, Total Inv: $132,000-$181,350 (including franchise fee & operating capital) - Financing: Yes third party.

HOME HELPERS
H.H. Franchising Systems, Inc
10700 Montgomery Rd., Ste. 300, Cincinnati, OH, 45242. Contact: Franchise Department - Tel: (800) 216-4196, (513) 563-8339, Fax: (513) 563-2691. We are the #1 franchise providing non-medical in-home companion care to the elderly, new mothers & those recuperating from illness or injury. Established: 1997 - Franchising Since: 1997 - No. of Units: Franchised: 106 - Franchise Fee: $13,900-$23,900 - Royalty: 6% deslining to 4% with rebates - Financing: In-house financing up to 50%.

HOME INSTEAD SENIOR CARE
Home Instead, Inc.
604 N 109th Ct, Omaha, NE, 68154-1716. Contact: Franchise Development Mgr. - Tel: (402) 498-4466, (888) 484-5759, Fax: (402) 498-5757, Web Site: www.homeinstead.com. Home Instead Senior Care is a successful, non-medical companionship and home care franchise. The elderly market we serve is the fastest growing segment of the population. Services such as companionship, light housework, errand and meal preparation assist the elderly in remaining in their homes rather than being institutionalized. Established: 1994 - Franchising Since: 1995 - No. of Units: Company Owned: 1 - Franchised: 205 - Franchise Fee: $15,500 - Royalty: 5% - Total Inv: $22,000-$28,000 (incl. fran. fee) - Financing: No.

HOMECARE AMERICA
Homecare America Holding, Inc.
5 Wellwood Ave., Farmingdale, NY, 11735. Contact: Linda Richards, Director/Marketing - Tel: (516) 454-6664, Fax: (516) 454-8572, E-Mail: lrichards@homecare.com, Web Site: www.homecareamerica.com. Healthcare products retail store, resource centers. Established: 1996 - Franchising Since: 1996 - No. of Units: Company Owned: 1 - Franchised: 17 - Franchise Fee: $100,000, $30,000 conversion - Royalty: 8% yrs. 1-3 , 6% yrs 4-5, 5% thereafter - Total Inv: $730,000-$1,370,000 - Financing: Yes.

JOANNE'S BED & BACK SHOPS
Joanne's Bed & Back Stores, Inc
564 Sunnyside Ave, Beltsville, MD, 20705, IN. Contact: "Skip" Schatz, CEO - Tel: (301) 220-4256, (888) SOS-BACK (767-2225), Fax: (301) 513-5774, E-Mail: joannesbednback@mindspring.com, Web Site: www.backfriendly.com. Specialty retail stores selling products for (1) back and neck pain relief and (2) good - sleep. Shops offer over 1000 back friendly products for office, home, car/ travel that give proper support yet are stylish and affordable. Established: 1989 - Franchising Since: 1996 - No. of Units: Company Owned: 11 - Franchised: 2 - Franchise Fee: $10,000 - Royalty: 2% 1st $2,000, 3% $2,000,000-$10,000,000, 2% over $10,000,000 - Total Inv: $267,200-$377,3000 - Financing: No.

JOSLIN DIABETES AFFILIATED CENTERS
Joslin Diabetes Center, Inc.
One Joslin Place, Boston, MA, 02215. - Tel: (617) 732-2666, Fax: (617) 732-2562. Works with leading health care facilities to establish regional diabetes treatment centers of excellence that annually, on average, achieve significant growth, improved health outcomes, and attract payors. Established: 1898 - Franchising Since: 1987 - No. of Units: Company Owned: 7 - Franchised: 17 - Franchise Fee: Negotiable - Royalty: Negotiable - Total Inv: Proprietary.

LOTUSEA WELLNESS GROUP
Lotusea Franchising Group, Inc.
150 View Bend, Johnson City, TN, 37601. Contact: Sandra Breeding - Tel: (423) 915-0852, (800) 914-2598, Fax: (423) 282-1489, E-Mail: Lotusea@hotmail.com, Web Site: www.Lotusea.com. We offer a corporate wellness program dedicated to reducing the cost of health care and enabling more people to make informed decisions regarding health care. Our company offers a solution rather than a bandaid to employers. Our goals for a company are to increase the quality and length of lives of people. The result is the incrase in the quality and length of lives of companies. Established: 1990 - Franchising Since: 2000 - No. of Units: Company Owned: 1 - Franchised: 6 - Franchise Fee: $35,000 - Royalty: 8% for first $10,000; 7.5% for the second $10,000; and 7% thereafter (monthly) - Total Inv: $98,000 - Financing: No.

MASSAGE ENVY *
4835 E. Cactus Rd., #260, Scottsdale, AZ, 85254. Contact: Franchise Department - Tel: (602) 889-1090, Fax: (602) 889-1086, Web Site: www.massageenvy.com. Membership pricing in echange for on-going monthly membership fee. Established: 2001 - Franchising Since: 2003 - No. of Units: Franchised: 12 - Franchise Fee: $29,000-$39,000 - Royalty: 5% - Total Inv: $145,200-$234,500 - Financing: No.

MEDICAP PHARMACY
Medicap Pharmacies Inc.
4350 Westown Parkway, Suite 400, West Des Moines, IA, 50266-1061. Contact: Calvin C. James, V.P. Fran. Dev. - Tel: (515) 224-8400, (800) 445-2244, Fax: (515) 224-8494, E-Mail: cjames@medicaprx.com, Web Site: www.medicap.com. Professional apothecary-styled pharmacy franchise specializing in prescriptions, pharmacy care initiatives and healthcare-related items. Established: 1971 - Franchising Since: 1974 - No. of Units: Company Owned: 12 - Franchised: 174 - Franchise Fee: New store = $15,000; Conversion = $8,500 - Royalty: New store 3.9% plus 1% national marketing fund - Total Inv: Approx $94,000 - Financing: Assistance.

MEDIPOWER
P.O. Box 335, San Marcos, TX, 78667. - Tel: (830) 629-1400, Fax: (512) 353-5333. Offering unique patented toothbrush for retail sales. Total Inv: $200 Approx .

MILLICARE ENVIRONMENTAL SERVICES
201 Lukken Industrial Dr. W, La Orange, CA, 30240. Contact: Pete Franetovich, Franchise Development - Tel: (706) 880-3377, Fax: (706) 880-3279, E-Mail: pete_franetovich@millicare.com, Web Site: www.millicare.com. Our system includes a variety of services provided to commercial facility managers including carpet maintenance, carpet installation, carpet recycling, panel and upholstery cleaning and entryway systems. Initial headquarters training, technical, sales training etc. Established: 1986 - Franchised: 70 - Total Inv: $77,775-$166,900.

MIRACLE-EAR HEARING SYSTEMS
Dahlberg, Inc
4101 Dahlberg Drive, Golden Valley, MN, 55422. Contact: Franchise Department - Tel: (612) 520-9749, (800) 234-7714, Fax: (612) 520-9520, E-Mail: miracle-ear.com. Manufacturing and retailer of hearing systems with 1500 + offices nationally and 20+ master franchises in foreign countries. Established: 1948 - Franchising Since: 1984 - No. of Units: Company Owned: 162 - Franchise Fee: $28,000 + - Royalty: 47/aid - Total Inv: $82,825-$223,625 - Financing: No.

MOTHER'S HELPMATES FRANCHISING, INC
4320 Fincastle Ct, Tampa, FL, 33624-5418. Contact: Cora H. Thomas - Tel: (813) 681-5183, (800) 221-5183, Fax: (813) 681-5176. In home child care and also elderly care. Established: 1983 - Franchising Since: 1997 - No. of Units: Company Owned: 1 - Franchise Fee: $7,500 - $20,000 - Financing: Yes.

NATIONAL SCREENING ASSOCIATES
Medical Screening Foundation
3680 North Abbey, Fresno, CA, 93726. - Tel: (909) 699-4027. National screening associates provides medical painless non invasive screening tests for osteoporosis, cholesterol, peripheral artorial disease and stroke. Mobile testing with locations convient to our customers, complete training and support, no need to be a doctor, immediate revenue and high

return. Established: 1997 - Franchising Since: 1997 - No. of Units: Company Owned: 1 - Franchised: 2 - Franchise Fee: $50,000 - Royalty: 12% - Total Inv: $125,000 - Financing: Yes.

NATIONAL TUB SAFETY
SPR International Inc.
4492 Acworth IndustrialDrive, #102, Acworth, GA, 30101. Contact: Sandy Stevens, Sales - Tel: (800) 476-9271, Fax: (770) 975-4647, E-Mail: anomia@netzero.com, Web Site: www.oak.org. Safety tub mats for all types of tubs. White, almond, clear, all sizes available. Established: 1973 - Franchising Since: 1999 - No. of Units: Franchised: 60 - Franchise Fee: $2,000 - Total Inv: $2,000 - Financing: No.

NATURE'S SOAP DISH, INC
P.O. Box 1625, Riverview, FL, 33568. - Tel: (813) 672-8571, Fax: (813) 354-3428, E-Mail: info@naturessoapdish.com, Web Site: www.naturessoapdish.com. Franchise retailer of high quality bath, body and spa products that help people feel good and relaxed at a reasonable price. Established: 2000 - Franchising Since: 2002 - No. of Units: Franchised: 500 - Franchise Fee: $25,000 - Total Inv: $70,000.

NU-BEST® DIAGNOSTIC LABS
VF-Works, Inc®
4159 A Corporate Court, Palm Harbor, FL, 34683. Contact: Sales & Franchise Rep - Tel: (727) 942-8324, (800) 839-6757, Fax: (727) 943-7198, E-Mail: nubest@mindsprings.com, Web Site: www.vf-works.com. We offer DMX™ (Dynamic Motion X-ray®) as a complete turn-key, business opportunity. This is a medical lab sold as a complete mobile clinic and can travel from office to office or city to city. This mobile opportunity known as NU-BEST® diagnostic labs is a growing health care franchise in the country. Franchise opportunity comes complete with a protected territory, national advertising and intensive training in protocols, marketing, billing and collection. Established: 1991 - Franchising Since: 1996 - No. of Units: Company Owned: 1 - Franchised: 24 - Franchise Fee: $25,000 - Royalty: $500.00 or 5% of collections which ever is greater - Total Inv: Avr= $200,000 (mobile lab $132,000, franchise $25,000, operations $43,000) - Financing: Leasing available 5 year term.

NU-CONCEPT BODY WRAP, INC.
603 Cleveland St., Elyria, OH, 44035. Contact: Dennis Doman, Vice President - Tel: (216) 365-7378. Inch loss, cellulite, centroll European style wrap and solutions. Established: 1980- Franchising Since: 1981- No. of Units: Company Owned: 1 - Franchised: 7 - Franchise Fee: $10,000 - Royalty: None - Total Inv: $10,000 - Financing: Yes. NOT FRANCHISING AT THIS TIME.

NURSEFINDERS
1701 E Lamar Blvd #200, Arlington, T X, 76006-7303. - Tel: (800) 445-0459, (817) 460-1181, Fax: (817) 462-9146, Web Site: www.nursefinders.com. National provider of temporary staffing for hospitals, nursing homes and other health care facilities. Also provide a complete range of home health care services and products. Established: 1974 - Franchising Since: 1978 - No. of Units: Company Owned: 65 - Franchised: 55 - Franchise Fee: $29,000 - Royalty: 7% - Total Inv: $123,000-$225,500 - Financing: Yes, financing for working capitals and accounts receivable.

NUTRITIONARY
3635 Boardman Canfield Rd, Canfield, OH, 44406. Contact: David Mihalik - Tel: (866) 882-8470, Fax: (330) 702-3778, E-Mail: dmihalik@nutritionary.com, Web Site: www.nutritionary.com. Nutritionary is a retail kiosk offering upscale supplements for weight loss, energy, body-building and anti-aging. Established: 1979 - Franchising Since: 2001 - No. of Units: Company Owned: 22 - Franchised: 2 - Franchise Fee: $25,000 - Total Inv: Capital requirements; $90,000-$150,000 - Financing: Yes.

ON-SITE HEALTH & SAFETY PROFESSIONALS (OHSP)
OHS Health & Safety Services, Inc.
1500 Quail St., Fifth Floor, Newport Beach, CA, 92660. - Tel: (714) 263-5928, (800) 456-4647, Fax: (714) 852-1020, E-Mail: edpoole@ohsinc.com, Web Site: www.ohsinc.com. OHSP business owners arrange for medical, drug-testing, health and safety services to be performed for other companies. Since OHSP business owners simply "arrange" for

such services, medical experience is not necessary. Established: 1991 - Franchising Since: 1995 - No. of Units: Company Owned: 1 - Franchised: 64 - Franchise Fee: $18,700 - Royalty: None - Total Inv: $18,700 plus minimum of 3 months personal living expenses - Financing: With excellent credit.

OPTION CARE
Option Care, Inc.
485 Half Day Road #300, Buffalo Grove, IL, 60089. Contact: Franchise Department - Tel: (800) 879-6137, Fax: (847) 913-89763. Home I.V. and nutritional services. Established: 1979 - Franchising Since: 1984 - No. of Units: Company Owned: 20 - Franchised: 160 - Franchise Fee: $2,500-$35,000 - Royalty: 9% $1 M, 7% $2M, 5% over $2M per year.

ORIGINAL HERB CO ., THE
2960 Shallowford Rd Suite 110, Marietta, GA, 30066. Contact: Bart Rene, President - Tel: (404) 261-4372, (888) 357-4372, Fax: (770) 579-0609. Retail of herbs, vitamins, minerals, homeopathics and other nutritional suppliments. Locations available in malls "strip-centers" nationwide. Established: 1993 - Franchising since: 1993 - No. of Units: Company Owned: 1 - Franchised: 122 - Total Inv: $10,000 and up - Financing: Yes.

PAIN PHYSICIANS OF AMERICA
P.O. Box 4384, Portsmouth, NH, 03802-4384. Contact: Robert Tortorello, Dir. of Franchising - Tel: (603) 431-5900, Fax: (603) 431-5900, E-Mail: franchise@franchise2000.com, Web Site: www.painmd.com. The ultimate in pain management in a unique surgicenter facility. Full training and support. Need not be an MD to own this business. Established: 1992 - Franchising Since: 1999 - No. of Units: Company Owned: 3 - Franchise Fee: $40,000 - Royalty: 5% of gross, 4%-6% advertising - Total Inv: $107,000-$134,000 - Financing: Yes third party.

PASSPORT HEALTH
Passport Health, Inc
845 E. Fort Ave, Baltimore, MD, 21230. Contact: Peter Savage, V.P - Tel: (410) 727-0556, (888) 499-7277, Fax: (410) 727-0696, E-Mail: fran@passporthealthusa.com, Web Site: www.passporthealthusa.com. Travel medicine clinic where international travelers get vaccinations and counseling for international traveling. Established: 1996 - Franchising Since: 1996 - No. of Units: Company Owned: 1 - Franchised: 44 - Franchise Fee: $25,000-$50,000 - Royalty: 7% - Total Inv: $70,000-$100,000 - Financing: No.

PEAK PERFORMERS
Peak Performers Franchise Corp.
34020 W. Seven Mile, #102, Livonia, MI, 48152. Contact: Franchise Development - Tel: (248) 477-5777, Fax: (248) 477-7032. Dentistry's first on call human resource dept. Temporary and contract staffing, direct placement, temp-hire consulting, personnel manual services exclusively for dentistry. Established: 1991 - Franchising Since: 1994 - No. of Units: Company Owned: 2 - Franchised: 1 - Franchise Fee: $22,500 - Royalty: 6% gross rev., 1% adv. - Total Inv: $60,000-$100,000 - Financing: N/A.

RAINSTAR MASSAGE THERAPY CENTERS
Edward Companies
P.O. Box 7495, Phoenix, AZ, 85011-7495. Contact: Edward R. Richards, CEO - Tel: (602) 279-3315, (888) RAIN-STAR, E-Mail: franchiseinfo@rainstargroup.com, Web Site: www.rainstaruniversity.com. Full-service massage therapy center. Established: 1994 - Franchising Since: 1997/98 - No. of Units: Company Owned: 1 - Franchise Fee: $22,500 - Royalty: 5% & 5% - Total Inv: $45,000-$95,000 - Financing: None, possible SBA.

RELAX THE BACK STORE
Relax the Back Corp.
10350 Heritage Park Dr Ste 202, Santa Fe Springs, CA, 90670-7313. - Tel: (800) 290-2225. Specialty retail stores offering products for relief and prevention of back pain and discomfort. Established: 1988 - Franchising Since: 1989 - No. of Units: Company Owned: 8 - Franchised: 71+ - Franchise Fee: $25,000 - Royalty: 4%, 1% adv. - Total Inv: $126,100-$239,100 - Financing: No.

RESPECT YOUR ELDERS
Respect Your Elders, Inc
2351 Sunset Blvd #170-133, Rocklin, CA, 95765-4338. - Tel: (916) 363-7200, (800) 994-0043, Fax: (916) 363-9305. Elderly housing placement referral service. Established: 1994 - Franchising Since: 1997 - No. of Units: Company Owned: 1 - Franchised: 2 - Franchise Fee: $12,500 - Royalty: 6% of gross income - Total Inv: $24,000-$49,000 - Financing: Outside financing.

RESPOND FIRST AID SYSTEMS
P.O. Box 1809, Wheat Ridge, CO, 80034-1809. Contact: Gary Green, General Manager - Tel: (303) 371-6800, Fax: (800) 453-0198. Selling first aid cabinets and supplies, safety equipment and emergency care training classes to the industrial and office markets. Operating from customized, fully-stocked vans. Established: 1984 - Distributing Since: 1984 - No. of Units: 58 - Total Inv: $35,000 - Financing: No.

RIGHT AT HOME
Right at Home Inc
2939 S. 120th St, Omaha, NE, 68144. Contact: Ron Schuller, Director of Sales - Tel: (402) 697-7537, (877) 697-7537, Fax: (402) 697-7536, E-Mail: info@rightathome.net, Web Site: www.rightathome.net. Right at Home is one of the most exciting concepts in franchising today. Right at Home serves the fast growing senior and health care industries by providing in home care and assistance for seniors and supplemental staffing for hospitals, nursing homes and other medical settings. Established: 1995 - Franchising Since: 2000 - No. of Units: Company Owned: 1 - Franchised: 44 - Franchise Fee: $16,500 - Royalty: 5% - Total Inv: $28,000-$64,000 - Financing: No.

RIGHT WAY BY POLLY, THE
The Right Way by Polly Inc
416 New London Rd., Newark, DE, 19711. - Tel: (302) 454-1970. A business designed to augment a physician or chiropractor's existing practice by offering the patient lifestyle changes in addition to conventional treatment. This comprehensive program is based on nutrition, exercise and stress management giving the franchisee the opportunity to increase both services and revenues. Established: 1984 - Franchising Since: 1994 - No. of Units: Company Owned: 1 - Franchised: 2 - Franchise Fee: $37,500 - Royalty: 10% of monthly gross revenue with a min. of $200 - Total Inv: $37,500 initial fee, $1,850 initial inventory, $6,000 security deposit - Financing: Yes.

SARAAHCARE ADULT DAY SERVICES
Sarah Adult Day Services, Inc
800 Market Ave, N. Suite 1230, Canton, OH, 44702. Contact: Dr. Stanley E. Brody - Tel: (330) 454-3200, (800) 472-5544, Fax: (330) 454-6708, E-Mail: franchises@sarahcare.com, Web Site: www.sarah care.com. According to Entrepreneur Magazine, Adult Day Services is one of the top 10 hottest growing businesses. Become a part of Sarah Adult Day Services. Know the pleasure of both running a successful business and making a difference in your community. Established: 1985 - Franchising Since: 2000 - No. of Units: Company Owned: 2 - Franchised: 6 - Franchise Fee: $19,500 - Royalty: 5% - Total Inv: $170,000 - Financing: Assistance available.

SAV-MOR DRUG STORES
43155 West Nine Mile Road, Novi, MI, 48376. Contact: Gerald Katchman, Executive V.P. - Tel: (248) 348-1570, Fax: (248) 348-4316. Drug Store. Established: 1968 - Franchising Since: 1995 - No. of Units: Franchised: 73 - Franchise Fee: $1,000.00 - Royalty: Full line $420.00/mo, Apothacary $210.00/mo - Financing: No.

SERENITY COVE HEALTH & NUTRITION CENTERS
207 N. Cedar, Abilene, KS, 67410. - Tel: (785) 263-2084,. Dietary supplements, massage, etc. Established: 1995 - Franchising Since: 1995 - No. of Units: 2 - Franchised: 2 - Franchise Fee: $12,000 - Financing: No.

SHAPE UP SISTERS INC
Town Cednter W #116, St. Augustine, FL, 32092. - Tel: (904) 940-9331. Fitness boutique for women. Established: 2002 - Franchising Since: 2002 - No. of Units: Company Owned: 1 - Franchise Fee: $19,800 - Total Inv: $36,000-$47,000 - Financing: No.

SMOOTHIE KING
Smoothie King Franchises
2400 Veterans Blvd., Ste. 110, Kenner, LA, 70062. Contact: Michael Powers - Tel: (504) 467-4006, (800) 577-4200, Fax: (504) 469-1254, E-Mail: mikep@smoothieking.com, Web Site: www.smoothieking.com. Frozen nutritional fruit drinks, vitamin and protein supplements, and all the latest trends in sports nutrition. Established: 1973- Franchising Since: 1989 - No. of Units: Company Owned: 1 - Franchised: 282 - Franchise Fee: $25,000 - Royalty: 6% - Total Inv: $130,000-$200,000.

SONA LASER CENTERS, INC.
Sona International Corporation
1025 Executive Blvd., Suite 112, Chesapeake, VA, 23320. - Tel: (757) 436-0333, Fax: (757) 436-7444, E-Mail: franchise@sonalaser centers.com, Web Site: www.sonalasercenters.com. Sona offers laser hair removal, with better results and at fees that are affordable to the general public. Established: 1997 - Franchising Since: 2002 - No. of Units: Company Owned: 3 - Total Inv: $305,000-$369,000.

SPECTRUM HOME SERVICES *
SHS Franchising, LLC
7107 S. 400 West #8, Midvale, UT, 84047. Contact: Tony Nelson, President - Tel: (801) 562-5883, (800) 496-5993, Fax: (801) 255-4663, E-Mail: spectrumhomeservice.com, Web Site: www.spectrumeservice.com. Spectrum Home Services gives assistance to seniors and busy home owners by providing Personal care, Homemaking, Cleaning, Maintenance & Yard Care. Spectrum Home Services is the most unique senior care company in the industry. Our business is about caring, but it is also about providing the necessary services seniors need to stay in their home. No other non-medical in home care franchise can come close to full spectrum of services we provide. Established: 2000 - Franchising Since: 2004 - No. of Units: Company Owned: 1 - Franchise Fee: $25,000 - Royalty: 5% - Total Inv: $58,000-$99,950 (includes franchise fee) - Financing: No.

SUPERIOR SENIOR CARE
Superior Senior Care Franchises
101 N. 10th St, Ste. A, Fort Smith, AR, 72901. Contact: Timothy Taylor - Tel: (479) 783-1206, Fax: (479) 783-1232. Non-medical home care. Established: 1985 - Franchising Since: 2000 - No. of Units: Company Owned: 9 - Franchised: 2 - Franchise Fee: $15,000 - Total Inv: Min $18,771 - Financing: No.

TEXAS TEAS
Teaxas Tea Co.
P.O. Box 7101, Houston, TX, 77248. Contact: Nancy Spradley, President - Tel: (713) 683-8700, Fax: (713) 683-8796, E-Mail: RENCO2000@mail.com, Web Site: www.texasteas.com. Private label flavored herbal teas. Established: 1995 - Franchising Since: 2002 - No. of Units: Company Owned: 3 - Total Inv: Varies.

TLC LOW CARB STORES *
Totally Low Carb Stores Inc.
2620 Regetta Dr #102, Las Vegas, NV, 89128. Contact: Bruce Benson - Tel: (800) 631-2272, Fax: (702) 736-8621, E-Mail: bruce@tlcstores.com, Web Site: www.tlcstores.com. We franchise low carb stores. TLC treats which all feature low carb products. Established: 2003 - Franchising Since: 2003 - No. of Units: Franchised: 12 - Franchise Fee: $19,500 - Royalty: 3% - Total Inc: $50,000 - Financing: SBA.

UNWIND
4218 N. Surf Rd, Hollywood, FL, 33019. Contact: Tiffany Field, President - Tel: (954) 929-2876, Fax: (954) 262-3886, E-Mail: field@nsv.nova.edv. Wellness Centers, massage therapy, and movement therapies (Yoga, Tai Chi). Established: 1997 - Franchising Since: 1998 - No. of Units: Company Owned: 1 - Franchised: 3 - Franchise Fee: $5,000 - Royalty: 4%, (2% company, 1% marketing, 1% res.) - Financing: No.

VISIONS SENIOR PROGRAMS
P.O. Box 51 New Suffolk Ave, Laurel, NY, 11948. Contact: Robert Costanzo - Tel: (800) 870-5184, Fax: (631) 298-1997, Web Site: www.seniorumbrella.com. Home support program. Established: 1992 - Franchising Since: 1999 - No. of Units: Company Owned: 1 - Franchised: 9 - Total Inv: $12,900.

VISITING ANGELS LIVING ASSISTANCE SERVICES
Living Assistance Services
P.O. Box 630, Haverton, PA, 19083. Contact: Lawrence Meigs - Tel: (610) 642-4663, Fax: (610) 642-3877. Senior Care offering protected territories. Established: 1998 - Franchising Since: 1998 - No. of Units: Company Owned: 1 - Franchised: 13 - Franchise Fee: $9,950-$11,950 - Royalty: 15% - Total Inv: Upto $15,000.

VITAMIN LOGIC
Healthy Holdings
301 E 57th Ave., Ste D, Denver, CO, 80216-1352. Contact: Sales/Development - Tel: (303) 438-1600, Fax: (303) 438-0700, Web Site: www.vitaminlogic.com. Retail concept providing private label as well as name brand products. Vitamin Logic specializes in the niche market of high quality nutritional supplements. Established: 1997 - Franchising Since: 1997 - No. of Units: Company Owned: 4 - Franchised: 5 - Franchise Fee: $27,500 - Royalty: 6%+2% adv. fee - Total Inv: $67,000-$130,000 includes (FFE, RI, INV, DEPOSIT) - Financing: Financing available for franchise fee.

WESTERN MEDICAL SERVICES
220 N. Wiget Lane, Walnut Creek, CA, 94598. Contact: Bobbi George, Franchise Development - Tel: (510) 256-1561, (800) 872-8367. Full service home health and staffing agency. Established: 1967 - Franchising Since: 1975 - No. of Units: Company Owned: 30 - Franchised: 24 - Franchise Fee: $30,000-$40,000 - Total Inv: $100,00 + Fran Fee.

WHITE GLOVE PLACEMENT, INC *
We Know How, Inc.
155 Lorimer Street, Brooklyn, NY, 11206. Contact: Sarah Karper - Tel: (718) 387-6168, (866) 862-8994, Fax: (718) 387-8359, E-Mail: sarah@whiteglovecare.com, Web Site: www.whiteglovecare.com. White Glove franchises provide professional nursing personnel to hospitals and other healthcare facilities. Established: 1995 - Franchising Since: 2004 - No. of Units: Company Owned: 2 - Franchise Fee: $25,000 - Royalty: 5% - Total Inv: $89,000-$242,900 - Financing: Optional.

WOMEN'S HEALTH BOUTIQUE
Women's Health Boutique Franchise System, Inc.
12715 Telge Rd., Cypress, TX, 77429. Contact: Fran. sales consultant - Tel: (888) 280-2053, (281) 256-4100, Fax: (281) 373-4450. One stop shopping for women with special needs in a tasteful environment, attended by knowledgeable, highly trained, compassionate saleswomen. Retail products and services for post-mastectomy, compression therapy, hair loss, incontinence, pre and postnatal, skin care, wigs and turbans, personal care and post breast surgery. Established: 1988 - Franchising Since: 1993 - No. of Units: Company Owned: 4 - Franchised: 13 - Franchise Fee: $20,800 - Royalty: 4%-7% - Total Inv: $143,000-$240,600 - Financing: Third party financing.

WOODHOUSE DAY SPA *
203 E. Stayton Ave, Victoria, TX, 77901. Contact: Lamar Garrett - Tel: (361) 570-7772, Fax: (361) 578-7116, Web Site: www.woodhouse spas.com. Day spa services & retail body products. Established: 2003 - Franchising Since: 2003 - No. of Units: Company Owned: 1 - Franchised: 1 - Franchise Fee: $10,000 - Royalty: 6% - Total Inv: $153,675-$254,625.

HOME FURNISHINGS: RETAIL, SALES, RENTAL AND SERVICE

A SHADE BETTER, INC.
3615 Superior Ave., Cleveland, OH, 44114. Contact: Franchise Department - Tel: (800) 722-8676, (216) 391-5267. Distinctive retail stores selling beautiful lamp shades, lamps and accessories. Franchisees will also have the opportunity to develop and service the wholesale market in their exclusive territory. A Shade Better, Inc. has combined streamlined operating systems, efficient distribution and high profile marketing techniques. And we've put them together with support from a management team bolstered by 20 years in the industry. Established: 1989 - Franchising Since: 1994 - No. of Units: Company Owned: 9 - Franchised: 10 - Franchise Fee: $35,000 - Royalty: 6% - Total Inv: $115,500-$147,000 - Financing: No.

AFFORDABLE WINDOW COVERINGS
Affordable Window Coverings, Inc.
39075 Corte de Ollas, Murrieta, CA, 92562. Contact: Lisa Thompson, Dir. of Franchise Operations - Tel: (909) 698-1391, (800) 700-4947, Fax: (909) 677-2324, E-Mail: info@affordablewindow.com, Web Site: www.affordablewindow.com. Home-based, mobile window covering sales, specializing in at home presentations of quality, name brand manufactured blinds, drapes, shades and shutters. Established: 1995 - Franchising Since: 1998 - No. of Units: Company Owned: 1 - Franchised: 4 - Franchise Fee: $12,500 - Royalty: 4%-6% - Total Inv: $18,500-$35,000 -Financing: N/A.

AMERICA'S CARPET GALLERY
Magic Marketing, Inc.
P.O. Box 21737, Roanoke, VA, 2401. Contact: Sands Woody, Pres. - Tel: (800) 344-7557, (540) 772-1729, Fax: (540) 776-9281. Retail floor covering and home decorating stores catering to middle-to upper income households. Established: 1986 - Franchising Since: 1992 - No. of Units: Company Owned: 4 - Franchised: 12 - Franchise Fee: $15,000 - Royalty: 2% - 4% depending on sales - Total Inv: $85,000-$185,000 depending on store size and location - Financing: No.

ART SOURCE AND DESIGN
Decorative Arts, Inc.
200 E. Hill Street, Oklahoma City, OK, 73105. - Tel: (405) 524-0055, Fax: (405) 524-0066. Art Source And Design is a framed art showroom selling exclusively to "The Trade" combining over 200 framed pictures, several thousand loose prints and hundreds of frame profiles on display allows for endless design possibilities. Established: 1969 - Franchising Since: 1992 - No. of Units: Franchised: 5 - Franchise Fee: $20,000 - Royalty: 4% first year, 6% 2nd through 10th year - Total Inv: Inventory $30,000. equipment $15,000, other to $25,000 - Financing: Equipment leasing possible.

BLIND MAN OF AMERICA
Keller Corporation
606 Freemant Circle, Colorado Springs, CO, 80919. Contact: Linda Keller, Owner - Tel: (719) 260-8989, (800) 547-9889, Fax: (719) 272-4105, E-Mail: blindmanofamerica@msn.com, Web Site: www.blindman ofamerica.com. Sell custom-made blinds, shades, shutters, and more. Our home-based, mobile showroom concept makes it easy for customers to do business with us. The Blind Man's unique approach of offering both interior as well as exterior window coverings sets up apart from the competition. Not only that, but our territory sizes are normally double that of other window coverings franchises. We will teach you everything you need to know from sales to installation to office management. Established: 1991 - Franchising Since: 1996 - No. of Units: Company Owned: 1 - Franchised: 6 - Franchise Fee: $15,000 - Royalty: 4.25% - Total Inv: $26,800-$50,400 - Financing: No.

BOX OFFICE BLINDS
All American Blinds
23052 Alicia Pkwy, #H202, Mission Viejo, CA, 92692. Contact: Steven K. Dale - Tel: (949) 459-8931, Fax: (949) 364-3475. Mobile blinds, drapes and shutters. Established: 1985 - Franchising Since: 2001 - No. of Units: Company Owned: 1 - Franchise Fee: $4,995 - Financing: Yes.

BUDGET BLINDS, INC.
733 W Taft Ave, Orange, CA, 92865-4229. - Tel: (714) 637-2100, Fax: (714) 637-1400. Window coverings. Established: 1992 - Franchising Since: 1994 - No. of Units: Company Owned: 1 - Franchised: 163 - Franchise Fee: $14,950 - Royalty: 4%-5% - Total Inv: $14,950, plus van - Financing: Yes outside.

CARPET MASTER
CM Franchise Corp.
179 Christopher St., New York, NY, 10014. - Tel: (662) 299-1117. America's fastest growing carpet franchise stressing service, selection and savings. Complete training and site selection provided. If you are good with people this is great for you. Established: 1994 - Franchising Since: 1995 - No. of Units: Franchised: 12 - Franchise Fee: $25,000 - Royalty: 5% gross - Total Inv: $67,000 - Financing: Third party.

CERTA PROPAINTERS LTD.
150 Green Tree Rd., Ste. 1003, Oaks, PA, 19456. - Tel: (800) 462-3782. Painting (interior and exterior), wallpaper, decorative finishes such as rag rolling, sponge painting, polychrome products etc. Established: 1991 - Franchising Since: 1991 - No. of Units: Franchised: 35 - Franchise Fee: $25,000 - Royalty: $1,000 per month - Total Inv: $22,000; fran. fee plus $7,000 capital investment - Financing: Yes.

CLOSETS BY DESIGN
13151 South Western Avenue, Gardena, CA, 90249. Contact: Jerry Egner, President - Tel: (310) 965-2040, (800) 377-5737, Fax: (310) 527-8955, Web Site: www.closets-by-design.com. 18 years as industry leader of custom closet organizers, enterainment centers, in-home office systems and more. Huge market demand. Large exclusive territories available. Technical skills not necessary. Complete on-site training. Established: 1981 - Franchising Since: 1998 - No. of Units: Company Owned: 3 - Franchised: 13 - Franchise Fee: $19,500-$34,900 - Royalty: 6% - Total Inv: $88,000-$220,000 - Financing: Yes.

DECOR & YOU
Decor & You, Inc.
900 Main St South, Bldg. 2., Southbury, CT, 06488. - Tel: (203) 264-3500, (800) 477-3326, Fax: (203) 264-5095, E-Mail: info@decorandyou.com, Web Site: www.decorandyou.com. The industry's newest decorating franchise, featuring state-of-the-art computerized sampling, personalized services from professionally trained interior decorators who go to their clients. Regional opportunities also available. No experience needed, We provide complete training. Established: 1994 - Franchising Since: 1998 - No. of Units: Franchised: 22 - Franchise Fee: $14,500 (Inddividual); $75,000 (Regional) - Royalty: 13% (10% CSF, 3% Nat'l Ad Fund) - Total Inv: Starting at $30,000 (Individual); $105,000 (Regional) - Financing: None.

DECOR-AT-YOUR-DOOR INTERNATIONAL
P.O. Box 2290, Pollock Pines, CA, 95726. - Tel: (916) 644-6056, (800) 936-3326, Fax: (916) 644-3326. One of the best franchises in America. Blinds and carpet business, selling from a custom mobile showcase to your customers at great prices. Royalty only $100 mo. or 1%, no quotas, no renewal charge, no transfer charge. No experience necessary, we train you, great part or full time job. Established: 1983 - Franchising Since: 1995 - No. of Units: Franchised: 35 - Franchise Fee: $4,000 - Royalty: $100/mo. or 1% - Total Inv: $4,000 - Financing: No.

DOTI DESIGN STORES
DOTI Franchising, Inc
1226 W. Northwest Hwy, Palatine, IL, 60067. Contact: Jim Evanger, Franchise Dev - Tel: (847) 776-7477, (888) 382-7488, Fax: (847) 776-7459, E-Mail: info@doti.com, Web Site: www.DOTI.com. DOTI Design Stores is the worlds only upscale home furnishings and design retail franchise system. $200 billion industry with opportunity for single or multiple store development. No experience in industry is neccessary. Established: 1983 - Franchising Since: 1998 - No. of Units: Company Owned: 2 - Franchised: 4 - Franchise Fee: $24,000 - Royalty: 6% - Total Inv: $190,000-$250,000 - Financing: Third party.

EURO-WALL STYLES
Rol-A-Decor
10022 Iroquois St., Apple Valley, CA, 92308. Contact: Martin Logan, Owner - Tel: (760) 247-1900. Design wall printing (European). The wallpaper look with paint. Home decorating. Established: 1979.

FLOOR COVERINGS INTERNATIONAL
5182 Old Dixie Highway, Forest Park, GA, 30297. Contact: Karen Childers, Market Development Coordinator - Tel: (800) 955-4324, (404) 361-5047, Fax: (404) 366-4606. Floor Coverings International is a mobile floor covering retailer that brings the carpet store to the customer's front door. FCI's mobile service concept means that there are no high overhead costs. Our Carpet van is loaded with a store full of colorful, name brand styles that customers coordinate with their existing decor and lighting. Established: 1985 - Franchising Since: 1988 - No. of Units: Franchised: 330 - Franchise Fee: $16,000 - Royalty: 5%, 2% ad. fund - Total Inv: $24,000: fran. fee plus $4,500-$5,500 start up costs - Financing: Yes.

FUNCTION JUNCTION
Function Junction Enterprises, Inc.
306 Delaware, Kansas City, MO, 64105. Contact: Avery Murray, Franchise Rep. - Tel: (816) 471-6000, Fax: (816) 471-3220. Things for the home from the store you can believe in. Unique product mix of lifestyle, kitchen, and housewares. Established: 1977 - Franchising Since: 1997 - No. of Units: Company Owned: 13 - Franchise Fee: $40,000 for a new store, $30,000 for a conversion franchise - Royalty: 4% up to $500,000, 3.5% of sales over $500,000 - Total Inv: $188,200-$308,000 - Financing: No.

INTERIOR DOOR REPLACEMENT
IDRC Franchising Corp.
231 South Whisman Rd, #D, Mountain View, CA, 94041. Contact: Dave Winter - Tel: (650) 965-IDRC (4372), (866) 315-IDRC (4372), Fax: (650) 938-6879, E-Mail: franchiseinfo@idrcfranchise.com, Web Site: www.idrcfranchise.com. Low cost retrofit interior door replacement service specializing in raised panel molded doors in a variety of styles including custom painting, locksets, door knobs, handles with 1 week turnaround. Established: 1997 - Franchising Since: 2001 - No. of Units: Company Owned: 1 - Franchise Fee: $10,000 - Royalty: 6% - Total Inv: $126,500-$178,000 - Financing: Third party.

INTERIORS BY DECORATING DEN
Decorating Den Systems, Inc.
19100 Montgomery Village Ave., Montgomery Village, MD, 20886. Contact: Victoris Jenkins, Vice President of Franchise Marketing - Tel: (301) 272-1500, (800) DEC-DENS, Fax: (301) 272-1520, E-Mail: decoratingden@decoratingden.com, Web Site: www.decoratingden.com. Provides an affordable, shop-at-home full decorating service. Our owners bring thousands of samples to the customers home in our ColorVan®. Free consultation. Established: 1969 - Franchising Since: 1970 - No. of Units: Franchised: 477 - Franchise Fee: $23,900 - Royalty: 9% upto 1 million; 8% upto 2 million; 7% over 2 million - Total Inv: $23,900 and $12,0000-$15,000 for working capital - Financing: Yes.

KITCHEN WIZARDS
World Wide Cabinet Systems, Inc.
1020 North University Parks Dr., Waco, TX, 76712. - Tel: (800) 893-6777. The most exciting and fastest growing kitchen business in the world today. We make kitchens beautiful for new or remodel. We have the right solution to fit budgets from $2,000 to $40,000. New Cabinets, reface, recolor, revive and much more. Established: 1991 - Franchising Since: 1995 - No. of Units: Franchised: 25 - Franchise Fee: $12,500 per 100,000 population - Royalty: 7%-3% - Total Inv: $65,000-$300,000. NOT FRANCHISING AT THIS TIME.

MINI-BLINDS N'MORE
23052 Alicia Parkway #H202, Mission Viejo, CA, 92692. Contact: Steve Dale, Owner - Tel: (949) 459-8931, Fax: (949) 888-9942. Established: 1985 - Franchising Since: 2001 - No. of Units: Company Owned: 1 - Franchise Fee: $4995 - Royalty: $150 per month, $150 National Advertising Fee - Total Inv: $7,400-$15,000 - Financing: No.

MOUNTAIN COMFORT FURNISHINGS
Mountain Comfort Furnishings, Inc.
507 Summit Blvd., Frisco, CO, 80443. Contact: Mr. Bill Jarski, Owner - Tel: (970) 668-3661, Fax: (970) 668-5329. Home furnishings featuring solid woods such as oak and pine. Upholstered custom and specialty casual mountain contemporary. Established: 1985 - Franchising Since: 1990 - No. of Units: Company Owned: 2 - Franchised: 3 - Franchise Fee: $22,500 - Royalty: Yearly license fee $10,000, mktg. fund .5% - Total Inv: $165,955-$356,825.

NAKED FURNITURE
Summit-Naked Furniture, Inc.
P.O. Box F, 1157 Lackawanna Trail, Clarks Summit, PA, 18411. Contact: Bruce C. MacGowan, President - Tel: (570) 587-7800, (800) 352-2252, Fax: (570) 586-8587, Web Site: www.nakedfurniture.com. Home furnishings retailer featuring custom-finished and ready-to-finish real wood furniture. Established: 1972 - Franchising Since: 1976 - No. of Units: Company Owned: 2 - Franchised: 39 - Franchise Fee: $19,500 - Royalty: 4%, 0% adv. - Total Inv: $143,000-$245,000 with $75,500-$122,500 in available cash - Financing: $30,000-$40,000.

NATIONWIDE FLOOR & WINDOW COVERINGS
Nationwide Floorcovering, Inc.
111 E. Kilbourne Ave, Ste. 2400, Milwaukee, WI, 53202. - Tel: (414) 765-9900, (800) 366-8088, Fax: (414) 765-1300, Web Site: www.floorsandwindows.com. America's premier mobile floor and window coverings franchise. We provide a free shop at home service to today's time-starved consumers. We bring carpet, vinyl, hardwood, laminates, ceramic tile, area rugs, and a huge selection of name brand window treatments right to our customer's home or office. Low overhead, national account pricing, comprehensive training, an extensive product line, largest exclusive territory and our unique marketing programs are just the beginning. Established: 1992 - Franchising Since: 1995 - No. of Units: Franchised: 98 - Franchise Fee: $24,000-$39,000 - Royalty: 5%.

NORWALK - THE FURNITURE IDEA
Norwalk Furniture Corp.
100 Furniture Parkway, Norwalk, OH, 44857. Contact: Dir. of Fran. - Tel: (419) 744-3200, (800) 837-2565, Fax: (419) 744-3212, Web Site: www.norwalkfurnitureidea.com. Custom upholstered furniture specialty stores. Offers consumers choice of 2,000 fabrics and leathers available on any of 500 styles with delivery in just 35 days. Established: 1902, Franchising Since: 1987 - No. of Units: Company Owned: 15 - Franchised: 77 - Franchise Fee: $50,000 - Initial Inv: $400,000 - Financing: Third party affiliation.

ROCHE-BOBOIS U.S.A. LTD.
183 Madison Ave., New York, NY, 10016. Contact: Michael Lerner, Pres. - Tel: (212) 889-5304, Fax: (212) 779-8950. Exclusive high-fashion contemporary retail furniture. Established: 1974 - Franchising Since: 1974 - No. of Units: 27 - Franchise Fee: $20,000 - Royalty: 6% - Total Inv: $350,000-$400,000.

ROLLAWAY STORM & SECURITY SHUTTERS
1061 Oak Street, East, St. Petersburg, FL, 33716. Contact: Bill Salin, V.P. Franchise Development - Tel: (888) 765-5292, Fax: (727) 579-9410, E-Mail: commercial@roll-a-way.com, Web Site: www.roll-a-way.com. Manufacturers of PVC and Aluminum security and storm roll down shutters. Established: 1955 - Franchising Since: 1994 - No. of Units; Company Owned: 3 - Franchised: 52 - Franchise Fee: $19,605-$42,680 - Roaylty: None - Total Inv: $40,000-$80,000 - Financing: None.

SCREENMOBILE, THE
The Screenmobile Corp.
72050A Corporate Way, Thousand Palms, CA, 92276. Contact: Monty M. Walker, Vice President - Tel: (909) 394-4581, Fax: (909) 394-0273, E-Mail: mmwal@screenmobile.com, Web Site: www.sceenmobile.com. Mobile window and door screening service. Established:1980 - Franchising Since: 1984 - No. of Units: Company Owned: 1 - Franchised: 52 - Franchise Fee: $43,300 - Royalty: 5% of gross sales - Total Inv: $49,300 - Financing: No.

SLUMBERLAND INTERNATIONAL
Slumberland, Inc
3060 Centerville Rd., Little Canada, MN, 55117. Contact: Keith Freeburg, Dir. of Franchising - Tel: (651) 482-7500, (888) 482-7500, Fax: (651) 490-0479, Web Site: www.slumberland.com. Furniture, bedding and mattresses. Established: 1968 - Franchising Since: 1968 - No. of Units: Company Owned: 26 - Franchised: 42 - Franchise Fee: $15,000 - Royalty: 3% - Total Inv: Varies - Financing: No.

SMART HOUSE INC.
8410 Falls of Neuse Rd Ste F, Raleigh, NC, 27615-3536. Contact: Jack Gallagher - Tel: (919) 872-8553, Fax: (919) 790-9670. Home automation. Established: 1997 - Franchising Since: 1997 - No. of Units: Franchised: 8 - Franchise Fee: $17,500 - Total Inv: $100,250-$131,250 (includes Franchise Fee) - Financing: No.

SOFA SOLUTIONS
North 480 Willow Rd, Whetaon, IL, 60187. Contact: Marianne Barrtkowski, Vice President - Tel: (630) 588-1744, Fax: (630) 588-1754, Web Site: www.sofasolutions.com. Concept is unique in offering quality custom furniture at warehouse prices. We are a people focused organization providing consistent, concise & steady franchise

involvement. Established: 1994 - Franchising Since: 1997 - No. of Units: Company Owned: 1 - Franchised: 3 - Franchise Fee: $24,900 - Royalty: 6% - Total Inv: $100,000-$125,000.

SOLARMASTERS
1100 NW Loop 410, Ste. 700, San Antonio, TX, 78213. Contact: Michael Eakman - Tel: (210) 492-9222, (866) SOLARMASTER, Web Site: www.solarmasters.com. Own your own Awning, Shade and Shutter store. Established: 1995 - Franchising Since: 2002 - Franchise Fee: $34,000 - Financing: No.

STAINED GLASS OVERLAY
Stained Glass Overlay, Inc
1827 North Case Street, Orange, LA, 92865. Contact:Mike Cassidy - Tel: (714) 974-8124, (800) 944-4746, Fax: (714) 974-6529, E-Mail: mcassidy@stainedglassoverlay.com, Web Site: www.stainedglassoverlay.com. Proven decorative glass franchise operating in 30 countries. Work with a remarkable product product creating beautiful glass. A complete business system. Established: 1981- Franchising Since: 1982 - No. of Units: Franchised: 180 - Franchise Fee: $45,000 - Royalty: 5% - Total Inv: $90,000 - Financing: No.

TERRI'S CONSIGN & DESIGN FURNISHINGS
Consign & Design Franchise Corp
1375 W Drivers Way, Tempe, AZ, 85204-1040. Contact: Marcus Curtis, President - Tel: (480) 969-1121, (800) 455-0400, Fax: (480) 969-5052, Web Site: www.Terrisconsign.com. Consignment home furnishings retailer dealing in furnishings acquired from model homes, estates, factory liquidations, skilled craftsman and fine homes. Quality brand name furnishings, accessories, office, art and antiques. Established: 1979 - Franchising Since: 1995 - No. of Units: Company Owned: 8 - Franchised: 7 - Franchise Fee: $28,000 - Royalty: 3%, 1% advertising - Total Inv: $74,000-$170,000 - Financing: No.

U-PAINT DESIGN STUDIO
7855 E. Evans, Ste. C, Scottsdale, AZ, 85260. Contact: John Hall, VP - Tel: (480) 483-2194, Fax: (480) 922-7283. Painting Pottery. Customers enjoy unique experience in painting pottery. Pottery, paint and included in price of pottery. Custom paint at the store in great store environment. Established: 1998 - Franchising Since: 1999 - No. of Units: Company Owned: 1 - Franchise Fee: $17,500 - Royalty: 5% - Total Inv: $75,000-$125,000 - Financing: No.

UNIVERSITY PAINTERS
JZA Development Corp.
P.O. Box 549, Alexandria, VA, 22314. Contact: Josh Jablon, Pres. - Tel: (703) 836-8000. Franchisor of residential house painting franchises. Franchises are owned primarily by college student business owners for a one to three year period. Established: 1990 - Franchising Since: 1991 - No. of Units: Franchised: 90 - Franchise Fee: Varies - Royalty: Varies - Total Inv: Under $2,000 - Financing: Yes.

V2K THE VIRTUAL WINDOW FASHION STORE
1127 Auraria Pkwy, #204, Denver, CO, 80204. Contact: Victor Yosha, President - Tel: (30) 202-1120, Fax: (303) 202-5201, Web Site: www.v2k.com. V2K can go to a customer's home an d on a lap top display the custmoer's walls and windows so the customer can see their windows. Established: 1997 - Franchising Since: 1997 - No. of Units: Franchised: 80 - Franchise Fee: $34,500 - Royalty: 8-6.5% - Total Inv: $$40,000-$50,000.

VERLO® MATTRESS FACTORY STORES
Verlo®Mattress Factory Stores, LLC
W3130 State Road 59, Whitewater, WI, 53190. Contact: James M. Young, V.P. of Franchising - Tel: 262) 473-8957 ext 104, (800) 229-8957, Fax: (262) 473-4623, E-Mail: franchise@verlo.com, Web Site: www.verlofranchise.com. 44-year-old manufacturer direct to consumers (retail opportunity). Verlo Mattress Factory Stores is the nation's largest Craftsman Direct mattress/bedding retailer, offering consumers personalized, handcrafted bedding at a substantail cost savings. Established: 1958 - Franchising Since: 1986- No. of Units: Company Owned: 7 - Franchised: 64 - Franchise Fee: $30,000 trdaitional model; $22,500 Chicago retail-only model - Royalty: 5% - Total Inv: $178,000 traditional model; $83,500 chicago model - Financing: SBA approved third party only.

WALL-AH! BY WALLPAPER DEPOT
D.W. Wallcovering
9300 Shelbyville Rd. Ste. 709, Louisville, KY, 40222. Contact: David Owen - Tel: (502) 412-4361, (800) USA-WALL, Fax: (502) 412-6622. Retail wall covering specialty store. Established: 1989 - Franchising Since: 1999 - No. of Units: Company Owned: 4 - Franchised: 5 - Franchise Fee: $15,000 - Total Inv: $49,000-$108,000.

WALLPAPERS TO GO
Wallpapers To Go, Inc.
P.O. Box 340698, Austin, TX, 78743-0012. - Tel: (800) 843-7094, (972) 503-8616, Fax: (972)644-2441. Large national chain of in-stock wallcoverings, special order wallcoverings, window treatments, fabrics, paint supplies and decorative accessories. Stores designed, stocked and merchandised to appeal to growing do-it-yourself market. Established: 1986 - Franchising Since: 1986 - No. of Units: Company Owned: 16 - Franchised: 56 - Franchise Fee: $15,000 - Royalty: 8% - Total Inv: $139,000-$194,000 - Financing: Assistance in securing financing.

WINDOW PERFECT
Window Dressing International Inc.
5 Dunwoody Park #110, Atlanta, GA, 30338. Contact: Franchise Dev. - Tel: (770) 723-9991. Home based window covering sales, providing customers with shop at home convenience, high quality products and life time service. Established: 1995 - Franchising Since: 1996 - No. of Units: Franchised: 3 - Franchise Fee: $15,000 - Royalty: 3% - Total Inv: $20,000 - Financing: Yes.

WINDOW & WALL CREATIONS
Home Services
2000, 1016 E Brittany Creations, Highlands Ranch, CO, 80126-3024. Contact: Nat'l Marketing Director - Tel: (303) 741-5073, (800) 461-5180, Fax: (303) 741-9710, E-Mail: infodesk@windowandwallcreations.com, Web Site: www.windowandwallcreations.com. Interior decorating service shop at home. Custom window treatments bedroom access, wall paper, area rugs. Established: 1996 - Franchising Since: 1996 - No. of Units: Franchised: 20 - Franchise Fee: $7,900 - Royalty: 9% reduces to 6% , 2% nat, 2% local - Total Inv: $2,000-$3,000 - Financing: No. NOT FRANCHISING AT THIS TIME.

WINDOW WORKS
Window Worls International, Inc.
3601 Minnesota Dr Suite 800, Edina, MN, 55435. Contact: Scott Thompson, President - Tel: (952) 943-4353, Fax: (952) 921-5801, E-Mail: info@windowworks.net, Web Site: www.windowworks.net. Retail showrooms specializing in custom made draperies, blinds, shades and shutters. Offering complimentary shop at home appointments. Training and support as well as exclusive software. Established: 1978 - Franchising Since: 1979 - No. of Units: Franchised: 5 - Franchise Fee: $30,000 - Royalty: 4% continuing, 1% adv. - Total Inv: $44,000-$84,000 - Financing: No.

YESTERDAY'S FURNITURE AND COUNTRY STORE, INC
2000 S. 7Hwy, Blue Springs, MO, 64014. Contact: Chris Belcher, President - Tel: (816) 228-7227, (888) 228-0800, Fax: (816) 229-1233. Furniture and country store. Established: 1993 - Franchising Since: 1997 - No. of Units: Company Owned: 1 - Franchised: 1 - Franchise Fee: $27,500.00 - Royalty: 5% - Total Inv: $150,000-$175,000 - Financing: No.

HOME INSPECTION

ALLSTATE HOME INSPECTION AND HOUSEHOLD ENVIRONMENTAL TESTING. LTD
Allstate Home Inspection and Environmental Testing Ltd.
2907 N. Randolph Rd., Randolph Center, VT, 05061. Contact: Executive Assistant - Tel: (800) 245-9932, Fax: (802) 728-5534, E-Mail: karen@allstatehomeinspection.com, Web Site: www.allstatehomeinspection.com. We are a recognized world leader and innovator in the home inspection and environmental testing industries. With the most comprehensive service offerings in the industry, it's AHI's mission to help homeowners around the country achieve the level of safety, security

and peace of mind that they deserve. Established: 1984 - No. of Units: Company Onwed: 1 - Franchised: 15 - Franchise Fee: $23,900 - Royalty: 7.5% - Total Inv: $28,000-$47,000 - Financing: Yes.

BRICKKICKER, THE
Ronlen Enterprises, Inc.
849 N Ellsworth St, Naperville, IL, 60563-3150. Contact: Ron Ewald, Pres. - Tel: (800) 821-1820, Fax: (630) 420-2270, Web Site: www.brickkicker.com. Home and building inspections. Established: 1989 - Franchising Since: 1995 - No. of Units: Company Owned: 20 - Franchised: 117 - Franchise Fee: $7,500-$25,000 - Royalty: 6% - Total Inv: From $13,950-$52,100 - Financing: 50% of fran. fee.

HOUSE PRO INSPECTIONS®
1406 E. 14th St, Des Moines, IA, 50316-2406. Contact: Dane J. Shearer, Pres. - Tel: (515) 265-6667, (800) 288-7437, Fax: (515) 278-2070. Home, commercials and environmental inspections. Established: 1998 - Franchising Since: 1998 - No. of Units: Company Owned: 1 - Franchise Fee: $9,800 - Royalty: 6% + 2% adv Co-op - Total Inv: $15,000 = fran fee. $9,800 + capital reg $5,200 - Financing: Yes.

NATIONAL PROPERTY INSPECTIONS, INC.
11620 Arbor St., Ste. 100, Omaha, NE, 68144. Contact: Julie Erickson, Dir. of franchise sales - Tel: (800) 333-9807, (402) 333-9807, Fax: (800) 933-2508, Web Site: www.npiweb.com. Franchisor of home inspection business in U.S. and Canada. Franchise includes exclusive territory, 2 weeks training, hand held computer, equipment and apparel. Established 1987 - Franchising Since: 1987 - No. of Units: Franchised: 130 - Franchise Fee: $21,800 - Royalty: 8% - Total Inv: $25,000 with working capial - Financing: SBA/home equity most popular.

HORTICULTURAL

FOLIAGE DESIGN SYSTEMS
Foliage Design Systems Franchise Co.
4496 35th St., Orlando, FL, 32811. Contact: John S. Hagood, Chairman/Founder - Tel: (800) 933-7351, (407) 245-7776, Fax: (407) 245-7533, Web Site: www.foliagedesign.com. Interior plant design, installation and maintenance; sale and lease programs and short-term rentals. Established: 1971 - Franchising Since: 1980 - No. of Units: Company Owned: 3 - Franchised: 45 - Franchise Fee: $20,000-$100,000 - Royalty: 6% - Total Initial Inv: $35,000-$150,000 - Financing: No.

JIM'S GREENERY
Interium Landscape Management Corp.
28 West Elm St., Townsend, MA, 01474. Contact: Jim Gerry, Owner - Tel: (978) 343-6000, (800) 249-7600, (978) 597-3060, E-Mail: www.jgreenery@net1plus, Web Site: www.interiorplants.com. Interior plant design and maintenance of tropical plants. Established: 1986 - Franchising Since: 1994 - No. of Units: Company Owned: 2 - Franchised: 1 - Franchise Fee: $15,000 - Royalty: 5% - Total Inv: $35,000-$40,000 - Financing: No.

MR. PLANT
Mr. Plant Inc.
1106 2nd Street, Encinitas, CA, 92024. Contact: Larry McCarthy, Vice President - Tel: (760) 944-0438, (800) 974-0488, Fax: (760) 295-5629, E-Mail: mcplant@adnc.com, Web Site: www.mrplant.com. Interior indoor plants, sales, leasing and service maintenance for commercial & residential. Office buildings, restaurants, hotels, hospitals, airports, malls, model homes , etc. Established: 1980 - Franchising Since: 1990 - No. of Units: Company Owned: 2 - Franchised: 33 - Franchise Fee: $14,950 - Royalty: 4% - Total Inv: $20,000 - Financing: No.

PARKER INTERIOR PLANTSCAPE
1325 Terrill Rd, Scotch Plains, NJ, 07076. Contact: Rich Parker, President - Tel: (908) 322-5552, (800) 526-3672, Fax: (908) 322-4818, E-Mail: rich@parkerplants.com, Web Site: www.parkerplants.com. Interior plantscaping. Established: 1948 - Franchising Since: 1995 - No. of Units: Company Owned: 2 - Franchised: 3 - Franchise Fee: $35,000 - Total Inv: $35,000 - Financing: No.

HOUSE/PET SITTING SERVICES

CRITTER CARE OF AMERICA
1519 Kirkwood Ave., Nashville, TN, 37212. Contact: Stan Bumgarner, Pres.- Tel: (800)256-3014, Web Site: www.crittercare.com. Professional in-home pet care service, plant and homecare. Product sales home-based. Offering the franchisees the service of a professional public relations firm, franchise management software, and area development agreements. Established: 1980 - Franchising Since: 1984 - No. of Units: Company Owned: 2 - Franchised: 18 - Franchise Fee: $15,000 - Royalty: 6% - Total Inv: $25,000-$30,000 - Financing: No.

FETCH! PET CARE INC
701 Grizzly Peak Blvd, Berkley, CA, 94708. - Tel: (510) 527-6420, Fax: (510) 525-4054, Web Site: www.fetchpetcare.com. Pet-sitting and dog walking services. Establishe: 2002 - Franchising Since: 2003 - No. of Units: Company Owned: 1 - Franchise Fee: $3,000-$8,000 - Royalty: 5% - Total Inv: $13,500-$30,000 - Financing: No.

HOMEWATCH
Homewatch International
2865 S. Colorado Blvd., Ste. 203, Denver, CO, 80222. Contact: Paul Sauer, Pres. - Tel: (303) 758-7290 or (800) 777-9770, Fax: (303) 758-1724, Web Site: www.Homewatch-Intl.com. Over 25% of the population is over 55 years of age and this market is rapidly growing. The elderly and recuperating often need supervising and assistance with personal services to remain in their own home where they are happiest. We provide personal care services to the aging, convalescing, recuperating, rehabilitating population in their homes. These services are non-medical, private pay care and companionship services. This is a rewarding and compassionate franchise opportunity. Established: 1973 - Franchising Since: 1986 - No. of Units: Company Owned: 1 - Franchised: 12 - Franchise Fee: $13,500-$25,000 determined by area - Royalty: 5% - Total Inv: $50,000 - Reserve of $20,000 + franchise fee - Financing: Yes to multiple units.

PET NANNY®
Pet Nanny of America, Inc.
310 North Clippert, Suite 5, Lansing, MI, 48912. Contact: Rebecca Brevitz, Pres. - Tel: (517) 336-8622, Fax: (517) 336-8624. Professional in-home pet care service. Established: 1987 - Franchising Since: 1987 - No. of Units: Franchised: 22 - Franchise Fee: $2,500 - Royalty: 5% - Financing: $1,000 down, $1,500 financed by franchisor.

PET-TENDERS®
Pet-Tenders® International, Inc.
P.O. Box 23622, San Diego, CA, 92193. Contact: Cheryl Dagostaro, Pres.- Tel: (619) 298-3033. In-home pet/housesitting service. Established: 1983 - Franchising Since: 1990 - No. of Units: Company Owned: 1 - Franchised: 4 - Franchise Fee: $8,500 - Royalty: 5%, 2% adv.- Total Inv: $10,500-$13,900 - Financing: Qualified applicants.

PETS ARE INN
Pets Are Inn, Inc.
7723 Tanglewood Court #150, Minneapolis, MN, 55439. - Tel: (248) 557-2784. Pet boarding, pets that are "a part of the family" are our customers. The pets' personality is matched to an appropriate host family. Pets Are Inn arranges for round trip pickup and delivery. The worry and fear of our customer's concern for their pet is taken care of. Established: 1982 - Franchising Since: 1992 - No. of Units: Franchised: 17 - Franchise Fee: $15,000 - Royalty: 5%-10% - Total Inv: $20,000-$25,000 - Financing: Yes.

SITTERS UNLIMITED
25381-G Alicia Parkway, #215, Laguna Hills, CA, 92653. Contact: Sharon Gastel, Owner - Tel: (949) 643-8148, Fax: (949) 448-5946. Childcare, elderly companion care, home and pet care services on both a temporary and permanent basis. Convention services available. Established: 1979 - Franchising Since: 1983 - No. of Units: Company Owned: 1 - Franchised: 10 - Franchise Fee: $8,000-$15,000 - Royalty: 5%-4% - Total Inv: $8,000-$15,000 + work. cap. - Financing: Yes.

JEWELRY

ACCESSORIES FOR HER
P.O. Box 2302, Brandon, FL, 33509-2302. Contact: Bill Henry, Consultant - Tel: (954) 214-0338. We offer earrings and other jewelry accessories at unbelievable savings. Our 216 earring displays are exceptionally profitable in retail stores. For those interested in an accessory boutique - 500 to 1,000 sq. ft. is required and all inventory is guaranteed to sell. Established:1975 - Total Inv: $4,950 plus.

AMERICAN NAME-JEWELRY
Lasting Impressions, Inc.
P.O. Box 22065-Dept. FA, Lake Buena Vista, FL, 32830. Postal inquiries only. Easy to make custom-made bead jewelry. Unlimited market with profits to 1000%. No special jewelry training needed. Free color catalog and details available. Established:1991 - Distributing Since: 1991 - No. of Units: Company Owned: 1 - Distributed: 100+ - Royalty: N/A - Total Inv: $299 for complete starter kit - Financing: Visa, MC, Amex, Optima, C.O.D.

B. ROBERTS & CO. - FACTORY DIRECT JEWELERS
Premier Treasures Holdings, LLC
915 Broadway., Suite 1607, New York, NY, 10010. Contact: Robert Schwartz, Executive Office - Tel: (212) 995-0522, Fax: (212) 995-9130, Web Site: www.broberts.com. Factory direct jewelry outlet store, offering fine jewelry (including diamonds, gemstones, gold and watches) at savings of up to 70% off traditional retail prices. Established: 1998 - Franchising Since: 1999 - No. of Units: Company Owned: 2 - Management Service Fee: $35,000 plus licensing fee: $50,000 - Royalty: 10% - Total Inv: $400,000-$500,000 - Financing: No.

FAST-FIX JEWELRY REPAIRS ®
Jewelry Repair Enterprises, Inc
1750 N. Florida Mango Rd., Ste. 103, West Palm Beach, FL, 33433. Contact: V.P. Franchise Development - Tel: (561) 478-5292, (800) 359-0407, Web Site: www.fastfix.com. Jewelry and watch repairs in the mall while you watch or shop. Established: 1984 - Franchising Since: 1987 - No. of Units: Franchised: 98 - Franchise Fee: $25,000 - Royalty: 5% on gross sales - Total Inv: $95,000-$150,000 - Financing: Third party.

GOLD BY THE INCH
The Gold Factory
100 Corporate Drive - Dept 23, Yonkers, NY, 10701. Contact: Phil Ross, VP - Tel: (914) 376-8700, (888) 442-8800, Fax: (914) 376-7580, E-Mail: TheGoldFactory.com, Web Site: www.Thegoldfactory.com. Gold by the inch is a unique method of making custom jewelry in seconds. The 14 kt gold layered chain comes in a variety of popular styles. The chain comes in an attractive display. There is also a full line of gold layered bracelets and rings. Franchise Fee: $199.00 & up - Total Inv: $199.00 & up.

HANNOUSH JEWELERS
Hannoush Franchise Corp.
134 Capital Drive, West Springfield, MA, 01089. - Tel: (413) 846-4640, Fax: (413) 788-7588, Web Site: www.hannoush.com. Offers stores for the retail sale of diamonds, gold jewelry, giftware, watches and related merchandise and products. Established: 1980 - Franchising Since: 1995 - No. of Units: Company Owned: 33 - Franchised: 8 - Franchise Fee: $20,000 - Royalty: 4%, 2.5% adv. - Total Inv: $290,000 ($100,000 liquid cash needed) - Financing: No.

HI FASHION JEWELRY
1743 Deer Park Avenue, Deer Park, NY, 11729. Contact: Bruce Kravis - Tel: (631) 582-1508, Fax: (631) 582-1508. Manufacturing and selling of 10kt gold diamond jewelry. Established: 1978 - Franchising Since: 1999 - No. of Units: Company Owned: 1 - Franchised: 1 - Franchise Fee: $150 - Total Inv: $150.

JEWELRY DIRECT INTERNATIONAL
399 North Main ., Suite 333D, Logan, UT, 84321. Contact: Richard Ballam, President - Tel: (435) 753-5619, (800) 563-4339, Fax: (801) 753-5619, E-Mail: orders@jewelry-direct.com, Web Site: www.jewelry-direct.com. Our marketing strategy is to dispute the typical 300% retail jewelry markup and sell a superior product at less than 50% markup through non-traditional overhead structure. Established: 1994 -

Franchising Since: 1994 - No. of Units: Franchised: 45 - Franchise Fee: $8,900 - Total Inv: $8,900 fee, $1,299 for tools. $10,199 total - Financing: Yes.

JEWELRY KLEER & SEE KLEER
Color Seal Inc
P.O. Box 2302, Brandon, FL, 33509-2302. Contact: Bill Bonneau - Tel: (813) 643-0320, (888) 801-0333, Fax: (813) 689-7522. Jewelry and eye glass cleaner. Established: 2000 - Franchising Since: 2001 - No. of Units: Franchised: 33 - Total Inv: Dealer = $1,657 - Distributor = $7,000 - Financing: Yes.

JEWELRY-BY-THE-INCH
Lasting Impressions, Inc.
962 Northlake Blvd #160, Lake Park, FL, 33403. - Tel: (561) 333-8087, Fax: (561) 753-5443. Gold-layered chains made into custom jewelry including neck, wrist, waist and ankle chains. Also, crystal by-the-inch, rainbows, charms, etc. Free details and color catalogue available. Established: 1980 - Distributing Since: 1980 - No. of Units: Company Owned: 1 - Distributed: 1200+ - Total Inv: $399 - Financing: Visa, M.C., Amex. or ship C.O.D.

MAGIC RICE, INC
P.O. Box 592457, Orlando, FL, 32859. Contact: Adnan M. Aksu, Owner - Tel: (407) 370-9074, (800) 376-8791, Fax: (407) 888-4447, E-Mail: aol@magicrice.com, Web Site: www.magicrice.com. Personalized rice jewelry. Established: 1994 - Franchising Since:1996 - No. of Units: Company Owned: 10 - Franchised: 67 - Total Inv: $500-$1000 - Financing: N/A.

PRECIOUS ART JEWELERS
6015 University Ave #4, Cedar Falls, IA, 50613-5239. - Tel: (319) 277-0717, Fax: (319)277-0717. Fine gold, diamond and colored gemstone jewelry complete from lease, const., training and start up. Multi-option contracts from 0% no royalty, hire as consultant basis or standard royalty relationship, inline mall or kiosk or free standing locations. Established: 1988 - Franchising Since: 1990 - No. of Units: Company Owned: 1 - Franchised: 1 - Franchise Fee: $35,000-$55,000 - Royalty: 6% - Total Inv: Variable inventory from $75,000-$350,000 - Financing: Yes.

PRIMAL URGE
Primal Franchise Corp.
28 W. Bridge St, New Hope, PA, 18938. Contact: Ron Rotatori - Tel: (215) 862-3242. Body jewelry, piercing. Established: 1993 - Franchising Since: 1998 - No. of Units: Company Owned: 1 - Franchised: 3 - Franchise Fee: $15,000 - Total Inv: $59,900-$104,000 - Financing: Yes.

QUICKSILVER INTERNATIONAL, INC.
618 State Street, P.O. 2118, Bristol, TN, 37621-2118. Contact: Bill King - Tel: (423) 652-2677, Fax: (423) 764-0234. Cleaning system for silver, jewelry, etc. Established: 1927 - Franchising Since: 2000 - No. of Units: Company Owned: 1 - Franchise Fee: Less than $1000 - Financing: N/A.

THE WATCH DEPOT
The Watch Depot
7762 E. Gary Rd, Scottsdale, AZ, 85260. Contact: T. Hackett, National Marketing Director - Tel: (480) 922-7795, Fax: (480) 951-5761, E-Mail: tomh@watchdepot.com, Web Site: www.watchdepot.com. Watch Depot offers luxury and fine watches in retail market at a discount with optional diamond accessories and repair services. Established: 1990 - Franchising Since: 2002 - No. of Units: Company Owned: 5 - Franchise Fee: $48,000 - Royalty: Optional - Total Inv: $235,000 - Financing: Not at this time.

LAUNDRY & DRY CLEANING

AWC COMMERCIAL WINDOW COVERINGS
AWC Commercial Window Coverings, Inc.
825 W. Williamson Way, Fullerton, CA, 92832. Contact: Lee Daniels, President - Tel: (714) 879-3880, (800) 252-2280, Fax: (714) 879-8419. Mobile non-toxic drapery dry cleaning services provided on location for commercial customers; as well as sales, installation and repairs of all types of window coverings at competitive prices through centralized buying. Nation-wide accounts will be serviced by the franchisees as they

are established. Utilizing the customer base, references and reputation of the franchisor, developed over the past 35 years makes this an exceptional opportunity with endless possibilities and immediate credibility. Established: 1963 - Franchising Since: 1992 - No. of Units: Company Owned: 4 - Franchised: 10 - Distribution: U.S.A. 10 - Franchise Fee: $25,000 - Royalty: 5%-12.5%, 2.5% adv. - Total Inv: $112,520-$181,350 (Equity capital required: $25,000-$50,000) - Financing: Yes, third party.

CHAMPION CLEANERS
Champion Cleaners Franchise, Inc.
2305 Hickory Valley Rd, Suite 1A, Chattanooga, TN, 37421. Contact: Lew Waddey - Tel: (423) 296-1150, (800) 357-0797, Fax: (423) 296-1170, Web Site: www.championcleaners.com. Champion Cleaners is an upscale drycleaning and laundry establishment that is dedicated to a customer driven focus. The company displays this by providing customers with same day service, drive through service, alterations, VIP bags and all work is done on premises. Established: 1994 - Franchising Since: 1996 - No. of Units: Company Owned: 2 - Franchised: 25 - Franchise Fee: $25,000 - Royalty: 2% of gross sales - Total Inv: $450,000-$470,000 - Financing: Third Party.

CLEAN N' PRESS AMERICA
Vallejo Corporation
500 Airport Blvd., Ste. 100, Burlingame, CA, 94010. Contact: Alan Block, Pres. - Tel: (650) 344-2377, Fax: (650) 344-2545. Multiple outlet dry cleaning, "professional dry cleaning for less". Established: 1985 - Franchising Since: 1987 - No. of Units: Franchised: 38 - Franchise Fee: $35,000 - Royalty: 5% - Total Inv: $330,000-$390,000 - Financng: Third party.

COMET CLEANERS
Jack Godfrey & Sons
406 West Division Street, Arlington, TX, 76011. Contact: Jack Godfrey, Jr - Tel: (817) 461-3555, Fax: (817) 861-4779, E-Mail: info@cometcleaners.com, Web Site: www.cometcleaners.com. Comets are uniquely designed to provide dry cleaning, fast service & com.petitive prices. We offer a basic, comprehensive dry cleaning and laundry plant at minimal cost without expensive frills. A complete turnkey operation including site evaluation, market analysis, floor plan design & layout. Established: 1957 - Franchising Since: 1967 - No. of Units: Company Owned: 12 - Franchised: 340 - Franchise Fee: $25,000 - Royalty: 0 - Total Inv: $250,000 + - Financing: Third party.

DRY CLEANING STATION
8301 Golden Valley Rd., #240, Golden Valley, MN, 55427-4410. Contact: John Campbell, C.E.O. - Tel: (763) 541-0832. Discount dry cleaning stores located in high drive-by traffic locations in medium to larger cities. Full franchising services available. Established: 1987 - Franchising Since: 1990 - No. of Units: Company Owned: 3 - Franchised: 21- Franchise Fee: $22,500 - Royalty: 5% if own one store, 4%-3%-2% for multiple stores - Total Inv: $40,000-$250,000 - Financing: Up to $250,000 SBA or lease financing.

DRY CLEANING TO-YOUR-DOOR FRANCHISE CORPORATION
4491 N.W. Hidden Lake Loop, Waldport, OR, 97394. - Tel: (800) 318-1800, Fax: (541) 563-6938. Residential free pick-up and next day delivery dry cleaning service. Established: 1994 - Franchising Since: 1995 - No. of Units: Franchised: 41 - Franchise Fee: $15,500 includes all supplies - Royalty: 3.5% gross/1% national advertising - Total Inv: $15,500 plus van - Financing: No.

DRYCLEAN USA
Dryclean USA Inc.
290 NE 68th St, Miami, FL, 33138. Contact: Mr. Jaime Remond, Director of Operations - Tel: (305) 754-9966, (800) 746-4583, Fax: (305) 754-8010, Web Site: www.drycleanusa.com. DRYCLEAN USA is one of the largest, most respected and recognizable names in the drycleaning industry. Over 400 stores world wide. This is a turn key business. Training on, emp, operations, sales, marketing and technical. $25,000 license fees for plants with royalties of $5,000 per year, with no %. $12,500 license fee for drop stores with royalties of $2,500 per year with no %. Established: 1977 - Franchising Since: 1978 - No. of Units:

Franchised: 450 - Franchise Fee: $25,000 for plants and $12,500 for drop stores - Royalty: $5,000 per year for plants and $2,500 per year for drop stores - Total Inv: $78,300-$445,000 - Financing: Yes.

EAGLE CLEANERS
Great American Cleaners Inc.
1500 University Dr., Ste. 208, Coral Springs, FL, 33071. Contact: V.P. Fran. Dev.- Tel: (954) 346-9501, Fax: (954) 346-9505.Drycleaning and laundry using state of the art, EPA approved equipment and stylish designs in an industry with history of high profitability...training, field operations and marketing support...turnkey. Established: 1991 - Franchising Since: 1993 - No. of Units: Company Owned: 1 - Franchised: 66 - Franchise Fee: $19,000 - Royalty: Sliding scale up to 5% - Total Inv: $164,500-$306,000 - Financing: Yes.

EVERCLEAN LAUNDRY CENTERS
Dept. E.C., Block B, P.O. Box 24, Fayetteville, AR, 72702. Contact: Henry Nwauwa, Licensing Dir. - Tel: (501) 443-6791, Fax: (501) 443-4024. Self-service laundry centers with optional dry cleaning and entertainment center. Complete floor design and equipment selection. Established: 1987 - Franchising Since: 1997 - Franchise Fee: $15,000 - Royalty: None - Total Inv: $150,000-$1,000,000 - Financing: Yes, equipment lease financing. Training Equipment set-up and assistance provided.

HANGERS CLEANERS
Micell Technologies
7516 Precision Dr, Raleigh, NC, 27617. Contact: Jamie Flora, Franchise Development Coor - Tel: (919) 313-2102, (877) 642-3551, Fax: (919) 313-2103, E-Mail: www.hangersdrycleaners.com, Web Site: www.micell.com. Hangers Cleaners is an environmentally friendly, consumer-oriented franchise utilizing carbon dioxide. Established: 1996 - Franchising Since: 1998 - No. of Units: Company Owned: 1 - Franchised: 17 - Franchise Fee: $25,000 - Royalty: 5% of gross sales or revenues.

HARVEY WASHBANGERS®
Harvey Washbangers® Franchise Corporation
P.O. Box 50582, Nashville, TN, 37205. Contact: Postal only. A high tech blend of laundry, restaurant and bar facilities. Award-winning menu and friendly atmosphere make a comfortable, neighborhood place that people come back to again and again. Established: 1986 - Franchising Since: 1994 - No. of Units: Company Owned: 1 - Franchised: 4 - Franchise Fee: $20,000 - Royalty: 5% of gross sales, 2% adv. - Total Inv: Equip. $210,000; Leasehold Inv. $123,000; Working cap. $120,600 - Financing: Third party leasing avail. on laundry equip.

HIS & HERS IRONING SERVICE
Mairs, Inc.
P.O. Box 480066, Kansas City, MO, 64148-0066. Contact: Kenneth Mairs, V.P. - Tel: (913) 814-9000. Ironing and laundry featuring pick-up and delivery. Serving commercial and residential customers. Established: 1983 - Franchising Since: 1985 - No. of Units: Company Owned: 1 - Franchised: 1 - Franchise Fee: $10,000 - Royalty: 5% + 2% adv. - Total Inv: Additional $10,000-$25,000 start-up capital - Financing: No.

LAPELS
962 Washington St, Hanover, MA, 02339. - Tel: (866) 695-2735, Fax: (781) 829-9546, Web Site: www.mylapels.com. Dry cleaning services. Established: 2000 - Franchising Since: 2001 - No. of Units: Franchised: 11 - Franchise Fee: $20,000 - Royalty: 5% - Total Inv: $66,200.

LAUNDROMAX
Laundromax Franchising Company
201 West Sunrise Blvd., Ste. 200, Fort Lauderdale, FL, 33311. Contact: Gloria Chabot, Director Of Franchise Sales - Tel: (954) 764-1400, (800) 600-0015, Fax: (954) 764-2202. Full laundry service. Established: 1997 - Franchising Since: 1999 - No. of Units: Company Owned: 38 - Franchised: 4 - Franchise Fee: $25,000 - Total Inv: $100,000.

LUCY'S LAUNDRYMART
LaundryMart, Inc
3812 Sepulveda Blvd., Suite 510, Torrance, CA, 90505. Contact: Robert Levin, Dir. of Franchising - Tel: (310) 378-2620, (877) GO-LUCYS, Fax: (310) 378-6264, E-Mail: laundryMart@earthlink.com, Web Site:

www. lucyslaundrymart.com. Lucy's is the predominant laundromat operator and convenience services provider. Established: 1993 - Franchising Since: 1999 - No. of Units: Company Owned: 6 - Franchise Fee: $30,000 - Royalty: 6% - Total Inv: $100,000-$150,000 (start-up), total $450,000-$500,000.

MARTINIZING DRY CLEANING
Martin Franchises Inc.
422 Wards Corner Road, Loveland, OH, 45140. Contact: Jerald Laesser - Tel: (513) 699-4252, (800) 827-0345, Fax: (513) 731-0818, E-Mail: cleanup@martinizing.com, Web Site: www.martinizing.com Complete training program, no experience needed. Site selection and financing assistance. On-going marketing and operations support. Established: 1949 - Franchising Since: 1949 - No. of Units: Franchised: 667 - Franchise Fee: $30,000 - Royalty: 4% - Total Inv: $220,000-$305,000 - Financing: Assistance.

MAYTAG HOMESTYLE LAUNDRIES
Amerivend Corp.
4101 S.W. 73rd. Ave., Miami, FL, 33155. - Tel: (954)704-4920, Fax: (954) 704-7850, E-Mail: Rgeronimo@macgray.com, Web Site: www.mac-gray.com. Maytag Homestyle Laundry stores built over 1000. Selling in 26 states -North + South America and the Carribbean. Selling to exporters, seeking associates and distributors too. Established: 1927 - Franchising Since: 1960 - No. of Units: Franchised: Over 1,000 - Franchise Fee: None - Royalty: None - Total Inv: $30,000-$500,000 - Financing: Yes in the USA.

NU-LOOK 1HR CLEANERS
NLF, Inc.
5970 SW 18th St, #331, Boca Raton, FL, 33433-7197. Contact: Karl Dickey, President/CEO - Tel: (561) 362-4190, (800) 413-7881, Fax: (561) 362-4229, E-Mail: marketing@nu-look.com, Web Site: www.nulookcleaners.com. Retail dry cleaners seek franchisees and area developers.. Established: 1967 - Franchising Since: 1967 - No. of Units: Franchised: 47 - Franchise Fee: $20,000 initial - Royalty: 5% - Total Inv: $200,000-$1 million - Financing: Third party.

ONE PRICE DRY CLEANERS
One Price Concepts, Inc.
1943 University Dr, Coral Springs, FL, 33071. Contact: Irv Rosenblatt, V.P. - Tel: (954) 575-3960, (877) 788-1405, Fax: (954) 575-3965 Professional dry cleaning using the very latest 6th generation EPA approved equipment. Any garment dry cleaned for $1.99. High volume due to One Price Concept. No experience necessary. Full and complete training program, location and site assistance, turnkey operation, grand opening package and in-store training. Established: 1985 - Franchising Since: 1985 - No. of Units: Company Owned: 6 - Franchised: 94 - License Fee: $5,000 - Total Inv: $199,900-$297,900 - Financing: Up to 75% financing available.

PREMIER ONE LOW PRICE CLEANERS
Premier One Price Dry Cleaner, Inc
4822 N University Dr, Sunrise, FL, 33351-4509. Contact: Michael Gorman - Tel: (954) 748-8383, (800) 800-5919, Fax: (954) 748-8382. Dry cleaning and laundry service. Established: 1995 - Franchising Since: 1997 - No. of Units: Company Owned: 1 - Franchised: 2 - Franchise Fee: $9,950, Capital requirements = $60,000 + cash; $212,380-$229,200 total incl. working capital.

PRESSED 4 TIME
Pressed 4 Time, Inc.
124 Boston Post Rd., Sudbury, MA, 01176. Contact: Randy Erb, Director of Franchising - Tel: (800) 423-8711, (978) 443-9200, Fax: (978) 443-0709, E-Mail: franchiseinfo@pressed4time.com. Web Site: www.pressed4time.com. Dry cleaning laundry & shoe repair pick-up & delivery service, catering to the consumer at home or office. Established: 1987 - Franchising Since: 1990 - No. of Units: Franchised: 125 - Franchise Fee: $17,500 - Royalty: 6% - Total Inv: $15,100-$23,000 - Financing: None.

SILVER HANGER CLEANERS
Silver Hanger Systems, Inc
8638 Phillips Hwy Ste #3, Jacksonville, FL, 32256. Contact: Michael Donziger, President - Tel: (904) 367-8620, (800) 779-6503, Fax: (904) 367-8856, E-Mail: silhang@concentric.net. Turnkey drycleaning plants. Established: 1993 - Franchising Since: 1993 - No. of Units: Company Owned: 53 - Total Inv: $150,000 complete turnkey - Financing: SBA.

SUNDAY BEST
Centrix Group
P.O. Box 697169, Boston, MA, 02269. - Tel: (617) 984-0405. Dry cleaning, and/or laundromats. Established: 1991 - Franchising Since: 1995 - No. of Units: Company Owned: 1 - Franchised: 9 - Franchise Fee: Included in package - Total Inv: Packages range from $135,000-$195,000 - Financing: Yes.

SUPREME USA CLEANERS
Suprema USA Cleaners, Inc
2300 W. Sample Road, Suite-106, Pompano Beach, FL, 33073. Contact: George Esquivel, President - Tel: (954) 978-0099, (800) SUPREMA, Fax: (954) 974-0726, E-Mail:supreme-USA-cleanera@wordnet.att.net, Web Site:www.supreme-usa.com. International developers of dry cleaning and laundry plants. Equipment distributors. Established: 1991 - No. of Units: Franchised: 180 - Total Inv: $109,900. Down payment $19,900 - Financing: $90,000-$100,000 financing for quality individuals.

VALET EXPRESS
Valet Express Franchising Inc.
10151 University Blvd., Ste. 224, Orlando, FL, 32817. Contact: Darrell New, Pres. - Tel: (407) 316-0277. Executive drycleaning delivery service, catering to professionals at home and at work. Customers receive computerized monthly billing service, personal liaison service, and a 100% satisfaction guarantee on all work, all at no additional charges. Established: 1988 - Franchising Since: 1993 - No. of Units: Company Owned: 2 - Franchised: 18 - Franchise Fee: $7,500 - Royalty: $120 per month - Total Inv: $5,000-$7,000 plus fran. fee - Financing: None.

LAWN & GARDEN CARE

EMERALD GREEN LAWN CARE
E. G. Systems, Inc.
14111 Scottslawn Rd., Marysville, OH, 43040-9506. Contact: Jim Miller, V.P. Fran. Dev. - Tel: (800) 334-7336. As a result of a unique licensing agreement, Emerald Green, with Scotts as its partner, is capitalizing on the multi-billion dollar green industry. The dynamic combination of Emerald Green's experienced support staff and the strongest brand name in the business - Scotts, is the foundation for America's premier lawn care company. Established: 1984 - Franchising Since: 1984 - No. of Units: Company Owned: 5 - Franchised: 27 - Franchise Fee: $18,000 - Royalty: 6.5% to 8.5% - Total Inv: $49,000-$84,800 - Financing: Franchise fees and inventory. NOT FRANCHISING AT THIS TIME.

JIM'S MOWING
210 Lerk Lane, Aulass, TX, 76051. - Tel: (817) 684-0192, (888) 900-JIMS, Web Site: www.jimsint.com. Complete lawn and garden care services. Calls taken and dispatched via regional offices, allowing same day service. This full office support includes initial and ongoing training, all advertising. Established: 1982 - Franchising Since: 1989 - No. of Units: Company Owned: 2 - Franchised: 1200 - Franchise Fee: $8,000 - Royalty: Variable: average 4-9% royalty plus 2.1% advertising - Total Inv: $7-12,000 - Financing: Yes.

LADYBUG ORGANICS
LadyBug Organics, L.L.C.
P.O. Box 5404, Tyler, TX, 75712. Contact: Jolene Rogers - Tel: (903) 593-3158, (903) 593-6158, Fax: (903) 535-9919. Organic specialty store and lawn service. Established: 1999 - Franchising Since: 1999 - No. of Units: Company Owned: 1 - Franchise Fee: $5,000 - Total Inv: $250,000.

LANDSCAPERS SUPPLY FRANCHISE CORP.
Landscapers Supply
750 Chestnut Ridge Road, Spring Valley, NY, 10977. Contact: Robert B. Mytalka - Tel: (845) 356-8300, (800) 222-4303, Fax: (845) 356-8593, E-Mail: rbm@landscapersupply.com, Web Site: www.landscaper supply.com. The Landscapers Supply Corp. concept provides an opportunity that will give everyone from commercial contractors to home garden enthusiasts the quality equipment and supplies they need, when they need it - all at affordable prices. as a franchisee, you'll be on the front line of the vast gardening industry, offering topnotch products, tools and supplies - with a rock solid reputation of quality, dependability and value. Established: 1985 - Franchising Since: 2000 - No. of Units: Company Owned: 8 - Franchise Fee: $25,000 - Royalty: Yes - Total Inv: $65,000 - Financing: Yes.

LAWN DOCTOR
Lawn Doctor, Inc.
142 State Route 34, Holmdel, NJ, 07733. Contact: Edward L. Reid - Tel: (732) 946-0029, (800) 631-5660, Fax: (732) 946-9089, E-Mail: edreid@lawndoctor.com, Web Site: www.lawndoctor.com. Lawn Doctor is a leader in the lawn, tree & shrub care industry. Lawn Doctor designs and manufactures patented, state-of-the-art equipment, which provide nutrients landscapes need to maintain peek health and appearance. Established: 1967 - Franchising Since: 1967 - No. of Units: Franchised: 430 - Franchise Fee: None - Royalty: 10% - Total Inv: $27,500 - Financing: 50% available for qualified applicants.

LAWNTAMERS
LawnTamers Franchising, Inc
2644 W. Barrow Dr, Chandler, AZ, 85224. Contact: C. L. Jackson - Tel: (602) 919-4896, (602) 527-5227, Web Site: www.lawntamers.com. LawnTamers is a high quality weekly and bi-weekly lawn and landscape maintenance company, operating 52 weeks a year. Training and support provided. Established: 1988 - Franchising Since: 1999 - No. of Units: Company Owned: 1 - Franchised: 1 - Franchise Fee: $14,000 - Total Inv: $31,000-$39,000.

LIQUI-GREEN LAWN CARE CORP.
9601 North Allen Rd., Peoria, IL, 61615. Contact: C.M. Dailey, Dir. - Tel: (309) 243-5211, Fax: (309) 243-5247. Lawn and tree care. Established: 1953 - Franchising Since: 1971 - No. of Units: Company Owned: 1 - Franchised: 25 - Franchise Fee: $5,000 - Royalty: $6,000 annually - Total Inv: Option 1 $20,900 - Option 2 $23,900 - Financing: Lease for qualified buyers.

LIVING GREEN
P.O. Box 1579, Cottonwood, CA, 96022-1579. Contact: Frank Bramante, Pres. - Tel: (530) 347-4300, Web Site: www.elmago.com. Hydroponic growing systems and supplies. Specialty nutrients. Established: 1977 - Franchising Since: 1985 - No. of Units: Company Owned: 30 - Franchised: 65 - Total Inv: $12,500-$25,000 - Financing: Yes. Direct Distributing.

NATURALAWN OF AMERICA
1 E Church St, Frederick, MD, 21701-5444. Contact: Randy Loeb, V.P. Franchise Development- Tel: (301) 694-5440, (800) 989-5444, Fax: (301) 846-0320, E-Mail: franchise@nl-amer.com, Web Site: www.nl-amer.com. NaturaLawn of America is the only nation wide natural, organic-based lawn care franchise opportunity offering a safer and healthier alternative to harsh chemicals and pesticides. Established: 1987 - Franchising Since: 1989 - No. of Units: Company Owned: 3 - Franchised: 71 - Franchise Fee: $29,500 - Royalty: 7-9% - Total Inv: Varies.

NITRO-GREEN PROFESSIONAL LAWN & TREE CARE
All Green Corporation
99 Weatherstone Dr #920, Woodstock, GA, 30188. Contact: Randy Caldararo, Dir. Fran. Dev. - Tel: (678) 494-5000, (888) 233-0734, Fax: (770) 928-1074, E-Mail: nitrogreen@mindspring.com, Web Site: www.nitrogreen.com. Professional lawn and tree care services. Established: 1977 - Franchising Since: 1977 - No. of Units: Company Owned: 16 - Franchised: 40 - Franchise Fee: $19,500 - Royalty: 8.5%-7% based on annual revenues - Total Inv: $50,000-$19,500 initial fee $30,000 for startup - Financing: Possible.

OUTDOOR LIGHTING PERSPECTIVES FRANCHISE INC.
1122 Industrial Dr., Ste. 103, Matthews, NC, 28105. Contact: Thomas Fenig - Tel: (704) 849-8808, (877) 898-8808, Fax: (704) 841-1822, E-Mail: outdoorlights@mindspring.com, Web Site: www.outdoor lights.com. Design and installation of landscape lighting. Established: 1995 - Franchising Since: 1998 - No. of Units: Company Owned: 1 - Franchised: 38 - Franchise Fee: $35,000-$130,000 - Financing: No.

SCOTTS LAWN SERVICE
The Scotts Company
14111 Scottslawn Rd., Marysville, OH, 43041. Contact: Rick Gruber, Dir. of Franchising - Tel: (937) 644-7297, (800) 221-1760, ext. 7297, Fax: (937) 644-7422, E-Mail: jim.miller@scotts.com, Web Site: www.scotts.com. Lawn and landscape fertilization and pest management using high quality, well known, Scotts products. Strong brand recognition and powerful marketing programs drive an excellent return on investment. Established: 1998 - Franchising Since: 1998 - No. of Units; Company Owned: 70 - Franchised: 75 - Franchise Fee: $30,000-$250,000 - Royalty: 10%-6% - Total Inv: $85,700-$405,900 - Financing: Yes, franchise fee.

SHARP-N-LUBE
Ray Enterprises Inc.
3245 St., Route 589, Cass Town, OH, 45312. Contact: Stan Ray, President - Tel: (800) 842-2782. Mobile lawn equipment service co. - we come to you! Full training and support provided. Established: 1989 - Franchising Since: 1993 - No. of Units: Company Owned: 1 - Franchsied: 4 - Franchise Fee: $7,900 - Total Inv: $17,900.

SOS MOLE TRAPERS
5309 Palisades Dr, Cincinnati, OH, 45238. Contact: Craig A. Stevens - Tel: (513) 922-4419, (513) 922-2922, Fax: (503) 210-7831. Residential & commercial mole trapping service. Established: 1996 - Franchising Since: 2001 - No. of Units: Franchised: 2 - Franchise Fee: $5,000 - Total Inv: Capital requirements' $21,000-$76,000 - Financing: No.

SPRING-GREEN LAWN CARE
Spring-Green Lawn Care Corp.
11909 Spaulding School Dr., Plainfield, IL, 60544. - Tel: (800) 435-4051, E-Mail: nancysg@ix.netcom.com, Web Site: www.spring-green.com. 25 years experience offering professional lawn and tree care services. Established: 1977 - Franchising Since: 1977 - No. of Units: Company Owned: 25 - Franchised: 99 - Franchise Fee: $21,900 - Royalty: Low of 6% - Total Inv: $84,000 - Financing: Yes.

SUPERLAWNS
Super Industries, Inc.
P.O. Box 5677, Rockville, MD, 20855. - Fax: (301) 990-6202. Profitable concept of lawn care performed with automated equipment, seeding, aerating, fertilizing, etc. No mowing, low overhead and low labor costs. Renewal factor of 70% or better and excellent annual growth for this recession proof business. Established: 1976 - Franchising Since: 1976 - No. of Units: Company Owned: 2 - Franchised: 21 - Franchise Fee: $17,500 - Royalty: 10% first $150,000 annually, then 5% - Total Inv: $62,000 - Financing: Assistance.

TERRA SYSTEMS
Terra Systems Franchise Corp.
1714 Orr Industrial Ct, Charlotte, NC, 28213-6300. Contact: Kevin G. Robke, Owner - Tel: (704) 597-5800, Fax: (704) 597-0840. Provide natural organic turf and shrub care, concentrating on the unique approach of integrated pest management. Established: 1991 - Franchising Since: 1994 - No. of Units: Company Owned: 1- Franchised: 1 - Franchise Fee: $22,000 - Royalty: 5% of the gross - Total Inv: $45,000-$60,000 including franchise fee - Financing: No.

TREE FACTORY
5639 Brookshire Blvd., Charlotte, NC, 28216. Contact: Lewis Lavine, CEO - Tel: (704) 399-4446, Fax: (704) 399-0140. A specialty retailer of artificial silk plants, trees, floral arrangements and other related home furnishings. The operations of the stores also include commercial service. The manufacturing company has a central design center which constantly develops new products, the individual store can provide custom arrangements, professional decorating, installation and consulting

to businesses. Established: 1987 - Franchising Since: 1993 - No. of Units: Company Owned: 2 - Licensed 2 - License Fee: $5,000 - Royalty: None - Total Inv: $40,000-$6,000 - Financing: No.

U.S. LAWNS
U.S. Lawns
4407 Vineland Rd, Suite D-15, Orlando, FL, 32811. Contact: Paul Wolbart - Tel: (407) 246-1630, (800) USLAWNS, Fax: (407) 246-1623, E-Mail: info@uslawns.com, Web Site: www.uslawns.com. Commercial landscape maintenance service. Established: 1986 - Franchising Since: 1986 - No. of Units: Franchised: 120 - Franchise Fee: $29,000 - Royalty: 4% - Total Inv: Up to $75,000 - Financing: Yes, third party.

MOTELS, HOTELS AND CAMPGROUNDS

AMERICA'S BEST INNS, INC.
1205 Skyline Dr., Marion, IL, 62959.Contact: Jim Haidet, Dir. of Franchising - Tel: (618) 997-5454, Fax: (618) 993-5974. Development and franchising of motel inns and suites. Established: 1968 - Franchising Since: 1982 - No. of Units: Company Owned: 14 - Franchised: 17 - Franchise Fee: 0-75 rooms $12,000, $75 per additional room - Royalty: 2% royalties, 1% reservation fee, 1% marketing, total = 4% of gross revenues - Total Inv: $20,000-$43,000 - Financing: N/A.

AMERICINN
AmericInn International, LLC
250 Lake Drive East, Chanhassen, MN, 55317. Contact: Jon Kennedy, Senior V.P., Mktg. & Fran. Dev - Tel: (952) 294-5000, Fax: (952) 294-5001, E-Mail: franchise@americinn.com, Web Site: www.americinn. com. The AmericInn Lodging System is one of the fastest growing upscale limited lodging chains in the world. The success and savvy growth of the AmericInn Lodging System is due to its unique product and market niche. AmericInn competes across the luxury-economy and mid-market segments. The AmericInn Lodging System is dedicated to the concept of providing the best lodging value for its guests. Established: 1984 - Franchising Since: 1984 - No. of Units: Company Owned: 6 - Franchised: 214 - Franchise Fee: $35,000 - Royalty: 5% - Financing: Referral.

BAYMONT INNS & SUITES
250 E. Wisconsin Ave., #1750, Milwaukee, WI, 53202. Contact: Gilbert S. Simon, Nat'l Director Franchise Sales & Development - Tel: (414) 905-2000, Fax: (414) 905-2496, Web Site: www.baymontinns.com. A recgonized leader in limited service hotels as an owner and franchisor. Established: 1974 - Franchising Since: 1986 - No. of Units: Company Owned: 96 - Franchised: 76 - Franchise Fee: $35,000 - Royalty: 5%, 2% mktg, 1% reservation - Total Inv: $43,000-$53,000 per room complete - Financing: Referrals.

BEST WESTERN
Best Western International, Inc.
6201 N. 24th Parkway, Phoenix, AZ, 85016. Contact: Public Relations - Tel: (602) 957-5751, Fax: (602) 957-5505. Best Western International, Inc. is the world's largest single hotel brand with more than 3,700 hotels in 75 countries throughout North America, Europe, South America, Asia, Africa, the Middle East and the South Pacific. All Best Western hotels are independently owned and operated. Established: 1946 - Franchise Fee: (Entrance fee) $32,000 for 100 rooms; $42,000 for 200 rooms - Annual Dues: $3,096 for 100 rooms - Membership Fee: $23,634 - Reservation Fee: $12,045 first year - Total Inv: Varies according to size - Financing: No.

BUDGET HOST INNS
Budget Host International
P.O. Box 14341, Arlington, TX, 76094-1341. Contact: Ray Sawyer, Pres. - Tel: (817) 861-6088, Fax: (817) 861-6089. A referral chain of affiliated independent inns, providing full chain services. Prospective affiliates must have a lodging facility either in operation or under construction. Established: 1976 - Franchising Since: 1976 - No. of Units: Franchised: 178 - Franchise Fee: $5,000 - Royalty: $75 per room per year; reservations, $40 per unit per year (approx.) - Total Inv: $9,000 and up depending on number of rooms.

CAMBRIDGE SUITES
Candlewood Hotel Company
8621 E. 21st Street N., Ste. 200, Wichita, KS, 67206. Contact: Chuck Armstrong - Tel: (316) 631-1361, (888) CANDLEWOOD, Fax: (316) 631-1333, E-Mail: bgordon@candlewoodsuites.com, Web Site: www.candlewoodsuites.com. Cambridge Suites presents an opportunity for you to build or convert your existing hotel into the newest concept in upscale lodging. Established: 1998 - Franchising Since: 1999 - No. of Units: Company Owned: 1 - Franchised: 1 - Franchise Fee: $30,000 - Royalty: 4% first 2 years, 5% thereafter - Financing: No.

CANDLEWOOD SUITES
Candlewood Hotel Company, Inc.
8621 E 21st Street N. Ste.#200, Wichita, KS, 67206. Contact: Chick Armstrong, VP-Franchise Sales - Tel: (316) 631-1361, (888) candlewood, Fax: (316) 631-1333, E-Mail: bgordon@candlewoodsuites.com, Web Site: www.candlewoodsuites.com. Candlewood Suites is a leading, national, mid-priced hotel brand delivering exceptional quality and value to business travelers and franchisees. Cambridge Suites presents an opportunity for you to build or convert your existing hotel into the newest concept in upscale lodging. Established: 1995 - Franchising Since: 1996 - No. of Units: Company Owned: 77 - Franchised: 59 - Franchise Fee: Greater of $40,000 or $400/room - Royalty: 4% RR first 24 months, 5% RR thereafter - Total Inv: $7,000,000-$10,000,000 - Financing: No.

CARLSON WAGONLIT TRAVEL ASSOCIATES
Carlson Leisure Group
P.O. Box 59159, Minneapolis, MN, 55459. Contact: Lori Langenhahn/ Lori Moreno, Start-Up Rep./Conversions Rep. - Tel: (888) 523-2200, Fax: (763) 212-2302, Web Site: resultstravel.com. Startup and conversion franchise agreements available. Preferred supplier program, national and local marketing and advertising, newsletters, brochures, assistance with commercial business development, regional meetings, participation in the Carlson Selling System, Associate Consulting Service, hotel program, 24-hour service center, centralized support services department, international rate desk, and professional development programs. Established: 1888 - Franchising Since: 1984 - No. of Units: Company Owned: 416 worldwide - Franchised: 1,388 in the US - Franchise Fee: Start-up: $34,500 - Conversion: $3,950 - Royalty: Start-up: $400 per month to $750 per month, Conversion: $0.5%-4.55% - Total Inv: Start-up: $79,985-$156,160, Conversion: $6,560-$17,735 - Financing: No.

CENDANT
1 Sylvan Way, Parsippany, NJ, 07054. Contact: Exec. V.P. Fran. Sales - Tel: (973) 496-8490, (800) 758-8999, Fax: (973)496-5360. Hotels, Inns and resorts throughout the United States. Established: 1954 - Franchising Since: 1990 - No. of Units: Franchised: 550 - Franchise Fee: $30,000 or $300 per room - Royalty: 4%, 4.5% adv./reserv. - Financing: None.

CLARION INNS
Choice Hotels International
10750 Columbia Pike, Silver Spring, MD, 20901. Contact: Steve Schultz, Executive VP of Franchise Operations - Tel: (301) 592-5000, (800) 547-0007, Fax: (301) 592-6113, Web Site: www.choicehotels.com. Choice Hotels Internationl (NYSE:CHH) franchises more than 4000 hotels, inns, all-suite hotels and resorts open and under development in 33 countries under the brand names of Comfort, Quality, Sleep, Rodeway Inn, Econo Lodge and Main Stay Suites. Established: 1941 - Franchising Since: 1941 - No. of Units: Franchised: Over 4000 in 33 countries - Franchise Fee: Varies by brand - Royalty: Varies by brand - Total Inv: Varies by brand - Financing: Choice will assist with preparing and presenting mortgage applications.

CLUB REGENT
Carlson Vacation Ownership, Inc. (CVO)
1405 Xenium Lane N., Minneapolis, MN, 55441-8254. Contact: V.P. of Operations and Development - Tel: (612) 212-2052. Multi tiered, multi brand franchiser of Carlson Hotels' brands. Established: 1998 - Franchising Since: 1998 - No. of Units: Franchised: 1 - Franchise Fee: Initial = greater of $50,000 or $150.00 per unit - Royalty: 3.5% of net interval sales, rent royalty of $5 of gross rental revenue - Financing: No.

CLUBHOUSE INNS OF AMERICA, INC.

10610 Marty St., Ste. 500, Overland Park, KS, 66212-2595. Contact: David H. Aull, Pres. - Tel: (214) 863-1000, Fax: (214) 863-1627. Very high-quality, garden style hotel with a club-like atmosphere; sized from 120-148 rooms and suites. Features full complete breakfast and cocktails. 1993 systemwide occupancy 73.9%. Established: 1984 - Franchising Since: 1984 - No. of Units: Company Owned: 11 - Franchised: 8 - Franchise Fee: $25,000 - Royalty: 4% + 1.5% - Total Inv: $6,000,000 - Financing: From financial lending institutions.

COMFORT INNS
Choice Hotels International

10750 Columbia Pike, Silver Spring, MD, 20901. Contact: Steve Schultz, Executive VP of Franchise Operations - Tel: (800) 547-0007, (301) 592-0007, Web Site: www.choicehotels.com. Choice Hotels International (NYSE:CHH) franchises more than 4000 hotels, inns, all-suites hotels and resorts open and under development in 33 countries under the brand names of Comfort, Quality, Sleep, Rodeway Inn, Econo Lodge and MainStay Suites. No. of Units: Franchised: Over 4000 in 33 countries - Franchise Fee: Varies by brand - Royalty: Varies by brand - Total Inv: Varies by brand - Financing: Choice will assist by preparing and presenting morgage applications.

CONDOTELS
Condotels International, Inc.

2000 Hwy. 17 S, N. Myrtle Beach, SC, 29582. Contact: Tom Taylor, Owner - Tel: (800) 852-6636 US; (800) 845-0631 CAN. Franchisees act as rental manager for condo owners. Operates much like a hotel franchisor except that the lodging provided is condos rather than hotel rooms. Established: 1982 - Franchising Since: 1989 - No. of Units: Franchised: 7 - Franchise Fee: $25,000-$75,000 - Royalty: 4% - Total Inv: $45,000-$193,000 - Financing: No.

COUNTRY HEARTH INN
Buckhead America

7000 Central Parkway NE, Ste. 850, Atlanta, GA, 30328. Contact: Chetan Patel, Senior Vice President - Tel: (770) 393-2662, (800) 432-7992, Fax: (770) 393-2480. E-Mail: cpatel@buckheadamerica.com, Web Site: www.countryhearth.com. Hospitality franchise company and management company. Established: 1985 - Franchising Since: 1995 - No. of Units: Company Owned: 28 - Franchised: 24 - Franchise Fee: $30,000 or $300.00 per room which ever is greater - Royalty: 4%, 1.5% marketing, 1% reservations.

COUNTRY INN VACATION VILLA
Carlson Vacation Ownership, Inc. (CVO)

1405 Xenium Lane North, Minneapolis, MN, 55441-8254. Contact: V.P. Operations and Development - Tel: (612) 212-2052, Fax: (612) 212-0235. Multi-brand franchisor of Carlson Hotels. Established: 1998 - Franchising Since: 1998 - No. of Units: Franchised: 1 - Franchise Fee: Initial greater of $50,000 or $150.00 per units - Royalty: 3% of net interval sales, rent royalty of 4% of gross rental revenue - Financing: No.

COUNTRY INNS & SUITES BY CARLSON

701 Carlson Parkway, Minneapolis, MN, 55305. Contact: Nancy Johnson, S.R V.P. Development - Tel: (763) 212-2525, (800) 477-4200, Fax: (763) 212-1338, E-Mail: njohnson@countryinns.com, Web Site: www.countryinns.com. Franchise upscale, mid-tier, limited services lodging w/o food or beverage. Established: 1987 - Franchising Since: 1987 - No. of Units: Company Owned: 4 - Franchised: 309 - Franchise Fee: $40,000 - Royalty: 4.5% of gross room revenues- Total Inv: $3,173.600-$5,480,400 - Financing: Referrals.

DAYS INNS WORLDWIDE
Days Inns Of America, Inc

1 Sylvan Way, Parsippany, NJ, 07054. Contact: Tom Bernardo, Exec. V.P. of Franchise Sales - Tel: (973) 428-9700, (800) 952-3297, Fax: (973) 496-7658, Web Site: www.daysinn.com. Days Inn founded the economy lodging segment 30 years ago and is consistently ranked as one of the world's largest franchised lodging systems. With over 1900 hotels worldwide, Days Inns targets seniors, leisure and business travelers who are looking for quality accommodations at an affordable price. Established: 1970 - Franchising Since: 1972 - No. of Units: Franchised: 1,911 - Franchise Fee: Greater of $35,000 or $350.00 per guest room - Royalty: 6.5% - Total Inv: $389,600-$6.2 million (includes franchise fee) - Financing: Yes.

DOUBLETREE HOTELS
Doubletree Hotel Systems, Inc.

9336 Civic Center Drive, Beverly Hills, CA, 90210. - Tel: (800) 222-TREE. Provides a full range of management and franchise services for individual and institutional owners of full service traditional hotels, full service all -suite hotels and limited service hotels under the Doubletree brand. Established: 1989 - Franchising Since: 1989- No. of Units: Company Managed: 142 - Franchised: 37 - Franchise Fee: $25,000-$50,000 + room costs- Royalty: 2% - year 1, 3% - year 2, 4% for remaining license term.- Total Inv: $7,000,000-$21,000,000 - Financing: No.

ECONO LODGES OF AMERICA, INC.
Choice Hotels International

10750 Columbia Pike, Silver Spring, MD, 20901. Contact: Steve Schultz, Executive VP of Franchise Operations - Tel: (301) 592-5000, (800) 547-0007, Fax: (301) 592-6113, Web Site: www.choicehotels.com. Choice Hotels International (NYSE:CHH) franchises more than 4000 hotels, inns, all-suite hotels and resorts open and under development in 33 countries under the local manes of Comfort, Quality, Clarion, Rodeway Inn, Econo Lodge and MainStay Suites. Established: 1941 - Franchising Since: 1941 - No. of Units: Franchised: Over 4000 in 33 countries - Franchise Fee: Varies by brand - Royalty: Varies by brand - Total Inv: Varies by brand - Financing: Choice will assist in preparing and presenting mortgage applications.

EMBASSY SUITES HOTELS
Promus Hotel Corp.

755 Crossover Lane, Memphis, TN, 38117. Contact: Franchise Department - Tel: (901) 374-5000, Fax: (374) 6330. Hotel chain. Established: 1983 - Franchising Since: 1984 - No. of Units: Company Owned: 55 - Franchised: 47.

FIRST INTERSTATE INNS

925 L St, Lincoln, NE, 68508-2229. Contact: Jack L. Rediger, President - Tel: (402) 434-5620, (800) 865-2378. First Interstate Inns provides a value or mid-priced lodging facility. Established: 1960 - Franchising Since: 1997 - No. of Units: Franchised: 20 - Franchise Fee: $15,000-$25,000 - Royalty: 3% plus 2% nat. adv., plus 2% reservations and mktg. - Total Inv: $600,000-$2,500,000 - Financing: Indirect.

FOUR POINTS HOTELS
Starwood Hotels & Resorts

1111 Westchester Ave, White Plains, NY, 10604. Contact: Franchise Department - Tel: (919) 640-8100, Fax: (919) 640-8310, Web Site: www.starwoodhotels.com. Franchising midscale & upscale full service. Established: 1937 - Franchising Since: 1962 - No. of Units: Company Owned: 538 - Franchised: 247.

GUESTHOUSE INN, GUEST HOTEL, GUESTHOUSE SUITES
Suburban Lodges of America, Inc

300 Galleria Parkway, Suite 1200, Atlanta, GA, 30339. - Tel: (888) 951-2100, Fax: (770) 951-0307, E-Mail: rwilson@ghicorp.com, Web Site: www.guesthouseintl.com. National brand of mid-market inns, hotels and suites with an owner-friendly license agreement. Highlights include: low flat fees, short 5-year term, a designated areas of protection and personalized franchisee support. Established: 1994 - Franchising Since: 1994 - No. of Units: Franchised: 75 - Franchise Fee: $30,000 - Royalty: $1.50 room/day * 1.75 years; Marketing: $.50 room/day 3-5 years - Total Inv: $150,000-$6,000,000 - Financing: No.

HAMPTON INN HOTELS
Promise Hotel Corp.

755 Crossover Lane, Memphis, TN, 38117. Contact: V.P., Fran. - Tel: (901) 374-5000. One of the fastest growing moderately-priced chains. Development opportunities exist with our standard prototype, our modified prototype designed for communities of 75,000 people or less, and conversions. Hampton Inn is a division of The Promus Companies Inc. Established: 1983 - Franchising Since: 1984 - No. of Units: Company Owned: 15 - Franchised: 302 - Franchise Fee: $300 per room (min. $35,000) - Royalty: 4%; Mktg./reserv. - Total Inv: $2,500,000-$7,000,000.

HILTON HOTELS

9336 Civic Center Dr., Beverly Hills, CA, 90210. Contact: Fran. Dept. - Tel: (310) 205-7696. Hotels and inns. Established: 1965 - Franchising Since: 1965 - No. of Units: Franchised: 500 - Franchise Fee: $250 1st 100 rooms, $150 per room thereafter - Royalty: 5% room sales - Total Inv: $60,000-$75,000 per room - Financing: No.

HOLIDAY PLAZA

3 Ravinia Dr., #2900, Atlanta, GA, 30346-2149. Contact: Vicki Gordon, President - Tel: (770) 604-2000, Fax: (770) 604-8588. National hotel chain. Established: 1953 - Franchising Since: 1954 - No. of Units: 1,700.

HOMEWOOD SUITES HOTELS
Promese Hotel Corp.

755 Crossover Lane, Memphis, TN, 38117. - Tel: (901) 374-5000. Chain of extended-stay, all suite hotels geared to today's business travel market. Offer guests a 100% satisfaction guarantee. Homewood Suites is a division of The Promus Companies Inc. Established: 1989 - Franchising Since: 1989 - No. of Units: Company Owned: 8 - Franchised: 16 - Franchise fee: $300 per guest suite with min. $35,000 - Royalty: 4%; mktg./reservations - Total Inv: $3,000,000-$8,000,000.

HOWARD JOHNSON FRANCHISE SYSTEMS
Hospitality Franchise Systems

339 Jefferson Rd., Parsippany, NJ, 07054. - Tel: (973) 496-8439, Fax: (973) 496-5231. Hotels, lodges, resorts and Ho Jo Inns in the U.S., Canada, and Mexico. Established: 1925 - Franchising Since: 1954 - No. of Units: Franchised: 450 - Franchise Fee: $30,000 min. or $300 per room - Royalty: 5%, 1% adv., 1.5% reserv. fee - Financing: No.

INNSUITES HOTELS
Hospitality Corporation International

1651 W. Baseline Rd., Tempe, AZ, 85283. - Tel: (602) 944-1500. Studio and 2-room suite hotels. Established: 1980 - Franchising Since: 1986 - No. of Units: Company Owned: 8 - Franchised: 6 - Franchise Fee: Zero to $15,000 - Royalty: 1.5% of gross or percent of reservations sent - Total Inv: Conversion and new - Financing: N/A.

KAMPGROUNDS OF AMERICA, INC.

P.O. Box 30558, Billings, MT, 59114-0558. - Tel: (406) 248-7444, Fax: (406) 248-7414, Web Site: www.koa.com. Campgrounds/RV resort development and support. Established: 1961 - Franchising Since: 1962 - No. of Units: Company Owned: 10 - Franchised: 566- Franchise Fee: $25,000 (New) $20,000 (conversion) - Royalty: 2% adv. + 8% royalty fee - Total Inv: $$250,000 to start development - Financing: Yes.

KNIGHTS INN, KNIGHTS COURT
Knights Franchise Systems, Inc.

1 Sylvan Way, Parsippany, NJ, 07054. Contact: Chip Ohlsson, SVP. Franchise Sales - Tel: (973) 496-5581, (800) 932-3300, Fax: (973) 496-1359, Web Site: www.knightsinn.com. Knights Franchise Systems, Inc. franchises more than 230 Knights Inn® properties in the United States and Canada. The chain's clear positioning in the limited-service, budget segment attracts value-conscious families, seniors, business travelers, construction workers and truckers. Established: 1972 - Franchising Since: 1995 - No. of Units: Franchised: 233 - Franchise Fee: $15,000 and up. Royalty: 4.5%, Total Inv: $215,000-$5.6M - Financing: Yes.

LASUITE INN & SUITES
LaSuite World Wide Inc.

P.O Box 2340, Windermere, FL, 34786-2340. - Tel: (888) LAS-UITE. Hotel Franchise. Established: 1994 - Franchising Since: 1997 - No. of Units: Company Owned: 2 - Franchise Fee: In process - Financing: No. NOT FRANCHISING AT THIS TIME.

LEES INN
Lees Inns Of America, Inc.

130 N. State St., P.O. Box 86, North Vernon, IN, 47265. Contact: Franchise Department - Tel: (812) 346-5072, Fax: (812) 346-7521. Hotel/Motel. Franchisor for partnerships or joint ventures only. Builder/developer. Franchisor is an equity investor in each franchise. Franchisor performs as general managing partner of each franchise. Established: 1985 - Franchising Since: 1987 - No. of Units: Company Owned: 17 - Franchise Fee: $35,000-$45,000 - Royalty: 7% royalty/reservation fee - Total Inv: $6,000,000 for 120 rooms - Financing: Negotiable.

MAINSTAY SUITES
Choice Hotels International

10750 Columbia Pike, Silver Spring, MD, 20901. - Tel: (301) 592-5000, (800) 547-0007, Fax: (301) 592-6113, Web Site: www.choicehotels.com. Choice Hotels International (NYSE:CHH) franchises more than 4000 hotels, inns, all-suite hotels and resorts open and under development in 33 countries under the brand names of Comfort, Quality, Clarion, Sleep, Rodeway Inn, Econo Lodge and Main Stay Suites. Established: 1996 - Franchising Since: 1996 - No. of Units: Franchised: Over 4000 in 33 countries - Franchise Fee: Varies by brand - Royalty: Varies by brand - Total Inv: Varies by brand - Financing: Choice will assist with preparing and presenting mortgage applications.

MARRIOTT CORP.

1 Marriott Dr. Dept 851.07, Washington, DC, 20058. Contact: VP Franchising - Tel: (301) 380-8735, (800) 638-8108-ext. 88735, Fax: (301) 380-1401. Franchise Residence Inn By Marriott and Townplace Suites by Marriott. Established: 1927 - Franchising Since: 1980, No. of Units: Company Owned: 2000 - Franchised: 50% - Franchise Fee: $50,000 - Royalty: 5%.

MICROTEL INN & SUITES, HAWTHORN SUITES, HAWTHORN SUITES LTD, BEST INNS & SUITES.
US Franchise Systems, Inc

13 Corporate Square, Ste. 250, Atlanta, GA, 30329. Contact: Steve Romoniello, S.V.P. Fran. - Tel: (404) 321-4045, Fax: (404) 321-4482, Web Site: www.usfsi.com. Hotel franchise with 3 concepts. 1 Microtel, all new construction budget brand, Hawthorn, an upscale suite oriented brand, and Best, an upper economy limited service brand. Established: 1995 - Franchising Since: 1995 - No. of Units: Franchised: 1200 - Franchise Fee: $35,000 - Royalty: 5-6% - Total Inv: $1.500,000-$10,000,000 - Financing: Assistance.

MOTEL 6
Accor Economy Lodging

14651 Dallas Pkwy, Ste. 500, Dallas, TX, 75254. Contact: Dean Savas, Senior VP / Franchise - Tel: (972) 702-6951, (888) 842-2942, Fax: (972) 702-3610, E-Mail: arcinfo@airmail.net, Web Site: www.motel6.com. Motel 6 has a quality product proven operational results and easy to operate. Many open markets are available. Motel 6 is a well established brand. Part of Accor North America. Established: 1962 - Franchising Since: 1996 - No. of Units: Company Owned: 688 - Franchised: 132 - Franchise Fee: $25,000 - Royalty: 4%, marketing fee 3.5% - Total Inv: $1.8 M-$2.2M.

NATIONAL 9 INNS, SUITES, MOTELS

2285 S. Main St., Salt Lake City, UT, 84115. Contact: Kevin Howell, V.P. Oper. - Tel: (801) 466-9826, Fax: (801) 466-9856. Franchising existing properties, enabling them to compete with larger franchises. Established: 1984 - Franchising Since: 1984 - No. of Units: Company Owned: 7 - Franchised: 169 - Franchise Fee: $3,500 - Royalty: $5 monthly per room - Total Inv: $3,500 F.F., $5,000 R.F., $3,500 sign - Financing: OAC.

NENDELS CORPORATION

P.O. Box 942, Lebanon, OR, 97355. Contact: V.P. Dev. - Tel: (800) 547-0106, (541) 451-1414, Fax: (541) 259-3835. Hotel inns and resorts franchise company. Established: 1934 - Franchising Since: 1986 - No. of Units: Company Owned: 35 - Franchised: 50 - Franchise Fee: $100/room ($10,000 min) - Royalty: 2% + 10 cents/room/day reservations fee + - 50 cents/room/day mktg. - Financing: No.

QUALITY INNS
Choice Hotels International

10750 Columbia Pike, Silver Spring, MD, 20901. Contact: Steve Schultz, Executive V.P. of Franchise Operations - Tel: (301) 592-5000, (800) 547-0007, Fax: (301) 592-5000, Web Site: www.choicehotels.com. Choice Hotels International (NYSE:CHH) franchises more than 4000 hotels, inns, all-suite hotels and resorts open and under development in 33 countries under the brand names of Comfort, Quality, Clarion, Rodeway Inn, Econo Lodge and Main Stay Suites. Established: 1941 - Franchising Since: 1941 - No. of Units: Franchised: Over 4000 in 33 countries - Franchise Fee: Varies by brand - Royalty: Varies by brand - Total Inv: Varies by brand - Financing: Choice will assist with preparing and presenting mortgage applications.

RADISSON HOTELS WORLDWIDE

Carlson Pky., P.O. Box 59159, Minneapolis, MN, 55459-8204. - Tel: (212) 540-5335, Fax: (212) 449-3400. Radisson Hotels International caters to the upscale business travel and leisure destination markets. Radisson offers five hotel products plazas, hotels, suites, inns and resorts. Established: 1983 - Initial Fee: $30,000 - Royalty Fee: 4% gross room sales - Adv./Mktg. Fee: 3.5% gross room sales - Reservation Fee: Included in Adv/Mktg. fees - Locations Outside of the US: Initial Fee: $200 per room with a min. of $40,000 - royalty: 4% gross room rev. - Adv./Mktg. Fees: 2.5% gross room sales - Reservation Fee: $11 per reservation booked through the Radisson system.

RADISSON VACATION VILLAS
Carlson Vacation Ownership

1405 Xenium Lane North, Minneapolis, MN, 55441-8254. Contact: V.P. of Operations and Development - Tel: (612) 212-2052. A multi-tiered, multi-brand franchisor of Carlson Hotels'. Established: 1998 - Franchising Since: 1998 - No. of Units: Franchised: 1 - Franchise Fee: Initial greater of $50,000 or $150.00 per units, Royalty: 3.5% of net interval sales, rent royalty of 4% of gross rental revenue - Financing: No.

RED CARPET INN, SCOTTISH INNS, PASSPORT INN
Hospitality International, Inc.

1726 Montreal Cir., Tucker, GA, 30084. Contact: Franchise Development Coordinator - Tel: (770) 270-1180, (800) 247-4677, Fax: (770) 270-1077, E-Mail: franchise-sale@reservahost.com, Web Site: www.reserva host.com. Franchisor of recognizable brand names which allows investors to obtain widespread exposure through marketing programs, reservation centers and group sales. Established: 1982 - Franchising Since: 1982 - No. of Units: Franchised: 239 - Franchise Fee: $10,000-$15,000 - Royalty: 3 1/2%-4% marketing 1% - reservations $300 - Total Inv: Varies by size of project - Financing: No.

RED ROOF INNS, INC
Accor Economy Lodging

14651 Dallas Parkway, Ste. 500, Dallas, TX, 75240. Contact: Dean Savas, Senior VP / Franchise - Tel: (972) 702-6951, (888) 842-2942, Fax: (972) 702-3610, E-Mail: arcinfo@airmail.net, Web Site: www.redroof.com. Red Roof has quality product proven operational results and easy to operate. Many open markets are available. Red Roof is a well established brand. Part of Accor North America. Established: 1972 - Franchising Since: 1996 - No. of Units: Company Owned: 260 - Franchised: 98 - Franchise Fee: $30,000 - Royalty: 5%; marketing fee: 4% - Total Inv: $2.6M-$3.4M.

RESIDENCE INNS, THE

1 Marriott Dr., Dept. 851.07, Washington, DC, 20058. Contact: V.P. Fran. Dev. - Tel: (301) 380-8735, Fax: (301) 380-1401. Extended stay all-suite hotels featuring sleeping quarters, living rooms, fireplaces, fully equipped kitchens and breakfast bars, recreational facilities and swimming pools. Established: 1985 - Franchising Since: 1985 (when system was purchased from Brock Residence Inns, Inc.) - No. of Units: Company Owned: 30 - Franchised: 88 - Franchise Fee: $50,000 or $400/ suite (whichever is greater) - Total Inv: $3,400,000-$5,600,000 (for a 64-suite Inn) - Royalty: 4% gross sales - Financing: Advisory assistance only.

RODEWAY INNS INTERNATIONAL
Choice Hotels International

10750 Columbia Pike, Silver Spring, MD, 20901. Contact; Steve Schultz, Executive VP of Franchise Operations - Tel: (301) 592-5000, (800) 547-0007, Fax: (301) 592-6226, Web Site: www.choicehotels.com. Choice Hotels International (NYSE:CHH) franchises more than 4000 hotels, Inns, all-suite hotels and resorts open and under development in 33 countries under the brand names of Comfort, Quality, Sleep, Rodeway Inn, Econo Lodge and MainStay Suites. Established: 1941 - Franchising Since: 1941 - Franchised: Over 4000 in 33 countries - Franchise Fee: Varies by brand - Royalty: Varies by brand - Total Inv: Varies by brand - Financing: Choice will assist with preparing and presenting mortgage applications.

SHERATON HOTELS AND INNS
Starwood Hotels & Resorts

100 Galleria Pkwy., Ste. 1350, Atlanta, GA, 30339. Contact: Sam Winterbottom, President, Franchise - Tel: (770) 857-2050, Fax: (770) 857-2040, E-Mail: sam.winterbottom@starwoodhotels.com, Web Site:

www.starwoodhotels.com. Full service hotels - Upscale and Midscale. Established: 1938 - Franchising Since: 1962 - No. of Units: Company Owned: 479 - Franchised: 246 .

SLEEP INNS
Choice Hotels International

10750 Columbia Pike, Silver Spring, MD, 20901. Contact: Steve Schultz, Executive V.P. of Franchise Operations - Tel: (301) 592-5000, (800) 547-0007, Fax: (301) 592-6113, Web Site: www.choicehotels.com. Choice Hotels International (NYSE:CHH) franchises more than 4000 hotels, inns, all-suite hotels and resorts open and under development in 33 countries under the brand names of Comfort, Quality, Clarion, Sleep, Rodeway Inn, Econo Lodge and MainStay Suites. Established: 1941 - Franchising Since: 1941 - No. of Units: Franchised: Over 4000 in 33 counries - Franchise Fee: Varies by brand - Royalty: Varies by brand - Total Inv: Varies by brand - Financing: Choice will assist with preparing and presenting mortgage applications.

STUDIO 6

14651 Dallas Pkwy, #500, Dallas, TX, 75254. Contact: Dean Savas, Senior VP Franchising - Tel: (972) 702-6951, (888) 842-2942, Fax: (972) 702-3610, E-Mail: arcinfo@airmail.net, Web Site: www.staystudio6.com. Hotelier - economy business lodging. Established: 1998 - Franchising Since: 1999 - No. of Units: Company Owned: 36 - Franchised: 2 - Franchise Fee: $25,000 - Royalty: 5%, 2% marketing fee - Total Inv: $2,700,000-$3,400,000 - Financing: System lenders reference contact available.

SUBURBAN LODGE
Suburban Lodges of America, Inc.

300 Galloria Parkway Suite 1200, Atlanta, GA, 30339. Contact: Brand President - Tel: (888) 951-2100, Fax: (770) 951-0307, E-Mail: dberman@slacorp.com, Web Site: www.suburbanlodge.com. The nation's leading economy extended stay hotel brand. The Suburban Lodge franchising concept features low construction and operating costs, 6-10 employees per hotel, an average guest stay of 3-4 weeks, and occupancies that were 16% higher than the hotel industry average last year. Established: 1987 - Franchising Since: 1991 - No. of Units: Company Owned: 65 - Franchised: 61- Franchise Fee: $30,000 or $225 per room - Royalty: 5% - Total Inv: $3,000,000-$6,000,000 - Financing: No.

SUNDOWNER INNS
Hospitality International

1726 Montreal Circle, Tucker, GA, 30084-6809. - Tel: (770) 270-1180, (800) 247-4677, Fax: (770) 270-1077. Economy motel. Established: 1996 - Franchising Since: 1996 - No. of Units: 9 under development - Franchise Fee: $20,000 - Royalty: 4% + 1% adv. + reservation support - Total Inv: Varies - approx. $20,000-$25,000 per unit in most areas - Financing: Assistance.

SUPER 8 MOTELS

1 Sylvan Way, Parsippany, NJ, 07054. Contact: SR. V.P. Sales - Tel: (973)496-2956, Fax: (973) 496-0581. Franchise economy motels. Operate extensive franchise services, supply and management division. Established: 1973 - Franchising Since: 1976 - No. of Units: Franchised: 1,800+ - Franchise Fee: $20,000 - Royalty: 5% + 3% adv. - Financing: Assistance in loan preparation.

TRAVELODGE
HFS Incorporated

1 Sylvan Way, Parsippany, NJ, 07054. Contact: Franchise Dept. - Tel: (973) 428-9700, Web Site: www.travelodge.com. Travelodge is a brand of economy lodging for accommodations owned and operated by the most profitable hotel and catering company in the world. Franchises are available in all lodging segments. Established: 1935 - Franchising Since: 1966 - No. of Units: Company Owned: 50 - Franchised: 300 - Franchise Fee: $30,000 or $300/room, whichever is greater - Royalty: 4% - Financing: No.

VILLAGER LODGE, VILLAGER PREMIER
Villager Franchise Systems, Inc.

1 Sylvan Way, Parsippany, NJ, 07084. Contact: Anthony Falor, SVP Franchise Sales - Tel: (973) 496-5859, (800) 694-6428, Fax: (973) 496-2055, E-Mail: anthony.Falor@cendant.com, Web Site: www.villager. com. Villager Franchise Systems, Inc. franchises extended stay properties

under two tiers: Villager Lodge® and Villager Premier(SM). This extended stay chain has over 175 locations open or under development throughout the US, Mexico and Canada that offer from furnished mini-apartments to traditional hotel amenities. Villager's strategy has been built on serving the traditional transient traveler with addition of the extended stay customer. That's why—by the day or extended stay Villager offers the best of both worlds. Established: 1989 - Franchising Since: 1996 - No. of Units: Franchised: 117 - Franchise Fee: $15,000 and up - Royalty: 5% - Total Inv: $197,000-$4.9 million - Financing: Yes.

WELLESLEY INN & SUITES
Prime Hospitality Corp.
700 Route 46 East, Fairfield, NJ, 07007. Contact: Jeff Williams - Tel: (973) 244-7555, (888) 778-3111, Fax: (973) 882-1991, Web Site: www.wellesleyinnandsuites.com. Value-priced hotel with elegany lobby areas, beautiful guest rooms. We provide complimentery continental breakfast, facsimile services, remore-control televisions, in-room coffee makers and clock radios. Established: 1985 - Franchising Since: 1998 - No. of Units: Company Owned: 66 - Franchise Fee: $30,000.

WESTIN HOTELS
Starwood Hotels & Resorts
100 Galleria Pkwy, Suite 1350, Atlanta, GA, 30339. Contact: Sam Winterbottom, President, Franchise - Tel: (770) 857-2050, Fax: (770) 857-2040, E-Mail: Sam.winterbottom@starwoodhotels.com, Web Site: www.starwoodhotels.com. Full service hotels - upscale and midscale. Established: 1938 - Franchising Since: 1968 - No. of Units: Company Owned: 479 - Franchised: 246.

WINGATE INN HOTELS
Wingate Inns International, Inc
1 Sylvan Way, Parsippany, NJ, 07054. Contact: Franchise Department - Tel: (973) 428-9700, (800) 567-4283, Fax: (973) 496-1354, Web Site: www.wingateinns.com. Upper mid-market hotel chain that features high tech amenities for business and leisure travelers. Established: 1995 - Franchising Since: 1995 - No. of Units: Franchised: Over 100 - Franchise Fee: Min of $36,000 - Royalty: 4.5% - Total Inv: 5 million - 5.2 million - Financing: Mezzanine financing.

YOGI BEAR'S JELLYSTONE PARK CAMP-RESORTS
Leisure Systems, Inc.
50 W Techne Center Dr Ste G , Milford, OH, 45150-9798. Contact: Rob Schutter, Pres./COO - Tel: (513) 232-6800, (800) 626-3720, Fax: (513) 231-1191, Web Site: www.campjellystone.com. Family oriented camping resorts. Established: 1969 - Franchising Since: 1970 - No. of Units: Franchised: 70 - Franchise Fee: $18,000 - Royalty: 6% + 1% adv. Total Inv: $25,000 + conversion/$800,000 + new - Financing: No.

MOVING SERVICES

APARTMENT MOVERS ETC.
KS Investmentn Inc
403G Miller Rd, Greenville, SC, 29607. Contact: Kim Swanson, President - Tel: (843) 573-0350, (800) 847-2861, Fax: (843) 767-3834, E-Mail: apartmentmovers@mindspring.com, Web Site: www.apartmentmovers etc.com. Residential and commercial moving company. Specializing in guaranteed lowest price, move quotes given by phone, guaranteed in writing. Bold logo. Exclusive computerized software for all your business needs. Established: 1995 - Franchising Since: 1999 - No. of Units: Company Owned: 2 - Franchised: 4 - Franchise Fee: $19,500 - Royalty: 5% royalty, 1% adv - Total Inv: $75,000 - Financing: Available.

CROWNING TOUCH
Senior Moving Services
6704 Williamson Rd, NW, Roanoke, VA, 24019. Contact: Linda Balentine - Tel: (888) 982-5800, Fax: (540) 982-3903, E-Mail: crowningtouch@msn.com, Web Site: www.crowningtouchusa.com. Detailed moving services include: Computerized furniture floor plans, estate purchasing, detailed packing, unpacking, storage, utility changes, resetting, shelf & picture hanging, cleaning the vacated property. Established: 1996 - Franchising Since: 2000 - No. of Units: Company Owned: 1 - Franchise Fee: $26,000-$50,000 - Total Inv: $77,500-$138,600.

MINUTEMAN MOVING & STORAGE INC.
3259 Alden Starnes Rd., Granite Falls, NC, 28630. - Tel: (704) 322-7999, (704) 495-3113. Home-based moving and storage services. Full training and support provided. Established: 1995 - Franchising Since: 1996 - No. of Units: Company Owned: 1 - Franchised: 2 - Franchise Fee: $15,000 - Total Inv: $25,000 - Financing: Yes.

THE RESETTLERS
The Resetters Franchise Group, LLC
5811 Kennett Pike, Centreville, DE, 19807. Contact: Len Adams - Tel: (302) 658-9110, (800) 730-0900, Fax: (302) 658-5809, E-Mail: resettlers@att.net, Web Site: www.resettlers.com. Successful combination of service and retailing as you manage the transition from a client's home to retirement living. Increase your personal wealth through the estate purchase segment of the business. Established: 1985 - Franchising Since: 1997 - No. of Units: Company Owned: 2 - Franchised: 1 - Franchise Fee: $20,000 - Royalty: 5% of sales - Total Inv: $50,000-$100,000, depending on the extent of your initial inventory and store location - Financing: No.

OPTICAL AID & SERVICE

BEI POLAR CLIPS *
2525 Miller Road, Kalamazoo, MI, 49001. - Tel: (866) 765-2740. Custom polarized clip-on sunglasses. Established: 2002 - Franchising Since: 2003 - No. of Units: Franchised: 15 - Franchise Fee: $20,000.

D.O.C OPTICAL
D.O.C Optics Corp.
19800 West Eight Mile Rd., Southfield, MI, 48075. Contact: Charles M. Males, Sr. V.P. & Fran. Dir. - Tel: (248) 354-7100 Ext. 279, Fax: (248) 353-3570. Retail optical business. Established: 1961 - Franchising Since: 1986 - No. of Units: Company Owned: 69 - Franchised: 43 - Franchise Fee: $12,500 - Royalty: Based on sales - Total Inv: Varies.

EYEGLASS EMPORIUM
6097 US Highway 6, Portage, IN, 46368-5046. Contact: Franchise Department - Tel: (219) 736-1366. Retail optical stores - eye exams, frame and glass adjustments. Established: 1979 - Franchising Since: 1990 - No. of Units: Company Owned: 9 - Franchise Fee: $20,000 for 1st store, $15,000 subsequent - Royalty: 8% - Total Inv: Exam store (no lab) $136,000, with lab $288,000 - Financing: No.

OPTIM EYES
Henry Ford Optim Eyes
655 W 13 Mile Rd., Madison Heights, MI, 48071. Contact: Jonathan Raven, C.E.O. - Tel: (248) 588-9300, (888) 655-2020, (877) 678-4639, Fax: (248) 588-3355, Web Site: www.optimeyes.com. Full eye care fashion eyewear and contact lens. Service by licensed optometrists and opticians. Affiliated with Henry Ford Eyecare Services. Ophthalmologist Network. Established: 1980 - Franchising Since: 1981 - No. of Units: Company Owned: 22 - Franchised: 13 - Franchise Fee: $10,000 - Total Inv: 7% Royalty - 5% Advertising. - Royalty: 7% - Financing: Yes.

PEARLE VISION
Pearle, Inc.
1965 Enterprise Pkwy, Twinsburg, OH, 44087. Contact: Franchise Operations - Tel; (800) 732-7531, Fax: (330) 486-3425. Optical retailer. Established: 1960 - Franchising Since: 1981 - No. of Units: Company Owned: 328 - Franchised: 330 - Franchise Fee: $30,000 - Royalty: 7% - Total Inv: $104,200-$696,600 - Financing: Yes.

PROCARE VISION CENTERS INC.
926 North 21 St., Newark, OH, 43055. Contact: Eva Pound-Bickle, Ph.D., Vice Pres. - Tel: (800) 837-5569, Fax: (740) 366-1919. Retail eye and vision care franchises only sold to licensed eye care professionals. Established: 1981 - Franchising Since: 1985 - No. of Units: Company Owned: 1- Franchised: 18 - Franchise Fee: $8,000 - Royalty: 5%, 1% adv.- Total Inv: $150,000 - Financing: Through financial institutions.

STERLING OPTICAL INC.
Sterling Vision Inc.
100 Quentin Roosevelt Blvd., Ste. 508, Garden City, NY, 11530. - Tel: (516) 390-2100, (800) 856-9664, Fax: (516) 390-2110. Retail - One hour optical service. Established: 1992 - Franchising Since: 1992 - No. of Units: Company Owned: 21 - Franchised: 180 - Franchise Fee: $20,000 - Royalty: 10%, 4% adv. - Total Inv: $175,000-$250,000 - Financing: Referral only.

TEXAS STATE OPTICAL
TSO, Inc.
5858 Westheimer #330, Houston, TX, 77057. - Tel: (877) 953-7600, Fax: (801) 881-1192. Franchised professional optical practice/retail optical dispensary. Established: 1934 - Franchising Since: 1972 - No. of Units: Company Owned:5 - Franchised: 115 - Franchise Fee: Varies - Royalty: 4% - Total Inv: $92,500-$438,500 - Financing: No.

PACKAGE PREPARATION/SHIPMENT/MAIL SERVICE

AD COM EXPRESS
R.F.F. Enterprises, Inc.
Box 390048, Minneapolis, MN, 55439. Contact: Ward Peterson, Dir. Mktg. Sales. - Tel: (612) 829-7990, Fax: (952) 829-9124. National network of overnight small package air express, pick-up and delivery stations offering multi-level personalized services. Established: 1979 - Franchising Since: 1981 - No. of Units: Company Owned: 3 - Franchised: 21 - Franchise Fee: $10,000 - Total Inv: $30,000 - Royalty: 8%.

AIM MAIL CENTERS
Amailcenter Franchise Corporation
15550-D Rockfield Blvd., Irvine, CA, 92618. Contact: David Wiener, Franchise Development - Tel: (949) 837-4151, (800) 669-4246, Fax: (949) 837-4537, E-Mail: franchiseinfo@aimmailcenters.com, Web Site: www.aimmailcenters.com. AIM Mail centers based in Irvine, CA. has developed a unique and attractive franchise opportunity designed for motivated professionals. AIM Mail centers are complete business service centers offering a wide array of products and services to small buisnesses and the general consumer. This includes shipping services with UPS, FedEx, and the US Postal Service. Established: 1985 - Franchising Since: 1989 - No. of Units: Franchised: 123 - Franchise Fee: $26,900 - Royalty: 5% - Total Inv: $109,950-$179,250 - Financing: Yes third party.

CRAFTERS & FREIGHTERS
7000 E. 47th Ave, Ste. 100, Denver, CO, 80216. - Tel: (303) 399-8190, Specialty freight handlers. Established: 1990 - No. of Units: Company Owned: 1 - Franchised: 49 - Franchise Fee: $24,800 - Total Inv: $76,000.

HANDLE WITH CARE PACKAGING STORE
The Packaging Store, Inc.
5675 DTC Blvd. Ste. 280, Englewood, CO, 80111. - Tel: (800) 293-7415, Fax: (303) 741-6653, E-Mail: info@gonavis.com, Web Site: www.gonavis.com. Custom packaging and shipping from 1 to 1500 pounds domestically and internationally with insurance available. Small load specialist shipping small prepacked items as well as expertly packaging and shipping the fragile, large awkward and valuable items that range from teddy bears to an antique grandfather clock, original Picaso, roomful of furniture, or a computer. Established: 1980 - Franchising Since: 1983 - No. of Units: Franchised: 157 - Franchise Fee: $22,500 - Royalty: 5% - Total Inv: $69,500-$114,500 - Financing: None.

HOTLINE DELIVERY SYSTEMS
Hotline Delivery Systems, Inc
2124 Farrington Ste 100, Dallas, TX, 75207. Contact: Robert Wakefield - Tel: (502) 244-1858, (800) 288-6247, Fax: (502) 254-7196, E-Mail: sales@franchise-one.com, Web Site: www.hotlinedeliverysystems.com. We provide same-day and next-day delivery and courier services requiring expidited handling. We offer everything from evelopes to large palletized orders delivered door to door or desk to desk. Established: 1989 - Franchising Since: 2001 - No. of Units: Company Owned: 1 - Franchise Fee: $35,000 - Total Inv: $50,000-$100,000 - Financing: Third party.

LASER COURIER
Laser Franchise Systems, Inc.
7927 Jonesbranch Dr., Ste 150N, McLean, VA, 22102. Contact: Ted Goodenov, Franchise Development - Tel: (703) 761-9030 x8102. Fast and reliable courier service. Full training and support provided. Established: 1986 - Franchising Since: 1997 - No. of Units: Company Owned: 8 - Franchise Fee; $15,000 - Total Inv: $67,000-$113,000.

MAIL & MORE
4305 State Bridge Rd., Suite 103, Alpharetta, GA, 30022. - Tel: (877) 214-1444, Fax: (770) 518-9650, Web Site: www.mailandmore franchise.com. Mail & More...is a complete one-stop center for all your shopping, copying and business communication needs. Mail and More is a one-stop store for black & white copies, color copies, faxing, shipping, mail box rentals, binding and laminating. Established: 1997 - Franchising Since: 2001 - No. of Units: Franchised: 7 - Franchise Fee: $25,000 - Total Inv: $90,000-$165,000 - Financing: Yes.

NAVIS PACK & SHIP
5675 DTC Blvd., Suite 280, Greenwood Village, CO, 80111. Contact: Director of Franchise Dev. - Tel: (303) 741-6626, Fax: (303) 741-6653. Retail packaging and shipping of fragile, large, awarkward and valuable items. Established: 2000 - Franchising Since: 2001 - No. of Units: Company Owned: 1 - Franchised: 157 - Franchise Fee: $24,000 - Total Inv: $69,500-$114,500.

PACK MART INC.
13529 U.S. Highway #1, Sebastian, FL, 32958. Contact: V.P., Mktg. - Tel: (800) 234-7411, (561) 589-0680, Fax: (561) 589-0680. Pack and shipping of packages, next day letters, etc. by UPS, Federal Express and U.S. Mail. Established: 1993 - Franchising Since: 1995 - Franchise Fee: Mini Center $4,500, Full Store $15,000 - Royalty: Flat rate of $200-$400 monthly - Total Inv: Between $10,000 for mini center to $70,000 for full store - Financing: Yes, to qualified buyers.

PACKAGING AND SHIPPING SPECIALISTS
5211 85th St., Ste. 104, Lubbock, TX, 79424. Contact: Mike Gallagher/ Wendi Mohl - Tel: (806) 794-9996, (800) 877-8884, Fax: (806) 794-9997, E-Mail: mike@packship.com, Web Site: www.packship.com. Complete packing/shipping/copy center/with retail products and sign center. Our high tech look along with all of our services make us unique to our competitors. So much more than just a mailing center. "No Royalties". Established: 1981 - Franchising Since: 1985 - No. of Units: Company Owned: 6 - Franchised: 704 - Franchise Fee: $28,900 - Total Inv: $91,000-$138,000 - Financing: Yes.

PACKY THE SHIPPER/ PACK 'N SHIP
PNS, Inc.
409 Main St., Racine, WI, 53403. - Tel: (414) 504-2490. Complete packaging and shipping service centers set up as an addendum to currently existing businesses. Established: 1981 - Franchising Since: 1981 - No. of Units: 1,400 - Total Inv: $495 - Financing: No.

PAK MAIL
Pak Mail Centers Of America, Inc
7173 S. Havana St., Ste 600, Englewood, CO, 80112. Contact: Chuck Prentner, Dir. of Fran. Dev. - Tel: (303) 957-1000, (800) 833-2821, Fax: (303) 790-9445, E-Mail: sales@pakmail.org, Web Site: www.pakmail.com. Convenient retail centers offering residential and commercial customers freight movement, crating, custom packaging, domestic and international shipping, business support services including copies, fax, business printing, private mailbox rental, logistics and fulfillment services. Established: 1984 - Franchising Since: 1984 - No. of Units: Franchised: 400+ - Franchise Fee: $27,950 - Royalty: Up to 5%, 2% advertising - Total Inv: $60,000-$115,000 including franchise fee - Financing: Yes, third party, SBA franchise registry.

PARCEL PLUS
Parcel Plus, Inc.
12715 Telge Road, Cypress, TX, 77429. - Tel: (800) 662-5553, Fax: (281) 373-4450, E-Mail: rhadfield@inotes.iced.net. Shipping, packaging, business support and computer services. Established: 1986 - Franchising Since: 1988 - No. of Units: Franchised:102 - Franchise Fee: $25,000 - Royalty: 4%, 1% nat'l. adv. - Total Inv: $115,000-$174,000 - Financing: None.

PONY MAIL BOX & BUSINESS CENTER
1645 Dunlawton Ave Apt 3813, Port Orange, FL, 32127-7933. Contact: R. E. Howell, Pres. - Tel: (615) 826-1901, E-Mail: ponymailbox@aol.com. Postal, shipping and business communication services. See our home page at www. ponymailbox.com. Established: 1982 - Franchising Since: 1986 - No. of Units: Company Owned: 1 - Franchised: 16 - Franchise Fee: $19,950 - Royalty: $3,500 1st yr., $3,000 rest of contract annually - Total Inv: $56,950-$76,000 incl. fran. fee - Financing: No.

POSTAL ANNEX
Postal Annex, Inc.
7580 Metropolitan Dr #200, San Diego, CA, 92108-4417. Contact: Rhonda ward - Tel: (800) 456-1525, (619) 563-9800, Fax: (619) 563-9850, E-Mail: info@postalannex.com, Web Site: www.postalannex.com. Provide postal packaging & shipping, business & communication support, high-speed copying & web site e-commerce. Services to consumer & business in a convenient service oriented environment. Established: 1985 - Franchising Since: 1985 - No. of Units: Franchised: 295 - Franchise Fee: $29,950 - Royalty: 5% - Total Inv: Up to $160,000 - Financing: Yes.

POSTNET POSTAL & BUSINESS CENTERS
PostNet International Franchise Corp.
181 North Arroyo Grande #A-100, Henderson, NV, 89014. Contact: Brian Spindel, Exec. Vice President - Tel: (702) 792-7100, (800) 841-7171, Fax: (702) 792-7115, E-Mail: info@postnet.net, Web Site: www.postnet.net. Business and communication center offering shipping, packaging, fax, copies, business services and much more. Established: 1992 - Franchising Since: 1993 - No. of Units: Franchised: 650 - Franchise Fee: $26,900 - Royalty: 4% + 1% ad - Total Inv: $91,000-$125,000 US - Financing: Yes.

PRIVATE POSTAL CENTERS
Salsbury Industries
1010 E. 62nd St., Los Angeles, CA, 90001. Contact; Dir. of Mktg. - Tel: (800) Salsbury, Web Site: www.salsbury.com. A one-stop postal, communication and business service center. A center is based around mailbox rentals plus the optional services of package wrapping and shipping, faxing, notarizing, photocopying, telephone answering, word processing and/or a host of other service oriented ideas. Established: 1936 - Franchising Since: 1978 - Franchise Fee: Equipment sales only - Total Inv: $15,000-$20,000.

SHIPPING CONNECTION
1601 Belvedere Rd., Ste. 402 East, West Palm Beach, FL, 33406. - Tel: (561) 640-5998, (800) 727-6720, Fax: (561) 640-5580. Shipping Connection is quickly becoming a leader in one of the fastest growing industries. We offer our customers a wide variety of services, including, packaging, shipping, mail box rentals, faxing, copying, conference room rentals. Our slogan says it all "Your Home For Business Services". Established: 1986 - Franchising Since: 1986 - No. of Units: Company Owned: 1 - Franchised: 19 - Franchise Fee: $22,500 - Royalty: Flat monthly fee, max. $500/month - Total Inv: $22,500 franchise fee, $30,400 equipment ($52,900) - Financing: Yes, up to 60% of total investment.

SHIPPING DEPT.INC., THE
5800 Siegen Ln., Baton Rouge, LA, 70809. Contact: Robert X Hafele, Franchise Development - Tel: (504) 295-1085. Packing and shipping services under 2000 lbs. - fast and reliable. Full training and support. Established: 1985 - Franchising Since: 1988 - No. of Units: Company Owned: 2 - Franchised: 1 - Franchise Fee: $12,000 - Total Inv: $22,000.

SUNSHINE PACK & SHIP
Sunshine Pack & Ship Franchise
548, 48th St Ct, E, Bradenton, FL, 34208. Contact: Douglas Roper - Tel: (941) 746-9825, (877) 751-1513, Fax: (941) 746-9897, E-Mail: marketing@sunshinepackandship.com, Web Site: www.sunshinepack andship.com. Sunshine Pack & Ship retail centers are full service stores that offer custom packaging & crating with multiple shipping options. Wev also have logistics centers for commercial customer needs. Established: 1993 - Franchising Since: 2000 - No. of Units: Company Owned: 1 - Franchised: 24 - Franchise Fee: $19,900 - Royalty: 4% - Total Inv: $50,795-$148,945 - Financing: Third party.

SUREWAY AIR EXPRESS
24-30 Skillman Ave, Long Island, NY, 11101. Contact: Steven Dorfman - Tel: (718) 937-7600, (800) 221-0157, Fax: (718) 361-7937. Air courier/air freight. Established: 1963 - No. of Units: Company Owned: 6 - Franchised: 10 - Total Inv: $7,000-$37,5000 - Financing: No.

SYSTEMAX PARCEL SHIPPING CENTER
Systemax Network Inc.
6115 Washington Ave., Racine, WI, 53406. - Tel: (414) 504-2490, (800) 547-2259, Fax: (414) 504-2499. Parcel shipping and packaging services to the general public through existing retail store's customer service desk. Established: 1978 - Franchising Since: 1980 - No. of Units: Company Owned: 1 - Franchised: 450 - Franchise Fee: Dealership Program $165 - Financing: N/A.

TARGET DIRECT USA
Target Direct USA, Inc
107 8th St, Augusta, GA, 30901. Contact: Matthew Korb - Tel: (706) 724-7980. Provide targeted customer base-custom design, layout, address, fold, weight, seal and meter direct mailings for clients. Established: 1999 - Franchising Since: 1999 - No. of Units: Franchised: 12 - Franchise Fee: 5% of gross sales - Total Inv: $20,000 - Financing: Will provide up to 100% equipment financing for franchisees and agents.

WORLDWIDE EXPRESS
CGI Franchise Systems, Inc.
P.O. Box 132518, Dallas, TX, 75313. Contact: David Kiger, Franchise Development - Tel: (214) 965-9965, (800) 758-7447, Fax: (214) 220-1046, Web Site: www.cgi-express.com. Overnight air express reseller offering franchises throughout the USA. Franchisees offer small to medium sized companies savings of up to 40% on their overnight packages. Established: 1992 - Franchising Since: 1995 - No. of Units: Franchised: 58 - Franchise Fee: $25,000-$100,000 - Total Inv: Variable - Financing: Yes.

PEST CONTROL

A ALL ANIMAL CONTROL *
P.O. Box 80233, Northglennm CO, 80233. - Tel: (540) 815-7992, E-Mail: info@aallanimalcontrol.com. We specialize in removing wildlife in the home or office to reduce the risk of serious structural damage. Established: 1995 - Franchising Since: 2000 - No. of Units: Franchised: 4 - Franchise Fee: $5,000 - Royalty: 8% - Total Inv: $10,000-$20,000 - Financing: No.

CRITTER CONTROL
Wildlife Management Supplies
9435 E. Cherry Bend Rd, Traverse City, MI, 49684. - Tel: (800) 451-6544, Fax: (231) 947-9440, E-Mail: info@crittercontrol.com, Web Site: www.crittercontrol.com. Wildlife management and animal pest control services. Established: 1983 - Franchising Since: 1988 - No. of Units: Company Owned: 50 - Franchised: 50 - Franchise Fee: $12,000-$18,000 - Royalty: 6%-16% plus 2% adv. - Total Inv: $15,000-$50,000 - Financing: N/A.

EARTH TOUCH ORGANIC PEST CONTROL
Earth Touch Franchise Corp
4203 Lead Southeast, Albuquerque,NM, 87108. Contact: Al Gonzales, President - Tel: (505) 265-0338, Fax: (505) 266-0727. Organic pest control for residential and commercial customers. Established: 1994 - Franchising Since: 1994 - No. of Units: Company Owned: 1 - Franchised:

2 - Franchise Fee: $5,800 - Royalty: $150 / mnth first 12 mnths, $275/ mnth 2nd 12 mnths, $385/mnth for 60 months - Total Inv: $34,000 - Financing: Yes.

FLEAPRUF 365
AllerClean Inc.
6400 Black Horse Pike, Egg Harbor Township, NJ, 08234-4521. Contact: Ray Hurley, Fran. Dept. - Tel: (609) 641-7005, Fax: (609) 641-0988. Hypo-allergenic pest control services. Established: 1992 - Franchising Since: 1995 - No. of Units: Company Owned: 1 - Franchised: 8 - Franchise Fee: $15,000 - Royalty: 8%, 2% adv. - Total Inv: $35,000-$75,000 - Financing: None.

KNOCKOUT PEST CONTROL INC.
Knockout Inspections
1009 Front St., Uniondale, NY, 11553. - Tel: (212) 425-7378. Pest control inspections. Established: 1975 - Franchising Since: 1993 - No. of Units: Company Owned: 1 - Franchised: 2 - Franchise Fee: $15,000 - Royalty: 10%, 2% adv. - Total Inv: $10,000 - Financing: No.

MASTERSHIELD PEST MANAGEMENT, LLC
MasterShield Franchise Systems LLC
1875 Thomaston Avenue, Waterbury, CT, 06704. Contact: Dir. of Fran. Operations - Tel: (203) 756-1814, (800) 462-3366, Fax: (203) 754-1694. Complete pest control-specializing in termites and ants, currently covering all of Connecticut. Established: 1988 - Franchising Since: 1996 - No. of Units: Company Owned: 1 - Franchised: 4 - Franchise Fee: $5,000 - Royalty: 5% of total gross rev. monthly - Total Inv: $44,000-$87,000 excluding fran. fee - Financing: No.

NATURZONE PEST CONTROL INC. *
1899 Porter Lake Dr., #103, Sarasota, FL, 34240. - Tel: (941) 378-3334, Fax: (941) 378-8584, Web Site: www.naturzone.com. Pest control services. Established: 1982 - Franchising Since: 1998 - No. of Units: Company Owned: 1 - Franchised: 5 - Franchise Fee: $20,000 - Royalty: 5% - Total Inv: $19,000-$25,000.

PESTMASTER
Pestmaster Services
137 E. South St., Bishop, CA, 93514. Contact: Terry Walker - Tel: (760) 873-8100, (800) 525-8866, Fax: (760) 873-5618, E-Mail: pfn@pest master.com, Web Site: www.pestmaster.com. Pestmaster Services is dedicated to the utilization of Integrated Pest Management. We will assist you to expand your menu of services into new fields of pest, weed, aquztic and landscape pest control. Pestmaster's Technical Directors can cross train you in order to build up your experience level and expertise in these new areas, which will add gross sales to your Petsmaster Service Center. Pestmaster has a very wide vision of what pest control is and likes to "think outside of the box". Established: 1989 - Franchising Since: 1990 - No. of Units: Company Owned: 13 - Franchised: 14 - Franchise Fee: $15,000-$30,000 - Royalty: 4%-7% - Financing: No.

SEARS TERMITE & PEST CONTROL
6359 Edgewater Dr, Orlando, FL, 32810. Contact: Tom Dubnicki - Tel: (407) 445-2174, (800) 528-7287, Fax: (407) 445-2118. Offering residential customers total home protection against termites and general pests. Established: 1982 - Franchising Since: 1997 - No. of Units: Company Owned: 125 - Franchised: 7 - Franchise Fee: $35,000-$70,000 - Royalty: Varies - Total Inv: $50,000 - Financing: Up to 50% if intial franchise fee by allowing you to pay in installments.

TERMINIX
Terminix International Co. L.P.
860 Ridge Lake Blvd., Memphis, TN, 38120. Contact: Willian A. Cochran, Manager Franchise Operations - Tel: (800) TERMINIX. Residential and commercial termite and pest control service. Established: 1927 - Franchising Since: 1927 - No. of Units: Company Owned: 278 - Franchised: 208 - Franchise Fee: $25,000-$50,000 - Royalty: 7% fees,1% renewals, 2% advertising - Total Inv: $75,000-$105,000 - Financing: Yes, with approved credit, up to 70% of initial fran. fee.

PET PRODUCTS AND SERVICES

ANIMAL ADVENTURE
Animal Adventure, Inc
5453 S. 76th St, Greendale, WI, 53129. Contact: Mike Edwards, President - Tel: (800) 289-5665, Fax: (414) 423-7351, Web Site: www.animaladventurepets.com. Retail pet store specializing in birds, tropical fish, small animals and pet supplies. Established: 1980 - Franchising Since: 1999 - No. of Units: Company Owned: 3 - Franchised: 3 - Franchise Fee: $25,000 - Royalty: 4% first million in sales, 2% second million in sales, 1% sales over 2 million - Total Inv: $245,000-$348,000 - Financing: No.

AQUA ZOO *
3001 Hartley Rd., Jacksonville, FL, 32257. - Tel: (904) 880-8858, Fax: (904) 880-0105, Web Site: www.aquazoopets.com. Unique mix of live pets, pet-realted equipment & supplies. Established: 1969 - Franchising Since: 2003 - No. of Units: Franchised: 2 - Franchise Fee: $25,000 - Royalty: $5.57/sq.ft. - Total Inv: $191,100-$280,000.

AUSSIE PET MOBILE
34189 Pacific Coast Hwy, Ste. 203, Dana Point, CA, 92629. Contact: David Louy - Tel: (949) 234-0680, Fax: (949) 234-0688, E-Mail: corp@aussiepetmobile.com. Using a uniquely designed Aussie Pet Mobile trailer, franchisees provide a convenient 15-step grooming service to pet owners in a low stress environment for pets. Established: 1996 - Franchising Since: 1996 - No. of Units: Company Owned: 1 - Franchised: 88 - Franchise Fee: $20,000 - Total Inv: $120,000 - Financing: Third party.

BARK BUSTERS HOME DOG TRAINING
Dingo
3881 E. Mallard St, Highlands Ranch, CO, 80126. Contact: Andrew Brooke, President & CEO. - Tel: (877) 280-7100, E-Mail: liamcrowe@msn.com, Web Site: www.barkbusters.com. Unique dog training system developed in Australia. We go to clients home to adress any behaviorial problems. Established: 1989 - Franchising Since: 1994 - No. of Units: Company Owned: 1 - Franchised: 53 - Franchise Fee: $40,000-$55,000 - Total Inv: Capital requirements; $12,000.

BONE APPETIT BAKERY, THE
925 L St, Lincoln, NE, 68508-2229. - Tel: (402) 434-5888, Fax: (402) 434-5624. Bone Appetit is a unique business concept, providing wholesome all-natural treats for your dog or cat. The treats are hand-cut and freshly baked! Established: 1996 - Franchising Since: 1997 - No. of Units: Company Owned: 1 - Franchised: 14 - Franchise Fee: $17,500 - Royalty: 6%, 1% adv. - Total Inv: $29,000-$68,000 - Financing: Indirect.

CAMP BOW WOW™
Camp Bow Wow™ Branding, LLC
1660 17th Street, Ste. 450, Denver, CO, 80202. Contact: Heidi Flammang, President - Tel: (866) 821-0409, Fax: (866) 821-0412, E-Mail: franchise@ campbowwowusa.com, Web Site: www.campbow wowusa.com. Dog Day Camp overnight boarding franchise - A Dog Gone great business opportunity and a Howlin! Great Time! Established: 2000 - Franchising Since: 2003 - No. of Units: Company Owned: 2 - Franchised: 4 - Franchise Fee: $25,000 - Royalty: 5% - Total Inv: $108,000-$307,000 - Financing: Assistance available.

CANINE COUNSELORS
Canine Counselors Inc.
1660 Southern Blvd., West Palm Beach, FL, 33406. Contact: Dir. of Fran. Promotions - Tel: (561) 640-3970. Professional animal behaviour and on-site dog training company offering all levels of training services on a contract basis, specializing in correcting destructive behaviour. Established: 1975 - Franchising Since: 1987 - No. of Units: Company Owned: 3 - Franchised: 4 - Franchise Fee: $19,000 - Royalty: 7% of gross, 2% nat'l. adv. contribution - Total Inv: $33,500-$39,500 - Financing: Yes.

CATS INN™, THE
557 Western Ave., P.O. Box 480, Manchester, ME, 04351. - Tel: (207) 622-9915, (877) CAT-SINN, Fax: (207) 623-6299. Full service cat boarding facility. Established: 1997 - Franchising Since: 1998 - No. of Units: Company Owned: 1 - Franchise Fee: $20,000-$25,000 - Total Inv: $75,000-$190,000 - Financing: No.

DOG GONE PORTRAITS
DGP Enterprises Inc
45 Brown Hill Road, Bow, NH, 03304. - Tel: (603) 774-6030, (800) 414-1492, Fax: (603) 226-4212. Home based pet portrait photography. On location through sponsor outlets. Established: 1990 - Franchising since: 1998 - No. of Units: Company Owned: 1 - Franchise Fee: $15,000 - Royalty: $5.00 per sitting - Total Inv: $22,000 min - Financing: No.

DOG WASH
Southwest Pet, Inc.
5724 S.W. Green Oaks Blvd., Arlington, TX, 76017. - Tel: (817) 561-1801. A do-it-yourself pet care centerthat offers affordable pet care and vaccinations. Established: 1972 - Franchising Since: 1988 - No. of Units: Company Owned: 1 - Franchised: 1 - Franchise Fee: $17,500 - Royalty: 5.5% - Total Inv: Fee, $20,000 equip./fixtures - Financing: No.

HAYNES PET CENTER
Haynes Pet Centre Franchising, Inc.
12460 Crabapple Road, Suite 403, Alpharetta, GA, 30004. Contact: Randy Trotter, Owner/President - Tel: (404) 570-4200, Fax: (770) 751-5891. Pet supply and grooming shop located in niche markets. Customer service specialist with over 10 years experience. Training program and continuous support. Established: 1988 - Franchising Since: 1996 - No. of Units: Company Owned: 1 - Franchised: 6 - Franchise Fee: $15,000 - Royalty: $140/wk., no percentages - Total Inv: $45,000-$59,000 (including franchise fee) - Financing: No.

HYDO-GROOM MOBILE PET WASH
3820 Premier Avenue, Memphis, TN, 38118. Contact: Bob Richey, President - Tel: (901) 368-3333, Fax: (901) 368-1144, E-Mail: franmark@msn.com. Mobile Pet Wash franchise. Complete trailer set-up with special hydro-wash system. Full training and support provided. Established: 1999 - No. of Units: Company Owned: 1 - Franchised: 10 - Franchise Fee: $10,000 - Total Inv: $25,000.

HYDRO-GROOM
1515 Coleman Street, Reidsville, NC, 27320. Contact: Franchise Director - Tel: (901) 368-3361, Fax: (901) 368-1144. A mobile pet bathing and grooming service. Established: 1998 - Franchising Since: 2001 - No. of Units: Company Owned: 1 - Franchised: 1 - Franchise Fee: $18,941.

JIM'S DOG WASH
Jim's Dog Wash Inc.
4017 Whitby Ln., Grapevine, TX, 76051. Contact: Anthony Silverman, Franchise Development - Tel: (888) 900-5467, Fax: (817) 251-4585. Mobile dog washing service. Full training and support provided. Established: 1997 - Franchising Since: 1998 - Franchised: 80+ - Total Inv: $15,000, masters from $100,000.

JUST DOGS! GOURMET INC. *
5101 Cyrus Cir., Birmingham, AL, 35242. - Tel: (888) 332-0307, Fax: (205) 453-0132, Web Site: www.justdogsgourmet.com. Gourmet dog treats & related merchandise. Established: 2001 - Franchising Since: 2003 - No. of Units: Company Owned: 1 - Franchised: 8 - Franchise Fee: $11,300-$22,500 - Royalty: 8% - Total Inv: $94,000-$159,500 - Financing: No.

LAUND-UR-MUTT, THE PREMIER PET CENTERS
Pet Pioneers, Inc.
8854 S. Edgewood St., Highlands Ranch, CO, 80130. Contact: Scott D. Southworth, Pres. - Tel: (303) 470-1540, Fax: (303) 470-8669, E-Mail: muttman@laundurmutt.com, Web Site: www.laundurmutt.com. Self-service, full service, wash-while-u-wait, premium per foods and supplies. Established: 1992 - Franchising Since: 1994 - No. of Units: Franchised: 7 - Franchise Fee: $25,000 - Royalty: 5% monthly - Total Inv: $150,000-$200,000 - Financing: None in-house assistance available.

PET PANTRY, THE
Pet Pantry International, Inc., The
3719 North Carson St, Carson, NV, 89706. Contact: Franchise Department - Tel: (775) 841-9722, Fax: (775) 841-9732. Complimentary delivery of super premium pet food. Established: 1995 - Franchising Since: 1995 - No. of Units: Company Owned: 1 - Franchised: 4 - Franchise Fee: $20,000 - Royalty: None - Total Inv: $60,000 approx. includes franchise fee and van - Financing: No.

PET PEOPLE - PET FOOD & SUPPLIES
Pet People Franchise Systems, Inc.
722 Genevieve Street, Ste. E, Solana Beach, CA, 92075. Contact: Gregory S. Morris, President - Tel: (619) 481-3335 x12, (800) 655-6595, Fax: (619) 481-3337, Web Site: www.petpeople.com. Pet People is a 3000 sq. foot pet food and supply store format. We don't sell any live animals!. Established: 1990 - Franchising Since: 1999 - No. of Units: Company Owned: 11 - Franchised: 1 - Franchise Fee: $25,000 - Royalty: 4% of gross - Total Inv: $141,000-$165,000 - Financing: No.

PET SUPPLIES PLUS
Pet Supplies Plus/USA, Inc.
37720 Amrhein, Livonia, MI, 48150. Contact: Harold Cavney, V.P. - Tel: (734) 464-2700. Fax: (734) 464-7500. This franchise is licensed to operate a retail pet food and supply store under the Pet Supplies "Plus" system. Established: 1988 - Franchising Since: 1989 - No. of Units: Company Owned: 6 - Franchised: 153 - Franchise Fee: $25,000 - Royalty: $2,000 per month plus 2% gross sales in excess of $1,000,000 per year - Total Inv: Estimated low - $306,500, high - $481,000 - Financing: Franchisees must arrange their own financing.

PET X USA
707 Kansas Ave., Kansas, KS, 66061. Contact: Rob Boone, President - Tel: (402) 484-7100, (800) 249-1618. Pet food resale service - full training and support provided. Established: 1990 - Franchising Since: 1997 - No. of Units: Company Owned: 5 - Franchised: 2 - Franchise Fee: $25,000 - Total Inv: $5,000 cash - $25,000 capital investment - Financing: Yes.

PETLAND
Petland, Inc.
250 Riverside St., Chillicothe, OH, 45601. - Tel: (800) 221-5935, Fax: (740) 775-2575. Full service retail pet stores carrying pets and pet supplies, specializing in innovative pet care, housing, and customer education. Established: 1967 - Franchising Since: 1972 - No. of Units: Company Owned: 1 - Franchised: 149 - Franchise Fee: $25,000 - Royalty: 4.5% paid twice a month - Total Inv: $125,000-$450,000 based on size of the store - Financing: No, but will assist.

SHAKE A PAW
Shake A Paw Associates Inc
91 Knollwood Rd., Whiteplains, NY, 10607. - Tel: (914) 997-7877. Shake A Paw is a retail store that exclusively features purebred puppies, related pet supplies and accessories. Puppies are the most popular and profitable pets sold today. Shake A Paw franchise offers over seventy different breeds of the highest quality purebred puppies. Established: 1997 - Franchising Since: 1997 - No. of Units: Franchised: 4 - Franchise Fee: $25,000 - Royalty: 5% of sales - Total Inv: $120,000-$170,000 - Financing: Third party.

STEIN-WAY DOG TRAINING
1 Sarah Wells Trail, Goshen, NY, 10924. Contact: Linda Stein, President - Tel: (845) 636-7171, Fax: (845) 294-8613, Web Site: www.stein-way.com. Stein-Way Dog Training offers franchises to people who would love to spend their work week training dogs and the people who love them. Established: 1980 - Franchising Since: 2002 - No. of Units: Company Owned: 1 - Franchise Fee: $12,500 - Royalty: $500-$700 per month - Total Inv: $21,500-$47,500.

THREE DOG BAKERY
1627 Main St, Suite 700, Kansas City, MO, 64108. - Tel: (816) 474-3647, Fax: (816) 474-2171, E-Mail: info@threedog.com, Web Site: www.threedog.com. Three Dog Bakery fresh-bakes over 150 all natural wholesome bakery treats and food for your dog. Presents them in a fun whimsical retail format. Dog loving and dog friendly, this concept also sells related doggie accessories. Established: 1990 - Trademark Licensing Since: 1997 - Trademark Licensed: 12 - Total Inv: $100,000-$200,000.

TOP DOG DAYCARE *

3116 Karen Place, Colorado Springs, CO, 80907. Contact: Franchise Department - Tel: (719) 448-9600, Fax: (719) 448-0496, Web Site: www.topdogdaycare.com. Day care, boarding, grooming & training services for dogs. Established: 1999 - Franchising Since: 2004 - No. of Units: Company Owned: 1 - Franchise Fee: $30,000 - Royalty: 4% - Toltal Inv: $71,500-$182,300 - Financing: No.

U-WASH DOGGIE
The Pet Wash Corporation

1056 W. Alameda, Burbank, CA, 91506. Contact: Francisco Gamero, President - Tel: (818) 846-9600, (888) 820-7900, E-Mail: uwashdoggie @petwash.com, Web Site: www.petwash.com. Full and self service pet grooming and accessories. Established: 1992 - Franchising: 1997 - No. of Units: Company Owned: 5 - Franchise Fee: $12,500 - Royalty: 6%-2% Adv - Total Inv: $65,000-$95,000 - Financing: Third party.

WAG'N TAILS
Wag'n Tails Mobile Pet Grooming

12634 Industrial Dr, Granger, IN, 46530. - Postal inquiries only. Do You Love Animals? Wag'n Tails can provide you with a great business that will "Put Your Dreams In Motion". We provide the latest technology in the pet industry with each unit. The fully enclosed units are well equipped for both warm and cold climates providing air conditioning and heating. Established: 1975 - Franchising Since: 1996 - No. of Units: Franchised: 247 - Franchise Fee: No Fee! - Royalty: No Fee! - Total Inv: $31,000-$76,000 - Financing: Yes.

WHISKERS & PAWS CATERING
Whiskers & Paws Catering, Inc

896 West NYE Ln., Ste 201, Carson City, NV, 89703. Contact: Kenneth N. Wright, Chairman/CEO - Tel: (775) 841-6000, (877) 583-9800, Fax: (775) 841-6420, Web Site: www.whiskersandpaws.com. We offer FREE home delivery of super premium pet food and supplies. Our franchisees have exclusive marketing areas. They receive ongoing training and support along with management support. They also receive advertising and marketing support. Established: 1998 - Franchising Since: 1998 - No. of Units: Franchised: 35 - Franchise Fee: $19,500 - Total Inv: Approx $60,000 including fran. fee. - Financing: No.

WHOLLY CRAP *

392 Seaburn St, Brookfield, OH, 44403. Contact: Franchise Department - Tel: (330) 448-1700, Web Site: www.whollycrap.com. Pet waste removal services. Established: 2001 - Franchising Since: 2003 - No. of Units: Company Owned: 1 - Franchise Fee: $12,500 - Royalty: $100-150. monthly - Total Inv: $14,800-$16,800 - Financing: No.

PHOTO, FRAMING AND ART

ACTION SPORTS PHOTOS
Action Sports Photos Incorporated

4220 N. May Ave., Oklahoma City, OK, 73112. Contact: Gary L. Fearnow, Pres. - Tel: (405) 942-7007, Fax: (405) 942-0555. Photography business specializing in action photos and team portrait photos. Package is complete including all business materials, cameras, photographic supplies and training. Established: 1985 - Franchising Since: 1992 - No. of Units: Franchised: 3 - Franchise Fee: $17,500 - Total Inv: $25,000-$37,650 - Financing: No.

BIG PICTURE FRAMING *

855 Highland Ave, Needham, MA, 02494. - Tel: (800) 315-3589, Fax: (781) 444-3589, Web Site: www.bigpictureframing.com. We are a picture framing store that frames while you wait. Established: 2000 - Franchising Since: 2003 - No. of Units: Franchised: 129 - Franchise Fee: $30,000 - Total Inv: $147,000-$267,000.

BRUSHSTROKES - WORKS OF ART

3744 Pennsylvania Ave, Cincinnati, OH, 45226. - Tel: (888) 844-3676, Web Site: www.brushstrokescompany.com. Homebased business that turns favorite pictures into beautiful paintings. Established: 1999 - Franchising Since: 2000.

CASI - CREATIVE NAMES

602 South Third Ave, Mount Vernon, NY, 10701. - Tel: (914) 668-7200, Fax: (914) 668-2080, E-Mail: info@creativenames.com, Web Site: www.creativenames.com. A revolutionary technology that turns photos into beautiful keepsakes by glazing them onto porcelain plates, frames, music boxes, baby shoes aand more. Work from home doing mail order, fund raising, private parties and order fulfillment or if you prefer set up a retail location. With Photo-Creations you will turns pictures into profits. Established: 1977 - Total Inv: $495 and up - Financing: No.

CASI-PHOTO-CREATIONS
Creative Amusement Services, Inc

100 Corporate Drive, Yonkers, NY, 10701. Contact: Department 61 - Tel: (914) 376-7400, (888) 787-7754, Fax: (914) 376-7580, E-Mail: info@photo-creations.com, Web Site: www.photo-creations.com. A revolutionary technology that turns photos into beautiful keepsakes by glazing them onto porcelalin plates, frames, music boxes, baby shoes and more. Work from home doing mail order, fund raising, private parties and order fulfillment or if you prefer set up a retail location. With Photo-Creations you will turn pictures into profits! Established: 1977 - Total Inv: $5995.

CONTEMPO PORTRAITS
CP Enterprises Inc.

1235 S. Gilbert Rd., Ste. 16, Mesa, AZ, 85204. Contact: Patrick Silard, Pres. - Tel: (480) 926-2216, Fax: (480) 926-2382. Contemporary portrait studio offering a whole new concept in portraiture. Established: 1987 - Franchising Since: 1993 - Franchise Fee: $25,000 - Royalty: 7%, 1% adv. - Total Inv: $65,000 plus fran. fee - Financing: Will assist.

CYGNUS SYSTEMS INC.

1719 Zartman Rd, Kokomo, IN, 46902-3258. Contact: Greg Swartz, Fran. Dir. - Tel: (765) 453-7077, Fax: (765) 854-0647. Computer portrait systems that produces prints that transfer by a heating process. Established: 1974 - No. of Units: 150 - Total Inv: $5,100-$22,000 - Financing: No.

DECK THE WALLS
Franchise Concepts

12707 North Freeway, Houston, TX, 77060. Contact: Ann Nance - Tel: (800) 543-3325, Web Site: www.deckthewalls.com. We are North America's largest franchised mall-based retailer & selective shopping centers offering affordable & fashionable home furnishing solutions through art, custom framing & related wall decor. Established: 1979 - Franchising Since: 1981- No. of Units: Company Owned: 2 - Franchised: 156 - Franchise Fee: $30,000 - Royalty: 6% - Total Inv: $180,000-$245,000.

FASTFRAME
Fastframe USA, Inc.

1200 Lawrence Dr., #300, Newbury Park, CA, 91320. Contact: Franchise Dev. - Tel: (888) TO FRAME, (805) 498-4463, Fax: (805) 498-8983, E-Mail: brenda@fastframe.com, Web Site: www.fastframe.com. Fastframe provides high quality custom framing in art sales in both retail and commercial markets. The fastframe package offers a complete turn-key service from site from selecting to final store build out. Established: 1986 - Franchising Since: 1987 - No. of Units: Company Owned: 7 - Franchised: 197 - Franchise Fee: $25,000 - Royalty: 7.5%, 3% adv. - Total Inv: Turn key $194,500-$124,000 - Financing: Assistance with financing approved by the SBA.

FINE ART RENTALS
Fine Art Rentals Franchising Inc.

1638 Via Tulipan, San Clemente, CA, 92673-3722. - Tel: (949) 831-0222. Have rented quality art work to business and professional offices for 31 yrs. Oldest and largest art rental service in CA, now offering a limited number of exclusive franchise territories. Included in franchise fee are 100 tastefully framed original serigraphs, watercolors, etchings and other limited edition works, complete training program, support of a parent company. Established: 1959 - Franchising Since: 1987 - No. of Units: Company Owned: 1 - Franchised: 3 - Franchise Fee: $30,000 - Royalty: 5% gross rentals per mth. - Total Inv: $30,000 - Financing: No.

FLOATOGRAPH TECHNOLOGIES
2021 Seville Dr., Napa, CA, 94559. - Tel: (707) 253-0485, (800) 236-9259, Fax: (707) 252-1436, E-Mail: float@floatograph.com, Web Site: www.floatograph.com. Blimp aerial photography. Blimp raises camera and remote controlled positioner up to 250 feet. Ground based control console has monitor for viewing camera frame, remote shutter. Established: 1989 - No. of Units: Company Owned: 1 - Franchised: 50 - Franchise Fee: Free - Royalty: None - Total Inv: Starting at $2,990 - Financing: None.

GLAMOUR SHOTS LICENSING, INC.
1300 Metropolitian Ave, Oklahoma City, OK, 73108. Contact: Kim McElroy - Tel: (405) 951-7343, (800) 336-4550, Fax: (405) 951-7343, E-Mail: kim@glamourshots.com, Web Site: www.glamourshots.com. We offer a makeover, hairstyling & wardrobe to enhance the portrait. Our instant proofing system allows custmers to view their proofs, place their order, and pay at the time of session. Established: 1988 - Franchising Since: 1992 - No. of Units: Company Owned: 2 - Franchised: 115 - Franchise Fee: $20,000 - Financing: Third party.

GREAT FRAME UP, THE
Franchise Concepts, Inc.
P.O. Box 1187, Houston, TX, 77251-1187. - Tel: (281) 775-5262, (800) 543-3325, Fax: (281) 872-1646, E-Mail: anance@fcibiz.com, Web Site: www.thegreatframeup.com. Specializes in custom framing in a hands-on, artistic environment. Located in non-mall shopping centers. Each store offers a wide selection of custom frame moulding and mat styles, and features patented framing systems and design areas. Easy to learn and operate with exceptional training and on-going support. National buying power and proven marketing programs. Single and multi-units available. Established: 1971 - Franchising Since: 1975 - No. of Units: Franchised: 152 - Franchise Fee: $30,000 - Royalty: 6% - Total Inv: $138,425-$188,150 - Financing: Third party.

HOT LOOKS HIGH FASHION PORTRAITS
Hot Looks International, Inc.
724 Old York Rd., Jenkintown, PA, 19046. - Tel: (215) 572-8900. Rapidly growing specialty chain featuring high fashion glamour photography, cosmetic makeovers plus wedding and special event photography and videos. Established: 1968 - Franchising Since: 1992 - No. of Units: Company Owned: 6 - Franchised: 3 - Franchise Fee: $19,500 - Royalty: 7%, 1% adv. - Total Inv: $70,000-$120,000 - Financing: No.

I.N.V.U. PORTRAITS
563 W. 500 S. Ste. 250, Bountiful, UT, 84010. Contact: Mark R Gilleland, V.P. Franchise Sales - Tel: (801) 292-4688, Fax: (801) 299-1625, E-Mail: markg@invuportraits.com, Web Site: www.invuportraits.com. INVU Portraits combines photography with fun. We provide imaginative props, clothing, hats and backdrop. We do all types of photography but specialize in the production of unique portraits in creative settings and offer sepia (brown-tone), black and whites and hand colored portraits in sepia and black and white. Established: 1995 - Franchising Since: 1997 - No. of Units: Franchised: 36 - Franchise Fee: $12,000 - Royalty: 6%, 1% Nat'l adv. - Total Inv: Low $29,950 - high $66,000 - Financing: No.

IMAGE ARTS ETC.
8340 Camino Santa Fe, Ste. F, San Diego, CA, 92121. - Tel: (858) 453-4200, (800) 865-4333, Fax: (858) 453-4218, E-Mail: djacobssen@IAETC.com, Web Site: www.IAETC.com. Digital Image center that combine the latest digital photography and imaging print technology all under one roof. Established: 1999 - Franchising Since: 1999 - No. of Units: Franchised: 30 - Franchise Fee: $22,750 - Financing: In-house available.

INSTA-PLAK, INC.
IPI (Insta-Plak, Inc.)
5025 Dorr St., Toledo, OH, 43615. Contact: Steve Hardin, President - Tel: (419) 537-1555, (800) 444-7525, Fax: (419) 537-1511, E-Mail: info@i-p-i.com, Web Site: www.I-P-I.com. IPI, Inc. is a photography and award franchise company. IPI presently services over 1000 sporting events yearly, inlcuding 100 events on the PGA, LPGA, and senior tours. We are looking for potential franchisees in large metropolitan markets.

Established: 1985 - Franchising Since: 1997 - No. of Units: Franchised: 4 - Franchise Fee: $20,000 - Royalty: 6% - Total Inv: $100,000 - Financing: No.

KENNEDY STUDIOS, INC.
140 Tremont St., Boston, MA, 02111. - Tel: (617) 542-0868, Fax: (617) 695-0957. Art gallery carrying limited edition prints and posters offering custom framing. Unique arrangement with franchisor which is also an art publishing company supplying images to the new franchise territory. Established: 1973 - Franchising Since: 1983 - No. of Units: Company Owned: 15 - Franchised: 38 - Franchise Fee: $15,000-$25,000- Royalty: 3%, (no ad fee) - Total Inv: $45,000-$100,000 work cap., fran. fee incl. - Financing: No.

LIL' ANGELS PHOTOGRAPHY
Lil' Angeles, LLC
6080 Quince Rd, Memphis, TN, 38119. Contact: Mark Lewis, Dir. of Franchising - Tel: (901) 682-9566, (800) 358-9101, Fax: (901) 682-2018. Daycare photography. Established: 1996 - Franchising Since: 1997 - No. of Units: Franchised: 26 - Franchise Fee: $25,000 - Total Inv: $25,000 includes all equipment and training - Financing: Partial (not through Lil' Angels).

LINDELLE STUDIOS
Fineman Marketing Corp.
724 Old York Rd., Jenkintown, PA, 19046. Contact: Barry Fineman, Pres. - Tel: (215) 572-8900, ext. 114, (800) 925-6657, Fax: (215) 572-7054. Social and wedding photography and video services. Established: 1948 - Franchising Since: 1998 - No. of Units: Company Owned: 6 - Franchised: 2 - Franchise Fee: $9,900 - Royalty: 10% - Total Inv: $19,900 - Financing: Yes.

MALIBU GALLERY
925 L St, Lincoln, NE, 68508-2229. Contact: Jack L. Rediger, President - Tel: (402) 434-5620, (800) 865-2378. Malibu Gallery offers high-quality custom framing, as well as a customer-friendly and reasonably-priced art gallery. Established: 1986 - Franchising Since: 1994 - No. of Units: Company Owned: 4 - Franchised: 3 - Franchise Fee: $20,000 - Royalty: 6%, 2% adv. - Total Inv: $59,500-$137,000 - Financing: Indirect.

MARAD FINE ART
992 High Ridge Rd, Stamford, CT, 06905. Contact: Dick Fierstein - Tel: (203) 322-7666, Fax: (203) 322-7666. Commercial framed art business. Established: 1938 - Franchising Since: 2001 - No. of Units: Company Owned: 1.

MASTER PHOTOGRAPHY
Master Photo Franchising Corp.
P.O. Box 2239, Aspen, CO, 81612. Contact: Gary Crabtree, President - Tel: (970) 927-2505, (800) 482-2505, Fax: (970) 927-2522. Wedding and event photo business - complete training and support provided. Established: 1993 - Franchising Since: 1998 - No. of Units: Company Owned: 1 - Franchised: 5 - Franchise Fee: $15,000 - Total Inv: $45,000-$60,000.

MILFORD HEIRLOOM INC.
403 New Haven Ave., Milford, CT, 06460-6649. Contact: Dennis Brown, Pres. - Tel: (203) 877-8334, Fax: (203) 877-8629. Manufacturer of photoglazing equipment wholesaler of china plates and novelties to entrepreneurs who wish to start a photo plate business. Established: 1982 - No. of Units: Company Owned: 1 - Dealers: 594 - Total Inv: $4,995-$6,995 package price.

MOTOPHOTO®
Moto Photo, Inc.
4444 Lake Center Dr., Dayton, OH, 45426. Contact: Jan Henline - Tel: (937) 854-6686 ext 313, (800) 733-6686, Fax: (937) 854-0140, E-Mail: franchise@motophoto.com, Web Site: www.motophoto.com. MotoPhoto stores are self-contained, on-site photo imaging stores providing 35mm, advanced photo system, uploads to internet, digital imaging services, and merchandise. Established: 1981 - Franchising Since: 1983 - No. of Units: Company Owned: 25 - Franchised: 254 - Franchise Fee: $35,000 - Royalty: 6% - Total Inv: $250,000-$300,000 - Financing: No.

MUD SLIDE POTTERY
207 East Main Street, El Dorado, AR, 71730. - Tel: (901) 368-3361, Fax: (901) 368-1144, E-Mail: franmark@msn.com. Contemporary ceramic studio, offering training in pottery making, art instruction and sales of pottery and related items. Established: 1995 - Franchising Since: 2001 - No. of Units: Company Owned: 1 - Franchise Fee: $15,000 - Royalty: 5% - Financing: Yes.

PHOTOLAND
Photo Images, Inc.
3115 N. Roemer Rd, Appleton, WI, 54911. Contact: Franchise Department - Tel: (920) 731-5461, Fax: (920) 731-5713. Photofinishing lab with 1 hour processing digital imaging, professional and consumer portrait photography plus accessories (frames, albums, camera accessories etc.). Established: 1992 - Franchising Since: 1996 - No. of Units: Company Owned: 2 - Franchised: 1 - Franchise Fee: $25,000.

PHOTVIDEO NETWORK
201 Willowbrooke Blvd, Wayne, NJ, 07470-7025. Contact: Nicholas Mosseau, Partner - Tel: (973) 256-2000, (800) 942-0056, Fax: (973) 256-6333. Professional photography and video services for weddings and other events. Established: 1985 - Franchising Since: 1997 - No. of Units: Company Owned: 2 - Franchised: 2 - Franchise Fee: $5,000 - Royalty: 6% - Total Inv: $32,500 - Financing: No.

PIXARTS
Picture Arts, Inc
9420 - C Mira Mesa Blvd, San Diego, CA, 92126. Contact: Anthony M. Napoli, V.P. Franchise Development - Tel: (800) 865-4333, Fax: (858) 578-2750, E-Mail: anapoli@pixarts.com, Web Site: www.pixarts.com. Founded by Tony DeSia, founder of Mail Boxes ect. Pixarts is a digital imagimg center, combined with commercial sign and graphic, frame shop and art gallery all under one roof. Established: 1999 - Franchising Since: 2000 - No. of Units: Company Owned: 1 - Franchised: 6 - Franchise Fee: $19,500 - Royalty: 6% plus, 2% advertising + 1% marketing - Total Inv: $125,000 - Financing: Yes, plus full training provided.

SPECIAL DELIVERY PHOTOS
P.O. Box 34905, Bartlett, TN, 38134. Contact: Dan Leach, President - Tel: (901) 829-3555. Provide hospitals with newborns 1st picture - full training and support provided. Established: 1984 - Franchising Since: 1991 - No. of Units: Company Owned: 1 - Franchised: 6 - Franchise Fee: $10,000 - Total Inv: $16,850-$22,050 (incl fran. fee).

SPORTS SECTION, THE
2150 Boggs Rd #200, Dulth, GA, 30096. Contact: Franchise Department - Tel: (800) 321-9127, Fax: (770) 622-4949, Web Site: www.sports-section.com. Youth and sports photography is great business... join in this explosive niche market. Protected territory, no royalties, no photography experience necessary. Established: 1983 - Franchising Since: 1984 - No. of Units: Company Owned: 2 - Franchised: 125 - Franchise Fee: $9,900 and up depending on territory - Total Inv: Fran. fee plus $3,500 equipment package - Financing: No.

VISUAL IMAGE
Visual Image, Inc., The
100 E Bockman Way, Sparta, TN, 38583-2011. Contact: Paul Holman, Pres. - Tel: (423) 981-1270, (800) 344-0323, Fax: (423) 681-0279. On location pre-school and pet photography. Established: 1984 - Franchising Since: 1994 - No. of Units: Company Owned: 5 - Franchised: 14 - Franchise Fee: $23,500 - Total Inv: $35,000 - Financing: Yes.

PRINTING AND COPYING SERVICES

ALLEGRA NETWORK LLC
21680 Haggerty Rd, Suite 105S, Northville, MI, 48167. Contact: Meredithz Zielinski, Development Program Manager - Tel: (248) 614-3700, (888) 258-2730, E-Mail: meredithz@allegranetwork.com, Web Site: www.allegranetwork.com. Our owners operate full service communications centers marketing a range of products including copying, desktop publishing, two-four color printing and digital capabilities. Established: 1976 - Franchising Since: 1977 - No. of Units: Franchised: 490 - Franchise Fee: $25,000 - Royalty: 3.6%-6% - Total Inv: $256,000-

$358,500 - Financing: Third party available. Two weeks of training at the home office, one week on-site training and continous on-going support.

ALLEGRA PRINT & IMAGING
AMERICAN SPEEDY PRINTING
INSTY-PRINTS
QUIK PRINT
SPEEDY PRINTING
ZIPPY PRINT

ALLEGRA NETWORK LLC
21680 Haggerty Raod, Suite 105S
Northville, MI, 48167
Tel: 888.258.2730   Fax: 248.614.3719
Web Site: www.allegranetwork.com
Contact: Meredith Zielinski
E-Mail: meredithz@allegranetwork.com
Our owners operate full service communications centers marketing a range of products including copying, desktop publishing, two-four color printing and digital capabilities.
Established: 1976 - Franchising Since: 1977
490 Franchised Units - Franchise Fee: $25,000
Royalty: 3.6%-6% - Total Investment including working capital: $256,000-$358,500. Third party financing available. Two weeks of training at the home office, one week on-site training and continous on-going support.

ALLEGRA PRINT & IMAGING
Allegra Network LLC
21680 Haggerty Road, Suite 105S, Northville, MI, 48167. Contact: Meredith Zielinski, Development Program Manager - Tel: (248) 614-3700, (888) 258-2730, E-Mail: meredithz@allegranetwork.com, Web Site: www.allegranetwork.com. Allegra Network links nearly 500 locations in the U.S, Canada, Poland and Japan. The company ranked 54th among Entrepreneur Magazine's Annual Franchsie 500 and was named the 20th fastest growing franchise. Allegra Print & Imaging, offers full-service print and graphic communications services including full-color printing, graphic design, digital color copying, high speed copying and online file transfer. Established: 1976 - Franchising Since: 1977 - No. of Units: Franchised: 490 - Franchise Fee: $25,000 - Royalty: 6%-3.6% - Total Inv: $256,000-$358,500 - Financing: Third party.

ALPHAGRAPHICS® PRINTSHOPS OF THE FUTURE
AlphaGraphics, Inc.
268 South State St., Suite 300, Salt Lake City, UT, 84111. Contact: Keith M. Gerson, V.P., Global Development - Tel: (801) 595-7270, (800) 955-6246, Fax: (801) 595-7271, E-Mail: opportunity@alphagraphics.com, Web Site: www.alphagraphics.com. The AlphaGraphics® Network is the leading provider of print-related and digital publishing services for businesses worldwide. All our digital centers provide a wide range of business communication services; design, copying, printing, binding, the latest digital technology (color & B&W), high speed internet connections, digital document, etc. The AlphaGraphics global intranet links AlphaGraphics locations in 15 countries. Established: 1970 - Franchising Since: 1980 - No. of Units: Company Owned: 1 - Franchised: 345 (nat'l & int'l) - Franchise Fee: $25,900 - Royalty: 1.5%-8% - Total Inv: $256,000-$448,000 - Financing: SBA, local bank, third party leasing.

AMERICAN WHOLESALE THERMOGRAPHERS
American Wholesale Thermographers, Inc.
12715 Telge Rd., Cypress,TX, 77429. Contact: Bob Dolan, Exec. Dir.Franchise Sales - Tel: (888) 280-2053, Fax: (281) 373-4450, E-Mail: awtsales@awt.com, Web Site: www.awt.com. Wholesale printing providing next day raised-letter printed materials to retail printers, copy centers and business service centers. Products include quality business cards, stationery, announcement and invitations. Training for 2 people, 216 hours in class room, 48 hours on the job. Established: 1980 - Franchising Since: 1981 - No. of Units: 20 - Franchise Fee: $30,000 - Royalty: 5% - Minimum Cash Required: $90,000 - Financing: Assistance, Yes.

BCT (BUSINESS CARDS TOMORROW)
Business Cards Tomorrow, Inc.
3000 NE 30th Pl., 5th Flr., Fort Lauderdale, FL, 33306. - Tel: (954) 563-1224, Fax: (954) 565-0742. Wholesale printing franchise specializing in next-day delivery of thermographed and offset printed products and rubber stamps. Our extensive wholesale product line includes business cards, letterhead, envelopes, announcements, stationery and rubber stamps. Established: 1975 - Franchising Since: 1977 - No. of Units: Company Owned: 3 - Franchised: 97 - Franchise Fee: $35,000 - Royalty: 6% - Total Inv: $35,000 fran. fee, $50,000 inven., $175,000 equip. plus work. cap. - Financing: Third party outsourced.

FRANKLIN'S PRINTING, DIGITAL IMAGING & COPYING
Franklin's Systems, Inc.
5045 Memorial Drive, Stone Mountain, GA, 30082. - Tel: (404) 296-9504, Fax: (404) 296-9150. Part of the ICED family of franchises, now in our 30th year, with over 1,000 franchises in 21 countries. As a memebr of the ICED family of franchises we maintain a position of leadership with our traditional printing and digital publishing, including Website design and maintenance as well as legendary outside sales consultant training. Your corporate management skills are transferable in our business to business environment. 4 weeks of classroom training and 2 weeks in your store training. Outside sales consultant training for 1, selling techniques/systems and product knowledge. Established: 1971 - Franchising Since: 1977 - No. of Units: Franchised: 65 - Franchise Fee: $25,000 - Royalty: 4%-8% - Equity Capital Required: $80,000 - Financing: Assistance, yes.

INK WELL, THE
Ink Well of America, Inc., The
12715 Telge Rd, Cypress, TX, 77429. - Tel: (888) 280-2053, Fax: (281)-373-4450, E-Mail: iwasales@iwa.com, Web Site: www@iwa.com. Part of the ICED family of franchises, now in our 30th year, with over 1,000 franchises in 21 countries. As a member of the ICED family of franchises we maintain a position of leadership with our traditional printing and digital publishing, including WebSite design and maintenance as well as legendary outside sales, consultant training. Your corporate, management skills are transferable in our business to business environment. Four weeks of classroom training and 1 1/2 weeks in your shop. Outside sales consultant training for 1, selling techniques/systems and product knowledge. Established: 1972 - Franchising Since: 1981 - No. of Units: Franchised: 42 - Franchise Fee: $25,000 - Royalty: 4%-6% - Equity Capital Required: $80,000 - Financing: Assistance, Yes.

INSTY-PRINTS
Insty-Prints , Inc.
8091 Wallace Rd., Eden Prairie, MN, 55344. Contact: Robert Warmka, V.P. Franchise Services - Tel: (952) 975-6200, (800) 779-1000, Web Site: www.insty-prints.com. Provides high quality printing and copying services. Emphasis on fast, convenient service in a friendly, professional atmosphere. Established: 1965 - Franchising Since: 1967 - No. of Units: Company Owned: 2 - Franchised: 233 - Franchise Fee: $40,000 - Royalty: 4.5% - Total Inv: $283,000-$340,000 - Financing: No.

INTERNATIONAL LEGAL IMPRINTS
3820 Premier Ave., Memphis, TN, 38118. Contact: Franchise Director - Tel: (901)368-3361, Fax: (901)368-3724. Copying services and litigation support services for law firms, legal departments. Established: 1991- No. of Units: Company Owned: 5 - Franchised: 4 - Franchise Fee: $25,000 - Royalty: 8%, 1% adv. - Total Inv: $138,875-$231,375 - Financing: Partial available. NOT FRANCHISING AT THIS TIME.

INVENTORY MANAGEMENT SOLUTIONS
Quadco Printing
2535 Zanella Way, Chico, CA, 95928. Contact: Michelle Mitchell, Dir. - Tel: (530) 894-0654, Fax: (530) 894-0709. This company offers "one-call does it all" convenience for you and your franchisees. Services include: design, electronic prepress, modem service, printing, one-color to full-color, packaging, mailing, bindery operations, warehousing and distribution, on-line order processing and shipment tracking, management reports and inventory financing. Established: 1896.

KWIK KOPY BUSINESS CENTER
Kwik Kopy Business Center
12715 Telge Road, Cypress, TX, 77429. Contact: Bob Dolan, Exec. Dir. Franchise Sales - Tel: (800) 746-9498, (281) 256-4100, Fax: (281)256-4178, E-Mail: kksales@kwikkopy.com, Web Site: www.www.kkbconline.com. Kwik Kopy provides a full range of printing, copying, pack-and-ship and cargo services. Established: 2001 - Franchising Since: 2001 - No. of Units: Franchised: 8 - Total Inv: $161,500-$206,700 - Financing: Assistance, yes.

LAZERQUICK ®
Graphic Information Systems, Inc.
27375 SW Parkway Ave. #200, Wilsonville, OR, 97070. Contact: V.P Franchising - Tel: (503) 682-1322, (800) 477-2679, Fax: (503) 682-7816, Web Site: www.lazerquick.com. Lazerquick Centers are complete, one-stop printing and copying centers. All centers feature state-of-the-art electronic publishing and digital graphics and imaging services that support our wide range of quality, fast-service offset printing, high speed copying, color copying and related bindery and finishing services. Established: 1968 - Franchising Since: 1990 - No. of Units: Company Owned: 23 - Franchised: 29 - Franchise Fee: $25,000 - Royalty: Start up 5% of gross first 48 months, 3% of gross remaining 36 months, renewals: 3% of base line increase in sales - Total Inv:Start up $172,500-$275,000/conversion $16,300-$35,200 - Financing: AT&T small business lending corp.

MINUTEMAN PRESS
Minuteman Press International
61 Executive Blvd, Farmingdale, NY, 11735. - Tel: (631) 249-1370, Fax: (631) 249-5618, Web Site: www.minutemanpress.com. Full service printing and graphic's franchise with 24 regional support offices for technical, marketing, and ongoing business management support. Established: 1973 - Franchising Since: 1975 - No. of Units: Franchised: 890 - Franchise Fee: $44,500 - Royalty: 6% of gross sales, with cap of $21000 in monthly sales - Total Inv: $44,500 lic.fee, equip pk $60,000-$70,000 =$105,000-$115,000 - Financing: Yes various.

PIP PRINTING
26722 Plaza Dr., Ste. 200, Mission Viejo, CA, 92691. Contact: Karen Brock, Fran. Dev. Spec. - Tel: (800) 894-7498, Fax: (800) 747-0679. PIP Printing provides a full range of business communications services from initial concept to finished printed product. Established: 1965 - Franchising Since: 1968 - No. of Units: Franchised: 554 - Franchise Fee: $20,000 - Royalty: Sliding scale 7%-1% - Total Inv: $232,850-$465,840 - Financing: Third party.

POSTAL INSTANT PRESS INC.
PIP Printing
27001 Agara Rd., Ste. 200, Agara Hills, CA, 91301. Contact: Franchise Development - Tel: (818) 880-3887, (800) 292-4747, Fax: (818) 880-3989, E-Mail: fransales@pip.com, Web Site: www.pip.com. PIP locations provide a full range of business communications from initial concept to finished printed product. PIP service menu includes: short run full/multi color printing, high colume copying, DTP, layout, design and finishing. Also unique opportunity to own your own print broker business. Established: 1965 - Franchising Since: 1968 - No. of Units: Franchised: 501 - Franchise Fee: $5,000-$22,000 - Royalty: 7% flat rate - Total Inv: $21,000-$220,000 - Financing: No.

PRINTING ONE
Printing One Corporation
740 Hillcrest Rd., Mobile, AL, 36695. - Tel: (334) 633-3006. Printing franchise emphasizing marketing and customer service. Franchisor provides centralized production facility. Owners devote majority of their time to developing a strong customer base. Established: 1990 - Franchising Since: 1990 - No. of Units: Franchised: 4 - Franchise Fee:

$25,000 - Royalty: 5% - Total Inv: $33,000 to open, plus $24,000 oper. cap. - Financing: $5,000 of franchise fee deferred. Corporate will finance that amount only.

PRINTSOURCE CORPORATION
969 Park Ave., Craanston, RI, 02910. Contact: Edward Tavares, Franchise Development - Tel: (401) 943-6601, (800) 341-6300. Printing, copying and related services. Established: 1969 - Franchising Since: 1999 - No. of Units: Company Owned: 5 - Fraanchised: 2 - Franchise Fee: $25,000 - Total Inv: $40,000 - Financing: Yes.

SCREEN PRINTING USA
Screen Printing USA, Inc.
534 W. Shawnee Ave., Plymouth, PA, 18651. Contact: Russ Ownes, Pres. - Tel: (717) 779-5175. Silk screen printing with state-of-the-art equipment for T-shirts, signs, posters, metal, + ASI, wood, hats, jackets, etc. Established: 1989 - Franchising Since: 1989 - No. of Units: Company Owned: 1 - Franchised: 30, 2 in Canada - Franchise Fee: $25,000 - Royalty: 6% - Total Inv: $25,000-$48,000 - Financing: Yes. NOT FRANCHISING AT THIS TIME.

SIR SPEEDY PRINTING CENTERS
Sir Speedy, Inc.
26722 Plaza Dr. P.O. Box 9077, Mission Viejo, CA, 92691. Contact: Franchise Department - Tel: (949) 348-5000, Fax: (949) 348-5066. Printing, copying, digital network services provided to businesses and individuals. We are the small business communications network. Established: 1968 - Franchising Since: 1968 - No. of Units: Company Owned: 20 - Franchised: 830 - Franchise Fee: $20,000 - Royalty: 4% first yr., 6% thereafter - Total Inv: $20,000 fee; $36,000 start-up; $74,000 equip., $100,000 working cap. - Financing: Yes.

SMALL CITY BUSINESS JOURNALS INC.
110 Merchants Row, Rutland, VT, 05701. Contact: Richard S. Rohe, Pres. - Tel: (802) 775-9500, Fax: (802) 775-0658. Newspaper business journal. Established: 1986 - Franchising Since: 1986 - No. of Units: Company Owned: 4 - Franchised: 1 - Franchise Fee: $30,000 - Royalty: 7% of gross sales - Total Inv: $100,000 - Financing: Yes.

SPEEDPRO COLOR IMAGING CENTERS
Speedpro Systems, Inc.
605 S. Sherman, Ste. J, Richardson, TX, 75081. Contact: Blair Gran - Tel: (800) 775-6355, E-Mail: blair@speedpro.com. High resolution digital imaging setup, with multiple printing systems. Established: 1992 - Franchising Since: 2002 - No. of Units: Franchised: 43 - Franchise Fee: $20,000 - Total Inv: $97,500 - Financing: Third party.

UNITED PRINTING UNLIMITED
United Printing Unlimited Inc.
P.O. Box 2020, Davenport, IA, 52809. - Tel: (407) 246-0160, Fax: (407) 246-0207. Full service printing centers. Complete support, 3 wks. training, covering all aspects of printing and business. Established: 1985 - Franchising Since: 1986 - No. of Units: Company Owned: 2 - Franchised: 13 - Franchise Fee: $25,000 - Royalty: 5% of gross profit - Total Inv: $25,000 fee, $75,000 equip. - Financing: Yes, 90%.

PUBLICATIONS

ABOUT MAGAZINES
Strategic Publishing Franchising Corp.
576 Sigman Rd., Ste. 200, Conyers, GA, 30013. Contact: Greg Tanner - Tel: (770) 761-3331, (877) 607-4768, Fax: (770) 761-9889, E-Mail: gtanner@strategicpub.com. We publish digest size community advertising publications anywhere in the U.S. Established: 1999 - Franching Since: 2000 - No. of Units: Company Owned: 3 - Franchised: 14 - Franchise Fee: $12,500 - Total Inv: $20,000 min.

BINGO BUGLE NEWSPAPER
K & O Publishing, Inc.
P.O. Box 527, Vashon, WA, 98070. - Tel: (206) 463-5656, Fax: (206) 463-5630. Monthly publication for bingo players. Franchisee is responsible for sales, publishing, and distribution. A 2-day training is provided to franchisees, along with manuals and start-up materials. Established: 1981 - Franchising Since: 1983 - No. of Units: Franchised:

68 - Franchise Fee: $1,500-$10,000 - Royalty: 10% of monthly gross revenues, except first month of publication - Total Inv: $2,500-$10,000, plus cost of telephone, camera, automobile, typewriter and/or computer if franchisee doesn't own.

BOOKS ARE FUN
A Readers Digest Company
1680 Hwy. 1 North, Fairfield, IA, 52556. Contact: Lidia Saldivar - Tel: (800) 966-8301, Fax: (888) 625-6812, E-Mail: busops@booksarefun.com, Web Site: www.booksarefun.com. Sell high quality books, gifts, jewelry and art to customers in the work place. All inventory on consignment. Established: 1990 - No. of Units: Franchised: 800 - Franchise Fee: $500.-$5,000 - Financing: Yes.

BUSINESS MONTHLY
245 W. Saginaw Box 26, Hemlock, MI, 48626. - Tel: (517) 642-NEWS, Fax: (517) 642-3600. Monthly business newspaper. Established: 1996 - No. of Units: Company Owned: 1 - Total Inv: $14,900 - Financing: No.

BUYING & DINING GUIDE
Community Publications of America, Inc.
80 8th Ave., New York, NY, 10011. Contact: Allan Horwitz, Pres. - Tel: (212) 243-6800. Buying and Dining Guide is a unique money-maker for the publisher and the advertiser offering total market coverage of the active buyers and diners throughout the area. Publishing and distribution costs are minimal, and the advertiser receives 14 days of effective advertising, for the price of a single ad. Established: 1980 - Franchising Since: 1989 - No. of Units: 4 - Franchise Fee: $29,900 with money-back guarantee - Royalty: $200+ per issue - Total Inv: $29,900 incl. fran. fee plus $3,000 work. cap. - Financing: No.

CATHEDRAL DIRECTORIES FRANCHISES, INC.
1401 W. Girard Ave., Madison Heights, MI, 48071. Contact: Bob Austin, Fran. Sales Dir. - Tel: (800) 544-6903, (248) 545-1415, Fax: (248) 544-1611. U.S. publisher of church, homeowners and organization directories. Franchisee will offer the service on a no-charge basis to the church and will sell advertisements to support it. No royalties. No competition. Enjoy 95% renewal. Build a long term, profitable, home-based business. Established: 1948 - Franchising Since: 1993 - No. of Units: Company Owned: 4 - Franchised: 3 - Franchise Fee: $14,500 - Total Inv: $50,000 - Financing: Third party assistance, SBA.

COFFEE NEWS, USA
Ergonomic Consulting Services, Inc.
P.O. Box 8444, Bangor, ME, 04402-8444. Contact: William A. Buckley, President - Tel: (207) 941-0860, Fax: (207) 941-01050, Web Site: www.coffeenewsusa.com. Coffee News is a weekly restaurant publication for patrons to read while eating. It is a fun, entertaining paper containing short stories, jokes, trivia, local events, activities and weekly horoscopes. Established: 1994 - Franchising Since: 1996 - No. of Units: Company Owned: 3 - Franchised: 279- Franchise Fee: $2,000 1st area, $1,000 for each additional - Royalty: $75/wk 1st, $20/wk for each additional area - Total Inv: $2,500 - Financing: No.

CREATE-A-BOOK
Create-A-Book, Inc
1232 Paula Circle., Gulf Breeze, FL, 32561. Contact: John Hefty, President - Tel: (850) 934-1599, Fax: (850) 934-8903, Web Site: www.hefty.com. Personalize children's books using your computer and inkjet printer. 400% markup on products. Established: 1981 - No. of Dealerships: 2,000 - Franchise Fee: $500.00 - Royalty: None - Financing: No.

DISCIPLE'S DIRECTORY
Disciple's Directory, Inc
10 Fiorenza Drive, Wilmington, MA, 01887. Contact: Kenneth Dorothy, President - Tel: (978) 657-7373, (800) 696-2344, Fax: (978) 657-5411, E-Mail: kadorothy@yahoocom, Web Site: www.disciplesdirectory.com. Christian business and ministry directory. Established: 1984 - Franchising Since: 1999 - No. of Units: Company Owned: 3 - Franchised: 3 - Franchise Fee: $5,000 - Royalty: None - Total Inv: None - Financing: No.

EASYCHAIR MAGAZINE
EasyChair Media, LLC
800 Third Street, Windsor, CO, 80550. Contact: Kristie Melendez, Manager - Tel: (970) 686-5805, (800) 741-6308, Fax: (970) 686-7335, E-Mail: kristie@easychairmedia.com, Web Site: www.easychair media.com. A community, family magazine that delivers postive "good" news to prime households in the market through controlled direct mail. Established: 2000 - Franchising Since: 2002 - No. of Units: Company Owned: 5 - Franchised: 1 - Franchise Fee: $10,000-$20,000 - Total Inv: $35,000-$45,000 - Financing: No.

FRANCHISEWORKS.COM
1501 Nevare Rd, Warminster, PA, 18974. Contact: Maria Ponentre - Tel: (215) 672-9048, (877) 824-4411, Fax: (215) 672-1878, E-Mail: advertise@franchiseworks.com, Web Site: www.franchiseworks.com. Directory of franchise and business opportunities. If you are looking to buy a franchise or business go to www.franchiseworks.com. Established: 1999.

H.O.M.E. - FOR SALE BY OWNER
60 Madison Ave., Suite 1206, New York, NY, 10010. - Tel: (888) 933-8900. Publishing FSBO magazine, listings on internet, published monthly. Established: 1990 - Franchising Since: 1993 - No. of Units: Franchised: 1 - Franchise Fee: $15,000 - Royalty: 5% (3% fees + 2% adv.) - Total Inv: Includes complete set up, computer and $1,000 allowance for 3 day training in Daytona Beach, FL - Financing: No.

HOME INC - FOR SALE BY OWNER - F.S.B.O.
Biro and Associates
6348 Palmas Bay Circle, Port Orange, FL, 32127. Contact: M.V. Biro, President - Tel: (904) 767-7523. Publication, advertising of For Sale By Owner magazine. Full training and support provided. Established: 1990 - Franchising since: 1990 - No. of Units: Company Owned: 1 - Franchised: 2 - Franchise Fee: $1,500 - Total Inv: $ 1,650 and up - Financing: Yes.

HOMES & LAND PUBLISHING, LTD.
1600 Capital Circle., S.W., Tallahassee, FL, 32310. - Tel: (850) 574-2111. Pictorial community real estate advertising magazine. Established: 1973 - Franchising Since: 1984 - No. of Units: Company Owned: 6 - Franchised: 248 - Total Inv: $49,000- $95,000 working capital - Financing: None.

HOMESTEADER®, THE
Homesteader Enterprises, Inc.
P.O. Box 2824, Framingham, MA, 01703. Contact: Allen Nitschelm, Pres. - Tel: (508) 820-4311, (800) 941-9907, Fax: (508) 820-0280, E-Mail: homestea@tiac.net, Web Site: www.thehomesteader.com. Publish a monthly newspaper mailed to new homeowners, offering local businesses the opportunity to target their advertising to this market. Publish a edition of the Homesteader in your area! Established: 1989 - Franchising Since: 1993 - No. of Units: Company Owned: 3 - Franchised: 13 - Franchise Fee: $3,400 - Royalty: 10% on gross revenues - Total Inv: $8,000-$22,000 includes f.f. - Financing: Yes, $400.00 down and $3,000 in 6 months.

INDUSTRY MAGAZINE
317 S. Northlake Blvd., Ste. 1020, Altamonte Springs, FL, 32701. Contact: Susan Summey - Tel: (407) 253-9972, (866) 256-9550, Fax: (407) 532-9180, E-Mail: industrymag2004@aol.com, Web Site: www.industrymagazine.com. Own & publish your own high fashion/ entertainment magazine without the risk involved in spending a million dollars. Established: 2003 - Franchising Since: 2004 - No. of Units: Company Owned: 1 - Franchise Fee: $25,000 - Total Inv: $34,000-$43,000.

PENNYSAVER
Community Publications of America, Inc.
80 Eighth Ave., New York, NY, 10011. Contact: Allan Horwitz, Pres. - Tel: (212) 243-6800, Fax: (212) 243-7457. America's favourite shopping guide, offering advertisers total market coverage by direct mail to all households and most businesses in the community. Established: 1973 - Franchising Since: 1979 - No. of Units: 20 - Franchise Fee: $29,900 with money-back guarantee - Royalty: $200+ per issue - Total Inv: $29,900 plus $10,000 work cap.- Financing: No.

REACH MAGAZINE
Reach Publishing Systems, Inc.
9933 Alliance Rd, Cincinnati, OH, 45242-5642. Contact: Franchise Dept. - Tel: (513) 794-4100, (800) 945-0050 #119, Fax: (513) 794-4140, E-Mail: jsander@reachusa.com. Reach Magazine is a direct response magazine franchised to an exclusive geographic area (min. 100,000 pop.). The franchisee sells ads, advertorials and classified to local and national clients. Established: 1989 - Franchising Since: 1991 - No. of Units: Company Owned: 2 - Franchised: 8 - Franchise Fee: $10,000 - Royalty: None - Total Inv: $24,000 - Financing: $125,000.

RENTAL GUIDE MAGAZINE
Homes & Land Publishing, Ltd.
1600 Capital Circle., SW, Tallahassee, FL, 32310. - Tel: (800) 726-6683, ext 252. Color community advertising magazine for rental properties and apartment complexes, free to consumers. Franchisee handles advertising, sales and distribution; franchisor offers production, printing, training and marketing support services. Established: 1973 - Franchising Since: 1988 - No. of Units: Company Owned: 2 - Franchised: 28 - Royalty: Varies 6%-16% - Total Inv: $55,800-$94,000 - Financing: No.

SNITCH *
4229 Bardstown Rd., #315, Louisville, KY, 40218. - Tel: (502) 779-3073, E-Mail: franchising@snitch.com, Web Site: www.snitch.com. Free weekly crime-focused newspaper with a mix of local and nationally syndicated content. Established: 2001 - Franchising Since: 2004 - No. of Units: Company Owned: 1 - Franchise Fee: $15,000-$40,000 - Royalty: 10% - Total Inv: $57,300-$171,700 - Royalty: No.

STUDENT SUPER-SAVER®
Pendant Publishing
P.O. Box 2933, Grand Junction, CO, 81502. - Tel: (970) 243-6465, Fax: (970) 241-0771. Advertising publications that target high school and college students. Established: 1982 - Franchising Since: 1995 - No. of Units: Company Owned: 2 - Franchise Fee: $9,999 - Royalty: 10% - Total Inv: $25,000 - Financing: Yes.

SUBFINDERS. COM PUBLICATION
Subfinders. Com
3275 Hillmont Cir., Orlando, FL, 32817. Contact: Jess Gendron, President - Tel: (407) 681-0400, Fax: (407) 681-0403, E-Mail: info@subfinders. com, Web Site: www.subfinders.com. Construction publication for commercial and residential. "An exciting and fun magazine". Established: 1998 - Franchising Since: 1999 - No. of Units: Company Owned: 2 - Franchise Fee: $10,000/$15,000 - Royalty: 5% - Total Inv: $20,000-$30,000 - Financing: None.

TELEVISION & ENTERTAINMENT PUBLICATIONS, INC
Liberty Square, Danvers, MA, 01923. Contact: VP, Franchise Director - Tel: (978) 777-4666, (888) 977-4666, Fax: (781) 595-9237, Web Site: www.tventmag.com. Home based publishing business. On going regional support. Established: 1995 - Franchising Since: 1997 - No. of Units: Company Owned: 1 - Franchised: 4 - Total Inv: $28,800 ($25,500 start-up).

TV FACTS MAGAZINE
TV Facts of North America, Inc.
Liberty Square, Danvers, MA, 01923. Contact: Ronald S. Rubin, President - Tel: (508) 777-9225. Free weekly TV magazine and shoppers guide - training and support provided. Established: 1987 - Franchising Since: 1988 - No. of Units: Franchised: 170 (14 states, 2 countries) - Franchise Fee: $24,500 - Total Inv: $30,500 (fran fee + $4,000-$6,000 work cap) - Financing: No.

TV NEWS MAGAZINE
Community Publications of America, Inc.
80 Eighth Ave., New York, NY, 10011. Contact: Allan Horwitz, Pres. - Tel: (212) 243-6800, Fax: (212) 243-7457. An award winning free community publication combining the 7-day readership of a TV guide, with the total market coverage of a penny saver, and the efficiency of scale of a major national publication. The exciting editorial attracts readers, and the excellent response attracts advertisers. Established: 1973 - Franchising Since: 1979 - No. of Units: Company Owned: 1 -

Franchised: 9 - Franchise Fee: $29,900 with money-back guarantee - Royalty: $150+ per week - Total Inv: $29,900 fran. fee plus $5,000 work. cap. - Financing: Yes, with min. 20% down.

REAL ESTATE SERVICES

ADVANTAGE RADON CONTROL CENTERS
804 Second St. Pike, Southampton, PA, 18966. - Tel: (215) 953-9200, Fax: (215) 953-8837. Offers a franchisee the opportunity to tap into the growing market of home and business owners seeking a safer environment. Our centers provide radon detection, testing and reduction services. Customer-oriented, spotting and solving radon problems quickly and efficiently. Comprehensive two-week training and support package is included, which qualifies you for EPA listing and state certification. Established: 1984 - Franchising Since: 1990 - No. of Units: Company Owned: 1 - Franchise Fee: $17,500 - Royalty: 8% - Financing: Will assist. Not currently offering franchises at this time.

AMERICA'S CHOICE® CANADA'S CHOICE®
America's Choice International Inc.
636 N. French Rd., Ste. 10, Amherst, NY, 14228. Contact: David Schembri, Co-Founder - Tel: (800) 831-2493 (US/Canada), (716) 691-0596 (Erie County), Fax: (716) 691-0650, E-Mail: accorporate@ sprintmail.com. Formerly Preferred Realty Concepts, Inc. Leading International Owner-Assisted Real Estate Marketing Company with 59 franchise units in several states and 3 provinces. Full service real estate/ home owner shows home. Established: 1992 - Franchising Since: 1994 - No. of Units: Franchised: 59 - Franchise Fee: $7,000 - (option 1- Limited availability) or $16,000 (option 2) - Master Franchises available (option 3): $2,500/100,000 households - Royalty: 7/10%+ 1% nat'l adv. (revenue splits with master franchisees) - Total Inv: $2,000-$16,000 depending on option purchased.

AMERICORP REALTY NETWORK
Americorp Marketing Inc.
185 Hillside Ave., Williston Park, NY, 11596. Contact: Anthony J. Biancaniello, President - Tel: (516) 248-4080, (877) 248-4080, Fax: (516) 248-4091, E-Mail: info@americorp.net, Web Site: www.americorp.net. ARN is a home based, turnkey franchise combining on-line real estate listings with local advertising from related businesses. Established: 1998 - Franchising Since: 1998 - Franchise Fee: $29,000 - Royalty: 80/20 - Total Inv: $47,500-$87,950 including franchise fee - Financing: No.

APARTMENT SEARCH INTERNATIONAL
Apartment Search, Inc
7900 Xerxes Ave S. Ste, 2250, Bloomington, MN, 55431. Contact: Franchise Department - Tel: (952) 830-0509, (800) 989-3764. Apartment locator business. Established: 1965 - Franchising Since: 1990 - No. of Units: Company Owned: 25 - Franchised: 8 - Franchise Fee: $40,000 (capital requirement $80,000-$150,000).

ARTHUR RUTENBERG HOMES, INC.
13922 58th St. N., Clearwater, FL, 33760. Contact: Raja Jaghab, Sr. V.P. - Tel: (727) 536-5900, (800) 274-6637, Fax: (727)538-9089, E-Mail: rjaghab@arhomes.com, Web Site: www.arhomes.com. Custom home building franchisor. Established: 1980 - Franchising Since: 1980 - No. of Units: Company Owned: 3 - Franchised: 25 - Franchise Fee: $30,000 - Royalty: 4% - Total Inv: $350,000-$500,000 - Financing: No.

ASSET VERIFICATION, INC
Asset Verification, Inc
510 S. Batavia Avenue, Batavia, IL, 60510. Contat: Mr. Randy Forman - Tel: (630) 406-8874, (800) 335-0513, Fax: (630) 406-9793, E-Mail: rforman@assetverification.com, Web Site: www.assetverification.com. AVI provides, appraisal, and asset management (bar-coding) systems on CD-ROMS for residential, commercial, and religious properties. Our patent-pending software, voice-activated technology, and digital imaging define AVI as an industry leader. Clients are able to confirm that insurance coverage is adequate, complete estate plans, manage the movement of assets, and conduct real estate transactions and other legal proceedings with ease. We also offer aggregate valuations of property contents, individual certified appraisals, and document scanning.

Established: 1998 - Franchising Since: 1999 - No. of Units: Company Owned: 1 - Franchised: 14 - Franchise Fee: $25,000 - Royalty: 10% of gross - Total Inv: $40,000-$55,000 - Financing: No.

ASSIST-2-SELL
Assist-2-Sell, Inc.
1610 Meadow Wood Lane, Reno, NV, 89502. Contact: Lyle Martin, V.P. - Tel: (775) 688-6060, (800) 528-7816, Fax: (775) 828-8823, E-mail: info@assist2sell.com, Web Site: www.assist2sell.com. America's "Full Service with $avings!" real estate company. A Pioneer in the "menu of services" discount real estate concept. Franchise available nationwide, protected areas, low fees. Established: 1987 - Franchising Since: 1994 - No. of Units: Franchised: 120 - Franchise Fee: $10,000 - Royalty: 5% - Total Inv: Available - Financing: No.

BETTER HOMES AND GARDENS REAL ESTATE
Meredith Corporation
2000 Grand Ave., Des Moines, IA, 50312. Contact: Franchise Department - Tel: (800) 274-7653. Franchising of real estate companies in all 50 states with a full-service support system. Established: 1977 - Franchising Since: 1978 - No. of Units: Company Owned: 2 - Franchised: 680 - Franchise Fee: $11,000 and up - Royalty: From 6% - Total Inv: Varies - Financing: Deferred payment plan for one year.

BETTER HOMES REALTY
Better Homes Realty, Inc.
1777 Botelho Dr., #380, Walnut Creek, CA, 94596. Contact: V.P. of Operations - Tel: (925) 937-9001, (800) 642-4428, Fax: (925) 988-2770. Real estate franchisor of independently owned and operated offices. Established: 1964 - Franchising Since: 1964 - No. of Units: Franchised: 48 - Franchise Fee: $9,950 - Royalty: 6% royalty/service per transaction - Total Inv: $9,950 for existing brokerages; up to $40,000 start-up - Financing: $4,000 down payment; franchisor may agree on deferred payment.

BETTER LIFESTYLES
P.O. Box 540912, Flushing, NY, 11354. Contact: Maury S. Jazzetti, President - Tel: (718) 461-9000. Professional real estate franchise system. Established: 1995 - Franchising Since: 1995 - No. of Units: Franchised: 7 - Franchise Fee: $5,000 - Financing: No.

BUY OWNER INTERNATIONAL
5757 N. Andrews Way, Ft. Lauderdale, FL, 33309. Contact: Scott A. Eckert, Pres. - Tel: (954) 771-7777, (800) 940-7777, Fax: (954) 771-8187, Web Site:www.byowner.com. A real estate advertising service where sellers pay an up front advertising fee to appear on our computer matching system, TV show, and magazine. Buyers receive free information of properties that meet their requirements. Established: 1984 - No. of Units: Company Owned: 1 - Franchised: 6 - Franchise Fee: $15,000 - Royalty: 5% - Total Inv: $75,000-$300,000.

BUYER'S AGENT, THE
Buyer's Agent, Inc., The
1255 Lynnfield Ste. 273, Memphis, TN, 38119. Contact: Franchise Department - Tel: (901) 767-1077, (800) 766-8728, Fax: (901) 767-3577, E-Mail:rebuyragt@aol.com, Web Site: www.forbuyers.com. The oldest, largest and most successful franchisor of exclusive buyer agency. Our offices represent the real estate and home buyers only. Franchises are purchased by successful business people changing careers, real estate brokers, appraisers, accountants and attorneys. Established: 1988 - Franchising Since: 1988- No. of Units: Franchised: 88 - Franchise Fee: $14,900 - Royalty: 5%, 1% adv., franchisor matches 1% nat'l. adv. fee - Total Inv: $14,900 franchise fee, $5,000-$15,000 operational funds, $5,000-$15,000 starting fee - Financing: Short term available.

CASTLES UNLIMITED
Castles Unlimited International, Inc
837 Beacon Street, Newtson Centre, MA, 02459. Contact: James Lowenstern, Franchise Director - Tel: (617) 964-3300, Fax: (617) 244-5847, E-Mail: franchise@castlesunlimited.com, Web Site: www.castlesunlimited.com. 100% PLUS Commission System. Established: 1985 - Franchising Since: 1995 - No. of Units: Company Owned: 1 - Franchised: 1 - Franchise Fee: $5,000 - Royalty: 5% - Total Inv: $5,000.

CASTLETON
Castleton Home Corp.
1960 Congressional Dr., St. Louis, MO, 63146. - Tel: (314) 567-1500, (800) 908-0706, Fax: (314) 567-0304. Provider of full service corporate apartments for relocation and project assignment individuals in leased units. Established: 1987 - Franchising Since: 1994 - No. of Units: Company Owned: 2 - Franchised: 4 - Franchise Fee: $20,000 - Royalty:4% - Total Inv: $100,000+ - Financing: No.

CENTURY 21 REAL ESTATE
6 Sylvan Way, Parsippany, NJ, 07054. Contact: Rick Del Sontro, SR VP Fran. Sales - Tel: (973) 496-7221, (800) 826-8083, Fax: (973) 496-4981, Web Site: www.century 21.com. Residential real estate franchising organization. Provides a marketing support system for independently owned and operated real estate brokerage offices, offering international advertising, VIP referral system, residential and commercial sales training and other real estate related services. Established: 1971 - Franchising Since: 1972 - No. of Units: Franchised: 6,200 - Franchise Fee: $25,000 - Royalty: 6% of gross revenue - Total Inv: $50,000-$200,000 - Financing: No.

COLDWELL BANKER REAL ESTATE CORPORATION
6 Sylvan Way, Parsippany, NJ, 07054. Contact: Ernie Kerns, Sr. VP Fran. Sales - Tel: (973) 428-9700, Fax: (973) 496-0199, Web Site: www.coldwellbanker.com. Established in 1906, the company has 91 years of real estate experience. The system includes over 2,565 franchised offices and more than 52,000 sales associates and employees in North America, International Real Estate Franchising. Established: 1906 - Franchising Since: 1982 - No. of Units: Franchised: 2,565 - Franchise Fee: $7,500-$20,000 - Royalty: 6% of gross revenue - Total Inv: $15,100-$56,750 - Financing: No.

ELLIOTT & COMPANY APPRAISERS
7-C Oak Branch Dr., Greensboro, NC, 27407. Contact: Charlie Elliott,, President - Tel: (800) 854-5889, (336) 854-3075, Fax: (336) 854-7734, Web Site: www.elliottco.com. The franchisor provides a comprehensive package of services designed to assist the franchisee in marketing residential and commercial appraisals and managing the appraisal office. Established: 1985 - Franchising Since: 1993 - No. of Units: Company Owned: 4 - Franchised: 7 - Franchise Fee: $7,500 - Royalty: 8%, 2% adv. - Total Inv: $5,250-$17,000 - Financing: Yes.

GMAC HOME SERVICES
2021 Spring Rd., #300, Oak Brook, IL, 60523. - Tel: (800) 274-7653, Fax: (630) 214-1693, Web Site: www.gmacrealestate.com. GMAC is one of the nation's largest real estate organizations, delivering premier service to home sellers and buyers. Established: 1998 - Franchising Since: 1998 - No. of Units: Company Owned: 100 - Franchised: 1100 - Franchise Fee: $20,000 - Royalty: 5%.

HELP-U-SELL REAL ESTATE
6800 Jericho Turnpike Suite 208E, Syosset, NY, 11791. Contact: Ann Reynolds, V.P./ Franchise Sales Director - Tel: (516) 364-9650, (800) 366-1177, Fax: (516) 364-8757, E-Mail: husoffice@aol.com, Web Site: www.helpusell.net. Help-U-Sell is one of the largest and oldest fee for service franchise system. It is a full service real estate company offering the consumer choices and savings. Established: 1976 - Franchising Since: 1978 - No. of Units: Company Owned: 24 - Franchised: 105 - Franchise Fee: $10,500 - Royalty: 7.5% - Financing: Yes.

HOMELIFE REALTY SERVICE
4100 Newport Place, Ste. 730, Newport Beach, CA, 92660. Contact: Andrew Cimerman, President - Tel: (800) 755-1910, (949) 250-6789, Fax: (949) 660-1910. Real estate office. Established: 1985 - Franchising Since: 1985 - No. of Units: Franchised: 180 - Franchise Fee: $9,000 - Royalty: $575 per month - Total Inv: $10,000 - Financing: In some cases.

HOMEOWNERS CONCEPT, INC.
611 North Mayfair Rd., Milwaukee, WI, 53226. Contact: Peter Skenevis, President - Tel: (414) 258-7778, (800) 800-9890, Fax: (414) 258-8276, Web Site: www.homeownersconcept.com. High volume operation of real estate consulting/sales. Extremely efficient program, no showings, no open houses and minimum driving. Established: 1982 - Franchising Since: 1985 - No. of Units: Franchised: 31 - Franchise Fee: $7,500 - Royalty: 2% - Total Inv: $18,700-$24,550 - Financing: Yes.

HOMETEAM INSPECTION SERVICE, THE
6355 E. Kemper Rd., Ste. 250, Cincinnati, OH, 45241-2300. Contact: Franchise Dept. - Tel: (800) 598-5297, Fax: (513) 469-2226, Web Site: www.hmteam.com. A Home Inspection Service that emphasizes marketing and ongoing support. As one of our franchisees said, "With our marketing, image and value to our customers, I found that my competition was doing nothing but helping me build my business. People were so accustomed to the 'typical inspection', they just couldn't believe how different we are". Established: 1991 - Franchising Since: 1992 - No. of Units: Franchised: 330 - Franchise Fee: $11,900-$29,900 - Royalty: 6%, 3% nat'l. adv. - Total Inv: Cap. Inv: $18,450-$45,550 - Financing: Yes, up to 50% of franchise fee.

HOUSEMASTER - "THE HOME INSPECTION PROFESSIONALS"
421 W. Union Ave, Bound Brook, NJ, 08805. Contact: Dir. of Fran. Sales - Tel: (800) 526-3939, Fax: (732) 469-7405. Home inspection and environmental testing. Established: 1971 - Franchising Since: 1979 - No. of Units: Franchised: 326 - Franchise Fee: $12,500-$29,000 - Royalty: 7.5%, 2.5% adv. - Total Inv: $15,75-$51,500 - Financing: No.

IOWA REALTY MEMBERS
Iowa Realty Company, Inc.
3501 Westown Parkway, W. Des Moines, IA, 50265. - Tel: (515) 224-6222, Fax: (515) 453-5786. Franchising real estate companies. Established: 1952 - Franchising Since: 1978 - No. of Units: Company Owned: 27 - Franchised: 60 - Franchise Fee: $4,500 - Total Inv: $2,500 signs, tapes, printed material - Royalty: 5% - Financing: Yes.

KEY TREND, INC.
Key Associates
973 N. North Reo Dr., Rockport, IN, 47635. Contact: Don Schultz, President - Tel: (812) 649-9716, (800) 288-8539, Fax: (812) 649-9496, Web Site: www.keyassociates.com. Real estate memberships. Established: 1977 - Licensing Since: 1977 - No. of Units: Licensed: 22 - Fee: $4,000 - Royalty: Flat monthly fee - Total Inv: $4,000 - Financing: Yes.

MORTGAGE TECH GROUP
186 W Montauk Hwy Ste. D7, Hampton Bays, NY, 11946-2347. Contact: Donald Henig, President - Tel: (516) 723-2218, Fax: (516) 348-0705, Web Site: www.mtgweb.com. Franchisor of mortgage origination business. Established: 1992 - Franchising Since: 1995 - No. of Units: Franchised: 70 - Franchise Fee: $5,000 - Royalty: None - Total Inv: $500 investigation fee plus franchise fee - Financing: Yes.

NATIONAL HOME BUYERS ASSISTANCE *
6600 E. Hampden Ave., Suite 300, Denver, CO, 80224. Contact: Judy Wood, Franchise Development Manager - Tel: (303) 703-6422, (800) 905-6422, Fax: (303) 779-6422, E-mail: judyw@nhba.com, Web Site: www.nhba.com. The NHBA franchise provides an exceptional real estate investment opportunity for its franchisee partners. NHBA offers a proven process that minimizes the risk of real estate investing while increasing the potential return. NHBA partners do not buy a property unless they have a pre-qualified lessee ready to move in. The lessee actually selects the home of their choice which the NBHA franchise then buys for the lessee. Since the NHBA franchisee uses NHBA forms, systems, methods, processes and expertise, the NHBA franchisee is able to acquire a large real estate portfolio in a relatively short time frame and with minimum personal investment. Established: 2002 - Franchising Since: 2003 - No. of Units: Franchised: 70 - Franchise Fee: $30,000 - Royalty: 2% royalty, 1% advertising fee - Total Inv: $98,500 + - Financing: No. VetFran discount.

ONLY BUYERS-AMERICA REAL ESTATE ONLY BUYER, INC.
3661 S. Narcissus Way, Denver, CO, 80237-1235. Contact: Barry Miller, CEO - Tel: (303) 741-8644, (303) 713-1122, Fax: (303) 753-4616, E-Mail: harrymill@aol.com. Real Estate buyer protection and buying services provided by consumer-oriented real estate offices which are a part of the growing segment of real estate. Franchisee of Only Buyers America Real Estate, where each office has an affiliation with a licensed/certified appraiser assuring the buyer that valuations of their property are honest, fair and accurate. Established: 1996 - Franchising

Since: 1996 - No. of Units: Franchised: 26 - Franchise Fee: $8,900 - Royalty: 5% of a defined term known as gross commissions monthly - Total Inv: $10,000-$70,000 - Financing: Not more than about 75 days.

PICKET FENCE PREVIEW
1 Kennedy Dr., South Burlington, VT, 05403. - Tel: (802) 660-3167, Fax: (802) 863-8963. Published for sale by owner, real estate magazine, full color glossy publication, sell books, sign, necessary forms. Web publishing plus full service mortgage brokerage. (US direct mortgage). Established: 1993 - Franchising Since: 1994 - No. of Units: Company Owned: 1 - Franchised: 7 - Franchise Fee: $10,000-$25,000 - Royalty: 3% after 3 rd year - Total Inv: $10,000-$90,000 - Financing: Yes.

PROPERTY INVESTMENT GROUP SERVICES, INC
312 12th Street, NW, Canton, OH, 44703. Contact: Mike Kell, President - Tel: (330) 453-1672, (800) 949-7447, Fax: (330) 453-5420, Web Site: www.propertyinvestgroup.com. Urban redevelopment - purchasing, rehabing, and selling distressed properties for maximum profit. Complete training and support provided. Established: 1992 - Franchising Since: 1998 - No. of Units: Company Owned: 1 - Franchised: 1 - Franchise Fee: $35,000 - Royalty: $1,250 per home sales - Total Inv: $35,000, franchise fee + $65,000,$215,000 working capital, Total=$100,000-$250,000 - Financing: None. Not franchising at this time.

PRUDENTIAL REAL ESTATE AFFILIATES, INC., THE
3333 Michelson Dr., Ste. 1000, Irvine, CA, 92612. - Tel: (949) 794-7900, Fax: (949) 794-7031. Real Estate Services.

RE/MAX
Re/Max International, Inc.
P.O. Box 3907, Englewood, CO, 80155. Contact: Vinnie Tracey, V.P. Marketing - Tel: (303) 770-5531, Fax: (303) 796-3599, E-Mail: webmaster@remax.com, Web Site: www.remax.com. An international real estate network of independent member offices located throughout the U.S. and Canada. The concept is based upon a fair exchange: the highest possible compensation for the sales associate in return for shared common overhead expenses. Established: 1973 - Franchising Since: 1976 - No. of Units: Company Owned: 19 - Franchised: 4,076 - Franchise Fee: Varies - Total Inv: $5,000-$120,000 - Financing: No.

REAL ESTATE ONE LICENSING CO.
521 Randolph St., Traverse City, MI, 49684. - Tel: (248) 208-2954, Fax: (248) 263-0092, E-Mail: markjeffers@realestateone.com. Full service support system for real estate companies. Appropriate for new or existing businesses. Established: 1972 - Franchising Since: 1972 - No. of Units: Company Owned: 61 - Franchised: 40 - Franchise Fee: $9,800 - Royalty: 5% - Financing: Yes.

REALTY 500, INC.
500 Casazza Dr, Reno, NV, 89502-3316. - Tel: (775) 689-8545, Web Site: www.realty500inc.com. Complete real estate sales operation. We do conversion and start up, and continuing support. Agent training and continuing education. Discounts on retail supplies, services and staff support at corporate level. Established: 1979 - Franchising Since: 1979 - No. of Units: Franchised: 12 - Franchise Fee: Call for quote - Royalty: 5% of gross commissions - Total Inv: $5,000-$10,000 - Financing: Yes.

REALTY EXECUTIVES
Realty Executives International, Inc.
4427 North 36th St., #100, Phoenix, AZ, 85018. - Tel: (800) 252-3366, (602) 957-0747, Web Site: www.RealtyExecutives.com. Originator of the 100% Commission Concept in real estate, which attracts the top producing agents in the industry and ends the revolving door syndrome that is so common with traditional brokerages. Established: 1965 - Franchising Since: 1987 - No. of Units: Franchised: 584 - Franchise Fee: $5,000-$25,000 - Royalty: $25-$35/agent/month - Total Inv: $15,000-$100,000 - Financing: Yes.

REALTY ONE
Realty One Corp.
7310 Potomac Dr., Boise, ID, 83704. - Tel: (208) 322-2700, Fax: (208) 322-2756. Full service real estate franchise company offering a new and proven concept to the small broker providing a large office image and support system featuring maximum income and minimum overhead.

Established: 1985 - Franchising Since: 1987 - No. of Units: Franchised: 2 - Franchise Fee: $15,000 - Royalty: Per agent monthly fee - Total Inv: $50,000-$100,000 - Financing: None.

REGAL MORTGAGE. COM
125 E Palace Ave Ste 44, Santa Fe, NM, 87501-2304. Contact: David Ware, CEO - Tel: (505) 983-1206, (888) 236-0051, Fax: (505) 983-1223, E-Mail: regalusa@aol.com, Web Site: www.regal-mortgage.com. Mortgage loans for residential and commercial. On line. Established: 1996 - Franchising Since: 1999 - No. of Units: Company Owned: 1 - Franchised: 3 - Franchise Fee: $15,000 - Royalty: $100 per transaction - Total Inv: $15,000 + computer + office space - Financing: Yes.

REMERICA
Remerica Real Estate Corp.
40500 Ann Arbor Rd., Ste. 102, Plymouth, MI, 48170. Contact: James Courtney, Robert Hutchinson, CEO, Pres, - Tel: (800) REMERICA, (734) 459-4500, Fax: (734) 459-1566, E-Mail: remerica@remerica.com, Web Site: www.remerica.com. Real estate franchises. Established: 1989 - Franchising Since: 1990 - No. of Units: Franchised: 26 - Franchise Fee: $7,200 - Royalty: 6% to $36,000, 0% thereafter, 2% adv. to $7,200, 0% thereafter - Financing: None. Regions now available throughout the U.S.

RYAN REALTY
Ryan Properties, Inc
8212 Thomas Drive, Panama City Beach, FL, 32408. - Tel: (850) 233-7926, (800) 238-7926, Fax: (850) 234-0551. Real Estate Company. Established: 1991 - No. of Units: Company Owned: 1.

SALE BY OWNER SYSTEMS®
4740 Newland St, Wheat Ridge, CO, 80033-3639. - Tel: (303) 449-2838. Marketing and support to sell homes without the use of a real estate agent. Services provided: market analysis, advertising, professional signage, buyers qualification and computerized loan origination. Established: 1992 - Franchising Since: 1994 - No. of Units: Company Owned: 1 - Franchised: 6 - Franchise Fee: $15,000 - Royalty: 6%, 2% adv. - Total Inv: Fran. fee plus $11,000-$30,000 - Financing: No.

SELL YOUR OWN HOME
Sell Your Own Home of America
P.O. Box 14804, Lenexa, KS, 66285-4804. Contact: Arvin Zwick, Pres./Founder - Tel: (913) 492-SAVE, Fax: (913) 492-9552. Offering a broad range of real estate products and services at discount prices. Unique services include: Talking Home, By Owner Referral Network, nationally recognized How to manual, and much more. The SYOH programs and value are unequalled. Established: 1987 - Franchising Since: 1992 - No. of Units: Company Owned: 1- Franchise Fee: None - Royalty: None - Total Inv: $495. plus working capital - Financing: MC/V. Offering license and joint venture programs.

UNITED CAPITAL MORTGAGE ASSOCIATION L.L.C.
1300 Mercantile Ln. Ste. 126-C, Largo, MD, 20774. Contact: Richard Ballou, Franchise Development - Tel: (301) 386-8803, (800) 474-1407, Fax: (301) 386-8803. Homeowner foreclosure service - full training provided. Established: 1996 - Franchising Since: 1998 - No. of Units: Company Owned: 1- Franchise Fee: $9,995 includes training - Total Inv: $18,500-$27,000 (includes francise fee). Financing: No.

UNITED COUNTRY
First Horizon Corp.
1600 N. Corrington Ave., Kansas City, MO, 64120. Contact: Louis F. Francis, President - Tel: (816) 231-4212, (816) 444-5044, Fax: (816) 231-5599, Web Site: www.unitedcountry.com. Sale of real estate franchises and providing of marketing services to franchisees in small town and rural markets. Established: 1925 - Franchising Since: 1988 - No. of Units: Company Owned: 2 - Franchised: 302 - Franchise Fee: $5,900 - Royalty: 1% of sales price in transactions on which franchisee receives a sales commission or referral fee adjusted for co-brokers. Cap on residential sales - Total Inv: Estimated initial investment from $6,690-$12,410 for franchisee already operating real estate office or $15,500-$?8,250 for new office - Financing: Negotiable.

WEICHERT REAL ESTATE AFFILIATES INC

225 Littleton Rd, Morris Plains, NJ, 07950. - Tel: (973) 359-8377, Fax: (973) 292-1428, Web Site: www.weichert.com. Real estate brokerage. Established: 1969 - Franchising Since: 2001 - No. of Units: Company Owned: 200 - Franchise Fee: $25,000 - Royalty: 6% - Total Inv: $45,000-$254,000 - Financing: No.

WHY USA REAL ESTATE
Why USA North America, Inc

1421 N Broadway, Suite 108, Menomonie, WI, 54751. - Tel: (715) 235-9546, (888) 990-7355, Fax: (715) 235-9738, Web Site: www.whyusa.com. National franchise real estate organization offer opportunities to join national organization and still maintain independently owned and operated status. Established: 1987 - Franchising Since: 1988 - No. of Units: Franchised: 85 - Franchise Fee: $9,800 - Royalty: $95.00 per transaction - Total Inv: Beyond franchise fee; Eat: equip - $4,500, rent - $2,500 per month, licenses - $500, inventory - $3,500 - Financing: Yes.

WORLD INSPECTION NETWORK
World Inspection Network International, Inc.

6500 6th Ave NW, Seattle, WA, 98117-5015. Contact: Tee Houston-Aldridge, VP Franchise Development - Tel: (800) 967-8127, Fax: (206) 441-3655, E-Mail: joinwin@wini.com. Professional home based business providing inspection services to sellers, buyers, real estate professionals, lenders and homeowners. As North America's leader in home inspection services, World Inspection Network provides franchisees the most aggressive marketing approach and unique business operating system available. We have a comprehensive 2 week training program that includes inspection marketing and business development, conducting the inspection, and operational procedures for managing your own franchise. Established: 1993 - Franchising Since: 1994 - No. of Units: Company Owned: 1 - Franchised: 75 - Franchise Fee: $19,900 - Royalty: 7%, 3% adv. - Total Inv: $26,000-$43,000-$36,000 average - Financing: Yes, fran. fee.

RENTAL SERVICES

AARON'S RENTAL PURCHASE

309 E. Paces Ferry Rd. N.E., Atlanta, GA, 30305-2377. Contact: VP Fran. Dev. - Tel: (404) 240-6534. Fax: (404) 240-6540. One of the nation's largest publicly held furniture, electronics and appliance rental and sales chains. Established: 1955 - Franchising Since: 1992 - No. of Units: Company Owned: 129 - Franchised: 47 - Franchise Fee: $35,000 - Royalty: 5% gross revenue - Total Inv: $175,500-$385,900 - Financing: Inventory financing available.

ALL AROUND RENTAL

20091 Hamburg Street, Detroit, MI, 48205. Contact: Mike or Belinda - Tel: (313) 521-7032. Rental of portable toilets, tents and chairs. Established: 2000 - No. of Units: Franchised: 1 - Franchise Fee: $12,500 - Financing: Yes.

APARTMENT SELECTOR
Apartment Selector Corp.

8600 NW Plaza Dr., Ste. 2C, Dallas, TX, 75228. Contact: Kendall A. Laughlin, CEO - Tel: (214) 361-4420, (800) 324-3733, Fax: (214) 361-8677, E-Mail: apts@aptselector.com, Web Site: www.aptselector.com. Free rental referral service. Established: 1959 - Franchising Since: 1985 - No. of Units: Franchised: 20 - Franchise Fee: $7,500 - Royalty: 5% - Total Inv: $9,000-$25,000 - Financing: None.

BABY'S AWAY
Baby's Away International, Inc.

P.O. Box 308, Breckenridge, CO, 80424-0308. - Tel: (303) 394-3777. Baby's Away rents baby/child equipment to travelling families at destination locations throughout the U.S. and Canada. Established: 1990 - Franchising Since: 1993 - No. of Units: Company Owned: 8 - Franchised: 17 - Franchise Fee: $8,000 - Royalty: 7% plus 3% nat'l. adv. - Total Inv: $12,000-$15,000 - Financing: 50% of franchise fee.

BATES MOTOR HOME RENTAL NETWORK
Bates Int'l Motorhome Rental System, Inc.

3690 S. Eastern Ave., Ste. 220, Las Vegas, NV, 89109. Contact: Michael Williams, VP of Operations - Tel: (702) 737-9050, (800) 732-2283, Fax: (702) 737-9149, E-Mail: headquarters@batesintl.com, Web Site: www.batesintl.com. Bates rents motorhomes as a broker. Providing motorhomes to our clients from all over the world. Established: 1973 - Franchising Since: 1998 - No. of Units: Company Owned: 2 - Franchised: 16 - Franchise Fee: $16,000-$45,000 - Royalty: 8% royalty, 2% advertising - Total Inv: $30,000-$60,000 - Financing: Yes.

COLORTYME

5700 Tennyson Pkwy #180, Plano, TX, 75024-3556. Contact: Mitch Fadel, Pres. - Tel: (972) 608-5376, (800) 411-8963, Fax: (972) 403-4935. Appliance/television video furniture rentals. Established: 1978 - Franchising Since: 1981 - No. of Units: Franchised: 320- Franchise Fee: $25,000 - Royalty: 4%-3%, nat'l. adv. $250./month.- Total Inv: $254,616-$466,480 - Financing: Thru third party.

CONDOMINIUM TRAVEL ASSOCIATES, INC.

2001 W. Main St., Ste. 140, Stamford, CT, 06902. Contact: Richard H.Fisher, Pres. - Tel: (203) 975-7714, Fax: (203) 964-0073, E-Mail: rickf@cta, Web Site: www.condotravel.com. Business Opportunity: Condo vacation rental business; home or storefront; part-time or full-time. Includes quality product inventory source, sales training program, marketing plan, educational trips and seminars, and national convention. Established: 1989 - Franchising Since: 1989 - Franchise Fee: $495. first year. initial member. fee ($250.00 annual renewal fee) - Royalty: None - Total Inv: Start-up approx. $2,500 - Financing: None.

GUARANTEED CHRISTMAS
Christmas Concepts

3960 South Higuera St., Suite 8, San Luis Obispo, CA, 93401. Contact: Pamela Dorn - Tel: (805) 782-0128, Fax: (805) 782-0127, Web Site: www.christmasconcepts.com. Rent Christmas decorations to hotels, banks, shopping centers and homes. Very high net profit. Established: 1982 - Franchising Since: 1990 - No. of Units: Company Owned: 279 - Franchised: 139 - Franchise Fee: One time fee - Royalty: None - Total Inv: $1500. - Financing: No.

GUARANTEED GREEN
Green Concepts

3960 South Higuera Suite 8, San Luis Obispo, CA, 93401. Contact: Pamela Dorn - Tel: (805) 782-0128, Fax: (805) 782-0127, Web Site: www.green-concepts.com. Rent plants to banks, restaurants, offices and homes. Fun and easy. Established: 1990 - Franchising Since: 1990 - No. of Units: Company Owned: 97 - Franchised: 297 - Franchise Fee: One time fee - Royalty: None - Total Inv: $500. - Financing: No.

ICE MAGIC
Ice Magic Franchising, Inc.

11124 Satellite Blvd, Orlando, FL, 32837. Contact: Joe Bornstein, Vice President - Tel: (407) 816-1905, Fax: (407) 816-7150, E-Mail: info@icemagic.biz, Web Site: www.icemagic.biz. Ice Magic is a specialty decor vendor within the meeting and event industry. Our innovation and affordable products redefine traditional decor. Patented products such as our crystal clear ice centerpieces and remote controlled illuminated tables called "LighTables", allow lighted decor to flow from top to bottom for unforgettable events. Established: 1996 - Franchising Since: 2001 - No. of Units: Company Owned: 1 - Franchised: 7 - Franchise Fee: $30,000-$48,000 - Royalty: 6% of gross revenues - Total Inv: $414,950-$684,150 - Financing: No.

INFLATE INC

15800 Strathern St, Van Nuys, CA, 91406. - Tel: (818) 786-7573, (888) BLOWAIR, Fax: (818) 786-7576. Manufacture, sales and rentals of inflatable moon bouncers. Established: 1993 - Franchising Since: 1997 - No. of Units: Company Owned: 200 - Total Inv: Negligible - Financing: Yes.

NATIONAL EDUCATIONAL MUSIC COMPANY

1181 Route 22, Mountainside, NJ, 07092. Contact: Gene Garb, Vice President - Tel: (908) 232-6700, (800) 526-4593, Fax: (908) 789-3025. Rental of school band and orchestra instruments on a rent to own plan.

Dealer receiving commissions paid monthly on collections. Established: 1957 - Franchising Since: 1967 - No. of Units: Franchised: 209 - Franchise Fee: $2,500.

PODS (PORTABLE ON DEMAND STORAGE)
PODs, LLC
6061 45th St N St., Petersburg, FL, 33714. Contact: Bill Ash, Vice President - Tel: (727) 592-0222, (888) 776-7637, Fax: (727) 556-2955, E-Mail: pods_storage@msn.com, Web Site: www.putitinapod.com. Mobil storage for residential and business, 8x8x12 and 8x8x16 pods delivered to your home or business and then transported to our climate controlled warehouse. Established: 1998 - Franchising Since: 1999 - No. of Units: Company Owned: 4 - Franchised: 5 - Franchise Fee: $30,000 - Royalty: 2%, 8% royalty (includes central call centre) - Total Inv: $350,000-$400,000 - Financing: Banks, financial institutions.

PRESIDENT TUXEDO
32185 Hollingsworth, Warren, MI, 48092. - Fax: (586) 264-7119. Rentals and sales of men's and women's formalwear and accessories. Established: 1970 - Franchising Since: 1984 - No. of Units: Company Owned: 16 - Franchised: 5 - Franchise Fee: $18,000 - Royalty: 7% - Total Inv: $115,000 - Financing: Yes.

RENT-A-COMPUTER
Professional Processing Systems
2424 S. 120th Street, Omaha, NE, 68144. - Tel: (402) 330-7368, Fax: (402) 330-8218, E-Mail: rentrpc@earthlink.net. Personal computer renting, leasing, and sales. We specialize in the purchase, remanufacturing and resale of used PC equipment and peripherals and large number PC rentals. Established: 1985 - Franchising Since: 1996 - No. of Units: Company Owned: 3 - Franchise Fee: $24,500 - Royalty: 6% total gross - Total Inv: $102,500-$146,500 - Financing: Limited.

TALKING BOOK WORLD
Talking Book Inc.
26211 Central Park Blvd Suite 415, South Field, MI, 48076. - Tel: (248) 945-9999. Talking book store - rentals and sales of talking books in retail strip centers. Established: 1993 - Franchising Since: 1995 - No. of Units: Company Owned: 14 - Franchised: 15 - Franchise Fee: $25,000 development, training, site selection & territory - Royalty: 5% of gross revenues, 2% NH adv. fund - Total Inv: $90,000 inven., $25,000 fee, $15,000 signs & fixtures, $5,000 misc. $15,000 work. cap., $5,000 deposit - Financing: No.

TAYLOR RENTAL
Tru Seerv Corporation
203 Jandus Road, Cary, IL, 60013. Contact: Phil Agee - Tel: (773) 695-5310, (800) 833-3004, Fax: (847) 516-9921, E-Mail: pagee@truserv.com, Web Site: www.taylorrental.com. Retail rental business providing tools, equipment and party rental items to homeowners and contractors. Established: 1925 - Franchising Since: 1985 - No. of Units: Franchised: 1250 - Total Inv: $225,000-$275,000.

TUBS TO GO
P.O. Box 1132, Edmonds, WA, 98020. Contact: Ron Tosh, Owner - Tel: (425) 672-7816, (800) 882-7864, Fax: (425) 776-2157, E-Mail: tubman@wa.net, Web Site: www.tubstogo.com. Overnight spa rental service. Established: 1986 - Franchising Since: 1998 - No. of Units: Company Owned: 2 - Franchise Fee: $15,000-$25,000 - Royalty: Ranges from 2%-8% - Total Inv: $20,000-$40,000 - Financing: No.

14 KARAT PLUM, THE
Plum International, Inc.
P. O. Box 1977, Kaulua, HI, 96734-8977. Contact: Sandy Gottesman, V.P. - Tel: (808) 247-1127. A fine 14 karat gold gift boutique. Established: 1984 - Franchising Since: 1989 - No. of Units: Company Owned: 1 - Franchise Fee: $25,000 - Royalty: 7%, 1% adv. - Total Inv: $165,000-$225,000 incls. inven. - Financing: No.

RETAIL

ABBEY CARPET CO.
Abbey Carpet Co, Inc
3471 Bonita Bay Blvd., Bonita Springs, FL, 34134-4364. Contact: Stephen Silverman, Pres. - Tel: (941) 948-0900, (800) 873-2223, Fax: (941) 948-0999, Web Site: www.abbeycarpet.com. Retail floor covering specialty store franchising to people already in the retail floor covering business. Established: 1958 - Franchising Since: 1962 - No. of Units: Franchised: 750 - Franchise Fee: $18,000 - Financing: Yes.

ACE HARDWARE CORPORATION
2200 Kensington Court, Oakbrook, IL, 60523-2100. Contact: Randy Hook, Corp. Mgr. New Business - Tel: (630) 472-4688 or (630) 990-6528. Ace's Mission: to be a retail support company providing independent Ace dealers with quality products, program and services that focus on retail success. Ace 2000 strategic plan, national advertising, Ace Rental place, store planning, retail computer services, commercial industrial program, retail training, manufacturer of Ace Quality Paint. Established: 1924 - Franchising Since: 1924 - No. of Units: 5,100 stores in 50 states; 58 countries.

AGWAY, INC.
P.O. Box 4746, Syracuse, NY, 13221. Contact: Dave Menapace, Dir. of Reps. - Tel: (800) 248-0810, Fax: (315) 449-7268. Farm, home and garden supplies. Established: 1964 - No. of Units: Company Owned: 182 - Franchised: 320 - Total Inv: Varies.

AIR TRAFFIC RETAIL FRANCHISE SYSTEMS
451 Cliff Rd., E #106, Burnsville, MN, 55337. - Tel: (952) 895-5555, Fax: (952) 707-9900, E-Mail: ted@airtrafficinc.com, Web Site: www.airtrafficinc.com. Air Traffic offers the customer a retail atmosphere that offers unique products that are fun to play with, Example: flying toys, kites, juggling equipment etc... Established: 1993 - Franchising Since: 2003 - No. of Units: Company Owned: 2 - Franchised: 2 - Franchise Fee: $25,000 - Royalty: 5% - Total Inv: $161,175-$212,850 - Financing: No.

ALL AMERICAN MOBILE MINI-BLIND SALES
23052 Alicia Parkway, #H202, Mission Viejo, CA, 92692. Contact: Steven K. Dale, Owner - Tel: (949) 459-8931, (888) 922-5463, Web Site: www.allamericanblind.com. Become a competition killer using our tight wand marketing plan. Own your own discount shop at home window covering business. Established: 1985 - Biz. Op Since: 1996 - No. of Units: Company Owned: 1 - Biz Opportunities: 282 - Fee: $1,695 - Total Inv: $1,695 - Financing: Yes.

ALL NATIONS FLAG CO., INC.
Patriot Enterprises L.L.C.
118 W. 5th St., Kansas City, MO, 64105. Contact: Gregory J. Wald, President - Tel: (816) 842-8798, (800) 533-3524, Fax: (816) 842-3995, E-Mail: gwald@allnationsflags.com, Web Site: www.allnations flags.com. Retail and commercial sales of flags, banners, flag poles and any related products i.e. US, state, foreign, historical, holiday, sports flags and kites, windsocks, globes and much more. Established: 1924 - Franchising Since: 1997 - No. of Units: Company Owned: 1 - Franchise Fee: $15,000 - Royalty: 5% - Total Inv: $75,000-$125,000 - Financing: No.

ALMOST HEAVEN, LTD.
10 Thieriot Ave, Chestertown, NY, 12817. - Tel: (518) 494-7777, Fax: (518) 494-7779. World's leading manufacturer of hot tubs, spas, saunas, steamrooms and whirlpool baths. Established: 1976- Franchising Since: 1978 - No. of Units: Franchised: 1,983 - Total Inv: $5,000-$10,000 - Financing: Yes.

AMERICAN HERITAGE SHUTTERS
American Heritage Shutters Inc.
6655 Poplar Ave., Ste. 204, Memphis, TN, 38138-0643. Contact: W. Thomas Crutcher, President - Tel: (901) 213-1001. Custom interior and exterior shutters. Established: 1972 - Franchising Since: 1983 - No. of Units: Franchised: 11 - Franchise Fee: $7,500 - Royalty: 5%, 1% adv. - Financing: Negotiable.

ASHLEY AVERY'S COLLECTABLES

100 Glenborough Dr., 14th Floor, Houston, TX, 77067. Contact: Bob Kirschner, V.P. Franchise Dev. - Tel: (281) 775-5262 (800) 543-3325, Fax: (281) 775-5250, E-Mail: franinfo@fcibiz.com, Web Site: www.ashleyaverys.com. Largest chain of collectables and gift stores in the country. Located nationwide in upscale regional malls. Features an elegant, gallery-like atmosphere filled with fascinating works. Offering merchandise ranging from whimsical, inexpensive and impulse items to prestigious, name brand and limited production pieces. Easy to learn and operate with exceptional training and on-going support. National buying power and proven marketing programs. Single and multi-units available. Established: 1981 - Franchising Since: 1981 No. of Units: Company Owned: 1, Franchised: 41 - Franchise Fee: $30,000 - Royalty: 6%, 2% adv. - Total Inv: $266,000-$397,000- Financing: Yes, third party.

BARNIES COFFE & TEA COMPANY

Barnie's Coffee & Tea Company, Inc

7001 Lake Ellenor Dr Ste 250, Orlando, FL, 32809-5772. Contact: Michael Daigle - Tel: (407) 854-6600, Fax: (407) 854-6666, E-Mail: franchise@barniescoffee.com, Web Site: www.barniescoffee.com. Mall based retailer of gourmet coffees, teads, food items and related hard goods. (Coffee makers, cups, mugs, etc). Established: 1981 - No. of Units: Company Owned: 68 - Franchised: 17 - Franchise Fee: $25,000 - Royalty: 6% - Total Inv: $216,500-$354,000 - Financing: None provided.

BASKET CONNECTION, INC., THE

20959 S. Springwater Rd., Estacada, OR, 97023. - Tel: (503) 631-7288, Fax: (503) 631-7289, E-Mail: winthrop@zzz.com. Gift baskets and basket parties. Established: 1978 - Franchising Since: 1995 - Total Inv: $4,000 - Financing: Yes.

BATTERIES PLUS - AMERICA'S BATTERY STORES

Batteries Plus, LLC

925 Walnut Ridge Dr #100, Hartland, WI, 53029-9389. Contact: Richard Zimmerman, Dir. of Fran.Marketing - Tel: (414) 369-0690, (800) 274-9155, E-Mail: batplus@batteriesplus.com, Web Site: www.batteries plus.com. Retailer and distributor of "1,000's of batteries for 1000's of items". Established: 1988 - Franchising Since: 1992 - No. of Units: Company Owned: 20- Franchised: 120 operational, 74 under development - Franchise Fee: $25,000 - Royalty: 4% - Total Inv: $185,000-$225,000: $25,000 fee, equip. & fix's. $50,000, inventory and supplies $60,000, initial advertising $20,000, working cap. $30,000 - Financing: Assistance only.

BATTERY PATROL

John Willemsen Corp

1901 E. University Ave, Des Moines, IA, 50316. Contact: Jim Goodman, President - Tel: (515) 266-8207, (800) 203-6549, Fax: (800) 246-1024. A system to sell over 5,000 different types of batteries to businesses and retail customers. Established: 1981 - Franchising Since: 1997 - No. of Units: Company Owned: 5 - Franchised: 43 - Franchise Fee: $25,000 - Royalty: 5% first 500, 4.5%-$750, 4% L/M, 3.5% L/M, Total Inv: $150,000-$250,000.

BEAUTY BY SPECTOR, INC.

1 Spector Place, Dept. FADQ-01, McKeesport, PA, 15134-0502. - Tel: (412) 673-3259, Fax: (412) 678-3978. Internationally known fashion authority offers dealerships in men's hairpieces, women's wigs, women's intimate and fashion wear, and continental-designed fine and fashion jewelry. These dealerships, successfully field-tested for over 3 decades, offer a high return with little or no investment. The firm was established in 1958, and began offering dealerships in 1967. Dealerships are available at no cost.

BIG BOB'S NEW & USED CARPET SHOPS

Big Bob's Used Carpet Shops of America, Inc.

9320 W 75th St, Shawnee Mission, KS, 66204-2233. - Tel: (913) 789-7773, Fax: (913) 789-7126. Big Bob's New and Used Carpet sells used carpet, mill seconds, and new carpet at the entry level price point in a warehouse atmosphere. Our operation captures a unique niche in the market that is virtually untapped and has proven successful in a variety of metro areas greater than 250,000 people throughout North America. Established: 1984 - Licensing Since: 1989 - Franchising Since: 1993 - No. of Units: Company Owned: 4 - Franchised: 30 - Franchise Fee:

$7,500 - Royalty: 1%-5% sliding scale based on gross sales - Total Inv: $60,000-$100,000 turn key - Financing:assistance in obtaining an SBA loan by providing a complete business plan and loan package.

BIG ENTERTAINMENT

Big Entertainment, Inc., Nasdaq:Big E

2255 Glades Rd., #237-W, Boca Raton, FL, 33431. - Tel: (561) 998-8000, Fax: (561) 998-2974. Super regional mall based "specialty" entertainment retail. Retail sale of science fiction, fantasy, comic and entertainment related merchandise, what's hot and best of best. Established: 1993 - Franchising Since: 1996 - No. of Units: Company Owned: 30 - Franchise Fee: $20,000 - Royalty: 4% of gross sales - Total Inv: $170,000 - Financing: Not from franchisor.

BIKER'S DREAM SUPERSTORES

1420 Village Way, Santa Ana, CA, 92705. - Tel: (714) 835-8464, Fax: (714) 835-2414. Sale of Harley Davidson motorcycles, accessories, clothing, custom bikes. Established: 1990 - Franchising Since: 1993 - No. of Units: Company Owned: 4 - Franchised: 2 - Franchise Fee: $20,000 - Royalty: 4% - Total Inv: $300,000; 6,000 sq. ft. bldg. - Financing: SBA.

BREAD BASKET, THE

539 Northern Avenue, Signal Mountain, TN, 37377. - Tel: (800) 863-8380, Web Site: www.breadbasket.com. We offer you the opportunity to own and operate a Bread Basket franchise for the operation of specialty retail stores which feature gift baskets containing "hand-made" baked goods including breads, muffins, cakes, pies and confectionary bars. Established: 1990 - Franchising Since: 2003 - No. of Units: Company Owned: 1 - Franchised: 1 - Franchise Fee: $20,000 - Royalty: 5% - Total Inv: $172,400-$294,450.

BUDGET FRAMER

Budget Framer, Inc

4313 E. Tradewinds Ave, Ft. Lauderdale, FL, 33308. Contact: T.L. Haddan, CEO - Tel: (954) 491-0129, (866) 491-0124, Fax: (954) 491-0129, E-Mail: THaddan@aol.com, Web Site: www.budgetframer inc.com. Complete turn-key custom picture framing, art, prints and posters - all work done on premises. All training in franchisee's store. Established: 1986 - Franchising Since: 1992 - No. of Units: Company Owned: 1 - Franchised: 18 + 5 licensed - Franchise Fee: $30,000 - Royalty: 4% on gross monthly sales - Total Inv: $95,000 - Financing: Available.

BUTONIQUE THE BUTTON BOUTIQUE

SAR Franchises, Inc.

8971-B Metcalf Avenue, Overland Park, KS, 66212. - Tel: (913) 649-0700, (800) 585-8971, Fax: (913) 649-0700. Retail/service store which sells clothing buttons from around the world. Along with providing a button sewing service. Turnkey, hobby-like business, full training and support. Established: 1995 - Franchising Since: 1997 - No. of Units: Company Owned: 1 - Franchise Fee: $15,000-$18,000 - Royalty: 3% mo. sales - Total Inv: $50,000-$82,000 - Financing: No. Not franchising at this time.

CANDLEMAN

Candleman Corp.

1021 Industrial Pk. Rd., P.O. Box 731, Brainerd, MN, 56401. Contact: Sara Wise, V.P. - Tel: (218) 829-0592, (800) 328-3453, Fax: (218) 825-2449, E-Mail: info@candleman.com, Web Site: www.candleman.com. Upscale retail candle store located in high traffic shopping malls offering candles, candle holders and related accessories. Established: 1991 - Franchising Since: 1992 - No. of Units: Company Owned: 2- Franchised: 62- Franchise Fee: $25,000 - Royalty: 6% - Total Inv: $127,500-$397,250 - Financing: Will assist in obtaining third party financing.

CANDY EXPRESS

Candy Express Franchising, Inc.

10480 Little Patuxent Pkwy., #400, Columbia, MD, 21044-3506. - Tel: (410) 964-5500, Fax: (410) 964-6404. Specialty retail candy stores located in regional shopping centers. Self serve format that is easy to operate and profitable. Franchisor offers total turnkey including site selection, lease negotiation, store design and construction, training and grand opening. Established: 1988 - Franchising Since: 1990 - No. of

Units: Company Owned: 6 - Franchised: 55 - Franchise Fee: $35,000 - Royalty: 6% gross sales per wk., 1% adv. fee - Total Inv: $175,000 - Financing: Yes.

CARPET NETWORK
Carpet Network, Inc.
109 Gaither Dr, Mt. Laurel, NJ, 08054. Contact: Christine Rankin, Director of Franchise Development - Tel: (800) 428-1067, (856) 273-9393, Fax: (856) 273-0160, E-Mail: info@carpetnetwork.com, Web Site: www.carpetnetwork.com. Carpet Network is a mobile business. Bring our floorcovering & window treatment store directly to the home or business in a professional, informitive, conceinent manner. Established: 1992 - Franchising Since: 1993 - No. of Units: Franchised: 48 - Franchise Fee: $17,500 - Royalty: 2%-7%, Total Inv: $29,000 - Financing: Yes.

CARPETERIA
Carpeteria, Inc.
25322 Rye Canyon Rd., Valencia, CA, 91355. Contact: Bryan Haserjian, Senior V.P. - Tel: (661) 295-1000. Retail floor and window coverings business operating from a network of inventory stores, sample showrooms and shop at home vans. Established: 1960 - Franchising Since: 1972 - No. of Units: Company Owned: 39 stores, 10 vans - Franchised: 34 stores, 12 vans - Franchise Fee: $25,000-$100,000 - Royalty: 3%-4% adv. - Total Inv: $100,000-$500,000 - Financing: Yes, fran. fee.

CARTOON CLASSICS
1004 Wicksteed Ct, Apex, NC, 27502-5215. Contact: Lisa Sands, Owner/Pres. - Tel: (865) 531-8865. Sells licensed Cartoon Merchandise from Mickey Mouse, Bugs Bunny to Underdog. The shops also carry classic merchandise that features the likes of Elvis, Marilyn Monroe, James Dean, the 3 Stooges and more. Established: 1992 - Franchising Since: 1994 - No. of Units: Company Owned: 7.

CASH CONVERTORS
Cash Converters USA, Inc.
1450 E. American Lane, Ste. 1350, Schaumburg, IL, 60173. Contact: Franchise Department - Tel: (847) 330-1122, (888) 910-2274, Fax: (847) 330-1660. A retail franchise business that buys and sells quality preowned merchandise. Our stores trade within the local community and strive to provide the best value for customers. We pay the customer fair market value for goods, warranty the product and resell it to other customers. Established: 1987 - Franchising Since: 1995 - No. of Units: Franchised: 500 in 22 countries - Franchise Fee: $50,000 - Royalty: $400/wk 1st yr, $600/wk 2nd yr, $800/wk 3rd yr, $1000/wk 4th year and on - Total Inv: $220,000-$400,000 - Financing: Third party.

CATHOLIC STORE
3398 S. Broadway, Englewood, CO, 80110. - Tel: (303) 762-8385, (800) 776-4569, Fax: (303) 789-2754. Catholic bible, book and gift store. Established: 1981 - Franchising Since: 1994 - No. of Units: Company Owned: 1 - Franchise Fee: $15,500 - Royalty: 4%, 1% adv. - Total Inv: $71,000-$137,500.

COLOR-CHANGING WONDERMUGS
Wondermugs
902 S. Main Street, Point Marion, PA, 15474. Contact: Jim Simpson, Exec. Director - Tel: (724) 725-9602, (888) 296-6337, Fax: (724) 725-3311, E-Mail: wholesale@wondermugs.com, Web Site: www.wondermugs.com. Wondermugs are porcelain mugs that change design and/or color when a hot beverage is added. Top sellers at fairs and festivals and at kiosks in shopping malls. Great income potential prt or full time. Established: 1994 - No. of Units: Company Owned: 6 - Franchised: 50 - Total Inv: $2,500-$4,000 average - Financing: No.

COMPUTER IMAGES IN TIME
Martek Ltd.
P.O. Box 15160, Dept. IFN, Charlotte, NC, 28211. Contact; P.T. Muckler, Mgr. - Tel: (704) 357-3910, Fax: (704) 357-3891. Novel business card clocks using your computer, good family oriented business. Established: 1980 - Franchising Since: 1997 - Franchise Fee: $50-$295.

CONNOISSEUR, THE
Connoisseur Franchise Corp.
201 Torrance Blvd., Redondo Beach, CA, 90277. Contact: Sandy French, Pres. - Tel: (310) 374-9768, (877) 261-3111, Fax: (310) 372-9097, Web Site: www.giftsofwine.com. Personalized gifts including wines, champagnes, gourmet foods, crystal stemware, etc. Established: 1975 - Franchising Since: 1995 - No. of Units: Company Owned: 1 - Franchised: 7 - Franchise Fee: $29,500 - Royalty: 6% - Total Inv: $200,000 approx - Financing: No.

CONSUMER CASKET USA
Consumer Casket USA Franchise Systems Corp.
354 Eisenhower Pkwy, Livingston, NJ, 07039-1022. Contact: James M. St. George, President/CEO - Tel: (814) 866-7777, E-Mail: info@ccusa.com, Web Site: www.ccusa.com. Retail funeral merchandise sales and memorial tribute items. Established: 1995 - Franchising Since: 1997 - No. of Units: Company Owned: 1 - Franchised: 7 - Franchise Fee: $25,000 - Royalty: 4% on gross and 1% adv. - Total Inv: $89,064-$144,420 - Financing: Yes. NOT FRANCHISING AT THIS TIME.

COUNTRY CLUTTER
Country Visions
3333 Vaca Valley Pkwy., #900, Vacaville, CA, 95688. Contact: Terry Odneal, V.P. Franchise Development - Tel: (800) 425-8883, Fax: (707) 451-0410. A charming country store for gifts, collectibles and home decor. A unique business that offers old fashioned quality, selection and customer service. A complete franchise program that is professionally designed, computerized and planned to sell a perfected blend of country merchandise made up of primarily American manufacturers and crafters. Rich arrangements and displays of textures, colors and aromas make shopping at Country Clutter a true sensory delight. Established: 1991 - Franchising Since: 1992 - No. of Units: Franchised: 60 - Franchise Fee: $25,000 - Royalty: 5.5% - Total Inv: $175,950-$297,100 - Financing: Will assist.

DE ELLA ENTERPRISES INC.
1201 S.W. 141 Ave., Unit 111, Hollywood, Fl, 33027. Contact: Ms. Ella, President - Tel: (954) 450-0556, Web Site: www.deella.com. Sell Words in Neighborhood Franchises, no competition, no comparisons, no spoilage, and no seasonal mdse. Proud markets waiting. Remember: "It's 'The Word' that makes the Difference". Established: 1998 - Franchising Since: 2000 - No. of Units: Company Owned: 1 - Franchise Fee: $25,000 - Total Inv: $35,000-$200,000.

DISC-GO-ROUND
Grow Biz International
204 NW Redwood Ct, Lee's Summit, MO, 64064. - Tel: (816) 373-8345, Fax: (816) 350-1105. A retail store that buys, sells and trades new and used compact discs, accessories and CD-ROM. Established: 1990 - Franchising Since: 1992 - No. of Units: Company Owned: 3 - Franchised: 135 - Franchise Fee: 20,000 - Royalty: 5% of gross sales - Total Inv: $86,000-$115,000 - Financing: Yes, through business plan development.

DOLLAR DISCOUNT
Dollar Discount Stores of America™
1362 Naamans Creek Rd., Boothwyn, PA, 19061. Contact: Fran. Dir. - Tel: (610) 497-1991, (800) 227-5314, Fax: (610) 485-6439, E-Mail: info@dollardiscount.com, Web Site: www.dollardiscount.com. Dollar stores. Established: 1982 - Franchising Since: 1987 - No. of Units: Franchised: 165 - Franchise Fee: $20,000 - Royalty: 3% of gross sales - Total Inv: $99,000-$195,000 - Financing: Will assist in preparing loan pkg.

DOLLAR MORE OR LESS
Dollar More Or Less
1061 E. Flamingo Road Suite 516, Las Vegas, NV, 89119. Contact: Ted Tepsich - Tel: (702) 737-9228, Fax: (702) 737-9218, E-Mail: 123store@dollarmoreorless.com, Web Site: www.adollarmoreorless.com. Develop custom dollar-type discount stores - not "junky" dollar stores. Established: 1992 - Franchising Since: 1993 - No. of Units: Company Owned: 1 - Franchised: 26 - Franchise Fee: $26,500 - Royalty: Zero if merchandise is purchased through DMOL - Total Inv: $125,000-$300,000 - Financing: None.

DOLLAR STORE EXPRESS

4528 W. Craig Rd #120, N. Las Vegas, NV, 89032.. Contact: L Fredrich - Tel: (702) 631-6075, Fax: (702) 631-3603, E-Mail: ifdollarstore@ aol.com, Web Site: www.ifdollarstoreexpress.com. Complete turnkey package from $49,900. Includes inventory/merchandise, fixtures, site locations and lease negotiation. Hot selling merchandise at wholesale prices. Established: 1999 - Franchising Since: 2002 - No. of Units: Company Owned: 1 - Franchise Fee: $49,900 - Financing: Will refer to SBA lender or broker.

DRAPERY FACTORY, THE

80 Tanforan Ave., Ste. 10, South San Francisco, CA, 94080. Contat: Vic Brown, Fran. Dir. - Tel: (415) 583-1300 or (800) 637-2731. Custom window coverings, custom drapery, blinds and bedspreads. Established: 1980 - Franchising Since: 1988 - No. of Units: Franchised: 27 - Franchise Fee: $25,000 - Royalty: 6% - Total Inv: $50,000-$60,000- Financing: Yes.

EARFUL OF BOOKS

907 W 5th St # 203, Austin, TX, 78703-5428. Contact: Jim Grant, V.P. - Tel: (512) 343-2620, (888) 327-3857, Fax: (512) 343-2751. Audiobook store with over 7500 titles available on cassette tape and cd. Available for rental as well as for sale. Established: 1992 - Franchising Since: 1998 - No. of Units: Company Owned: 6 - Franchised: 5 - Franchise Fee: $25,000 - Royalty: 4%, 1% nat'l adv. - Total Inv: $210,000-$275,000 - Financing: Nationwide.

EASYRIDERS

Easyriders Franchising, Inc.

28210 Dorthy Drive, Agoura Hills, CA, 91301. Contact: Franchise Dev. - Tel: (818) 879-6114, Fax: (818) 889-5214. Sale of new, used and custom motorcycles, service, parts/accessories and fashion motorcycle apparel. Established: 1993 - Franchising Since: 1994 - No. of Units: Company Owned: 2 - Franchised: 28 - Franchise Fee: $25,000 - Royalty: 3%, 2% adv. - Total Inv: $770,000-$1,100,000- Financing: No.

ELEPHANT WALK, A GALLERY OF LIFE

I.E.L. Franchising Group

318 North Carson Street, Ste, 214, Carson City, NV, 89701. Contact: John "Jack" D. Pomeroy, President - Tel: (775) 882-1963, (800) 654-5156, Fax: (800) 654-5161. Naturally Beautiful! Elephant Walk, America's most unique hand craft gift gallery features gifts, sculpture, jewelry and home decorative products of exceptional value. All in a retail environment that reflects the beauty of nature. Outstanding purchasing and inventory systems. Complete training, start up and ongoing support provided. Established: 1983 - Franchising Since: 1996 - No. of Units: Company Owned: 9 - Franchise Fee: $25,000 - Royalty: 6% weekly, 1% adv weekly - Total Inv: $200,000 - Financing: No.

ELITE BUSINESS DESIGNS INC

1334 Buffalo Road, Rochester, NY, 14624. Contact: President - Tel: (716) 934-7166, Web Site: www.elitebd.com. Greeting card distributorship; involves restocking cards at various locations, mainly retail. Established: 1996 - Franchising Since: 1996 - No. of Units: Company Owned: 6 - Franchised: 75 - Franchise Fee: $5,500-$11,000 - Total Inv: $11,000-$13,000 (includes locations).

EMBROID IT!

Embroid It! Company, The

10859 Shady Trail, Ste. 102, Dallas, TX, 75220. Contact: Gino Mortola, President - Tel: (214) 350-2505, Fax: (214) 350-1310, E-Mail: info@embroidit.com, Web Site: www.embroidit.com. Retail embroidery positioned in high traffic malls. Established: 1994 - Franchising Since: 1994 - No. of Units: Company Owned: 4 - Franchised: 5 - Franchise Fee: $5,000 - Royalty: $400 or 3% of gross - Total Inv: $55,000 - Financing: Yes.

EMPOWERED WOMEN'S GOLF SHOPS

Dixon International Inc

5344 Belt Line RD, Dallas, TX, 75240. Contact: V.P Operations - Tel: (972) 233-8807, (800) 533-7309. Women's only golf retail. Established: 1993 - Franchising Since: 1997 - No. of Units: Company Owned: 1 - Franchised: 4 - Franchise Fee: $25,000 - Royalty: 3% gross revenue - Total Inv: $305,000 - Financing: Through S.B.A.

FAN-A-MANIA

Fantastic Inc.

3855 S. 500 W. #R, Salt Lake City, UT, 84115. Contact: Dir. Fran. Sales - Tel: (801) 288-9120, (800) 770-9120. Specialty retailer products are Disney, Warner Bro., Pro & College Sports. All licensed product. Established: 1993 - Franchising Since: 1995 - No. of Units: Company Owned: 5 - Franchised: 12 - Franchise Fee: $19,500 - Royalty: 3.5% of gross sales, 1% adv. - Total Inv: Inventory $65,000, improvements $46,000, working capital $7,5000, miscellaneous $7,500 - Financing: SBA approved.

FAUX PAS

Faux Pas International, Inc.

5817 Kavanaugh Blvd, Little Rock, AR, 72207. - Tel: (501) 225-4848, (888) 854-3289. A stylish alternative to fine jewelry. Spectacular faux jewelry along with fine pieces, placed in beautiful mounting of 14k gold, sterling silver, or vermeil. Faux Pas customers want the right look, not the high price. We search the world for jewelry your customers seek. Extensive training in marketing store design, sales techniques and much more. Established: 1996 - Franchising Since: 1996 - No. of Units: Company Owned: 1 - Franchised: 4 - Franchise Fee: $20,000-$60,000 - Royalty: No royalty fees - Total Inv: $20,000-$60,000 - Financing: No.

FIELD OF DREAMS®

Dreams Franchise Corp.

5017 Hiatas Rd, Sunrise, FL, 33351. Contact: Louis D. Novak, Franchise Sales Director - Tel: (800) 959-0956, Fax: (954) 742-8544, E-Mail: dreamsmail@aol.com, Web Site: www.field-of-dreams.com. Retail outlets with the ultimate sports personality and celebrity gifts. Established: 1990 - Franchising Since: 1991 - No. of Units: Franchised: 29 - Franchise Fee: $32,500 ($25,000 area development) - Royalty: 3% marketing/advertising, 6% royalty - Financing: Assistance available.

FIT AMERICA STORES, LTD

Fit America

401 Fairway Drive, #200, Deerfield Beach, FL, 33441. - Tel: (954) 570-3211, (800) 221-1186, Fax: (954) 570-8608. Natural weight loss. Established: 1992 - Franchising Since: 1996 - No. of Units: Franchised: 54 - Franchise Fee: $8,400 - Royalty: Flat rate $400 per month per store - Total Inv: $35,000 - Franchise fee, adv commitment, normal business expenses - Financing: No.

FLICKERS

Flickers Franchising, Inc

811 East Las Olas Boulevard, Fort Lauderdale, FL, 33301-2265. Contact: Dave Wild, President - Tel: (954) 563-9744, (877) 563-9744, Fax: (954) 563-9755, E-Mail: flickers@bellsouth.net. Retailer of quality candles from basic to sculptured & designer. Established: 1999 - Franchising Since: 2001 - No. of Units: Company Owned: 2 - Total Inv: $190,000-$295,000.

FLOOR TO CEILING STORE, THE

MRM Inc.

216 N. River Ridge Circle, Burnsville, MN, 55337. Contact: Steve Sindinge, Franchise Development - Tel: (612) 890-8979, Fax: (612) 890-3818. Retail store - home interior products. Established: 1990 - Franchising Since: 1994 - No. of Units: Company Owned: 1 - Franchised: 51 - Franchise Fee: $5,000.

FLOORS TO GO

4295 Business Dr, Shingle Spring, CA, 95682. Contact: Jake Kimmel, Owner - Tel: (530) 676-1882, (800) 313-5667, Fax: (530) 676-1573. Retail floor covering. Group together floor dealers in key areas. Together they combine their advertising thusly lowering their adv. cost by 95%. Also they are able to save between 10%-25% on purchasing. Established: 1976 - Franchising Since: 1990 - No. of Units: Franchised: 15 - Franchise Fee: $1,500/month - Financing: None.

FOOT SOLUTIONS

Foot Solutions, Inc

2359 Windy Hill Road, Marietta, GA, 30067. Contact: Betty Hubauer, Administrative & Franchise Support - Tel: (770) 955-0099, (866) 338-2597, Fax: (770) 951-2666, E-Mail: fscorp@footsolutions.com, Web Site: www.footsolutions.com. A unique concept that focuses on health/wellness and meets the demands and needs of a rapidly growing segment of our population (the forty and older market). Using computer technology we scan our customer's feet and make custom comfort inserts, as well as custom orthitics. Established: 2000 - Franchising Since: 2000 - No. of Units: Franchised: 122 - Franchise Fee: $25,000 - Royalty: 5% - Total Inv: $150,000-$200,000 - Financing: No.

FURLA *
Furla Licensing (USA), Inc
389 5th Avenue, Ste. 700, New York, NY, 10016-3320. - Tel: (212) 213-1177, Fax: (212) 685-5910, Web Site: www.furlausa.com. Furla sells women's handbags, shoes, belts, small leather goods, watches, jewelry & accessories. Established: 1927 - Franchising Since: 1998 - No. of Units: Company Owned: 8 - Franchised: 11 - Franchise Fee: $15,000-$25,000 - Royalty: 0-2% - Total Inv: $ 284,000-$480,000.

FURNITURE WEEKEND
Furniture Weekend Franchising Inc.
2 Margaret St, Plattsburgh, NY, 12901-2925. Contact: Larry Kriff, Franchise Development - Tel: (518) 483-1328, (800) 562-1606, Fax: (217) 328-0785. Limited hours retail furniture store. Training and support provided. Established: 1982 - Franchising Since: 1990 - No. of Units: Company Owned: 2 - Franchised: 6 - Franchise Fee: $15,000 - Total Inv: $89,000 (including fran fee).

GAME PLAYER
925 L St, Lincoln, NE, 68508-2229. Contact: Jack L. Rediger, President - Tel: (402) 434-5620, (800) 865-2378, Fax: (402) 434-5624, Web Site: www.franchisedeveloper.com. At Game Player, we have taken a new approach to video game stores by buying, selling, and trading new or used titles and systems. Established: 1993 - Franchising Since: 1996 - No. of Units: Franchised: 1 - Franchise Fee: $20,000 - Royalty: 6%, 1% adv. - Total Inv: $47,000-$120,000 - Financing: Indirect.

GAMETOWN USA
HobbyTown USA
6301 South 58th Street, Lincoln, NE, 68516. Contact: Nichole Ernst - Tel: (402) 434-5064, (800) 858-7370, Fax: (402) 434-5055, E-Mail: dfo@hobbytown.com, Web Site: www.hobbytown.com. Specializing in all types of games, including family games, strategy games and miniature games. Established: 1979 - Franchising Since: 2002 - No. of Units: Company Owned: 1 - Total Inv: $135,000-$155,000.

GCO CARPET OUTLETS
GCO, Inc.
210 Townpark Dr., Kennesaw, GA, 30144-5514. - Tel: (334) 279-8345, Fax: (334) 279-0536, Web Site: www.gcocarpet.com. GCO Carpet Outlet stores is devoted primarily to the sale of discount floor covering products on a "cash and carry" basis to the do-it-yourself or price conscious consumer market.The outlets do not offer installation, instead customers requiring installation and services are provided a list of recommended independent installers. Established: 1988 - Franchising Since: 1989 - No. of Units: Company Owned: 6 - Franchised: 102 - Franchise Fee: $25,000 - Royalty: 5% for first $500,000 then 3% - Total Inv: $260,100-$502,100 including fran. fee. - Financing: No.

GENERAL NUTRITION CENTERS
General Nutrition Centers, Inc.
300 Sixth Avenue, Pittsburgh, PA, 15222. Contact: Bruce Pollock, Senior Franchise Director - Tel: (800) 766-7099, Fax: (412) 402-7105, E-Mail: livewell@gncfranchising.com, Web Site: www.gnc franchising.com. National specialty retailer of vitamins, minerals, herbs, and sports nutrition supplements, personal care and related products and holds the largest share of the nutritional market. Established: 1935 - Franchising Since: 1988 - No. of Units: Company Owned: 2,872 - Franchised: 1,916 - Franchise Fee: $40,000 - Royalty: 6% - Total Inv: $132,700-$182,500 - Financing: Yes.

GENERAL STORE, THE
The General Store Franchise, Corp
15446- Bel Bed Rd., Suite 310, Redmond, WA, 98052. Contact: Glen Easthorpe, CEO - Tel: (888) 292-8288, Fax: (604) 669-2711, E-Mail: info@genstore.com, Web Site: www.genstore.com. Online home shopping/home delivery business. Flagship product line; groceries not a delivery job, not multi level 1 not high pressure sales. Franchise home based business. Established: 1996 - Franchising Since: 1999 - No. of

Units: Company Owned: 1 - Franchised: 99 - Franchise Fee: $6,000-$10,000 - Royalty: 7.5% of overall gross sales go to franchise - Financing: Yes.

GNC FRANCHISING, INC
General Nutrition Companies, Inc
300 Sixth Avenue, 4th Floor, Pittsburgh, PA, 15222. Contact: Director of Franchising - Tel: (412) 288-2043, (800) 766-7099, Fax: (412) 288-2033, E-Mail: franchising@gnc-hq.com, Web Site: www.bison1.com/gnc. GNC is the only national specialty retailer of vitamins, minerals, herbs and sports nutrition supplements and is uniquely positioned to capitalize on the accelerating trend toward self care. Established: 1935 - Franchised Since: 1988 - No. of Units: Company Owned: 2,336 - Franchised: 1,220 - Franchise Fee: $30,000 - Royalty: 6% - Total Inv: $114,931-$200,431 - Financing: Direct financing available to qualified candidates.

GOLD CAST PRODUCTS
130 Welsco Rd, Smackover, AR, 71762. - Tel: (870) 546-2598, Fax: (870) 725-3563, E-Mail: goldcast@cei.net, Web Site: www.goldcast products.com. Manufactured store opportunity. Established: 1989 - No. of Units: Franchised: 80 - Franchise Fee: $12,000 - Financing: No.

GOLF USA
Golf USA, Inc.
3705 W. Memorial Rd., Ste. 801, Oklahoma City, OK, 73134. Contact: Rick Benson, VP Franchise Sales & Operations - Tel: (405) 751-0015, (800) 488-1107, Fax: (405) 755-0065, E-Mail: franchise@gusahq.com, Web Site: www.golfusa.com. We franchise the operation of off-course specialty retail stores offering golf equipment, supplies, related clothing and accessories, swing analyzer and club repair under the name GOLF USA® (the "Store"). Established: 1986 - Franchising Since: 1989 - No. of Units: Company Owned: 5 - Franchised: 97 - Franchise Fee: $34,000-$44,000 - Royalty: 2% royalty; 1% advertising - Total Inv: $189,900-$285,750 for a one store location excluding rent - Financing: Third party.

GREAT EARTH VITAMIN STORES
Great Earth Companies, Inc.
140 Lauman Lane, Hicksville, NY, 11801. Contact: Chris Barr, Director, National Development - Tel: (800) 374-7328, (310) 571-0571, Web Site: www.greatearth.com. Specialty retailer of vitamins, herbs, homeopathics, fitness products and other supplements, focusing on high quality, high margin and superior customer service. Established: 1971 - Franchising Since: 1978 - No. of Units: Company Owned: 1 - Franchised: 125 - Franchise Fee: $22,000 - Royalty: 3% first six (6) months, 6% therafter - Total Inv: $90,000-$115,000, including buidout and inventory - Financing: On partial fee and opening inventory; third party balance.

HALLOWEEN EXPRESS
1860 Georgetown Rd, Owenton, KY, 40359. Contact: Holly Hutchinson, Director - Tel: (828) 670-9588, (888) 670-9444, Web Site: www.halloweenexpress.com. Temporary seasonal retail. Established: 1992 - Franchising Since: 1993 - No. of Units: Company Owned: 4 - Franchised: 69 - Franchise Fee: $10,000 - Royalty: 5% of gross sales - Total Inv: $15,000-$20,000 - Financing: No.

HAPPI-NAMES
Happi-Stores, Inc.
Rosana Square, 7508 W. 119th Street, Overland Park, KS, 66213. - Tel: (913) 327-1699, Fax: (913) 327-1283. Personalized gift store. Established: 1982 - No. of Units: 9 - Approx. Inv: $30,000 - Financing: None. NOT FRANCHISING AT THIS TIME.

HAT ZONE, THE
Hat Zone Franchising Co. Ltd., The
1036 A NE Jib Court, Lee' Summit, MO, 64064. Contact: Franchise Department - Tel: (816) 795-8702, Fax: (816) 795-9159. A specialty headware and appareal store. Established: 1993 - Franchising Since: 1995 - No. of Units: Company Owned: 10 - Franchised: 6 - Franchise Fee: $20,000-$25,000 - Royalty: 6% - Total Inv: $87,370-$234,300 - Financing: None.

HOBBYTOWN UNLIMITED INC
HobbyTown Unlimited, Inc
6301 S. 58th St., Lincoln, NE, 68516. Contact: Nichole Ernest - Tel: (402) 434-5064, (800) 858-7370, Fax: (402) 434-5055, Web Site: www.hobbytown.com. HobbyTown USA® is a retail franchise selling toys, hobby products and entertainment products. Established: 1980 - Franchising Since: 1985 - No. of Units: Company Owned: 1 - Franchised: 153 - Franchise Fee: $19,500 - Royalty: 2.5% monthly - Total Inv: $175,000 - Financing: Third party.

HOMETOWN THREADS
Hirsch International Corp.
3200 Univeristy Dr., Ste. 210, Coral Springs, FL, 33065. Contact: Franchise Development - Tel: (954) 255-3393, Fax: (954) 255-3389, E-Mail: leads@hometownthreads.com, Web Site: www.hometownthreads.com. Threads is a retail embroidery and personalization store that comes with everything you need to open your doors for business. Established: 1999 - Franchising Since: 2000 - No. of Units: Company Owned: 3 - Franchise Fee: $25,000 - Total Inv: $125,000.

HYCITE CORPORATION
Royal Prestiges
333 Holtzman Rd., Madison, WI, 53713. Contact: Rita Congdon, CEO - Tel: (608) 273-3373, Fax: (800) 678-9608. Complete line of cookware, cutlery, china, stonewear, casual and formal crystal and premium items for direct sales industry, together with financial package, sales promotion and incentive program. Established: 1961 - No. of Units: Company Owned: 3 - Franchised: 68 - Approx. Initial Inv: $500-$1,000 - Approx. Total Inv: $3,000-$5,000.

IT'S A BUCK
1036 Old Smithfield Rd., Goldsboro, NC, 27530. Contact: Philip Britt - Tel: (919) 731-4320, Fax: (919) 731-4328, E-Mail: info@itsabuck.com. A dollar store offering one of the most exciting retail concepts available. Offer customers the widest variety and products mix in the industry. Established: 1993 - Franchisig Since: 1999 - No. of Units: Franchised: 7 - Franchise Fee: $15,000 - Total Inv: $110,000-$195,000 - Financing: Will assist in obtaining.

JOHN SIMMONS
STS, Inc.
678 Phelan Ave, Memphis, TN, 38126-4047. - Tel: (901) 526-5567. Retail gift shops. Established: 1970 - Franchising Since: 1970 - No. of Units: Company Owned: 1 - Franchised: 1 - Franchise Fee: $15,000 - Royalty: 3.5% - Total Inv: $110,000-$185,000 - Financing: No.

JOHN T'S UNIQUE GIFTS
1018 Garden St., Ste. 206, Santa Barbara, CA, 93101. Contact: George Antonaros, Pres. - Tel: (800) 782-8988, (805) 564-6943, Fax: (805) 564-6953. Games, gifts, cigars and tobacco products retail sales. Established: 1967 - Franchising Since: 1991 - No. of Units: Company Owned: 7 - Franchised: 1 - Franchise Fee: $20,000 - Royalty: 5% - Total Inv: $125,000-$215,000 - Financing: No.

JUST ROSES
5428 W. Clearwater Ave., Kennewick, WA, 99336-1905. Contact: Lisa Koons, V.P. - Tel: (509) 783-2223, (877) 9-ROSES-9, Fax: (509) 783-7003, E-Mail: franchising@jroses.com, Web Site: www.jroses.com. Just Roses uses the highest quality roses and sells them at the lowest possible price. Roses are available in a large selection of colors, varieties and stems lengths. By emulating this concept we can create successful franchises. Established: 1989 - Franchising Since: 1993 - No. of Units: Company Owned: 6 - Franchised: 3 - Franchise Fee: $12,500 - Royalty: 2% of gross - Total Inv: $25,000-$50,000 - Financing: No.

JUST-A-BUCK
301 N. Main St., Suite 5, New City, NY, 10956. - Tel: (800) 332-2229, (845) 638-4111, Fax: (845) 638-3878, E-Mail: one_buck@sprynet.com, Web Site: www.just-a-buck.com. A dollar store of distinction, offering merchandise that would cost many times more anywhere else. The stores are beautifully maintained. Most of our franchisees own more than one store. Established: 1988 - Franchising Since: 1992 - No. of Units: Company Owned: 10 - Franchised: 36 - Franchise Fee: $25,000 - Royalty: 4% - Total Inv: $126,000-$260,000 (incl. fran. fee) - Financing: Assistance.

KIDS TEAM
Kids Franchise Corp.
7050 E 116th St, Fishers, IN, 46038-1727. Contact: Rory Underwood, Pres. - Tel: (800) 875-5439. Retailer of children's licensed sports apparel featuring professional and collegiate apparel in sizes ranging from infant to youth size 20. Established: 1972 - Franchising Since: 1993 - No. of Units: Company Owned: 2 - Franchised: 5 - Franchise Fee: $10,000 - Royalty: 4% - Total Inv: $56,000-$101,500 - Financing: None.

KING KOIL BEDQUARTERS
King Koil Sleep Products
770 Transfer Rd., Ste. 13, St. Paul, MN, 55114. - Tel: (612) 646-6882, Fax: (612) 646-8864. Sleep shop mattress retail strategy. Free standing or business expansion of furniture or appliance operation - or electronics store expansion. Established: 1898 - Franchising Since: 1982 - No. of Units: Franchised: over 100 - Total Inv: Upon request - Financing: N/A.

LATEX CITY
1814 Franklin St, #820, Oakland, CA, 94612. Contact: Jeffe Hoser, President - Tel: (510) 839-5462, Fax: (510) 839-2104, Web Site: www.latexnovelty.com. Ground floor specialty retailing opportunity in booming latex novelty aid business. Complete line of proprietary products. Latex City is deal for aggressive couples. Established: 1972 - Franchising Since: 1986 - No. of Units: Company Owned: 4 - Franchised: 26 - Franchise Fee: $15,000 - Royalty: 6% - Total Inv: $85,000-$235,000.

LE GOURMET
Le Gourmet Gift Basket Inc
516 W 8th Ave, Denver, CO, 80204. Contact: Cynthia McKay, Customer Service Rep or CEO - Tel: (303) 623-0500, (800) 93-GIFT-6, Fax: (303) 623-0559, E-Mail: Cynthia@intellink.net, Web Site: www.legift.com. Complete setup, training and referrals for gift basket business. Established: 1992 - Franchising Since: 1997 - No. of Units: Company Owned: 1 - Franchised: 340 - Franchise Fee: $3,500 - Total Inv: $3,500 - Financing : Yes.

LEARNING EXPRESS
29 Buena Vista St., Ayer, MA, 01432-5026. - Tel: (800) 924-2296. Learning Express is an exciting approach to the traditional toy store, with a hands-on philosphy and innovative products that stimulate a curious mind. Established: 1987 - Franchising Since: 1987 - No. of Units: Franchised: 160 - Franchise Fee: $30,000 - Royalty: 5% - Total Inv: $203,000-$354,000 (includes inventory) - Financing: No.

LEMSTONE BOOKS
Lemstone, Inc.
311 S. Country Farm Rd, Ste. E, Wheaton, IL, 60187. - Tel: (630) 682-1400, Fax: (630) 682-1828, E-Mail: sales@lemstone.com, Web Site: www.lemstone.com. Christian book/gift/music and cards with stores located in large enclosed malls and major strip centers. Established: 1981 - Franchising Since: 1982 - No. of Units: Company Owned: 1 - Franchised: 56 - Franchise Fee: $20,000 - Royalty: 4% - Total Inv: $185,000-$270,000 - Financing: No.

Let's Make Wine
Great Time. Great Wine.

LET'S MAKE WINE *
Let's Make Wine, LLC
1560 SW 14th Drive, Boca Raton, FL, 33486. Contact: Ann Rosenberg - Tel: (561) 416-9096, (888) 416-9755, Fax: (561) 416-9098, E-Mail: franchisesales@letsmakewine.com, Web Site: www.letsmakewine.com. Let's Make Wine franchises are upscale retail stores where franchisees offers customers the opportunity to make their own great tasting wine. Perfect for corporate events, parties, or private reserves. The process is simple and fun to do! Customers select bottles, corks and customers design their own labels. Wine related giftware provides multiple revenue streams. Immediate opportunities in FL, Co, TX, WY, OH, AR,

DC, KS, NE, and IN. Established: 2003 - Franchising Since: 2004 - No. of Units: Company Owned: 4 - Franchise Fee: $35,000 - Royalty: 6% - Total Inv: $226,500-$405,000 - Financing: No.

LITTLE PROFESSOR BOOK CENTER / LITTLE PROFESSOR BOOK COMPANY
Little Professor Book Centers, Inc.
405 Little Lake Dr., Ste. C, Ann Arbor, MI, 48103-6206. Contact: Franchise Department - Tel: (800) 899-6232, Fax: (734) 663-8738, Web Site: www.littleprofessor.com. Full-line, full-service community book stores carrying a complete selection of books, magazines and book related sidelines. Franchisor provides complete assistance and counsel needed to open and operate a book store from site selection to store opening, through the life of the agreement. Established: 1964 - Franchising Since: 1969 - No. of Units: Franchised: 62 - Franchise Fee: $37,000 - Royalty: 3% - Total Inv: $330,000 and up - Financing: Yes.

MEDICINE SHOPPE, THE
Medicine Shoppe International Inc., The
1100 N. Lindbergh Blvd., St. Louis, MO, 63132. - Tel: (800) 325-1397, Fax: (314) 872-5370. Retail prescription and health centers. Emphasis on the counselling pharmacist/manager being an integral part of screenings and delivery in the market area. Approx. 90% prescription and 10% non-prescription ethical medicines and Medicine Shoppe brand products. Established: 1970 - Franchising Since: 1970 - No. of Units: Company Owned: 9 -Franchised: 1065 - Franchise Fee: $10,000-$18,000 - Royalty: 2% conversion, 5.5% on growth, 5.5% on new - Total Inv: $117,000 - Financing: Yes.

MISTER MONEY - USA
Mister Money-USA, Inc
2057 Vermont Dr, Fort Collins, CO, 80525. Contact: Franchise Sale Director - Tel: (970) 493-0574, (800) 827-7296, Fax: (970) 490-2099, Web Site: www.mistermoney.com. USA franchises offer pawn loans, payday laons, check cashing, money orders and other financial services. Franchisees operate full-service retail stores or loan only outlets. Mister Money - USA stores are modern, customer-friendly and located in solid blue collar areas. Established: 1976 - Franchising Since: 1995 - No. of Units: Company Owned: 15 - Franchised: 34 - Franchise Fee: $21,500-$24,500 - Royalty: 3-5% - Total Inv: $65,000-$200,000 - Financing: Inventory.

MOBILITY SCOOTERS FRANCHISING LLC
1329 N. University Dr., Ste. E2, Nacoghoches, TX, 75965. Contact: Nick Hajdusiewicz - Tel: (936) 559-5522, (877) 953-6328, Fax: (936) 559-5144, E-Mail: mobilityscooters@yahoo.com, Web Site: www.mobility-scooters.net. We are a retail operation specializing in the sales and rentals of electric wheelchairs and scooters. Established: 2000 - No. of Units: Franchised: 6 - Franchise Fee: $19,500 - Total Inv: capital requirement; $48,700-$89,7000 - Financing: No.

MORE SPACE PLACE
More Space Place, Inc.
12555 Enterprise Blvd, Largo, FL, 33773. - Tel: (727) 539-1611, (888) 731-3051, Fax: (727) 524-6382, E-Mail: cwilliams@morespace place.com, Web Site: www.morespaceplace.com. More Space Place showrooms feature the world famous Murphy Bed as well as a host of other space saving wall beds and cabinets. Also available is a full line of closet, utility and garage products. Stores provide design service, including a computer design program that allows the customer to visualize the products in their space. The stores also provide professional installation of the products in the customers home or office. Established: 1996 - Franchising Since: 1996 - No. of Units: Company Owned: 3 - Franchised: 21 - Franchise Fee: $22,500 - Royalty: 4.5% of retail sales - Total Inv: $85,000-$195,000 depending on size of store - Financing: Third party.

MRM MARKETING NETWORK
2999 W County Road 42 #145, Burnsville, MN, 55306.Contact: Dir. Fran. Sales - Tel: (612) 890-8979, Fax: (612) 890-3818, E-Mail: mrmnet@minn.net. The MRM Marketing Team has established programs to increase dealer profitability in three major lines: floor covering, kitchen and bath and decorative (window treatments, wallpaper). Members can utilize any one or combination of the three lines...Includes

comprehensive advertising and support. Established: 1990 - Franchising Since: 1995 - No. of Units: Franchised: 47 - Franchise Fee: $500-$5,000 - Royalty: None - Total Inv: Varies - Financing: No.

MUNCHABLE BOUQUET
Candy Magic, Inc.
14321 Nicollete Court, Burnsville, MN, 55306. Contact: Thomas Lee, Pres. - Tel: (612) 898-5111, Fax: (208) 330-6453. We design and sell floral-looking bouquets made with edible products such as candy, gourmet coffees, teas and biscuits. Established: 1991 - Franchising Since: 1994 - No. of Units: Company Owned: 1 - Franchised: 1 - Franchise Fee: $7,500 - Royalty: 6% - Total Inv: $40,000-$55,000 - Financing: No. Unfortunately Munchable Bouquet is not offering franchises at the present time.

MUSIC GO ROUND®
Winmark Corporation
4200 Dahlberg Dr., Suite 100, Minneapolis, MN, 55422-4837. Contact: Franchise Development - Tel: (763) 520-8582, (800) 269-4076, Fax: (763) 520-8501,Web Site: www.musicgoround.com. Music Go Round stores sell, buy, trade quality used and new musical instruments. Our stores carry brand-name guitars, keyboards, drums, amps, studio and P.A. equipment. Established: 1986 - Franchising Since: 1994 - No. of Units: Company Owned: 6 - Franchised: 57 - Franchise Fee: $20,000 - Royalty: 3% of gross sales - Total Inv: $186,560-$280,802.

NATURE BLUE
Hemingway Unimpex Corp.
PO Box 360949, Los Angeles, CA, 90036. - Tel: (323) 936-9186, Fax: (323) 851-0854. Natural cosmetics, hair and body care retail store. Established: 1993 - Franchising Since: 1993 - No. of Units: Franchised: 12 - Franchise Fee: Franchising foreign territories only.

NATURE OF THINGS STORE, THE
NOTS, Inc.
10700 W. Venture Dr., Franklin, WI, 53132. Contact: Franchise Director - Tel: (414) 529-2192, (800) 283-2921, Fax: (414) 529-2253. Retail sales of science and nature, environmental, educational and gift items. Established: 1989 - Franchising Since: 1991 - No. of Units: Company Owned: 2 - Franchised: 12- Franchise Fee: $25,000 - Royalty: 5% - Total Inv: $125,000-$275,000 - Financing: No.

OAK CREEK VILLAGE
Associated Retailers Group
2221 E. Lamar Blvd., Suite 790, Arlington, TX, 76006. Contact: Richard A. Carver, President - Tel: (817) 695-0100, Fax: (817) 695-0150. Franchisor established retail sales centers specializing in the sale of new manufactured homes. Established: 1991 - Franchising Since: 1997 - No. of Units: Company Owned: 137 - Franchised: 80 - Franchise Fee: $10,000 - Total Inv: Varies - Financing: Yes.

OFFICE 1 SUPERSTORE INTERNATIONAL
P.O. Box 5093, East Hampton, NY, 11937. - Tel: (516) 537-4290, Fax: (516) 537-4293. Office supply retail. Established: 1989 - Franchising Since: 1989 - No. of Units: Franchised: over 200 - Franchise Fee: Master fee to de determined - Royalty: To be determined - Total Inv: $1,500,000 - Financing: No.

PAPER WAREHOUSE
7630 Excelsior Blvd., Minneapolis, MN, 55426. Contact: V.P. of Franchising - Tel: (800) 229-1792, (952) 936-1000, Fax: (952)936-9800. Retail party stores. Three store profiles: 4,000, 6,500 and 8,500 square feet. Established: 1983 - Franchising Since: 1987 - No. of Units: Company Owned: 97 - Franchised: 55 - Franchise Fee: $35,000 - Royalty: 4% - Total Inv: $165,000-$400,000 - Financing: No.

PARTY AMERICA
PA Acquisitions Corp
980 Atlantic Ave., Suite 103, Alameda, CA, 94501. Contact: Claude B. Hagopian, Director of Franchise Development - Tel: (510) 747-1800, Fax: (510) 747-1810, E-Mail: franchising@partyamerica.com, Web Site: www.partyamerica.com. Party America specialty retail stores capture the "Party Experience" by offering the most comprehensive everyday and seasonal merchandise needed to throw a great party. Our fun and customer centric stores offer atremendous selection of balloons, gift ware, table ware, decorations, party favors, and greeting cards for

virtually every special or seasonal theme. Established: 1997 - No. of Units: Company Owned: 63 - Franchised: 51 - Franchise Fee: $35,000 - Royalty: 4% - Total Inv: $250,000-$480,000 - Financing: TBD.

PARTY CENTRAL
203 Jandus Rd, Cary, IL, 60013. - Tel: (800) 833-3004. Established: 1910 - Franchising Since: 1985 - No. of Units: Franchised: 475 - Franchise Fee: $1,500.

PARTY LAND
Party Land Inc
5215 Militia Hill Rd., Plymouth Meeting, PA, 19462. Contact: John Barry, V.P., Sales - Tel: (610) 941-6200, (800) 778-9563, Fax: (610) 941-6301, E-Mail: jbarry@partyland.com, Web Site: www.party land.com. World's largest retail party supply chain with over 250 stores in 40 countries. Specializing in service and selection. Established: 1986 - Franchising Since: 1988 - No. of Units: Franchised: 250 - Franchise Fee: $35,000 - Royalty: 5% - Total Inv: $240,000-$299,000 - Financing: No.

PARTY ON!
Party On Franchise Corp.
210 Navajo Road, Pittsburgh, PA, 15241. - Tel: (412) 835-1824, (800) 254-8073, Fax: (412) 835-1824. Party On! Retail stores specialize in balloons, cards, decorations, costumes, gag gifts, stationery, gift wrap, tableware, and other party supplies, at a mix of deep discount and retail prices. Stores are unique to the industry in size, fixture layout, and merchandising. Full support is given to franchisees for store design, training, opening assistance, merchandising, buying (including substantial discount), promotions, and operations. Established: 1990 - Franchising Since: 1996 - No. of Units: Company Owned: 1 - Franchised: 2 - Franchise Fee: $15,000 - Royalty: 3% of gross sales royalty, 1% ad fee - Total Inv: $95,000 (2000 sf) - $165,000 (3500 sf) - Financing: No.

PARTY UNIVERSE
Party Warehouse Franchising, Inc
7630 Excelsoir Blvd, Minneapolis, MN, 55426. Contact: Mike Anderson - Tel: (952) 936-1000, (800) 229-1792, Fax: (952) 936-9800, E-Mail: franchise.leads@paperwarehouse.com, Web Site: www.paperware house.com. Retailer featuring party supplies, balloons and greeting cards at a discount price. Established: 1983 - Franchising Since: 1987 - No. of Units: Company Owned: 87 - Franchised: 55 - Total Inv: $184,400-$478,500.

PAWSENCLAWS & CO.
1055 Parsippany Blvd, Parsippany, NJ, 07054. Contact: Steven Mandell, President - Tel: (973) 335-0100, (866) 797-6259, Fax: (973) 335-2225, E-Mail: smandell@pawsenclaws.com. An interactive experience of stuffing, naming and dressing stuffed animals. A shopping mall based concept. Established: 2001 - Franchising Since: 2002 - No. of Units: Company Owned: 2 - Franchised: 1 - Total Inv: $535,500-$814,000.

PINCH A PENNY, INC.
Porpoise Pool & Patio
14480 62nd St., N., Clearwater, FL, 33760. Contact: John Thomas, President & C.E.O. - Tel: (727) 531-8913, Fax: (727) 536-8066. Retail pool and patio supply store. Established: 1975 - Franchising Since: 1976 - No. of Units: Company Owned: 5 - Franchised:115 - Franchise Fee: $15,000-$250,000 - Total Inv: $100,000-$500,000 - Royalty:10% - Financing: N/A.

POOL CENTERS U.S.A. INC.
1844 N Nob Hill Rd #615, Plantation, FL, 33322-6548. Contact: Michael Coleman, President - Tel: (305) 587-1574. Retail pool supplies, spas and patio furniture. Full training and support provided. Established: 1989 - Franchising since: 1990 - No. of Units: Company Owned: 2 - Franchised: 8 - Franchise Fee: $18,000 - Total Inv: $40,000-$55,000 - Financing: Yes.

RAILROADTOWN USA
HobbyTown USA
6301 South 58th Street, Lincoln, NE, 68516-3676. Contact: Nichole Ernst, Franchise Sales - Tel: (402) 434-5064, (800) 858-7370, Fax: (402) 434-5055, E-Mail: dfo@hobbytown.com, Web Site: www.hobby town.com. Part of HobbyTown USA. RailRoadTown USA specializes in all types of model railroad sets, engines, supplies and gifts. Established: 1979 - Franchising Since: 2002 - No. of Units: Company Owned: 1 - Total Inv: $155,000-$175,000.

RETOOL
Grow Biz International, Inc
4200 Dahlberg Drive, Minneapolis, MN, 55422-4837. Contact: Franchise Department - Tel: (612) 520-8500, (800) 645-7299, Web Site: www.growbiz.com. Retail store that buys and sells new, refurbished and used tools and accessories. Established: 1998 - Franchising Since: 1998 - No. of Units: Company Owned: 3 - Franchised: 4 - Franchise Fee: $20,000 US stores, $23,000 Canadian stores - Royalty: 4% gross sales - Total Inv: US approx $160,000, Canadian approx $180,000 - Financing: No.

ROBBIN'S RAINY DAY GIFT
P.O. Box 129, Putnam, CT, 06260. Contact: Robbin Peterson - Tel: (877) 928-2083. Selling of gifts. Established: 2000 - No. of Units: Company Owned: 1 - Total Inv: Capital requirements; $25.00 - Financing: No.

ROCKY MOUNTAIN CHOCOLATE FACTORY, INC.
265 Turner Drive, Durango, CO, 81303. - Tel: (800) 438-7623, Fax: (970) 259-5895, Web Site: www.rmcf.com. Retail packaged and bulk chocolates, truffles, cocoas, carmels, and fudges. Established: 1981 - Franchising Since: 1982 - No. of Units: Company Owned: 8 - Franchised: 200 - Franchise Fee: $24,000 - Royalty: 5% - Total Inv: $88,500-$447,686.

ROCS CARDS AND GIFTS
Recycled Paper Greetings
3636 N. Broadway, Chicago, IL, 60613. - Tel: (773) 348-6410, (800) 777-3331, Fax: (773) 244-8173. Fun and exciting card and gift stores. Established: 1984 - No. of Units: Company Owned: 3 - Licensed: 90 - Total Inv: $100,000-$150,000 - Financing: No.

ROLLING PIN KITCHEN EMPORIUM LLC
Aropi Inc.
P.O. Box 21798, Long Beach, CA, 90801. - Tel: (949) 221-9399. Retail gourmet Kitchen Store. Established: 1978 - Franchising Since: 1982 - No. of Units: Company Owned: 17 - Franchised: 18 - Royalty: 5% gross + .5% adv. - Total Inv: $200,000-$250,000 - Financing: No.

ROMAY SKIN CARE
Romay Inc
41 Anchor Dr, Lake Tapiwingo, MO, 64015. Contact: Robyn Sumner, President - Tel: (816) 478-4900, (800) 279-3402, Fax: (816) 478-1214. 800-1200 square foot retail outlets offering Romay skin care, body care and cosmetics. Specialty products. Established: 1989 - Franchising Since: 1996 - No. of Units: 2 - Franchise Fee: $5,000 - Royalty: 3% (1% of 3% goes towards adv. production) - Total Inv: $60,000-$130,000 includes working capital - Financing: Assistance available. NOT FRANCHISING AT THIS TIME.

RUG PLACE, THE
Rug Place, The
6485 Perkins Rd, Baton Rouge, LA, 70808. Contact: Yvonne Kelleher - Tel: (225) 766-0599, (866) 666-0784, Fax: (225) 766-0655, E-Mail: yvonne@rugplace.com, Web Site: www.rugplace.com. Retail -affordable rugs answering the demand created by the popularity of hard flooring. Established: 1997 - Franchising Since: 2000 - No. of Units: Company Owned: 2 - Franchised: 1 - Franchise Fee: $25,000 - Royalty: 5% - Total Inv: $150,000-$275,000 - Financing: No.

SANTA'S CLAUSET
The Visions Group LLC
3333 Valley Parkway, Ste. 900, Vacaville, CA, 95688. - Tel: (707) 421-5308, (800)425-8883, Fax: (707) 451-0410, E-Mail: info@santas clauset.com, Web Site: www.santasclauset.com. Seasonal or temporary retail store operating from mid October to mid January retail offering includes 60% Christmas merchandise and 40% general gifts. Established: 1997 - Franchising Since: 1998 - No. of Units: Company Owned: 3 - Franchise Fee: $2,000 - Royalty: 5% - Total Inv: Pre-opening cash, working capital, pre-paid rent for season, complete inventory and fixtures package: $95,000-$120,000 - Financing: Third party provides up to $60,000.

SEEN ON SCREEN, INC
Seen On Screen
4017 Colby Ave, Everett, WA, 98201. Contact: Antoine Jarjour, President - Tel: (425) 258-5960, (800) 780-1012, Fax: (425) 258-6789, E-Mail: seenonscreen@aol.com, Web Site: www.ontelevision.com. Retail store As Seen On TV products. Established: 1994 - Franchising Since: 1994 - No. of Units: Company Owned: 11 - Franchised: 7 - Franchise Fee: $7,500-$15,000 - Royalty: 6% - Total Inv: $150,000 - Financing: No.

SGO DESIGNER GLASS OF...
Stained Glass Overlay, Inc.
1827 North Case St., Orange, CA, 92865. Contact: Michael A. Cassidy, President - Tel: (714) 974-6124, Fax: (714) 974-6529. SGO is a rapidly growing international franchise company, featuring the unique process of manufacturing solid, seamless, one piece decorative or beveled glass products in any design. Established: 1974 - Franchising since: 1981 - No. of Units: Franchised: 332 - Franchise Fee: $34,000 - Royalty: 5% + 2% adv. - Total Inv: $34,000FF, $8,000 start up pkg., $3,000 training. Additional capital required $10,000-$30,000 studio set up - Financing: No.

SMOKERS EXPRESS
31275 Northwestern Hwy, #150, Farmington Hills, MI, 48334-2558. - Tel: (248) 932-0600, Fax: (248) 932-1333. Franchising of retail tobacco stores. Established: 1994 - Franchising Since: 1996 - No. of Units: Company Owned: 9 - Franchised: 3 - Franchise Fee: $12,500 - Royalty: 5 cents per carton, 2% on general merchandise - Total Inv: $50,000-$100,000.

SNAPPY AUCTIONS *
2014 Glen Echo Rd, Nashville, TN, 37215. Contact: Franchise Department - Tel: (615) 463-7355, Web Site: www.snappyauctions.com. EBay consignment outlets/drop-off stores. Established: 2003 - Franchising Since: 2003 - No. of Units: Company Owned: 1 - Franchised: 2 - Franchise Fee: $15,000 - Royalty: 4% - Total Inv: $34,000.

SOCCER POST
111 Melrose Drive, New Rochelle, NY, 10804. Contact: Steve Tunis, Franchise Director - Tel: (732) 578-1377, Fax: (732) 578-1399, Web Site: www.soccerpost.com. Retail soccer specialty business. Largest sellers retail of soccer equipment in the U.S. Established: 1978 - Franchising Since: 1991 - No. of Units: Company Owned: 1 - Franchised: 23 - Franchise Fee: $19,500 - Royalty: 5% retail, 3% team - Total Inv: $150,000-$200,000 - Financing: Yes.

SPRING CREST DRAPERY CENTERS
Spring Crest Company, Inc.
4375 Prado Rd Unikt 104, Corona, CA, 91720. - Tel: (800) 552-5523. Custom window fashions, including exclusive products. Established: 1955 - Franchising Since: 1968 - No. of Units: Franchised: 148 - Franchise Fee: $15,000 - Royalty: 3%-5% - Total Inv: $65,000.

STAR VALLEY INSTALLATIONS
Cazier Enterprises
2253 Linda St., Saginaw, MI, 48603. Contact: Monty Cazier, Owner - Tel: (517) 776-0733, Fax: (517) 790-9195. Franchisee will be provided with the products and training to install flagpoles, mailboxes, landscape lighting, and much more. Established: 1987 - Franchising Since: 1992 - No. of Units: Company Owned: 1 - Franchise Fee: $3,000 - Royalty: 8%, no advertising fee - Total Inv: $3,000 initial package plus $3,000-$5,000 misc. expenses - Financing: None.

STORAGE USA
165 Madison Ave, Memphis, TN, 38103. Contact: Ed Ansbro - Tel: (901) 252-2000, Fax: (901) 252-2060. Franchise and management of self storage units. Established: 1984 - Franchising Since: 1996 - No. of Units; Company Owned: 500 - Franchised: 50 - Franchise Fee: $40,000 - Royalty: 4% - Total Inv: $35,000-$50,0000 - Financing: Yes.

STREET CORNER NEWS
2945 S.W. Wanamaker Drive, Topeka, KS, 66614. Contact: Marci Daugherty - Tel: (785) 272-8529, Fax: (785) 272-2384, Web Site: www.streetcornernews.com. We are the "Convenience Store in the Mall". We offer the things that mall employees and mall patrons want during their shopping experiences; Aspirin, Fountain & Bottled Drinks, Coffee & Tea. Magazines & Newspspers, Lottery, Snacks, Candy &

Gum, Fax & Copy services, Cigarettes & Cigars, Souvenirs & Gifts, Office & Desk supplies and other incidentials. Established: 1988 - Franchising Since: 1995 - No. of Units: Franchised: 32 - Franchise Fee: $19,900 - Royalty: 4.5% of gross - Total Inv: $80,000-$120,000 - Financing: Will help to find outside financing.

SUCCESSORIES
Successories, Inc.
2520 Diehl Road, Aurora, IL, 60504. Contact: Walter Wollnik, Dir. of Fran. Operations - Tel: (630) 820-7200 Ext. 5542, (800) 621-1423, Fax: (630) 820-3856. Successories sells products for business and personal motivation, including over 500 proprietary products and from other sources such as audio tapes, time management systems and self improvement books. Our objective is to provide one stop shopping for all motivational resources. Established: 1985 - Franchising Since: 1992 - No. of Units: Company Owned: 57 - Franchised: 47 - Franchise Fee: $35,000 - Royalty: 2% - Total Inv: $144,000-$238,000 - Financing: No.

TALKING BOOKS
Talking Book World
26211 Central Park, #415, Southfield, MI, 48076. Contact: V.P. Franchising - Tel: (248) 945-9999. Retail chain of audiobook stores. We rent sell, and trade audiobooks. Carry a large selection of over 7,000 titles per location and access to over 70,000 titles. Established: 1993 - Franchising Since: 1996 - No. of Units: Company Owned: 20 - Franchised: 20 - Franchise Fee: $25,000 for 1st store, $10,000 each additional location - Royalty: 5% twice a month - Total Inv: $150,000-$225,000 per location - Financing: Not at this time.

THE CAR PHONE STORE
Automotive Technologies, Inc.
1807 Berlin Turnpike, Wethersfield, CT, 06109. - Tel: (860) 571-7600, Fax: (860) 257-1818. Retail sales, service and installation of cellular telephones and other wireless communications products and services. Established: 1988 - Franchising Since: 1989 - No. of Units: Company Owned: 1 - Franchised: 76 - Franchise Fee: $7,500-$25,000 - Royalty: Percentage of activation commissions and residuals - Total Inv: $22,900-$125,750 - Financing: Yes.

THE NUTRITION CLUB
1540 Omega Drive, Pittsburgh, PA, 15205. Contact: Bob Montanari, President/CEO - Tel: (412) 490-2929, (877) 474-2582, Fax: (412) 490-2955, Web Site: www.thenutritionclub.com. The Nutrition Club operates and franchises nutritional retail stores with a highly experiential environment and open architecture design, utilizing internet, in-store information systems and state-of-the-art retail technology. With their free membership, customers receive product education, informed guidance, price incentives and awards through a unique Customer Loyalty Program. Much of the franchise fee of $25,000-$30,000 is offset by ROI programs. Established: 1999 - Franchising Since: 2000 - No. of Units: Company Owned: 6 - Franchise Fee: $25,000-$30,000 - Royalty: 6% - Total Inv: TBD - Financing: Yes through third party.

TOTALLY WIRELESS
47241 Bayside Parkway, Fremont, CA, 94538. Contact: Franchise Department - Tel: (510) 651-3555 ext. 204, (800) 969-4735, Fax: (510)651-5995, E-Mail: jakewbrown@aol.com. Totally Wireless is the nation's first retail chain dedicated exclusively to wireless communications, with products ranging from cellular phones and pagers to wireless E-Mail and Internet services. In addition to developing a unique concept and a rigorous training program. Totally Wireless has negotiated preferential carrier contracts that will keep it competitive with other large national retailers. Established: 1993 - Franchising Since: 1997 - No. of Units: Company Owned: 20 - Franchise Fee: $25,000-$75,000 - Royalty: 7% - Total Inv: $126,750-$225,500 - Financing: Third Party.

TRUE FRIENDS
I.E.L. Franchising Group
P.O. Box 1278, Cumming, GA, 30028. - Tel: (770) 887-7815, Fax: (770) 781-9598. Unconditional Love! That's one of the things that makes pets so adorable. Own the store that offers America's largest selection of gifts for pet lovers. It's not a pet store; it's a gift store like none you've ever seen before. Volume buying power, computer inventory management and other support services help simplify your ownership in this fast-growing, multi-billion dollar industry. Established: 1993 - Franchising

Since: 1996 - No. of Units: Company Owned: 1 - Franchise Fee: $25,000 - Royalty: 6% weekly, 1% adv. weekly - Total Inv: Approximately $200,000 - Financing: No.

TRUE VALUE
Truserv Corp.
8600 West Bryn Mawr, Chicago, IL, 60631-3505. Contact: Retail Development & Operations Manager - Tel: (773) 695-5151, Fax: (773) 695-6534, E-Mail:dlange@truevalue.com. Member owned co-operative that supplies merchandise and support services to over 6,000 retailers world-wide. Offering made by prospects only. Established: 1948 - Franchising Since: 1948 - No. of Units: Franchised: 6,000 - Franchise Fee: $1000 stock purchase - Royalty: 0 - Total Inv: $150,000 min. - Financing: Yes.

TRUSTWORTHY HARDWARE STORES
Emery Waterhouse Co., The
P.O. Box 659, Portland, ME, 04104. Contact: Steve Frawley, Pres. - Tel: (207) 775-2371, Fax: (207) 775-5206. Retail hardware stores. Established: 1840 - Franchising Since: 1963 - No. of Units: Company Owned: 20 - Franchised: 160 - Franchise Fee: $60,000 - Total Inv: $120,000.

UNIFORMS FOR AMERICA
Uniforms For America, Inc.
1965 Vaughn Rd NW #B, Kennesaw, GA, 30144-7006. Contact: Roger Flynn, VP of Marketing - Tel: (770) 590-0199, (800) 908-0199, Fax: (770) 252-9793. Franchisor of turn-key, high profit retail stores that provide a wide selection, competitive pricing and unique customer service for the healthcare industry, businesses, and any organizations that require uniforms. (Healthcare, career, sports, schools, food service, security, etc.)   Established: 1995 - Franchising Since: 1995 - No. of Units: Franchised: 65 - Franchise Fee: $25,000 - Royalty: 12% on product reorders - Total Inv: $95,000 - Financing: Yes.

WHISKEY DUST
526 Hudson St., New York, NY, 10014. Contact: Mervin Bendewald, Owner - Tel: (212) 691-5576, Fax: (212) 675-1157. Vintage western apparel and western oddities. Established: 1989.

WICKS 'N' STICKS
Wicks 'N' Sticks, Inc.
16825 Northchase Dr., #900, Houston, TX, 77060. Contact: William McPherson, V.P. Fran. Dev. - Tel: (800)231-6337, (281) 874-0800. Large retailer of candles, fragrancing and related home decorative products. We offer outstanding name recognition, comprehensive training and extensive merchandising support. Established: 1968 - Franchising Since: 1968 - No. of Units: Franchised: 218 - Franchise Fee: $25,000 - Royalty: 6% - Total Inv: $169,000-$282,600 - Financing: Third party financing.

WILD BIRD CENTER
Wild Bird Centers of America, Inc.
7370 MacArthur Blvd., Glen Echo, MD, 20812. Contact: George Petrides, Jr., Director of Franchise Development - Tel: (301) 229-9585, (800) wildbird, Fax: (301) 320-6154, E-Mail: info@wildbird.com, Web Site: www.wildbird.com. Our full service stores carry a complete line of birding products such as seed, suet, feeders, baths, houses, books, hardware, and garden accessories. You'll also find a variety of exciting nature-oriented gifts for any occasion as well as a variety of unique local specialties, hand-selected by the owner of your store. Established: 1985 - Franchising Since: 1989 - No. of Units: Company Owned: 2 - Franchised: 99 - Franchise Fee: $15,000 - Royalty: 4% - Total Inv: $90,000-$135,000 - Financing: No.

WILD BIRD CROSSING
Wild Bird Centers of America, Inc.
7370 MacArthur Blvd., Echo, MD, 20812. Contact: George Petrides, Pres. - Tel: (301) 229-9585, Fax: (301) 320-6154, E-Mail: info@wild birdcenter.com, Web Site: www.wildbirdcenter.com. Franchising and supporting the ultimate wild bird specialty shops for people who want succesful businesses they can be proud to call their own. Established: 1985 - Franchising Since: 1993 - No. of Units: Franchised: 18 - Franchise Fee: $19,500 - Royalty: 3% - Total Inv: $75,000-$131,000 - Financing: No.

WILD BIRD MARKETPLACE
AF&G Supply Inc.
4317 Elm Tree Rd, Bloomfield, NY, 14469-9740. Contact: John F. Gardner, Pres. - Tel: (585) 229-5897, Fax: (585) 229-5448. Retail specialty store, serving the needs of the birder, the gardener and the naturalist. Established: 1988 - Franchising Since: 1990 - No. of Units: Franchised: 32 - Franchise Fee: $15,000 - Royalty: 4% on gross sales - Total Inv: $75,000-$95,000 - Financing: No.

WILD BIRDS UNLIMITED
Wild Birds Unlimited, Inc.
11711 N. College Ave, Suite 146, Carmel, IN, 46032. Contact: Paul Pickett - Tel: (317) 571-7100, (888) 730-7108, Fax: (317) 208-4050, E-Mail: pickettp@wbu.com, Web Site: www.wbu.com. The original and leading franchise system specializing in the hobby of backyard bird feeding. Wild Birds Unlimited functions as a true community resource: we provide valuable knowledge about the bird-feeding hobby, and represent a unique and pleasant shopping experience. Established: 1981 - Franchising Since: 1983 - No. of Units: Franchised: 281 - Franchise Fee: $18,000 - Royalty: 4% of gross sales - Total Inv: $82,000-$142,000 - Financing: Not direct.

@WIRELESS
@Wireless Enterprises, Inc
50 Methodist Hill DR #1500, Rochester, NY, 14623-4265 - Tel (585) 359-3390, (800) 613-2355, Fax: (858) 359-3253, E-Mail: info@shopatwireless.com, Web Site: www.shopatwireless.com Complete "Click and Brick" in one of today's hottest markets. Products include wireless phones/services, satelite tv's, high speed internet, high-tech toys and more. Use of full service e-commerce site is also included. Established: 1994 - Franchising Since: 2000 - No. of Units: Company Owned: 7 - Franchised: 48 - Franchise Fee: $15,000 - Royalty: 6-10% - Total Inv: $70,000-$131,000 - Financing: Third party options available.

WOODCRAFT FRANCHISE
Woodcraft Franchise Corporation
5300 Briscoe Road, Parkersburg, WV, 26102. Contact: William T. Carroll, Dir. of Franchise Operations - Tel: (304) 422-5412, Fax: (304) 422-5417, Web Site: www.woodcraft.com. A woodcraft retail store is a woodworker's paradise of over 6,000 different woodworking products, including hand and power tools, hardware and books, finishing and project supplies, carving tools, workbenches, domestic and imported handwoods and educational facilities. Established: 1928 - Franchising Since: 1997 - No. of Units: Company Owned: 28 - Franchised: 34 - Franchise Fee: $40,000 - Royalty: 5% - Total Inv: $425,000-$525,000 - Financing: No.

RETAIL: CLOTHING AND SHOES

ANGELICA IMAGE APPAREL
700 Rosedale Ave., St. Louis, MO, 63112. - Tel: (314) 889-1111 ext. 1126, Fax: (314) 889-1234. Designers and manufacturers of image apparel and custom designed uniform programs. Established: 1878.

AROUND YOUR NECK
15103 Canyon Crest, Dallas, TX, 75248. Contact: Bob Baumann - Tel: (972) 490-9797, (800) 601-3770, Fax: (972) 490-9798. Direct sales of men's clothing. Established: 1991 - No. of Units: Company Owned: 1 - Franchise Fee: $25,000 - Financing: Yes.

ATHLETE'S FOOT, THE
Athlete's Foot Group Inc., The
1950 Vaughn Rd., Kennesaw, GA, 30144-7017. Contact: Jeff Shafritz, National Sales Manager - Tel: (800) 524-6444, (770) 514-4718, Fax: (770) 514-4903, E-Mail: jshafritz@theathletesfoot.com, Web Site: www.theathletesfoot.com. Step into the action with the World's Leading Athletic Footwear Specialist, sporting more than 750 stores in 43 countries. Keep on the cutting-edge of footware technology. Become a "Fit Technician" through our exclusive training programs and benefit from our tremendous buying power and vendor selection. Established: 1971 - Franchising Since: 1972 - No. of Units: Company Owned: 253 - Franchised: 480 - Franchise Fee: $25,000 - Royalty: 5% + .6% marketing - Total Inv: $200,000-$350,000 - Financing: Third party.

BAGS & SHOES

P.O. Box 2302, Brandon, FL, 33509-2302. Contact: W.H. Bonneau, Pres. - Tel: (800) 405-2688. Offers over 3,000 current designer and brand name fashions and shoes and bags and accessories at 25% to 75% savings. Site selection, lease negotiation, design, construction, fixturing, merchandising, computerization, training and all inventory is guaranteed to sell. Established: 1980 - No. of Units: Franchised: 137 - Franchise Fee: $5,000 per $25,000 of investment - Royalty: None - Total Inv: $50,000-$150,000 - Financing: No.

EDUCATIONAL OUTFITTERS

8002 East Brainerd Rd, Chattanooga, TN, 37421. Contact: Brian Elrod - Tel: (423) 894-1222, (877) 814-1222, Fax: (423) 894-9222, E-Mail: info@eschoolclothes.com, Web Site: www.eschoolclothes.com. Offering high quality school uniforms and dress code apparel to private, christian and public schools. Established: 1999 - Franchising Since: 2001 - No. of Units: Company Owned: 1 - Franchised: 1 - Franchise Fee: $25,000 - Financing: No.

FASHION, LTD.

P.O. Box 2302, Brandon, FL, 33509-2302. - Tel: (954) 214-0338. Designer and brand name clothes at savings of up to 70%. Current season styles that are all guaranteed to sell. We set up stores in high traffic malls and shopping centers. Site selection, design, layout, fixturing, merchandising, computerization, and training at your location in your city. Established: 1985 - Franchising Since: 1985 - Franchise Fee: $5,000-$20,000 - Total Inv: $25,000-$100,000 - Financing: No.

FINE LINE LINGERIE

P.O. Box 7315, Laguna Niguel, CA, 92677. - Tel: (949) 448-7010. Ladies and men's lingerie lounge wear. Established: 1986 - Total Inv: $12.00 for catalog.

FLEET FEET, INC.

110 East Main Street #200, Carrboro, NC, 27510. - Tel: (919) 942-3102, Fax: (919) 932-6176. Specialty retailer of athletic footwear, apparel and accessories. We are the leader in specialty running stores with focus on technical product, knowledgeable staff and superior customer service. We are committed to our sport and our local communities. Established: 1976 - Franchising Since: 1979 - No. of Units: Franchised: 28 - Franchise Fee: $20,000 - Royalty: 4%-1% on a declinig scale - Total Inv: $150,000 - Financing: SBA.

HIDDEN AGENDA CLOTHING
Hidden Agenda Industries, Inc

4965 N. 42nd St, Milwaukee, WI, 53209. Contact: Clifton Davis - Tel: (414) 536-0517, (414) 527-1938. Mail order designer clothing lines. Established: 1997 - Total Inv: $500,000 - Financing: No.

JOS. A. BANK CLOTHIERS
Bell French & Associates

1 Boston Way, Asheville, NC, 28803. - Tel: (828) 274-1238, Fax: (828) 274-1973. Men's classic clothier. Established: 1905 - Franchising Since: 1991 - No. of Units: Company Owned: 74 - Franchised: 8.

LIBERTY FASHIONS INC.
Liberty Opportunities

2395 Prince Street, Conway, AR, 72032. - Tel: (501) 327-8031, Fax: (501) 327-0593. Business Start up for retail stores. Programs include inventory (you choose-apparel, shoes, bridal, lingerie, crystal/gift or $1 variety), fixtures, supplies, buying trip, grand opening co-ordination, training and in-store set up. Established: 1983 - Total Inv: Programs vary. Investment start at $18,900 with complete store starting at $27,900.

MAINSTREAM FASHIONS, INC

13877 Elkhart Rd, Apple Valley, MN, 55124. Contact: Marie Deniola, President - Tel: (612) 423-6254, Fax: (612) 322-3013, Web site: www.mainstreamfashions.com. Mainstream Fashions is a home based business. We provide todays busy woman with fun, comfortable fashions in the convenience of their home or office. Established: 1991 - Franchising Since: 1998 - No. of Units: Company Owned: 1 - Franchised: 4 - Franchise Fee: $9,500 - Royalty: 8% of sales - Total Inv: $26,000-$35,000 - Financing: No.

PICKLES AND ICE CREAM FRANCHISING, INC

203 Main St, Thomson, GA, 30824. Contact: Caroline Yort - Tel: (706) 595-9779, Fax: (706) 595-9560, E-Mail: franchise@pickles maternity.com, Web Site: www.picklesmaternity.com. Owned and started by mothers, it is the fastest growing maternity franchise. Established: 1997 - Franchising Since: 1999 - No. of Units: Company Owned: 1 - Franchised: 13 - Franchise Fee: $20,000 - Total Inv: $110,400-$302,100 - Financing: No.

PLATO'S CLOSET
Winmark Corporation

4200 Dahlberg Dr. Suite 100, Minneapolis, MN, 55422-4837. Contact: Franchise Department - Tel: (763) 520-8581, (800) 269-4081, Fax: (763) 520-8501, E-Mail: pc-franchise-development@platoscloset.com, Web Site: www.platoscloset.com. Plato's Closet stores buy and sell and trade quality used and brand-named apparel and accessories for teens and young adults. Established: 1998 - Franchising Since: 1999 - No. of Units: Company Owned: 1 - Franchised: 111 - Franchise Fee: $20,000 - Royalty: 4% of gross sales - Total Inv: $121,043-$211,389.

RED WING SHOES

314 Main St., Red Wing, MN, 55066. - Tel: (651) 388-8211, Fax: (651) 388-8211. Casual and work shoes. Established: 1976 - No. of Units: Company Owned: 2 - Franchised: 4.

SHOES FOR HER/SHOES FOR HIM

P.O. Box 2302, Brandon, FL, 33509-2302. Contact: W.H. Bonneau, Pres. - Tel: (954) 214-0338. Designer and name brand bags, shoes, belts, briefcases and accessories at affordable prices. Complete program, site selection, lease negotiation, design, construction, fixturing, inventory, one week on-site training, hiring of personnel, computer programming, grand opening, advertising and continued management support. Established: 1985 - Franchising Since: 1987 - No. of Units: 74 - Franchise Fee: $20,000 - Total Inv: $100,000-$250,000 - Financing: None.

SOX APPEAL
Sox Appeal Franchising

7167 Shady Oak Rd, Eden Prairie, MN, 55344-3516. Contact: Mike Jurgensen, CEO/President - Tel: (612) 943-1011, (800) 899-8478, Fax: (612) 943-9050. Retail sock and hosiery stores. Established: 1984 - Franchising Since: 1986 - No. of Units: Franchised: 7 - Franchise Fee: $20,000 - Royalty: 5% sales, 1% advertising - Total Inv: $125,000-$200,000 - Financing: No.

SPORT SHOE, THE
Sport Shoe Marketing, Inc., The

1770 Corporate Dr., Ste. 500, Norcross, GA, 30093. Contact: Dir. of Fran. - Tel: (770) 279-7494, (800) 944-7463. Athletic shoe store - selling athletic foot wear, apparel and accessories. Established: 1974 - Franchising Since: 1989 - No. of Units: Company Owned: 19 - Franchised: 5 - Franchise Fee: $25,000 - Royalty: 4% of gross sales - Total Inv: $212,750 - Financing: No.

T-SHIRTS PLUS
TSPN Inc

3209 Earl Rudder Frwy (Upstairs), College Station, TX, 77845. Contact: Randy Lee, CEO - Tel: (979) 485-0521, (800) 880-0721, Fax: (979) 694-3130, E-Mail: TSPN2001@aol.com, Web Site: www.t-shirtsplus.com. Franchise retail specialty chain offering the very best in imprinted sportswear and customized activewear. Located in regional malls. Established: 1974 - Franchising Since: 1975 - No. of Units: Franchised: 65 - Franchise Fee: $25,000 - Royalty: 6% Retail, 4% Group - Total Inv: $111,700-$213,800: Fran. fee+ $5,000-$25,000 inven; $12,000-$30,000 equip.; $29,000-$83,000 constr.; $1,000-$2,000 train.; $2,700-$18,000 init. rent - $10,000-$15,000 work. cap. - Financing: SBA.

TEN TOES SHOE WAREHOUSE
Ten Toes International

P.O. Box 770091, Coral Springs, FL, 33077-0091. Contact: Bruce Parker, President - Tel: (561) 689-8399, (800) 210-8637, Fax: (561) 688-1823. Retail discount shoes. One price shoes. Franchising Since: 1975 - No. of Units: Franchised: 2 - Franchise Fee: $25,900 - Royalty: None - Total Inv: $135,000 - Financing: No.

TOTALLY KOOL

1599 Fence Row Drive, Fairfield, CT, 06430. Contact: Bill Glazer, President - Tel: (203) 256-9944. Retail children's clothing store carrying a broad range of contemporary styles for boys and girls, and a secondary line of clothing called totally next (junior sizes). Established: 1993 - Franchising Since: 1996 - No. of Units: Company Owned: 1 - Franchise Fee: $24,500 - Royalty: 5% - Total Inv: $260,200 - Financing: No. NOT FRANCHISING AT THIS TIME.

WALK & JOG/WALK & ATHLETIC FOOTWEAR

P.O. Box 2302, Brandon, FL, 33509-2302. - Tel: (954) 214-0338. Offering over a 100 designer brand name footwear and accessories with 25% to 70% savings. We will design a store to fit your budget. All inventory is guaranteed to sell in 90 days. Established: 1987 - Franchising Since: 1988 - No. of Units: Franchised: 37 - Franchise Fee: $5,000 plus.

WINESTYLES INC. *

3000 N.E. 30th Pl., #308, Ft. Lauderdale, FL, 33306. - Tel: (954) 561-6545, fax: (954) 565-4045, Web Site: www.winestyles.net. Offers consumers a conveniently organized by tast styles shopping experience. Established: 2002 - Franchising Since: 2003 - No. of Units: Franchised: 1 - Franchise Fee: $25,000 - Royalty: 6% - Total Inv: $122,300-$200,500.

SCHOOLS AND TEACHING

ABC PHONETIC READING SCHOOL INC.
Phx. Ed. Franchise Sys. Inc.

3625 North 16th St., Ste. 130, Phoenix, AZ, 85016. Contact: John Cahal, Pres. - Tel: (800) 538-7323, Fax: (602) 265-2283. Tutoring. Established: 1986 - Franchising Since: 1993 - No. of Units: Company Owned: 9 - Licensed: 1 - Licensing Fee: $10,000 - Royalty: None - Total Inv: $6,500 - Financing: No.

ACADEMY OF LEARNING

5 Bank St., Ste. 202, Attleboro, MA, 02703-2351. Contact: Richard Brown, C.O.O. - Tel: (800) 750-TYPE, (508) 222-000, Richard Brown (508) 672-6888, Fax: (508) 222-0005. State of the art computer and business skills training. Unique, self paced Integrated Learning System. Established: 1987 - Franchising Since: 1987 - No. of Units: Company Owned: 2 - Franchised: 118 - Franchise Fee: $35,000 - Total Inv: $112,600-$147,800 - Financing: No.

AMERICAN INSTITUTE OF SMALL BUSINESS

7515 Wayzata Blvd., Ste. 129, Minneapolis, MN, 55426. Contact: Max Fallek, Director - Tel: (800) 328-2906, (953) 545-700, Web Site: www.aisbofmn.com. Seller of books, videos and software on small business start up and business operation. Offers workshops on setting up and operating a small business. Established: 1985 - Franchising Since: 1991 - No. of Units: Company Owned: 1 - Franchised: 6 - Franchise Fee: $2,000 - Total Inv: $5,000 - Financing: Yes.

AMRON SCHOOL OF THE FINE ARTS
John & Joe Fashions, Inc.

1315 Medlin Rd., Monroe, NC, 28112. Contact: Norma Williams, Pres. - Tel: (704) 283-4290. A franchise system to teach modeling, acting, do portfolios for models and actors, cosmetic sales (Amron Cosmetics). Established: 1979 - No. of Units: Company Owned: 1 - Franchise Fee: $15,000-$25,000 depending upon population - Royalty: Based on a sliding scale of gross . NOT FRANCHISING AT THIS TIME.

BARBIZON INTERNATIONAL, INC.

2240 Woolbright Rd., Ste. 300, Boynton Beach, FL, 33426. - Tel: (561) 369-8600, Fax: (561) 369-1299. Courses in modeling, fashion and acting. Established: 1939 - Franchising Since: 1968 - No. of Units: Franchised: 75 - Franchise Fee: $35,000 - Total Inv: $50,000 - Financing: Portion of franchise fee.

BOSTON BARTENDERS SCHOOL OF AMERICA
Boston Bartenders School Associates Inc.

P.O. 176, Wilbraham, MA, 01095. - Tel: (800) 357-3210, Fax: (413) 596-4630. Bartender training school. Established: 1968 - Franchising Since: 1994 - No. of Units: Company Owned: 3 - Franchised:6 - Franchise Fee: $6,999 - Royalty: 5% - Total Inv: $21,799 - Financing: Yes.

CAREER BLAZERS LEARNING CENTERS

175 Pinelawn Rd., Ste. 307, Melville, NY, 11747. - Tel: (631) 756-2400. Computer training schools designed to cater to the adult learner. We teach you all that you'll ever need to know about how to successfully operate a profitable business school. Established: 1949 - Franchising Since: 1994 - No. of Units: Company Owned: 4 - Franchised/Licensed: 147 - Franchise Fee: $25,000 - Royalty:12% - Total Inv: $90,000-$150,000 not incl. fran. fee.

CLUB Z INC

15310 Amberly Dr., #185, Tampa, FL, 33647. Contact: Franchise Department - Tel: (813) 931-5516, (800) 434-2582, Fax: (813) 932-2485, Web Site: www.clubztutoring.com. Direct a staff of qualified teachers that tutor children in the comfort of the child's home. We offer a proven operating system that's financially and personally rewarding. Individuals with business or education backgrounds excel. Established: 1995 - Franchising Since: 1997 - No. of Units: Company Owned: 1 - Franchised: 220 - Franchise Fee: $19,500 - Total Inv: $20,000 - Financing: No.

COMPUQUEST EDUCATIONAL SERVICES

1570 Lancelot Ave, Highland Park, IL, 60035-2219. - Tel: (847) 831-4105. On location computer classes for children age 3 1/2 through the sixth grade. Established: 1991 - Franchising Since: 1991 - No. of Units: Company Owned: 1- Franchised: 37 - Franchise Fee: $25,000 - Royalty: Up to 10% - Total Inv: $33,400-$71,600 - Financing: No.

COMPUTER U
Computer U Learning Centers

75-850 Osage Trail, Indian Wells, CA, 92210. Contact: Russ Beckner, V.P. - Tel: (760) 340-2453, (888) 708-7877, Fax: (760) 340-0306, E-Mail: info@computer.com, Web Site: www.computeru.com. Computer U provides computer training to mature adults through classroom instruction and private tutoring. Established: 1992 - Franchising Since: 1997 - No. of Units: Company Owned: 4 - Franchised: 9 - Franchise Fee: $20,000 - Royalty: 6% - Total Inv: $40,000 - Financing: No.

COMPUTERMOMS INTERNATIONAL CORP.

3925 W. Baker Lane, Ste. 1000, Austin, TX, 78758. Contact: Carol Evanicky, Franchise Dev. Manager - Tel: (512) 477-MOMS, (888) HIRE-MOMS, Fax: (512) 305-0132, Web Site: www.computer moms.com. Franchisee's provide one-on-one on-site computer training and support. Established: 1994 - Franchising Since: 1998 - No. of Units: Franchised: 52 - Franchise Fee: $9,750 - Royalty: 14% of Gross Sales - Total Inv: $9,750 - Financing: Up to $5,000.

CTI FRANCHISES, INC.
CTI Computer Training Institutes

5748 Bixbywoods, Columbus, OH, 43232. Contact: Franchise Director - Tel: (614) 860-0662, Fax: (614) 860-9722. Self paced flexible schedule computer applications training school. 100% hands-on, personal training. Established: 1996 - Franchising Since: 1997 - No. of Units: Company Owned: 1 - Franchised: 6 - Franchise Fee: $30,000 - Royalty: 6% - Total Inv: $90,000-$250,000 - Financing: No.

DREAMCATCHER LEARNING CENTERS
Dreamcatcher Franchise Corp.

427 Main Street, Windsor, CO, 80550. Contact: Stacy Swift, Fran. Consultant - Tel: (970) 686-9282, (888) 937-3121, Fax: (970) 686-7045, Web Site: www.dreamcatcherlearning.com. Educating America's children with a guaranteed year of academic progress with each 30 hours of instruction. Utilizing the only research validated instructional method in reading, writing, spelling and math. This is as good as education gets! No education degree required. Liquid assets $50,000. Established: 1995 - Franchising Since: 1997 - No. of Units: Company Owned: 3 - Franchised: 27 - Franchise Fee: $25,000 - Royalty: 8% - Total Inv: $29,650-$61,350 - Financing: Will provide only assistance/documents to lending organization, SBA approved.

ECHOLS INTERNATIONAL TRAVEL/TRAINING COURSES/INTERNATIONAL TRAVEL TRAINING COURSES,INC.

140 S. Dearborn St., Ste. 320, Chicago, IL, 60603-5202. Contact: Evelyn Echols, Pres. - Tel: (312) 697-6240. Training personnel for all facets of the travel industry including airlines. Established: 1962 -

Franchising Since: 1972 - No. of Units: Company Owned: 2 - Franchised: 2 - Franchise Fee: $50,000 - Total Inv: $125,000 - Royalty: 10% first 5 yrs., 7% thereafter. NOT FRANCHISING AT THIS TIME.

ELS LANGUAGE CENTERS
ELS Educational Services
400 Alexander Park, Princeton, NJ, 08450. Contact: Charles Gilbert, Vice President - Tel: (609) 750-3508, Fax: (609) 750-3596, E-Mail: international@els.com, Web Site: www.els.com. English as a second language schools. Franchises are sold internationally, USA schools are company-owned. Established: 1956 - Franchising Since: 1978 - No. of Units: Company Owned: 26 - Franchised: 50 - Franchise Fee: $30,000 - Royalty: 5% - Total Inv: $150,000-$300,000 (excl. fran./train.fees) - Financing: None.

GWYNNE LEARNING ACADEMY
Gwynne Systems, Inc.
1432 W. Emerald Ave., Unit 735, Mesa, AZ, 85202-3220. Contact: Penny Gwynne, Treasurer - Tel: (480) 644-1434. Video-based educational courses. Established: 1981 - Franchising Since: 1992 - No. of Units: Company Owned: 1 - Franchised: 13 - Franchise Fee: $45,000 - Royalty: 7% - Total Inv: $9,800-$14,000 plus fran. fee - Financing: Yes.

HAMMETT LEARNING
J.L. Hammett Co.
P.O. Box 859057, Braintree, MA, 02185-9057. Contact: Fran. Dept. - Tel: (781) 848-1000, Fax: (781) 356-5021. J.L. Hammett Co. is a supplier of educational and early learning material. The product line has been supplemented to include office supplies and craft products. Established: 1863 - Franchising Since: 1986 - No. of Units: Company Owned: 31 - Franchised: 38 - Franchise Fee: $25,000 - Royalty: 6% + 1% adv. - Total Inv: $96,000-$216,500 excld. fran. fee - Financing: No.

HONORS LEARNING CENTER, THE
5959 Shallowford Rd., Ste. 517, Chattanooga, TN, 37421. Contact: Gary Miller, Pres. - Tel: (423) 892-1803, Fax: (423) 892-1803, Web Site: www.honorslearningcenter.com. After-school supplemental education services for grades K-12 in reading, math, study-skills, ACT/SAT prep with individualized programs and academic testing. Corporately approved by CITA and SACS. Established: 1987 - Franchising Since: 1992 - No. of Units: Franchised: 1 - Franchise Fee: $19,500 - Royalty: 7% - Total Inv: $69,000-$136,000 - Financing: None.

HUNTINGTON LEARNING CENTER, THE
Huntington Learning Centers, Inc.
496 Kinderkamack Rd., Oradell, NJ, 07649. Contact: Russ Miller/Rich Pittus - Tel: (201) 261-8400, (800) 653-8400, Fax: (201) 261-3233, E-Mail: franchise@huntingtonlearningcenter.com, Web Site: www.huntingtonlearning.com. Supplemental educational services provider helping K-12 students do better in school. Provides tutoring in reading, writting, math and study skills in a learning center environment. Established: 1977 - Franchising Since: 1985 - No. of Units: Company Owned: 33 - Franchised: 181 - Franchise Fee: $38,000 - Royalty: 8% - Total Inv: $65,000 - Financing: Third party.

IVY LEARNING CENTERS, INC
5 Wilshire Dr., Sharon, MA, 02067. - Tel: (781) 793-0123, (877) 463-9489. IVY Learning Centers provide quality school-age child care enrichment programs for children ages 5 through 12. Hands on enrichment activities and homework help in a safe and nurturing environment. Tutoring services for students of all ages. Established: 1995 - Franchisng Since: 1998 - No. of Units: Company Owned: 2 - Franchised: 1 - Franchise Fee: $15,000-$25,000 - Total Inv: $25,000-$104,000 - Financing: No.

JOHN CASABLANCAS MODELING & CAREER CENTER
Model Merchandising International, L.P.
111 East 22nd St., New York, NY, 10010. Contact: Charyn K. Urban, Dir. of Fran. Dev. - Tel: (212) 420-0655, Fax: (212) 473-2725, mmilllzz@aol.com, Web Site: www.jc-centers.com. Our franchised schools & in-house modeling agencies provide cutting-edge professional modeling, personal image development and film & TV acting programs & workshops. Established: 1979 - Franchising Since: 1979 - No. of Units: Franchised: 49 - Franchise Fee: $40,000 - Royalty: 7% + 3% = 10% - Total Inv: $150,000 - Financing: N/A.

JOHN ROBERT POWERS FINISHING, MODELING, AND CAREER SCHOOLS
John Robert Powers School System, Inc.
9220 Sunset Blvd., Ste. 100, West Hollywood, CA, 90069. Contact: Franchise Dept. - Tel: (310)858-3300, (888) 41 model, Fax: (310) 777-3696. Schools specializing in training for men and women in self-improvement, modelling, executive grooming, drama, fashion merchandising, interior design, etc. Established: 1923 - Franchising Since: 1950 - No. of Units: Company Owned: 7 - Franchised: 18 - Franchise Fee: $10,000-$30,000 - Royalty: 10% on cash collected plus $150/mo. adv fee - Total Inv: $50,000-$75,000 depending on territory - Financing: 50% of fran. fee.

KIDS "R" KIDS QUALITY LEARNING CENTERS
Kids "R" Kids International
1625 Executive Drive South, Deluth, GA, 30096. Contact: Franchise Sales - Tel: (770) 279-8500, (800) 279-0033, Fax: (770) 279-9699, E-Mail: Kids@KidsRKids.com, Web Site: www@KidsRKids.com. We build from the ground up, never buy existing. 14,000 sq ft, our schools are on the internet so parents can dial up, log on, + visit their child's class room anytime. We're a privately owned company. Established: 1985 - Franchising Since: 1988 - No. of Units: Franchised: 80 in 15 states and San Juan, P.R - Franchise Fee: $37,500 - Royalty: 5%, 1% adv - Total Inv: Approx 1.5 million - Financing: Yes.

KIDSPEAK
Kidspeak International, L.C.
112 Hurt, Atlanta, GA, 30307. - Tel: (404) 222-9855, Fax: (404) 222-9914. Spanish and French instruction for children. Established: 1990 - Franchising Since: 1991 - No. of Units: Company Owned: 1 - Francished: 3 - Franchise Fee: $5,000 - Royalty: 10% of gross revenues - Financing: No.

LADO INTERNATIONAL COLLEGES
Lado Enterprises, Inc.
2154 Wisconsin Ave., NW, Washington, DC, 20007. - Tel: (202) 338-3179, Fax: (202) 338-2941, Web Site: www.lado.com. English Language schools. A 10 months program to teach students with little or no English language knowledge to pass the TOEFL with a score of 550 or better. Established: 1977 - Franchising Since: 1986 - No. of Units: Company Owned: 3 - Franchised: 6 - Franchise Fee: $50,000 - Royalty: 6% of gross sales - Total Inv: $250,000 ($50,000 fee, $20,000 buildout, $180,000 first year) - Financing: No.

LANGUAGE LEADERS *
3N503 Townhall Rd, Elburn, IL, 60119. - Tel: (877) 532-3370, Fax: (630) 578-0948, Web Site: www.language-leaders.com. Successfully teach Spanish, French and German to more than 6,000 children per year. Esrtablished: 1992 - Franchising Since: 2004 - No. of Units: Company Onwed: 1 - Franchise Fee: $10,000-$98,000.

MILE HIGH KARATE, LLC
2555 East Jamison Ave, Littleton, CO, 80211. Contact: Stephen Oliver, President - Tel: (303) 740-9467, Fax: (303) 796-7181, E-Mail: info@milehighkarate.com, Web Site: www.milehighkarate.com. Martial Arts schools catering primarily to children and their families. Established: 1983 - Franchising Since: 2002 - No. of Units: Franchised: 12 - Total Inv: $67,500-$165,000.

NEW HORIZONS COMPUTER LEARNING CENTER
New Horizons Computer Learning Centers, Inc.
1900 S. State College Blvd, Ste. 200, Anaheim, CA, 92896. Contact: V.P. Franchise - Tel: (714) 940-8230, Fax: (714) 938-6008. A complete PC, Macintosh, Windows NT, Novell, Unix and Sun training and support company for businesses and individuals. Franchise locations throughout the world. Established: 1982 - Franchising Since: 1992 - No. of Units: Company Owned: 27 - Franchised: 224 - Franchise Fee: $25,000-$50,000-$75,000 - Royalty: Continuing 6% of gross rev., adv. 1% of gross rev. - Total Inv: $450,000-$500,000, liquid assets minimum - Financing: 50% of the franchise fee.

ODYSSEY ART CENTERS
Odyssey Art Centers LLC
Box 512, Tarrytown, NY, 10591. Contact: Linda Perlmutter, President - Tel: (914) 631-7148, E-Mail: odysseyart@aol.com, Web Site: www.odysseyart.com. Creative art schools for children and adults. Can

be done from home studio. Established: 1974 - Franchising Since: 1995 - No. of Units: Company Owned: 1 - Franchised: 3 - Franchised Fee: $24,000 - Royalty: 6% gross sales, 2% gross sales - advertising - Total Inv: $28,000-$54,000 - Financing: No.

PC PROFESSOR COMPUTER TRAINING & REPAIR
7056 Beracasa Way, #208, Boca Raton, FL, 33433. Contact: Dir. - Tel: (561) 750-7879, (888) PC-12345, Fax: (561) 750-9872. Provides quality, personalized computer training in a relaxed, hands-on manner. Our formula works! Includes thorough training package and software authorizations. Established: 1989 - Franchising Since: 1995 - No. of Units: Company Owned: 2 - Franchised: 1 - Franchise Fee: $25,000 - Total Inv: $125,000 - Financing: Yes.

PRIMROSE SCHOOL
Primrose School Franchising, Co.
3660 Cedarcrest Rd, Acworth, GA, 30101. Contact: Franchise Development - Tel: (770) 529-4100, Web Site: www.primroseschools.com. Quality educational childcare with proven curriculum and lesson plans for infants through kindergarden. Comprehensive operations manual, thorough training, ongoing support from professional staff. Established: 1982 - Franchising Since: 1989 - No. of Units: Company Owned: 1 - Franchised:141 - Franchise Fee: $50,000 - Royalty: 7%, 1% adv./dev. - Approx. Total Inv: $1,000,000 ($150,000) - Financing: Assistance available.

PRINCETON REVIEW, THE
Princeton Review Management Corp., The
2315 Broadway, New York, NY, 10024. Contact: Linda Nessim, V.P. - Tel: (212) 874-8282, Fax: (212) 874-0775. Offers courses and tutoring programs for standardized tests. These include the SAT, The College Board Achievements, The ACT, GRE, GMAT and the LSAT. Established: 1981- Franchising Since: 1985 - No. of Units: Company Owned: 4 - Franchised: 37 - Franchise Fee: Differs for each location - Royalty: Differs for each location - Total Inv: Differs for each location.

SANDLER SYSTEMS INC.
10411 Stevenson Rd., Stevenson, MD, 21153. Contact: Ron Taylor, Dir.of Fran - Tel: (800) 669-3537, Fax: (410) 358-7858, Web Site: www.sandler.com. Sales, management and human relations training company. Our target market is small to medium size businesses. Established: 1967 - Franchising Since: 1984 - No. of Units: Franchised: 160 - Franchise Fee: $50,000 - Royalty: Monthly fee $908 - Financing: Minimal.

SHOW ME PCS
Show Me PS's, Inc
12010 Bammel North Houston Rd Ste L, Houston, TX, 77066-4773. - Tel: (281) 880-8766, Fax: (281) 880-8847. Teaching of computer skills, at home or at the office. Established: 1998 - Franchising Since: 1999 - No. of Units: Company Owned: 2 - Franchised: 2 - Franchise Fee: $5,000 - Total Inv: $49,400 - Financing: No.

SLEEPING GIANT WITHIN, THE
Sleeping Giant Within, Inc., The
3697 Hwy. C, Leslie, MO, 63056. - Tel: (573) 764-3920, Fax: (573) 764-4420. Leadership, management and human development training specialist. Established: 1990 - Franchising Since: 1995 - No. of Units: Company Owned: 4 - Franchised: 1 - Franchise Fee: $25,000 - Royalty: 8% gross sales - Total Inv: $25,000 fran. fee - Financing: Yes.

SPEAKFIRST
Speakeasy Development Co.
401 W Baseline Rd Ste 108, Tempe, AZ, 85283-5349. - Tel: (602) 839-4811. Language and cultural training franchise. Established: 1992 - Franchising Since: 1998 - No. of Units: Company Owned: 1 - Franchise Fee: $17,500 - Royalty: Call for details - Total Inv: Call for details - Financing: Yes.

STANFIELD EDVANCEMENT CENTERS
Stanfield Educational Alternatives, Inc
1025 S. Semoran Blvd., Ste. 1093, Winter Park, FL, 32792. Contact: Kevin Price/Marlene Bremont, COO/Franchise Development - Tel: (877) 732-9162, E-Mail: aero2000@email.msn.com, Web Site: www.helpingkids.com. Stanfield offers both stand alone and satelite centers that incorporate proprietary ciriculum. Established: 1998 -

Franchising Since: 2000 - No. of Units: Company Owned: 1 - Franchise Fee: Stand alone $35,000, Satelite $25,000 - Financing: Through approved companies.

SUDDENLY YOU'RE SEWING SCHOOL
1350 Broadway Ste. 1601, New York, NY, 10018. Contact: Donna Pierson, Director - Tel: (212) 714-1633, Fax: (212) 714-1655, E-Mail: dpierson@sewing.org, Web Site: www.suddensewing.org. One and two class rooms for 5 students to be taught sewing. Small class size and solid 16 week course provide a good foundation to learning to sew. Established: 1998 - Franchising Since: 1998 - Franchise Fee: $12,000 - 1 room school, $18,000 2 room class - Royalty: 5% monthly net, advertising fee not to exceed .5% of net sales monthly - Total Inv: $43,65-$65,600 - Financing: Yes.

SUNBROOK ACADEMY
Sunbrook Franchising Inc
2933 Cherokee St, Kennesaw, GA, 30144. Contact: Neil Gass - Tel: (770) 426-0619, Fax: (770) 426-0724, E-Mail: info@sunbrook academy.com, Web Site: www.sunbrookacademy.com. We offer the opportunity to provide quality educational childcare programs. Established: 1984 - Franchising Since: 1999 - No. of Units: Company Owned: 4 - Franchised: 6 - Franchise Fee: $40,000 - Total Inv: $15,000-$20,000 - Financing: Third party.

SYLVAN LEARNING CENTERS
Sylvan Learning Systems, Inc.
1001 Fleet Street, Baltimore, MD, 21202. Contact: Dir. Fran. System Dev. - Tel: (410) 843-8880, Fax: (410) 843-6265, Web Site: www.sylvan.com. Leading provider of supplemental education to children and adults. Individualized programs in reading, mathematics, writing, study skills, SAT/ACT prep. Instruction by certified teachers. Established: 1979 - Franchising Since: 1980 - No. of Units: Company Owned: 140 - Franchised: 1010 - Franchise Fee: $32,000-$46,000 - Royalty: 8%/9%, - Total Inv: Cash $66,060-$94,500; Total: $76,060-$137,500 - Financing: In some instances.

TRAINAMERICA®
TrainAmerica Corporation
1 Lafayette Cir., Ste. 203, Bridgeport, CT, 06604. - Tel: (203) 372-4836, (203) 372-4853. Computer Training. Established: 1992 - Franchising Since: 1999 - No. of Units: Company Owned: 1 - Franchise Fee: $24,995 - Royalty: 8% (5% royalty, 2% local, 1% national) - Total Inv: $74,995-$119,995 - Financing: Yes.

TUTORING CLUB, INC
6964 Almaden Expressway, San Jose, CA, 95120-3201. Contact: Chad Schwartz, V.P - Tel: (408) 997-7590, (888) 674-6425, Fax: (408) 997-7024, E-Mail: tutoringclub@aol.com, Web Site: wwwTutoringClub.com. Private individualized education services for students from kindergarten through adults. Established: 1991 - Franchising Since: 1999 - No. of Units: Company Owned: 1 - Franchised: 25 - Total Inv: $48,000-$74,900.

UNIVERSITY INSTRUCTORS
P.O. Box 17415, Richmond, VA, 23226. Contact: James Popp, President - Tel: (804) 741-7515, E-Mail: univinstr@aol.com, Web Site: www.universityinstructors.com. University Instructors offers individual academic tutoring, one-to-one and small group sports instruction for high school, middle school, and elementary school students. Established: 1994 - Franchising Since: 1997 - No. of Units: Company Owned: 3 - Franchised: 1 - Franchise Fee: $5,000-$8,000 - Royalty: 6% of revenue - Total Inv: $12,000-$22,000 (includes franchise fee) - Financing: No.

SIGN PRODUCTS & SERVICES

AMERICAN SIGN SHOPS
All American Signs Shops Inc.
3803-B Computer Dr., Ste. 200, Raleigh, NC, 27609. Contact: Bruce Harabes, Dir. Franchise Dev - Tel: (919) 787-1557, (800) 966-2700, Fax: (919) 787-3830, E-Mail: info@amerisign.com, Web Site: www.american.com. Retail sign shops giving fast service with computer technology, producing quality vinyl signage and the latest capabilities in full color graphics. A business to business marketing opportunity.

Established: 1984 - Franchising Since: 1987 - No. of Units: Franchised: 49 - Franchise Fee: $20,000 - Royalty: 6% of gross sales - Total Inv: $66,795-$91,595 including franchise fee - Financing: Third Party.

ANYTHING A CUSTOMER WISHES
Thrifty Impressions
853 Bryan Rd, Pocatello, ID, 83201. Contact: John Savage, President - Tel: (208) 235-7573, E-Mail: directory@thriftyimpressions.com, Web Site: www.thriftyimpressions.com. Developers of over 18 home based or store front businesses specializing in personlization. Full or part time. Established: 1972 - No. of Units: Company Owned: 1 - Franchised: 143 - Total Inv: $18,000-$29,000.00 - Financing: Yes.

ASI SIGN SYSTEMS, INC
3890 W. Northwest Highway, Ste. 102, Dallas, TX, 75220. Contact: Jason Killough, Dir. of Franchise Development - Tel: (214) 352-9140, (800) 274-7732, Fax: (214) 352-9741, Web Site: www.asisign systems.com. Leading supplier of architectural sign systems and planning services in North America. A business-to-business opportunity where by franchisees consult with business and design professionals. Established: 1965- Franchising Since: 1977 - No. of Units: Company Owned: 1 - Franchised: 33 - Franchise Fee: $50,000-$105,000 - Royalty: 5%, 1% marketing fee - Total Inv: $297,100-$372,100 - Financing: Yes, third party financing available.

FASTSIGNS
Fastsigns International, Inc
2550 Midway Road, Ste. 150, Carrollton, TX, 75006. Contact: Bill McPherson, VP Domestic Franchise Sales - Tel: (800) 827-7446, (214) 346-5600, Fax: (972) 248-8201, E-Mail: bill.mcpherson@fastsigns.com, Web Site: www.fastsigns.com. FASTSIGNS is one of the industry's leading sign and graphic franchises. Using a computer-based design technique, our concept emphasizes sign and graphic solutions. We offer fast turnaround, business-to-business environment, and top-quality signs and graphics for corporate, professional, and retail clients. Established: 1985 - Franchising Since: 1986 - No. of Units: Franchised: 451 - Franchise Fee: $20,000 - Royalty: 6%, 2% advertising - Total Inv: $152,360 (plus working capital) - Financing: Yes third party.

MAIN EVENT LAWN SIGN INC.
911 E. Brookwood Dr., Arlington Heights, IL, 60004. Contact: Denise Paine, Pres. - Tel: (847) 670-7777. Announcement signs and pink flamingo's to rent and display in yard for new babies, birthdays and more. A fun, easy business that can be run from home. Established: 1986 - Franchising Since: 1988 - No. of Units: Company Owned: 1 - Franchised: 62 - Royalty: None - Total Inv: $299. and up - Financing: No.

SIGN BIZ, INC.
24681 La Plaza Suite 270, Dana Point, CA, 92689. - Tel: (800) 633-5580. Computer-aided business-to-business sign stores, independently owned. Store owners use high-tech equipment to create text, logos, and custom graphics. These sign business owners receive exclusive territories, full training, marketing support, conventions, hot lines and deep discounts. Established: 1989 - No. of Units: Approximately 145 dealers Individually owned - Franchise Fee: None - Royalty: None - Total Inv: $78,500 plus $40 to $50,000 to get up and running - Financing: Yes.

SIGN IT QUICK
Sign It Quick International, Inc.
3155 Savannah Hwy., Charleston, SC, 29414. Contact: Frank Au Coin, Pres. - Tel: (843) 763-3155, Fax: (843) 769-6982. Regular and super sign stores. Menu ranges from basic signs to awnings and more elaborate, depending on type of shop. Best marketing and promotion programs. Owner and president was awarded Small Business Person of the Year, South Carolina, 1994. Established: 1987 - Franchising Since: 1988 - No. of Units: Company Owned: 1 - Franchised: 8 - Franchise Fee: $15,500 - Royalty: 5% gross sales (excluding media trades), 1% adv. 1st yr., 2% thereafter - Total Inv: Approx. $125,000.

SIGN-A-RAMA
1801 Australiian Ave South, West Palm Beach, FL, 33409. Contact: Chris Simnick, V. P. Franchise Development - Tel: (800) 286-8671, E-Mail: signinfo@sign-a-rama.com, Web Site: www.sign-a-rama.com. Sign franchise with nearly 500 locations in 18 countries. Full service sign center utilizing the latest in computerized sign making technology into everything from banners and vehicle lettering to neon and large outdoor electrical signs. Established: 1986 - Franchising Since: 1987 - No. of Units: Franchised: Nearly 500 - Franchise Fee: $37,500 - Royalty: 6% with a cap - Total Inv: Approx. $101,000 plus working capital - Financing: Yes.

SIGNS BY TOMORROW
6460 Dobbin Rd., Columbia, MD, 21045. Contact: Robert Nunn, Marketing Director - Tel: (410) 992-7192, (800) 765-7446, Fax: (410) 992-7675, Web Site: www.signsbytomorrowusa.com. Computerized one day retail sign business. Established: 1986 - Franchising Since: 1987 - No. of Units: Company Owned: 1 - Franchised: 82 - Franchise Fee: $19,500 - Royalty: 5%/2.5% - Total Inv: $80,000-$150,000 - Financing: Yes.

SIGNS FIRST
Monotag Corp.
813 Ridge Lake Blvd., Ste. 390, Memphis, TN, 38120. Contact: Karen Warr, Franchise Development - Tel: (800) 852-2163, (901) 682-2264, Fax: (901) 682-2475. Retail one-day computerized sign service with a strong show room design and service focus. We offer the only Franchise with over 25 years experience in the sign industry. Established: 1966 - Franchising Since: 1989 - No. of Units: Franchised: 41 - Franchise Fee: $5,000-$10,000-$15,000 - Royalty: 6% - Total Inv: $15,000-$50,000 not including franchise fee - Financing: Franchisor will assist with leasing, SBA, or bank financing.

SIGNS NOW
Signs Now Corporation
4900 Manatee Ave. W., Ste. 201, Bradenton, FL, 34209. Contact: Dennis Staub, Dir. Fran. Development - Tel: (800) 356-3373, (941) 747-7747, Fax: (941) 750-8604, E-Mail: franchiseinfo@signsnow.com, Web Site: www.signsnow.com. Signs Now centers are America's professional graphics solution. The originator of the "Quick Sign Concept", Signs Now maintains its leadership position providing service to a wide range of business clients worldwide. Signs Now centers are the 'One Stop' source for all signs and graphics. Established: 1983 - Franchising Since: 1986 - No. of Units: Company Owned: 2 - Franchised: 260 - Franchise Fee: $25,000 - Royalty: 5% to franchisor, 2% to marketing - Total Inv: $150,000 - Financing: Third party available.

SIGNS ON SITE, INC
5350 Corporate Grove Blvd, S.E., Grand Rapids, MI, 49512. Contact: Jeffrey R. Lewis, CEO / President - Tel: (616) 656-9770, (888) 715-7446, Fax: (616) 656-9775, E-Mail: mail@signsonsite.con, Web Site: www.signsonsite.com. Facility signage - sales - installation - maintainance. Established: 1996 - Franchising Since: 1999 - No. of Units: Company Owned: 1 - Franchised: 7 - Franchise Fee: $25,000 - Royalty: 6%/, 1% - Total Inv: $75,000-$100,000 - Financing: Yes.

SPEEDPRO SIGNS PLUS
Signs Plus USA Ltd
188 Technology Dr Ste L, Irvine, CA, 92618-2403. Contact: Blair M. Gran, President - Tel: (949) 450-0685, (800) 775-6355, Fax: (949) 450-0686, Web Site: www.speedpro.com. One stop advertising center. Established: 1990 - Franchised: 85 - Franchise Fee: $82,500 - Royalty: 6% of gross revenue and 2% advertising - Total Inv: $82,500 - Financing: Yes.

VAC SET SIGN SHOP
Universal Products Co.
108 N. Archer St., Norton, KS, 67654. Contact: R. L. Eldridge, Mgr. of Sales - Tel: (785) 877-3816. Complete sign shop package for making plastic signs of all kinds for indoor and outdoor use. Established: 1941 - Franchising Since: 1958 - Total Inv: $1,995 - Financing: No.

YARD CARDS®
Yard Cards® LLC
49 Alta Vista Rd, Tuscola, TX, 79562. - Tel: (915) 572-5488, Fax: (915) 698-1000. Yard Cards® is a low investment franchise designed to be operated as a home-based business, or it could be added on to a balloon, party, floral, rental business. Yard Cards® offers for rent, 8-foot tall greeting cards for special occasions. Established: 1983 - Franchising Since: 1986 - No. of Units: Company Owned: 1 - Franchised: 8 - Franchise Fee: .03 per person based on territory to service; min. of

$1,000 - Royalty: 5% of gross sales paid bi-monthly - Total Inv: Based on population as stated above - Start Up Costs: Approx. $3,300 for inventory - Financing: No.

SPORTS AND RECREATION

A CORPORATE A'FAIR, INC
1922 Lynn Brook Pl., Memphis, TN, 38116. Contact: David F. Martin, Sr. - Tel: (901) 398-4386, (800) 783-8386. Full service corporate events planner. Established: 1993 - No. of Units: Company Owned: 1 - Franchised: 4 - Franchise Fee: $20,000 - Total Inv: $25,000-$50,000.

ADVANTAGE GOLF
Advantage Golf Franchising Corp.
3728 Realty Rd, Addison, TX, 75001. Contact: Michael Price, Dir.of Franchise Development - Tel: (972) 243-6209, (800) 659-2815, Fax: (972) 243-4688, Web Site: www.advantagegolf.com. Advantage Golf is a one-stop source for companies, organizations and individuals planning golf tournaments. Featuring a beautiful golf tournament showroom. Tournament clients can select their tournament awards, gifts, logo merchandise, signs and more. Established: 1996 - Franchising Since: 1998 - No. of Units: Company Owned: 1 - Franchised: 11 - Franchise Fee: $25,000-$50,000 - Royalty: The greater of $500.00 per month or 3% of gross sales - Total Inv: $65,495-$159,285 - Financing: No.

AJ BARNES BICYCLE EMPORIUM
14230 Stirrup Lane, Wellington, FL, 33414. Contact: Franchise Director - Tel: (901) 368-3361, Fax: (901) 368-1144, E-Mail: franmark@msn.com. Retail business offering bicycle sales, services, accessories, clothing and rentals in "showroom store". Full training for 3 weeks with ongoing support. Established: 1989 - Franchised: 27 - Total Inv: $82,250-$116,000.

AJ BARNES BICYCLES
9014 Rocky Point, Cordova, TN, 38018. Contact: Rob Richey, Marketing Director - Tel: (901) 368-3333, Fax: (901) 368-1144, E-Mail: bikebiz@AOL.com, Web Site: www.ajbarnes.com. Retail sales/service/rental of bicycles, skateboards, bladeskates, etc. Training and support provided. No. of Units: Franchised: 27 - Franchise Fee: $15,000 - Total Inv: $100,000.

AMATEUR BOWLERS TOUR
Amateur Bowlers Tour, Inc.
6422 Industry Way, Westminster, CA, 92683-3695. Contact: Ken Daleiden, Pres. - Tel: (714) 898-7874, or 3822, Fax: (714) 903-2518, E-Mail: abtinc@eathlink.net, Web Site: www.amateurbowlerstour.com. Conduct bowling tournaments on a weekly basis for non-professional bowlers. Two divisions, classic 199 and under averages. Masters 200-225 average bowlers. Guarenteed prizes. Established: 1977 - Franchising Since: 1987 - No. of Units: Franchised: 14- Franchise Fee: $60,000 - Royalty: Based on expense portion of entry fee + membership - Total Inv: $94,100.00 - Financing: Up to 50% of initial franchise fee.

AMERICAN POOL/PLAYERS ASSOCIATION, INC.
1000 Lake St. Louis Blvd., Ste. 325, Lake St. Louis, MO, 63367. Contact: Fran. Dev. Mgr. - Tel: (800) 372-2536, (636) 625-8611, Fax: (636) 625-2975, Web Site: www.poolplayers.com. Recreational billard league which utilizes trademark handicapp system known as the Equalizer. Established: 1979 - Franchising Since: 1982 - No. of Units: Company Owned: 0 - Franchised: 225 - Franchise Fee: $6,000-$10,000 - Royalty: 20% - Total Inv: $10,000-$13,000 - Financing: Yes.

AQUA-CYCLE INTERNATIONAL, INC.
Post Office Box 2129, Yoba Linda, CA, 92885-1329. Contact: Howard Parker, President - Tel: (714) 970-2668, Fax: (714) 970-0467, E-Mail: fad@aqua-cycle.com, Web Site: www.aqua-cycle.com. "Ride a tricycle on water". Aqua-cycle watersport products for water recreation rentals, Fun, safe, durable, low maintenance and profitable. Established: 1983.

ARNOLD PALMER GOLF MANAGEMENT INT., LLC
6751 Forum Dr Suite 200, Orlando, FL, 32821. - Tel: (407) 926-2500, Fax: (407) 926-2550. Franchises public and private golf courses. Established: 1984 - Franchising Since: 1997 - No. of Units: Company Owned: 20 - Franchised: 1 - Franchise Fee: $35,000 - Royalty: Year 1-3%, year 2-3.5%, year 3 thru end of term 4% - Total Inv: Estimated initial investment, $99,000-$315,000 - Financing: No.

ARTHUR MURRAY DANCE STUDIO'S
Arthur Murray International, Inc.
1077 Ponce De Leon Blvd., Coral Gables, FL, 33134. Contact: Tony K. Cardinali, First V.P. Franchise Relations - Tel: (305) 445-9645, Fax: (305) 445-0451, Web Site: www.arthurmurray.com. Ballroom, dance studios. Established: 1912 - Franchising Since: 1938.

BABBITT BASEBALL CAMPS
Babbitt Baseball Camps, Inc.
14801 Perrywood Dr., Burtonsville, MD, 20866. Contact: Todd Babbitt, V.P. - Tel: (800) 253-3014. Instructional baseball camps for youth. Established: 1983 - Franchising Since: 1995 - No. of Units: Company Owned: 50 - Franchised: 8 - Franchise Fee: $1,000-$3,000 - Royalty: 8%, 1% nat'l. adv. per camper - Total Inv: $3,000-$5,000 - Financing: No. NOT FRANCHISING AT THIS TIME.

BIKE LINE
Paoli Bike & Sports
1035 Andrew Dr., West Chester, PA, 19380. Contact: Chris Zorger, Dir. of Franchise Dev. - Tel: (800) 537-2654, (610) 429-4370, Fax: (610) 429-4295. Bicycle and fitness equipment sales and service. Established: 1983 - Franchising Since: 1991 - No. of Units: Company Owned: 17 - Franchised: 55 - Franchise Fee: $24,500 - Royalty: 4%, 1% nat'l adv., 2% local adv. - Total Inv: $130,000-$176,000 inclusive of franchise fee - Financing: No, help with obtaining funds from third party sources.

BLACK DIAMOND GOLF *
4963 Stahl Rd., #112, San Antonio, TX, 78284. - Tel: (210) 590-2384, fax: (210) 590-2386, Web Site: www.theclubpolisher.com. A fully automated machine designed to accomadate up to 10 irons in a single cycle and cleans in less than 90 seconds. Established: 2001 - Franchising Since: 2003 - No. of Units: Franchised: 55 - Franchise Fee: $3,000-$50,000 - Royalty: 0 - Total Inv: $25,000-$100,000.

BUFFALO STIX GOLF COMPANY
5526 Main Street, Williamsville, NY, 14221. Contact: Jeffrey S. VanFossen, Pres. - Tel: (716) 634-7860, (800) 684-5934, Fax: (716) 204-0106. Built to order golf clubs. Established: 1995 - Franchising Since: 1999 - No. of Units: Company Owned: 1 - Franchised: 85 - Franchise Fee: $99.00-$1,499. - Financing: No.

CHAMPIONSHIP MINIATURE GOLF
Amusement Products
5954 Brainerd Rd., Chattanooga, TN, 37421. Contact: Dutch Magrath, President - Tel: (423) 892-7264, Fax: (423) 855-0432, Web Site: www.amusepro.com. Miniature golf courses that include a theme to make a unique setting. Established: 1960 - No. of Units: Company Owned: 2 - Total Inv: $100,000-$300,000 - Financing: No.

CLUB NAUTICO INTERNATIONAL POWERBOAT RENTALS
Adventurent, Inc.
3149 JP Curci Dr. #1A-1, Pembroke Park , FL, 33009-3834. Contact: Gina A. Durnak, Exec. V.P. - Tel: (954) 927-9800, Fax: (954) 893-9802. Powerboat rental operation. Franchisee maintains fleet and rents powerboats to the general public, and to members of an international boating club. Club Nautico Centers are located throughout the U.S., Caribbean, Mexico and in Asia. Established: 1984 - Franchising Since: 1986 - No. of Units: Company Owned: 7 - Franchised: 45 - Franchise Fee: $5,000 - Royalty: 5% + 2% adv. - Total Inv: $220,000-$262,000 which includes 6 month working cap. & fran. fee - Financing: None.

COLLEGE PROSPECTS OF AMERICA®
College Prospects of America, Inc
12682 College Prospects Dr., P.O. Box 269, Logan, OH, 43138. Contact: Tracy LiJackson - Tel: (740) 385-6624, (888) 275-2762, Fax: (740) 385-9065, E-Mail: homeoffice@cpoa.com, Web Site: www.cpoa.com. Marketers of high school student athletes to colleges helping them to get

the best college education at the best price and allowing them to continue participating in a sport they enjoy. Established: 1986 - Franchising Since: 1989 - No. of Units: Franchised: 85 - Franchise Fee: From $6,000-$50,000 - Financing: Some.

COLLEGIATE SPORTS OF AMERICA
Collegiate Sports of America, Inc
22900 Ventura Blvd., Suite 100, Woodland Hills, CA, 91364. Contact: Roy Reeves, VP - Tel: (818) 225-7300, (800) 600-7518, Fax: (818) 225-1098, E-Mail: rreeves @ csasports.com, Web Site: www.csasports.com. College recruiting services - provide services to help student - athletes receive athletic scholarships and other opportunities to play their sport at the college level. Established: 1996 - Franchisng Since: 1998 - No. of Units: Company Owned: 5 - Franchised: 6 - Franchise Fee: $11,000 - Royalty: Franchisor/franchisee = 45% / 55% split on sales - Total Inv: $15,000-$25,000 depending on size of territory - Financing: Yes.

CONTINENTAL INDOOR SOCCER LEAGUE
15821 Ventura Blvd., #520, Encino, CA, 91436-2946. - Tel: (818) 906-7627. 15 team professional indoor soccer league in markets throughout the United States and Mexico. Established: 1993 - Franchising Since: 1991 - No. of Units: Company Owned: 1 - Franchised: 15 - Franchise Fee: $1,000,000 - Financing: No.

CROWN TROPHY, INC.
9 Skyline Dr, Hawthorne, NY, 10532-2100. Contact: Scott Kelly, Executive VP - Tel: (914) 347-7700, (800) 583-8228, Fax: (914) 347-0211, E-Mail: Scott@crowntrophy.com, Web Site: www.crown franchise.com. The only franchise of its kind, crown trophy is the largest supplier and fastest growing retailer in the awards recognition industry. Established: 1978 - Franchising Since: 1987 - No. of Units: Franchised: 129 - Franchise Fee: $35,000 - Royalty: 5% - Total Inv: $135,000-$145,000 - Financing: Third party.

DEK STAR HOCKEY CENTERS
1106 Reedsdale Street, Pittsburgh, PA, 15233. Contact: Larry Gaus, Franchise Development - Tel: (412) 231-1660. Turnkey dek hockey and roller hockey rink and pro shop. Full training and support provided. Established: 1990 - Franchising Since: 1992 - No. of Units: Company Owned: 2 - Franchise Fee: $10,000 - Total Inv: $70,000 - Financing: Yes.

DIXIE DIVERS
800 Virginia Ave Ste 11, Fort Pierce, FL, 34982-5887. Contact: Nestor Palmero, Pres. - Tel: (561) 466-3388, Fax: (561) 466-9329. A chain of professional retail dive stores. Established: 1979 - Franchising Since: 1991 - No. of Units: Company Owned: 10 - Franchised: 6 - Franchise Fee: $15,000 - Royalty: 4%, 2% nat'l. adv. - Total Inv: Varies - Financing: No. NOT FRANCHISING AT THIS TIME.

DRYJECT
DryJect, LLC
1001 Deal Rd, Ocean, NJ, 07712. Contact: Chris des Garennes, V. President - Tel: (732) 493-3555, (800) 270-TURF, Fax: (732) 493-3255, E-Mail: info@dryject.com, Web Site: www.dryject.com. Aeration service to Golf Courses, Sports turf etc. using unique patented DryJect machine. The Dryject aerates, fills the holes continuously with sand and leaves a smooth and playable surface. Service is presently used by all types of golf courses from US open type courses to small family owned courses. Established: 2002 - Franchising: 2002 - No. of Units: Company Owned: 1 - Franchised: 25 - Franchise Fee: $19,500 - Royalty: $3,600 first year - Total Inv: Approx $85,000 - Financing: Yes.

FORMACOURSE
SGD Company
P.O. Box 8410, Akron, OH, 44320. Contact: Donald Nelson, Chairman - Tel: (330) 239-2828, Fax: (330) 239-2668. An 18 hole Formacourse provides unique hole designs with low initial cost. Formacourse can be installed on areas of 10,000 square feet or larger. Formacourse includes pre-positioned pressure treated lumber for sideboards to insure low maintenance. Established: 1964 - Franchising Since: 1989 - No. of Units: Franchised: 7 - Franchise Fee: Built into basic construction package - Royalty: None - Total Inv: 50M- 95M plus land - Financing: None.

GOLF AUGUSTA PRO SHOPS
217 Bobby Jones Expressway, Augusta, GA, 30907. Contact: Franchise Development - Tel: (706) 863-9905, (800) GOLF-051, Fax: (706) 863-9909, Web Site: www.GolfAgustaproshops.com. Golf Augusta Pro Shops are industry leading custom clubs fitting/indoor teaching/ and golf retailing centers. Gaps specializes in helping golfers maximize ability through properly fit golf clubs and lessons. Established: 1994 - Franchising Since: 1995 - No. of Units: Company Owned: 1 - Franchised: 12 - Franchise Fee: $40,000 - Royalty: 3% royalty, 1% adv. - Total Inv: $395,000-$700,000 - Financing: Third party assistance.

GOLF ETC
Golf Etc of America Inc.
710 E. Hwy. 377, Granbury, TX, 76048. - Tel: (817) 279-7888, (800) 806-8633, Fax: (817) 279-9882. Golf supplies and equipment. Established: 1992 - Franchising Since: 1995 - No. of Units: Company Owned: 1 - Franchised: 23 - Franchise Fee: 10% - Total Inv: $105,000 - Financing: SBA.

GOLFPRO INTERNATIONAL, INC.
851 Martin Ave, Santa Clara, CA, 95050. - Tel: (408) 235-8001, Fax: (408) 235-8055. Fully automated robotic golf caddy. The world's first. Established: 1993 - Franchising Since: 1998 - No. of Units: Franchised: 5 - Franchise Fee: $250,000 - Toatal Inv: $250,000-$500,000 - Financing: No.

GOLFTEC *
5555 DTC Pkwy, #A4000, Greenwood Village, CO, 80111. Contact: Franchise Department - Tel: (877) 446-5383, Fax: (303) 741-1751, Web Site: www.golftec.com. Indoor golf instruction centers. Established: 1995 - Franchising Since: 2003 - No. of Units: Company Owned: 17 - Franchised: 4 - Franchise Fee: $30,000 - Royalty: 5% - Total Inv: $116,500-$275,500.

GROVE RECREATIONS INC.
1207 Hillside Drive N. N. Myrtle Beach, SC, 29578. Contact: Charles H. Grove, Pres. - Tel: (843) 236-4733. Designer/builder of exquisitely beautiful and elaborate miniature golf courses - themed with a great deal of mounding/contours, waterfalls, lakes, streambeds, bridges, tunnel systems, lush landscaping, and very unique playable holes. Established: 1977 - Franchising Since: 1977 - No. of Units: Company Owned: 4 - Franchised: 15 - Franchise Fee: Negotiable - Total Inv: $250,000-$400,000 - Financing: Grove Recreations will work with the client to help secure same.

HOOP MOUNTAIN
Hoop Mountain Development, Inc.
7A McDermott Farm Rd., Danvers, MA, 01923. - Tel: (978) 774-7730, (800) 519-8445, Fax: (978) 750-0187. Basketball camps and counseling services. Federally registered trademark, professional training and continuous support. Office may be home based, full or part time opportunity. Established: 1985 - Franchising Since: 1995 - No. of Units: Company Owned: 1 - Franchised: 3 - Franchise Fee: $20,000 - Royalty: 5% on gross sales - Total Inv: $12,400-$16,750 excluding fran. fee - Financing: No.

I9 SPORTS
i9 Sports Corporation
1463 Oakfield Drive-Suite 135, Brandon, FL, 33511. Contact: Frank V. Fiume, Franchise Director - Tel: (813) 662-6773, (800) 9-PLAYER, E-Mail: franchisesupport@i9sports.com, Web Site: www.i9sports.com/corporate. i9 Sports is an amateur sports franchise for both youth and adult recreational and competitive athletes. i9 Sports offers franchise opportunites for people to own and operate local amateur sports leagues, tournamants, camps, clinics, special events, and corporate outings in over two dozen sports for people of all ages in their community. Established: 2002 - Franchising Since: 2003 - No. of Units: Company Owned: 2 - Franchised: 17 - Franchise Fee: $16,000-$36,000 - Royalty: 7.5% - Total Inv: $28,000-$68,000 - Financing: Yes, In-House and third party.

INTERNATIONAL GOLF DISCOUNT
International Golf Enterprises, Inc.
9101 N. Thornydale Rd, Tucson, AZ, 85742. Contact: Director of Operations - Tel: (520) 744-1840, (800) 204-2600, Fax: (520) 744-2076, Web Site: www.intlgolf-ent.com. Off-course retail golf store specializing

in equipment, supplies, clothing and accessories. May complement with tennis and / or ski. Established: 1976 - Franchising Since: 1981 - No. of Units: Company Owned: 6 - Franchised: 59 - Franchise Fee: $42,000 - Royalty: 5% of total gross sales - Total Inv: $300,000-$400,000 - franchise fees opening, inventory & start-up costs - Financing: Indirectly.

JUGS RANGE PRO BATTING CAGES
Amusement Products LLC
5954 Brainerd Rd, Chattanooga, TN, 37421. Contact: Tony Hunnicutt, Sales Manager-VP - Tel: (423) 892-7264, (800) 438-3558, Fax: (423) 855-0432, E-Mail: tony@amusepro.com, Web Site: www.amuse pro.com. Commercial batting cages for both indoor and outdoor use including lazerball, batting cages and the ultimate trainer 2000 commercial multi-speed pitching machine. Established: 1998 - Franchising Since: 2000 - No. of Units: Company Owned: 2 - Total Inv: $20,000-$150,000.

L A BOXING *
L A Boxing Franchise Corporation
6 Journey Suite 170, Aliso Viejo, CA, 92656. Contact: Anthony Geisler - Tel: (949) 362-1464, (866) LA-BOXING, Fax: (949) 362-1465, E-Mail: franchise@laboxing.com, Web Site: www.laboxing.com. Cardio boxing and kick boxing fitness training. See www.laboxing.com. Established: 1992 - Franchising Since: 2004 - No. of Units: Company Owned: 3 - Franchised: 2 - Franchise Fee: $25,000 - Royalty: 6% - Total Inv: $87,000-$96,000 - Financing: Particial.

LAS VEGAS GOLF & TENNIS
Las Vegas Golf & Tennis, Inc.
2701 Crimson Canyon Dr, Las Vegas, NV, 89128. Contact: Franchise Manager - Tel: (800) 873-5110 ext.139, (702) 798-5500 ext.139, Fax: (702) 798-6847, Web Site: www.lvgolf.com. Country club atmosphere at the off course price. Our stores specialize in all pro-line golf and tennis equipment and apparel. As well as our own golf and tennis merchandise called "VISION". Our corporate buying programs and in-house advertising agency and operational support places our franchise program well ahead of the rest. Established: 1974 - Franchising Since: 1984 - No. of Units: Company Owned: 7 - Franchised: 42 - Franchise Fee: $39,000 for first franchise, $19,500 for additional stores - Royalty: 3% weekly gross sales - Total Inv: $537,000-$774,000 - Financing: We are an approved SBA Franchisor and assist with SBA approved lending institutions.

LASERBALL INDOOR SHOOTING GAME
Amusement Products LLC
5954 Brainerd Rd, Chattanooga, TN, 37421. Contact: Geoff Lee - Tel: (423) 892-7264, Fax: (423) 855-0432. A game of laser tag and paintball. Established: 2000 - Franchising Since: 2001 - No. of Units: Company Owned: 1 - Franchise Fee: $6,000 - Total Inv: $35,000 - Financing: No.

LOMMA GOLF
Lomma Enterprises, Inc.
1120 S. Washington Ave., Scranton, PA, 18505. - Tel: (570) 346-5559, Fax: (570) 346-5580. Lomma Golf is the world's oldest and largest designer and builder of prefab, portable miniature golf courses, indoors and outdoors. Also a complete line of upscale concrete courses including mountains, waterfalls, ponds, caves, themes, etc. Established: 1963 - Each Lomma Golf is individually owned - Total Inv: From $5,900-$100,000 - Financing: Some.

LUYE AQUAFIT INTERNATIONAL, INC.
310 East 23rd St., New York, NY, 10010. Contact: Mitch Bogage, Exec.V.P. - Tel: (212) 505-2400. Offer professional, complete, safe and fun cardiovascular and musculoskeletal water aerobics workouts suitable for almost everyone regardless of age, level of fitness, physical capabilities and swimming ability. Other offerings include fitness evaluation, youth and adult swimming classes, workout gear and related products. Established: 1984 - No. of Units: Company Owned: 1 - Franchised: 12 - Franchise Fee: $20,000 - Royalty: 8%, 2% adv. - Financing: Training and operations support.

MAC BIRDIE GOLF GIFTS
Mac Birdie Golf Gifts, Inc.
7399 Bush Lake Rd, Edina, MN, 55439-2027. Contact: Chuck Lunde, Pressident / CEO - Tel: (952) 830-1033, Fax: (952) 830-1055. Retail shops offer more than 300 items in a wide range of golf apparel, novelties, gifts and accessories. Exclusive MacBirdie catoulogue for

direct sales and direct mail. Established: 1989 - Franchising Since: 1994 - No. of Units: Company Owned: 1 - Franchised: 7 - Franchise Fee: $12,500 - Royalty: 5% of gross sales - Total Inv: $55,000-$115,000 - Financing: No.

MASTERFIT GOLF LTD.
9400 Atlantic Blvd Ste 63, Jacksonville, FL, 32225-8245. Contact: Phil Lanza, President - Tel: (904) 726-9984, Web Site: www.masterfit golfltd.com. Golf retail, all equipment sold is custom built, fitted and designed on site for each individual customer. Established: 1997 - Franchising Since: 1997 - No. of Units: Company Owned: 4 - Franchised: 3 - Franchise Fee: $10,000 - Royalty: 5% gross - Total Inv: $50,000 ($10,000 fran. fee, $15,000 inventory, $25,000 furnishing fixture and equipment).

MILLION DOLLAR HOLE-IN-ONE®
AMK Service, Corp.
8930 W State Road 84, Davie, FL, 33324-4456. - Tel: (954) 423-4355, (800) 595-6466, Fax: (954) 423-2392. Golf contest. Established: 1990 - Franchising Since: 1990 - No. of Units: Franchised: 126 - Franchise Fee: $15,000 - Royalty: 5% - Total Inv: $20,000 - Financing: No.

MINI-GOLF, INC.
202 Bridge St., Jessup, PA, 18434. Contact: Joseph J. Rogari, V.P./ Mktg. - Tel: (570) 489-8623, Fax: (570) 383-9970, E-Mail: jrogari@epix.net, Web Site: www.minigolfinc.com. Manufacture portable, pre-fab miniature golf courses for indoor or outdoor use. Established: 1981- No. of Units: Franchised: 2,160 - Total Inv: $5,900-$27,900 - Financing: None.

MODY COMPANY SPEED PITCHING BOOTH
Mody Company
8 Northrup Ave, Norwich, NY, 13815. Contact: Thomas A. Mody, Owner - Tel: (607) 336-6233, (888) 828-MODY, Fax: (607) 336-6232, E-Mail: mody@norwich.net, Web Site: www.speedpitch.com. Speed timing booth for income opportunity or youth fundraising. Established: 1992 - Franchising Since: 1993 - No. of Units: Company Owned: 3 - Franchised: 30 - Total Inv: $1,400-$4,000 - Financing: No.

MUNCHVILLE- BILLIARDS & ARCADE
Winco Window Cleaning
Colonial Terrace #27, Knoxville, IA, 50138. - Tel: (515) 828- 7794. Fun and entertainment for the whole family. Utilizing unique and exciting concepts. Assistance with building selection, inventory, promotions, wholesale contacts, regulations. Established: 1986 - Franchising Since: 1993 - Franchise Fee: $5,000 - Royalty: None - Financing: No.

NATIONAL COLLEGE RECRUITING ASSOC. INC. (NCRA)
Sport Star Marketing, Inc.
5275 DTC Parkway, #110, Englewood, CO, 80111. - Tel: (303) 804-0155, (888) 302-6272, Fax: (303) 804-0315. Connecting quality high school student-athletes, in all 49 competitive mens and womens sports, with college coaches seeking athletes in positions they need - resulting in a scholarship. Established: 1992 - Franchising Since: 1993 - No. of Units: Company Owned: 12 - Franchised: 18- Franchise Fee: By population: $15,000-$50,000 - Royalty: 30% for services - Total Inv: $18,000-$55,000 - Financing: Yes.

NEVADA BOB'S PROFESSIONAL GOLF SHOPS
4043 S. Eastern Ave., Las Vegas, NV, 89119. Contact: Don Schafer, Fran. Dir. - Tel: (702) 451-3333, (800) 348-2627, Fax: (214) 360-9329, E-Mail: nevadab@nevadabob.com, Web Site: www.nevadabob.com. World's largest network of specialty golf shops serving the golfing community with the finest professional golf equipment at guaranteed lowest prices. Established: 1974 - Franchising Since: 1978 - No. of Units: Company Owned: 43 - Franchised: 254 - Franchise Fee: $37,500-$57,500 - Royalty: 2% - Total Inv: $295,000 - Financing: No.

ON TARGET GOLF CENTERS
On Target, Inc.
501 Airport Rd., Bentonville, AR, 72712. - Tel: (501) 273-1316, (800) 264-1316, Fax: (501) 271-7964. An On Target Golf Center is a standard range with the addition of the unique and patented game of On Target (4 large, 2,300 sq.ft., tents at 70, 100, 130 and 160 yards), electronic

signals. Established: 1993 - Franchising Since: 1994 - No. of Units: Franchised: 7 - Franchise Fee: $9,500 - Royalty: Flat fee, varies - Total Inv: $50,000-$250,000 - Financing: Partial.

OUTDOOR CONNECTION
Outdoor Connection, Inc
424 Neosho, Burlington, KS, 66839. Contact: Marc Glades - Tel: (620) 364-5500, Fax: (620) 364-5563, E-Mail: franchise@outdoor-connection.com, Web Site: www.outdoor-connection.com. Specializing in worldwide fishing and hunting travel. Established: 1988 - Franchising Since: 1990 - No. of Units: Company Owned: 3 - Franchised: 81 - Franchise Fee: $9,500 - Royalty: 3%-5% - Total Inv: $12,500 - Financing: On franchise fee (minus $2,500 minimum).

PACER GO KARTS
Amusement Products LLC
5954 Brainerd Rd., Chattanooga, TN, 37421. Contact: E K Magrath, President - Tel: (423) 892-7264, (800) 438-3558, Fax: (423) 855-0432, E-Mail: dutch@amusepro.com, Web Site: www.amusepro.com. Design layout family fun centers with mini golf, go-karts, batting cages, bumper boats and paint ball. Established: 1960 - Franchising Since: 1975 - No. of Units: Company Owned: 3 - Total Inv: $50,000-$500,000 - Financing: No.

PAR T J GOLF
4747 Morena Blvd, #355, San Diego, CA, 92117. Contact: Marketing Director - Tel: (619) 273-0370. Indoor golf, utilizing the double eagle golf simulator. Established: 1989 - Franchising Since: 1989 - No. of Units: Franchised: 250 - Total Inv: $35,000 min - Financing: Yes.

PARMASTERS GOLF TRAINING CENTERS
Parmasters Golf Training Centers LLC
N67 W26918 Argyle Drive, Sussex, WI, 53089. Contact: Tom Matzen - Tel: (800) 663-2331, Fax: (800) 416-6325, E-Mail: info@parmastersgolf.com, Web Site: www.parmastersgolf.com. We are the world's year round indoor golf training center franchise and combine two growing, proven successful industries - golf training and franchising - to create a fun and unique business opportunity. Established: 2000 - Franchising Since: 2000 - Franchise Fee: $25,000 - Royalty: 8% - Total Inv: $381,900-$1,100,000 - Financing: No.

PERSONAL BEST KARATE
250 E. Main Street, Norton, MA, 02766. Contact: Christopher Rappold - Tel: (508) 285-5425, (866) 400-KICK, Fax: (781) 285-7064, E-Mail: founder@personalbestkarate.com, Web Site: www.personalbestkarate.com. Personal best karate is a profession and a business opportunity designed to build character and enhance lives. Support services include comprehensive training, operations manual, site selection, marketing support, ongoing service & support, and market exclusivity. Established: 1991 - Franchising Since: 1999 - No. of Units: Company Owned: 2 - Franchised: 3 - Franchise Fee: $34,000 - Royalty: 10% - Total Inv: $63,000-$113,000 - Financing: As needed.

PLAY IT AGAIN SPORTS
Winmark Corporation
4200 Dahlberg Dr., Suite 100, Minneapolis, MN, 55422. Contact: Franchise Department - Tel: (763) 520-8480, (800) 453-7752, Fax: (763) 520-8501, Web Site: www.playitagainsports.com. Play It Again Sports stores sell, buy, trade quality used and new sporting gear and equipment. Established: 1983 - Franchising Since: 1988 - No. of Units: Franchised: 500 - Franchise Fee: $20,000 - Royalty: 5% of gross sales - Total Inv: $205,660-$307,252.

POOL CLEAR
2124 Citation Dr, Arlington, TX, 76017-4530. Contact: Franchise Director - Tel: (901) 368-3361, Fax: (901) 368-3724. Swimming pool service using special techniques, equipment processes, standards and specifications at budget prices. Established: 1988 - No. of Units: Franchised: 2 - Total Inv: $31,500-$37,500.

POWER KICKBOX
6800 Westgate #119, Austin, TX, 78745. Contact: Steve Doss, President - Tel: (512) 447-KICK, (800) 758-3122, (512) 447-7011, Web Site: www.powerkickbox.com. Power Kickbox is a group fitness training business. Classes are often held in community and recreation centers, or in a leased space. Franchisees are thoroughly trained in everything

required to own, teach, operate and market this service. Established: 1983 - Franchising Since: 1999 - No. of Units: Company Owned: 2 - Franchised: 14 - Franchise Fee: $900.00 - Total Inv: $2,500-$7,500 - Financing: No.

PRO GOLF DISCOUNT
32751 Middlebelt Rd., Farmington Hill, MI, 48334. Contact: Jeff Griffith, Director Franchise Development - Tel: (248)737-0553, (800) 521-6388, Fax: (248)737-9077, E-Mail: jgriffith@progolfamerica.com, Web Site: www.progolfamerica.com. The oldest and largest golf only retail franchise, creating highly satisfied customers with a large selection of merchadise, informed one-on-one customer service, and our low price guarantee. We provide a 40 year proven system, execellent training, and continued support. No previous golf equipment or retail experience needed. Established: 1962 - Franchising Since: 1975 - No. of Units: Franchised: 135 - Franchise Fee: $49,500 - Royalty: 2.5% - Total Inv: $250,000 - Financing: Third party.

PRO IMAGE FRANCHISE, LC
563 W. 500 S., Ste 330, Bountiful, UT, 84010. Contact: Ryan Laws/Burr Calopp, Franchise Development - Tel: (801) 296-9999, Fax: (801) 296-1319, E-Mail: ryan@proimage.net/burr@proimage.net. Licensed sports apparel, miscellaneous products. Training and support provided. Established: 1985 - Franchising Since: 1985 - No. of Units: Franchised: 140 - Franchise Fee: $19,500 1st/$12,500 2nd.

PURSUIT PACK POINTBALL FIELDS
Amusement Products
5954 Branard Rd, Chattanooga, TN, 33942. Contact: Mr. Magrath, President - Tel: (923) 892-7264, (800) 438-3558, Fax: (923) 855-0432, E-Mail: info@amusepro.com, Web Site: www.amusepro.com. A commercialized paintball playing facility that takes only $5,000 to $15,000 square feet outdoors or inside. Specializing in safe, competitive comercialized paintball playing fields and equipment. Established: 1998 - Franchising Since: 1999 - No. of Units: Company Owned: 1 - Franchised: 15 - Franchise Fee: $1,500 per year - Royalty: None - Total Inv: $50,000-$100,000 - Financing: No.

PUTT-PUTT® GOLF & GAMES
Putt-Putt® Golf Courses of America, Inc.
P.O. Box 35237, Fayetteville, NC, 28303. Contact: Scott Anderson, Nat'l Fran. Dir. - Tel: (866) PUTT-PUTT, Web Site: www.Putt-Putt.com. Uniquely designed miniature golf courses testing the player's skill, not luck. Established: 1954 - Franchising Since: 1955 - No. of Units: Company Owned: 9 - Franchised: 225 US, 36 International - Franchise Fee: $30,000 - Royalty: Golf 3% service fee, 2% adv.; Other attractions 2% service fee, 1% adv. - Total Inv: $100,000-$3 million - Financing: Assistance with financing.

PUTT-R-GOLF
PRG Inc.
2390 Medina Rd., Medina, OH, 44256. Contact: Don Nelson, Pres. - Tel: (330) 239-2828, Fax: (330) 239-2668, Web Site: www.5gdgolf.com. Provide CA drawings to construct minature golf courses. Franchising Since: 1997 - No. of Units: Company Owned: 1 - Franchised: 1 - Total Inv: Drawings $3,900 - Financing: N/A.

SCORECARD PLUS
1101 Portage St. NW, North Canton, OH, 44720-2353. - Tel: (330) 493-9900, (800) 767-9273. A combination scorecard and full-color yardage book which replaces the traditional cardboard scorecard at public and semi-private golf courses throughout the US. The books also include advertising which allows businesses to target the golfer and it decreases the cost of the program to the golf course. Established: 1990 - Franchising Since: 1992 - No. of Units: Company Owned: 6 - Franchised: 16 - Franchise Fee: $22,500 - Royalty: 8% of gross revenues - Total Inv: $59,000-$80,000 - Financing: On everything except the fran. fee.

SCUBA NETWORK
Scuba Network Stores
3170 N. Federal Hwy Suite 210, Lighthouse Point, FL, 33064. - Tel: (954) 946-9595. Scuba lessons, equipment, dives, tours. Established: 1989 - Franchising Since: 1989 - No. of Units: Company Owned: 5 - Franchised: 5 - Franchise Fee: $15,000 - Royalty: 7% - Total Inv: $80,000-$120,000 - Financing: No.

SIDE POCKETS
Side Pockets Franchise Systems, Inc.
13320 W. 87th St., Pkwy, Lenexa, KS, 66215. Contact: Richard Hawkins, Vice President - Tel: (913) 888-POOL, Fax: (913) 888-8869, E-Mail: info@sidepockets.com, Web Site: www.sidepockets.com. Upscale restaurant, bar and billards parlor. Established: 1994 - Franchising Since: 1997 - No. of Units: Company Owned: 1 - Franchised: 4 - Franchise Fee: $25,000 - Royalty: $700.00 per week - Total Inv: $800,000 - Financing: No.

SIR GOONY MINIATURE GOLF
Golf Players Inc.
5954 Brainerd Rd., Chattanooga, TN, 37421. Contact: E.K. "Dutch" Magrath III, V.P. - Tel: (423) 892-7264, Fax: (423) 855-0432. Miniature golf courses utilizing large and colourful figures. Established: 1960 - No. of Units: Company Owned: 4 - Franchised: 44 - Total Inv: $100,000 - Financing: No.

SKATETIME SCHOOL PROGRAMS
Skatetime Inc.
16194 E. Lincoln Hwy, Box 265, Morrison, IL, 61270. - Tel: (815) 772-5644, (800) 557- SKATE (5283), Fax: (815) 772-7178, Web Site: www.skatetime.com. Roller and inline skating rental program provider to K-12 public and non-public schools. Established: 1985 - Franchising Since: 1994 - No. of Units: Company Owned: 4 - Franchised: 11 - Franchise Fee: $20,000 - Royalty: 7% royalty, 1% marketing fee - Total Inv: $75,000-100,000 - Financing: No.

SOUTHERN LEAGUE OF PROFESSIONAL
One Depot Street., Suite 300, Marietta, GA, 30060. Contact: Arnold D. Fieltern, Pres. - Tel: (770) 428-4749, Fax: (770) 428-4849. Professional baseball league - AA level minor league. Established: 1964 - No. of Units: Franchised: 10 - Franchise Fee: Market value-currant AA clubs for in excess of 5 million.

STROKES
Strokes Franchisng, Inc
777 2nd Ave., Unit C, Redwood City, CA, 94063. Contact: Franchising Director - Tel: (800) 973-1111. Custom built, custom fit golf clubs. Established: 1995 - Franchising Since: 1996 - No. of Units: Company Owned: 3 - Franchised: 25 - Franchise Fee: $35,800-$61,500 start-up - Total Inv: $60,800-$86,500 - Financing: Several lending institutions.

STROKES GOLF INTERNATIONAL, INC
3223 Crow Canyon Road #240, San Ramon, CA, 94593. Contact: Douglas Perkins - Tel: (925) 355-1152, (888) 847-9796, Fax: (925) 355-1153. Custom club & lesson centers. Established: 1999 - Franchising Since: 2000 - No. of Units: Franchised: 8 - Franchise Fee: $37,500 - Total Inv: $72,000-$123,500 - Financing: Yes.

SUPERBROKERS, THE YACHT BROKERS FRANCHISE
3920 N US Highway 31 S #A, Traverse City, MI, 49684. Contact: Franchise Department - Tel: (231) 922-3002, (800) 968-2628, Fax: (231) 922-3016, Web Site: www.superbrokers.com. Boat/ yacht brokers. Established: 1991 - Franchising: 1992 - No. of Units: Company Owned: 1 - Franchised: 7 - Franchise Fee: $10,000-$20,000 - Royalty: Varies - Total Inv: $25,000-$75,000 - Financing: Yes.

TEAM GOLF
1776 Woodstead Ct., Ste. 213, The Woodlands, TX, 77380. Contact: VP Fran. Dev. - Tel: (281) 362-7777, Fax: (281) 362-8888. Corporate turn-key golf and special events. Established: 1993 - Franchising Since: 1994 - No. of Units: Company Owned: 1 - Franchised: 4 - Franchise Fee: $15,000 - Royalty: Fixed - Financing: No.

THEMED PUTTING COURSES
Grove Recreations, Inc.
P.O. Box 2435, Highway 544, Myrtle Beach, SC, 29578-2435. Contact: Charles H. Grove, Pres. - Tel: (843) 236-4733, Fax: (843) 236-0336. Designer/builders of miniature golf courses with waterfalls, caves, props and lush landscaping. Established: 1975 - Franchising Since: 1977 - No. of Units: Company Owned: 3 - Franchised: 5 - Total Inv: $300,000-$350,000 - Financing: Will help with financial info.

TRIPLE CROWN SPORTS
3930 Automation Way, Fort Collins, CO, 80525. Contact: Dave King/ Brent Amick - Tel: (970) 223-6644, Fax: (970) 223-3636, E-Mail: brent@triplecrownsports.com, Web Site: www.triplecrownsports.com. A quality national tournament series in the sports of softball, baseball, hockey and fastpitch. Own a protected territory and operate tournaments where your participants qualify for the nationally recognized Triple Crown Sports Championships. Established: 1982 - Franchising Since: 1997 - No. of Units: Company Owned: 1 - Franchised: 3 - Franchise Fee:$14,500-$30,000 - Royalty: 10%-14% - Total Inv: $19,500 and up - Financing: Third party & company.

ULTRAZONE, INC.
2880 E. Flamingo Rd., Ste. E, Las Vegas, NV, 89121. Contact: Sales Director - Tel: (702) 734-3617. Ultrazone, the ultimate laser adventure is the most exciting investment in franchising's newest industry, live-action laser games. An American company offering the most advanced laser game technology on the planet, backed by 7 years of research and development and operations. Ultrazone offers franchise owners service & support unequaled in the industry. No. of Units: Company Owned: 1 - Franchised: 4 - Franchise Fee: $15,000 - Royalty: 5% of gross or $2,000 per mo. - Total Inv: $320,000-$480,000 - Financing: No.

UNITED STATES BASKETBALL LEAGUE, INC.
46 Quirk Road, Milford, CT, 06460. - Tel: (203) 877-9508, Fax: (203) THE-USBL (878-8109). Franchisor of professional basketball teams. Established: 1985 - Franchising Since:1988 - No. of Units: Franchised: 12 - Franchise Fee: $300,000 plus $200,000 working capital - Royalty: $20,000 per year - Total Inv: $500,000 liquid assets - Financing: Partial.

UNITED STUDIOS OF SELF DEFENSE
United Studios of Self Defense, Inc.
26826 Vista Terrace, Bldg. 18, Lake Forest, CA, 92630. - Tel: (949) 588-7925. A chain of martial arts studios teaching a modern system of karate/ kung-fu with more than 108 locations nationwide and a membership of more than 30,000. America's self defense leader and largest franchised martial arts studio organization. Established: 1968 - Franchising Since: 1988 - No. of Units: Franchised: 108 - Franchise Fee: $27,000 - Royalty: 5% of total gross sales - Total Inv: $110,000: fran. fee plus $83,000 set-up/operations costs - Financing: None. Not franchisng at this time.

VELOCITY SPORTS PERFORMANCE FRANCHISE SYSTEMS, LLC
2125 Corporate Drive, Suite 101, Marietta, GA, 30067. Contact: Franchise Development Department - Tel: (866) 955-0400, Fax: (770) 955-1021, E-Mail: info@velocitysp.com, Web Site: www.velocitysp.com. Velocity is a fast-paced, exciting new sporrts business concept that's in a league all its own. Developed initially for student athletes, Velocity Sports provides training programs that improve the strength, power and agility of athletes at all ages and levels. Velocity Sports Performance Centers provide local athletes of all ages and skill levels with a bright, safe and friendly environment in which to train. Established: 1999 - Franchising Since: 2002 - No. of Units: Company Owned: 1 - Franchise Fee: $25,000 - Royalty: 8% - Total Inv: $254,300-$461,900 - Finaincng: Will assist.

WASHINGTON GOLF CENTER
Worldwide Washington Golf Center, Inc.
2625 Shirlington Rd., Arlington, VA, 22206. Contact: Joe McOwen, Dir. of Fran. - Tel: (703) 979-7639, Fax: (703) 521-5440. Retail supplier of discount golf equipment. Established: 1978 - Franchising Since: 1992 - No. of Units: Franchised: 4 - Franchise Fee: Range: $45,000-$80,000 - Royalty: 2% of gross sales plus 1% adv. - Total Inv: Range: $500,000-$800,000 - Financing: No.

WHEEL FUN RENTALS
Freetime, Inc
802 E. Yanonali Street, Santa Barbara, CA, 93101. Contact: Jim Colitz, Vice President - Tel: (805) 962-1234, (877) WHEELFUN, Fax: (805) 962-2464, E-Mail: info@wheelfunrentals.com, Web Site: www.wheelfun rentals.com. Franchisor of unique recreational rental outlets including quadricycle surreys, "Deuce Coupe", "Slingshot", and "Choppers". Locations available in leisure time and tourist destinations. Established: 1988 - Franchising Since: 2000 - No. of Units: Company Owned: 5 - Franchise Fee: $20,000-$40,000 - Royalty: 9% - Total Inv: $139,000-$328,500 - Financing: Yes, third party

ZAP WORLD
Zap World. Com
117 Morris St., Sebastopol, CA, 95472. Contact: Dir. of Marketing - Tel: (707) 824-4150, (800) 251-4555, Fax: (707) 824-4159, Web Site: www.zapworld.com. Manufacturer of electric bikes, electric scooters, and other personal transportation products. Established: 1994 - Franchising Since: 1997 - Franchise Fee: $12,500 - Royalty: 2% - Total Inv: $50,000-$100,000 - Financing: Yes.

TANNING SALONS

BARE BOTTOM TANNING
Bare Bottom Franchising, Inc
P.O. Box 4384, Portsmouth, NH, 03802-4384. Contact: Dir. of Franchising - Tel: (603) 431-5900, Fax: (603) 431-5900. Upscale safe tanning. Oriented tanning salons and retail stores. A simple highly lucrative cash business. Full training and support with certification after initial training. Established: 1992 - Franchising Since: 1998 - No. of Units: Company Owned: 1 - Franchised: 9 - Franchise Fee: $15,000 - Royalty: Flat fee based on season, 5% adv. - Total Inv: $41,000-$62,000 includes operating capital and franchise fee - Financing: Yes - leasing and financing through third party.

BEACH BUMS TANNING CENTERS
5514 metro Pkwy, Sterling Heights, MI, 48310. - Tel: (586) 303-0040, (800) 837-1388, Fax: (856) 303-0050. Tanning Salon. Established: 1994 - Franchising Since: 1999 - No. of Units: Company Owned: 4 - Franchised: 1 - Franchise Fee: $25,000 - Total Inv: $165,000-$300,000 - Financing: Yes.

CELSIUS TANNERY
Celsius Franchising, Inc
12142 State Line Rd, Leawood, KS, 66209. - Tel: (913) 451-7000, (866) 826-7400, Fax: (913) 451-7001. Tanning salon. Established: 1995 - Franchising Since: 2000 - No. of Units: Company Owned: 5 - Franchised: 17 - Franchise Fee: $20,000-$35,000 - Total Inv: Capital requirements; $300,000-$600,000 - Financing: Yes.

CITY LOOKS SALONS INTERNATIONAL
The Barbers Hairstyling For Men & Women, Inc.
7201 Metro Blvd, Edina, MN, 55439-2130. - Tel: (952) 947-7328, Fax: (952) 947-7301. Full service, upscale hair care salon offering a broad range of hair care services and products in tasteful, comfortable surroundings, filling a need for clients who place a strong emphasis on full-service, personalized hair care. Established: 1963 - Franchising Since: 1967 - No. of Units: Company Owned: 1 - Franchised: 45 - Franchise Fee: $19,500 for 1st salon; $12,500 for each consecutive salon - Royalty: 4%, 4% adv. - Total Inv: $95,000-$172,000 - Financing: Counseling available.

CLUB TAN
7537 E. McDowell Rd, #121, Scottsdale, AZ, 85257. Contact: Nick Nikias, President/CEO/Franchisor - Tel: (480) 423-1031, Fax: (480) 940-9538, E-Mail: clubtan2@aol.com, Web Site: www.clubtan salon.com. Nick and Amy Nikias opened their first Club Tan salon in 1995, and fater two kids, 3 salons of their own and 21 franchise salons signed (they have only been a franchise since 2001), they managed to still be married! Club Tan is a captivating and enhancing tanning franchise that has taken the industry to a whole new perspective. With an established name, monumental purchasing power, freedom for the franchisee (not at all a cookie cutter corporate franchise). Club Tan is a refreshing change for Tanning industry, as well as the Franchise industry. Established: 1994 - Franchising Since: 2001 - No. of Units: Company Owned: 3 - Franchised: 21 - Franchise Fee: $20,000 - Royalty: Minimul $900 per month, $300 per month for advertising - Total Inv: $140,000 franchise fee, build outs, tanning equipment, to working capital - Financing: No.

COPACATANA TANNING SALONS
CopacaTana Franchise Company LLC
222 N. Sepulveda Blvd., Ste 2000, El Segundo, CA, 90245. Contact: Franchise Sales - Tel: (310) 364-5245, (877) juice-99, Fax: (570) 824-5273, Web Site: www.copacatant.com. Full service tanning salons offering the latest in tanning technology. Also sell full line of lotions (including Copacatana brand) and accessories. Can be co-branded with Juice Cabana. Established: 1996 - Franchising Since: 1999 - No. of Units: Company Owned: 7 - Franchise Fee: $22,000 for individual brands or $30,000 for co-brands - Royalty: 5% of weekly gross sales or 8% for co-brands - Total Inv: $151,400 including franchise fee = $206,000 - Financing: Third party.

EVERLASTING TAN CLUB
709 Johnnie Dodds Blvd, Mt. Pleasant, SC, 29464. Contact: Michael Mason, President - Tel: (856) 849-3000, (888) 826-2582, Fax: (856) 856-0210, E-Mail: mrmason@aol.com, Web Site: www.tan-club.com. Large scale indoor tanning centers with ten or more tanning units. Our clubs offer "no appointment tanning" at all times. Established: 1992 - Franchising Since: 1997 - No. of Units: Company Owned: 1 - Franchise Fee: $10,000 - Royalty: $600.00/month - Total Inv: $114,000-$246,000 - Financing: Third party - equipment.

EXECUTIVE TANS
Executive Tans USA
165 S. Union Blvd #780, Lakewood, CO, 80228. - Tel: (303) 988-9999, (877) 393-2826, Fax: (303) 988-5390, E-Mail: sales@executivetans.com, Web Site: www.executivetans.com. Franchise indoor tanning salons. Established: 1991 - Franchising Since: 1995 - No. of Units: Company Owned: 1 - Franchised: 47 - Franchise Fee: $20,000 - Royalty: $795.-$1895 - Financing: Yes, third party.

EXOTIC TAN SUN CLUB
Mid-Atlantic Tanning, Inc
405 Silver Creek Trl, Chapel Hill, NC, 27514-1850. - Tel: (919) 401-6979, Fax: (919) 401-8113, Web Site: www.exotictansunclub.com. The Sun Club offers long-term memberships for year round unlimited low-pressure tanning as well as single and package sessions for non-club tanners. Established: 1997 - Franchising Since: 1999 - No. of Units: Company Owned: 1 - Franchised: 1 - Franchise Fee: $35,000 - Total Inv: $322,600 - Financing: Through third party.

IMAGE SUN TANNING CENTERS *
5514 Parkway Meter, Sterling Heights, NY, 48310. Contact: Sarah Conroy, Franchise Department Specialist - Tel: (800) 837-1388, (800) 837-1388, Fax: (586) 303-0050, E-Mail: franchise@imagesun tanning.com, Web Site: www.imagesun tanning.com. Tanning Salon Franchise expanding Nationwide and throughout Canada. Join our exploding concept with as little as $25,000-$50,000 down. Single unit and Area Developments available. Established: 1994 - Franchising Since: 1999 - No. of Units: Company Owned: 4 - Franchised: 23 - Franchise Fee: $25,000 - Royalty: 5.5% of gross revenue - Total Inv: $25,000-$50,000.

MIRAGE TANNING CENTERS, INC.
Tan Fran, Inc.
1401 N. U.S. Hwy 31 N., Traverse City, MI, 49686. Contact: Franchise Director - Tel: (248) 559-1415, Fax: (248) 557-7931. Upscale state of the art tanning center specializing in bright, spacious rooms, no appointment necessary and computer controlled system which controls both overall operations and the time a person tans for. Established: 1989 - No. of Units: Company Owned: 2 - Franchised: 12 - Franchise Fee: $15,000 - Royalty: 8% - Total Inv: $150,000-$250,000 - Financing: No.

PALMS TANNING RESORT *
8577 E. Arapahoe Rd., #A, Greenwood Village, CO, 80112. - Tel: (866) 725-6748, Fax: (303) 688-3789, Web Site: www.thepalmstanning resort.com. Upscale resort concept featuring private bungalow's prepared with all the tanning amenities your clients will need. Established: 2003 - Franchising Since: 2003 - No. of Units: Company Owned: 1 - Franchise Fee: $25,000 - Royalty: 6% - Total Inv: $542,500-$636,500.

PLANET BEACH TANNING SALON
Planet Beach Franchising Corp.
5161 Taravella Rd, Marrero, LA, 70072. Contact: Russ Smith, SR. VP., Franchise Development - Tel: (504) 361-5550, (888) 2901-8266 (TANN), Fax: (504) 3641-5540, E-Mail: franchise@planetbeach.com, Web Site: www.planetbeach.com. Planet Beach is the earth's largest & fastest growing tanning salon franchise with over 400 awarded locations throughout the U.S., Canada & Australia. Established: 1995 - Franchising

Since: 1996 - No. of Units: Company Owned: 1 - Franchised: 172 - Franchise Fee: $30,000 - Royalty: 6% - Total Inv: $179,000-$299,000 - Financing: Yes.

SOLAR PLANET CORPORATION
856 Folsom St, San Francisco, CA, 94107. - Tel: (800) 886-8486, Fax: (415) 908-6860, E-Mail: solarplanet@qdmco.com, Web Site: www.solarplanet.com. Tanning salon and spa. Established: 1995 - Franchising Since: 1997 - No. of Units: Company Owned: 1 - Franchised: 17 - Franchise Fee: $25,000 - Total Inv: $120,000-$275,000.

SUNCHAIN TANNING CENTERS
8102 E. McDowell, #2C, Scottsdale, AZ, 85257. Contact: Edward Chaney, Chief Executive Officer - Tel: (480) 421-9630, Fax: (480) 421-1505, Web Site: www.sunchain.com. Sunchain has put together a proven program that offers a great return with incredible ease of operation. With Sunchain's membership, your start-up is made easy with existing customer traffic. Established: 1992 - Franchisiing Since: 1996 - No. of Units: Company Owned: 1 - Franchised: 2 - Franchise Fee: $12,500 - Royalty: 4% - Total Inv: $75,000-$150,000.

TAN & TONE AMERICA
6444 NW Expressway, Ste. 245E, Oklahoma City, OK, 73132. Contact: Franchise Department - Tel: (405) 720-8519, Fax: (405) 728-1242. Taning salon. Established: 1986 - Franchising Since: 1998 - No. of Units: Company Owned: 11 - Franchised: 7 - Franchise Fee: $15,000 - Total Inv: $165,000-$250,000. T

TAN WORLD
925 L St, Lincoln, NE, 68508-2229. Contact: Jack L. Rediger, President - Tel: (402) 434-5620, (800) 865-2378. Tan World offers full-service tanning and tanning products in an air-conditioned, consumer-oriented environment. Established: 1995 - Franchising Since: 1996 - No. of Units: Company Owned: 2 - Franchised: 3 - Franchise Fee: $20,000 - Royalty: 6% plus 2% adv. - Total Inv: $168,000-$247,000 - Financing: Indirect.

TROPI-TAN
Tropi-Tan, Inc.
5152 Commerce Rd., Flint, MI, 48507. - Tel: (810) 230-6789, Fax: (810) 230-1115, Web Site: www.tropitan.biz. Indoor tanning salons. Established: 1979 - Franchising Since: 1985 - No. of Units: Company Owned: 7 - Franchised: 3 - Franchise Fee: $25,000 - Royalty: 4.5%, 3.5% adv. - Total Inv: $75,000-$250,000 - Financing: No.

ULTIMATE TAN, THE
New Business Investment Corp.
408 Warren Ave., Ste. AA, Normal, IL, 61761. Contact: Lawrence Pritts, Pres. - Tel: (309) 661-2223, Fax: (309) 661-2222. Tanning salons. Established: 1984 - No. of Units: Franchised: 6 - Franchise Fee: $35,000 - Royalty: 7% weekly - Total Inv: $200,000-$300,000 - Financing: No but assistance with obtaining. NOT FRANCHISING AT THIS TIME.

WE CARE HAIR
The Barbers a Division of Regis Corp
7201 Metro Blvd, Edina, MN, 55439. Contact: Franchise Sales - Tel: (800) 858-2266, (612) 947-7382, Fax: (612) 947-7300. High quality, moderately priced, beauty supplies and tanning. Established: 1985 - Franchising Since: 1986 - No. of Units: Franchised: 63 - Franchise Fee: $12,500-$19,500 - Royalty: 6%, 4% nat'l adv, 1% local adv.- Total Inv: $73,150-$151,800 - Financing: Yes.

TRAVEL

ADMIRAL OF THE FLEET CRUISE CENTERS
Cruise Centers of America
3430 Pacific Ave. S.E., Ste. A-5, Olympia, WA, 98501. - Tel: (360) 438-1191, Fax: (360) 438-2618. Specialized travel agency selling cruises only. Established: 1983 - Franchising Since: 1986 - No. of Units: Company Owned: 4 - Franchised: 3 - Franchise Fee: $25,000 - Royalty: 5% of gross margin - Total Inv: $75,00-$125,000 - Financing: No.

CAREY INTERNATIONAL
4530 Wiscousin Ave., NW, Washington, DC, 20016. - Tel: (202)895-1204, Fax: (202) 895-1209. Chauffeur driven transportation in sedans, limousine, vans and minibuses. Established: 1927 - Franchising Since: 1980 - No. of Units: Company Owned: 8 domestic, 1 international - Franchised: 41 domestic, 24 international - Franchise Fee: $15,000 min. - Royalty: 5% system fee, 2 1/4% marketing fee - Total Inv: Varies - Financing: Yes.

CARIBBEAN CRUISE LINES
P.O. Box 842, Brookhaven, MS, 39602. Contact: William E. Thomas - Tel: (601) 833-5746, (877) 493-5746, Fax: (520) 222-2174, E-Mail: thomas@golfahoy.com, Web Site: www.golfahoy.com. A home-based office focusing on sales & marketing of a selective niche product. Our products focus on golf... We use the fabulous cruise as transportation & off-course fun & entertainment. Established: 1998 - Franchising Since: 1999 - No. of Units: Company Owned: 1 - Franchised: 10 - Franchise Fee: $9,995 - Total Inv: $9,995.

CEQUIS INTERNATIONAL
4809 E. Mossman Rd, Phoenix, AZ, 85054. Contact: Marisa Hsu - Tel: (480) 585-5383, Fax: (509) 753-6142, E-Mail: marisa@cequis.com, Web Site: www.cequis.com. We are the only franchise of its kind in the vacation rental industry. Manage and rent homes in popular vacation destinations. Established: 1985 - Franchising Since: 2001 - No. of Units: Company Owned: 1 - Franchise Fee: $14,950 - Total Inv: $30,000.

CRUISE HOLIDAYS
Cruise Holidays International, Inc.
701 Carlson Pkwy, Minnetonka, MN, 55305. - Postal inquires only. Cruise specialty store. Cruise into business with the largest franchisor of cruise and vacation agencies. Cruises are the fastest growing segment of leisure travel and the most profitable. Established: 1984 - Franchising Since: 1984 - No. of Units: Franchised: 206 - Franchise Fee: $29,500 - Royalty: 6%-1% - Total Inv: $100,000-$140,000 incl. fran. fee - Financing: Third party sources.

CRUISE LINES RESERVATION CENTER
2 Emily Ct, Moriches, NY, 11955-1817. Contact: Bernard Korn, Pres. - Tel: (567) 482-9557. Cruise and travel agency. Established: 1989 - Franchising Since: 1990 - No. of Units: Company Owned: 10 - Royalty: 1% gross sales - Total Inv: $2,000-$5,000.

CRUISE PLANNERS
CP Franchising, Inc.
3300 University Drive, Ste. 602, Coral Springs, FL, 33065. Contact: Marilyn Davis, Director of Marketing - Tel: (954) 344-8060, (888) 582-2150, Fax: (954) 344-4479, E-Mail: mpdavis@cruiseplanning.com, Web Site: www.cruiseplanners.com. Leading user friendly home based cruise agency franchise. Established: 1994 - Franchising Since: 1994 - No. of Units: Franchised: 216 - Franchise Fee: $7,995 - Royalty: 3% reduced by volume - Total Inv: $10,000-$15,000 - Financing: None.

CRUISEONE
1415 NW 62ND Street, #205, Fort Lauderdale, FL, 33309. - Tel: (954) 958-3701, (800) 892-3928, Fax: (954) 958-3697, E-Mail: franchise@cruiseone.com, Web Site: www.cruiseone.com. CruiseOne is the largest franchisor of independent cruise agents throughout North America. As a division of Travel Services International the largest seller of cruises in the world, CruiseOne specialsts capitalize on some of the highest commissions in the industry. Established: 1992 - Franchising Since: 1992 - No. of Units: Franchised: 405 - Franchise Fee: $9,800 - Royalty: 3% - Total Inv: $10,000 - Financing: Limited.

EAGLE TRAVEL SERVICES, INC
8647 Hall Blvd, Loxahatchee, FL, 33470. - Tel: (561) 683-4622, (800) 811-3553, Fax: (561) 753-5977. The original home based travel agency. Can be operated part time or full time from home or office. Unique tax benefits, free or low-cost travel, great income. Established: 1989 - Franchising Since: 1989 - No. of Units: Affiliates: 1000+ - Total Inv: $7900. - Financing: Yes.

EMPRESS TRAVEL LP
465 Smith Street, Farmingdale, NY, 11735. Contact: Elizabeth Beutel, Dir. Sales Marketing - Tel: (631) 845-7000, Fax: (631) 420-0511. Travel agency franchise company specializing in tour cruise and group travel

retailing. Franchising is only available to existing licensed travel agencies. Program benefits include extensive consumer advertising, incentive commissions, exclusive territories, affiliation with one of America's leisure travel wholesalers. Established: 1956 - Franchising Since: 1974 - No. of Units: Franchised: 93 - Franchise Fee: $3,000 - Total Inv: Include one time franchise fee plus monthly payments - Royalty: Sliding scale starting at $1,055 per month. - Financing: No.

ENCHANTED HONEYMOONS
2925 S 108th Street, Omaha, NE, 68144. Contact: Kem Matthews, President - Tel: (402) 390-9291,(800) 253-2863, Fax: (402) 393-8096, E-Mail: ehmoons@aol.com, Web Site: www.enchantedhoneymoon.com. Enchanted honeymoon is the only full service travel agency that specializes in leisure and honeymoon travel. Established: 1996 - Franchising Since: 1997 - No. of Units: Company Owned: 1 - Franchised: 5 - Franchise Fee: $21,500 - Royalty: .5% - Total Inv: $25,500-$35,500 - Financing: Partial.

FIRST DISCOUNT TRAVEL & DISCOUNT TRAVEL
First Discount Travel
5665 Highway 9 N Ste 103, Alpharetta, GA, 30004-3932. Contact: Elizabeth Yancey, Pres. - Tel: (770) 394-1434, Fax: (770) 394-1434. Full service travel agencies. Established: 1988 - Franchising Since: 1989 - No. of Units: Franchised: 37 - Franchise Fee: $29,500 - Royalty: $500 per month - Total Inv: $29,500 plus $35,000 work. cap. - Financing: Short term only.

GALAXSEA CRUISES & TOURS
North American Gaming and Entertainment
5710 Cancun Dr, North Richland Hills, TX, 76180-6126. Contact: Ms. Tanna Hodges, Franchise Development - Tel: (972) 671-7245, (800) 820-4710, Fax: (972) 671-1151. Cruise and vacation business. Full training and support provided. Established: 1986 - Franchising Since: 1988 - Franchise Fee: $2,500-$25,000 - Financing: No.

GOLD COAST LTD
P.O. Box 568508 10 West Pineloch Ave, Orlando, FL, 32856. - Tel: (407) 857-3645, (800) Train21, Fax: (407) 857-3649, Web Site: www.royalrail.com. Operator of private railcars on Am Trak Trains. Established: 1985 - Franchising Since: 1997 - No. of Units: Company Owned: 10 - Franchised: 2 - Franchise Fee: Each situation is different - Royalty: None - Total Inv: $350,000 min - Financing: Through approved sources & lenders.

IN HOUSE TRAVEL GROUP, LLC
190 E. Westminister Ave., Lake Forest, FL, 60045. - Tel: (847) 234-8750, (800) 863-1606, Fax: (847) 234-8774, E-Mail: inhouse @hometravel.com, Web Site: www.hometravel.com. Premier network of independently owned travel companies. We support home-based professional travel agents and inhouse corporate travel offices. Established: 1995 - Franchising Since: 1995 - No. of Units: Company Owned: 1 - Franchised: 160 - Franchise Fee: $500-$3,950 - Royalty: 1-4% - Total Inv: $2,250-$9,700 - Financing: Yes.

INTERNATIONAL TOURS, INC.
5270 Neil Road, Reno, NV, 89502. - Tel: (972) 671-1100, (800) 233-0695, Fax: (972) 385-1591. Full service retail travel agencies. Established: 1968 - Franchising Since: 1970 - No. of Units: Company Owned: 3 - Franchised: 278 - Franchise Fee: $28,000 - Royalty: Less than 1% - Total Inv: $75,000-$95,000 - Financing: No.

KIRBY TOURS
Kirby Tours, Inc.
719 Griswold, Suite 100, Detroit, MI, 48226. Contact: Shakil A. Khan, Pres. - Tel: (313) 278-2000, Fax: (313) 963-1699, E-Mail: info@kirbytours.com, Web Site: www.kirbytours.com. Sightseeing tours, airport shuttle service, family reunion planning, bus/van/limo charters and convention and meeting planning. Established: 1919 - Franchising Since: 1993 - No. of Units: Company Owned: 3 - Franchise Fee: $15,000-$25,000 - Royalty: 5% - Total Inv: $15,000-$40,000 - Financing: Yes.

SHIPS & TRIPS
22802 Ne 189th St, Woodinville, WA, 98072-6717. Contact: Kenneth Beebe, President / CEO - Tel: (206) 306-7520, (800) 689-8674. Vacation dealerships offering a very limited line of branded vacation cruise and tour packages from kiosks located in high traffic malls. Established: 1996 - Franchising Since: 1999 - No. of Units: Company Owned: 2 - Franchise Fee: $22,500 - Royalty: 1% of gross - Total Inv: $22,500 franchise - $25,000 kiosk - $40,000-$60,000 operating capital - Financing: No.

SUMMIT TRAVEL
Summit Travel Group, Inc.
200 Brookstown ave #301, Winston Salem, NC, 27101-5202. - Tel: (336) 896-1010, (800) 7-SUMMIT, Fax: (336) 896-0555. Home based travel business. Complete training and materials necessary to own and operate a successful air, cruise and tour business. Established: 1993 - Franchising Since: 1993 - No. of Units: Company Owned: 1 - Franchised: 100+ - Franchise Fee: $5,875 - Royalty: 0 - Total Inv: $5,875 - Financing: N/A.

TEAM TRAVEL
Team Travel, Inc.
2920 S Rainbow Blvd Ste 170, Las Vegas, NV, 89146-6227. - Tel: (702)248-8838,(800) 960-TEAM, Fax: (702)248-8874, Web Site: www.teamtravel.com. Home based travel. Established: 1994 - Franchising Since: 1994 - No. of Units: Company Owned: 1 - Franchised: 1.200 - Franchise Fee: $6,995 - Royalty: None - Total Inv: $6,995 - Financing: None.

TIX TRAVEL & TICKET AGENCY, INC
TIX Travel & Ticket Agency, Inc.
201 Main Street, Nyack, NY, 10960. Contact: R. Klein, Manager - Tel: (845) 358-1007, (800) 872-8849, Fax: (845) 358-1266, E-Mail: infokit@tixtravel.com, Web Site: www.tixtravel.com. Start your own full service travel agency and Concerts, Sports & Theater ticket business. From storefront, office, home or web. Established: 1982 - Franchising Since: 1992 - No. of Units: Company Owned: 1 - Franchised: 400 - Franchise Fee: $3,495 - Total Inv: $3,495 - Financing: Credit cards.

TPI TRAVEL SERVICES
Travel Pros Inc.
10012 N Dale Mabry Hwy Ste 203, Tampa, FL, 33618-4425. - Tel: (813) 281-5670. Full service travel agency. Can be run from home or office. We provide reservations, software, training and support. Established: 1987 - Franchising Since: 1987 - No. of Units: Company Owned: 1 - Franchised: 385 - Franchise Fee: $4,995 - Royalty: $99 - Financing: No.

TRAVEL CENTERS OF AMERICA
24601 Center Ridge Rd Ste. 200, Westlake, OH, 44145-5677. Contact: John Holahan, President - Tel: (440) 808-9100, Fax: (440) 808-4458, Web Site: www.TPOA.com. Full service travel plazas incorporating motels, diesel fuel for trucks, gas stations,full service restaurants with fast food outlets and retail stores for the traveling public. Established: 1979 - Franchising Since: 1998 - No. of Units: Company Owned: 18 - Franchise Fee: Fuel- $50,000 initial, 2%-4% of retail sales, Rest-$25,000 initial, 4% of sales - Royalty: Additional ad fee as required - Financing: No.

TRAVEL NETWORK
560 Sylvan Ave., Englewood Cliffs, NJ, 07632. Contact: Stephanie Abrams, Executive VP - Tel: (800)TRAV-NET,(201)567-8500, Fax: (201) 567-4405, E-Mail: info@travnet.com, Web Site: www.travelnetwork.com. Travel agencies specializing in leisure/vacation and business travel. Fully computerized. Comprehensive training/on-going support services. Award-winning marketing programs, customer loyalty and lead generation programs. Over $1 billion sales volume creates comprehensive advantages and services. Established: 1982 - Franchising Since: 1983 - No. of Units: Company Owned: 1 - Franchised: 455 - Franchise Fee: $29,900 - Royalty: Flat service fee: $350/mo. 1st yr, $550/mo. 2nd yr, $750/mo. 3rd yr, CPI add on years 4+ - Total Inv: Approx. $15,000 buildout cost, fran fee, $45,000 - $50,000 work cap. - Financing: Yes, third party, SBA lender. Prime sites available in Wal-Mart superstores.

TRAVEL PROFESSIONALS INTERNATIONAL
Travel Professionals International, Inc.
1100 Park Central Blvd S Ste 2500, Pompano Beach, FL, 33064-2232. Contact: V.P., Fran. Dev. - Tel: (800) 626-2469, (502) 423-9966, Web Site: www.travelprof.com. Franchisor of travel resource offices, the

next generation of consumer travel delivery. Established: 1982 - Franchising Since: 1983 - No. of Units: Company Owned: 1 - Franchised: 80 - Franchise Fee: $27,500 - Royalty: 5% - Total Inv: $120,000-$160,000 - Financing: No.

TRAVELHOST TRAVEL AGENCY
Travelhost Agencies, Inc.
10701 N. Stemmons Fwy., Dallas, TX, 75220-2419. Contact: V.P. Fran. Sales - Tel: (214) 691-1163. Travel agency turn-key franchise includes: Complete int. furnishings, computer equip., signage and adv. materials along with comprehensive sales and operations training and an array of on-going support programs. Established:1988 - Franchising Since:1988 - No. of Units: Company Owned: 1 - Franchised: 30 - Franchise Fee: $50,000 - Royalty: Flat fee of $175 /wk - Total Inv: $42,900 - Financing: Yes.

WORLDWIDE MARKETING CORP
P.O Box 647, Rosebuck, SC, 29376-0647. Contact: Pat Tibbitts, CEO - Tel: (864) 472-5900, Fax: (864) 472-3035, E-Mail: flyfre42@mind spring.com, Web Site: www.worldwidemarketingcorp.com. Travel certificates. Established: 1967 - No. of Units: Company Owned: 20.

VIDEO/AUDIO SALES & RENTALS

DVD PLAY *
750 University Ave, #280, Los Gatos, CA, 95032. - Tel: (408) 395-1727, Fax: (408) 395-1997, E-Mail: info@dvdplay.net, Web Site: www.dvd play.com. The world's first automated machine that rents and sells the latest blockbuster movies. Established: 1999 - Franchising Since: 2003 - No. of Units: Company Owned: 4 - Franchise Fee: $10,000 - Total Inv: $154,750 - Financing: No.

HANCOCKS HOME VIDEO
450 Southland Dr., Ste. E, Lexington, KY, 40503. Contact: Franchise Dept. - Tel: (859) 278-1341. Video rental and sales. Established: 1987 - Franchising Since: 1987 - No. of Units: Company Owned: 4 - Franchised: 44 - Franchise Fee: $20,000 - Royalty: 5% rentals; 2% sales - Total Inv: $180,000-$250,000 - Financing: No.

INFINITY VIDEO PRODUCTIONS, INC.
1028 W. Maude Ave. Ste 403, Sunnyvale, CA, 94086. Contact: Clifton Hildreth, Franchise Development - Tel: (408) 720-0281, Fax: (408) 720-0282. Video production services. Training and support provided. Established: 1978 - Franchising Since: 1995 - No. of Units: Company Owned: 8 - Franchised: 4 - Franchise Fee: $18,500 - Total Inv: $2,500-$5,000. Financing: No.

INTERACTIVE VIDEOCONFERENCING CENTERS (IVC)
45 Braintree Hill Park, Ste. 401, Braintree, MA, 02184. Contact: Charlie Olminsky, Franchise Development - Tel: (781) 843-1400, Fax: (781) 843-1400. Video conferencing centers. Full training and support provided. Established: 1996 - Franchising Since: 1996 - No. of Units: Franchised: 6 - Franchise Fee: $25,000 - Total Inv: $50,000-$175,000 (includes fran. fee).

MARBLES ENTERTAINMENT
United Business Group, Inc
10351 Santa Monica Blvd., Ste 430, Los Angeles, CA, 90025. - Tel: (800) 669-2221. Retail store; video, games and CD's. Established: 1969 - Franchising Since: 1988 - No. of Units: Company Owned: 12 - Franchised: 7 - Franchise Fee: $20,000 - Financing: Yes.

MR. MOVIES
Mr. Movies, Inc.
7625 Parklawn Ave., #200, Edina, MN, 55435.Contact: David Kaiser, V.P. Franchising - Tel: (612) 835-3321, Fax: (612) 835-1144. Video sales and rental outlets featuring a "neighborhood superstore" concept. Professionally decorated, computerized, up-to-date store design set Mr. Movies apart from other video retailers. Established: 1985 - Franchising Since: 1985 - No. of Units: Company Owned: 14 - Franchised: 76 - Franchise Fee: $19,500 - Royalty: 4% + 4% adv - Total Inv: $200,000-$260,000 - Financing: No.

PREPLAYED *
9 West Aylesbury Rd Suite F-G, Timonium, MD, 21093. Contact: Ed Gieske - Tel: (410) 560-0551, (888) 640-7529, Fax: (410) 5600-6355, E-Mail: info@preplayed.com, Web Site: www.preplayed.com. PrePlayed is a chain of franchised stores that does more than just sell to its customers...it also buys directly from them. In fact, the majority of the CDs, movies, video/computer games, electronics and the gear that goes with it, all that we sell, has been obtained directly from our customers. Established: 2003 - Franchising Since: 2003 - No. of Units: Franchised: 5 - Franchise Fee: $25,000 - Royalty: 4% - Total Inv: $222,000-$322,000 - Financing: N/A.

VIDEO GAME SWAPPERS
Video Game Swappers, Inc.
3008 E. Hammer Ln., Ste. 119, Stockton, CA, 95212-2829. - Tel: (209) 474-1052, Fax: (209) 474-8225. We buy, sell and trade new and used home video game systems and games. Established: 1990 - Franchising Since: 1994 - No. of Units: Company Owned: 6 - Franchised: 3 - Franchise Fee: $10,000 - Royalty: 5% on annual gross sales - Total Inv: $32,000-$72,000 - Financing: No.

VIDEO GAMER
15965 Jeanette St., Southfield, MI, 48075. - Tel: (248) 557-2784, Fax: (248) 557-7931. Video games, sales, rentals and resale. Established: 1988 - Franchising Since: 1993 - No. of Units: Company Owned: 2 - Franchised: 2 - Franchise Fee: $16,000 - Royalty: 5% - Total Inv: $77,000-$96,000 - Financing: Yes.

VIDEO IMPACT
Video Active , Inc
1100 Hammond Dr Suite 220, Atlanta, GA, 30328. - Tel: (707) 206-9889, (800) 544-6139. Video communications centers, offering video tape duplicating, editing and film, picture and slide transfer to video. Located in retail outlets, providing user friendly enviroment using latest equipment. Established: 1985 - Franchising Since: 1997- No. of Units: 3 - Franchise Fee: $25,000 - Royalty: 6% gross revenue - Total Inv: $150,000-$180,000 - Financing: Third party equipment financing available.

VIDEO STOP
Video Stop Unlimited Inc.
3303 E. Memorial Dr., Muncie, IN, 47302. Contact: Fran. Dir. - Tel: (765) 288-7800, Fax: (765) 282-2863. Video and Nintendo game rental. VCR and nintendo system rental. Video sell-thru. Family oriented video rental with full line of video rental. Play area for children. Arcade room for adolescents. Established: 1988 - Franchising Since: 1990 - No. of Units: Company Owned: 3 - Franchise Fee: $17,500 - Royalty: 5% - Total Inv: Video software-$50,000; computers-$10,000; improvements are determined on location; display- $30,000-$40,000; misc.- $5,000-$15,000 - Financing: No.

VIDEOMASTERS INC
2200 Dunbarton Dr Ste. D, Chesapeake, VA, 23325. Contact: Roy Graham - Tel: (800) 836-9461, Fax: (757) 424-8693, E-Mail: corporate @videomasteronline.com, Web Site: www.videomasters.org. Video opportunity built around eight profit centers. Established: 1980 - No. of Units: Franchised: 80 - Franchise Fee: $950. annually - Total Inv: $29,950 - Financing: No.

WATER TREATMENT

AMERICA'S BEST WATER TREATERS, INC.
3808 South Concord Street, Davenport, IA, 52802. - Tel: (319) 322-4120, Fax: (319) 322-0890, E-Mail: abwt@h2otreaters.com, Web Site: www.h2otreaters.com. Industrial and municipal water treatment products and equipment. Established: 1992 - Franchising Since: 1996 - No. of Units: Franchised: 1 - Franchise Fee: $15,000 - Royalty: 2% of net sales - Total Inv: $25,000-$50,000 - Financing: No.

ASTRO-PURE WATER PURIFIERS
3025 SW 2nd Ave., Ft. Lauderdale, FL, 33315-3309. Contact: R.L. Stefl, Pres. - Tel: (954) 832-0630, Fax: (954) 832-0729. Complete line of water treatment equipment, purifiers, filters, decalcifies, reverse

osmosis, iron filters, chemical feed equipment. Sizes for portable, point-of-use, central, commercial and industrial. Established: 1971 - Franchising Since: 1981 - Total Inv: $10,000 inventory.

BYOB WATER STORE
1288 W. Main #103, Old Orchard Village East, TX, 75067. - Tel: (972) 219-1551. A retail store concept which refines its own product water. The product is sold to the customer in his own bottle. Other sales items include dispensers, coolers, bottles, etc. Established: 1984 - Licensing Since: 1985 - No. of Units: Licensed: 12 - Inv: $48,000+.

CULLIGAN USA
One Culligan Parkway, Northbrook, IL, 60062-6209. - Tel: (847) 205-6000. Sales and delivery of 5-gal. bottles of water, sales of water treatment and other high purity water production systems. Established: 1936 - Franchising Since: 1939 - No. of Units: Company Owned: 53 - Franchised: 704 in 50 states - Franchise Fee: $5,000 - Royalty: 5% on bottled water products, 0% on others - Total Inv: $103,000-$342,000 - Financing: Franchisee must provide from their own funds.

ECOWATER SYSTEMS
Ecowater Systems, Inc.
1890 Woodland Drive, P.O. Box 64420, St. Paul, MN, 55164-0426. - Tel: (651) 739-5330, Fax: (651) 739-5293. Manufacturer of water treatment equipment for residential, commercial and industrial softening and drinking water systems. Established: 1945 - Franchising Since: 1950 - No. of Units: Franchised: 1,000 - Franchise Fee: None - Royalty: None - Total Inv: $50,000-$100,000 - Financing: None.

HOME ENVIRONMENT CENTER FRANCHISE, INC.
Environmental Health Services
310 T. Elmer Cox Dr, Greenville, TN, 37743. Contact: Fran. Dir. - Tel: (423) 798-6405. ATR and water purification units and service in a retail store plus a retail water store. Network marketing and air purification products. Established: 1995 - Franchising Since: 1995 - No. of Units: Company Owned: 2 - Franchise Fee: $25,000 - Royalty: 2% avg. - Total Inv: $120,000 - Financing: None.

LA PURE WATER MANUFACTURING
Satmarketing.com
8414 17th St N St. Petersburg, FL, 33702-2846. Contact: Thomas Carson, V.P. Sales - Tel: (727) 865-9502, (800) 784-7122, Fax: (727) 864-0186. Manufacture of water filtration systems for home and office. Established: 1989 - Franchised Since: 1990 - No. of Units: Franchised: 100 + International - Total Inv: Product only from $330.00-$675.00 - Financing: No.

PURE WATER INC.
3725 Touzalin Ave., Lincoln, NE, 68507. Contact: Dir. of Sales - Tel: (402) 467-9300, Fax: (402) 467-9393. In business providing fresh, high-quality drinking water using the state-of-the-art Pure Water Ultima™, which purifies the water and dispenses hot, room or cold temperature water. Established: 1968 - Franchising Since: 1995 - No. of Units: Franchised: 10 - Franchise Fee: None - Royalty: None - Total Inv: Approx. $75,000 - Financing: None.

PURIFIED WATER TO GO
Purified Water To Go Corp.
5160 S. Valley View, Ste. 110, Las Vegas, NV, 89118-1778. Contact: V.P Franchise Development - Tel: (800) 976-9283, (702) 895-9350, Web Site: www.watertogo.com. We retail fresh purified water for drinking and other purposes. We sell our water the lowest price, for the purest product, and the highest quality service. Nationally and internationally. We also sell containers, such as 5 gallon bottles to half liter sizes. Crocks and coolers as well. Area development contracts for cities and/or stores available. "Full size and express locations available". Established: 1992 - Franchising Since: 1995 - No. of Units: Franchised: 55 - Franchise Fee: $24,500 - Royalty: 7% - Total Inv: $53,000-$99,000 - Financing: Yes.

RAINBORN, INC.
702 S. Thornton Ave., Ste. C, P.O. Box 2766, Dalton, GA, 30722. Contact: Greg Greene, Pres. - Tel: (706) 277-7779, (800) 360-5537, Fax: (706) 277-0814. Manufactures the RainBorn Point-of-Use Drinking Water Purification System which replaces the bottle on standard bottle water coolers. Patented technology makes tap water up to 99.99% pure.

Designed for convenience, can be manually filled or pumped in. Produces three types of water to drink: two mineralized and one purified. This product is marketed in the U.S. exclusively through franchises. Established: 1993 - Franchising Since: 1994 - No. of Units: Franchised: 3 - Franchise Fee: $15,000 - Royalty: 10% - Total Inv: $46,000-$54,000 initial investment (incl. fran. fee $100,000 required) - Financing: No.

RAINSOFT WATER TREATMENT SYSTEMS
RainSoft Water Treatment Systems
2080 East Lunt Ave., Elk Grove Village, IL, 60007. Contact: Richard Dayton - Tel: (847) 437-9400, (800) 642-3426, Fax: (847) 437-1594, E-Mail: rdayton@rainsoft.com, Web Site: www.rainsoft.com. Sales and rentals of water purification equipment for homes, businesses, light industry and municipalities from $299-$200,000. Established: 1953 - Franchising Since: 1960 - No. of Units: Franchised: 300 - Total Inv: $25,000-$100,000 - Financing: SBA assistance.

RAYNE CORPORATION
3775 Market St., 2nd Floor, Ventura, CA, 93003-5133. Contact: Robert E. Denne, President - Tel: (800) 550-8510, Fax: (805) 676-3095. Water conditioning and water filtration for domestic and light commercial applications. Established: 1930 - Franchising Since: 1951 - No. of Units: Company Owned: 6 - Franchised: 34 - Approx. Inv: $20,000+ - Financing: No.

UNITED WORTH HYDROCHEM CORP.
413 E. Magnolia, P.O. Box 366, Ft. Worth, TX, 76101. Contact: Roy Coleman, Pres. - Tel: (817) 332-8146, Fax: (817) 429-6843. Chemical water treatment of commercial and industrial water systems (boilers, heat exchangers, cooling towers, etc). Established: 1957 - Franchising Since: 1960 - No. of Units: Company Owned: 2 - Franchised: 10 - Franchise Fee: $500 - Royalty: Purchase contract - Total Inv: $1,000 - Financing: No.

WATER RESOURCES INTERNATIONAL
2800 E. Chambers St., Phoenix, AZ, 85040. Contact: Chris Bower Exec. V.P. - Tel: (602) 268-2580, Fax: (602) 268-8080. Manufacturing and distribution of water treatment and water purification equipment, both residential and commercial to it's nationwide network of franchisees who retail to the public. Established: 1966 - Franchising Since: 1990 - No. of Units: Company Owned: 1 - Franchised: 35 - Franchise Fee: $15,000 - Royalty: 1% - Total Inv: $38,000 - Financing: No. NOT FRANCHISING AT THIS TIME.

WATERCARE CORPORATION
1025 East Albert Drive, Manitowoc, WI, 54220-1717. Contact: Wm. Granger, Pres. - Tel: (920) 682-6823, Fax: (920) 682-7673. Retail, sale, rental and lease of water conditioning equipment for residential, institutional, commercial and industrial. Established: 1946 - Franchising Since: 1967 - No. of Units: Company Owned: 2 - Franchised: 135 - Franchise Fee: $10,000-$15,000 - Approx. Inv: Varies.

WEDDING RELATED SERVICES

A DAY TO CHERISH WEDDING VIDEOS *
A Day To Cherish Wedding Videos, Inc.
10174 South Memorial Drive, South Jordan, UT, 84095. Contact: Murray Dalton, President - Tel: (801) 253-2450, E-Mail: weddingvideosutah@msn.com, Web Site: www.adaytocherish.com. This is a low cost ground floor opportunity to own your own wedding video franchise business. No experience necessary. We will train on camera work, editing, marketing, setting up your office and producing a professional wedding video. Established: 2004 - Franchising Since: 2004 - No. of Units: Company Owned: 1 - Franchise Fee: $24,000 - Royalty: 6% - Total Inv: $41,000-$47,000 - Financing: No, but have contacts that can help.

A WONDERFUL WEDDING
A Wonderful Wedding Franchising Inc.
3 McDougall Dr, Charleston, SC, 29414-7345. Contact: Ken Thomason, Pres. - Tel: (843) 556-1500, (800) 661-9135, Fax: (843) 769-0269, E-Mail: krt@awonderfulwedding.com, Web Site: www.awonderful wedding.com. Produce a semi-annual bridal guide and produce an annual bridal show. The guide and show are two highly targeted

marketing mediums for wedding-related businesses in your market. Their effectiveness builds customer loyalty and steady revenues for you as a franchisee. Established: 1993 - Franchising Since: 1997 - No. of Units: Company Owned: 1 - Franchise Fee: $15,000 - Royalty: 10% of gross sales - Total Inv: $26,450-$40,400 (includes franchise fee) - Financing: No.

ALL ABOUT HONEYMOONS *
950 S. Cherry St., #108, Denver, CO, 80246. Contact: Clay Gibbons - Tel: (888) 845-4488, Web Site: www.aahfranchise.com. Travel agency specializing in honeymoon packages. Established: 1994 - Franchising Since: 2003 - No. of Units: Franchised: 11 - Franchise Fee: $7,000-$19,000 - Royalty: 1-3% - Total Inv: $9,100-$28,100 - Financing: No.

BRIDE'S DAY MAGAZINE
Bride's Day Franchise Corp.
750 Hamburg Tpk., Ste. 208, Pompton Lakes, NJ, 07442. Contact: David A. Gay, Publisher - Tel: (973) 299-1600. Free community bridal magazine designed to assist brides-to-be with planning while offering quality, affordable, local exposure to wedding related businesses in a given area. Established: 1987 - Franchising Since: 1990 - No. of Units: Company Owned: 2 - Franchised: 8 - Franchise Fee: $14,900 - Royalty: 6% - Total Inv: $5,000 in work cap. - Financing: Yes.

DISCOUNT BRIDAL SERVICE
1583 Sulpher Spring Road, #108, Baltimore, MD, 21227. Contact: Kim Strauss - Tel: (410) 595-0140, (800) 441-0102, Fax: (410) 595-0139, E-Mail: gowns@ix.netcom.com, Web Site: www.discountbridal service.com. Retails at discount prices. Established: 1985 - Franchising Since: 1985 - No. of Units: Company Owned: 1 - Dealers: 500 - Franchisee Fee: $495-$895 - Royalty: N/A - Total Inv: N/A - Financing: No.

FOR THE BRIDE TO BE
P.O. Box 4437, Cordova, TN, 83088.Contact: John Ferrante,CEO-Franchise - Tel: (901) 753-9867, (866) 843-7378, Fax: (901) 624-6810, E-Mail: john@forthebridetobe.com, Web Site: www.forthebrideto be.com. Retail boutique that specializes in the sale of gifts, invitations and specialty wedding items. Established: 1994 - Franchising Since: 2001 - No. of Units: Company Owned: 1 - Franchise Fee: $25,000 - Royalty: 6% - Total Inv: $150,000-$270,000.

LITTLE WEDDING CHAPEL, THE
Wedding Belles, Inc.
27857 Orchard Lake Rd., Farmington Hills, MI, 48334. - Tel: (248) 489-1144, Fax: (248) 489-0209. World's only wedding chapel franchise. We have created an entirely new segment in the wedding industry by providing an elegant and romantic setting that offers value and convenience to the consumer. Our franchisees have experienced a tremendous rate of return on their investment while working in an enjoyable and rewarding business. We provide our franchisees with all the important design, operational and administrative procedures necessary as well as an exclusive territory. Established: 1989 - Franchising Since: 1990 - No. of Units: Company Owned: 1 - Franchised: 4 - Franchise Fee: $16,500 - Royalty: 6% gross sales - Total Inv: $90,900-$158,900 - Financing: None.

PERFECT WEDDING GUIDE, INC, THE
1206 N. CR 427, Longwood, FL, 32750. Contact: Patrick J. McGroder, President - Tel: (407) 331-6212, (888) 222-7433, Fax: (407) 331-5004, E-Mail: patrick@thepwg.com, Web Site: www.thepwg.com. The Perfect Wedding Guide is a comprehensive buyers guide to wedding and honeymoon services. You will be trained to publish your own wedding magazine, utilizing the systems that have been time tested for over nine years. Established: 1991 - Franchising Since: 1998 - No. of Units: Company Owned: 3 - Franchised: 29 - Franchise Fee: $25,000-$35,000 - Royalty: 6% - Financing: Yes.

STATICE FRANCHIISNG, LLC
3872 Roswell Rd., Ste. B3, Atlanta, GA, 30342. Contact: Sue Everets - Tel: (404) 237-9911, (888) 237-9911, Fax: (404) 237-8385. Wedding gowns in plus sizes. Established: 1994 - Franchising Since: 2002 - No. of Units: Franchised: 1 - Franchise Fee: $35,000 - Financing: No.

WEDDING EXPRESSIONS
1275 Country Walk, Wichita, KS, 67206-4104. - Tel: (316) 681-0121. Full service bridal retailer (gowns, bridesmaid dresses, mothers dresses, tuxedos, cake, flowers, photography, invitations, candelabra rental, accessories). Established: 1982 - Franchising Since: 1988 - No. of Units: Company Owned: 1 - Franchised: 7 - Franchise Fee: $12,000-$16,000 - Royalty: 3 1/2 + 1/2 adv. - Total Inv: $75,000-$150,000 - Financing: Business bank.

WEDDING GOWN SPECIALISTS RESTORATION LABS
Websco, Inc.
1270 Cedars Rd, Lawrenceville, GA, 30045-5121. Contact: Gary Webster, Founder - Tel: (800) 543-8987, (770) 998-3111. Restores discolored and stained wedding, christening and debutante gowns to true color. Established: 1987 - Licensing Since: 1987 - No. of Units: Company Owned: 1 - Franchised: 115 - Franchise Fee: $1,000+ - Royalty: 20% annual renewal - Financing: No. NOT FRANCHISING AT THIS TIME.

WEDDING PAGES, THE
Weddingpages, Inc.
11106 Mockingbird Dr., Omaha, NE, 68137. - Tel: (800) 843-4983, (402) 331-7755, Fax: (402) 331-2887. Complete databased bridal marketing system designed to locate brides 8-10 months before their wedding. It involves sales and marketing to wedding professionals. Established: 1982 - Franchising Since: 1987 - No. of Units: Company Owned: 35 - Franchised: 53 - Franchise Fee: $15,000 - Royalty: 10% - Total Inv: $25,000-$50,000 work. cap. - Financing: None.

WEIGHT LOSS CENTERS

BEVERLY HILLS WEIGHT LOSS & WELLNESS
Beverly Hills Weight Loss & Wellness, Inc.
300 International Parkway, #100, Heathrow, FL, 32746. - Tel: (407) 333-8998, (800) 886-1301. Weight loss clinics. Franchising Since: 1989 - No. of Units: Franchised: 44 - Franchise Fee: $15,000 - Royalty: 8% of weekly gross - Total Inv: Fran. fee, buildout, clinic supplies - Financing: No.

CONTOURS EXPRESS
Contours Express, Inc
156 Imperial Way, Nicholasville, KY, 40356. Contact: Daren Carter, President - Tel: (859) 885-6441, (877) 227-2282, Fax: (214) 242-2234, E-Mail: daren@contoursexpress.com, Web Site: www.contours express.com. Ladies Fitness and Weight Loss Studio. Established: 1998 - Franchising Since: 1998 - No. of Units: Franchised: 320 - Franchise Fee: $9,995 - Royalty: $395.00 per month - Total Inv: $33,000-$49,500 - Financing: Limited.

CUTS FITNESS FOR MEN *
1120 Raritan Rd Bldg 2, Clark, NJ, 07066. - Tel: (732) 381-9300, Fax: (732) 574-1130, Web Site: www.cutsfitness.com. Private environment exclusivley for men. Total body strength training through the use of hydraulic resistance. Established: 2003 - Franchising Since: 2003 - No. of Units: Company Owned: 15 - Franchise Fee: $29,500 - Royalty: $400/monthly - Total Inv: $47,100-$70,900 - Financing: No.

DIET LIGHT WEIGHT LOSS SYSTEM
Diet Light Inc.
300 Market St., Ste. 101, Lebanon, OR, 97355. Contact: Kathy Bengtson, Pres. - Tel: (541) 259-3573, (800) 248-7712, Fax: (541) 259-3506, E-Mail: dietlight@proaxis.com., Web Site: www.dietlight.webvalley.com. Weight loss counseling on an individual basis with portion controlled meals, and lifetime maintenance. Established: 1983 - Franchising Since: 1988 - No. of Units: Company Owned: 10 - Distributorships: 5 - Distributorship Fee: $5,000 - Royalty: None - Total Inv: $15,000 ($5,000 fran. fee, $5,000 products & literature, $5,000 signs, furnishings) - Financing: No.

FORM YOU 3 WEIGHT LOSS CENTERS
Health Management Group
395 Springside Drive, Akron, OH, 44333. Contact: Ken Massey, Dir. of Franchise Dev. - Tel: (800) 525-6315, (330) 668-1461, Fax: (330) 666-2197, Web Site: www.formyou3.com. Weight loss counseling and sales of related weight loss products. Established: 1982 - Franchising Since: 1984 - No. of Units: Company Owned: 2 - Franchised: 70 - Franchise Fee: $4,900 - Royalty: 6% - Total Inv: $23,100-$33,700 - Financing: No.

INCHES-A-WEIGH
P.O. Box 59346, Birmingham, AL, 35209. Contact: Scott Simcik, President - Tel: (800) 241-8663, (205) 879-8614, Fax: (205) 879-2106, E-Mail: iawcorp@aol.com, Web Site: inchesaweigh.com. Inches-A-Weigh Centers extend a new nutrition and onsite exercise formula to the "larger" middle class. It's simple....nutrition and exercise classes that are easy and affordable. Established: 1986 - Franchising Since: 1992 - No. of Units: Company Owned: 1- Franchised: 60 - Franchise Fee: $29,500 - Royalty: 3% - Total Inv: $45,000-$65,000 - Financing: Yes.

JENNY CRAIG WEIGHT LOSS CENTERS
Jenny Craig International Inc.
5770 Fleet St, Carlbad, CA, 92008. - Tel: (760) 696-4000. Weight loss centers. Established: 1983 - Franchising Since: 1986 - No. of Units: Company Owned: 524 - Franchised: 191 - Franchise Fee: $50,000 - Royalty: 7% - Total Inv: $152,500-$295,500 incl. fran. fee - Financing: None.

L A SHAPES *
L A Shapes
747 Dresher Road, Suite 150, Harsham, PA, 19044. Contact: Tim Britt, VP of Franchise Development - Tel: (215) 346-4302, (888) 258-7099, Fax: (215) 356-8810, E-Mail: franchiseleads@laweightloss.com, Web Site: www.lashapes.com. L A Shapes is the complete body workout exclusively for women. In only 30 minutes three times a week clients can shape up and slim down with easy-to-use hydraulic equipment in a comfortable environment. L A Shapes is a division of L A Weight Loss, one of the world's most successful weight loss companies with a 15 year history of helping clients lose weight. Established: 2004 - Franchising Since: 2004 - No. of Units: Company Owned: 20 - Franchised: 5 - Franchise Fee: $29,990 - Royalty: $275/month - Total Inv: $52,073-$72,065 - Financing: Yes, third party.

L A WEIGHT LOSS CENTERS
L A Weight Loss
747 Dresher Road Suite 150, Horsham, PA, 19044. Contact: Tim Britt, VP of Franchise Development - Tel: (215) 346-4302, (888) 258-7099, Fax: (215) 346-8810, E-Mail: tbritt@laweightloss.com, Web Site: www.laweightloss.com. LA Weight Loss Centers combine personalized meal plans, using everyday foods, with professional one-on-one counseling and a line of proprietary products to create one of the hottest new business opportunities. Featured the industries leading marketing, training operations systems. Established: 1989 - Franchising Since: 1998 - No. of Units: Company Owned: 365 - Franchised: 300 - Franchise Fee: $20,000 - Royalty: 7% - Total Inv: $67,175-$120,400.

LIGHTEN UP! WEIGHT LOSS PROGRAM INC., THE *
2608 3rd Ave., N.E., Seattle, WA, 98121. - Tel: (206) 441-8550, (888) 311-1998, Fax: (206) 448-5938, Web Site: www.lighten-up.com. Weight-loss program. Established: 1987 - Franchising Since: 2003 - No. of Units: Company Owned: 1 - Franchising Since: 3 - Franchise Fee: $10,000-$15,000 - Royalty: $395 - Total Inv: $34,800-$67,400 - Financing: No.

LITE FOR LIFE *
Lite For Life Franchise Corpoation, Inc
388 Second Street, Los Altos, CA, 94022. Contact: Chris Bruno - Tel: (650) 941-3200, Fax: (650) 559-3111. Weight loss and nutrial consulting. Established: 1978 - Franchising Since: 2003 - No. of Units: Company Owned: 4 - Franchied: 2 - Franchise Fee: $20,000.

OUR WEIGHT
3637 Park Ave., Ste. 201, Memphis, TN, 38111-5614. Contact: Helen K. Seale, Owner - Tel: (901) 458-7546. A unique weight control group consisting of thirty minute meetings, behaviour modification, exercise and most important, a nutritional diet that allows members to eat only foods they like. First in the field to introduce "food rewards", free weekly weigh in upon reaching desired weight. Established: 1974 - Franchising Since: 1974 - No. of Units: Company Owned: 8 - Franchised: 4 - Franchise Fee: $1,500 - Total Inv: $1,500 - Financing: No.

PHYSICIANS WEIGHT LOSS CENTERS
Health Management Group
395 Springside Dr., Akron, OH, 44333-2496. Contact: Dir. Franchise Dev. - Tel: (330) 666-7952, (800) 205-7887, Fax: (330) 666-2197. Weight loss Center and related products. Established: 1979 - Franchising Since: 1981 - No. of Units: Company Owned: 1 - Franchised: 63 - Franchise Fee: $4,900 - Royalty: 5.5%-3.5 % - Total Inv: $20,340-$39,800 - Financing: No.

SLIMMER IMAGE WEIGHT LOSS CLINICS
P.O Box 26562, Shawnee Mission, KS, 66225-6562. - Tel: (816) 356-4000, (800) 723-6258, Fax: (816) 356-4981. Physician supervised weight loss programs using grocery store food. Established: 1986 - Franchising Since: 1996 - No. of Units: Company Owned: 7 - Franchised: 6 - Franchise Fee: $5,000 - Royalty: 4% total sales - Total Inv: $50,000 - Financing: Partial.

WEIGH USA *
Lakeview Mall, 15 1st Ave South, Buffalo, MN, 55313. - Tel: (828) 743-1000, Fax: (828) 743-1799. Weight loss center. Established: 2000 - Franchising Since: 2002 - No. of Units: Company Owned: 1 - Franchise Fee: $12,000.

MISCELLANEOUS

1 (800) TRAPPER
P.O. Box 266, Oyster Bay, NY, 11771. Contact: Andrew Mihlstn - Tel: (516) 624-2126, (800) TRA-PPER. Wildlife animal damage control. Established: 1996 - No. of Units: Company Owned: 1 - Franchised: 12 - Total Inv: capital requirements; $1,000-$20,000 - Financing: No. NOT FRANCHISING AT THIS TIME.

1ST PROPANE
1st Propane Franchising, Inc
14670 Cantova Way, Ste. 208, Rancho Murieta, CA, 95683. Contact: William Thacher, President - Tel: (916) 354-4022, Fax: (916) 354-1533, E-Mail: info@1st-propane.com, Web Site: www.1st-propane.com. Bulk distribution of propane gas to rural homeowners. Established: 1997 - Franchising Since: 1998 - No. of Units: Franchised: 13 - Franchise Fee: $30,000 - Royalty: 6% - Total Inv: $176,500-$440,500 - Financing: Third party.

A CUSTOM TILE MANUFACTURING OPPORTUNITY
Olde World Enterprises, Inc
1517 Moccasin Creek Rd., P.O. Box 531, Murphy, NC, 28906. Contact: John McKenzie Panagos - Tel: (828) 837-0357, Fax: (828) 837-1458, E-Mail: Info@Oldeworld.com, Web Site: www.Oldeworld.com. Custom tile manufacturing business opportunity can be started at home, and grows as desired. Complete Mfg. & Mktg. Training Course on CDs and video include 8 FREE bonuses, (business plan template, invoicing program, molds, sample forms/letters, etc.) all for less than $500! Established: 1991 - Franchising Since: 1995 - No. of Units: Company Owned: 1 - Franchised: 40+ - Total Inv: Under $1,000-$10,000.

A HOME CHECK
6348 Palmas Bay Circle, Port Orange, FL, 32127. - Tel: (904) 767-7523, Fax: (904) 756-4980. Professional inspection services, residential, commercial, industrial, for purchasers, insurance companies and financial institutions. Established: 1987 - Franchising Since: 1998 - No. of Units: Franchised: 1 - Franchise Fee: $7,000 - Total Inv: $7,000-$35,000 - Financing: Available for large franchises or master franchises.

AGRONICS INC

7100-C Second NW, Albuquerque, NM, 87107. Contact: Colonel Taylor, CEO - Tel: (505) 761-1454, Fax: (505) 761-1458, E-Mail: Linvent@aol.com. The originators of total soil management by completely, affordable remineralizing and biologically reactivating soils, the enviromental friendly farming method. Established: 1966 - Franchising Since: 1987 - No. of Units: Company Owned: 1 - Franchised: 31 - Franchise Fee: $5,000 - Financing: No.

AIR CARE
DPL Enterprises Inc.
3868 East Post Rd #89120, Las Vegas, NV, 89118. Contact: Richard F. Papaleo, Pres. - Tel: (702) 454-5515,(800) 322-9919, Fax: (702) 454-5225. Indoor air quality test and air system cleaning. Established: 1979 - Franchising Since: 1979 - No. of Units: Company Owned: 1 - Dealerships: 125 - Franchise Fee: None - Royalty: None - Total Inv: $20,500 - Financing: Yes.

AIT FREIGHT SYSTEMS, INC.
701 N. Rohlwing, Itasca, IL, 60143. Contact: Herb Cohan, Sr. V.P. - Tel: (630) 766-8300, (800) 669-4248, Fax: (630) 766-0305. International/domestic/ocean freight forwarder. Established: 1979 - Franchising Since: 1988 - No. of Units: Company Owned: 6 - Franchised: 18 - Franchise Fee: $6,000 - Royalty: 12.75% domestic and 32% international - Total Inv: $18,000-$25,000 - Financing: On initial franchise fee only.

ALPHA CHECKPOINT DRUG + ALCOHOL TESTING SERVICES
National Compliance Alliance, Inc
725 East Jericho Turnpike, Turnpike Plaza, Huntington Station, NY, 11746. Contact: Jay Howard - Tel: (516) 643-7700, (877) NOD-RUGS, Fax: (516) 491-1155. Drug testing for employers. Established: 1997 - Franchisng Since: 1998 - No. of Units: Company Owned: 2 - Franchise Fee: $27,500-$57,500 - Total Inv: $50,450-$103,600 (includes fran. fee) - Financing: Yes.

AMERICAN ASPHALT SEALCOATING
American Ashphalt Sealcoating Franchise, Corp
P.O. box 600, Chesterland, OH, 44026. Contact: Todd Tornstrom, CEO - Tel: (440) 729-8080, Fax: (440) 729-2231, Web Site: www.american-sealcoating.com. Driveway and parking lot maintenence. Established: 1988 - Franchising Since: 1998 - No. of Units: Company Owned: 2 - Franchised: 5 - Fraanchise Fee: $12,500 - Royalty: 8% to $100,000, 7% to $80,000, 6% all a base - Total Inv: $25,000-$45,000 - Financing: Yes.

AMERICAN LEAD CONSULTANTS
American Lead Consultants, Inc.
1400 112th Ave, SE #100, Bellevue, WA, 98004. - Tel: (425) 646-7226, Fax: (425) 646-6681. Residential lead inspection for paint, water and soil. Established: 1993 - Franchising Since: 1994 - No. of Units: Company Owned: 1 - Franchised: 14 - Franchise Fee: $25,000 - Royalty: 9% - Total Inv: $50,000 - Financing: Partial.

AMERICAN OUTDOOR ADVENTURES
Hill Country Unlimited LLC
4611 Sinclair Ave, Austin, TX, 78756. Contact: David Dahill - Tel: (512)467-7421, Fax: (512)467-7421, E-Mail: ddahill@aoanetwork.com, Web Site: www.aoanetwork.com. American Outdoor Adventures is a network of internet based outdoor & social clubs. Established: 2000 - Franchising Since: 2002 - No. of Units: Company Owned: 3 - Franchise Fee: $10,000 - Capital Requirement: $50,000 - Financing: Third party.

AMERICAN RAMP SYSTEMS *
202 West First Street, South Boston, MA, 02127-1110. Contact: Ron Dimitrik - Tel: (617) 269-5679, (800) 649-5215, Fax: (617) 268-3701, E-Mail: info@americanramp.com, Web Site: www.americanramp.com. Manufacturer of wheelchair ramps. Established: 2002 - Franchising Since: 2003 - No. of Units: Company Owned: 2 - Franchised: 10 - Franchise Fee: $32,250 per million population - Royalty: 12% - Total Inv: $100,000 - Financing: No.

AMERICAN SECURITY FINANCE
4132 Shoreline Dr. Ste. J, Earth City, MO, 63045. Contact: John Weigel, National Sales Mgr. - Tel: (314) 344-1111 ext: 101, Fax: (314) 298-9110, E-Mail: credit@creditpluscard.com, Web Site: www.creditpluscard.com for personal credit or www.nabl.com for business credit.

provide customer financing for credit rejected installment finance and revolving credit customers. Dealer financing. Established: 1976 - Franchising Since: 1976 - No. of Units: Company Owned: 1 - Franchised: 210 - Total Inv: $495 - Financing: Yes.

ANDY ONCALL
Andy Oncall Franchising, Inc.
921 East Main St., Chattanooga, TN, 37408. Contact: Franchise Department - Tel: (877) 263-9662, Fax: (423) 622-0580, E-Mail: info@andyoncall.com, Web Site: www.andyoncall.com. Handy Man, small home repair service. Established: 1993 - Franchising Since: 1999 - No. of Units: Franchised: 9 - Franchise Fee: $15,000-$30,000 - Royalty: 4% - Total Inv: $23,550-$43,650 - Financing: 50% of franchise fee.

ARMOR FUELING
Armor International, Ltd
1900 Country Road., #1, Wrenshall, MN, 55797. - Tel: (218) 384-3504, (888) 827-1122, Fax: (218) 384-3087, Web Site: www.armorfuel.com. An Armor Fueling franchise is an unattended retail fueling facility that accepts cash or credit cards 24 hours a day, 365 days a year. Established: 1999 - Franchising Since: 2000 - No. of Units: Company Owned: 5 - Franchised: 5 - Franchise Fee: $30,000 - Total Inv: $75,000.

AURA SHOP INC
520 Washington Blvd PMB 907, Marina del Rey, CA, 90292. - Tel: (310) 390-7090, Fax: (310) 390-8167, Web Site: www.aurashop.com. Self-empowerment wellness products and services. Established: 1994 - Franchising Since: 2000 - No. of Units: Franchised: 1 - Franchise Fee: $3,950 - Royalty: 495/month - Total Inv: $21,700-$27,500.

AUTO DRIVEAWAY CO.
310 S. Michigan Ave., Chicago, IL, 60604. Contact: Drew Little, V.P. - Tel: (312) 939-3600, Fax: (312) 341-1900. Transporting automobiles, trucks and motor homes via driveaway or truckaway. Established: 1952 - Licensing Since: 1954 - No. of Units: Company Owned: 4 - Licensed: 88 - Franchise Security Deposit: $5,000 - Total Inv: $10,000 - Royalty: Varies - Financing: No.

BALLOON CAFE - GOURMET BALLOON DELIVERY
P.O. Box 398, Providence, UT, 84332. - Tel: (435) 752-5729, Fax: (435) 787-8654, Web Site: www.ballooncafe.com. Home-based balloon delivery franchise. Established: 1999 Franchising Since: 2002 - No. of Units: Company Owned: 1 - Franchise Fee: $6,000-$30,000 - Financing: No.

BATH GENIE, INC.
20 River St., Marlborough, MA, 01752-3242. Contact: John Foley, Pres. - Tel: (508) 481-8338, Fax: (508) 624-6444. Porcelain repair and resurfacing. Established: 1974 - Franchising Since: 1984 - No. of Units: Company Owned: 1 - Franchised: 26 - Total Inv: $24,500 - Financing: No.

BEECHWOOD AND COMPANY
77 Huguenot Rd., Oxford, MA, 01540. - Tel: (508) 987-3900, Fax: (508) 987-9686. Financial services business oportunity. Turn-key programs that allow clients to broker residential and commmercial mortgages as well as leasing factoring and retail installment contracts. Established: 1995 - Total Inv: $1,500 - Financing: Yes.

BERLITZ FRANCHISING CORP.
Berlitz International, Inc.
400 Alexander Park, Princeton, NJ, 08540. Contact: Frank J. Garton, V.P. Fran. Worldwide - Tel: (609) 514-3046, Fax: (609) 514-9675. Worlds largest provider of language instruction and translation services with 117 years of experience. Other businesses: Interpretation Services, Publishing Products, Self-Teaching Language and Travel Guides. Also Dictionaries. Established: 1878 - Franchising Since: 1995 - No. of Units: Company Owned: 323 - Franchise Fee: $30,000 - Royalty: 10% - Total Inv: $150,000-$300,000 - Financing: None.

BIOLOGIX
BioLogix F.M.C.
1561 Fairview Ave, St. Louis, MO, 63132. - Tel: (314) 423-1945, (800) 747-1885, Fax: (314) 423-4394, Web Site: www.biologix.com. Guaranteed environmental waste elimination services for the food service hospitality industry. Business to business sales, renewable

income and a positive environmental impact. Established:1989 - Franchising Since: 1995 - No. of Units: Company Owned: 2 - Franchised: 19 - Franchise Fee: $12,000 - Royalty: 4% - Total Inv: $11,400-$31,100 - Financing: No.

BLUE MAGIC POOL SERVICE
Rix Pool Service Dev. Corp.
2496 W. Shore Rd., Warwick, RI, 02886. Contact: Richard Thompson, President - Tel: (401) 737-1533, (800) 640-5528. Complete swimming pool cleaning and repair - quickly and conveniently - full training and support provided. Established: 1994 - Franchising Since: 1995 - No. of Units: Company Owned: 1 - Franchised: 5 - Franchise Fee: $22,500 - Total Inv: $31,700-$35,000 (incl. fran. fee).

BURKE. BURKE & EDWARDS
Road #3 Box 221A1, Smithfield, PA, 15478-8705. Contact: David Burke - Tel: (724) 569-1003, Fax: (724) 569-0203. Credit/debit consulting businesses and or consumers. Established: 1995 - Franchising Since: 2001 - No. of Units: Company Owned: 1.

CENTER COURT CONCIERGE
76-947 Desi Drive, Indian Wells, CA, 92210. - Tel: (619) 360-2325, Fax: (619) 360-7175. Info center located in malls, includes ATM'S, fax, copying etc. Established: 1994 - Franchising Since: 1995 - No. of Units: Company Owned: 12 - Franchise Fee: $25,000-$32,500 - Total Inv: $75,000 + working capital - Financing: Yes.

CHIMNEY FIX-IT
15965 Jeanette, Southfield, MI, 48075. - Tel: (248) 559-1415. Home based business. Professional chimney, brick and mortar repair. Established: 1976 - Franchising Since 1998 - No. of Units: Company Owned: 1 - Franchise Fee: $15,000-$17,000 - Total Inv: $31,500 (includes $6,000 working capital) - Financing: Outside financing available. Home Based business.

CHRISTMAS DECOR
Christmas Decor Inc.
206 23rd St, Lubback, TX, 79404. - Tel: (806) 722-1225, (800) 687-9551, Fax: (806) 722-9627, E-Mail: info@thedecorgroup.com, Web Site: www.christmasdecor.net. Installation of christmas holiday and special event decorations. Established: 1991 - Franchising Since: 1996 - No. of Units: Franchised: 342 - Franchise Fee: $9,500-$15,900 - Royalty: 2%-4.5% - Total Inv: Varies - Financing: Yes.

CITIZENS EQUALITY TELECOMMUNICATIONS
26A Barnes Park Rd.-N., Wallingford, CT, 06492. Contact: Glenn D. Sloenko, Sr. VP. - Tel: (800) 221-1511. L.D. paging, internet and cellular - full training and support provided. Established: 1992 - Franchising Since: 1993 - No. of Units: Company Owned: 1 - Franchised: 871 - Franchise Fee: $79-$20,000 - Total Inv: Franchise and/or license fee.

CLICKTOWN INTERNATIONAL
20 Hales Drive, Kenilworth, NJ, 07033. - Tel: (908) 259-0500, Fax: (908) 241-9654, E-Mail: info@clicktown.com, Web Site: www.clicktown.com. We offer a franchise for the 21st century. We are dedicated to being the ultimate portal for local news, information and businesses. Established: 2000 - Franchising Since: 2001 - No. of Units: Company Owned: 1 - Franchise Fee: $7,500 - Total Inv: $20,000.

COLOR ME MINE
5140 Lankershim Blvd, North Hollywood, CA, 91601. Contact: Mike Mooslin - Tel: (818) 505-2100, Fax: (818) 509-9778, Web Site: www.colormemine.com. Paint-your-own ceramics studios. Established: 1991 - Franchising Since: 1996 - No. of Units: Franchised: 54 - Franchise Fee: $ 20,000 - Royalty: 5% - Total Inv: $97,500-$185,000 - Financing: Third party.

COLOR SPECIALTIES, INC.
6405 Cedar Ave., S., Richfield, MN, 55423. Contact: Ron Toupin, CEO - Tel: (612) 861-1555. Reconditioning, repairing, refinishing of auto interiors, boat interiors, furniture, commercial and restaurant. Service business that is completely mobile. Established: 1976 - Franchising Since: 1977 - No. of Units: Company Owned: 2 - Franchised: 571 - Total Inv: $18,600, equip., chemicals, supplies, training - Financing: No.

COLOR YOUR CARPET
Color Your Carpet, Inc
767 Blanding Blvd., Suite 112, Orange Park, FL, 32065. Contact: Connie D'Imperio, President - Tel: (904) 272-6567, (800) 321-6567, E-Mail: cdimperio@carpetcolor.com, Web Site: www.coloryour carpet.com. The only on site fulltime, 100% carpet dying restoration service in the world. Our unique services are providing property owners with a cost-effective alternative to costly and usually unnecessary carpet replacement. Carpet dyeing, as a business, as a untapped, unlimited opportunity. Established: 1979 - Franchising Since: 1990 - No. of Units: Company Owned: 1 - Franchised: 218 - Franchise Fee: $15,000 - Royalty: 3% on gross sales - Total Inv: $49,800 ($15K=franchise fee, $8K=Inventory & equipment, $5K to $10K=Start-up costs, Protected territory=included, $15K-$20K for mini-van) - Financing: No, third parrty assistance available.

COMFORT ZONE
Prism Enterprises, Inc.
P.O. Box 680728, San Antonio, TX, 78268. - Tel: (210) 520-8051, Fax: (210) 520-8039. No. of Units: Independently Owned: Approx. 80 - Franchise Fee: N/A - Royalty: N/A - Total Inv: $12,500 = intial start-up - Financing: N/A.

COMMERCIAL WATER & ENERGY
CW&E Franchise Corp
11926 S.W. 8th Street, Miami, FL, 33184. Contact: Richard Ley, Director of Sales - Tel: (305) 436-6050, (888) 77- METER, Fax: (305) 436-6020, E-Mail: info@commercialwater.com, Web Site: www.commercialwater.com. Utility billing and metering company. Sub-meters utilities for apartments, shopping centers, mobile home parks and condominiums. We provide reading, billing and collecting service. Established: 1994 - Franchising Since: 2000 - No. of Units: Company Owned: 1 - Franchise Fee: $20,000 - Royalty: 5% gross sales - Total Inv: $60,000-$180,000 - Financing: No.

COMMUNICATIONS CONSULTING INTERNATIONAL
1889 Monroe Drive, Atlanta, GA, 30324. Contact: Jim Valentine, Franchise Development - Tel: (404) 874-5587, Fax: (404) 815-7255 Telecom consulting and auditing service. Full training and support provided. Established: 1995 - Franchising Since: 1997 - No. of Units: Company Owned: 1 - Franchised: 4 - Franchise Fee: $6,000.

CONCRETE GRINDING COMPANY
Concrete Grinding Company
188 Civic Circle #109, Lewisville, TX, 75067. - Tel: (972) 353-9220, (800) 922-2488, Fax: (800) 474-6332, E-Mail: info@concrete grinding.com, Web Site: www.concretegrinding.com. Specializing in the repair of raised sidewalk trip hazards with an innovative grinding repair technique, instead of costly replacement. Additional services include surface preparation, graffiti removal and scabbling. Established: 1986 - Franchising Since: 1998 - No. of Units: Company Owned: 11 - Franchised: 4 - Franchise Fee: $15,000 - Royalty: 12% - Total Inv: $27,000-$74,000 - Financing: Yes 75% of franchise fee.

CORNERSTONE FUELS
Cornerstone Fuels International, Inc.
515 Eaton St., St. Paul, MN, 55107. - Tel: (952) 831-0114. Sale of franchise to pump self serve fuel on airports for aircraft. Established: 1989 - Franchising Since: 1993 - No. of Units: Company Owned: 8 - Franchised: 6 - Franchise Fee: $5,000 - Royalty: Flow fee 11¢-25¢ per gallon based on volume - Total Inv: Varies by site - Financing: Yes.

CORPORATE MINUTES MADE FRANCHISING
5631 E. Le Mauche Ave, Scottsdale, AZ, 85265. Contact: Dale Smith, President - Tel: (480) 510-9000, Fax: (480) 473-2323. Sell corporate minutes to their clients. No inventory, employees, leases or franchisor performance reporting necessary. Established: 1995 - Franchising Since: 1995 - No. of Units: Franchised: 17 - Franchise Fee: $12,5000 - Royalty: $250. per month - Total Inv: $12,500-$17,500.

CRATERS & FREIGHTERS
Craters & Freighters Franchise Company
7000 E 47th Avenue Dr., Ste. 100, Denver, CO, 80216-3450. Contact: Franchise Department - Tel: (303) 399-8190, (800) 949-9931, Fax: (303) 393-7644. As "Specialty Freight Handlers" Craters & Freighters is the exclusive source for reliable, affordable specialty shipping services

for pieces that are too big for UPS and too small for movers. We provide high demand crating and shipping with ironclad insurance to a loyal, upscale clientele. Established: 1990 - Franchising Since: 1991 - No. of Units: Franchised: 56- Franchise Fee: $24,800 - Royalty: 5%, 1% adv. - Total Inv: $65,000-$76,000 includes fran.fee - Financing: Assistance available.

CREATIVE ETCHINGS
Sherwood Enterprises, Inc
4122 123rd Trail N, West Palm Beach, FL, 33411-8927. Contact: Robert Woods, President - Tel: (561) 798-2657, (800) 226-3824, Fax: (561) 798-0013. Complete on-site glass etching service, training, equipment and support. Established: 1986 - Franchising Since: 1997 - No. of Units: Company Owned: 1 - Franchised: 1 - Franchise Fee: $18,500 (business opportunity - complete pkg) - Royalty: 0 - Total Inv: $15,000 opening operating capital.

CUSTOM CASE SUPPLY CO.
9329 De Soto Ave., Dept. 783, Chatsworth, CA, 91311. Contact: Joanne Schmickel - Tel: (818) 882-5121, Fax: (818) 998-1967. Direct sales, mail order. Build custom cases for salesmen. Established: 1945 - Inv. $9.95 to start. Training and support provided. NOT FRANCHISING AT THIS TIME.

CUTIE PIES CO
United Bronze Inc
181 Greenwood Ave, P.O. Box 4799, Rumford, RI, 02916. Contact: John Walters - Tel: (401) 434-4444, (401) 438-5550. Bronzed baby hand/footprint keepsakes. Established: 1972 - No. of Units: Company Owned: 1 - Franchised: 21 - Total Inv: Capital requirements; $2,995 - Financing: No.

DEBT DOCTORS
2472 Glick St., Lafayette, IN, 47905. - Tel: (765) 474-9887, (800) 733-3287. Debt management and credit counseling, we help people get out of debt using their own money, not borrowed money. Established: 1966 - Franchising Since: 1993 - No. of Units: Company Owned: 2 - Franchised: 1 - Franchise Fee: $10,000 - Royalty: 7.5% - Total Inv: $10,000 franchise fee, $5,000 start up advertising, up to $10,000 furniture and equipment - Financing: No, unless prospect is already in the business.

DIAL-A-TILE
1604 Hwy. 35, Box 71, Oakhurst, NJ, 07755. Contact: Robert Ballack, Pres. - Tel: (732) 517-0575, Fax: (732) 531-7347. Mobile shop at home ceramic tile showroom. Established: 1990 - Franchising Since: 1991 - No. of Units: Company Owned: 3 - Franchise Fee: $20,000 - Total Inv: $40,000-$50,000 - Financing: Will assist.

DINER-MITE
diners, inc
Monarch Plaza, 3414 Peachtree Rd, #105, Atlanta, GA, 30326-1164. Contact: Director of Marketing - Tel: (404) 237-5221, Fax: (404) 237-4481, E-Mail: info@dinermite.com, Web Site: www.dinermite.com. New 1950's style stainless steel "modular" diners starting at $139.500 fully equipped. Established: 1959 - Financing: SBA + leasing.

DISPLAY DOC
Display Doc Inc.
P.O. Box 64, Lincoln, IL, 62656. Contact: Greg Potratz, Franchise Development - Tel: (217) 737-4187, Fax: (217) 732-8240. Storage and service of trade show displays. Training and support provided. Established: 1997 - Franchising Since: 1999 - No. of Units: Company Owned: 1 - Franchised: 1 - Franchise Fee: $500 - Total Inv: $500-$1,000.

DOAN & COMPANY AUTO APPRAISING
Doan & Co. Franchising Corp.
5090 Highway 212, Covington, GA, 30016. Contact: Peter Sciandra, Senior Vice President - Tel: (877)7411-DOAN, Fax: (877) DOAN-FAX. Doan & Co. is one of the fastest growing auto damage appraisal companies in the U.S. Founded in 1981, Doan & Co. provides quality appraisal services based on accuracy, speed, integrity and professionalism. Doan & Co. provides service to over 300 clients through 45 franchised offices covering 20 states. Established: 1981- Franchising Since: 1991- No. of Units: Franchised: 45 - Franchise Fee: None - Royalty: 12% of gross sales - Total Inv: Approx $5,000-$20,000 - Financing: No.

ECOSMARTE PLANET FRIENDLY, INC.
1600 east 78th St, Richfield, MN, 55423. - Tel: (612) 866-1200, (800) 466-7946, Fax: (612) 866-0152. Enviromental technology store with propiertary ecosafe products for home, pool, spa or business as seen at http://ecosmarte.com. Franchising Since: 1996 - No. of Units: Company Owned: 2 - Franchised: 2 - Royalty: None - Total Inv: $145,000-$225,000.

EMBROIDME
1801 Australian Ave, South, West Palm Beach, FL, 33409. - Tel: (561) 640-7367, (800) 727-6720, Fax: (561) 478-4340, Web Site: www.embroidme.com. Embroidery and promotional products. Established: 2000 - Franchising Since: 2000 - No. of Units: Company Owned: 2 - Franchised: 150 - Franchise Fee: $37,500 - Total Inv: $115,000 - Financing: Yes.

ENCOUNTERS CORPORATION
1800 Second Street, Ste. 725, Sarasota, FL, 34236. Contact: Carl Bennett, Pres. - Tel: (941) 955-8855. The franchisee through a unique method of introduction, provides a quicker, easier, more effective, and safer way than other means available for single professionals to meet their compatible counterpart. Established: 1993 - Franchising Since: 1997 - No. of Units: Company Owned: 1 - Franchise Fee: $7,500 - Royalty: 7% on first $300,000, 5% over $300,000 - Total Inv: $44,666-$64,818 - Financing: No.

ENECON
Enecon Corporation
700 Hicksville Rd., #110, Bethpage, NY, 11714-3496. - Tel: (515) 349-0022, Fax: (516) 349-5522. Repair and protection products for fluid flow systems performance enhancement. Appoints exclusive distributors. Established: 1990 - No. of Units: Franchised: 30 - Total Inv: $35,000 - Financing: No.

ENERGY MISER WINDOWS
P.O. Box 187, Conshohocken, PA, 19428. - Fax: (410) 727-4534. Energy Miser offers an efficient low cost method to reduce energy cost, and noise infiltration in homes, commercial buildings and historic properties. Included along with the exclusive Energy Miser product line is proven training in marketing, sales and installation developed by Richard Kaller, a nationally recognized speaker and authority. Established: 1964 - Franchising Since: 1991 - No. of Units: Company Owned: 1 - Franchise Fee: $25,000 includes training - Royalty: 8% - Total Inv: $60,000 - Financing: Yes.

ENVIRONMENTAL ASSESSMENTS FRANCHISE
431 East Main St., Brownsburg, IN, 46112. - Tel: (317) 858-3090, Fax: (317) 858-3090. Phase 1 site assessments. Established: 1992 - Franchising Since: 1995 - No. of Units: Company Owned: 1 - Franchise Fee: $14,000 - Royalty: 7% - Total Inv: $18,050-$44,750 - Financing: Negotiable.

EXPRESS ONE
8160 South Highland Dr, Suite A, Sandy, UT, 84093. - Tel: (801) 944-1661, (800) 399-3971. An authorized national provider of DHL worldwide services along with reselling other transportation companies. Established: 1995 - Franchising Since: 1996 - No. of Units: Company Owned: 4 - Franchised: 25 - Franchise Fee: $15,000 & up - Royalty: 6% - Total Inv: Minimal start up cost - Financing: Yes.

FAMILY TREE VIDEO
Family Tree Video Inc.
2966 Wildwind Dr., El Cajon, CA, 92019. - Tel: (619)444-9401. Transforming photographs, slides and old home movies into a heartwarming music video. Incorporating titles, music, live testimony, voice over, so a family can see 100 years in less than an hour. Established: 1986 - Franchising Since: 1991 - No. of Units: Company Owned: 1 - Franchised: 100+ - Franchise Fee: None - Royalty: None - Total Inv: $46,500 includes all equipment and training - Financing: Some/partial.

FINANCIAL SERVICES
Mid-States Financial Group
55 Meridian Pkwy, 101, Martinsburg, WV, 25401. Contact: Thomas L. Burke - Tel: (304) 263-1000, (866) 258-6190, Fax: (304) 263-1001, E-Mail: msfg@intrepid.net, Web Site: www.msfgloans.com. MSFG provides training and support for those interested in owning their own residential mortgage lending business. Detailed instruction includes

loan officer training and recruitment, compliance, licensing, investor relations, loan products, processing, marketing, advertising, etc. This program will eliminate or significantly reduce the time it takes to enjoy the financial success of owning a business which there is a never ending demand for the product... money. Established: 1997 - Franchising Since: 1999 - No. of Units: Company Owned: 3 - Franchised: 1 - Franchise Fee: $10,000 - Royalty: 2% - Total Inv: $40,000 - Financing: No.

FLAMINGO A FRIEND
648 Rumson Rd., Birm, AL, 35209. Contact: Victor Kepic, President - Tel: (205) 870-1315. We put plastic animals, flamingos, cows, pig, etc. in yards for special events, birthdays, anniversary, graduation, includes a large sign. Established: 1994 - Franchising Since: 1998 - No. of Units: Company Owned: 2 - Franchised: 8 - Royalty: 6% on gross sales paid monthly - Total Inv: $4,995.00 - Financing: Yes.

FLASH-IN-THE-PAN
FIP Franchising, Inc
P.O. Box 159, Leola, PA, 17540-0159. Contact: Harlan Krok, President - Tel: (717) 656-4681, Fax: (717) 656-4681, E-Mail: kilgore1959@aol.com, Web Site: www.flashinthepan.bigstep.com.The Flash-in-the-Pan franchise is a ground floor opportunity that puts you on the cutting edge of a revolutionary new trend and enables you to harness the most sophisticated emerging technology to meet the needs of today's time-starved and cash-rich consumers. Established: 2000 - Franchising Since: 2001 - No. of Units: Company Owned: 1 - Franchised: 1 - Franchise Fee: $30,000 - Royalty: 6% of gross sales, 1% of advertising - Total Inv: $45,000 ($30,000 franchise fee, $10,000 equipment/supplies, $5,000 working capital) - Financing: No. NO LONGER FRANCHISING.

FORTUNE PRACTICE MANAGEMENT
9888 Carroll Centre Rd, 3100, San Diego, CA, 92126. - Tel: (800) 628-1052, Fax: (858) 535-6387. Our franchisees consult with health care practitioners in the business and management areas of their practices. Established: 1990 - Franchising Since: 1990 - No. of Units: Franchised: 40 - Franchise Fee: $60,000 - Royalty: 15% - Total Inv: $60,000-$114,000 - Financing: Yes, up to 75% of fran. fee. NOT FRANCHIISING AT THIS TIME.

FRANCHISE CHINA CONFERENCE & EXHIBITION
Asian Sources
901 Sneath Lane, Ste. 212, San Bruno, CA, 94066. Contact: Chuck Armitage, General Manager - Tel: (650) 742-7900, Fax: (650)742-7962. Provides international franchisors an opportunity to meet face to face with China's entrepreneurs and interact with individuals keen on investing in a franchise. Established: 1971.

FRENCH COMPANY, THE
French Developments Corp., The
31005 Bainbridge Rd., Solon, OH, 44139. - Tel: (440) 349-4344, (800) 321-8875, Fax: (440) 349-5872. Business to Business Service franchise specializing in shopping cart repair and pressure cleaning. Franchise owners manage service crews and sell accounts to grow. Franchise comes with existing trained employees and established client base for an excellent headstart. Established: 1985 - Franchising Since: 1995 - No. of Units: Company Owned: 16 - Franchised: 2 - Franchise Fee: $34,900 - Royalty: 8%, 5% adm. and marketing fee - Total Inv: $78,000 working capt., franchise fee, inv. and equip. - Financing: Equipment leasing.

FRIENDLY FOLKS, INC
426 Hudson St, Hackensack, NJ, 07601. Contact: Janice Guarneri - Tel: (973) 751-5800, Fax: (973) 751-0050, Web Site: www.friendlyfolks.com. Personalized cartoon pictures, 500% mark up. make keychains, magnets, mousepads, etc. from your PC. Established: 1996 - Total Inv: $495.

FUTURE BUSINESS INC
477 Shoup Ave., Ste. 105, Idaho Falls, ID, 83402. Contact: Ken Draper - Tel: (208) 227-0385, Fax: (208) 529-6990. Customer follow up/referral generation. Established: 2001 - Franchising Since: 2001 - No. of Units: Company Owned: 2 - Franchised: 6 - Franchise Fee: $25,000 - Financing: Yes.

GARAGETEK
Garage Tek, Inc,
5 Aerial Way, Ste.200, Soyosset, NY, 11791. Contact: Skip Barrett - Tel: (516) 621-4300, Fax: (516) 992-8600. Residential garage organization. Established: 1999 - Franchising Since: 2000 - No. of Units: Franchised: 15 - Franchise Fee: $50,000 - Total Inv: Capital requirements; $150,000 - Financing: No.

GECKO HOSPITALITY
Gecko Development Corp.
119 East Ogden Ave, Suite 10, Hinsdale, IL, 60521. Contact: Robert Krzak - Tel: (630) 390-1000, (866) 604-3256, Fax: (630) 390-0232, E-Mail: franchise@geckohospitality.com, Web Site: www.gecko hospitality.com. Recruiting firm dedicated to the restaurant industry. Establsihed: 2000 - Franchising Since: 2003 - No. of Units: Company Owned: 2 - Franchised: 2 - Franchise Fee: $25,000-$35,000 - Royalty: 10% - Total Inv: $53,000-$83,000 - Financing: No.

GEMINI TUB REPAIR
2592 River Rd, Bainbridge, PA, 17502. Contact: Sandy Richardson - Tel: (800) 365-2807, Fax: (717) 367-7266. Bath refinishing and repair franchise. Home based business which offers potential for return on your investment. Established: 1984 - Franchising Since: 2003 - No. of Units: Company Owned: 1 - Franchise Fee: $15,000 - Total Inv: $40,000.

GLASS MAGNUM
17815 Shawnee Trail, Tualatin, OR, 97062. - Tel: (503) 641-6926, Fax: (503) 612-9441. Glass and crystal reconstruction, bullet proof glass repair, crack repair in plate glass, windshield chip and crack repair, and foreign matter removal from glass. Established: 1982 - Franchising Since: 1990 - No. of Units: Company Owned: 1 - Franchised: 20 - Franchise Fee: $6,000 - Royalty: 5% and 1% adv. - Total Inv: $7,500-$14,000 - Financing: SBA.

GOLD/CHROME BRUSH PLATING
American Instruments Corp
1844 N. Nob Hill Rd, PMB 170, Fort Lauderdale, FL, 33322. Contact: James Caron - Tel: (954) 341-6656, E-Mail: info@ameracar.com, Web Site: www.ameracar.com. Brush selective electroplating of 60 metals and alloys, (gold chrome) on any chemicals, sale, service. Manufacturer ISO9002, chemicals, sales, service. Established: 1989 - No. of Units: Company Owned: 4 - Franchised: 1298 - Total Inv: $895-$5,500 - Financing: Yes, also leasing.

GRAND GATHERINGS
Partners in Franchising, Inc
417 Commercial Ct, #F, Venice, FL, 34292. Contact: Marianne Bedard - Tel: (941) 484-1312, (866) 484-7263, Fax: (941) 484-5531, E-Mail: GrandGatherings@aol.com, Web Site: www.aboutgrandgatherings.com. We provide an event-planning service that is based on the concept of "NO FEE" to the client. Established: 1993 - Franchising Since: 2000 - No. of Units: Company Owned: 1 - Franchise Fee: $16,500 - Total Inv: Capital requirements; $26,000-$34,500.

GRANITKABLOOM E TRANSFORMATIONS
11098 Inland Ave, Mira Loma, CA, 91752. - Tel: (866) 685-5300, (909) 685-5300, Fax: (909) 685-5464, Web Site: www.granitetrans formations.com. We offer new and exciting alternatives to traditional countertop and surfacing choices. We import Mosaics, Cristallino and Rocksolid Granit slabs from Italy. Established: 1995 - Franchising Since: 1997 - No. of Units: Company Owned: 1 - Franchised: 31 - Franchise Fee: $25,000 - Royalty: 2% - Total Inv: $107,000-$345,000 - Financing: No.

GREAT!GUMBALLS
11081 Zaring Court, Cincinnati, OH, 45241. - VP Franchising - Tel: (513) 936-6799, Fax: (702) 995-3723, E-Mail: info@greatgumballs.com, Web Site: www.greatgumballs.com. Unique self-service franchise vending concept. Exotic flavored gumballs offered in a stunning pyramid. Established: 2002 - Franchising Since: 2002 - No. of Units: Company Owned: 2 - Franchise Fee: $10,000 - Royalty: 0% - Total Inv: $25,000-$30,000.

GREEN CARD USA
Data Systems USA
2901 S Highland Dr Ste 14-C, Las Vegas, NV, 89109-1055. - Tel: (727) 529-6380, Fax: (202) 318-0679, Web Site: www.greencardusa.com. Immigration consultants, business brokers and developers of hotel and motel investments for foreign nationals which enable "green card" acquisition. Established: 1998 - Franchising Since: 1998 - No. of Units: Company Owned: 2 - Franchise Fee: $10,000 - Royalty: 10% of gross turnover - Financing: None.

GROUPADVANTAGE®
Consumer Insurance Services of America Inc.
100 Cummings Center, Ste. 206C, Beverley, MA, 01915. Contact: John F. McCarthy Jr., Franchise Development - Tel: (978) 927-6633, (888) 772-2472, Fax: (978) 927-6688. Insurance sales - full training and support provided. Established: 1996 - Franchising Since: 1998 - No. of Units: Company Owned: 7 - Franchised: 20 - Franchise Fee: $28,000 - Total Inv: $120,000.

GUM BUSTERS
Gumbusters North America, Inc
1041 Sterling Road, Unit 106, Herndon, VA, 20170. - Tel: (877) GUM-BUST, Fax: (703) 668-0602, E-Mail: information@gumbusters.com, Web Site: www.gumbusters.com. GumBusters has developed a unique patented method of gum removal that can be used on concrete, asphalt, carpets, furniture, walls, etc. No. of Units: Company Owned: 1 - Franchised: 6.

GUMBALL GOURMET
1460 Commerce Way, Idaho Falls, ID, 83401. Contact: Jeff Callis - Tel: (208) 524-4969, (866) GUM-BALL, Fax: (208) 524-0783, Web Site: www.gumballgourmet.com. A kiosk with 47 individual different flavor gumball machine's. Established: 2001 - Franchising Since: 2001 - No. of Units: Company Owned: 15 - Franchise Fee: $17,200-$313,960 - Royalty: $100. per month - Total Inv: $24,620-$462,081 - Financing: No.

HAKKY INSTANT SHOE REPAIR
Hakky, Inc.
1739 Sands Place, Ste. F, Marietta, GA, 30067. - Tel: (770) 956-8651, Fax: (770) 951-0355. European instant shoe repair. Established: 1983 - Franchising Since: 1989 - No. of Units: Company Owned: 1 - Franchised: 72 - Franchise Fee: $9,000-$12,500 - Royalty: 4%, 1% adv. - Total Inv: $40,000-$100,000 - Financing: Assistance.

HEEL QUIK!
Heel Quik!, Inc.
1730 Cumberland Point Dr., Ste. 5, Marietta, GA, 30067. Contact: Betty Hubauer, Administrative & Franchise Support - Tel: (770) 951-9440, (800) 255-8145, Fax: (770) 933-8268, E-Mail: hqcorp@bellsouth.net, Web Site: www.heelquick.com. Heel Quik is a foot and shoe care personal services and specialty retail franchise with over 700 operations in over 30 countries. Established: 1984 - Franchising Since: 1985 - No. of Units: Franchised: 710 - Franchise Fee: $15,000-$17,500 - Royalty: 4% of monthly net sales - Total Inv: $8,000-$155,000 - Financing: No.

HISTORICAL RESEARCH CENTER
HRC Int. Inc.
2019 Corporate Drive, Boynton Beach, FL, 33426. Contact: Fran. Dir. - Tel: (561) 740-0122, (800) 940-7991, Fax: (561) 740-0497. Specialty retailer of family name histories and a unique line of heraldic (coat-of-arms) products. Established: 1988 - Franchising Since: 1992 - No. of Units: Company Owned: 73 - Franchised: 502 - Franchise Fee: None - Royalty: Varies - cost of goods 25% - Total Inv: $6,995-$12,000 - Financing: No.

HOME SAFETY SERVICES
1680 Lark Avenue, Redwood City, CA, 94061. Contact: Roger Albrecht, Franchise Development - Tel: (650) 365-7300, Fax: (650) 365-7365. General home safety - safety items sold and installed - full training and support provided. Established: 1997 - Franchising Since: 1999 - No. of Units: Company Owned: 1 - Franchised: 5 - Franchise Fee: $25,000 - Total Inv: $75,000.

HOT N' FAST
Global Franchise Corporation
3820 Premier Ave., Memphis, TN, 38118. Contact: Franchise Director - Tel: (901) 368-3361, Fax: (901) 368-1144. Electronic food cooking and serving equipment. Established: 1993 - Franchising Since: 1997 - No. of Units: Company Owned: 1 - Franchised: 101 - Franchise Fee: $37,500-$250,000 - Royalty: 6%, 1% adv - Total Inv: $54,100-$362,000 - Financing: Yes.

HYDROSHIELD
2255 N. Tuweap Dr #16, St. George, UT, 84770. Contact: Franchise Department - Tel: (435) 688-8787, Fax: (435) 628-8434, Web Site: www.hydroshield.net. The new latest technology in protecting glass. Established: 1996 - Franchising Since: 2002 - No. of Units: Company Owned: 1 - Franchised: 19 - Franchise Fee: $5,950-$19,500 - Financing: Yes.

INNER CIRCLE ®
3320 Louisianna Ave S Suite 305, Minneapolis, MN, 55426. Contact: Norm Stoehr, Founder/CEO - Tel: (612) 933-6629, Fax: (612) 935-5269. Peer groups exclusively for business owners. Established: 1985 - Franchising Since: 1997 - No. of Units: Company Owned: 1 - Franchised: 6 - Franchise Fee: $57,500 initial - Royalty: 10% - Total Inv: $68,500-$85,500 - Financing: No.

INTELLIGENT OFFICE, THE
4450 Arapahoe Ave, Suite 100, Boulder, CO, 80303. - Tel: (303) 447-9000, (800) 866-2702, Fax: (303) 415-2500, E-Mail: franchise@intelligentoffice.com, Web Site: www.intelligentoffice.com. Highly-evolved alternative to the traditional office, providing a prestigious address, a live receptionist for businesses, corporate executives, etc. Established: 1999 - Franchising Since: 1999 - No. of Units: Company Owned: 17 - Franchised: 3 - Franchise Fee: $38,000 - Royalty: 5% - Total Inv: $350,000-$500,000.

INTERIOR MAGIC *
107 Black Forty Drive, Winston-Salem, NC, 27127. Contact: Shane Loman - Tel: (336) 788-2775, (888) 227-6826, Fax: (336) 788-9775, E-Mail: info@myinteriormagic.com, Web Site: www.myinterior magic.com. Mobile business that offers expert repair and redyeing of leather, vinyl, plastic and carpet. Established: 2001 - Franchising Since: 2003 - No. of Units: Company Owned: 6 - Franchise Fee: $14,900-$29,000 - Financing: No.

INTERNATIONAL CENTER FOR ENTREPRENEURIAL DEVELOPMENT (ICED)
12715 Telge Road, Cypress, TX, 77429. Contact: V. P. Franchise Sales - Tel: (888) 280-2053, (281) 256-4100, Fax: (281) 373-4450, E-Mail: info@iced.net, Web Site: www.iced.net. A franchising parent company with six separate franchises. ICED has over 1,000 franchises in 21 countries, with it's first company, Kwik Kopy Printing, now 30 years old. Known for its premier and legendary training/support facility, on a 125 acre campus, with over 150 employees. The purpose of ICED is entrepreneurial and franchising development.

ISOLD IT *
129 N. Hill Ave., #202, Pasadena, CA, 91106. - Tel: (626) 584-0440, Fax: (626) 584-6540, Web Site: www.i-soldit.com. A chain of ebay drop off stores that makes it easy for anyone to sell their things on ebay. Established: 2003 - Franchising Since: 2003 - No. of Units: Company Owned: 1 - Franchised: 7 - Franchise Fee: $15,000 - Royalty: 4% - Total Inv: $57,300 - Financing: Third party.

ITEX *
3625 132nd Ave, SE, Suite 200, Bellevue, WA, 98006. - Tel: (425) 463-4000, Fax: (425) 463-4040, Web Site: www.itex.com. Largest retail trade and barter exchange. Over 14,000 businesses in over 80 offices in the U.S. and Canada have discovered how ITEX helps them increase sales, reduce cash expenses, open new markets, move idle inventory, and build cash profits. Established: 1982 - Franchising Since: 2003 - No. of Units: Company Owned: 4 - Franchise Fee: $10,000 - Royalty: Varies - Total Inv: $15,900-$31,000.

JET-BLACK SEALCOATING & REPAIR
Jet-Black International, Inc.
25 Cliff Rd W #103, Burnsville, MN, 55337-1690. Contact: Fran. Dev. - Tel: (952) 890-8343, (888) 538-2525, Fax: (952) 890-7022. Blacktop driveway maintenance service (sealcoating, hot crack filling, heat treat oil spots, and patching). Established: 1988 - Franchising Since: 1992 - No. of Units: Franchised: 65 - Franchise Fee: $20,000 - Royalty: 8% - Total Inv: $23,000 incl. fran. fee - Financing: Will finance equipment.

KOTT KOATINGS INC.
27161 Burbank, Foothill Ranch, CA, 92610. Contact: John M. Kott - Tel: (714) 770-5101. Porcelain and fiberglass refinishing on location of tub, sinks, tile, counters, showers and fiberglass. Established: 1955 - Franchising Since: 1973 - No. of Units: Company Owned: 1 - Franchised: 400 - Franchise Fee: $10,000 - Total Inv: $19,995 - Financing: O.A.C.

LEATHER MEDIC
11532 Mahogany Run, Ft. Myers, FL, 33913. - Tel: (888) 561-0423, Fax: (239) 561-2136, Web Site: www.leathermedic.com. Mobile service specializing in leather repair and refinishing. Established: 1988 - No. of Units: Company Owned: 7 - Franchised: 35 - Franchise Fee: $29,500.

LOGAN FARMS HONEY GLAZED HAMS
Logan Farms, Inc.
10560 Westheimer, Houston, TX, 77042. - Tel: (713) 781-4335, Fax: (713) 977-0532. Retail gourmet meats. Established: 1984 - Franchising Since: 1985 - No. of Units: Company Owned: 2 - Franchised: 7 - Franchise Fee: $25,000 - Royalty: 4% - Total Inv: $362,900-$413,900 - Financing: No.

LYONS & WOLIVAR INVESTIGATIONS
23332 Mill Creek R., #200, Laguna Hills, CA, 92653. - Tel: (949) 305-7383, Fax: (949) 305-7864, E-Mail: scottc@lyonswolivar.com, Web Site: www.lyonswolivar.com. Private investiagtion services. Established: 2002 - Franchising Since: 2002 - No. of Units: Company Owned: 1 - Franchised: 1 - Franchise Fee: $105,000-$210,000 - Royalty: 7% - Total Inv: $100,000-$200,000 - Financing: No.

M & A SHAW, INC.
P.O. Box 22271, Houston, TX, 77227-2271. Contact: Marvin Shaw, President - Tel: (713)728-3882, Fax: (713)721-5177, E-Mail: AShaw1026@aol.com. Importing/exporting program for people without any experience or very little experience that want to start from home part or full time. The program teaches in simple every day language and gives them contacts (leads) and exposure in 120 countries. Established: 1984 - Total Inv: The membership includes a complete program. Total most expensive investment under $400 US. - Financing: No.

MARGIES CUSTOM BASKETS
May Wright Co., Inc.
3330 W. Court, Ste. L, Pasco, WA, 99301. - Tel: (509) 544-2864, (877) 544-2864, Fax: (509) 545-3110, E-Mail: margiesbasket@juno.com. Design and wrap baskets for car dealers and other businesses. Established: 1995 - Franchising Since: 1997 - No. of Units: Company Owned: 1 - Franchised: 2 - Franchise Fee: $7,500 - Royalty: $1 per basket - Total Inv: $9,500 - Financing: In some cases.

MARTEK LTD.
P.O. Box 15160, Dept. IF, Charlotte, NC, 28211. - Tel: (704) 364-7213, (704) 364-7253. Market the guide book web site tips for smartie pants. Established: 1980 - Franchising Since: 1991 - No. of Units: Company Owned: 1 - Franchised: 10 - Franchise Fee: $49.95 - Royalty: None - Total Inv: $49.95 - Financing: No.

MATS, FLOORS & MORE
978 Hermitage Rd., NE, Rome, GA, 30161. Contact: John C. Hoglund, President - Tel: (706) 295-4111, (800) 328-9203, Fax: (706) 295-4114, E-Mail: johnc@roman.net, Web Site: www.matsfloorsmore.com. Selling mats & matting & specialty flooring. Established: 1998 - Franchising Since: 1998 - No. of Units: Company Owned: 1 - Franchise Fee: $15,000 - $26,000 - Royalty: 5% - Total Inv: None - Financing: Possible.

MELCO EMBROIDERY SYSTEMS
1575 W. 124th Ave., Denver, CO, 80234. - Tel: (303) 457-1234, Fax: (303) 252-0508. Manufacturer and supplier of computerized personalization equipment and supplies: embroidery, chenille, and digitizing, scanning and editing of designs, for entrepreneurs who want to start their own businesses in home, retail store, or wholesale shop. Established: 1972 - Total Inv: From $10,000 up for equipment - Financing: Lease purchase plans available.

METAL SUPERMARKETS
Metal Supermarkets International
700 Sarasota Quay, Sarasota, FL, 34236. Contact: Peter Rutledge, Manager-Franchise Development - Tel: (941) 951-1320, (888) 734-1828, Fax: (941) 954-0364, E-Mail: rutledgep@compuserve.com, Web Site: www. metalsupermarkets.com. World franchise leader in the small quantities metal business. Established: 1985 - Franchising Since: 1987 - No. of Units: Company Owned: 18 - Franchised: 50 - Franchise Fee: $38,000 - Royalty: 6% gross sales - Total Inv: $220,000 total, $100,000-$110,000 cash - Financing: No.

MOBILE CONTAINER SERVICE
Mobile Container Service, Inc.
3820 Premier Ave., Memphis,TN, 38118. Contact: Fran. Dir. - Tel: (901) 368-3361, Fax: (901) 368-1144. A business specializing in refurbishing, repainting, and refinishing waste recycling,trash dumpsters and containers. Established: 1983 - Franchising Since: 1991 - No. of Units: Company Owned: 1 - Franchised: 42 - Franchise Fee: $15,000 - Total Inv: $29,800-$52,000 - Royalty: 6%, 1% adv. - Financing: Yes..

MOBILE-MECHANIC
2329 N. 500 W, Layton, UT, 84041. Contact: Denis Thurgood - Tel: (801) 564-3311, Fax: (801) 774-6400. Mobile repair center. Established: 2001 - Franchising Since: 2001 - No. of Units: Franchised: 2 - Franchise Fee: $38,500-$49,900.

MR.CIGAR, INC
International Industries, Inc
6413 Congress Ave. St.240, Boca Raton, FL, 33487. - Tel: (561) 988-0819, (888) 82-cigar. Cigar vending humidor-cedar lined and kept at approx 70 degress for freshness. Mr.Cigar is the worlds first franchised vending humidor with the ability to offer fresh quality cigars 24 hours a day. Prices range from $2.00-$25.00 per cigar. Established: 1997 - Franchising Since: 1998 - No. of Units: Company Owned: 31 - Total Inv: $5,000-$100,000 - Financing: Yes.

MY GIRL FRIDAY *
My Girl Friday
1776 Mentor Avenue, Cincinnati, OH, 45212. Contact: Julie Hagenmaier, CEO - Tel: (513) 531-4475, Fax: (513) 631-3693, E-Mail: franchise@egirlfriday.com, Web Site: www.egirlfriday.com. We provide services that take care of the tedious and time consuming portion of your day. A Girl Friday will do your laundry, pick up your groceries and prep your dinner all while waiting for the cable guy or your furniture to be delivered. Picking up your dry-cleaning, taking your car in for an oil change or the cat to the vet are all requests that make your life easier. With the true concept of the personal assistant, My Girl Friday works with each individual to develop a plan of action that enables a client to feel as if they have accomplished the task themselves. Established: 1999 - Franchising Since: 2004 - No. of Units: Franchise Fee: $31,500 - Royalty: 6% roylaty; 2% national marketing fund - Total Inv: $46,000-$86,000 - Financing: No.

NATGO, INC.
15965 Jeanette St., Southfield, MI, 48075. - Tel: (248) 557-2784. If you are a marina or current business owner and are looking for an extra product line, Natgo Inc. invites you to join them in an exciting new adventure as natural gas, the fuel of the future, is introduced into American boats and automobiles through innovative technology. Established: 1991 - Franchising Since: 1993 - No. of Units: Franchised: 1 - Franchise Fee: $25,000 - Royalty: 7% - Total Inv: $230,000-$1,000,000 - Financing: No.

NATIONAL AUTO/TRUCKSTOPS INC.
24601 Center Ridge Rd., Ste. 300, WestLake, OH, 44145-5600. Contact: Franchise Department - Tel: (800) 688-1276, Fax: (800) 688-1276. Full service interstate travel plazas. Established: 1950 - Franchising Since: 1993 - No. of Units: Company Owned: 97 - Franchised: 105 - Franchise Fee: $80,000 - Royalty: Variable - Financing: Yes.

NATIONAL TELE-COMMUNICATIONS
Parcel Consultants Inc.
300 Broadacres Dr., Bloomfield, NJ, 07003. Contact: Mark Allen DeLanay, Franchise Development - Tel: (201) 338-1200, Fax: (201) 338-0222. Access discounts on all major carriers. Established: 1984 - Franchising Since: 1988 - No. of Units: Company Owned: 1 - Franchised: 350 - Franchise Fee: $14,500 - Financing: No.

NATIONAL TRADE EXCHANGE
P.O. Box 180325, Dallas, TX, 75218-0325. - Tel: (214) 320-8227, Fax: (214) 328-6990. Barter and trading among businesses using computerized network select and approve. Established: 1981 - Franchising Since: 1983 - Franchise Fee: $5,000 - Total Inv: $5,000 - Financing: Yes.

NATURE'S REFLECTIONS
Nature's Reflections Inc.
3375 Buckinghammock Trail, Vero Beach, FL, 32960. - Tel: (561) 778-8343, Fax: (561) 778-8343. Established: 1995 - Franchising Since: 1995 - No. of Units: Franchised: 1 - Franchise Fee: $15,000 - Royalty: 5% - Total Inv: Low-$60,000; high-$120,000.

NITE TIME DECOR
Nite Time Decor, Inc
P.O. Box 5183, Lubbock, TX, 79408. - Tel: (806) 722-4242, (800) 987-9551, Fax: (806) 722-9627, E-Mail: info@nitetimedecor.com, Web Site: www.nitetimedecor.com. Landscape and architectural lighting design and installation services, offering premium quality products. Established: 1999 - Franchising Since: 1999 - No. of Units: Franchised: 60 - Franchise Fee: $9,500-$15,900 - Royalty: 2%-4.5% - Total Inv: $15,900-$31,900 - Financing: Yes.

NORTH AMERICAN FLORAL, INC
1154 Audubon Rd, Grosse Pointe Farms, MI, 48230-1439. Contact: Faye Gmeiner, President - Tel: (313) 885-3581. Recyclers of pottery, glass, plastic, ceramic and wicker floral containers. Established: 1996 - Franchising Since: 1998 - No. of Units: Company Owned: 1 - Franchise Fee: $8,000 - Royalty: 10% of gross revenues - Total Inv: $13,000-$17,000 Franchise Fee/Included .

NORTHWEST AQUIFER SURVEYING
P.O. Box 123, Adna, WA, 98522. Contact: Christine E. Kraemer, President - Tel: (360) 740-6446, (866) 740-6446, Fax: (866) 422-5357, E-Mail: ckraemer@findwellwater.com, Web Site: www.findwellwater.com. Franchises map & locate well water (aquifer depth, yield and quality) before a well is drilled using state of the art proven electrosiesmic technology developed in England by two BP geologist. Our franchises are the authority in ground water assesment mapping and location. Established: 2001 - Franchising Since: 2002 - No. of Units: Company Owned: 1 - Franchised: 14 - Franchise Fee: $15,000-$25,000 - Royalty: $300.00 minimum or 4% 1st yr, 5% 2nd yr, 6% remainder of 10 year contract - Total Inv: Franchise fee, depending on location, equipment $38,000-$80,000 - Financing: No.

NOVA CULTURAL DIVERSITY TESTING INC.
Nova Media Unit
1724 N. State, Big Rapids, MI, 49307-9073. - Tel: (231) 796-4637. Racial attitude testing and racial diversity training. Plus cultural diversity testing (sexual harrassment, vulnerability) Racial attitude test (reviewed in Mental Measurements Yearbook 1990) and Racial Attitude survey PC windows 3.1 the software version. Data can be used as legal evidence in racial discrimination and sexual harrassment cases. Also internet/intranet testing capability. Established: 1987 - Franchising Since: 1996 - No. of Units: Company Owned: 1 - Franchised: 1 - Franchise Fee: $10,000 - Royalty: 5% - Total Inv: $50,000 - Financing: Yes.

NUMARKETS *
816 Tennessee Ave., Etowah, TN, 37331. Contact: David Boehm, Franchise Director - Tel: (423) 263-5211, Fax: (423) 263-5499, Web Site: www.numarkets.com. Numarkets is the pioneer of eBay selling and shipping. Centers help the public and business with a new way of selling items. Established: 2002 - Franchised: 2004 - No. of Units: Company Owned: 1 - Franchised: 5 - Franchise Fee: $28,900 - Royalty: 4.7% - Total Inv: $103,000-$150,000.

OMNI PRODUCTS
Chronomite Laboratories, Inc
1420 West 240th Street, Harbor City, CA, 90710. Contact: Robert Russell Jr., Marketing Director - Tel: (310) 534-2300, (800) 447-4962, Fax: (310) 530-1381. Water and energy conservation distributorships. Established: 1966 - Franchising Since: 1997 - No. of Units: Franchised: 125 - Total Inv: $2000 - Total Inv: $15,000 - Financing: Yes.

PARADISE WIRELESS
The Paradise International Connections, Inc.
10582 Grove Place, Cooper City, FL, 33328. Contact: Ed/Sharon Pudleine, Owners - Tel: (954) 434-9971, Fax: (954) 983-1966. Telecommunication sales and services. Full training and support provided. Established: 1993 - Franchising Since: 1996 - No. of Units: Company Owned: 2 - Franchised: 1 - Franchise Fee: $29,900 for license - Financing: Yes.

PARAGRAVE CORP.
507 Commerce Rd, Orem, UT, 84058-5899. Contact: Franchise Department - Tel: (800) 624-7415, (801) 225-8300. Ultra high speed engraving system that turns even non-artists into engraving professionals. Established: 1983 - No. of Dealers: 4000+ - Franchise Fee: None - Royalty: None - Total Inv: $2,999 - Financing: None.

PARTY 123
Eventscape America
400 Perrine Rd., Ste. 400B, Oldbridge, NJ, 08857. Contact: John Murphy, Franchise Development - Tel: (732) 316-0665, Fax: (732) 316-0673. We can make any party a success - we supply DJ, Video and photo - full training and ongoing support provided. Established: 1996 - Franchising since: 1998 - No. of Units: Company Owned: 1 - Franchised: 2 - Franchise Fee: $19,500 - Total Inv: $68,000-$99,000 - Financing: None.

PARTY AMERICA
980 Atlantic Ave, 103, Alameda, CA, 94501. - Tel: (516) 747-1800, Fax: (510) 747-1810, E-mail: franchising@partyamerica.com.. Party supplies and balloons at discount prices - full training and support provided. Established: 1976 - Franchising Since: 1978 - No. of Units: Company Owned: 18 - Franchised: 15 - Franchise Fee: $25,000 - Royalty: 4% - Total Inv: $250,000-$300,000.

PAWN MART, INC
6300 Ridglea Pl #724, Fort Worth, TX, 76116-5730. Contact: Robert Bourland, President - Tel: (817) 569-9305, (800) 729-6261, Fax: (817) 569-1062, E-Mail: rbourlan@gte.net, Web Site: www.pawnmart.com. Pawn Mart is a public traded specialty retail enterprises that: 1) sells pre-owned merchandise, 2) buys pre-owned merchandise, 3) loans money secured by the pledge of merchandise. Established: 1995 - No. of Units: Company Owned: 24 - Franchise Fee: $25,000 - Royalty: 5% of gross revenues - Total Inv: $250,000-$450,000 - Financing: Yes.

PERFORMAHOME
Intellitricity, Inc.
317 HWY, 620 S. 2nd Floor, Austin, TX, 78734. - Tel: (512) 267-2672, (800) 944-6873, Fax: (512) 263-5499. Home automation dealership network. Comprehensive training, one-stop and on-going support of dealers. Total remote and automatic control of lighting, HVAC, security, home theatre, computers, etc by push button, phone or voice! Established: 1987 - Franchising Since: 1991 - No. of Units: Company Owned: 1 - Franchised: 2047 - Franchise Fee: $6,900-$9,900 - Total Inv: $10,000-$15,000 - Financing: Some.

PLANET EARTH RECYCLING OIL FILTER RECYCLING INC.
7928 State Rd., P.O. Box 65311, Philadelphia, PA, 19155-5311. Contact: Barry Guss, Pres. - Tel: (800) 471-4684, Fax: (800) 471-4684. Mobile antifreeze recycling. Established: 1990 - Franchising Since: 1995 - No. of Units: Company Owned: 1 - Franchised: 2 - Franchise Fee: $10,000 - Royalty: 3% of gross sales - Total Inv: $60,000-$85,600 - Financing: With good credit & $20,000, balance can be financed.

PLUMBING M.D.
Fast Aid Franchise Corp.
752 L Stree, Davis, CA, 95616-3942. Contact: Mike Farias, Pres. - Tel: (916) 658-8483. Plumbing service and repair, sewer and drain cleaning. Established: 1984 - Franchising Since: 1995 - No. of Units: Franchised: 1 - Franchise Fee: $10,000-$15,000 - Royalty: 7% - Total Inv: $15,000-$50,000 - Financing: No.

POOL FRANCHISE SERVICE (PFS)
P.O. Box 18877, San Jose, CA, 95156-8877. - Tel: (408) 321-8483, (800) 399-4070. The nations only franchised swimming pool service and repair franchise. Established: 1983 - Franchising Since: 1995 - No. of Units: Franchised: 30 - Franchise Fee: $14,950 - Royalty:4%-8% - Total Inv: $5,000-$15,000 - Financing: No.

PORT-A-PITT FOOD SERVICE SYSTEM
T.G. Corp.
602 Maple Ln, Wakarusa, IN, 46573-9302. Contact: Tod Gongwer - Tel: (219) 862-2184, Fax: (219) 862-2434. Full service catering and fund raising operations. Full training and support provided. Established: 1968 - Franchising Since: 1995 - No. of Units: Company Owned: 1 - Franchised: 2 - Franchise Fee: $10,000-$30,000 - Total Inv: $30,000-$160,000 - Financing: No.

POSITIVE CHANGES HYPNOSIS *
192 Ballard Court, Suite 305, Virginia Beach, VA, 23462. - Tel: (757) 499-0047, Fax: (757) 499-1029, Web Site: www.positivechanges.com. Only organized franchise network of centers specifically designed to utilize hypnosis in bringing about lasting behavior modification and lifestyle changes for consumers seeking weight loss, smoking cancellation, pain control, stress reduction, phobia management and more. Established: 2002 - Franchising Since: 2003 - No. of Units: Company Owned: 1 - Franchised: 35 - Franchise Fee: $29,500 - Total Inv: $150,000-$250,000.

PROFESSIONAL POLISH
Professional Polish Inc.
5450 E. Loop 820 S., Fort Worth, TX, 76119. Contact: Carren Cavanaugh, Pres. - Tel: (817) 446-9696, Fax: (817) 315-4660, Web Site: www.professionalpolish.com. Commercial cleaning services, lawn maintenance and light building maintenance. Established: 1982 - Franchising Since: 1986 - No. of Units: Company Owned: 2 - Franchised: 34 - Franchise Fee: $4,500 - Royalty: 15% - Total Inv: $20,000 - Financing: Yes.

PROPERTY DAMAGE APPRAISERS
Property Damage Appraisers, Inc.
6100 Southwest Blvd., Ste. 200, Ft. Worth, TX, 76109. - Tel: (800) 749-7324, Fax: (817) 731-5565. Provide automobile and property appraisals for insurance companies and self-insureds. Automobile damage appraising experience a prerequisite. National marketing support and ongoing management assistance. Established: 1963 - Franchising Since: 1963 - No. of Units: Franchised: 258 - Royalty: 15% - Total Inv: $9,250-$23,450 start up costs.

PROTEAM
Safe Not Sorry
421 West Union Ave., Bound Brook, NJ, 08805. Contact: Dir. Fran. Sales. - Tel: (888) 469-3900, Fax: (732) 469-7405, E-Mail: jgranito@safenotsorry.com, Web Site: www.safenotsorry.com. The home safety people - child proofing, senior well being home care and pet control. Established: 1988 - Franchising Since: 1997 - No. of Units: Franchised: 22 - Franchise Fee: $10,000 - Royalty: 8%, 2% adv - Total Inv: $20,750-$49,000 - Financing: Yes - 100% in most states.

PROTECT PAINTERS
831 Beacon Street, #322, Newton Center, MA, 02459. Contact: Wayne Scherger - Tel: (800) 824-8881, (888) 464-4242, Fax: (800) 746-8563. Painting business. Established: 1995 - No. of Units: Franchised: 7 - Franchise Fee: $12,500 - Financing: Yes.

PROTOCOL
1370 Mendota Hts. Rd., Mendota Hts., MN, 55120. Contact: Brett McKay, V.P. - Tel: (800) 227-5336, (651) 454-0518, Fax: (651) 454-9542. Manufacture four models of personal product vending machines that can dispense any combination of more than 30 products, i.e., condoms, aspirins, tampons, fragrances, etc. Established: 1987 - Franchising Since: 1987 - No. of Units: Franchised: 18,000 - Franchise Fee: None - Royalty: None - Total Inv: $10,000 equip. & products - Financing: Yes, lease program following initial investment.

R.J. PERSSON ENTERPRISES, INC
P.O. box 2069, Montrose, CO, 81402-2069. Contact: Richard J. Persson, President - Tel: (970) 249-6000, Fax: (970) 249-0800. Mailing lists of opportunity seekers. Established: 1982.

RAINSHADOW LABS
P.O. Box 1125 Seappoose, OR, 97056. Contact; Casey Kellar - Tel: (503) 543-3413, Fax: (503) 543-3416, E-Mail: ckellar@colcenter.org, Web Site: www.rainshadowlabs.com. Private label manufacturer of bath/body, spa/salona romatherapy Products. R&D customizing available. Establised: 1983.

RASPBERRY JUNCTION™
R.J. Ventures, Inc.
417 Norwich Westerly Rd.. P.O. Box 306, N. Stononington, CT, 06359. Contact: Ann/Dwight Ketelhut, Franchise Development - Tel: (860) 535-0324, Fax: (860) 535-8057. Landlord to various artisans and craftsmen. Established: 1991 - Franchising Since: 1996 - No. of Units: Company Owned: 1 - Franchised: 1 - Franchise Fee: $17,000 - Total Inv: $95.00-$225.00.

REGUS BUSINESS CENTRES
555 North Point Centre E., 4th Fl., Alpharetta, GA, 30022. - Tel: (866) 734-8748, (678) 366-5000, Fax: (678) 366-5001, Web Site: www.regus.com. Office space an business support centers. Established: 1989 - Franchising Since: 2001 - No. of Units: Company Owned: 409 - Franchise Fee: $50,000 - Royalty: 6% - Total Inv: $243,000-$989,800.

RELOCATION STRATEGIES
Relo Franchise Services/Relocation Strategies
17 East 8th Street, Suite 100, Cincinnati, OH, 45202. Contact: Timothy Haines - Tel: (513) 651-2332, Fax: (513) 651-0860, E-Mail: relostrat1@aol.com, Web Site: www.relocationstrategies.net. Commercial relocation, move project management and consulting services. Established: 1994 - Franchising Since: 2002 - No. of Units: Company Owned: 1 - Franchised: 3 - Franchise Fee: $18,500-$32,500 - Royalty: .5%-6% - Financing: Yes.

RICH PLAN
Rich Plan Corp.
4981 Commercial Dr., Yorkville, NY, 13495. Contact: R. Bruce Evans, Chairman - Tel: (800) 243-1358, Fax: (315) 736-7597. Each franchisee provides its customers with various food analysis services and offers a line of high quality, prepackaged, perishable frozen food items ordered from a price list, food guide or menu planner and delivered directly to the customer at home. A franchisee also markets freezers and cookware for use by its customers. Established: 1946 - Franchising Since: 1952 - No. of Units: Franchised: 19 - Franchise Fee: $10,000 - Royalty: $10 each new customer for 100 each month, $5 on 101st and each thereafter each month - Total Inv: $25,000-$50,000: $10,000 fran. fee, $15,000 inven. - Financing: None.

ROBINSON EXPOSITIONS
17670 Heron Ln, Fort Myers, FL, 33907. - Tel: (941) 415-7911, Fax: (941) 415-7912. Franchised producers of regional expose. Established: 1995 - Franchise Fee: $9,995.

SAFE-STRIDE INTERNATIONAL INC.
6549 Golden Horseshoe Dr, Largo, FL, 33777-4729. Contact: R.E. Colfels, President - Tel: (800) 646-3005, Fax: (727) 399-0188. Slip resistive safety floor treatment. Slip resistive cleaner degreasers. Established: 1985 - Franchising Since: 1995 - No. of Units: Company Owned: 1 - Franchised: 18 - Franchise Fee: $11,500 - Royalty: 5% gross sales - Total Inv: $11,500 plus inventory $904 - Financing: Yes, $5,000.

SALSBURY MAILBOXES
125 Louis St, South Hackensack, NJ, 07606-1735. - Tel: (201) 229-5897, Fax: (201) 329-7272. Manufacturer of mailboxes for private mail/postal centers that offer mailbox rentals. Established: 1936 - Total Inv: $500-$5,000 - Financing: No.

SEAGA MANUFACTURING CORPORATION
700 Seaga Drive, Freeport, IL, 61032. - Tel: (813) 297-9500, Fax: (815) 297-1700. Manufacturer and supplier of vending equipment (specifically Super Vend 2000, Super Snack 900C, Super Snack 1800, Super Snack 2700, Super Bite, and Double Play.) Established: 1987 - Financing: Yes.

SEALMASTER
SealMaster
P.O. Box 2218, Sandusky, OH, 44870. Contact: Franchise Department - Tel: (419) 626-4375, (800) 395-7325, Fax: (419) 626-5477. Manufacture pavement sealers and supply pavement maintenance products and equipment. Established: 1969 - Franchising Since: 1993 - No. of Units: Company Owned: 2 - Franchised: 17 - Franchise Fee: $35,000 - Royalty: 5% - Total Inv: $225,500-$426,000 - Financing: Possible on start-up equip.

SHOESMITH/SHOEFIXERS
1884 Breton Rd. S.E., #201, Grand Rapids, MI, 49506. - Tel: (800) 335-5894, (616) 785-5140. Instant shoe repair and shoe care. Established: 1987 - Franchising Since: 1987 - No. of Units: Franchised: 45 - Franchise Fee: $12,500 - Royalty: 5% - Total Inv: $32,000-$90,000 (excl. fran. fee) - Financing: None - will assist.

SIGNATURE LANDSCAPE LIGHTING
P.O. Box 355, Novi, MI, 48376. - Tel: (248) 347-1117, Fax: (248) 344-1761, Web Site: www.signaturelights.com. Exterior residential lighting systems. Established: 1995 - Franchising Since: 2001 - No. of Units: Company Owned: 1 - Franchise Fee: $40,000 - Royalty: 5% - Total Inv: $59,500.

SOMETHING SPECIAL
20 Douglas Ave, Wilmington, MA, 01887. - Tel: (978) 658-8484, Fax: (978) 658-7215. Seasonal home craft parties. Established: 1981 - No. of Units: Franchised: 5 - Franchise Fee: $8,000.

SPECIALTY DATA
Specialty Data, Inc
273 E. Lanier Ave, Fayetteville, GA, 30214. Contact: Kaylene Canfield Director - Tel: (770)719-8338, Fax: (770)716-8322, E-Mail: franchise@specialtydata.com, Web Site: www.specialtydata.com. Data collection and management for registries. Established: 1993 - Franchising Since: 1999 - No. of Units: Company Owned: 1 - Franchise Fee: $15,000 - Royalty: 8% of gross revenue or $250.00 per month whichever is greater - Total Inv: $15,000 franchise fee plus $3,000-$5,000 start-up - Financing: No.

STARR GIFT BASKETS
7135 W. Tidwell #114, Houston, TX, 77092. Contact: Carol Starr - Tel: (713) 956-5190. Hame based gift basket business. Established: 1987 - Franchising Since: 2001 - No. of Units: Company Owned: 1 - Franchised: 1 - Franchise Fee: $500.

STENCIL HOME GALLERY
2300 Pilgrim Rd., Brookfield, WI, 53005, Contact: Sandra Barker, Franchise Development - Tel: (414) 797-9974. Decorative stencils, home furnishings. Full training and support provided. Established: 1988 - No. of Units: Company Owned: 2 - Franchise Fee: $15,000 - Total Inv: $50,000-$100,000.

SUPPLY MASTER USA
Master Supply Systems International, Inc
6C White Deer Plaza, Sparta, NJ, 07871. Contact: Bert Owens, President - Tel: (973) 729-5006, (800) 582-1947, Fax: (973) 729-1975, E-Mail: supplymasterusa@juno.com, Web Site: www.supplymasterusa.com. Unique mobile distribution service providing unlimited commercial and industrial product opportunities. Provides the freedom, rewards and personal satisfaction of being "Your Own Boss" on a full or part-time bases. Established: 1989 - Franchising Since: 2001 - No. of Units: Company Owned: 1 - Franchised: 2 - Franchise Fee: $4,500-$10,000 - Total Inv: $4,950-$18,900 - Financing: No.

SURVEY AMERICA, INC
1440 Gene St, Winter Park, FL, 32789. Contact: Reg Shrigley, President - Tel: (407) 644-POLL, Fax: (407) 644-1USA, E-Mail: shrigley@att.net, Web Site: www.survey-america.com. Market research, survey software/hardware allowing faster, more accurate data gathering with instant reporting capability. Established: 1976 - Franchising Since: 1990 - No. of Units: Company Owned: 1 - Franchised: 24 - Franchise Fee: $25,000-$100,000 (site dependent) - Royalty: Varies - Total Inv: $25,000-$100,000 - Financing: 100%.

SUSPENDED IN TIME
225 S. 600 East, Alpine, UT, 84004. Contact: Lee Gerlach - Tel: (866) 756-0059, (801) 772-0377, Fax: (801) 756-0059. Preserving flower arrangements. Established: 1997 - No. of Units: Company Owned: 1 - Franchised: 5 - Franchise Fee: $18,000 - Financing: Yes. NOT FRANCHISING AT THIS TIME.

SWIM EEZY USA, INC
Division of Swim Eesy, USA
P.O. Box 42506, Portland, OR, 97242-0506. Contact: John George - Tel: (503) 848-6447, (503) 701-6170, Fax: (503) 848-6447. Sun and swim safety products. Established: 1989 - No. of Units: Company Owned: 1 - Franchised: 8 - Total Inv: From $500.00 depending on area - Financing: None.

SWING SYNC
Business Golf Assc.
4711 NE 50th St, Seattle, WA, 98105-2907. Contact: James W. Smith, Pres. - Tel: 206) 524-5958, Fax: (206) 524-7826. Swing Sync licenses their system of custom golf club manufacturing. Service includes sales, marketing, custom fitting, club making and promotion. Established: 1985 - Franchising Since: 1985 - No. of Units: Company Owned: 2 - Franchised: 10 - Franchise Fee: $5,000-$15,000 depends on territory - Royalty: 2% adv. fund - Total Inv: $5,000-$15,000 - Financing: No.

T & G CRAFTS
597 Rock St., New Braunfels, TX, 78130. Contact: Geraldine Webb, Mgr. - Tel: (830) 629-6469. Specialty name plaques. Established: 1992 - Licensing Since: 1992 - No. of Units: 1 - Total Inv: Cost of plaques at wholesale - Financing: No.

TAT GONE INK
40 Fourth St #211, Petaluma, CA, 94952. Contact: Dave Rosprim - Tel: (707) 765-6091, Fax: (707) 765-1091. Reverse of tattoos. Established: 2000 - Franchising Since: 2001 - No. of Units: Franchised: 800 - Total Inv: $600.00.

TEMPACO
Tempaco, Inc.
1701 Alden Road, Orlando, FL, 32803. - Tel: (407) 898-3456, (800) 868-7838, Fax: (407) 898-7316, Web Site: www.tempaco.ca. Controls and instrumentation distributor. Established: 1946 - Franchising Since: 1968 - No. of Units: Company Owned: 5 - Franchised: 3 - Franchise Fee: $25,000 plus - Royalty: 4% of sales - Total Inv: $25,000 base - $100,000 total - Financing: No. NOT OFFERING FRANCHISES AT THIS TIME.

THE TRADES GUILD.COM
2476 Verna Court, San Leandro, CA, 94577-4223. Contact: Seth Wiles, Vice President - Tel: (888) 733-3739, Fax: (510) 875-7697, E-Mail: peter@contractonline.com, Web Site: www.ContractOnline.com. Contractor and Trader referral service. Established: 1998 - Franchising Since: 2000 - No. of Units: Company Owned: 30 - Franchise Fee: $32,800 - Total Inv: $69,790. NO LONGER FRANCHISING.

THEE CHIMNEY SWEEP, INC.
36 Vernon Rd., N.E., Rome, GA, 30165. Contact: Garry Trotter, Owner/Pres. - Tel: (706) 232-5261, E-Mail: trotters2000@earthlink.net, Web Site: www.theechimneysweep.com. Chimney cleaning and sales of wood heaters, chimney relining and accessories.

TIME + TEMPERATURE, DATELINE HOTEL, COMMUNITY INFO LINE
Electronic Voices Services, Inc
5816 Covehaven Dr, Dallas, TX, 75252. Contact: Richard Hardgrove, President - Tel: (972) 713-6622, (800) 713-8353, Fax: (972) 713-8364. Automated phone systems for advertising, information, + entertainment. Established: 1993 - Total Inv: $995-$1,995 - Financing: No.

TIPS

55 Main Street, Little Falls, NJ, 07424. Contact: Al Inga - Tel: (973) 256-5399, (888) 564-6847, E-Mail: tips@tipsdirectory.com, Web Site: www.tipsdirectory.com. NO MORE COUPONS! Patent Pending! Merchants pay only for advertising results! Free Tips issued. Magnetic swipe saving cards are used by consumers to get discounts and free rewards. Established: 1996 - No. of Units: Company Owned: 41 - Franchised: 63 - Franchise Fee: $5,000 - Total Inv: $5,000 licence fee and $2,500 working capital - Financing: Three month payout.

TOIKS CHOPPERS, INC

16869 West Sierra Hwy, Canyon Country, CA, 91351. Contact: Todd Hallberg - Tel: (310) 962-1268, Web Site: www.toikschoppers.com. Custom motorcycles. Established: 1990 - No. of Units: Company Owned: 1 - Franchised: 1 - Franchise Fee: $4,000 - Financing: No.

TRAK-1 *

6060 Richmond Ave, Suite 170, Houston, TX, 77057. - Tel: (800) 600-8999. We specialize in packaging and delivering public data background information to specific markets. Such as credit reports, criminal reports, driving records, etc. Established: 1997 - Franchising Since: 2003 - No. of Units: Company Owned: 4 - Franchised: 6 - Franchise Fee: $35,000 - Financing: Third party.

TRANSTITLE CORP.

4926 Johnson Dr, Roeland Park, KS, 66205-2902. Contact: Harold Kaseff, President - Tel: (913) 236-8051, (888) 483-4253, Fax: (913) 236-6018. Tinting of all types of vehicles. Established: 1981 - Franchising Since: 1997 - No. of Units: Franchised: 2 - Franchise Fee: $35,000 - Royalty: 6.5% - Financing: Negotiable.

TREND COATINGS, INC.

1850 Porter Lake Dr Ste 107, Sarasota, FL, 34240-7806. - Tel: (941) 923-6292, (800) 632-2063, Fax: (941) 923-5563, Web Site: www.trendsafety.com. A non-slip coatings manufacturer/applicator coatings are water based acrylic coupled with quartz and pomex aggregate. Designed for use on walkways, stairs, pool decks, patios, parking garages and anywhere a person can slip and fall. Established: 1946 - Franchising Since: 1997 - No. of Units: Company Owned: 1 - Franchised: 3 - Franchise Fee: $4,000-$100,000 - Royalty: None - Total Inv: $4,000-$100,000 - Financing: Yes.

TRIVIDEOM PRODUCTIONS INC

4754 Shavano Oak, Suite 103, San Antonio, TX, 70249. Contact: Kenneth J. Kwit, CEO - Tel: (210) 479-3456, (888) 490-8360, Fax: (210) 492-2256, E-Mail: sales@trivideom.com, Web Site: www.trivideom.com. Country's only franchise system to produce and market affordable custom video keepsakes, video greeting cards and other personal media products. New computer technology utilized to clean and restore photographs which together with slides and home movies are transformed into entertaining videos. Music, titles and proprietary effects are added. Established: 1998 - Franchising Since: 1998 - No. of Units: Company Owned: 1 - Franchised: 10 - Franchise Fee: $15,000-$97,500 - Royalty: 5% - Total Inv: From $46,550 - Financing: Third party leasing of equipment / software = $19,000.

TRULY NOLEN OF AMERICA

1126 N. Scottsdale Rd, Ste. 11, Tempe, AZ, 85281. Contact: Director of Franchising - Tel: (480) 894-0289, (800) 458-3664, Fax: (480) 894-5280, Web Site: www.trulynolen.com. Service business and pest prevention. Established: 1938 - Franchising Since: 1996 - No. of Units: Company Owned: 88 - Franchised: 14 - Franchise Fee: $35,000 - Royalty: 7% - Total Inv: $35,000 fee $25,000 equipment - Financing: Third party.

TSW, THE SIGN WASHERS INC.

P.O. Box 1907, Ferndale, WA, 98248. Contact: Doug Wilson, President - Tel: (360) 647-8545. Awning maintenance and repair - full training and support provided. Established: 1985 - Franchising Since: 1987 - No. of Units: Company Owned: 1 - Franchised: 14 - Franchise Fee: $10,000 - Financing: Yes.

TURBO LEADERSHIP SYSTEMS
Turbo Management Systems

36280 NE Wilsonville Rd, Newberg, OR, 97132. Contact: Franchise Department - Tel: (800) 574-4373, (503) 625-1867, Fax: (503) 625-2699, E-Mail: turbo@turbomgmt.com, Web Site: www.turbomgmt.com. Turbo Management Systems is a leadership development and training organization specializing in helping client companies create an empowered team where they maximize the utilization of their single most important resource, their human resource. Established: 1985 - Franchising Since: 1997 - No. of Units: Company Owned: 1 - Franchised: 2 - Franchise Fee: $29,000 - Royalty: 10% - Total Inv: $29,000-$35,000 - Financing: No.

UNCLE JOHNS & SEPTICS
M&M Sons Enterprise

20091 Hamburg, Detroit, MI, 48205. Contact: Mike Messing - Tel: (877) 489-0714, (313) 521-7032, Fax: (734) 397-2388. Servicing port johns and septic tanks. Established: 1950 - Franchising Since: 2000 - No. of Units: Company Owned: 1 - Franchised: 2 - Franchise Fee: $25,000 - Total Inv: $200,000.

UNIVERSAL TRAINING
Universal Training

900 Skokie Blvd., Ste. 104, Northbrook, IL, 60062-4014. Contact: Mary D Carolan, Senior V.P., Sales & Marketing - Tel: (847) 498-9700, (800) 726-9700, Fax: (847) 498-9608, E-Mail: information@universal training.com, Web Site: www.universaltraining.com. Universal Training provides made-to-order performance improvement solutions to companies with specialized training needs including franchises. We provide technical, interpersonal, and basic job skills training for more than 300 client organizations, many of them Fortune 1000 companies. Founded in 1968, United Training is an active member in Instructional Systems Association, the American Society for Training and Development, and the International Society for Performance Improvement.

UNLIMITED RESULTS, INC

P.O. Box 579, West Long Branch, NJ, 07764. - Tel: (732) 229-3609, Fax: (732) 229-5293, E-Mail: sales@unlimikted-results.com, Web Site: www.unlimikted-results.com. Suppliers to franchise & distributors of printing, logo apparel, imprinted promotional merchandise, office supplies, signs and banners.

VALDCO T-SHIRTS

P.O. Box 18170, Dept. FAD, 3334 W. Montrose, Chicago, IL, 60618-0170. - Tel: (773) 583-4423, Fax: (773) 583-7341. Silk screening of all imprintables (t-shirts, caps, poly bags, sweats, signs, flags, banners, P.O.P.'s). Established: 1982 - Franchising Since: 1982 - No. of Units: Company Owned: 4 - Franchised: 2 - Franchise Fee: Varies - Total Inv: Varies - Financing: No.

WESTLAND OF (NAME OF TERRITORY)
Westland Services Corporation

18 Lyman Street, Ste. K, Westborough, MA, 01581-1431. Contact: Philip G. Haddad, Peter Abdelmaseh, Pres., Mktg. Cons. - Tel: (508) 836-2600, (800) 622-0772. Westland is awarding franchises for exclusive territories to market and sell beautification and maintenance services for individual family cemetery plots anywhere in the U.S. and soon the world - for a one time fee with services performed for 25 years (shorter term contracts also available). Established: 1987 - Franchising Since: 1994 - No. of Units: Company Owned: 1 - Franchise Fee: From $19,000-$57,000 - Royalty: None - Total Inv: $50,000-$140,000 - Financing: Assistance available.

WIRELESS TOYZ

23399 Commerce Dr, B-1., Farmington Hills, MI, 48335. Contact: Richard Simtob - Tel: (866) 2-franchise, Fax: (248) 426-8440. Wireless phone accessories & satellite TV. Established: 1995 - Franchising Since: 2001 - No. of Units: Company Owned: 4 - Franchised: 13 - Franchise Fee: $20,000 - Total Inv: $85,000-$145,000.

WORKSMART INTERNATIONAL INC.
595 Blossom Road, Rochester, NY, 14610. Contact: Dir. of Fran. Dev. - Tel: (716) 654-7420, (800) 836-9948, Fax: (716) 654-9973. International supplier of training and development programs and services to local and multi-national businesses. Training, exclusive territories, curriculum and national training contracts for franchisees. Established: 1982 - Franchising Since: 1995 - No. of Units: Company Owned: 1 - Franchised: 20 - Franchise Fee: $100,000 - Royalty: 5% on all Worksmart business, 5% commission on national contracts -Total Inv: $15,000-$50,000 - Financing: Initial instalment is $10,000 balance at 10% due quarterly.

WORLD CLASS PARKING
WCP Franchising Inc.
525 Plymouth Rd Suite 319, Plymouth Meeting, PA, 19462. Contact: Gerald Eicke, Vice President - Tel: (610) 828-1908, (888) 680-7275, Fax: (610) 834-2937. World Class Parking provided parking management and valet parking services to establishments such as hotels, hospitals, condominiums, restaurants, banquet facilities, country clubs etc. Established: 1991 - Franchising Since: 1995 - No. of Units: Company Owned: 1 - Franchised: 21 - Franchise Fee: $14,500-$39,500 - Royalty: $50/wk. to a cap of $150/wk. after 3 years - Financing: No. NOT FRANCHISING AT THIS TIME.

WORLD TRAVEL PARTNERS AFFILIATE GROUP
400 Skokie Blvd, 8th Floor, Northbrook, IL, 60062. Contact: Misti Cornelius, V.P. and G.M - Tel: (847) 753-6700, (800) 775-7702, Fax: (847) 753-6730, Web Site: www.worldtravel.com. WTP Affiliates provide support programs and resources to established, market-leading agencies across the United States, that are seeking to enhance profit, gain local prestige, increase cutting-edge technology and elevate operational capabilities. Established: 1977 - Franchising Since: 1991 - No. of Units: Franchised: 53 - Franchise Fee: $5,000-$10,000 - Royalty: Based on volume - Total Inv: Based on volume - Financing: No.

WORLDWIDE INFORMATION SERVICES, INC.
P.O. Box 2302, Brandon, FL, 33509-2302. Contact: W.H. Bonneau, Pres. - Tel: (800) 581-4651. Become an information consultant, gateway to 1,000's of data sources from credit, criminals, motor vehicle and many more. Attorneys, private investigators, human resources, realtors and individuals who are seeking to find someone or check the background of the one you love before marriage. Established: 1990 - No. of Units: Company Owned: 1 - Total Inv: $12,500 - Financing: No.

YACHT SALES DEALERSHIP
Majestic Yachts Inc.
1831 NE 38th St., Apt. 402, Fort Lauderdale, FL, 33308-6203. Contact: Ray Tankersley, Pres. -Tel: (954) 537-3334. Yacht sales 46-75ft. Established: 1985 - Franchising Since: 1985 - No. of Units: Franchised: 6 - Franchise Fee: Buy 46 yacht approx. $880,000 - Total Inv: 46 ft. motoryacht less 50% - Financing: 0 down 15-20 years amortization.

CANADIAN LISTINGS

ACCOUNTING AND TAX SERVICES

ACCOUNTAX SERVICES
Accountax International Inc.
32-499 Raylawson Blvd., Brampton, ON, L6Y 4E6. Contact: General Manager - Tel: (905) 453-3220, (800) 336-2001, Fax: (905) 453-9562. Accounting, bookkeeping, taxation and financial planning. Established: 1979 - Franchising Since: 1981 - No. of Units: Company Owned: 2 - Franchised: 4 - Franchise Fee: $5,000 and sign up bonus - Royalty: 5% + 2% advertising - Total Inv: $10,000.00 Min (Depends + Flexible) - Financing: Yes.

BRIEF ROTFARB WYNBERG CAPPE
3845 Bathurst St., Ste. 402, Toronto, ON, M3H 3N2. Contact: M. Rotfarb, Partner - Tel: (416) 635-9080, Fax: (416) 635-0462. Chartered Accountant services include preparation of business plans, financing proposals, exploring business opportunities and accounting and tax planning services. Established: 1980 - No. of Units: One head office.

COLLINS BARRROW CHART. ACCOUNTANT
418 Sheridan Street, Peterborough, ON, K9H 3J9. Contact: Wes Stripling, Partner - Tel: (705) 742-3418, Fax: (705) 742-9775. Accounting, auditing, tax and business advisory services to franchisors and franchisees. Established: 1922.

COMPREHENSIVE BUSINESS SERVICES
Comprehensive Business Services of Canada
8500 Leslie St., Ste. 520, Thornhill, ON, L3T 7M8. Contact: Coleltte M. Hessenauer, V.P. Field Oper. - Tel: (905) 771-1200, (800) 561-1200, Fax: (905) 771-9060. Accountants (designation of CA, CMA, CPA, or CGA required) provide monthly accounting, tax and business consultation services to business clients. The Comprehensive Marketing System can deliver up to $75,000 in repetitive annualized (monthly) client fees. Currently processing over 20,000 monthly business clients in North America. Established: 1949 (US), 1991 (CAN) - Franchising Since: 1963 (US), 1991 (CAN) - No. of Units: Franchised: 45 - Franchise Fee: $59,500 - Royalty: 9%, 2% adv. - Total Inv: $30,000 balance of $29,500 can be financed, plus marketing services if needed - Financing: Yes.

DELOITTE & TOUCHE
181 Bay Street, Bay Wellington Tower BCE Place #1400, Toronto, ON, M5J 2V1 - Tel: (416) 601-6150, Fax: (416) 601-6151. Rajiv Mathur, Tel: (416) 512-3460. Deloitte & Touche provides a broad range of specialized services to both franchisors and franchisees, including: due diligence and franchise acquisition support, public offerings, assistance with regulatory requirements, business planning, financial planning, operations manuals, technology selection and implementation, litigation support, re-engineering, supply chain management, audit and tax planning.

DONE RIGHT ACCOUNTING
410 Registration Drive, Kelowna, BC, V4B 4T5. Contact: Susan Harrison, Fran Dev. - Tel: (888) 573-1136, Fax: (866) 957-0265. The only way to have all your accounting needs addressed is the right way. Done Right Accounting is the first and best choice for you. Established: 1985 - Franchised: 1987 - No. of Units: Company Owned: 2 - Franchised: 16 - Franchise Fee: $38,500.

E. K. WILLIAMS & CO. LTD.
EKW Systems
15 Springlake Circle, Ottawa, ON, K2S 1E2. Contact: Wayne Deane-Freeman, Pres. - Tel: (613) 836-5130, Fax: (613) 836-4637. Manual and computerized bookkeeping, accounting and tax preparation systems for small to medium sized businesses (industry specific). Financial and operational management consulting and training services. Established: 1968 - Franchising Since: 1969 - No. of Units: Company Owned: 3 - Franchised: 19 - Franchise Fee: $10,000-$25,000 - Royalty: 5% of sales - Total Inv: $50,000-$250,000 (depending on established client list and volume of business) - Financing: Yes, 50% of franchise fee; up to 50% of client list.

EAGLE TAX SERVICE
Eagle Tax Service Inc.
299 Bonnechere St., W., P.O. Box 630, Eganville, ON, K0J 1T0. Contact: Ron Watson, Pres. - Tel: (613) 628-2500, Fax: (613) 628-1259, Web Site: www.eagletax.com. Computerized income tax preparation, exclusive tax programs, full training and support backed by 30 years experience, providing reliable, accurate and friendly service to repeat

clientele. Established: 1988 - Franchising Since: 1990 - No. of Units: Company Owned: 3 - Franchised: 7 - Franchise Fee: $7,500-$12,500 depending on population - Royalty: 8% on gross sales - Total Inv: Franchising Fee + $2,500 working cap. - Financing: Some to qualified applicants.

GARY SAUL CHARTERED ACCOUNTANT
68 Prince Edward Blvd., Thornhill, ON, L3T 7E8. - Tel: (905) 886-6330, Fax: (905) 707-5763. Chartered accountant available for financial planning, accounting and tax services. Membership: CICA, OICA. Established: 1976.

GRANT THORNTON
200 Bay Street 19th Floor, Toronto, ON, M5J 2P9. Contact: Grant Thornton - Tel: (416) 366-0100, Fax: (416) 360-4949, Web Site: www.drgt.ca. Chartered accountants/business advisors, management consultants.

H & R BLOCK CANADA, INC.
4720-50 Ave, Leduc, AB, T9E 6Y6. - Tel: (780) 986-1606, Fax: (780) 986-1695. Preparation of individual tax returns and related services. Established: 1955 - Franchising Since: 1962 - No. of Units: Company Owned: 487 - Franchised: 384 - Approx. Inv: Varies - Royalty: 50/30 with items furnished by the company for operating the franchise.

HARRIS & PARTNERS, LLP
30 Wertheim Ct, Unit 20, 2nd Floor, Richmond Hill, ON, L4B 1B9. Contact: Jack Hertzberg, Partner - Tel: (905) 764-8004, Fax: (905) 764-8323, E-Mail: finestca@aol.com. Harris & Partners is a full service accounting firm, offering audit accounting, taxation and advisory services. Both franchise and independent business alike will benefit from the firms experienced and insight into a strategic approach to business management for success. Established: 1952.

HORWATH ORENSTEIN LLP
595 Bay St., Ste. 300, Toronto, ON, M5G 2C2. Contact: Dennis Epstein, Partner - Tel: (416) 596-1711, Fax: (416) 596-7894, E-Mail: depstein @hto.com, Web Site: www.hto.com. A full service accounting and auditing firm servicing entrepreneurial clients; evaluating domestic and international business and franchise opportunities; planning growth strategies and assisting financial needs. Established: 1926.

KPMG LLP
95 Mural Street, Suite 300, Richmond Hill, ON, L4B 3G2. - Tel: (905) 707-2828, Fax: (416) 777-8818. International firm offering specialized tax, financial reporting and business advisory services to both franchisors and franchisees. Member of the Canadian Franchise Association. Established: 1869.

LACE
Accountax International Inc.
32-499 Raylawson Blvd., Brampton, ON, L6Y 4E6. Contact: Mr. Vijay Kapur, General Manager - Tel: (905) 453-3220, (800) 336-2001, Fax: (905) 453-9562. Accounting, bookkeeping, taxation and financial planning. Established: 1979 - Franchising Since: 1981 - No. of Units: Company Owned: 2 - Franchised: 4 - Franchise Fee: $5,000 and sign up bonus - Royalty: 5% + 2% advertising - Total Inv: $10,000.00 Min (Depends + Flexible) - Financing: Yes.

LEDGERS PROFESSIONAL - BOOKKEEPING
P.O. Box 93067, Newmarket, NS, L3Y 8K3. Contact: Director of Operations - Tel: (905) 898-6320, E-Mail: info@ledgers.com, Web Site: www.ledgers.ca. Ledgers represents the future in accounting, taxation and business advisory services franchises. Developed by practicing Canadian chartered accountants for Canadians, our concept is simple,"professional quality service at affordable prices". Established: 1997 No. of Units: Franchised: 13 - Franchise Fee: $15,000.

LIBERTY TAX SERVICE
Tax Depot Inc.
800 Denison St, #18, Markham, ON, L3R 5M9. Contact: Jeff Dusza, Fran. Dev. Mgr. - Tel: (416) 231-0945, Fax: (416) 231-7691. Income tax preparation for individuals, including small business, farming, investments and real estate. Also operating an income tax preparation school under trade name Liberty Tax Schools. Established: 1972 - Franchising Since: 1973 - No. of Units: Company Owned: 13 - Franchised:

185 - Franchise Fee: $10,000 per territory - Royalty: 14% plus 3% advertising fee - Total Inv: $10,000-$15,000 working cap - Financing: Yes for income tax refund purchasing.

MARKET LEADERSHIP INC.
155 Rexdale Blvd., Suite 704, Etobicoke, ON, M9W 5Z8. - Tel: (416) 744-0596, Fax: (416) 744-0186. Growth strategy consulting and financial services including financing proposals, business plans, small business loans, term loans, operating lines, commercial and personal mortgages, investors/bank presentations and marketing devices. Established: 1994.

PADGETT BUSINESS SERVICES
Padgett Business Services of Canada, Ltd.
5580 Kennedy Rd., Ste. 2, Mississauga, ON, L4Z 2A9. Contact: Greg Williams, Franchise Development Mgr. - Tel: (888) 723-4388, (888) 723-4388, Fax: (514) 733-9725, E-Mail: padgett@generation.net, Web Site: www.smallbizpros.com. Accounting, counsulting and tax services for small businesses. Established: 1966 - Franchising Since: 1975 - No. of Units: Franchised: 423 - Franchise Fee: $37,500 - Royalty: 9% decreasing to 4.5% - Total Inv: $50,000 - Financing: No.

PARTNERS IN SMALL BUSINESS
50 Ronson Dr., #140, Etobicoke, ON, M9W 1B3. Contact: Jason R. Price, Glenn Lott - Tel: (416) 247-4388, Fax: (416) 247-1570. Accounting and business services. Business planning, financial planning services. Corporate and personal income tax preparation. Credit management services. Business management systems. Established: 1991 - Franchising Since: 1992 - No. of Units: Franchised: 12 - Franchise Fee: From $14,500-$40,000 full concept - Royalty: 8% services, 4% office products - Total Inv: $50,000 - Financing: Yes.

PRECISE ACCOUNTING PROFESSIONALS
1820 Lexington Drive, Suite 200, Winnipeg, MB, R1K 3A7. Contact: Shane Ross, Dir of Finance - Tel: (905) 625-2896, Fax: (905) 625-9076. We represent the finest in accounting services for all of your financial needs. If you want it done right have it done by a professional. Established: 1971 - No. of Units: Company Owned: 3 - Franchised: 12 - Total Inv: $35,000.

SMALL BUSINESS SOLUTIONS INC.
745 Mt. Pleasant Rd. Suite 203, Toronto, ON, M4S 2N4. - Tel: (416) 482-0567, Fax: (416) 482-8438. Small Business Solutions offers accounting services, business and financing plans, management consulting, tax and estate planning, Personal and Corporate financial planning and advisory services. Established: 1993.

TAAG INTERNATIONAL, INC
2420 Paliswood Rd., S.W., Calgary, AB, T2V 3P8. - Tel: (403) 238-5370. Property and business tax appeal. Established: 1987 - Franchising Since: 1995 - No. of Units: Company Owned: 1 - Franchised: 6 - Franchise Fee: $35,000 - Financing: No.

ADVERTISING AND DIRECT MAIL

4 SEASONS PUBLISHING INC.
Ste 112-9-3151, Lakeshore Road, Kelowna, BC, V1W 2S9. Contact: Glenn Thompson, Publisher - Tel: (250) 868-0728, Fax: (250) 868-0730. Publish free coupon books for tourists and residents. Established: 1997 - Franchising Since: 1998 - No. of Units: Company Owned: 6 - Franchise Fee: $50,000 - Total Inv: $50,000 - Financing: 50% at prime plus 3.

ACTION VIEW
Action View Advertising Systems Inc.
2323 Quebec Street, Ste. 210, Vancouver, BC, V5T 3A3. Contact: Chris Stringer, President - Tel: (604) 878-0200, Fax: (604) 879-8224, Web Site: www.222.actionview.ca. Sales and marketing of advertisements on franchise owned scrolling billboard signs which are situated in malls and similar high pedestrian traffic locations. Established: 1994 - Franchising Since: 1996 - No. of Units: Company Owned: 1 - Franchised: 2 - Franchise Fee: $15,000 = licence to operate 5 signs - Royalty: $230 per sign per month - Total Inv: $15,000 (F.Fee) $20,000 cost per sign - Financing: S.B.L. loans or leasing on signs.

ADCOM ADVERTISING & DESIGN
440 Reynolds St., Oakville, ON, L6J 3M4. Contact: Janice Johnston, President - Tel: (905) 845-3715, Fax: (905) 845-9515. Advertising agency providing award winning creative services to the industry. Specializing in web development. Established: 1982.

BADGE MAKER, LE BADGE
Canadian Badge Maker Ltd., The
2806 West King Edward Ave., Vancouver, BC, V6L 1T9. Contact: Paul McCrea, Pres. - Tel: (604) 733-4323, Fax: (604) 736-8419. Manufacturers of badges, award plaques and personalized corporate recognition products. Established: 1978 - Franchising Since: 1978 - No. of Units: Franchised: 16 - Franchise Fee: $25,000 incl. fee, inven., training and all equip. - Royalty: 6%, 2% adv. - Total Inv: $25,000 - Financing: 50%.

BUNGEE BANNER
671 County Road, Plantagenet, ON, K0B 1L0. Contact: Patrick Molla, Vice President - Tel: (613) 673-2672, (800) 928-6433, Fax: (613) 673-1445. Bungee Banner signs are the origination of patents in Canada and the United States that have made them successful in the sign industry estimated at over eight billion a year. Established: 1988 - Franchising Since: 1998 - No of Units: Company Owned: 1 - Franchised: 2 - Franchise Fee: $45,000 - Royalty: 10% - Total Inv: $275,000.

CAMPBELL & COMPANY STRATEGIES INC.
23195 96th Avenue, P.O. 770, Langley, BC, V1M 1Z7. Contact: Steve Campbell, APR President - Tel: (604) 888-5267, Fax: (604) 888-5269, E-Mail: mail@campbellpr.bc.ca, Web Site: www.campbellpr.bc.ca. With over 17 years experience, we are a full-service marketing, communications and public relations firm providing services to its clients in the corporate, government and association sectors.

CHC THE CHRIS HUGHES COMPANY
169 Brunswick Ave, Toronto, ON, M5S 1L6. Contact: Julie Hughes, Div of Acct Services - Tel: (416) 921-9699, Fax: (416) 921-8606, E-Mail: hughesj@globalservice.net. Full service marketing agency with special affinity for franchised businesses, the principals owned and operated a franchise. We pride ourselves in creating communicative, strategically sound brandbuilding campaigns. The majority of our clients are national franchisors such as New York Fries, First Choice Haircutters, Kernels and Proshred. Established: 1979.

COUPON BOOK, THE
4 Seasons Publishing, Inc
9-112-3151 Lakeshore Rd, Kelowna, BC, V1W 2S9. Contact: Glenn Thompson, Franchise Relations - Tel: (250) 868-0728, (877) 868-0729, Fax: (250) 868-0730, E-Mail: wwtc@silk.net, Web Site: www.thecouponbook.com. Direct mail advertising. Established: 1997 - Franchising Since: 1998 - No. of Units: Company Owned: 5 - Franchise Fee: Negotiable - Total Inv: $50,000 - Financing: Yes.

CVC PRODUCTIONS
110 Sudbury Street, Toronto, ON, M6J 3S6. - Tel: (416) 588-1445, Fax: (416) 588-3793, Web Site: www.cucprod.ca. Corporate communications including T.V. commercials, radio, training programs, corporate videos, conventions and print. Member: CFA - Established: 1976.

ECOM COMMUNICATIONS CORPORATION
501-1202 Centre Street South, Calgary, AB, T2G 5A5. - Tel: (403) 261-5000, Fax: (403) 261-4999, Web Site: www.secretshopnet.com. Marketing Research. Established: 1992.

GOOD NEWS ADVERTISING & MAILING INC.
100 The East Mall #13, Etobicoke, ON, M8Z 5X2. Contact: Fran. Dir. - Tel: (416) 503-1900, Fax: (416) 503-1210. Delivery and sales of local advertising. Provision of graphics, printing and mailing services. Coupons and flyers sent with first class mail. Established: 1984 - Franchising Since: 1989 - No. of Units: Company Owned: 4 - Franchised: 29 - Total Inv: $7,500-$25,000 depending on size of area - Financing: No.

HI-RISE COMMUNICATIONS
3-1010 Polytek St., Gloucester, ON, K1J 9H8. Contact: Diane Stuemer, President - Tel: (613) 742-6341, Fax: (613) 745-7586. Advertising in billboard displays in high rise elevators. Established: 1988 - Franchising

Since: 1996 - No. of Units: Company Owned: 1 - Franchised: 7 - Franchise Fee: $25,000-$40,000 - Royalty: None - Total Inv: $50,000-$75,000 incl. initial fee - Financing: No.

JAG COMMUNICATIONS INC.
3365 Harvester Road, Burlington, ON, L7N 3N2. Contact: Fran. Dev. - Tel: (905) 681-2177, Fax: (905) 681-6603, E-Mail: gord@jagcom.com. Advertising, public relations corporate publishing - cost effective solutions that deliver results. Established: 1988.

LOUD ADVERTISING INC.
55 King St. Suite 606, St.Catharines, ON, L2R 3H5. Contact: Fran. Dev. - Tel: (905) 682-8933, Fax: (905) 682-3951, E-Mail: loud@niagara.com. Full service advertising agency: marketing, advertising, public relations, market research, event management. Established: 1995.

MAIN MARKETING
405-625 Benton Road, Brandon, MB, R2J 4ZF. Contact: Franchise Dept. - Tel: (204) 235-0010, Fax: (204) 235-0116. A marketing group with unique strategies and approaches. Established: 1996.

MILLENNIUM RIDGE CORPORATION
6900 Airport Road, Suite 277, International Centre, P.O.Box 88, Mississauga, ON, L4V 1E8. Contact: Peter Servenis, Fran. Dev. - Tel: (905) 671-8084, Fax: (905) 671-4803, Web Site: www.millenium ridge.com. Millennium Ridge is a one-stop, full service marketing and advertising firm. A talented team of multi-disciplined experts work in partnership with their clients to effectively market their products and services and help achieve greater profitability. Established: 1996.

MJM PRODUCTIONS
44 King Street West, Hamilton, ON, L8P 1B7. Contact: Karrie Ross, Sales Director - Tel: (905) 529-9901, Fax: (905) 529-6322, E-Mail: sales@mjm-productions.com, Web Site: www.mjm.productions.com. MJM is an award-winning audio and video production house specializing in the creation of radio and television commercials and corporate videos. Established: 1983.

MOBIL' AMBITION CANADA LTD.
200 Finch Ave., West, Ste. 333, North York, ON, M2R 3W4. Contact: Victor Steinberg, Gen. Mgr. - Tel: (416) 243-6666, Fax: (416) 243-3183. A revolutionary mobile "Billboard" advertising display system that captures your markets attention as it cruises around town - "The Ad-Van". Established: 1996 - Franchising Since: 1996 - Financing: Yes.

RESULTS PROMO MARKETING, INC.
2928 Crosscurrent Drive, Mississauga, ON, L5N 6K4. Contact: Joanne Hillier, President - Tel: (905) 824-3772, Fax: (905) 824-2382. Provides full marketing services including design, print, P.O.P. promotional items and premium and incentive programs. Established: 1995.

RETAIL IMAGE & DESIGN
2300 Yonge Street, Suite 1901, Toronto, ON, M4P 1E4. Contact: Fran. Dev. - Tel: (416) 486-0551, Fax: (416) 495-1577, E-Mail: info@retailimage.com. Full service Retail Advertising Agency providing Retail Communication Strategies and Solutions to the franchising industry. Identity Programs, Image Building, Marketing, Advertising and Design, Franchise marketing kits, Point of Sale, Collateral Materials, Promotions, Direct mail, Store opening, Public relations. Established: 1998.

THE B.C. NEWSPAPER GROUP
1405 Broadway Street, Port Coquitlam, BC, V3C 6L6. - Tel: (604) 941-9696, Fax: (604) 944-0617, E-Mail: readers@metrovalleynews.com. Publishes community newspapers throughout B.C. and Alberta. Also distribution company distributing fliers and samples.

THE METRIC SYSTEM
80 Ronald Avenue, 2nd Floor, Toronto, ON, M6E 5A2. Contact: Lawrence Metrick, President - Tel: (416) 781-0151, Fax: (416) 781-8455, E-Mail: laurence@metricksystem.com, Web Site: www.metrick system.com. We develop concise marketing strategies with advertising creativity that is intriguing, powerful and relevant.

TV SHOWCASE PRODUCTS & DEMONSTRATION STORES

As Seen On TV Showcase Inc.
4917-99 Street, Edmonton, AB, T6E 4Y1. Contact: Jim R. Thomson, Marketing Dir. - Tel: (780) 430-9098, (888) 413-0088, Fax: (870) 430-9644, Web Site: www.tvshowcase.com. TV advertising products. Established: 1994 - Franchising Since: 1996 - No. of Units: Company Owned: 6 - Franchised: 11 - Franchised Fee: $15,000 - Royalty: 2% of gross - Total Inv: $120,000 - Financing: OAC.

VCR ACTIVE MEDIA

3055 Lenworth Drive, Mississauga, ON, L4X 2G3. - Tel: (905) 629-2553, Fax: (905) 629-3437, E-Mail: sales@vcractive.com, Web Site: www.vcractive.com. VCR Active Media has been an active and successful service bureau since 1985 providing clients with top quaality products, expertise and fast, reliable service. Our goal is to provide duplication, post production computer graphics, animation and multi media services by establishing a client relationship which develops into a partnership of mutual benefit and growth. Established: 1985.

WALSH & ASSOCIATES ADVERTISING INC.

One Greensboro Drive, Suite 405, Toronto, ON, M9W 1C8. Contact: Nick Bank, VP Bus. Dev. - Tel: (416) 245-6865, Fax: (416) 245-7144. Agency combines extensive experience in corporate packaged goods and retail marketing with franchise operation expertise. This integration results in creating successful marketing and advertising campaigns that build our clients business. Established: 1992.

ZIP SIGNS LTD.

5040 North Service Road, Burlington, ON, L7L 5R5. Contact: Richard Nelson, Marketing Manager - Tel: (905) 332-8332, Fax: (905) 332-9994, E-Mail: info@zipsigns.com, Web Site: www.zipsigns.com. Zip Signs has been in business for over 25 years. We operate from a 16,000 sq. ft. manufacturing facility. We design, build and service all types of signs and specialize in serving the franchise industry.

ALLERGY CONTROL

MITEBUSTERS CLEANING SERVICE

Mitebusters Cleaning Service, Inc
P.O. Box 1029, Cobourg, ON, K9A 4W5. Contact: Alan Powley, Managing Director - Tel: (905) 342-9424, (866) 377-9334, E-Mail: mitebusters@mitebusters.net, Web Site: www.mitebustersinfo.net. Mitebusters Cleaning Service removes harmful mite dust from mattresses, carpets, drapes & upholstery in residential and commercial establishments. After extraction has taken place a Dust Mite Anti Allergen treatment is applied. Established: 2001 - Franchising Since: 2001 - No. of Units: Franchised: 25 - Total Inv: $19,900 - Financing: Yes.

AUTOMOBILE RENTAL & LEASING

ASSOCIATED CANADIAN CAR RENTAL OPERATORS

A.C.C.R.O.
1 Crayton Place, Gowanstown, ON, N0G 1Y0. Contact: Sid Kenmir, Gen.Mgr. - Tel: (519) 291-3668, Fax: (519) 291-2633, E-Mail: sidk@golden.net. Help for car rental operators. Rental supplies and forms. Rental fleet insurance, loss prevention, rental procedure consultant. Group volume bonus for GM purchases and rental software programs. Established: 1986 - Franchising Since: 1986 - No. of Units: Member: 150 - Royalty: Small monthly fee.

AUTOHIRE RENT-A-CAR

Autohire Rent-A-Car Inc.
110 Skyway Ave, Toronto, ON, M9W 4Y9. Contact: Steve Reynar/ Bruce McGivern, President - Tel: (416) 213-0782, (888) 635-5372, Fax: (416) 578-9035, E-Mail: sreynar@autohire.ca, Web Site: www.auto hire.ca. Local car & truck rental company specializing in insurance replacement with a range of units from minis to hummers. Established: 1998 - Franchising Since: 2000 - No. of Units: Company Owned: 1 -

Franchised: 20+ - Franchise Fee: From $15,000-$35,000 - Royalty: $29.00 per unit - Total Inv: $100,000-$150,000 - Financing: Some financing is available.

AUTOMATED RUSTPROOF OF QUEBEC

2005 Du Centre, Ste-Rosalie, QC, J0H 1X0. Contact: Fran. Dev. - Tel: (450) 799-5336, Fax: (450) 799-4846. Automated system for rust-proofing treatments on cars, trucks and more. For automotive business. Established: 1987 - Franchising Since: 1988 - No. of Units: Company Owned: 1 - Franchised: 21 - Franchise Fee: $3,500 - Royalty: 8% - Total Inv: $50,000-$55,000. Financing: Assistance site selection, lease negotiations and advisory council provided.

BUDGET RENT A CAR OF CANADA LTD.

2501 Kenworth Rd, Nanaimo, BC, V9T 3M4. - Tel: (250) 729-2400, Fax: (250) 729-2410. Rental of cars and trucks. Established: 1962 - Franchising Since: 1962 - No. of Units: 375 - Franchise Fee: $15,000 ($500,000 credit line) - Royalty: 10% gross revenue - Total Inv: Varies.

BYWAYS RENT A CAR

Byways Automotive Group Ltd.
219 Wyse Rd, Dartmouth, NS, B3A 1N1. Contact: Brian Hicks, Franchise Manager - Tel: (902) 469-2620, Fax: (902) 463-5413. Daily car and truck rental. Market specialist, volume purchasing programs for fleet, insurance, supplies, advertising etc. Established: 1980 - Franchising Since: 1992 - No. of Units: Company Owned: 3 - Franchised: 3 - Franchise Fee: $1 - Royalty: 2.5% + admin. fee - Region/Area: Master franchise rights available - Financing: No.

DELTA RENT A CAR LTD.

279 Rothersay Ave., Saint John, NB, E2L 2L4. Contact: Fran. Dev. - Tel: (506) 634-1125, Fax: (506) 658-0665. Car sales and service rental. Full training and support provided. Established: 1979 - No. of Units: Franchised: 2 - Total Inv: Varies.

DIRECT CAR RENTALS

155 Toryork Drive Suite 7, North York, ON, M9L 1X9. - Tel: (416) 744-6989, (888) 835-0338, Fax: (416) 744-6987, E-Mail: northyork@ directcarrentals.com, Web Site: www.directcarrentals.com. Specializing in insurance replacement. We provide a wide selection of late model import and domestic vehicals to insurance companies. Established: 1998 - Franchising Since: 1999 - No. of Units: Franchised: 1 - Franchise Fee: $15,000-$40,000.

DISCOUNT CAR AND TRUCK RENTALS

Discount Car & Truck Rentals Ltd.
720 Arrow Rd., North York, ON, M9M 2M1. Contact: John Stanaitis, Dir. of Fran. Oper. - Tel: (416) 744-0123, ext. 225, Fax: (416) 744-9829. Car and truck rental, daily, weekly, monthly. Established: 1980 - Franchising Since: 1984 - No. of Units: Company Owned: 40 - Franchised: 160 - Franchise Fee: Varies by size of market - Royalty: Canada 8%, U.S.A. 6% - Total Inv: Varies - Financing: Yes.

DRIVER'S DELIGHT AUTO RENTALS

414 Autobohn Drive, Mississauga, ON, L3B 2L9. Contact: Rachel Hudson, Sales Executive - Tel: (905) 625-2896, Fax: (905) 625-9076. Drive in and check out our wide selection of cars and trucks for rent. We've got the perfect vehicle for you!! Full training and support provided. Established: 1990 - No. of Units: Company Owned: 3 - Franchised: 18 - Franchise Fee: $20,000.

FLEET RENT A CAR

1111 Finch Ave. West, Toronto, ON, M3J 2P7. Contact: Fran. Dev. - Tel: (416) 227-0249, (888) 873-3310, Fax: (416) 661-3290. Used auto leasing and business leasing. Full training and support provided. Established: 1996 - No. of Units: Franchised: 72 - Total Inv: $50,000 - Financing: 60% of total investment.

HERTZ CANADA LTD.

5403 Eglinton Ave. West, Etobicoke, ON, M9C 5K6. Contact: Charlie Mete, Franchise Director - Tel: (514) 631-7035, Fax: (514) 636-6327. Car and truck, leasing and rental. Established: 1960 - No. of Units: 170.

HOJ CAR AND TRUCK RENTALS/LEASING
HOJ Franchise Systems Ltd.
10 Strada Dr #16, Woodbridge, ON, L4L 5W2. - Tel: (905) 850-8278. Short term car and truck rentals and long term leasing. Established: 1966 - Franchising Since: 1984 - No. of Units: Franchised: 37 - Franchise Fee: $10,000-$50,000 - Royalty: 6% - Total Inv: $80,000-$150,000 - Financing: Fleet financing available.

NATIONAL CAR RENTAL
280 Attwell Dr., Etobicoke, ON, M9W 5B2. Contact: Mark Lindsey, Manager Franchise Operations - Tel: (416) 798-8802, Fax: (416) 798-4363, E-Mail: lindseym@nationalcar.com, Web Site: www.national car.com. Automobile rental. Established: 1947 - Franchising Since: 1947 - No. of Units: Company Owned: 50 - Franchised: 300 - Franchise Fee: Varies according to market area - Royalty: 8% cars, 4% trucks - Total Inv: Varies - Financing: No.

PHOENIX CAR & TRUCK RENTALS AND LEASING
328367 Alberta Corporation
207-4808 Ross Street, Red Deer, AB, T4N 1X5. Contact: William Thielle, President - Tel: (403) 314-3963, Fax: (403) 343-2623. Renting and leasing, both short and long term of vehicles. Established: 1985 - Franchising Since: 1987 - No. of Units: Company Owned: 1 - Franchised: 1 - Franchise Fee: $5,000-$100,000 - Royalty: 5% of gross - Total Inv: $75,000-$700,000 - Financing: Phoenix assists in helping to arrange financing.

RENT FOR LESS
961 Circle Drive #55, Winnipeg, MB, R3C 2K2. Contact: Fran. Dev. - Tel: (204) 235-0113. Car and truck rentals. Full training and ongoing support provided. Established: 1996 - No. of Units: Franchised: 9 - Total Inv: $35,000 min cash required.

RENT-A-WRECK
Practicar Systems,Inc.
204, 7710 5th Street, S.E., Calgary, AB, T2H 2L9. Contact: Dave Forseth - Tel: (403) 259-6666, (800) 668-8591, Fax: (403) 259-6776, E-Mail: psi@rentawreck.ca, Web Site: www.rentawreck.ca. National franchise specializing in the rental & sale of high quality, clean and dependable used vehicles at affordable rates. Established: 1976 - Franchising Since: 1978 - No. of Units: Franchised: 60 - Franchise Fee: $30,000 - Royalty: 6% - Total Inv: $100,000 unencumbered cash.

THRIFTY CAR RENTAL
Thrifty Canada, Ltd.
6050 Indian Line, Mississauga, ON, L4V 1G5. Contact: Jack Forrester, Mgr, Franchise Sales - Tel: (905) 612-1881, (800) 667-5925, Fax: (905) 612-1893. Long and short term car and truck rental and leasing. Full service franchisor supplying franchisees with fleet lease and insurance programs, a worldwide reservation system, local and national sales and marketing assistance as well as initial and ongoing training. Established: U.S. 1975, CDN. 1986 - Franchising Since: 1975 - No. of Units: Company Owned: 28 - Franchised: 129 - Franchise Fee: $8,000-$150,000 - Royalty: 5% admin., 3% nat'l. adv. - Total Inv: $80,000-$250,000 minimum capital required - Financing: Vehicle fleet leasing program.

WHEELS 4 RENT USED CAR RENTALS
Wheels 4 Rent Corp
77 Nassau Street, Toronto, ON, M5T 1M6. Contact: President - Tel: (416) 585-7782, (877) 707-2500, Fax: (416) 585-4797. Rental of used automobiles, daily, weekly and monthly. Established: 1991 - Franchising Since: 1995 - No. of Units: Company Owned: 1 - Franchised: 5 - Franchise Fee: $5,000 - Royalty: $25/vehical per month - Total Inv: $15,000-$200,000 - Financing: Yes.

AUTOMOTIVE: LUBRICATION & TUNE UP

GREAT CANADIAN OIL CHANGE
Great Canadian Oil Change Ltd., The
#9-8337 Young Road, Chilliwack, BC, V2P 4N8. Contact: Mr. Trev Weflen, President - Tel: (604) 792-6686, Fax: (604) 792-6639, Web Site: www.gcocltd@imag.net. Great Canadian Oil Changes gives having your oil changed a year "2000" experience. Affiliated with PetroCanada

+ our franchises are CAA approved. Established: 1978 - Franchising Since: 1990 - No. of Units: Franchised: 14 - Franchise Fee: $44,000 - Royalty: 6% - Total Inv: $90,000-$140,000 - Financing: Some, Royal Bank.

JIFFY LUBE
Minit-Lube Ontario Inc.
130 Dearborn Place, Waterloo, ON, N2J 4N5. Contact: Joanne Lewis, Fran. Dir. - Tel: (519) 886-0561, Fax: (519) 886-8752. Franchising Since: 1977 - No. of Units: Company Owned: 19 - Franchised: 10 - Franchise Fee: $25,000 - Royalty: 5% - Total Inv: $145,000 - Financing: Yes.

LUBEMASTER
1989 Dundas St. East, Mississauga, ON, L4M 1X1. Contact: Andrew Wanie, Pres. - Tel: (905) 629-3773, Fax: (905) 629-3864. Portable oil change units. Quick oil and lube units. Established: 1985 - Franchising Since: 1985 - No. of Units: Company Owned: 2 - Franchised: 25 - Franchise Fee: 0 - Royalty: $250/mo. - Total Inv: $100,000-$115,000 - Total Inv: $50,000 - Financing: Yes.

MINIT-TUNE & BRAKE AUTO CENTRES
Minit-Tune International Corp.
#305-1488 Hornby St., Vancouver, BC, V6Z 1X3. - Tel: (604) 684-5515, Fax: (604) 684-5517, Web Site: www.minit-tune.com. Tune-ups, lube/oil/filter, brakes and minor engine repairs. Established: 1976 - Franchising Since: 1976 - No. of Units: Franchised: 35 - Franchise Fee: $20,000 - Royalty: 5% service fee + 5% adv. - Total Inv: $95,000, fran. fee plus $50,000 equip. - Financing: On equipment.

MR. LUBE
Mr. Lube Canada Inc.
3535 Laird Rd, #4, Mississauga, ON, L5L 5Y7. Contact: Dave Blundell, V.P. Franchise Business - Tel: (905) 828-0909, Web Site: www.mr lube.com. Quick oil change and convenient, preventative automotive maintenance services. Established: 1976 - Franchising Since: 1981 - No. of Units: Company Owned: 34 - Franchised: 51 - Franchise Fee: $50,000 - Royalty: 7% - Total Inv: $250,000 ($50,000 lic. fee, $75,000 tools and equipment, $25,000 inventory, $75,000 working capital, $25,000 furniture and fixtures - Financing: Yes.

OIL CHANGERS
The Lube Factory International Inc.
A13-2285 St. Laurent Blvd, Ottawa, ON, K1G 4Z4. - Tel: (613) 224-6105, Fax: (613) 225-0704, E-Mail: headoffice@oilchangers.ca, Web Site: www.oilchangers.ca. Fast oil change. Established: 1981 - Franchising Since: 1981 - No. of Units: Franchised: 10 - Franchise Fee: $20,000 - Royalty: 5%, 2% adv. - Total Inv: $80,000-$150,000 equipment & leaseholds - Financing: Yes.

AUTOMOTIVE: MUFFLER SHOPS

MINUTE MUFFLER AND BRAKE
Muffler House Canada Ltd.
1600 - 3rd Ave., S., Lethbridge, AB, T1J 0L2. Contact: R. Sloan, V.P. Sales & Mktg. - Tel: (403) 329-1020, Fax: (403) 328-9030. Retail exhaust, brake and shock absorber business. Great emphasis on customer service, quality and more than competitive prices. Established: 1968 - Franchising Since: 1977 - No. of Units: Company Owned: 4 - Franchised: 122 - Franchise Fee: $5,000-$25,000 - Royalty: 0% of sales, 4% of purchase price - Total Inv: $120,000-$150,000 on average - Financing: Protections, 5 year business plans etc.

MONSIEUR MUFFLER
4840 Boul Des Grandes Prairies, St. Leonard, QC, H1R 1A1. Contact: Yvon Jutras, Fran. Dir. - Tel: (514) 955-7511, (888) 833-7511, Fax: (514) 955-3531. Mufflers, brakes, alignment, tires, shocks, sales and installation. Established: 1956 - Franchising Since: 1976 - No. of Units: Franchised: 81 - Franchise Fee: $10,000 - Royalty: 5% & 2% - Total Inv: $300,000-$500,000 - Financing: No. NOT OFFERING FRANCHISES AT THIS TIME.

OCTO FREINS SILENCIEUX, OCTO BRAKES MUFFLERS
Groupe MMO
4840 Boul. Des Grandes Praires, Suite 200, St-Leonard, QC, H1R 1A1. Contact: Pierre Valiquette, Operation Manager - Tel: (514) 955-6286 ext 326, (888) 833-7511, Fax: (514) 955-3531. Specialist in repairing brakes, mufflers, shock absorbers, front-end and under the car repairs. Established: 1971 - Franchising Since: 1971 - No. of Units: Franchised: 46 - Total Inv: $150,000 - Financing: Bank.

SPEEDY MUFFLER KING CANADA LTD.
Speedy Muffler King Inc.
365 Bloor St. East, Toronto, ON, M4P 1V3. Contact: C. Noble, Dir. - Tel: (416) 961-1133, (800) 387-1410, Fax: (416)960-7971. Established: 1956 - Franchising Since: 1990 - No. of Units: Company Owned: 150 - Franchised: 5 - Franchise Fee: $20,000 - Royalty: 5%, 5% adv. - Total Inv: $180,000 - Financing: Through chartered banks.

THRUWAY MUFFLERCENTRE
Maremont Exhaust Products
3600A Lakeshore Blvd. W., Etobicoke, ON, M8W 4Y8. Contact: Sandy Bragg, Franchise Dev. - Tel: (416) 255-9555, Fax: (416) 255-2308. Muffler specialty shop, independently owned and operated coast to coast, offering a lifetime guarantee, nationwide. Established: 1954 - Franchising Since: 1976 - No. of Units: Associates: 90 - Development Fee: $5,995 - Royalty: None - Total Inv: $50,000 cash - Financing: Balance by bank financing.

AUTOMOTIVE: PRODUCTS AND SERVICES

ACTIVE GREEN + ROSS TIRE & AUTOMOTIVE CENTRE
Active Tire & Auto Centre Inc.
580 Evans Ave., Toronto, ON, M8W 2W1. Contact: Ralph Chiodo, President - Tel: (416) 255-5581, Fax: (416) 255-4793. Tire and automotive sales and services. Established: 1982 - Franchising Since: 1983 - No. of Units: Company Owned: 5 - Franchised: 25 - Franchise Fee: $25,000 - Royalty: 5%, 2.5% adv. - Total Inv: $115,000-$200,000 - Financing: None.

ALEX PNEU ET MECANIQUE
Groupe Alex Pneu et Mecanique
6000 Street Sherbrooke, Montreal, QC, H1N 1B8. Contact: Claude Goyal, Dir. of Fran. - Tel: (514) 254-6006. Car and light truck automotive services. Established: 1977 - Franchising Since: 1980 - No. of Units: Company Owned: 4 - Franchised: 8 - Franchise Fee: $20,000 - Royalty: 4% net sales - Total Inv: $250,000 turnkey - Financing: Yes.

APPLE AUTO GLASS
Apple Auto Glass Ltd.
360 Applewood Cres., Concord, ON, L4K 4V2. Contact: Roger Williams, VP. Gen. Mgr. - Tel: (905) 669-7800, (800) 267-6105, Fax: (905) 669-6334, E-Mail: rogerw@tcgi.com. Auto glass amd accessory franchisor. Established: 1983 - Franchising Since: 1983 - No. of Units: Company Owned: 5 - Franchised: 115 - Franchise Fee: $5,000 - Royalty: 5% of the first $500,000 of annual gross revenue and 4% of annual gross revenue in excess of $500,000 per year - Total Inv: $75,000-$100,000 - Financing: 60 day terms on product purchases.

ARMORTHANE COATINGS INC.
10350 176 St., Edmonton, AB, T5S 1L3. - Tel: (403) 444-6200, (800) 363-6100, Fax: (403) 444-9405. Protective polyurethane coatings for truck bed liners. Industrial, commercial and marine applications. Established: 1991 - Franchising Since: 1991 - Franchised: Approx. 35 - Franchise Fee: Depends on type and size of territory - Total inv: $20,000-$60,000 - Financing: No.

AUTOPRO REPAIR CENTRE
UAP Inc.
7025 Ontario St., E., Montreal, QC, H1N 2B3. Contact: Denis Bellemore, Nat'l. Dir. - Tel: (514) 899-0044, Fax: (514) 256-5497. A perfect add-on program on under-the-car specialties for a regular service station or independent repair shop. Offers marketing and advertising assistance along with lifetime warranties in brakes, mufflers, suspensions, front-end and front wheel drive parts. UAP Inc. Established: 1926 - Franchising Since: 1983 - No. of Units: Franchised: 600 - Franchise Fee: $4,995 - Adv: $1,800 adv. fee per year - Total Inv: $8,000-$10,000 - Financing: No.

BREAK-AWAY WINDSHIELD REPAIR CENTRES
101-273 Third Ave., Timmins, ON, P4N 1E2. Contact: Marc R.Brazeau, Principal - Tel: (705) 267-2447, (800) 452-0053, Fax: (705) 267-7283. Repair of chips and cracks up to 20 inches of windshield. Also just added new product line of glass repair - scratches and nicks (home and auto). Established: 1995 - Franchising Since: 1995 - No. of Units: Franchised: 5 - Franchise Fee: $15,000 includes complete turnkey operations - Royalty: Including billings and reporting 15% - Total Inv: $15,000 - Financing: Yes.

BUDGET BRAKE & MUFFLER
104-1750 Hartley Ave, Coquitlam, BC, V3K 7A1. Contact: Lane Vance, Franchise Sales - Tel: (604) 523-1239, Fax: (604) 523-1470, E-Mail: info@budgetbrake.com. Retail automotive service. Brake and muffler specialists. Established: 1969 - Franchising Since: 1972 - No. of Units: Franchised: 30 - Franchise Fee: $25,000 - Royalty: 4% and 4% adv. - Total Inv: Approx $200,000 - Financing: Thru financial institutions.

CANABUF MFG. CO.
344 Dupont St., Ste. 202, Toronto, ON, M5R 1V9. Contact: Gordon Krofchick, President - Tel: (416) 292-3612, (800) 616-8403, Fax: (416) 292-7813. Mobile units equipped with automotive and industrial products. Providing service and products to exclusive territories. High profit product lines. Established: 1965 - No. of Units: Company Owned: 2 - Franchised: 1 - Franchise Fee: $20,000 - Total Inv: $45,000 - Financing: Yes.

CAP-IT- ACCESSORY CENTRES
Cap-It Franchise International Inc.
2620A Barlow Trail N.E., Calgary, AB, T1Y 1A1. Contact: Henry Funk, Fran. Dev. - Tel: (403) 250-5927, Fax: (403) 230-0212. Retailers and installers of light truck accessories and truck caps. Wholesale and distribution of these products is a portion of the business. Training and support provided. Established: 1973 - No. of Units: Company Owned: 1 - Franchised: 8 - Franchise Fee: $25,000 - Royalty: 5% - adv. fee 2%.

CARSMETICS®
27 Nihan Dr, St.Catharines, ON, L2N 1L2. Contact: John Finley, Fran. Dev. - Tel: (877) 883-CARS. Carmetics® provides automobile touch-up services to commercial and retail customers. Offering superior techniques and procedures couples with the most comprehensive training program in the industry. Established: 1990 - No. of Units: Franchised: 20 - Total Inv: $25,000.

CARSTAR COLLISION CENTRE
Carstar Automotive Canada
1124 Rymal Rd., East, Hamilton, ON, L8W 3N7. Contact: Franchise Department - Tel: (905) 388-2264, (800) 665-2264, Fax: (905) 388-1124, Web Site: www.carstar.com. Provide "collision management services". Automotive collision repair - proven system and consultative services. We are consolidating the collision repair industry. Established: 1992 - Franchising Since: 1993 - No. of Units: Company Owned: 7 - Franchised: 47 - Franchise Fee: $6,000 - Royalty: 2%-4% of gross collision sales - Total Inv: Variable based on gross sales - Financing: Yes.

CERTIGARD (PETRO-CANADA)
Petro-Canada
105-6th Ave SW, P.O. 2844, Calgary, AB, T2P 3E3. Contact: Peter Bridger, Category Manager - Tel: (403) 296-4040, Fax: (403) 296-3061, Web Site: www.certigard.com. Petro-Canada's national auto repair franchise, offering terms up to 10 years. Proven by management system, enhanced customer service techniques, local and national advertising programs. National warranty program. Established: 1973 - Franchising Since: 1987 - No. of Units: Franchised: 160 - Franchise Fee: $20,000 - Royalty: 5%, 2% business development fee - Total Inv: $100,000-$150,000 - Financing: No, but assistance is provided.

CHIPMASTER AUTO PAINT SYSTEM *
Chipmaster Auto Paint System Ltd.
25 Rayborn Cresc., St. Albert, AB, T8N 5B9. Contact: Ivan Mayer/Lyle Robson - Tel: (780) 460-4246, (888) 349-2729, Fax: (780) 460-4251, E-Mail: fixcrack@incentre.net, Web Site: www.chipmasterscanada.com. Chipmaster is a new & innovative breakthrough in paint & spot repairs. Capable of matching every possible color including metallics and pearls, polishing and detailing, bumper repair, PDR. Ability to offer same day service & full start up kit included. Full training & support. Potential payback on investment over $60,000.00. Established: 2004 - Franchising Since: 2004 - No. of Units: Corporate: 1 - Dealerships: 20 - Franchise Fee: $25,000, include all equipment, product and training - Royalty: $300.00/mth - Total Inv: $25,000 - Financing: Available assistance in financial, accounting, computer and administrations.

COAST TO COAST COLLISION CENTERS
120 King Edward Street East, Winnipeg, MB, R3H 0N8. Contact: Terry Smith, Fran. Dev. - Tel: (204) 895-1244, Fax: (204) 895-1283, E-Mail: info@boydgroup.com, Web Site: www.boydgroup.com. Collision repairs. Established: 1990 - No. of Units: Company Owned: 32 - Franchised: 21 - Total Inv: Varies.

COBRA CAR PROTECTION CENTRES
1075 Queensway Ave. E., Unit #12, Mississauga, ON, L4Y 4C8. - Tel: (905) 848-0010, Fax: (905) 273-7686, E-Mail: info@cobral.com, Web Siye: www.cobral.com. Automotive appearance services and accessories, featuring Protectoil rustproofing and related services and Cobra Truck Accessories. Established: 1989 - Franchising Since: 1992 - No. of Units: Company Owned: 1 - Franchised: 3 - Franchise Fee: $12,500 - Royalty: None - Total Inv: Franc. fee plus $30,000 equip. & inven., $7,500 leaseholds - Financing: Yes.

COLORWORKS
1461-27 th Street, West Vancouver, BC, V7V 4K8. Contact: Don Konantz, Fran. Dev. - Tel: (604) 926-1329, Fax: (604) 926-0534. Mobile business specializing in automobile paint repairs - Locations: Prairies and Maritimes. Full training and support provided. Established: 1991 - Total Inv: Varies.

CRACKMASTERS WINDSHIELD REPAIR AND REPLACEMENT
Crackmaster Dist., Ltd.
25 Rayborn Cresc., St. Albert, AB, T8N 5B9. Contact: Ivan Mayer/Lyle Robson - Tel: (780) 460-4246, (888) 349-2729, Fax: (780) 460-4251, E-Mail: fixcrack@incentre.net, Web Site: www.crackmasters canada.com. Guaranteed repairs of chips and cracks up to 36" with patented Ultra-Bond System. Windshield Replacement, Auto Graphics, 3M Paint Protection, PDR, Auto Detailing, plus many other retail opportunities. Full training and support start up kit included with enough materials to recoup entire investment. No experience required. Established: 1994 - Franchising Since: 1994 - No. of Units: Corporate: 1 - Dealerships: 75 - Franchise Fee: $15,000, incl. all equipment & product - Royalty: $150.00 per month - Total Inv: $10,000-$15,000 - Financing: Available assistance in financial, accounting, computer and administration.

DEE-RO VITRES D'AUTO'S
Belron Canada
8288 Boul Pie IX, Montreal, QC, H1Z 3T6. Contact: Claude Lamiel, Dir. - Tel: (514) 593-8000. Sales and installation of windshields, car radio, alarm system, anti-theft system, upholstery, cellular phone, sunroofs, engine remote starter. Established: 1947 - Franchising Since: 1980 - No. of Units: Company Owned: 37 - Franchised: 35 - Franchise Fee: $30,000 - Royalty: 5% plus 2% publicity - Total Inv: $150,000 excl. land and building - Financing: No.

DENT CLINIC
#7-770 11th Street S.E., Calgary, AB, T2H 2W8. Contact: Fran. Dev. - Tel: (403) 650-5277, Fax: (403) 258-3555, Web Site: www.dent clinic.com. Paint free dent repair. Full training and ongoing support provided. Established: 1993 - No. of Units: Franchised: 7 - Total Inv: $50,000-$100,000.

DYNAMIC TIRE
155 Delta Park Blvd, Brampton, ON, L6T 5M8. Contact: Bill Bagg, Retail Sales Mgr. - Tel: (905) 595-5558. Tire and automotive repair shop. Established: 1992 - Franchising Since: 1992 - No. of Units: Company Owned: 2 - Franchised: 8 - Franchise Fee: $25,000 - Royalty: 4%.

FIBRENEW INTERNATIONAL
Box 33, Site 16, RR# 8, Calgary, AB, T2J 2T9. Contact: Michael Wilson, Pres. - Tel: (403) 278-7818, Fax: (403) 278-1434. #1 Home-Based business servicing the aviation, auto, commercial furniture, marine and residential markets. Established: 1986 - Franchising Since: 1987 - No. of Units: Franchised: 83 - Franchise Fee: $25,000 - Royalty: $220 per month plus - Total Inv: $35,000 - Financing: No.

FIBREPRO INTERNATIONAL INC
205-610 Ford Drive, Oakville, ON, L6J 7W4. Contact: John R. Allen - Tel: (905) 829-5325, (888) 532-5349, Fax: (905) 849-9320, E-Mail: info@fibrepro.com, Web Site: www.fibrepro.com. Specialists in leather, vinyl, velour, plastic repair, recolouring and reconditioning and deodorizing. Mobile service, serving Automotive dealers, body shops, insurance companies and commercial, residential and industrial customers. Established: 2002 - Franchising Since: 2002 - No. of Units: Company Owned: 1 - Franchised: 2 - Franchise Fee: $15,000 - Royalty: 6% monthly and 1% to be spent in franchisees territory - Total Inv: $34,950 total turn key - Financing: Yes, third party through TD Canada Trust.

FINE DETAILS INC.
3200 Ridgeway Drive Suite #3, Mississauga, ON, L5L 5Y6. Contact: Scott Weller, President - Tel: (905) 820-9274, (888) THE-WASH, Fax: (905) 820-4179, E-Mail: finedetails@finedetails.org, Web Site: www.finedetails.org. Services vary from full hand car wash to a total interior and exterior cleaning, waxing and fine detailing, including engine shampoo. Established: 1995 - Franchising Since: 1998 - No. of Units: Franchised: 17 - Franchise Fee: $10,000.

FIRESTONE TIRE & AUTOMOTIVE CENTRE
5770 Hurontario St., Ste. 400, Mississauga, ON, L5R 3G5. Contact: Lou Monico, Manager Retail Operations - Tel: (905) 568-5258, Fax: (905) 890-9022, E-Mail: lmonico@bridgestone-firestone.ca. Sale of tires and automotive service to the public. Established: 1919 - Franchising Since: 1974 - No. of Units: 115 - Total Inv: $100,000 - Financing: Yes.

GOLDPRO
GoldPro Canada, Inc.
300 Steelcase Road West, Unit 25, Markham, ON, L3R 2W2. Contact: Marc Gordon, President - Tel: (905) 475-1010, (888) 816-9996, Fax: (905) 475-1777, E-Mail: goldpro@goldpro.ca, Web Site: www.goldpro.ca. Offering high margin aftermarket services to car dealerships. These services include gold plating, windshield repair, wood dash trim, and paint protection. Established: 1990 - Franchising Since: 1996 - No. of Units: Company Owned: 1 - Franchised: 50 - Total Inv: Less than $5,000 - Financing: Yes.

GOODTURN RIDE CENTRES
Goodturn Management, Inc.
2345 Barton St. East, Hamilton, ON, L8E 2W8. Contact: Don McLaughlin, Pres. - Tel: (905) 573-2224, Fax: (905) 573-1221. Under car care specialists. Quality workmanship at fair prices. Experts in brakes, alignments, shocks, tires, exhaust, steering and frame straightening. Original inventor of lifetime warranty on brakes and mufflers. Established: 1978 - Franchising Since: 1990 - No. of Units: Company Owned: 1 - Franchised: 6 - Franchise Fee: $7,500 - Royalty: 6% gross sales, franchisor pays national advertising - Total Inv: $100,000 - Financing: Yes.

INSTANT WINDSHIELD REPAIR
363 Lilac Street, Suite 312, Winnipeg, MB, R1B 2N4. Contact: Jordan Halstead, Fran. Dev. - Tel: (204) 235-0010. Mobile windshield repair. Full training and support provided. Established: 1994 - No. of Units: Franchised: 17 - Total Inv: $8,500 min cash required.

LEAKPRO INTERNATIONAL INC.

205-610 Ford Drive, Oakville, ON, L6J 7W4. Contact: John R. Allen, President - Tel: (905) 829-LEAK, (888) LEAKFIX, Fax: (905) 849-9320, E-Mail: info@leakpro.com, Web Site: www.leakpro.com. #1 network of automotive water leak, air leak and wind noise repair specialists. Mobile service OEM approved, and very high demand. Servicing new car dealers, used car lots and body shops and fleets. Established: 1996 - Franchising Since: 1996 - No of Units: Company Owned: 2 - Franchised: 18 - Franchise Fee: $20,000 - Royalty: 6% monthly and 1% to be spent in franchisees territory - Total Inv: $39,950 total turn key - Financing: Third party through TD Bank.

MAACO AUTO PAINTING & BODYWORKS

MAACO Systems Canada, Inc.
10 Kingsbridge Garden Cir., #501, Mississauga, ON, L5R 3K6. Contact: Hermann Delisle, Nat. Sales Mgr. - Tel: (800) 387-6780, (905) 501-1212, Fax: (905) 501-1218. Production retail auto painting and body works. Established: 1972 - Franchising Since: 1972 - No. of Units: Company Owned: 1 - Franchised: 42 in Canada, 460 in US - Franchise Fee: $25,000 - Royalty: 8% - Total Inv: $232,500 - Financing: Yes.

MASTER MECHANIC

Master Mechanic Inc., The
1989 Dundas St. E., Mississauga, ON, L4X 1M1. Contact: Andrew Wanie, Pres. - Tel: (905) 629-3773, (800) 383-8523, Fax: (905) 629-3864, E-Mail: mastermcn@aol.com, Web Site: www.mastermechanic.org. General automotive repair. Established: 1983 - Franchising Since: 1983 - No. of Units: Company Owned: 1 - Franchised: 33 - Franchise Fee: $25,000 - Royalty: 6% advtg up to 3% - Total Inv: $150,000 - Financing: Yes.

MINI-TANKERS

#215-9440, 202 Street, Langley, BC, V1M 4A6. Contact: Laura Rayner, Franchise Coordinator - Tel: (604) 513-0386, Fax: (604) 513-0397, Web Site: www.mini-tankers.com. Mini-Tankers service offers direct refuelling to diesel powered equipment in the construction, transportation, rail, marine and stand by power industries. Established: 1987 - Franchising Since: 1987 - No. of Units: Company Owned: 12 - Franchised: 88 - Franchise Fee: $35,000 - Royalty: 0 - Total Inv: F.F.$35,000, Tanker $75,000-$100,000, Mix $10,000 - Financing: Comprehensive business plan preparation and guidance on approaching lenders.

MISTER FRONT-END LTD.

192 N. Queen St., Etobicoke, ON, M9C 1A8. Contact: Gerry R. Jones, Pres. - Tel: (416) 622-9999, Fax: (416) 622-9999. Automotive and truck alignment, suspension repair and power steering box rebuiding. Established: 1973 - Franchising Since: 1980 - Franchise Fee: $15,000 - Royalty: 5% - Total Inv: $120,000 - Financing: Yes.

MR. FRONT END

192 North Queen St, Etobicoke, ON, M9C 1A8. Contact: Gerry Jones, President - Tel: (416) 622-9998, Fax: (416) 622-9999. Mr. Front End specializes in Spring-suspension laser alignment, fram straightening and rebuilding. Established: 1973 - Franchising Since: 1993 - No. of Units: Company Owned: 1 - Franchised: 1 - Franchise Fee: $10,000 - Royalty: 4% - Total Inv: $150,000.

MR. GAS TANK / M. RESERVOIR

490 McGeachie Drive, Milton, ON, L9T 3Y5. Contact: Howard Kennedy, Fran. Dev. - Tel: (905) 878-8863, Fax: (905) 878-1449. Gas tank repair and replacement service - 2 weeks training and ongoing support. Established: 1985 - No. of Units: Franchised: 13.

NOVUS AUTO GLASS REPAIR & REPLACEMENT

550330 Main Gate D U, Mississauga, ON, L4W 1N5. Contact: Fran. Dev. - Tel: (905) 624-5161, Web Site: 905) 624-7339. Novus invented windshield repair in 1972. Novus' state-of-the-art repair technology and factory training enables its technicians to repair up to 75% of stone damaged windshields when damage first occurs, plus cracks over 12 inches long. Established: 1972 - No. of Units: Franchised: 525 - Total Inv: $15,000 - fran fee and set-up costs.

O.K. TIRE STORES

O.K. Tire Stores, Inc.
9430-198 St., Langley, BC, V1M 3C8. Contact: Denis Marshall, V.P. Fran. - Tel: (604) 888-3000, Fax: (604) 888-4511, Web Site: www.oktire.com. Tires and mechanical services, brakes, wheel alignments, shocks, exhaust, suspension, front end repair. Established: 1953 - Franchising Since: 1953 - No. of Units: Franchised: 212 - Franchise Fee: $4,000 - Total Inv: $120,000 equip., inv. - Financing: No.

OIL GARD ANTI-RUST CANADA LTD.

Oil Gard Anti-Rust Canada Ltd
779 Wonderland Rd N., London, ON, N6H 4L1. Contact: Donald F. Hawken, Pres. - Tel: (519) 471-6311, Fax: (519) 471-7281, E-Mail: fenix@gardgroup.com, Web Site: www.gardgroup.com. With over 24 years of providing proven rust prevention formulas to a national chain of retail outlets we are seeking master licensees for national development. All of our franchisees are provided with leading edge technology supported by customized training and marketing packages. Established: 1976 - Franchising Since: 1983 - Franchise Fee: $500-$25,000 - Royalty: None - Total Inv: $5,000-$25,000 c/w equipment, supplies, products and license fee - Financing: On approved applicants.

OIL-TECH INDUSTRIES, LTD.

9 Gowan St., Barrie, ON, L4N 2N9. Contact: John Robb, Pres. - Tel: (705) 721-0058. Automotive rust control and appearance for vehicles. Established: 1982 - Franchising Since: 1984 - Franchise Fee: None - Royalty: None - Total Inv: $7,200 and up - Financing: None. NOT OFFERING FRANCHISES AT THIS TIME.

OILTRELL AUTO COSMETIC CENTERS

5 Peacock Bay, St. Catharines, ON, L2M 7N8. Contact: George Kelmer, Owner - Tel: (905) 714-9275, Fax: (905) 714-9276. Automotive detailing centres specializing in annual rustproofing (The Neutralizer) and guaranteed five-year acrylic print glazing (The Shine), plus a host of other exclusive premium quality car care products for the marine and the used and new markets. Established: 1984 - Franchising Since: 1986 - No. of Units: Company Owned: 1 - Franchised: 12 - Franchise Fee: $5,000 - Total Inv: $10,000 - Financing: Yes.

PERMA-SHINE

Perma-Shine, Inc.
P.O. Box 21129-6677, Meadowvale Town Ctr. Cir., Mississauga, ON, L5N 2W0. Contact: Brian Batstone, Pres. - Tel: (905) 877-2403, Fax: (905) 877-8127. Car detailing including permanent shine and rust-protection including oiling. Established: 1974 - Franchising Since: 1976 - No. of Units: Company Owned: 1 - Franchised: 46 - Franchise Fee: $5,000 - Royalty: $200 flat fee monthly - Total Inv: Varies - Financing: No.

RUST CHECK CENTER

Rust Check Canada Inc.
6175 Danville Rd, Mississauga, ON, L5T 2H7. Contact: Dale Moneghan, Dir. of Finance - Tel: (905) 670-5411, Fax: (905) 670-5174. Rust inhibiting and vehicle detailing. Established: 1973 - Franchising Since: 1981 - No. of Units: Company Owned: 3 - Franchised: 277 - Franchise Fee: $15,000-$40,000 - Royalty: None - Total Inv: $20,000-$50,000 - Financing: Limited.

SCORPION CANADA INC

Scorpion Canada Inc
25 Rayborn Cres., St. Albert, AB, T8N 5B9. Contact: Ivan Mayer, Lyle Robson, President, Sales & Marketing Mgr - Tel: (780) 460-4246, (888) 349-2729, Fax: (780) 460-4251, E-Mail: scorpios@incentre.net, Web Site: www.scorpioncanada.com. The most versatile polyurethane spray on protective coating on the market. Tough enough to protect truck boxes and durable enough for residential decks and commercial safety flooring. Can be used in shop and mobile situations. Simply to use and no spray booth needed. Very user friendly. Full color range of UV resistant tones. Established: 1997 - Franchising Since: 1997 - No. of Dealerships: Corporate: 1 - Dealerships: 48 - Franchise Fee: $5,000.00 including all equipment and startup equipment - Royalty: $100.00 per month - Total Inv: $5,000 - Financing: Financial, computer, accounting/administration, training/profile-full technical marketing.

SHINE FACTORY
Shine Factory Systems, Inc.
320 Monument Place S.E., Calgary, AB, T2A 1X3. Contact: Bruce Cousens, Pres. - Tel: (403) 243-3030, Fax: (403) 243-3031, E-Mail: shines@telus.net, Web Site: www.shinefactory.ca. Automotive polishing and detailing, complete turnkey operation. Established: 1979 - Franchising Since: 1979 - No. of Units: Franchised: 21 - Franchise Fee: $40,000 - Royalty: 8% - Total Inv: $45,000 w/equipment - Financing: No.

SNAP-ON TOOLS OF CANADA LTD.
2325 Skymark Avenue, Mississauga, ON, L3W 5A9. - Tel: (905) 624-0066, Fax: (905) 238-9658, (800) 268-8477. Snap-on Tools of Canada Ltd. is the Canadian subsidiary of Snap-on Incorporated, the world's largest independent manufacturer of tools and equipment for the professional technician. We are an established company, with a comprehensive product line, that developed the concept of a "showroom on wheels". A Snap-on franchise offers some unique features: a low initial franchise fee, a low fixed monthly fee, no advertising fee, financing assistance, ongoing training and assistance. Dealer business software and credit assistance programs. Established: 1931 - Franchising Since: 1993 - No. of Units: Company Owned: 34 - Franchised: 337 - Non-franchised: 45 - Franchise Fee: $6,000 - Royalty: No royalty fee, $50 monthly admin. fee - Total Inv: $115,650-$207,000 - Financing: Financing available for certain components of initial investment.

STOP 'N STEER SHOPS
Northern Investments Ltd.
2841 E. Arthur St., Thunder Bay, ON, P7E 5P5. Contact: George Giba, Owner - Tel: (807) 623-4700, Fax: (807) 626-9197. Automotive repair centres specializing in high profit required areas of automotive maintenance, brakes, steering, suspension and alignments. Offers owner training support packages, ongoing training and purchasing power. Management experience or license technician an asset. Established: 1978 - No. of Units: Company Owned: 1 - Franchised: 1 - Franchise Fee: $16,500 - Royalty: 5% - Total Inv: $150,000-$175,000 - Financing: Assistance.

SUPERIOR TIRE AUTO FITNESS CENTRES
Superior Tire Corp.
5070 Sheppard Ave. E., Scarborough, ON, M1S 4N3. - Tel: (416) 291-9291, Fax: (416) 291-9302. Tires and automotive service. Established: 1942 - Franchising Since: 1991 - No. of Units: Company Owned: 4 - Franchised: 3 - Franchise Fee: $25,000. NOT OFFERING FRANCHISES AT THIS TIME.

SURE STOP BRAKE CENTERS
Motorcade Industries Ltd.
90 Kincourt St., Toronto, ON, M6M 5G1. Contact: Joel Klein, General Sales Manager - Tel: (416) 614-6118, Fax: (416) 614-6130, Web Site: www.motorcade-ind.com. Sale of complete brake systems, suspension systems, shocks, etc. Established: 1952 - Franchising Since: 1972 - No. of Units: Franchised: 45 - Total Inv: $10,000 - Financing: Third party.

THE GREAT CANADIAN OIL CHANGE LTD.
P.O. Box 10716, Lloydminster, AB, T97 3A7. Contact: T. Wefler, Fran. Dev. - Tel: (780) 875-0040, Fax: (780) 875-0065. Our all-glass building brings to the oil change industry a bright open look - and with our added services and fair pricing Great Canadian Oil Change is ready for the new millennium. Full training and support provided. Established: 1978 - No. of Units: Franchised: 13 - Total Inv: Up to $90,000.

THE LAW OF TINTING
2638-6243 Que. Inc.
6087 St-Jacques, Montreal, QC, H4A 2G4. Contact: Howard Nadler, Owner - Tel: (514) 489-9591, Fax: (514) 489-0896. Window tinting/auto accessories. Established: 1999 - Franchising Since: 1999 - No. of Units: Company Owned: 1 - Franchised: 23 - Franchise Fee: $25,000 - Royalty: 7% - Total Inv: $50,000 - Financing: Yes.

TINT KING AUTO WORLD SUPER MARKETS
Tint King of California Inc.
136 Castle Rock Dr., Richmond Hill, ON, L4C 5K5. Contact: Mr. Allan Starkman - Tel: (416) 464-TINT (8468). Tint, accessory and detail shop(s). Automotive aftermarket service. Now expanding worldwide. Enter the knighthood today! Established: 1979 - Franchising Since:

1983 - No. of Units: Franchised: 29 - Franchise Fee: From $10,000 - Royalty: 5% of gross sales - Total Inv: $25,000 includes territory, training, supplies, tools, advertising, field support - Financing: Yes.

TINT MASTER AND AUTO GLASS
6033 Shawson Dr., Unit 9, Mississauga, ON, L5T 1H8. Contact: James Formosa, Pres. - Tel: (905) 670-TINT (5181), Fax: (905) 670-8468. Automotive window film - energy saver for the 90's. Comfort, image, safety are three important needs for every driver. Film processing technology and highest quality materials provide optical clarity of film and provide years of comfort and good looks for millions of drivers. Established: 1981 - Franchising Since: 1995 - No. of Units: Company Owned: 1 - Franchised: 5 - Franchise Fee: $15,000 - Royalty: 6% - Total Inv: $80,250 which includes fran. fee - Financing: We assist in obtaining financing.

TRENT AUTOBODY
45 Sutton Place, Suite 304, Vancouver, BC, V9L 1B3. Contact: Franchise Dept. - Tel: (250) 744-1662, Fax: (250) 744-1337. An autobody repair shop, two weeks full training, support ongoing. Locations available in B.C. Established: 1983 - No. of Units: Franchised: 4 - Total Inv: $350,000.

UNI PRO
Uni-Select, Inc.
170 boul. Industriel, Boucherville, QC, J4B 2X3. Contact: Luc Charlebois, Dir. - Tel: (450) 641-2440, Fax: (450) 449-1619. Automobile parts. Established: 1969 - Franchising Since: 1980 - No. of Units: 160 - Franchise Fee: $2,995 - Royalty: 3% adv.

VITAL PROTECTION SYSTEMS INC.
17 McEwan Dr., Bolton, ON, L7E 1H5. Contact: Curtis D. Johnson, Pres. - Tel: (905) 951-3600, Fax: (905) 951-3636. Anti corrosion (rust proofing) of automobiles including undercoating, sound guard, fabric and paint protection plus liquid truck bed liner. Established: 1969 - Franchising Since: 1970 - No. of Units: Company Owned: 3 - Franchised: 15 - Franchise Fee: Variable - Royalty: Based on purchases - Total Inv: $25,000-$50,000 - Financing: Yes.

WYNN'S X-TEND AUTO LINK
Wynn's Canada Ltd.
170 Traders Blvd., E., Mississauga, ON, L4Z 1W7. Contact: Mr. Douglas Stewart, Fran. Mgr. - Tel: (905) 507-9966, (800) 668-5626, Fax: (905) 507-2265. Automotive aftermarket chemicals and equipment. Franchisee is offered a protected territory within a defined region to sell and service automotive repair outlets. Established: 1939 - Franchising Since: 1996 - No. of Units: Franchised: 8 - Franchise Fee: $15,000-$20,000 - Royalty: 2.5% on purchases - Total Inv: $0.10 per registered vehicle approx. $15,000-$20,000 - Financing: None.

XPRESS WINSHIELD REPAIRS
1200 Speers Road, Unit 16, Oakville, ON, L6L 2X4. Contact: Hugh Tulk, President - Tel: (905) 815-1121, (800) 603-4665, Fax: (905) 815-1196, Web Site: www.xpressho.com. Windshield repair, now operating at 48 Canadian Tire locations nation wide. Established: 1993 - Franchising Since: 1994 - No. of Units: Company Owned: 2 - Franchised: 28 - Franchise Fee: $30,500 turn key - Total Inv: $30,500 - Financing: OAC.

AUTOMOTIVE: TRANSMISSION REPAIR

AALL-TECH TRANSMISSION
Aall Tech Transmission Systems, Inc.
5651 #3 Rd., Richmond, BC, V6X 2C7. Contact: Bill Byrd, Gen. Mgr. - Tel: (604) 644-0257, Fax: (604) 270-9759. Automotive transmission service. Established: 1975 - Franchising Since: 1995 - No. of Units: Company Owned: 3 - Franchised: 2 - Franchise Fee: $25,000 - Royalty: 6% + 6% adv. - Total Inv: $150,000 - Financing: Through bank arrangement.

MISTER TRANSMISSION
Mister Transmission (International) Ltd.
9675 Yonge Street, 2nd Floor, Richmond Hill, ON, L4C 1V7. Contact: Kevin Brillinger, V.P.- Corporate Development - Tel: (905) 884-1511, (800) 373-8432, Fax: (905) 884-4727, Web Site: www.mistertrans

mission.com. Canada's largest transmission repair franchise, in business for over 36 years, Mister Transmission is the leader in its category. Join the All-Canadian Mister Transmission team. "Hey Mister, You're A Friend of Mine!" Established: 1963 - Franchising Since: 1969 - No. of Units: Franchised: 90 - Franchise Fee: $25,000 - Royalty: 7% - Total Inv: $100,000-$125,000 - Financing: Third party assistance.

TRANSMISSION DEPOT
Transmission Depot Franchising Inc
126 Tyco's Drive, Toronto, ON, M6B 1W8. Contact: Rick Keene - Tel: (416) 785-7118, Fax: (416) 783-4902, E-Mail: rkeene@attcanada.ca, Web Site: www.transmissiondepot.ca. The sales and marketing of transmission repair. Franchisees do not need a technical or an automotive background but must be comfortable selling. Established: 1996 - Franchising Since: 2000 - No. of Units: Company Owned: 1 - Franchised: 7 - Franchise Fee: $25,000 - Royalty: 7% - Total Inv: $90,000-$130,000 - Financing: Assistance is provided in SBL application.

BEVERAGES

BITTERS & GRAPES
Bitters & Grapes Enterprises Ltd
1212 Hwy. 2 East., Kingston, ON, K7L 4V1. Contact: Bill Amodeo - Tel: (613) 547-5630, (888) 549-4727, Fax: (613) 547-2166, E-Mail: headoffice@bittersandgrapes.com, Web Site: www.bittersand grapes.com. Bitters & Grapes is a chain of franchise-operated businesses offering services and merchandise to both the home-brewer and wine-maker. On premise wineries and breweries are included in those franchises located where laws permit. Nowhere can you find as complete a venue for both the amateur and seasoned enthusiast in an ambient and professional environment. We offer a wide variety of high quality products from many respected vendors, not limiting our wares to in-house products only. This enables us to volume purchase the best products of the year, passing the savings directly onto the franchises. Established: 1994 - Franchising Since: 1995 - No. of Units: Franchised: 5 - Franchise Fee: $25,000 - Royalty: 5% gross - Total Inv: $80,000 - Financing: No.

CARAFE WINE MAKERS
Carafe International, Inc
339 Olivewood Rd., Etobicoke, ON, M8Z 2Z6. Contact: Stewert Petrie, Pres. - Tel: (416) 236-4990, (800) 236-4999, (416) 236-4995, E-Mail: sp@carafe.ca, Web Site: www.carafe.ca. Join our team of successful franchises. Carafe Wine Makers are setting the standard in wine-making excellence. Clean, inviting, friendly and fully automated. Carafe is the Ultimate Wine Making Experience! Established: 1990 - Franchising Since: 1992 - No. of Units: Franchised: 14 - Franchise Fee: $25,000 - Royalty: 5% - Total Inv: Equipment/Furnishing $40,000, Improvements $30,000, Start-up $15,000 - Financing: To qualified franchisees.

D'VINE WINE
D'Vine Wine International Inc.
44 Charles St., West Suite 3603, Toronto, ON, M4Y 1R8. Contact: George Fluter - Tel: (416) 944-2200, Fax: (416) 944-3555, E-Mail: george.fluter@dvinewine.com. Web Site: www.dvinewine.com. Wine making with a difference. Customers come in and make over 50 varieties "DVineWiners of The World" and wine accessories gift shop. Established: 1995 - Franchising Since: 1996 - No. of Units: Franchised: 38 world wide - Franchise Fee: $25,000 - Royalty: 5% - Total Inv: $85,000-$115,000 - Financing: No.

JUGO JUICE *
Bay 8A, 416 Meridian Rd S.E, Calgary, AB, T2A 1X2. - Tel: (403) 207-5850, Fax: (403) 207-5875, E-Mail: information@jugojuice.com, Web Site: www.jugojuice.com. Jugo Juice offers premiere made to order smoothies and juices. Jugo's product offering is supplemented with signature food items such as wraps, paninis and salads. Established: 1998 - Franchising Since: 2004 - No. of Units: Company Owned: 4 - Franchise Fee: $25,000 - Royalty: 6% of gross sales paid weekly - Total Inv: $134,000-$245,000.

MAXI BROUE BREWING CENTRE INC.
Centre Brassicole Maxi-Broue Inc.
11720, 4th Ave., Montreal, QC, H1E 5Y2. - Tel: (514) 881-8920, Fax: (514) 881-8920. Maxi-Broue offers a warm atmosphere that is the perfect backdrop for its unique gourmet beer recipes of the highest quality. Store also offers fine glassware, promotional items (caps, t-shirts, sweaters, etc). Established: 1994 - Franchising Since: 1996 - No. of Units: Company Owned: 2 - Franchised: 6 - Franchise Fee: $15,000 - Total Inv: $75,000 - Financing: Assistance with business plan.

THE ARROW NEIGHBOURHOOD PUB
The Arrow Neighbourhood Pub Group
173 Woolwich St., Suite 201, Guelph, ON, N1H 3V4. Contact: J. Perry Maisonneuve - Tel: (905) 804-9711, (888) 667-8449, Fax: (905) 804-9713, E-Mail: northernlights@interhop.net. The Arrow Neighbourhood Pub captures the atmosphere of a traditional British Pub but in a distinctly Canadian fashion, designed to appeal to the whole family with emphasis on locally produced beverages and culinary specialties. Established: 1991 - Franchising Since: 1991 - No. of Units: Company Owned: 1 - Franchised: 3 - Franchise Fee: $35,000 - Royalty: 5% + 2% ad fee - Total Inv: $350,000-$400,000 - Financing: No.

TIMOTHY'S WORLD COFFEE
Timothy's World Coffees
400 Steeprock Dr., Toronto, ON, M3J 2X1. Contact: Susan Jack, Franchise/Lease Representative - Tel: (416) 638-3333 x338, (800) 827-1038, Fax: (416) 638-5603, E-Mail: franchise@timothys.com, Web Site: www.timothys.com. Timothy's World Coffee selects only the top 1-5% of the world's best coffee beans, freshly roasts the beans in small batches in our roasting plant and serves brewed and whole bean coffee within 20 days of roasting. Our inviting stores provide a comfortable environment for guests to enjoy our selection of pure origin coffees, exclusive blends, decaffeinated and specialty drinks. Freshly made baked goods, sandwiches, salads and soups complement our guests' "best cup of the day". Established: 1975 - Franchising Since: 1982 - No. of Units: Company Owned: 16 - Franchised: 118 - Franchise Fee: $25,000 - Royalty: 9%, 1% adv. - Total Inv: Will vary - Financing: No.

VINTNER'S CELLAR CANADA, INC
101-4093 Meadowbrook Drive, London, ON, N6L 1G4. Contact: Franchise Department - Tel: (519) 652-1782, Fax: (519) 652-1781, Web Site: www.vintnerscellar.com. On premises wine making, supplies and accessories in our modern inviting retail stores. Established: 1994 - No. of Units: Company Owned: 2 - Franchised: 30 - Franchise Fee: $25,000 Unit - $150,000-$300,00 Master Franchise - Total Inv: $100,000 Unit Franchise.

WINE CRAFT LTD.
1 Tarton Drive, Nepean, ON, K2J 2W7. Contact: Scott Ecclestone, Fran. Dev. - Tel: (613) 823-1331, Web Site: www.winecraft.com. Wine Craft is a complete state-of-the-art, do-it-yourself wine making facility. The business is simple, appealing to a large upscale clientele with no accounts receivable problem. Full training and support. Established: 1992 - No. of Units: Franchised: 12 - Total Inv: $40,000.

WINE KITZ
Wine Kitz Canada Inc.
309 Execter Rd., Ste. 51, London, ON, N6L 1C1. Contact: John R. DeHondt, Pres. - Tel: (519) 471-5144, Fax: (519) 649-6798. Retail outlet for beer and wine making ingredients, related equipment and giftware. Established: 1992 - Franchising Since: 1993 - No. of Units: Company Owned: - Franchised: 30 - Under Development: 2 Franchise Fee: $22,500 - Royalty: Flat fee $420 per month offset by buying group rebates - Total Inv: $110,000 turnkey with stock - Financing: No.

WINE NOT, INC.
Wine Not International Inc.
P.O Box 80, Kimberly, ON, N0C 1G0. - Tel: (519) 599-7400, (889) WINENOT, Fax: (519) 599-7300, E-Mail: global@winenot.com, Web Site: www.winenot.com. Franchisor of Micro Wineries and U-Unit stores. Established: 1993 - Franchising Since: 1995 - No. of Units: Franchised: 47 - Franchise Fee: $30,000-$50,000 - Royalty: 5% - Total Inv: $15,000 - Financing: SBL or SBA.

BUILDING PRODUCTS AND SERVICES

AMERILOK CANADA
110 Chain Lake Dr., Vantage Point 3, Unit 3I, Halifax, NS, B3S 1A9. Contact: A. Peter Feron, Pres./Owner - Tel: (902) 450-5144, Fax: (902) 450-5339. Two business opportunities available: (1) Manufacture fiberglass wicker furniture; (2) Coved-Wal seamless one-piece custom formed bathtub enclosure. Established: 1988 - Franchise Fee: $34,900 - Financing: No.

BASEMENT BOSS®
10078 Longwoods Rd., RR#1, Chatham, ON, N7M 5J1. Contact: Chuck Tomecek, President - Tel: (519) 354-4336, (800) 641-0058, Fax: (519) 354-8569, E-Mail: bboss@ctm.auracom.com, Web Site: www.basement boss.com. We fix leaky basements with our proven methods of internal water control. Established: 1995 - Franchising Since: 1996 - No. of Units: Company Owned: 3 - Franchised: 6 - Franchise Fee: $35,000 - Royalty: None - Total Inv: $35,000 includes equipment and supplies - Financing: OAC.

BATHTUB DOCTOR, LE DOCTEUR BAIGNOIRE
Respo-Technik of North America, Ltd.
2814-C Leigh Rd., Victoria, BC, V9B 4G3. Contact: W.C. (Chuck) Parsons, Pres. - Tel: (250) 478-3900, Fax: (250) 478-0045. Bathtub resurfacing and chip repair. Established: 1952 - Franchising Since: 1952 - No. of Units: Company Owned: 1 - Franchised: 36 - Franchise Fee: $15,000 - Royalty: 5% gross - Total Inv: $20,000 min. - Financing: No.

BATHTUB KING REFINISHING
109 Meg Drive Unit 11, London, ON, N6E 3T2. - Tel: (519) 681-5140, Fax: (519) 649-0555. Reglazers bathroom renovation and refinishing. Established: 1975 - Franchising Since: 1976 - No. of Units: Company Owned: 16 - Franchise Fee: $25,000 - Financing: No.

CALIFORNIA CLOSETS
The Franchise Company
391 Edgeley Blvd Ste, 5, Concord, ON, L4K 4G7. Contact: Tom Wood, Franchise Recruiting - Tel: (905) 669-1599, E-Mail: twood@certa pro.com, Web Site: www.thefranchisecompany.com. Custom designed and installed storage systems for both residential and commercial applications. Closets and garage systems, office systems and more. Established: 1974 - Franchising Since: 1978 - Franchise Fee: Varies - Royalty: Call for details - Total Inv: Varies - Financing: No.

CONFEDERATION LOG HOMES
Box 9, R.R. #3, Bobcaygeon, ON, K0M 1A0. Contact: Rick Kinsman, Owner - Tel: (705) 738-5131, Fax: (705) 738-5283. Canada's leading log home manufacturer. Established: 1980 - Franchising Since: 1981 - No. of Units: Company Owned: 3 - Franchise Fee: To be negotiated depending on area and size of building required.

DEC-K-ING
Coast Sundecks Waterproofing Ltd.
19292 60th Ave., Ste. 108, Surrey, BC, V3S 3M2. Contact: Roland P. Houle, Pres. - Tel: (604) 530-0050, Fax: (604) 530-4466. Reinforced vinyl sheeting for waterproofing sundecks, roof decks, garage decks, pool decks, patios. Also aluminum/glass railings. Established: 1978 - Franchising Since: 1981 - No. of Units: Franchised: 96 - Franchise Fee: $2,500-$15,000 (Initial inv. $1,500) - Total Inv: $5,000-$15,000 - Financing: No.

DO-IT CENTER STORES
D.H. Howden & Co. Limited
3232 White Oak Rd., P.O. Box 5485, London, ON, N6A 4G8. Contact: Ernie Bruce, Franchise Marketing Mgr. - Tel: (519) 686-2200, Fax: (519) 686-2202. Complete marketing programme (merchandising, store decor, advertising, etc.) for independent retail building supply dealers. Established: 1901 - Franchising Since: 1984 - No. of Units: Franchised: 60 - Total Inv: Variable - Financing: Will assist in obtaining.

ECI ENVIROCOATINGS, INC
Envirocoat Technologies Inc.
#200-20351 Duncan Way, Langley, BC, V3A 7N3. Contact: Roland Langset, Managing Director - Tel: (604) 532-5311, (888) 792-4411, E-Mail: eci@axionet.com, Web Site: www.eci-coatings.com. Manufacturer and distributor of high performance exterior ceramic-filled surface coatings including the amazing ceramic insulcoat RE permanent coating system. Established: 1960 - Franchising Since: 1998 - No. of Units: Company Owned: 1 - Franchised: 1 - Franchise Fee: $9,800 - Royalty: No royalty - product purchase only - Total Inv: $9,800.00 + per capital charge - Financing: Yes.

ENVIRO-SHEILD ENERGY SYSTEMS
6033 Shawson Dr., Unit 9, Mississauga, ON, L5T 1H8. Contact: John Formosa, Pres. - Tel: (905) 670-5181, Fax: (905) 670-8468. There are millions of square feet of commercial, institutional and residential glass which needs to be retrofitted with our high tech environmental solar film. The retrofit of glass with film results in a reduction of energy usage that surpasses dollar for dollar any other system. Established: 1995 - Franchising Since: 1995 - No. of Units: Company Owned: 1 - Franchise Fee: $20,000 - Royalty: 6% - Total Inv: $79,500 which incl. fran. fee - Financing: We assist in obtaining financing.

EUROPEAN SHARPENING, INC.
457-42 Ave. S.E., Calgary, AB, T2G 1Y3. Contact: Doug McKay, Pres. - Tel: (403) 287-0850, Fax: (403) 287-1622. ESI provides sharpening services to wood working, metal, ice arena, paper industry and general public. New tooling in the woodworking, ice arena, paper industry. Established: 1975 - Franchising Since: 1991 - No. of Units: Company Owned: 1 - Franchised: 4 - Franchise Fee: $30,000 - Royalty: 10% incl. adv. - Total Inv: Start up $140,000-$300,000 - Financing: None at this time.

HANDYMAN CONNECTION
Newbridge Management Group Inc.
Unit C-1836 Ness Avenue, Winnipeg, MB, R3J 0Y4. Contact: Bruce McKenzie, President - Tel: (204) 895-1744, Fax: (204) 895-1773, E-Mail: brucem@icenter.net, Web Site: www.handymanconnection.com. You will administer an efficient, high volume operational and marketing program on behalf of skilled tradespeople who perform small to medium-sized home repairs and remodeling in a $12 billion industry. Established: 1990 U.S./1995 Can. - Franchising Since: 1992 - No. of Units: Company Owned: 5 US/1 Can. - Franchised: 80 U.S. / 22 Can. - Franchise Fee: $10,000-$50,000 - Royalty: 5% & 2% marketing fund - Total Inv: $30,000-$75,000 - Financing: Yes.

IN'FLECTOR CONTROL SYSTEMS INC.
3088 Jefferson Blvd., Windsor, ON, N8T 3G9. Contact: Mr. Guy Hamel, President - Tel: (800) 954-7598, (519) 944-1110, Fax: (519) 944-6146. Manufacturer and franchisor of In'flector Window Insulating Panels: An innovative, successful, patented system to provide homeowners and business with energy savings and comfort 365 days a year. Established: 1983 - Franchising Since: 1993 - No. of Units: Company Owned: 1 - Franchised: 26 - Franchise Fee: $25,000 - Royalty: $400-$100 monthly - Total Inv: Approximately $31,000 - Financing: 50% of franchise fee.

IN-LINE STORE FIXTURES INC.
111 Industrial Drive, Unit 11-14, Whitby, ON, L1N 5Z9. Contact: Albert Appleby, V.P. Marketing & Sales - Tel: (905) 665-1226, Fax: (905) 665-1617. Manufacturing of commercial store fixtures and custom cabinets. Established: 1990.

INDUSTRIAL PLASTICS AND PAINTS
3944 Quadra Street, Victoria, BC, V8X 1J6. Contact: Franchise Department - Tel: (800) 667-1757, Fax: (250) 727-7066, E-Mail: ipp@ippnet.com, Web Site: www.ippnet.com. Retail, wholesale and commercial sales of plastic materials, paint, coatings and other related products. Established: 1991 - No. of Units: Company Owned: 2 - Franchised: 9 - Franchise Fee: $30,000.

JOJACKS
JoJacks Inc
RR#2, Essex, ON, N8W 2X6. Contact: Joe Nardella or Robert Soulliere - Tel: (519) 948-1266, (877) 565-2257, Fax: (519) 945-1868, E-Mail: info@jojacks.com, Web Site: www.jojacks.com. Using the method of concrete leveling as an alternative to removing & replacing cement. Established: 1999 - Franchising Since: 2000 - No. of Units: Company Owned: 3 - Franchised: 2 - Franchise Fee: $20,000 - Total Inv: $25,000-$35,000 - Financing: Yes.

KITCHEN SAVER OF CANADA & RENUIT
Nubold Industries Inc.
420 Newbold Street, London, ON, N6E 1K1. Contact: Jeanette McDougall, Office Manager - Tel: (519) 686-8820, (800) 265-0933, Fax: (519) 685-7283, E-Mail: renuit@nuboldinc.com. Cabinet door manufacturer-specializing in laminated door and thermo-foil styles. Ever expanding colours and designs. Established: 1986 - Franchising Since: 1986 - No. of Units: Franchised: 15 - Franchise Fee: $10,000-$20,000 - Total Inv: Variable - Financing: Some.

LAPRISE, MAISONS 4E DIMENSIONMAISONS
Laprise Inc.
240 Des Ateliers, Montmagny, QC, G5V 4G4. - Tel: (418) 248-0401, Fax: (418) 248-8415. Structure Laprise is a builder of new houses. Established: 1989 - Franchising Since: 1996 - No. of Units: Company Owned: 2 - Franchised: 10 - Franchise Fee: $4,000-$15,000 - Royalty: None - Total Inv: $15,000-$120,000 - Financing: $45,000.

MARBELITE
1028 Deer Run, Mississauga, ON, L5C 3N4. - Tel: (905) 897-9211. 3-function concrete resurfacing coating (1) restore, (2) preventative maintenance, (3) beautify, for existing concrete or any cemintitious surface indoor or outdoor - Established: 1975 US - Franchising Since: 1975 - Franchisee Fee: Negotiable - Royalty: Negotiable - Total Inv: $10,000-$80,000 - Financing: Most of Canada.

MAX PIES HOME IMPROVEMENTS *
Max Pies Home Improvements
809 Eaglemount Ct, Mississauga, ON, L5C 1H2. Contact: Leo Dos Reis, Franchise Sales - Tel: (416) 999-9659, E-Mail: leo@maxpies.ca, Web Site: www.maxpies.ca. 18 different types of home improvement franchises, one stop shopping for the client www.maxpies.ca. Established: 1978 - Franchising Since: 2004 - No. of Units: Company Owned: 1 - Franchised: 4 - Franchise Fee: $25,000 - Royalty: $500. per month - Total Inv: $5,000-$50,000 - Financing: Yes.

MEASURE MASTERS FLOOR PLANNING & BLUEPRINT SERVICE
Measure Masters Inc.
2974 Folkway Dr., Mississauga, ON, L5L 1Z6. Contact: John McPhail, Pres. - Tel: (905) 608-0000. Provide computerized floor plan blue prints of existing buildings, residential and commercial. Bonded measurements and certified square footage. All franchises operate from home. Established: 1989 - Franchising Since: 1990 - No. of Units: Franchised: 28 - Franchise Fee: $30,000-$50,000 - Royalty: 8% - Total Inv: $30,000-$50,000 - Financing: Third party possible. NOT OFFERING FRANCHISES AT THIS TIME.

MONSIEUR DISMAT
Dismat, Inc.
1250 Nobel St., Boucherville, QC, J4B 5K1. Contact: Robert Dutton, Pres. - Tel: (514) 599-5100, Fax: (514) 599-5138. Building supplies. Established: 1966 - No. of Units: 125. NOT OFFERING FRANCHISES AT THIS TIME.

MR. SQUEEEEKY
Mr. Squeeeeky Inc.
Millcreek Country Club, Suite 34, RR #3, Guelph, ON, N1H 6H9. Contact: James A. McKellar, President - Tel: (519) 763-7007, (888) 778-3359, Fax: (519) 763-2244, Web Site: www.mr-squeeeeky.com. Unique patented squeeeeky floor product that repairs squeeeeky floors, from the top through carpet, ceramic, hardwood and vinyl. No need to remove any floor covering. Established: 1997 - Franchising Since: 1997 - No. of Units: Company Owned: 1 - Franchised: 4 - Franchise Fee: $6,500 includes fee, tools, materials & training - Royalty: Yearly fee $1,000 - Financing: Yes.

NASCOR INCORPORATED
1212-34th Avenue. S.E., Calgary, AB, T2G 1V7. Contact: Fran. Dev. - Tel: (403) 243-8919, Fax: (403) 243-3417, Web Site: www.nascor.com. Nascor licenses companies to manufacture wooden l-beams. We offer design software, marketing support, technical 2 week training and ongoing support. Established: 1982 - No. of Units: Franchised: 13 - Total Inv: $250,000 US funds. Locations: Southern B.C. and U.S.

NORTHERN SHIELD
827 Danforth Place, Burlington, ON, L7T 1S1. Contact: John S. Luckanuck, President - Tel: (905)522-7949, (800)913-9299, Fax: (905) 528-4585, E-Mail: northernshield@cogeco.ca. Fire retardant coatings for wood construction, steel, wallboards, aircraft, auto's, etc. Established: 1989 - Franchising Since: 1994 - No. of Units: Company Owned: 1 - Franchised: 2 - Franchise Fee: $25,000 - Royalty: 5% - Total Inv: $50,000 - Financing: Yes.

PAL LUMBER AND BUILDING
5 rue Montclair, Hull, QC, J8Y 2E3. Contact: Ronald Lavoie, Pres. - Tel: (819) 771-5841, Fax: (819) 771-6319. Wood and construction materials. Franchisee must currently own an establishment. Franchising Since: 1958 - No. of Units: Company Owned: 12 distribution centers - Franchised: Over 100.

PAUL'S RESTORATIONS
Paul's Restorations Management Inc.
1640 Upper Ottawa St., Hamilton, ON, L8W 3P2. Contact: David Sebastianutti, Controller - Tel: (800) 363-7285, (905) 388-7285, Fax: (905) 388-7478. Property restoration and cleaning services for the insurance industry. Established: 1980 - Franchising Since: 1995 - No. of Units: Company Owned: 2 - Franchised: 6 - Franchise Fee: $20,000 base territory fee adjusted for population - Royalty: Flat monthly fee + 1% corp. adv. - Total Inv: Territory fee + start up costs.

PERMACRETE
Permacrete Systems Ltd.
85 Main Street, Dartmouth, NS, B2W 3V1. Contact: William G. Cole, Pres. - Tel: (902) 468-1700 , (800) 565-LEAK (5325), Fax: (902) 468-7474, Web Site: www.permacrete.ca. Unique system of basement waterproofing concrete repair and restoration, offering protected territories and water control systems (license-franchise). Two week in-house and on-site training with supervision and ongoing support. Established: 1980 - Franchising Since: 1990 - No. of Units: Company Owned: 1 - Franchised: 19 - Franchise Fee: $18,000-$30,000 - Royalty: 5% gross - Financing: No.

QUARTZ COAT CANADA
Quartz Coat Protective Coatings
25 Rayborn Cres, St. Albert, AB, T8N 5B9. Contact: Ivan Mayer or Lyle Robson - Tel: (780) 460-4246, (888) 349-2729, Fax: (780) 460-4251, E-Mail: quartzcoat@incentre.net, Web Site: www.quartzcoatcanada.com. Quartz Coat coatings beautifies as well as protects wood and concrete surfaces with a rock hard coating on exterior and interior applications. 8 new coating products included. Established: 2002 - Franchising Since: 2002 - No. of Units: Corporate Units: 1 - Franchised/Dealers: 30 - Franchise Fee/ Dealership Fee: $8,000 including equipment & start up product - Total Inv: $8,000 - Royalty: $100 monthly - Financing: Financial & business start up.

STUCCO DOCTOR
Stucco Doctor Corp.
#18-1780 McLean Ave., Port Coquitlam, BC, V3C 4K9. Contact: Ken Brandon, Pres. - Tel: (250) 474-3037, Fax: (250) 474-3056. A stucco care and restoration company with 50 years experience. We feature products and services unique to this industry, from cleaning and maintenance through to refinishing with stucco. Established: 1990 - Franchising Since: 1991 - No. of Units: Company Owned: 1 - Franchised: 8 - Franchise Fee: $24,500 - Royalty: 7%, 2% nat. and reg. adv. - Total Inv: $69,500 (fee $24,500/training $13,000/equip. $20,000/opening $12,000) - Financing: No.

STUDENT WORKS PAINTING
Works Corps.
144 Main Street North, Markham, ON, L3P 5T3. Contact: Chris Thompson, Pres. - Tel: (905) 201-1477. Student operated residential maintenance painting business. Entire business/marketing plans and materials provided, along with ongoing support. Operates only during the summer. Established: 1981 - Franchising Since: 1983 - No. of Units: Approx. 1,000 (Incl. Canada & U.S.) - Royalty: 10% of sales - Total Inv: $2,000 an average for summer vehicle - Financing: Yes, depending upon regional gov't programs.

SUPER SEAMLESS STEEL SIDING OF CANADA, LTD.

560 Henderson Dr., Regina, SK, S4N 5X2. Contact: Nestor Mryglod, Dir. of Franchise - Tel: (800) 565-4334, (306) 721-8000, Fax: (306) 721-2532. Exclusive franchisor of the ABC Super Seamless siding machines in Canada. Machines job-site or in-plant manufacture siding in 14 profiles, in custom lengths up to 200 ft. For commercial and residential application. Company provides PVC Steel Coil for manufacture and supply all necessary trims and accessories. Training, comprehensive business operations and procedures manuals, counselling and sales aids. Established: 1978 - Franchising Since: 1985 - No. of Units: Company Owned: 2 - Franchised: 12 - Franchise Fee: $19,500 - Royalty: Yearly fee - Total Inv: $55,000-$120,000. Equipment leasing available.

SUPERGARD CANADA LTD.

4056 Meadowbrook Dr. Ste. #102, London, ON, N6L 1E4. Contact: Donald F. Hawken, Pres. - Tel: (800) 682-6943, Fax: (519) 652-9614. The long lasting answer for your outside and inside protection needs. Industrial strength coatings for commercial, agricultural and residential use. Sales, service and application for concrete, masonry, wood, metal, interlocking and natural stone. Automotive Rust Prevention System. Established: 1988 - No. of Units: Company Owned: 1 - Dealers: 100+ - Dealership Fee: Based on territory - Total Inv: Opportunities start at $1,000 - Financing: Yes, on approved applicants.

UNIVERSITY FIRST CLASS PAINTERS
University Contractors Corp. Ltd.

5687 West St., Ste. 200, Halifax, NS, B3K 1H6. Contact: Mike Benteau, Pres. - Tel: (888) 724-6888, E-Mail: ufcp@ufcp.ca, Web Site: www.ufcp.ca. Offering franchises for a full range of painting and cleaning services. We provide marketing, training, leases for equipment, accounting and payroll services and all forms for the operation of the business. Established: 1982 - Franchising Since: 1986 - No. of Units: Company Owned: 1 - Franchised: 40 - Franchise Fee: None - Royalty: 16%-24% depends on area and experience - Total Inv: $3,000-$5,000 - Financing: Yes.

WINDSOR PLYWOOD

10382 176th Street, Surrey, BC, V4N 4H5. Contact: S.R. Jones or A.Wightman, Pres. /Mgr., Mktg.& Opers. - Tel: (604) 581-4661, Fax: (604) 581-8886. The wholesale and retail distribution of building material products. Established: 1960 - Franchising Since: 1970 - No. of Units: 61 - Franchise Fee: $35,000.

WINMAR
Winmar Franchise Corp.

175 Stronach Crescent, London, ON, N5V 3G5. Contact: John White, Owner - Tel: (519) 451-0000, Fax: (519) 451-4279. General contracting, disaster restoration, insurance work specialists. Established: 1977 - Franchising Since: 1991 - No. of Units: Franchised: 11 - Franchise Fee: $20,000 - Royalty: 3% to million gross, 1% over million, .25% adv. - Total Inv: $50,000 - Financing: Yes.

WISE CRACKS®
Wise Cracks Concrete Technologies Inc.

2 Lakeside Place, Unit 9, Halifax, NS, B3T 1L7. Contact: Franchise Director - Tel: (902) 835-6763, (800) 587-7325, Fax: (902) 876-8863, E-Mail: wisecracks@aol.com, Web Site: www.wisecracksrestoration.com. Foundation waterproofing and concrete repair system. No leak too BIG!! Established: 1991 - Franchising Since: 1994 - No. of Units: Company Owned: 2 - Franchised: 8 - Franchise Fee: $5,000 - Royalty: 4.5% - Total Inv: Varies by population of exclusive terr - Financing: No.

BURGLAR & FIRE PREVENTION

ALARMFORCE
AlarmForce Industries Inc.

98 Scarsdale Rd., Don Mills, ON, M3B 2R7. Contact: Joel Matlin, President - Tel: (416) 445-2001, (800) 267-2001, Fax: (416) 445-1482, Web Site: www. alarmforce.com. Home alarm business. Proprietary technology with alarm voice 2-way voice. Established: 1988 - Franchising

Since: 1991 - No. of Units: Company Owned: 4 - Franchised: 34 - Franchise Fee: $25,000 - Royalty: None - Total Inv: $25,000 - Financing: No.

INTERNATIONAL LOSS PREVENTION SYSTEMS INC.

1350 E. 4th Ave. Vancouver, BC, V5N 1J5. Contact: Ian Abramson, CEO - Tel: (604) 255-5000, (800) 633-4577, Fax: (604) 254-2575, E-Mail: info@ilps.com, Web Site: www.ilps.com. Manufacturer of Loss Prevention Products, Services and Educational programs. Established: 1988 - Franchising Since: 1987 - No. of Units: Company Owned: 15 - Franchised: 8 - Franchise Fee: $25,000 - Total Inv: $25,000 - Financing: Yes.

SAFETECH ALARM SYSTEMS

121 Willowdale Ave., Unit 202, Toronto, ON, M2N 6A3. Contact: Sean O'Leary, Pres. - Tel: (416) 229-9902, Fax: (416) 229-9400, (888) 939-3733. Install and monitor residential and commercial alarm systems, c.ctv and card access also. Established: 1995 - Franchising Since: 1996 - No. of Units: Company Owned: 1 - Franchise Fee: $10,000-$15,000 - Royalty: 6% + 3% prov. adv. - Total Inv: $5,000 setup fee + $10,000 inventory - Financing: Yes.

X-RAY EYES

473 Bowsman Road, #234, Winnipeg, MB, R2X 1M6. Contact: Fran. Dev. - Tel: (204) 235-0010. Residential and commercial security systems. Full system training and ongoing support. Established: 1990 - No. of Units: Franchised: 22 - Total Inv: $32,000 min cash.

BUSINESS PRODUCTS AND SERVICES

A-2-Z MONEY IDEAS INC.

351 Parkridge Cres, Oakville, ON, L6M 1A8. Contact: Daniel J. Hebert, Pres. - Tel: (905) 337-2600. #1 team offers proven blueprints, strategies and distributorships to earn biggest profit ever! Showing America how to capitalize on the trend of economic insecurity. Established: 1993 - Franchising Since: 1993 - No. of Units: Company Owned: 2 - Franchised: 417 - Franchise Fee: $55 - Total Inv: Under $500 - Financing: No. NOT OFFERING FRANCHISES AT THIS TIME.

ADVOCATE PARALEGAL SERVICES LTD.

12 Ottawa Street North, Hamilton, ON, L8H 3Y7. Contact: Robert Thomson, Dir. of Fran. - Fax: (519) 752-4297. Paralegal services dealing with gov't agencies such as U.I.C.,Workmans Comp., etc. Established: 1991 - Franchising Since: 1996 - No. of Units: Company Owned: 4 - Franchise Fee: $5,000 - Royalty: 4%, 2% adv. - Total Inv: $25,000 - Financing: Yes.

BARTER WORLD INC.

230 Harwood Ave South Ste 2, Ajax, ON, L1S 2H6. Contact: Ken Yeomans, Pres. - Tel: (800) 668-5915, Fax: (905) 426-7117. A brokerage firm overseeing business owners trading goods and services between each other. Established: 1993 - No. of Units: Company Owned: 1 - Franchised: 1 - Franchise Fee: $5,000-$45,000 - Royalty: 2.5% - Total Inv: $10,000-$55,000 - Financing: Yes.

BEVINCO
Bevasco Corporation

505 Consumers Rd., #510, Toronto, ON, M2J 4V8. Contact: Vanessa Ziskos-Decarie - Tel: (416) 490-6266, (888) 238-4626, Fax: (416) 490-6899, E-Mail: vanessa@bevinco.com, Web Site: www.bevinco.com. Bevinco provides "on-premise" owners with a more effective method to end liquor loss. Bevinco has grown internationally to become the leading profit control service available today. Bevinco will help you find more profit in very bottle, guaranteed less shrinkage", more profit, better business with Bevinco. Established: 1987 - Franchising Since: 1991 - No. of Units: Company Owned: 1 - Franchised: 250 - Franchise Fee: $39,500 (US) - Royalty: 12% + 4% advert - Total Inv: $40,000 (US) - Financing: Not provided.

BUSINESS ROUND TABLE

5 Pacific Ave, Moncton, NB, E1E 2G2. Contact: Rick DesBrisay, President - Tel: (506) 389-7030, E-Mail: rick@businessroundtable.com, Web Site: www.businessroundtable.com. Guided mutual mentoring for

small-business owners. People are placed in a group of about ten others and they meet regularly to help each other have more successful businesses. Established: 1991 - Franchising Since: 2001- No. of Units: Company Owned: 1 - Franchised: 3 - Franchise Fee: $20,000 Cdn - Royalty: 10% - Total Inv: $20,000 - Financing: Yes.

CADET PLUS BUSINESS CENTRE
Grayker Corporation
290 Old Weston Rd., Toronto, ON, M6N 3A4. Contact: Don Schell, G.M. Franchise Operation - Tel: (416) 656-5601, Fax: (416) 656-4519, E-Mail: grayker@home.com, Web Site: www.cadetclean.com. Dry cleaning depot combined with copying machines, fax machines, printing services, computer time rental, mailbox receiving and desk publishing. Established: 1999 - Franchising Since: 1999 - No. of Units: Company Owned: 3 - Total Inv: Starting at $149,500 - Financing: Will assist.

CANADA POST CORPORATION
2701 Riverside Dr., Ste. N0551, Ottawa, ON, K1A 0B1. Contact: Mgr., Fran. Dev. - Tel: (416) 204-4245. Retailing of postal products through existing established retail businesses. Franchising Since: 1987 - No. of Units: Franchised: 1,000 urban outlets & 1,200 rural - Royalty: 2%+1% adv. - Total Inv: Approx. $65,000 - Financing: No.

CANADIAN TRAINING & DEVELOPMENT GROUP, INC.
7170 W. Credit Ave., Mississauga, ON, L5N 5Z3. Contact: Gary Prenevost, Nat'l Development Director - Tel: (800) 387-8301, Fax: (905) 542-0235. C.T.D.G. offers business opportunities in the form of distributorships. This national educational/training company has been providing Canadian businesses with an integrated source for all their training and development needs for over 20 years. Distributor support includes extensive training in sales/mktg, facilitation, training skills, product knowledge. Two annual conferences and conventions, monthly training schools, bi-monthly support mailings, personal coaching, full-time marketing directors, a 1-800 support line etc. Established: 1974 - Offering Distributorships Since: 1975 - No. of Distributorships: 138 - Total Inv: $38,950 - Financing: Yes.

CENTER FOR PERFORMANCE DEVELOPMENT
1600 Merivale Road, Suite 216, Ottawa, ON, K2G 5J8. - Tel: (613) 225-0083, (877) 611-7587, Fax: (613) 225-8469, E-Mail: cpd@persprod plus.com, Web Site: www.persprodplus.com. Become a licensed practitioner of a Time Management program. Part of the Queen's University Executive MBA program in Ottawa. Add to your present services or build a rewarding second career. Help executives, managers and professionals Work and Live Smarter... Not Harder. Help organizations achieve measurable increases in productivity. Established: 1991 - Franchising Since: 1999 - Franchise Fee: $12,500 - Total Inv: Varies.

CERIDIAN CANADA LTD.
125 Garry St., Winnipeg, MB, R3C 3P2. - Tel: (204) 946-0770, (877) 237-4342, Fax: (888) 311-2117, E-Mail: sales@ceridian.ca, Web Site: www.ceridian.ca. Ceridian Canada, the nation's HR and payroll specialists, delivers innovative solutions to more than 40,000 businesses of all sizes, in virtually every industry. From payroll by phone and web ideal for small businesses, to integrated payroll and HR solutions, employee assistance programs, training, recruitment and managed payroll administration for larger companies, Ceridian Canada provides unique solutions to help you save valuable time and achieve your buisness goals. With a commitment to service excellence and a dedicated franchise team, Ceridian Canada can give you the freedom to succeed.

CHRISELLE CONFERENCE MANAGEMENT
383 Richmond Street, #1000, London, ON, N6A 3C4. Contact: Robyn Abbey, President - Tel: (519) 679-6962, Fax: (519) 679-7495, E-Mail: robyn@chriselle.com. Specializes in turnkey operation, regional/national/ international conference management, incentive travel trade show management, creative/communication services, registration information/ data management, complete budget management. Established: 1992.

CMC COLLATERAL MANAGEMENT CANADA LTD.
104-630 Columbia St., New Westminster, BC, V3M 1A5. Contact: Robert M. Fletcher, Pres. - Tel: (604) 522-8618, Fax: (604) 522-9896. Specialized financial service company offers third party assessments to financial institutions on the assets pledged as collateral for loans. Successful preparation of financing requests and loan placements. Established: 1983 - No. of Units: Company Owned: 1 - Franchise Fee: $25,000 - Royalty: 5%, 10% adv. - Total Inv: $75,000.

CRANKPOTS CERAMIC STUDIOS
2025 West Broadway, Suite 405, Vancouver, BC, V6J 1Z6. Contact: M.A. Hannah, Fran. Dev. - Tel: (604) 739-7161, Fax: (604) 734-8333. Paint your own ceramics. Customers choose ceramics to paint, studio supplies paint and brushes, then glaze and fire the customers creation. Training and support provided. Support: 2 weeks - site selection, lease negotiations. Established: 1994 - No. of Units: Company Owned: 1 - Franchised: 9 - Franchise Fee: $15,000 - Royalty: 6% - adv. fee 2% - Total Inv: $60,000-$80,000.

DISTRIO *
1418 Maisonneuve Street, Mont-Joli, QC, G5H 2J3. Contact: Gaston St-Pierre - Tel: (418) 775-8311, (877) 258-0852, Fax: (418) 775-7388, E-Mail: mail@sport-fest.info, Web Site: www.sport-fest.com. New formula allowing to do commerce in franchisor's premises. No overhead, no risk. Lot of fun and profits. Established: 2004 - Franchising Since: 2004 - No. of Units: Company Owned: 12 - Franchise Fee: $5,000-$10,000 - Total Inv: $200,000 - Financing: No.

ENVOY BUSINESS SERVICES
Envoy Business Services Inc.
91 Rylander Blvd., Ste. 7, Toronto, ON, M1B 5M5. Contact: John Reynolds & Ken West, Managing Partners - Tel: (416) 283-6897, (800) 26 ENVOY, Fax: (416) 283-9502, E-Mail: kenwest@envoy.ca, Web Site: www.envoy.ca. Retail outlets providing integrated range of business services including mailbox rentals, courier and postage, printing, copying, fax and e-mail, computer use, internet services, desktop and word processing. Established: 1990 - Franchising Since: 1990 - No. of Units: Company Owned: 1- Franchised: 39 - Franchise Fee: $25,500 CDN - Royalty: 6% on high margin only of gross - Total Inv: $75,000 intial plus operating funds - Financing: Assistance, business planning.

EXPENSE REDUCTION ANALYSTS
Expense Reduction Analysts International/Canada Inc
703 Evans Avenue., Suite 307, Toronto, ON, M9C 5E9. Contact: Ross Pinkerton, President - Tel: (416) 622-7720, (877) 859-8146, Fax: (416) 622-4501, Web Site: www.expense-reduction.net. ERAI today operates an office network providing clients in eighteen countries with a vital business service dedicated to keeping client costs down and profits up. ERAI franchisees are trained to analyze a company's expenditure opportunities for cost reduction. ERAI seeks franchisees with a professional or commercial background, an ability to communicate effectively with business decision-makers, deliver a professional service and communicate and process information productively. Established: 1998 - Franchising Since: 1998 - Franchise Fee: $34,500 - Royalty: $700/monthly membership fee - Total Inv: Franchise fee $34,500 + say 6 months living expenses $54,500 - Financing: No.

GEORGIAN OAKS INTERNATIONAL
1952 Ludgate Cres., Ottawa, ON, K1J 8L2. Contact: Bill Marsden, C.E.O. - Tel: (613) 741-0267. Business consultants in selling, buying business and franchises. Established: 1984 - Franchising Since: 1984 - No. of Units: Company Owned: 2 - Total Inv: $10,000 and up - Financing: No.

IB YOUR OFFICE BUSINESS CENTERS
MG & Bal Business Service
3300 Bloor St. W. #3140, Toronto, ON, M9A 1A4. Contact: President - Tel: (416) 207-2070, (800) 806-1167, Fax: (416) 207-2071, E-Mail: canada@youroffice.com, Web Site: www.yourofficecanada.com. "International Franchising," International network features flexibility in providing comprehensive office facilities for home-based businesses and cost conscious corporations. We will provide services to small

bussinesses and new entrepreneurs without overhead. Established: 1996 - Franchising Since: 1996 - No. of Units: Company Owned: 1 - Franchised: 5 - Franchise Fee: $38,000 - Royalty: 6%, 2% ad fund - Total Inv: $250,000 (capital $200,000; operating $50,000) - Financing: Yes.

IMAGE CONTROL
Recycled Toner Cartridges
3-489 Brimley Rd, Toronto, ON, M1J 1A3. - Tel: (416) 694-7509, Fax: (416) 694-7929, E-Mail: toner@idirect.com, Web Site: www.image-control.com. Canada's largest inventory of toner cartridges - new, compatible, remanufactured - all at discount from 'Depot' type store prices. Trademark regd. #728213. No royalties, recurring fees or fancy lawyers. Associates receive: 2 days training, on-going support, existing base of corporate and retail customers in protected area. Solid accounting, marketing and dignified proven, telemarketing systems. Meticulously detailed cross reference and guides. You will be the Laser and Jet Printer, fax and small copier toner expert in your area. Inclusion in all national corporate advertising and the most advanced web site in the industry. Associates must have sales experience to gain corporate accounts and close leads supplied. Currently 2 retail locations, 3 other home based associates. License fee $12,500. Initial inventory min. $5,000. Image Control will assist with up to 35% financing. Member of Metro To. Better Business Bureau.

INFO-CHIP COMMUNICATIONS LTD.
3137 Kingsway, 2nd Floor, Vancouver, BC, V5R 5J9. Contact: Bob Stewart, Dealer Division Manager - Tel: (604) 439-7561, (800) 881-2833, Fax: (604) 439-7562, E-Mail: dealer@info-chip.com, Web Site: www.info-chip.com. Manufacture the DPV-2000 digital on-hold marketing system. Provide creative and production services for telephone on hold marketing. Established: 1993 - No. of Units: Company Owned: 1 - Franchise Fee: Negotiable - Royalty: Negotiable - Total Inv: Negotiable - Financing: Negotiable.

INTERFACE FINANCIAL GROUP, THE
Interface Group Ltd., The
#205-444 Victoria St, Kamloops, BC, V2C 2A7. Contact: David Banfield, Pres. - Tel: (888) 819-3289, Fax: (250) 372-3289. Provides short term working to small businesses by purchasing invoices (accounts receivable) for cash at a discount on a recourse basis. Established: 1970 - Franchising Since: 1990 - No. of Units: Franchised: 30 Canada, 19 USA - Franchise Fee: $25,000 - Royalty: 10% of gross income or 1% of sales - Total Inv: $25,000 fee + $5,000 equip., working capital - Financing: On franchise fee only.

INTERNATIONAL BUSINESS OPPORTUNITIES
Worldwide Canadian Management Consultants, Inc.
P.O. Box 639, Pickering, ON, L1V 3T3. Contact: Dr. K. Rogers or Dr. Dar, Dir. - Tel: (905) 686-0469, Fax: (905) 686-0469. Over 25 years of great success the businesses covered by the company are: product promotion, marketing, import/export, joint ventures, investment, business tours, business acquistions, real estate, franchising and training. Established: 1976 - Franchising Since: 1980 - No. of Units: Company Owned: 2 - Franchised: 37 - Franchise Fee: Home office: $6,599 US, Full franchise: $20,000-$60,000 US- Total Inv: Home office: $15,000 US, Full: $25,000 US - Financing: Yes in 23 different countries and expanding.

INTERNATIONAL BUSINESS REFERRALS INC.
1653 Greenfield Road, Cambridge, ON, N1R 5S5. Contact: Terry Hunter, Gen. Mngr. - Tel: (519) 740-9074, Fax: (519) 740-9237. An organization dedicated to helping small and medium-sized business, including self employed individuals increase their sales and profits thru business referrals. Its business helping business. Established: 1997 - Franchising Since: 1999 - No. of Units: Franchised: 1 - Franchise Fee: $35,000.

INTERNATIONAL HOME OFFICE
1053311 Ontario Inc.
10 Royal Orchard Blvd., P.O. Box 53037, Thornhill, ON, L3T 7R9. Contact: Vladimir Machlis, Pres. - Tel: (905) 764-7058, Fax: (905) 709-9596. Service of office machines (copiers, fax, printers); sales of supplies for office machines. Established: 1989 - Franchising Since: 1992 - No. of Units: Company Owned: 1 - Franchise Fee: $15,000 - Total Inv: $15,000.

ISLAND INK-JET SYSTEMS INC.
244 Fourth Street, Courtenay, BC, V9N 1G6. - Tel: (877) 446-5538, E-Mail: pacton@islandinkjet.com, Web Site: www.islandinkjet.com. The Refill Guys. Regional shopping mall inkjet cartridge refill kiosks. Established: 2000 - Franchising Since: 2000 - No. of Units: Company Owned: 1 - Franchised: 43 - Franchise Fee: $29,900 - Total Inv: $59,900-$159,900.

LEASE SAVERS LTD.
Lease Savers Ltd.
10 Queen Elizabeth Blvd., Toronto, ON, M8Z 1L8. Contact: Jack Fishman - Tel: (416) 252-1330, (888) 888-5912, Fax: (416) 252-8278. Business Opportunity. Incorrect administration of leases by landlords is costing commercial and retail tenants millions of dollars. Profit from proven lease auditing and cost recovery techniques. Established: 1986 - Franchising Since: 1996 - Total Inv: $3,770 U.S.

LIGHTNING CAPITAL
1 Bartley Bull Parkway, Suite 18, Brampton, ON, L6W 3T7. Contact: Fran. Dev. - Tel: (905) 459-6122, Fax: (905) 459-5155, Web Site: www.lightningcapital.com. Franchise Concept: We purchase receivables from companies who cannot wait the normal thirty to sixty days it takes to receive payment from their clients. We also offer other financial services such as letters of credit and purchase ordering funding. Established: 1998 - No. of Units: Franchised: 12 - Total Inv: $100,000.

MARSH CANADA LIMITED
70 University Ave. Suite 800, Toronto, ON, M5J 2M4. Contact: Fran. Dev. - Tel: (416) 349-4359, Fax: (416) 349-4521. The country's largest insurance broker with 19 offices from St.Johns to Vancouver, specializes in the development of high quality programs for all classes of property and casualty insurance. Established: 1914.

MATCH'N "MONEY WITH MOXY"
Match'n "Money With Moxy" Services Inc.
#1-1949 West 8th Ave., Vancouver, BC, V6J 1W2. Contact: Donald M. Burdeny, Pres/CEO - Tel: (604) 737-8233, Fax: (604) 737-8233, E-Mail: moxy@mrmoxy.com, Web Site: www.mrmoxy.com. Opportunity for affiliate to join, sell advertising, loan, franchise, consulting, boat brokering & more. Established: 1998 - Franchising Since: 1998 - No. of Units: Company Owned: 1 - Franchise Fee: $4,900 - Royalty: 3.5% - Financing: No.

MICROCREDIT TECHNOLOGIES CORP.
144 Front Street West, Ste. 470, Toronto, ON, M5J 2L7. Contact: V.P. Sales - Tel: (416) 977-9993, Fax: (416) 977-6893. Manufacture of Internet Access Terminals for public and commercial locations. The units, resembling a traditional arcade-type amusement game, can be used by the public for countless applications. Accepts coins, bills, and credit cards. Established: 1996 - Franchising Since: 1996 - No. of Units: Company Owned: 230 - Franchised: 14 - Franchise Fee: $9,200 per unit - Royalty: None - Total Inv: Minimum $11,000 - Financing: O.A.C.

MIND THE STORE INC.
869 Gana Street, Mississauga, ON, L5S 1N9. Contact: Christine Korda, Corp. Comm/Marketing Div. - Tel: (905) 670-5704, Fax: (905) 670-7697, Web Site: www.mindthestore.com. We are an award winning advanced software development and marketing company that provides affordable total merchant management solutions for business around the world. Established: 1985.

MONEY CONCEPTS (CANADA) LTD.
180 Attwell Dr., Ste. 501, Toronto, ON, M9W 6A9. Contact: Franchise Department - Tel: (416) 674-0450, Fax: (416) 674-4785. Money Concepts is in the business of bringing personal financial planning to the middle income market through individually owned financial planning centres purchased by entrepreneurs under the franchise system. Money Concepts provides a comprehensive business system embodying all aspects of business establishment and continuation. Established: 1984 - Franchising Since: 1985 - No. of Units: Franchised: 99 - Franchise Fee: $43,000 - Total Inv: Fee plus $15,000 start up costs - Financing: None.

MUTUAL EXCHANGE INTERNATIONAL, INC.
#706-1155 Robson Street, Vancouver, BC, V6E 1B5. Contact: Fran. Dev. - Tel: (604) 685-8750, (800) 720-3388, Fax: (604) 681-2648, E-Mail: corp_office@mutual.com, Web Site: www.mutual.com. Canada's

first fully automated commercial barter, exchange, company. Our members are some of Canada's leading corporations. Are you comfortable dealing at the corporate level and have the drive and commitment to capitalize on a first class business opportunities in a 10.2 billion dollar growth industry. Established: 1994 - No. of Units: Franchised: 7 - Total Inv: $75,000-$200,000.

PARALEGAL INVESTIGATION
P.O. Box 270, Campbellford, ON, K0L 1L0. - Tel: (705) 778-3863. We investigate global business opportunities, you operate from home. Example: world investments, information broker with numerous job openings for self employment. Established: 1989 - Franchising Since: 1992 - Franchise Fee: $3,800 - Royalty: None - Total Inv: $3,800 - Financing: Yes.

PAYSTATION CRIME CONTROLL CENTRES
Paystation Inc
5155 Spectrum Way, Unit 17, Mississauga, ON, L4W 5A1. Contact: Robert Warner, Pres. - Tel: (905) 625-8500, (800) 268-1440, Fax: (905) 625-6254, Web Site: www. paystation.ca. Our business is controlling criminal activities involving cheque fraud, computer fraud and corporate espionage crimes. Established: 1955 - Licensing Since: 1995 - No. of Units: Company Owned: 9 - Licensed: 15 - Franchise Fee: $7500.00 - Royalty: None - Total Inv: $7500.00 - Financing: No.

PRAIRIE PACIFIC FRANCHISING, INC
8793 Pender Park Dr, Sidney, BC, V8L 4B4. Contact: Dale Stewart - Tel: (250) 656-7686, (888) 522-4567, Fax: (250) 656-7618. Research, financing and start-up in franchises and home based businesses, offering a variety of opportunities including coffee, bakery, business services, day care, computer training on-line and legal services. Established: 1989 - No. of Units: Company Owned: 1 - Franchised: 1 - Franchise Fee: $25,000 - Total Inv: $25,000-$200,000.

PREVUE ASSESSMENT
Prevue Resource Group
1896 West 1st Ave., Vancouver, BC, V6J 1G5. Contact: Eric Hoover, President - Tel: (604) 730-1232, Fax: (604) 730-1298. Prevue Resource Group is a distributor of four automated systems or software packages that help corporations and individuals maximize people performance. Our products facilitate improved selection coaching, training and succession planning decisions. Established: 1994 - Offering Dealerships Since: 1994 - No. of Units: Company Owned: 1 - Dealerships: 30 - Dealership Fee: $7,500 - Royalty: Fee includes initial inventory- Financing: None.

PRODUCTIVITY POINT INTERNATIONAL CANADA INC.
99 Metcalfe St. Ste. 405, Ottawa, ON, K1P 6l7. Contact: Bob Crozier, V.P. - Tel: (613) 230-3391. PPI is a powerful consortium of conversion-computer-training franchises across Canada and U.S. Major benefit to conversion - franchisees include: 1) networked national training delivery 2) comprehensive instructor-led courseware portfolio - 300 course title 3) mgmt. support systems 4) save money on ATC applications. Established: 1985 - Franchising Since: 1991 - No. of Units: Company Owned: 1 - Franchised: 52 - Franchise Fee: $15,000 - Royalty: 8% up to $500,000, 7.5% up to $1 million, 7% up to $1.5 million etc. - Total Inv: $15,000 plus monthly royalties based on revenues - Financing: Qualification: must be an existing established instructor-led computer training company to be considered.

PROSHRED SECURITY
Proshred Inc.
2200 Lakeshore Blvd. W., Ste. 102, Toronto, ON, M8V 1A4. Contact: Sean O'Dea, Fran. Dev. - Tel: (800) 461-9760, Fax: (416) 251-7121. Large mobile document shredding service operating in U.S.A., Canada and Europe. Business to business service for executive types with good management skills. Established: 1986 - Franchising Since: 1990 - No. of Units: Franchised: 18 - Franchise Fee: $35,000 - Royalty: 8% of sales - Total Inv: $218,000: $80,000 cash plus work. cap. - Financing: Third party: $110,000.

RIBBON XCHANGE
Rynker Ribbon Xchange Inc
#200-8566 Fraser St, Vancouver, BC, V5X 3X3. Contact: Pete Benson, President - Tel: (604) 322-9421, Fax: (604) 322-1658, E-Mail: rynker@dowco.com, Web Site: www.rynker.com. Franchisees recycle computer, fax and photo copier printer cartridges: inkjet, ribbon and laser cartridges. Established: 1991 - Franchising Since: 1991 - No. of Units: Company Owned: 3 - Franchised: 25 - Franchise Fee: $25,000 - Royalty: $600.00 month - Total Inv: $85,000 - Financing: No.

RISK TAKER INVESTMENT STRATEGIES
Oasis Publishing Of Canada Corp
2344 Valleyview Drive, Courtenay, BC, V9N 8S5. Contact: Clinton Beck, CEO - Tel: (250) 897-0044, (800) 265-6332, Fax: (250) 334-3456, E-Mail: ceo@risktaker.net, Web Site: www.risktaker.net. Educating entrepreneurs on how to technically trade commodities and stocks on line. Established: 1992 - Franchising Since: 1998 - No. of Units: Company Owned: 2 - Franchised: 192 - Franchise Fee: $700 U.S. - Royalty: $65.00 + tax, $69.55 US /month - Total Inv: $5,000 - computer - internet - advertising.

ROSS DIXON FINANCIAL SERVICES
Ross Dixon Holdings Ltd.
110 Pinnacle Dr., Kitchener, ON, N2P 1C5. Contact: Dave Velanoff, Pres. - Tel: (519) 895-1513, Fax: (519) 895-2346. Offers personal service in financial planning with a broad range of financial products. RDFS shops the markets for GIC's, RSP's, mutual funds, mortgages, insurance, RIF's, annuities, self directed plans and more. Established: 1978 - Franchising Since: 1989 - No. of Units: Franchised: 24 - Franchise Fee: None, cost of start up only, variable - Royalty: 20% of gross commissions (reduces by volume) - Total Inv: Varies, $25,000 and up work. cap. - Financing: Available through bank facility.

SANDLER SALES INSTITUTE
Sandler Sales Institute (Canada) Ltd
3625 McGill Street, Vancouver, BC, V3V 5B7. Contact: Ron Taylor, Director of Franchise Sales - Tel: (604) 254-4341, (800) 669-3537, Fax: (6041) 251-8060, E-Mail: rtaylor@sandler.com, Web Site: www.sandler.com. The Sandler Sales Institute provides ongoing incremental reinforced sales and management training for individuals and companies. Coaching and one on one counselling are the key element required to ensure positive change and growth. The Sandler selling system is proprietary and non-traditional. Established: 1992 - Franchising Since: 1992 - No. of Units: Franchised: 12 Canada, 167 US - Franchise Fee: $58,000 - Royalty: $908.00 monthly - Total Inv: $75,000 - Financing: No.

SHRED-TECH
Shred-Tech
295 Pinebush Rd., Cambridge, ON, N1T 1B2. - Tel: (519) 621-3560, (800) 465-3214, Fax: (519) 621-0688, E-Mail: mobile@shred-tech.com, Web Site: www.shred-tech.com. Shred-Tech is the original manufacturer of document destruction vehicles for the on-site security shredding industry, and serves business start-ups accounts. Established: 1976 - Franchising Since: 1976 - No. of Units: Franchised: 350+ - Total Inv: $50,000 U.S., Cash equity required - Financing: Yes.

SKY.LINK INTERNET ACCESS
30 Greenboro Crescent, Ottawa, ON, K1T 1W5. Contact: Joe Simpson, Senior VP of Marketing - Tel: (613) 738-1374, Fax: (613) 738-0809, E-Mail: joe.simpson@skylink.ca, Web Site: www.skylink.ca. Provide stand-alone public internet kiosks to hotels, airports, train stations etc., to be used on a pay-per-use basis. Established: 1996 - Franchising Since: 1997 - No. of Units: Company Owned: 7 - Franchise Fee: $500 per unit - Royalty: 8% - Financing: No.

SOURCE IMAGING
1110 Finch Ave. West, Suite 524, Toronto, ON, M3J 2T2. Contact: Joe Osiel, President - Tel: (416) 650-1588, Fax: (416) 650-1722. Franchisees provide services of printing, packaging and promotions without investing in equipment, staff or store front, as they purchase products directly from manufacturers. Business operates from home or small office. Training and support provided. Established: 1997 - No. of Units: Franchised: 12 - Franchise Fee: $12,500 total turnkey - Total Inv: $17,500 (FF $12,500+$5,000 cap).

SUCCESS HIGHWAY INTERNATIONAL
3950, 14th Ave., Ste. 405-407, Markham, ON, L3R 0A9. Contact: Franchise Manager - Tel: (905) 305-1850, (888) 722-2118, Fax: (905) 305-8960. Prepaid calling cards, cellular phones, reduced long distance equal access, IDD service and internet, security monitoring system. Established: 1998 - Franchising Since: 1998 - No. of Units: Company Owned: 1 - Franchise Fee: $15,000 - Royalty: 5% of gross sales, 2% adv. on gross sales - Total Inv: $45,000 turnkey - Financing: Yes.

SUSSEX INSURANCE AGENCY INCORPORATED
136 West 3 Street, Vancouver, BC, V7M 1E8. Contact: Ken Armstrong, President / CEO - Tel: (604) 988-6344, Fax: (604) 986-5293, E-Mail: sussex@direct.ca. We are general insurance agents specializing in government and private auto insurance from offices located inside the Real Canadian Superstores in BC, AB, MAN. Full range of insurance for homeowners, condos, tenants, business/commercial. Established: 1976 - No. of Units: Company Owned: 7 - Franchised: 20 - Franchise Fee: $75,000-$150,000 - Total Inv: $200,000-$300,000.

TGD (INTERNATIONAL INVESTMENT CONSULTANT)
P.O. Box 270, Campbellford, ON, K0L 1L0. Contact: Agent on Duty, Consultant - Tel: (705) 778-3863, Fax: (705) 778-3863. World markets, international investment rate 80% ROI, research advocate. $100,000, per year income guarantee. Information free, S.A.S.E. mandatory. Established: 1990 - Franchising Since: 1996 - Franchise Fee: $5,000 - Royalty: None - Total Inv: $10,000 - Financing: Numerous sources available.

TIME + PLUS´®
Time + Plus Canada, Inc
2B -17705B Leslie St, Newmarket, ON, L3Y 3E3. Contact: Hermann Delisle, Director of Franchise Sales - Tel: (905) 836-6697, (800) 836-6697, Fax: (905) 836-5689, E-Mail: timeplus.ca, Web Site: www.timeplus.com. Business to business electronic timekeeping and payroll service. Possible home base. Established: 1992 - Franchising Since: 1992 - No. of Units: Franchised: 14 - Franchise Fee: $11,000 - Royalty: 300 / month fix fee after 3 month - Total Inv: $11,000 franchise fee, $11,000 hardware and software, $1,000 accessories - Financing: Yes.

TINT KING MOBILE SOLAR WINDOW TINTING
136 Castle Rock Dr, Richmond Hill, ON, L4C 5K5. - Tel: (416) 464-TINT. Great home based business. Mobile, office, marine and commercial window tinting, reduces heat upto 78%, reduces glare upto 85% and reduces fading harmfull UV rayes by 99%. Established: 1979 - Franchising Since: 1983 - No. of Units: Franchised: 29 - Franchise Fee: From $10,000 - Royalty: 5% - Total Inv: $15,000 - Financing: Third party.

VAL-PAK OF CANADA LIMITED
40 Wynford Dr., Ste. 301, Don Mills, ON, M3C 1J5. Contact: David Elmer, Dir. Franchise Sales - Tel: (800) 237-6266 ext 3200, Fax: (727) 392-0049, Web Site: www.valpak.com. Established: 1968 - Franchising Since: 1978 - No. of Units: Company Owned: 2 - Franchised: 220 - Royalty: 0 - Total Inv: Beginning at $30,000.

VIGILANT BUSINESS SOFTWARE
181 Eglinton Ave. E, Toronto, ON, M4P 1J4. Contact: Fran. Dev. - Tel: (800) 668-2200, Fax: (416) 332-5744, Web Site: www.vigilant.com. Vigilant sets standards for POS solutions, providing retailers with the ultimate control required to succeed. Retail, mail order and manufacturing are accomodated with comprehensive solutions. Multi-site polling attracts multi-location and chain stores. With year 2000 compliance, we are ready for the next millenium.

WOMEN WHO EXCEL
P.O. Box 3533, Station 'C', Hamilton, ON, L8H 7M9. Contact: Christine Whillock, President/Publisher - Tel: (905) 547-7135, Fax: (905) 547-7135. Local business women's networking organization, monthly dinner meetings, mini trade shows, fashion shows, a yearly members directory financed by advertising, speakers roster, link to website for members, referral service. Training and support provided. Established: 1989 - Total Inv: $500.

WSI
WSI Internet
5915 Airport Road, Suite 300, Mississauga, ON, L4V 1T1. Contact: Robert Alvarado, Marketing Director - Tel: (905) 678-7588, (888) 678-7588, Fax: (905) 678-9974, E-Mail: vmjuarez@wsicorporate.com, Web Site: www.wsicorporate.com. WSI is one of the most profitable franchise opportunities in the world today, with over 700 franchises in 87 countries. No specific business experience is required. WSI offers its franchises one of the most complete and comprehensivce training & certification programs available among franchise companies today, and a dynamic on-going support program tailored to meet the needs of each new franchisee. Established: 1995 - Franchising Since: 1996- No. of Units: Company Owned: 1 - Franchised: 800 - Franchise Fee: $39,700 us - Royalty: 10% - Total Inv: $39,700-$50,000 - Financing: No.

CARPET, DRAPERY AND UPHOLSTERY CLEANING

CHEM-DRY® CARPET & UPHOLSTERY CLEANING
Chem-Dry Canada Ltd
8472 Harvard Place, Chilliwack, BC, V2P 7Z5. Contact: Trudy Miller, Franchise Marketing & Licensing - Tel: (604) 795-9918, (888) 243-6379, (800) 665-9090, Fax: (604) 795-7071, E-Mail: franchisesales@chemdry.ca, Web Site: www.chemdry.ca. Carpet and upholstery cleaning franchise. Patented, fast drying hot carbonating process. Ongoing research, training and support. Established: 1977 - Franchising Since: 1978 - No. of Units: Franchised: 130 - Franchise Fee: $17,950+ taxes - Royalty: Flat monthly fee $300 - Total Inv: $35,700 - Financing: Yes.

DOCTOR STEAM CLEAN
2345 Wyecrost Rd #29, Oakville, ON, L6L 6L8. - Tel: (905) 877-1964. Carpet and upholstery cleaning, flood and fire restoration, area rug plant. Established: 1982 - Franchising Since: 1992 - No. of Units: Company Owned: 1 - Franchised: 2 - Franchise Fee: $5,000 - Royalty: $250 per month - Total Inv: $10,000-$15,000 - Financing: No.

FABRI-ZONE CLEANING SYSTEMS
Fabri-Zone Canada, Ltd.
3135 Universal Dr. Unit#6, Mississauga, ON, L4X 2E2. Contact: David S. Collier, Pres. - Tel: (888) 781-1123, (416) 201-1010, Fax: (905) 602-7821. Fabri zone offers a home based franchised service business with a turnkey package. Patented carpet dry cleaning and purification process, upholstery and ceiling cleaning. Water and smoke damage restoration, indoor air quality systems and product sales. Ongoing technical, marketing, sales and financial support. Established: 1981 - Franchising Since: 1985 - No. of Units: Company Owned: 1 - Franchised: 23 - Franchise Fee: $2,000-$5,000 - Royalty: 6% - Total Inv: $2,500-$30,000 - Financing: Yes.

GOOD LOOKIN' CARPET CLEANING
GLCC Franchising Inc.
40 Burnbank St., Nepean, ON, K2G 0H4. Contact: Luigi F. Orlando, Fran. Sales - Tel: (613) 831-2604, Fax: (613) 831-3784, E-Mail: good@cyberus.ca, Web Site: www.goodlookin.com. Carpet and upholstery cleaning; carpet repairs and sales; fire and water damage restoration. A full service company. Make it your business. Established: 1990 - Franchising Since: 1995 - No. of Units: Company Owned: 1 - Franchise Fee: $10,000 - Royalty: Flat monthly fee - Total Inv: Approx $30,000 - Financing: Not at this time.

INTERIOR CARE

174 Wicksteed Ave, Toronto, ON, M2N 1A1. Contact: Randall Linton - Tel: (416) 467-0200, Fax: (416) 467-7626, E-Mail: randall@interior care.com, Web Site: www.interiorcare.com. Be the only owner of the one and only Interior Care franchise in your city. Our services include commercial carpet & upholstery cleaning, residential carpet & upholstery cleaning. Insurance Restoration and Janitorial Services. Established: 1963 - Franchising Since: 2002 - Franchise Fee: $30,000-$80,000.

RAM CARPET SERVICES

3611 27 Street NE, Suite 1, Calgary, AB, T1Y 5E4. Contact: Frank Goodman, Manager - Tel: (403) 291-1051, Fax: (403) 291-0553, Web Site: www.ramcleaningservices.com. Specializing in residential and commercial carpet cleaning, upholstery cleaning, window coverings cleaning, furnace and duct cleaning, carpet repair and emergency floor and odor control. Established: 1967 - Franchising Since: 1999 - Franchise Fee: $9,900.

ROTO-STATIC INTERNATIONAL
Robben Industries, Ltd.

90 Delta Park Blvd #A, Brampton, ON, L6T 5E7. Contact: Greg Inkster - Tel: (905) 458-7002, Fax: (905) 458-8650. Excellent business opportunity in the growing services field. Carpet and upholstery cleaning, ceiling and wall cleaning, water damage restoration and more. Low overheads, low investment and high returns. A caring organization. Established: 1977 - Franchising Since: 1977 - No. of Units: Franchised: 146 - Franchise Fee: $14,500 - Royalty: 5% - Total Inv: $40,000 Fee inclusive of training, equipment package @ $24,000 .

RUG DOCTOR RENTS
Rug Doctor Canada Ltd.

14 Trottier Bay, Winnipeg, MB, R3T 3Y5. Contact: Gerald Hochman, Exec. V.P. - Tel: (204) 284-1444, Fax: (204) 453-2324. Rug Doctor Rents is at the forefront of carpet and upholstery cleaning systems for the Do-It-Yourself market throughout the world. Exclusiveness is granted for territory in which Rug Doctor Rents rental stations may be set up. Area development is accomplished with the assistance of the franchisor. Full training and support programs are also provided. Many national accounts are available into which the machines may be placed. Established: 1975 - Franchising Since: 1978 - No. of Units: Company Owned: 10 corp. territories - Franchised: 42 - Royalty: 6-8% - Total Inv: Dependent on number of machines and size of territory - Financing: Assistance with banking, but no direct financing.

STEAMATIC
Steamatic Canada Inc.

7750 Jarry East, Anjou, QC, H1J 2M3. Contact: Claude Berube, Development Manager - Tel: (514) 351-1234, (800) 215-8621, Fax: (514) 351-3423, E-Mail: stmcanada@steamatic.ca, Web Site: www.steamatic.ca. Fire and flood restoration; dehumidification; decontamination; duct cleaning; carpet and upholstery cleaning. Exclusive territories. Patented systems. Complete training and support. Established: 1967 - Franchising Since: 1967 - No. of Units: Company Owned: 1 - Franchised: 49 - Franchise Fee: $10,000-$25,000 - Royalty: 8% declining to 5% - Total Inv: $40,000-$60,000 - Financing: Yes.

VONSCHRADER ASSOCIATE
Vonschrader Canada

9 Antares Dr., Nepean, ON, K2E 7V5. Contact: Douglas Conner, Pres. - Tel: (800) 267-7422, Fax: (613) 225-1090. Patented and worldwide manufacturer of state-of-the-art and industry rated #1 dry foam carpet, upholstery, wall and ceiling cleaning systems. Far superior to steam cleaning. Established: 1989 - Franchising Since: 1990 - No. of Associates: 484 - Franchise Fee: $550 - Total Inv: $2,500-$15,000 - Financing: Yes.

ZIPPY-CLEAN
Derek's Ltd.

299 Paul Martin Dr, Pembroke, ON, K8A 6W4. -Tel: (613) 732-1196, Fax: (613) 732-8498. Carpet and upholstery cleaners offering rental mat service. Established: 1990 - Franchising Since: 1990 - No. of Units: Company Owned: 1 - Financing: Yes.

CHILDREN'S PRODUCTS AND SERVICES

CHILDREN'S MARKETPLACE, THE

P.O. Box 1078, Tottenham, ON, L0G 1W0. Contact: Joan McDonald, Pres. - Tel: (905) 936-2092, Fax: (905) 936-9686. A great children's specialty store selling baby furniture, nursery accessories, educational toys, books, wonderful gifts and specially selected clothes. Offers designer consignment of children's items, a great service to parents. Established: 1974 - Franchising Since: 1980 - No. of Units: Franchised: 3 - Franchise Fee: $25,000 - Royalty: 6%+1% adv. - Total Inv: $110,000.

COMPUCHILD
CompuChild Services of Canada, Inc.

239 Lisa Marie Drive, Orangeville, ON, L9W 2V5. Contact: Toni Lugano, President - Tel: (519) 942-9988, (888) 835-6654, Fax: (519) 942-1034, Web Site: www.compuchild.ca. CompuChild is an leader in early-age computer training for preschool children 2-6 years of age. CompuChild offers a business start-up package, complete with 3 days on-site training, field training, ongoing support, market development and continuous technology development. Established: 1997 - Franchising Since: 1997 - No. of Units: Franchised: 30 - Franchise Fee: $15,000 - Royalty: $250.00 - Total Inv: Complete business package including 3 days on-site and field training - franchise private forum - Financing - Yes.

HAND ME DOWNS, INC

3201 Tooley's Rd, Courtice, ON, L1E 2K7. Contact: Stephanie Jukes, Owner/Founder - Tel: (905) 720-3328, Fax: (905) 720-3328, Web Site: www.handmedowns.com. Consignment children's clothing, toys, equipment and nursery furniture and maternity wear. Established: 1991 - Franchising Since: 1993 - No. of Units: Company Owned: 3 - Franchised: 8 - Franchise Fee: $15,000 - Royalty: 5% of gross sales - Total Inv: $30,000-$40,000 - Financing: Yes.

IDENTIFICATION SERVICES OF CANADA INC.

Ste. 238, 150 Clark Blvd., Brampton, ON, L6T 4Y8. Contact: Paul Marr, Marketing Manager - Tel: (905) 796-2211, Fax: (905) 455-7273, E-Mail: isi@idirect.com. Provide laminated child I.D. cards containing a child's photograph, fingerprint, and physical description, on a yearly basis to parents. The program is marketed through public and private schools, using a unique video presentation. Established: 1988 - Franchising Since: 1988 - No. of Units: Company Owned: 1 - Franchised: Can. 43/USA 298 - Franchise Fee: Zero no charge - Royalty: Nil - Total Inv: $25,000 all inclusive - Financing: Yes.

INFO TECHKIDS
Info TechKids International, Inc

279 Broadway Ave, Suite 3, Orangeville, ON, L9W 1L2. Contact: Director of Franchising - Tel: (519) 942-9077, (877) 8-it-kids, Fax: (519) 942-1034, Web Site: www.infotechkids.com. Info TechKids provides complete training to children at basic to advanced levels at local learning centers, now located in a learning neighbourhood. Full curriculum plus program. Established: 1998 - Franchising Since: 1998 - No. of Units: Company Owned: 2 - Franchised: 4 - Franchise Fee: $40,000-$60,000 - Royalty: Percentage - Total Inv: Full turn key operation, full training, on-going support and internet access - Financing: No.

INFOTECHKIDS CANADA INC.

3325 North Service Road, Suite 108, Burlington, ON, L7N 3G2. Contact: Fran. Dev. - Tel: (905) 319-7695, (877) 697-KIDS, E-Mail: barbara@infotechkids.ca, Web Site: www.infotechkids.ca. Provides computer learning solutions for children. Computer training is offered to children aged 2-12 years of age on a seasonal basis. Children are encouraged and guided by trained I.T.KIDS instructors in our carefully designed learning centres using our high scope curriculum which offers a caring and interactive learning environment. Children are certified upon completion of each I.T.K. level.

KIDDIE KOBBLER
Kiddie Kobbler Limited

68 Robertson Rd., #106, Nepean, ON, K2H 8P5. Contact: Fred Norman, Pres. - Tel: (613) 820-0505, Fax: (613) 820-8250. Childrens shoe stores. Proven concept over 45 years complete training and support. Will appeal

to independent, service oriented couples with good people skills, who enjoy working with children in clean friendly family business. Established: 1951 - Franchising Since: 1968 - No. of Units: Franchised: 31 - Franchise Fee: $20,000 - Royalty: 4%, .5% adv. - Total Inv: $100,000-$120,000 - Financing: Through banks upion credit approval.

KIDS COACH
Kids Coach Inc
7-3331 Viking Way, Richmond, BC, V6V 1X7. - Tel: (604) 270-2360, (604) 270-6560, Fax: (604) 220-6442. Services for children. Established: 1992 - Franchising Since: 2001 - No. of Units: Company Owned: 4 - Franchised: 2 - Franchise Fee: $15,000 - Total Inv: $20,000 - Financing: No.

MAD SCIENCE GROUP, THE
8360 Bougainville St, @201, Montreal, QC, H4P 2G1. Contact: Joel Lazarovitz, Marketing Co-ordinator - Tel: (800) 586-5231, (514) 344-4181, Fax: (514) 344-6695, Web Site: www.madscience.org. Entertaining and educational hands-on science for children age 4-12. After school programs, workshops, birthday parties and special events. Complete training, on-going support. Home based. Established: 1985 - Franchising Since: 1995 - No. of Units: Franchised: 95 - Franchise Fee: $23,500 - Royalty: 8% - Total Inv: $23,500 fran. fee, $25,000 equipment - Financing: Yes (Att SBA loans).

OUR BABY IMPRESSIONS
Associated Baby Impressions Ltd.
437 Duke Court, Kelowna, BC, V1W 3A2. Contact: Sal or Darlene Del Buono, Owners - Tel: (250) 764-4888, Fax: (250) 764-4830, Web Site: www.ourbabyimpressions.com. Imprints of baby's hands or feet, 3 dimensional in a frame. Established: 1987 - Franchising Since: 1987 - No. of Units: Franchised: 33 - Franchise Fee: $6,000 and up - Royalty: 2% - Total Inv: $6,000 and up - Financing: No.

PACER CUB KARTING
601-650 Waterloo Street, London, ON, N6B 2R4. Contact: Franchising Department - Tel: (519) 433-9658, Fax: (519) 433-6123. Children's karting activity. Established: 1996 - No. of Units: Company Owned: 1 - Franchised: 100 - Franchise Fee: $8,000 - Total Inv: $30,000.

PANDA SHOES
Panda Franchises Ltd.
305 Marc-Aurele-Fortin Blvd., Laval, QC, H7L 2A3. Contact: Linda Goulet, President - Tel: (450) 622-4833 ext 201, Fax: (450) 622-2939, E-Mail: info@pandashoes.com. Children shoe specialist, greatest selection of children footwear and accessories, volume buying, exclusivities, full training. Established: 1972 - Franchising Since: 1974 - No. of Units: Company Owned: 5 - Franchised: 42 - Franchise Fee: $25,000 - Royalty: 4% - Total Inv: Store $60,000, inventory $100,000 - Financing: No.

PAR-T-PERFECT *
2615 Kilmarnock Cres, North Vancouver, BC, V7J 2Z3. - Tel: (604) 985-0105, Fax: (604) 985-0142, E-Mail: info@par-t-perfect.com, Web Site: www.par-t-perfect.com. Par-T-Perfect is a full service, year round children's event and party company. Let us do it for you with our unique themes, fun inflatables and complete party packages. Established: 1988 - No. of Units: Company Owned: 9 - Franchise Fee: $24,500 - Total Inv: $44,500.

PEANUT CLUB
Peanut Club Franchise Group, The
36 Cranfield Rd., Toronto, ON, M4B 3H3. Contact: Don McBride, Pres, G.M - Tel: (416) 751-5292, Fax: (416) 750-8766. Party and play centre-indoor for children, infant - 7 yr, indoor playground and children's parties. Sale of related party goods, toys and balloons. Established: 1991 - Franchising Since: 1993 - No. of Units: Company Owned: 2 - Franchised: 1- Franchise Fee: $25,000 - Royalty: 5%, 2% adv. - Total Inv: Franchise fee $25,000 lease + equipment $50,000-start-up & misc $20,000, Financing: No. NOT OFFERING FRANCHISES AT THIS TIME.

SIMPLY KIDS
The Gramcor Franchising Co.
30 Jim Ashton Street, London, ON, N5V 2A9. Contact: Danny Grammenopoulos, President - Tel: (519) 451-9004, Fax: (519) 451-6609. Canadian made clothing for children ranging from newborn to 6X. Usually co-branded with sweet-retreat. Established: 1991 - Franchising Since: 1999 - No. of Units: Franchised: 1 - Franchise Fee: $19,900 - Royalty: 4.9% - Total Inv: $80,000-$170,000 - Financing: Third Party.

STRETCH-N-GROW OF CANADA INC.
Stretch-n-Grow of Canada Inc
136 Main Street S, Brampton, ON, L6W 2C9. Contact: Myra Myre, Director - Tel: (416) 220-1031, (800) 892-5742, Fax: (866) 892-9902, E-Mail: info@workoutwithticker.com, Web Site: www.stretch-n-grow.com. We are the leading fitness program for young children.. Our program is now running with independent owners all around the worls. An ideal low-investment business for someone who enjoys exercise and working with children High earning potential!!. Established: 1993 - Franchising Since: 1993 - No. of Units: Company Owned: 1 - Franchised: 5 - Franchise Fee: $13,600-$15,600 (U.S.) - Royalty: $100 Canadian dollars monthly - Total Inv: Franchise fee + $1,000 start up costs (includes 1 year of liability insurance) - Financing: No.

TECHNOKIDS
2232 Sheridan Garden Dr, Oakville, ON, L6J 7T1. Contact: Scott Gerard, Pres. - Tel: (905) 829-4171, (800) 221-7921, Fax: (905) 829-4172, E-Mail: info@technokids.com, Web Site: www.technokids.com. Distributing proprietary theme based curriculum to educators which teaches technology skills to children. Established: 1993 - Franchising Since: 1994 - No. of Units: Company Owned: 1 - Franchised: 104 - Franchise Fee: Varies $5,000-$50,000 - Royalty: Varies - Total Inv: $15,000-$60,000 including franchise fee - Financing: Yes.

THEATER FUN
3400 Jean Talonm West, Ste. 101, Montreal, QUE, H3R 2E8. - Tel: (514) 344-4181, (800) 586-5231, Fax: (514) 344-6695, E-Mail: sales@theaterfun.com, Web Site: www.theaterfun.com. We instill self esteem and confidence in children through the performing arts. A full time, year round business - home based or run out of an office. Established: 1997 - Franchising Since: 2001 - No. of Units: Company Owned: 1 - Franchise Fee: $23,500 - Total Inv: $35,000-$40,000 - Financing: Third party.

TODDLER TIME
14 Dawson Road, Winnipeg, MB, R4J 3X1. Contact: Franchise Development - Tel: (204) 235-0091. A daycare centre for children from ages one to four, offering a safe and enjoyable environment. One week training and ongoing support provided. Established: 1994 - No. of Units: Franchised: 3 - Total Inv: $150,000-$200,000.

WEE PIGGIES & PAWS INC
Wee Piggies & Paws Inc.
166 St. Augustine Drive, St. Catharines, ON, L2P 3W1. Contact: Debbie Cornelius - Tel: (905) 988-5437, E-Mail: debbie@weepiggies.com, Web Site: www.weepiggies.com. Original franchise concept designed by a work-at-home mom. Features bronze plaques of children's hand & footprints and LifeCast Statues. Offers parents a unique business opportunity to work from their homw without the need for daycare. No additional franchise or royalty fees. All stsrt-up supplies, materials and tools included with initial fee. Established: 2001 Franchising Since: 2002 - No. of Units: Company Owned: 1 - Frachised: 3 - Franchise Fee: $8,000-$12,000 - Total Inv: $11,000-$14,000 - Financing: N/A.

WEE WATCH DAY CARE
Wee Watch Day Care Systems, Inc.
105 Main St., Unionville, ON, L3R 2G1. Contact: Leslie Wilson - Tel: (905) 479-4274, (800) 663-6072, Fax: (905) 479-9047, E-Mail: Leslie@weewatch.com, Web Site: www.weewatch.com. Quality private home day care, full & part time. Established: 1985 - Franchising Since: 1987 - No. of Units: Franchised: 55 - Franchise Fee: $17,500 - Royalty: 8% - Total Inv: $27,500 - Financing: No.

WHIPPER SNAPPER "THE FUN TOY STORE"
Whipper Snapper Inc.
134 Kent St., Charlottetown, PEI, C1A 6E3. Contact: Barb MacLeod or Kim Cudmore, Owners - Tel: (902) 566-9188, Fax: (902) 368-8659. A specialty toy store that mixes up toys like no other! Offering a great

childrens shopping experience, fun entertaining atmosphere, experienced staff and lots to choose from. Established: 1988 - Franchising Since: 1998 - No. of Units: Company Owned: 1 - Franchise Fee: $20,000 - Royalty: 1st yr. 2% of sales, 2nd yr. 3% of sale, 3rd yr. 4% of sales - Total Inv: $120,000 - Financing: No.

CLEANING PRODUCTS AND SERVICES

ACTION WINDOW CLEANERS
ASI - Academic Systems Inc.
476 Evans Ave., Unit 1, Etobicoke, ON, M8W 2T7. Contact: Rodney Larmand, V.P. - Tel: (416) 291-9990, Fax: (416) 259-9350. Seasonal network of student-run residential window cleaning franchises. Franchisor provides full training, administrative/consulting support and established customer base. Established: 1986 - Franchising Since: 1986 - No. of Units: Company Owned: 1 - Franchised: 50 - Royalty: 18.5%-22.5% of gross sales.

AIRKEM DISASTER SERVICES
100 Huntington Park, Sault Ste. Marie, ON, P6A 3P5. Contact: Jack/Marty Moore, Owners - Tel: (705) 759-2255, (888) 247-5365, Fax: (705) 946-2992, E-Mail: airkem@soonet.ca. Insurance restoration work pertaining to floods, fire, smoke etc. Established: 1987 - Franchising Since: 1994 - No. of Units: Company Owned: 1 - Royalty: $5,000-$10,000 - Total Inv: $15,000-$25,000 - Financing: No.

ALL AMERICAN SHADE CARE SYSTEM
25 Coronet Rd. Unit 3, Etobicoke, ON, M8Z 2L8. Contact: Dieter Micheletti, Dir. - Tel: (416) 234-8069, Fax: (416) 234-9718. The company provides a blind cleaning service for all hard window coverings such as venetians, verticals, sunscreens and parabolic louvers. A patented variable hydromatic system cleans more thoroughly so spotting and shrinkage can be controlled. Established: 1989 - Franchising Since: 1995 - No. of Units: Company Owned: 1 - Franchise Fee: $15,000 - Royalty: 5% - Total Inv: $52,500 incl. fran. fee - Financing: For qualified prospects. NOT OFFERING FRANCHISES AT THIS TIME.

ARODAL SERVICES
Arodal International Inc.
6171 Conin Dr., Mississauga, ON, L4V 1N8. Contact: Mr. A.E. Fisher, Pres. - Tel: (905) 678-6888, Fax: (905) 678-6967. Contract cleaning of industrial and commercial office buildings. Established: 1971 - Franchising Since: 1990 - No. of Units: Company Owned: 2 - Franchised: 2 - Franchise Fee: $20,000 - Royalty: 7% of gross sales - Total Inv: $80,000; fran. fee plus $60,000 furn., leaseholds and computer - Financing: 50%.

BEE-CLEAN
Bee-Clean Building Maintenance, Inc.
375 Naire Ave, Winnipeg, MB, R2L 0W8. Contact: Jim Malott, Pres. - Tel: (204) 668-4420, Fax: (204) 663-0402. Janitorial service. Established: 1967 - Franchising Since: 1972 - No. of Units: Company Owned: 7 - Franchised: 25 - Franchise Fee: $12,500 - Royalty: Scale from 5%-2% - Total Inv: $15,000 - Financing: Yes.

BIO-SAFE® SKIN PRODUCTS, INC.
619 Pineridge Rd., Waterloo, ON, N2L 5N6. Contact: Fran. Dev. - Tel: (800) 667-0520, Fax: (519) 746-9392, Web Site: www.bisafe-inc.com. We distribute antibacterial polymer lotions that stay on the hands for four hours despite frequent hand washing. Protects agaainst dermatitis, cross contamination and dermal absorption of latex protein and carcinogens. Established: 1980.

BRUNMAC SERVICES INC
106-1515 Broadway Street, Port Coquitlam, BC, V3C 6M2. Contact: Bob Burnham - Tel: (604) 941-3041, Fax: (604) 944-7993, Web Site: www.burnmac.com. Burnmac is a flood and retsoration, carpet and upholstery and home repair service. Established: 1976 - Franchising Since: 2000 - No. of Units: Company Owned: 1 - Franchised: 1 - Franchise Fee: $15,000 - Royalty: 6.5% of gross sales - Total Inv: $29,925.00

CAN-CLEAN PRESSURE WASHERS
450 Matheson Blvd. E., #56, Mississauga, ON, L4Z 1R5. Contact: John Drummond, President - Tel: (905) 568-4868, (888) 568-8001, Fax: (905) 568-0611, E-Mail: canclean@pathcom.com, Web Site: www.can cleanpressurewashers.com. Set up of pressure washers for siding cleaning, truck washing and 65 other related types of cleaning. Established: 1991 - Total Inv: $5,000-$10,000 plus vehical - Financing: Lease available.

CLEAN UP SYSTEMS
P.O. Box 86310, North Vancouver, BC, V7L 4K6. Contact: Fran. Dev. - Tel: (604) 980-4561, Fax: (604) 980-4561. Specialty cleaning: walls, ceiling and office equipment. Established: 1981.

CLEAN-BRITE
Clean Brite Canada Ltd.
1201 Osler St, Regina, SK, S4R 1W4. Contact: Steve Yang, Pres. Franchise operations in janitorial supply and service. Commercial and residential accounts. Established: 1981 - Franchising Since: 1986 - No. of Units: Company Owned: 2 - Franchised: 3 - Franchise Fee: $5,000-$25,000 - Royalty: Min. 5%, max. 10% - Total Inv: $10,000-$60,000 - Financing: Yes.

COTTAGECARE CANADA
105-816 Willow Park Dr., S.E., #105, Calgary, AB, T2J 5S1. Contact: Brian Murphy, President - Tel: (403) 225-3441, (800) 718-8100, Fax: (403) 225-3502 , Web Site: www.cottagecare.com. General house cleaning services. Established: 1996 - Franchising Since: 1996 - No. of Units: Franchised: 9 - Franchise Fee: $16,500-$19,500 - Royalty: 6.5% - Total Inv: $65,000-$85,000 - Financing: No.

COVERALL OF CANADA
2969 Sheppard Ave East, Toronto, ON, M1T 3J5. - Tel: (416) 431-7911 Web Site: www.coverall.com. Commercial office cleaning services provided by franchisees who have received full training, equipment and guaranteed customers from Coverall. Established: 1985 - Franchising Since: 1985 - No. of Units: 14 (US parent) - Franchised: 3,100 internationally - Franchise Fee: Six programs, min. $2,550 - Royalty: 10% service, 5% royalty - Total Inv: $6,000-$17,000 - Financing: Yes.

DISTINCTION SERVICE PLUS, INC.
7750 Garry East, Anjou, QC, H1J 2M3. - Tel: (514) 351-7744, Fax: (514) 351-5793, E-Mail: cmercier@distinction.ca. Janitorial service. Established: 1998 - Franchising Since: 1998 - No. of Units: Franchised: 25.

FIBRECLEAN SUPPLIES LTD.
#101-3750-19th Street N.E., Calgary, AB, T2E 6V2. Contact: Kathy Brown, Operations Manager - Tel: (403) 291-3991, Fax: (403) 291-2295. Cleaning supplies wholesale to carpet cleaners, restoration companies and janitor services. Established: 1976 - Franchising Since: 1996 - No. of Units: Company Owned: 4- Franchised: 4- Franchise Fee: Varies - Royalty: 5% franchise, 1.25% nat'l advertising - Financing: No.

HYGENICOMP
Hygenicomp Technology Maintenance Inc.
Ste. 600, 900 West Hasting St., Vancouver, BC, V6C 1E5. Contact: Kevin Gibbs, President - Tel: (866) 666-8006, Fax: (866) 666-8004. Cleaning and tune-up of computers and other electronics. ATM cleaning, air filtration, mainframe cleaning, fire restoration. Established: 1989 - Franchising Since: 1991 - No. of Units: Franchised: 21 - Franchise Fee: $15,000 - Royalty: 8% gross - Total Inv: $30,000 includes equip. & supplies - Financing: Yes.

JANI-KING CANADA
Renfrew Group Ltd. (c/o)
23 Cornwallis St., Kentville, NS, B4N 2E2. Contact: Bruce Tupper, President - Tel: (800) 565-1873, (902) 678-3200, Fax: (902) 678-3500, Web Site: www.janiking.ca. World's largest commercial cleaning franchise with over 30 years of experience. Franchise fee includes training, equipment starter package, training and uniforms. Initial customer contracts are available with franchise. Franchisees provide commercial cleaning services to clients on a long term contract basis. Continuous training and ongoing support provided to the franchisees along with the administrative support, billing and collections performed by the regional office make this a very popular franchise. This program has proven itself many times over producing hundreds of successful

franchises worldwide each year. Established: 1969 - Franchising Since: 1974 (in Canada since 1986) - No. of Units: Company Owned: 30 - Franchised: 400 Canada, (7,000 worldwide) - Franchise Fee: $9,900-$24,900 - Total Inv: $9,900 + - Financing: Partial, available to qualified individuals.

JDI CLEANING SYSTEMS INC.
OIA Janitorial Design and Innovations
3390 South Service Rd., Burlington, ON, L7N 3J5. Contact: Joseph Imbrogno, Pres. - Tel: (905) 634-5228, Fax: (905) 634-8790. Commercial janitorial services. Initial contracts, equipment, training, supplies and administrative support to qualified individuals seeking the opportunity to own and operate their own janitorial business. Master franchises available. Established: 1992 - Franchising Since: 1992 - No. of Units: Company Owned: 1 - Franchised: 40 - Franchise Fee: $10,500 - Total Inv: Varies - Financing: Yes.

MAID TO PERFECTION
Donar Cleaning
2419 Park Street, Regina, SK, S4N 2H1. - Tel: (301) 790-3949, Web Site: www.maidtoperfectioncorp.com. Residential and commercial cleaners. Established: 1970 - Franchising Since: 1980 - No. of Units: Company Owned: 10 - Franchised: 220 - Franchise Fee: $6,995.00 (U.S Funds) - Royalty: 7% - Total Inv: $25,000 - Financing: Yes.

MAPLE LEAF SERVICE
2424 Bloor St. West, Toronto, ON, M6S 1P9. Contact: Fran. Dir. - Tel: (416) 762-6330, Fax: (416) 762-3557. Commercial janitorial services. Full training and support. Franchising in greater Toronto area. Established: 1984 - No. of Units: Franchised: 49.

MASTER CARE JANITORIAL
International Master Care Janitorial Franchising Inc.
P.O. Box 189, New Westminster, BC, V3L 5H1. Contact: Gerhard Hoffmann, Pres. - Tel: (604) 526-4867, (800) 889-2799, Fax: (604) 526-2235, E-Mail: info@mastercare.com. Provide professional janitorial services to offices, banks and medical centers, via franchising. Established: 1981 - Franchising Since: 1987 - No. of Units: Company Owned: 1 - Franchised: 159 - Franchise Fee: $4,000 to $75,000 - Royalty: 7%-15% - Total Inv: $7,500-$150,000 - Financing: Yes.

MERRY MAIDS
ServiceMaster of Canada
6540 Tomken Rd., Mississauga, ON, L5T 2E9. Contact: Franchise Department - Tel: (800) 798-8000, Fax: (901) 537-8140. Merry Maids the largest residential cleaning service in the world. Ranked the #1 cleaning service in North America by Entrepreneur magazine. Merry Maids offers regular hours, steady clientele, exceptional growth, low investment and an excellent return. Training and support is provided with 10 days at Merry Maids worldwide head office plus ongoing support from Canadian Home Office. Established: Can 1991, US 1980 - Franchising Since: Can 1989, US 1980 - No. of Units: Company Owned: 40+ in Canada over 1200 worldwide - Franchise Fee: $17,500-$24,500 - Total Inv: $40,000 - Financing: Yes.

MINI-MAID SERVICES
MiniMaid Service Systems
192 Shorting Rd., Scarborough, ON, M1S 3S7. Contact: David Dugas, Pres. - Tel: (800) 363-MAID, Fax: (416) 298-8445. Residential housecleaning performed by 4-person teams in uniforms and identified company car. Professional advertising, training, and ongoing support ensures profitable success. Established: 1979 - Franchising Since: 1979 - No. of Units: Company Owned: 11 - Franchised: 78 - Franchise Fee: $11,950 - Royalty: 6,5,4% + 2% adv. - Total Inv: $16,000 ($4,000 min. work cap) - Financing: No.

MISS MILLY HOUSE CLEANING
2273-129 St., Surrey, BC, V4A 7V7. Contact: Peter Myddleton - Tel: (604) 531-5449, Fax: (604) 535-6397. BC based franchise offering franchises only in BC. Support and training is ongoing. Personalized approach towards franchise owners and clients needs. Established: 1991 - Franchising Since: 1992 - No. of Units: Franchised: 12 - Franchise Fee: $10,500 - Royalty: 6% advertising 2% - Total Inv: $25,000-$10,500 f.f., $14,500 op.cap.- Financing: OAC.

MITEX MATTRESS HYGIENICS
SCS Marketing International, Inc
Box 10, Site 15, RR#3, Olds, AB, T4H 1P4. Contact: Wolfgang Struebel - Tel: (403) 556-7160, Fax: (403) 556-1336, E-Mail: mitex@telus planet.net, Web Site: www.mitex.org. Unique mattress cleaning business, removing dust, dust mite excrement from inside the mattress. Established: 1991 - Franchising Since: 1998 - No. of Units: Company Owned: 3 - Franchised: 52 - Total Inv: $21,000 - Financing: Upto $15,000 OAC.

MOLLY MAID INTERNATIONAL, INC.
100 Bronte Rd., Oakville, ON, L6L 6L5. Contact: Kevin Hipkins, Vice-President & GM - Tel: (905) 847-6243, (800) 663-6243 Fax: (905) 847-6255, E-Mail: khipkins@onramp.ca, Web Site: www.mollymaid.com. Canadian leader in residential cleaning industry. Most recognized trademark and comprehensive training and support program. Established: 1978 - Franchising Since: 1980 - No. of Units: Franchised: 160 - Franchise Fee: $14,000 - Royalty: 6% - Total Inv: $14,000 plus working cap. $4,000 - Financing: No.

NATURE TECH SYSTEMS
Nature Technologies Inc.
1166 Hyde Park Rd., London, ON, N6H 5K5. Contact: Larry Boyd, Pres. - Tel: (519) 657-6793. Environmentally friendly process for the maintenance, restoration and preservation for exterior wood, brick, aluminum, vinyl and concrete surfaces. Established: 1994 - Franchising Since: 1994 - Franchise Fee: $20,000 - Royalty: Nil - Total Inv: $20,000 - Financing: No.

NEAT AS A PIN
462 Edward Street, Suite 303, Winnipeg, MB, R2L 1M3. Contact: Fran. Dev. - Commercial and residential cleaaning company - full training and support. Established: 1992 - No. of Units: Franchised: 13 - Total Inv: $15,000 min cash.

NEWBROOK CLEANING SERVICES
3060 Cedar Hill Road, Ste. 300, Victoria, BC, V8T 3J5. Contact: John Carter, President - Tel: (877) 639-2766, Fax: (250) 595-4863, E-Mail: franchise@newbrook.com, Web Site: www.newbrook.com. Enjoy the safety and stability of a steady demand for your services. Newbrook Cleaning Services delivers professional cleaning services in a wide range of commercial buildings. Training and support includes: comprehensive instruction, ongoing managerial support, nationwide discounts on supplies, internet based supply ordering and easy to use management software. Established: 1991 - Franchising Since: 1999 - No. of Units: Company Owned: 1 - Franchise Fee: $15,000-$25,000 - Royalty: 5.5% on gross sales - Total Inv: $25,000-$40,000 - Financing: Yes.

NO SKIDDING PRODUCTS, INC.
266 Wildcat Rd., Toronto, ON, M3J 2N5. - Tel: (416) 667-1788, (800) 375-0571, Fax: (416) 667-1783. Supply and application of slip injury prevention products to industry, hospitality and residential. The largest range of slip injury prevention products in the world. Strong technical support. Established: 1991 - Franchising Since: 1999 - No. of Units: Franchised: 30 - Franchise Fee: $1,000 - Total Inv: $5,000, (inventory + tools) - Financing: No.

ONTARIO DUCT CLEANING LTD.
5635 Finch Ave. E., Ste. 5, Scarborough, ON, M1B 5K9. Contact: Peter Townend, V.P. - Tel: (416) 292-9700, Fax: (416) 292-7600. Residential/commercial high technology duct cleaning. Established: 1979 - Franchising Since: 1988 - No. of Units: Company Owned: 1 - Franchised: 15 - Franchise Fee: $20,000 - Royalty: 7% - Total Inv: $80,000 - Financing: Yes.

POWER KING CLEANING SYSTEMS
P.O. Box 364, Sutton West, ON, L0E 1R0. Contact: Brenda Payton, Office Mgr. - Tel: (905)722-9956, Fax: (905) 722-9956. Pressure wash exhaust systems in restaurants. Established: 1986 - Franchising Since: 1994 - No. of Units: Company Owned: 1 - Franchised: 3 - Franchise Fee: $60,000+ - Royalty: 7%, 1% adv. - Total Inv: $60,000+$10,000 working credit line.

PRIORITY BUILDING SERVICES LTD.
9001 Shaughnessy Street, Vancouver, BC, V6P 6R9. Contact: Randy Zimmerman, Pres/CEO. - Tel: (604) 327-1123, Fax: (604) 327-2510, E-Mail: rzimmers@direct.ca. A janitorial company offering a unique blend of quality workmanship and customer satisfaction unparalleled in the industry. Established: 1994 - No. of Units: Franchised: 50 - Franchise Fee: $5,000-$30,000 - Total Inv: min $5,000.

RESTORX - PEEL REGION
Restorx Canada Incorporated
2355 Royal Windsor Dr., Unit 4, Mississauga, ON, L5J 4S8. Contact: Gordon Hufnagel, Pres. - Tel: (905) 855-3573, Fax: (905) 855-9913. Canada's foremost disaster restoration company utilizing patented products and proprietary systems. Established: 1946 - Franchising Since: 1985 - No. of Units: Franchised: 15 - Franchise Fee: $21,900-$32,900 - Royalty: $700/month - Total Inv: Approx. $60,000 plus fran. fee - Financing: Small amount available.

SANIBRITE INC.
Sanibrite Inc.
3145 Southcreek Rd #19, Mississauga, ON, L4X 2E9. - Tel: (905) 624-4290, Web Site: www.sanibrite.on.ca. Sanibrite is a unique company that is embarking on one of the most dynamic and totally new ideas in Canada. We have combined the success rate of franchising with a profitable and growing field of commercial cleaning. As a weary investor Sanibrite will provide you with the best business investment available for your money. It is a business that will be immune to economic problems, such as depreciation, recession and inflation. Established: 1987 - Franchising Since: 1989 - No. of Units: Company Owned: 1 - Franchised: 41 - Franchise Fee: $2,500-$17,000 (vary) - Royalty: 6%, 3%, 12% - Total Inv: Vary $2,500-$17,000 - Financing: Yes.

SERV-U-CLEAN LTD.
207 Edgeley Blvd., Unit 5, Concord, ON, L4K 4B5. Contact: Rick Katz, Gen. Mgr. - Tel: (905) 660-0899, Fax: (905) 660-0550, Web Site: www.serv-u-clean.com. Providing commercial janitorial services. Established: 1990 - Franchising Since: 1992 - No. of Units: Company Owned: 18 - Franchised: 64- Franchise Fee: $5,500 + up to $20,000 - Financing: Partial financing available.

SERVICESTAR INDUSTRIES
260 Hearst Way, Kanata, ON, K2L 3H1. Contact: Derek Artichuk, Area Mgr. - Tel: (613) 599-6344, Fax: (613) 736-9407, E-Mail: studdenham@svcstar.com, Web Site: www.svcstar.com. Commercial cleaning. Established: 1992 - Franchising Since: 1992 - No. of Units: Company Owned: 2 - Franchised: 39 - Franchise Fee: $25,000 - Royalty: 10%, 3% adm., 1% adv.(14%) - Total Inv: $25,000 (includes $3,500 equipment and guaranteed $36,000 in first year) - Financing: Yes.

SILO CLEAN INTERNATIONAL
1054 Centre Suite 174, Thornhill, ON, L4J 8E5. Contact: Marvin Lee, Mktg. Dir. - Tel: (905) 660-7022, Fax: (905) 660-1755. World's safest and fastest clean out of industrial silos, tanks, bins and hoppers. Services over 80 industries, worldwide. Company is the inventor and developer of a cleaning process which enables cleaning done by remote control from the outside without sending men in. Avoids all confined space legislation and liability for companies using service as well as providing significant cost savings. Dry cleaning, no water or chemicals used. Established: 1984 - Licensing Since: 1993 - No. of Units: Company Owned: 1 - License Fee: $150,000 approx. depending on size of territory - Royalty: 6% - Total Inv: $150,000 incl. tech. training program, equip., mktg. training - Financing: No.

SPOTLESS OFFICE SERVICES, INC.
1959 Marine Dr., Ste. 1061, N. Vancouver, BC, V7P 3G1. Contact: Bob Mussio - Tel: (604) 985-6569, Fax: (604) 985-6569. Building maintenance broker. No trucks, cleaning equipment or office needed. Janitors use own equipment. Can be operated from home, contacting office buildings and sign them up to a janitorial cleaning contract. Established: 1978 - Franchising Since: 1980 - No. of Units: Company Owned: 1 - Franchised: 17 - Total Inv: $3,000 - Royalty: 5% - Financing: No.

UNICLEAN SYSTEMS
Uniclean Systems, Inc.
236 Brooksbank Ave., N. Vancouver, BC, V7J 2C1. Contact: Jack Karpowicz, Pres. - Tel: (604) 986-4750, Fax: (604) 987-6838. Professional office cleaning on the long term contract basis. Established: 1976 - Franchising Since: 1981 - No. of Units: Company Owned: 1 - Franchised: 346 - Franchise Fee: $7,500-$15,000 - Royalty: 10% - Total Inv: $8,000-$15,000 - Financing: No.

WINCH ENTERPRISES
48 Riverside Cr. S.E., Calgary, AB, T2C 3Y1. Contact: Brian Winch, Pres. - Tel: (403) 236-7551, Fax: (403) 246-0582. Earn big money in commercial outdoor clean-up. So simple even a child can be successful. Work full or part time from home or office. One year money back guarantee. Established: 1981 - No. of Units: Company Owned: 1 - Total Inv: $30 for business manual - Financing: No.

COMPUTER/ELECTRONICS/INTERNET SERVICES

BEYOND SIGNS
Beyond Vinylgraphics, Inc
36 Apple Creek Boulevard, Markham, ON, M6M 3W7. Contact: Glenn Kerekes, President - Tel: (800) 265-7446, (905) 415-9809, Fax: (905) 415-9424, Web Site: www.beyondsigns.com. Beyond Signs-Imaging Centres is a retail store and manufacturing facility that incorporates an easy-to-use desktop computer system to design and precision-cut signs out of versatile, weather-resistant vinyl. Through the National Franchise Support Centre, you are linked to over $5 million worth of additional signmaking hardware and software that puts you way ahead of the competition. Established: 1988 - Franchising Since: 1990 - No. of Units: Franchised: 12 - Franchise Fee: $25,000 - Royalty: 8% first two years - then 6% - Total Inv: $100,000 plus working capital.

COMPUCENTRE
Hartco Enterprises, Inc.
9393 Louis H. Lafontaine, Anjou, QC, H1J 1Y8. Contact: Franchise Dept. - Tel: (514) 354-0580, ext. 309, Fax: (514) 354-2299, E-Mail: dtaylor@hartco.com. Retail stores located in regional malls selling personal computers to home and small businesses, peripherals, software, calculators, TV games and related products to the above. Established: 1976 - Franchising Since: 1982 - No. of Units: Company Owned: 7 - Franchised: 48 - Franchise Fee: $25,000 - Royalty: None - Total Inv: Approx. $275,000 - Financing: Bank franchise packages with 2 mjaor banks.

DIGITCOM TELECOMMUNICATIONS
Digitcom Canada, Inc.
1 Yorkdale Road Suite 220, Toronto, ON, M6A 3A1. Contact: J. Wiener, Pres. - Tel: (416) 783-7890, Fax: (416) 783-8962. Call processing, telecommunications, voice mail, interactive voice response, computer telephone integration. Established: 1991 - Franchising Since: 1993 - No. of Units: Company Owned: 1 - Franchised: 1 - Franchise Fee: $40,000 - Total Inv: $75,000 - Financing: Yes.

FEGAN SERVICES
P.O. Box 755, St. Catharines, ON, L2R 6Y3. Contact: Joseph Fegan, Founder/Owner - Tel: (905) 688-5880, Fax: (905) 688-7728, E-Mail: feganj@cogeco.ca. Specializing in Contingency Planning, Web Design & Hosting, Computer & Network Consulting. Established: 2002 - No. of Units: Company Owned: 2 - Franchise Fee: $15,000 - Total Inv: Varies.

IBC COMPUTER DISTRIBUTORS
86 Howard Place, Kitchener, ON, N2K 2Z4. Contact: Fred Hastings, Director of Franchising - Tel: (519) 571-8269, Fax: (519) 571-9319. Retail outlet that sells and services custom built computer systems and related accessories. Established: 1993 - Franchising Since: 1996 - No. of Units: Company Owned: 6 - Franchised: 1 - Franchise Fee: $40,000 - Royalty: 11% of gross, marketing 1% of gross - Total Inv: $110,000 - Financing: Available.

KING'S COMPUTERS

1191 Aster Street, Unit 5, Winnipeg, MB, R1P 2B2. Contact: Marv Hammerstein, Fran. Dev. - Tel: (204) 235-0091. Used computers, scanners, monitors, etc. Full training and support provided. Established: 1991 - No. of Units: Franchised: 21 - Total Inv: $35,000.

LE SUPERCLUB VIDEOTRON

Le Superclub Videotron Ltd
6455 Jean Talon East., 500, St. Leonard. QC, H1S 3E8. - Tel: (514) 259-6000, Fax: (514) 259-3232, E-Mail: rsoly@superclub.videotron.com, Web Site: www.superclub.videotron.com. Rental and sales of home video and electronic games. Distribute services related to the cable operation company. Established: 1989 - Franchising Since: 1991 - No. of Units: Company Owned: 48 - Franchised: 94 - Royalty: 0-8% - Total Inv: $220,000 - Financing: 60%.

MIBARSOFT INC.

4950 Yong Street, Suite 512, Toronto, ON, M2N 6K1. Contact: Shaun Minett, President - Tel: (416) 226-6607, Fax: (416) 730-8060, E-Mail: solution@mibarsoft.com, Web Site: www.mibarsoft.com. Offers a fully integrated exception based reporting solution that tracks Advertising and Royalty funds by location from the franchisees point-of-sale system to the franchisor's head office. Our software application supports EDI to the bank for electronic funds transfer and generates weekly operating reports.

MOBILWORLD

3 St. Mary's Road, Winnipeg, MB, R3G 2N1. - Tel: (204) 233-4135, Fax: (204) 233-2125, Web Site: www.mobilworld.com. A high-tech store specializing in cellular paging computers and laptops for the mobile professional. Small business computer needs networking internet server installations and configuration. Service contracting Cantel, AT&T approved agent. Authorized IBM business partner. Full training and support. Established: 1999 - No. of Units: Franchised: $30,000 - Total Inv: $50,000.

PLANET SATELLITE

729 Corydon Ave., Ste. E, Winnipeg, MB, R3M 0W4. - Tel: (204) 284-9060, (204) 792-9356, Fax: (204) 284-9004. Audio + satellite specialist, sale + servicing of 18" mini dish satellites + audio video equipment. Established: 1996 - Franchising Since: 1999 - No. of Units: Company Owned: 1 - Franchise Fee: $140,000 - Total Inv: $140,000 - Financing: No.

QUIK INTERNET

19086 Mitchell Rd, Pitt Meadows, Maple Ridge, BC, V2X 7E9. Contact: Fran. Dir. - Tel: (888) 584-9226, (604) 671-6543, Fax: (604) 465-1768, Web Site: www.quik.com. Provide internt access and web hosting services through locally owned franchises. Full training and ongoing support. Established: 1996 - No. of Units: Franchised: 150 - Total Inv: $60,000-$65,000.

RADIO BLASTER

310 Harbour Street, Winnipeg, MB, R3B 1N6. Contact: Fran. Dev. - Tel: (204) 235-0010. Retail sales of computers, radios, CD players and much more. 6 days of training with on-going support. Established: 1992 - No. of Units: Franchised: 15.

RMS LTD.

Tv Net Marketing
191 Munro Street, Toronto, ON, M4N 2B8. Contact: Gene Schmidt, Founder - Tel: (416) 778-1739, Fax: (416) 360-6863. Retail and wholesale of set top internet and e-mail access devise. No inventory required. All orders drop shipped. Full professional training program provided. Established: 1996 - Franchising Since: 1998 - No. of Units: Company Owned: 2 - Franchised: 10 - Franchise Fee: $990 plus taxes - Total Inv: $1,138 Demo unit, literature, presentation material and order forms - Financing: Third party.

SCHOOLEY MITCHELL TELECOM CONSULTANTS

187 Ontario Street, Stratford, ON, N5A 3H3. Contact: Dennis Schooley, President - Tel: (519) 273-4145, (800) 465-4145, Fax: (519) 273-7979, E-Mail: ho@schooleymitchell.com, Web Site: www.schooley mitchell.com. Professional telecommunications consulting business with complete training and support, easy to use computer tools, no inventory, helping business make their best telecom decisions. Excessive training and ongoing support. Established: 1996 - No. of Units: Franchised: 50 - Total Inv: $25,000.

SKILLSET TRAINING

SKILLSET Training Systems Inc.
365 Bloor St., East, Ste. 1902, Toronto, ON, M4W 3L4. Contact: Ted Turner, Pres. - Tel: (416) 920-4141, Fax: (416) 920-7285. Corporate computer training centers. Established: 1990 - Franchising Since: 1994 - No. of Units: Company Owned: 2 - Franchise Fee: $15,000-$30,000 depending on market - Royalty: 10% reducing to 5% - Total Inv: $100,000 - Financing: No, hardware might be leased if qualified.

SKY LINK INTERNET PLUS

30 Greenboro Crescent, Ottawa, ON, K1T 1W5. - Tel: (613) 738-1374, Fax: (613) 738-0809. Public internet kiosks. Established: 1996 - Franchising Since: 1997 - No. of Units: Company Owned: 7 - Franchised: 3 - Franchise Fee: $500.00 per kiosk.

SYSTEMWAY ™

Distribution Tandem Ltée
1418 Maisonneuve Street, Mont Joli, QC, G5H 2J3. Contact: Gaston St-Pierre, Dir. Of Marketing - Tel: (418) 775-8311, (877) 347-8746, Fax: (418) 775-5799, E-Mail: gaston@reporters.net, Web Site: www.system way.com. Internet assisted general store and order desk combined. Protected territories, regional or city district. Lowest overhead of all store concepts. No inventory financing at all. Systemway Distributors ship it to stores, staff supplied. Excellent profit potential. Established: 1999 - Franchising Since: 1999 - No. of Units: Company Owned: 1 - Franchise Fee: Approx. $30,000 for store set up - Total Inv: Approx. $50,000 Canadian.

THE WORLD CO.

2505-11 Avenue, Suite 301, Regina, SK, S4P 0K6. Contact: Jason Friend, President - Fax: (306) 352-3133 - E-Mail: info@theworldco.com, Web Site: www.theworldco.com. Business and corporate website design and hosting; logo, graphics, on-line shopping carts, secured credit card transactions, professional award-winning designs. Established: 1997.

VRS SYSTEMS INC.

VRS Systems Inc.
15-1600 Regent Ave West, Winnipeg, AB, R2C 3B5. Contact: Len Herbach, VP Operations - Tel: (204) 474-1531, Fax: (204) 474-1531, Web Site: www.videorefitshop.com. Repair of consumer electronics, VCR, TV camcorders, audio equipment, microwave ovens, compact disc players, computer monitors and more. Established: 1983 - No. of Units: Franchised: 5 - Franchise Fee: $15,000-$25,000 - Royalty: 5%, 5% adv. - Total Inv: $75,000-$105,000 - Financing: Portion of Franchise Fee.

WORLDSITES

Worldsite International
5915 Airport Road., Suite 300, Toronto, ON, L4V 1T1. Contact: Franchise Department - Tel: (905) 678-7588, (888) 678-7588, Fax: (416) 213-8025, E-Mail: franchise@worldsites.net, Web Site: www.worldsites.net. World's largest Internet Consultancy Franchise with 500+ locations in 78 countries. Our franchises provide small to medium sized business a one stop service for Internet Solutions. Not being a technical expert, our franchises depend on our full training/ support and 10 production centers around the world for effective/ efficient web solutions. Established: 1995 - Franchising Since: 1996 - No. of Units: Franchised: 500+ - Franchise Fee: $34,700 US - Royalty: 10% - Financing: No.

WSI

5915 Airport Rd Suite 300, Mississauga, ON, L4V 1T1. Contact: Roberto Alvarado, Marketing Director - Tel: (905) 678-7588, (888) 678-7588, Fax: (905) 678-9974, E-Mail: vmjuarez@wsicorporate.com, Web Site: www.wsicorporate.com. WSI is one of the most profitable franchise opportunities in the world today, with over 700 franchises in 87 countries. No specific business experience is required. WSI offers its franchises one of the most complete and comprehensivce training & certification programs available among franchise companies today, and a dynamic on-going support program tailored to meet the needs of each new franchisee. Established: 1995 - Franchising Since: 1996- No. of Units: Company Owned: 1 - Franchised: 800 - Franchise Fee: $39,700 us - Royalty: 10% - Total Inv: $39,700-$50,000 - Financing: No.

CONSUMER BUYING SERVICES

MAKE YOUR MARK ONSITE COMPUTER SECURITY
Make Your Mark Onsite Computer Security
P.O. Box 2000, Squamish, BC, V0N 3G0. Contact: Mary Jane Charman, President - Tel: (604) 519-7566, (888) 282-6275, Fax: (604) 898-5107, E-Mail: mj@makeyourmark.net, Web Site: www.makeyourmark.net. Loss Prevention s Our Goal!! Our system permanetly and visably marks valuable office and computer equipment with your company name/logo to reduce exposure to break-ins and theft. Our customer findings show losses reduce by 91%. Make Your Mark also carries a variety of harware proucts such as computer lockdowns, cables, T-Locks, etc. Established: 1996 - Franchising Since: 2000 - No. of Units: Company Owned: 1 - Franchised: 5 - Franchise Fee: $25,000 (including equipment and supplies) - Royalty: 8% - Total Inv: $25,000 - Financing: N/A.

DISTRIBUTORS

ACTUAL REALITY / LASER EXTREME
Actual Reality International Inc.
34 Sioux Rd, Sherwood park, AB, T8A 4X1. - Tel: (780) 449-6918, Fax: (780) 416-9302. Actual Reality specializes in the design, manufacture and worldwide distribution of interactive laser tag systems. Established: 1993 - Licensor Since: 1994 - No. of Units: Company Owned: 1- Licenced: 47 - Total Inv: $150,000-$350,000 - Financing: Yes upon approval.

ADVANCED COATING, INC.
15288 Hwy 12, P.O. Box 670, Midland, ON, L4R 4P4. Contact: Les Shannon, Marketing Manager -Tel: (705) 534-7219, (800) 787-8059, Fax: (705) 534-4125, E-Mail:LShannon@atlasblock.com, Web Site: www.advancedcoating.on.com. Distributor of liquid applied coatings for foundations water proofing, air/vapour barriers and retrofit roofs. Established: 1994 - Franchising Since: 1994 - No. of Units: Company Owned: 1 - Franchised: 33 - Franchise Fee: $1,000 - Royalty: 0% - Total Inv: $15,000-$25,000 - Financing: None.

ALLSTAR DISTRIBUTING INC.
240 Voyageur, Point-Claire, QC, H9R 6A8. Contact: Myrna Dorfman, Pres. - Tel: (514) 426-1690, Fax: (514) 426-5644. Manufacturer of "Typhoon" spiral gumball machine, "Typhoon" spiral $2 capsule machine and "Allstar" sticker vending machines. Also manufacturer of licensed prismatic stickers, tattoos and beanie babies with key chains. Established: 1981- No. of Units: Company Owned: 500 - Total Inv: Minimum $995.00.

AMERACAR ELECTROPLATING W/O IMMERSION
Ameracar Instruments Canada
1990 Chareft West Blvd., Quebec, QC, G1N 4K8. - Fax: (954) 472-0041. Portable electroplating system w/o immersion also call brush plating. We have all preparatory solutions and 60 liquid metal. We offer machine tools aeronautic, marine and decoration training. Marketing and sales included in training. Established: 1989 - Offering Dealerships Since: 1995 - No. of Units: Company Owned: 4 - Dealers: 481 - Fee: None - Total Inv: $2,500 + - Financing: Yes.

BLOCKSUN INTERNATIONAL, INC.
4300 Drummond Rd., Ste. 202, Niagara Falls, ON, L2E 6C3. Contact: Ken McKee, President - Tel: (905) 357-3614, (888) Burn Free, Fax: (905) 357-3117, E-Mail: info@blocksun.com, Web Site: www.block sun.com. Manufacture and market the world's first package free sunscreen vending unit. We offer exclusive territories, and dealer support. Our product line includes; hand cream vending, liquid laundry vending. Established: 1996 - Distributorships Since: 1996 - No. of Units: Company Owned: 1 - Distributors: 3 - Distributorship Fee: Accessed on an individual basis - Royalty: None - Total Inv: $6,000 - Financing: Partial. Also located at P.O. Box 1434, Lewiston, NY, 14092-8434.

BREATHPATROL INC.
P.O. Box 22113, Waterloo, ON, N2L 6J7. Contact: Gerhard Zielinsky, Pres. - Tel: (800) 361-3284, Fax: (800) 278-8507, E-Mail: gmzi@breath patrol.com, Web Site: www.breathpatrol.com. Vending and distributor of breath lozenges for eliminating alcohol and other bad breath to bars, restaurants etc. Established: 1993 - Offering Dealerships Since: 1993 - Vending Since: 1995 - No. of Dealers: 20 - Investment: $400-$15,000 - Financing: No.

BUSINESS OPPORTUNITY SALES & SERVICE
Biovite Inc.
26 Livingston Rd., Unit #128, Scarborough, ON, M1E 4S4. Contact: Michael Helbig, President - Tel: (416) 266-4622, Fax: (416) 266-6653. Cart vending etc. Stickers and collectables. Established: 1987 - Franchising Since: 1988 - No. of Units: Franchised: 500 - Franchise Fee: $5,000-$100,000 - Total Inv: $5,000-$30,000 - Financing: Yes.

DICKIE DEE ICE CREAM
Good Humor - Dickie Dee Ice Cream
1585 Cliveden Ave W #6, Delta, BC, V3M 6M1. Contact: Andy Barish, G.M. Sales - Tel: (604) 519-0600, Fax: (604) 519-0606. Mobile street vending of frozen novelties. Equipment (tricycles, carts, freezers etc.) is leased to a contracted distributor who then leases to vendors. Ice cream and water ice novelties are sold to the distributor by the company. The company provides training and support. Established: 1959 - Distributorships Since: 1960 - No. of Distributors: 240 - Total Inv: Approx. $700 per unit leased - Financing: No.

DRUG TRADING CO. LTD.
131 McNabb St., Markham, ON, L3R 5V7. Contact: Neil Jorgensen, Mgr. - Tel: (905) 943-9499, Fax: (905) 943-4504. Company is engaged in the wholesale of drugs. Mfg. opers. carried out in small plant in Scarborough. Franchised opers. carried out through IDA, Guardian and Custom Pharmacy stores. Established: 1904 - Offering Distributorships Since: 1933 - No. of Units: 2250.

ELEPHANT COMPANY, THE
3100 Ridgeway Drive, #40, Mississauga, ON, L5L 5M5. Contact: Amit Karia, President - Tel: (905) 569-2273, (800) 591-4218, Fax: (905) 569-2938, Web Site: www.elephanthouse.com. Franchised distributor of fine greeting cards. Franchises are awarded territories and are assisted in finding retailers to carry fresh new and exciting greeting cards. Established: 1995 - Franchising Since: 1996 - No. of Units: Company Owned: 1 - Franchised:11 - Franchise Fee: $4,950 - Royalty: None - Total Inv: $29,950 + gst - Financing: No.

FABRICLAND/FABRICVILLE
444 Adelaide St. W., Toronto, ON, M5V 1S7. Contact: Ron Kimel, Co-Owner - Tel: (416) 703-1877. Fabric, drapery, upholstery, sewing notions, crafts, patterns, etc. Established: 1968 - Distributing Since: 1968 - No. of Units: Company Owned: 110 - Franchised: 16 - Franchise Fee: $35,000 - Royalty: 5% - Total Inv: $110,000 - Financing: No.

FREEWAY 100 INTERNATIONAL
Box 332, Waverly, NS, B0N 2S0. Contact: Ken and Rose Davidson, Independent Representative - Tel: (902) 462-2945, Fax: (902) 462-2985. Home based business offering a wide variety of affordable products. Established: 1996.

GALAXY CRYSTAL & CHINA, INC.
11 Latonia Dr., Rexdale, ON, M9W 2J1. Contact: Jake Rumph, Pres. - Tel: (416) 741-1758, Fax: (416) 741-1769. Direct sales of cookware, chinaware crystal, oil cure skillets, woks, extra large pans to 20 quart. Ideal business to operate from home. Low overhead. Established: 1983 - Franchising Since: 1984 - No. of Units: Company Owned: 1 - Franchised: 20 - Franchise Fee: Min. $300 - Total Inv: Avg. $2,300 secured by inventory - Financing: Yes. NOT OFFERING FRANCHISES AT THIS TIME.

GENUINE PARTS COMPANY LTD.
7025 Ontario Street East, Montreal, QC, H1N 2B3. Contact: Brian Johnson, Mktg. - Tel: (514) 256-5031, Fax: (514) 256-8469. Auto parts. Established: 1947 - No. of Units: Company Owned: 17 - Associates: 163 - Distribution Centers: 4.

GODDEN
R.A. Godden Company Limited
344 Dupont St., Ste. 202, Toronto, ON, M5R 1V9. Contact: Gordon Krofchick, President - Tel: (416) 922-9889, (800) 616-8403, Fax: (416) 922-3056. Direct distribution of industrial, automotive, marine products. Servicing chemical and product needs. Training, technical assistance, and accounting assistance available. Established: 1965 - Franchising Since: 1987 - Total Inv: $40,000 - Financing: Yes.

GUARANTEED MUFFLER SHOPS
Motorcade Industries, Ltd.
90 Kincourt St., Toronto, ON, M6M 5G1. Contact: Joel Klein, General Sales Manager - Tel: (416) 614-6118, Fax: (416) 614-6130, Web Site: www.motorcade-ind.com. Auto parts warehouse distributor presently operating in Ontario only. Established: 1950 - Franchising Since: 1972 - No. of Units: Franchised: 45 - Total Inv: $10,000 - Financing: Yes.

HORIZON MANAGEMENT SYSTEMS
P.O. Box 21044, 35 Harvard Rd., Guelph, ON, N1G 4T3. Contact: Jeff Axson, V.P. - Tel: (519) 767-9983. Provides personal management tools and workshops to improve the effectiveness of management and sales people. Many business people are now using this system to organize their activities and information. Established: 1986.

I.L.P.S.
International Loss Prevention Systems Corp.
1350 E. 4th Ave., Vancouver, BC, V5N 1J5. Contact: Ian Abramson, President - Tel: (604) 255-5000, (800) 663-4577, Fax: (604) 254-2575, E-Mail: ilps@msn.com, Web Site: www.ilps.com. Manufacturer of shoplifting employee theft prevention products. Established: 1986 - Offering Distributorships Since: 1988 - No. of Units: Company Owned: 5 - Distributors: 41 - Distributorship Fee: $25,000 - Total Inv: $25,000 - Financing: Yes.

IRLY BIRD BUILDING CENTRES
Irly Distributors Ltd.
7846-128th St., P.O. Box 9010, Surrey, BC, V3T 4X7. Contact: Stuart Joyle, Gen Mgr. - Tel: (604) 596-1551, Fax: (604) 597-3693. Wholesale distribution centre for member stores carrying a complete assortment of building materials and hardware. Established: 1963 - Franchising Since: 1963 - No. of Units: Franchised: 56 - Franchise Fee: $2500.

KEN-CO INDUSTRIES, LTD.
1070 Heritage Rd., Burlington, ON, L7L 4X9. Contact: Larry Minaker, Pres./G.M. - Tel: (905) 335-1828, Fax: (905) 335-1829. Direct marketing of garage supplies and auto parts to the general repair garage and service station industries. Established: 1963 - Distributing Since: 1963 - No. of Distributorships: 31 - Distribution Fee: Varies 0-$10,000 - Total Inv: $15,000-$30,000 equip., $15,000-$25,000 inven.

MAC TOOLS CANADA
Division of Stanley Canada, Inc.
1294 South Service Rd. West, Oakville, ON, L6L 5T7. Contact: Steve Eyre, Oper. Mgr. - Tel: (905) 825-9630, Fax: (800) 422-0565. Manufactures and distributes tools for the industrial and automotive aftermarket. Our products are only available from authorized mobile distributors. Each distributor has a protected territory assignment. Investment in inventory is also protected by a buy back agreement. Established: 1938 - Distributing Since: 1938 - No. of Distributorships: 2000 Worldwide, 135 Canada - Total Inv: $112, 298 - Financing: Yes, for approved applicants.

METAL SUPERMARKETS INTERNATIONAL
170 Wilkinson Rd., Unit 18, Brampton, ON, L6T 4Z5. - Tel: (905) 459-0466, (800) 807-8755, Fax: (905) 459-6684, E-Mail: headoffice@ metalsupermarkets.com, Web Site: www.metalsupermarkets.com. Wholesale distributor of metals. Established: 1985 - Franchising Since: 1987 - No. of Units: Company Owned: 8 - Franchised: 56 - Franchise Fee: $38,000 - Total Inv: $180,000 - Financing: No.

MISTER MINI POST
Box 131 Place Bonaventure, Montreal, QC, H5A 1A6. Contact: Murray Black, Pres. - Tel: (450) 688-6443, Fax: (450) 688-6491, Web Site: www.mrminipost.com. Private postal terminal manufacturer and distributor. Each module contains 60 postal boxes. Ideal traffic builder for supermarkets, drug stores, convenience stores and other mass merchandisers. Self contained, free standing, lockable and private. Brings increased traffic and sales. You can also create your own route using other peoples stores. Comes complete with everything needed to run as a seperate business. Total Inv: $6,000 per 60 box unit. No franchise fee or royaltys payable.

NOAH'S ARK LEASING, INC
5796 Byng Ave., Niagara Falls, ON, L2G 5E2. Contact: Herb Cowan, Pres. - Tel: (905) 371-1724. Lawn ornaments for special occasions such as birthdays, just arrived, happy retirement, welcome home, congratulations. Established: 1994 - Franchising Since: 1994 - No. of Units: Company Owned: 3 - Franchised: 1 - Franchise Fee: $20,000 - Royalty: None - Total Inv: $20,000 - Financing: None.

NORTHWEST SAFETY PRODUCTS, LTD
800-15355-24th Ave., #117, Surrey, BC, V4A 2H9. Contact: Sean Russell, President - Tel: (604) 538-3471, Fax: (604) 538-3458. Pepper spray bear and dog repellent. Established: 1994 - Franchising Since: 1994 - No. of Units: Company Owned: 1 - Franchised: 392 - Franchise Fee: None - Royalty: None - Total Inv: $500-$1,000 - Financing: None.

PRO-TECT ASPHALT LTD.
100 Buchanan St., Cobourg, ON, K9A 1Z1. Contact: Jim Hartford, Pres. - Tel: (905) 372-3902, Fax: (905) 372-8204. Manufacture of driveway sealing equipment and distributor of related asphalt maintenance equipment. Support and assistance given to purchaser in establishing driveway sealing business. Established: 1980 - No. of Distributors: 25 - Total Inv: $2,275 - Financing: No.

PROVINCIAL TABLE PADS
Provincial Table Pads Ltd.
321 Anchor Rd., Unit 1A, Hamilton, ON, L8W 3R1. Contact: Ross DePalma, Pres. - Tel: (905) 383-1343, Fax: (905) 692-0972. Shop at home service for custom table pads. Established: 1982 - Franchising Since: 1983 - No. of Units: Company Owned: 2 - Franchised: 5.

ROTHSTEIN DESIGN WORLD PRODUCTS CORPORATION
9105 Shaughnessy St, Vancouver, BC, V6P 6R9. Contact: Arlen Rothstein, President - Tel: (604) 713-8340, (888) 296-3034, Fax: (604) 713-8344. Home based business specialist - marketing 7 different programs, hot dog carts, counter space products, snack foods, internet kiosk, spa beds, smoke masks and hot dog kiosks. Established: 1988 - Franchising Since: 1993 - Total Inv: $5,995.00-$24,995.00 - Financing: OAC total amount.

SERVICEMASTER
Servicemaster Res/Comm.
5462 Timberlea Blvd, Mississauga, ON, L4W 2T7. Contact: David Messenger, V.P. Sales & Mktg. - Tel: (905) 670-0000, (800) 263-5928, Fax: (905)670-0077. Professional cleaning services for businesses, government and institution buildings and residences. Cleaning and re-construction after fire or flood damage. Established: (Can) 1953, (US) 1947 - Franchising Since: (Can) 1953, (US) 1952 - No. of Units: Franchised: 160 in Can. - Franchise Fee: $11,500-$28,500 - Royalty: 4%-9% depending on type of business - Total Inv: $21,500-$46,500 - Financing: Yes.

SHUR-GAIN
Maple Leaf Foods, Inc.
150 Research Lane #200, Guelph, ON, N1G 4T2. Contact: Jerry Vergeer, Regional Manager - Tel: (519) 823-7000. Livestock and poultry feeds, pet foods, animal health products, birdseed, horse feed. Established: 1929 - Distributing Since: 1938 - No. of Units: Company Owned: 20 - Distributors: 200 - Total Inv: $50,000-$200,000 - Financing: Yes.

SOFTUB CANADA
967 Falconbridge Rd, Sudbury, ON, P3A 5K8. - Tel: (800) 668-8827. Manufacturer/distributor of lightweight, portable, full featured hydrotherapy hot tub. Softubs plug into standard 110V outlet, and weighing only 60lbs empty adds to the portability. Established: 1990 - Franchising Since: 1990 - No. of Units: Franchised: 120 - Financing: No.

SUNITRON INC.
40 Pippin Rd. Unit 4, Concord, ON, L4K 4M6. Contact: Jerry Pappa, Pres. - Tel: (416) 630-8811, Fax: (416) 781-5140. Distributor of all kinds of computerized bill board for indoor or outdoor (LED message signs).

Established: 1986 - No. of Dealers: Over 350 - Total Inv: Up to negotiation - Financing: No.

TOPLINE PAINT & COLOUR
Weather-Bos Canada Ltd.
555 Bat Street, Midland, ON, L4R 1L4. Contact: Eric J. Bos, Pres. - Tel: (705) 526-7563. Manufacturers of enviro safe stains and paints. Established: 1989.

TOTALLY TROPICAL INTERIORS LTD
4310 12st NE, Calgary, AB, T2E 3K9. - Tel: (403) 291-5802, Fax: (403) 291-3362. Totally Tropical designs, manufactures and distributes an exclusive collection of silk plants, trees and decorating accessories. We bring warmth and beauty to offices and homes. Established: 1985 - Franchising Since: 1985 - No. of Units: Company Owned: 1500 - Franchised: 1500 - Franchise Fee: $500.00 - Royalty: None - Total Inv: $500.00 - Financing: Yes.

UAP/NAPA ASSOCIATE PROGRAM
7025 Ontario St., E., Montreal, QC, H1N 2B3. Contact: Benoit Bouchard, Coordinator, Jobber Programs - Tel: (514) 256-5031, Fax: (514) 256-8469. Wholesale and retail stores for distributing automotive parts and supplies including body shop supplies. UAP Inc. Established: 1926 - Franchising Since: 1955.

WEBER SECURITY DISTRIBUTION
Weber Supply
675 Queen St. S., Kitchener, ON, N2G 4H6. Contact: Donald Young, Exec. V.P. - Tel: (519) 744-04300, (800) 387-4290, Fax: (519) 888-4207. Importer and distributor of security, access control and surveillance systems and equipment. Established: 1992 - Franchising Since: 1992 - Total Inv: Demo kit $800.

EMPLOYMENT & PERSONNEL

HUNT PERSONNEL, TEMPORARILY YOURS
Business Aid, Inc.
330 Bay St. Suite 403, Toronto, ON, M5H 2S8. Contact: Ted Turner, Pres. - Tel: (416) 920-4141, Fax: (416) 860-9410, E-Mail: info@hunt.ca, Web Site: www.hunt.ca. Personnel services, temporary and permanent. Industry experience preferred. Established: 1967 - Franchising Since: 1974 - No. of Units: Franchised: 12 - Franchise Fee: $10,000 min. - Total Inv: $100,000 minimum - Royalty: Varies with volume and services.

RESUME HUT, THE®/ TRH BUSINESS CENTRE™
Gandalf Enterprises, Inc.
743 View St., Victoria, BC, V8W 1J9. Contact: Mr. C. Dalgarno, President - Tel: (250) 383-3983, (800) 441-6488, Fax: (250) 383-1580, E-Mail: info@resume-hut.com, Web Site: www.resume-hut.com. Exciting varied consultancy business. Ideally positioned to capitalize on the employment environment and small business sectors. Provides professional resumes, career assessment testing, interview skills training etc. Established: 1986 - Franchising Since: 1993 - No. of Units: Company Owned: 1 - Franchised: 1 - Franchise Fee: $15,000 - Royalty: Flat Fee - Total Inv: $25,000-$62,500 includes fran. fee - Financing: No.

THE CENTRE FOR CORPORATE RESOURCES
615-133 Richmond Street West, Toronto, ON, M5H 2L3. Contact: Richard Fernandes, President & CEO - Tel: (416) 364-2900, Fax: (416) 364-1575, Web Site: www.corporate-resources.com. Recruits talented individuals using our exclusive M.C.L.S.™ system for leading corporations in North America. Full training and support provided. Established: 1991 - Franchising Since: 1995 - No. of Units: Company Owned: 1 - Franchised: 4 - Franchise Fee: $49,500 - Royalty: 10% - Total Inv: $65,000 - Financing: Yes.

ENTERTAINMENT

CANADIAN POOL LEAGUE
208 Scott Street, Walkerton, ON, N0G 2V0. Contact: Lindsay Dobson, Pres. - Tel: (519) 881-2196, Fax: (519) 881-2520. Amateur pool leagues, organize tournaments. Established: 1989 - Franchising Since: 1989 - No. of Units: Franchised: 13 - Royalty: $5 per team or 20%, whichever is greater - Total Inv: $4,500 approx. - Financing: No.

DAVOLI OF NORTH AMERICA
Sunitron Inc. Holding Corp.
40 Pippin Road, Building #4, Concord, ON, L4K 4M6. Contact: Jerry Pappa, Pres. - Tel: (416) 630-8811, Fax: (416) 781-5140. Davoli of North America imports from Italy hi fi sound systems for mobile D.J., night clubs and discoteques. Established: 1986 - Royalty: None - Total Inv: To be negotiated - Financing: To be negotiated.

DOOLY'S
dooly's inc
795 Main Street Suite 200, Moncton, NB, E1C 8P9. Contact: Pierre Lariviere, VP - Tel: (506) 857-8050, Fax: (506) 858-7039, E-Mail: info@doolys-inc.com, Web Site: www.doolys.ca. Our customers say DOOLY'S is their favorite place to play, relax and have fun. We've been in buisness for 10 years and now have 91 locations in 7 provinces. Whether you come to play pool or site back in a leather sofa in front of the fireplace to catch up at Dooly's you're always in good company. Established: 1993 - Franchising Since: 1995 - No. of Units: Company Owned: 18 - Franchised: 73 - Franchise Fee: $25,000 - Royalty: 6% - Total Inv: $350,000.

GARY ROBERTSON MUSIC SERVICES
75 Stillwater Road, Winnipeg, MB, R2J 2R2. Contact: Franchise Director - Tel: (204) 255-8871, Fax: (204) 255-8871. Professional disc jockey services and mobile music entertainment. Full training and support provided. Established: 1971 - No. of Units: Company Owned: 5 - Franchised: 28 - Total Inv: $15,000-$20,000.

GONE HOLLYWOOD VIDEO LTD
20085-96th Ave, Langley, BC, V1M 2P8. Contact: Paul Sanders, V.P. - Tel: (604) 881-2450, (800) 567-7710, Fax: (604) 881-2451, Web Site: www.gonehollywoodvideo.com. Specializing in neighborhood video rental stores. Turnkey set-up, ongoing support, steady rotation of product. Best selection of movies, games, DVD, music, apparel and more. Established: 1990 - Franchising Since: 1994 - No. of Units: Company Owned: 6 - Franchised: 72 - Franchise Fee: $10,000 - Royalty: 8% - Total Inv: $180,000-$250,000 - Financing: Yes.

ONTARIO CONSERVATORY OF MUSIC
Ontario Conservatory Of Music, Inc
1515 Britannia Rd East 235, Mississauga, ON, L4W 4K1. Contact: Paul Johnston, General Manager - Tel: (905) 670-7888, (800) 739-3828, Fax: (905) 696-7298. Music-teaching-examinations-concerts-recitals-musical instrument sales, pianos, guitars, keyboards and etc. Established: 1938 - Franchising Since: 1970 - No. of Units: Company Owned: 15 - Franchised: 30 - Franchise Fee: Varies - Royalty: 6% lesson revenue - Total Inv: Varies minimum $50,000 - Financing: Partial if required.

THE BEAT GOES ON
385 Fairway Road South, Kitchener, ON, N2C 2N9. - Tel: (905) 804-9711, (888) 667-8449, Fax: (905) 804-9713, E-Mail: northernlights @interhop.net. The Beat Goes On retail stores sell previously enjoyed c.d's for music lovers at a fraction of the price of regular retail. Proven systems, great bottom line and terrific returns on investment. Established: 1991 - Franchising Since: 1999 - No. of Units: Company Owned: 8 - Franchised: 2 - Franchise Fee: $20,000 - Royalty: 5%, 3% ad fund - Total Inv: $95.500-$128.500 - Financing: No.

TOP FORTY / TFM
Top Forty Music Ltd.
10333-174 St., Edmonton, AB, T5S 1H1. Contact: A.J. Herfst, V.P. - Tel: (780) 483-3217, Fax: (780) 486-7528, E-Mail: tfminquiries@ totalsound.org. Retailer of pre-recorded music (cassette, compact disc and DVD) products, accessories, video and other paraphenalia. Established: 1975 - Franchising Since: 1983 - No. of Units: Company

Owned: 4 - Franchised: 12 - Franchise Fee: $15,000 - Royalty: 5% of sales, 1% of advertising - Total Inv: $120,000-$160,000 - Financing: 60% thru bank.

WEST SIDE CHARLIES BAR AND BILLARDS
10641 Newfoundland Limited
Suite 380, Cabot Place, 100 New Gower Street, St.Johns, NF, A1C 6K3. Contact: Wade Gravelle, Vice President - Tel: (709) 738-4747, Fax: (709) 726-4849, E-Mail: westside@nfld.net. West Side Charlies is your local neighborhood bar that is set in a upscale billiards room, catering to those who enjoy good times and fun. Established: 1996 - No. of Units: Franchised: 13 - Franchise Fee: $25,000 - Royalty: 6% - Total Inv: $225,000.

YUK - YUKS INTERNATIONAL
13 Balmuto Street, #200, Toronto, ON, M4Y 1W4. Contact: D. Jae Gold CA, Fran. Dev. - Tel: (416) 967-6431, Fax: (416) 925-9298, Web Site: www.yukyuks.com. Stand up comedy nightclub. Yuk-Yuks is the world's largest chain of comedy clubs. Extensive training and ongoing support. Established: 1978 - No. of Units: Franchised: 13 - Total Inv: Varies.

FINANCIAL SERVICES

CANADIAN CHEQUE CASHING CORP.
1075 Granville St, Vancouver, BC, V6Z 1L4. - Tel: (604) 684-2333, Fax: (604) 684-9818. Cheque cashing business, foreign exchange, money orders, Western Union agents. Established: 1985 - Franchising Since: 1995 - No. of Units: Company Owned: 2 - Franchise Fee: $15,000 - Royalty: Negotiable - Total Inv: Applicant should have $100,000 unencumbered capital.

CASH MONEY
28 Windsor Road, Etobicoke, ON, M9R 3G1. Contact: VP of Franchising - Tel: (416) 240-0082, Fax: (416) 240-8564, E-Mail: rpreston@cashmoney.ca, Web Site: www.cashmoney.ca. Cash money is a producer of retail financial services, including: cheque cashing, payday advances, money transfer, currency exchange. Established: 1992 - Franchising Since: 2000 - Franchise Fee: $35,000 - Total Inv: $135,000-$150,000 for buildout, $60,000 cash flow.

CASH NOW - USA
3100 Steeles Ave. E., Ste. 906, Toronto, ON, L3R 8T9. - Tel: (905) 470-6100, Fax: (905) 470-0084, E-Mail: staff@cashnow.com, Web Site: www.cashnow.com. Payday advanced loans and check cashing products are juust a few of the services that Cash Now provides. Established: 1998 - Franchising Since: 2001 - No. of Units: Company Owned: 2 - Franchised: 50 - Franchise Fee: $18,500.

CASH-A-CHEQUE/FOREIGN EXCHANGE
Cash Plus Services
360 Bayfield St., Unit 3, Barrie, ON, L4M 3C4. Contact: General Manager - Tel: (705) 725-7680, Fax: (705) 725-7687. Cheque cashing, foreign exchange and related financial services. Established: 1991 - Franchising Since: 1992 - No. of Units: Company Owned: 1 - Franchised: 11 - Franchise Fee: $95,000 turnkey - Royalty: None - Total Inv: $150,000 - Financing: Some.

CASHQUEST
Cashquest Limited
145 Rodeo Drive, Thornhill, ON, L4J 4Y6. Contact: B M Bloch, Director - Tel: (416) 878-4128, Fax: (905) 709-9176, E-Mail: cashquest2002@yahoo.co.uk. Payday advances, cheque cashing & money exchange. Established: 2002 - Franchising Since: 2003 - No. of Units: Company Owned: 1 - Franchise Fee: $30,000 - Royalty: $500 per month plus $1250 per month for advertising - Total Inv: $75,000-$150,000.

INSTA CASH ATMS INC.
16 Northwestern Avenue, Toronto, ON, M6M 5E5. - Tel: (416) 240-9900, (800) 523-3077, Fax: (416) 240-9904, E-Mail: instacash@sprint.ca. ATM machines & direct debit terminals. Established: 1998 - Franchising Since: 2002 - No. of Units: Company Owned: 3 - Franchised: 1.

LIQUID CAPITAL
Liquid Capital Corp.
5734 Yonge Street, Suite 400, Toronto, ON, M2M 4E7. Contact: Jan Golland - Tel: (416) 222-5599, (877) 228-0800, Fax: (416) 222-0166, E-Mail: golland@liquidcapitalcorp.com. Factoring services and accounts receivable funding. Established: 1999 - Franchising Since: 2000 - No. of Units: Franchised: 13 - Franchise Fee: $25,000 - Royalty: 8% + advertising - $400/mth - Total Inv: $150,000 working capital - Financing: Yes.

MONEY MART
National Money Mart, Inc.
2940 Jutland Street, #201, Victoria, BC, V8T 5K6. Contact: Bruce Marshall, V.P. Operations - Tel: (250) 595-5211, Fax: (250) 595-0410, Web Site: www.moneymart.ca. Money Mart provides convenient cash-based financial services across Canada. Services include cheque cashing, small loans, small business cheque cashing, money transfers, currency exchange, bill payments, and mailbox rentals. Established: 1982 - Franchising Since: 1982 - No. of Units: Company Owned and/or Operated: 150 - Franchised: 80 - Franchise Fee: $35,000 - Royalty: 6.75% gross rev., 2% adv. - Total Inv: $250,000 - Financing: No.

NATIONAL MONEY MART COMPANY
1640 Oak Bay Avenue, 3rd Floor, Victoria, BC, V8R 1B2. Contact: Fran. Dev. - Tel: (250) 595-5211, Fax: (250) 595-0410. Retail financial service, cheque cashing, currency exchange, cash wire, cash advances, money orders, bill payment service and mailbox rentals. Established: 1982 - No. of Units: Franchised: 185 - Franchise Fee: $35,000 - Total Inv: $250,000.

PREMIERE CASH ADVANCE
45923 Airport Road, Chilliwack, BC, V2P 1A3. Contact: Rick Lobb - Tel: (604) 702-0727, Fax: (604) 795-7145, E-Mail: franchise@money tilpayday.com, Web Site: www.moneytilpayday.com. Premiere Cash Advanced is the only franchised dedicated payday advance company in Canada. Proven autimated systems and business plan. Established: 1997 - Franchising Since: 2001 - No. of Units: Company Owned: 1 - Franchised: 24 - Franchise Fee: $22,900 - Royalties: 1.00% of gross sales financing services.

UNICASH
Unicash Franchising Inc.
1 First Canadian Place, Suite 5100, Toronto, ON, M5X 1K2. Contact: Ed Stivelman, Franchising Director - Tel: (416) 250-8661, Web Site: www.unicash.com. Check cashing and other related financial services. Established:1990 - Franchising Since: 1997 - No. of Units: Company Owned: 4 - Franchised: 2 - Franchise Fee: $19,800 - Royalty: 5% - Total Inv: $80,000-$110,000 - Financing: Yes.

FITNESS CENTERS

GOODLIFE FITNESS CLUBS
355 Wellington Rd., PO Box 122, London, ON, N6A 3N7. Contact: Director of Franchising - Tel: (519) 661-0190, Fax: (519) 434-6701. Fitness clubs. Established: 1979 - Franchising Since: 1989 - No. of Units: Company Owned: 22 - Franchised: 15 - Franchise Fee: $50,000 - Royalty: 10% of gross revenue - Total Inv: $300,000-$1,000,000 - Financing: No.

GYMNASIA
P.O. Box 3402, Main Station, Tracadie-Sheila, NB, E1X 1G5. Contact: Alain Champoux, Director - Tel: (506) 394-7433, (506) 395-7376, Fax: (506) 393-1888. Fitness and health club. Established: 1995 - No. of Units: Company Owned: 7 - Franchise Fee: $15,000 - Total Inv: $100,000 +.

MUSCLEMAG INTERNATIONAL
Musclemag International Corporation
5775 McLaughlin Road, Mississauga, ON, L5R 3P7. Contact: Marianne Butler, Dir. of Franchise Op. - Tel: (905) 507-354-5111. Exercise stores selling to the skyrocketting fitness, health and bodybuilding market: Supplements, sportswear, weight equipment accessories, books and videos. Established: 1974 - Franchising Since: 1993 - No. of Units: Company Owned: 5 - Franchised: 12 - Franchise Fee: $20,000 - Royalty: 5% monthly - Total Inv: $125,000-$350,000 - Financing: No.

THE FIX WORKOUT *
719 Central Parkway West Unit 202, Mississauga, ON, L5B 4L1. - Tel: (877) 843-3496, Fax: (416) 946-1182, E-Mail: info@thefixworkout.com, Web Site: www.thefixworkout.com. We offer a great franchise package for entrepreneurs interested in opening a co-ed circuit training, fitness club. We'll provide everything you'll need to start, grow & successfully operate your own club. Established: 2003 - Franchising Since: 2004 - No. of Units: Company Owned: 1 - Franchise Fee: $10,000 - Royalty: $600. monthly - Total Inv: $75,000-$100,000.

FLORISTS

GROWER DIRECT FRESH CUT FLOWERS LTD.
#301, 4220-98 Street, Edmonton, AB, T6E 6A1. Contact: John Paton, V.P. of Oper. - Tel: (780) 436-7774, (800) 567-7258, Fax: (780) 436-3336, E-Mail: grow1@grower.com, Web Site: www.grower.com. Grower Direct Fresh Cut Flowers is the supplier of a wide range of quality fresh cut flowers to its franchised retail flower shops who, in turn by maintaining an affordable price point to their customers, make the enjoyment of fresh cut flowers an affordable everyday event. Established: 1991 - Franchising Since: 1991 - No. of Units: Company Owned: 1 - Franchised: 122 - Franchise Fee: $25,000 - Royalty: $240 per week flat rate - Total Inv: $55,000 - Financing: No.

VIOLET BLOOM'S FRESH FLOWERS
705 Kingston Rd., Unit 14, Pickering, ON, L1V 6K3. Contact: Robert Trimbee, Pres. - Tel: (905) 839-6035, Fax: (905) 839-1899. Ninety years of experience have gone into creating a fresh flower retailing concept that replaces the traditional florist as the convenient source of quality flowers. Member of Canadian Franchise Association. Established: 1900 - Franchising Since: 1995 - No. of Units: Company Owned: 1 - Franchised: 1 - Franchise Fee: $18,000 - Royalty: 5% of sales - Total Inv: $90,000-$100,000 - Financing: $60,000-$70,000.

FOOD: BAKED GOODS/DONUTS/PASTRY

"ARTFUL COOKIE", THE
Sampson & Associates
45 B West Wilmot Street, Suite 211, Richmond Hill, ON, L4B 1K1. Contact: Lee Sampson/Steve Leavens - Tel: (905) 764-8922, Fax: (905) 764-9341. An exciting and revolutionary concept in "ALL OCCASION GIFT GIVING". A combination of cookie arrangements in floral-like bouquets, guaranteed to bring a smile to that special someone's face. 800-1000 Sq.ft retail space. Established: 1992 - Franchising Since: 1992 - No. of Units: Company Owned: 1 - Franchised: 5 - Franchise Fee: $20,000 - Royalty: 3% of gross sales paid monthly - Total Inv: $50,000-$70,000 Turnkey. Includes construction, equipment, inventory, deposits, opening promo, training, store setup, site selection, account setups, ongoing marketing support - Financing: Yes.

BAGEL BOYS
7181 Woodbine Avenue, Suite 222, Markham, ON, L3R 1A3. Contact: Mark Halpern, Director of Sales/Marketing - Tel: (905) 470-1517, Fax: (905) 470-8112, E-Mail: saintcinnamon.com, Web Site: www.saintcinnamon.com. Featuring fresh-baked gourmet bagels in a variety of flavours. Also offering gourmet sandwiches, salads, soups and specialty beverages. We offer a fresh healthy high-quality menue - reasonably priced. Established: 1990 - No. of Units: Company Owned: 1 - Franchised: 7 - Franchise Fee: $25,000 - Royalty: 6%, 2% of gross - Total Inv: $150,000.

BAKER'S DOZEN DONUTS
Baker's Dozen Donuts Corporation
1224 Dundas Street East, Mississauga, ON, L4Y 4A2. Contact: Joe Farrugia, Fran. Dir. - Tel: (905) 272-1825, (905) 272-0140, Fax: (905) 272-0140. Coffee shops. Established: 1977 - Franchising Since: 1984 - No. of Units: Company Owned: 2 - Franchised: 110 - Royalty: 5%, 2% adv. - Total Inv: From $65,000 - Financing: Yes.

BEAVERTAILS PASTRY
Beavertails International Inc.
112 Nelson Street, Suite 101-C, Ottawa, ON, K1N 7R5. Contact: Robert Libbey, President - Tel: (613) 789-4940, (800) 704-0351, Fax: (613) 789-5158, E-Mail: info@beavertailsinc.com, Web Site: www.beavertailsinc.com. A unique wholesome pastry cooked fresh at leisure sites. Low entry investment, interesting locations, excellent stategic support. We are interested in development opportunities at amusement parks, sporting venues, tourist destinations and ski hills across North America. Established: 1978 - Franchising Since: 1991 - No. of Units: Company Owned: 3 - Franchised: 70 - Franchise Fee: $20,000 US - Royalty: 5% royalty, 3% advertising (monthly) - Total Inv: $70,000-$150,000 us - Financing: No (but assistance is provided in securing financing).

BREAD KING BAKERIES
2 Addley Cres., Ajax, ON, L1T 1R8. Contact: Abdul Rahim, Director - Tel: (905) 686-7087, Fax: (905) 686-4136. Bakery and deli. Established: 1981 - Franchising Since: 1981 - No. of Units: Franchised: 2 - Franchise Fee: $15,000 - Royalty: 5% - Total Inv: $200,000 - Financing: No.

BUNS MASTER BAKERY
Maple Leaf Foods Franchising
2 East Beaver Creek Rd., Bldg. 1, Richmond Hill, ON, L4B 2N3. Contact: Peter Mertens, Pres. - Tel: (905) 764-7066, Fax: (905) 764-7634. Merchandise unique quality buns, rolls, bread and other bakery products on a self-serve basis. Established: 1972 - Franchising Since: 1977 - No. of Units: Franchised: 110 - Franchise Fee: $25,000 - Royalty: 4% + 1%-3% adv. - Total Inv: $275,000-$300,000 - Financing: Through chartered banks.

CAROLE'S CHEESECAKE COMPANY
Carole's Cheesecake Company Ltd.
1272 Castlefield Ave., Toronto, ON, M6B 1G3. Contact: Michael Ogus, Exec. V.P. - Tel: (416) 256-0000. Manufacturer, retailer and food service supplier of 100 flavours of premium brand cheesecakes + 20 other gourmet baked cakes and pies. Manufacturer and retailer of a line of low fat salad dressings and marinades. Established: 1972 - Franchising Since: 1979 - No. of Units: Company Owned: 1 - Franchised: 7 - Franchise Fee: $25,000 - Royalty: None - Total Inv: $125,000-$200,000 - Financing: Assistance thru Cdn. chartered banks.

CHEESECAKE CAFE, THE
CheesecakeLicensing Inc.
#232, 8625-109 Street, Edmonton, AB, T6G 1E7. - Tel: (780) 406-1700, Fax: (780) 437-2250. Bakery restaurants. Established: 1988 - Franchising Since: 1995 - No. of Units: Company Owned: 5 - Franchised: 2 - Franchise Fee: $40,000 - Royalty: 5% of gross sales - Total Inv: $600,000-$700,000 in leased premises - Financing: Through banks.

CINNAMON CITY
Cinnamon City Bakery-Cafe Inc.
2265 West Railway St., P.O. 490, Abbotsford, BC, V3S 5Z5. Contact: Byron Hildebrand, President - Tel: (604) 859-1014, Fax: (604) 859-1711, E-Mail: rolls@cinnamoncityinc.com, Web Site: www.cinnamoncityinc.com. Cafe's that specialize in cinnamon rolls, scones, soups, coffee, etc. Established: 1991 - Franchising Since: 1991- No. of Units: Company Owned: 5 - Franchised: 16 - Franchise Fee: $20,000 - Royalty: 6% - Total Inv: Approximately $100,000; (Equipment $60,000, Leaseholds $40,000) - Financing: Assistance for third party.

COFFEE TIME DONUTS
Coffee Time Donuts Inc.
477 Ellesmere Rd., Scarborough, ON, M1R 4E5. Contact: Dir. of Fran. - Tel: (416) 288-8515, Fax: (416) 288-8895. Coffee, donuts, muffins, sweet baked goods, soups, sandwiches and salads. Established: 1982 - Franchising Since: 1989 - No. of Units: Company Owned: 2 - Franchised: 240 - Franchise Fee: $15,000 - Royalty: 4.75%, 1% adv. - Total Inv:

$100,000-$140,000 kiosk locations, $140,000-$190,000 satellite store, $190,000-$240,000 full producing - Financing: Arranged through financial institutions.

COFFEE WAY
Coffee Way, Inc., The
123 Rexdale Blvd., Rexdale, ON, M9W 1P3. Contact: Roger G. Garneau, Dir. of Franchise - Tel: (416) 741-4144, Fax: (416) 741-5878. Coffee, donuts, muffins, pastries, soup and sandwiches. Established: 1982 - Franchising Since: 1985 - No. of Units: Franchised: 22 - Franchise Fee: Included in turnkey pkg. - Royalty: 5% of gross sales - Total Inv: $160,000-$225,000 turnkey package - Financing: No.

COMPANY'S COMING BAKERY CAFE
Comac Food Group Inc.
Ste. 440, 1121 Centre St. N., Calgary, AB, T2E 7K6. Contact: Director of Franchising - Tel: (403) 230-1151, (800) 361-1151, Fax: (403) 230-2182. Featuring over 65 varieties of freshly baked goods including mini loaves, carrot cake, brownies, tarts and over 20 varieties of gourmet coffee. Established: 1987 - Franchising Since: 1989 - No. of Units: Franchised: 21 - Franchise Fee: $25,000 - Royalty: 8% - Total Inv: $125,000-$175,000 - Financing: Royal Bank of Canada.

COUNTRY STYLE DONUTS
Country Style Donuts CSD
2 East Beaver Creek Rd., Bldg. One, Richmond Hill, ON, L4B 2N3. Contact: Girts Steinhards, Fran. Mgr. - Tel: (905) 764-7066, Fax: (905) 764-78426. Donut shops featuring freshly ground and brewed coffee and a full variety of donuts, pastries, luncheon sandwiches, soups, salads and specialty products. Established: 1962 - Franchising Since: 1963 - No. of Units: Company Owned: 2 - Franchised: 160 - Franchise Fee: $35,000 - Royalty: 4.5% of gross sales - Total Inv: $235,000 (fran.fee $35,000; equip. $105,000; leaseholds $95,000) - Financing: No.

CROISSANT TREE, THE
Box 20, 595 Bay Street, Toronto, ON, M5G 2C2. Contact: Andrew Chamot, Executive - Tel: (416) 925-3705, Fax: (416) 920-9297. Bakery-café, specializing in gourmet hand-rolled croissants. Upscale design and decor. Established: 16 - Franchising Since: 1992 - No. of Units: Franchised: 9 - Franchise Fee: $25,000 - Royalty: 5%, 2% adv. - Total Inv: Minimum $100,000 - Financing: Yes.

DELI SANTÉ
Cup Java
174 St-Joseph, Hull, QC, J8Y 3W9. - Tel: (780) 423-8500, Fax: (780) 423-2870. Upscale coffee house and bakery, specializing in french baked goods, croissants, baquettes, home made style sandwiches and salads, gourmet coffees international flavors. Established: 1992 - Franchising Since: 1996 - No. of Units: Company Owned: 3 - Franchised: 1 - Franchise Fee: $15,000 - Royalty: 5% monthly - Total Inv: $50,000 - Total $125,000 - Financing: No.

DER BROTKORB BAKERY & CAFE
Der Brotkorb Inc.
1334 Kerrisdale Blvd., Newmarket, ON, L3Y 7V1. Contact: Mr. Donath, Owner - Tel: (905) 830-0657, Fax: (905) 830-9677. Old world style of bakery/café. Emphasis on bakery as opposed to café - 120 different products, a selection of which are baked fresh daily. Established: 1991 - Franchising Since: 1992 - No. of Units: Company Owned: 3 - Franchised: 12 - Franchise Fee: $30,000 - Royalty: No royalty - Total Inv: Approx. $180,000-$220,000 - Financing: Will assist obtaining financing.

DUNKIN' DONUTS (CANADA) LTD.
Allied Domecq Retailing International, Canada Ltd.
405 The West Mall, 6th Floor, Toronto, ON, M9C 5J1. Contact: Anna Colacchio, Ass.Fran. Mngr. - Tel: (800) 937-8686, Fax: (905) 814-9741. Donut shops, serving coffee, donuts, muffins, croissants, etc. Established: 1950 - Canada 1961 - No. of Units: Franchised: 210 - Franchise Fee: $25,000 - Total Inv: $350,000 including franchise fee - Royalty: 4.9% plus 5.5% adv.

GOURMET CUP
Gourmet Cup Foods Ltd., The
P.O. Box 490, 2265 W. Railway St., Abbotsford, BC, V2S 5Z5. Contact: T. Hartford, Dir. of Fran. - Tel: (604) 852-8771, Fax: (604) 859-1711, E-Mail: shefield @uniserve.com, Web Site: www.shefieldgourmet.com. Retail sale of gourmet coffees and teas, beverages (cappuccinos, espressos, juice, hot chocolate), pastries and coffee/tea accessories (grinders, pots, mugs). Established: 1985 - Franchising Since: 1986 - No. of Units: Franchised: 33 - Franchise Fee: $25,000 - Royalty: 8% - Total Inv: $110,000-$250,000 - Financing: No.

GREAT CANADIAN BAGEL, THE
Great Canadian Bagel, Ltd., The
1270 Central Pkwy #301, Mississauga, ON, L5C 4P4. - Tel: (905) 566-1903, Fax: (905) 566-1402, Web Site: www.greatcanadianbagel.com. Bakery café featuring 24 varieties of fresh baked bagels, 21 flavours of cream cheese spreads, soups, salads and made to order sandwiches. Catering available. Established: 1993 - Franchising Since: 1994 - No. of Units: Company Owned: 13 - Franchised: 153 - Franchise Fee: $30,000 - Royalty: 6% of gross sales paid monthly - Total Inv: $260,000-$300,000 - Financing: No.

GREAT COOKIES BY GEORGE, INC.
8 Edmonton Centre, Edmonton, AB, T5J 2Y7. Contact: Don Landon, President - Tel: (780) 477-6853, (800) 250-9557, Fax: (780) 474-6689, Web Site: www.cookiesbygeorge.com. Bakery café featuring great cookies, muffins and specialty coffee, great gift ideas in cookie tins and flower boxes. Established: 1983 - Franchising Since: 1986 - No. of Units: Company Owned: 3 - Franchised: 13 - Franchise Fee: $25,000 - Royalty: 6%, 1.5% adv. - Total Inv: $110,000 - Financing: No.

JUBILATION BAKERY
Catalyst Investments
601 Bertsford Ave., Toronto, ON, M6S 3C2. Contact: Jim Aoam, President - Tel: (416) 762-2396, Fax: (416) 762-7082. Bakery of top quality dairy free all natural baked goods and easy entry level business that quickly develops steady clientele. Established: 1976 - No. of Units: Company Owned: 1 - Franchise Fee: $2,500 - Royalty: None - Total Inv: $10,000 - fee $2,500, equipment $5,000, supplies $2,500 - Financing: Yes.

KETTLEMAN'S BAGEL CO.
Kettleman's Bagel Corp.
12 Inverary Drive, Ottawa, ON, K2K 2R9. Contact: Bill Armour, Franchise Development - Tel: (613) 592-2211, (866) 422-4435, Fax: (613) 592-9162, E-Mail: armour.t@sympatical.ca, Web Site: www.kettlemansbagel.com. Take-out, eat-in, catering & wholesale. With so many bagel franchises, kettleman's stands alone with its wood-burning, hand-rolled, authentic Montreal-style bagels & original open concept. At Kettleman's we "Roll in Dough all day." Established: 1993 - Franchising Since: 1996 - No. of Units: Company Owned: 1 - Franchised: 5 - Franchise Fee: $25,000 - Royalty: 6% - Total Inv: $300,000-$475,000 - Financing: OAC - Bank franchise programs.

LES BOULANGERIE CANTOR
8575 8th Ave., Montreal, QC, H1Z 2X2. Contact: Mr. Cantor, Fran. Dept. - Tel: (514) 374-2700, Fax: (514) 374-5501. Wholesale baker with bakery/convenience retail outlets. Established: 1950 - Franchising Since: 1964 - No. of Units: Company Owned: 5 - Franchised: 75 - Royalty: 2% - Total Inv: $80,000-$150,000. Financing: Through bank.

LIL' MISS MUFFINS
15943 Airport Rd., Caledon East, ON, L0N 1E0. Contact: Bruno Marino, President - Tel: (905) 584-1861, Fax: (905) 584-1862. Muffins - coffee- bagels- soups- salads- yogen fruz- sandwiches and cappuccino. Established: 1995 - Franchising Since: 1996 - No. of Units: Company Owned: 1 - Franchised: 6 - Franchise Fee: $15,000 - Royalty: 3%+ 2% - Total Inv: $110,000-$125,000 - Financing: Yes.

LONDON PIE CO.
100 Upper Madison Ave. Suite 1704, North York, ON, M2N 6M4. Contact: Fran. Dev. - Tel: (416) 201-0357, Fax: (416) 250-8783. The largest and fastest growing pie company in the world, offering eat in or take out meat pies, soups and salads. Located in malls and street front stores. Full training and support provided. Established: 1997 - No. of Units: Franchised: 4 - Total Inv: $139,000.

MICHEL'S BAGUETTE
mmmuffins Canada Corporation
400 Steeprock Dr, Toronto, ON, M3J 2X1. Contact: Tim Grech, Director Global Development - Tel: (416) 236-0055, Fax: (416) 236-0054. Combination French café and bakery for either take-out or dine-in consumption includes a sit-down cappuccino bar. Established: 1980 - Franchising Since: 1984 - No. of Units: Company Owned: 5 - Franchised: 10 - Franchise Fee: $25,000-$40,000 - Royalty: 6%, 2% adv. - Total Inv: $250,000-$900,000 - Financing: We will set up bank contacts for potential franchisees.

MMMUFFINS
mmmuffins Canada Corporation
400 Steeprock Drive, Toronto, ON, M3J 2X1. Contact: Susan Jack, Franchise/Lease Representative - Tel: (416) 236-0055 ext 338, (800) 890-7322, Fax: (416) 236-0054, E-Mail: franchise@mmmuffins.com, Web Site: www.mmmuffins.com. mmmuffins products are freshly baked on-site every day, using only the finest quality ingredients and served with freshly roasted, delicious coffee. Our modern store design temptingly showcases the fresh baked goods, sandwiches & soups. Established: 1979 - Franchising Since: 1980 - No. of Units: Company Owned: 11 - Franchised: 67 - Franchise Fee: $25,000 - Royalty: 8% - Total Inv: Varies by location - Financing: No.

MONSIEUR FELIX & MR. NORTON CANADA INC.
5650 Rue Cypihat, Ville St.Laurent, PQ, H4S 1V7. Contact: Fran. Dev. - Tel: (514) 334-8203, Fax: (514) 333-4656, Web Site: www.sweet-factory.com. A name associated with the best cookies money can buy - our cookies are made with the finest ingredients and sold in mouth watering varieties, available in gift packages in special designed tins to cookie bouquets. Established: 1985 - No. of Units: Franchised: 20 - Total Inv: $35,000.

MRS. POWELL'S BAKERY EATERY
Mrs. Powell's Inc.
C/O 3380 South Service Rd., Burlington, ON, L7N 3J5. Contact: Director of Franchising - Tel: (905) 681-8448, Fax: (905) 637-7745, E-Mail: mrspowells@aftonfood.com, Web Site: www.aftonfood.com. Features our signature cinnamon rolls and other freshly baked products. Add in delicious custom sandwiches, soups and a full gourmet coffee line. Established: 1984 - Franchising Since: 1984 - No. of Units: Franchised: 30 - Franchise Fee: $25,000 (plus area and master available) - Royalty: 5% - Total Inv: $120,000-$195,000 - Financing: Third party.

MUFFIN PLUS
393 St. Jacques West, Ste. 370, Montreal, QC, H2Y 1N9. - Tel: (514) 281-2067, Fax: (514) 281-6405. Specializing in muffins baked on site plus sandwiches, gourmet salads, specialized coffees, desserts, cookies, juices. Established: 1982 - Franchising Since: 1983 - No. of Units: Company Owned: 3 - Franchised: 22 - Franchise Fee: $20,000 - Royalty: 7% - Total Inv: $130,000-$220,000 - Financing: Program with Royal Bank.

OPEN WINDOW BAKERY
Open Window Bakery Ltd.
1125 Finch Ave., W., Downsview, ON, M3J 2E8. Contact: Gail Agasi, Vice President - Tel: (416) 665-8241, Fax: (416) 665-9528, Web Site: www.owbakery.com. Manufacturer, wholesaler, retailer of over 250 quality baked products from bagels,, buns, breads to cakes, pastries, cookies. Traditional recipes, family run company. Established: 1953 - Franchising Since: 1960 - No. of Units: Company Owned: 11 - Franchised: 5.

ROBIN'S DONUTS®
Afton Food Group
3380 South Service Rd, Burlington, ON, L7N 3J5. Contact: Richar Straker, Director of Franchise Development - Tel: (905) 681-8448, (877) 241-0241, Fax: (905) 637-7745, E-Mail: rstraker@aftonfood.com, Web Site: www.aftonfood.com. Coffee house serving coffee and donuts, muffins and pastries, submarines, sandwiches, soups, stews and salads, hot and cold beverages, homemade bagels, pies and cheesecake. Established: 1993 - Franchising Since: 1997 - No. of Units: Company Owned: 10 - Franchised: 350 - Franchise Fee: $25,000 - Royalty: 4% of gross sales - Total Inv: $330,000 - Financing: No.

ROBIN'S DONUTS®
Afton Food Group
3380 South Service Rd, Burlington, ON, L7N 3J5. Contact: VP Franchising & R.E.Development - Tel: (905) 681-8448, (877) 241-0241, Fax: (905) 637-7745, E-Mail: corporate@aftonfood.com, Web Site: www.aftonfood.com. Coffee house serving coffee and donuts, muffins and pastries, submarines, sandwiches, soups, stews and salads, hot and cold beverages, homemade bagels, pies and cheesecake. Established: 1975 - Franchising Since: 1978 - No. of Units: Franchised: 250 - Franchise Fee: $25,000 - Royalty: 4% gross sales - Total Inv: $260,000 (equip. $180,000, leaseholds $55,000) - Financing: Yes.

ROBIN'S DONUTS & DELI
Robin's Foods Inc.
2001-715 Hewitson St, Thunder Bay, ON, P7B 6B5. Contact: Claudio Foresta, Franchise Administration - Tel: (807) 623-4453, Fax: (807) 623-4682, E-Mail: robins@aftonfood.com. Coffee house with drive-thru opportunity serving fresh baked goods, donuts, muffins, bagels, made-to-order sub sandwiches, soups/stews, salads, hot and cold beverages and other assorted products. 7 day - 24 hour operation. Established: 1975 - Franchising Since: 1978 - No. of Units: Company Owned: 30 - Franchised: 213 - Franchise Fee: $25,000 - Royalty: 4% gross sales - Total Inv: $260,000: equip $180,000; leaseholds $55,000 - Financing: Yes.

SAINT CINNAMON BAKE SHOPPE
Saint Cinnamon Bakery Ltd.
350 Esna Park Drive, Markham, ON, L3R 1H5. Contact: M. Halpern, Exec V.P. - Tel: (905) 470-1517, Fax: (905) 470-8112, E-Mail: info@saintcinnamon.com, Web Site: www.saintcinnamon.com. Fast food, freshly baked cinnamon rolls and baked products with our freshly brewed coffee. Established: 1986 - Franchising Since: 1986 - No. of Units: Company Owned: 1 - Franchised: 124 - Franchise Fee: $25,000 - Royalty: 6%, 3% adv. - Total Inv: $80,000-$100,000. Require master franchisees.

SARATOGA BAGEL & BEAN CO.
Bru-Laur Franchise Corp. Ltd.
1638 Bank Street, Ottawa, ON, K1V 7Y6. - Tel: (613) 226-2311. Bagel bakery and cappuccino café. Established: 1997 - Franchising Since: 1997 - No. of Units: Company Owned: 1 - Franchise Fee: $25,000 - Royalty: 5%, 1.5% advertising contribution - Total Inv: $240,000 - Financing: No.

SWEET ROSIE'S
Sweet Rosie's Corporation
362 Sumach Street, Toronto, ON, M4X 1V4. Contact: Rosie Gumieniak, Fran. Dept. - Tel: (416) 923-9113, (800) 923-9113, Fax: (416) 532-9576. Gourmet coffee bar, bake shoppe, sandwiches, muffins, salads, etc. European concepts. Established: 1978 - Franchising Since: 1981 - No. of Units: Company Owned: 2 - Franchised: 14 - Franchise Fee: $25,000 (CAN) - Royalty: 5%, 2% adv. - Total Inv: $135,000-$165,000 turnkey average - Financing: Up to $50,000 min. investments $45,000.

THE SAUCY BREAD COMPANY
Bay #1 920 28th Street N.E., Calgary, AB, T2A 6K1. Contact: Fran. Dev. - Tel: (888) 565-7810, Fax: (403) 215-7821, Web Site: www.saucybread.com. A retail bakery café specializing in the sale of all things bread! Customers enjoy gourmet soft hand-rolled pretzels to eat on the run, artisan bread to take home for dinner, sweets, soups, and classic sandwiches to enjoy in the café. Locations available in Alberta and B.C. Established: 1996 - No. of Units: Franchised: 6 - Total Inv: $140,000-$330,000.

TIM HORTONS
The TDL Group Ltd.
874 Sinclair Rd., Oakville, ON, L6K 2Y1. Contact: Anne Marie Cresswell, Mgr. of Fran. - Tel: (905) 845-6511, Fax: (905) 845-0265. Retail coffee, donuts, and specialty baked goods. Established: 1964 - Franchising Since: 1965 - No. of Units: Company Owned: 145 - Franchised: 1,553 - Franchise Fee: $50,000 - Royalty: 3% - Total Inv: $350,000-$400,000 Cdn. - Financing: Yes.

TREATS
Treats International
418 Preston St., Ottawa, ON, K1S 4N2. Contact: J. Deknatel, C.O.O. - Tel: (613) 563-4073, (800) 461-4003, Fax: (613) 563-1982, E-Mail: info@treats.com, Web Site: www.treats.com. Micro bakery operations from 100 - 1800 square feet. Established: 1977 - Franchising Since: 1979 - No. of Units: Company Owned: 5 - Franchised: 140 - Franchise Fee: $10,000 - Royalty: 8%, 2% adv. - Total Inv: $150,000-$250,000 - Financing: O.A.C.

FOOD: CANDY/POPCORN/SNACKS

CHOCOLATERIE BERNARD CALLEBAUT, LTD.
1313 1st St. S.E., Calgary, AB, T2G 5L1. Contact: Robert Ingles, Dir. of Oper. - Tel: (403) 266-4300, Fax: (403) 262-6070. High quality chocolates and chocolate related products. Manufactured in Calgary and sold exclusively at Callebaut outlets. Established: 1983 - Franchising Since: 1984 - No. of Units: Company Owned: 2 - Franchised: 34 - Total Inv: $170,000-$190,000 - Financing: No.

KERNELS EXTRA ORDINARY POPCORN CART
Kernels Popcorn Limited
40 Eglinton Ave., E., Ste. 250, Toronto, ON, M4P 3A2. Contact: Bernice Sinopoli, Oper. Adm. - Tel: (416) 487-4194, Fax: (416) 487-3920. Kernels Carts are an affordable turnkey package that are also flexible and mobile. The carts will carry a selection of Kernels Extraordinary Popcorn and will pop up in areas like, the "subway", the airport, the train station, university campus's, etc. Established: 1996 - Franchising Since: 1996 - Royalty: 8% + 1% adv. fund - Total Inv: $35,000-$40,000 -

KERNELS POPCORN (CAN)
Kernels Popcorn, Limited
40 Eglinton Ave., E., Ste. 250, Toronto, ON, M4P 3A2. Contact: Bernice Sinopoli, Dir. of Cndn Fran. - Tel: (416) 487-4194, Fax: (416) 487-3920, Web Site: www.kernelspopcorn.com. Kernels Popcorn Limited is the world's largest retail popcorn chain in the world. We make the most extraordinary popcorn, from "Kernals Low Fat" and "Air-Popped" varieties for the health conscious to "Kernals Jalapeno Jack" for those that dare a hot and spicy treat! There's a Kernals treat to please any palate and nutritional guideline. Established: 1983 - Franchising Since: 1984 - No. of Units: Company Owned: 8 - Franchised: 59 - Franchise Fee: $25,000 - Royalty: 8%, 1% promo fund - Total Inv: $125,000 - Financing: No.

PAULINE JOHNSON CHOCOLATES & CANDIES
113-7400 MacPherson Ave, Richmond, BC, V5J 5B6. Contact: Franchise Directors - Tel: (604) 432-9458, Fax: (604) 432-9494. Full line of chocolates and candies, from soap candy to jelly beans. Will co-brand. Established: 1932 - Franchise Fee: $10,000 - Total Inv: $60,000.

RICHARD'S FINE CHOCOLATES
4120 Ridgeway Drive, Unit 38, Mississauga, ON, L5L 5S9. Contact: Niels Lund, Vice President - Tel: (905) 607-5120, Fax: (905) 607-9007. Belgian chocolate retail. Everything hand-made. Established: 1990 - Franchising Since: 1993 - No. of Units: Company Owned: 2 - Franchised: 5 - Franchise Fee: $45,000 - Royalty: 2%-5% - Total Inv: $100,000 Turnkey.

SCHNEIDERS POPCORN PARTIES
2406 Wheaton Ave., Unit 2, Saskatoon, SK, S7L 5Z4. Contact: Fran. Dev. - Tel: (800) 665-6484, Fax: (306) 653-4272. Spices, popcorn, kaktus chips and other snack foods-full training and ongoing support. Established: 1988 - No. of Units: Franchised: 7 - Total Inv: Varies.

SUCKERS CANDY CO
I Love Recess
1111 Flint Road Unit 36, Downsview, ON, M3J 3C7. Contact: Franchise Development - Tel: (416) 665-3471, Fax: (416) 665-8839. Candy's and toy's. Established: 1998 - Franchising Since: 1998 - No. of Units: Company Owned 4 - Franchise Fee: $25,000 - Royalty: 6% - Total Inv: $120,000-$200,000 - Financing: No.

SURF CITY SQUEEZE
Surf City Squeeze Franchise Corp.
198 Glengrove Ave West, Toronto, ON, M4R 1P3. Contact: George S. Panos, President - Tel: (416) 699-7886, Fax: (416) 698-2907, E-Mail: surfcity@idirect.ca. Surf City Squeeze is a new Canadian retail concept that offers a wide variety of Fresh Fruit Smoothies, Sweet Smoothies and Fruit Quenchers. Specializes in a wide array of health snacks and bottled water. Located throughout the country in movie theaters in Vancouver, Montreal, Toronto and Ottawa. Established: 1998 - No. of Units: Company Owned: 1 - Franchised: 15 - Franchise Fee: $15,000 - Total Inv: $90,000-$150,000.

SWEET FACTORY INC., THE
5650 Cypihot, St. Laurent, QC, H4S 1V7. Contact: P. Friedmann, Pres. - Tel: (514) 334-8203, Fax: (514) 333-4656. Retail confectionary. Established: 1988 - Franchising Since: 1989 - No. of Units: Company Owned: 4 - Franchised: 54 - Franchise Fee: $25,000 store, $20,000-$25,000 kiosk - Royalty: 6% - Total Inv: $50,000-$120,000.

SWEET RE-TREAT
The Gramcor Franchising Co.
16715-12 Yonge Street, Suite 909, Newmarket, ON, L3X 1X4. Contact: Danny Grammenopoulos, President - Tel: (416) 603-6306, Fax: (416) 603-9012. Retail sale of candy, whether in bulk or prepackaged, loot bags and other party supplies, popcorn and a complete ice cream bar. Established: 1999 - Franchising Since: 1999 - No. of Units: Company Owned: 1 - Franchised: 4 - Franchise Fee: $19,900 - Royalty: 4.9% - Total Inv: $90,000-$200,000 - Financing: Third Party.

FOOD: CONVENIENCE STORES

AJORA
Hudon et Deaudelin Ltee.
11281 Albert-Hudon Blvd., Montreal-Nord, QC, H1G 3J5. Contact: Gaetan Dufresne, Dir. Dev. - Tel: (514) 324-5700. Voluntary wholesaler supplying affiliated food markets and convenience stores. Established: 1873 - Franchising Since: 1953 - No. of Units: Company Owned: 2 - Affiliated: 855.

AMI GEM METRO RICHELIEU SUPER CARNAVAL
Metro Richelieu
11011 Maurice Duplessis Blvd., Montreal, QC, H1C 1V6. Contact: Claude Brunetta, Franc. Dir. - Tel: (514) 643-1000, Fax: (514) 643-1269. Grocery and convenience stores. Established: 1976 - No. of Units: 628.

COUNTRY BULK INC.
332 Wellington Road South, London, ON, N6C 4P6. - Tel: (519) 434-9298, Fax: (519) 434-3500. We buy in bulk then package at random sizes for our customer's. Our philosphy is "In service we are fulfilled." Established: 1982 - Franchising Since: 1995 - No. of Units: Company Owned: 1 - Franchised: 6 - Franchise Fee: $25,000 - Royalty: 3%, 2/3 for advertising and promotion - Toal Inv: Inventory $65,000+$65,000 for shelving and equipment - Financing: No.

GOOD NEIGHBOUR STORES
75 Barbour Drive, Mount Pearl, NF, A1N 2X3. Contact: Fran. Dev. - Tel: (709) 368-6355, Fax: (709) 368-6047. Convenience stores. Full training and support provided. Established: 1996 - No. of Units: Franchised: 120.

MOHAWK OIL CO, LTD.
Mohawk Oil Co Ltd.
Ste. 325, 6400 Roberts St., Burnaby, BC, V5G 4G2, Contact: Gina Poschner, Fran. Coord. - Tel: (604) 293-4114. Service station and convenience store. Established: 1961 - No. of Units: Company Owned: 34 - Franchised: 304. NOT OFFERING FRANCHISES AT THIS TIME.

WINKS
C Corp. (Ontario) Inc. Western Division
#102-10335 172st, Edmonton, AB, P2S 1J9. Contact: Joe Nemeth, Mgr., Winks Admin. - Tel: (780) 483-8201, Fax: (780) 484-7896. Winks Convenience Stores focus on food service. Hot chicken program - in

store bakery - 24 hr - full video and game rentals. Established: 1988 - Franchising Since: 1988 - No. of Units: Company Owned: 5 - Franchised: 22 - Franchise Fee: $25,000 - Royalty: 12.5% - Total Inv: $25,000 fran. fee, $40,000 inven., $10,000 small equip. - Financing: No.

FOOD: ICE CREAM AND YOGURT

BASKIN ROBBINS
Allied Domeaq Retailing International, Canada
60 Bristol Road East, Mississauga, ON, L4Z 3K8. Contact: Karen Kraus - Tel: (905) 270-2571, Fax: (905) 270-2795, E-Mail: kkraus@adrus.com. Ice cream and frozen desserts and beverages. Established: 1945 - Franchising Since: 1971(Canada) - No. of Units: Franchised: 211- Franchise Fee: $25,000 - Royalty: 1%, 5% adv. - Total Inv: Fee $225,000-$250,000 - Financing: No.

BRAVO GELATO "THIS COUNTRY'S BEST ICE CREAM"
7-331 Viking Way, Richmond, BC, V6V 1X7. Contact: Franchise Directors - Tel: (604) 270-2360, Fax: (270) 6560. Ice cream and yogurt at it's best. Made from same family recipe for 100 years. All low fat and no fat. Will co-brand. Established: 1998 - Franchising Since: 1998 - No. of Units: Franchised: 4 - Franchise Fee: $10,000 - Royalty: None - Total Inv: $80,000-$150,000 - Financing: No.

DAIRY QUEEN CANADA, INC.
5245 Harvester Rd., P.O. Box 430, Burlington, ON, L7R 3Y3 . Contact: L. Carver / W. Vanderhorst, Fran. Dev. Mgr. - Tel: (905) 639-1492, Fax: (905) 681-3623, Web Site: www.dairyqueen.com. Franchising of quick service restaurants specializing in fast food and frozen dairy treats. Established: 1940 - Franchising Since: 1950 - No. of Units: Franchised: 520 - Franchise Fee: $35,000 - Royalty: 4% - Total Inv: $450,000-$1,200,000.

G. WILLIKERS - OLDE WORLD FUDGE
Olde World Fudge Co. Ltd.
#207, 7475 Hedley Ave., Burnaby, BC, V5E 2R1. Contact: Wanye Wright, Pres. - Tel: (604) 432-9908, Fax: (604) 432-9980. On site candy/yogurt/ice cream manufacturer and retailer. Established: 1982 - Franchising Since: 1984 - No. of Units: Company Owned: 2 - Franchised: 8 - Franchise Fee: $10,000 - Royalty: 8%, 2% adv. - Total Inv: $75,000-$100,000 depending on size - Financing: No. NOT OFFERING FRANCHISES AT THIS TIME.

GOOD FOR YOU FRUIT & YOGURT LTD.
24-4567 Lougheed Hwy, Burnaby, BC, V5C 3Z6. Contact: Karim Rahemtulla, President - Tel: (604) 299-2797, E-Mail: karim@goodfor youyougurt.com, Web Site: www.goodforyouyogurt.com. Frozen yogurt and fresh food including breakfast items. Established: 1983 - Franchising Since: 1985 - No. of Units: Franchised: 15 - Franchise Fee: $20,000 - Royalty: 6%-7% - Total Inv: $70,000 - Financing: Yes.

LA CREMIERE
Matoyee Enterprises Inc.
3465 Thimens, Ville St-Laurent, QC, H4R 1V5. Contact: Claude St-Pierre - Tel: (514) 336-8885, Fax: (514) 336-9222, E-Mail: info@mtygroup.com, Web Site: www.mtygroup.com. Ice cream parlour offering delicious soft and hard ice cream, frozen yogurts, sherbets, ice crea, cakes and other specialties such as la Cremiere Famous "Spirel" and "Tofrui". Established: 1970 - Franchising Since: 1971 - No. of Units: Company Owned: 1 - Franchised: 90 - Franchise Fee: $25,000-$40,000 - Total Inv: $150,000-$175,000.

MINI MELTS® ICE CREAM
Empire Pacific Trade
7-3331 Viking Way, Richmond, BC, V6V 1X7. Contact: Duncan Williams, Director - Tel: (604) 207-8711, Fax: (604) 270-2360, Web Site: www.rayray.com. Ice cream from Japan. New 21st century ice cream. Little pearls of ice cream taste delicious, very appealing to adults and children. Will co-brand. Established: 1998 - Franchising Since: 1998 - No. of Units: Franchised: Thousands - Franchise Fee: One time charge $60,000 - Royalty: None - Total Inv: 1000 cases at $100 each - Financing: No.

PEERLESS ICE CREAM STORES
459 Erie Street, East, Windsor, ON, N9A 3X6. Contact: Fran. Dev. - Tel: (519) 254-9333. Ice cream, yogurt, snacks, candy and lottery. Full 2 weeks training and ongoing support provided. Established: 1936 - No. of Units: Franchised: 3 - Total Inv: $75,000.

SHAKE SHOPPE
22 Ashwarren Road, Downsview, ON, M3J 1Z5. Contact: Fran. Dev. - Tel: (416) 631-0601, (800) 263-1455, Fax: (416) 631-7687. A dairy bar featuring ice cream, frozen yogurt and fruit slushes. Ideal for an add-on or stand alone concept. One week training and ongoing support. Established: 1979 - No. of Units: Franchised: 50+ - Total Inv: $20,000.

STEVE'S ICE CREAM/ICE CREAM CHURN/ HONEYHILL/JAVA COAST COFFEES
Yogen Fruz World Wide Inc
8300 Woodbine Ave, 5th Floor, Markham, ON, L3R 9Y7. Contact: Aaron Serruya, President - Tel: (905) 479-8762, Fax: (905) 479-5235, E-Mail: aarons.yogenfruz.com, Web Site: www.yogenfruz.com. Fast food outlet - sales of frozen yogurt blended with real fruit, soft server yogurt, ice cream, smoothies, cake, pie, novelties, and sundaes. Established: 1986 - Franchising Since: 1987 - No. of Units: Company Owned: 108 - Franchised: 4654 - Franchise Fee: $15,000-$25,000 - Royalty: 6%, 2% adv - Total Inv: $100,000-$150,000 - Financing: Third party.

TCBY TREATS FROZEN YOGURT & ICE CREAM
TCBY Ontario Operations
4 Lakeshore Rd., West, Oakville, ON, L6K 1L5. Contact: Mark Kemper, Director - Tel: (416) 376-9437, Fax: (905) 278-5017. Largest international frozen yogurt franchise. Premium frozen yogurt soft-serve and hard scooped. Established: 1981 - Franchising Since: 1981 - No. of Units: Company Owned: US - 21 - Franchised: US 2,572, Can 14 - Franchise Fee: $5-$25,000 - Royalty: 5%, 2% adv. - Total Inv: $60-$130,000 - Financing: No.

THE LI'L ICE CREAM SHOP
42 Newcombe Crescent, Winnipeg, MB, R2J 3T6. Contact: Fran. Dept. - Tel: (203) 992-2730, Fax: (204) 255-1373, Web Site: www.lilice creamshop.com. Full service mobile ice cream shops serving over 70 premium desserts. These self contained shops are great at beaches, parks and busy downtown sidewalks. One week hands on training and full support provided. Established: 1996 - No. of Units: Franchised: 6 - Total Inv: $58,000.

THE NUTTY CHOCOLATEUR
182 Queen Street, Port Perry, ON, L9L 1B8. Contact: Fran. Dev. - Tel: (905) 985-2210, Fax: (905) 985-4373. An old fashioned candy and ice cream store. Full training and support. Established: 1988 - No. of Units: Franchised: 5 - Total Inv: $200,000.

YOGEN FRUZ /BRESLER ICE CREAM/I CAN'T BELIEVE IT'S YOGURT/SWENSEN'S ICE CREAM/ GOLDEN SWIRL
Yogen Fruz World Wide Inc.
8300 Woodbine Ave. 5th Floor, Markham, ON, L3R 9Y7. Contact: Aaron Serruya, President - Tel: (905) 479-8762, Fax: (905) 479-5235, E-Mail: aarons.yogenfruz.com, Web Site: www.yogenfruz.com. Fast food outlet - sales of frozen yogurt blended with real fruit, soft server yogurt, ice cream, smoothies, cake, pie, novelties, and sundae. Established: 1986 - Franchising Since: 1987 - No. of Units: Company Owned: 108 - Franchised: 4654 - Franchise Fee: $15,000-$25,000 - Royalty: 6%, 2% adv. - Total Inv: $100,000-$150,000 - Financing: Third party.

WAFFLE WORLD
73 Railside Rd., Unit 3, Don Mills, ON, M3A 1B2. Contact: Lorne Solish, Pres. - Tel: (416)447-0031, (800)923-3530, Fax: (416) 447-6174, E-Mail: isolish@waffleworld.com, Web Site: www.waffle world.com. Unique, mobile, low investment, specialty food franchise, selling freshly made hot waffle and ice cream sandwiches, from an amazing cart set-up, at all kinds of both indoor and outdoor events and attractions. Established: 1994 - Franchising Since: 1998 - No. of Units: Company Owned: 1 - Franchised: 1 - Franchise Fee: Nil - Royalty: $300/month - Total Inv: $39,000 US-$67,750 US - Financing: No.

FOOD: RESTAURANTS

2 FOR 1 SUBS
P.O. Box 492, Whitby, ON, L1N 5V3. Contact: Fran. Dev. - Tel: (905) 579-2275, Fax: (905) 579-2275. Proven value added, buy 1 get 1 free submarine sandwich concept plus scoop ice cream. Expanding only in Ontario. Established: 1991 - No. of Units: Franchised: 3 - Total Inv: $98,500.

241 PIZZA
Afton Food Group
3380 South Service Rd., Burlington, ON, L7N 3J5. Contact: Richar Straker - Tel: (905) 681-8448, (877) 241-0241, Fax: (905) 637-7745, E-Mail: rstaker@aftonfood.com, Web Site: www.aftonfood.com. A unique concept of pizza takeout and delivery (home and business). Established: 1997 - Franchising Since: 1997 - No. of Units: Company Owned: 10 - Franchised: 350 - Franchise Fee: $25,000 - Royalty: 4% of gross sales - Total Inv: $170,000 - Financing: No.

3 FOR 1 PIZZA & WINGS
3 Pizzas 3 Wings Ltd.
10 Bay Street, Ste. 802, Toronto, ON, M5J 2R8. - Tel: (416) 360-0888, (888) 693-8888, Fax: (416) 360-5543. Unique pizza and wings delivery and take out. 3 pizzas and/or 3 wings for the price of one. 100% complete turnkey operation. Established: 1991 - Franchising Since: 1991 - No. of Units: Franchised: 100 - Franchise Fee: No franchise fee for a limited time - Royalty: 4% - Total Inv: $35,000 initial investment - Financing: Yes.

A & W FOOD SERVICES OF CANADA INC.
#300-171 West Esplanade, North Vancouver, BC, V7M 3K9. Contact: J. Graham Cooke, V.P. Mktg. & Oper. - Tel: (604) 988-2141, Fax: (604) 988-5531. Quick service hamburger restaurant chain. Established: 1956 - Franchising Since: 1957 - No. of Units: Company Owned: 11 - Franchised: 491- Franchise Fee: $50,000 initial fee - Royalty: 2.5% service fee, 2.5% dist. fee - Total Inv: Varies by concept - Financing: Program available with 4 major Canadian lenders.

ABC COUNTRY RESTAURANTS
ABC Country Restaurants
Ste. 202, 15373 Fraser Hwy., Surrey, BC, V3R 3P3. Contact: Joan Overin, Director of Marketing - Tel: (604) 583-2919, Fax: (604) 583-8488, E-Mail: info@abccountry.ca, Web Site: www.abcweb.ca. Family casual style restaurants. Established: 1972 - Franchising Since: 1972 - No. of Units: Company Owned: 3 - Franchised: 32 - Franchise Fee: $50,000 - Royalty: 4% + 2% adv. - Total Inv: $250,000-$400,000 - Financing: No.

AIDA'S FALAFEL
Aida's Falafel (1995) Ltd.
3410 Sheppard Ave. E., Ste. 302, Scarborough, ON, M1T 3K4. Contact: Asif Khan, President - Tel: (416) 299-4888, Fax: (416) 299-1322, E-Mail: aidas@ilap.com. Middle Eastern fast food, delicious, nutritious sandwiches and combo platters, prepared fresh daily. Established: 1976 - Franchising Since: 1986 - No. of Units: Company Owned: 2 - Franchised: 9 - Franchise Fee: $20,000 - Royalty: 6% - Total Inv: $50,000 - Financing: Yes.

ALBERT'S FAMILY RESTAURANT
Albert's Franchise Inc.
10550-115 Street, Edmonton, AB, T5H 3K6. Contact: Mark Siderson, V.P. of Franchising - Tel: (780) 429-1259, Fax: (780) 426-7391. Successful family restaurant chain, good cash flow, we have a complete training program. We are successful because we have excellent on-going support and a value priced menu. Established: 1980 - Franchising Since: 1989 - No. of Units: Company Owned: 8 - Franchised: 12 - Franchise Fee: $25,000 - Royalty: 5%, 2% adv. - Total Inv: $350,000-$450,000 - Financing: No.

ALIBI CAFE BAKERY AND PIZZERIA
Grandma Lee's Inc.
2059 Lakeshore Blvd., Burlington, ON, L7R 1E1. Contact: Alix Box, Exec Vice Pres. - Tel: (905) 634-4111, (800) 894-7063, Fax: (905) 634-1101. A mediterranean style cafe featuring fresh baked breads and desserts, gourmet pizzas and fresh pasta, salads and hot entrees, mineral and fresh squeezed juices, and an espresso and coffee bar. Established: 1981 - Franchising Since: 1995 - No. of Units: Company Owned: 1 - Franchised: 1 - Franchise Fee: $25,000 - Royalty: 5 1/2% - Total Inv: $280,000 - Financing: No.

ARBY'S ROAST BEEF RESTAURANT
Arby's Canada, Inc.
6299 Airport Rd., #200, Mississauga, ON, L4V 1N3. Contact: Mike Brown, Dir. of Operations - Tel: (905) 672-2729, Fax: (905) 672-2755. Roast beef sandwich based fast food concept. Established: 1981 - Franchising Since: 1981 - No. of Units: Franchised: 116 - Franchise Fee: $42,500 - Royalty: 4% plus adv. - Total Inv: $400,000.

AU VIEUX DULUTH EXPRESS *
Matoyee Enterprises Inc.
3465 Thimens, St-Laurent, QC, H4R 1V5. Contact: Claude St-Pierre - Tel: (514) 336-8885, Fax: (514) 336-9222, E-Mail: info@mtygroup.com, Web Site: www.mtygroup.com. Delicious Greek specialities such as chicken, pork and beef brochettes & yeros, served with fries, rice & salad and our special sauces. Established: 2002 - No. of Units: Company Owned: 1 - Franchised: 10 - Franchise Fee: $25,000-$40,000 - Royalty: 5% - Total Inv: $150,000-$175,000.

AUNTIE FANNY'S
205-3131 29th Street, Vernon, BC, V1T 5A8. Contact: Barry Laughren - Tel: (250) 558-6723, Fax: (250) 558-9901, Web Site: www.auntie fannys.com. Auntie Fanny's is a retailer of quality priced wood living room, dining room and bedroom furniture. Established: 1985 - Franchising Since: 2003 - No. of Units: Company Owned: 2 - Franchised: 2 - Franchise Fee: $40,000.

BADASS JACK'S SUBS & WRAPS CO.
303 - 4220 98th St., Edmonton, AB, T6E 6A1. Contact: Fran. Dev. - Tel: (780) 468-3452, Fax: (780) 431-0247, E-Mail: gary_a@powersurfr.com, Web Site: www.badassjacks.com. One of Canada's fastest growing franchises. Our food is distinctly different. No processed meats or cheeses. Everything fresh-made before your eyes. Fun invironment and atmosphere. Turn-key operation. Established: 1997 - No. of Units: Franchised: 14 - Total Inv: $200,000-$250,000.

BAGEL STOP, THE
Zonin Food Corp. Ltd.
601 Magnetic Dr., Unit 24, Downsview, ON, M3J 3J2. - Tel: (416) 663-7579, Fax: (416) 663-5539, Web Site: www.bagelstop.com. The sale of bagels and bagel sandwiches, soups, salads, hot and cold non-alcoholic beverages. Established: 1987 - Franchising Since: 1988 - No. of Units: Company Owned: 1 - Franchised: 32 - Franchise Fee: $20,000 - Royalty: 6%, 2% adv. - Total Inv: $130,000-$250,000 - Financing: Will assist.

BAKEWORKS
Bagels Franchise, Inc.
8241 Keele Street, Units 9 and 10, Concord, ON, L4K 1Z5. - Tel: (905) 761-5266, (800) 95-BAGEL, Fax: (905) 761-9127. Bagel and baked goods manufactured. Operates franchise stores under Bakeworks - Hot Bagels and Basics and Bakeworks Bagel Cafe. Established: 1993 - Franchising Since: 1993 - No. of Units: Company Owned: 1 - Franchised: 13 plus - Franchise Fee: $15,000-$25,000 depending on store size and concept - Royalty: 4%/6% larger stores - Financing: Yes.

BAROLI CAFFÉ
Svelto Foods Inc.
32 Atamic Ave, Suite 200, Toronto, ON, M8Z 5L1. Contact: Edward Durate, President - Tel: (416) 503-8036, Fax: (416) 503-3241, Web Site: www.barolicaffe.com. Quick-food service offering grilled and cold panini, fresh salads and juices, pizzettas, pastries and cakes, and the best European coffee specialties. We also offer catering. Established: 1997 - Franchising Since: 1997 - No. of Units: Company Owned: 3 - Franchised: 6 - Franchise Fee: $30,000 - Royalty: 6%- Total Inv: 275,000 - Financing: No.

BOSTON PIZZA
Boston Pizza International Inc.
708-1 City Centre Drive, Mississauga, ON, L5B 1M2. Contact: Andrew Diveky - Tel: (905) 848-2700, Fax: (905) 848) 1440, E-Mail: divekya@ bostonpizza.com, Web Site: www.bostonpizza.com. Mid-scale, full

service, casual dining restaurant and sports bar featuring gourmet pizza nad pasta, salads, ribs and much more. Established: 1963 - Franchising Since: 1968 - No. of Units: Company Owned: 2 - Franchised: 185 - Franchise Fee: $50,000 - Royalty: 7% food sales - Total Inv: $1.8-$1.9 million - Financing: Yes, third party.

BURGER KING
Burger King Restaurants of Canada Inc.
401 The West Mall, Ste. 700, Etobicoke, ON, M9C 5J4. Contact: George Heos, Manager, Fran. Dev. - Tel: (416) 626-7423, Fax: (416) 626-6691, E-Mail: gheos@whopper.com. Second largest hamburger restaurant in the world with over 11,000 restaurants in 54 country's. Opportunities exist for new franchisees throughout Canada. Established: 1954 - Franchising in Canada Since: 1969 - No. of Units: Company Owned: 110+ - Franchised: 190+ - Franchise Fee: $55,000 - Royalty: 4%, 4% adv - Total Inv: Average $700,000 with 20%-35% equity - Financing: Through financial banks.

CAFE SUPREME
Cafe Supreme F&P Ltd.
1233 Rue de la Montagne, Suite 201, Montreal, QC, H3G 1Z2. Contact: Raymond Croubalian, Franchise Dept. - Tel: (514) 875-9803, Fax: (514) 875-7413. A European style cafe bistro. Established: 1980 - Franchising Since: 1980 - No. of Units: Company Owned: 5 - Franchised: 35 - Franchise Fee: $35,000 - Royalty: 6% - Total Inv: $150,000-$250,000 - Financing: Through bank.

CAFE VIENNE
Cafe Vienne Canada Inc.
1422 Notadam West, Montreal, QC, H3C 1K9. Contact: Franchise Director - Tel: (514)935-5553, Fax: (514) 395-0391. Cafe/Bistro offer coffee and cakes muffins, croissants along with sandwiches, salads, and hot dishes. Established: 1995 - Franchising Since: 1995 - No. of Units: Company Owned: 1 - Franchised: 7 - Franchise Fee: $25,000 - Royalty: 6%, 1.5% adv. - Financing: Yes.

CAFERAMA *
Matoyee Enterprises Inc.
3465 Thimens, St-Laurent, QC, H4R 1V5. Contact: Claude St-Pierre - Tel: (514) 336-8885, Fax: (514) 336-9222, E-Mail: info@mtygroup.com, Web Site: www.mtygroup.com. Specialty: Fresh quality gourmet coffee, muffins, tasty cookies and homemade pastries. Also offers breakfast, panini & wrap sandwiches as well as a variety of salads. Established: 1999 - No. of Units: Franchised: 3 - Franchise Fee: $25,000-$40,000 - Royalty: 5% - Total Inv: $150,000-$175,000.

CAFES-BISTROS A.L. VAN HOUTTE
A.L. Van Houtte Ltee
8300, 19th Avenue, Montreal, QC, H1Z 4J8. Contact: Stephane Breault President - Tel: (514) 593-7711, (800) 361-5628, Fax: (514) 593-1293. Cafes-bistros offer healthy, no-fry meals, served at any time of the day with a cup of the distinctive, high-quality coffee that has given A.L. Van Houtte cafes and bistros the refinement of an European breakfast and the freshness of a light meal or well-deserved coffee break. Established: 1919 - Franchising Since: 1983 - No. of Units: Company Owned: 1 - Franchised: 58 - Franchise Fee: $25,000 - Royalty: 5%, Advertising: 2% - Financing: Financial assistance provided.

CAGNEY'S RESTAURANTS
128 Queen St. S., Mississauga, ON, L5M 1K8. Contact: Tom/Gus Lassos, Pres./V.P. - Tel: (905) 826-2311, Fax: (905) 826-2307. Casual family restuarants, rich warm decor, broad menu. Established: 1978 - Franchising Since: 1986 - No. of Units: Company Owned: 1 - Franchised: 2 - Franchise Fee: $20,000 - Royalty: 4% - Total Inv: $250,000 - Financing: Nil.

CAMILLE'S BAR & GRILL, CAMILLE'S SEAFOOD EXPRESS
Camille's Restaurant Systems
111 Chain Lake Dr., Halifax, NS, B3S 1B3. Contact: Dir. Franchise Mktg. - Tel: (902) 450-1478, Fax: (902) 450-1520, Web Site: www.camillesresturants.com. Camilles is a theme restaurant featuring authentic Maritime Flare, predominately seafood with fresh village and lighthouse, incorporated in the leaseholds. Established: 1997 - Franchising

Since: 1997 - No. of Units: Franchised: 1 - Franchise Fee: $25,000 - Royalty: 5%, 3% ad fund - Total Inv: $600,000-$800,000 - Financing: Chartered Banks.

CANADIAN 2 FOR 1 PIZZA
Sarpinos Enterprises (Canada) Ltd.
9591-128th Street Surrey, BC, V3B 6T2. Contact: Fran. Dev. - Tel: (604) 599-0950, E-Mail:canadian2for1@ebfast.com, Web Site: www.canadian2for1.ebfast.com. Pizza, pasta, barbeque, take-out and delivery. Established: 1989 - Franchising Since: 1990 - No. of Units: Company Owned: 2 - Franchised: 43 - Franchise Fee: $15,000 Cdn. - Royalty: 4%, 1.5% adv. - Total Inv: $100,000 - Financing: Special bank financing.

CASEY'S GRILLHOUSE
Prime Restaurant Group Inc.
10 Kingsbridge Garden Cir., Ste. 600, Mississauga, ON, L5R 3K6. Contact: Lori McNicol - Tel: (905) 568-0000, (800) 361-3111, Fax: (905) 568-0080, E-Mail: lmcnicol@primerestaurtants.com, Web Site: www.primerestaurant.com. The adult "neighborhood" focus of Casey's draws patrons to the bar to meet with friends or to enjoy watching a sports game. Casey's restaurants offer fresh, high quality, "grilled foods" like AAA steak house burgers and AAA steaks, and fresh cut fries. Casey's offers "fresh not frozen" steaks and burgers. Established: 1979 - Franchising Since: 1982 - No. of Units: Company Owned: 10 - Franchised: 27 - Franchise Fee: $40,000 - Royalty: 5% - Total Inv: $1-1.2 million - Financing: 60%.

CAZ'S FISH & CHIPS
Caz's International Canada Ltd.
4034 Mainway Dr, Suite 202B, Burlington, ON, L7M 4B9. Contact: John Woodburn, Franchise Director - Tel: (905) 335-4627, (877) 322-2153, Fax: (905) 335-4649, E-Mail: woodburnassoc@on.aibn.com, Web Site: www.woodburnassociates.com. Caz's Gourmet Fish & Chips is one of the oldest seafood chains in Canada. We have gained critical aclaim for our unique concept and development of an upscale product now termed "Gourmet Fish & Chips" while maintaining a reasonably priced family takeout and dine-in restaurant. Caz's has become synonymous with quality fish and chips and delicious seafood. Established: 1973 - Franchising Since: 1987 - No. of Units: Company Owned: 1 - Franchised: 6 - Franchise Fee: $25,000 - Royalty: 6% - Total Inv: $250,000 - Financing: No.

CHARLEY'S STEAKERY
12 Welland Drive, Welland, ON, L3C 6M3. Contact: Fran. Dev. - Tel: (905) 732-6030, Fax: (905) 735-4249. Quick service restaurant specializing in Philly-style fresh grilled steak and chicken subs, hand-cut fries, salads and fresh squeezed lemonade. Established: 1991.

CHEZ CORA DÉJEUNERS/ CORA'S BREAKFAST AND LUNCH
Franchises Cora Inc.
3820 Alfred Laliberte, Boisbriand, QC, J7H 1P8. Contact: Robert Longtin, Dir. Development - Tel: (905) 673-2672, E-Mail: rlongtin@chezcora.com, Web Site: www.chezcora.com. Famous for our great food, Cora's offers it's customers original breakfasts where plates are generously filled with fresh fruits and where omelets and crepes have the place of honor. Established: 1987 - Franchising Since: 1994 - No. of Units: Franchised: 40 - Franchise Fee: $35,000 - Royalty: 5 - Total Inv: $400,000 - Financing: Help building the business plan.

CHICK 'N' CHICK
Mayotee Enterprises Inc.
3465 Thimens Blvd., St.Laurent, QC, H4R 1V5. Contact: Claude St. Pierre - Tel: (514) 336-8885, Fax: (514) 336-9222, E-Mail: info@mtygroup.com, Web Site: www.mtygroup.com. Fried chicken & BBQ chicken, in nuggets, burger & more. Also offers an extensive menu complemented by french fries and hot & cold salad delicacies. Established: 1995 - Franchising Since: 1995 - No. of Units: Franchised: 7 - Franchise Fee: $25,000-$40,000 - Royalty: 6% - Total Inv: $150,000-$175,000.

CHICKEN CHEF
Chicken Chef Canada Ltd.
97 Plymouth St., Winnipeg, MB, R2X 2V5. Contact: Fred Thorgilsson Pres. - Tel: (204) 694-1984, Fax: (204) 694-1964. Full service, family restaurant. Established: 1978 - Franchising Since: 1984 - No. of Units: Franchised: 37 - Franchise Fee: $12,000 - Royalty: 3% - Financing: No.

CHICKEN DELIGHT
Chicken Delight of Canada, Ltd.
395 Berry St., Winnipeg, MB, R3J 1N6. Contact: Devon Kashton or Gus Murray, Marketing Mgr. or Dir. of Finance - Tel: (204) 885-7570, Fax: (204) 831-6176. Fast food: Specializing in pressure cooked chicken and fresh dough pizza; dine-in/take-out, drive thru and delivery. Established: 1958, 1952 U.S.A. - Franchising Since: 1952 - No. of Units: Company Owned: 16 - Franchised: 40 - Franchise Fee: $20,000 - Royalty: 5% - Total Inv: $150,000-$600,000 - Financing: No.

CITY SUBMARINE
SABSCO-Afaf Corp.
720 Broadway Suite #207, Winnipeg, MB, R3G 0X1. Contact: Steve Sabbagh, Pres. - Tel: (204) 786-8696, Fax: (204) 783-1749, E-Mail: koya-jp@pangea.ca. Sandwiches, soups, and salads. Established: 1978 - Franchising Since: 1983 - No. of Units: Franchised: 7 - Franchise Fee: $10,000 - Royalty: 6% - Total Inv: $90,000-$120,000 - Financing: No.

COCO BROOKS
32nd Ave NE #2020, Calgary, AB, T2E 6T4. - Tel: (888) 249-2626, Fax: (403) 250-2681, Web Site: www.cocobrooks.com. Fast casual pizza. Established: 1999 - Franchising Since: 2002 - No. of Units: Company Owned: 2 - Franchise Fee: $30,000.

CRABBY JOE'S TAP AND GRILL
The Obsidian Group
2780 Skymark Avenue, Suite One, Mississauga, ON, L4W 5A7. Contact: John Woodburn, Franchise Department - Tel: (905) 335-4627, (877) 322-2153, Fax: (905) 335-4649, E-Mail: woodburnassoc@on.aibn.com, Web Site: www.crabbyjoes.com. We're a 4500 sq. ft. restaurant and bar designed for family dining. Reasonable prices, good quality food, warm pleaseing decor and fun-filled service combine to capture new customers and make for regular return visits. Contact us to see pictures of our restaurant interior and outside patio and learn more about us. Established: 1996 - Franchising Since: 1996 - No. of Units: Franchised: 15 - Franchise Fee: $30,000 - Royalty: 4%; 2% advertising - Total Inv: $375,000 and up - Financing: Business pan assitsance provided.

CROISSANT PLUS
Matoyee Enterprises Inc.
3465 Thimens, St-Laurent, QC, H4R 1V5. Contact: Claude St-Poerre - Tel: (514) 336-8885, Fax: (514) 336-9222, E-Mail: info@mtygroup.com, Web Site: www.mtygroup.com. European style concept offering specialized coffees and a wide variety of croissants, pastries, soups, salads, sandwiches & hot baked items. Established: 1980 - Franchising Since: 1981 - No. of Units: Franchised: 16 - Franchise Fee: $25,000-$40,000 - Royalty: 5% - Total Inv: $150,000-$175,000.

DA GIOVANNI RESTAURANT
576 Ste. Catherine Street East, Ste. 111, Montreal, QC, H2L 2E1. Contact: Dir. Development - Tel: (514) 845-3345, Fax: (514) 845-3412. Italian Restaurant. Established: 1954 - Franchising Since: 1996 - No. of Units: Company Owned: 5 - Franchised: 5 - Franchise Fee: $50,000 - Royalty: 5%, 3% Pub. - Total Inv: $800,000-$1,000,000 average - Financing: Yes.

DE DUTCH PANNEKOEK HOUSE
De Dutch Pannekoek House Restaurants Inc.
Unit 108, 8484 162nd St., Surrey, BC, V4N 1B4. Contact: Bernie Skene Franchise Development Manager - Tel: (604) 543-3101, Fax: (604) 543-3107. Full service breakfast specialty, menu features many signature items in an ethnic Dutch theme. Emphasis on quality over price. Seating capacity 60 inside, 24 patio (where applicable). The company is currently seeking qualified area developers outside British Columbia and Washington State. Established: 1975 - Franchising Since: 1978 - No. of Units: Franchised: 18 - Franchise Fee: $37,500 - Royalty: 5%, adv. 2% - Total Inv: $230,000-$270,000.

DINKYS
Madi International
2020 St. Patrick, Montreal, QC, H3K 1A9. - Tel: (514) 931-5550, Fax: (514) 931-3749. Fast food restaurant serving bagels and submarines with chips, fries, salads and beverages. Established: 1980 - Franchising Since: 1981 - No. of Units: Company Owned: 8 - Franchised: 25 - Franchise Fee: $10,000 - Royalty: 5% plus 3% for promotions - Total Inv: $100,000-$120,000 - Financing: Will assist through the banks.

DIXIE LEE FRIED CHICKEN & SEAFOOD
Dixie Lee Food Systems Ltd.
497 Dundas Street West, Belleville, ON, K8P 1B6. Contact: Dave Silvester, Pres. - Tel: (613) 962-1299, Fax: (613) 962-3182. Fast food chicken franchise. Low investment in smaller communities. Established: 1964 - Franchising Since: 1964 - No. of Units: Company Owned: 3 - Franchised: 117 - Franchise Fee: $20,000 - Royalty: 3% - Total Inv: Equipment, lease holds $100,000 - Financing: Financial assistance available.

DOMINO'S PIZZA
Domino's Pizza of Canada Ltd.
1121 Centre St., North, Ste. 440, Calgary, AB, T2E 7K6. Contact: Suzanne Dyal - Tel: (403) 230-1151, (800) 420-4667, Fax: (403) 230-2182, E-Mail: info@dominos.ca, Web Site: www.dominos.ca. Domino's pizza is an efficient operations focused delivery system. It starts with a proprietary pizza sauce, dough and cheese blend that gives each Domino's pizza a consistent taste and quality. The Domino's Pizza store of the 90's is a model of efficiency. Established: 1983 - No. of Units: Company Owned: 20 - Franchised: 225 - Franchise Fee: $25,000 - Royalty: 5.5% - Total Inv: $200,000 - Financing: N/A.

DON CHERRY'S SPORTS GRILLS
Don Cherry's Grapevine Restaurants Inc
500 Ray Lawson Blvd, Brampton, ON, L6Y 5B3. - Tel: (905) 451-5197, Fax: (905) 451-1980. Sports grill - roadhouse menu, licensed. We now have a licensing program. Established: 1985 - Franchising Since: 1987 - No. of Units: Licensed: 19 - License : $50,000.00 - License Fee: 2 1/4% - Financing: No.

DOUBLE
Dixie Lee Food Systems Ltd.
428 Preston St., Unit 200, Ottawa, ON, K1S 4N2. Contact: Dave Silvester, Pres. - Tel: (613) 236-7497, Fax: (613) 565-4792. Fast food chicken franchise. Low investment in smaller communities. Established: 1964 - Franchising Since: 1964 - No. of Units: Company Owned: 3 - Franchised: 117 - Franchise Fee: $20,000 - Royalty: 3% - Total Inv: Equipment, lease holds $100,000 - Financing: Financial assistance available.

DOUBLE DOUBLE PIZZA & CHICKEN
1 Greensboro Dr., Ste. 200, Toronto, ON, M9W 1C8. Contact: Sheila Jalili - Tel: (416) 241-0088, Fax: (416) 241-0001, E-Mail: sheila@doubledouble.ca, Web Site: www.doubledouble.ca. Fast food franchise of take-out, delivery & some sit down locations. Handeling many items of pizza & a full line of chicken & wings prepared on the premises. Established: 1989 - Franchising Since: 1989 - No. of Units: Company Owned: 5 - Franchised: 55 - Franchise Fee: $15,000 - Royalty: 5% - Total Inv: Depends on location - Financing: Available for qualified purchasers.

DOUGHBOYS PIZZA SHOPS - INC.
109-1100 Concordia Ave., Winnipeg, MB, R2K 4B8. - Tel: (204) 667-6237, Fax: (204) 669-8567. Our franchise package is for anyone considering the pizza business. Our restaurant package is truly unique.

We utilize large scale high quality marketing systems at a small business price. Take out and delivery, pizza, salads and wings. Established: 1998 - No. of Units: Franchised: 3 - Total Inv: $40,000-$50,000.

DRUXY'S FAMOUS DELI SANDWICHES
Druxy's Inc.
1200 Eglington East Suite 802, North York, ON, M3C 1H9. Contact: Peter Druxerman, V.P. Mktg. - Tel: (416) 385-9500, Fax: (416) 385-9501, Web Site: www.droxys.com. Chain of New York style delicatessen restaurants designed as cafeterias. The philosophy is to offer customers the highest quality, service and product possible. Druxy's prides itself on going beyond where other fast food operators would venture, giving customers a unique and unforgettable experience. Established: 1976 - Franchising Since: 1990 - No. of Units: Company Owned: 26 - Franchised: 24 - Franchise Fee: $30,000 - Royalty: 6.5%, 2% adv. - Total Inv: $210,000; $150,000 construction, $30,000 fran. fee, $30,000 work. cap. - Financing: No.

EAST SIDE MARIO'S
Prime Restaurant Group Inc.
10 Kingsbridge Garden Cir., Ste. 600, Mississauga, ON, L5R 3K6. Contact: Lori McNicol - Tel: (905) 568-0000, (800) 361-3111, Fax: (905) 568-0080, E-Mail: lmcnicol@primerestaurnts.com, Web Site: www.primerestaurants.com. Offering quality food at affordable prices in a unique and fun atmosphere. The menu offering is 75% Italian with a touch of American cuisine East Side Mario's restaurants were inspired by the busting energy of manhattan's Lower East Side, otherwise known as "Little Italy". The decor is themed on the sights and sounds of New York and has been designed to appeal to a wide demographic group including baby boomers, young adults, teens and children. Established: 1979 - Franchising Since: 1982 - No. of Units: Company Owned: 6 - Franchised: 103 - Franchise Fee: $50,000 - Royalty: 5% - Total Inv: $1-1.2 million - Financing: 60%.

EDELWEISS DELI EXPRESS
Edelweiss International Franchise Corp.
#7-3331 Viking Way, Richmond, BC, V6V 1X7. Contact: Regional Directors - Tel: (604) 270-2360, Fax: (604) 270-6560. Quality food served and catered. Sandwiches, Subs, Soups, Salads and Philly's. Established: 1973 - Franchising Since: 1989 - No. of Units: Franchised: 20 - Franchise Fee: $20,000 - Royalty: 6%, 2% advertising - Total Inv: $80,000-$150,000 - Financing: Bank.

EDO JAPAN
Sono Food Service Corporation
4838 32nd Street, S.E., Calgary, AB, T2B 2S6. Contact: Simon Lileikis, Mgr. Oper. Programs - Tel: (403) 215-8800, Fax: (403) 215-8801, E-Mail: edo@edojapan.com, Web Site: www.edojapan.com. Franchisor of Japanese Teppan-style fast food, serving customers in food courts all over N.A. and Australia. Established: 1977 - Franchising Since: 1986 - No. of Units: Company Owned: 9 - Franchised: 93 - Franchise Fee: $20,000 - Royalty: 6% monthly gross sales - Total Inv: $180,000-$260,000 - Financing: No.

EGGSPECTATIONS INTERNATIONAL
7101 Park Ave., Suite 500, Montreal, PQ, H3N 1X9. Contact: Enzo Renda - Tel: (514) 282-0677, Fax: (514) 282-8115, E-Mail: info@egg spectation.ca, Web Site: www.eggspectation.ca. All day breakfast and brunch. Eggspectaion provides a relaxed, personable approach to eating. Established: 1993 - Franchising Since: 2003 - No. of Units: Company Owned: 12 - Franchise Fee: Please call - Total Inv: $500,000 minimum.

ELEPHANT & CASTLE PUB RESTAURANT
Elephant & Castle Group Inc.
1190 Hornby St 12th Floor, Vancouver, BC, V6Z 2K5. - Tel: (604) 684-6451, (800) 527-8273, Fax: (604) 684-8595, Web Site: www.elephant castle.com. A public company that operates restaurants in major malls and hotels under three brand names: Elephant & Castle, an English style pub concept; Rosie's New-York style delis, and Alamo Grill a steakhouse concept. The company has also aquired the Canadian development rights for Rainforest Cafe, and has opened three Rainforest Cafes in Vancouver and Toronto with plans to open five units in the next two or three years. Established: 1977 - Franchising Since: 1997 - No. of Units:

Company Owned: 23 - Franchised: 4 - Franchise Fee: $35,000 - Royalty: 5%, 2% marketing fee - Total Inv: $500,000 for remodels; 1,200,000 for new construction. Financing: Introduction to lenders.

EXTREME PITA
2191-B Dunwin Drive, Mississauga, ON, L5L 1X2. Contact: Franchise Department - Tel: (905) 820-7887, Fax: (905) 820-8448, E-Mail: corporate.cda@extremepita.com, Web Site: www.extremepita.com. Outlet offering a full array of freshly prepared pitas cooked to order in front of guests. Lunch, dinner, late night offerings include surf N turf, grilled chicken smoked meat. 3 weeks comprehensive and 1 week on site training and continuous support. Established: 1997 - No. of Units: Franchised: 5 - Total Inv: $85,000.

FAMILY PIZZA
Family Pizza Inc.
Bay 10 - 318-105 St. East, Saskatoon, SK, S7N 1Z3. Contact: Hal Schmidt, President - Tel: (306) 955-0215, Fax: (306) 955-0215, Web Site: www.familypizza.ca. 2 for 1 gourmet pizza take out and delivery business. Our menu includes 29 selections of pizzas and 6 varieties of pastas. Free delivery in 39 minutes or it is free. Fifteen locations in Western Canada. Established: 1983 - Franchising Since: 1988 - No. of Units: Company Owned: 1 - Franchised: 14 - Franchise Fee: $15,000 - Royalty: 4% on gross - Total Inv: $100,500 - Equipment: $59,500 - Leasehold: $15,000 - Financing: No.

FAST EDDIE'S
129 Wellington Street, Suite 102, Brantford, ON, N3T 5Z9. Contact: Fran. Dept. - Tel: (519) 758-0111, Fax: (519) 758-1393. Free standing fast food restaurant with double drive-thru hamburger concept - full training at corporate and home office locations. Established: 1987 - No. of Units: Franchsied: 9 - Total Inv: $100,000 min cash required.

FAT ALBERT'S RESTAURANTS/RALPH'S NEIGHBOURHOOD SPORTS BAR
80 Presland Rd W, Ottawa, ON, K1K 2C3. Contact: Pres. - Tel: (613) 260-3574. Fat Albert's: Now opening combo units in convenience and retail stores, specializing in submarines and pizzas, licensed, seating 40-60 people; Ralph's: neighborhood licensed lounges (adjacent to Fat Albert's), comfortable atmosphere seating 50-90 people. Established: 1969 - Franchising Since: 1974 - No. of Units: Company Owned: 1 - Franchised: 6 - Franchise Fee: $10,000 - Total Inv: Approx $50,000-$150,000 - Royalty: 5%.

FEAST DINNER THEATRE
P.O. Box 418, Summerside, PEI, C1N 4K2. Contact: Fran. Dev. - Tel: (902) 436-7674, Fax: (902) 888-3860. Unique concept dinner theater where performers serve the food. Sales and marketing support. Established: 1971 - No. of Units: Franchised: 4.

FIONN MAC COOL'S *
Prime Restaurant Group Inc.
10 Kingsbridge Garden Cir., Ste. 600, Mississauga, ON, L5A 3K6. Contact: Lori McNicol - Tel: (905) 568-0000, (800) 361-3111, Fax: (905) 568-0080, E-Mail: lmcnicol@primerestaurtants.com, Web Site: www.primerestaurant.com. Authentic Irish Pub, offering a superior culinary program, premium beer and spirit brands, authentic design and decor with the same 'craic' (The friendly, welcoming atmosphere) as experienced in Ireland, and traditional Celtic and Canadian East Coast live entertainment. These pubs are identified under such trade-marks as Fionn MacCool's Irish Pub, D'Arcy, McGee's Irish Pub, Slainte, Tir nan Og and Paddy Flaherty's Irish Pub. Established: 1979 - Franchising Since: 1982 - No. of Units: Company Owned: 7 - Franchised: 6 - Franchise Fee: $40,000 - Royalty: 5% - Total Inv: $1-1.2 million - Financing: 60%.

FIT FOR LIFE
P.O. Box 41065, Winnipeg, MB, R3T 5T1. Contact: Franchise Dir. - Tel: (800) 889-9989, Fax: (204) 488-4903. Healthy and nutritious fast food creating a variety of sandwiches with traditional and exotic fillings. Downtown business cores to shopping centre food courts ranging from 200-800 sq. ft. Established: 1989 - Franchising Since: 1991 - No. of Units: Company Owned: 1 - Franchised: 8 - Franchise Fee: $25,000 - Royalty: 5% of gross sales - Total Inv: $110,000-$180,000 - Financing: Assistance in obtaining financing available.

FONTAINE SANTE
450 rue Deslauriers, St. Laurent, QC, H4N 1V8. Contact: Serge Renauld, President Franchise Div. - Tel: (514) 956-7730, franchise (519) 472-6967, ext. 243, Fax: (514) 956-7734. Health fast food. Established: 1981 - Franchising Since: 1983 - No. of Units: Company Owned: 4 - Franchised: 16 - Franchise Fee: $25,000 - Total Inv: $145,000: $60,000 equip.; $60,000 leasehold - Royalty: 5%+1% promotion - Financing: By small business loan.

FRANS'
21 St.Clair Ave. West, Toronto, ON, M4V 1K6. Contact: Fran. Dev. - Tel: (416) 972-9490, Fax: (416) 925-7662. Casual dining, full service restaurant open 24 hours. Training - approx 2 months. Ongoing support. Locations available in Southern Ontario. Established: 1940 - No. of Units: Company Owned: 1 - Franchised: 3 - Total Inv: $300,000-$500,000.

FRANX SUPREME
Maytoyee Enterprises Inc.
3465 Thimens Blvd., St-Laurant, QC, H4R 1V5. Contact: Claude St-Pierre, Controller - Tel: (514) 336-8885, Fax: (514) 336-9222, E-Mail: info@mtygroup.com, Web Site: www.mtygroup.com. Specialty: Hot dogs, fries, poutine, chicken nuggets, hamburgers and assorted sandwiches. A concept in which quality, cleanliness, service and ambiance is comparable with major quick service restaurants in North America. Established: 1989 - Franchising Since: 1990 - No of Units: Franchised: 17 - Franchise Fee: $25,000-$40,000 - Royalty: 5% - Total Inv: $150,000-$175,000.

FRIENDLY BANNERS RESTAURANTS
Banners Restaurants of Canada, Ltd.
5000 Dufferin St, Unit B, Toronto, ON, M3H 5T5. - Tel: (416) 739-7748, Fax: (416) 736-9676. A family-oriented restaurant open for breakfast, lunch and dinner featuring ice cream products. Established: 1972 - Franchising Since: 1972 - No. of Units: Franchised: 7 - Franchise Fee: $30,000 - Royalty: 4%, 2% adv. - Total Inv: Equip., leaseholds $400,000; work. cap. $100,000 - Financing: Will assist franchisee in obtaining financing.

GALAXIE DINER
121 Willowdale Ave. #104, Toronto, ON, M2N 6A3. Contact: Fran. Dev. - Tel: (416) 346-8899, Fax: (416) 223-1145. Galaxie Diner is a full service casual family restaurant with a retro 50's-60's theme. One million dollars plus sales per location. Established: 1999 - Franchise Fee: $22,500 - Total Inv: $300,000 full cost.

GOLDEN GRIDDLE FAMILY RESTAURANTS
The Golden Griddle Corporation
10 Allstate Parkway, Marham, ON, L3R 5Y1. Contact: Bill Hood, President - Tel: (905) 947-1100, Fax: (905) 947-1200, E-Mail: general@goldengriddlecorp.com, Web Site: www.goldengridlecorp.com. Full service, licensed, sit-down family restaurant, serving all day parts. Established: 1964 - Franchising Since: 1976 - No. of Units: Franchised: 38 - Franchise Fee: $25,000 - Royalty: 5% - Total Inv: $150,000-$500,000 - Financing: No.

GOLDEN GRIDDLE (WESTERN) INC.
4711-91 Avenue, Edmonton, AB, T6B 2M7. Contact: Fran. Dev. - Tel: (780) 461-0460, Fax: (780) 465-5124. Full service, sit-down licensed restaurant with particular emphasis on breakfast - 4 weeks training, ongoing support. Locations available: B.C. Saskatchewan, Alberta. Established: 1964 - No. of Units: Franchised: 55 - Total Inv: $125,000.

GRANDMA LEE'S RESTAURANT AND BAKERY
Grandma Lee's Inc.
2059 Lakeshore Blvd., Burlington, ON, L7R 1E1. Contact: Karen Mulholand, Director - Tel: (905) 634-4111, (800) 894-7063, Fax: (905) 634-1101. Restaurants featuring homestyle baked products, chili, stews, soups, sandwiches made on fresh baked bread on the premises. A full line of desserts and specialty products are also available. Established: 1972 - Franchising Since: 1976 - No. of Units: Franchised: 80 - Franchise Fee: $25,000 - Royalty: 6.5% - Total Inv: $150,000 - Financing: Yes.

GREAT CANADIAN SOUP COMPANY, THE
Grandma Lee's Inc.
2059 Lakeshore Blvd., Burlington, ON, L7R 1E1. Contact: Sharron Armstrong, Franchise Sales - Tel: (905) 634-4111, (800) 894-7063, Fax: (905) 634-1101. Soup and sandwich concept featuring hearty soups made from scratch on the premises. Established: 1972 - Franchising Since: 1976 - No. of Units: Franchised: 3 - Franchise Fee: $25,000 - Royalty: 6 1/2% - Total Inv: $150,000 - Financing: Yes.

GRECO PIZZA DONAIR
Grinner's Food Systems Ltd.
105 Walker St., P.O. Box 1040, Truro, NS, B2N 5G9. Contact: Guy Gallant, Dir. of Dev. - Tel: (902) 893-4141, Fax: (902) 895-7635, E-Mail: grinners@greco.ca, Web Site: www.greco.ca. Pick-up and delivery restaurant chain, specializing in pizza, donair, salads, oven sub sandwiches and pita wrap sandwiches. Established: 1977 - Franchising Since: 1981 - No. of Units: Company Owned: 2 - Franchised: 54 - Franchise Fee: $15,000 - Royalty: 5%, 3% adv. - Total Inv: $140,000-$160,000 - Financing: No.

HARVEY'S RESTAURANT
Cara Operations Ltd.
6303 Airport Road, Mississauga, ON, L4V 1R8. Contact: Claus Etzler, Mgr. of Franchising - Tel: (905) 405-6500, Fax: (905) 405-6777. Fast food restaurant serving charbroiled hamburgers, hot dogs, chicken fingers, salads, chicken sandwiches and breakfast items. Established: 1883 - Franchising Since: 1962 - No. of Units: Company Operated: 18 - Franchised: 352 - Franchise Fee: $50,000 - Harvey's Plus $75,000 - Royalty: 5%, nat adv. 4%, local adv. 1% - Total Inv: $300,000 for kiosk, $550,000-$650,000 for full size unit depending on format - Financing: Bank financing packages available.

HEAVY DUTY PIZZA
Heavy Duty Pizza Inc.
14 Northrup Cres., Unit 4, St. Catharines, ON, L2M 7N7. Contact: Julia Blanchard, Pres. - Tel: (905) 646-5717, Fax: (905) 646-1912. Retail pizza and subs, commissary at head office. Established: 1975 - Franchising Since: 1975 - No. of Units: Company Owned: 4 - Franchised: 6 - Franchise Fee: $10,000 - Royalty: 4%, 3% adv. - Total Inv: $70,000-$80,000 - Financing: No.

"HECTOR"
Casse Croute "Hector" Inc.
270, 76ieme Rue Est, Charlesbourg, QC, G1H 1G7. Contact: Georges Fontaine - Tel: (418) 623-8849. Fast foods (Cuisine rapide same as Burger King, etc.) Our speciality is Pain a La Viande. Meat in hotdog bread with special sauce. Franchise or Licence available. Established: 1954 - Franchising Since: 1984 - No. of Units: Company Owned: 1 - Franchised: 2 - Franchise Fee: $25,000/ Licensor/ $5,000.- Fournitore sauce and photo menu and operator manuel - Total Inv: $150,000-$200,000 - Royalty: 3%/400,000, 4%/500,000.

HO-LEE-CHOW
GCF Food Services Inc.
658 Danforth Avenue, Ste. 201, Toronto, ON, M4J 5B9. Contact: Jake Cappiell, Pres. - Tel: (416) 778-8028, Fax: (416) 778-6818, Web Site: www.holeechow.com. Great Chinese food delivered fast and fresh. Pick-up available too. Each entré cooked to order - Hot! - Fast! and Fresh! Established: 1989 - Franchising Since: 1989 - No. of Units: Company Owned: 4 - Franchised: 26- Franchise Fee: Included in turnkey package - Royalty: 6% - Total Inv: $150,000 complete turnkey operation - Financing: Yes.

HONEY GARLIC BUFFET RESTAURANT
Honey Garlic Buffet, Inc.
80 Acadia Ave., Ste. 300 A, Markham, ON, L3R 9V1. Contact: Ray Sit, Corporate Consultant - Tel: (905) 940-8922, Fax: (905) 477-6403. An all you can eat buffet restaurant with emphasis in oriental delicacies.

Established: 1995 - Franchising Since: 1995 - No. of Units: Franchised: 4 - Franchise Fee: $25,000 - Royalty: 4% - Total Inv: $300,000-$800,000 - Financing: Yes.

HOUSTON PIZZA FAMILY RESTAURANT
Houston Pizza Franchises Ltd.
3422 Hill Ave., Regina, SK, S4S 0W9. Contact: John Kolitsas, Pres. - Tel: (306) 584-0888, Fax: (306) 586-0414. Family restaurant, specializes in pizza, pasta and steak house, eat-in, take out and delivery. Established: 1970 - Franchising Since: 1983 - No. of Units: Company Owned: 1 - Franchised: 10 - Franchise Fee: $10,000 - Royalty: 7%, 3% for adv. included - Total Inv: $200,000 - Financing: No. NOT OFFERING FRANCHISES AT THIS TIME.

HUMPTY'S FAMILY RESTAURANTS
Humpty's Restaurants International, Inc.
2505 Macleod Tr. S., Calgary, AB, T2G 5J4. Contact: Don Koenig, Pres. - Tel: (403) 269-4675, Fax: (403) 266-1973. A full service family restaurant providing large portions of quality food at reasonable prices. A unique menu provides extensive selection and a 24 hour breakfast. Established: 1977 - Franchising Since: 1986 - No. of Units: Company Owned: 7 - Franchised: 53 - Franchise Fee: $25,000 - Royalty: 5% - 2% adv. - Total Inv: $495,000 turnkey for 4000 sq. ft. location - Financing: No.

HUSKY HOUSE RESTAURANT
Husky Oil Marketing Co.
707-8th Ave. S.W., Calgary, AB, T2P 3G7. Contact: C. Perry Bloxom, Restaurant Mgr. - Tel: (403) 298-6111. Restaurants. Franchising Since: 1990 - No. of Units: Company Owned: 42 - Franchised: 2 - Franchise Fee: Varies - Royalty: Varies - Total Inv: Varies.

J.B. SUBMARINE
22 Ashwarren Road, Downsview, ON, M3J 1Z5. Contact: Fran. Dept. - Tel: (416) 631-0601, Fax: (416) 631-7687. A submarine concept with soups, subs, etc. One week full training with ongoing support. Established: 1980 - No. of Units: Franchised: 65 - Total Inv: $15,000.

J. KWINTER GOURMET
3130 Bathurst Street, Suite 214, Toronto, ON, M6A 2A1. Contact: Fran. Dev. - Tel: (416) 781-4299, Fax: (416) 781-5405. Fast food outlet featuring 4 types of premium hot dogs - full training and ongoing support provided. Established: 1984 - No. of Units: Company Owned: 13 - Total Inv: $135,000.

JACK SPRATT PREMIUM SUB™
271 Hamilton Road, London, ON, N5Z 1R4. - Tel: (519) 455-7746. Submarine sandwiches and salads. Established: 1996 - No. of Units: Company Owned: 2 - Franchised: 23 - Franchise Fee: $10,000 - Total Inv: $75,000.

JIMMY THE GREEK FOOD
5307 Yonge Street, 2nd Floor, Toronto, ON, M2N 5R4. Contact: Fran. Dev. - Tel: (416) 362-6783, (416) 250-8369, Fax: (416) 250-1242, (416) 362-0827. Greek fast food restaurant. Full training and support provided. Established: 1985 - No. of Units: Franchised: 25 - Total Inv: $200,000.

JOEY'S ONLY SEAFOOD RESTAURANTS
Joey's Only Franchising Ltd.
514-42 Avenue S.E., Calgary, AB, T2G 1Y6. Contact: David Mossey, Senior Executive - Tel: (403) 243-4584, (800) 661-2123, Fax: (403) 243-8989. "Joey's Only" is a warm, friendly, full service family style seafood restaurant. A welcoming atmosphere awaits seafood lovers who return time and time again for generous servings of our famous fish and chips and to sample our vast array of seafood delights. Established: 1985 - Franchising Since: 1992 - No. of Units: Company Owned: 1 - Franchised: 1967 - Franchise Fee: $25,000 - Royalty: 4.5% - Total Inv: $187,000-$232,500 (Franchise fee, opening promo fee, leasehold improvement, smallwares, furniture fixtures and kitchen equipment, food and supplies, opening supplies, training: Pre-opening. Deposits) - Financing: No.

JUNGLE JIM'S RESTAURANTS CANADA INC.
P.O. Box 71553, Hill Crest, White Rock, BC, V4B 5J5. Contact: Dave Malenchuk, President - Tel: (604) 541-8559, Fax: (604) 541- 8535. Franchising family style tropical decor restaurants in a casual atmosphere. Kiddie friendly. Established: 1991 - Franchising Since: 1992 - No. of

Units: Franchised: 11- Franchise Fee: $25,000 - Royalty: 4% royalty plus 2% ad fund - Total Inv: $350,000 leaseholds, $200,000 equipment, $150,000 start-up and decor - Financing: None.

KEG RESTAURANTS LTD.
10100 Shellbridgeway, Richmond, BC, V6X 2W7. - Tel: (604) 276-0242, Fax: (604) 276-2681, Web Site: www.kegsteakhouse.com. Full service, full menu, licensed steak houses. Actively pursuing franchise opportunities. Established: 1971 - Franchising Since: 1973 - No. of Units: Company Owned: 68 - Franchised: 17 - Franchise Fee: $50,000 - Royalty: 5% gross, 2.5% mktg. - Total Inv: $1,250,-$2.500 - Financing: No.

KELSEY'S RESTAURANTS
450 South Service Rd. W., Oakville, ON, L6K 2H4. Contact: Larry Santolini, Dir. of Fran. - Tel: (905) 842-5510, (800) 982-1682, Fax: (905) 842-9048. Casual dining dinner house with lounge. "Your neighbourhood bar and grill." Established: 1978 - Franchising Since: 1985 - No. of Units: Company Owned: 77 - Franchised: 28 - Franchise Fee: $40,000 - Royalty: 5% - Total Inv: $600,000-$750,000 - Financing: Assistance through bank financing package.

KFC, KENTUCKY FRIED CHICKEN
Tricon Global Restaurants Canada
101 Exchange Ave, Vaughan, ON, L4K 5R6. - Tel: (416) 664-5200, Fax: (416) 739-7762. Quick service chicken restaurant serving both on and off-the-bone products and side items. Established: 1937 - Franchising Since: 1956 - No. of Units: Company Owned: 216 - Franchised: 646 - Franchise Fee: $30,000 (food court or in-line), $75,000 (free standing) - Royalty: 6% on net sales, 5% adv. - Total Inv: $300,000-$450,000 (f/c or i/l), $80,000-$1,000,000 (f/s) - Financing: Through financial institution, not thru KFC. Limited opportunities available in Canada.

KOJAX
Kojax Souvlaki
8150 Marco Polo, Montreal, QC, H1E 5Y7. Contact: Giovanni Fiorino, Pres. - Tel: (514) 494-2526, Fax: (514) 494-8988. Greek fast food specializing in souvlaki and yero (donair). Established: 1977 - Franchising Since: 1985 - No. of Units: Company Owned: 2 - Franchised: 15 - Franchise Fee: $38,500 - Royalty: 5%, 2% adv. - Total Inv: $250,000 turn key - Financing: No.

KOYA JAPAN
Koya Japan, Inc.
720 Broadway St., Ste. 207, Winnipeg, MB, R3G 0X1. Contact: Steve Sabbagh, Pres. - Tel: (204) 783-4433, Fax: (204) 783-1749, E-Mail: koya-jp@pangea.ca. Japanese fast food restaurants. Established: 1985 - Franchising Since: 1986 - No. of Units: Franchised: 20 - Franchise Fee: $25,000 - Royalty: 7% - Total Inv: $150,000-$200,000 - Financing: No.

LA TORTILLERIA
145-1669 Johnson Street, Vancouver, BC, V6H 3R9. Contact: Fran. Dept. - Tel: (604) 889-0511, Fax: (604) 874-5570. Authentic, freshly made Mexican cuisine that offers popular items in a fast food setting. Full training and support provided. Established: 1984 - No. of Units: Franchised: 3 - Total Inv: $80,000-$150,000.

LES BERGES
Les Restaurants Les Berges Inc.
129 Rus. Princpale, St. Sauver, QC, J0R 1R0. Contact: Jean St-Amour, Pres. - Tel: (514) 594-3893. Restaurants specialized in "fondues" and "clams". Established: 1990 - Franchising Since: 1993 - No. of Units: Company Owned: 2 - Franchised: 8 - Franchise Fee: $25,000 - Royalty: Appx. 15 t./Year - Total Inv: $75,000-$85,000 - Financing: Yes.

LES COMMENSAL
3737 Grande-Allee, Boisbriand, QC, J7H 1M6. Contact: Fran. Dev. - Tel: (450) 979-3311, Fax: (450) 979-3369. Health food services, self serve buffet, pricing by weight take out products. Three franchise formulas 1) Original Commensal, 2) Mini-Commensal, 3) Commensal Express. Full training and ongoing support. Established: 1977 - No. of Units: Franchised: 10.

LES RESTAURANTS SPORTSCENE INC.
20 Boulevarde de Mortagne, Local S, Boucherville, QC, J4B 5K6. Contact: Sylvia Paradis, Dir. Fran. Corp. Affairs - Tel: (450) 641-3011, Fax: (450) 641-9742, E-Mail: sparadis@cage.ca, Web Site: www.cage.ca.

Chain of family restaurants with sports entertainment and/or decor - specializing in the sales of steak, chicken and ribs - 6 weeks of training and ongoing support provided. Franchise Fee: $75,000 - Total Inv: $850,000.

LICKS
Ice Cream & Burger Shops
1962 A Queen St. East, Toronto, ON, M4L 1H8. Contact: Frank Peruzzi, Fran. Dir. - Tel: (416) 362-5425, Fax: (416) 690-0504, Web Site: www.lickshomeburgers.com. Gourmet fast food and ice cream. Established: 1979 - Franchising Since: 1991 - No. of Units: Company Owned: 5 - Franchised: 16 - Franchise Fee: $45,000 - Royalty: 6%, 2% mktg., 1% accounting - Total Inv: $395,000-$500,000 - Financing: No.

LIL JULIE FRANCHISE LTD.
84 Linden Road, Linden Park Mall, Brantford, ON, N3L 5E4. Contact: Fran. Dept. - Tel: (519) 753-1097. Shopping mall food outlet/court featuring fresh cut fries, hot dogs, etc. Full training and support provided. Established: 1972 - No. of Units: Franchised: 2 - Total Inv: Varies.

LIL'JULI FRIES COMPANY
84 Lynden Rd, Brantford, ON, N3R 6B8. Contact: Victor Bielik President - Tel: (519) 753-1097. Fast Food. Established: 1972 - Franchising Since: 1974 - No. of Units: Company Owned: 1 - Franchised: 2 - Franchise Fee: $25,000 - Total Inv: $40,000-$60,000 - Royalty: 3%.

LITTLE CAESARS
Little Caesar of Canada Inc.
2301 Royal Windsor Dr., Mississauga, ON, L5N-8C1. Contact: Wendy J. MacKinnon, Development Manager - Tel: (905) 822-7899, (888) 822-7981, Fax: (905) 822-9808, E-Mail: wendymac@sprint.ca, Web Site: www.littlecaesars.com. One of the owrld's largest carry-out and delivery pizza chains. Established: 1959 - Franchising Since: 1962 - No. of Units: Company Owned: 1 - Franchised: 150+ - Franchise Fee: $20,000 - Royalty: 5% payable weekly - Total Inv: $125,000-$225,000 - Financing: Through a lending institution.

MADE IN JAPAN - TERIYAKI EXPERIENCE
Made In Japan Japanese Restaurants Limited
700 Kerr Street, Oakville, ON, L6K 3W5. - Tel: (905) 337-7777, (800) 555-5726, Fax: (905) 337-0331, E-Mail: info@donatogroup.com, Web Site: www.madein-japan.com. Over the counter quick service restaurants, Japan style cooking, prepared in front of customers. Teriyaki style dishes, located in high traffic settings. A full support franchise system with ongoing support. A team oriented system. Established: 1986 - Franchising Since: 1987 - No. of Units: Franchised: 61- Franchise Fee: $25,000 - Royalty: 6% - Financing: Will assist in financial presentation.

MANDARIN RESTAURANT
Mandarin Restaurant Franchise Corp.
8 Clipper Court, Brampton, ON, L6W 4T9. Contact: George Chiu, Vice President - Tel: (905) 451-4100, Fax: (905) 456-3411, E-Mail: info@mandarinbuffet.com, Web Site: www.mandarinbuffet.com. Buffet style Chinese and Canadian restaurant. Established: 1979 - Franchising Since: 1989 - No. of Units: Company Owned: 1 - Franchised: 12 - Franchise Fee: 10% - Royalty: 5% - Total Inv: $1.6 million.

MARY BROWN'S FAMOUS CHICKEN & TATERS
Mary Brown's Inc
250 Shields Crt., Unit 7, Markham, ON, L3R 9W7. Contact: Nigel Beattie, V.P. Oper. Dev. - Tel: (905) 513-0044, Fax: (905) 513-0050, E-Mail: nigel@marybrowns.com. A chain of chicken restaurants with stores in 5 provinces. Looking to expand in the maritimes, Ontario and Western Canada. Established: 1969 - Franchising Since: 1969 - No. of Units: Franchised: 65 - Franchise Fee: $20,000 - Royalty: 4% - Total Inv: $150,000-$275,000 - Financing: Bank.

MCDONALD'S RESTAURANTS OF CANADA LTD.
McDonald's Place, Toronto, ON, M3C 3L4. Contact: John Piper, Franchising Mgr - Tel: (416) 443-1000, Fax: (416) 446-3443. Quick service restaurant providing quality, service, cleanliness and value. Franchising information line (416) 446-3870. Established: 1967 - Franchising Since: 1968 - No. of Units: Company Owned: 344 - Franchised: 771 - Franchise Fee: $45,000 - Royalty: 17% includes rent, service fees and advertising - Total Inv: $600,000-$800,000 - Financing: No.

MELODIE'S HEALTHY MEDITERRANEAN CUISINE INC
103 Hidden Trail Ave., Richmond Hill, ON, L4C 0H1. Contact: Noelle Daher, President - Tel: (905) 884-8511, Fax: (905) 764-9341. Serving healthy Mediterranean food menu primarily focuses on grilled or baked less fat foods. Established: 1998 - Franchising Since: 2000 - No. of Units: Company Owned: 1 - Franchise Fee: $20,000 - Total Inv: $140,000 turnkey - Financing: No.

MERV'S PITCHFORK FONDUE
P.O. Box 190, Craven, SK, S0G 0W0. Contact: Merv Brandt, Owner - Tel: (306) 543-3388, Fax: (306) 543-3388. Outside caterer. Established: 1992 - Franchising Since: 1995 - No. of Units: Company Owned: 2 - Franchised: 2 - Franchise Fee: $30,000 - Royalty: 4% Gross - Total Inv: $75,000-$100,000 - Fianance: Partialy.

MIKE'S RESTAURANTS
M-Corp., Inc.
8250 Decarie Blvd., Ste. 310, Montreal, QC, H4P 2P5. - Tel: (514) 341-5544, Fax: (514) 341-5635, Web Site: www.mikes.ca. Italian style restaurant with full table service. A complete menu featuring pizzas, hot and cold sandwiches and pastas. Established: 1967 - Franchising Since: 1969 - No. of Units: Company Owned: 24 - Franchised: 113 - Franchise Fee: $45,000 - Royalty: 8% incl. adv. - Total Inv: $225,000-$575,000 - Royalty: 8% adv. incl. - Financing: Yes with chartered bank.

MINI DONAL LTD.
71 Main St., Ste. Anne de Mad, NB, E7E 1B6. Contact: Hermel Cormier, Pres./Owner - Tel: (506) 445-2742, Fax: (506) 445-2411. Franchise for small restaurant. Established: 1979 - Franchising Since: 1979 - No. of Units: Company Owned: 32 - Franchise Fee: $1,000 per yr.

MONTANA'S COOKHOUSE SALOON
450 S. Sarvis Rd., W, Oakville, ON, L6K 2H4. Contact: VP Franchise Development - Tel: (913) 696-0815, Fax: (913) 696-0815. Montana's offers a rustic, western lodge setting with great country-style cooking. Established: 1978 - Franchising Since: 1983 - No. of Units: Company Owned: 83 - Franchised: 36 - Franchise Fee: $35,000 - Royalty: 4% - Total Inv: $800,000.

MOSS BISTRO BEIGE
255, rue St-Paul, Quebec, QC, G1K 3W5. - Tel: (418) 692-0233. Restaurant with specialty of mussels and European cuisine. Established: 1987 - Franchising Since: 1994 - No. of Units: Company Owned: 1 - Franchise Fee: $25,000 - Royalty: 4% - Total Inv: $225,000 - Financing: Yes.

MOUNTAIN BOY CHICKEN AND TATERS
22 Ashwarren Rd, Downsview, ON, M3J 1Z5. Contact: Paul LeClerc - Tel: (416) 631-0601, (800) 263-1455, Fax: (416) 631-7687. Eat-in or take-out fried chicken with full complimentary menu. Established: 1979 - No. of Units: Company Owned: 5 - Franchised: 100 - Franchise Fee: $25,000.

MOXIE'S CLASSIC GRILL
31 Hopewell Way N.E. Calgary, AB, T3J 4B7. Contact: John Covello, Dir. of Real Estate and Franchise Development - Tel: (403) 543-2600, Fax: (403) 543-2646, Web Site: www.moxie's.ca. Upper-tier casual dining restaurant. Established: 1986 - Franchising Since: 1986 - No. of Units: Company Owned: 35 - Franchised: 20 - Royalty: 5% - Total Inv: $1,400,000.

MR. GREEK MEDITERRANEAN GRILL
Mr. Greek Restaurants Inc
18 Wynford Drive., Suite 504, Toronto, ON, M3C 3S2. Contact: Peter Georgopoulos, Dir. Franchise Dev. - Tel: (416) 444-3266, (888) 674-7335, Fax: (416) 444-3484, E-Mail: franchising@mrgreek.com, Web Site: www.mrgreek.com. MR. GREEK Restaurants, Inc. is a privately-held company that is the owner and franchisor of MR. GREEK MEDITERRANEAN GRILL and MR. GREEK JR. restaurants specializing in Greek and Mediterranean cuisine. MR. GREEK JR is a smaller version of the traditional style MR. GREEK restaurant offering a limited menu of the most popular specialties, counter-service with seating and take-out. Established: 1988 - Franchising Since: 1994 - No. of Units: Franchised: 13 - Franchise Fee: $50,000 - Royalty: 4% of sales - Advertising - 2% of sales - Total Inv: $550,0000 - Financing: No.

MR. MIKE'S GRILL
Megalicious Food Corp.
631 Camarvon, New Westminster, BC, V3M 1E3. - Tel: (604) 515-1190, Fax: (604) 515-1197. Unique full service, casual dining restaurants with a prominent west coast decor, surrounded by warm autumn colors, our guests enjoy the world famous Mikeburger, premium quality steaks and much more, all served from our open kitchens that encompasses a colorful salad bar offering fresh fruits, salads, soups and breads. Established: 1960 - Franchising Since: 1962 - No. of Units: Company Owned: 1 - Franchised: 17 - Franchise Fee: $37,500.00 - Royalty: 5% - Total Inv: $250,000-$300,000 - Financing: No.

MR. MUGS
Mr. Mugs Canada, Inc.
P.O. Box 20019 Global Courier, Brantford, ON, N3P 2A4. Contact: Paul Cleave, Pres. - Tel: (519) 752-9890, Fax: (519) 752-0978. Gourmet coffee shop featuring a deli bar with fresh made soup, sandwiches and chili. Bagels, donuts and baked goods prepared on premises. Established: 1986 - Franchising Since: 1986 - No. of Units: Company Owned: 4 - Franchised: 20 - Franchise Fee: $20,000 - Royalty: 4% - Total Inv: $130,000-$195,000.

MR. SUB
Mr. Submarine Ltd.
4576 Young St Suite 600, Toronto, ON, M2N 6P1. Contact: Carl Maynard, Director of Franchise Development -Tel: (416) 225-5545, (800) 688-7827, Fax: (416) 225-5536, Web Site: www.mrsub.ca. Submarine sandwich franchise. Complete training and on-going operations support. Menu consists of hot and cold submarine sandwiches, soups, salads, beverages and desserts, and on premises baked goods. Established: 1968 - Franchising Since: 1972 - No. of Units: Company Owned: 1 - Franchised: 550 - Franchise Fee: Up to $15,000 - Royalty: 5%, 3% adv. - Total Inv: $160,000 - Financing: Financing presentation assistance.

MR. TUBE STEAK
Mr. Tube Steak Canada, Inc
155 West Kent Ave. N., Vancouver, BC, V5X 2X4. Contact: Roxanne Colby, V.P. - Tel: (604) 322-6943, Fax: (604) 322-6973, Web Site: www.mrtubesteak.com. Hot dog cart franchise, exclusive products, manufacture own equipment, food services, master territories available across North America and Internationally. Established: 1988 - Franchising Since: 1989 - No. of Units: Company Owned: 30 - Franchised: 100+ - Franchise Fee: $9,000 - Royalty: $125/month - Total Inv: $75 month - Financing: OAC.

MRS. VANELLIS
Mrs. Vanellis Restaurant Ltd.
7885 Tranmere Dr #28, Mississauga, ON, L5S 1V8. Contact: Steve Bailey - Tel: (905) 672-7777, Fax: (905) 672-5999, E-Mail: steveba@mtygroup.com Web Site: www.mtygroup.com. We offer a large selection of pizza & pastas, fresh prepared salads also french fries, onion rings and sandwiches. Established: 1981 - Franchising Since: 1983 - No. of Units: Franchised: 105 - Franchise Fee: $25,000-$40,000 - Royalty: 6% - Total Inv: $150,000-$175,000.

MY FAMILY FOOD COURT
Wok To U Express Corp
3331 Viking Way, Unit 7, Richmond, BC, V6V 1X7. Contact: Duncan Williams, Director - Tel: (604) 270-2360, Fax: (604) 270-6560. Four franchises in one location. Edelweiss Deli Express, Wok Tu U Express (Stirfry), My Favourite Munches, Bravo Gelato (This country's best ice-cream). Low overhead, high profit. Industrial areas, strip malls, major food chains etc. Low overhead, high profit in major food chains, strip malls, industrial areas. Established: 1998 - Franchising Since: 1999 - No. of Units: Franchised: 2 - Franchise Fee: $10,000 - Royalty: 6% or $600.00 per month which ever is greater - Total Inv: $120,000-$180,000 - Financing: Bank.

MY FAVOURITE MUNCHIES
7-3331 Viking Way, Richmond, BC, V6V 1X7. - Tel: (604) 270-2360, Fax: (604) 270-6560. A concept featuring burgers, hotdogs, pizza, golden french fries, chicken strips etc. We love to co-brand. Established: 1998 - Franchising Since: 1998 - No. of Units: Franchised: 1 - Franchise Fee: $10,000 - Royalty: $600 or 6% , 2% advertising - Total Inv: $80,000 - Financing: No.

NANDO'S CHILCKENLAND
Blundell Centre, P.O. Box 26567, Richmond, BC, V7C 5M9. Contact: Dan Isserow, CEO. - Tel: (604) 303-0881, Fax: (604) 303-0882, E-Mail: disserow@nandoscanada.com, Web Site: www.nandos.com. Casual dining restaurant chain specializing in flame grilled chicken. Part of an international franchise company with over 400 stores in 22 countries around the world. Established: 1994 - Franchising Since: 2000 - No. of Units: Company Owned: 3 - Franchised: 7 - Franchise Fee: $35,000.

NEIGHBORHOOD PUB GROUP OF COMPANIES
173 Woolwich St., Ste. 201, Guelph, ON, N1H 3V4. Contact: Bob Desautels, President - Tel: (519) 836-3948, Fax: (519) 836-6749. A group of pubs/restaurants which specilize in locally produced beers and foods. The company has a signature line of foods called Taste Of Ontario. The company operates by co-op principles. Established: 1991 - Franchising Since: 1995 - No. of Units: Company Owned: 2 - Franchised: 2 - Franchise Fee: $35,000 - Royalty: 5% - Total Inv: $400,000 - Financing: N/A.

NEW ORLEANS PIZZA
New Orleans Pizza Canada, Inc
150 Hurron St, Upper Unit, Stratford, ON, N5A 5S9. Contact: John Cosse, President - Tel: (519) 273-5422, Fax: (519) 273-3824, E-Mail: nop@golden.net, Web Site: www.neworleanspizza.ca. 100% Canadian owned and operated specializing in pizza and submarines. Full franchise support; company-owned distribution centre. Full marketing support. Established: 1978 - Franchising Since: 1982 - No. of Units: Company Owned: 2 - Franchised: 44 - Franchise Fee: $7,000 - Royalty: 3% - Total Inv: $75,000-$100,000 - Financing: Yes.

NEW YORK FRIES
122164 Canada Inc.
1220 Yonge St., Ste. 400, Toronto, ON, M4T 1W1. Contact: Warren Price, Exec. V.P. - Tel: (416) 963-5005, Fax: (416) 963-4920, E-Mail: mail@newyorkfries.com, Web Site: www.newyorkfries.com. A quick service concept providing consumer with a fresh cut fried potato with skins on and the nutritional value intact. Offer a high quality product cooked according to a unique recipe and served in a clean, fresh environment. Established: 1984 - Franchising Since: 1984 - No. of Units: Company Owned: 11 - Franchised: 125 - Franchise Fee: $30,000 - Royalty: 6%, 1.5% nat'l. ad fund - Total Inv: Fran. fee $25,000; leaseholds & equip. $100,000-$150,000 - Financing: No.

NEW YORK PIZZA & CHICKEN
New York Pizza & Chicken Ltd.
Ste. 205, 805 Middlefield Road, Scarborough, ON, M1V 4Z6. - Tel: (416) 292-6060, Fax: (416) 321-2030. Pizza and wings take out and delivery. Established: 1990 - Franchising Since: 1990 - No. of Units: Company Owned: 52 - Franchised: 24 - Royalty: 4% - Total Inv: $75,000. NOT OFFERING FRANCHISES AT THIS TIME.

NIAKWA PIZZA
3140 St.Mary's Road, Winnipeg, MB, R0G 2A0. Contact: Fran. Dev. - Tel: (204) 257-5469, Fax: (204) 257-6540. Pizza restaurant franchise - 2 weeks to 1 month training and ongoing support. Established: 1963 - No. of Units: Franchised: 7 - Total Inv: $50,000.

NICKELS RESTAURANTS
Nickels Restaurants Inc.
1955 Cotede-Liesse, St. Laurent, QC, H4N 1W5. Contact: Lawrence Mammas, Vice-President - Tel: (514) 856-5555, Fax: (514) 856-6050, E-Mail: comments@nickels.ca, Web Site: www.nickels.ca. Superstar Celine Dion's chain of family restaurants. Nickels is a thematic restaurant concept based in the 50's. It incorporates three major cornerstones of the era: good food, good value and good times. Established: 1990 - Franchising Since: 1991 - No. of Units: Company Owned: 2 - Franchised: 36 - Royalty: 5% plus 3% Advertising equals 8% total - Total Inv: $650,000 - Financing: $400,000.

NOODLE DELIGHT
85 W. Wilmot Street, Unit 6, Richmond Hill, ON, L4B 1K7. Contact: Fran. Dev. - Tel: (905) 886-9700, Fax: (905) 886-9702, E-Mail: noodles@noodledelight.com, Web Site: www.noodledelight.com. Authentic Chinese dishes served in a western theme restaurant. Full training and support provided. Established: 1983 - No. of Units: Franchised: 3 - Total Inv: Varies.

O'DONALS FAMILY RESTAURANTS
O'Donals Restaurants of Canada Ltd.
104-5900 Ferrway Rd., Delta, BC, V4K 5C3. Contact: Don Michel, Pres. - Tel: (604) 946-6606, Fax: (604) 946-0444. Family style full service restaurant featuring quality menu items including senior and kids menus. Offer support and purchasing programs. Established: 1981 - Franchising Since: 1987 - No. of Units: Company Owned: 4 - Franchised: 3 - Franchise Fee: $25,000 - Royalty: 4% + 2% adv. - Total Inv: $150,000 cash, total cost $500,000 - Financing: Package through Royal Bank.

ONIT CYBER-CAFE
Hopkins Inc.
P.O. Box 269, Concord, ON, L4K 1B4. - Tel: (416) 562-8833, Fax: (905) 824-9806. This is the earth's first cyber-cafe and internet service provider. To dine at Onit Cyber-cafe is more divine. Its an experience to remember and resistance is futile atmospheric conditions within Onit Cyber-Cafe are ideal for relaxation and indulgence while surfing the net. Established: 1996 - Franchising Since: 1996 - No. of Units: Company Owned: 1 - Franchised: 3 - Franchise Fee: $35,000 - Royalty: 5%, 3% local adv., 2% nat'l adv. - Total Inv: $250,000 - Financing: Yes 60% financing, 40% down payment.

ORANGE JULIUS CANADA LTD.
905 Century Drive, P.O. Bov 430, Burlington, ON, L7R 3Y3. - Tel: (905) 639-1492. Fast food franchisor with restaurants in enclosed malls, specializing in orange fruit drinks and hot dogs. Established: 1977 - Franchising Since: 1977 - No. of Units: Franchised: 106 - Franchise Fee: $20,000 - Royalty: 6% - Total Inv: $150,000-$200,000.

ORIENTAL WOK INC.
2900 Warden Avenue, Scarborough, ON, M1W 2S8. Contact: Fran. Dev. - Tel: (416) 492-8833, Fax: (905) 474-0482. A taste of the Orient! Specialty dishes include Cantonese style noodles, hot and spicy chicken and our famous crispy chicken wings - catering for special functions and events . Full training and ongoing support provided. Established: 1983 - Total Inv: $125,000-$250,000.

ORIGINAL PANZEROTTO AND PIZZA
Il' Panzerotto and Pizza Ltd., The
234 Parliament St., Toronto, ON, M5A 3A4. Contact: Joe Schiavone, Fran. Dir. - Tel: (416) 362-5555, Fax: (416) 362-8217. Fast food take out specializing in pizza, panzerotto, Italian sandwiches and wings ordered through a central number. Established: 1976 - Franchising Since: 1980 - No. of Units: Franchised: 36 - Franchise Fee: $20,000 - Royalty: 5% + 3% adv. - Total Inv: $145,000 turn-key - Financing: Yes.

PANAGO PIZZA
Panago Pizza Franchises
33149 Mill Lake Road, Abbotsford, BC, V2S 2A4. Contact: Stojan Ninkovic, Fran. Dev. - Tel: (877) 310-0001, Fax: (604) 850-1244, E-Mail: Panago@direct.ca. Panago is Western Canada's leading delivery/takeout pizza franchise with over 140 locations. Panago is currently enjoying tremendous growth, average store sales have grown over 20% in each of the last two years with further expansion plans in place across Western Canada. Established: 1994 - Franchising Since: 1994 - No. of Units: Company Owned: 4 - Franchised: 133 - Franchise Fee: Average $20,000 - Royalty: 5% charge to franchisees - Total Inv: $80,000 unencumbered ($240,000-$280,000) - Financing: Assistance provided.

PANINI - PIZZA PASTA
Matoyee Enterprises, Inc.
3465 Thimens Blvd., St-Laurent, QC, H4R 1V5. Contact: Claude St-Pierre, Controller - Tel: (514) 336-8885, Fax: (514) 336-9222, E-Mail: info@mtygroup.com, Web Site: www.mtygroup.com. Offers the best pizza & pasta specialities and compliments its menu with a wide variety of fresh garden salads and with fresh fries, onion rings, club sandwiches & submarines. Established: 1995 - Franchising Since: 1995 - No. of Units: Company Owned: 4 - Franchised: 8 - Franchise Fee: $25,000-$40,000 - Royalty: 6% - Total Inv: $150,000-$175,000.

PANTRY RESTAURANT, THE
The Pantry Hospitality Corporation
#203-1812 152 Street, South Surrey, BC, V4A 4N5. Contact: Mike Hoffmann, President - Tel: (604) 536-4111, Fax: (604) 536-4103. A BC owned franchise since 1975. We are a franchise restaurant chain well known for our motto " we guarantee to give you our best". Established: 1975 - No. of Units: Company Owned: 2 - Franchised: 23 - Franchise Fee: $40,000 or $50,000 (out of town) - Royalty: 4.5% gross sales plus further 2.5% advertising - Total Inv: Varies with location and area ($400,000-$500,000) - Financing: No.

PASTEL'S CAFE
Comac Food Group Inc.
#440, 1121 Centre St. N., Calgary, AB, T2E 7K6. - Tel: (403) 230-1151, (800) 361-1151, Fax: (403) 230-2182. Pastel's features a full menu of the finest quality gourmet sandwiches, mouth watering array of specialty salads and hearty homemade soups, all prepared with fresh, healthy ingredients. Established: 1980 - Franchising Since: 1982 - No. of Units: Franchised: 20 - Franchise Fee: $25,000 - Royalty: 5%, 1% adv. - Total Inv: $175,000-$235,000 for store development costs - Financing: Bank of Montreal.

PATIO VIDAL RESTAURANT
2452 Marie Victoria, Vareness, QC, J3X 1R4. Contact: Fran. Dev. - Tel: (450) 929-2490, Fax: (450) 929-2507. Family-style restaurant offering breakfast 24 hours a day, full training and support provided - Hands-on training. locations available in Quebec. Established: 1982 - No. of Units: Franchised: 20.

PIAZZETTA - FINE PIZZA
125 Rue Dal Housie #215, Quebec, QC, G1K 4C5. Contact: C. Montrevil, D.G. - Tel: (418) 521-4393, Fax: (418) 529-3645. Fine pizza, European style. Fine square pizza. Established: 1989 - Franchising Since: 1992 - No. of Units: Company Owned: 3 - Franchised: 15 - Franchise Fee: $25,000, formation $10,000 - Royalty: 5%+3% publicity - Total Inv: $250,000-$300,000.

PIE'S THE LIMIT, THE
145 Rodeo Dr., Thornhill, ON, L4J 4Y6. Contact: Barry M. Bloch, CEO - Tel: (905) 709-2614, Fax: (905) 709-9176. 50 flavours of premium quality savoury, vegetable and dessert pies (individual and large sizes), soups, salads, snacks and speciality coffees and drinks. Established: 1996 - Franchising Since: 1998 - No. of Units: Company Owned: 2 - Franchise Fee: $20,000 - Royalty: 6% or set fee - Total Inv: $139,000 - Financing: Yes, but minimum $50,000 required.

PITA PAZZAZ GRILL HOUSE & ROTISSERIA
Pita Pazzaz Inc.
4200 South Service Rd, Burlington, ON, L7L 4X5. Contact: Ray Gauthier, Pres. - Tel: (905) 639-8369, Fax: (905) 639-8387. On the Grill pita and wrapped sandwiches. Food court and street locations.Sizzling Souvlaki, flambroiled fajitas, chargrilled vegetarians. Established: 1991 - Franchising Since: 1992 - No. of Units: Company Owned: 2 - Franchised: 20 - Franchise Fee: $20,000 - Royalty: 6%-2% adv. fund - Total Inv: $150,000-$300,000 - Financing: Assistance in arranging financing.

PIZZA DELIGHT, LE COQ ROTI
Pizza Delight Corp. Ltd.
774 Main Street 4th Floor, Moncton, NB, E1C 9Y3. Contact: Bernard Imbeault, Chief Executive officer - Tel: (506) 853-0990, Fax: (506) 853-4131. Family style restaurants specializing in pizza, pasta, salads and rotisserie chicken in most locations, also offer take out and delivery services. Established: 1967 - Franchising Since: 1968 - No. of Units: Company Owned: 3 - Franchised: 209 - Franchise Fee: From $10,000-$35,000 according to type of operation- Royalty: 6% for pizza restaurant, 5% pizza delivery, 4% chicken.

PIZZA DONINI
Pizza Donini Inc.
4555 DeGrandes Prairies Blvd Ste 30, St. Leonard, QC, H1R 1A5. Contact: Peter Deros, President - Tel: (514) 327-6006, (877) 327-6006, Fax: (514) 327-0782. Full service restaurants with delivery featuring pizza, pasta, salads, wings and other menu items. One number centralized delivery order system and 30 min. guarantee. Established: 1987 - Franchising Since: 1987 - No. of Units: Franchised: 32 - Franchise Fee: $30,000 - Royalty: 5%, adv. 4% - Total Inv: $235,000-$395,000.

PIZZA HUT CANADA
Tricon Global Restaurants Canada
101 Exchange Ave, Vaughan, ON, L4K 5R6. Contact: Humphrey Kadaner, Dir. Franchise - Tel: (866) 664-5696. Family dine-in, carryout and delivery pizza restaurant. Established: 1958 - Franchising Since: 1968 - No. of Units: Company Owned: 239 - Franchised: 148 - Franchise Fee: $40,000 - Royalty: 5%, 4% adv. - Total Inv: Excluding land/lease costs, Inline - $575,000, Free standing - $925,000 - Financing: No. No longer offering franchises in Canada. Contact name for Pizza Hut U.S. Wilma Jarboe, Tel: (316) 681-9806.

PIZZA NOVA
Pizza Nova Take-Out Ltd.
2247 Midland Ave, Scarborough, ON, M1P 4R1. Contact: Frank Macri, Fran. Dir. - Tel: (416) 439-0051, Fax: (416) 299-3558. Take-out and delivery of pizza and pasta. Established: 1963 - Franchising Since: 1968 - No. of Units: Company Owned: 1 - Franchised: 90 - Franchise Fee: $8,000 - Royalty: 6% - Total Inv: $135.000.

PIZZA PATIO
Box 23070, 331 Elmwood Drive, Moncton, NB, E1A 6S8. Contact: C. Tom Rollert, VP Dev & Oper. - Tel: (506) 853-0990, Fax: (506) 853-4131, E-Mail: trollert@nb.aibn.com. Family style restaurants specializing in pizza, pasta, salads and rotisserie chicken with take-out and delivery. Established: 1967 - No. of Units: Franchised: 7 - Franchise Fee: Varies.

PIZZA ROYALE
650 Graham Bell, Ste. 217, Ste. Foy, QC, G1V 4G8. Contact: Rejean Samson, Pres. - Tel: (418) 682-5744, Fax: (418) 682-2684. Italian restaurant. Pizza cooked in an open-fire wood oven in the serving area with salad and pasta bar, take-out orders and delivery available. Established: 1980 - Franchising Since: 1985 - No. of Units: Company Owned: 3 - Franchised: 12 - Franchise Fee: $30,000 - Total Inv: $150,000: $290,000 leasehold, equip, $30,000 fees + others. - Royalty: 3%-1.8% adv. - Financing: Yes.

PIZZA SHACK
Pizza Shack Holdings
9600 Main Street, Unit 1, Richibucto, NB, E4W 4E6. Contact: Raymond Bourque, CEO - Tel: (506) 523-9283, Fax: (506) 523-6341, E-Mail: pshack@nbnet.nb.ca, Web Site: www.pizza-shack.com. We specialize in pizza, garlic fingers, donuts, sub. Pizza Shack is an excellent add-on to an existing restaurant or business. Established: 1980 - Franchising Since: 1991 - No. of Units: Company Owned: 2 - Franchised: 38- Franchise Fee: $9,500-$15,000 - Royalty: 5% - Total Inv: $30,000-$85,000 - Financing: Yes.

PIZZALINO
Madi International
2020 St. Patrick, Montreal, QC, H3K 1A9. Contact: Tony Vanvari, President - Tel: (514) 931-5550, Fax: (514) 931-3749. Fast food restaurant serving pizza (no crust), salads, soup, Italian food, pastries, beer and wine, desserts, gourmet coffees and teas. Established: 1980 - Franchising Since: 1981 - No. of Units: Company Owned: 8 - Franchised: 25 - Franchise Fee: $30,000 - Royalty: 5% plus 3% promotions - Total Inv: $150,000-$180,000 - Financing: Will assist thru the banks.

PIZZAVILLE
Pizzaville Inc
741 Rowntree Dairy Rd., Unit 1, Woodbridge, ON, L4L 5T9. Contact: Mr. John Gillespie - Tel: (905) 850-0070, Fax: (905) 850-0339, E-Mail: jgillespie@pizzaville.ca, Web Site: www.pizzaville.ca. Pizza take out and delivery. Established: 1963 - Franchising Since: 1979 - No. of Units: Company Owned: 1 - Franchised: 60 - Franchise Fee: $10,000 - Royalty: Flat Fee - Total Inv: $140,000 - Financing: Yes through our approved lenders.

PIZZEDELIC
Gestion Pizzedelic
9015 Rue Meilleur, Montreal, QC, H2N 2A3. Contact: M. Martindale, Fran. Dept. - Tel: (514) 382-4343, Fax: (5141) 382-4313, E-Mail: mmartindale@pizzedelic.qc.ca. Trendy thin crust pizza place with contemporary topping and design. Established: 1991 - Franchising Since: 1991 - No. of Units: Franchised: 20 - Franchise Fee: $35,000 - Royalty: 6% - Total Inv: $2501,000 - Financing: Available through franchise program.

PIZZERIA DI LORENZO'S
2201 Arch St., Ottawa, ON, K1G 2H5. - Tel: (613) 737-3737, Fax: (613) 737-0432. Italian/Canadian restaurant with Ottawa's favourite pizza. Established: 1976 - Franchising Since: 1990 - No. of Units: Company Owned: 2 - Franchised: 5 - Franchise Fee: $25,000 - Royalty: 6% (First year free of royalties) - Total Inv: $50,000-$100,000 depending on location - Financing: Some.

POULTRY KING
Poultry King International, Inc
30 E. Beaver Creek Rd, Ste. 206, Richmond Hill, ON, L4B 1J2. Contact: Michael Aychental, C.E.O. - Tel: (905) 886-8900, Fax: (905) 886-8904. BBQ'D + smoked poultry + deli products. Established: 1995 - Franchising Since: 1995 - No. of Units: Company Owned: 1 - Franchised: 3 - Franchise Fee: $35,000 - Financing: Yes.

PUMPERNICKEL'S DELI
Unit 411-1315 Lawrence Ave. East, North York, ON, M3A 3R3. Contact: C. John Woodburn, Fran. Dev. - Tel: (416) 447-9499, Fax: (416) 447-3974. Full service delicatessan operation-located in malls and office tower locations. Features hot and cold breakfasts, lunches, and snacks, deli sandwiches, soups and salads, plus beverages. Full pre-opening and grand opening training of 6-8 weeks, plus ongoing support. Established: 1991 - No. of Units: Franchised: 8 - Total Inv: $ 75,000.

RESTAURANT LA CAGE AUX SPORTS
Restaurants Sportscene Inc.
20, boul. De Mortagne, Local S, Boucherville, QC, J4B 5K6. Contact: Sylvie Paradis, Director Franchise - Tel: (450) 641-3011, (800) 413-2243, Fax: (450) 641-9742. Sports bar and restaurant. Food specialties include chicken, ribs, steak and salads, chicken wings. Established: 1984 - Franchising Since: 1988 - No. of Units: Company Owned: 5 - Franchised: 34 - Franchise Fee: $75,000 - Royalty: 5%, 3% national adv. - Total Inv: $850,000.

RESTAURANT NORMANDIN
2335 Boul. Bastien, Quebec City, QC, G2B 1B3. Contact: Denis Pigeon, Gen. Mgr. - Tel: (418) 842-9160, Fax: (418) 842-8916. Family restaurant. Established: 1969 - Franchising Since: 1990 - No. of Units: Company Owned: 3 - Franchised: 25 - Franchise Fee: $30,000 - Royalty: 3%.

RESTAURANT PUB O'TOOLE
Corporation O'Toole Quebec (1994) Inc.
258 Boul Rideau, Rouyn-Noranda, QC, J9X-1P1. - Tel: (819) 762-2255. Restaurant - bar. Established: 1990 - Franchising Since: 1990 - No. of Units: Franchised: 6 - Franchise Fee: $50,000 - Royalty: 5%, 3% publicity - Total Inv: Variable - Financing: Yes.

RICKY'S RESTAURANTS
1901 Rosser Ave, Burnaby, BC, V5C 6S3. Contact: Dean Petrone, Exec. V.P. - Tel: (604) 597-7272, Fax: (604) 597-8874. Family dining. Established: 1979 - Franchising Since: 1981- No. of Units: Company Owned: 6 - Franchised: 33 - Franchise Fee: $45,000 - Royalty: 3% monthly f.f. based on performance 2.5% monthly advertising - Total Inv: $10,000 site reservation deposit (50% refundable) - Financing: $35,000 balance paid to Ricky's for brand name and operating system.

RISTORANTE GIORGIO / LE STEAK FRITES ST PAUL / COQ & BROUE
Restaurants Giorgio (Amerique) Ltee.
222 Saint-Laurent Blvd., Montreal, QC, H2Y 2Y3. Contact: Franchise Department - Tel: (514) 845-4221, Fax: (514) 844-0071. Restaurants. Established: 1977 - Franchising Since: 1985 - No. of Units: Company Owned: 14 - Franchised: 20 - Franchise Fee: $30,000 - Royalty: 5%, 4% adv. - Total Inv: $300,000 - Financing: None.

ROOSTER'S B.B.Q.
P.O. Box 23070, Moncton, NB, E1A 6S8. Contact: Fran. Dev. - Tel: (506) 853-0990, Cell: (418) 561-1364, Fax: (506) 853-4131. Fast food restaurant featuring chicken. Full training and support provided. Established: 1968 - No. of Units: Franchised: 14 - Total Inv: Varies.

RUFFAGE RESTAURANTS
3380 South Service Road, Burlington, ON, L7W 3J5. Contact: Fran. Dev. - Tel: (905) 681-8448, Fax: (905) 637-7745, E-Mail: ruffage@aftonfood.com, Web Site: www.aftonfood.com. Upscale soups,

salads and sandwiches, baked goods and gourmet coffees. Three weeks in classroom and store training. Established: 1979 - No. of Units: Franchised: 10 - Total Inv: $115,000-$200,000.

SALVATORE
Les Franchises Salvatore GA., Inc.
980 Rue Bouvier, 2nd Floor, Quebec, QC, G2J 1A3. Contact: Development Agent - Tel: (418) 624-8888, (888) 400-3232, Fax: (418) 624-8626. Pizza Delivery, dine-in and takeout. Established: 1964 - Franchising Since: 1986 - No. of Units: Franchised: 18 - Franchise Fee: $12,000 - Royalty: 8% - Financing: Yes.

SANDWICH BOARD, THE
Nova Corp. Ltd.
10 Plastics Ave., Toronto, ON, M8Z 4B7. Contact: R.D. Hoefel, Pres. - Tel: (905) 271-9353. Gourmet style sandwich bar serving a wide variety of salads, sandwiches, baked goods and catering. Established: 1981 - Franchising Since: 1985 - No. of Units: Company Owned: 2 - Franchised: 20 - Franchise Fee: $25,000 - Royalty: 5% of sales weekly, 2% of sales weekly for advertising - Financing: Up to 25% of construction costs.

SANDWICH TREE
Rest-Con Management Systems Ltd.
#600-535 Thurlow St, Vancouver, BC, V6E 2L2. - Tel: (604) 220-4566, Fax: (604) 463-2955. Soup, sandwich, and catering. Established: 1978 - Franchising Since: 1978 - No. of Units: Franchised: 35 - Franchise Fee: $10,000 & up - Royalties: 5% royalties, 3% advertising - Total Inv: Variable - Financing: No.

SARKU / SAKKIO JAPAN
95 Royal Crest Court, Bldg. 5, Markham, ON, L3R 9X5. Contact: Fran. Dev. - Tel: (905) 474-0710, Fax: (905) 474-1939. The largest and most successful Japanese fast food chain in food courts in super-regional malls in U.S. and East Coast.Four weeks training on-site and ongoing support. Established: 1987 - No. of Units: Franchised: 110 - Total Inv: $160,000-$240,000 US.

SARPINO'S PIZZERIA
3690 Shelbourne #202, Victoria, BC, V8P 4H2. - Tel: (250) 881-8733, Fax: (250) 881-7573, Web Site: www.sarpinos.com. We offer the highest-quality traditional and gourmet pizzas and a wide variety of authentic pastas, chicken wings, salads, garlic bread and more. Established: 2000 - Franchising Since: 2001 - No. of Units: Company Owned: 2 - Franchised: 11 - Franchise Fee: $15,000 - Royalty: 6% - Total Inv: $165,000-$207,000.

SELECT SANDWICH
Select Food Services, Inc.
23 Lesmill Rd #200, Toronto, ON, M3B 3P6. Contact: Brian Kahn - Tel: (416) 391-1244, (866) 567-5648, Fax: (416) 391-5244, Web Site: www.selectsandwich.com. Established brand-leader operating quick-casual gourmet sandwich restaurants. Established: 1979 - Franchising Since: 1980 - No. of Units: Company: 1 - Franchised: 29 - Franchise Fee: $20,000 - Financing: Capital required = $75,000.

SHOELESS JOE'S
c/o 121 Willowdale Avenue, #104, Toronto, ON, M2N 6A3. Contact: Ron Scribner, Fran. Dev. - Tel: (905) 760-1295. We are a full service casual family restaurant and bar with a sports theme. One million dollars plus sales per location. Established: 1985 - No. of Units: Franchised: 20 - Franchise Fee: $25,000 - Total Inv: $500,000.

SHOPSY'S DELI & RESTAURANT
Shopsy's Hospitality Inc.
33 Yonge St., Toronto, ON, M5E 1G4. Contact: Lewis Allen, President & CEO - Tel: (416) 365-3333, Fax: (416) 365-7264, Web Site: www.shopsy.com. Deli restaurants from kiosks to 10,000 sq ft. Established: 1921 - Franchising Since: 1992 - No. of Units: Company Owned: 3 - Franchised: 3 - Franchise Fee: $25,000-$40,000 - Royalty: 6% - Total Inv: $150,000-$750,000.

SIZZLING WOK
Sizzling Wok Intl. Inc.
P.O. Box 2183, Vancouver, BC, V6B 3V7. Contact: G. Jeff Mack, Pres. - Tel: (604) 738-8998. Chinese fastfood restaurants in shopping centre food courts. Established: 1986 - Franchising Since: 1987 - No. of Units: Franchised: 32 in Canada, 36 Flaming Wok in US - Franchise Fee: $25,000 - Royalty: 5% of gross - Initial Inv: $100,000; Approx - Total Inv: $200,000 - Financing: Available OAC.

SJ FRANCHISING INC.
Sakkio/Sarku Japan
7650 Birchmount Rd, Markham, ON, L3R 6B9. Contact: Danny Cheung, Mgr. of Recruiting & Fran. - Tel: (905) 474-0710, (800) 668-3858, Fax: (905) 474-1939. Japanese Fast-food chain with 1000 + stores in 24 states in USA and in Ontario Canada. Established: 1987 - Franchising Since: 1993 - No. of Units: Company Owned: 80 - Franchised: 20 - Franchise Fee: $30,000 - Royalty: 6% - Total Inv: $160,000-$250,000 - Financing: Yes.

SMITTY'S FAMILY RESTAURANT AND LOUNGE
Smitty's Canada Ltd.
#600-501 18th Ave., S.W., Calgary, AB, T2S 0C7. Contact: Director of Franchising - Tel: (403) 229-3838, Fax: (403) 229-3899, E-Mail: franchiseinquiry@smittys.ca, Web Site: www.smittys.ca. Established in 1960, Smitty's is Canada's largest family restaurant chain with more than 115 restaurants currently open, and several more in development. Smitty's is truly a natioanl chain, operating from coast to coast. We provide great variety to our customers in a comfortable environment for the whole family. Established: 1960 - Franchising Since: 1960 - No. of Units: Company Owned: 10 - Franchised: 105 - Franchise Fee: $35,000 - Royalty: 5% - Total Inv: Equioty required $150,000 - Financing: No.

SOLY'S DINER
1315 Lawrence Ave E, Unit 411, North York, ON, M3A 3R3. Contact: C. John Woodburn - Tel: (416) 447-9949, Fax: (416) 447-3974, E-Mail: gwassociates@ibm.net. Delicious homemade hamburgers and combos plus healthy style additions, complimented with a breakfast menu. Located in high traffic areas such as food courts. Established: 1993 - No. of Units: Franchised: 4 - Total Inv: $70,000.

SOMETHING FISHY
314 Dowell Street, Winnipeg, MB, R6B 3B7. Contact: John Horowitz, Fran. Dev. - Tel: (204) 235-0113. Fast food seafood restaurant - 3 to 5 days training at corporate office, 1 week at store opening. Ongoing support provided. Established: 1992 - No. of Units: Franchised: 6 - Total Inv: $50,000 min cash required.

SOUP MAN, THE
38 Place DuCommerce, Suite #607, Iles Des Soeurs, QC, H3E 1T8. Contact: Martin Greenspon, President - Tel: (514) 214-3297, Fax: (514) 765-3799. A unique fast food system specializing in international gourmet soups for both "Eat In" and "Take Out". In step with present trend to all natural food. Prepared with authentic premium quality ingredients. Manufacturer of its own proprietary soup line - 50 patented recipes. Established: 1997 - Franchising Since: 1997 - No. of Units: Company Owned: 1 - Franchised: 16 - Franchise Fee: $20,000 - Royalty: $200 per week - Total Inv: $50,000 - Financing: No.

SQUARE BOY PIZZA AND SUBS
Waymar Food Service
700 Oxford St., Oshawa, ON, L1J 3V9. Contact: Ted Crandall, General Manager - Tel: (905) 434-4445, Fax: (905) 433-1111. Pizza and submarine take-out and delivery only. Established: 1979 - Franchising Since: 1980 - No. of Units: 35 - Franchise Fee: $10,000 - Total Inv: $85,000 - Royalty: 5% - Financing: Assistance.

ST. HUBERT BAR-B-Q
St. Hubert Bar-B-Q Ltd.
1515 Chomedey Blvd., Ste. 250, Laval, QC, H7V 3Y7. Contact: Jacques Guilbert, Vice President, Development - Tel: (450) 688-6500, Fax: (450) 688-3900. Family style restaurant offering roasted chicken and Bar-B-Q ribs. Table service, take-out and home delivery. Established: 1951 - Franchising Since: 1967 - No. of Units: Company Owned: 6 - Franchised: 86 - Franchise Fee: $60,000 - Royalty: 4% - Total Inv. $800,000-$2,000,000 - Financing: No.

ST. LOUIS BAR & GRILL
2050 Yonge Street, Toronto, ON, M4S 1Z9. Contact: Brent Poulton - Tel: (416) 485-1094, Fax: (416) 480-1837. Serving signature chicken wings and more in a inviting warm and friendly atmosphere. Established: 1994 - Franchising Since: 1999 - No. of Units: Company Owned: 8 - Franchise Fee: $35,000 - Royalty: 6% of gross.

ST. VIATEUR ARAHOVA SOUVLAKI
Arahova Network Inc.
1115 Sherbrooke St., West, Ste. 2802, Montreal, QC, H3A 1H3. - Tel: (514) 289-8718, Fax: (514) 8553. A 25 year tradition, Arahova's menu consists of delectable Greek dishes all served with their famous Tzatziki sauce, souvlaki, chicken platters, grilled meats and seafoods. Exquisite desserts and coffees. Outstanding value, generous portions all at reasonable prices. Estabished: 1971 - Franchising Since: 1996 - No. of Units: Company Owned: 1 - Franchised: 4 - Franchise Fee: $25,000 - Royalty: 6% - Total Inv: $300,000-$400,000.

SUBGARDEN FRANCHISE CORP
100 West Pender (Sunlife Tower) Suite 307, Vancouver, BC, V6B 1R8. - Tel: (604) 684-2274, Fax: (604) 904-0984, E-Mail: cormac@ subgarden.com, Web Site: www.subgarden.com. A wesome gourmet sub sandwiches with three inviting interior garden design themes as part of the fresh approach to this quick service food establishment. Established: 1998 - No. of Units: Company Owned: 5 - Total Inv: $150,000.

SUBS PLUS
Subs Plus Inc.
173 Queenston St., St. Catharines, ON, L2R 3A2. Contact: Robert Dumas, Pres. - Tel: (905) 641-4404, Fax: (905) 641-3696. Fast food outlet specializing in submarine sandwiches along with delicious cakes and pastries baked fresh on the premises. Eight weeks training with ongoing support. "We will train you in the skills you need to succeed!". Established: 1985 - Franchising Since: 1990 - No. of Units: Company Owned: 1 - Franchised: 4 - Franchise Fee: $12,000 - Royalty: 3.5%, 2% adv. on gross sales - Total Inv: $120,000 ($30,000 min. cash required) - Financing: Presentation assistance to chartered banks.

SUBWAY
Restaurants Subway Quebec Ltee
4473 rue Sainte - Catherie Quest, Westmount, QC, H3Z 1R6. Contact: Julie Galaise, Development Coordinator - Tel: (514) 939-1171, Fax: (514) 939-0212. Sandwiches and salads. Established: 1989 in Quebec, 1965 in the U.S. - Franchising Since: 1989 - Franchise Fee: $10,000 - Royalty: 8%, 2.5% adv. - Total Inv: $150,000.

SUKIYAKI - A JAPANESE DELIGHT
Matoyee Enterprises Inc.
3465 Timmins Ville, Ville, St. Laurant, QC, H4R 1V5. Contact: Claude St-Pierre, Controller - Tel: (514) 336-8885, Fax: (514) 336-9222, E-Mail: info@mtygroup.com, Web Site: www.mtygroup.com. Tappan-style Japanese food: Combination platters of beef, chicken, seafood and pork teriyaki, with sauteed mixed vegatables and rice. Also offers a variety of noodles, sushi and soup noodles. Established: 1988 - Franchising Since: 1979 - No. of Units: Company Owned: 1 - Franchised: 29 - Franchise Fee: $25,000-$40,000 - Royalty: 6% - Total Inv: $150,000-$175,000.

SWISS CHALET CHICKEN & RIBS
Cara Operations Ltd.
6303 Airport Rd., Missisauga, ON, L4V 1R8. Contact: Claus Etzler, Mgr. of Franchising - Tel: (866) 450-2903. Licensed family restaurant serving char-broiled chicken and barbecued pork ribs. Established: 1883 - Franchising Since: 1980 - No. of Units: Company Operated: 29 - Franchised: 121 - Franchise Fee: Swiss Chalet $75,000, Swiss Chalet Plus $90,000 - Royalty: 5%, nat. adv. 4%, local adv. 1% - Total Inv: $1,100,000 -1,350,000 depending on size of unit and format - Financing: Bank financing packages available.

TACO TIME
#105, 7500 MacLeod Trail S., Calgary, AB, T2H 0L9. Contact: Ken Pattenden, Pres. - Tel: (403) 543-3490, Fax: (403) 543-3499. Franchising quick service Mexican fast food. Established: 1977 - Franchising Since: 1977 - No. of Units: Franchised: 120 - Franchise Fee: $20,000 - Royalty: 5%, 5% adv. - Total Inv: Food Court $150,000 Free Standing $225,000-$275,000 - Financing: No.

TACO VILLA
Taco Villa Inc.
3710 Chesswood Drive, Ste. 220, Toronto, ON, M3J 2W4. Contact: Wendy J. Mackinnon, Franchise Director - Tel: (416) 636-9348, (800) 608-Taco, Fax: (416) 636-9162, E-Mail: tacovilla@on.aibn.com. Mexican quick service restaurant featuring tacos, burritos, nachos, salads, wraps, platters and combos. An original Canadian company based in Ontario with locations found primarily in high traffic shopping centres. Established: 1983 - Franchising Since: 1985 - No. of Units: Company Owned: 2 - Franchised: 23 - Franchise Fee: $20,000 - Royalty: 6%, 2 % adv. - Total Inv: $150,000-$170,000 - Financing: Assistance thru a lending institution.

TASTEE-DAWGS HOT DOG CARTS
P.O. Box 252, Dewinton, AB, T0L 0X0. Contact: Tony Sansotta - Tel: (403) 861-8638, Fax: (403) 938-9424. Selling of hotdogs and smookies. Established: 1998 - No. of Units: Company Owned: 1 - Franchise Fee: Varies.

THAI EXPRESS *
Matoyee Enterprises Inc.
3465 Thimens St-Laurent, QC, H4R 1V5. Contact: Claude St-Pierre - Tel: (514) 336-8885, Fax: (514) 336-9222, E-Mail: info@mtygroup.com, Web Site: www.mtygroup.com. Freshly prepared Thai authrntic food prepared right before your eyes. From delicious variety of flavors to chose from, noodles, rice, soup and much more. No. of Units: Franchised: 12 - Franchise Fee: $25,000-$40,000 - Royalty: 6% - Total Inv: $150,000-$175,000.

THE COFFEE WAY INC.
123 Rexdale Blvd., Rexdale, ON, M9W 1P1. Contact: Fran. Dev. - Tel: (416) 741-4144, Fax: (416) 741-5878. Coffee shop offering a variety of donuts and muffins as well as hot and cold dishes, salads, soups and sandwiches. No. of Units: Franchised: 14 - Total Inv: $80,000.

THE FIRKIN GROUP OF PUBS
20 Steele Gate Road #1C, Markham, ON, L3R 1B2. Contact: Larry Isaacs, Marketing Director - Tel: (905) 305-9792, Fax: (905) 305-9719, Web Site: www.firkenpubs.com. We have 21 pubs (1 in Vancouver) 8 under construction. Our pubs are based on a traditional English theme and are all built with a British motif. We have an extensive menu and a large variety of imported and domestic draft beer and liquor on our menu.

TIKI MING
Matoyee Enterprises Inc.
3465 Thimens Blvd., St-Laurent, QC, H4R 1V5. Contact: Claude St.Pierre, Controller - Tel: (514) 336-8885, Fax: (514) 336-9222, E-Mail: info@mtygroup.com, Web Site: www.mtygroup.com. #1 Oriental chain in Quebec, featuring the "Best" in Chinese Fast Food. Thinking of Chinese Food? Think Tiki Ming! Established: 1983 - Franchising Since: 1983 - No. of Units: Company Owned: 4 - Franchised: 54 - Franchise Fee: $25,000-$40,000 - Royalty: 6% - Total Inv: $150,000-$175,000.

TOBY'S GOODEATS
The Goodeats Corporation
8 Richmond West #808, Toronto, ON, M5H 2A4. Contact: Johnathon Yen, Manager - Tel: (416) 304-1010, Fax: (416) 440-0756. The original gourmet hamburger restaurants featuring table service in an atmosphere of comfort and nostalgia. Established: 1976 - Franchising Since: 1997 - No. of Units: Company Owned: 6 - Franchise Fee: $35,000 - Royalty: 5% gross sales + 2% adv. - Total Inv: $350,000 (approx.) turn-key includes fran.fee.

TOGO'S GREAT SANDWICHES
50 Ronson Drive, Suite 131, Toronto, ON, M9W 1B3. Contact: Franchise Dept. - Tel: (416) 245-3131, (888) 760-8548, (800) 361-5830, Fax: (416) 245-3040. Togos great sandwiches is a "premium value" sandwich, salad and soup concept that has been built with uncompromising standards for its ingredants, food preparation and service techniques. Full training and support on marketing and operations. Established: 1998 - No. of Units: Franchised: 2 - Total Inv: $225,000-$250,000.

TOM'S HOUSE OF PIZZA
7730 MacLeod Trail S., Calgary, AB, T2H 0L9. Contact: John H. Windle, Pres. - Tel: (403) 252-0111, Fax: (403) 255-3209. Thin crust pizza, special sauces and recipes, dine-in, take-out, delivery. Established: 1963 - Franchising Since: 1963 - No. of Units: Company Owned: 2 - Franchised: 4 - Franchise Fee: $10,000 - Financing: Possible.

TOPPER'S PIZZA
Mr. Toppers Pizza Limited
311 Elm St., West, Unit 3, Sudbury, ON, P3C 1V6. Contact: Franchise V.P. - Tel: (705) 674-0703, Fax: (705) 674-5302, E-Mail: keith@top pizza.com, Web Site: www.toppizza.com. Carry-out and delivery pizza business. Bright new concept specializing in great tasting pizzas at a competitive price. Established: 1982 - Franchising Since: 1985 - No. of Units: Company Owned: 6 - Franchised: 5 - Franchise Fee: $15,000 - Royalty: 5% + 1% - 3% adv fund - Total Inv: $182,000-$202,000 equipment leaseholds operating capital - Financing: Preferred client relationship with chartered bank.

TROLL'S FRANCHISE RESTAURANTS LTD.
14597 Marine Dr., White Rock, BC, V4B 1B7. Contact: Stewart Peddemors, Pres. - Tel: (604) 531-7877, Fax: (604) 536-3728, E-Mail: eat@trolls.ca, Web Site: www.trolls.ca. Highly successful fresh food concept (500-2,500 sq. ft). Features high quality fish and chips, chowders and salads. Established: 1946 - Franchising Since: 1984 - No. of Units: Company Owned: 1 - Franchised: 5 - Franchise Fee: $25,000 - Royalty: 5% - plus 2% adv. - Financing: Through bank.

UPPER CRUST BAKERY/EATERY
c/o J.F. Schmitz Associates, P.O. Box 58025, 500 Rossland Road, Oshawa, ON, L1J 8L6. Contact: Fran. Dev. - Tel: (905) 579-7252, (905) 579-0285, Fax: (905) 579-7513. Joint venture, affiliated owner/operator. Bakery/eatery concept. Intensive 4 weeks training with ongoing support. Established: 1982 - Total Inv: $140,000-$260,000 - depending on unit size.

VALENTINE
Groupe Valentine, Inc.
6495 Boul. Choquette, St. Hyacinthe, QC, J2S 8L2. Contact: Jean-Pierre Robin, Pres. - Tel: (450) 773-1276, Fax: (450) 773-2677. Fast food operation serving hot dogs, hamburgers and french fries. Established: 1979 - Franchising Since: 1984 - No. of Units: Company Owned: 3 - Franchised: 105 - Franchise Fee: $25,000 - Royalty: 5%, 2.5% adv. - Total Inv: $150,000.

VEGGIRAMA
Matoyee Enterprises Inc.
3465 Thimens Blvd., St. Laurent, PQ, H4R 1V5. Contact: Claude St-Pierre, Controller - Tel: (514) 336-8885, Fax: (514) 336-9222, E-Mail: info@mtygroup.com, Web Site: www.mtygroup.com. Offers healthy and delicious daily freshly prepared variety of specialities such as hot dishes, panini, salads, soups and sandwiches. Established: 1979 - Franchising Since: 1979 - No. of Units: Franchised: 30 - Franchise Fee: $25,000-$40,000 - Royalty: 5% - Total Inv: $150,000-$175,000.

VILLA MADINA *
Matoyce Enterprises Inc.
3465 Thimens, St-Laurent, QC, H4R 1V5. Contact: Claude St-Pierre - Tel: (514) 336-8885, Fax: (514) 336-9222, E-Mail: info@mtygroup.com, Web Site: www.mtygroup.com. The best of Mediterranean cuisine featuring Shawarma, Falafel, Shish Taouk, vine leafs, brochettes & yeros, rice, salads & sandwiches. Established: 2003 - Franchising Since: 2004 - No. of Units: Franchised: 4 - Franchise Fee: $25,000-$40,000 - Royalty: 5% - Total Inv: $150,000-$175,000.

WENDY'S OLD FASHIONED HAMBURGERS
Wendy's Restaurants of Canada, Inc.
874 Sinclair Rd, Oakville, ON, L6K 2Y1. Contact: Dave Carter, Dir. of Dev. - Tel: (905) 849-7685, Fax: (905) 849-5545, E-Mail: dave_carter @wendys.com, Web Site: www.wendys.com. Quick service restaurants serving hamburgers, fresh salad, baked potatoes, chili, chicken sandwich, fresh stuffed pitas. Wendy's offers the widest variety of menu choices, the most nutritous selections and the highest quality food. Established: 1975 - Canada - Franchising Since: 1979 - Canada - No. of Units: Company Owned: 105 - Franchised: 200 - Franchise Fee: $40,000 - Royalty: 4% of monthly sales + 4% adv. - Total Inv: $590,000-$1,520,500 - Financing: No, but have finance packages with 4 national banks.

WESTERN PIZZA & FAMILY RESTAURANTS
Western Pizza & B.B.Q. Chicken 1979 Ltd.
6 Wood Cres., Regina, SK, S4S 6J7. Contact: Jim or Spiro Bonis, Pres. & V.P. Mktg. - Tel: (306) 924-8391, Fax: (306) 545-3112. Pizza, pasta, chicken, take-out, delivery and dining. One of the top franchises in Saskatchewan looking to expand in Manitoba. Established: 1976 - Franchising Since: 1979 - No. of Units: Company Owned: 2 - Franchised: 14 - Franchise Fee: $25,000 a portion which goes to the promotion of the new location - Royalty: 5% of gross sales - Total Inv: $100,000.

WHITE SPOT RESTAURANTS
White Spot Ltd.
1126 S.E. Marine Dr., Vancouver, BC, V5X 2V7. Contact: Jim Devitt, VP - Tel: (604) 321-6631, Fax: (604) 325-1499. White Spot is an up-scale family style restaurant business in the west. Established: 1928 - Franchising Since: 1993 - No. of Units: Company Owned: 15 - Franchised: 35 - Franchise Fee: $75,000 - Royalty: 5%, 2% adv., 1% local mktg. - Total Inv: $500,000-$750,000 - Financing: No.

WILLY DOG®
120 Clarence Street, #1141, Kingston, ON, K7L 4Y5. Contact: Will R. Hodgskiss, Fran/Sales - Tel: (613) 389-6118, (800) 915-4683, Fax: (613) 549-4108, E-Mail: willrhodgskiss@aol.com, Web Site: www.willy dogs.com. Fully self-contained hot dog, sausage and drink carts to wable behind a car, has built in ice box, BBQ, hot and cold water, propane, etc. Lots of support provided in this turn-key money maker. Established: 1989 - Franchising Since: 1993 - No. of Units: Company Owned: 15+ - Franchised: 106 - Franchise Fee: $ 5,000 - Royalty: $500 yearly - Total Inv: $5500 - Financing: Sometimes.

WILLY'S OLD STYLE HAMBURGERS
3916 McLeod Trail S., Calgary, AB, T2G 2R5. Contact: Will Danek, Pres. - Tel: (403) 243-1175, Fax: (403) 233-7205. Fast food restaurant. Established: 1977 - Franchising Since: 1989 - No. of Units: Company Owned: 2 - Franchised: 6 - Franchise Fee: $20,000 - Royalty: 4% - Total Inv: $150,000-$180,000 - Financing: No.

WIMPY'S DINERS INC.
20 Rivermede Rd Unit 1, Vaughan, ON, L4K 2H2. Contact: Fran. Dev. - Tel: (888) 594-6797, Fax: (416) 269-8484. Family style diner - full training and support. Established: 1986 - No. of Units: Franchised: 23 - Total Inv: Varies.

WINCHESTER ARMS
4181 Sladeview Cres. Unit 43, Mississauga, ON, L5L 5R2. Contact: Fran. Dept. - Tel: (905) 569-2610, Fax: (905) 569-3108. British-style pub restaurant. Complete training and ongoing support. Locations available: Mid to Southern Ontario. Established: 1981 - No. of Units: Franchised: 24 - Total Inv: $375,000.

WING MACHINE, INC.
246 Parliament Street, Toronto, ON, M5A 3A4. Contact: Frank Schiavone, Mgr. - Tel: (416) 961-1000, Fax: (416) 362-5555. Fast food service specializing in chicken wings, pizza and ribs. Currently serving the Metro Toronto area. Recently opened our first location in Shanghai China. Established: 1986 - Franchising Since: 1987 - No. of Units: Company Owned: 2 - Franchised: 13 - Franchise Fee: $15,000 - Royalty: 6% of gross sales. - Total Inv: $95,000 - Financing: Yes.

WOK TO U EXPRESS
Wok to U Express Corp.
7-3331 Viking Way, Richmond, BC, V6V 1X7. - Tel: (604) 270-2360, Fax: (604) 270-6560. Healthy Mongolian food. Choice of meat, fries, fresh vegetables and sauces. Thai rice with coconut milk. Will co-brand. Established: 1998 - Franchising Since: 1999 - No. of Units: Franchised: 1 - Franchise Fee: $10,000 - Royalty: 6%, 2% advertising - Total Inv: $80,000-$150,000.

WRAP DADDY'S
2789 Hwy 97 North Suite 6, Kelowna, BC, V1X 4J8. - Tel: (250) 491-9727, Fax: (250) 491-9652. Fresh stir fry with veggie's, chicken, beef or vegetarian stuffed into a tortilla. Established: 1995 - Franchising Since: 2002 - No. of Units: Franchised: 4 - Franchise Fee: $15,000.

XELA ENTERPRISES LTD.
2225 Sheppard Ave. East, Suite 1200, Toronto, ON, M2J 5J2. Contact: Nancy Criconet, Manager Special Projects - Tel: (416) 494-5111, Fax: (416) 494-5177, E-Mail: ncriconet@xela.com, Web Site: www.xela.com. Toronto based holding company with diverse interests around the world. One of our major investments is in food services. Xela owns and operates Venezuela's premier quick service chicken concept, restaurant chain Arturo's. Franchise info @ www.arturos.com. Established: 1987 - No. of Units: Company Owned: 40 - Franchise Fee: $35,000 - Total Inv: Varies.

ZESTO'S SUBS & WRAPS
Zesto's OFLI & Restaurant Canada Ltd.
22-6782 Veyaness Rd., Saanichton, BC, V8M 2C2. Contact: Gerry Koutougos, Pres. - Tel: (250) 544-2361, (888) 922-2294, Fax: (350) 544-2349. Zesto's oven baked subs and california style wraps. Established: 1998 - Franchising Since: 1999 - No. of Units: Company Owned: 1 - Franchised: 4 - Franchise Fee: $15,000 - Royalty: 5% - Total Inv: 2.5% - Financing: Yes.

ZYNG, ASIAN NOODLERY
Zyng Inc.
4710 St Ambroise, 320, Montreal, QC, H4C 2C7. Contact: VP. Franchise Development - Tel: (888) 9-noodle, Fax: (514) 939-8808, Web Site: www.zyng.com. A new and unique Asian inspired casual dining restaurant with an eclectic decor featuring nutritious " design your own meal-in-a-bowl " noodle dishes. Appetizers, deserts, beer and wine and a specialty retail section round out the offerings. Established: 1997 - Franchising Since: 1998 - No. of Units: Company Owned: 1 - Franchised: 4 - Franchise Fee: $25,000 - Royalty: 6%, 3% advertising - Total Inv: $100,000-$125,000 - Financing: No.

FOOD: SPECIALTY SHOPS

ARENA MEATS FINE QUALITY FOOD STORES
22 White Oak Ct., Markham, ON, L3P 3Y1. Contact: Amedeo Arena, Pres. - Tel: (905) 294-7640. Meat shops. Established: 1980 - Franchising Since: 1993 - No. of Units: Company Owned: 1 - Franchise Fee: $25,000 - Royalty: 3% - Total Inv: $100,000 - min. cash required $35,000 - Financing: Canada and USA.

ARIZONA BLENDS
Pot Pourri Systems Inc.
4699 Keele St., Unit 1, Downsview, ON, M3J 2N8. Contact: V.P. Franchising & Leasing - Tel: (416) 661-9916, Fax: (416) 661-9706. Arizona blends is a specialty coffee and tea cafe serving select specialty foods such as bagels, soups and desserts. A charming southwestern design. Full training and support is provided. Established: 1995 - Franchising Since: 1997 - No. of Units: Franchised: 1 - Franchise Fee: $25,000 - Royalty: 6% - Total Inv: $90,000-$100,000 - Financing: Available through financial institutions.

BLENZ COFFEE
Blenz Coffee Ltd.
Ste. 300, 535 Thurlow St., Vancouver, BC, V6E 3L2. Contact: Mgr. Franchise Development - Tel: (604) 682-2995, Fax: (604) 684-2542. Specialty coffee, whole beans, pastries. Established: 1992- Franchising Since: 1992- No. of Units: Franchised: 23 - Franchise Fee: $25,000 - Royalty: 8%, 2% adv. - Total Inv: approx. $200,000 - Financing: No.

BOOSTER JUICE
#205, 8915-51 Ave, Edmonton, AB, T6E 5J3. Contact: Dale Wishewan - Tel: (780) 440-6770, Fax: (780) 461-7161, Web Site: www.booster juice.com. Fastest growing juice bar in Canada. The Canadian Dietary Association recommends 5 servings of fruits and vegetables per day and that's just what we bring you in one of our 24 oz. smoothies. Established: 2000 - Franchising Since: 2000 - Franchise Fee: $20,000 - Royalty: 6% of gross sales; 2% advertising.

CARROTHEADS RESTAURANTS
The Gramcor Franchising Co.
16715-12 Yonge St., Suite 909, Newmarket, ON, L3X 1X4. Contact: Danny Grammenopoulos, President - Tel: (416) 603-6306, Fax: (416) 603-9012, E-Mail: gramcoi@home.com. Full service food operations serving fresh squeezed juices, smoothies, sandwiches, healthy pizzas and baked products. All items are portioned for maximum bodily performance. Established: 1996 - Franchising Since: 1997 - No. of Units: Franchised: 7 - Franchise Fee: $19,900 - Royalty: 4.9% - Total Inv: $70,000-$200,000 - Financing: Through third party.

CUPPS COFFEE HOUSE
7181 Woodbine Avenue, Suite 222, Markham, ON, L3R 1A3. Contact: Mark Halpern, V.P. of Marketing - Tel: (905) 470-1517, Fax: (905) 470-8112, E-Mail: info@saintcinnamon.com, Web Site: www.cupps coffeehouse.com. Coffee house and eatery featuring specialty coffees, deluxe desserts and gourmet sndwiches on freshly baked asorted bagels and baquettes. Training and support provided. Established: 1995 - Franchising Since: 1999 - No. of Units: Company Owned: 1 - Franchise Fee: $25,000 - Total Inv: $155,000-$250,000 turnkey.

DAYBERRIES CAFE
1875 Leslie Street Suite 11, Toronto, ON, M3B 2M5. Contact: Bernie Pramama - Tel: (416) 385-1488, Fax: (416) 385-1499, E-Mail: cafe@dayberries.com, Web Site: www.dayberries.com. Cafe featuring fresh pastries, specialty breads, gourmet coffees and baguetts. Established: 2001 - Franchising Since: 2002 - No. of Units: Company Owned: 3 - Franchise Fee: $30,000.

DEATH BY CHOCOLATE
Death By Chocolate Franchise Ltd.
207 West 4th Ave #103, Vancouver, BC, V6J 1M9. Contact: Shakil Adam, Director - Tel: (604) 684- 2462, Fax: (604) 684- 2562. Licensed designer dessert restaurant also serving speciality coffees, baked goods and savouries. Established: 1996 - Franchising Since: 1997 - No. of Units: Company Owned: 2 - Franchised: 7 - Franchise Fee: $30,000 - Royalty: 6%, ad fund 1.5% - Total Inv: $200,000 - Financing: Assistance in acquiring.

ESQUIRES COFFEE HOUSE INC.
1959 152 St., Ste. 237, White Rock, BC, V4E 9E3. Contact: Dir. of Fran. - Tel: (604) 541-1004, (888) 551-6611, Fax: (604) 535-1411. Esquires is a vibrant new retailer serving gourmet coffee and bagels to communities outside of the city. Established: 1992 - Franchising Since: 1994 - No. of Units: Company Owned: 2 - Franchised: 17 - Franchise Fee: $25,000 - Royalty: 6%, 4% adv. - Total Inv: $186,500 - Financing: Yes.

EVERYTHING GARLIC
Everything Garlic Corp
2148 Kings Ave, West Vancouver, BC, V7V 2B8. Contact: Jeff Oates, President - Tel: (604) 990-1610, (800) 668-6299, Fax: (604) 990-1648, Web Site: www.everythinggarlic.com. Garlic specialty shops and garlic hot foods and high end kitchenware shops. Best selection of garlic related items available anywhere, Canada and USA. Established: 1994 - Franchising Since: 1997 - No. of Units: Company Owned: 1 - Franchised: 4 - Franchise Fee: $15,000 - Royalty: 5%, 1% advertising - Total Inv: $60,000.

GATEWAY NEWSTANDS/ GATEWAY CIGAR STORES
Tobmar Investments
9555 Yonge Street, Richmond Hill, ON, L4C 9M5. Contact: Michael Aychental, C.E.O. - Tel: (905) 737-7755, Fax: (905) 737-7757, E-Mail: info@gatewaynewstands.com, Web Site: www.gatewaynewstands.com. Tobacco/newstands and gifts in large office buildings and shopping malls, transit locations from coast to coast. Established: 1983 - Franchising Since: 1983 - No. of Units: Franchised: 306 - Franchise Fee: $25,000-$75,000 - Royalty: 3% gross sales - Total Inv: $60,000-$275,000 - Financing: Yes.

GRABBAJABBA
Comac Food Group Inc.
Ste. 440, 1121 Centre St. N., Calgary, AB, T2E 7K6. Contact: Franchise Department - Tel: (403) 230-1151, (800) 361-1151, Fax: (403) 230-2182. Upscale European coffee house featuring over 50 varieties of Arabica coffee and over 12 varieties of specialty coffee plus European style sandwiches, soups, salads, freshly baked goods and decadent desserts. Established: 1988 - Franchising Since: 1990 - No. of Units: Company Owned: 5 - Franchised: 54 - Franchise Fee: $25,000 - Royalty: 8%, Advertising: 1% - Total Inv: $175,000-$225,000 - Financing: Bank of Montreal. NOT FRANCHISING AT THIS TIME.

JAVA JOE'S
Java Joe's Inc.
5160 Explorer DR #13, Mississauga, ON, L4W 4T7. - Tel: (905) 602-0008. Specialty coffee concept with freshly prepared food, baked goods and exotic desserts, includes unique gift gallery - all served in a warm jazzy environment. Established: 1991 - Franchising Since: 1991- No. of Units: Company Owned: 3 - Franchised: 9 - Franchise Fee: $25,000 - Royalty: 5%, 2% adv. - Total Inv: $125,000 - Financing: No.

JUICE FARE
1 Whitby Place, St. Albert, AB, T8N 3N6. Contact: Cynthia Storme - Tel: (780) 418-5431, Fax: (780) 418-5491, E-Mail: info@juicefare.com, Web Site: www.juicefare.com. Features fresh fruit juices and smoothies. Established: 1999 - Franchising Since: 2003 - No. of Units: Company Owned: 6 - Total Inv: $175,000.

M & M MEAT SHOPS
M & M Meat Shops Ltd.
P.O. Box 2488, 640 Trillium Dr., Kitchener, ON, N2H 6M3. Contact: Johanna Jamnik, Admin. Assistant - Tel: (519) 895-1075, Fax: (519) 895-7062, E-Mail: johannaj@mmms.ca, Web Site: www.mmmeat shops.com. Sale of frozen foods at the retail level including barbeque items, vegetables, desserts and party items. Established: 1980 - Franchising Since: 1981 - No. of Units: Company Owned: 3 - Franchised: 297 - Franchise Fee: $30,000 - Royalty: 3% + 1.5% adv. - Total Inv: $300,000 turn-key - Financing: $150,000 bank.

MCBEANS
Midwest Coffee Systems Inc.
1560 Church Ave., Unit 6, Victoria, BC, V8P 2H1. Contact: Arne Andersson, Pres. - Tel: (250) 721-2411, Fax: (250) 721-3213. Gourmet coffee, tea and related accessories. Established: 1983 - Franchising Since: 1985 - No. of Units: Company Owned: 1- Franchised: 17 - Franchise Fee: $25,000 - Royalty: 7% - Total Inv: $135,500-$173,500 incl. fran. fee - Financing: Will assist through conventional methods.

ORIGINAL BASKET BOUTIQUE, THE
20 Larkspur Place, Sherwood Park, AB, T8H 1G3. Contact: Pat Lamourex, Owner - Tel: (780) 416-2530, Fax: (780) 416-2531, E-Mail: z-brower@home.com, Web Site: www.originalbasket.ca. Custom gift basket franchise. Established: 1989 - Franchising Since: 1989 - No. of Units: Company Owned: 1 - Franchised: 22 - Franchise Fee: $10,000 and up - Royalty: 7% on gross monthly sales - Total Inv: $20,000 - Financing: No.

P.A.M.'S COFFEE & TEA CO.
P.A.M.'S Coffee & Tea Co. Inc.
1 Atkinson Street, Richmond Hill, ON, L4C 0H5. Contact: Greg MacCormack, Fran. Dir. - Tel: (905) 780-0296. Specialty coffee chain. Established: 1981 - Franchising Since: 1991 - No. of Units: Company Owned: 1 - Franchised: 20 - Franchise Fee: $25,000 - Royalty: 8%, 2% adv. - Total Inv: $165,000-$200,000 - Financing: No.

PISTOL & BURNES COFFEE & TEA HOUSE
Pistol & Burnes Coffee Roastery Corp.
#10-8005 Alexander Rd., Delta, BC, V4G 1C6. Contact: Roy Hardy, Owner - Tel: (604) 946-5767, Fax: (604) 946-5761. Retailers of specialty coffees and teas in pleasant, comfortable surroundings. Selling cupped and bulk coffees and teas, panini sandwiches and bagels. Roasters and wholesalers since 1978. Canadian owned. Established: 1978 - Franchising Since: 1994 - No. of Units: Franchised: 10 - Franchise Fee: $20,000 - Royalty: Nil - Total Inv: From $250,000 - Financing: Some O.A.C.

ROCKY MOUNTAIN CHOCOLATE FACTORY
Immaculate Confection Ltd.
5284 Still Creek Avenue, Burnaby, BC, V5C 4E4. Contact: Lloyd Shears - Tel: (604) 298-2462, (800) 567-2207, Fax: (604) 298-7212, E-Mail: franchise@rockychoc.com, Web Site: www.rockychoc.com. Retail sale of confectionary, chocolate and ice cream. Stores are located in regional malls, power centers and tourist markets. Most locations have onsite production for many of the items. Established: 1988 - Franchising Since: 1992 - No. of Units: Company Owned: 8 - Franchised: 20 - Franchise Fee: $25,000 - Royalty: 8% - Total Inv: Leaseholds-$75,000-$1252,000, Inventory-$15,000-$25,000, Working Capital-$20,000-$25,000 - Financing: No.

SECOND CUP COFFEE CO.
Second Cup, Ltd., The
6303 Airport Road, Mississauga, ON, L4V 1R8. Contact: Roy Benin, Vice President, Franchising - Tel: (800) 569-6318, Fax: (905) 405-6615. Specialty gourmet coffees and teas. Established: 1975 - Franchising Since: 1979 - No. of Units: Company Owned: 6 - Franchised: 400 - Franchise Fee: $25,000 - Royalty: 9%, 2% marketing co-op fee - Total Inv: $300,000-$350,000 - Financing: Introduction to bank.

TABATOUT INC.
1 Place Du Commerce, Nun's Island, Montreal, QC, H3E 1A4. Contact: Jean-Gilles Boisvert, Pres. - Tel: (514) 768-7678, Fax: (514) 768-4988. Franchises, newstands, variety and tobacco shops. Established: 1984 - Franchising Since: 1986 - No. of Units: Company Owned: 3 - Franchised: 27- Franchise Fee: $30,000 - Royalty: 3% - Total Inv: $85,000-$150,000, franchise fee, $30,000, leasehold and equip $40,000-$80,000, stock $15,000-$35,000 - Financing: $40,000-$100,000.

TOUCH OF EUROPE COFFEE SYSTEMS, INC.
2775 Sabourin, St. Laurent, QC, H4S 1M9. Contact: VP Marketing - Tel: (514) 333-3235, (800) 759-3235, Fax: (514) 333-0830. Providers of specialty coffees to the office environment. Complete training available along with financial support. Established: 1995 - Franchising Since: 1995 - Franchise Fee: None - Royalty: None - Total Inv: Please contact for further information - Financing: Yes.

WILLIAMS COFFEE PUB
198 King St. W, Suite 202, Kitchener, ON, N2G 1B1. - Tel: (888) 741-7417, Fax: (519) 744-5229, E-Mail: www.williamscoffeepub.com. Coffee cafe with light meals + specialty desserts. No. of Units: Franchised: 18 - Franchise Fee: $35,000 - Total Inv: $150,000.

FOOD: SUPERMARKETS

ACHILLE DE LA CHEVROTIERE LTEE.
333 Ave. Montemurro, P.O Box 940, Rouyn-Noranda, QC, J9X 5E1. - Tel: (819) 797-1900, Fax: (819) 797-1271. Food retailer (grocery, meat, fruit and vegetables). Established: 1956 - Franchising Since: 1963 - No. of Units: 8.

AG FOODS
Div. of the Overwaitea Food Group
7100 44th St S.E., Calgary, AB, T2C 2Y7. Contact: Larry Chmielewski, Dir. of Sales and Operations - Tel: (800) 242-3182, Fax: (800) 461-8876. Retail-oriented wholesaler supplying full product listing (grocery, frozen, produce, meat, deli, confectionery, HBA, cigarettes and tobacco) to all types of operations, including gas bars, C-stores, full-line grocery stores. (5,000-50,000 sq. ft). Established: 1918 - Franchising Since: 1992 - No. of Units: Company Owned: 1 - Franchised: 49 AB & BC, over 600 Independent accounts.

BULK BARN
55 Leek Cres., Beaver Creek Bus. Pk., Richmond Hill, ON, L4B 3Y2. - Tel: (905) 886-6756, Fax: (905) 886-3717. Canada's largest bulk food retailer. Established: 1982 - No. of Units: 70 - Total Inv: $375,000-$475,000.

BUY LOW FOODS, BUDGET FOODS, G&H SHOP & SAVE, GIANT FOODS
Buy Low Foods Ltd.
19580 Telegraph Trail, Surrey, BC, V4N 4W2. Contact: Bob Mills, President - Tel: (604) 888-1121, Fax: (604) 888-2696. Retail-oriented wholesaler supplying a full product listing (grocery, frozen, meat, deli, confectionary, HBA, cigarettes and tobacco) to all types of operations including gas bars, C-stores, grocery stores (5,000-20,000 sq.ft.). Established: 1978 - Franchising Since: 1980 - No. of Units: Company Owned: 14 - Franchised: 13 and over 450 independent accounts - Total Inv: Varies - Financing: Introduction to financial institutions.

FOODLAND
LUMSDEN BROS.
P.O .Box 3100, Brantford, ON, N3T 6K2. Contact: Franchise Dir. - Tel: (519) 751-6000, Fax: (519) 751-4467. Grocery and convenience stores. No. of Units: Owner Operator: 500 - Franchised: 60.

METRO - RICHELIEU - AMIX - GEM
Alimentation A.D.L. Enr.
333 Montemurro Ave., P.O. Box 940, Rouyn-Noranda, QC, J9X 5E1. - Tel: (819) 797-1900, ext. 206, Fax: (819) 797-1271. Food retailer. Established: 1927 - Franchising Since: 1950 - No. of Units: Franchised: 48 - Royalty: Purchasing Agreement - Total Inv: Depending on store size - Financing: Yes. NOT OFFERING FRANCHISES AT THIS TIME.

NUTTER'S BULK & NATURAL FOODS
107-1601 Dunmore Rd., S.E., Medicine Hat, AB, T1A 1Z8. Contact: Donald Cranston, President - Tel: (403) 529-1664, Fax: (403) 529-6507. Nutter's, largest bulk and natural food franchise, offers a unique retail opportunity in one of North America's fastest growing industries. Our unique combination of bulk foods, deli, natural foods and gourmet gift baskets has made Nutter's a leading edge food retailer. Established: 1982 - Franchising Since: 1984 - No. of Units: Company Owned: 3 - Franchised: 32 - Franchise Fee: $15,000-$30,000 - Royalty: 2%-4% - Total Inv: $120,000-$250,000 - Financing: No.

SAVE-EASY, FOODMASTER, RED & WHITE, QUIK MART, VALU MART AND THE PHARMACY
Atlantic Wholesalers Ltd.
120 Eileen Stubbs Ave. Ste. 101, Dartmouth, NS, B3B 1Y1. Contact: Bill Witman - Tel: (902) 468-8866, Fax: (902) 481-4283. Food, GM and health and beauty pharmacies in The Pharmacy group. Established: 1903 - Franchising Since: 1954 - No. of Units: Company Owned: 16 - Franchised: 434.

VALU-MART/FRESHMART/MR. GROCER/YOUR INDEPENDENT GROCER
National Grocers Co. Ltd.
6220A Yonge Street, North York, ON, M2M 3X4. Contact: Leo Bugeja, Vice-President - Tel: (416) 218-7713, Fax: (416) 218-8046. Stores featuring in-store bakery and delicatessen within a conventional supermarket format. Established: 1925 - Franchising Since: 1929 - No. of Units: 180.

FRANCHISE CONSULTANTS AND FRANCHISE SERVICES

ACCOUNTING & CONSULTING SERVICES OF CANADA INC.
1454 Dundas St. E., Ste. 125, Mississauga, ON, L4X 1L4. Contact: Douglas Steen, V.P. - Tel: (905) 848-6202, Fax: (905) 848-0755. Professional accounting and consulting expertise for the franchisee and franchisor. Financial business planning statements. Franchise analysis, assistance for financing, evaluation and selection services. Established: 1984.

ACT ONE FRANCHISING
5 Roberta Crescent, Nepean, ON, K2J 1G5. Contact: Ted MacMillan, Owner - Tel: (613) 825-5615, Fax: (613) 825-5615. Franchise development service. Concept evaluation, franchising the business, marketing setup, consultations and support. Established: 1975.

ANDREW L. CHIN, C.A.
7220-6 Kennedy Road, Suite 1002, Markham, ON, L3R 0N4. - Tel: (416) 609-9663, Fax: (416) 297-8454. Assistance to prospective and existing franchisees in the following areas: Business plans, franchise assessments, cash flow forecasts, preparation of financial statements, tax returns and computerization of accounting systems.

ARAHOUA SOUVLAKI NETWORK INC.
266 St. Viateur West, Montreal, QC, H2V 1X9. Contact: Nector Koutroumanis, President - Tel: (514) 272-4681, Fax: (514) 272-4592. Franchising of Restaurants. Established: 1970 - Franchising Since: 1997 - No. of Units: Company Owned: 1 - Franchised: 2 - Franchise Fee: $25,000 - Royalty: 5% , 2% adv. - Total Inv: $150,000-$650,000 - Financing: Yes.

ASSANTE CAPITAL MANAGEMENT INC.
320 Bay St. Suite 1100, Toronto, ON, M5H 4A6. Contact: Fran. Dev. - Tel: (416) 216-6588, Fax: (416) 216-6534, Web Site: www.equion.com. Comprehensive financial planning services and solutions for people in the franchise industry. Established: 1980 - Member: Cndn. Assoc. of Financial Planners.

B & B CONSULTANTS
26 Chateau Kirkland St., Kirkland, QC, H9J 3Y6. Contact: Robert Brideau, Pres. -Tel: (514) 426-5859, Fax: (514) 426-4826. Specializing in franchise recruitment for the Quebec and Ontario markets. Established: 1985.

BAKER-BLAIS MARKETING
1000 St. Charles Ave., Ste. 1100, Vaudreuil, QC, J7V 8P5. Contact: Michel Auigliano, Intern Consultant - Tel: (450) 424-2400, (888) 654-6277. Franchise Consultants and services. Site location and market studies. Established: 1987.

BAUM, FALLENBAUM ATTORNEYS
5415 Queen Mary Rd., Ste 2, Montreal, QC, H3X 1V1. - Tel: (514) 486-2003, (888) LAW 5850, Fax: (514)486-8474. Full service franchise attorneys.

BENE*PEN SERVICES LTD.
25 North Rivermede Rd Unit 9, Concord, ON, L4K 5V4. Contact: Zeke Oudeh, Owner - Tel: (905) 660-0572, (800) 567-0156, Fax: (905) 660-4199. Specialists in implementing and administering group benefit packages for franchisees. Endorsed agents of the Canadian Franchisee Association and providers of the Canadian Franchisee Benefit Plan. Established: 1991.

BIZDEV
328 North Rivermede Rd #10, Concord, ON, L4K 3N5. Contact: Jeffrey Sugarman, President - Tel: (905) 760-1977, Fax: (905) 760-2977. Management consulting firm specializing in business development, franchising (franchisee, franchisor) leasing/site development and in financial services. Established: 1984.

BUSINESS CONNECTIONS INT'L.
1454 Dundas St. E., Ste. 125, Mississauga, ON, L4X 1L4. Contact: William Gay, Franc. Dir. - Tel: (905) 848-6202, Fax: (905) 848-0755. Offering professional, comprehensive franchise services to the franchisor and franchisee with an experienced staff, covering all services, representing different opportunities. Established: 1983.

BY LAW TRADENAME, CLEARANCE INC.
Box 12109 - Ste. 2200, 555 West Hastings, Vancouver, BC, V6B 4N6. Contact: Sandra Wright or Trisha Dore - Tel: (604) 669-6023, (800) 663-1444, Fax: (604) 687-3478. Trade mark searching and development for Canada and foreign countries. Trade mark registration referral. Established: 1985.

C. ANTHONY WILSON LAW CORPORATION
Suite 1700-1188 West Georgia Street, Vancouver, BC, V6E 4A2. - Tel: (604) 684-1800, Fax: (604) 684-3350. Law firm with a specialization in franchise, licensing and intellectual property, representative franchisors in British Columbia. Registered Canadian trade agent. Established: 1998.

C.J. WOODBURN & ASSOCIATES
4034 Mainway Drive, Suite 202B, Burlington, ON, L7M-4B9. Contact: John Woodburn, President - Tel: (905) 335-4627, (877) 322-2153, Fax: (905) 335-4649, E-Mail: woodburnassoc@on.aibn.com, Web Site: www.woodburnassociates.com. Franchise consulting firm providing full services to assist emerging and existing franchisors locate & select new franchisees. Special projects undertaken for individuals and groups to select single area or master franchise. Over 30 years experience. Canada, U.S. & Off shore. Established: 1994.

CANADIAN ALLIANCE OF FRANCHISE OPERATIONS
1201 Bayfield Street North, Midhurst, ON, L0L 1X1. Contact: Les Stewart, President - Tel: (705) 737-4635, Fax: (705) 737-4950, E-Mail: lstewart@cafo.net, Web Site: www.cafo.net. The Canadian Alliance of Franchise Operators (CAFO) is Canada's only trade association for

small business franchise investors. CAFO works to bolster the climate for franchising while seeking to protect and enhance franchisees' economic investment. Established: 1997.

CANADIAN ASSOCIATION OF FRANCHISEE OPERATORS
P.O. Box 7, Midhurst, ON, L0L 1X0. Contact: Les Stewart, Founder - Tel: (705)737-4635, Fax: (705) 737-4950, E-Mail: lstewart@sympatico.ca, Web Site: www.cafo.net. The Canadian Alliance of Franchisee Operators (CAFO) is Canada's only trade association for small business franchise-investors. CAFO works to bolster the climate for franchising while seeking to protect and enhance franchisees' economic investment. Established: 1997.

CANADIAN FRANCHISE ASSOCIATION
2585 Skymark Ave., Suite 300, Mississauga, ON, L4W 4L5. Contact: Kim Divell, Dir. of Member Services - Tel: (800) 665-4232 or (905) 625-2896, Fax: (905) 625-9076, E-Mail: info@cfa.ca, Web Site: www.cfa.ca. Established: 1967. The Canadian Franchise Association is the national trade association representing the franchising community. The CFA is dedicated to promoting and strengthening ethical franchising in Canada. As a condition of membership, companies agree to abide by the CFA code of ethics and undergo the scrutiny of their peers. The CFA provides educational programs, tradeshows, and networking opportunities to assist franchisors. For prospective franchisees, the CFA provides publications and seminars to help in the process.

CASTELANE CONSULTING
78 Highland Crescent, Toronto, ON, M2L 1G9. Contact: Karen Castelane, Pres. - Tel: (416) 226-9850, Fax: (416) 226-1430, E-Mail: karen@pathcom.com. Development of franchise/licensing programs, franchise system improvement, alternate expansion strategies. Established: 1992.

CHOICE CORPORATION
1100 Queens Ave. Suite 23, Oakville, ON, L6H 2B5. - Tel: (800) 689-81175, Fax: (905) 339-3313. Consulting firm specializing in marketing of franchises. Professional handling of dispositions of existing locations for franchisees, as well as expert third party representation for franchisors. We arrange financing to complete the purchase. Established: 1996.

COMMERCIAL CONSULTANTS INC.
2911 A Cleveland Ave., Saskatoon, SK, S7K 8A9. Contact: Lorne Horning, Pres. - Tel: (306) 931-2131, Fax: (306) 931-2323. Act as advisor to franchisors in establishing program, operation of the system and sales of franchises. Established: 1983.

COMPUSEARCH MICROMARKETING DATE & SYSTEMS
330 Front Street West, Ste. 1100, Toronto, ON, M5V 3B7. Contact: Ian Caminsky, Nat'l Mktg. Mgr. - Tel: (416) 348-9l95, Fax: (416) 348-9195. Compusearch has been providing vital market analysis tools and geodemographic information to over 4,000 Canadian businesses across all industry sectors. Compusearch has one-stop shopping for demographic, georgraphic and marketing data, including Census data, Estimates & Projections etc. Established: 1974.

CONTEMPORARY COMMUNICATIONS
Contemporary Communications Ltd.
1663 West 7th Ave, Vancouver, BC, V6J 1S4. Contact: Perry Goldsmith, Pres. - Tel: (604) 734-3663, Fax: (604) 734-8906. Public relations and communications. Services for franchisors. Established: 1974.

DAREN, MARTENFELD, CARR, TESTA & CO., CHARTERED ACCOUNTANTS
20 Eglinton Ave. W., Ste. 2100, Toronto, ON, M4R 1K8. Contact: Marvin B. Martenfeld, FCA, Partner - Tel: (416) 480-0160, Fax: (416) 480-2646. Franchise consultants, accounting, audit and taxation services. Acquisitions and private investment banking. Established: 1970.

DYNAMIC PERFORMANCE SYSTEMS INC.
478 Valerno Drive, Etobicoke, ON, M8W 2M7. - Tel: (416) 201-0202, Fax: (416) 201-0808, E-Mail: fberni@franchise-profiles.com, Web Site: www.franchise-profiles.com. We help franchisors select great franchisees and retail managers with our Franchise Profile™ and Manager PROfile™. Unlike personality profiles, our performance based profiles

assess a candidate's core values and compare them to successful franchisees and/or retail managers. This eneables us to predict the candidates eventual performance with unprecedented accuracy." Established: 1988. Member: CFA, IFA, Council of Suppliers.

ENTREPRENEUR COACH INC
9600 Cameron Street., #314, Burnaby, BC, V3J 7N3. Contact: Tom Matzen, Entrepreneur Coach - Tel: (604) 422-8677, (800) 955-1345, Fax: (604) 422-8699, Web Site: www.entrepreneur-coach.com. A franchise development company specializing in long term joint ventures with socially responsible, cutting edge franchises. Established: 1995.

ETZLER FRANCHISE CONSULTING
405 Bartley Bull Pkwy, Brampton, ON, L6W 2M2. Contact: Claus Etzler - Tel: (905) 866-7013, Fax: (905) 796-9288, E-Mail: cetzler@franchiseconnexion.com, Web Site: www.franchise connexion.com. Completely independent service specializing in in-depth research on franchisors and helping clients secure the best possible franchise business for themselves. Established: 2002.

F.D.C. (FRANCHISE DEVELOPMENT CORP.)
100 Upper Madison Ave., Ste. 1704, North York, ON, M2N 6M4. Contact: Kim Berry, General Manager - Tel: (416) 250-8887, Fax: (416) 250-8783. A complete franchise management and marketing program for franchisors including financing proposals for franchisees. Established: 1979.

FHG INTERNATIONAL INC.
14 Glengrove Ave W, Toronto, ON, M4R 2H7. Contact: Doug Fisher, M.Sc, CMC, Pres. - Tel: (416) 489-6996, Fax: (416) 489-7792, Web Site: www.fhgi.com, E-Mail: doug@fhgi.com. Management consulting firm specializing in food service and retail franchise development including: strategic planning, manual development, promotional material, business plans, litigation support and arbitration. Established: 1984.

FINANCIAL FOCUS, INC.
P.O. Box 1735, 23 Cashin Ave., St. John's, NF, A1C 5P5. Contact: Terence W. Pike, Pres. - Tel: (709) 754-1847, Fax: (709) 579-0432. Management consultants specializing in franchise search and evaluation. Established: 1989 - No. of Units: Company Owned: 1.

FRANCHISE AFFAIRES 1701, INC.
648 Laurie, Greenfield Park, QC, J4V 2A6. Contact: Norbert Lemieux, Pres. - Tel: (450) 466-9538, Fax: (450) 466-9430. Specialized franchise development and franchisees' recruitment for the Quebec market and marketing consultation. Established: 1986 - Franchising Since: 1987.

FRANCHISE CANADA DEVELOPERS INC.
514 Riverside Dr., Ste. 3, Toronto, ON, M6S 4B5. Contact: Frank A. Rush, Pres. - Tel: (416) 769-6430, Fax: (416) 769-6429. Franchise Consultant. Established: 1981.

FRANCHISE COMPANY, THE
5397 Eglinton Ave., West, Ste. 108, Etobicoke, ON, M9C 5K6. Contact: Tom Wood, Franchise Recruiting - Tel: (416) 620-4700, Fax: (416) 620-9955, E-Mail: twood@certapro.com, Web Site: www.thefranchise company.com. Franchise consulting firm representing service sector franchise systems.

FRANCHISE RECRUITERS
William J. Coke and Associates Ltd.
20 Holly St., Ste. 203, Toronto, ON, M4S 3B1. Contact: George Kinzie, Pres. - Tel: (416) 322-5730, Fax: (416) 322-0648, E-Mail: franchise@att.net, Web Site: www.franchiserecruiters.com. Twenty-six years of franchising experience. An international executive search corporation dedicated exclusively to franchising. Unconditional one-year guarantee. Excellent client references. Placement of professional in sales, operations, executive, marketing, training, finance, legal and international development. Contigency search only. Franchise Recruiters Ltd. is a strategic partner with the iFranchise Group. Established: 1984 - No. of Locations: 2.

FRANCHISE REGISTRY & EXCHANGE, INC.
P.O. Box 888, Black Diamond, AB, T0L 0H0. Contact: Douglas J. Queen, C.A., Pres. - Tel: (403) 933-3711, E-Mail: queend@huey.c advision.com, Web Site: www.cadvision.com. Author of Low-Risk Franchising and franchise consultant with particular emphasis on the

assistance to franchisees in the evaluation of franchise opportunities in Canada and preparation of filings for franchisors to the Alberta Securities Commission in the province of Alberta.

FRANCHISE SPECIALISTS
410-2551 Parkview Lane, Port Coquitlam, BC, V3G 6J8. Contact: Wayne Maillet, President - Tel: (604) 941-4361, Fax: (604) 941-4315, Web Site: www.members.aol.com/wmaillet. Franchise Specialists implements franchise strategies to develop new or existing brands, based on 14 years of practical experience. Services include feasibility studies to complete franchise program development and implementation. Existing concepts are reviewed and provided with strategies to build market share and grow. Established: 1997.

FRANCHISE SUPPORT SERVICE
Box 2000, Squamish, BC, V0N 3G0. Contact: Mary Jane Charman, Pres. - Tel: (604) 898-5157, Fax: (604) 898-5107. Assisting franchisors in establishing their systems and networking in Canada. In depth experience in Operational Support Systems for franchisors and franchisor/franchisee relations. Established: 1988.

FRANCHISE WIZARD DATA BASE
Francon Consulting Ltd.
100 -1 The East Mall, Toronto, ON, M8Z 5X2. Contact: Gord Metcalfe, President - Tel: (416) 232-2411, (800) 506-6669, Fax: (416) 232-2418. Preparing of detailed franchise corporate background reports, feasibility studies, franchise industry and category overview studies. Established: 1992 - Franchising Since: 1997 - No. of Units: Company Owned: 1 - Franchised: 1 - Franchise Fee: $20,000 - Royalty: None - Total Inv: $25,000 - Financing: Yes.

FRANNET
Franchise Network
1177 Hornby St Main Floor, Vancouver, BC, V6Z 2E9. Contact: Fred Hopkinson, Pres. - Tel: (604) 883-5671, Fax: (604) 689-2013. Franchise Consultants, prospective franchisees looking for the right fit, for franchisors looking to improve or develop their systems. Established: 1984 - Franchising Since: 1987 (US) - No. of Units: Franchised: 60 Worldwide offices.

GEOMARKETING™
831 Millwood Rd, Toronto, ON, M4G 1W5. Contact: Don Baker, V.P. Sales - Tel: (905) 337-3202, Fax: (905) 845-7387. Demographics, site evaluation, market analysis, mapping services and database marketing service. Established: 1988.

GOLDMAN, SLOAN, NASH & HABER
250 Dundas St. West, Ste. 700, Toronto, ON, M5T 2Z5. Contact: Ron Miller - Tel: (416) 597-9922, Fax: (416) 597-3370. Franchisor Consultant.

GROUPE FRANCHISE MULTI SERVICES
6300 Auteuil Ave., Brossard, QC, J4Z 3P2. Contact: Robert Vaillancourt, President - Tel: (450) 445-9555, Fax: (450) 445-9322. Structure, translation, operational manuels, site selection, selection of qualified franchisees, Quebec market realities. Franchisor introduction. Established: 1980.

HERTZBERG & ASSOCIATES LTD.
30 Wertheim Ct., Unit 20, Richmond Hill, ON, L4B 1B9. Contact: Jack Hertzberg, Pres. - Tel: (905) 764-8569, Fax: (905) 764-8323, E-Mail: finestca@aol.com. Franchise and business advisors who work with franchisors and franchisees to conduct and prepare feasibility assessments and business plans; design and implement control systems including tailored manuals; and provide training in the use of these systems. Established: 1982.

INFORMATION PLUS
925 Yonge St., Ste. 154, Toronto, ON, M4W 2H2. Contact: D.C. Sawyer, Pres. - Tel: (416) 968-1062, in the US call (716) 852-2220, Fax: (416) 968-2591. Provides qualitative research to support business location decisions, industry and market trends information and related business development data, for Canada and the U.S. Established: 1979.

INTERFRAN INC.
Interfran Inc.
1001 Bay Street, Suite 3502, Toronto, ON, M5S 3A6. Contact: George Fluter, Chairman, CEO - Tel: (416) 944-2200, Fax: (416) 944-3555, E-Mail: Gfluter@hotmail.com, Web Site: www.interfran.com. Franchise consulting development marketing nationally and internationally. Established: 1967.

J. F. SCHMITZ ASSOCIATES..THE FINDERS
390 Rossmount Ave., Oshawa, ON, L1J 3K6. Contact: Joseph Schmitz, Pres. - Tel: (905) 579-7252, Fax: (905) 579-7513. In depth consulting service to both franchisor and franchisee. Franchisor: franchise, site development and operations. Franchisee: franchise acquisitions, specializing in new franchises and out of Canada franchise representation. Established: 1963 - Franchising Since: 1989.

JAMES R. DUBROY LTD.
270 MacLaren St., Ottawa, ON, K2P 0M3. Contact: James Dubroy, President - Tel: (613)235-6166, Fax: (613) 235-2523. Business broker, valuator and consultant (confidential).

JEAN H GAGNON
Jean H. Gagnon
370 Chemin de Chambly, Suite 230, Longueuil, QC, J4H 3Z6. Contact: Jean H, Gagnon - Tel: (450) 670-0411, Fax: (450) 670-0811, E-Mail: jhgagnon@jeanhgagnon.com. Accredited Expert in Franchising, Certified Mediator, Arbitrator and Lawyer. With more than 30 years of experience in franchising, Jean H. Gagnon offers a full range of consulting and legal services to franchisors operating or wishing to develop their franchise systems in Quebec.

LARKIN INVESTMENTS LTD.
932 Cobblestone Lane, Victoria, BC, V8Y 3G3. Contact: Richard Larkin, Pres. - Tel: (604) 658-1258, Fax: (604) 658-1904, Web Site: www.dynamic-essentials.net/visionbuilders. Marketing one of the best opportunities today "The People's Franchise". Free information package available. Established: 1988.

M-FOUR INTERNATIONAL
38 Place Du Commerce., Suite #607, Iles Des Soeurs, QC, H3E 1T8. Contact: Martin Greenspon, Pres. - Tel: (514) 214-3297, Fax: (514) 765-3789. North America's most comprehensive franchise marketing strategists, providing consultancy services to franchisors planning to expand in Canada or Internationally. Specializing in franchise development, feasibility projections, marketing plans and franchisee recruiting. Master Licensees, Area Franchisees, Multiple Unit Networks, Site location and lease negotiation services. Established: 1981 - Franchising Since: 1991 - No. of Units: Company Owned: 1 - Franchised: 4 - Franchise Fee: $50,000 - Royalty: Varies.

MARTIN INTERNATIONAL
500 Place d'Armes, Ste. 2910, Montreal, QC, H2Y 2W2. Contact: Serge Martin, Pres. - Tel: (514) 288-3931, Fax: (514) 288-0641. Organizer of the Franchise and Start-Up Show held in Montreal (75,000 visitors) and in Quebec City (25,000 visitors) each year in January. Also organizer of the Business World Exhibition with its section on Franchises & Business Opportunities each year at the end of September (30,000 visitors). Established: 1967.

MCGOVERN, HURLEY, CUNNINGHAM
#3002005 Sheppard Ave. E., Toronto, ON, M2J 5B4. Contact: W. David Sanderson, C.A., Partner - Tel: (416) 496-1234, Fax: (416) 496-0125. Public accounting firm providing consulting services to franchisors and franchisees, taxation, accounting and financial planning to entrepreneurial companies and individuals. Established: 1984.

MEDIA THREE MARKETING SERVICES LTD.
145 Main St., Unionville, ON, L3R 2G7. Contact: Brock Weir, Pres. - Tel: (905) 475-6611, Fax: (905) 475-0636, E-Mail: media3@media threegroup.com, Web Site: www.mediathreegroup.com. Offers expert marketing and communication planning, video and audio productions, interactive video training and speciality programming, event management and graphic design. Established: 1973.

NATIONAL FRANCHISE CONSULTANTS

51 Hurricane Rd., Fonthill, ON, L0S 1E3. Contact: Andre Champagne, President - Tel: (905) 892-8404, Fax: (905) 892-9934. Full service franchise consulting, development, marketing and sales, US and Canada. Home of "Do It Yourself" franchise kit. Established: 1987 - No. of Offices: 2.

NETWORK FRANCHISING INTERNATIONAL

1 Concorde Gate Suite 201, Toronto, ON, M3C 3N6. Contact: Cliff D. Richler, President - Tel: (416) 447-9499, (800) 293-4929, Fax: (416) 447-3974. Single source - Total Resources for franchising sales, marketing, packaging, bank loans, site selection, real estate services, legal documents. Complete self employment assessment program. Established: 1978 - No. of Units: 2.

OFF THE BEATEN PATH MARKETING

Main St., Box 1138, Osoyoos, BC, V0H 1V0. Contact: W. Schmidt, Pres. - Tel: (250) 446-2455, Fax: (250) 446-2862, E-Mail: wschmidt@direct.ca. Consulting to establish master franchises in Canada and the USA. Includes packaging first step marketing efforts with advertising and screen interview, arranging local supply, feasibility studies and marketing research. Specializing in small and home based business franchises. Established: 1967.

PARKER & ASSOCIATES

303 Bagot Street, #501, Kingston, ON, K7K 5W7. Contact: Pat Parker, President - Tel: (613) 545-3303, Fax: (613) 545-1154. Consulting firm specializing in franchise concept development, strategic planning and marketing, systems development, and organizational analysis with a focus on getting franchisors through new growth plateaus. Also professional franchise mediation and legal expert witness work. Established: 1991.

PRICE WATERHOUSE

5700 Younge St., Ste. 1900, North York, ON, M2M 4K7. Contact: Terry Hogan, Partner - Tel: (416) 218-1500, Fax: (416) 365-8215. A national accounting and consulting firm providing an extensive range of professional services to franchisors and franchisees. Services include accounting and management information systems; preparation of forms and policies with respect to royalties and advertising; preparation of operation and training manuals; business plan development; feasibility studies; consultation with solicitors, financing packages, tax planning and review; audit and accounting services.

QUALITY CREDIT SERVICES LTD.

111 Granton Drive, #105, Richmond Hill, ON, L4B 1L5. - Tel: (905) 762-0740, Fax: (905) 762-9410, E-Mail: info@qcsl.com. Licensed consumer reporting agency providing financial background reports on both individuals and corporations to franchisors and franchisees alike. Established: 1992.

RETAILINK

200, 270 Midpark Way S.E., Calgary, AB, T2X 1M2. Contact: Ken Purvis, Pres. - Tel: (403) 543-1044, Fax: (403) 543-1046. Retailink is multi-disciplined franchise development and management consulting firm specializing in all aspects of franchising in Western Canada and the Pacific Northwest United States. Established: 1994.

SAMPSON & ASSOCIATES

45 B West Wilmot Street, Ste. 211, Richmond Hill, ON, L4B 1K1. - Tel: (905) 764-8922, Fax: (905) 764-9341. A full franchise service offering needs analysis, franchise structuring, marketing and business planning. Established: 1981 - Franchising Since: 1982 - No. of Units: Representing a variety of franchise offers - Total Inv: $100,000-$350,000 - Financing: Available.

SEARCH COMPANY INC., THE

1410-439 University Ave., Toronto, ON, M5G 1Y8. Contact: Gabor Horvath, Principal - Tel: (416) 979-5858, Fax: (416) 979-5857. Credit and background reporting on both franchisors and franchisees. Public record searching, incorporation services. Established: 1993 - Total Inv: $100-$1,000.

SMITH, NIXON & CO.

390 Bay St., Ste. 1900, Toronto, ON, M5H 2Y2. Contact: John C. Sinclair, Manager - Tel: (416) 361-1622, Fax: (416) 367-1238. Full range of accounting, taxation and business advisory services to franchisors

and franchisees. Established: 1961.

SOCIETE NATIONALE DE LA FRANCHISE INC.

2800 Rue Einstein, Ste.145, Sainte-Foy, QC, G1X 4N8. Contact: Julien Riou, Pres. - Tel: (418) 652-0898, Fax: (418) 652-2866. Franchise Consultant. Specialist of development for English franchisees in Quebec. Established: 1986 - Franchising Since: 1990 - No. of Units: Company Owned: 1 - Franchise Fee: $5,000 - Royalty: 10% - Total Inv: $20,000 - Financing: No.

SUMIDA & ASSOCIATES

528510 BC Ltd.
Ste. 409-1441 Craigflower Road, Victoria, BC, V9A 2Y9. Contact: Reed Sumida, President - Tel: (250) 595-8934, Fax: (250) 595-8935. Franchise consultant systems development, master franchising, feasibilities, purchasers advocate, public offerings.

SYNERGY MANAGEMENT GROUP LTD.

201 Selby Street, Nanaimo, BC, V9R 2E2. Contact: Fran. Dev. - Tel: (800) 838-4808, Fax: (250) 755-7711, Web Site: www.synergy-mana gement.com. Busines development consulting - money, marketing, planning. Help businesses grow with proven Synergy business techniques. Established: 1990.

TARGET MARKETING SERVICES

1035 McNicoll Ave, Main Floor, Scarborough, ON, M1W 3W6. Contact: Raymond Chan, President - Tel: (416) 756-9328, Fax: (416) 756-3589, E-Mail: cic@NAchinese.com, Web Site: www.NAchinese.com. Target Marketing Servies is a company to help the main stream company to expand their business in the Chinese community in North America and Asia. Established: 1993 - No. of Units: Company Owned: 1.

TORONTO FINANCIAL & BUSINESS CONSULTANTS

3410 Midland Ave., Ste. 12, Scarborough, ON, M1V 4V5. Contact: Mr. M. Hafeez, Pres. - Tel: (416) 609-1526, Fax: (416) 609-1529. Business and financial consultants specializing in financing, business analysis and turn-around, acquisitions, resolving serious operational problems, personnal motivation, etc. Established: 1982 - No. of Units: Company Owned: 1.

VR BUSINESS BROKERS (CANADA) INC.

2 Lansing Square, Ste. 101, North York, ON, M2J 4P8. Contact: Serge DeConinck, Pres. - Tel: (416) 497-1545, Fax: (416) 497-4988. Business and franchise professionals specializing in the design and development of the complete franchise program for your business. Services include: business plan development, financial analysis, franchise marketing evaluation of franchise opportunities, etc. Established: 1984.

W.H. PUNT ENTERPRISES INC.

356 King St. W., Kingston, ON, K7L 2X4. Contact: W. H. Punt, Pres. - Tel: (613) 549-4475, Fax: (613) 549-4475. Franchise consulting, system development and marketing. Business review, evaluation and interim management. Established: 1983.

WSI

5915 Airport Rd Suite 300, Mississauga, ON, L4V 1T1. Contact: Roberto Alvarado, Marketing Director - Tel: (905) 678-7588, (888) 678-7588, Fax: (905) 678-9974, E-Mail: vmjuarez@wsicorporate.com, Web Site: www.wsicorporate.com. WSI is one of the most profitable franchise opportunities in the world today, with over 700 franchises in 87 countries. No specific business experience is required. WSI offers its franchises one of the most complete and comprehensivce training & certification programs available among franchise companies today, and a dynamic on-going support program tailored to meet the needs of each new franchisee. Established: 1995 - Franchising Since: 1996- No. of Units: Company Owned: 1 - Franchised: 800 - Franchise Fee: $39,700 us - Royalty: 10% - Total Inv: $39,700-$50,000 - Financing: No.

ZAREX CONSULTING GROUP

225 East Beaver Creek Rd., Ste. 300, Richmond Hill, ON, L4B 3P4. Contact: Les Rupf or Robin Wilson, Pres./V.P. - Tel: (905) 886-0215, Fax: (905) 886-1705. Franchise consultants specializing in strategic planning for established franchisors, franchise system design, franchise selling, franchise system trouble shooting, operations manuals, franchisor financing and assisting in the purchase or sale of franchisor companies. Established: 1978.

FRANCHISE CONSULTANTS - FINANCIAL

ALLIANCE CAPITAL LEASING
2 Cullen Dr., St. Catharines, ON, L2T 3H1. Contact: Scott Hinsperger, Pres. - Tel: (905) 687-8554, (888) 895-3273, Fax: (905) 687-9050. Equipment financing for franchisors and franchisees. Established: 1987. NOT OFFERING FRANCHISES AT THIS TIME.

BANK OF MONTREAL
55 Bloor Street West 14th Floor, Toronto, ON, M4W 3N5. Contact: Ian K. Hamilton or Stephen Z. Iskierski, Senior Mgr., Mgr. Senior Accts. - Tel: (416) 927-6026, Fax: (416) 927-6369, E-Mail: lhamiltonpassport.ca, Web Site: www.bmo.com. Major Canadian chartered bank, providing a full range of domestic and international financial services, including a specialized group which deals exclusively with franchisors and their franchise networks. Established: 1817.

BUSINESS DEVELOPMENT BANK OF CANADA
5 Place Ville Marie, Suite 400, Montreal, QC, H3B 5E7. Contact: Account Manager - Tel: (877) 232-2269, Fax: (877) 329-9232. Providing consulting and financial services to small and medium sized businesses.

CANADA TRUST
55 King St. West, Toronto, ON, M5K 1A2. Contact: Frank Dinino, Senior Manager-Franchise Banking - Tel: (416) 983-4397, Fax: (416) 307-9290, Web Site: www.canadatrust.com. CANADA TRUST provides a full range of financial services through a variety of convenient service options, including financial products and services tailored to the needs of franchisors and their franchisee network.

CANADIAN IMPERIAL BANK OF COMMERCE
Commerce Court West, 3rd Floor, Toronto, ON, M5L 1A2. Contact: Charles Scrivener, General Mgr. National Franchising - Tel: (416) 980-2211, Fax: (416) 363-5347. One of Canada's largest full service banks, CIBC provides specialized financial services to franchise businesses. Franchise Services.

EQUION SECURITIES CANADA LTD.
320 Bay Street, Suite 1100, Toronto, ON, M5H 4A6. Contact: John DeGoey, Bus / Fin. Mngr. - Tel: (416) 216-6588, Fax: (416) 216-6534, E-Mail: jdegoey@equion.com, Web Site: www.equion.com. A franchise problem-solver specializing in helping mature franchisees maximize their client specific risk-adjusted, after-tax long-term investment returns. Qualified, customized service and advice. Established: 1980.

MALTON FINANCIAL SERVICES CORP.
7955 Torbran Road, Unit 5, Brampton, ON, L6T 5B9. - Tel: (905) 799-9150, Fax: (905) 799-9381, Web Site: www.maltonfinancial.com. Malton Financial is a brokerage that facilitates loans for people looking to buy a franchise. If you are inexperienced with banking protocol, we can help you.

PROGRAMMED INSURANCE BROKERS INC.
49 Industrial Drive, Elmira, ON, N3B 3B1. Contact: Bruce Burnham, President - Tel: (519) 669-1631, Fax: (519) 669-1923. As a multi-line insurance and financial service brokerage, we have teams of professionals developing financial programs, estate planning strategies, innovative employee benefits, commercial and personal lines solutions. Established: 1980.

RBC ROYAL BANK
Royal Bank
320 Front Street West, 9th Floor, Toronto, ON, M5V 3B6. Contact: Luella Stephens or Annie Wong, Manager and Senior Manager - National Franchise Market - Tel: (416) 974-8301 or (416) 974-8299, Fax: (416) 974-8320, E-Mail: luella.stephens@rbc.com, or aanie.wong@rbc.com, Web Site: www.rbcroyalbank.com/franchise. Provider of financial services meeting the unique needs of the franchising market since 1973. Wide variety of financial services provided by dedicated franchising network across the country. Download "Buying a Franchise - Doing It Right" from our web site.

SCOTIABANK
Bank of Nova Scotia
44 King St. W., Toronto, ON, M5H 1H1. Contact: R.D. (Roger) Roy, Manager, Franchising - Tel: (416) 866-4377. Established: 1832 - One of North America's premiere financial institutions with assets of more than $107 billion. Scotiabank offers a full spectrum of services in retail, commercial, corporate and investment banking including financing for franchisors and their franchisees. For more information and your free copy of our "Business Plan Writer" - Contact: R.D. (Roger) Roy, Manager Franchising - No. of Branches: 1,400.

TD BANK FINANCIAL GROUP
TD Bank and Canada Trust
55 King Street West, 20th Floor, Toronto, ON, M5K 1A2. Contact: Frank Dinino, Senior Manager - Tel: (416) 983-4397, Fax: (416) 307-9290, Web Site: www.tdbank.ca. TD BANK provides a full range of financial services through a variety of convenient service options, including financial products and services tailored to meet the need of franchisors and their franchisee network.

FRANCHISE CONSULTANTS - LEGAL

ADESSKY POULIN
999 de Maisonneuve Blvd West, Suite 1800, Montreal, QC, H3A 3L4. - Tel: (514) 288-9797, Fax: (514) 288-2697, E-Mail: lcianci@adessky poulin.com. A law firm providing legal service to businesses, institutions and individuals in the greater Montreal area, US and overseas. Specialties include corporate and commercial law, civil and commercial litigation, alternate dispute resolutionn, real estate law, tax law and estate planning, intellectual property, bankruptcy and insolvency law etc. Established: 1962.

ARTHUR J. TREBILCOCK
56 Sycamore Dr., Thornhill, ON, L3T 5V6. Contact: Arthur Trebilcock, Owner - Tel: (416) 977-0007, Fax: (416) 977-0717. Practicing general commercial law with special emphasis on franchising. Franchising Since: 1979 - Trade mark agent since: 1982.

AYLESWORTH, THOMPSON, PHELAN, O'BRIEN
P.O. Box 124, 18th Floor, 222 Bay Street, Toronto, ON, M5K 1H1. - Tel: (416) 777-0101, Fax: (416) 865-1398, Web Site: www.aylesworth.com. Legal services. Established: 1861.

BLAKE, CASSELS & GRAYDON LLP
Box 25, Commerce Court West, Toronto, ON, M5L 1A9. - Tel: (416) 869-5300, Fax: (416) 360-8877. Barrister and solicitors, patent and trade-mark agents. Established: 1857. Offices also located in Ottawa (Tel: (613) 788-2200), Calgary (Tel: (403) 260-9600), Vancouver (Tel: (604) 631-3300) and London, England (Tel: (0171) 374-2334). Other office locations in Ottawa, Calgary, Vancouver, London- England and China.

BORDEN & ELLIOT
Scotia Plaza, 40 King St., West, Ste. 4400, Toronto, ON, M5H 3Y4. Contact: Mr. John Hall, Partner - Tel: (416) 367-6643, Fax: (416) 361-7379. Providing full legal services to franchisors/franchisees including franchise agreements, real estate, litigation and intellectual property.

BULL, HOUSSER & TUPPER BARRISTERS & SOLICITORS, PATENT AND TRADE-MARK AGENTS
3000-1055 West Georgia St., P.O. Box 11130, Vancouver, BC, V6E 3R3. Contact: Grant Weaver or Andrew Jackson, Partner, Associate - Tel: (604) 687-6575, Fax: (604) 641-4949, E-Mail: gkw@bht.com. Bull, Housser & Tupper is one of Canada's oldest and largest law firms. Its franchising legal services encompass all aspects of franchising agreements, trade-mark issues, acquisitions and real estate. Established: 1890.

BURCHELL MACDOUGALL
710 Prince St. P.O. Box 1128, Truro, NS B2N 5H1. Contact: Robert B. MacLellan, Partner - Tel: (902) 895-1561, Fax: (902) 895-7709, E-Mail: truro@burmac.ns.ca. We have provided legal services for over 50 year in all major area of the law. We have many years of experience in legal

aspects of franchising having represented regional franchisors as well as a national franchise association of a major food service franchisor and individual/national/international franchisors.

CAMPNEY & MURPHY

1111 West Georgia Street, Suite 2100, Vancouver, BC, V7X 1K9. Contact: Andrew Kadler, Partner - Tel: (604) 688-8022, Web Site: www.campney.com. We are a full service law firm. Our clients include leading corporations, financial institutions, independent entrepeneurs, government organizations, trusts and individuals. We are proud of our continuing commitment to excellence in the services which we provide to our clients.

CASSELS BROCK & BLACKWELL

Scotia Plaza, Ste. 2100, 40 King St. W., Toronto, ON, M5H 3C2. Contact: Frank P. Monteleone, Partner - Tel: (416) 869-5300, Fax: (416) 360-8877, Web Site: www.casselsbrock.com. A full service law firm offering specialty advice to franchisors and franchisees in all areas of franchise law. Established: 1870.

CHIDLEY-HILL, JOHN W.

220 Duncan Mill Rd., Suite #519, Toronto, ON, M4N 2T3. Contact: John W. Chidley-Hill, Barrister and Solicitor - Tel: (416) 443-9440, Fax: (416) 443-9422. Practicing since 1982, a full service law firm representing franchisors and franchisees. Legal and Practical advice for your ongoing needs. Accessible location, convenient to highways 401, 404 and Don Valley Parkway.

COHEN, MARKUS, Q.C., LL.M.

Ste. 1010, 22 St. Clair Ave. E., Toronto, ON, M4T 2S3. Contact: Mark Cohen, Owner - Tel: (416) 413-9822, Fax: (416) 961-7011, E-mail: virtual@interlog.com, Web Site: www.thevirtuallawfirm.com. Legal franchise consultant concentrating on franchise law matters since the early 80's. Trade-mark agent since 1969.

COMPESCI & WEBBOLT

586 Browns Line, Etobicoke, ON, M8W 3V5. Contact: Mark LaRochelle, Managing Partner - Tel: (416) 253-0888, Fax: (416) 251-6368. Full service law firm: we assist both franchisors and franchisees with no-nonsense, dependable, experienced and affordable help. We are also starting to franchise our law firm to lawyers. Several other offices throughout Southern Ontario. Established: 1987 - No. of Units: Company Owned: 8 - Franchise Fee: $25,000 - Royalty: Annual (one time) - Total Inv: Varies.

CONNELL LIGHTBODY

1055 West Georgia St., Ste. 1900, Vancouver, BC, V6E 4J2. Contact: Philip G. Ferber - Tel: (604) 684-1181, Fax: (604) 641-3916. Full service law firm, including franchising and trade marks. Established: 1961.

CONWAY, KLEINMAN, KORNHAUSER & GOTLIEB

390 Bay Street, Ste. 502, Toronto, ON, M5H 2Y2. Contact: David Kornhauser, Partner - Tel: (416) 368-5400, Fax: (416) 368-5454. Professional and practical advice for both franchisors and franchisees.

DAVID N. KORNHAUSER

Conway, Kleinman, Kornhauser & Gotlieb
390 Bay St., 5th Fl., Toronto, ON, M5C 2W7. Contact: David Kornhauser, Lawyer - Tel: (416) 368-5400, Fax: (416) 368-5454. Full service law firm. Practical advice for both franchisors and franchisees.

DAVID WIZINSKY

450-800 West Pender St., Vancouver, BC, V6C 2V6. Contact: David Wizinsky, Principal - Tel: (604) 805-6114, Fax: (604) 688-3818, E-Mail: wiz@uniserve.com. Franchise legal services with emphasis on public financing of franchise concepts. Established: 1989.

DOUGLAS, SYMES & BRISSENDEN

2100-505 Burrard St., Vancouver, BC, V7X 1R4. Contact: John L. Rogers, Partner - Tel: (604) 683-6911, Fax: (604) 669-1337. Our Franchise and Distribution Law Group handles all aspects of franchising, from inception to termination. Our affiliated law firms in Calgary, Toronto, Montreal and Mexico City also have expertise in franchising. Established: 1925.

EKLIND, LIPTON & JACOBS

1 Queen St. E., Ste. 1900, Toronto, ON, M5C 2W6. Contact: S.W. Eklind, Sr. Partner - Tel: (416) 367-0871, Fax: (416) 367-9388. Attorneys representing franchisors and franchisees on an international basis.

EYRE, GEORGE C.

36 Toronto Street, Suite 850, Toronto, ON, M5C 2C5. Contact: George C. Eyre, Barrister & Solicitor & Trade Mark Agent - Tel: (416) 362-0495, Fax: (416) 962-9818. Legal and consulting services for franchisors and franchisees.

FASKEN CAMPBELL GODFREY

4200 TD Bank Tower, Toronto, ON, M5K 1N6. Contact: Fran. Dev. - Tel: (416) 868-3444, Fax: (416) 364-7813, E-Mail: mark-stinson.fasken.com, Web Site: www.fasken.com. As a law firm, we provide services for franchises. Member CFA, IFA.

FELLER DRYSDALE

1550-400 Burrard St, Vancouver, BC, V6C 3A6. Contact: Del Feller, Managing Partner - Tel: (604) 689-2626, Fax: (604) 681-5354. Franchise Lawyer. Established: 1976 - No. of Units: Company Owned: 4.

FLEMING KAMBEITZ

1500, 736-6th Ave. S.W., Calgary, AB, T2P 3T7. Contact: Larry Yuzda, Partner - Tel: (403) 266-5550, Fax: (403) 265-6910. Lawyers. Established: 1955.

FRASER MILNER CASGRAIN

30th Fl., Fifth Ave. Pl., 237-4th Avenue S.W., Calgary, AB, T2P 4X7. Contact: Gail L. Harding, Partner - Tel: (403) 268-7000, Fax: (403) 268-3100. Law firm.

GARY J. MATALON, BARRISTER & SOLICITOR

540 Cranbrooke Avenue, 1st Floor, Toronto, ON, M5M 1N8. Contact: Gary J. Matalon - Tel: (416) 789-9372, Fax: (416) 789-9373, E-Mail: gm@LegalAdviceforBusiness.com. Recognized in Lexpert as one of Canada's leading franchise lawyers. Unique practice: in-house counsel for businesses on a transaction basis, not on contract. Former associate of Osler, Hoskin & Harcourt. Served as Law Clerk to the Chief Justice of Ontario Court of Appeal (after Call to the Bar of Ontario in 1984). Part-time instructor for businesws law, negotiation and legal ethics, Ontario Bar Admission Course. CFA Affiliate Recognition Award, 1999.

GOLDMAN ROSEN BARRISTERS

121 King St., West, Ste. 1100, Toronto, ON, M5H 3T9. Contact: Scott A. Rosen, Steven H. Goldman, Partner - Tel: (416) 867-9100, (416) 867-9500, Fax: (416) 867-9091, E-Mail: shgold@goldmanrosen.com or sarosen@goldmanrosen.com, Web Site: www.goldmanrosen.com. A law firm with extensive experience in complex franchise litigation and dispute resolution. Established: 1998.

GOODMAN AND CARR

Goodman and Carr
200 King St. W., Ste. 2300, Toronto, ON, M5H 3W5. Contact: Sheldon Disenhouse, Partner - Tel: (416) 595-2300, Fax: (416) 595-0567, E-Mail: sdisenhouse@goodmancarr.com. Goodman and Carr is a full-service law firm providing a full range of professional services to the franchise industry, including structural consultations, advising with respect to document package, drafting of franchise agreements and other documentation, ligitation services and other legal elements of franchising.

GORMAN NASON LUNGSTROM

121 Germain St., P.O. Box 7286, Station A, Saint John, NB, E2L 4S6. Contact: Frank Hamm - Tel: (506) 634-8600, Fax: (506) 634-8685, E-Mail:hammf@mi.net. Full service law firm providing complete legal services for franchisors and franchisees.

GOWLING, LAFLEUR, HENDERSON LLP

1055 Dunsmuir Street, Suite 2300, Vancouver, BC, V7X 1J1. Contact: Leonard H. Polsky, Partner - Tel: (604) 683-6498, Fax: (604) 683-3558, E-Mail: leonard.polsky@gowlings.com, Web Site: www.gowlings.com. Gowling, Lafleur, Henderson LLP is a legal consulting firm with national and international offices and relationships providing a full range of professional services to the franchise industry, including structural consultations, advising with respect to document package, intellectual property protection and other legal elements of franchising. One of Canada's oldest and largest full service law firms. Established: 1877.

HORLICK LEVITT
100 Sheppard Ave East, Suite 870, Toronto, ON, M2N 6N5. Contact: Brian J. Horlick, Barrister & Solicitor - Tel: (416) 512-7440, Fax: (416) 512-8710, E-Mail: info@horlicklevitt.com, Web Site: www.horlicklevitt.com. Our practice has focused on franchise law since 1984., includes the preparation of Disclosure Documents, the negotiating and drafting of Franchise Agreements and Leases as well as related Security Agreements. We are actively involved in franchise Arbitration and Mediation and we vigorously represent of our clients in franchise Litigation.

J. JOHN O'DONOGHUE
2200 Yonge St., Ste. 1301, Toronto, ON, M4S 2C6. Contact: John O'Donoghue, Lawyer - Tel: (416) 932-4945, Fax: (416) 932-0541, E-Mail: jod@stn.net, Web Site: www.odonoghue-law.com. Legal consultant to franchisors and franchisees in connection with franchise agreements, leasing, dispute resolution, security issues, purchase and sale of franchises. Established: 1967 - Franchising Since: 1967. Twenty year member of CFA.

JAMIESON STERNS
5475 Spring Garden Rd #503, Halifax, NS, B3J 3T2. Contact: Heather Sanford, Fran Dev. - Tel: (902) 429-3123, Fax: (902) 429-3522. Law firm with a focus on advocacy. Partners focus practice in the areas of litigation, labour and employment, immigration, franchising and intellectual property. Established: 1998.

LAFLEUR BROWN, BARRISTERS & SOLICITORS
1 First Canadian Place, Ste. 920, Toronto, ON, M5X 1E1. Contact: John Papadakis - Tel: (416) 869-0994, Fax: (416) 362-5818, E-Mail: jpapadakis@tor.lafleurbrown.ca. Advising franchisors and franchisees locally and internationally. Drafting and negotiating franchise agreements, master franchise agreements, territrorial agreements and leases.

LANG MICHENER
181 Bay Street, Ste. 2500, BCE Place, P.O. 747, Toronto, ON, M5J 2T7. Contact: Robert Glass, Partner - Tel: (416) 360-8600, Fax: (416) 365-1719, E-Mail: rglass@toronto,langmichener.ca, Web Site: www.langmichener.ca. Full service law firm experienced in franchising and distribution including: structuring agreements, disclosure compliance, system acquisitions, protecting intellectual property, licensing, real estate, advertising and dispute resolution. Established: 1890's.

LAPOINTE ROSENSTEIN
1250 Rene-Levesque Blvd., W., Ste. 1400, Montreal, QC, H3B 5E9. Contact: Alex S. Konigsberg, Q.C., Partner - Tel: (514) 925-6300, Fax: (514) 925-9001, E-Mail: general@lapros.qc.ca. Lapointe Rosenstein was founded in 1966 and currently has a team of 50 lawyers. The firm prides itself on offering a full range of legal services with an entrepreneurial outlook that is fully responsive to the commercial need of its clients. The practice is broad and diverse, encompassing all of the substantive areas of law necessary for today's business leaders, including expertise in cross border and international affairs.

LARSEN & FORESTER
1015 4th St., S.w., Ste. 1230, Calgary, AB, T2R 1J4. Contact: Kim Larsen, Partner - Tel: (403) 262-8888, Fax: (403) 262-3292. General practise of law including franchising, acquisitions, financing, leasing, trade marks, corp. and commercial.

LEASEMASTER NATIONAL
3109 Bloor St. West, Toronto, ON, M8X 1E3. Contact: Fran. Dev. - Tel: (416) 207-3004, (800) 465-1174, Fax: (416) 236-3490. Leasing all makes and models of vehicles, new and used, fleet rate vehicle aquisition; low interest rates. Established: 1963.

LENOX, DEMSEY
103-343 Richmond Street, London, ON, N6A 3C2. - Tel: (519) 433-5233, Fax: (519) 433-5281. Barristers and solicitors. Established: 1993.

LEVITT, BEBER
Scotia Plaza, 40 King St. W., Ste. 3001, Toronto, ON, M5H 3Y2. Contact: Edward N. Levitt, Partner - Tel: (416) 865-6701, Fax: (416) 865-6720, E-Mail: nlevitt@levitthoffman.com, Web Site: www.levitthoffman.com. Franchise law for franchisors and franchisees. Established: 1975.

MICHAEL LUDWICK - ATTORNEY
580 Corix Suite 100, Saint-Laurent, QC, H4L 3X5. Contact: Michael Ludwick, Attorney - Tel: (514) 744-9117, Fax: (514) 744-4041, E-Mail: ludwickmichael@hotmail.com. A business-oriented, full service lawyer providing franchising, licensing and general corporate/commercial services in English and French, to one man, medium and large local, national and international clients.

MILLER THOMSON LLP
20 Queen St. W, P.O. Box 27, Ste. 2500, Toronto, ON, M5H 3S1. Contact: Paul Jones, Lawyer - Tel: (416) 595-8500, Fax: (416) 595-8695, E-Mail: toronto@millerthomson.ca, Web Site: www.millerthomson.com. Miller Thomson LLP is a national full service law firm with over 335 lawyers located in Toronto, Vancouver, Calgary, Edmonton, Markham, Waterloo Region, Whitehorse, and Washington, D.C. Our lawyers are experienced in start-up and master franchising, regulatory affairs, liquor licensing, Food And Drug Act compliance, trade-marks and trade secrets, marketing and distribution law. One of our lawyers, Paul Jones, chairs the American Bar Association Sub-Committee on Canadaian Franchising Developments. Member: CFA-Aff., IFA, ISOF, ABA-Forum on Franchising, IBA Committee on International Franchising, Intellectual Property Institute X, and INTA. In Business Since: 1957. Contacts: Toronto: Paul Jones - Tel: (416) 595-2639; Vancouver: Gord Plottel - Tel: (604) 643-1245; Calgary: Michael Hayduk - (403) 298-2410; Edmonton: Bruce Geiger - (780) 429-9774; Waterloo Region: John Griggs - (519) 579-3660.

MORRIS ROSE LEDGETT
161 Bay Street, Suite 2600, Canada Trust Tower, BCE Place, Toronto, ON, M5J 2S1. - Tel: (416) 981-9400, Fax: (416) 863-9500. Barristers and solicitors. Established: 1968.

MORRISON BROWN SOSNOVITCH
P.O. Box 28 1 Toronto Street, Suite 910, Toronto, ON, M5C 2V6. Contact: Kevin Gallagher - Tel: (416) 368-0600, Fax: (416) 368-6068, E-Mail: kgallagher@businesslawyers.com. Corporate and commercial law firm with extensive experience acting on behalf of franchisors and franchisees. Our clients include some of Canada's largest franchisors. Kevin Gallagher of our firm is a member of the Legal and Legislative Affairs Committee of the Canadian Franchise Association.

NESKER, JERRY M.
5255 Yonge Street, Ste. 703, Toronto, ON, M2N 6P4. Contact: Jerry M. Nesker, Barrister & Solicitor - Tel: (416) 221- 5521, Fax: (416) 226-2242-8306, E-Mail: jmnesker@msn.com. Barrister, Solicitor and trademark agent franchise associate. Established: 1974.

OGILVY RENAULT
1981 McGill College Ave., Ste. 1100, Montreal, QC, H3A 3C1. Contact: Leanne Souquet, Associate - Tel: (514) 847-4747, Fax: (514) 286-5474, E-Mail: info@ogilvyrenault.com, Web Site: www.ogilvy renault.com. The firm, which has offices in Montreal, Ottawa, Quebec, Toronto and London (England), provides legal services in both official languages, in all areas of interest to those involved in franchising including corporate organization, contracts, copyright and trade-marks, real estate, taxation, employment, government assistance, public offerings and disclosure documentation. Established: 1879.

OSLER, HOSKIN & HARCOURT
P.O. Box 50, 1 First Canadian Place, Toronto, ON, M5X 1B8. Contact: Frank Zaid, Senior Partner - Tel: (416) 362-2111, Fax: (416) 862-6666. Law Firm. Franchise Law Group specializes in advising CDN/US and

international franchisors, as well as franchise investors and franchise associations in all aspects of franchise law. Members of Canadian Franchise Assoc., International Franchise Assoc., International Bar Assoc. (Franchise Committee) and American Bar Assoc. Franchise Forum. General Counsel to Canadian Franchise Association.

PARLEE MCLAWS
1500 Manulife Place , 10180-101 St., Edmonton, AB, T5J 4K1. Contact: Michael B. Witt, Lawyer - Tel: (780) 423-8500, Fax: (780) 423-2870. Parlee McLaws provides legal services to both franchisors and franchisees, including advice regarding compliance with Alberta's unique franchise legislation. We also have expertise in areas relating to franchising including leasing, trademarks and the resolution of franchise disputes. Established: 1883.

PITBLADO
2500-360 Main St., Winnipeg, MB, R3C 4H6. Contact: Andrew D.M. Ogaranko, Q.C., Partner - Tel: (204) 956-0560, Fax: (204) 957-0227, E-Mail: ogaranko@pba-law.com. Law firm. Established: 1882.

POULIOT MERCURE, G.P.
CIBC Tower, 1155 West Rene Levesque Blvd., 31st Flr., Montreal, QC, H3B 3S6. Contact: Jean H. Gagnon, Lawyer/Partner - Tel: (514) 875-5210, Fax: (514) 875-4308, E-Mail: jhgagnon@pouliotmercure.com, Web Site: www.pouliotmercure.com. A major Canadian law firm practicing mainly in the field of commercial and civil law comprising a group of lawyers which specialized itself in the fields of franchising (both domestic and international) and intellectual property matters. Affiliated with Cassels Brock & Blackwell (Toronto), Douglas Symes & Brissenden (Vancouver), and Noriegay Escobedo (Mexico). Established: 1952.

RICHARDS & RICHARDS
10325 150th St., Surrey, BC, V3R 4B1. Contact: Jeffrey Andrews, George Richards, Lawyer - Tel: (604) 588-6844, Fax: (604) 588-8800. Full service law firm with expertise in franchising. Established: 1967.

SCARLETT MANSON ANGUS
1200-777 Hornby St., Vancouver, BC, V6Z 1S4. Contact: Douglas W. Scarlett, Partner (Lawyer) - Tel: (604) 684-4777, Fax: (604) 684-7773. Law firm. Established: 1992.

SHIBLEY RIGHTON LLP
250 University Ave #700, Toronto, ON, M5H 3E5. Contact: Jonathan H. Flanders, Lawyer, Mediator - Tel: (416) 214-5200, Fax: (416) 214-5400, E-Mail: jonathan.flanders@shibleyrighton.com. Counsel on franchising. Providing mediation, arbitration, business law and litigation services in all aspects of franchising. Established: 1964.

SHIELDS HARNEY
1285 West Pender Street 9th Floor, Vancouver, BC, V6E 4B1. Contact: Gregory N. Harney - Tel: (604) 682-7770, Fax: (604) 682-1822, E-Mail: gharney@implaw.com, Web Site: www.shieldsharney.com. Shields Harney provides strategic advice to avoid and resolve disputes in franchise relationships. Office also located at 401-915 Fort Street, Victoria, BC, V8R 3N1, (250) 405-7616, Fax: (250) 405-7619, E-Mail: gnhlawcorp@pacificcoast.net.

SISKINDS FRANCHISE LAW GROUP
680 Waterloo Street, London, ON, N6A 3V8. Contact: Peter Macrae Dillon - Tel: (519) 672-2121, (800) 816-9596, Fax: (519) 672-6065, E-Mail: peter.dillon@siskind.com, Web Site: www.franchiselaw.ca. Specializing in advising start-up franchisors in the conversion and early stages of franchising, and in franchise default and termination situations. Author of the Annotated Franchise Act of Ontario and Alberta. Our group represents mature Canadian and American franchise systems operating internationally. Established: 1883.

SOTOS, ASSOCIATES BARRISTERS AND SOLICITORS
Ste. 1250, 180 Dundas St. W., Toronto, ON, M5G 1Z8. Contact: John Sotos, Partner, Solicitor - Tel: (416) 977-0007, Fax: (416) 977-0717. Law Firm. Sotos Associate's franchise lawyers provide a full range of services to franchisees and franchisors with a focus on structuring co-operative relationships. Our range of services includes: development of new franchise systems to ensure success; registration of trademarks; master and conversion franchising; alternate dispute resolution and

litigation including injunctions; all aspects of leasing and development agreements; protection of intellectual property rights; franchise acquisitions/sales of new/existing franchises; taxation matters and dispute avoidance and restructuring. Executive member of the Canadian Bar Association, Business Law Section, American Bar Association, Franchise Law Forum, Canadian Franchise Association, International Franchise Association. Established: 1980.

STEINBERG MORTON FRYMER
5255 Yonge Street, Suite 1100, North York, ON, M2N 6P4. Contact: Darryl Singer, Fran Law Group - Tel: (416) 225-2777, Fax: (416) 225-7112. Providing legal services and business consulting to franchisees and franchisors.

STEPHEN LEVINSON
390 Bay Street, Suite 500, Toronto, ON, M5H 2Y2. Contact: Fran. Dev. - Tel: (416) 363-6166, Fax: (416) 362-1404, E-Mail: levinson @interlog.com, Web Site: www.interlog.com/~levinson. Providing comprehensive cost effective commercial legal services and practical advice on franchise law including preparation of custom tailored franchise agreements, leases and dispute resolution. membership: Law Society of Upper Canada, Canadian Franchise Association. Established: 1985.

STEVEN F. TROSTER
40 Sheppard Ave., West, Ste. 710, Toronto, ON, M2N 6K9. Contact: Steven Troster - Tel: (416) 250-6401, Fax: (416) 250-6403. I can provide legal services in the French language. Established: 1973 - Franchising Law Since: 1986.

TEPLITSKY, COLSON
70 Bond Street, Suite 200, Toronto, ON, M5B 1X3. Contact: Ivan N. Roher - Tel: (416) 365-9320, Fax: (416) 365-0695. A boutique litigation firm practicing virtually all forms of advocacy with particular emphasis on commercial litigation. The firm has developed a significant practice in franchise related issues. Established: 1983.

TORKIN, MANES, COHEN & ARBUS
151 Yonge St., Ste. 1500, Toronto, ON, M5C 2W7. Contact: Jeffrey Cohen, Partner - Tel: (416) 863-1188, Fax: (416) 863-0305, Web Site: www.torkinmanes.com. Full service law firm with expertise in corporate and litigation matters relating to franchising, licensing and distribution arrangements. Established: 1976.

TUOVI • LARMOUR
934 The East Mall, Toronto, ON, M9B 6J9. Contact: Peter E. Tuovi, Partner - Tel: (416) 258-8422, Fax: (416) 352-5960. Full service law firm. Trade mark agents representing franchisors and franchisees in all legal aspects odf their business. Will assist franchisors and franchisees with preparing financing packages and negotiating financing.

WALTON ADVOCATES
820 Mount Pleasant Rd., Toronto, ON, M4P 2L2. Contact: Fran. Dev. - Tel: (416) 489-3171, Fax: (416) 489-9973. Barristers and solicitors. Established: 1993.

WEIR & FOULDS

130 King Street West, Suite 1600, Toronto, ON, M5X 1J5. Contact: John Wilkinson, Partner - Tel: (416) 947-5010, Fax: (416) 365-1876, E-Mail: wilkinsj@weirfoulds.com. We are a full-service law firm which includes among its clients both franchisees and franchisors in a wide variety of businesses.

WITTEN LLP

Ste. 2500 10303 Jasper Ave., Edmonton, AB, T5J 3N6. Contact: Daniel Zalmanowitz, Partner - Tel: (780) 428-0501, Fax: (780) 429-2559, Web Site: www.wittenlaw.com. Full service Alberta law firm, Franchise and Master Franchise and related agreements. Alberta Franchise Act compliance, franchise litigation, employment, law, trademark. Established: 1925.

FURNITURE REFINISHING AND REPAIR

FURNITURE MEDIC OF CANADA
ServiceMaster of Canada

5462 Timberlea Blvd, Mississauga, ON, L4W 2T7. Contact: Market Expansion Manager - Tel: (905) 670-0000, (800) 263-5928, Fax: (905) 670-0077, Web Site: www.servicemaster.com. Furniture Medic is a furniture restoration and repair service franchise with an unlimited market. Manufacturers, hotels, restaurants, office buildings, furniture retailers, as well as the residential market and many others have a need for furniture restoration. Furniture Medic is commited to research and development and uses the latest technological advancements to repair furniture on site at a cost that is much less than refinishing or replacement. Established: 1992 - Franchising Since: 1993 - No. of Units: Franchised: 40 - Franchise Fee: $15,400 - Royalty: 7%+1% national adv - Total Inv: $19,900-$15,400+$4,500 equipment - Financing: Yes.

STRIPPERS!, FURNITURE REFINISHING, THE
MBR Creations Inc.

427 Gage Ave., Unit 2, Kitchener, ON, N2M 5E1. Contact: Mktg. Dir. - Tel: (519) 836-8310, Fax: (519) 579-6711, E-Mail: maggie@the-strippers.com, Web Site: www.the-strippers.com. High quality furniture refinishing, touch-up and repair service using exclusive stripping process with complete training of 4 weeks at head office, and continuous support. Established: 1982 - Franchising Since: 1991 - No. of Units: Company Owned: 1 - Franchised: 7 - Franchise Fee: $39,500 - Royalty: None.

GREETING SERVICES

CREATIVE CARDS

594 Thompson Drive, Winnipeg, MB, R1S 2T4. - Tel: (204) 235-0113. Greeting cards for all occasions. Established: 1996 - No. of Units: Franchised: 8 - Total Inv: $12,500.

NORTHERN CARD PUBLISHING COMPANY
Northern Card Publishing Company Ltd.

5694 Ambler Dr., Mississauga, ON, L4W 2K9. Contact: Hugh Clarkson, Pres. - Tel: (905) 625-4944, Fax: (905) 625-5995. A greeting card publisher and distributor, distributing their own cards in the Toronto area and with protected territories available across Canada for wholesalers/distributors. Established: 1992 - Franchising Since: 1992 - No. of Units: Company Owned: 7 - Franchised: 26 - Total Inv: $20,000-$100,000 dependent on territory size - Financing: Yes.

PARTY HUT
922928 Ontario Inc.

6625 Kitimat Rd., Unit 49, Mississauga, ON, L5N 6J1. Contact: Luigi Chiarella, Pres. - Tel: (905) 542-1555, Fax: (905) 542-7314. Party Hut is the source for unique, outrageous and humourous gifts. Whether it's a birthday, anniversary or office party, Party Hut stocks t-shirts, hats, mugs, games, jokes and greeting cards that reflect the occasion. Plus there's a wide assortment of "over the hill" gags and age-related merchandise that's sure to put a smile on everyone's face. Established: 1987 - Franchising Since: 1990 - Franchised: 7 - Franchise Fee: $35,000 - Royalty: 6%, 2% adv. - Total Inv: $100,000-$125,000 - Financing: No.

TEDDY BEAR GRAM CORPORATION

2880 Sheffield Rd., #3, Ottawa, ON, K1B 1A4. Contact: Noel Perera, President - Tel: (613) 745-2327, Fax: (613) 747-0520. Designer teddy bears sent worldwide with personalized message. Hand delivered to any where in this world. Established: 1989 - Franchising Since: 1991 - No. of Units: Company Owned: 2 - Franchised: 1000+ - Franchise Fee: $1,000 - Royalty: None - Financing: No.

HAIRSTYLING & COSMETICS

AEVA'S BEAUTY SPA CORP.

7701 Lundy's Lane, Ste. 200, Niagara Falls, ON, L2H 1H3. Contact: Erika A. Szijarto, President - Tel: (905) 356-4242, Fax: (905) 356-9373. Balneotherapy - eyelash tinting - facials - manicures - pedicures - geland acrylic nails - make-up - reflexology - tanning and waxing. Established: 1997 - Franchising Since: 1997 - No. of Units: Company Owned: 1 - Franchised: Taking applications - Franchise Fee: $5,000 - Royalty: 5% monthly gross in the first year plus 3% advertising and promotion - Total Inv: Basic $17,000, $5,000 franchise fee plus $3,000 stock + $9,000 equipment, Advanced $27,000, $5,000 franchise fee plus $6,000 stock plus $16,000 equipment - Financing: Can Assist.

BEANERS FUN CUTS FOR KIDS
Beaners Enterprises

#1200, 407 2nd Street SW, Calgary, AB, T2P 2Y3. Contact: Saundra Sharpio, President - Tel: (403) 261-8600, Fax: (403) 264-2197. Children's hair salon. Established: 1987 - Franchising Since: 1996 - No. of Units: Franchised: 7 - Franchise Fee: $20,000 - Royalty: 6%, 3% advertising - Total Inv: $55,00 ($20,000 fees, inventory $5,000, interior $30,000) - Financing: No.

BEAUTY SUPPLY OUTLET, THE
Tree-O Marketing

30 West Beaver Creek Rd #3, Richmond Hill, ON, L4B 3K1. Contact: Monty Koffman, Owner - Tel: (905) 731-7622, Fax: (905) 731-7244. Retailer of professional hair care products and salon. Established: 1992 - Franchising Since: 1995 - No. of Units: Company Owned: 1 - Franchised: 11 - Franchise Fee: $25,000 - Royalty: 5% plus 2% advertising - Total Inv: $25,000 franchise fee/ $25,000 fixtures plus inventory - Financing: No.

CALL N' CUT
Call N' Cut Inc.

1106 Wilson Ave., P.O. Box 66129, North York, ON, M3M 1G7. Contact: Joseph Pampena, Exec. Pres. - Tel: (416) 630-5001, (800) 866-2887, Fax: (416) 638-2442. In-home hairdressing services. Full turn key operation, training, support and all marketing systems included. Established: 1980 - Franchising Since: 1989 - No. of Units: Company Owned: 50 - Franchised: 4 - Franchise Fee: $25,000.

CARYL BAKER VISAGE SALONS
Visage Cosmetics Ltd.

31 Wingold Ave, Toronto, ON, M6B 1P8. Contact: Alan Baker, V.P. - Tel: (416) 789-7141, Fax: (416) 789-2594, Web Site: www.carylbaker visage.com. Franchisee salons across Canada that retail our own professional line of over 300 mskin care and cosmetics. We also provided facial treatment services. Established: 1969 - Franchising Since: 1974 - No. of Units: Franchised: 30 - Franchise Fee: $20,000 - Total Inv: $150,000-$175,000 - Financing: No.

CHATTERS SALON & REFILL CENTER
Chatters Canada Limited

#1-7429-49th Ave, Red Deer, AB, T4P 1N2. Contact: Jason Volk, Dir. of Operations - Tel: (403)342-5055, (888) 944-5055, Fax: (403) 347-7759, E-Mail: jasonv@city.red-deer.ab.ca, Web Site: www.chatters salons.com. Hair salons, retail and refill centers. Established: 1988 - Franchising Since: 1992 - No. of Units: Company Owned: 3 - Franchised: 54 - Franchise Fee: $15,000-$30,000 - Royalty: 4%, 2% adv - Total Inv: $130,000 ($1000,000 store, $30,000 inventory) - Financing: Yes, Royal Bank.

FACES

Faceco Inc.

30 Machintosh Blvd, Unit 6, Vaughan, ON, L4K 4P1. - Tel: (905) 760-0110, Fax: (905) 760-0901. Retailing top quality private label cosmetics at affordable prices. Established: 1983 - Franchising Since: 1983 - No. of Units: Company Owned: 1 - Franchised: 38 - Franchise Fee: $10,000 - Royalty: 6% - Total Inv: Kiosk $52,500 - Financing: At 60% of the total cost loaned by a financial institution.

FACES COSMETICS

Faces Inc

3425 Laird Rd #5, Mississauga, ON, L5L 5R8. - Tel: (905) 569-8989, Fax: (905) 569-8998, E-Mail: stevensont@faces-cosmetics.com, Web Site: www.faces-cosmetics.com. In mall boutique featuring cosmetics in an atmosphere of ease and accessibility. Our people help you look your best. Visit our playground of colour. Established: 1974 - Franchising Since: 1982 - No. of Units: Company Owned: 14 - Franchised: 69 - Franchise Fee: $16,250 - Royalty: 5% of gross sales - Total Inv: Franchise fee $16,250; training $3,250; inventory $5,000-$8,000; kiosk $36,500-$46,500; pos $8,000 - Financing: Yes., fixtures through alliance capital leasing.

FANTASTIC SAM

Fantastic Sams - Quebec

15710 Boul. Pierrefonds, Pierrefonds, QC, H9H 3P6. Contact: Michel B. Dulone, V.P. - Tel: (514) 620-2557. Family hair care services. Coiffure pour la famille. Established: 1980 in U.S. - Franchising Since: 1987 in Quebec - No. of Units: Company Owned: 1 - Franchised: 2 - Franchise Fee: $25,000 - Royalty: $150 per week - Total Inv: $75,000-$85,000 - Financing: Support provided to obtain financing. Not offering franchises at the present time.

FIRST CHOICE HAIRCUTTERS

First Choice Haircutters, Ltd.

6465 Millcreek Dr., Ste. 210, Mississauga, ON, L5N 5R6. Contact: Martha Lawrence, Franchise Sales Rep - Tel: (905) 821-8555, Fax: (905) 567-7000, E-Mail: martha@firstchoice.com, Web Site: www.firstchoice.com. We're a cutting-edge chain of price-value family haircare salons with over 300 locations across Canada and the states. Since 1980, we've built a strong base of customer loyalty. You don't have to have any hair experience or become a stylist to own a single unit, multiple salons or even a territory. We will provide you with all the tools and training you'll need to effectively manage your business. At First Choice Haircutters our philosophy is simple: your success is our success. Established: 1980 - Franchising Since: 1982 - No. of Units: Company Owned: 124 - Franchised: 177 - Franchise Fee: $10,000-$25,000 - Royalty: 5%-7% - Total Inv: $70,000-$80,000 - Financing: Third party.

FRAGRANCE

La Parfumerie Duquin Ltd.

9610 F. Ignace, Brossard, QC, J4Y 2R4. Contact: Alain Quintal, Pres. - Tel: (514) 444-1806. Perfumes and cosmetics stores. Established: 1972 - Franchising Since: 1986 - No. of Units: Company Owned: 3 - Franchised: 17 - Franchise Fee: $15,000 - Royalty: 3%, 1.5% adv. - Total Inv: $150,000 - Financing: Yes.

HEAD SHOPPE, GOLDEN CLIPPER, THE

Box 8, 1465 Brenton St., Halifax, NS, B3J 3T3. Contact: Peter Mahoney, Pres. & Owner - Tel: (902) 455-1504, Fax: (902) 425-1947. Hairstyling salons. Established: 1977 - No. of Units: 15 Head Shoppes, 2 Golden Clippers.

JOSEPH'S HAIR SALONS (JOSEPH COIFFURES)

18 Hollywood Ave., Ste. 303, North York, ON, M2N 6P5. Contact: Franc. Dir. - Tel: (416) 733-3525. Hairstyling salons. Established: 1955 - No. of Units: Company Owned: 11 - Franchised: 5.

LASER STOP INC

4800 Leslie Street Suite 206, Toronto, ON, M2J 2K9. - Tel: (416) 756-3335, Fax: (416) 756-3345, E-Mail: info@laserstop.com, Web Site: www.laserstop.com. Laser hair removalk and skin rejuvenation. Established: 1999 - Franchising Since: 2003 - No. of Units: Company Owned: 1 - Franchise Fee: $25,000.

NAIL QUEEN / NAIL ACADEMY, INC

Nail Queen Ltd.

199 Advance Blvd., Unit #7, Brampton, ON, L6T 4N2. Contact: Hala Anderson, President - Tel: (905) 799-3344, (800) 235-6007, Fax: (905) 799-3044, E-Mail: intnail@on.aibn.com, Web Site: www.nailqueen.net. Complete nail care salon and retail. Established: 1985 - Franchising Since: 1994 - No. of Units: Company Owned: 5 - Franchised: 4 - Franchise Fee: $5,000 - Royalty: 3% royalty 2% advertising - Total Inv: $55,000 - Financing: Yes.

NAILS 'N LASHES STUDIOS

P.O. Box 254, Brechin, ON, L0K 1B0. Contact: Irving Fine, Pres. - Tel: (705) 484-9994, Fax: (705) 484-9994. Application of acrylic fingernails. Established: 1970 - Franchising Since: 1972 - No. of Units: Franchised: 16 - Franchise Fee: $5,000-$15,000 - Total Inv: $35,000-$40,000 - Financing: Subject to credit.

PARFUMERIES DANS UN JARDIN

Parfumeries Dans Un Jardin Canada Inc.

1351-B Ampere Street, Boucherville, QC, J4B 5Z5 - Tel: (450) 449-2121, Fax: (450) 641-1322. Retail sales of distinctive bath, skin care products and accessories for the whole family. Established: 1986 - Franchising Since: 1988 - No. of Units: Franchised: 65 - Franchise Fee: $30,000 - Total Inv: $185,000.

PERFUMES ETC. LTD.

871 Islington Ave., Unit #2, Toronto, ON, M8Z 4N9. Contact: Sanjay Bawa, President - Tel: (416) 253-7717, Fax: (416) 253-7757, (888) 253-7757, Web Site: www.perfums.com. Retail of brand name fragrances and perfumes at discount prices. Established: 1992 - Franchising Since: 1995 - No. of Units: Company Owned: 3 - Franchised: 4 - Franchise Fee: $1000 - Royalty: $150-$300 per month - Total Inv: $7,000-$50,000 - Financing: Yes.

QUICK STOP HAIR SHOP

Chatters Canada Ltd.

153 Dowler Street, Red Deer, AB, T4R 2M3. Contact: Jason Volk, Director - Tel: (403) 341-6609, Fax: (403) 347-7759. Hair and retail salon. Established: 1996 - Franchising Since: 1996 - No. of Units: Company Owned: 1 - Franchised: 8 - Franchise Fee: $15,000 - Royalty: 6% - Total Inv: $60,000-$45,000 store, $15,000 inventory.

SCISSORS SALON

349 Melon Street, Winnipeg, MB, R2L 4B2. Contact: Fran. Dev. - Tel: (204) 235-0091. Full service hair salon. One week training and ongoing support. Locations available in Western Canada. Established: 1993 - Franchised: 12 - Total Inv: $47,000.

THE BODY SHOP

469A King Street West, Toronto, ON, M5V 3M4. Contact: Fran. Dev. - Tel: (800) 387-4592, Web Site: www.TheBodyShop.com. Seller of retail products for the body, face and hair, including cosmetics. Complete nine weeks training and ongoing support provided. Established: 1980 - No. of Units: Franchised: 122 - Total Inv: $300,000.

HEALTH AIDS AND SERVICES

911 EMERGENCY LOCATOR ALERT SYSTEMS

#16, 24 Viceroy Rd, Concord, ON, L4K 2L9. Contact: Chuck Gilder, General Manager - Tel: (905) 738-8688, (888) 213-6888, Fax: (905) 738-9543. Exclusive territories to market and install electronics telephone interfaces, which automatically activates strobe light when householder dials 911. Established: 1997 - Franchising Since: 1997 - No. of Units: Company Owned: 1 - Franchised: 1 - Franchise Fee: $6,000 - Royalty: None - Total Inv: $8,000 - Financing: No.

A1 NUTRITION

300-1120 Grant Ave., Winnipeg, MB, R3M 2A6. Contact: Valerie Wylychenko - Tel: (204) 475-7255, (800) 341-7719, Fax: (204) 284-9212, E-Mail: a1nutrit@sprint.ca. Full service health food store offering a wide range of health foods, supplements, herbs, cosmetics and sports nutrition. Established: 1990 - Franchising Since: 1997 - No. of Units: Company Owned: 1 - Franchised: 5 - Franchise Fee: $20,000 - Royalty: 5% - Total Inv: $100,000-$149,000.

ALTERNATIVE CHOICES
429 St. Clair Street, Chatham, ON, N7L 3K4. Contact: Rob Clarke, President - Tel: (579) 351-1246, (888) 877-6861, Fax: (579) 436-2449, Web Site: www.alternativechoices.on.ca. We specialize in customer service and product knowledge for todays alternative needs. Each location provides selections in vitamins, herbs, body and skin care, sports nutrition, specialty foods and educational books. Full training and support provided. Established: 1997 - No. of Units: Company Owned: 1 - Franchised: 5 - Franchise Fee: $25,000 - Total Inv: $11,500.

BODY NUTRITION FRANCHISE CORP
2100 Bloor St. West,. Suite# 6193, Toronto, ON, M6S 5A5. Contact: Franchise Department - Tel: (416) 256-1429, (877) BODY NUT, E-Mail: mlambe@bodynutrition.com. Web Site: www.bodynutrition.com. Retail health food and sports nutrition. Established: 1994 - No. of Units: Company Owned: 1 - Franchised: 7 - Franchise Fee: $45,000 (Eastern Canada), $55,000 (Western Canada) - Total Inv: $1,000,000.

CENTRE DE SANTE MINCEUR / HEALTH AND SLIM CENTER
Idem
1000 Victoria, Office 37, St-Lambert, QC, J4R 2T1. Contact: V.P. Business Development - Tel: (450) 923-5559, Fax: (450) 923-5545. The Health and Slim Center is a health concept that makes a rapid and safe weight loss. Established: 1994 - Franchising Since: 1995 - No. of Units: Company Owned: 8 - Franchised: 52 - Franchise Fee: Between $25,000 & $40,000 - Royalty: None - Total Inv: $100,000 - Financing: Small business loan.

DENTRIX DENTAL CARE
Ste. 300, 222 - 58th Ave., S.W., Calgary, AB, T2H 2S2. Contact: Dr. Roger Watson, Pres. - Tel: (403) 255-6211, Fax: (403) 253-5014. Dental centres. Established: 1984 - No. of Units: 6.

ENORMO CLINIC
Energy Medicine Developments (N.A.) Inc.
104-630 Columbia St., New Westminster, BC, V3M 1A5. Contact: Bob Fletcher, V.P. - Tel: (604) 522-8618, Fax: (604) 522-9896, Web Site: www.intergate.bc.ca. Non invasive relief of migraine pain and multiple sclerosis symptoms. Electro magnetic medical device which is used to suppress pain. Established: 1994 - No. of Units: Company Owned: 2 - Franchise Fee: $25,000 - Royalty: 10% of sales, incl. adv. - Total Inv: $50,000-$75,000 - Financing: Major Canadian cities. Would need to be an R.N. or have medical background.

FRESH AIR
2921 Crocus Drive, Winnipeg, MB, R3K 1T3. Contact: Fran. Dev. - Tel: (204) 235-0010. Air purification systems - 1 week training at corporate headquarters. Full support provided. Established: 1996 - No. of Units: Franchised: 6 - Total Inv: $15,000 min. cash required.

GOOD HEALTH MART
847 Magnolia Ave, Newmarket, ON, L3Y 5H5. Contact: Murray Mcmahon, CEO - Tel: (905) 895-3630, Fax: (905) 895-0656, E-Mail: GHM@DCSnet.com, Web Site: www.goodhealthmart.com. Natural pharmacy/health food store. Buying group membership. Established: 1993 - Franchising Since: 1996 - No. of Units: Company Owned: 3 - Franchised: 7 - Royalty: Based on purchases not sales - Total Inv: Turnkey store $49,000, inventory $50,000 + - Financing: Will assist in preparing documents and making contacts.

GREAT EARTH VITAMIN STORES
1500 Fisher Street, Unit 116, North Bay, ON, P1B 2H3. Contact: Fran. Dev. - Tel: (705) 472-7344, (800) 352-6622, Fax: (705) 472-8635, Web Site: .www.greatearthcanada.com. Vitamins and nutritional supplement retailer offering exclusively high quality, high margin line of Great Earth products. Comprehensive training at our Vitamin University - in house creative marketing support. Full 3 week training course in California and strong marketing support ongoing. Established: 1972 - No. of Units: Franchised: 146 - Total Inv: $50,000.

ISLAND HEARING SERVICES
645 Fort Street, Suite 309, Victoria, BC, V8W 1G2. Contact: Mark Hambley, Pres/CEO. - Tel: (800) 563-4327, Fax: (250) 383-6664, Web Site: www.ihs.ca. Canada's largest integrated company dedicated to providing audiological and aural rehabilitative services including the testing of hearing and prescription fitting and the repair of hearing instruments and related assistive devices. Training and ongoing support provided. Established: 1978 - No. of Units: Company Owned: 15 - Franchised: 4 - Franchise Fee: $15,000 - Total Inv: Varies.

JEAN COUTU GROUP
530 Beriault, Longueuil, P.Q, J4G 1S8. Contact: Mr. Yvon Bechard, Sr. Exec. V.P. - Tel: (450) 646-9760, Fax: (450) 646-5649. Drug stores. Established: 1969 - No. of Units: 146.

KLEEN AIR SYSTEMS
190 Industrial Ave. P.O. Box 402, Truro, NS, B2N 6V4. Contact: Fran Dev. - Tel: (902) 893-7666, (800) 565-7264, Fax: (902) 893-4586, E-Mail: kleenair@ns.sympatico.ca, Web Site: www.EasternKleenAir.com. Residential and commercial air purification process. Full training and support provided. Established: 1988 -No. of Units: Franchised: 6 - Total Inv: $40,000.

MEDICHAIR LTD.
1410-28 Street N.E., Calgary, AB, T2A 7W6. Contact: Harry Mykolaishyn, CEO - Tel: (403) 204-1419, (800) 667-0087, Fax: (403) 204-1409, Web Site: www.medichair.com. Retailer of durable and home medical equipment such as wheelchairs, scooters, stairlifts, lift and recline chairs, bath lifts, bathroom safety equipment, and aids to daily living. Established:1985 - Franchising Since: 1988 - No. of Units: Company Owned: 2 - Franchised: 43 - Franchise Fee: $15,000-$25,000 - Royalty: 5% - Total Inv: $125,000-$200,000 - Financing: No.

MY SPECIAL NANNY & PERSONNEL INC.
186 Morrison Rd, East Oakville, ON, L6J 4J3. Contact: Executive Director - Tel: (905) 845-3878, Fax: (905) 845-5843. We are a service industry franchise in licensed home daycare, licensed nanny programs, geriatric homecare and helping hands. Established: 1993 - Franchising Since: 1998 - No. of Units: Company Owned: 2 - Franchised: 4 - Franchise Fee: Depending on territory $9,500.00-$22,000.00 - Royalty: 7% - Total Inv: $9,000.00-$22,000.00 - Financing: Yes.

NATIONAL HEALTH STORES
111 heritage Road, Suite 103, Chatham, ON, N7M 5W7. Contact: Stephan McElrany/Roy Cleves, CEO/Operations Manager - Tel: (519) 358-1119, Fax: (519) 358-7530, Web Site: www.nhs.on.ca. Retail/clinical health store. Each store offers at least four practitioners and sells water, vitamins, body building, weight loss, candles and grocery. Established: 1999 - No. of Units: Franchised: 12 - Total Inv: $150,000.

NEWAYS INC. INDEP CONSULTANTS
2279 Stafford Ave, Port Coquitlam, BC, V3C 4X5. Contact: Tracey Depaoli / Loris Depaoli, CEO - Tel: (604)464-7902, Fax: (604) 464-7450, Web Site: www.biofactsors.com/ths/wealth. Advanced cutting edge formulations, premiere anti-aging/life extension Co. only company endorsed by the cancer prevention coalition for products free of cancer - causing agents, over 300 products ranging from anti aging oral spray, noni. aromatherapy, cosmetics. athletic sport line, toiletries, arthritis/joint aid, tanning, weightloss, anti-cellulite, toning, nutritionals, etc. Established: 1986 - Franchising: 1986 - Franchise Fee: N/A - Royalty: 2 pay centers (1st pays 5%-16%, 2nd pays 5%-25%0 + $1,000 car bonus) - Total Inv: $150-$500 per month.

NEWFOUND HEALTH
11420A 170th Street, Edmonton, AB, T5S 1L7. Contact: Fran. Dev. - Tel: (877) 682-6395, Fax: (780) 452-9619. A dynamic growing retail health food franchise. Leaders in providing customer service - franchise training - 3 weeks an corporate office and on-site. Established: 1990 - No. of Units: Franchised: 13 - Total Inv: $120,000-$130,000.

SANGSTER'S HEALTH CENTRES
2218 Hanselman Ave, Saskatoon, SK, S7l6A4. Contact: Wendy Sangster, Fran. Dir. - Tel: (306) 653-4481, Fax: (306) 653-4688, E-Mail: franchise@sangsters.com, Web Site: www.sangsters.com/franchise.shtml. Retail health stores located mostly in malls. We sell private label vitamins, minerals, herbs, natural cosmetics and sports nutrition. Conversions available. Established: 1971 - Franchising Since: 1978 - No. of Units: Company Owned: 3 - Franchised: 44 - Franchise Fee: $25,000 - Royalty: 5% - Total Inv: $125,000-$160,000 - Financing: Will assist.

SENIOR WATCH INC.
33 Hanover St, Saint John, NB, E2L 3G1. Contact: Jean E. Porter, President & CEO - Tel: (506) 634-8906, (800) 561-2463, Fax: (506) 633-2992, E-Mail: senior@nbnet.nb.ca, Web Site: www.senior watch.com. Home care services dedicated exclusively to senior care, care management, family teaching, training curriculum for families and workers. Established: 1987 - Franchising Since: 1996 - No. of Units: Company Owned: 2 - Franchised: 2 - Franchise Fee: $35,000 - Royalty: 10% on home care revenues includes corporate advertising - Total Inv: $50,000 guarantee for start up - Financing: No.

SILVER CROSS
Privax International Ltd.
1195 North Service Rd., West, Unit B5, Oakville, ON, L6M 2W2. Contact: Robert Harvey, Pres. - Tel: (416) 755-1164, (905) 847-5837, Fax: (905) 847-5837, Web Site: www.silvercross.com. Recycled and new health care equipment. Established: 1993 - Franchising Since: 1995 - No. of Units: Company Owned: 2 - Franchised: 4 - Franchise Fee: $25,000 - Royalty: Fixed monthly fee - Total Inv: $90,000.

SUPER THRIFTY DRUG MARTS
381 Park Ave., E., Brandon, MB, R7A 7A5. Contact: Greg Skura, Pres. - Tel: (204) 728-1522, Fax: (204) 727-8680. Drug stores. Established: 1978 - Franchising Since: 1980 - No. of Units: 11.

THE CENTRE FOR PERFORMANCE DEVELOPMENT
885 Meadowsland Drive East, Suite 506, Ottawa, ON, K2C 3N2. Contact: Jim Moir/Christine Lamothe-Moir, Partners/Owners - Tel: (613) 225-0083, Fax: (613) 225-8469, E-Mail: jmoir@persprodplus.com, Web Site: www.persprodplus.com. Become a licensed practitioner of the proven "Personal Productivity Plus" system training program. Build a rewarding second career, profitable home-based business helping people work and live smarter, not harder. Help organizations achieve measurable increases in productivity. Support ongoing, full 10 days training. Established: 1991 - No. of Units: Company Owned: 1 - Total Inv: $5,000-$35,000.

THE GREAT AMERICAN BACK RUB
12 Challister Court, Toronto, ON, M2K 1X2. Contact: Fran. Dev. - Tel: (416) 512-0120, Fax: (416) 512-0103. Retail store providing massage therapy in specially designed chairs. Massages administered by RMT's in 10, 20, 40, minute sessions. Stress reduction products also sold. full training provided. No. of Units: Franchised: 7 - Total Inv: $120,000.

WE CARE HEALTH SERVICES INC
We Care Health Services Inc.
151 Bloor St. West, Suite 602, Toronto, ON, M5S 1S4. Contact: C. John Woodburn, Dir. Fran. Sales - Tel: (416)922-7601, (800) 316-2212, Fax: (416) 922-6280, Web Site: www.wecare.ca. We Care Health Services is now Canada's largest franchise system in the health care industry. We Care franchises benefit from exploding demand for our services due to aging populations and government cutbacks, as well as the extensive support and infrastructure to supply that demand. Member of CFA. Established: 1984 - Franchising Since: 1984 - No. of Units: Company Owned: 2 - Franchised: 51 - Franchise Fee: $40,000 - Royalty: 5%, 2% advertising - Total Inv: $100,000 - Financing: Varies, depending upon individual.

HOME FURNISHINGS

BETONEL LTEE.
8600 De L'Epee, Montreal, QC, H3N 2G6. Contact: Franchise Director - Tel: (514) 273-8855, Fax: (514) 273-7391. Paint, wallpaper, stain, varnish. Established: 1959 - Franchising Since: 1985 - No. of Units: Company Owned: 8 - Franchised: 18 - Franchise Fee: $5,000 - Total Inv: $50,000 - Financing: For half inventory.

CERTA PROPAINTERS CANADA
5397 Eglinton Ave., W., Ste. 108, Etobicoke, ON, M9C 5K6. Contact: Scott Mossip, VP - Tel: (416) 620-4700, Fax: (416) 620-9655. Painting and decorating service company. Residential and commercial and industrial maintenance work. Basic painting, wallpapering, spraying and decorative finishes. Established: 1989 - Franchising Since: 1991 - No. of Units: Franchised: 40 - Franchise Fee: $16,000 - Royalty: $700-$1,200/month depends on size of the territory - Total Inv: $35,000: $16,000 fee, $19,000 start up & equip. - Financing: Some; with Certa ProPainters and Suppliers.

COLOR YOUR WORLD, CORP.
2600 Steele Ave. West, Concord, ON, L4K 3C8. Contact: Robert Crookston, Franchise Sales Manager - Tel: (905) 738-7477, (800) 387-7311, Fax: (905) 738-9723. Retailers of paint and wallcoverings, blinds and carpet. A one-stop decorating shop. Also servicing commercial and industrial accounts. Established: 1912 - Franchising Since: 1973 - No. of Units: Company Owned: 130 - Franchised: 41 - Authorized Dealers: 65 - Franchise Fee: $25,000 - Royalty: 7%, adv. 4% - Total Inv: $160,000-$300,00 - Financing: Assist in obtaining.

DECOR DISTINCTION
422 Masson Street, Oshawa, ON, L1G 4Z8. Contact: Gaetane Montreuil President - Tel: (905) 725-0385, Web Site: www.decordistinction.com. Decor Distinction is our threshold to success in decorating. With Decor Distinction your customer can shop for a new couch while sitting on the old one. Aptly known as The Store To Your Door. Decor Distinction is the largest Canadian franchise network to provide mobile interior decoration service with a strong emphasis on Canadian merchandise and materials. Established: 1981 - Franchising Since: 1989 - No. of Units: Company Owned: 2 - Franchised: 10 - Franchise Fee: $12,000-$23,600 - Royalty: 9.5%, adv 2.5%- Total Inv: $15,000-$30,000 - Financing: No.

DECORATING DEN INTERIORS
23 Lore Court, Cambridge, ON, N3C 3S2. Contact: Linda Fagg, Regional Director - Tel: (519) 658-9300, (800) 263-0242, Fax: (519) 658-9055, E-Mail: linda@decoratingden.ca, Web Site: www.decoratingden.com. Largest international decorating service. Our home based interior decorators provide convenient in-home appointments. We are a full service decorating business. Established: 1969 - Franchising Since: 1972 - No. of Units: Franchised: 90 CDN, 750 US - Franchise Fee: $21,900-$29,900 - Royalty: 11%-7% - Total Inv:$15,000 working capital. Financing: Yes.

FERPLUS DECORATION, FERPLUS QUINCAILLERIE, FERPLUS RENOVATION
Marchands Unis, Inc.
915 Paradis St., Duberger, QC, G1N 4E3. Contact: Geston Legare, Director of Sales - Tel: (418) 687-3050, Fax: (418) 687-5317. Retail stores specializing in wallpaper, paint and hardware. Established: 1950 - No. of Units: 125.

LEON'S FURNITURE LTD.
45 Gordon MacKay Rd., P.O. Box 1100, Station B, Weston, ON, M9L 2R8. Contact: Bruce Stevens, Mgr. Franc. Div. - Tel: (416) 243-7880, Fax: (800) 267-6981. Furniture, appliances and carpet retail. Established: 1909 - Franchising Since: 1983 - No. of Units: 16 - Franchise Fee: $10,000.

MANOOCHEHR ZANDI
Zandi International
134 A Cartwright Ave, North York, ON, M6A 1V2. Contact: Mr. Zandi, President - Tel: (416) 787-8632, Fax: (416) 8787-6691, E-Mail: zandi@zandiinternational.com, Web Site: www.zandiinternational.com. Zandi International has been manufacturing and importing Persian & Oriental Rugs & Kilims, crafts and paintings of the highest quality since 1955. Established: 1955 - Franchising Since: 2003 - No. of Units: Company Owned: 50 - Franchised: 10 - Franchise Fee: $20,000 - Royalty: $40,000 materials - Total Inv: $60,000 - Financing: Yes.

MASTERBEDROOM INC.
1606 Charles Street, Whitby, ON, L1N 1B9. Contact: Valerie Lett, Franchise Director - Tel: (905) 430-0100, Fax: (905) 430-2134, Fran Div: (905) 899-5029. Recognized for 18 years as one of Canada's foremost sleep and bedroom specialists. We showcase major lines of quality mattresses at outlet prices. Fashionable "one stop" outlets offer classic and trendy head boards, bedroom furniture, bed linens, pillows, protective coverings, window dressings and exclusive sleep products. Established: 1982 - No. of Units: Company Owned: 2 - Franchised: 4 - Franchise Fee: $25,000 - Total Inv: $145,000.

PAINT SHOP
P.S. Paint Shop, Inc.
102 Clyde Ave., Donovan Industrial Park, Mount Pearl, NF, A1N 4S2. Contact: Paul Burt, Pres. - Tel: (709) 747-5432, Fax: (709) 747-3425. Home decorating retail,offering paint, wallpaper, blinds and related products. Servicing retail and contractor. Established: 1973 - Franchising Since: 1975 - No. of Units: Company Owned: 1 - Franchised: 30 .

PANHANDLER, THE
Liv Group Incorporated
4699 Keele St., Ste. 2, North York, ON, M3J 2N8. Contact: V.P. Franchising & Leasing - Tel: (416) 661-9916, Fax: (416) 661-9706. An array of interesting gift, gourmet ideas and kitchen accessories. Full training and support is provided. Established: 1968 - Franchising Since: 1972 - No. of Units: Company Owned: 1 - Franchised: 27 - Franchise Fee: $25,000 - Royalty: 6% - Total Inv: $105,000-$150,000 - Financing: Available through financial institutions.

POT POURRI
Pot Pourri Systems Inc.
4699 Keele St., #2, Downsview, ON, M3J 2N8. Contact: Michael Mayerson, V.P. Franchising & Licensing - Tel: (416) 661-9916, Fax: (416) 661-9706. Wide range of kitchen and gift products, full line of housewares, volume purchasing prices. Established: 1970 - Franchising Since: 1970 - No. of Units: Company Owned: 6 - Franchised: 20 - Franchise Fee: $25,000 - Royalty: 6% - Total Inv: $110,000-$150,000 - Financing: Available through financial institutions.

ST. CLAIR PAINT & WALLPAPER, WALLPAPER WORLD
2600 Steeles Ave., W., Concord, ON, L4K 3C8. Contact: Jack Mady, V.P., Real Est. and Fran. - Tel: (905) 738-0080, Fax: (905) 738-9723. Retail sale of paint, wallpaper and other decorating accessories. Established: 1939 - Franchising Since: 1970 - No. of Units: 146 St. Clair - 1 Wallpaper World.

STAINED GLASS OVERLAY
The Franchise Company, Inc.
1827 North Case St, Orange, CA, 92865. Contact: Tom Wood, Franchise Recruiting - Tel: (714) 974-6124, Fax: (714) 974-6529, E-Mail: twood@certapro.com, Web Site: www.thefranchsiecompany.com. Features the unique process of manufacturing solid seamless, one piece decorative or bevelled glass products in any design. Established: 1974 - Franchising Since: 1981 - No. of Units: Franchised: 332 - Franchise Fee: Call for details - Royalty: Varies - Total Inv: Varies.

HOME INSPECTION SERVICE

AMERISPEC HOME INSPECTION SERVICE-CANADA
Service Master of Canada
6540 Tomken Dr, Mississauga, ON, L5T 2E9. Contact: Edmond Kett, Market Expansion Manager - Tel: (905) 670-0000, (800) 263-5928, Fax: (905) 670-0077, Web Site: www.servicemaster.com. Provider of home inspection and related services in an exploding industry. Superior marketing, training, computer applications and support make this low capital, home-based franchise an exceptional opportunity. Established: 1987 - Franchising Since: 1988 - No. of Units: Franchised: 53 - Franchise Fee: $14,900-$24,900 - Royalty: 7%+3% national adv - Total Inv: $14,900-$24,9000 - Financing: Yes.

CANADIAN RESIDENTIAL INSPECTION SERVICES LTD
P.O. Box 2121 D.E.P.S., Dartmouth, NS, B2W 3Y2. Contact: Russell Cook, President - Tel: (902) 499-0999, (888) 499-0999, Fax: (902) 435-1984. Pre-purchase home inspections. Established: 1990 - Franchising Since: 1995 - No. of Units: Company Owned: 1 - Franchised: 3 - Franchise Fee: $10,000 minimum - Royalty: $300 per month minimum - Total Inv: Approx $20,000 - Financing: On approval.

GRASSROOTS® THE HOME INSPECTION SPECIALISTS
PAIRS Reporting Service, Inc.
214 Martindale Rd., St. Catharines, ON, L2R 6P9. Contact: Graham Ashdown, President - Tel: (800) 774-2538, (905) 687-1925, Fax: (905) 685-8125, E-Mail: info@grassroots.ca, Web Site: www.grassroots.ca. Residential/commercial/building and enviromental inspection service with full support, marketing materials, strategy, training, customer service, bookkeeping, and procedures on how to run your own business successfully. Quick generation of inspection reports using our unique, easy-to-use computerized system. Our report is narrative style, not just a checklist. Established: 1991 - Franchising Since: 1991 - No. of Units: Franchised: 9 - Franchise Fee: $10,000 - Royalty: 7%, 3% adv. - Total Inv: $17,500 incl. fran. fee and $2,500 training fee (may be greatly reduced if operating from existing office) - Financing: To qualified candidates - $2,500 prime + 2% (over 24 months).

PILLAR TO POST
5805 Whittle Rd., Ste. 211, Mississauga, ON, L4Z 2J1. Contact: Franchise Department - Tel: (905) 568-86085, (800) 294-5591, Fax: (905) 568-8137. The Pillar To Post professional home inspection program was developed by specialists for persons wanting to be in a business for themselves that is home based and does not require a large capital investment, expensive inventories, accounts receivable or employees. Extensive technical, marketing and operations training provided at company's training facility. Strong ongoing corporate support. Established: 1994 - Franchising Since: 1994 - No. of Units Franchised: 92 - No. of Area Developers: 5 - Franchise Fee: $10,900-$20,900 - Royalty: 7% - Total Inv: Unit Franchise: $16,000-$30,000; Area Developer: $40,000-$70,000 - Financing: OAC.

HOUSE/PET SITTING SERVICES

CUSTOM HOME WATCH INTERNATIONAL INC.
2094 Tomat Ave., Kelowna, BC, V1Z 3C5. Contact: Terry Bates, Pres. - Tel: (250) 769-4329, (800) 713-2888, Fax: (250) 769-4329. Looking after absent home-owner's premises, pets, plants, yard, mail, repairs, maintenance, maid service. Franchisees receive all start up supplies, training, equipment and operations manual. Established: 1988 - Franchising Since: 1989 - No. of Units: Franchised: 45 - Franchise Fee: $2,950-$7,950 (depending on population) - Royalty: 3% + 2% nat'l adv. - Total Inv: $4,000-$10,000 - Financing: No.

HAWKEYE'S HOME SITTERS
Hawkeye's Home Sitters of Canada Ltd.
14920-95A Street, Edmonton, AB, T5E 4A6. Contact: Dennis Pysyk, Pres. - Tel: (888) 247-2787, Fax: (780) 988-8948, E-Mail:hawkeyes @homesitter.com, Web Site: www.homesitter.com. A full, professional service for homeowners while they are away on business or vacation. Caring for their pets, plants, homes, picking up mail, cutting lawns, shoveling walks, etc. form part of the day to day activities. Offering franchisees a proven, turnkey, business opportunity with ongoing assistance and continious support. Established: 1987 - Franchising Since: 1996 - No. of Units: Franchised: 7 - Franchise Fee: $3,495-$6,995 (depending upon population) - Royalty: 4% plus 2% national advertising - Total Inv: $5,000-$10,000 - Financing: No.

JEWELRY

CULTURE CRAZE IMPORTS
#304, 1363-56 Street, Delta, BC, V4L 2P7. Contact: Mike Williams, President - Tel: (604) 948-5131, Fax: (604) 948-5130, E-Mail: info@culturecraze.com. Culture Craze offers a turn-key business opportunity with proven success in the body jewellery market. Call, write or e-mail to find out more information on this innovative alternative to the basic franchise business. Established: 2000 - Franchising Since: 2001 - No. of Units: Company Owned: 1 - Franchised: 4 - Franchise Fee: $2,000.

DISTINCTIVE DESIGNS JEWELLERY

P.O. Box 25026, Halifax, NS, B3M 4H4. Contact: Melvin Slade, President - Tel: (902) 445-1768, E-Mail: info@distinctivedesigns jewellry.com, Web Site: www.distinctivedesignsjewellery.com. Personal selling sterling silver jewellery company. Established: 2003 - Franchising Since: 2003 - No. of Units: Company Owned: 25 - Franchise Fee: No investment.

SIMPLY CHARMING / RODAN JEWELLERS
Rodan Enterprises (1994) Ltd.

102-4180 Lougheed Hwy, Burnaby, BC, V5C 6A7. - Tel: (604) 438-1625, Fax: (604) 438-1635. Fine jewellery stores on key corner locations in major regional shopping centres - British Columbia, Canada only. Established: 1976 - Franchising Since: 1982 - No. of Units: Franchised: 11 - Franchise Fee: $50,000 Simply Charming, $75,000 Rodan Jewellers - Royalty: 5% - Total Inv: $250,000 Simply Charming, $500,000 Rodan - Financing: Yes.

TANDY LEATHER CO.
Tandy Crafts Ltd.

P.O. Box 13000, 120 Brock St., Barrie, ON, L4M 4W4. Contact: Doug Black, Pres. - Tel: (705) 728-2481, (800) 387-9815, Fax: (705) 721-1228, E-Mail: tandy@tandy leather.ca, Web Site: www.tandy leather.ca. Complete supplies for leathercrafts, jewellery making, native crafts. Established: 1956 - Franchising Since: 1975 - No. of Units: Company Owned: 8 - Franchised: 80 - Franchise Fee: $1,000.00 - Total Inv: $1,000.00 (franchise fee/dealer fee) $2,000.00 + (inventory) - Financing: None.

TIMECRAFT
Timecraft Company Limited

4500 Chesswood Drive, Suite 2031, North York, ON, M3J 2E3. Contact: Anthony Barbosa, CEO. - Tel: (416) 782-7377, Fax: (416) 782-8057. Retail: Sales and service of all types of timepieces, weather stations, timing devices and all the above acessories. Established: 1971 - No. of Units: Company Owned: 6 - Franchised: 5 - Franchise Fee: $30,000 - Royalty: 6% of total sales - Total Inv: $150,00-$175,000.

VIVAH JEWELRY
Vivah Franchise, Inc.

995 Finch Ave West, North York, ON, M3J 2C7. Contact: Mr. Z. Goodbaum, Pres. - Tel: (416) 661-7188, Fax: (416) 661-8748. Retail sale of exclusive fashion jewelry namely earrings, pins, necklaces and bracelets with a strong emphasis on sterling silver jewelry, fashion watches and bridal lines. Established: 1976 - Franchising Since: 1989 - No. of Units: Company Owned: 9 - Franchised: 1 - Franchise Fee: $25,000 - Total Inv: $20,000-$25,000 merch., $40,000-$75,000 store fix. - Financing: $80,000 min. invest. with bal. thru bank. NOT OFFERING FRANCHISES AT THIS TIME.

LAUNDRY & DRY CLEANING

CADET CLEANERS
Grayker Corporation

290 Old Weston Rd., Toronto, ON, M6N 3A4. Contact: Don Schell, G.M. Franchise Operation - Tel: (416) 656-5601, Fax: (416) 656-4519, E-Mail: grayker@home.com, Web Site: www.cadetclean.com. Dry cleaning and shirt laundry depots. Established: 1962 - Franchising Since: 1994 - No. of Units: Company Owned: 22 - Franchised: 78 - Royalty: 53% production - royalty - advertising - Total Inv: $55,000 and up - Financing: Will assist.

CAVALIER FACTORY OUTLET CLEANERS

165 Eileen Ave., Toronto, ON, M6N 1W3. - Tel: (416) 767-8991, Fax: (416) 767-2012. Dry cleaning, turn-key retail outlets. Established: 1983 - Franchising Since: 1994 - No. of Units: Company Owned: 2 - Franchised: 7 - Franchise Fee: Included in total investment - Royalty: 0% - Total Inv: $35,000 - Financing: $5,000 down the rest can be financed. NOT OFFERING FRANCHISES AT THIS TIME.

CHATEL VOTRE NETTOYEUR (YOUR CLEANER)

1200 boul. Rome, Local M, Brossard, QC, J4W 3H3. Contact: Andre Demers, Pres. - Tel: (514) 671-5642, Fax: (514) 671-5243. Drycleaning and related services. Established: 1984 - Franchising Since: 1984 - No.

of Units: Company Owned: 6 - Franchised: 70 - Franchise Fee: $15,000 - Royalty: $310.00 per month - Total Inv: $135,000-$145,000 - Financing: Via S.B.L.

FACTORY OUTLET DRYCLEANERS

2450 Finch Ave., West, Unit #11, Toronto, ON, M9M 2E9. Contact: Jim Karagiannis, President - Tel: (416) 745-7189, Fax: (416) 745-7954. Turn-key drycleaning depot and plants, full training and year round support. Established: 1994 - Franchising Since: 1994 - No. of Units: 1 - Franchised: 12 - Royalty: 2% - Total Inv: $50,000-$500,000 - Financing: On approved credit.

HILLARY'S CLEANERS

1235 Bank Street, Ottawa, ON, K1S 3Y2. Contact: David Hillary, President - Tel: (613) 733-3070, Fax: (613) 733-3398. One of the most innovated dry cleaning plants in the country. All same day service. Totally environmentally sound. Established: 1949 - No. of Units: Company Owned: 6 - Franchised: 6 - Total Inv: Depends on location.

LONDON CLEANERS
London Cleaners Inc.

45 B West Wilmost Street, Richmond Hill, ON, L4B 1K1. Contact: Mark Kuzu, Exec. Secretary - Tel: (905) 771-1024. Dry cleaners and alteration franchise. Established: 1929 - Franchising Since: 1982 - No. of Units: Company Owned: 2 - Franchised: 23 - Franchise Fee: $20,000 - Royalty: 5% - Total Inv: $40,000 and up - Financing: CIBC.

MAXI-BRITE-DAOUST-MICHEL FORGET
Groupe Multinet

1695 B. Laval Ste. 420, Laval, QC, H7S 2M2. Contact: Anthony Ciarlo, V. P. - Tel: (514) 990-1699, (800) 668-9080, Fax: (514) 668-7769. Dry cleaners plant fully equipped for work done on premises. Established: 1980 - Franchising Since: 1980 - No. of Units: Company Owned: 140 - Franchised: 140 - Franchise Fee: $264.26 / mnth adv. - Royalty: $320/month - Total Inv: $125,000-$140,000 - Financing: Yes.

MAYTAG
Lavoir Libre-Service Maytag

10301 Ray Lawson, Anjou, QC, H1J 1L6. Contact: Pierre Bourcheix, Pres. - Tel: (514) 351-1212, Fax: (514) 351-7296. Self-service laundry. Franchising Since: 1958 - No. of Units: 400 Canada, 2,500 US, - Approx. Inv: $80,000 - Financing: Partial.

SKETCHLEY
Three Penguins Inc.

290 Old Weston Rd., Toronto, ON, M6N 3A4. Contact: Don Schell, Fran. Dir. - Tel: (416) 656-5601, Fax: (416) 656-4519, E-Mail: grayker@home.com, Web Site: www.cadetclean.com. Service/dry cleaning. Established: 1956 - Franchising Since: 1987 - No. of Units: Franchised: 70 - Royalty: 53% prod-royalty-adver - Total Inv: $55,000 and up Financing: Will assist.

LAWN AND GARDEN CARE

BOBBY LAWN CARE / BOBBY PEST CONTROL
Bobby Lawn, Inc.

P.O. Box 35082, London, ON, N5W 5Z6. - Tel: (519) 455-5912. We offer the finest lawn care services available using the exclusive Bobby Lawn Care System designed and manufactured exclusively by Bobby Lawn Inc, and supplemented by a broad range of cultural provided services to produce a healthy, beautiful lawn with enhanced sales. We practice Integrated Pest Management and environmentally responsible lawn care services for weed and insect control as well as structural pest control. Established Since: 1979 - Restricted Number of Licensees Issued Since: 1981 - No. of Units (trucks) Company Owned: 45 - Licensed 52 - Royalties: 5% - Total Inv: $15,000-$25,000 - Financing: No.

CLINTAR GROUNDSKEEPING SERVICES
Truserve GroundsCare Inc.

70 Esna Park Drive Unit #1, Markham, ON, L3R 1E3. Contact: Robert Wilton, President - Tel: (905) 943-9530, (800) 361-3542, Fax: (905) 943-9529, E-Mail: info@clintar.com, Web Site: www.clintar.com. A large "Business To Business" format. Average business size is $1.5

million, selling landscape services to fortune 500 companies. Established: 1973 - Franchising Since: 1984 - No. of Units: Company Owned: 1 - Franchised: 15 - Franchise Fee: $30,000 - Royalty: 8% - Total Inv: $150,000 - Financing: No.

CURB KING
Curb KIng Borderline Edging Inc.
17025 104 Ave., Surrey, BC, V4N 4L9. - Tel: (604) 584-9882, Fax: (604) 584-9886. Continuous concrete machinery package to install curbing for garden beds, driveways, walkways, and parking lots. Established: 1994 - Franchising Since: 1994 - No. of Units: Company Owned: 2 - Franchised: 28 - Total Inv: $42,000 Can./ $27,800 US - Financing: No.

E - Z LANDSCAPING
891 Lynden Blvd., Winnipeg, MB, R1B 5S2. Contact: Fran. Div. - Tel: (204) 235-0113. Complete residential and commercial landscaping - 5 days training and ongoing support. Established: 1992 - No. of Units: Franchised: 23 - Total Inv: $40,000.

ENVIROMASTERS LAWN CARE
P.O.Box 178, Caledon East, ON, L0N 1E0. Contact: Martin Fielding, Pres. - Tel: (905) 584-9592. Organic and Environmentally considerate lawn care. Enjoy the great outdoors and be part of a great new approach to lawn care. Full training with ongoing support. Established: 1987 - Franchising Since: 1994 - No. of Units: Company Owned: 2 - Franchised: 16 - Franchise Fee: $15,000-$25,000 - Royalty: 5% - Total Inv: $25,000-$35,000 - Financing: Yes.

EVERGREEN LAWN & GARDEN SUPPLIES
355 Adelaide Street W, 5th Floor, Toronto, ON, M5V 1S2. Contact: Franchise Director - Tel: (416) 596-1495, Fax: (416) 596-1443. Landscaping services with a garden centre. Extensive training and support. Established: 1987 - No. of Units: Franchised: 12 - Total Inv: $250,000-$300,000.

GARDENER LANDSCAPE MAINTENANCE & SNOW REMOVAL, INC., THE
300 John St., Ste. 329, Thornhill, ON, L3T 5W4. Contact: Sean French, Pres. - Tel: (905) 889-1532, Fax: (905) 889-3265, Web Site: www.the-gardener.com. Residential and commercial lawn and garden maintenance and snow removal service. Guaranteed gross weekly sales of $1200 per week, home based business. Established: 1994 - Franchising Since: 1994 - No. of Units: Company Owned: 1 - Franchised: 22 - Franchise Fee: $15,000 - Royalty: 6%, 1% adv. - Total Inv: $30,000 - Financing: Assistance available. Master franchise territories available.

GREENLAND IRRIGATION
150 Ambleside Dr., London, ON, N6G 4R1. Contact: Barry Smith, Pres. Lawn sprinkler installation and maintenance - commercial / residential/ turn-key / clients, equipment provided. Established: 1986 - Franchising Since: 1993 - No. of Units: Company Owned: 10 - Franchised: 6 - Franchise Fee: $25,000 - Royalty: 13% all inclusive - Financing: Yes.

HERBU
Herbu, Inc.
100 Fisher, Mount Saint Hilaire, QC, J3G 4S6. Contact: Claude Gagnon, Pres. - Tel: (450) 464-7093, Fax: (450) 446-4336. Lawn care. Franchised: 15 - Franchise Fee: $12,500 - Royalty: Fixed (to be determined) - Total Inv: $45,000 - Financing: No.

JIM'S MOWING CANADA, INC.
105-1515 Pemberton Ave., N. Vancouver, BC, V7P 2S3. Contact: Fran. Dev. - Tel: (604) 878-0787, Fax: (604) 990-0724, E-Mail: jimsmowing bc@msn.com, Web Site: www.jims.com.au/www.jimsmowing canada.com. World's largest lawn and garden care fraanchise organization providing multiple services 12 months of the year. offers same day service to clients and provides training, office support, computerized manaagement system. Established: 1989 - No. of Units: Franchised: 30 - Total Inv: $25,000 (includes equipment, trailor, work availability guarantee).

KWIK KERB
Kwik Kerb Edgemaster Inc.
101-20050 Stewart Cres., Maple Ridge, BC, V2X 0T4. Contact: Don Regewig - Tel: (604) 465-2703, (866) 459-4553, Fax: (604) 465-2704, E-Mail: canada@kwikkerb.com, Web Site: www.kwikkerb.com. Be

your own boss in this home based decorative landscape concrete edging business. Join the world leaders in this lucrative growth industry and receive a complete turnkey business system with all equipment, marketing & promotional items. Training and on-going support. Change your lifestyle by calling us today. Established: 1992 in canada - Franchising Since: 1987 - No. of Units: Franchised: 1200+ - Royalty: None - Total Inv: $55,595 - Financing: Yes.

LAWN CARE THE PROFESSIONAL WAY
Nutrite Inc.
P.O. Box 1000, Brossard, QC, J4Z 3N2. - Tel: (450) 462-2555, Fax: (450) 462-3634. Lawn care. Nutrite Inc. is also a manufacturer of fertilizer. Established: 1984 - Franchising Since: 1984 - No. of Units: Franchised: 42 - Franchise Fee: $15,000 - Royalty: $3,550 per year - Total Inv: $40,000 - Financing: No.

MISTER AERATOR
Mister Aerator Inc
9 Dooley Place, Guelph, ON, N1G 4M7. Contact: Michael E. Sloopka, V.P. Sales & Operations - Tel: (519) 836-6105, Fax: (519) 836-6937. Mister Aerator is North America's only home based business system specializing in professional lawn aeration services. Mister Aerator owner/operator's use specialized equipment to mechanically remove plugs of soil and thatch from lawns to improve health and appearance without the use of chemicals. Established: 1997 - Franchising Since: 1998 - No. of Units: Company Owned: 1 - Independent Owner/Operators: 3 - Franchise Fee: No franchise fee - Royalty: No royalties - Total Inv: $24,900 complete turn key business system, all startup equipment, supplies and materials included - Financing: Not available.

NUTRI-LAWN ECOLOGY FRIENDLY LAWN CARE
Nutri-Lawn International
Ste. 110, 5397 Eglinton Ave. W., Toronto, ON, M9C 5K6. Contact: Larry Maydonik, President - Tel: (416) 620-7100, (800) 396-6096, Fax: (416) 620-7771, E-Mail:nli@istar.ca, Web Site: www.nutri-lawn.com. Residential and commercial lawn care with an approach of reduced pesticide usage and a goal to be pesticide free. Many added services to fertilization, trees, shrubs, irrigation, seeding, etc. Established: 1985 - Franchising Since: 1987 - No. of Units: Franchised: 38 - Franchise Fee: $25,000 - Royalty: 6% -Total Inv: $55,000: $25,000 fran. fee, $15,000 equip., $15,000 working cap. - Financing: No.

NUTRITE HYDRO AGRI CANADA
7005 Taseherean Blvd, Brossard, PQ, J4Z 1A7. Contact: Dir. of Franchising - Tel: (450) 462-2555, Fax: (450) 462-3634, Web Site: www.nutrite.com. Nutrite Lawn Care franchise. Established: 1967 - Franchising Since: 1984 - No. of Units: Franchised: 43 - Franchise Fee: $18,000- Royalty: $3,550 per year - Total Inv: $40,000.

O'TOOLE LAWN CARE
82 Woolwich St., North, Box 283, Breslau, ON, N0B 1M0. Contact: Patrick O'Toole, Owner - Tel: (519) 648-3838, Fax: (519) 648-3810. Ecology friendly lawn care with minimial use of pesticides including fertilizing aerating, seeding and pest control. Established: 1993 - Franchising Since: 1997 - No. of Units: Franchised: 5 - Franchise Fee: $15,000 - Royalty: 5% - Total Inv: Truck - $10,000 equipment - Financing: Yes.

PAYSAGISTE BONZAI
Paysagiste Bonzai Junior Inc.
79 Chemin de la Petit Cote, Laval, QC, H7L 1K5. Contact: Courtemanche, Pres. - Tel: (450) 963-6686, Fax: (450) 963-6687. Specialiste en application eugrais de pelouse 100% natural. Eutretien des espace vert et deneigement. Established: 1988 - Franchising Since: 1995 - No. of Units: Company Owned: 3 - Franchised: 1 - Royalty: 4% - Total Inv: $35,000 - Financing: Yes.

WEED MAN
Turf Management Systems, Inc.
2399 Royal Windsor Dr., Mississauga, ON, L5J 1K9. Contact: Michael J. Kernaghan, V.P. - Tel: (905) 823-8550, Fax: (905) 823-4594, E-Mail: weedman@netcom.ca, Web Site: www.weed-man.com. Lawn care. Established: 1970 - Franchising Since: 1976 - No. of Units: Company Owned: 1 - Franchised: 140 - Franchise Fee: $25,000 - Royalty: 6% - Total Inv: $30,000 - Financing: No.

MOTELS, HOTELS AND CAMPGROUNDS

BASS HOTELS & RESORTS, INC.
2167 Alconbury Crescent, Burlington, ON, L7P 3C5. Contact: Fran. Dev. - Tel: (905) 331-9264, Fax: (905) 331-9396, E-Mail: holiday-inn.com, Web Site: www.holiday-inn.com. 7 franchise opportunities. Training and support in advertising, marketing, architectural assistance, central purchasing, central reservation, quality control. Established: 1952 - No. of Units: Franchised: 2698 - Total Inv: $500/room, $40,000 min.

BEST WESTERN INTERNATIONAL
5915 Airport Road, Ste. 412, Mississauga, ON, L4V 1T1. - Tel: (905) 673-0555, Fax: (905) 673-5061. Hotels, motels and resorts. Established: 1946 - Franchising Since: 1946 - No. of Units: Franchised: 135 Canada - Franchise Fee: 100 rooms - entrance fee - $43,514 - Total Inv: $54,214 Canadian - Financing: None.

CHOICE HOTELS CANADA
5090 Explorer Dr.,Suite 500, Mississauga, ON, L4W 4T9. Contact: Scott Duff, V.P., Fran. Dev. - Tel: (905) 602-2222, Fax: (905) 624-7796, E-Mail: franchising@choicehotels.ca, Web Site: www.choicehotels.ca. Choice Hotels Canada has 250 locations coast to coast representing over 21,000 rooms. Choice franchise has seven different hotel brands; Clarion, Quality, Comfort, Sleep, Econo Lodge, Rodeway Inn and Mainstay Suites. Established: 1993 - Franchising Since: 1949 - No. of Units: Franchised: 248 - Franchise Fee: $25,000-$50,000 - Royalty: 2.5%-5% - Total Inv: Varies - Financing: No.

DAYS INNS - CANADA
Realstar Hotel Services Corp.
77 Bloor St., West, Ste. 2000, Toronto, ON, M5S 1M2. Contact: Irwin Prince, President & C.O.O. - Tel: (800) 840-8162, ext 387, (416) 923-5424, Fax: (416) 923-5424. Hotel/motel franchises - establishing franchised properties in all major cities across the country in the moderate priced segment of the market. Providing extensive and dedicated franchise services to franchisees, including a reservation system. Established: 1992 - Franchising Since: 1992 - No. of Units: Franchised: 74 - Royalty: 5% of gross room revenue (grr), adv. 1.5% grr, reservation 2.3% grr - Franchise Fee: $350/room + $10,000 - Financing: No.

GOUVERNEUR HOTELS
1000 Sherbrooke West., Office 2300, Montreal, QC, H3H 3R3. Contact: Jean-Pierre Kerten, Vice-President Franchises - Tel: (514) 875-8822, Fax: (514) 875-6711. Full service hotel chain offering deluxe accommodation, restaurants, bars, meeting facilities and swimming pools, located throughout Quebec. Established: 1963 - Franchising Since: 1969 - No. of Units: Company Owned: 6 - Franchised: 10.

HOME ALYZE
5160 Skyline Way N.E., Caalgary, AB, T2E 6V1. Contact: Franchise Director - Tel: (800) 831-6272, (403) 730-9986, Fax: (403) 274-4821, Web Site: www.homealyze.com. Home inspection service developed in the Canadian enviroment. Unique inspection and reporting system adaptable for regional differences. The best opportunity to build a successful future. Established: 1978 - Franchising Since: 1999 - No. of Units: Franchised: 3 - Total Inv: $20,900 plus working capital.

HOWARD JOHNSON HOTELS IN CANADA
Accommodex Franchise Management, Inc.
36 Toronto Suite 3750, Toronto, ON, M5C 2C5. Contact: Paul Blake, V.P. - Tel: (416)361-1010, (800) 249-4656, Fax: (416) 361-9050. Hotels, motor lodges, restaurant. Established: 1971 - Franchising Since: 1971 - No. of Units: Franchised: 37 - Franchise Fee: $15,000 - Royalty: 5% gross room revenue - Total Inv: Varies - Financing: Varies.

RAMADA
Franchise Canada Inc
36 Toronto Suite 750, Toronto, ON, M5C 2C5. Contact: Timothy Whitehead, V.P. - Tel: (416) 361-1010, Fax: (416) 361-9577. Franchisor of Ramada Limited Inns, Hotels and Plaza Hotels for Canada. Established: 1992 - Franchising Since: 1992 - No. of Units: Franchised: 43, 7 under construction - Franchise Fee: $35,000 for 1st 100 rooms, $350.00 per room after that - Royalty: 4% mktg. assessment, 4% (calc. on room revenue) - Financing: No.

SUPER 8 MOTELS, INC.
Royop Hospitality
30-1015 4th street, S.W., Calgary, AB, T2R 1J4. Contact: Fran. Dev. - Tel: (403) 543-8800, Fax: (403) 543-8803. Franchisor of Super 8 Motels. Full training and support provided. Established: 1992 - No. of Units: Franchised: 1825 - Total Inv: Varies.

TRAVELODGE / THRIFTLODGE
Travelodge Canada
500, 5940 Macleod Tr. S., Calgary, AB, T2H 2G4. Contact: Robin Cumine, Dir. Fran. Ser/Oper. - Tel: (403) 259-9800, (800) 646-2435, Fax: (403) 255-6981, E-Mail: rcumine@travelodge.ca. Sales and development of Travelodge and Thrift Lodge franchise. Established: 1992 - Franchising Since: 1996 - No. of Units: Franchised: 90 - Franchise Fee: $36,000 - Financing: Assistance available.

VENTURE INNS INC.
1250 Eglinton Ave East, Toronto, ON, M3C 1J3. Contact: Steven James, Director Of Operations - Tel: (416) 441-4140, Fax: (416) 441-9609. To manage, market, license and grow a chain of hotels in the luxury budget sector of the hospitality business. Established: 1983 - Franchising Since: 1986 - No. of Units: Franchised: 9 - Franchise Fee: $100 per room, $20,000 minimum - Royalty: 1.5% gross guest room revenues, 2.4% adv.

WANDLYN INNS
58 Prospect St., P.O. Box 430, Fredericton, NB, E3B 5P8. Contact: Gary Llewellyn, Pres. - Tel: (506) 462-4417, Fax: (506) 452-7658. Mid-market motor inns, highway locations, 50-150 units per location, full facility. Established: 1955 - Franchising Since: 1970 - No. of Units: Company Owned: 6 - Franchised: 12.

MOVING SERVICES

TWO SMALL MEN WITH BIG HEARTS
11089B Ravine Rd, Surrey, BC, V3T 3X5. - Tel: (800) 727-6255, Fax: (604) 581-9244. Independent moving network. Local or long distance moving and storage. Established: 1979 - Franchising Since: 1985 - No. of Units: Company Owned: 8 - Franchised: 19 - Franchise Fee: $5,000 and up - Royalty: 2-4% - Total Inv: $10,000 and up for equipment.

OPTICAL AID/SERVICE

DR. SPECS OPTICAL
C & G Optical
2280A Leckie Road, Kelowna, BC, V1X 6G6. Contact: Cathy Goheen, Pres. - Tel: (250) 861-7731, Fax: (250) 861-3166. Chain of retail optical outlets. Established: 1987 - Franchising Since: 1994 - No. of Units: Company Owned: 7 - Franchised: 7 - Franchise Fee: $15,000 - Royalty: 5% of gross sales (monthly) - Total Inv: $89,000 - Financing: No.

FORT OPTICAL LTD.
814 Broughton Street, Victoria, BC, V8W 1E4. Contact: Fran. Dev. - Tel: (250) 383-7412, Fax: (250) 385-7500. Retail optical sales. Established: 1928.

HALE OPTICAL EYE-CRAFTERS/ LONDON OPTICAL / PRESCRIPTION OPTICAL
Prescription Optical Company Ltd.
7495 132nd Street Ste. 2010, Surrey, BC, V3W 1J8. Contact: Ron Phillip, Franc. Dir. - Tel: (604) 501-0811, Fax: (604) 501-0911. Established: 1924 - No. of Units: 45.

PACKAGE PREPARATION/SHIPMENT/MAIL SERVICE

FASTWAY COURIERS
Abbott Canada Courier Ltd
104-131 Water Street, Vancouver, BC, V6B 4M3. Contact: Doug Faulkner - Tel: (604) 739-2520, Fax: (604) 739-2560, E-Mail: info@fastway.ca. Courier franchise. Fastway operates on the philosophy of extremely cost effective courier services utilizing a simple pre-paid label system. Established: 2003 - Franchising Since: 2003 - No. of Units: Franchised: 2 - Franchise Fee: $Region = $50,000-$300,000; Courier = $20,500 - Royalty: Region = 9%; Courier = 0% - Total Inv: Region = $150,000-$750,000; Courier = $50,000-$60,000 - Financing: No.

MAIL BOXES ETC.
MBEC Communications Inc.
505 Iroquois Shore Rd., Unit 4, Oakville, ON, L6H 2R3. Contact: Mario Sita, Dir. of Fran. Development - Tel: (905) 338-9754, (800) 661-MBEC, Fax: (905) 338-7491. Business and communications services. Established: 1990 - Franchising Since: 1990 - No. of Units: Company Owned: 1 - Franchised: 210 - Franchise Fee: $29,950 - Royalty: 6% - Total Inv: $120,000 - Financing: Yes.

PACK 'N' SHIP MAILING CENTERS
718 Circle Dr., East, Saskatoon, SK, S7K 3T7. Contact: Jerry Gilchrist, Pres. - Tel: (306) 931-8881, Fax: (306) 931-8833. Custom packing and shipping service in addition to mail preparation. Limited retail of packing supplies. Established: 1981 - Franchising Since: 1981 - No. of Units: Company Owned: 6 - Franchised: 225 - Franchise Fee: $25,000 - Royalty: None - Total Inv: $60,000-$100,000.

POSTNET
189 Hymus Blvd., Ste. 205, Pointe Claire, QC, H9R 1E9. - Tel: (514) 426-0660, Fax: (514) 426-4244. Business and communication center offering shipping, packaging, fax, copies, business services and much more. Established: 1994 - Franchising Since: 1992 - No. of Units: Company Owned: 1 - Franchised: 15 (350 in US) - Franchise Fee: $25,000 - Royalty: 6%, 2% adv. - Total Inv: $95,000 - Financing: Yes.

PET PRODUCTS AND SERVICES

ANIMAL TRANSPORTATION SERVICES
1599 Canadore Crescent, Oshawa, ON, L1G 8A6. Contact: Ellen Holmes, President - Tel: (905) 725-9626, Fax: (905) 721-9729. Pet Taxi to veterinarians, groomers, kennels, airport. Also in-home pet sitters and dog walkers. Established: 1995 - Franchise Fee: $6,250 - Royalty: 5% - Total Inv: $10,000 - Financing: No.

AQUARIUM WAREHOUSE OUTLETS
2800-14th Ave., Unit 2 & 3, Markham, ON, L3R 0E4. Contact: Allan Saul, President - Tel: (905) 944-2404, Fax: (905) 944-2405, E-Mail: bigals@home.com, Web Site: www.aquariumservices.com. Retail of tropical and marine fish and related dry goods. Ongoing support provided. Established: 1985 - No. of Units: Franchised: 15 - Franchise Fee: $50,000 - Total Inv: $350,000.

CANUSA (BRANT) PET PRODUCTS
Canusa Distribution Inc.
175 Ashgrove Ave., Brantford, ON, N3R 7C6. Contact: John Di Sabatino, Executive Director - Tel: (519) 752-7866, (877) 241-6443, Fax: (519) 752-2752. We are a pet nutrition company that markets across North America, through a distribution base of its own creation along with franchises and master franchises, plus a new concept called (concept 2000) call for more information. Established: 1993 - Franchising Since: 1993 - No. of Units: Franchised: 45 - Franchise Fee: $4,000-$10,000 - Royalty: Call for more info - Total Inv: $1,000-$5,000 - Financing: No.

GLOBAL PET FOODS
Global Pet Food Stores Inc.
4699 Keele Street, Ste. 2, Downsview, ON, M3J 2N8. - Tel: (416) 661-9716, Fax: (416) 661-9706. Global Pet Foods has grown to become one of the leading retailers in the specialty pet foods and supplies business in Ontario. The pet foods and supplies industry has estimated annual sales in the U.S.A. of $18 billion. We specialize in National, Premium and Private label brands, with a complete range of accessories. We are currently expanding throughout Ontario and in select markets across Canada. Full training and support is provided. Established: 1973 - Franchising Since: 1986 - No. of Units: Company Owned: 9 - Franchised: 20 - Franchise Fee: $25,000 - Royalty: Flat monthly fee - Total Inv: $88,500 - Financing: Available through financial institutions.

HAPPYPAWS FRANCHISES INC.
137 Skinner Street, Victoria, BC, V9A 6X4. Contact: Neil Fimrite, Marketing Director - Tel: (250) 361-3230, (888) 217-7297, Fax: (250) 361-3240, E-Mail: nfimrite@happypaws.com, Web Site: www.happypaws.com. Franchising distributor of high quality natural pet food for dogs and cats. Established: 1996 - No. of Units: Franchised: 5 - Franchise Fee: $30,000-$75,000 - Royalty: N/A - Total Inv: $115,000 - Financing: N/A.

MULTI MENU PET FOOD SYSTEMS
3200 1ere Rue, Suite #510, St. Hubert, PQ, J3Y 8Y5. - Tel: (450) 462-0056, (877) 462-0056, Fax: (450) 462-0206, E-Mail: multimenu @sid.com, Web Site: www.multimenu.ca. A unique "home based" distribution system of superior quality brand name pet food products and asseories, for home delivery to "pet owners". Established: 1996 - Franchising Since: 1998 - No. of Units: Company Owned: 1 - No. of Units: Franchised: 102 - Franchise Fee: $8,500 - Royalty: 3%; Advertising $100/Mo. - Total Inv: $14,000 - Financing: No.

NUTRI ZOO
50 Sicard Local 118, Ste. Therese, QC, J7E 5R1. Contact: Jean Desjardins, V.P. - Tel: (514) 434-4499, (800) 774-4499, Fax: (514) 434-4694. Specialist in home delivery of pet food and accessories. Established: 1991 - Franchising Since: 1994 - No. of Units: Company Owned: 2 - Franchised: 102- Franchise Fee: $10,000 - Royalty: None required - Total Inv: $10,000 fran. fee, $8,000 truck, $2,000 cash flow for one month - Financing: No.

PAMPERED PAWS LIMITED
201 Davenport Road, Toronto, ON, M5R 2E8. Contact: Lesley Weeks, President - Tel: (416) 962-7877, Fax: (416) 962-5168, E-Mail: pamperedpaws.com, Web Site: www.pamperedpaws.com. We are a business school which teaches the art of animal grooming. Training up to 16 weeks - ongoing support provided. Established: 1969 - No. of Units: Company Owned: 2 - Franchise Fee: $25,000 - Total Inv: $100,000.

PAULMAC'S PET FOOD, PAULMAC'S PLUS
Pet Value Canada Inc.
2365 Whittington Dr., RR#3, Peterborough, ON, K9J 6X4. Contact: Wade D. Jamieson - Tel: (888) 254-7824, Fax: (905) 946-0659. Sale of pet food, pet supplies and pets. Established: 1983 - Franchising Since: 1987 - No. of Units: Company Owned: 10 - Franchised: 39- Franchise Fee: $25,000 (10 years) - Royalty: 3% - Total Inv: $135,000+ - Financing: No.

PET HABITAT
International Bio Research Ltd.
6921 Heather St., Vancouver, BC, V6P 3P5. Contact: Ernest Ang, Pres. - Tel: (604) 266-2721, Fax: (604) 266-5880, E-Mail: pethabitat@aol.com. Upscale retail pet shop. Established: 1979 - Franchising Since: 1981 - No. of Units: Company Owned: 1 - Franchised: 7 - Franchise Fee: $15,000 and up - Royalty: 5% on gross sales - Total Inv: $125,000 and up - Financing: Yes.

PET VALU
Pet Valu Canada Inc.
130 Royal Crest Ct, Markham, ON, L3R 0A1. Contact: Wade D. Jamieson, Vice President, Franchise Sales - Tel: (905) 946-1200. Sale of pet foods and pet supplies. Established: 1976 - Franchising Since: 1987 - No. of Units: Company Owned: 32 - Franchised: 215 - Franchise Fee: $12,000 (6 years) - Royalty: 6%, 10% rent - Total Inv: $75,000 - Financing: No.

PETLAND
Petland Canada Inc
4895 boul des Forges, Trois-Rivieres, QC, G8Y 4Z3. Contact: Robert Brissette, Pres. - Tel: (819) 378-6434, Fax: (819) 378-6012. Petland has over 30 years of experience developing unique specialty pet retail stores. Turn key development programs available, real estate and site selection service, custom store design and animal habitats, comprehensive training program, complete operational and marketing system. Established: 1969 - Franchising Since: 1990 - No. of Units: Franchised: 49 in Canada - Franchise Fee: $25,000 - Royalty: 4.5% of sales - Total Inv: $75,000 cash or equivalents plus - Financing: Pledgeable assets of $125,000 to secure bank financing.

PETLAND
Petland Quebec
7400, boul. Taschereau, bur. 105, Brossard, QC, J4W 1M9. Contact: Jean Picard, Vice-President - Tel: (450) 465-4989, Fax: (450) 465-6085. Franchise network of 24 petshops, full line livestock included. Established: 1997 - Franchising Since: 1997 - No. of Units: Franchised: 24 - Franchise Fee: $25,000 - Royalty: 4.5% - Total Inv: $175,000.

PETS BEAUTIFUL
371 Hamilton Road, London, ON, N5Z 1R7. Contact: Barb Mathison - Tel: (800) 565-8446, Fax: (519) 432-9744, E-Mail: petsbeautiful @serix.com, Web Site: www.petsbeautiful.ca. Pet grooming school. Established: 1996 - No. of Units: Company Owned: 3 - Total Inv: $50,000 - Financing: No.

PETS FIRST
Pets first Products & Services, Inc.
106-12824 78th Ave., Surrey , BC, V3W 8E7. Contact: Nat Monachese, V.P. - Tel: (604) 590-7387, (800) 738-7178, Fax: (604) 590-5578, E-Mail: pets1st@pro.net, Web Site: www.pets1st.com. Direct selling of pet food and supplies over 100 products, home delivered. Established: 1994 - Franchising Since: 1994 - No. of Units: Company Owned: 2 - Franchised: 7 - Franchise Fee: Depends on demographic numbers - Financing: Yes.

RUFFIN'S PET CENTER, INC.
109 Industrial Dr., Dunnville, ON, N1A 2X5. Contact: Mark Reynolds, President - Tel: (905) 774-7079, Fax: (905) 774-1096, E-Mail: franchise@ruffinspet.com, Web Site: www.ruffinspet.com. A progessive and fun franchise combining the best aspects of a pet store with those of a pet food outlet. A reasonable startup cost along with great support and programs make Ruffin's the ideal franchise for anyone looking to establish their own business but want the support Ruffin's can provide. Established: 1981 - Franchising Since: 1987 - No. of Units: Franchised: 14 - Franchise Fee: $20,000 - Royalty: 4%, 1% adv. - Total Inv: $75,000-$90,000 - Financing: No, Assistance in obtaining.

RYAN'S PET FOODS
Ryan's Pet Food Inc.
4699 Keele Street, Ste. 2, Downsview, ON, M3J 2N8. Contact: Ted Loyst, Jim Walker, Chairman, President - Tel: T. Loyst - (416) 661-9916, J. Walker - (905) 771-9227, Fax: (416) 661-9706. Ryan's Pet Food Inc. is a specialty pet food and accessory business. By providing the consumer with guidance on pet care and nutrition, as well as quality pet food and accessories, we provide a complete service to our customers. Ryan's is geared for people who love animals and desire to convert this enthusiasm into a business. Ryan's is a low-investment and successful business for operating a retail specialty pet food store. Full training and support. Established: 1979 - Franchising Since: 1993 - No. of Units: Company Owned: 13 - Franchised: 9 - Franchise Fee: $25,000 - Royalty: Flat monthly fee - Total Inv: $95,000 est. - Financing: Available through financial institutions.

SLINKY SAM'S PETS
453 Parot Road, Brandon, MB, R0L 1S7. Contact: Fran. Dev. - Tel: (204) 235-0113. Retailer of pets, pet foods and supplies. Full 2 weeks training and ongoing support. Established: 1987 - No. of Units: Franchised: 32 - Total Inv: $5,750 min cash required.

THE GLOBAL FAMILY OF PET FOOD STORES
70 Doncaster Avenue, Thornhill, ON, L3T 1L3. Contact: Fran. Dev. - Tel: (905) 771-9227, Fax: (905) 771-1032. Retail, franchise and distribution of pet food, accessories, related supplies and services. Training ongoing throughout 10 year term. Established: 1976 - No. of Units: Franchised: 50 - Total Inv: $50,000-$100,000.

PHOTO, FRAMING AND ART

ARTS' STUDIO
244 Brooklyn Blvd., Winnipeg, MB, R1L 2N4. Contact: Fran. Dev. - Tel: (204) 235-0010. Portrait studio photography. On-site 5 days training, ongoing support. Established: 1995 - No. of Units: Franchised: 9 - Total Inv: $25,000 min cash required.

ECONO COLOR
170 Townsend Street, Sydney, NS, B1P 5E2. - Tel: (902) 455-0479, Fax: (902) 445-3147. Photofinishing, photography and retail. Locations available in Nova Scotia. Full training and support provided. Established: 1998 - No. of Units: Franchised: 5 - Total Inv: $50,000.

FRAMING & ART CENTRE
Franchise Concepts
1800 Appleby Line, Burlington, ON, L7L 6A1. Contact: Diane Howatt, Dir of Franchise Development/Operations - Tel: (905) 332-6116, (800) 563-7263, Fax: (905) 335-5377, Web Site: www.framingand artcentre.com. FRAMING & ART CENTRE, is Canada's only national art and custom framing franchise and the only framing retailer in Canada licensed to offer Air Miles®. Located in neighborhood shopping centers, each store offers an attractive, creative atmosphere featuring custom framing. We offer exceptional training and support, national buying power and proven marketing programs. Established: 1974 - Franchising Since: 1974 - No. of Units: Franchised: 54 - Franchise Fee: $25,000 - Royalty: 6%, 2% adv. - Total Inv: $96,000-$141,000 and franchise fee - Financing: Third party.

FUTURE STARS SPORTS PHOTOGRAPHY
325 Barton St. E., Stoney Creek, ON, L8E 2K8. Contact: Joe Bruno, Pres. - Tel: (905) 664-9511 or (800) 461-6575, Fax: (905) 664-9520, E-Mail: joebruno@future-stars-sp.com, Web Site: www.future-stars-sp.com. Photography services for youth sports organizations. Offering exciting products like trading cards, photo pennants, digital clocks, calenders, mouse pads and more. New action photography division now available. Established: 1987 - Franchising Since: 1991 - No. of Units: Company Owned: 7 - Franchised: 17 - Franchise Fee: $5,000 and up - Royalty: N/A - Total Inv: $10,000-$15,000 - Financing: No.

JAPAN CAMERA 1 HOUR PHOTO
Japan Camera Centre Ltd.
178 Main Street, Unionville, ON, L3R 2G9. Contact: Franchise Department - Tel: (416) 445-1481, (800) 268-7740, Fax: (416) 445-0519, Web Site: www.japancamera.com. In business for over 40 years of memories. We are the originators of the 1 hour photo franchise. We help you provide up to date photo imaging products and services that will help your customers capture and enjoy a lifetime. Established: 1959 - Franchising Since: 1981 - No. of Units: Company Owned: 20 - Franchised: 94 - Franchise Fee: $20,000 - Royalty: 5%, advertising 2.5% - Total Inv: $350,000 - Financing: Assistance to qualified applicant.

MAGNI FRAME CUSTOM FRAMING & ART STUDIOS
3401 Dufferin Street, Toronto, ON, M6A 2T9. - Tel: (416) 785-2161, Fax: (416) 785-4639. Custom framing, art conservation and restoration, memorabilia conservation and framing. Specializing in all custom framing of specialty items such as tapestries, needlework, silk screens. Established: 1988 - Franchising Since: 1989 - No. of Units: Company Owned: 1 - Franchised: 3 - Franchise Fee: $25,000 - Royalty: 5% + 2% - Total Inv: Depending on location - Financing: Yes.

MOTO PHOTO
CIS Franchising Limited
4-44 East Beaver Creek Rd, Richmond Hill, ON, L4B 1G4. Contact: Patricia Lambie - Tel: (905) 889-0889, (877) 299-6686, Fax: (905) 889-1680, E-Mail: franinfo@motophoto.ca, Web Site: www.motophoto.ca. Motophoto is the largest franchise of photo imaging stores, offering

complete imaging services and merchandize from digital cameras, memory cards to film, frames & albums. Established: 1987 - Franchising Since: 1987 - No. of Units: Company Owned: 3 - Franchised: 30 - Franchise Fee: $35,000 - Royalty: 3%-6% - Total Inv: $95,000 cash - Financing: Assistance.

NORTHERN IMAGES
Arctic Cooperative
1645 Inkster Blvd., Winnipeg, MB, R2X 2W7. Contact: Dave Wilson, Marketing Director - Tel: (204) 697-1625, Fax: (204) 697-1880. Arts and crafts. Established: 1972 - No. of Units: 5.

PICTURES
85 Chambers Drive, Unit 1, Ajax, ON, L1Z 1E2. Contact: Henry Lee, Dir. Fran. - Tel: (905) 683-9935, Fax: (905) 683-1960. A unique wall decor store featuring framed art, gallery prints, limited-edition prints and custom framing. Established: 1981 - Franchising Since: 1990 - No. of Units: Company Owned: 5 - Franchised: 30 - Royalty: 5% - Total Inv: $35,000-$75,000 - Financing: Financial, realty, comp., full training.

REGIS PICTURES & FRAMES
Regis Pictues & Frames Ltd
102 SE Marine Drive, Vancouver, BC, V5X 2S3. Contact: Jane Dew - Tel: (604) 327-3447, (877) 711-2233, Fax: (604) 327-5223, E-Mail: franchise@regispictures.com, Web Site: www.regispictures.com. Located in major malls throughout BC providing complete custom framing and home decor items including premade frames, prints, framed art and giftware. Established: 1979 - Franchising Since: 2001 - No. of Units: Company Owned: 19 - Franchise Fee: $25,000 - Royalty: 6% - Total Inv: $140,000-$150,000 - Financing: Yes; third party.

SOOTER STUDIOS LTD.
88 Sherbrook St., Winnipeg, MB, R3C 2B3. Contact: John Kresz, Pres. - Tel: (204) 775-8188, Fax: (204) 786-7708. Portrait studios, photofinishing and photo related products. Established: 1960 - Franchising Since: 1966 - No. of Units: Company Owned: 142 - Franchised: 180 - Franchise Fee: $1.50 per population, Royalty: 5% + - Total Inv: $30,000-$60,000 - Financing: Yes.

ZELLERS PORTRAIT STUDIO
St- A Photo Corp.
3 Picardie, Gatineau, QC, J8T 1N3. Contact: J. St. Amour, V.P. - Tel: (819) 669-6022. Personalized family portraits as well as children, graduation etc. Complete photo studio service plus lamination, framing and photographic restoration. Established: 1988 - Franchising Since: 1989 - No. of Units: Franchised: 32 - Franchise Fee: $25,000 - Royalty: 2.5 % Sales - Total Inv: $85,000 - Financing: Yes.

PRINTING AND COPYING SERVICES

AD CRAFT
The Professional Card Exports
855 Hilton Blvd, Newmarket, ON, L3X 2H7. Contact: Marketing Department - Tel: (905) 953-1256. Printed promotional products for franchisors & franchisees, specializing in full color business cards, brochures and display and direct mail items. Established: 1997.

ANGEL'S PRINTING
718 Elvy Place, Suite 238, Winnipeg, MB, R4S 4N2. Contact: Fran. Dev. - Tel: (204) 235-0091. Full service print shop. Full training and ongoing support. Established: 1988 - No. of Units: Franchised: 7 - Total Inv: $80,000 min cash required.

HENRY ARMSTRONG'S INSTANT PRINTING
Armstrong Printing Ltd.
955 Portage Ave., Winnipeg, MB, R3G 0R2. Contact: Greg Armstrong, V.P. Mktg. - Tel: (204) 958-4230, Fax: (204) 783-7963. Instant printing and copying. Established: 1968 - Franchising Since: 1982 - No. of Units: 14 - Franchise Fee: $12,500.

KWIK-KOPY DESIGN & PRINT CENTERS
Kwik Kopy Printing Canada Corp.
1550, 16th Avenue, Richmond Hill, ON, L4B 3K9. Contact: Linda Budway, Franchise Development -Tel: (416) 798-7007, (800) 387-9725, Fax: (905) 780-0575, E-Mail: kkpcc@kwikkopy.ca, Web Site: www.kwikkopy.ca. Franchisor of full service print/color & black & white high speed digital copying/design franchise centres, servicing business communities. Established: 1979 - Franchising Since: 1979 - No. of Units: Company Owned: 3 - Franchised: 67 - Franchise Fee: $29,500 - Royalty: 6%, 3% adv. - Total Inv: $200,000 + working capital - Financing: Portion of franchise fee + bank small buisness loan applicable.

LASERNETWORKS
785 Pacific Rd., Unit #1, Oakville, ON, L6L 6M3. Contact: Chris Stoate, President - Tel: (905) 847-5990, (800) 461-4879, Fax: (905) 847-5991, Web Site: www.lasernetworks.com. A Laser printer sales and service and supply agreements or sales, services and supply of laser printers. Established: 1987 - Franchising Since: 1990 - No. of Units: Company Owned: 2 - Franchised: 34 - Franchise Fee: $0-$3,500 - Royalty: 5%-7.5% depending on volume and sales type - Total Inv: Nil-$10,000 - Financing: No.

LE PRINT EXPRESS
160 Nashdene Rd., Scarborough, ON, M1V 4C4. - Tel: (416) 754-8440, (800) 263-1723, Fax: (416) 754-2200, E-Mail: franchis@leprint.com, Web Site: www.leprint.com. Positioned in high-traffic areas, such as Wal-Mart supercenters and major shopping malls, Le Print Express provides high-quality graphic imaging services to retail and commercial clients. Business cards, colour copies, high-volume duplication, document creation, personalized retail gifts and much more. Established: 1989 - Franchising Since: 1993 - No. of Units: Company Owned: 5 - Franchised: 55 - Franchise Fee: $10,000 - Royalty: Varies - Total Inv: $54,500 + equipment package of $145,000 - Financing: Yes for equipment package.

MADE 'N-A-MINUTE PRINTERS
Made 'N-A-Minute Printers, Ltd.
2050 Rosser Ave., Burnaby, BC, V5C 5Y1. Contact: Paul McCrea, Sec/Treas. - Tel: (604) 688-2381, Fax: (604) 689-5388. Instant print shops. Established: 1979 - Franchising Since: 1985 - No. of Units: Company Owned: 1 - Franchised: 8 - Royalty: 4% 1st $250,000, then 3% - Total Inv: $35,000 - Financing: No.

MINUTEMAN PRESS
Minuteman Press International
6299 Airport Rd., Ste. 704, Mississauga, ON, L4V 1N3. Contact: Don Greeder, Regional V.P. - Tel: (905) 677-6015, (800) 645-3006, Fax: (905) 677-6061, Web Site: www.minuteman-press.com. Full service printing and graphics franchise. Established: 1973 - Franchising Since: in U.S.A. since 1975, in Canada since 1977 - No. of Units: Franchised: 900 - Franchise Fee: US$44,500 - Royalty: 6% of gross - Total Inv: US$110,000 + - Financing: Available.

PRINT THREE
Print Three Franchising Corporation
160 Nashdene Road, Scarborough, ON, M1V 4C4. Contact: John Johnson - Tel: (416) 754-8700, (800) 335-5918, Fax: (416) 754-8441, E-Mail: john@printthree.com, Web Site: www.printthree.com. Print Three centres are providers of digital printing, reproduction and finishing services to meet corporate and business requirements. All franchisees are professionally trained in customer service excellence. Established: 1971 - Franchising Since: 1981 - No. of Units: Franchised: 66 - Franchise Fee: $20,000 - Royalty: 6% for 10 years; 4% next 10 years and 3% last 5 years - Total Inv: $64,900 plus minimum $25,000 in working capital - Financing: Leasing from third party for equipment and cabinetry.

SIR SPEEDY
2800 Fourteenth Ave., #24, Markham, ON, L3R 0E4. - Tel: (905) 475-7627, Fax: (905) 475-7628, Web Site: www.sirspeedy.com. Full service printing and copy centres with desk top publishing facilities. Unique niche as "The Business Printer". Established: 1985 - Franchising Since: 1985 - No. of Units: Company Owned: 1 - Franchised: 6 - Franchise Fee: $20,000 - Royalty: 6%, 3% adv. - Total Inv: $110,000-$170,000 plus working capital - Financing: N/A.

SPEEDY PRINTING CENTERS

#115-32500 South Fraser Way, Box 405, Abbotsford, BC, V2T 4W1. Contact: Don Brenneman, Reg. Dir. - Tel: (604) 850-7726, Fax: (604) 850-7729. Full service printing, copying, business service centers. Full color printing, copying, desktop publishing, typesetting and faxing, local region support. Established: US 1986 - Franchising Since: US 1987 - No. of Units: Franchised: US 403, Canada 33 - Franchise Fee: $19,500 - Royalty: 6% on receipts - Total Inv: $150,000 turnkey - Financing: Yes.

SURE PRINT AND COPY CENTRES

Sure Print & Copy Centres Inc
#106-A12-1250 Eglinton Ave. W., Mississauga, ON, L5V 1N3. Contact: Par Amlani, Franchise Mgr. - Tel: (416) 910-6362, Fax: (416) 855-1279, Web Site: www.surecopy.com. Full service business centres. Servicing "SOHO" corporate clientelle since 1986. Full service B/W digital and color output, large format posters, engineering drawings, binding, laminating, etc. Established: 1986 - Franchising Since: 1991 - No. of Units: Company Owned: 2 - Franchised: 57 - Franchise Fee: $25,000 - Royalty: Flat monthly royalty fee - $450 (up to $1000) - Total Inv: $75,000 - Financing: Yes.

T.D.I. SYSTEMS CANADA

11-1393 Border St., Winnipeg, MB, R3H 0N1. Contact: Wilson Wong, Pres. - Tel: (204) 697-9612, Fax: (204) 697-9615. Large format printing (artist canvas, watercolor cloth, vinyl, translite, photo papers, etc.) from one printer. Enlarge images as small as 1"x2" into any size on any media. Established: 1994 - No. of Units: Company Owned: 120 - Total Inv: $40,000 - Financing: Yes. NOT OFFERING FRANCHISES AT THIS TIME.

PUBLICATIONS

AUGUST COMMUNICATIONS

Division of the PW Group
225-530 Century St, Winnipeg, MB, R3H 0Y4. Contact: Gladwyn Nickel, General Manager - Tel: (204) 957-0265, Fax: (204) 957-0217, E-Mail: august@escape.ca. We offer a full range of printing, graphic and publishing services. From catalogues and books to magazines - we do it all!

BINGO BUGLE NEWSPAPER

Shadow Publishing Corp.
P.O. Box 158, 26 Hale Road, Brampton, ON, L6W 3M1. Contact: Dawna Beatty, Master CDN. Fran. - Tel: (877) 272-8453 (ONT. only), (519) 938-8124, Fax: (519) 938-8120. Publish your own bingo newspaper - you provide local stories, we provide editorial from a staff of 14 writers. Established: 1979 (US),1991 (CAN) - Franchising Since: 1991 - No. of Units: Company Owned: 1 - Franchised: 4 - Franchise Fee: $5,000-$10,000 - Royalty: 8% monthly maintenance - Total Inv: $20,000-$30,000 (incl. computer equipment) - Financing: N/A.

CANADIAN BUSINESS FRANCHISE MAGAZINE

CGB Publishing Ltd
3388 A Tennyson Avenue, Victoria, BC, V8Z 3P6. Contact: Donna Kendell, Editor - Tel: (250) 383-8855, (800) 454-1662, Fax: (250) 383-8889, E-Mail: cgb@island.net, Web Site: www. cgb.ca. One of Canada's premiere publication, aimed at the growing market for franchisees, is a source of guidance, news and expertise from the industry. Produced bimonthly and distributed nationally, this is a quality, full color magazine. Published by CGB Publishing Ltd, along with the Canadian Franchise Directory, the Canadian Franchise Handbook and the International Franchise Investor. Members of the CFA and the IFA.

CANADIAN CREDIT REPORTING LTD.

200 Consumer Road, Suite 406, Toronto, ON, M2J 4R4. Contact: VP Sales - Tel: (416) 499-9936, (800) 567-4602, Fax: (416) 499-9703. We make freshly investigated credit reports on campanies and individuals. Franchisors use our comprehensive reports to aid in decisions regarding franchisee approval and to monitor existing franchisees.

DOLLARS & SENSE

183 King St., Ste. 201, London, ON, N6A 1C9. Contact: Kent Fletcher, Owner - Tel: (519) 645-8685, (800) 447-1826, Fax: (519) 645-1593. The best value, widely sold, and most useful directly distributed fundraising coupon book in your community. Established: 1991 - Franchising Since: 1996 - No. of Units: Company Owned: 3 - Franchise Fee: $9,000-$40,000 (variable to population) - Total Inv: $9,000 franchise fee + $33,000 stock - Financing: No.

HOME & OFFICE COMPUTING

4609 Crysler Ave., Niagara Falls, ON, L2E 3V6. - Tel: (905) 371-3115, (800) 668-5582, Fax: (905) 371-3117. A monthly magazine devoted to home based business, small business and technology. Established: 1995 - Franchising Since: 1997 - No. of Units: Company Owned: 1 - Franchised: 9 - Franchise Fee: $18,000 - Royalty: 0% - Total Inv: $18,000 plus $10,000 working capital - Financing: No.

MARKETINGPROFILE PUBLICATIONS *

The MarketingProfile Publications Company Inc.
Unit 1-1329 Niakwa Road East, Winnipeg, MB, R2J 3T4. Contact: Marc Beaudry, VP of Buisness Development - Tel: (204) 888-3709, (866) 888-3709, Fax: (204) 888-3813, E-Mail: contact@marketing profiles.com, Web Site: www.marketingprofiles.com. Learn how to quickly and easily tap into the high profits of custom publishing. Build your own profitable custom publishing buisness with no territorial restrictions or royalty fees. The MarketingProfile Publications Company has been supplying highly valued marketing magazines, at little or no cost to clients, since 1999. Established: 1999 - Franchising Since: 2004 - No. of Units: Company Owned: 1 - Franchised: 2 - Franchise Fee: $30,000 - Total Inv: $30,000 - Financing: No.

SANTA COMMUNICATIONS

1001 William St, Suite 300, Thunder Bay, ON, P7B 6M1. Contact: Fran. Dev. - Tel: (807) 623-8288, Fax: (807) 623-6213. Monthly publication of "Profile" magazine franchise. Established: 1991 - No. of Units: Franchised: 1 - Total Inv: $20,000.

REAL ESTATE SERVICES

ARJECO INDUSTRIES LTD.

418 Hanlon Rd., Unit 9, Woodbridge, ON, L4L 4Z1. Contact: Fran. Dev. - Tel: (905) 851-8782. Franchise/store construction offers complete turnkey realty operations. Established: 1982.

BAKER ASSOCIATES INC.

486 Albert St. c/o Doral Inn, Ottawa, ON, K1R 5B5. Contact: Fran. Dev. - Tel: (613) 230-8055, Fax: (613) 237-9660. Franchisor/franchisee consultant - Real Estate. Established: 1980.

CENTURY 21 CANADA LIMITED PARTNERSHIP

#700-1199 West Pender St., Vancouver, BC, V6E 2R1. Contact: C. Brian Rushton, Senior Vice President Franchise Sales & Development - Tel: (604) 606-2100, Fax: (604) 606-2125, E-Mail: thepower@century 21canada.com, Web Site: www.century21canada.com. CENTURY 21 Canada is the master franchisor in Canada for the CENTURY 21 real estate brand. CENTURY 21 is the world's largest real estate franchisor, actively operating in 41 countries and territories throughout the world. The System has over 6,600 offices and approximately 100,000 sales associates worldwide. Established: 1975 - Franchising Since: 1976 - No. of Units: Franchised: 345- Franchise Fee: $20,000 metro areas; $10,000 rural areas - Royalty: Various programs available - Total Inv: $50,000-$100,000 - Financing: N/A.

COLDWELL BANKER AFFILIATES OF CANADA

1 Richmond St. West, Ste. 701, Toronto, ON, M5H 3W4. Contact: Gary Hockey, Vice President - Tel: (416) 947-9229, (800) 268- 9599, Fax: (416) 777-4604, Web Site: www.coldwellbanker.ca. The most complete full service real estate franchise. Full management/sales training and support, extensive marketing system, and unsurpassed revenue generating capabilities. Established: 1989 - Franchising Since: 1989 - No. of Units: Franchised: 230 - Franchise Fee: Up to $18,000 - Royalty: Variable - Total Inv: Variable - Financing: No.

GELMON MCNEIL INC. (GMI)

1324-17 Avenue SW., Suite 330, Calgary, AB, T2T 5S8. Contact: Lewis Gelmon, Managing Director - Tel: (800) 459-3413, Fax: (403) 215-2519, E-Mail: gelbro@agt.net. GMI specializes in negotiating commercial tenant leases for industrial or multi-unit franchise operators. We also administer and perform lease audit recoveries from landlord overbilling. Other services include full-out service of real estate administration. GMI works for and only accepts fees from its clients (the tenant). Established: 1994.

GROUP TRANSACTION BROKERAGE SERVICES INC.

550 Sherbrooke W., #775, Montreal, QC, H3A 1B9. Contact: J.L. Bernard, Gen. Mgr. - Tel: (514) 288-6777, Fax: (514) 288-7543, E-Mail: trane.action@sympatico.ca, Web Site: www.trans-action.qc.ca. Complete Real Estate Services. Established: 1980 - Franchising Since: 1982 - No. of Units: Franchised: 56 - Franchise Fee: $6,000-$17,000 - Royalty: $95/month/agent service fee, $50/month/agent adv. fee - Total Inv: $15,000-$50,000 - Financing: Yes.

HOMELIFE

Homelife Realty Services, Inc.

28 Drewry Ave., Willowdale, ON, M2M 1C8. Contact: Dennis Goldberg, Franc. Sales & Mktg. - Tel: (416) 226-9770, Fax: (416) 226-0848, Web Site: www.homelife.com. Real estate offices. Established: 1985 - Franchising Since: 1985 - No. of Units: Franchised: 210, US office (CA-90, MI-65) - Franchise Fee: $9,000 - Royalty: $575 per month - Total Inv: $10,000 - Financing: In some cases.

HOMES CANADA OF ONTARIO

34 Dynasty Avenue, Unit28, Stoney Creek, ON, L8G 5C7. Contact: Fran. Dev. - Tel: (905) 664-4470, Fax: (905) 664-5326, Web Site: www.homes-canada.com. We are a Real Estate Marketing company specializing in private sales. We enable our clients to sell their property for a low flat fee and pay no commission. Full training including sales and administration plus ongoing support. Established: 1995 - No. of Units: Franchised: 2 - Total Inv: $25,000-$75,000 average investment.

LOCATIONS REALTY CORP.

8 Comden Street, Suite 200, Toronto, ON, M5V 1V1. - Tel: (416) 504-7100, (877) 704-7100, Fax: (416) 504-7359, E-Mail: info@locations realty.com. Locations is a full-serviced specialized retail leasing force. We are able to provide you with site selection based on your criteria, demographic needs, studies traffic counts, competitive market analyses and rental rate criteria and lease terms as required to fulfill your needs. We look forward to meeting your challange. Established: 1988.

MARSH & CO. HOSPITALITY REALTY INC.

121 Willowdale Avenue, Suite 104, North York, ON, M2N 6A3. Contact: Ron Scribner, VP - Tel: (416) 223-1600, Fax: (416) 223-1145, Web Site: www.interlog.com. We are a real estate broker specializing in the hospitality industry. We sell hotels, motels, restaurants, taverns, bars, fast food outlets, lease premises and develop franchises. Established: 1949.

PRO JET

Pro Jet Courtier, Inc.

2800 Einstein #145, Quebec City, QC, G1X 4N8. Contact: Julien Riou, Pres. - Tel: (418) 652-7887, Fax: (418) 652-7256. Real Estate. Established: 1987 - Franchising Since: 1990 - No. of Units: Company Owned: 1 - Franchised: 2 - Franchise Fee: $5,000 - Royalty: Variable - Total Inv: $5,000-$45,000 - Financing: Yes.

PROPERTYGUYS.COM

128 Highfield St #210, Moncton, NB, E1C 5N7. Contact: Ken LeBlanc - Tel: (506) 860-3433, (866) 666-9744, Fax: (506) 854-6918, E-Mail: kleblanc@propertyguys.com. PropertyGuys.com is a "For Sale By Owner" (FSBO) real estate marketing company that specializes in helping you sell your own home. By using traditional real estate marketing techniques, we offer For Sale By Owner home sellers flat fee marketing packages, saving For Sale By Owner clients "thousands of dollars" in real estate commissions on the private sale of their home. Established: 1998 - Franchising Since: 2002 - No. of Units: Company Owned: 1 - Franchised: 20 - Franchise Fee: $12,500-$17,500 - Royalty: 9% + 3% advertising - Total Inv: $20,000-$25,000.

REALTY WORLD CANADA

39 Wynford Dr, Don Mills, ON, M3C 3K5. Contact: Ken Halsey, Franchise Sales Manager - Tel: (416) 510-5827. Full service real estate franchisor. Established: 1974 - No. of Units: Franchised: 115 Canada, 465 U.S. and others - Franchise Fee: $1,000-$5,000 - Royalty: Variable.

S & H REALTY CORPORATION

130 King Street West #2810 Box 47, Toronto, ON, M5X 1A9. Contact: Danny Klempfner, Pres. - Tel: (416) 364-7810, Fax: (416) 364-9401. A real estate broker and consultant specializing in retail leasing and site selection on behalf of expanding franchisors. Services offered include finding a site and negotiating transactions as well as preparing market analysis reports. Established: 1982.

SMART SELLER HOME SALES

215 Advance Blvd., #5, Brampton, ON, L6T 4V9. Contact: Franchise Director - Tel: (905) 450-7863, (888) 383-SAVE, Fax: (905) 450-0871. Enable homeowners to sell their homes without paying real estate commissions. Get sold and save. Established: 1995 - Franchising Since: 1997 - No. of Units: Company Owned: 2 - Franchised: 9 - Franchise Fee: Variable - Total Inv: $15-$100,000 - Financing: Yes.

SUTTON GROUP

Canwest Marketing Ltd.

1700 Varsity Estates Dr. N.W., Calgary, AB, T3B 2W9. Contact: Chris Bolt, Pres. - Tel: (403) 286-5863, Fax: (403) 288-0610. 100% commission, fee for service real estate brokerage. Average franchise has 60 realtors. Established: 1989 - Franchising Since: 1989 - No. of Units: Company Owned: 2 - Franchised: 24 - Franchise Fee: $20,000 - Royalty: $75 per month per salesperson - Total Inv: $120,000-$150,000 - Financing: No.

THE LEASE COACH INC

1044-10303 Jasper Avenue, Edmonton, AB, T5J 3N6. Contact: Dale Willerton, Founder & CEO - Tel: (780) 448-2645, Fax: (780) 448-2670, E-Mail: dalewilleron@theleasecoach.com, Web Site: www.thelease coach.com A network of certified lease consultants execlusively helping tenants. Negotiations, lease renewals, site selection, document reviews, self help books, tapes and seminars. Established: 1993.

TRANS-ACTION REAL ESTATE SERVICES

Group Trans-Action Brokerage Service

550 Sherbrooke Street West, #795, Montreal, QC, H3A 1B9. - Tel: (514) 288-6777, Fax: (514) 288-7543, E-Mail: trans.action@sympatico. ca, Web Site: www.trans.-action.qc.ca. Complete real estate services. Established: 1980 - Franchising Since: 1982 - No. of Units: Franchised: 65 - Franchise Fee: $6,000-$17,000 - Royalty: $95/ per month, per agent - Total Inv: $12,000-$34,000 - Financing: Yes.

RENTAL SERVICES

INN TENTS

Inn Tents Canada Inc.

466 Elgin St., P.O. Box 2142, Brantford, ON, N3T 5Y6. Contact: Rick St. Amand, Co-Owner - Tel: (519) 756-2360, Fax: (519) 756-9451. Businesses are set up as home base operations. Franchises receive an inventory of party canopies to be rented out in the market that the franchise has bought the rights to. Established: 1993 - Franchising Since: 1993 - No. of Units: Company Owned: 1 - Franchised: 2 - Franchise Fee: $10,000 - Royalty: Per year is based on the amount of rental cost of each canopy in inventory - Total Inv: $25,000 - Financing: Possible.

JOE LOUE TOUT RENT ALL, INC.

28 Vanier St, Chateauguay, QC, J6J 3W8. Contact: J.M. Bissonnette, Pres. - Tel: (450) 692-6268, (800) 361-2020, Fax: (450) 692-2848. Tools and equipment, party goods, recreational vehicles and boats, etc. Established: 1982 - Franchising Since: 1982 - No. of Units: Franchised: 85 - Franchise Fee: $20,000 - Royalty: 4%+3% publicity - Financing: Yes.

RETAIL

A BUCK OR TWO STORES LTD.

8200 Jane St, Concord, ON, L4K 5A7. Contact: Audra Wosik, Fran. Dir. - Tel: (905) 738-3180, Fax: (905) 738-3176. 2,000 or 3,000 sq. ft. locations in enclosed shopping malls coast to coast selling general merchandise ranging from $1 to $2 with a bright and vibrant dollar store traffic oriented concept. Established: 1986 - Franchising Since: 1988 - No. of Units: Company Owned: 3 - Franchised: 160 - Franchise Fee: $50,000 - Royalty: 6% - Total Inv: $160,000 - Financing: Yes in-house.

ABINGTON'S (COLLECTIBLES)
Franchise Bancorp Inc

4699 Keele St, Unit 1, Downsview, ON, M3J 2N8. Contact: Mike Mayerson, V.P. Franchising/Leasing - Tel: (416) 661-9916, Fax: (416) 661-9706, E-Mail: mike@franchisebancorp.com. Quality collectibles in a unique market niche between the gift store and toy store. All merchandise in Abington's is an animal motif. Ceramics to wood, plush to crystal. Established: 1989 - Franchising Since: 1990 - No. of Units: Company Owned: 3 - Franchised: 3 - Franchise Fee: $25,000 - Royalty: 6% - Total Inv: $220,000-$270,000 - Financing: Through financial institutions.

ANIMATRIX
Cartoon Kingdom

250 The Esplanade, Suite 402, Toronto, ON, M5A 1J2. Contact: Viive Tamm - Tel: (416) 364-4441, Fax: (416) 304-0488. Unique and dazzling stores selling merchandise and apparel from Disney, Warner Bros, Sesame Street and much more in a bright, charming decor with service so friendly customers feel like guests. Established: 1998 - No. of Units: Company Owned: 2 - Franchise Fee: Depends on location.

AVORY IMPORTS

1653 Greenfield Road, Cambridge, ON, N1R 5S5. Contact: Terry R. Hunter, Gen. Mngr. - Tel: (519) 740-9074, Fax: (519) 740-9237, E-Mail: huntplace@golden.net. Unique retail giftware concept, kiosks located in regional shopping centres and malls. Kiosk retailing is rapidly becoming a trend in today's shopping invoronment. No. of Units: Company Owned: 5 - Franchise Fee: $24,950 - Total Inv: $25,000-$40,000 - Financing: Support available.

BASS RIVER CHAIRS
S.J. Rodd Trading Limited

11 Morris Dr. Ste 120, Dartmouth, NS, B3B 1M2. Contact: Susan Cranstoun, Franchise Director - Tel: (902) 468-1469, (905) 332-6898, Fax: (902) 468-1475, Web Site: www.bassriverchairs.com. Quality furnishings since 1860: Bass River is a leading Canadian chain of specialty furniture and household accessory shops. A unique collection of solid hardwood furniture is enhanced by a full line of quality cooks' tools, gifts, accent pieces and home decor accessories. Established: 1991 - Franchising Since: 1991 - No. of Units: Company Owned: 4 - Franchised: 7 - Franchise Fee: $25,000 - Royalty: 6% - 1% advertising - Total Inv: $250,000-$350,000 - Financing: No.

BEAVER LUMBER COMPANY LTD.

7303 Warden Ave., Markham, ON, L3R 5Y6. Contact: Doug Robinson, V.P. Oper. - Tel: (905) 479-2255, Fax: (905) 479-9607. Retail lumber, building materials and related hard goods. Established: 1906 - Franchising Since: 1977 - No. of Units: Company Owned: 35 - Franchised: 98 - Franchise Fee: $8,000-$20,000 - Financing: No.

BIJOUX & COMPAGNIE

5650 Cypihot Street, St. Laurent, PQ, H4S 1V7. Contact: Fran. Dev. - Tel: (514) 334-8203, Fax: (514) 333-4656. Retail sale of jewellery, principally composed of Quebecois creations, importations, as well as gift accessories. Selection and negotiation of sites, business and financial plans, administrative and technical support, promotion and start-up assistance. Established: 1997 - No. of Units: Franchised: 3 - Total Inv: $38,000-$43,000 cash - $105,000-$110,000.

BIRDERS NATURE STORE
The Global Ryans Pet Food Co, Ltd

70 Doncaster Ave, Thornhill, ON, L3T 1L3. Contact: Jim Walker, President - Tel: (905) 771-9227, Fax: (905) 771-1032. Wild bird centered nature gift stores, retailing bird feeders, bird houses, bird baths, bird seed, books, binoculars, garden accessories and gifts. Established: 1991 - Franchising Since: 1991 - No. of Units: Company Owned: 4 - Franchised: 2 - Franchise Fee: $10,000-$25,000 - Royalty: 3%, 2% adv. - Total Inv: $40,000-$120,000 - Financing: Some financing available.

BOOK BANK LTD.

5 Roberta Cres., Nepean, ON, K2J 1G5. Contact: Ted MacMillan, Pres. - Tel: (613) 825-4746, Fax: (613) 825-5615. Franchises bookstores new and used general inventory. Sold on a territory basis. Established: 1982 - Franchising Since: 1986 - No. of Units: Franchised: 4 - Franchise Fee: $16,500 - Royalty: 6% of sales to a capped maximum and minium - Total Inv: $46,500 average total turn key package - Financing: No.

BOUTIK ELECTRIK
Groupe VSRG

333 M Chemin du Tremblay, Boucherville, QC, J4B 7M1. Contact: Daniel Fournier, V.P., Dev. - Tel: (450) 449-4611, (800) 561-7750, Fax: (450) 449-7793, E-Mail: daniel-fournier@boutikelectrik.com, Web Site: www.boutikelectrik.com. Sales and services on shavers, personal care, scissors, gift and small appliances. We also repair all products we sell. Established: 1978 - Franchising Since: 1988 - No. of Units: Company Owned: 1 - Franchised: 25 - Franchise Fee: $20,000 - Royalty: 1% up to $400,000 volume - Total Inv: $125,000 - Financing: Yes.

BRITE LITE INDOOR GARDEN CENTER
Brite-Lite Group

1991 Francis Hughes, Lavel, QC, H7S 2G2. Contact: David Hodgson, President - Tel: (450) 669-3803, (800) 489-2215, Fax: (450) 669-9772, E-Mail: contact@hydroponix.com, Web Site: www.hydroponix.com. Retail store operations selling indoor gardening equipment and supplies - over 1300 products including gardens, lights, fertilizers and books. Established: 1969 - Franchising Since: 1998 - No. of Units: Company Owned: 6 - Franchised: 5 - Franchise Fee: $9,500-$15,000 - Royalty: 1st year, 1% gross sales, following years 2% - Total Inv: $90,000-$130,000.

BUSTERS BUY & SELL

56 Gordon Stree, Guelph, ON, N1H 4H3. Contact: Fran. Dev. - Tel: (519) 826-5963. We are a retail chain specializing in the buying and selling of quality pre-owned merchandise, providing customers with instant cash for the used merchandise and selling goods at "half the cost of regular retail prices", extensive computer product and customer service training and aadvertising support. Established: 1997 - No. of Units: Franchised: 8 - Total Inv: $180,000.

CANADIAN TIRE
Canadian Tire Corporation

2180 Yonge St., P.O. Box 770 Station K, Toronto, ON, M4P 2V8. Web Site: www.canadiantire.ca/dealers. Retailer of automotive, leisure home products and auto service. Established: 1923 - Franchising Since: 1927 - No. of Units: Franchised: 451 -Total Inv: $125,000 initial investment/ $100,000 training fee - Financing: Yes.

CANDLEMAN

24 Midtown Plaza, Saskatoon, SK, S7K 1J9. Contact: Franchise Director - Tel: (888) 260-2179, Fax: (306) 933-9667. Specialty retail stores located in major destination malls, selling candles, candle holders, and unique accessories - 1 week at corporate headquarters and on-site continuous support. Established: 1992 - No. of Units: Franchised: 94 - Total Inv: $150,000-$250,000.

CELLULAR SHOP INC., THE

1080 Adelaide St., N., #21, London, ON, N5Y 2N1. Contact: Ron Porter, Pres. - Tel: (519) 434-6196, (888) CEL SHOP, Fax: (519) 434-1314, Web Site: www.celshop.com. Cellular telephone, paging and wireless communications company, retail store front. Established: 1988 - Franchising Since: 1995 - No. of Units: Company Owned: 1 -

Franchised: 1 - Franchise Fee: $20,000 - Royalty: $1 per customer per month from franchisee residual base - Total Inv: $20,000 fran. fee, $30,000-$50,000, store setup, inv. etc.

CLAIR DELUNE
189 Hymus Blvd, Suite 207, Pointe-Claire, PQ, H9R 1E9. Contact: Fran. Dev. - Tel: (514) 695-8989, Fax: (514) 695-7868. Save at retail of oil lamps, aromatic candles, pot-pourris, wax and wax products, card holders, air freshners, bath oils, body gels and related accessories. Organizational training and development. Locations available in Montreal and Quebec City. Established: 1995 - No. of Units: Franchised: 12 - Total Inv: $125,000+.

CORBEIL ELECTROMENAGERS
Corbeil Electrique Inc
5100 Boul Des Grandes Prairies, St. Leonard, QC, H1R 1A7. Contact: Rene Deshaies, Development Manager - Tel: (514) 322-7726, Fax: (514) 322-8051. Retail sales of major appliances. Specialist offering largest variety at best prices in 8,000 sq. ft. locations. Over 600 models to choose from. Established: 1951 - Franchising Since: 1995 - No. of Units: Company Owned: 4 - Franchised: 11 - Franchise Fee: $25,000-$50,000 - Royalty: 0%-3.5% on a sliding scale - Total Inv: $250,000 - Financing: Through banks.

CRAFTS 'N MORE
Truserv Canada Coperative Inc
1530 Gamble Place, Winnipeg, MB, R3C 3A9. Contact: Hugh Matson, Recruitment & Operations Specialist - Tel: (800) 665-5085, (204) 453-9600, Fax: (204) 477-0445. Member owned cooperative serving 550 stores in Canada, including 34 Crafts 'N More locations coast to coast. Established: 1992 - Franchising Since: 1992 - Membership Fee: $2,000 - Royalty: None - Total Inv: $75,000-$100,000 - Financing: National bank packages.

CRAZY8'S BASIC ESSENTIALS
Crazy8's
Suite 234-810 Quayside Drive, New Westminister, BC, V3M 6B9. Contact: Cormac McCarthy - Tel: (604) 516-0203, Fax: (604) 516-0403, E-Mail: cormac@nornetco.com, Web Site: www.crazy-eights.com. Step above the proliferation of today's dollar store and take advantage of the new demographic retail trend, an upscale home variety store with its pricing based on increments ranging from .88¢-$288.00 offering a broad breadth of merchandise to capture a broad based demographic market in the communities. Established: 1994 - No. of Units: Company Owned: 2 - Franchised: 8 - Franchise Fee: $18,888 includes GST - Royalty: 5%; marketing find 2% - Total Inv: $160,000-$2000,000 - Financing: Franchisor will assist in document preparation.

DAKIN NEWS SYSTEMS, INC.
International News
2000 Argentia Rd., Plaza 1, Ste. 270, Mississauga, ON, L5N 1P7. - Tel: (905) 826-0826, (800) 319-5666, Fax: (905) 826-2105. News-stand with inventory on newspapers, magazines, cards and books, (at selected locations), gifts, souveniers, confection, pop, chips and lotterey tickets. Established: 1994 - Franchising Since: 1994 - No. of Units: Company owned: 9 - Franchised: 93 - Franchise Fee: $30,000 - Royalty: 3%/1% - Total Inv: $75,000-$150,000 - Financing: Assistance is provided. NOT OFFERING FRANCHISES AT THIS TIME.

DIGITAL SUPERSTORES
28 Raytec Road, Unit 6, Vaughan, ON, L4L 8E4. Contact: Franchise Director - Tel: (905) 264-9131, Fax: (905) 264-9132. Leading edge electronic retail superstores specializing in digital technologies. Direct to home satellite, high definition television , digital video, telephones, video conferencing. Residential and commercial applications. Full training and support. Established: 1995 - No. of Units: Franchised: 1 - Total Inv: $75,000.

DUFFERIN GAMES
Dufferin Games, Ltd
3770 Nashua Dr., #1, Mississauga, ON, L4V 1M6. Contact: Sarah Stone, Business Affairs Manager - Tel: (905) 677-7665, Fax: (905) 677-4977, (800) 268-2597, Web Site: www.dufferingames.com. A unique Family Fun concept specializing in Game Room products for the home. Canadian owned and operated, for 30 yrs, the Dufferin Group of Companies manufactures a complete line of billiard tables, cues and accessories as well as other recreation products such as bars and game tables. Franchising opportunities available across Canada. Owner operators preferred. Established: 1986 - Franchising Since: 1986 - No. of Units: Company Owned: 28 - Franchised: 9 - Franchise Fee: $25,000 - Royalty: 5%, 2% advertising and promotion - Total Inv: $250,000 - Financing: None.

ENGLISH BUTLER
88 Whitehall Rd, Toronto, ON, M4W 2C7. - Tel: (780) 406-1700, Fax: (780) 437-2250. Retail sale of giftware and home decor catering to traditional tastes. Established: 1984 - Franchising Since: 1994 - No. of Units: Company Owned: 6 - Franchised: 12 - Franchise Fee: $25,000 - Royalty: 6%, Adv. .5% - Total Inv: $220,000-$260,000, Min. of $75,000 cash.

FLAG SHOP, THE
International Flag & Banner Inc.
1755 W. 4th Ave., Vancouver, BC, V6J 1M2. Contact: Doreen Braverman, President - Tel: (604) 736-8161, (800) 663-8681, Fax: (604) 736-6439, E-Mail: franchise@flagshop.com, Web Site: www.flagshop.com. Retailer and manufacturer of flags, banners, flagpoles and related items - books, pins, crest, decals, games, charts — everything flag related. Established: 1974 - Franchising Since: 1987 - No. of Units: Company Owned: 2 - Franchised: 9 - Franchise Fee: $25,000 (CAN) - Royalty: 4% - Total Inv: $80,000 - Financing: Negotiable.

GIANT TIGER STORES LTD.
2480 Walkley Rd., Ottawa, ON, K1G 6A9. Contact: Greg Farreu, Director, Accounting and Finance - Tel: (613) 521-8222, Fax: (613) 521-4474. Family discount stores: clothing, shoes, health and beauty aids, toys, novelties. Established: 1961 - Franchising Since: 1965 - No. of Units: Company Owned: 2 - Franchised: 87.

GOLF OPTION
1754, rue Ste-Helene, Longueuil, QC, J4K 3T1. Contact: Claude Desautels, Pres. - Tel: (450) 670-2222, Fax: (450) 670-2220. Repair shop/retail store for custom made golf clubs. Established: 1990 - Franchising Since: 1994 - No. of Units: Company Owned: 6 - Franchised: 2 - Franchise Fee: $25,000 - Royalty: 2% adv. - Total Inv: $95,000-$115,000 - Financing: Yes.

GRAND & TOY LTD.
33 Green Belt Drive, Don Mills, ON, M3C 1M1. Contact: Anne MacPhee, Dir. Real Estate/Fran. - Tel: (416)391-8581, Fax: (416) 441-6084, Web Site: www.grandandtoy.com. Office supplies and services. Six weeks training and ongoing support. Licensee owns only the inventory. Established: 1882 - No. of Units: Company Owned: 43 - Franchised: 25 - Franchise Fee: $15,000 - Total Inv: $50,000-$80,000.

GREAT CANADIAN DOLLAR STORE
Great Canadian Dollar Store (1993) Ltd.
#302 - 31 Bastion Square, Victoria, BC, V8W 1J1. Contact: Kevin T. Walker, Dir. of Fran. - Tel: (250) 388-0123, (877) 388-0123, Fax: (250) 388-9763, E-Mail: franchise@dollarstores.com, Web Site: www.dollar stores.com. Great franchise opportunity offering retail in a vast range of extreme value items priced at $1.00-$3.00. Training available during set-up and on-going support provided. Established: 1993 - Franchising Since: 1993 - No. of Units: Franchised:140 - Franchise Fee: $15,000 - Royalty: 4% of gross sales - Total Inv: $100,000+.

GREAT WILDERNESS COMPANY, THE
Great Wilderness Co., Inc., The
3365 Harvester Rd., Burlington, ON, L7N 3N2. Contact: John Vaandering, President - Tel: (905) 631-5300, Fax: (905) 631-6303. Retail - giftwear and clothing with nature/wildlife theme. Established: 1989 - Franchising Since: 1992 - No. of Units: Company Owned: 2 - Franchised: 12- Franchise Fee: $30,000 - Royalty: 6% plus 1.5% advertising/promotion - Total Inv: $150,000 plus $150,000 trade credit - Financing: Assistance. NOT OFFERING FRANCHISES AT THIS TIME.

GREEN EARTH STORES LTD

452 Newbold Street, London, ON, N6E 1K3. - Tel: (519) 668-2188, Fax: (519) 668-5627, Web Site: www.greenearthstores.com. Retail stores specializing in nature oriented giftware. Established: 1990 - Franchising Since: 1999 - No. of Units: Company Owned: 14 - Franchised: 1 - Franchise Fee: $25,000.

HAPPYDAYS HANDBAG & LUGGAGE COMPANY
Happydays Franchises Inc.

222-4750 Rutherford Road, Nanaimo, BC, V9T 4K6. Contact: Reed Sumida, Dir. of Fran. Dev. - Tel: (250) 595-8934, Fax: (250) 595-8935. Handbag, wallets, briefcases, luggage, travel and leather accessories and backpack retailers. Products for all budgets. Established: 1993 - Franchising Since: 1996 - No. of Units: Company Owned: 3 - Franchised: 3 - Franchise Fee: $20,000 - Royalty: 6% decreasing to 4% - Franchise Fee: $20,000 leaseholds, $8,000 equipment, $30,000 inventory - Financing: Assistance.

HERBRAND TOOLS & EQUIPMENT
Herbrand Tools Corporation

340 Dufferin St., Toronto, ON, M6K 1Z9. Contact: E.D. Brooks, Mktg. Mgr. - Tel: (416) 534-7943, Fax: (416) 537-1642, E-Mail: herbrand1@aol.com. Hand tools, pneumatic tools, hydraulic equip, tool boxes, measuring tools, diagnostic equip., and specialized tools for automotive and industrial uses. Established: 1930 - Franchising Since: 1950 - No. of Units: Franchised: 100 - Total Inv: $30,000 - Financing: $15,000.

HOCK SHOP CANADA

400 Bayfield St., Box 245, Barrie, ON, L4M 5A1. Contact: William C.Hockley, Pres. - Tel: (705) 728-2274, (800)948-2274, Fax: (705)728-2288, E-Mail: Bill@hockshop.com, Web Site: www.hockshop.com. Buy, sell, trade and repair a vast array of quality products. Cheque cashing and money transfer services are also available. Established: 1981 - Franchising Since: 1992 - No. of Units: Company Owned: 6 - Franchised: 13 - Franchise Fee: $30,000-$50,000 - Royalty: $250. per week, includes advertising - Total Inv: $150,000-$200,000 - Financing: Yes.

HOME HARDWARE, HOME BUILDING CENTRE, HOME HARDWARE BUILDING CENTRE, HOME FURNITURE
Home Hardware Stores, Limited

34 Henry St., St. Jacobs, ON, N0B 2N0. Contact: Terry Davis, V.P. Mktg. - Tel: (519) 664-4913, Fax: (519) 664-2865. Canada's largest chain of independently owned hardware, home improvement and furniture retailers. Established: 1964 - Franchising Since: 1964 - No. of Units: Company Owned: 1 - Franchised: 936 - Franchise Fee: Investment in share/ownership - Royalty: Addition to purchases - Total Inv: Minimum $100,000 - Financing: Independantly arranged.

HOUSE OF KNIVES, THE EDGE
House of Knives Ltd.

61 McBrine Place, P.O. Box 9024, Kitchener, ON, N2G 4X2. Contact: David McCullagh, Leasing Mgr. - Tel: (519) 748-2211, Fax: (519) 748-2808. Established: 1979 - No. of Units: Company Owned: 28 - Franchised: 14 - Royalty: $100,000.

HUSQVARNA
Viking Sewing Machines of Canada, Inc.

1470 Birchmont Rd., Scarborough, ON, M1P 2G1. Contact: Richard Schell, President - Tel: (416) 759-4486, Fax: (416) 759-5475. Retailing of sewing machines and related products. Established: 1876 - Franchising Since: 1998 - Franchise Fee: None - Royalty: None - Total Inv: $40,000 - Financing: Yes.

IN CASE OF

P.O. BOX 2760, Cardston, AB, TOK OKO. Contact: Alan Klain, Div. of Mrktg. - Tel: (403) 653-2806, Fax: (403) 653-4409, E-Mail: incaseof@telusplanet.net, Web Site: www.incaseof.com. Rapidly growing worldwide in the field of emergency preparedness and food storage. Turnkey operation, site search, extensive training, startup and ongoing support systems. Providing unique water and food storage containers, emergency kits, non electric food storage packages. Established: 1997.

...IT STORE

1111 Flint Road, Unit 36, Downsview, ON, M3J 3C7. Contact: Jack Green, CEO - Tel: (416) 665-3471, Fax: (416) 665-8839. Gifts from the perfectly practical to the absolutely ridiculous. Established: 1981 - Franchising Since: 1981 - No. of Units: Company Owned: 19 - Franchised: 31 - Franchise Fee: $25,000 - Royalty: 6%, 2% adv. - Total Inv: $155,000+$70,000 leaseholds, $60,000 inventory, $25,000 fran. fee - Financing: No.

JACADI

87 Avenue Rd. Hazelton Lanes, Toronto, ON, M5R 3R9. Contact: Fran. Dev. - Tel: (416) 923-1717, Fax: (416) 322-0094. Retail clothing, clothing accessories, footwear and nursery bedding and accessories, furniture and accessories. Established: 1990 - No. of Units: Franchised: 2 - Total Inv: $250,000.

KING OF TRADE

302-5th Street South, Lethbridge, AB, T1J 3B5. Contact: Lou Pizzingrilli, President - Tel: (403) 329-9302, Fax: (403) 328-3128. A modern retail outlet specializing in the purchase and sale of quality second hand and new merchandise, specifically compact disscs, tapes, videos,music equipment, vcr, tvs, cameras, etc. Established: 1986 - No. of Units: Franchised: 2 - Total Inv: $115,000-$145,000.

LA BONBONNIÉRE SWEET FACTORY
La Bonbonniére Sweet Factory Inc.

5650 Cypihot, St. Laurent, QC, H4S 1V7. Contact: Jean-Guy LeBlanc, President - Tel: (514) 334-8203, Fax: (514) 333-4656, E-Mail: leblanc@colba.net, Web Site: www.sweetfactory.com. The Mission of the company is to bring Canadians confectionary and higher quality gift wrappings in a unique and amusing environment while putting together all the benefits they know and recognize from their signature projects: candies, cookies, ice creams,chocolate, coffees, popcorns, fudge etc. Established: 1990 - Franchising Since: 1990 - No. of Units: Company Owned: 6 - Franchised: 80 - Franchise Fee: $20,000 - Royalty: 5% - Total Inv: $110,000-$150,00 - Financing: Yes.

LA CLE DU PLAISIR
Les Entreprises K.S.K.

16 J.F. Kennedy, Ste. 700, St-Jerome, QC, J7Y 4B6. Contact: Johnny or Celine, Owner - Tel: (450) 431-3653, (800) 472-1304, Fax: (450) 431-3655. Specialize in sales of erotic lingerie and adult novelties. Our original concept had "a touch of class" into the erotic world and get our franchisee in a high profit business. Established: 1990 - Franchising Since: 1993 - No. of Units: Company Owned: 2 - Franchised: 108 - Franchise Fee: $25,000 - Royalty: None - Total Inv: $45,000-$75,000 - Financing: Yes.

LE NATURIST JEAN-MARC BRUNET

174 St. Foy Blvd., Longueuil, QC, J4J 1W9. Contact: Daniel Belanger, Director of Franchising - Tel: (450) 442-2244 , (800) 361-6521, Fax: (450) 442-2205. Natural products. Established: 1968 - Franchising Since: 1970 - No. of Units: Company Owned: 38 - Franchised: 14 - Approx. Inv: $5,000-$25,000 - Royalty: 1-2%.

LIVING LIGHTING
Franchise Bancorp Inc

4699 Keele St., Unit 1, Toronto, ON, M3J 2N8. Contact: Janine DeFreitas, Franchise Developments - Tel: (416) 661-9916, Fax: (416) 661-9706, E-Mail: janine@franchisebancorp.com, Web Site: www.franchisebancorp.com. Canada's largest chain of residential lighting stores. We can offer you an exceptional opportunity to own an exciting business that dominates a unique Fashion niche within the expanding home improvement market. Established: 1968 - Franchising Since: 1968 - No. of Units: Franchised: 21 - Franchise Fee: $25,000 - Royalty: 5%- Total Inv: $200,000-$350,000 - Financing: Admin. only.

LOONY LIZARD DOLLAR STORE
Loony Lizard Inc.

15 E Neilson Ave, St. Catharines, ON, L2M 5V9. - Tel: (905) 685-9655, Fax: (905) 685-9414. Dollar store, selling nothing over $1.00 plus tax. Established: 1992 - Franchising Since: 1995 - No. of Units: Company Owned: 1 - Franchised: 21 - Franchise Fee: $45,000 - Royalty: 2.5% - Total Inv: $145,000 (fee $45,000, fixtures $10,000, deposits $5,000, legal and bank fees $2,000, inventory $68,000, working capital $15,000) - Financing: No.

LOVE BOUTIQUES

17551-108 Ave, Edmonton, AB, T5S 1G2. Contact: David Miller, General Manager - Tel: (780) 486-0433, (888) 296-2588, Fax: (780) 486-5114, E-Mail: telford@sprint.ca, Web Site: www.thelove boutique.com. Adult lingerie, creams, lotions, marital aids, etc. Established: 1977 - Franchising Since: 1999 - No. of Units: Company Owned: 20 - Franchised: 2 - Franchise Fee: $25,000 - Royalty: 5% of sales - Total Inv: Turnkey operation including inventory. $125,000-$160,000.

MARCHANDS UNIS, INC.

915 Paradis St., Quebec City, QC, G1N 4E3. Contact: Jean-Pierre Drewitt, V.P. - Tel: (418) 687-3050, Fax: (418) 687-5317. Hardware, sporting goods, paint and wallpaper.

MEDIA ENCORE
Half Price Books And Music

1055 Yonge St., Ste. 304, Toronto, ON, M4W 2L2. Contact: Steve Gosewich, President - Tel: (416) 960-9339, Fax: (416) 960-3155. Offer a huge selection of used books, compact discs and publisher's overstocked books. Make offers on and pay cash for people's books and compact discs...all day every day. Established: 1994 - Franchising Since: 1996 - No. of Units: Company Owned: 2 - Franchised: 1 - Franchise Fee: $25,000 - Royalty: 6% on gross sales, 2% advertising fund - Total Inv: $65,000-$95,000 - Financing: No.

MIGHTY DOLLAR, INC

528 Hood Rd., Markham, ON, L3R 3K9. Contact: John MacKenzie, Pres. - Tel: (905) 513-8191, Fax: (905) 513-6387. Dollar store (Ontario only) with 20% of stock over a dollar. Established: 1992 - Franchising Since: 1992 - No. of Units: Company Owned: 19 - Franchised: 14 - Franchise Fee: $25,000 - Royalty: 5% - Total Inv: $100,000+ - Financing: Yes.

NICHOLBY'S FRANCHISE SYSTEMS INC.

3671 Victoria Park Avenue, Unit 6, Toronto, ON, M1W 3K6. Contact: Sandra B. Edwards, VP. Fran & Real Estate - Tel: (416) 492-6424, Fax: (416) 492-6843, E-Mail: sandra@nicholbys.com. Nicholby's has four store concepts, each offering merchandise suitable for each location in which it operates. The primary merchandise offerings include convenience, gift and souvenier products. Established: 1980 - Franchising Since: 1982 - No. of Units: Company Owned: 14 - Franchised: 4 - Franchise Fee: $24,900 (convenience) - $29,900 (other concepts) - Total Inv: $230,000.

NOVICO (HARDWARE)
Sidisco/Howden Group Inc.

3232 White Oak Rd., London, ON, N6A 4G8. - Tel: (519) 686-2200, Fax: (519) 686-2202. Retail hardware or lumber yard supported by marketing and advertising to compete in the retail environment of the 90's and beyond. Established: 1986 - Franchising Since: 1986 - No. of Units: Franchised: 215 - Royalty: No - Total Inv: Varies per location, average inventory $100,000-$150,000, fixt. and equip. $35,000-$50,000 - Financing: Will help with projections and assist in obtaining through financial institution.

OLD HIPPY WOOD PRODUCTS INC.

2415-80 Ave, Edmonton, AB, T6P 1N3. Contact: Richard Croft, Fran. Dev. - Tel: (888) 464-9700, Fax: (780) 435-5475, E-Mail: richard@oldhippy.com, Web Site: www.oldhippy.com. We manufacture high-quality solid wood furniture in Pine, Birch, Cherry, Maple and Oak. We supply Canadian franchise store outlets and we are proud to be a experienced exporter to Japan. Full training and support provided. Established: 1990 - No. of Units: Company Owned: 2 - Franchised: 9 - Franchise Fee: $10,000 - Total Inv: $100,000.

PET JUNCTION
Truserv Canada Cooperative, Inc

1530 Gamble Place, P.O. #6800, Winnipeg, MB, R3C 3A9. Contact: Hugh Matson, Recruitment of Operations - Tel: (204) 453-9511, (800) 665-5085, Fax: (204) 452-6615, E-Mail: hmatson@truserv.ca. Member owned cooperative, serving 600 independent retailers across Canada. Product assortment, competitive costing, professional advertising training and ongoing field support. Established: 1992 - Franchising Since: 1999 - No. of Units: Franchised: 50 - Memebership Fee: $2,000 - Total Inv: $150,000-$200,000 - Financing: National bank packages.

PHARM-ESCOMPTES JEAN COUTU
Services Farmico, Inc.

530 Beriault St. Longueuil, QC, J4G 1S8. Contact: Jacques Masse, Vice Chairman of Board - Tel: (450) 646-9760, Fax: (450) 646-5649. Retail pharmaceutical. Established: 1969 - Franchising Since: 1974 - No. of Units: 127 - Approx. Inv: $750,000/store stock, fixtures - Royalty: 5% 1st $2 million and 4% thereafter.

PHARMASAVE DRUGS LTD.
Forewest Holdings, Inc.

6350, 20 3rd St., Langley, BC, V2Y 1L9. - Tel: (604) 532-2250, Fax: (604) 532-2293, Web Site: www.pharmasave.com. Retail drug stores. Established: 1981 - No. of Units: Company Owned: 7 - Franchised: 250 - Total Inv: Variable - Royalty: Percentage of sales.

POT POURRI COFFEE & TEA FRANCHISE
Bancorp Inc.

401 Kent Street, W., #3N4, Lindsay, ON, K9V 4Z1. Contact: V.P. Franchising & Leasing - Tel: (705) 878-9141. Combination store and gourmet coffee cafe. Housewares and kitchenwares - warm friendly atmosphere to have a snack or light lunch and browse. Established: 1995 - Franchising Since: 1995 - Franchise Fee: $25,000 - Royalty: 6% - Total Inv: $110,000-$150,000 - Financing: Bank Assistance.

PRO HARDWARE
D.H. Howden & Co. Ltd.

3232 White Oak Rd., P.O. Box 585, London, ON, N6A 4G8. Contact: Jim Young, Banner Manager - Tel: (519) 686-2200, Fax: (519) 686-2202, E-Mail: key1@hay.net. Retail hardware supported by marketing and advertising to compete in todays market. Established: 1964 - Franchising Since: 1964 - No. of Units: Franchised: 250 plus - Total Inv: $50% unencumber capital, inventories, fixtures - Financing: Will assist in obtaining.

RADIO SHACK AUTHORIZED SALES CENTRE (CANADA)
A Division of Tandy Corporation

279 Bayview Dr., Barrie, ON, L4M 4W5. Contact: Joe Dombroski, Dir., Dealer Division - Tel: (705) 728-6242, Fax: (800) 265-7278. Retail electronics for the complete catalogue line of Radio Shack products including TVS-80 computers and peripherals. Established: 1972 - Franchising Since: 1972 - No. of Units: Company Owned: 492 - Authorized Sale Centers: 391 - Approx. Inv: Varies with size of market area.

RAFTERS HOME STORE/PANHANDLER
Franchise Bancorp Inc.

4699 Keele St., Ste. 1, Downsview, ON, M3J 2N8. Contact: Janine DeFreitas - Tel: (416) 661-9916, Fax: (416) 661-9706, E-Mail: janine@franchisebancorp.com, Web Site: www.franchisebancorp.com. Filled to the Rafters with the newest gift and decorative home accessory ideas. Each store varies in size from 1,000 to 8,000 sq. ft. All stores offer quality products that are priced to sell with many exclusive items and direct import lines. Established: 1975 - Franchising Since: 1975 - No. of Units: Franchised: 39 - Franchise Fee: $25,000 - Royalty: Max 6% - Total Inv: $140,000-$350,000 - Financing: Admin. only.

REDLINE RACING

111 Main Street, Campbellville, ON, L0P 1B0. Contact: Paul Yackman, Owner - Tel: (905) 854-7477, Fax: (905) 681-6845. Retail and mail order of licensed Nascar, NHRA, CART and FORMULA one racing souvenirs, die cast models and art. Established: 1995 - Franchising Since: 1995 - No. of Units: Company Owned: 1 - Franchised: 10 - Franchise Fee: None - Total Inv: Varies - Financing: No.

RO-NA L'ENTREPOT, RO-NA HOME CENTRE, RO-NA HARDWARE
Le Groupe Ro-Na Dismat, Inc.

220 Chemin Du Tremblay, Boucherville, QC, J4B 8H7. Contact: Michel Mérineau, Dev. Dir. - Tel: (514) 599-5124, Fax: (514) 599-5161. Retail chain, hardware, buying and selling group specialized in hardware, L.B.M. horticultural prod. Established: 1939 - No. of Units: Franchised: 450 - Franchise Fee: $6,000 for share + $90,000 investment - Royalty: No, advertising program - Total Inv: $96,000 (company shares) - Financing: Agreements with banks.

ROCKING HORSE, THE
843 2nd Ave., E., Owen Sound, ON, N4K 2H2. Contact: Dianne Mattice, Franc. Dir. - Tel: (519) 371-9921, Fax: (519) 371-6120. Trend setting toy boutique, exclusive products for tots and adults. Established: 1975 - Franchising Since: 1991 - No. of Units: Company Owned: 2.

SHEFIELD & SONS®
Shefield & Sons Tobacconists Inc.
P.O. Box 490, 2265 W. Railway St., Abbotsford, BC, V2S 5Z5. Contact: T. Hartford, Dir. of Fran. - Tel: (604) 859-1014, Fax: (604) 859-1711, E-Mail: shefield@uniserve.com, Web Site: www.shefieldgourmet.com. Retail sale of tobacco and related products, lottery (where available), reading material, confectionery, unique giftware and souvenirs. Established: 1976 - Franchising Since: 1976 - No. of Units: Company Owned: 2 - Franchised: 61 - Franchise Fee: $10,000 - Royalty: 2% - Total Inv: $69,000-$150,000 - Financing: No.

SHOPPERS DRUG MART
243 Consumers Road, North York, ON, M2J 4W8. Contact: Franchise Department - Tel: (800) 746-7737. Retail pharmacies. Shoppers Drug Mart associate program open and available only to licensed pharmacists. Established: 1968 - Franchising Since: 1968 - No. of Units: Approx. 715.

STEREO PLUS
5715 boul. Royal, Ste. 3, Trois-Rivieres, QC, G9A 4N9. Contact: Richard Roy, Pres. - Tel: (819) 378-2303, Fax: (819) 376-2554. Retail electronics. Established: 1982 - Franchising Since: 1982 - No. of Units: Company Owned: 7 - Franchised: 55 - Franchise Fee: $15,000 - Royalty: 2% of purchase - Total Inv: $60,000 - Financing: Bombardier Credit.

TELEMARK INTERNATIONAL
Telemark International
869 Gana Court, Mississauga, ON, L5S 1N9. Contact: John Thistlewaite, V.P. Business Development - Tel: (905) 670-6450 ext 241, (877) 413-3453 ext 241, Fax: (905) 670-6435, E-Mail: franchiseinfo@tvshowcase.com, Web Site: www.tvshowcase.com. A unique retail store specializing in products "As Seen On TV" infomercials. Located in major enclosed malls. Established: 1994 - Franchising Since: 1996 - No. of Units: Company Owned: 11 - Franchised: 21 - Royalty: 2% of gross sales - Total Inv: $180,000 store leasehold + fixtures, build-out, pos equip, $40,000 inventory - Financing: Yes.

THE HEMP CLOTHING STORE INC.
H & C Hemp & Company
1044 -10303 Jasper Ave., Edmonton, AB, T5J 3N6. Contact: Fran. Dev. - Tel: (780) 702-0367, Fax: (780) 448-2670, E-Mail: office@hempandcompany.com, Web Site: www.hempandcompany.com. Our retail stores offer the highest quality Canadian made hemp clothing available. A wide variety of other hemp based products including soaps, shampoos, writing paper and candles, available in our high end malls and street front locaations. Turnkey store with superior operational support. Established: 1998 - No. of Units: Franchised: 3 - Total Inv: $130,000.

THE MATTRESS KING
589 Eleventh Avenue, Thunder Bay, ON, P7B 2R5. Contact: Fran. Dev. - Tel: (807) 345-7222, Fax: (807) 345-9112, E-Mail: mattressking@norlink.net, Web Site: www.mattress-king.com. Sale of quality mattresses and related accessories. Full training and support provided. Established: 1980 - No. of Units: Franchised: 2 - Total Inv: $65,000.

THE PLUMBING MART
700 Dundas Street, East, Mississauga, ON, L4Y 3Y5. Contact: F r a n . Dev. - Tel: (905) 275-0574, Fax: (905) 275-8944. Retail full line of plumbing products and fixtures. Provide installed sales and service. Provide full bathroom and kitchen renovation services with full training and support. Established: 1959 - No. of Units: Franchised: 6 - Total Inv: $250,000.

TOP DOLLAR BARGAIN CENTRES
1157387 Ontario Ltd
P.O. Box 430, Stroud, ON, L0M 1B0. Contact: Randy Aylwin, V.P. of Sales & Marketing - Tel: (705) 431-1295, Fax: (705) 431-2077, E-Mail: topdollar.ho@sympatico.ca. Dollar stores. Established: 1993 - Franchising Since: 1995 - No. of Units: Company Owned: 6 - Franchised: 17 - Franchise Fee: $25,000 - Royalty: 3% - Total Inv: $68,500-$124,500.

TORONTO R.V. CENTRE
7200 Hwy 27, North, Woodbridge, ON, L4L 1A5. - Tel: (416) 743-1021, Fax: (905) 850-6219. Sales, service, rentals of motorhomes. Established: 1972 - Franchising Since: 1982 - No. of Units: Company Owned: 35 - Franchise Fee: $50,000 and up - Royalty: 60% to (owner) franchisee - Financing: Yes.

TRADE SECRETS
101 Jevlan Drive, Woodbridge, ON, L4L 8C2. Contact: Dave Warren - Tel: (905) 264-2799, Fax: (905) 264-2779, E-Mail: doug@trade secrets.ca, Web Site: www.tradesecrets.ca. Growing professional beauty product retailer. Established: 2002 - Franchising Since: 2003 - No. of Units: Company Owned: 37 - Total Inv: $110,000-$195,000.

TRUE VALUE HARDWARE STORES
Truserv Canada Cooperative Inc
1530 Gamble Place, P.O. Box 6800, Winnipeg, MB, R3C 3A9. Contact: Hugh Matson, Recruitment & Oper. Specialist - Tel: (8204) 453-9511, Fax: (204) 452-6615, E-Mail: hmatson@truserv.ca. Member owned Cooperative serving 600 independent retailers across Canada. Product assortment, competitive costing, professional advertising ,training and ongoing field support. Established: 1992 -Franchising Since: 1992 - No. of Units: Franchised: 600 - Membership Fee: $2,000 - Total Inv: Approx. $200,000-$250,000 - Financing: National Bank Packages.

U-PAWN & SMILE
Domphaff Corp. Ltd.
22-6780 Davand Dr., Mississauga, ON, L5T 2G4. Contact: Ralph Conty, Fran. Dir. - Tel: & Fax: (416) 252-8936. Pawnbroker and discount outlet for retailing, buying, selling and collateral lending. Dealing in a large variety of new, reconditioned and used consumer goods. Neighbourhood oriented operation doing all cash business by providing services to constant market demands. Low cost group purchasing power combined with inventory networking assures relatively quick merchandise turn-around at high profit margins. Training and operating manuals are provided along with ongoing market consultation. Franchise Fee: $5,000-$20,000 (depending on territory) - Royalty: 8%, 2% adv. of gross sales - Total Inv: $135,000-$175,000 (min. $100,000 unencumbered).

URBAN SOUND EXCHANGE
1592 Barrington St., Halifax, NS, B3J 1Z6. - Tel: (902) 422-8946, Fax: (902) 422-8556. E-Mail: usx00@ns.sympatico.ca, Web Site: www.urbansound.com. Retail sales/cd's. Established: 1992 - Franchising Since: 1991 - No. of Units: Company Owned: 8 - Franchised: 8 - Franchise Fee: $20,000.00 - Royalty: 5% - Financing: No.

URBAN TRAIL
210-10 Fort Street, Winnipeg, MB, R3C 1C4. Contact: Fran. Dev. - E-Mail: albert@quarkshoes.com, Web Site: www.urbantrail.com. Outdoor rugged footwear and clothing. Full training and support. Established: 1992 - No. of Units: Franchised: 3 - Total Inv: $250,000.

V & S DEPARTMENT STORES
Truserv Canada
1530 Gamble Place, Winnipeg, MB, R3C 3A9. Contact: Hugh Matson, Recruitment & Oper. Specialist - Tel: (800) 665-5085, (204) 453-9600, Fax: (204) 477-0445, E-Mail: hmatson@truserv.ca. 100% Membered owned Cooperative serving 600 stores across Canada Including 145 V & S Department stores. Established:1992 - Franchising Since:1992 - Membership Fee: $2,000 - Total Inv: $175,000 - Financing: National Bank Packages.

VANILLA ROMANCING THE SOUL
1111 Flint Road Unit 36, Downsview, ON, M3J 3C7. - Tel: (416) 665-3471, (888) vanilla, Fax: (416) 665-8839. Candles, candle accessories, scented oils and lamps. Established: 1997 - Franchising Since: 1998 - No. of Units: Company Owned: 2 - Franchise Fee: $25,000 - Royalty: 6% - Total Inv: $175,000 approx - Financing: No.

WATER DEPOT
56 Churchhill Drive Units 1-4, Barrie, ON, L4N 8Z5. - Tel: (705) 737-5606, Fax: (705) 722-6150, Web Site: www.waterdepotinc.com. Retail bottle water outlet. Established: 1989 - Franchising Since: 2001 - No. of Units: Company Owned: 2 - Franchised: 4 - Franchise Fee: $906.00.

RETAIL: CLOTHING AND SHOES

BIG BOLD AND BEAUTIFUL
1263 Bay Street, Toronto, ON, M5R 2C1. Contact: Fran. Dev. - Tel: (416) 923-4673, Fax: (416) 923-5673, E-Mail: info@bigboldand beautiful.com. Retail and womens apparel catalogue. Business for plus sizes. Full support. Established: 1985 - No. of Units: Franchised: 1 - Total Inv: $250,000-$500,000.

BIMINI
92 Water Street, Charlottetown, PEI, C1A 1A6. Contact: Fran. Dev. - Tel: (416) 484-4148, Fax: (416) 484-9296. Retail mens, ladies and kids denim based fashion product clothing. Name brands if its "hot we've got it". Medium price points. Finest quality available for the price. Established: 1978 - No. of Units: Franchised: 5 - Total Inv: $100,000.

DOG'S EAR T-SHIRT & EMBROIDERY CO., THE
524 Westview Place, Nanaimo, BC, V9V 1B3. Contact: Butts Giraud, Pres. - Tel: (250) 756-4433, Fax: (250) 756-4454, E-Mail: dogsear@ island.net, Web Site: www.dogsear.com. The Dog's Ear T-Shirt and Embroidery Co. has continually expanded its product line to include fast-selling fashion and corporate wear for today's growing sports wear market, on a retail, and wholesale level. Stores located in high traffic shopping centers and tourist locations. Established: 1973 - Franchising Since: 1981 - No. of Units: Franchised: 8 - Franchise Fee: $15,000 - Royalty: 5%, 1% adv. - Total Inv: $125,000 - Financing: No.

JUST LEGS
Just Legs Franchises Inc.
935 Richmond Ave, Victoria, BC, V8% 3Z4. Contact: Reed Sumida, Dir. of Fran. Dev. - Tel: (250) 595-8934. Retailer of women's, men's and children's hosiery, specialty lingerie, underwear, bodywear, slippers, leggings, tights, swimwear and other seasonal items. Established: 1989 - Franchising Since: 1995 - No. of Units: Company Owned: 2 - Franchised: 8 - Franchise Fee: $15,000 - Royalty: 5.5% declining to 3.5% - Total Inv: $90,000 - Financing: Assistance provided.

KETTLE CREEK CLOTHING CO.
100 Wingold Ave., Unit 7, Toronto, ON, M6B 4K7. Contact: Franchise Department - Tel: (416)256-1145. Womens and mens clothing in natural fabrics, Canadian design. Established: 1979 - Franchising Since: 1981 - No. of Units: Company Owned: 1- Dealers: 17 - Royalty: Included in the price of goods - Total Inv: Leaseholds - $40,000; Inventory - $85,000.

LA CACHE
Cornell Trading Ltd.
108 Gallery Square, Montreal, QC, H3C 3R3. Contact: Chris Cornell, Pres. - Tel: (514) 935-9295, Fax: (514) 933-4487. Ladies clothing collection, soft home furnishing, gifts, pottery, jewelry, etc. Established: 1973 - Franchising Since: 1986 - No. of Units: Company Owned: 16 - Franchised: 6 - Franchise Fee: $5,000 - Total Inv: $100,000-$150,000 turn-key (fix, inven., leasehold) - Financing: No.

LACEY'S
206-482 Barnes Avenue Brandon, MB, R2X 1M8. Contact: Franchise Department - Tel: (204) 235-0113, Fax: (204) 235-0655. An upscale lingerie boutique with sizes to fit all. Established: 1989 - No. of Units: Company Owned: 1 - Franchised: 3 - Total Inv: $250.

LEGS BEAUTIFUL HOSIERY BOUTIQUES
1903 Leslie St., Don Mills, ON, M3B 2M3. Contact: Ian Collins - Tel: (416) 449-7444, Fax: (416) 449-7612. Retailer of women's specialty hosiery. Established: 1978 - No. of Units: Company Owned: 23 - Franchised: 17 - Franchise Fee: $25,000 - Royalty: 8% - Total Inv: $120,000 - Financing: Assistance.

MODA ITALIA DIFFUSION - DISTINCTIVELY YOURS
1 Place Villa Marie, Ste. 1831, Montreal, QC, H3B 4A9. Contact: Vincent Governale, President - Tel: (514) 392-0505, Fax: (514) 392-1211. Business with Italian women apparels and accessories. Established: 1998 - Franchising Since: 1998 - No. of Units: Company Owned: 1 - Franchise Fee: None - Royalty: None - Total Inv: $150,000 - Financing: Yes by Royal Bank.

MONEYSWORTH & BEST QUALITY SHOE REPAIR
Moneysworth & Best Quality Shoe Repair, Inc
#222, 205 5th Ave, S.W., Calgary, AB, T2P 2V7. - Tel: (403) 225-0140, Fax: (403) 206-7233. While-you-wait shoe repair plus full line of branded shoe care merchandise with guaranteed customer satisfaction. Locations in major shopping malls. Established: 1984 - Franchising Since: 1986 - No. of Units: Company Owned: 4 - Franchised: 75 - Franchise Fee: $10,000 - Royalty: 8% - Total Inv: $80,000-$100,000 - Financing: No.

PEEK-A-BOO-TIQUE
Peek-A-Boo-tique (Port Dover) Ltd.
417 Main Street, Port Dover, ON, N0A 1N0. Contact: Nancy Wilkie, Owner - Tel: (519) 427-1624, Fax: (519) 583-1855, E-Mail: peekabout@ hotmail.com, Web Site: www.ontariotowns.on.ca. Lingerie, swimwear, adult novelties, massage oils, lotions and beach cover-ups. The store designs create an ambiance of romance and feminity, attracting both male and female clientele. Established: 1985 - Franchising Since: 1986 - No. of Units: Compnay Owned: 1 - Franchised: 2 - Franchise Fee: $15,000 - Royalty: None - Total Inv: $25,000 - Financing: None.

PETTICOAT BOX, THE
The Petticoat Box Franchise Corp
201-1050 West 14th St, North Vancouver, BC, V7P 3P3. Contact: Maria Cullen, President - Tel: (604) 985-4996, (888) 988-2444, Fax: (604) 985-3937. European style lingerie retail stores adapted to North American needs - carrying in house label at very competitive prices. Established: 1989 - Franchising Since: 1991 - No. of Units: Company Owned: 3 - Franchised: 5 - Franchise Fee: $25,000 - Royalty: 5% - Total Inv: $135,000-$200,000 - Financing: We advise and help obtain necessary financing.

WORK WORLD
Work World Enterprises Inc.
30, 1035-64th Avenue S.E., Calgary, AB, T2H 2J7. Contact: B.W. (Bernie) Bielby, Fran. Sales Dir. - Tel: (403) 640-5848, Fax: (403) 255-6005. Sale of safetywear, workwear, casualwear, footwear and apparel. Established: 1978 - Franchising Since: 1979 - No. of Units: Company Owned: 1 - Franchised: 155 - Franchise Fee: $35,000 - Royalty: 4.75% of gross sales - Total Inv: $300,000-$350,000 - Financing: Yes. NOT OFFERING FRANCHISES AT THIS TIME.

SCHOOLS AND TEACHING

A-LITTLE-EXTRA-HELP TUTORING SERVICE
108 Parnell Cres., Whitby, ON, L1R 1X1. Contact: Michael Peever, Pres. - Tel: (888) TUTOR-ME, (905) 668-2037, Fax: (905) 668-3365. We provide one-on-one tutoring by certified teachers in all grades and subjects in the students' home. Established: 1989 - Franchising Since: 1995 - No. of Units: Company Owned: 2 - Franchised: 22 - Franchise Fee: $15,000 - Royalty: 5% royalty, 4% adv. - Total Inv: $12,000 - Financing: None.

ACADEMY FOR MATHEMATICS
Academy For Mathematics & Science, Inc.
30 Glen Cameron Rd., Unit 200, Thornhill, ON, L3T 1N7. Contact: Steve Holler, V.P. Administration - Tel: (905) 709-3233, (800) 809-5555, Fax: (905) 709-3045, E-Mail: info@acadfor.com. Learning centres located in major malls across Canada providing tutoring in mathematics, science, english and study skills to students from kindergarten age to adult. Established: 1992 - Franchising Since: 1993- No. of Units: Company Owned: 6- Franchised: 37 - Franchise Fee: $29,500 - Royalty: 10%-12% - Total Inv: $40,000-$60,000.

ACADEMY OF LEARNING
100 York Blvd., Ste. 400, Richmond Hill, ON, L4B 1J8. Contact: Les Prosser, V.P. Administration - Tel: (905) 886-8973, Fax: (905) 886-8591, E-Mail: LPROSSER@academyol.com, Web Site: www.Academyol.com. Computer and business career college. A unique "Integrated Learning" system" of self paced, flex-time training. Established: 1987 - Franchising Since: 1987 - No. of Units: Company Owned: 4 - Franchised: 156 - Franchise Fee: $40,000 - Royalty: Nil - Total Inv: $130,000: $40,000 fran. fee; $30,000 equip. & furniture; $30,000 work. cap. - Financing: No.

FUTURESKILLS INTERACTIVE LEARNING CENTRES
CompuCollege Interactive Learning Centres Inc.
60 Yonge St., Toronto, ON, M5E 1H5. Contact: A. Ebedes, Pres. - Tel: (416) 862-9575, (800) 90-FUTURE, Fax: (416) 862-9893. Training in PC applications and HR development using fully interactive, self-paced multimedia courseware on a video-file server and/or CD ROM. Established: 1994 - Franchising Since: 1996 - No. of Units: Company Owned: 3- Franchise Fee: $50,000 - Royalty: 8% - Total Inv: $100,000 - Financing: Assistance.

GRADE EXPECTATIONS LEARNING CENTRES
Grade Expectations Learning Systems Inc.
105 Main St., Unionville, ON, L3R 2G1. Contact: Micheal Bateman, Gen.Mgr. - Tel: (800) 208-3826. Specializing in supplementary education from grades 1 through OAC. Established: 1994 - Franchising Since: 1994 - No. of Units: Company Owned: 1 - Franchised: 16 - Franchise Fee: $22,000 - Royalty: 10% - Total Inv: $75,000 - Financing: Yes.

GRADE MATH PROGRAMS
4174 Dundas St West Suite 210, Etobicoke, ON, M8X 1X3. - Tel: (800) 208-3826, Fax: (416) 236-0078, E-Mail: hq@gradeexpectations.on.ca, Web Site: www.gradeexpectations.on.ca. Grade Math Program is a Canadian math system, it assists children through ongoing math support. Established: 1998 - No. of Units: Company Owned: 7 - Franchise Fee: $9,000.

INTERNATIONAL INSTITUTE OF TRAVEL
907687 Ontario Inc.
1240 Bay Street., Suite 307, Toronto, ON, M5R 2A7. Contact: Rudolph Nareen, Pres. - Tel: (416) 924-4888, Fax: (416) 924-5667, E-Mail: iit@ica.net, Web Site: www.iitravel.com. The Institute offers a practical training program in travel and tourism and works together with instructors and course advisors from airlines and other travel related companies. Established: 1983 - Franchising Since: 1989 - No. of Units: Company Owned: 5 - Franchised: 6 - Franchise Fee: $35,000 - Royalty: 7% - Total Inv: $110,000 - Financing: Yes.

KEYIN TECHNICAL COLLEGE
KeyCorp Inc.
Suite 300, Atlantic Building, St. John's, NF, A1B 4G3. Contact: Craig Tucker, President - Tel: (709) 753-2284, Fax: (709) 753-2049, E-Mail: tuck@thezone.net, Web Site: www.keyin.com. Private Post-Secondary College providing education and training through educational programs along with specialized and contract training. Established: 1980 - Franchising Since: 1992 - No. of Units: Company Owned: 1 - Franchised: 13 - Franchise Fee: $30,500 - Royalty: 8%, 2% mktg, 1% R & D - Total Inv: $100,000 - Financing: Support for assistance available.

LITTLE SCHOLARS TRAINING CENTRE
901 Academy Street, Victoria, BC, V8X 2G1. Contact: Fran. Dept. - Tel: (250) 744-1661, Fax: (250) 744-1936. A training institute for young children with learning difficulties. All teachers are retired school teachers. 3 weeks training and ongoing support provided. Established: 1981 - No. of Units: Franchised: 3 - Total Inv: $150,000.

MILLENNIUM INFORMATION TECHNOLOGY SOLUTIONS INC.
Millennium Information Technology Solutions Inc.
1234 Main St., Suite 4002, Moncton, NB, E1C 8P2. Contact: Hal Butler, Director, Business to Business - Tel: (506) 854-7272, (877) 727-6487, Fax: (506) 388-2677, E-Mail: hbutler@millennium-it-solutions.com, Web Site: www.millennium-it-solutions.com. Information Technology Solution Provider specializing in Training Solutions and Consultations. Presently franchising a microsoft approved "Train The Trainer" course. Established: 1999 - Franchising Since: 2000 - No. of Units: Company Owned: 1 - Franchise Fee: $4,295 USD - Royalty: $100.00 USD per client trained - Total Inv: $4,295 USD .

MODEL MANAGERS INTERNATIONAL
Broadbelt & Fonte Model Centre, Inc.,
696 Dufferin St., Toronto, ON, M6K 2B5. Contact: Manuel Fonte, V.P. - Tel: (416) 588-8806, Fax: (416) 588-4984. Modelling school. Established: 1996 - Franchising Since: 1996 - No. of Units: Company Owned: 1 - Franchise Fee: $15,000 - Royalty: 10% - Total Inv: $5,000-$10,000 - Financing: No.

OXFORD LEARNING CENTRES
747 Hyde Park Rd, Ste. 230, London, ON, N6H 3S3. Contact: Anita Fisher, Fran. Dept. - Tel: (519) 473-1207, (888) 559-2212, Fax: (519) 473-6447, Web Site: www.oxfordlearning.com. Oxford Learning Centres is Canada's fastest growing education provider, specializing in improving students academic skills by teaching them how to think and learn by using unique Oxford designed materials and methods. We provide extensive training and support and lead the field in continuous research and development of new materials. Established: 1984 - Franchising Since: 1995 - No. of Units: Company Owned: 2 - Franchised: 40 - Franchise Fee: $35,000 - Royalty: 9% - Total Inv: $86,000-$130,000 - Financing: No.

PRIORITY MANAGEMENT SYSTEMS, INC.
13251 Delf Place, Suite 420, Richmond, BC, V6A 2A2. Contact: Dennis Lohrmon, Fran. Dev. - Tel: (604) 214-7772, (800) 665-5448, Fax: (604) 214-7773, Web Site: www.prioritymanagement.com. A worlwide training organization that reaches clients ranging from individuals to Fortune 500 companies through a global network of carefully selected highly trained Priority Associates. Established: 1984 - No. of Units: Franchised: 208 - Total Inv: $29,500.

SEARS DRIVER TRAINING
A. OK Road Safety Systems Ltd.
247 N. Service Rd., Ste. 301, Oakville, ON, L6M 3E6. Contact: Luba Castracane, Pres. - Tel: (416) 363-7483, Fax: (905) 842-4251. A full service driver training school with national name recognition. Turnkey operation with ongoing training and support. Low overhead, high traffic exposure with classrooms conveniently located in selected Sears stores. Established: 1976 - Franchising Since: 1994 - No. of Units: Company Owned: 12 - Franchised: 4 - Franchise Fee: $20,000 - Royalty: 6%, 5% nat'l. adv. - Total Inv: $25,000-$45.000 - Financing: No.

TECNIC DRIVING SCHOOL GROUP
583 Boulevard Henri-Bourassa Est, Montreal, QC, H2C 1E2. Contact: Donald O'Hara, Franchise Director - Tel: (514) 389-8237. Driving school. Established: 1957 - Franchising Since: 1984 - No. of Units: Company Owned: 1 - Franchised: 146 - Franchise Fee: $15,000 - Royalty: 4% + 2% adv. - Total Inv: $40,000 - Financing: Yes, in Quebec and Ontario, may expand elsewhere.

TORONTO SCHOOL OF BUSINESS, COMPUCOLLEGE SCHOOL OF BUSINESS
International Business Schools Inc.
5650 Yonge St., Ste. 1400, Toronto, ON, M2M 4G3. Contact: Mr. Sal Schipper, Exec. V.P. - Tel: (416)733-4452, Fax: (416) 733-4627. Private career training schools. Provides short term courses to enable students to obtain entry level job positions. Established: 1976 - Franchising Since: 1983 - No. of Units: Company Owned: 48 - Franchised: 26 - Franchise Fee: $50,000-$75,000 depending on size of location - Total Inv: $200,000-$300,000 incl. fran. fee - Royalty: 7% - Financing: No, but will assist in bank presentation.

U-CANDU LEARNING CENTRES
U-Candu Learning Centres, Inc.
130 Willowdale Ave., 2nd Floor, Toronto, ON, M2N 4Y2. Contact: Ernest Sneidzing, Director - Tel: (416) 225-0266, (888) U CANDU2 (82638), Fax: (416) 225-7869, E-Mail: syntality@ucandu.com, Web Site: www.vcandu.com. Accelerated virtual learning, ESL and personal development. Learn in 1/3 of the time, a language in 90 days, increase IQ by 9%, Syntality® and Mount Knowledge®. Established: 1986 - Franchising Since: 1994 - No. of Units: Company Owned: 2 - Franchised: 2 - Franchise Fee: $18,000 - Royalty: 6% plus 2% advertising - Total Inv: $72,000 - Financing: Yes if qualified.

YOUNG DRIVERS OF CANADA / YOUNG DRIVERS OF AMERICA/YOUNG DRIVERS OF FINLAND
Commerce Place Phase II, Box 38, 21 King St. W., Ste. 890, Hamilton, ON, L8P 4W7. Contact: Peter Christianson, Pres. - Tel: (905) 529-5501, Fax: (905) 529-5913. New driver training, plus collision free driver improvements programs. Established: 1970 - Franchising Since: 1970 - No. of Units: Franchised: 71 - 168 classrooms - Franchise Fee: $6,500 - Royalty: 4% of student fees, 3% of student fees for adv. - Total Inv: $25,000.

SIGN PRODUCTS & SERVICES

1 HOUR SIGNS
1 Hour Signs Inc.
485 Silvercreek Pkwy. N., Unit 4, Guelph, ON, N1H 7K5. Contact: Shan Jamal, Pres. - Tel: (519) 824-2832, Fax: (519) 824-1207. The most technologically advanced sign shop franchise - specializing in large or small signs. Ready made signs, screen printing and engraving. Established: 1991 - Franchising Since: 1992 - No. of Units: Company Owned: 1 - Franchised: 12 - Franchise Fee: $15,000 - Royalty: 5%, 1.5% adv. - Total Inv: $174,000; min. cash req. $80,000 including working capital - Financing: Assistance.

CALL-A-SIGN LTD.
R.R. #1, Belmont, ON, N0L 1B0. Contact: George Van Colen, Pres. - Tel: (519) 644-0272. Manufacture, sale, rental and long-term leasing of high quality illuminated, changeable copy, mobile signs equipped with a colored headliner section. Established: 1974 - Franchising Since: 1978 - No. of Units: Company Owned: 1 - Franchised: 1 - Franchise Fee: $35,000 - Total Inv: $100,000-$500,000 - Royalty: 3%-7% dep. on territory - Financing: Assistance. NOT OFFERING FRANCHISES AT THIS TIME.

COLOUR PRINTS CORP.
119 Vanderhoof Ave., Toronto, ON, M4G 4B4. Contact: Ron Benson, President - Tel: (416) 421-4136, Fax: (416) 421-4716. Digital imaging, we supply to a variety of clients, banners, durations, photo prints, inkjet prints and transparencies, full service lab. No. of Units: Company Owned: 1.

SIGN MASTER
Sign Master Training
16715 Yonge St. Bldg 12, Ste. 301, NewMarket, ON, L3X 1X4. Contact: Gary J. Brickell, President - Tel: (905) 836-2837, (800) 655-3620, Web Site: www.signmastertraining.com. Home-based sign shop business, includes latest generation digital color sign printing and vinyl cutting equipment, on-site training, supplies, inventory and toll-free support. Established: 1985 - Franchising Since: 1986 - No. of Units: Company Owned: 1 - Franchised: 60 - Franchise Fee: $1,500 - Royalty: None - Total Inv: $16,000 total (incl $14,500 equip and supplies, $1,500 training) - Financing: $399/per month, 4 year financing O.A.C.

SPEEDPRO SIGN & PRINT CENTERS
Speedpro Systems Inc.
Ste. 18, 18812 96th Ave., Surrey, BC, V4N 3R1. Contact: Rick Hiflop, District Manager - Tel: (604) 882-5115, Fax: (604) 882-3626. A one-stop advertising center, providing signs and printed products - produced same day. Established: 1991 - No. of Units: Franchised: 21 - Total Inv: $76,500.

VINYLGRAPHICS CUSTOM SIGN CENTRES
Vinylgraphics Inc.
2615 Lancaster Rd, Ottawa, ON, K1B 5N2. Contact: Glenn Kerekes, Pres. - Tel: (613) 523-7446, Fax: (416) 523-7234. Custom sign centres that offer full service interior/exterior signage, window lettering, vehicle and boat lettering, special event banners, magnetic signs, illuminated exterior signs, etc., to today's business community. The sign graphics are computer generated, utilizing state-of-the-art technology and proven vinyl films. Established: 1983 - Franchising Since: 1988 - No. of Units: Company Owned: 1 - Franchised: 13 - Franchise Fee: $25,000 - Royalty: 8% - Total Inv: $80,000 - Financing: Equipment Canadian Funds.

SPORTS & RECREATION

AROUND THE WORLD
373 Baltic Street, Winnipeg, MB, R3G 2N1. Contact: Fran. Dir. - Tel: (204) 235-0010. Full service travel agency. Full four weeks training and ongoing support. Established: 1994 - No. of Units: Franchised: 11 - Total Inv: $70,000 min cash required.

BOUNCE MANIA LEISURE PRODUCTS INC.
1431 Erin Drive, Airdrie, AB, T4B 2E9. Contact: Fran. Dev. - Tel: (403) 912-1726. A revolutionary inflatable play area rental business with unlimited potential. Specialty tailored for home based operation and adaptable to your lifestyle. Provides immediate market recognition. Affordable and fun to operate. Ongoing support and product development. Established: 1995 - No. of Units: Franchised: 4 - Franchise Fee: $7,500 - Total Inv: $30,000.

DALE'S HOUSE OF GOLF
12 Church Street., P.O. Box 755, St. Catharines, ON, L2R 6Y3. Contact: Franchise Department - Tel: (905) 688-2665. Manufacturing golf clubs and accessories. Established: 1990 - Franchising Since: 1994 - No. of Units: Company Owned: 1 - Franchised: 3 - Franchise Fee: $25,000 - Royalty: 4%, 2% adv. - Total Inv: $150,000 including franchise fee.

FLYAWAY INDOOR SKYDIVING
165417 Canada Ltd.
Box 1234, Cornwall, ON, K6H 5R9. Contact: Cliff Tessier, V.P. - Tel: (613) 933-2443, Fax: (613) 932-3518. Closed system vertical wind tunnel in which participants perform skydiving maneuvers. Spectator gallery can hold up to 60 people. Revenues derive from participants and spectators. Relatively simple business to operate. High returns possible. Exciting, fun, thrilling recreational activity. Established: 1980 - Franchising Since: 1984 - Franchise Fee: $50,000 - Royalty: 6% - Total Inv: $450,000 - Financing: Yes.

GOLD IN THE NET HOCKEY SCHOOL INC.
P.O. Box 414, Lantzville, BC, V0T 2H0. Contact: Perry Elderbroom, CEO - Tel: (250) 248-8143, (800) 661-2280, Fax: (250) 248-8162, E-Mail: gold@goldinthenet.com, Web site: www.goldinthenet.com. Hockey school for goaltenders and coaches. Includes summer hockey schools, traveling hockey clinics, seminars and private consultations. Other activities range from operating off-ice facilities to the sale of Gold in the Net instructional videos and other merchandise. Established: 1986 - Franchise Fee: $25,000 Turn-Key - Total Inv: $15,000 franchise fee, $10,000 equipment.

GOLF USA OF CANADA
Off Course Pro Shops Ltd.
9675 Macleod Tr. S., Calgary, AB, T2J 0P6. Contact: Dir. of Fran. - Tel: (403) 640-2000, Fax: (403) 640-2426. Golf equipment specialty store offering golf equipment and related clothing, accessories, supplies and services. Established: 1993 in Canada - Franchising Since: 1986 in U.S.A. - No. of Units: Company Owned: 1 - Franchised: 5 - Franchise Fee: $48,000 - Royalty: 3%, 1% ad. fund - Total Inv: $225,000-$300,000 - Financing: No.

NEVADA BOB'S GOLF AND RACQUETS
Dimarco Golf
1 First Canadian Place, Toronto, ON, M5X 1B1. - Tel: (416) 366-2221, Fax: (416) 361-0470. Franchise operation specializing in golf and racquet goods, repair services, footwear and athletic sportswear. Established: 1985 - Franchising Since: 1987 - No. of Units: Company Owned: 2 - Franchised: 10 - Franchise Fee: $15,000-$40,000 assessed on local population and potential sales volume - Royalty: 3.5% on first ($1M) gross sales - Total Inv: $150,000.

PAR T GOLF INT.
102A, 339-50 Ave. SE, Calgary, AB, T2G 2E3. Contact: Fran. Dir. - Tel: (403) 252-7777, Fax: (403) 252-3028. Double eagle golf simulators for year round play of world famous golf courses, lessons and practice. Ideally situated in retail golf stores featuring golf clubs, custom clubs, repairs and accessories. Established: 1979 - No. of Units: Franchised: 16 - Total Inv: $250,000.

PARMASTER GOLF TRAINING CENTERS
Parmaster Golf Training Centers LLC
1655 Broadway St., Ste. 102, 9600 Cameron Street, #314, Burnaby, BC, V3J 7N3. Contact: Tom Matzen, Co-Founder - Tel: (604) 444-0277, (800) 663-2331, Fax: (604) 422-8699, E-Mail: info@parmasters.com, Web Site: www.parmasters.com. We are the world's first year round indoor golf training center franchise and combine two growing, proven successful industries - golf training and franchising - to create a fun and unique business opportunity. Franchise opportunities available in golf

areas around North America. Established: 2000 - Franchising Since: 2000 - Franchise Fee: $25,000 - Royalty: 8% - Total Inv: $381,900-$1,100,000 - Financing: No, business plan assistance.

PRO GOLF
Pro Golf Of America
1293 Matheson Blvd., E., Mississauga, ON, L4W 1R1. Contact: Wilf Howson, Ass't Dir. of Canadian Operations - Tel: (905) 238-3320, (800) 463-7469, Fax: (905) 238-3301. Retail golf equipment and club repairs. Established: 1964 - Franchising Since: 1975 - No. of Units: Franchised: 17 (Canada), 165 (US) - Franchise Fee: $40,000 - Royalty: 3% gross sales - Total Inv: $200,000-$250,000 - Financing: None.

PROF. DE SKI®
Distributions Tandem Ltée
1418 Maisonneuve Street, Mont Joli, QC, G5H 2J3. Contact: Dir. of Marketing - Tel: (418) 775-8311, Fax: (418) 775-7388, Web Site: www.profdeski.com. Group of ski professionals. Six different categories. Work in destination areas worldwide for some. Established: 1998 - Franchising Since: 1999 - No. of Units: Company Owned: 1.

PUCKMASTERS HOCKEY TRAINING CENTERS
C/O Entrepreneur Coach Inc
1260 Hornby St, Suite 102, Vancouver, BC, V6Z 1W2. - Tel: (888) 775-7825, Fax: (604) 464-0138, E-Mail: pfry@puckmasters.com, Web Site: www.puckmasters.com. The world's first one-on-one personal hockey training center franchise and combine two growing proven successful industries - hockey training and franchising-to create a fun and unique business opportunity. Established: 1993 - Franchising Since: 1996 - No. of Units: Company Owned: 1 - Franchised: 8 - Franchise Fee: $20,000 - Royalty: 6% - Total Inv: $95,000-$135,000 - Financing: No.

RUCKERS FUN CENTRES
500-1110 Centre Street NE, Calgary, AB, T2E 2R2. Contact: Fran. Dir. - Tel: (403) 277-1332, Fax: (403) 277-1352. An upscale fun center concept offering the latest in video simulators, carnival games and sports games. Specializing in group parties. A flunky energizing environment housing the latest in interactive out-of-home fun for all ages. Established: 1992 - No. of Units: Franchised: 18 - Total Inv: $300,000-$100,000 unencumbered cash.

SPORT TIMES CORPORATION
71 King St., Ste. 202, St. Catharines, ON, L2R 3H7. - Tel: (905) 704-0228, Fax: (905) 704-0157, E-Mail: sports@sporttimes.com, Web Site: www.sporttimes.com. A sports marketing concept addressing the national level right down to the community grassroots. Established: 1995 - Franchising: 1996 - No. of Units: Company Owned: 1 - Franchised: 12 - Franchise Fee: $17,500-$45,500 - Royalty: $395.00 (mim.) - Total Inv: $29,500-$59,500.

SPORTS EXPERTS
Forzani Group Ltd.
824-41st Ave N.E., Calgary, AB, T2E 3R3. Contact: Paul Nowlan, Dir. of Fran. - Sporting goods and leisure products. Established: 1967 - Franchising Since: 1972 - No. of Units: Company Owned: 150 - Franchised: 130 - Franchise Fee: $30,000 - Royalty: 4.5% - Total Inv: $300,000-$400,000, fixed assets, $100,000-$250,000.

SPORTS RECRUITS INTERNATIONAL
Sports Recruits International Inc.
128 Queen St. S., Box 42277, Mississauga, ON, L5M 5Z5. Contact: Terry Glenister, Dir. of Fran. - Tel: (905) 821-0040. International recruiting organization which provides exposure of above average student/athletes to American/Canadian colleges/universities for purpose of obtaining a funded college/university education. Established: 1990 - Franchising Since: 1990 - No. of Units: Franchised: 10 - Franchise Fee: Varies according to location based on size of territory - Total Inv: Varies based on size of territory - Financing: No.

SPORTS TRADERS
Traders International
508 Discovery St., Victoria, BC, V8T 1G8. Contact: Patrick Mellett, Marketing Director - Tel: (250) 383-6443, (800) 792-3111, Fax: (250) 383-8481. Used and new sports equipment retail concept. Established: 1983 - Franchising Since: 1987 - No. of Units: Company Owned: 1 - Franchised: 32 - Franchise Fee: $25,000 - Royalty: First 6 months no

royalty, 7th-12th month $250/month, 2nd year $300/month, 3rd yr. 750/month, 4th yr. $1000/month - Total Inv: $25,000 franchise fee, $100,000 inventory, $30,000 lease hold - Financing: No.

WACKY PUTT
Le Rigol Feve Inc.
7 Boul. J.F. Kennedy Ste. 12, St. Jerome, QC, J7Y 4B4. Contact: Robert Longtin, V.P. Operations - Tel: (450) 438-2070, Fax: (450) 438-8478. Jokes 'n pranks electronic miniature golf with interchangeable cup, tee and platform. Established: 1993 - Franchising Since: 1994 - No. of Units: Company Owned: 1 - Franchised: 30 - Franchise Fee: $1,500 - Royalty: .50¢ per ball after 10,000/yr - Total Inv: $185,000 - Financing: No.

TANNING SALONS

FABUTAN SUN TAN STUDIOS
5925-3rd St., S.E., Calgary, AB, T2H 1K3. Contact: Will Hoes, Director of Franchising - Tel: (403) 640-2100, (800) 565-3658, Fax: (403) 640-2116, E-Mail: mail@fabutan.com, Web Site: www.fabu tan.com. Join over 130 other franchisees and brighten your future earning potential with an investment as low as $25,000. Fabutan provides indoor tanning and related services with a proven brand and operating system for over 20 years. Established: 1979 - Franchising Since: 1984 - No. of Units: Company Owned: 15- Franchised: 118 - Franchise Fee: $15,000 - Royalty: 6% of tanning sales - Total Inv: $100,000-$1150,000 - Financing: No.

ISLAND TAN
Island Tan Franchise Corp
Suite 234-810 Quayside Drive, New Westminister, BC, V3M 6B9. Contact: Cormac McCarthy, Key Account Manager Franchising - Tel: (604) 516-0203, Fax: (604) 516-0403, E-Mail: cormac@nornetco.com, Web Site: www.islandtan.ca. Island Tan is a tanning salon franchise that provides high quality tanning services along with realted tanning products, primarily tanning salons. Established: 1993 - No. of Uniuts: Franchised: 10 - Franchise Fee: $15,000 plus GST - Royalty: 5%; 3% marketing fund - Total Inv: $135,000-$150,000 - Financing: Franchisor will assist in document preparation.

R.X. SOLEIL, INC.
2466 Belanger St., Montreal, QC, H2G 1E5. Contact: Pres. - Tel: (514)729-8859, Fax: (514) 729-7510. Suntanning studio with accessory sale of complementary products such as sun-tanning gel and lotion, promotional material (e.g. lighters and garments) with logo. Established: 1981 - Franchising Since: 1981 - No. of Units: Company Owned: 6 - Franchised: 64 - Franchise Fee: $10,000-$30,000 - Approx. Total Inv: $75,000-$155,000 - Royalty: 5%, 5% adv. - Financing: Yes, bank package.

SUNBANQUE ISLAND TANNING
2533 A Yonge St., Toronto, ON, M4P 2H9. Contact: Joel Guisto, Pres. - Tel: (306) 653-4481. Suntanning salons, aesthetics and cosmetic/skin care products. Established: 1983 - Franchising Since: 1983 - No. of Units: Company Owned: 1 - Franchised: 12 - Franchise Fee: $10,000 - Royalty: 4% for adv. - Total Inv: $40,000 - Financing: Yes.

SUNSTREAM TAN & SKIN CARE
Sunstream Canada
44 Charles St., W., Ste. 2809, Toronto, ON, M4Y 1R7. Contact: Maurice Shpur, Pres. - Tel: (416) 964-6424, Fax: (416) 967-6837. Sun tan equipment. Established: 1984 - Franchising Since: 1984 - No. of Units: Company Owned: 3 - Franchised: 7 - Franchise Fee: $15,000 - Approx. Total Inv: $75,000 - Royalty: 5% - Financing: Yes.

THE TANNING SHOP
1370 Don Mills Road, Unit 300, Don Mills, ON, M3B 3N7. Contact: John Brennan, Fran. Dev. - Tel: (416) 381-4073, Fax: (416) 441-0591. Tanning salon operating with the new Hex Stand-Up Systems. Full training and ongoing support. Established: 1994 - No. of Units: Franchised: 3.

TRAVEL

CRUISE HOLIDAYS
44 Fitzwilliam Blvd., London, ON, N6H 5H6. Contact: Fran. Dev. - Tel: (519) 641-2203, Fax: (519) 641-2977. Retail cruise vacations store. Full three weeks training and ongoing support. Established: 1984 - No. of Units: Franchised: 0-Canada; 200-US - Total Inv: $100,000.

CRUISESHIPCENTERS
Cruise Ship Centers Canada Ltd.
1055 West Hastings Street #400, Vancouver, BC, V6E 2E9. Contact: Eunice LaRocque, Director of Franchise Sales - Tel: (604) 685-1221, (877) 791-7676, Fax: (604) 685-1245, E-Mail: eunice_Laroque@cruise shipcenters.ca, Web Site: www.cruiseshipcenters.com. Retail travel outlets specializing in the sale of cruise vacations. Established: 1989 - Franchising Since: 1989 - No. of Units: Franchised: 56 - Franchise Fee: $40,000 - Royalty: 9% of gross income - Total Inv: F.F $40,000, other $85,000 - Financing: Yes.

GLOBAL TRAVEL NETWORK
1027 Yonge Street, 3rd Floor, Toronto, ON, M4W 2K9. Contact: Jack Forrester, Fran. Dir. - Tel: (416) 969-9311, Fax: (416) 975-1636. Global Travel Network, Ltd. is a global franchise company that was formed in 1982 to provide an invester with a full service agency set-up. We offer a successful program with a proven track record which includes a complete start-up-turnkey package, intensive 4 week training, strong field support system, comprehensive marketing package etc. Established: 1982 - Franchising Since: 1982 - No. of Units: Franchised: Over 340 in 32 US States - Franchise Fee: Three investment opportunities: full service $29,900, store franchise fee $19,900, home based travel consultant franchise fee $4,995.

HAROLD SMITH TRAVEL
Algonquin Travel Corp.
10104-103rd Ave, Mezzanine Level, #205, Edmonton, AB, T5J 0H8. - Tel: (780) 429-3420, Fax: (780) 424-7144, E-Mail: info@haroldsmith travel.com, Web Site: www.haroldsmithtravel.com. Franchising of full service established travel agencys with a revenue guarantee for first 12 months. Full training provided. Established: 1964 - Franchising Since: 1979 - No. of Units: Franchised: 9 - Franchise Fee: $35,000 - Royalty: 6% of gross commissions net of discounts - Total Inv: $80,000-$200,000 - Financing: Upto 50% on OAC.

IDEAL CONCEPT TRAVEL, INC
151 Frobisher Dr., Ste. G116, Waterloo, ON, N2V 2E1. Contact: Joni Hartwick, President - Tel: (519) 725-7911, (888) 747-4968, Fax: (519) 725-8730. A home based travel business. All administration done by head office. Established: 1995 - Franchising Since: 1995 - No. of Units: Company Owned: 1 - Franchised: 19 - Franchise Fee: $10,000 - Royalty: None - Financing: Yes.

PEERLESS TRAVEL GROUP
7117 Bathurst Street, Ste 200, Thornhill, ON, L4J 2J6. Contact: Rick Keenie, Franchising - Tel: (905) 886-5610, (800) 294-1663, Fax: (905) 886-4019. A full service travel agency. Established: 1992 - Franchising Since: 1998 - No. of Units: Company Owned: 1 - Franchise Fee: $28,000 - Royalty: 0.9% - Total Inv: $90,000 - Financing: Available.

THOMAS COOK GROUP CANADA, MERLIN TRAVEL
5900A Rodeo Dr., Mississauga, ON, L5R 3S9. Contact: Jeff Chemeses, Director Franchise Sales - Tel: (905) 501-4653, (888) 823-7262, Fax: (905) 502-6367, E-Mail: jchemeres@thomascook, Web Site: www.thomascook.com. Travel industry. Established: 1993 - Franchising Since: 1993 - No. of Units: Company Owned: 148 - Franchised: 158 - Franchise Fee: Upon Request - Royalty: Upon request - Total Inv: Upon Request - Financing: Yes.

TIME LINES TRAVEL
667 Champlain St., Dieppe, NB, E1A 1P6. Contact: Mariner Black, President - Tel: (506) 854-3111, (800) 557-3111, Fax: (506) 384-3113. On-going training, support and administrative services to independent contractors. This is a home based business. Established: 1994 - No. of Units: Company Owned: 1 - Contractors: 28 - Franchise Fee: $10,000 - Royalty: $900/yr or less - Total Inv: Equipment plus fee $13,000 - Financing: Limited.

TRAVEL COUNTER, THE
Travel Counter Inc., The
5218 Yonge St., 2nd Floor, North York, ON, M2N 5P6. Contact: Benjamin Estreicher, Pres. - Tel: (416) 222-2929, Fax: (416) 223-4645, Web Site: www.travelcounter.on.ca. Full service travel agency operating in Loblaws supermarkets and affiliates. Low overhead, high income, exceptional visibility. "A lot of fun". Established: 1996 - Franchising Since: 1996 - No. of Units: Company Owned: 3 - Franchised: 16 - Franchise Fee: $19,500 - Royalty: 2% of gross sales - Total Inv: $49,500 for leasehold, equipment and signage - Financing: Yes.

TRAVEL EDGE, THE
The Travel Edge, Inc.
342 Delaware Ave., Toronto, ON, M5H 2T8. Contact: Garth Ballantyne, Executive V.P. - Tel: (416) 535-9908, (800) 419-4435, Fax: (416) 535-9879, Web Site: www.traveledge.com. Home office professional travel business using state of the art technology, professional reservation system, customized internet sites, training, support and very pro-active marketing programs. Established: 1996 - Franchising Since: 1996 - No. of Units: Company Owned: 1 - Franchised: 47 - Franchise Fee: $11,000 - Royalty: No - Total Inv: $11,000 - Financing: Yes.

TRAVEL PROFESSIONALS INTERNATIONAL
Travel One Corp.
2627 portage Ave, Winnipeg, MB, R3J 0P7. - Tel: (800) 799-9910, (204) 987-3322, Fax: (204) 788-1410, E-Mail: info@tpi.ca, Web Site: www.tpi.ca. Full service travel agency with unique national central support office linked to home, office or business based associates. Low overhead, high profit structure. Established: 1993 - Franchising Since: 1994 - No. of Units: Company Owned: 4 - Franchised: 200+ - Franchise Fee: $8,900-$12,900 - Royalty: None - Total Inv: $10,000 - Financing: Yes.

TRAVEL/MAX BRANCHISE
Travelwise Canada Ltd
1027 Younge Street, Suite 110, Toronto, ON, M4W 2K9. Contact: Mr. Amar, President - Tel: (416) 934-9991, (800) 930-7704, Fax: (416) 934-0119, E-Mail: info@travelmaxcanada.com, Web Site: www.travelmax canada.com. The perfect low cost home-based travel biz opportunity. Earn franchise income without the high start-up costs associated with a store front travel agency or franchise. Travel/Max Branchise = sun + fun + 100% commissions. Established: 1989 - Franchising Since: 1998 - No. of Units: Company Owned: 1 - Franchised: 15 - Franchise Fee: $5,000 - Total Inv: $5,000 - Financing: Yes.

UNIGLOBE TRAVEL
Uniglobe Travel (International) Inc.
1199 W. Pender St., Ste.900, Vancouver, BC, V6E 2R1. - Tel: (604) 718-2600, Fax: (604) 718-2678, Web Site: www.uniglobe.com. Uniglobe has consistently been a world leader in retail travel agency. Franchising for start-ups, conversions, cruise-only outlets and home-based agents. All franchisees benefit from programs and systems designed to handle the needs of corporate and leisure clients. Established: 1980 - Franchising Since: 1981- No. of Units: Franchised: 1000+ - Franchise Fee: Varies according to franchise product - Financing: Varies according to country.

VOYALGE VASCO
825 St-Pierre, Terrebonne, QC, J6W 1E6. Contact: Sylvain Lastere, Fran. Dir. - Tel: (450) 961-4242. The most affordable business trips, cruises and leisure travel. Established: 1994 - Franchising Since: 1994 - No. of Units: Company Owned: 1 - Franchised: 6 - Franchise Fee: $10,000 - Royalty: $400/mo. - Total Inv: $26,000 turn-key operation - Financing: Yes.

VIDEO/AUDIO SALES & RENTAL

2.4.1. VIDEO & GAMES
2.4.1. Video & Games, Inc.
62 Marmaduke Street, Toronto, ON, M9R 1T4. Contact: David Henriques, President - Tel: (416) 769-4241, (888) 241-2725, Fax: (416) 767-2059, Web Site: www.241.formovies.com. 2.4.1. video retailing. Stores feature a huge selection of new releases in videos, games and sell-thru. Established: 1995 - Franchising Since: 1995 - No. of Units: Company

Owned: 1 - Franchised: 13 - Franchise Fee: None - Royalty: Service fee $150.00-$500.00 per month - Total Inv: Turnkey $129,000-$30,000 - Financing: Third party.

JUMBO VIDEO
Jumbo Systems
5500 N. Service Rd, Burlington, ON, L7L 5H7. Contact: Doug Jacques, Director of Franchise Sales and Real Estate - Tel: (905) 634-4244, Fax: (905) 632-2964. Home video rental and sales, game rental, movie memorabilia, posters, movie related toys, and confectionery. Established: 1987 - Franchising Since: 1987 - No. of Units: Company Owned: 1 - Franchised: 60 - Franchise Fee: $25,000 J.V. new releases, $50,000 Jumbo video - Royalty: 5% Admin, 3% Nat'l Adv. - Total Inv: Total turn key investment from $150,000 - Financing: No.

STAR VIDEO
190 Harwood Ave., S., Ajax, ON, L1S 2H7. Contact: David Kang, Mgr. - Tel: (905) 427-7799, Fax: (905) 427-7799. Established: 1983 - Franchising Since: 1984 - No. of Units: Company Owned: 2 - Franchised: 6 - Franchise Fee: Negotiable - Total Inv: $300,000 - Financing: No. NOT OFFERING FRANCHISES AT THIS TIME.

TYME TO PARTY
Video Party Tyme
55 Northfield Dr., E., Waterloo, ON, N2K 3T6. Contact: Harvey Norris, Pres. - Tel: (519) 745-8274, Fax: (519) 745-4420. Video, sales and rentals. Established: 1982 - No. of Units: Company Owned: 2 - Franchised: 6.

VIDEOMATIC 24 HR
Videomatic 24 hr. Movie Rentals, Inc.
760 King Rd., Burlington, ON, L7T 3K6. Contact: David Cranston, Pres. - Tel: (905) 681-2484, Fax: (905) 681-1116, E-Mail: dcransto@cgocable.net, Web Site: www.videovending.com. Videomatic is a 24hr video store that operates without employees. Using fully patented video vending machines. Established: 1985 - Franchising since: 1986, No. of Units: Company Owned: 1 - Franchised: 41 - Total Inv: Leaseholds $15,000 venders leased, videos $10,000 - Financing: Yes.

VIDEOPLEX
165 Dundas Street West, Suite 1002, Mississauga, ON, L5B 2N6. Contact: Cliff Richler, Fran. Dev. - Tel: (888) 358-4336, Fax: (905) 276-5076. Videoplex features the newest video releases and multiple copies of Hollywood's greatest movies. We supply the movies at the best price, then we buy them back from you when they quit renting. Easy to own and operate. Established: 1997 - No. of Units: Company Owned: 1 - Franchised: 7 - Total Inv: $40,000 - full turnkey, $125,000 no royalties.

WATER TREATMENT

CULLIGAN OF CANADA LTD.
2213 N. Sheridan Way, Mississauga, ON, L5K 1A5. Contact: Carmine Scione, President - Tel: (905) 494-2100 , Fax: (905) 494-0262, E-Mail: tech@culligan.ca, Web Site: www.culligan.ca. Manufacturing and distributing of water conditioning equipment, domestic and commercial/industrial through franchised dealers. Established: 1947 - Franchising Since: 1952 - No. of Units: Company Owned: 1 - Franchised: 58 - Franchise Fee: $1,000-$20,000 - Royalty: 5%-10% Bottled Water - Total Inv: $75,000-$100,000 - Financing: Private.

GLACIER CLEARWATER
3291 Thomas Street, Thornton, ON, L0L 2N0. Contact: Fran. Dev. - Tel: (705) 436-6363, Fax: (705) 436-4949, Web Site: www.glacierclear.com. Commercial and residential treatment of water, spring water, coolers and filter softners. Established: 1985 - No. of Units: Franchised: 2 - Total Inv: $65,000-$85,000.

H20 COOL
Aquacell Of Canada
375 Wanyandy Rd, Edmonton, AB, T5T 4S4. - Tel: (403) 413-1670. Point-of-use water cooler system. Established: 1990 - No. of Units: Company Owned: 4 - Franchise Fee: $2500.00 - Total Inv: $2500.00 - Financing: Possible.

INTEGRA ENVIRONMENTAL, INC.
1430 Cormorant Rd, Ancaster, ON, L9G 4V5. Contact: Marc Bajzik, VP Sales - Tel: (905) 304-3713, (800) 661-6678, Fax: (905) 304-5742. Residential, commercial and industrial water treatments. Established: 1983 - Franchising Since: 1983 - No. of Units: Company Owned: 4 - Franchise Fee: None - Royalty: None - Total Inv: $5,000 - Financing: No.

ORIGINAL WATER CLUB, THE
The Original Water Club Ltd
P.O. Box 3412 22 East Lake Green, Airdrie, AB, T4B 2B7. Contact: Roy Lewis, President - Tel: (403) 948-1565, (888) 928-2582, Fax: (403) 948-1906, E-Mail: info@waterclub.com, Web Site: www.waterclub.com. The Original Water Club is an innovative aspiring company in the bottled water industry. The company has grown in involvement, structure, and market representation. Centralized communications and administration, configured hardware (laptop) and copyright software developed exclusively for TOWC have founded the "true value" service unprecedented in the bottled water industry. Established: 1996 - Franchising Since: 1998 - No. of Units: Franchised: 27 franchise operations, 3 master franchises - Franchise Fee: Master franchise: $250,000, Franchise operation: $14,900 - Royalty: 20% of equity ownership for master franchise, no royalty fee for franchise operation - Total Inv: Master franchise $250,000 - Franchise Operation, $24,900 - Financing: Yes up to $100,000 master franchise, $15,000 franchise operator.

PURIFIED WATER STORE
PWS Purified Water Store Corp.
Unit 108, 19070 Lougheed Hwy, Pitt Meadows, BC, V3Y 2M6. - Tel: (604) 465-8810, Fax: (604) 465-8057, E-Mail: opportunities@purified waterstore.com, Web Site: www.purfiedwaterstore.com. Premier bottled water retailer. Featuring high quality reverse osmosis bottled water for fill's, pick-up or delivery. We also provide the consumer option for purchasing your water dispensing equipment either through direct sale or rent to own. Established: 1999 - Franchising Since: 2000 - No. of Units: Company Owned: 1 - Franchised: 13 - Franchise Fee: $10,000 - Royalty: 5% - Total Inv: From $119,900 plus opening inventory.

WATER SOURCE, THE
Curetex Medical Devices Inc.
600 Ontario St., Unit 22, St. Catharines, ON, L2N 7H8. Contact: Michael Molnar, Pres. - Tel: (905) 646-4420, Fax: (905) 646-2583, E-Mail: mmolnar@thewatercource.com, Web Site: www.thewater source.com. Self serve water RETAIL store on site water purification by reverse osmosis and distillation. Also retail spring water. Complete line of water filtration and purification systems including water conditioners and water conservation products. Established: 1990 - Franchising Since: 1992 - No. of Units: Franchised: 14 - Franchise Fee: $15,000 - Royalty: 5¢ PER US gallon of reverse osmosis and distilled water dispensed plus $50/mo. admin. cost - Total Inv: $70,000-$90,000 - Financing: No. NOT OFFERING FRANCHISES AT THIS TIME.

WORLD OF WATER
World of Water International Ltd
326 Keewatin Street, Winnipeg, MB, R2X 2R9. Contact: Jarrett Davidson - Tel: (204) 774-7770, (866) 749-1146, Fax: (204) 772-5051, E-Mail: franchise@worldofwater.ca, Web Site: www.worldofwater.ca. Franchisor of retail bottled water stores. Established: 1976 - Franchising Since: 1996 - No. of Units: Company Owned: 1 - Franchised: 13 - Franchise Fee: $25,000 - Royalty: 5% - Total Inv: $165,000 - Financing: No.

WEIGHT LOSS CENTERS

BEVERLY HILLS WEIGHT LOSS CLINIC
Beverly Hills Weight Loss Clinics of Canada Inc.
23 Wellington St. East, Guelph, ON, N1H 3R7. Contact: Rhonda Bashton, Franchise Director - Tel: (519) 837-1177, Fax: (519) 837-1221. Weight loss services, offering a behavioral based program. Various weight management programs available, with all client programs selected by a doctor. Established: 1988 - Franchising Since: 1988 - No. of Units: Company Owned: 2 - Franchised: 60 - Franchise Fee: $25,000 - Royalty: 7.5% - Total Inv: $40,000 - Financing: Yes, must qualify.

HERBAL MAGIC SYSTEMS
Herbal Magic System International, Inc
1069 Wellington Rd. S, #108, London, ON, N6E 2H6. Contact: Dieter J. Decker, President - Tel: (519) 685-6294, (800) 850-1702, Fax: (519) 685-9157, E-Mail: magic@herbalmagicsystems.com, Web Site: www.magic@herbalmagicsystems.com. Weight management - counselling - retail sales - herbal/vitamin and mineral suppliments. Established: 1993 - Franchising Since: 1996 - No. of Units: Company Owned: 9 - Franchised: 150 - Franchise Fee: $16,500 - Royalty: $125.00 per wk - Total Inv: $50,000 - Financing: No.

POSITIVE CHANGES HYPNOSIS
P.C.H. Canada, Inc.
255 Rutherford Road, #102, Brampton, ON, L6W 3J7. Contact: George Fluter, Director Franchising - Tel: (416) 944-2200, Fax: (416) 944-3555, E-Mail: srpch@excite.com, Web Site: www.pchyponosis.com. Health and Wellness - to weight loss, stop smoking, stress management, sports enhancement. Established: US 1961-CAN 1998 - Franchising Since: 1998 - No. of Units: Company Owned: US 3 - CAN 3 - Franchised: US 100 - CAN 8 - Franchise Fee: $25,000 - Royalty: Flat $2,000 monthly. Total Inv: $90,000 - Fran. Fee: $25,000, Furniture: $18,000, Leaseholds: $30,000, Working Capital: $15,000, Monthly Fee: $2,000.

MISCELLANEOUS

1-800-GOT-JUNK ?
200-1523 West 3rd Ave, Vancouver, BC, V6J 1J8. Contact: Brian Scudamore, Founder - Tel: (604) 731-5782, (877) 408-5865, Fax: (801) 751-0634, Web Site: www.1800gotjunk.com. 1-800-GOT-JUNK? has revolutionized customer service in junk removal for over ten years. By setting the mark for service standards and professionalism, an industry that once operated without set rates, price lists, or receipts, now has top service standards. Established: 1989 - Franchising Since: 1999 - No. of Units: Company Owned: 1 - Franchised: 22 - Franchise Fee: $20,000 - Royalty: 8% of gross sales - Financing: No.

A WINNER EVERY TIME, INC.
144 Morningview Trail, Scarborough, ON, M1B 5L2. Contact: Mazen Jaafar, President - Tel: (416) 282-1478, (800) 915-9782, Fax: (416) 282-7640. Manufacturing, marketing, locating, servicing, training, consulting, and premixed product for "Snack Attacker", "Challenger", '"My Magic" Photo sticker machine, "Toy Zone" candy/toys/plush crane machines. Established: 1993 - Franchising Since: 1996 - No. of Units: Company Owned: 40 - Franchised: 10 - Franchise Fee: None - Royalty: None - Total Inv: $20,000 plus tax or min. $6,000 plus tax - Financing: Through banks/leasing companies.

ACCEL CAPITAL CORP.
100 Melville St. Suite 300, Vancouver, BC, V6E 4A6. Contact: Rod Hamilton, President - Tel: (604) 687-7155, Fax: (604) 646-2401, E-Mail: rod@accelcapital.com. Accel Capital Corp is a niche funding source for small ticket equipment leasing, specializing in transactions from $5,000-$200,000 in select industries such as franchising vending and laundry. Established: 1991.

ACTION PARALEGAL
109 Sheppard Ave, W, North York, ON, M2N 1M7. Contact: Wayne P. Morrison, Pres. - Tel: (416) 590-0253, Fax: (416) 733-9715. Paralegal services. Established: 1988 - Franchising Since: 1994 - No. of Units: Company Owned: 2 - Franchised: 2 - Franchise Fee: $10,000 - Royalty: 1st year nil, 2nd year 5% - Total Inv: $10,000 - Financing: Yes.

ADVANTAGE PROMOTIONAL RESOURCES
855 Hilton Blvd, Newmarket, ON, L3X 2H7. Contact: VP Marketing - Tel: (905) 953-1256. Corporate gifts, premiums, incentives and related programs for franchisees and franchisors. Established: 2001.

B COMMERCE TRADE EXCHANGE
2781 Highway 7, Concord, ON, L4K 1W1. Contact: John Tanti, President - Tel: (905) 660-3929, (866) 288-6148, E-Mail: john@bcommerce.ca, Web Site: www.bcommerce.ca. Leader in next generation barter trade

systems. EStablished: 2003 - No. of Units: Company: Owned: 1 - Franchise Fee: $40,000 - Royalty: 9% of transaction fees - Total Inv: $100,000.

BATHMASTER RESURFACING
BMR BathMaster Reglazing, Ltd.
4498 Trepanier Road, Peachland, BC, V0H 1X3. Contact: Trevor Dixon, Owner/President - Tel: (250) 767-2336, (877) 767-2336, Fax: (250) 767-2718, E-Mail: sales@bathmaster.com, Web Site: www.bathmaster.com. Bathtub, sink and tile reglazing. In home service. No mess or odour, same day use on most items. Counter top resurfacing, chip repairs, non slip systems for tubs and more. Established: 1989 - Franchising Since: 1993 - No. of Units: Company Owned: 1 - Franchised: 14 - Royalty: 5% - Total Inv: Starting at $24,000 - Financing: No.

BATTERY WORLD
Battery World Canada Corp
1229 Derwent Way, New Westminster, BC, V3M 5V9. Contact: Les Granholm, President - Tel: (604) 525-0391, Fax: (604) 525-0392, E-Mail: sales@bwsinc.com, Web Site: www.bwsinc.com. Specialty retailer and corporate reseller of battery products and mobile computing equipment. Established: 1996 - Franchising Since: 1997 - No. of Units: Company Owned: 2 - Franchised: 3 - Franchise Fee: $40,000 - Royalty: 3% of gross sales - Total Inv: $100,000-$150,000 - Financing: No.

CHECK ROOM SERVICES
1350 East 4th Ave., Vancouver, BC, V5N 1J5. Contact: Ian Abramson, CEO - Tel: (604) 255-5000, (800) 663-4577, Fax: (604) 254-2575, E-Mail: ian@ilps.com, Web Site: www.ilps.com. Manufacturer of Coat Check Express. A unique coin-operated automated Self-Service Coat Check System. Established: 1988 - Franchising Since: 1993 - No. of Units: Company Owned: 20 - Franchised: 4 - Franchise Fee: $25,000 - Total Inv: $25,000 - Financing: Yes.

CHEMWISE INC.
2175 Sheppard Avenue East, #307, North York, ON, H2J 1W8. Contact: J. David Carnie, Executive Vice President - Tel: (416) 493-9553, (800) 823-0193, Fax: (416) 493-3157, E-Mail: chemwise@idirect.com, Web Site: www.chemwise.com. Specialty chemicals. Advance technology is gathered from around the world and in many cases chemwise enters into an exclusive agreement to use this technology to produce products for Canada. Established: 1994 - Franchising Since: 1995 - No. of Units: Franchised: 20 - Franchise Fee: Varies with territory - Total Inv: Varies with exclusive territory - Financing: Yes.

CHRISTMAS DECOR
2399 Royal Windsor Drive, Mississauga, ON, L5J 1K9. Contact: Fran Dev. - Tel: (905) 823-8550, Fax: (905) 823-4594. Professional outdoor holiday and special event lighting and decorating fo both residential and commercial sites. Complete 3 days of training and ongoing training and full support. Established: 1986 - No. of Units: Franchised: 250 - Total Inv: $9,500-$15,900.

CLASSIXXX ENTERPRISES LTD
P.O. 72101, Kanata, ON, K2K 2P4. Contact: Michael Payuette - Tel: (613) 293-3741, Fax: (613) 523-8973, E-Mail: info@classixxx.com, Web Site: www.classixxx.com. Offering full range of adult toys, games, greeting cards and more. Established: 1993 - Franchising Since: 2002 - No. of Units: Company Owned: 3 - Franchised: 1 - Franchise Fee: $20,000.

CRD REGIONAL PLANNING SERVICES
2nd Floor-510 Yates Street, Victoria, BC, V8W 2S6. Contact: Fran. Dev. - Tel: (250) 360-3160, Fax: (250) 360-3159, Web Site: www.crd.bc.ca. Disseminates statistical data on population: housing, labour force, construction, business, building permits, tourism, traffic counts, demographics, income and household expenditures and other data used in typical market studies. Established: 1983.

DANICE PROFESSIONAL SERVICES INC.
5080 Timberlea Boulevard, Unit 24, Mississauga, ON, L4W 4M2. Contact: David Swan, President - Tel: (905) 602-8112, Fax: (905) 602-6273, E-Mail: danice@interlog.com. Danice provides custom business solutions that cover a full range of print needs, direct marketing, promotional materials and programs, as well as inventory and information

management. Danice provides every service from concept to delivery, working diligently to ensure total customer satisfaction. Established: 1989.

EDWARD JONES
Sussex Ctr., Ste. 902, 90, Burnhamthorpe Rd. W., Mississauga, ON, L5B 3C3. Contact: Jo-Anne Hiscock, Recruiting Administration - Tel: (905) 306-8600, Fax: (905) 306-8624. A full service investment firm specializing in single-representative, community-based branch offices. Established: 1994 (CAN), 1871 (US) - Branch offices: 3,500, 70 of these branch offices now in Canada.

ELITE TRADE PAINTING
Suite 200-5687 West Street, Halifax, NS, B3K 1H6. Contact: Fran. Dev. - Tel: (902) 422-7731, Fax: (902) 422-7742. Residential and commercial painting services. Training and support provided. Established: 1992 - No. of Units: Franchised: 21 - Total Inv: $30,000.

ELKIND, LIPTON & JACOBS, INTERNATIONAL ATTORNEYS
#1 Queen Street East, #1900, Toronto, ON, M5C 2W6. Contact: Stanley W. Elkind QC., Senior Partner - Tel: (416) 367-0871, Fax: (416) 367-9388, E-Mail: swelkind@eljlaw.com, Web Site: www.eljlaw.com. International Attorneys. Established: 1970.

FOUR SEASONS SUNROOMS
5005 Veterans Memorial Highway, Holbrook, NY, 11741. Contact: Fran. Dev. - Tel: (516) 563-4000, Fax: (516) 563-4010. Producers of quality sunrooms and solariums. Established: 1974 - No. of Units: Franchised: 15 - Total Inv: $50,000.

FRUITS & PASSION BOUTIQUE INC.
Hurteau & Associes Inc.
21 Paul-Gaugin Street, Candiac, QC, J5R 3X8. Contact: Sylvie Hudon, Adm. Assistant - Tel: (450) 638-2212, (800) 276-9952, Fax: (450) 638-2430, Web Site: www.fruits.passion.com. A line of high quality lifestyle products, based on the curative and regenerative properties of fruit, for body care, home ambiance and the gourmet. The products stand out by their uniqueness and esthetic appeal, all in keeping with the environmental concerns of our times. Established: 1992 - Franchising Since: 1995 - No. of Units: Company Owned: 3 - Franchised: 11 - Franchise Fee: $25,000 - Royalty: None - Total Inv: Capital Inv. $60,000-$75,000, Inventory $30,000-$50,000, Asset Acquisition $125,000-$150,000 - Financing: Yes with the Royal Bank of Canada.

FUTURE RECOVERY CENTRES
Future Recovery Canada Inc.
382 Queen St. West, Cambridge, ON, N3C 1G8. Contact: Dr. Gary T. Goodyear, President - Tel: (519) 658-5069, Fax: (519) 658-6935. Rehabilitation and coordination of treatment of injured workers or motor vehicle occupants. We offer access to and coordination of all employee services and injury management. Established: 1992 - Franchising Since: 1993 - No. of Units: Company Owned: 1 - Franchised: 5 - Franchise Fee: $85,000 - Royalty: 8.5% plus 3% adv. - Total Inv: $200,000 - Financing: Yes.

GOLD FINGER
136 Castle Rock Rd, Richmond Hill, ON, L4C 5K5. - Tel: (416) 464-8468. Great home based business. Mobile 24 karate gold electroplates, change chrome to gold in seconds. Life time guarantee, Make up to one thousand dollars a day. Established: 1995 - Franchising Since: 1995 - No. of Units: Franchised: 5 - Franchise Fee: $5,000 - Royalty: 5% or $300.00 monthly - Total Inv: $5,000 - Financing: Third party.

GUARDSMAN WOODPRO, CANADA
17075 Concession 10, Schomberg, ON, L0G 1T0. Contact: Michael F. James, Fran. Dir. - Tel: (905) 939-7721, (888) 966-3232, Fax: (905) 939-7480. Home based professional on site wood repair service. Franchise owners offer woodwork, furniture, upholstery, repairs as well as kitchen cabinet refurbishing, deck reconditioning and fabric protection to a wide selection of commercial and residential clients. Established: 1996 Canada, 1915 US - Franchising Since: 1996 Canada, 1994 US - No. of Units: Company Owned: 1 Canada - Franchised: 11 Canada, 80 US - Franchise Fee: $26,500 Canadian - Royalty: 8%, 1% adv. - Total Inv: $26,500 fran. fee/$500 van deposit/$2,500 misc. office, equip. - Financing: TDB.

HAGER & ASSOCIATES INC.
116 Spadina Avenue, Suite 402, Toronto, ON, M5V 2K6. Contact: Paula Gauici, Associate - Tel: (416) 703-5523, Fax: (416) 703-5526, E-Mail: dhagar416aol.com. Interior design services for multi-unit companies (hotels, restaurants, fast food and retail). Services include concept strategic positioning, working drawings, purchasing, project management from start to finish. Established: 1984.

HALL OF NAMES
Hall of Names Marketing, Inc
830 Development Dr., Kingston, ON, K7M 5V7. Contact: Jim Whidden, Sales Administrator - Tel: (613) 384-2257, (800) 265-7099, Fax: (613) 384-0606, E-Mail: jimw@hallofnames.com, Web Site: www.hallof names.com. Offers surname histories (600,000) first name histories (50,000) Scottish clan histories (35,000) coats of arms (2,000,000). Licensees can reproduce these products on their own computer using windows in any location. Established: 1988 - Franchising Since: 1988 - No. of Units: Company Owned: 2 - Franchised: 50 - License Fee: $5,000-$10,000 - Royalty: 20%- 30% - Total Inv: License fee $5,000 - Equipment $2,000 - Financing: N/A.

J&M COIN, STAMP & JEWELLERY LTD.
127 E. Broadway Ave, Vancouver, BC, V5T 1W1. - Tel: (604) 876-7181, Fax: (604) 876-1518. Coin, stamp, jewellery, foreign exchange buying and selling. Established: 1967 - No. of Units: Company Owned: 4 - Franchise Fee: $25,000 - Royalty: $1,000 per month - Total Inv: $25,000 fran. fee, $50,000-$150,000 furniture and equip., $150,000 and up inventory - Financing: Yes.

LEMPIBA INC.
Transtol Manufacturing Inc.
817 Brant St., Burlington, ON, L7R 2J4. Contact: Gord Olson, President - Tel: (905) 631-7000, (800) 465-0888, Fax: (905) 631-7107. Gravel and natural crushed surface repair and maintenance. Established: 1992 - Franchising Since: 1993 - No. of Units: Franchised: 8 - Franchise Fee: $10,000 in Canada, not established in the U.S. market.

LORMIT PROCESS SERVICES
Lormit Management Systems, Inc.
310, 10232-112 St., Edmonton, AB, T5K 1M4. Contact: Tim Haworth, Pres. - Tel: (403) 424-4442, Fax: (403) 426-4917, E-Mail: imsiho@ connect.ab.ca, Web Site: www.lormit.com. Delivery of notice in legal proceedings. Established: 1979 - Franchising Since: 1985 - No. of Units: Franchised: 70- Royalty: 20% of cash receipts inclusive of advertising and centralized accounts collection - Total Inv: Approx. $300 for stationery - Financing: No.

MAGI SEAL SERVICES
Magi Seal Corp
1065 Clarkside Rd., London, ON, N5V 3B3. Contact: James Harris, CEO - Tel: (800) 388-2640, (519) 455-8948. Furniture stores sell fabric protection to customers and contract Magi Seal to do the actual spraying of the furniture. Established: 1983 - Franchising Since: 1983 - No. of Units: Company Owned: 1 - Franchised: 22 - Franchise Fee: $10,000-$90,000 - Royalty: None - Total Inv: Typical $15,000 - Financing: 80% company financing.

MEDICINE SHOPPE
1702 Canada Trust Tower, 10104-103 Rd Avenue, Edmonton, AB, T5J 0H8. Contact: Geoff Sky/Orin Litman, Fran. Dev. - Tel: (780) 424-3096, Fax: (780) 425-3980, Web Site: www.medicineshoppe.ca. Pharmacy franchise group. A 1 week training course in St.Louis with strong marketing and operational support. Established: 1991 - No. of Units: Franchised: 47 - Total Inv: $25,000 cash min.

MR. CRISPY'S FRENCH FRY VENDING MACHINE
Pro Fries Inc.
640, 633 6th Avenue S.W., Calgary, AB, T2P 2Y5. Contact: Kenneth J. Small, Pres. - Tel: (403) 237-9758, Fax: (403) 262-9042. Design and manufacture of patented french fry vending machine that serves a 4.5 oz. of traditionally-cooked real potato fries in 35 seconds. CSA, UL, ULC and NAMA listed. Established: 1986 - Franchising Since: 1989 - No. of Units: Company Owned: 120 - Franchised/Sold: 550 - Franchise Fee: $15,600 - Royalty: 10¢ vend - Total Inv: $13,900 per machine - Financing: No.

PARALEGAL ASSOCIATES
Paralegal Associates Inc.
80 Bradford St., Ste. 551, Barrie, ON, L4N 6S7. Contact: Frank J. Laird, President - Tel: (705) 721-9442, Fax: (705) 721-9423. Providing full range of paralegal services including (highway traffic and provincial offences, small claims, landlord/tenant, family matters, business incorporation, criminal pardons). Established: 1987 - Franchising Since: 1987 - No. of Units: Company Owned: 2 - Franchised: 10 - Franchise Fee: $15,000 - Royalty: 5%, 1% adv. - Total Inv: $15,000 - Financing: Yes.

PAUL DAVIS SYSTEMS
5240 Finch Ave. E, Suite 10, Scarborough, ON, M1S 5A3. Contact: Fran. Dev. - Tel: (416) 299-8890, Fax: (416) 299-8510, E-Mail: wfrobin@pdscanada.com, Web Site: www.pds.ca. Provides estimating repair costs and full repair service for insurance claims for water, wind and fire damages. We serve the insurance industry across Canada. Established: 1986 - No. of Units: Franchised: 27 - Total Inv: $70,000.

PERSONAL PROTECTION SYSTEMS
200 Steelcase Rd., E., #3, Markham, ON, L3R 1G2. Contact: Helen Fischer, Franchising - Tel: (800) 861-4777, (905) 940-9777, Fax: (905) 940-9701. Women's personal protection courses. Established: 1993 - Franchising Since: 1995 - No. of Units: Company Owned: 1 - Franchise Fee: $7,500 - Royalty: 15% - Total Inv: $11,000 - Financing: No.

POINTTS
302 The East Mall, Suite 490, Toronto, ON, M9B 6C7. Contact: Fran. Dev. - Tel: (416) 234-9200, Fax: (416) 234-9203. Defense services for people facing traffic violations. Full training and support. Established: 1984 - No. of Units: Franchised: 31 - Total Inv: $70,000.

SAMINA NORTH AMERICA, INC
16 Goodrich Rd., Etobicoke, ON, M8Z 4Z8. Contact: Frank Heiverhate, President - Tel: (416) 521-6394, Fax: (416) 521-6397, E-Mail: samina1@interby.com. Web Site: www.samina.com. Samina specialty sleep shops, exclusive deals for the Samina sleep system. High and sleep systems plus accessories. Established: 1995 - Franchising Since: 1980 - No. of Units: Company Owned: 1 - Franchised: 50 - Franchise Fee: Yes - Royalty: No - Total Inv: $150,000.

SELECT COMMUNITY FUNERAL HOMES
111 Paradise Row, Saint John, NB, E2K 3H6. Contact: Fran. Dev. - Tel: (506) 632-1135, Fax: (506) 652-3251, Web Site: www.select funerals.com. A Canadian based funeral business franchise offering the widest range of funeral related services and products. Conversions and multi-home ownership are included as part of our extensive program. Extensive six months training and full support provided. Established: 1972 - Franchising Since: 1996 - No. of Units: Franchised: 7 - Total Inv: $42,700-$265,000 Cdn.

SHRED-IT
Shred-It Franchise, Inc.
2794 S. Sheridan Way, Oakville, ON, L6J 7T4. Contact: Franchise Development Representative - Tel: (905) 829-2794, Fax: (905) 829-1999, Web Site: www.shredit.com. Mobile paper shredding and recycling business serving hospitals, medical facilities, banks and financial institutions, government, large and small business. A mobile franchise operating business to business. Established: 1989 - Franchising Since: 1993 - No. of Units: Company Owned: 12 - Franchised: 56 - Franchise Fee: $55,000 U.S. - Royalty: 5%, 1.5% ad. fund - Total Inv: $350,000 net worth $150,000 cash - Financing: Yes.

SPRING CREST DRAPERY CENTERS
Unit 115-4471 No.6 Rd., Richmond, BC, V6V 1P8. Contact: Fran. Dev. - Tel: (604) 278-0773, Fax: (604) 278-0705. Window decor franchisor and distributor featuring Spring Crest/Spring Design drapery. Established: 1987 - No. of Units: Franchised: 12 - Fran. Fee: $50,000/ $12,000 distributor.

THE LEARNING NETWORK
Trocan Marketing Company
310 Ridge Road West, Grimsby, ON, L3M 4E7. Contact: Andy Trojner, President - Tel: (905) 945-1355, (800) 995-0796x0062, Fax: (905) 945-1356, Web Site: www.itsyourfuture.com. Direct sales of educational material for those who are concerned about wealth creation, preservation, privacy, liberty and free enterprise. We help people become prosperous. Established: 1996 - Franchising Since: 1998 - No. of Units: Company Owned: 1 - Franchised: 6 - Franchise Fee: $12,000.00 - Royalty: None - Total Inv: Working capital, inventory, start-up expenses approx. $20,000 - Financing: No.

THE RENOVATORS
474 Oxtail Road, Brandon, MB, R2X 3P4. - Tel: (204) 235-0091, Fax: (204) 234-0116. Student renovators available for homes and offices at reasonable rates. 10 days training and ongoing support. Established: 1996 - No. of Units: Franchised: 1.

UNA GLOBE ENVIRONMENTAL PRODUCTS
P.O. Box 1011, Stn. A, Delta, BC, V4M 3T2. Contact: Jim Ward, President - Tel: (604) 940-2213. Home business opportunity selling earth friendly septic tank-aid and non chemical insecticides/cleaners. Established: 1992 - Franchise Fee: None - Royalty: None - Total Inv: $3,000-$5,000.

UNIQUE MARKETING
3710 Main St, Niagara Falls, ON, L2G 6B1. Contact: Dave Barnes, Owner - Tel: (905)295-4381, Fax: (905) 295-4382. Manufacture of souvenirs and promotional items. Looking for comissioned reps. Established: 1982.

VTB BATHTUB LINERS & WALLS
VTB Bathtub Liners Inc.
24 Blackadder Ave., P.O. 2031, Cornwall, ON, K6H 6N8. Contact: David Pattinson, Owner - Tel: (613) 930-2135, (888) 930-2499, Fax: (613) 930-2136. Manufacturing of bathtub liners, wall systems, custom shower enclosures and accessories. Established: 1994 - Franchising Since: 1996 - No. of Units: Company Owned: 1 - Franchised: 28 - Franchise Fee: $7,000 - Total Inv: $7,000 - Financing: Yes.

WSI
5915 Airport Rd, Suite 300, Mississauga, ON, L4V 1T1. Contact: Roberto Alvarado, Marketing Director - Tel: (905) 678-7588, (888) 678-7588, Fax: (905) 678-9974, E-Mail: vmjuarez@wsicorporate.com, Web Site: www.wsicorporate.com. WSI is one of the most profitable franchise opportunities in the world today, with over 700 franchises in 87 countries. No specific business experience is required. WSI offers its franchises one of the most complete and comprehensivce training & certification programs available among franchise companies today, and a dynamic on-going support program tailored to meet the needs of each new franchisee. Established: 1995 - Franchising Since: 1996- No. of Units: Company Owned: 1 - Franchised: 800 - Franchise Fee: $39,700 us - Royalty: 10% - Total Inv: $39,700-$50,000 - Financing: No.

AUTOMOTIVE PRODUCTS AND SERVICES

AUTO 5
GB-INNO-BM sa, Ave. des Olympiades 20, Brussels Brabant, Belgium, 1140. Contact: H.J. Ruys, Expansion Manager - Tel: (02) 243-24 31 and 36. Sales of car accessories with workshop. Specializing in tires, exhausts, batteries, shock absorbers, lubricants, maintenance products. Established: 1966 - Franchising Since: 1986 - No. of Units: Company Owned: 42 - Franchised: 5 - Franchise Fee: 300.000 F - Royalty: 6.6% on turnover - Total Inv: 6.000.000+ BF - Financing: 1.700.000 BF.

AUTO COLORMATCH
P.A. Research Ltd.
28 Glen Road Boscombe, Bournemouth, Dorset, U.K., BH5 1HS. Contact: Peter Addison, M.D. - Tel: 0202-396002. Car paint shop in a small van repairing small dings, rust marks scratches etc. on cars for trade and public at 1/2 price of spraying whole panel. Established: 1986 - Franchising Since: 1988 - No. of Units: Franchised: 12 - Franchise Fee: Require area - Royalty: Master franchisees for Canada & US - Financing: Yes.

AUTOPREP LTD.
Old School, The Common, Redbourne, St. Albans, Herts, England, AL3 7NG. Contact: G. N. Hustings, Dir - Tel: 0805-770697. Car cleaning and valet service. Established: 1978 - Franchising Since: 1978 - No. of Units: 2 - Franchise Fee: £4,500 - Total Inv: £5,500 - Royalty: 15%.

AUTOSHEEN LIMITED
21-25 Sanders Rd., Finedon Rd. Ind. Estate, Wellingborough, Northants, England, NN8 4NL. Contact: Graham Bullock, Mktg. Dir. - Tel: 0933 272347. Mobile automotive valeting to private and corporate customers in U.K. Established: 1984 - Franchising Since: 1985 - No. of Units: Company Owned: 2 - Franchised: 55 - Franchise Fee: £4,995-£8,995 depending on area covered - Royalty: 8% management fee + 2.5% mktg. - Total Inv: Work. cap. £900, launch exps. £500 + fran. fee - Financing: Through major banks.

AUTOSMART LIMITED
Lynn Lane, Shenstone, Staffordshire, UK, WS14 0DH. Contact: Sophie Atkinson, Dir. - Tel: 0543 481616. Autosmart franchisees have a 'mobile showroom' from which they sell vehicle cleaning products to car dealers and haulers. Established: 1978 - Franchising Since: 1978 - No. of Units: Franchised: 85 - Franchise Fee: £4,000 - Royalty: None - Total Inv: £30,000-£65,000 work. cap. - Financing: From all big 5 banks.

AVIS RENT-A-CAR LTD.
Trident House, Station Rd., Hayes, Middlesex, England, UB3 4DJ. Contact: Tony Brewer, Lic. Rel. Mgr - Tel: (01) 848-8765. Auto rentals. Established: 1946 (in USA) - No. of Units: 3,500 locations in 110 countries, 90 in UK - Total Inv: £55,000.

BATTERYMAN BY CHLORIDE
Chloride Automotive Batteries Ltd.
Chequers Lane, Dagenham, Essex, England, RM9 6PX. Contact: Geoff Dean, Mktg. Mgr - Tel: 01-592-4560. Selling of dry batteries and allied products. Established: 1920 - Franchising Since: 1982 - No. of Units: 28 - Franchise Fee: £5,000/vehicle - Royalty: 1% gross - Financing: To suitable applicants through major banks.

BUDGET RENT A CAR
Budget Rent A Car Int. Inc.
41 Marlowes, Hemel Hempstead Herts., England, HP1 1XJ. Contact: Bernard Glover, Fran. Sales Mgr. - Tel: (44) 1442 276105, Fax: (44) 1442 276033. Car, van and truck rental (short term). Established: 1960 - Franchising Since: 1966 - No. of Units: Company Owned: 15- Franchised: 123 - Franchise Fee: £25,000 - Royalty: 7.5% + 2.5% adv. - Total Inv: £75,000 (£25,000 fee + £50,000 work. cap.) - Financing: Vehicle finance only.

CARNOISSEUR
Carnoisseur (Retail) Ltd.
Brittany Court, High St. S., Dunstable, Bedfordshire, England, LU6 3HR. Contact: Neville Crow, Chairman -Tel: (0582) 471700. Retail specialist car accessories. Established: 1986 - Franchising Since: 1993 - No. of Units: Company Owned: 2 - Franchised: 11 - Franchise Fee: £6,000 - Royalty: 6% sales - Total Inv: £38,980 - Financing: Yes.

CLEAN PARK
Clean Park GmbH
Amselweg 6/1, Winnenden, Germany, 71364. - Tel: 07195/6902-0. Selling and installation of franchised self service washing plants and additional installations for car care. Established: 1986 - Franchising Since: 1986 - Franchise Fee: DM 70, - per bay and month - Royalty: Approx. DM 50,000 per bay and year - Total Inv: Approx. DM 150,000- DM 1,200,000 - Financing: No, but support in obtaining and securing a credit.

COMPUTA TUNE
Oxford Street, Accrington, Lancashire, England, BB5 1QX. - Tel: (01254) 355 600, Fax: (01254) 355 609. Mobile vehicle servicing and fixed site motor centres. Established: 1981 - Franchising Since: 1986 - No. of Units: Company Owned: 1 - Franchised: 108 - Franchise Fee: £6,500 (mobile business) £15,000 (motor centre) - Royalty: 10% on sales - Total Inv: £15,000 + working capital (mobile business) £55,000 + working capital (mot centre) - Financing: Yes.

DENT MASTERS (NZ) LTD.
Dent Masters (NZ) Ltd
45 Mansfield Drivem, Kaiapo, North Canterburym, New Zealand. Contact: Keith Miller, Managing Director - Tel: (03) 327 4601, (0800) 422 766, Fax: (03) 327 4601. Paintless dent removal in motor vehicles. Established: 1994 - Franchising Since: 1995 - Franchised: 4 - Franchise Fee: $28,000 - Royalty: 16% - Total Inv: $39,750 - Financing: Negotiable.

ELEPHANT BLEU
Hypromat France S.A.
15, rue du Travail , BP 147, Hoerdt Cedex, France, 67720. - Tel: (33) 388 69 23 69, Fax: (33) 388 69 23 68, Web Site: www.elephantbleu.com. Self-service car wash centres under high pressure. Established: 1973 - Franchising Since: 1987 - No. of Units: Company Owned: 50 - Franchised: 500 - Franchise Fee: 580 FF per bay and per month - Royalty: 5100.000FF - Total Inv: 5 bays' centre: 1.400.000, FF + 5000.000 civil works + site.

FITTAPART LTD.
1 Southwell Rd., W., Mansfield, Nottinghamshire, England. Contact: J. R. Buckley, Dir. - Tel: 0623-759331. Retail auto parts and accessories. Established: 1977 - Franchising Since: 1978 - No. of Units: 4 - Approx. Inv: £25,000-£50,000 - Royalty: 5%.

HIGHWAY GLASS
Cathedral House, 16 Cathedral St., Norwich, Norfolk, U.K., NR1 1LX. Contact: Marianne Ashford, Assistant to the Board - Tel: 01603 667058, Fax: 01603 619292. 24 hour emergency glazing, frame repair and replacement, safety and security film installation, vehicle glass replacement. Established: 1973 - Franchising Since: 1980 - No. of Units: Company Owned:20 - Franchised: 36 - Franchise Fee: £15,000 - Royalty: 12.5 % reducing to 6.25% - Total Inv: £40,000 - Financing: Via banks subject to status.

HOMETUNE
Hometune Motoring Services Ltd.
Edward House, PrincesCourt, Barony Bus. Park, Nantwich, Cheshire, U.K., CW5 6PQ. Contact: Bryan Fretton, Fran. Dev. Mgr. - Tel: (0) 1270 6111 00. Mobile vehicle servicing and tuning services. On site work for vehicle maintenance and efficient running. Car security products fitting on site, caravan servicing, insured and guaranteed. Established: 1968 - Franchising Since: 1968 - No. of Units: Franchised: 110 - Franchise Fee: £5,000 plus tax - Royalty: 12.5% of labour.

IDENTICAR SECURITY SYSTEMS
Identicar Worldwide Ltd.
International House, Wolverhampton Rd., Warley, West Midlands, U.K., B69 4RJ. Contact: John Harris, C.E.O. - Tel: (021) 544-7022. Security marking systems. Established: 1980 - Franchising Since: 1980 - Franchise Fee: £5,000-£125,000 - Total Inv: £10,000-£150,000 (incl. equipment, depending on size of country) - Royalty: 3%-10% subject to market factors - Financing: 70% subject to status.

IMI MARSTON RADIATOR SERVICES.
Sandhill Dr., Narborough, Leicester, England. Contact: P. E. Richardson, Commercial Dir. - Tel: 0533-866551. Radiator sales and service. Established: 1969 - Franchising Since: 1982 - Franchise Fee: £12,000 - Total Inv: £20,000 - Royalty: 6% - Financing: Possible.

IMPALA BUSINESS SOLUTIONS
Unit 18, Ynyscedwyn Business Park, Ystradgynlais, Swansea, SSA9 1DT. Contact: David White - Tel: 01639 841256, Fax: 01639 841252, Web Site: www.impala-products.com. Impala provcides a select range of automotive chemical products, together with proven, systemised ways for customers to generate high profit margins from the products we supply. No royalties, no renewal fees, no stock holding.

LASALIGN AUTO-TEK
Lasalign Ltd.
O.S.B. House, 135 High St., Bromley Kent, England, Contact: Graham Ross, Bus. Dev. Dir. - Tel: (01) 4666021/2/3. Mobile laser assisted trailer axle alignment working with road haulage industry and companies running trailer fleets. Established: 1982 - Franchising Since: 1983 - No. of Units: Company Owned: 2 - Franchised: 7 - Franchise Fee: £2,200 - Total Inv: £10,500 - Royalty: 20%.

MIDAS
Midas N.V.
Belgielei 100- 2018 Antwerpen, Antwerpen, Belgium, 2018. Contact: Ronald Truyen, Development Manager - Tel: (03) 286-83-64, Fax: (03) 286-83-59, E-Mail: info@midasnv.ve, Web Site: www.midas.com. Fast auto repair replacement and repair of exhaust, shocks, brakes and tyres. General maintenance of cars. Established: 1973 - Franchising Since: 1997 - No. of Units: Company Owned: 28 - Franchised: 17 - Franchise Fee: 600.000 Bef - Royalty: 5% of turnover - Total Inv: 10,000 Bef.

MIDAS LE SILENCIEUX
108, Avenue Jean Moulin, 78170 La Celle Saint Cloud, France. Contact: Jean-Pierre Dassieu - Tel: (1) 30 82 56 56. Automotive repairs. Established: 1976 - Franchising Since: 1979 - No. of Units: Company Owned: 75 - Franchised: 162 - Franchise Fee: 100,000 FF - Total Inv: 1,000,000 FF - Royalty: 5% + 5% adv.

MOBILE RADIATOR SERVICES
80 Abbotsford Rd., Bowen Hills, Qsld., Australia, 4006. - Tel: (0011) 61 73252 4500. Specializes in exchanging, cleaning out and repairing automobile radiators, with free pick up and delivery. Each franchise has a central workshop, fully maintained and using the most up to date equipment and computers with control of a specified territory. Established: 1986 - Franchising Since: 1987 - No. of Units: Franchised: 6 - Franchise Fee: $10,000 - Royalty: Nil - Total Inv: $10,000-$80,000 - Financing: Yes.

MOBILETUNING LTD.
The Gate House, Lympne Industrial Park, Lympne, Hythe, Kent, England, CT21 4LR. Contact: Derrick Morley, Dir. - Tel: (0303) 48473 Mobile car engine tuning service. Established: 1976 - Franchising Since: 1976 - No. of Units: Company Owned: 2 - Franchised: 63 - Franchise Fee: £4,100 - Royalty: 10% - Total Inv: £10,500 - Financing: 70% to suitable applicants.

MR. CLUTCH
Clutch International Ltd.
2 Priory Rd., Strood, Rochester Kent, England, ME2 2EG. Contact: Managing Director - Tel: (01634) 717 747, Fax: (01634) 710 706, Web Site: www.mrclutch.com. Chain of garages specializing in the fast-fit replacement of clutches, brakes andgearboxes. Established: 1978 -

Franchising Since: 1986 - No. of Units: Company Owned: 20 - Franchised: 30 - Franchise Fee: £12,500 - Royalty: 10% of turnover - Total Inv: From £42,500 - Financing: Yes, details upon request.

PRACTICAL CAR & VAN RENTAL
Practical Car & Van Rental Ltd.
21-23 Little Broom St., Camp Hill, Birmingham, England, B12 OEU. Contact: Bolton Agnew, Mng. Dir. - Tel: (0121) 772-8599, Fax: (0121) 766-6229. System/insurance and vehicle based franchise using the rental experience and ability to offer competitive insurance and leasing rates. Applicable to all aspects of motor trade. Established: 1982 - Franchising Since: 1982 - No. of Units: Franchised: 200 - Franchise Fee: Various - Royalty: 7% of revenue - Financing: No.

SERCK MARSTON
International Radiator Services Ltd.
Silvertown House, Vincent Square, London, England, SW1P 2PL. - Tel: (0507) 510111. Supply of radiators for all types of vehicle and engine cooling systems, industrial heat exchangers, heater radiators, oil coolers, number plates, clutches, brake shoes, air brakes, power steering, water pumps, turbochargers, road springs and seat belts.

THRIFTY CAR RENTAL
Flightform Ltd.
The Old Court House, Hughenden Rd., High Wycombe, Bucks, England, HP1 35DT. Contact: Graham Burton, Franchise Manager - Tel: 01494 751500, Fax: 01494 464449, Web Site: www.thrifty.com. Car and van rental franchise covering corporate, retail, and international customers, with wide range of support functions from head office. Established: 1991 - Franchising Since: 1991 - No. of Units: Company Owned: 2 - Franchised: 68 - Franchise Fee: £17,500 + VAT - Royalty: 5% management fee, 2% adv levy - Total Inv: £80,000 working capital - Financing: Yes for vehicles,good contacts with major banks.

TYREFIX
Tyrefix Ltd.
Taylors Piece, 9-11 Stortford Rd., Dunmow, Essex, England, CM6 1DA. Contact: Carol Mackaoui, Dir. - Tel: (0371) 876640. Specialists in on-site plant puncture repairs. Offering within the hour service from time of call. Established: 1988 - Franchising Since: 1990 - No. of Units: Company Owned: 1 - Franchised: 9 - Franchise Fee: £10,000 - Royalty: 10% mgt., 1% adv. - Financing: Yes.

BUILDING PRODUCTS AND SERVICES

BOWLER GEOTECHNICAL
AJ Above
7/3359 Mt. Lindsey Highway, Brown Plains, QLD, 4118. Contact: David Bowler - Tel: (07) 3800 64 46, Fax: (07) 3800 08 16. Business format style franchise system for the provision of quality control testing services to the Civil Engineering Construction industry. These services are required to warrant construction of roads, dams, airports, railways, etc. Established: 1990 - Franchising Since: 1992 - No. of Units: Company Owned: 1 - Franchised: 8 - Franchise Fee: $55,000 standard - Royalty: 5% of monthly turnover - Total Inv: Approx. $135,000 if start from scratch - Financing: Commonwealth bank for approved applicants.

CICO CHIMNEY LININGS LTD.
Westleton, Suffolk, England, IP17 3EF. Contact: R. J. Hadfield, Mng. Dir. - Tel: (01) 728-648-608, Fax: (01) 728-648-428. The lining of domestic and non domestic chimneys using the Cico cast-in-site refractory lining system. No joints to work loose and non metallic so no corrosion. Established: 1980 - Franchising Since: 1982 - No. of Units: Franchised: 20 - Franchise Fee: £8,000 (sterling) - Royalty: 7.5% + 2.5% sales promo. - Total Inv: Fran. fee plus £8,000 equip., £6,000 working cap.

DREAMMAKER BATH & KITCHEN
Spectrum House, Lower Oakham Way, Oakham Business Park, Nansfield, NOTTS, NG18 5BY. Contact: Phil Else - Tel: 01623 422439, Fax: 01623 422466, E-Mail: phil@dreammaker-remodel.co.uk, Web Site: www.dreammaker-remodel.co.uk. #1 franchise in bathroom refinishing and remodeling with more than 30 years experience in

helping people achieve business success in America, and ten years experience in the UK. Our services are called upon daily by most major insurance companies, as well as homeowners and commercial clients. Initial Inv: £19,000.

ELECTRO CASH
European Franchise Federation
Boulesaido de l' Humaniki 116, Box 2, Brussels, Belguim, B-1070. Contact: Carol Chopra, Executive Director - Tel: (++32) 2 520 16 07, Fax: (++32) 2 520 17 35, E-Mail: eff-franchise@euronet.be. EEF - federates close to 20 national franchise associations from the European Union and other European Countries (non-eu). We defend the interests of franchising when it comes to negotiating European legislation in matter of competition law and the single market. Established: 1971 - Franchising Since: 1977 - No. of Units: Company Owned: 27 - Franchised: 25 - Franchise Fee: 450,000 FB - Royalty: 5% on buying turnover without tax - Total Inv: 10 - 13.5 MFB.

FIRST CALL LTD.
Chandos Mews, 34B Chandos Rd., Redland, Bristol, England, BS6 6PF. Contact: Clive Hughes, CEO - Tel: (01179) 232525, Fax: (01179) 445251. Building maintenance and repair covering all trades. Plumbing, carpentry, electrics, roofing, locks, glazing, small building work. Mainly commercial customers giving repeat business. National job control centre and sales account management. Established: 1986 - Franchising Since: 1990 - No. of Units: Franchised: 40 - Franchise Fee: £9,000-£12,000 - Royalty: 12% MSF, 3% adv.- Total Inv: £15,000-£30,000 (including working capital) - Financing: Business planning and finance advice available.

FLORENSE
Fabrica de Moveis Florense Ltda.
Rua John Kennedy, No 2509, Flores da Cunha, Rio Grande do Sul - RS, Brazil, 95270-000. - Tel: (054) 292-1300. Manufacturers of home and office furniture. Specialized in kitchen cabintes, closets and office furniture. Established: 1953 - Franchising Since: 1988 - No. of Units: Company Owned: 1 - Franchised: 119 - Franchise Fee: None - Royalty: None - Total Inv: US $80,000 in first six months - Financing: No.

GARAGE DOOR COMPANY,THE
Unit 7, Russell Rd. Industrial Estate, Edinburgh, Scotland, EH11 2NN. Contact: Allan MacReath, Fran. Mgr. - Tel: 0131-337-3332, 0800 889 777, Fax: 0131 313 2778, E-Mail: sales@garage-door.co.uk, Web Site: www.garage-door.co.uk. The supply, installation and repair of all types of garage doors, remote control operators and access systems to both the domestic and industrial markets. Automatic gates and wide sectional doors are a further service. Established: 1977 - Franchising Since: 1984 - No. of Units: Company Owned: 1 - Franchised: 9 - Franchise Fee: £500 (for legal agreement etc) - Royalty: 6% of total weekly sales (excl. VAT) - Total Inv: £20,000 - Financing: If required.

GSS
GSS (UK) Ltd.
2 Southernhay West, Exeter, Devon, England, EX1 4JG. Contact: Graham Sclater, Gen. Mgr. - Tel: (0392) 499889. Property maintenance specialists carrying out day to day reactive and planned maintenance in the commercial and retail property sector. Established: 1991 - Franchising Since: 1991 - No. of Units: Company Owned: 1 - Franchise Fee: £15,000 - Royalty: 7.5% - Total Inv: £40,000 - Financing: Yes.

INTOTO KITCHENS
Wakefield Road, Leeds, W. Yorkshire, England, LS27 7JZ. - Tel: (0113) 253 4800, Fax: (0113) 252-0154. Retailing of German fitted kitchens. Established: 1980 - Franchising Since: 1980 - No. of Units: Company Owned: 2 - Franchised: 31 - Franchise Fee: £5,000 - Total Inv: £40,000+ - Financing: Yes.

KIWI ALARMS
NSS
2163 6T North Rd. Avondale, Auckland, New Zealand. - Tel: (00)649-828-0-2302, Fax: (00)649-828-0-1676. Alarm sales, installation, and servicing franchise. Established: 1989 - Franchising Since: 1990 - No. of Units: Company Owned: 2 - Franchised: 4 - Franchise Fee: $16,500 - Royalty: 4% admin, 2% adv. - Financing: Yes.

SENSORTROL
197 Attercliffe Rd., Sheffield, England, S4 7XF. - Tel: (0114) 2701543. Energy management controls systems - a simple plug-in electronic controller for boilers of all sizes which cuts fuel consumption by as much as 30%. Established: 1983 - Franchising Since: 1992 - Franchise Fee: £900 U.K. Sterling - Royalty: None - Total Inv: £900 U.K. Sterling - Financing: No.

SOLAR-MESH® (SUN CONTROL DEVICES).
Solar-Mesh Pty, Ltd.
c/o P.O. Box 694 Archfield, Brisbane, Queensland, Australia, 4108. Contact: Kenneth Ivory, Mng. Dir. - Tel: (07) 32725157, (800) 700703, Fax: (07) 32725159. Sun control devices andquarantine insect screening, supply, manufacture and installations on site from mobile workshops. Established: 1985 - Franchising Since: 1992 - No. of Units: Company Owned: Multiple - Franchised: Multiple - Franchise Fee: Depends on area size to be operated - Royalty: On gross turnover - Total Inv: From A$150,000-A$1.2 million - Financing: For most countries.

STANAIR INDUSTRIAL DOOR SERVICES LTD.
Stanair House, The Crescent, Kettering, Northants, U.K., NN15 7HW. Contact: John Standoloft or Martin Wall, Chairman/Director - Tel: (0536) 82187. The repair and installation of industrial doors. Established: 1974 - Franchising Since: 1990 - No. of Units: Company Owned: 2 - Franchise Fee: £7,000-£12,000. Van operated or business franchise available - Total Inv: £22,000 (van, tools, adv., first 3 months salary) - Financing: Midland Bank.

BUSINESS PRODUCTS AND SERVICES

A.I.M.S.
A.I.M.S. Partnership Plc.
24 Red Lion St., London, England, WC1R 4SA. Contact: Henry Eidelbaum, Managing Director - Tel: 0171 831 1138, Fax: 0171 404 2325, Web Site: www.aims.co.uk. Provision of accountancy, taxation and general business advisory services for small - medium sized businesses. Established: 1992 - Franchising Since: 1992 - No. of Units: Company Owned: 1 - Franchised: 33 - Franchise Fee: £5,650 - Royalty: 12.5% reducing to 6.25% - Total Inv: £5,650 variable - Financing: Yes.

ACCOUNTING CENTRE,THE
Elscot House, Arcadia Ave., Finchley, London, England, N3 2JE. Contact: D.A. Ccouke, Managing Dir. - Tel: (0181) 349-3191. Provision of monthly management accounts to small / medium sized businesses. Franchisees generate clients on a local basis, supervise their bookkeeping, assist in interpreting their accounts and provide advice. Established: 1972 - Franchising Since: 1983 - No. of Units: Company Owned: 3 - Franchised: 3. Not franchising at this time.

ACTION INTERNATIONAL
15 Enggor Street #10-01 Realty Centre, Singapor, 079716. Contact: Paul Chieng - Tel: (+65) 622 11811, Fax: (+65) 622 11733, E-Mail: paulchieng@action-international.com, Web Site: www.action-international.com. Business Coaching franchise in the business of training business owners and supporting them through our various programs to enable them to have greater control over what their businesses provide to them. Established: 1992 - Franchising Since: 1999 - No. of Units: Franchised: 14 - Franchise Fee: SDG$55,000 - Royalty: SDG $1,500 per month.

ALFAL CONSULTANTS SA
6 Cours de Rive, Geneva, Switzerland, 1204. Contact: Al-Fallouji Ikbal, Chairman - Tel: (022) 28 84 39. Promotions, contacts, public relations; setting up and development of companies management, legal and fiscal advice and other activities. Established: 1984 - Franchising Since: 1987.

ALTA GESTION
ALTA Gestion Recursos Huhbnos S.A.
Pl. Manuel Gomez Moreno 3, Madrid, 28020. Contact: Joan Pinol Forcadell, Manager Expansion - Tel: (34) 1 555-53-53, Fax: (34) 1 597-17-98. Temporary work services. Established: 1985 - Franchising

Since: 1993 - No. of Units: Company Owned: 47 - Franchised: 73 - Franchise Fee: $47,000 US - Royalty: 5%, 2% marketing - Total Inv: $100,000 US.

AMTRAK EXPRESS PARCELS LTD.
Company House, Tower Hill, Bristol, England, BS2 0AZ. Contact: Franchise Dept. - Tel: 0990 456 456. Overnight parcel service throughout UK and international delivery service throughout the world. Established: 1987 - Franchising Since: 1987 - No. of Units: Company Owned: 1 - Franchised: 341 - Franchise Fee: From £12,500 - Total Inv: £19,000 incl. work. cap - Financing: Yes.

ANC
Parkhouse East Industrial Estate, Chesterton, Newcastle-Under-Lyme, Staffordshire, England, ST5 7RB. Contact: Antony Flood, Fran. Acct. Mgr. - Tel: (0782) 563322. Express parcel, freight and courier services - local, national and international. Established: 1981 - Franchising Since: 1981 - No. of Units: Company Owned: 3 - Franchised: 75 - Franchise Fee: P.O.A. - Royalty: Trunking charge - Total Inv: P.O.A. - Financing: Yes.

ASC
ASC Partnership PLC
3 Park Road, Regents Park, London, England, NW1 6AS. Contact: Louise Berwin, Sales and Marketing Manager - Tel: (0171) 616 6628, Fax: (0171) 616 6634. Specialists in finance for business. Large independent commercial mortgage brokers. Established: 1969 - Franchising Since: 1990 - No. of Units: Franchised: 30 - Franchise Fee: Varies - Royalty: Variable - Total Inv: Variable - Financing: Yes.

AUDIDCELL
CRA
65 Queens Walk, Ruislip, Middlesex, England, HA4 OLX. Contact: S. Harding, Sec. - Tel: 081 845 5993. Cost reduction consultancy aimed at telecoms expenditure. Established: 1993 - Franchising Since: 1993 - No. of Units: Company Owned: 1 - Franchise Fee: £5,950 - Royalty: None - Financing: No.

BOOK-KEEPING NETWORK, THE
90 Woodhall St., Stirling, Western Australia, 6021. Contact: Alex Polglaze, C.E.O. - Tel: (+619) 349-9189. Computerized book-keeping service for small and medium businesses and other organizations looking after payables, receivables, profit and loss etc. and payroll. Established: 1984 - Franchising Since: 1990 - No. of Units: Company Owned: 1 - Franchised: 7 - Franchise Fee: $AUD 13,500 - Royalty: 12% support, 3% adv. - Total Inv: $42,000 - Financing: Yes.

BUSINESS POST LTD.
Woiseley Drive, Heartlands, Erdington, Birmingham, England, B8 2SQ. Contact: Michelle Records, PA to Franchise Mgr. - Tel: (0121) 335 1115, Fax: (0121) 335 1160, E-Mail: michelle_recardo@business-post.com. Business post is one of the largest independent UK parcel and express mail delivery companies, delivering throughout the UK and worldwide. Established: 1971 - Franchising Since: 1988 - No. of Units: Company Owned: 21 - Franchised: 41 - Franchise Fee: £15000 + vat + business base fee - Total Inv: £100,000-£250,000 - Financing: Negotiable.

CARD LINE GREETINGS LTD.
Units 4/5 Hale Trading Estate,Tipton, West Midlands, DX4 7PQ. Contact: Michael Crapper, Managing Director - Tel: (0121) 522-4407, Fax: (0121) 522-4417. High quality greeting cards which franchisees distribute to retailers on a concession basis. Established: 1994 - Franchising Since: 1994 - No. of Units: Franchised: 35 - Franchise Fee: £750 - Royalty: None - Total Inv: £9,775 - Financing: Yes.

CNA INTERNATIONAL
Garden Court, Lockington Hall, Lockington, Derby,UK ,DE74 2RH. Contact: Jonathan Cullen - Tel: 01509 670022, Fax: 01509 670707. Executive recruitment. Established: 1994 - Franchising Since: 1995 - No. of Units: Company Owned: 1 - Franchised: 51 - Franchise Fee: £6,500 including training - Royalty: 12.5% - Total Inv: £12,000 inc. franchise fee - Financing: Yes.

DEFENSE PAK
High Performance Corporation
12 MacEwan Street, Leederville, Perth, W. Australia, 6007. Contact: Wayne Reed, Director - Tel: (618) 9382-3888, (800) 999-070, Fax: (618) 9388-9068. Marketing program for automotive aftermarket products and services within the dealerships. Established: 1972 - Franchising Since: 1985 - No. of Units: Company Owned: 3 - Franchised: 136 - Franchise Fee: To be arranged - Royalty: To be arranged - Total Inv: $50,000-$500,000 - Financing: No.

DRIVER HIRE
Driver Hire Group Services Ltd.
Progress House, Castlefields Lane, Bingley, W. Yorkshire, England, BD16 2AB. Contact: Alan Cawthorne, Marketing Director - Tel: (01274) 551166, Fax: (01274) 55 1165, E-Mail: info@driver-hire.co.uk, Web Site: www.driver-hire-.co.uk. Specialist employment agency supplying staff into transport and distribution industry. Established: 1984 - Franchising Since: 1985 - No. of Units: Company Owned: 1 - Franchised: 76 - Franchise Fee: £15,000 - Royalty: 8%- 5% royalty, 2% admin, 1% adv - Total Inv: £37,500-£15,000 fran. fee, £12,500 work. cap, £10,000 leasing - Financing: All major high street banks up to 70%.

ELLUS
Ellus Ind. E Com. Ltda.
Rua Coronel Luis Barroso 151, Sao Paulo S.P.,Brazil,04750. - Tel: (011) 521-9133, Fax: (011) 246-9984. A design enterprise. Creativity guided by a universal fashion concept, for fixed target, in each cycle or moment. Modern marketing based on the franchising and licensing systems. Selective marketing, based on the principle of line segmentation, products, public and life styles. Established: 1972 - Franchising Since: 1979 - No. of Units: Franchised: 115 - Royalty: 10% - Total Inv: Min. cash requirement - Financing: For qualified individuals.

EVERETT MASSON & FURBY
EMF Group Ltd.
3 Cornhill, Ottery, St. Mary, Devon, England, EX11 1DW. Contact: Kathie Carr, Dir. - Tel: (01404) 813762, Fax: (01404) 815236, E-Mail: emfgroup@eclipse.co.uk, Web Site: www.emf-group.co.uk. Business transfer agents. Sale of businesses and / or premises. Established: 1963 - Franchising Since: 1971 - No. of Units: Company Owned: 1 - Franchised: 19 - Franchise Fee: £15,000 - Royalty: 10% of commissions rec'd. - Total Inv: £15,000 plus WIP £20,000 - Financing: Yes.

FASTSIGNS
Fastsigns International, Inc.
2550 Midway Rd, Ste. 500, Carrollton, TX, 75006. Contact: Jenny Boreham - Tel: (800) 827-7446, (011) 0 800 093 4977, Fax: (011) 44 1245 477170, E-Mail: jenny.boreham@fastsigns.com, Web Site: www.fastsigns.com. FASTSIGNS is one of the industry's leading sign and graphic franchises. Using a computer-based design technique, our concept emphasizes sign and graphic solutions. We offer fast turnaround, business-to-business environment, and top-quality signs and graphics for corporate, professional, and retail clients. Established: 1985 - Franchising Since: 1986 - No. of Units: Franchised: 15 - Franchise Fee: £16,500 - Royalty: 7%, 2% advertising - Total Inv: $116,818 (includes working capital) - Financing: Yes third party.

FLAT SHOP FRANCHISING
Property Rentals
2 The Avenue, The Cross,Worcester, England, WR1 3QA. Contact: Mr. Mio Blagojevic, Fran. Dir. - Tel: 0905-24856. Residential letting agents and property management agents. Established: 1984 - Franchising Since: 1990 - No. of Units: Company Owned: 1 - Franchise Fee: $2,500 - Royalty: $1,000 mnth. service fee - Total Inv: $12,500 (equip., work cap., fran. fee, lease, etc.) - Financing: Yes.

GNUPO DOSDIN
Dosdin Rua torea's, Ribeino
US-10, Lisboa, Portugal, 1050 USBOA. Contact: Luis Nandin De Canvelho, Manager - Tel: (351-1)3552070, Fax: (351-1)3568560, E-Mail: dosdin@mail.telepoc.pt, Web Site: www.dosdin.pt. Consultancy activities for business and management. Established: 1985 - Franchising Since: 1996 - No. of Units: Company Owned: 1 - Franchised: 3 - Franchise Fee: $1200 cts - Royalty: Flexible according to invoicing - Total Inv: Depends - Financing: No.

HAYS APOLLO DESPATCH

28/30 Hoxton Sq., London, England, N1 6NN. Contact: Tony Edwards, Manager - Tel: 011-44-171-739-8444, Fax: 011-44-171-739-6463. Urgent delivery service including overnight, international, store/delivery services. Established: 1980 - Franchising Since: 1990 - No. of Units: Company Owned: 8 - Franchised: 11 - Franchise Fee: £20,000 - Royalty: 10% incl. adv. - Financing: 70%.

IB YOUR OFFICE
IB Your Office Int'l. Ltd.

Industriestr. 161c, 50999 Cologne, Germany. - Tel: (49) 02236-962460, Fax: (49) 02236-9624610. IB Your Office - is one of the largest business center networks worldwide. It offers not only office space, the clients can use the full supporting infrastructure and manpower. They can also use the international network that the system is based on. Established: 1989 - Franchising Since: 1990 - No. of Units: Company Owned: 1 - Franchised: 95 - Franchise Fee: Depending on county, US $50,000 - Royalty: 8% of turnover - Total Inv: US $300,000 - Financing: Yes.

INTERLINK EXPRESS

Wassell Grove Business Centre, Wassell Grove Lane, Stourbridge,DY9 9JH. - Tel: 01562 881030, Fax: 01562 881003, Web Site: www.interlinkexpress.com. Interlink Express is a locally-run parcel collection and delivery network operating nationally and worldwide. No. of Units: Company Owned: 1 - Franchised: 117.

LANS FÖR SÄKRINGAR WASA
WASA

Hemvärnsgata 9, Solna, Stockholm, Sweden, 17381. Contact: Krister Alpmar, Franchise Manager - Tel: (+46) 8 - 588-40441, Fax: (+46) 8 - 588-0402 48, E-Mail: krister.alpmar@wasa.se, Web Site: www.Lanstorakringar.se. Insurance for business. Established: 1828 - Franchising Since: 1984 - No. of Units: Company Owned: +100 - Franchised: 45 - Franchise Fee: £ 5.000 - Total Inv: £ 10.000.

LE SOIR
Rossel

Rue Royale 120, Bruxelles, Belgium, 1000. Contact: Jacqueline Lens, Manager - Tel: (32) 2-225.52.08, Fax: (32) 2-225.59.30, E-Mail: annonces.emploi@lesoir.be, Web Site: www.lesoir.be. Personal advertisements (franchising opportunities) in a french speaking newspaper in Belgium.

LEGAL & GENERAL ESTATE AGENCIES, LTD.

4 Bruntcliffe Way, Morley, Leeds, UK, LS27 0JG. - Tel: (0113) 253 9166, Fax: (0113) 252 4589. Estate agency, lettings and property management and financial services plus surveyors. Established: 1986 - Franchising Since: 1986 - No. of Units: Company Owned: 81 - Franchised: 103 - Franchise Fee: £10,000 - Royalty: Management fee 7.5% + 10% P.A. - Total Inv: Working cap. £50,000-£65,000, start-up cap. £75,000 - Financing: Dependent on individual.

LOCALGRAPEVINE

Newhey Mill, Two Bridges Road, Newhey, Rochdale, Lancashire, OL16 3SR. Contact: Paul Harding - Tel: (0871) 223-2011, Fax: (0871) 223-2012, E-Mail: paul@localgrapevine.co.uk, Web Site: www.localgrapevine.co.uk. Localgrapevine is where word of mouth meets the internet, a win-win for local business, local people and you. Established: 2002 - Franchising Since: 2003 - No. of Units: Company Onwed: 2 - Franchise Fee: £7,750 - Royalty: 10%.

MAIL BOXES ETC.
Mail Boxes Etc. (Thailand) Co. Ltd.

44/1-3 Sukhumvit 21 Asoke Rd., Bangkok, 10110, Thailand. - Tel: (66-2) 259-8456-7, Fax: (66-2) 259-8455. The world's largest franchisor of postal, business and communications franchise service network. Each MBE center provides the customer a total one stop shop, while the master franchisor provides product support, store design and layout, training, systems and procedures. Established: 1980 US - Franchising Since: 1980 US - No. of Units: Franchised: 3,300 centers in 50 countries - Total Inv: $20,000 US - Royalty: 6%, 2% adv. - Total Inv: US $ 80,000- US $120,000.

MAIL BOXES ETC.
Mail Boxes Etc. (Australia) Pty Ltd.

273 Alfred St., North Sydney, NSW, Australia, 2060. - Tel: (02) 9955 8922, Fax: (02) 9954-9556, E-Mail: hg@mailboxesetc.com.au, Web Site: www.mailboxesetc.com.au. World's largest network of postal, business and communications centers with over 3,300 centers in 50 countries. Established: 1980 USA, 1993 AUS - Franchising Since: 1993 Australia - No. of Units: Company Owned: 2 - Franchised: 38 - Franchise Fee: $25,000 - Royalty: 6%, 2% adv. - Total Inv: $150,000 incl. fran. fee - Financing: Yes.

MAIL BOXES ETC. BRAZIL

Rua Oscar Freire, 953, Cerquiera Cesar, Sao Paulo, SP Brazil, 01426-001. Contact: Jairo Adriano, President - Tel: (011) 3061-0214, Fax: (011) 280-0794, Web Site: www.mbe.com. MBE is the world's largest network of franchised postal, business and communication service centers . Established: 1992 - Franchising Since: 1995 - No. of Units: Company Owned: 1 (in Brazil) - Franchised: 9 (in Brazil) - Franchise Fee: P$22,500 - Royalty: 8% of gross sales. - Total Inv: P$75,000 - Financing: Only private.

MAIL BOXES ETC. FRANCE

69 Boulevard Saint Marcel, F-75013 Paris, France. Contact: Jacques Gentric, Director Gen. - Tel: 33-(0) 1 55 43 11 40, Fax: 33 (0)1 55 43 11 44, E-Mail: jgentric@mbefrance.com. MBE is the world's largest network of franchised postal, business and communication service centers with more than 3,300 centers in 50 different countries. Established: 1992 - Franchising Since: 1980 in the U.S. - Franchise Fee: Francs 200,000 (incl. training and site selection) - Royalty: 6%, 2% adv. - Total Inv: Francs800,000 incl. fran. fee - Financing: Yes.

MAIL BOXES ETC. ITALY

Piazza IV Novembre, 1, 20124, Milan, Italy. - Tel: 011-39-2-669-2661. MBE is the world's largest network of franchised postal, business and communication service centers with more than 3,300 centers in 50 different countries. Established: 1992 - Franchising Since: 1980 in the U.S. - Franchise Fee: Liras 28,000,000 (incl. training and site selection) - Royalty: 6%, 2% adv. - Total Inv: Liras 130,000,000 (incl. fran. fee).

MAIL BOXES ETC. MEXICO

Platero #39, C.P. 03900, Mexico, D.F., Mexico. - Tel: 011-525-598-0222. MBE is the world's largest network of franchised postal, business and communication service centers with more than 3,300 centers in 50 different countries. Established: 1990 - Franchising Since: 1980 in the U.S. - Franchise Fee: US $27,500 - Royalty: 6%, 2% adv. - Total Inv: US $70,000.

MAIL BOXES ETC. PHILIPPINES

#105, Twr. Ground 1st Fl., Makati Cinema Sq. Twr., Pasong Tamo, Cor. Pasay Rd., Makati, Metro Manilla, Philippines. - Tel: 011-632-811-1685. MBE is the world's largest network of franchised postal, business and communication service centers with more than 3,300 centers in 50 different countries. Established: 1994 - Franchising Since: 1980 in the U.S. - Franchise Fee: US $20,000 - Royalty: 6%, 2% adv. - Total Inv: US $85,000 incl. fran. fee.

MAIL BOXES ETC. TURKEY

Tarlabasi Bulvari Zambnak S0K. 33/1, Istanbul, Turkey, 80096. - Tel: (90)212-245-56-47 Fax: (90)212-245-56-85. Postal business and communications services. Established: 1993 (MBE Turkey) - Franchising Since:1980 in the U.S. - Franchise Fee: US$20,000 - Royalty: 6%, 2% adv. - Total Inv: US $80,000 (incl. fran. fee) - Financing: Leasing, yes.

MAIL BOXES ETC. VENEZUELA

Torre Centuria, Local Commercial N#2 P.B., Av. Venezuela con calle, Mohedano, Urb. El Rossal, Caracas, Venezuela. - Tel: 011-582-952-7444. MBE is the world's largest network of franchised postal, business and communication services centers with more than 3,300 centers in 50 different countries. Established: 1993 - Franchising Since: 1980 in the U.S. - Franchise Fee: US $32,600 - Royalty: 6%, 2% adv. - Total Inv: US $90,000 (incl. fran. fee).

MONEY CONCEPTS
M. Concepts Mexico
Chayiyicame 1 °B, Tecamachalco, Mexico, 53970. Contact: Abraham Yaffe, Master Franchise - Tel: (525) 2-93-08-78, (800) 326-1825, Fax: (525) 2-94-58-46, Web Site: www.moneyconcepts.com. Financial planning centres. No previous experience required. Established: 1979 - Franchising Since: 1983 - No. of Units: Company Owned: 1 - Franchised: 500 - Franchise Fee: $10,000 - Financing: Yes.

NATIONWIDE INVESTIGATIONS
Nationwide House, 86 Southwark Bridge Rd., London, England, SE1 0EX. Contact: Mr. K. Walker, Head of Fran. - Tel: 44-1-928-1799. Private investigation. Established: 1963 - Franchising Since: 1978 - No. of Units: Company Owned: 3 - Franchised: 22 - Franchise Fee: $10,500 min. - Royalty: 10% - Total Inv: $15,000 min. - Financing: Up to one third.

PITMAN TRAINING CENTRE
Pitman Training Ltd.
154 Southampton Row, London, England, WC1B 5AX. - Tel: (44) 0171 837 4481, Fax: (44) 0171 837 9272. The computer and office training network. Training in PC applications and office skills. Established: 1992 - Franchising Since: 1992 - No. of Units: Company Owned: 3 - Franchised: 67 - Franchise Fee: £10,000 min. - Total Inv: £50,000 incl. fran. fee, equip., materials and opening stock - Financing: Via UK banks.

PITMAN TRAINING LIMITED
Pitman House, Audby Lane, Wetherby, West Yorkshire, England, LS22 7FD. Contact: Mr. James O'Brein, Operations Director - Tel: (01937) 548500, Fax: (01937) 584067, Web Site: www.pitman-training.co.uk. Computer training and educational training centres. Established: 1977 - Franchising Since: 1992 - No. of Units: Company Owned: 2 - Franchised: 80 - Franchise Fee: £25.00 - Total Inv: £50,000 .

PRIORITY MANAGEMENT
Priority Benelux
Leuvensesteenweg 392(b), Zaventem, Belguim, 1932. Contact: Hugh Dow, Man. Dir. - Tel: (02) 7215744, Fax: (02) 7255009, Web Site: www.priority-management.com. Helping people to work more effectively through better organization and better choice in Belgium of Priorities. Established: 1989 - Franchising Since: 1991 - No. of Units: Franchised: 6 - Franchise Fee: $30,000 - Royalty: 10% on turnover - Total Inv: $40,000.

PRIORITY MANAGEMENT SYSTEMS PTY. LTD.
11 Averill St., Rhodes, Sydney, NSW, Australia, 2138. Contact: Greg Sparks, Mng. Dir. - Tel: (02) 9736-0000, Fax: (02) 9743-1399, E-Mail: adminqprioritymanagement.com.av, Web Site: www.prioritymanagement.com. Recognized as a leader in management training, and named the number one franchised training organization in North America, Priority Management helps all staff increase productivity and effectiveness. Established: 1988 - Franchising Since: 1988 - No. of Units: Company Owned: 1 - Franchised: 18 - Franchise Fee: $27,500 initial - Royalty: 10% of revenue - Total Inv: $50,000 - Financing: No.

QBVISION
qb Vision AG
2 Gayton Road, Harrow, Middx,England, HA1 2XU. Contact: Franchise Department - Tel: (0800) 169-4770, Fax: (0043) 316-763-0117, Web Site: www.gbvision.com. QBVision have created an internet-linked virtual workshop and marketplace for the development and sale of products, services and building design .Viewed as videos or stills, in CD-Rom or via the internet, they bring a cost-effective, new dimension to the world of 3D imaging. Total Inv: ƒ7,200.

RIBBON REVIVAL
Ribbon Revival Ltd.
Caslon Crt., Pitronnerie Rd., St. Peter Port, Guernsey, U.K., GY12RW. - Tel: (01481) 729552, Fax: (01481). Recycling of the full range of print technologies including photocopier, telefax, laser toner, ink jet cartridge and line printer, cash register and typewriter ribbons. Full technical training and support given. Established: 1993 - Franchising Since: 1993 - No. of Units: Company Owned: 1 - Franchised: 42 - Franchise Fee: £10,000-£30,000 - Royalty: 9% on gross turnover for UK, negotiable overseas - Total Inv: £40,000 plus - Financing: Major Banks.

SDR SVENSK DIREKTREKLAM
P.O. Box 1524, Uppsala, Sweden, SE-75145. Contact: Eva Ryss, Managing Director - Tel: (46) (0) 18-172100, Fax: +46(0) 18 154166, E-Mail: info@sdrgruppen.se, Web Site: www.sdrgruppen.se. Addressed and unaddressed direct mail to households in Sweden. Established Since: 1973 - Franchising Since: 1976 - No. of Units: Company Owned: 1 - Franchised: 53 - Franchise Fee: Not for sale, sold out - Royalty: 17.5% gross - Total Inv: SEK 1,000,000 - Financing: Yes.

SECURICOR PONY EXPRESS
Alexander Terrace Liverpool Gardens, Worthing, West Sussex, UK, BM11 1YH. Contact: Director of Franchising - Tel: (44)1903-821111, Fax: (44)1903-524279. Direct courier and overnight document and parcel delivery service. Currently U.K. only. Looking to expand worldwide. Established: 1975 - Franchising Since: 1994 - No. of Units: Company Owned: 34 - Franchised: 25 - Franchise Fee: From £19,000 - Royalty: 12% plus administration and marketing levy - Total Inv: From £40,000 including working capital - Financing: Through banks.

SIGNS NOW - UNITED KINGDOM
478 Stafford Rd., Oxley, Wolverhampton, UK, WV10 6AN. Contact: Bob Forsyth, Director - Tel: (01902) 398909, Fax: (01902) 398910, Web Site: www.signsnow.com. Sale and manufacture of a wide range of signs. Established: 1997 - Franchising Since: 1997 - No. of Units: Company Owned: 1 - Franchise Fee: £16,500 - Royalty: 7% service, 1% advertising - Total Inv: £68,000 inc. franchise fee - Financing: Yes.

TRAVAIL EMPLOYMENT GROUP
Travail Employment Group Ltd
24 Southgate St., Gloucester, Glos., England, GL1 2DP. Contact: Mr. Steve Mills, Fran. Mgr. - Tel: (01452) 420700, Fax: (01452) 420713, Web Site: www.travail.co.uk. Provision of temporary and permanent recruitment services to all types of companys. The role of the franchisee is predominantly a sales and marketing one. Substanial returns are possible. Established: 1977 - Franchising Since: 1986 - No. of Units: Company Owned: 13 - Franchised: 37 - Franchise Fee: £10,000 + vat - Royalty: 7.25%of sales - Total Inv: £40,000 + factoring; £ 70,000 w/o factoring - Financing: Yes, min personal investment £15,000.

V-KOOL FRANCHISE INTERNATIONAL *
3 Science Park Drive, Singapore, 118223. - Tel: (65) 6774 7077, Fax: (65) 6872 5461, E-Mail: info@v-kool.biz, Web Site: www.v-kool.com An energy conservation film product designed for use in the automotive and architectural markets. Established: 1992 - Franchising Since: 1997 - No. of Units: Company Owned: 4 - Franchised: 300 - Total Inv: $500,000.

VACATURE
Technologiestraat 1, Brussel, Belgium, 1082. - Tel: (32)2-482 03 63, Fax: (32) 2-469 08 31. Classified ad's about franchising in a product distributed with 4 newspapers and 2 magazine. Reach 1,810,000 readers and press and articles about franchising. Established: 1996.

WHITE KNIGHT FRANCHISING (U.K.) LTD.
Hi-Point, Thomas St., Taunton, Somerset, England, TA2 6HB. - Tel: (01823)332-331, Fax: (01823) 330-970. Opportunities in Vat Accounting (limited territories remaining) and business transfers/stocktaking throughout UK. Established: 1989 - Franchising Since: 1991 - No. of Units: Company Owned: 1 - Franchised: 19 - Franchise Fee: £8,000 Vat Accounting, £10,000 Business Transfers - Royalty: 10% of turnover - Total Inv: Fran. fee plus £400 working capital + £1200 computer hardware (Business transfer hardware included) = £10,400 - Financing: No.

CLEANING PRODUCTS AND SERVICES

ACOUSTIC CLEANING
Acoustic Cleaning Europe
C / Oropendola; 8, 28230 Las Rozas, Madrid(Spain). Contact: Gerard Darras, Managing Director - Tel: (34) 91 630 35 39, Fax: (34) 91 630 47 04, E-Mail: acoustic~arrakis.es, Web Site:www. arrakis.es/@acoustic. Restoration and cleaning of tiles, moquettes and carpets. We offer a high quality, at the earliest convenience and moderate prices. Established:

1991 - Franchising Since: 1993 - No. of Units: Company Owned: 4 - Franchised: 38 - Franchise Fee: 1.500.000 pesetas - Total Inv: 2.650.000 pesetas - Financing: Banco de Santander.

CHEMICAL EXPRESS
Chemical Express Group Ltd.
Spring Road, Smethwick, West Midlands, B66 4919. Contact: : Les Gray, Chairman -Tel: 0121 525 4040, Fax: 0121 525 4919. Mobile showrooms supplying full range of cleaning, maintenance and hygene chemicals plus janitorial supplies direct to every type of business and industry. Established: 1985 - Franchising Since: 1986 - No. of Units: Franchised: Over 105 - Franchise Fee: £7,900 - Royalty: 7.5% - Total Inv: £15,000 includes fee - Financing: Yes.

DIVERSEY MOBILE SALES
Weston Favell, Norhants, England, NN3 4PD. Contact: A.D.C. Wilding, Opers. Mgr. - Tel: 0604-405311. Supplying cleaning and maintenance materials to garages, factories and workshops. Established: 1958 - Franchising Since: 1983 - No. of Units: 4 - Franchise Fee: £2,500 - Royalty: 11% plus 1% adv. - Total Inv: £4,000 - Financing: Yes.

LIMPIDUS
Rua Helena 335 6 0, Sao Paulo, SP, Brazil, 04552.050. Contact: Fernando Sodre, President - Tel: (55) 11 820 8894, Fax: (55) 11 820 8894, E-Mail: info@limpidus.com.br, Web Site: www.limpidus.com.br. Janitorial service. Established: 1980 - Franchising Since: 1992 - No. of Units: Company Owned: 3 - Franchised: 103 - Franchise Fee: $ 4,500-$26,000 - Royalty: 9%- Total Inv: $4,500-$20,000 - Financing: Partial, depending on location.

MINSTER CLEANING SERVICES
Minster House, 948-952 Kingsbury Rd. Erdington, Birmingham, W.M., England, B24 9PZ. Contact: Alan Haigh, Managing Partner - Tel: 0121-386 1186, Fax: 0121 386 1191. Marketing and management of office cleaning serivces. Established: 1982 - Franchising Since: 1992 - No. of Units: Company Owned: 1 - Franchised: 33 - Franchise Fee: £14,000 - Royalty: 7% - Total Inv: £65,000 inc. £45,000 work. cap. - Financing: Subject to status.

MISTER KOOL'S
Joysound Limited
82 High St., Albrighton, Wolverhampton, England, WV7 3JA. Contact: Theo Kool, Dir. - Tel: 0902 374111. Carpet and upholstery cleaning service, using new process, no shampoos, dry powders or steam. Fibers dry and can be used minutes after cleaning. Established: 1990 (UK) - Franchising Since: 1987/88 (Continent) - No. of Units: Company Owned: 3 - Franchised: 50+ - Franchise Fee: £8500 plus vat per 1 million inhabitants - Royalty: £105 per month - Total Inv: £12000 (includes leased van and stock) - Financing: Various banks.

MOLLY MAID UK
Agostpolar, Ltd.
Vale House, 100 Vale Rd., Windsor, Berkshire, England, SL4 5JL. Contact: Richard Maidment, Operations - Tel: 01753 829 400, 0800 500 950, Fax: 01753 829 401. Domestic cleaning service. Established: 1984 - Franchising Since: 1985 - No. of Units: Franchised: 30 - Franchise Fee: £7.800 plus VAT - Royalty: 8% net sales, 2% net sales adv. - Total Inv: £7.800 franchise fee plus approx. £10,000 working capital - Financing: From clearing banks.

MOPPS CLEANING SERVICES
Mopps Plc.
P.O. Box 1055, Paisley, Renfrenshire, U.K., PA3 2SH. - Tel: 041 887 7848. Commercial and industrial contract cleaning. Established: 1988 - Franchising Since: 1992 - No. of Units: Company Owned: 4 - Franchised: 2 - Franchise Fee: £8,950 - Royalty: 7.5% reducing - Total Inv: £14,000 - Financing: Yes.

OVENU
Ovenu Franchising Ltd
67 Barkham Ride, Wokingham, Berks, RG40 4HA. - Tel: 0118 973 0734, Fax: 0118 973 1876, Web Site: www.ovenu.co.uk. We provide a professional oven valeting service using totally safe, caustic-free products. Established: 1994 - Franchise Fee: ƒ5,950.

PVC VENDO
Vendo plc
215 East Lane, Wembley, Middlesex, England, HA0 3NG. Contact: Ivan Calhoun, Mng. Dir. - Tel: (44) (0) 181 908 1234, Fax: (44) (0) 181 904 2698. Commercial vehicle powercleaning services to regular preplanned contract frequencies. Also the powercleaning of food carrying vehicles for hygiene-sanitation. Established: 1981 - Franchising Since: 1989 - No. of Units: Company Owned: 1 - Franchised: 86 - Franchise Fee: £1,000 sterling - Royalty: 12.5% continuous mktg. & mgmt. - Total Inv: £13,500 sterling - Financing: Yes.

RAINBOW CARPETS
Rainbow Corner Ltd.
140-142 Caversham Rd., Reading,Berkshire, England. Contact: David Staples, Mng. Dir. - Tel: 0734-585032. Retailing and supplying of carpets and floor coverings. Established: 1966 - Franchising Since: 1976 - No. of Units: Company Owned: 6 - Franchised: 1 - Franchise Fee: £5,000 - Total Inv: £20,000-£50,000 - Royalty: 7% plus 7.5% adv. - Financing: Yes.

RAINBOW INTERNATIONAL
Sprectrum Holdings Limited
Spectrum House, Lower Oakham Way, Oakham Business Park, Mansfield, Notts., NG18 5BY. Contact: Ron Hutton, Franchise Director - Tel: (01623) 675100, Fax: (01623) 422466, E-Mail: ron@rainbow-int.co.uk, Web Site: www.rainbow-int.co.uk. Carpet and upholstery cleaning and repair. fire and flood disaster restoration. Preferred service provider to most insurance companies and insurance loss adjusters in UK. Established: 1987 - Franchising Since: 1988 - No. of Units: Franchised: 135 - Franchise Fee: £228,500 - Royalty: 9% management fee, 2& national advertising - Total Inv: Exclusive Licence Fee; £14,000 - M/cy & equip £11,000 - Adv/sty/IT s/ware etc £3,500 - Financing: Yes via major banks to 70% of total investment.

FOODS AND BEVERAGES

7-ELEVEN CONVENIENCE STORES
7-Eleven Stores Pty. Ltd.
357 Ferntree Gully Rd., Mount Waverley, Victoria, Australia, 3149. Contact: Mr. Len Campbell, Fran. Mgr., - Tel: (03) 9541.0711, Fax: (03) 9541.0849. 24 hour convenience stores selling basic food and household needs such as newspapers and magazines, milk, bread, confectionery, soft drinks, take-away food and beverages, groceries, cleaning products etc. Many stores also offer self serve petrol. Established: 1977 - Franchising Since: 1978 - No. of Units: Company Owned: 3 - Franchised: 165 - Franchise Fee: $35,000-$250,000 - Royalty: 46% to franchisee, 54% to franchisor - Total Inv: Fran. fee, stock min. $45,000, goodwill (if applicable) $90,000-$450,000 - Financing: For part stock only.

ALFONSO'S
3 Prince Albert Rd., London, U.K., NW1 7SN. Contact: Philip Smith, Dir. - Tel: (071) 267-2828. Alfonso's offers the consumer a wide choice of eat-in or take-away high quality dairy soft serve ice cream treats in an entertaining store environment. Established: 1993 - Franchising Since: 1994 - No. of Units: Company Owned: 1 - Franchised: 1 - Franchise Fee: Dependent on territory - Royalty: 6%, 4% mktg. - Total Inv: From £70,000-£140,000.

ALPINE SOFT DRINKS (UK) LTD.
McAlpine House, Pytchley Lodge Rd., Kettering, Northants., England, NN15 6JN. Contact: M. Meredith, Deputy Mng. Dir. - Tel: (0536) 415115. Manufacturer and distributor of soft drinks and allied products direct to the customer's door. Established: 1975 - Franchising Since: 1987 - No. of Units: Company Owned: 20 approx. - Franchised: 180+ - Franchise Fee: Total cost between £1,000-£7,000.

AMPOL ROAD PANTRY
Ampol Road Pantry Pty Ltd.
620 Macauley St., Albury, NSW, Australia, 2640. Contact: Fran. Mgr. - Tel: (060) 582000. Convenience stores, always open, providing fuel and food at all hours. Established: 1987 - Franchising Since: 1987 - No. of Units: Company Owned: 1 - Franchised: 48 - Franchise Fee: $80,000 3+3+3 year tenure - Royalty: 5% of shop sales.

ARBY'S ROAST BEEF RESTAURANTS
Arby's U.K. Ltd.
24 Hay Market, London, England, SW1Y 4DG. Contact: Larry M. Lion - Tel: (071) 930-7171. America's largest and most successful roast beef restaurant chain. Established: 1992 - Franchising Since: 1992 - No. of Units: Company Owned: 1 - Franchised: 1 - Franchise Fee: £35,000 - Royalty: 6% - Financing: Possibly.

BANDIERA BLU
Gelito Spa
Via Del Greto 1/4, 40132 Bologna, ITALIA. Contact: Nicola Fabri, Chef Executive Manager - Tel: (051)619 42 01. Italian gourmet, small fast food selling lowfat ice cream with fifty different toppings, crepes (salted or sweet), Italian sandwiches ("Piadina") and espresso coffee. Established: 1975 - Franchising Since: 1991 - Franchise Fee: US $70,000 complete store corner/US $3,000 kiosk - Total Inv: About US $120,000 store - $70,000-$90,000 corner - $ 25,000 kiosk.

BARCELOS FLAMED CHICKEN
P.O. Box 8508 Centurion, South Africa, 0046. - Tel: (+27) 12 663 7657, Fax: (+27) 12 663 5122, Web Site: www.barcelos.co.za. Homestyle Portuguese chicken. No. of Units: Franchised: 75 - Franchise Fee: R240,000.

BEWLEY'S CAFES AND SHOPS
Bewley's Franchising Ltd.
Mary St., Dublin 1, Dublin, Ireland. Contact: C. O'Brien, Dev. Mgr. - Tel: 01-6776761. Cafes and shops with 150 year tradition offering full range of branded tea, coffee and confectionery products. Established: 1840 - Franchising Since: 1988 - No. of Units: Company Owned: 6 - Franchised: 22 - Total Inv: Approx. £350,000 - Financing: No.

BIERWINKEL
Idem 9uardia Civil 4-, Valencia (Spain), Valencia, 46020. Contact: Anabel Navas, Marketing Director - Tel: (96) 147-30-31, Fax: (96) 147-27-19, E-Mail: bierwinkel@accesosis.es, Web Site: www,mrbit.es/franquicias/hostel/bier.htm. We are a German Bier Franchise. We are specialized in beers, having more than 130 different brands from all over the world. We also deal with German food, which we include in all our restaurants. Our restaurants are decorated in a dd style which is a characteristic of our franchise. Established: 1992 - Franchising Since: 1994 - No. of Units: Company Owned: 4 - Franchised: 8 - Franchise Fee: $10,000 - Royalty: 25% in the first year to 5% in the seventh year - Total Inv: Approx. $200.000.

BJ'S
No 8., King Street, Randburg, South Africa, 2194. - Tel: (+27) 11 789 3535, Fax: (+27) 11 789 3538. A mixture of fast food such as burgers, sandwiches, milk shakes etc. Established: 1983 - No. of Units: Franchised: 35 - Franchise Fee: R50,000 - Royalty: 6% of gross.

BOCATTA
Frankfurt, S.A. C/ Lauria 5, 3 Planta, Barcelona, 08010. Contact: Mr. Juan Jose Sanz, Franchise Manager - Tel: (93) 301-34-05, Fax: (93) 301-93-26. Bread sandwiches and compliments. Established: 1986 - Franchising Since: 1989 - No. of Units: Company Owned: 19 - Franchised: 51 - Franchise Fee: 3.750.000 Ptas. - Royalty: 4.5% + 4% D&P - Total Inv: 30.000.000 Pts. - Financing: No.

BURGER KING
Auda De Europa, 26 Atica F, Edific. F, Pozuezo De Alaecon, Madrid, 28224. Contact: Ana Lledo Tarradell, Franchise Sales Manager - Tel: (91) 709-12.60, Fax: (91) 352-48.52. Venta de hamburguesas. Established: 1954 - Franchising Since: 1975 - No. of Units: Company Owned: 12 - Franchised: 132 - Franchise Fee: $40.000 - Royalty: 5% - Total Inv: $65,000.00 In line, $100,000.00 Drive thru - Financing Available: 40%.

BURGER STAR
206 Bath Rd., Cheltenham, Glos., U.K., GL52 7NE. Contact: Simon Daws - Tel: (0242) 528884. Fast food hamburger and pizza take-away. Established: 1981 - Franchising Since: 1989 - No. of Units: Company Owned:1 - Franchised: 3 - Franchise Fee: £6,000 - Royalty: 5% gross sales, 1% adv. levy - Total Inv: £50,000-£65,000 - Financing: Yes.

CAFE DO PONTO - CAFETERIE
Cafe Do Ponto S/A Ind. Com. e Exp.
Av. Cafe do Ponto, 336, Barueri, SP, Brazil, 06410-900. Contact: Franchising Dept. - Tel: (011) 7298.4122, Fax: (011) 7298.4122 Ramal 377. Coffee shops, specialty coffee. Established: 1950 - Franchising Since: 1977 - No. of Units: Company Owned: 11 - Franchised: 182 - Franchise Fee: $5.000 US - Royalty: Not informed - Total Inv: Aprox. $55.000 US.

CAFE LEFFE/CAFE HOEGAARDEN
Interbrew N.V. Vaartstraat 94, Leuven, Belgium, 3000. Contact: Luc Bastiaensen, Corp. Retailing Dev. Mgr. - Tel: (32) 16-24-7601, Fax: (32) 16-24-7448. Brand oriented pub concepts. Established: 1987 - Franchising Since: 1987 - No. of Units: Franchised: 66 - Franchise Fee: No - Royalty: No - Financing: Yes.

CAFE MADELAINE
Spiazzi (8) PTE Ltd
50 Playfair Road #06-03 Noel Building, Singapore, 367995. Contact: Leslie Sim, Director - Tel: (65) 487-7717, Fax: (65) 487-7789, E-Mail: spiazzi@email.com. A bakery cafe restaurant concept offering a wide range of pizzas, pastas and sandwiches, as well as a variety of coffee's. Established: 1998 - Franchising Since: 1998 - No. of Units: Franchised: 2 - Franchise Fee: S$50,000-S$80,000 - Royalty: Royalty based on gross sales, 4% net of withholding tax - Total Inv: S$300,000 - Financing: Refer to franchisor.

CANADIAN MUFFIN COMPANY, THE
19 Rotterdam Dr., London, England, E14 3JA. Contact: Garry Rowse, Mng. Dir. - Tel: (44) 0170 528 1667, Fax: (44) 0171 538 5490, Web Site: www.ids.co.uk/franchise/muffin. Large delicious, handmade freshly baked muffins, sandwiches, baked potatoes and soups, a truly healthy food concept. Established: 1989 - Franchising Since: 1991 - No. of Units: Company Owned: 2 - Franchised: 15 - Franchise Fee: £8,000.00 - Royalty: 5% of net turnover - Total Inv: £76,000 turnkey open for business - Financing: We advise.

CANTINA MARIACHI
Franchising Direct S.L.
1 Vilanova 26-28 Sitges, Barcelona, Spain, 08870. Contact: Jaime Berdejo, Gerente - Tel: (93) 894-4112, Fax: (93) 894-2654. Hosteleria mexicana tipo tradicional con servicio a mesas, precios populares. Gastronn mia tipica, animacion and delivery, venta de artesania and articulos de regalo mexicanos. Established: 1992 - Franchising Since: 1994 - No. of Units: Company Owned: 2 - Franchised: 50 - Franchise Fee: $23,400 US - Royalty: 3% - Total Inv: $133,000 US.

CARL'S JR. BIRD PARK
Carl's Jr. Asian Development (M) Sdn Bhd
Lot E1-2 Jalan Selaman 1/2 Dataran Palma, Jalan Ampang, Ampang, Selangor, 68000. Contact: Fiona Perera, Ex. Franchise Development - Tel: (603) 470 3191, Fax: (603) 470 3196. Master licensed developer for Carl's Jr. in 26 countries in the Pacific Rim. Established: 1996 - Franchised Since: 1993 - No. of Units: Franchised: 2 - Franchise Fee: Based on territory - Royalty: As per key terms on territory - Total Inv: Available in the franchise kit.

CHICAGO PIZZA PIE FACTORY
My Kinda Town Plc.
195-197 Kings Rd, Chelsea, London, England, SW3 5Ed. - Tel: 44 (0) 171 351 6996. The Chicago Pizza Pie Factory creates a feeling of actually being in Chicago. Every bit of wall space is covered with vast amount of authentic Chicago memorabilia, ie street signs, posters of cinema and theatre. Its menu offers a wide choice of deep dish pizzas and other classic dishes such as chicken, caesar salad, stuffed mushrooms, aubergine parmigiana and bruschetta. Established: 1977 - Franchising Since: 1985 - No. of Units: Company Owned: 20 - Franchised: 24 - Franchise Fee: £55,000-£85,000 - Royalty: 5%-7% - Total Inv: £300,000+ - Financing: No.

CHICKEN LICKEN
P.O. Box 38628, Booysens, South Africa, 2016. - Tel: (+27) 011 493 3703, Fax: (+27) 011 493 3571, Web Site: www.chickenlicken.co.za. Chicken Licken soul food. Established: 1981 - Franchise Fee: R80,000 - Royalty: 5%.

CREPELITO
Crepelito-Comercio de Maqs. Gen. Alimenticious Ltda.
Rua Oscar Freire, 1784, Sao Paulo, Brazil,05409. Contact: Cyro Augusto Baffi, Owner - Tel: (055) 011-280-1299. A fast food, which offers a product with no competitors. Crepes served on a pick with different kinds of stuffings such as sweets, fruit, ham, sausage and others as well as ice cream, espresso and soft drinks. Established: 1986 - Franchising Since: 1987 - No. of Units: Company Owned: 9 - Franchised: 32 - Franchise Fee: US $39,000 - Royalty: 7% - Financing: 4 x US $9, 750.

DELI FRANCE
Whitworths Restaurants Ltd.
166 Bute St. Mall, Arndale Centre, Luton, Beds., England, LU1 2TU. Contact: Mr. M.J.B. Ward, Mng. Dir. - Tel: 0582-422781. French-style coffee shop and retailer of bakery products. Established: 1991 - Franchising Since: 1992 - No. of Units: Company Owned: 1 - Franchised: 3 - Franchise Fee: £10,000 - Royalty: 6% - Total Inv: £140,000 - Financing: 75%.

DELICE DE FRANCE
Delice De France Plc.
11-13 Point Pleasant, Wandsworth, London, SW18 1NN. Contact: Franchise Dev. Mgr. - Tel: (081) 875 9966, Fax: (081) 875 1575. Boulangerie, patisserie, cafe francais. Established: 1985 - Franchising Since: 1985 - No. of Units: Company Owned: 2 - Franchised: 8 - Franchise Fee: £7.000 - Royalty: Marketing/advertising 2%, management services fee 5% - Total Inv: 3 options, Le Rapibe: £69.000, Le Cafe: £93.000, Le Duo: £118.000 - Financing: Yes.

DINKUM DOG
Plumcourt Ltd.
88-92 Wallis Rd., Hackney, London, U.K., E9 5LN. Contact: John Drage, M.D. - Tel: (081) 985-3623. Fast food sales and marketing. UK and European sites only. Established: 1986 - Franchising Since: 1990 - Franchise Fee: £10,900 - Royalty: 5% man. fee, 3% adv. levy - Financing: Yes.

DISTRIBUIDORA CORY
Industria De Prod. Alimenticios Cory Ltda
R: Antonio Fernandes Figueiroa, 1056, Ribeirao Preto, Brazil, 14095-280. Contact: Fran. Mgr. - Tel: 0055-16-6271550, Fax: 0055-16-6275647. Distributors of cookies, biscuits and candies. Established: 1969 - Franchising Since: 1991 - No. of Units: Company Owned: 1 - Franchised: 22 - Franchise Fee: US $10,000 - Royalty: 0.5% over gross sales - Total Inv: US $60,000 - Financing: No.

DIXY FRIED CHICKEN
Dixy Fried Chickens Euro Ltd.
185 Town Rd., Edmonton, London, U.K., N9 0HL. Contact: Mr. A. Mahmood, Mng. Dir. - Tel: 0181-345-6675, Fax: 0181-345-5733. Fast food franchise. Established: 1986 - Franchising Since: 1986 - No. of Units: Company Owned: 4 - Franchised: 34 - Franchise Fee: £5,000 - Royalty: 4% - Total Inv: £100,000 - Financing: Yes.

DOCE MANIA
Doceira & Confeitaria GNT Ltd.
R.Joao Cachoeira, 166, Sao Paulo, SP, 04535-000. Contact: Sergio Niski, Owner - Tel: (55) 11 280 6813, (800) 11 3623, Fax: (55) 11 3064 1384, E-Mail: niski@sti.com.br. Cake Shop, selling product by weight. Established: 1989 - Franchising Since: 1994 - No. of Units: Company Owned: 1 - Franchised: 3 - Franchise Fee: US $20,000 - Royalty: 4% of sales - Total Inv: US $100,000 - Financing: No.

DOMINOS
Dominos Pizza Group
Lasorough Road, Milton Keynes, England, MK10 0AB. Contact: Anthony Round, Franchise Sales Manager - Tel: 01908 580000, Fax: 01908 588000, Web Site: www.dominos.uk. Pizza home delivery and take-away. Established: 1985 - Franchising Since: 1985 - No. of Units: Company Owned: 11 - Franchised: 161 - Franchise Fee: ƒ8,000 per store - Royalty: 5.5% - Total Inv: £150,000 - Financing: Through leading lenders. Min 50,000 liquid.

DON MILLERS HOT BREAD KITCHENS
Whitworths Bakeries Ltd.
166 Bute Street Mall, Arndale Centre, Luton, England, LU1 2TL. Contact: Mr. M. J. B. Ward, Mng. Dir. - Tel: 0582-422781. Produce and retailer of bakery products including take-away. Established: 1973 - Franchising Since: 1983 - No. of Units: Company Owned: 92 - Franchised: 34 - Franchise Fee: £10,000 - Royalty: 8% - Total Inv: £70,000 - Financing: 75%.

DONUT MAGIC
International Marketing Systems P/L
26 Railway Street, Southport, QLD, 4215. Contact: Tony Williams, Dir. - Tel: 07 55 913 242, Fax: 07 55 919 021, E-Mail: rfga@rfg.com.au, Web Site: www.rfg.com.au. Retail sale of food systems that incorporate cake and yeast donuts, hot and cold beverages (including cappuccino), soft serve ice cream and hot dogs. Established: 1995 - Franchising Since: 1995 - No. of Units: Franchised: 3 - Franchise Fee: $50,000 (Aud) - Royalty: 9% - Total Inv: $245,000 (Aud) - Financing: Upon request.

EAGLE BOYS PIZZA
Eagle Boys Dial-A-Pizza Australia Pty Ltd
232 Arthur St., Fortitude Valley 4006, Brisbane, Queensland, Australia, 4006. Contact: Mr. Tom Potter, Mng. Dir. - Tel: (07) 3254-1799, Fax: (07) 3254 1960, Web Site: www.eagleboys.com. Franchising of retail pizza outlets. Established: 1986 - Franchising Since: 1990 - No. of Units: Company Owned: 2 - Franchised: 168 - Franchise Fee: $25,000 - Royalty: 6% of turnover - Total Inv: $190,000 - Financing: No.

EL RECINTO
El Recinto S.A.
12 N 1447, La Plata, Argentina, 1900. Contact: Julio Barrabino, CEO - Tel: (54) 21-51-1632, Fax: (54) 21-572707. Empanades souffle, typically Argentine food for delivery and store sales. Fast foods and meals. Established: 1987 - Franchising Since: 1993 - No. of Units: Company Owned: 4 - Franchised: 4 - Franchise Fee: $10,000 US - Royalty: 2.5% - Total Inv: $30,000-$40,000.

EPOCA'S
Contifarma, S.L
Avd, De Atenas, 75 Zoco rozas 1.154, Las Rozas, Madrid, 28230. Contact: Jose A. Bodega, Director Comercial - Tel: 916,317,916, Fax:916,319,907, E-Mail: epocas@cicom.es, Web Site: www.futurnet.es/asyensco/epocas. Restaurantes tematicos. Established: 1994 - Franchising Since: 1998 - No. of Units: Company Owned: 1 - Franchise Fee: 8.000.000-pts - Royalty: 5%, Total Inv: 85.000.000 -pts - Financing: BBV.

EXPRESSO PAO DE QUEIJO
Expresso Comércio E Industraa
Av Prendente Altino 19L - Jaguare, Sao Paulo, SP, 05323-000. - Tel: (011) 268 1444, Fax: (011) 819 0348, Web Site: www.exprenopodequeyo.com.br. A company which provides cheese bread, coffee cakes, juices and other "salt breads." Established: 1989 - Franchising Since: 1991 - No. of Units: Company Owned: 4 - Franchised: 26 - Franchise Fee: US $8,400 - Royalty: 2% - Total Inv: US $60,000.

FAST FOOD SYSTEMS LIMITED
Unit 1, Headley Park 9, Headley Road East, Woodley, Reading, Berkshire, RG5 4SQ. Contact: Andrew Withers - Tel: (01189) 441100, Fax: (01189) 411080, E-Mail: sales@fast-food-systems.co,uk, Web Site: www.southern-fried-chicken.co.uk. Fast Food Chicken franchise now in 70 countries worldwide. Franchises are available for all markets with an initial franchise fee of £10,000. Training and back-up assistance worldwide. Full design and menu systems available. Development and master franchises available. Established: 1980 - Franchising Since: 1982 - No. of Units: Company Owned: 0 - Franchised: 486 - Franchise Fee: £10,000 - Royalty: 3% of annual - Total Inv: Minimum £30,000.

FATTY ARBUCKLES AMERICAN DINERS
Laser House, Waterfront Quay,Salford Quays, Salford Quays, Manchester, England, M52XW. - Tel: 0161-877-0881, Fax: 0161-877-0882. Themed American style diner specializing in providing very generous portions of American Style food at affordable prices in a friendly relaxed atmosphere. The central theme being eating should be fun. Established: 1983 - Franchising Since: 1991 - No. of Units:

Company Owned: 20 - Franchised: 30 - Franchise Fee: £10,000 - Royalty: 7%+3% marketing. - Total Inv: £250,000-£300,000 - Financing: Most high street banks.

FAVORITE CHICKEN & RIBS
Favorite Fried Chicken Ltd.
7 Davy Rd., Clacton-On-Sea, Essex, U.K., C015 4XD. Contact: Frank Poole, Franishe Director - Tel: (+44)1255 222 568, Fax: (+44) 1255 430 423, E-Mail: favorite@netcomuk.co.uk. Fried chicken and bbq rib express units and quick service restaurants, throughout U.K. Also in Spain. Established: 1986 - Franchising Since: 1986 - No. of Units: Company Owned: 3 - Franchised: 71 - Franchise Fee: £7500 - Royalty: 4% - Total Inv: £90,000-£120,000 - Financing: Subject to status, up to 70%.

FISH & CO
O.B. Singapor Operations PTE Ltd
108 Robinson Road #03-01 GMG Building, Singapor, 068900. Contact: Joe Chiang - Tel: 65-622-444-80, Fax: 65-622-444-15, E-Mail: joe@fish-co.com. Seafood restaurant, fish & chips, mussel, spice, etc. Established: 1998 - Franchisinbg Since: 2001 - No. of Units: Company Owned: 9 - Franchised: 2 - Franchise Fee: Refer to franchisor.

GRAFFITI CAFE
Graffiti Cafe Sweden AB
V.Stoegatan 45, Kristianstad, Sweden, 29131. Contact: Anders Welander, MD - Tel: (46) 44-125967, Fax: (46) 44-109630, E-Mail: anders@graffiticafe.se, Web Site: www.graffiticafe.se. Fast food restaurants with take away baked potatoes, salads, baquettes. Established: 1985 - Franchising Since: 1987 - No. of Units: Company Owned: 1 - Franchised: 7 - Franchise Fee: $75,000SKR - Royalty: 5.5% - Total Inv: $500,000-$1000,000SKR.

GREAT AUSTRALIAN ICE CREAMERY
Ice Creameries of Australia
Ice Creamery Hse., 271 Bong Bong St., Bowral, NSW, Australia, 2576, Contact: John Berry, Operations Manager - Tel: (02) 486 22 299, Fax: (02) 48 61 41 79. Sit down or take-away ice cream parlours offering wide range of flavours, cones, sundaes and spiders plus milkshakes, hot drinks and hot food located around Australia. Franchisees are usually married couples. Established: 1977 - Franchising Since: 1982 - No. of Units: Company Owned: 1 - Franchised: 65 - Franchise Fee: $35,000 - Royalty: None, percentage rebate paid on stocks purchased - Total Inv: $160,000-$180,000 incl. fran. fee - Financing: Assistance with bank finance available.

HAN MONGOLIAN BARBECUE AG
Han Bar & Restaurant
Murtenstrasse 41, Bern, Bern, 3008. Contact: Herbert Gerencser, Manager - Tel: (41) 31 382 99 88, Fax: (41) 31 382 92 69. The idea is based on the Mongolian barbecue and a colonial cocktail bar. The fascinating Asian tradition of patron participation in the culinary arts has no equal and "cooking in the dining room" is an important component of the concept. It's a concept with well matured and contemporary food which manifests a strong trend for healthy vitamin and calorie conscious nourishment in a price range that finds acceptance. Established: 1992 - Franchising Since: 1992 - No. of Units: Company Owned: 6 - Franchised: 4 - Franchise Fee: Swiss Francs 30,000 - Royalty: 4% of turnover - Total Inv: 700,000 Swiss Francs - Financing: No.

HARRER MEINE EISDIELE
Toni Harrer Systemz Entrale
Ungargasse 8, 2700 Wr. Neustadt, Austria, 2700. - Tel: 02622/29084. Production and distribution of ice cream. Established: 1988 - Franchising Since: 1990 - No. of Units: Company Owned: 4 - Franchised: 4 - Franchise Fee: 5% - Total Inv: US$300,000 - Financing: No.

HARRY RAMSDEN'S
Harry Ramsden's PLC
Larwood House, White Cross, Guiseley, Leeds, W. Yorkshire, England LS20 8LZ. Contact: John Barnes, Chairman - Tel: 0943 879531. Fish and chip restaurants and takeaways. Established: 1928 - Franchising Since: 1991 - No. of Units: Company Owned: 1 - Franchised: 11 - Franchise Fee: $150,000 - Royalty: 7% of sales - Total Inv: Build. $1,200,000, Equip. $350,000.

HEMGLASS SVERIGE AB
Box 53, 64521 Strangnas, Sweden. Contact: Jan Hallgren, Mng. Dir. - Tel: 0152-18020, Fax: 0152-15704. Home delivery of ice cream. Established: 1968 - Franchising Since: 1968 - No. of Units: Company Owned: 22 - Franchised: 14 - Franchise Fee: SEK 5,000-20,000 - Total Inv: SEK 100,000-300,000.

HENRY J. BEANS, CHICAGO PIZZA PIE FACTORY, HAVANA
Capital Radio Restaurants Limited
30 Leicesher Square, London, England, WC2H 7LE. Contact: Douglas Smillie, Franchise Operations Director - Tel: (0171) 766-6450, Fax: (0171) 766-6460, Web Site: www.capitalradiorestaurant.co.uk. Themed American, Latin American and other restaurants. Established: 1977 - Franchising Since: 1986 - No. of Units: Company Owned: 18 - Franchised: 25 - Franchise Fee: 750,000 - Royalty: On application - Total Inv: On application - Financing: No.

HOGGIES
Hoggies Ltd.
Stowupland Hall, Stowmarket Suffolk, England, IP14 4BE. Contact: Chris Knock, Franc. Admin. - Tel: 0449 674289. Spit-roast and outside catering. Established: 1985 - Franchising Since: 1990 - No. of Units: Company Owned: 3 - Franchised: 3 - Franchise Fee: £4,000 - Royalty: £100 per month maintenance contract on equipment - Total Inv: £19,500 (equipment £15,500 franchise fee £4,000) - Financing: Yes, subject to status.

HOT BITE
Snackpoint Limited
Southwood Farm, Southwood Road, Shalden, Alton, United Kingdom, GU34 4EB. - E-Mail: enquires@hotbite.co.uk, Web Site: www.hotbite.co.uk. Toasted sandwiches, wraps, paninis, pizzas, popcorn and muffins. Established: 2002 - Franchising Since: 2003 - No. of Units: Company Owned: 1. Call for more details.

JACK'S PLACE STEAK HOUSE & RESTAURANT
Jack's Place Holdings Pte Ltd
123 Defu Lane 10, Jack's Place Building, Singapore, 539232. Contact: Mr. Jerry Lim - Tel: (65) 6282-1311, Fax: (65) 6288-1922, E-Mail: franchise@jacksplace.com.sg, Web Site: www.jacksplace.com.sg. Established since 1966, Jack's Place is the oldest and one of Singapore's most successful homegrown chain of steak house and restaurants with 12 steak house and restaurants. It has also diversified into retailing cake in 1986 and has a central bakery under the brand of Jack's Place Cake House. Established: 1966 - Franchising Since: 1997 - No. of Units: Franchised: 2 - Franchise Fee: $40,000 US (varies from country to country) - Royalty: 3%.

JAMAICA BLUE
Foodco Mamagement Pty, Ltd
Level 9 Trak Centre, 445 Toorak Rd, Toorak, Australia, 3142. Contact: James Fitzgerald - Tel: (61) 3 9827 8388, Fax: (61) 3 9827 6969, Web Site: www.jamaicablue.com.au. Jamaica Blue offers a wide range of gourmet coffee, sweet and savoury snacks, herbal and fruit teas. Designed in Australia. Established: 1990 - Franchising Since: 1992 - No. of Units: Franchised: 21 - Royalty: 6%, 2% advertising - Total Inv: $200,000-$265,000.

JAMAICA COFFEE SHOP
Jamaica Shareholding, S.L.
Dr. Dou, 17 Bajos, Barcelona, Spain, 08001. Contact: Jordi Torrents, General ManagerFranchise & Development Manager - Tel: (34) 933 041 890, Fax: (34) 933 178 499, E-Mail: jamaicab@jamaicacoffeeshop.es, Web Site: www.jamaicacoffeeshop.es. The main activity of the company is the taste and retail of origin coffees, teas and chocolates. Established: 1994 - Franchising Since: 1995 - No of Units: Company Owned: 10 - Franchised: 90 - Franchise Fee: $25.000 US - Royalty: 5% + 2% (both on monthly sales turnover of the establishment) - Total Inv: $200.000 US - Financing: 60% own resources - 40% financed (resources depend on franchisee decision).

JAVA COAST
Aarschotsesteenweg 157 -159, Wezemaal, Belgium, 3111. Contact: Dirk Bex, Marketing Mgr. - Tel: (00) 32 16 589900, Fax: (00) 32 16 58 9980. Coffee shops with a complete range of flavoured coffees and pure

origin coffees. Established: 1925 - Franchising Since: 1995 - No. of Units: Company owned: 1 - Franchised: 7 - Franchise Fee: 500,000 BEF - Royalty: 8% - Total Inv: 4500,000 BEF - Financing: Yes.

KFC
KFC (GB) Ltd.
88-97 High Street, Brentford, Mddx., England, TW8 8BG. - Tel: 081 569 7070. Fast food. Established: 1965 - Franchising Since: 1965 - No. of Units: Company Owned: 82 - Franchised: 215 - Franchise Fee: £10,000 - Royalty: 5% - Total Inv: £200,000 - Financing: No.

L'HERBIER DE PROVENCE, DISKONT - FRISEUR-BEDARF
I.M.T. Ges.m.b.H
Schumannpasse 38, Perchtoldsdorf, Austria, 2380. - Tel: 869-0934, Fax: 869-0935. Import and export of nutrition foods, cosmetics. Established: 1984 - Franchising Since: 1988 - No. of Units: Company Owned: 2 - Franchised: 8 - Franchise Fee: $10,000 - Royalty: 7% - Total Inv: $39,000 - Financing: 100%.

LA SIRENA
Congelats Reunits, S.A.
Joan Luis Vives, 13 Ai B, P.I. Can Tries, Viladecavalls, Barcelona, 08232. Contact: Manager Director - Tel: (93) 733 14 34, (900)21 06 21, Fax: (93) 733 15 96 ,E-Mail: lasirena@lix.intercom.es. A chain of frozen food stores spread out in Catalunya. This family business is the leading company in this specialty in Spain with 50 stores. Established: 1983 - Franchising Since: 1993 - No. of Units: Company Owned: 24 - Franchised: 26 - Franchise Fee: 3.000.000 Ptas - Royalty: 0.6% of sales - Total Inv: 40.000.000 Ptas - Financing: No.

LENARD'S
Lenard's Pty. Ltd.
4166 Annerley Rd W Gabba, QLD, Australia, 4102. Contact: Steve Patterson, System Development Manager - Tel: (07) 3217 4300, 1 800 068111, Fax: (07) 3217 4300, E-Mail: www.lenards.com.au, Web Site: www.lenards.com.au. Retailing of value added fresh poultry. Operate predominantly in shopping centres anchored by good supermarkets. Established: 1987 - Franchising Since: 1987 - No. of Units: Company Owned: 5 - Franchised: 145 - Franchise Fee: $40,000 - $50,000 depending on site - Royalty: 4% fran. fee, 3% mktg. fee - Total Inv: $40,000 fran. fee, plus $180,000-$250,000 for plant, equipment, etc. - Financing: Major banks.

LES ROIS MAGES
Turfait Et Cie S.A.
210 rue Louis Armand - Z-1- Aix en Provence, 13794 Aix. en. Pr. Cedex 3, France. Contact: Turfait Pierre, Directeur - Tel: 42.24.42.57. Torrefaction et degustation cafes thes chocolats. Established: 1950 - Franchising Since: 1977 - No. of Units: Company Owned: 10 - Franchise Fee: 70,000 FRS. - Royalty: 1% - Total Inv: 400,000 FRS-B.P. 132,000.

LIZARRAN TABERNAS SELECTAS
Tentapa, S.L.
Olerdola, 28, Vilanova i La Geltru, Spain, 08800. Contact: Mario Sala, Franchise Director - Tel: (34) 93 810 13 10, Fax: (34) 93 810 12 96, Web Site: www.lizarran.com. Bar-taverns. The success of our establishments is based on the wide offer in "tapas", more than 300, where the client helps himself picking them directly from the glass cases in the bar. We complete the offer with a wide range of carefully selected wines and beers. Established: 1988 - Franchising Since: 1996 - No. of Units: Company Owned: 2 - Franchised: 40 - Franchise Fee: 2.500.000 ptas - Royalty: 6% of total sales; 2% for publicity advertising - Total Inv: 19.700.000 ptas - Financing: Yes.

LOBSTER VILLAGE
Loeberenstreet 19, Z U G, Suisse, 8125. - Tel: (01) 391 9160, Fax: (01) 391-2796. Restaurant - the motto "Have fun - have Lobster". Diningroom/bar with service. Established: 1986 - Franchising Since: 1990 - No. of Units: Company Owned: 1 - Franchised: 4 - Franchise Fee: CH-Fr. 35,000 - Royalty: 4% - Total Inv: 80,000-250,000 Swiss Francs - Financing: Yes.

LOVE TOAST
Crepelito Com. Maqs. Gen. Alimenticios, Ltda.
Rua Oscar Freire, 1784, Sao Paulo, Brazil, 05409. - Tel: (055) 011-280-1299. Love Toast offers many different products such as waffles, sweet and salted picks, ice cream, espresso and soft drinks. Established: 1986 - Franchising Since: 1989 - No. of Units: Company Owned: 1 - Franchised: 3 - Franchise Fee: $39,000 US - Royalty: 7% - Total Inv: $39,000 US - Financing: 4 X $9,750 US.

MASTER BREW LTD.
Beverages House, 7 Ember Centre, Hersham, Surrey, England, KT12 3PT. Contact: Franchise Department - Tel: 01932 253787. Franchisees sell and deliver fresh roast and ground coffee and a complete range of beverage products to offices and catering outlets. Established: 1982 - Franchising Since: 1990 - No. of Units: Company Owned: 2 - Franchised: 64 - Total Inv: £9,900 + VAT + £7,000 work. cap. - Financing: Most banks.

MCDONALD'S
McDonald's Restaurants Ltd.
11-59 High Rd., East Finchley, London, England, N2 8AW. Contact: Wendy Ayling, Fran. Coord. - Tel: (0181) 700 7153, Fax: (0181) 700 7469. Quick service restaurants. Established: 1974 in UK - Franchising Since: 1986 in UK - No. of Units: Company Owned: 770 - Franchised: 200 - Franchise Fee: £30,000 - Royalty: 5% of turnover - Total Inv: Approx. £340,000 - Financing: Via traditional sources.

MISTER DONUT
353 North End Road, London, England, SW6 1NN. - Tel: (071) 386-9133. Fast food, donuts, pastry, muffins, cookies....brownies. Established: 1955 - Franchising Since: 1956 - No. of Units: Company Owned: 1 - Franchised: 1,000 - Franchise Fee: Based on the size of the region or country in Europe - Royalty: 3% and 2% adv. - Total Inv: £150,000, will depend on the size of region - Financing: The company may help finance through the banks.

MISTER PIZZA
Pizzarias Mister Pizza Ltd.
rue da Quitanda, 50 and/or 6 centro, Rio de Janerio - RJ, Brazil, 20011-030. Contact: Mrs. Eliane Bernardino, Vice-Pres. - Tel: (021) 224-4477, Fax: (021) 262-6364. Fast food pizza shops, thin and thick crust pizza as main menu item, special assorted sandwiches, giant hot-dogs with special sauces. Established: 1981 - Franchising Since: 1983 - No. of Units: Company Owned: 26 - Franchised: 59 - Franchise Fee: $15,000 U.S. - Royalty: 6% + 2% publicity - Total Inv: $120,000 U.S.

MONGOLIAN BARBEQUE
68 Home Park Rd., London, England, SW19 7HN. - Tel: 0181-947-7500. Restaurants/catering. Established: 1988 - No. of Units: Company Owned: 6 - Franchised: 3 - Franchise Fee: £10,000 sterling - Royalty: 6.5% mgmt. svc. fee, 1% adv. levy - Total Inv: Circa £25,000 sterling + fit out costs and property costs (£100,000 min.) - Financing: Assistance with preparation of business plan.

MR. BIG (UK) LTD.
18 Fairfax St., Coventry, England, CU1 5RY. Contact: Franchise Director - Tel: (0203) 57722/29238. Mr. Big giant sized hamburgers, counter or waitress service units.

MR. BIRD MYO
11 Preston Street Suite 3'1, Como, WA, 6152. - Tel: (61 8) 94774 5955, Fax: (61 8) 9474 2914, Web Site: www.mrbirdsmyo.com. Mr. Birds MYO is a make your own sandwich. Established: 2000 - Franchising Since: 2003 - No. of Units: Company Owned: 1 - Franchised: 2 - Franchise Fee: $35,000.

MR. COD
Mr. Cod Ltd.
6/7 High St., Woking, Surrey, England, GU21 1BG. Contact: J. Brewer, Mgr. Dir. - Tel: 01483-755407. Fast food. Established: 1980 - Franchising Since: 1985 - No. of Units: Company Owned: 1 - Franchised: 10 - Franchise Fee: On application - Total Inv: £35,000-£125,000 - Financing: Yes.

NEW ZEALAND NATURAL
Delinatural (Asia) Pte Ltd
179 River Valley Road, #05-12 River Valley Building, Singapore, 359396. Contact: Stanley Wong - Tel: (65) 6334 6977, Fax: (65) 6334 6649, E-Mail: delinatural@pacific.net.sg, Web Site: www.newzealand natural.com.sg. New Zealand Natural has a worldwide franchise network of more than 200 outlets in Australia, New Zealand, United Kingdom, Korea, Singapore and Indonesia selling world famous ice cream made in New Zealand using the finest dairy products amd 100% natural ingredients. Established: 2000 - Franchising Since: 2000 - No. of Units: Company Owned: 1 - Franchised: 4 - Franchise Fee: S$25,000 - Royalty: 5% - Total Inv: S$80,000-150,000.

O'BRIEN'S IRISH SANDWICH BARS
24 South William St., Dublin 2, Ireland, Contact: Olive Hipwell, Franchise Sales Manager - Tel: (+353)1 472 1400, (0800) 973 888, Fax: (+353)1 472 1401, E-Mail: franchise@obriens.ie, Web Site: wwwobriens.ie. Upmarket, strongly branded sandwich bar/coffee shop concept featuring unique thick bread, made to order sandwiches, and espresso based coffee drinks. Established: 1988 - Franchising Since: 1994 - No. of Units: Company Owned: 2 - Franchised: 59 - Franchise Fee: f9,000 - Royalty: 9% total, (6% management services/3% marketing) - Total Inv: £50,000-$100,000 varies - Financing: Yes.

OBI BAU- UND HEIMWERKERMARKTE
Hutteldorfer Straße 299, Vienna, 1140. Contact: Dr. Peter Langer, General Manager - Tel: (912) 57 10 ext. 609, Fax: (912) 57 10 ext. 699. Do it yourself markets. Established: 1995 - Franchising Since: 1995 - No. of Units: Company Owned: 2 - Franchised: 27 - Franchise Fee: 2.5% of the turnover - Royalty: No - Total Inv: AIS 150,000,000 up to AIS 200,000,000 - Financing: No.

PAN & CAFE
Franchidan SA 1 Vilanova 26-28 Sitges, Barcelona, Spain, 08870. Contact: Jaime Berdejo, Gerente - Tel: (93) 894-4112, Fax: (93) 894-2654. Fabricacion al momento de panei especialza dos, bolleria and degustacion de cafes, menus rapidos and services de delivery. Established: 1996 - Franchising Since: 1997 - No. of Units: Company Owned: 2 - Franchised: 4 - Franchsie Fee: $23,400 US - Royalty: 3% - Total Inv: $133,000 US.

PAO OF COMPANHIA
Pao & Companhia Servicos Ltda.
Rua Itapema, 326, Belo Horizonte, Brazil, 30310-490. Contact: Helio Valadao, President - Tel: (55) 31 287-7351, Fax: (55) 31 281 2316, Web Site: www.pasecia.com.br. Bakery franchising. Established: 1982 - Franchising Since: 1987 - No. of Units: Company Owned: 3 - Franchised: 41 - Franchise Fee: US $25 - US $35 for each square metter - Royalty: 3% on gross - Total Inv: Avg. US $120,000 - Financing: Possibility of banking financing up to 50%.

PERFECT PIZZA
Perfect Pizza House
The Forum, Hanworth Lane, Chertsey, Surrey, England, KT16 9JX. Contact: Martin Clayton, Fran. Sales Dir. - Tel: (01) 932-568000, Fax: (01) 932-570628, E-Mail: martin_clayton@perfectpizza.co.uk. Pizza delivery and take-away franchise. Established: 1978 - Franchising Since: 1982 - No. of Units: Company Owned: 10 - Franchised: 195 - Franchise Fee: £8,000 - Royalty: 5% + 4% main. - Total Inv: £81,000 - Financing: Through high street banks.

PICCOLO PIZZA
Fast Food Systems Ltd.
Unit 1, Headley Pk. 9, Headley Rd. E., Woodley Reading, England, RG5 4SQ. Contact: Director - Tel: (0118)9 44-1100, Fax: (0118) 9 44-1080. Piccolo pizza, complete turnkey store. Includes equipment, packaging and ingredients. Established: 1980 - Franchising Since: 1984 - No. of Units: Franchised: 50 - Total Inv: £8000 to 30,000 - Financing: Leasing.

PIERRE VICTOIRE, PIERRE LAPIN, CHEZ JULES, BEPPE VITTORIO
Pierre Victoire Ltd.
48 Albany St., Edinburgh, Scotland, Contact: Fran. Dir. - Tel (0131) 479-0011, Fax: (0131) 479-0012. French and Italian Bistro style restaurants offering excellent quality cuisine at value for money prices.

Established: 1988 - Franchising Since: 1992 - No. of Units: Company Owned: 17 - Franchised: 90 - Franchise Fee: £12,500 - Royalty: 5% turnover - Total Inv: £50,000-£80,000.

PIZZA 2/4
Franchise Development Services, Castle House, Castle Meadow, Norwich, England, NR2 1PJ. Contact: D. Mayers, Cons. - Tel: 0603-620301. Pizza restaurant with Italian style decor suitable for husband/ wife operation with part time staff. Established: 1978 - Franchising Since: 1985 - No. of Units: Company Owned: 1 - Franchised: 1 - Franchise Fee: £10,000 - Total Inv: £30,000 - Royalty: 5% - Financing: Possible.

PIZZA HUT (UK) LTD.
149 Earl's Court Rd., London, England. Contact: Peter A. Bassi, Area V.P. - Tel: 370 6443. Restaurants selling freshly prepared pizza, pasta, salad, desserts, wine and lager. Established: 1973 - Franchising Since: 1979 - No. of Units: Company Owned: 12 - Franchised: 1 - Franchise Fee: $25,000 US - Total Inv: £135,000 - Royalty: 5%.

PIZZAMANN
PizzaMann Restaurants GESMBH
Ruflinger Str.17, Leonding, Austria, A-4060, Contact: Mr. Adolf Platzl, Owner - Tel: 43/0732/67 06 46, Fax: 43/0732/68 03 58. Pizzamann is doing Pizza-business in Austria. We are an outdoor, indoor and delivery service. We are market-leader in that business in Austria. Established: 1986 - Franchising Since: 1988 - No. of Units: Company Owned: 30 - Franchised: 30 - Franchise Fee: 4%, 3% for advertising, 10% for property - Total Inv: $700,000 ATS - Financing: Yes.

POKIN'S
Alda Food S.A.
C/. Lauria 5. 3 Planta, Barcelona, 08010. Contact: Mr. Juan Jose Sanz, Franchise Manager - Tel: (93)301.34.05, Fax: (93)301.93.26. Fast food (burger). Established: 1979 - Franchising Since: 1984 - No. of Units: Company Owned: 2 - Franchised: 3 - Franchise Fee: 3,750,000Pts - Royalty: 4.5%+4% marketing - Total Inv: $35,000,000 Pts - Financing: No.

PRAWER
Prawer Fine Handmade Chocolate
RVA Gen. Souza Doca, 77 S. 403, Porto Alegre, RS, 90.630-050. Contact: Franchise Department - Tel: (051) 332-1030, Fax: (051) 331-8185. Fine hand made chocolate, coffee and ice cream commerce. It is the best and the first of hand made chocolates of the Gaúcha Mountains -A-region of German and Italian colonization in the state of Rio Grande Do Sul - South of Brazil. Established: 1976 - Franchising Since: 1995 - No. of Units: Company Owned: 5 - Franchised: 5 - Franchise Fee: $12,000 - Royalty: 5% over the total income - Total Inv: US$68,000 - Financing: No.

QUICK RESTAURANT
Grotesteenweg 224, bus 5, Berchem, Belgium, 2600. Contact: Guido De Paepe, Franchising & Expansion Director - Tel: (03)286 18 11, Fax: (03) 286 18 79. Hamburger, fast food chain. Established: 1971 - Franchising Since: 1978 - No. of Units: Company Owned: 36 - Franchised: 71 - Franchise Fee: 650,000 BF - Total Inv: 50,000,000 BF - Royalty: 5% - Financing: 3,000,000 BF.

RIBS, CASA DE LAS COSTILLAS
Ribs, La Casa De Las Costillas, S.A.
C/Atlantico, Naves 17-18, P.I. Los Olivas, Ajalvir, Madrid, 28864. Contact: Carlos Sanz, Manager - Tel: (34.91.)8843728, Fax: (34.91.) 8843687, Web Site: www.ribs-sa.es. Spanish chain of restaurants, specializes in American style food to enjoy in a great country atmosphere, with live rock music, country dancing and of course our famous BBQ ribs. Established:1995 - Franchising Since:1995 - No. of Units: Company Owned: 3 - Franchised: 4 - Total Inv: $800.000 .

SANTA FE TEX-MEX GRILL
Ampac Food Concepts PTE LTD
50 Playfair Road , #06-03, Noel Building, Singapore, 367995. Contact: Leslie, Director - Tel: (65) 487 7717, Fax: (65) 487-7789, E- Mail: spiazzi@email.com. A Texas-Mexican restaurant concept offering famed dishes such as Buffalo wings, fajitas and turkey quessidtas. Established:

1999 - No. of Units: Company Owned: 1 - Franchise Fee: Refer to franchisor - Royalty: Refer to franchisor - Total Inv: Refer to franchisor - Financing: Refer to franchisor.

SEVEN-ELEVEN CONVENIENCE STORES
Seven-Eleven (Japan) Co. Ltd.
4-14 Shibakoen 105, Tokyo, Japan. Contact: Tsumie Yamaguchi, Sec. - Tel: (03) 459-3711. Convenience stores. Established: 1973 - Franchising Since: 1974 - No. of Units: Company Owned: 68 - Franchised: 3327 - Franchise Fee: ¥3 million - Total Inv: ¥23 million (including ¥20 million for store construction) - Royalty: 45% gross profit - Financing: ¥20 million.

SOUTHERN FRIED CHICKEN EXPRESS
Fast Food Systems Ltd.
Unit 1, Headley Pk 9, Headley Rd. E., Woodley, Reading, England, RG5 4SQ. Contact: Andrew Withers, Mng. Dir. - Tel: (+44) 118 9441100, Fax: (+44)118 9441080, E-Mail: sales@fast-food-systems.co.uk, Web Site: www.southern-fried-chicken.co.uk. Chicken, burger, pizza, ribs restaurant and take away. We supply complete turnkey store, including equipment, supplies, packaging and seasoning. Established: 1980 - Franchising Since: 1980 - No. of Units: Franchised: 650 - Total Inv: £100,000- Financing: No.

SPUD MULLIGAN'S
Spud Mulligans Pm Ltd.
5 Plaza Parade, Maroochudore, QLD, Australia, 4556. - Tel: (07) 5479 - 2122, Fax: (07) 5443 - 7634. Irish themed restaurants and food court sites with optional mobile stores attached, selling oven roasted potatoes with wide range of fillings, plus tea, coffee, milk & fruit drinks, cakes, Etc. Established: 1992 - Franchising Since: 1994 - No. of Units: Company Owned: 2 - Franchised: 12 - Franchise Fee: $40,000 just (stores), masters negotiable - Royalty: 6% of turnover (stores), masters 50% negotiable - Total Inv: $180,000-$240,000 (stores) - Financing: Assistance through various banks, etc.

SPUDULIKE
Spudulike Ltd.
34/38 Standard Rd., Park Royal, London, England, NW10 6EU. Contact: Ron Snipp, Dir. - Tel: 081 965-0182, Fax: 081 965-6102. Specialist baked potato restaurants. Established: 1981 - Franchising Since: 1981 - No. of Units: Company Owned: 20 - Franchised: 23 - Franchise Fee: £10,000 - Royalty: 5% mgmt. 3% adv. - Total Inv: £80,000 - Financing: Up to 50%.

ST. PIERRE'S CORP.
1 Bidwell St., Wellington, New Zealand. - Tel: (04) 844-431. Specialty food retailer, specializing in gourmet seafood, poultry, and delicatessen. Established: 1985 - Franchising Since: 1989 - No. of Units: Company Owned: 3 - Franchised: 12 - Franchise Fee: $25,000 - Royalty: 7% - Total Inv: $180,000-$230,000 - Financing: Yes.

STROUD CREAMERY
Lansdown, Stroud, Glos., England. Contact: Pat Smith, Dir. - Tel: 04-536-2351. Dairy products. Established: 1967 - Franchising Since: 1967 - No. of Units: Company Owned: 10 - Franchised: 46 - Approx. Inv: £1,000 - Royalty: £9 per week.

SURTICASA / 5 MINUTOS
Operadora Suriticasa S.A.
Benito Juarez #226 Oficina 21 Col. Cedros, Metepec, Mexico, 52149. Contact: Franchise Management - Tel: (527) 2-19-83-53, Fax: (527) 2-17-48-29, E-Mail: almasur@toluca.podernet.com.mx. Surticasa - convenience store for Hispanic market. 5 Minutos - convenience store for any market. Established: 1970 - Franchising Since: 1995 - No. of Units: Company Owned: 9 - Franchised: 4 - Franchise Fee: Variable - Royalty: Variable - Total Inv: $100,000 US - Financing: Possible.

SUSHI-ITTO
ITTO Restaurantes Y Services Sa De Cv
Cuauhtemoc 158 Tizapan De San Angel, Mexico D.F., Mexico, 01090. Contact: Salvador Mejia, Franchise Sales and Promotion Assistant - Tel: (5) 616-47-80/83, Fax: (5) 616-46-49, Web Site: www.sushi-itto.com. Japanese restaurant with sushi bar, home delivery and take out. Established: 1988 - Franchising Since: 1991 - No. of Units: Company

Owned: 7 - Franchised: 34 - Franchise Fee: $35,000.00 USD - Royalty: 5% net sales monthly 4% local and institutional advertising fund - Total Inv: Varies in every case according to the size of the site. Financing: No.

TACO MARIACHI
Franqviciadora Del Fast Food
1 Vilanova 26-28 Sitges, Barcelona, Spain, 08870. Contact: Jaime Berdejo, Gerente - Tel: (93) 894 4112, Fax: (93) 894 2654. Gastrono mia mexicana tipo fast food. Established: 1996 - Franchising Since: 1997 - No. of Units: Company Owned: 1 - Franchise Fee: $23,400 US - Royalty: 3% - Total Inv: $250,000 US.

TAVERNERS FAYRE LTD.
RPL
21 Coopers Court, Newport Pagnell, Bucks, ENG, MK 168J5. Contact: Jim Mason - Tel: 01908-61900, Fax: 01908-611125, web Site: www.taverners-fayre.co.uk. We are a complete catering solution specifically designed for pubs/hotels. Operates easily from home. No stock required and your investment is protected through our unique business buy-back scheme. Total Inv: ƒ5,000.

TICKLE MANOR TEAROOM - LAVENHAM
Tickle Manor Tearoom Ltd.
18 High St., Lavenham, Sudbury, Suffolk, England, CO10 9PT. - Tel: (0787) 248216. Franchise tearooms, serving morning coffee, light lunch, and afternoon tea, of a very special kind. Professional catering. Service and ambiance with a curious theme which proves irresistible to customers new and regular. Established: 1988 - Franchising Since: 1990 - No. of Units: Franchised: 1 - Franchise Fee: £7,000 - Royalty: 5% total: 1% trouble shooting, 1.5% menu provision, 1% recipe dev., 1.5% mktg. - Total Inv: £7,000 fran. fee, £25,000 fixtures/fittings - Financing: No.

TOASTY KITCHENS
Old George Brewery, Rollestone St., Salisbury, Wiltshire, England, SP1 1BB. - Tel: (0722) 327456. Our specially designed gas operated cooking system enables franchisees to prepare, seal, and then sell thousands of crispy, freshly baked roasted sandwiches a day. The equipment is fitted in custom built catering trailers for use at all outdoor events and shows. Established: 1981 - Franchising Since: 1983 - No. of Units: Company Owned: 1 - Franchised: 14 - Franchise Fee: £12,000 + VAT incl. fully equip. catering unit - Royalty: £78 per mon. - Total Inv: £12,000+£3,000 work cap. - Financing: Yes, in UK.

VIVENDA DO CAMARAO
Great Food Prod. Alimenticios Ltda.
R. Dos Estudantes, 351, Cotia, Sao Paulo, Brazil, 06700-000. Contact: Dietmar Frank, Share holder/ Mng. Dir - Tel: (55)11 79 22 90 77, Fax: (55) 11 79 22 23 10, E-Mail: vivenda@sanet.com.br, Web Site: www.vivendadocamarao.com.br. Seafood /fast food, with emphasis on shrimp. Established: 1984 - Franchising Since: 1997 - No. of Units: Company Owned: 20 - Franchised: 6 - Franchise Fee: $20,000-$40,000 US - Total Inv: $150,000 US + Franchise Fee - Financing: No, only third party.

WEINERWALD RESTAURANTS GESELLSCHAFT MBH
Hinsenkampplate 1, Linz, Austria, 4040. Contact: Dr. Thomas Kainz, Signing Clerk - Tel: (732) 73-83-01-0, Fax: (732) 73-83-01-10. Restaurants. Established: 1955 - Franchising Since: 1970 - No. of Units: Company Owned: 162 - Franchised: 56 - Franchise Fee: 5% from sale.

WENDY'S SUPA SUNDAES
209 Fullarton Rd., Eastwood, South Australia, Australia, 5063. - Tel: (08) 373 3944. Wendy's Supa Sundaes is a chain of specialized impulse treat outlets. The bright shops and tempting range of products including ice cream, vitari, hot dogs, fruit salad and drinks promote on image of a "busy little ice cream shop". Established: 1979 - Franchising Since: 1980 - No. of Units: Company Owned: 24 - Franchised: 256 - Franchise Fee: Variable - Royalty: 6% , 3% adv. - Total Inv: $100,000-$300,000 - Financing: Package available.

WILTSHIRE FARM FOODS
Apetito Group Ladydown,
Trowbridge, Wiltshire, U.K., BA14 8RJ. Contact: Gary Rigby, Fran. Mgr. - Tel: 0225 753636, Fax: 0225 777085, E-Mail: apetitesales@compuseue. Ready made meals, home delivery service. Established:

1928 - Franchising Since: 1991 - No. of Units: Company Owned: 2 - Franchised: 46 - Franchise Fee: £8,000 plus vat - Royalty: None - Total Inv: £20,000 - Financing: All major banks.

WIMPY
Wimpy International Ltd
2 The Listons, Liston Road, Marlow, Bucks, Britain, SL7 1FD. Contact: Brian Crambac - Tel: 01628 891655, Fax: 016284 74025. Wimpy's is a table-service restaurant. Prospective franchisees do not require restaurant experience as full training is provided. Established: 1954 - Investment: £80,000-£200,000.

ZUSAL. SL-HOME JUICE
Poligono Industrial San Lorenzo, Bergara Gipuzkon, Spain, 20570. Contact: Isable Madina - Tel: (34) 943 967110, Fax: (34) 943 760050, E-Mail: export@zusal.com, Web Site: www.zusal.com. Orange juice vending machines. Established: 2002 - Franchising Since: 2002 - No. of Units: Company Owned: 1.

FRANCHISE CONSULTANTS

A F L DEESON PARTNERSHIP LTD., THE
Ewell House, Faversham, Kent, England, ME13 8UP. Contact: Dominic Deeson, Mng. Dir. - Tel: 0795 535468. Franchise Consultants. Established: 1959.

A.G.M., S.C.P.
AGM Lawyers Pau Clarisa
139, Paul, Barcelona, Spain, 08009. Contact: Francisco Lacasa, Legal Consultant - Tel: (343) 487 11 26, Fax: (343) 487 00 68. Legal Consultants specialized in franchise. Network all over Europe. Established: 1984.

ARENDORFF & PARTNERS
Amaliegade 37, 1256 Copenhagen K, Denmark. Contact: Peter A. Arendorff, Lawyer - Tel: (45) 33 91 00 60. International law firm that runs the secretariat of the Danish Franchisor's Association. Lawyers.

ARTHUR ANDERSEN
Arthur Andersen Y Cia S. Com.
Raimundo Fernandez Villaverde, 65, Madrid, Spain, 28003. Contact: Manuel Arranz, Manager - Tel: 34 1 514 51 00, Fax: 34 1 514 51 80. Franchising Advisory.

ASOCIATION MEXICANA DE FRANQUICIAS, A.C.
Insurgentes Sur 1783-202 Col. Guadalupe Inn, Mexico, D.F., 01020. Contact: Lorena Reynaud De Braune, General Director - Tel: (5) 66 0655/6632178/6622473. Mexican Franchise Association. Established 1998.

AVV. GIUSEPPE BERGAMASCHI
V. Pematteotti, N. 60, Florence, Italy. Contact: Dani Michela, Secretary - Tel: (55) 575270-588 988, Fax: (55) 575270 580 950. All problems concerning franchising, marketing, law, etc.

BARBADILLO & ASOCIADOS
Orense, 27-4 1ZQ, Madrid, Spain, 28020. Contact: Susana Ortega, Commercial Mgr. - Tel: 556 70 12, Fax: 556 02 12. Franchise Consultants. Established: 1992.

BUFETE QUILES
KMC Asesores S.L.
Avenida Blasco Ibanez, 41-5, Valencia, Spain, 46021. Contact: Carmen Quiles, Dir. - Tel: (96) 3619412, Fax: (96) 361-9242. Marketing and advertising advice, market studies, franchise consultants, legal advice. Established: 1992.

CALTAIN ASSOCIATES
Golitha Cottage, Draynes, Nr. Liskeard, Cornwall, England, PL14 6RX. Contact: Dick Crook, Chairman - Tel: (44-1579) 321 060. An American with 32 yrs. of franchise experience in European markets where he has the leading track record for building ethical, profitable and long-lasting franchises.

CFM CONSULTING
P.O. Box 748, Caterham, Surrey, England, CR3 7YQ. Contact: David C. Taube - Tel: (44) 1883 65 3178, Fax: 44 1883 65 3287, E-Mail: consult@uk.pi.net. Everything for the U.S. or Canadian franchisor with serious intentions on Europe: market studies, competitor search, outline recommendations, detailed business plans, finding master licensee, helping with start-up, problem solving. All counsellors are highly experienced and have many years of experience as CEO's of franchise businesses.

CHERTO FRANCHISING ,INC
Rua Fidencio Ramos, 100, San Paulo, Brazil, 04551-010. Contact: Marcelo Cherto, C.E.O - Tel: (5511) 820-1605, Fax: (5511) 829 9856, E-Mail: Marcelo@cherto.com.br, Web Site: www.cherto.com.br, Provides services to existing and prospective franchisors. The firm has 4 divisions: consulting courses and training, researches and studies and publications. Established: 1986.

CLAIRMONTS SOLICITORS
9 Clairmont Gardens, Glasgow, Scottland, G3 7LW. Contact: David Kaye, Partner - Tel: 0141 226-3020, Fax: 0141 221-0123. Legal.

CNA EXECUTIVE SEARCH LTD
4 Boundry Court, Wollow Farm Business Park, Castle Donington, Derby, DE74 2UD. Contact: Paula Reed - Tel: 01332 856 200, Fax: 01332 856 222, E-Mail: info@cnainternational.co.uk, Web Site: www.cnainternational.co.uk. We are the largest independently owned executive search franchise in Europe. Our clients have access to top-performing paople and we offer candidates excellent opportunities through-out the world. Total Inv: £20,000 plus working capital.

COMMERCIAL DEVICES
5 Farm Bldgs., Palmers Moor, Thornborough, North Bucks, England, MK18 2DJ. Contact: Derek Ayling and Alison Rushworth, Sr. Partners - Tel: (0280) 824100. Franchise and marketing counselling and trainers, specializing in bringing North American operations into Europe. Established: 1977 - Franchising Since: 1981.

CORRS CHAMBERS WESTGARTH
Bourke Pl., 600 Bourke St., Melbourne, Victoria, Australia, 3000. - Tel: (613) 672-3000, Fax: (613) 602-5544. Commercial law firm.

DAHLMAN MAGNUSSON / EFFECTUM
P.O. Box 7009, Stockholm, Sweden, 103 86. Contact: Anders Fernlund, Partner - Tel: (468) 679-8200, Fax: (468) 679-7565, E-Mail: a.fernlund@dma.se, Web Site: www.effectum.com. Commercial law firm specializing in franchising on both the domestic and international level.

DAVID BIGMORE & CO.
36 Whitefriars St., London, England, EC4Y 8BH. Contact: David Bigmore, Principal - Tel: 44-171-583-2277, Fax: 44-171-583-2288, E-Mail: db@dbigmore.demon.co.uk. Franchise Solicitors. Established: 1992 - Franchising Advice Since: 1985.

DONNET & VAES
Mechelse Steenweg 195, Antwerp, Belgium, 2018.Contact: O. Vaes, Lawyer - Tel: (03)289-2626, Fax: (03)239-3420. Specialized in set-up of franchising networks through a specialized team with lawyer (our office), bankers, tax and franchising consultant. We have also a international team of experts in franchising. Established: 1973 - Franchising: 1985.

DUBLER, LAW OFFICES
93 Zollikerstrasse, Zurich-Zollikon, Switzerland, 8702. Contact: Dr. Andreas M. Dubler, Partner - Tel: (41) 1 396 86 86 , Fax: (41) 1 396 86 96, E-Mail: dubler@access.ch. Law firm, franchise consultants - legal.

EDARA
#11, 26 July St, Midan Lobnan, Mohandessin, Cairo, Egypt, 12411. Contact: Mr. M. Azmi, Chairman - Tel: (202) 345-3340, Fax: 302-1870. Franchise consultants/brokers in the Middle East. Established: 1991.

EFFECTUM FRANCHISE CONSULTING
Adolf Fredriks Kyrkagata 2, S-11 37, Stockholm, Sweden. Contact: Curt Axberg Partner - Tel: (46) 8 652-1200, Fax: (46) 8 83-6640, Web Site: www.effectum.com. Effectum helps International franchisors entering the European community and especially the Scandinavian market.

EUROPE SERVICE
Via Risorgimento 11, Cologno 7.SE, Milano, 22093. Contact: Laura Missaglia - Tel: (02)253-8444. Franchise and marketing consultant.

EVERSHEDS
Senator House 85 Queen Victoria Street, London, England, EC4V 4JL. Contact: Martin Mendelsohn or Chris Wormald, Partners - Tel: (0171)919 4500, Fax: (0171)919 4919, E-Mail: mendelm@eversheds.com. Attorneys.

FIELD FISHER WATERHOUSE
41 Vine St, London, England, EC 3N 2AA. Contact: Mark Abell - Tel: (0171) 481-4841, Fax: (0171) 488-0084. Legal services.

FMM CONSULTANTS INTERNATIONS LTD.
83, Victoria Rd., Horley, Gatwick Airport, Surrey, England, RH6 7QH. Contact: Graham Tinsley, Int'l. Dir. - Tel: (44) 1293-820200, Fax: (44) 1293-821122. Europe's largest specialist franchise consultancy that has divisions for, property services, accountancy, information technology, public relations, management services, training, insurance, design, conferences and seminars, manual writing including ISO 9000. Established: 1981 - Franchising Since: 1963.

FRANCHISE ADVANTAGE, INC
12F Yebisu Garden Place Tower Bldg, 4-20-3, Ebisu, Shibuya-Ku, Japan. Contact: Masami Tajima, CEO - Tel: (81) 03 5424-1942, Fax: (81) 03 5424-1943, E-Mail: mtajma@tsutaya-net.or.jp. Franchise Advantage specializes in consulting franchisors in Japan. Established: 1996.

FRANCHISE CENTRE, THE
Suite 1A Level 2 802 Pacific Highway, Gordon, Australia, 2077. Contact: Garry Williamson, Mng. Dir. - Tel: (02) 482 7233, Fax: (02) 482 7339, E-Mail: contact@franchisecentre.com.au, Web Site: www.franchisecentre.com.au. Established: 1985 - Franchising Since: 1989 - No. of Units: Company Owned: 1 - Franchised: 3 - Franchise Fee: $35,000 - Royalty: 7% mgmt. fee, 2% adv. - Total Inv: $50,000 - Financing: No.

FRANCHISE DEVELOPMENT
2 Heathfield Rd., Sea Point, Cape Town, South Africa, 8001. Contact: Franchise Director - Tel: (021) 44 6710/44-2723. Franchise program developers, franchise marketing.

FRANCHISE DEVELOPMENT SERVICES
Franchise Development Services Limited
56 Surrey Street, Norwich, England, NR1 3FD. Contact: Mr. R. Seaman, Managing Director - Tel: (+44) 1 603-620301, Fax: (+44) 1 603-630174, E-Mail: enquires@fdsltd.com, Web Site: www.franchise-group.com Since 1981 our company has been providing a full range of services for established and prospective franchisors and franchisees nationwide and worldwide. We seek applications from experienced individuals and organizations seeking to become involved in all elements of national or international franchise developments. Established: 1981 - Franchising Since: 1985 - No. of Units: Company Owned: 1- Franchised: 14 - Franchise Fee: $50,000 - Royalty: Variable - Total Inv: $50,000 - Financing: Yes.

FRANCHISE DEVELOPMENTS PTY
464 St. Kilda Rd., Melbourne, Victoria, Australia, 3004. Contact: Franchise Director - Tel: (03) 2677666. Franchise Consultants.

FRANCHISE FINANCING AND MARKETING
27 Aetorahis St., Thessaloniki, 54640, Greece. Contact: M.H. Sarantoglou, Dir. Gen. - Tel: (**30) 31-821742, Fax: (**30) 31-819424, E-Mail: Interalex@hol.gr. Providing services to franchisors/parent companies as representatives. Broker. Finding areas, locations, (Master) franchisees, partners. Undertake expansion of firms through franchising, partnerships, branches. Personal experience of organizing approx. 2000 outlets, subsidiaries. Financing services to franchisors worldwide through direct lenders/funding. Marketing and sales of franchises, distributorships.

FRANCHISE KOLLEGIET
P.O. Box 6589, Stockholm, Sweden, S-113-83. Contact: Fran. Dir. - Tel: 46 (0) 8 612 30 50. Consultants in national and international franchising and licensing (Sweden). Established: 1988.

FRANCHISE RESOURCES
5 Glenwood Way, Castle Hill, NSW, Australia. Contact: Chris Dent, Partner - Tel: (02) 634-1634 or 868-4777. Consultancy for franchisors on aspects of franchising in Australia, including real estate selection, legal, manuals, staff selection, marketing, business plans, financing, etc. Established: 1982.

FRANCHISE SERVICES AB
Svennedalsvagen 200, 216 23 Malmo, Sweden, Contact: Kim Bachelder-Malmsjo, President - Tel: +46 - 40-13 68 25, Fax: +46 - 40 - 13 22 80. Franchise Services provides full service franchise consulting to both established franchise organizations and companies considering franchising. Over 10 years franchise experience in the U.S. and in Sweden. Established: 1993.

FRANCHISE SYSTEMS LIMITED
17A Jalan Sctiapuspa, Medan Damansara, Kuala Lumpur, Malaysia, 50490. Contact: Man. Dir. - Tel: (03) 255 9345, Fax: (03) 255-4750. Franchise consultants, marketing and accounting services, market evaluations, feasibility and research programs, franchise recruitment, activities and consultants throughout Australia and SE Asia.

FRANCHISING ADVISORS S.R.L.
Uruguay 667 Piso 8, 1015 Capital Federal, Argentina. Contact: Dr. Jorge D. Bliman, General Manager - Tel: (541)371-3502, Fax: (541) 373-8325. We are a consulting firm in franchising and also we have the only magazine in the country about franchising, also a tv-cable program, we do commercial and legal contract, marketing research, conferences, etc. Established: 1981 - Franchising Since: 1992.

FRANCORP ARGENTINA S.A.
Cerrito 1294, 5 Piso, 1010 Capital Federal, Argentina, 1010. Contact: Edward F. Chianea, General Manager - Tel: (541) 816-6130, Fax: (541)516-6127, E-Mail: edufch@yahoo.com, Web Site: www.francorpinc.com. Specialists in franchise partner development. Established: 1992 - Franchising Since: 1993 - No of Units: Company Owned: 4 - Franchise Fee: $20.000 - Royalty: 10% .

GENERALE DE BANQUE
Montagne Du Parc 3, Brussel, 1000. Contact: Patricia Flaba, Assistant - Tel: (32) 2 565 41 20, Fax: (32) 2 565 37 63. Bank operation. Franchising Since: 1989.

GOLDSMITH WILLIAMS
42-44 Stanley St., Liverpool, Merseyside, England, L1 6AL. Contact: Edward R. Goldsmith, Sr. Partner. Solicitors dealing in franchising. Established: 1984 - Franchising Since: 1984.

GRUPO CHERTO
Av. Paulista, 1337, Sao Paulo, Brazil, 01311-200. Contact: Marcelo Cherto - Tel: (55-11) 3171-0008, Fax: (55-11) 3171-0019, E-Mail: info@cherto.com.br, Web Site: www.grupocherto.com.br. Brazilian consulting firm specializing in Distribution Channels Strategies. Grupo Cherto has worked with the most successful Brazilian franchisors.

HAMBLEDEN GROUP, THE
P.O. Box 16980, London, UK, NW89WP. Contact: Mr Collins, CEO - Tel: (0171) 289-4443, Fax: (0171) 289-1943. Consultancy and training for prospective and practising franchisors, including international master licensing. Established: 1998.

HOBSON AUDLEY HOPKINS & WOOD
7 Pilgrim Street., London, England, EC4V 6DR. Contact: Robert Bond, Partner - Tel: (44) 171-450-4500, Fax: (44)171-450-4545. Legal advisers to domestic and cross border franchisors and franchisees; European and North America network; experienced in character merchandising, competition law and intellectual property issues. Established: 1983.

IMTIYAZ
Franchise Development and Marketing
P.O. Box 4520, Jeddah, Saudi Arabia, 21412. Contact: Khaled H. El-Zarka, Gen. Mgr. - Tel: (02) 660-7517. Developing sales, and marketing of franchise systems and distributorships in the Middle East. Established: 1988.

ING BANK
P.O. Box 1800, NL-1000 BV, Amsterdam, The Netherlands. Contact: Mgr. Fran. Finance - Tel: +31 20 652 2993, Fax: +31 20 652 2997. Ing Bank has unprecedented experience since 1962 and a leading position in franchise finance. It offers a comprehensive financial and insurance package to both franchisor and franchisee. Established: 1926 (successor of NMB Bank) - No. of Units: Company Owned: 400.

INTERNATIONAL CONSULTANT GROUP
P.O. Box 11-7711, Beirut, Lebanon. Contact: A.H. Zeidan, President - Tel: (961) 1-399-400, Fax: (961) 1-399-500, Web Site: www.ic-group.com.lb. Franchising and licensing services provided to International franchisors and national franchisees in Lebanan and Arab countries. Established: 1993.

INTERNATIONAL FRANCHISE BUSINESS MANAGEMENT
Pt. Inti Fokus Bina Management
Jl. Gandaria Tengah VI No. 41, Kebayoran Baru, Jakarta Selatan, DKI-Jakarta, 12160. Contact: Ms. Reni Chandriachsja, Mgr Partner - Tel: (62) 21-7266914, (62) 21-9226471, Fax: (62) 21-723-5738. Franchise business management consultant, franchise broker, franchise training cordinator, franchise business analyst, etc. Established: 1995 .

JOHN PERKINS & ASSOCIATES
Parade House, The Esplanade, Woolacombe, Devon, Warwickshire England, EX34 7DJ. Contact: John S. Perkins, Principal - Tel: 01271-870120. The only franchise advisor (not a consultant) in the U.K. Also involved with licensing and valuations to intellectual assets. Established: 1984.

KOELEWIJN & PARTNERS B.V.
Eemnesserweg 79, Baarn, The Netherlands, 3743 AG. Contact: A. Koelewijn, Managing Director - Tel: (31) 35 542-0828, Fax: (31) 35 541-8604, E-Mail: info@koelewijn.nl, Web Site: www.koelewijn.nl. Leader in franchise consulting in Holland. Established: 1988.

L.E.F. LICENTIE EN FRANCHISE
Herengracht 503, The Netherlands, Holland, 1017 BV. Contact: Picter Wiegman, Managing Partner - Tel: (020)6259915, Fax: (02)626-9287. Guidance for import and export of franchise concepts and licenses. How to expand in Europe. Member of the European Business Development Group. Established: 1989 - No. of Units: Franchised: 6.

LADAS & PARRY
52 High Holborn, London, U.K, WC1V 6RR. Contact: Iain C. Baillie, Partner - Tel: (+44) 20-7242-5566, Fax: (+44) 20-7405-1908. International intellectual property, licensing and franchising lawyers, U.K. and European Trademark Agents.

LEATHES PRIOR(SOLICITORS & NOTARIES)
74 The Close, Norwich, Norfolk, England, MR35 2JE. - Tel: (0603) 610911. Solicitors and notaries providing legal advice to the franchise industry on all aspects of franchising. Also, members of Eu-Lex network of European law firms, able to advise on European level. Advisors.

LUCAS NEALE
26 Station St., FernTree Gully, Victoria, Australia, 3156. Contact: David Lucas, Principal - Tel: (03) 9 758 7055, Fax: (03) 9758-2561, E-Mail: auslaw@lucasneale.com, Web Site: www.lucasneale.com.au. Lawyers. Established: 1977.

M K C -MICHEL KAHN CONSULTANTS
58 Avenue des Vosges, Strasbourg, France, 67000. Contact: Michel Kahn - Tel: (33) 3 88 36-56-16, Fax: (33) 3 88 362130. Consultant in franchise and partnership.

MACPHERSON & KELLEY SOLICITORS
229 Thomas St., Dandenong, Melbourne, Victoria, Australia, 3175. Contact: Stephen Giles, Partner - Tel: (613) 7916444. Legal practice providing a full range of legal services and specializing in franchise law and franchise consulting in Australia. Recognized as one of Australia's leading franchise law firms. Established: 1905 - Franchising Since: 1984 - No. of Units: Company Owned: 2 - Franchised: 2 - Franchise Fee: Depends upon location - Royalty: 50% of franchisee's net profit before personal drawings - Total Inv: $40,000-$200,000 depending upon location - Financing: Franchise or financed.

MACROBERTS
27 Melville St., Edinburgh, Scotland, EH3 7JF. Contact: Michael J. Bell, Partner - Tel: (031) 226-2552. Established for 130 years.

MASON SIER TURNBULL
5 Hamilton PLace, Mount Waverly, Victoria, Australia, 3149. Contact: John Sier, Partner - Tel: (61) 3-9807-8688, Fax: (61) 3-9807-8298, E-Mail: johns@mst.com.au, Web Site: www.mst.com.au. Franchising and licensing lawyers. Established: 1959.

MENZIES - CHARTERED ACCOUNTANTS
Ashby House, 64 High St., Walton-on-Thames, Surrey, England, KT12 1BW. Contact: Andrew Denley, Partner - Tel: (01932) 247611, Fax: (01932) 246457, E-Mail: adenley@menzies.co.uk. Chartered accountants advising business generally, financial planning, taxation advice and other specialist areas including franchising. Established: 1912 - Franchising Since: 1985.

MEXICAN FRANCHISE ASSOCIATION
Insurgentes Sur No. 1783-202 Col. Guadlupe Inn, Mexico City, Mexico, 01020. Contact: Lorena Reynaud, General Manager - Tel: (525) 661-0655/662 2473, Fax: (525) 663-2178, E-Mail: amfl prodigy.net.mx. Mexican Franchise Association. Established: 1989.

MUNDAY'S ATTORNEYS
Hamilton House 1 Temple Ave, London, England, ECAY OHA. Contact: Manzoor G.K. Ishani - Tel: (044) 171 8080, Fax: (044) 171 8180. Attorneys and notaries public.

N.V. KREDIETBANK
Havenlaan 2, Brussels, Belgium, 1080. Contact: Product Manager Franchising & Group Financing - Tel: (02) 422-82-11, Fax: (02) 422-81-66. Servicing to franchisors as well to franchisees by providing not only good financial arrangements but also consultancy- advice (included tax implications). Franchising Since: 1990.

NAT WEST BANK
Franchise Section, Level 10, Drapers Gdns., 12 Throgmorton Ave., London, EC2N 2DL, England. Contact: Peter Stern or Sandra Milburn, Sr.Fran.Mgr./Secretary - Tel: 171-920-5256, Fax: 171-920-5217. Largest retail bank in U.K. Providers of finance for franchisors and franchisees since 1981. Established: 1826 - Franchising Since: 1981 - No. of Units: Company Owned: 1800 - Financing: For franchisors and franchisees in UK.

NETHERLANDS FRANCHISE ASSOCIATION
Boomberglaan 12, Hilversum, The Netherlands, 1217 RR. Contact: A.W.M. Brouwer, Managing Dir. - Tel: +31(0)35 624 23 00, Fax: (031) 6249194, E-Mail: franchise@nfr.nl, Web Site: www.nfv.nl. Established 1972, the NFV is a non-profit national association, acting on behalf of all franchisers in representation to both national and international governmental bodies. Member of the European Franchise Federation and the World Franchise Council.

NEW CENTURY SOFTWARE LIMITED
Southampton, Hampshire, U.K., SO3 1LJ. Contact: Richard Pelly, Dir. - Tel: (+44) 962-771811. Develop and support computer software for business systems.Multi-lingual applications. Emphasis on single systems for use by both franchisor and franchisee. Established: 1980 - Franchising Since: 1982 - No. of Units: Company Owned: 1.

O.VAES

Van Rompaey & Vaes

Van Putlei 4, Antwerp, 2018.Contact: O.Vaes, Partner/Lawyer - Tel: 3-281-2626, Fax: 3-239-3420, E-Mail: o.vaes@vanrompaey-vaes.be, Web Site: www.vanrompaey-vaes.be. Advice, litigation and drafting for franchising outlets, licensing, sole distributorship agency. Established: 1973.

OFFICE KELLER-BURO FUR FRANCHISEBERATUNG

Rifferswilerstrasse 10, Hauptikon, ZH, CH-8926. - Tel: 01 764 11 11, Fax: 01 764 21 84. Office for franchise consulting. Established: 1997.

OPTIMAS HOLDING UND MANAGEMENT AG

Optimas

Ruchstuckstr. 19, CH-8306 Bruttisellen/Zurich, Contact: Lorenz A. Aries, CEO - Tel: (41) 01 834 04 54, Fax: (41) 01 834 04 53. Market treatment and sales optimizing program with more than 30 modules structured in seminars, trainings and workshops. Appliable for industrials - commercial - and service companies as well as financial services. Established: 1988 - Franchising Since: 1990 - No. of Units: Company Owned: 25 - Franchised: 17 - Franchise Fee: Regional partner (franchise partner) US$40,000, Master franchise for 1 country US$200,000 - Royalty: 17-12% - Total Inv: Max. US$10-15,000 dependent of the actual infrastructure - Financing: Approx. US$200,000 to 400,000 per year.

OWEN WHITE

Senate House, 62-70 Bath Rd., Slough, Berkshire, U.K., SL1 3SR. Contact: Anton Bates, Partner - Tel: (0753) 536846. Legal advice. Solicitors specializing in the provision of legal services to master licensors, franchisors and franchisees.

PAISNER & CO.

Bouverie House, 154 Fleet St., London, England, EC4A 2DQ. Contact: Linda Fazzani, Partner - Tel: 44 (0) 71 353 0299. Law firm advising on all aspects of franchising including document preparation, competition law, tax planning, intellectual property franchise litigation, EC law, property for franchisors and franchisees. Established: 1932.

PEAT MARWICK MAIN & COMPANY

England Branch Aquis Court, 31, Fishpool St., St. Albans, Hertfordshire, U.K., AL3 4RF. Contact: Gerry W. Hopkinson, Principal - Tel: 0727-43000. An international accounting, auditing, taxation and management consulting firm with over 300 offices worldwide. Established: 1895.

PERIBANEZ ASESORES

Ronda Universidad, 19, 1, Barcelona, Spain. - Tel: (34) 3 3189385, Fax: (34) 3 317 29 42. Consulting in franchising, export-import franchising. Established: 1929 - Franchising Since: 1990.

PRASETIO STRATEGIC CONSULTING

Wisma 46, Kota BNI, Level 27, JL Jend Sudirman Kev1, Jakarta, DKI, Indonesia, 10220. Contact: Suanning Tanardi, Manager - Tel: (021) 575-7125. Assist client to develop franchise system, to expand business overseas, to sell local franchise/international franchise locally, to do franchise feasibility assessment.

RAMBERG PR & INFORMATION

Berguddsv 52, 133 33 Saltsjobaden, Sweden. Editor of the Swedish franchise newsletter "Franchising". PR - consultant to franchise companys in Sweden. Established: 1996.

RECRUIT CO. LTD

BI Div., 2-12-11 9F, Higashi-Shinbashi, Ninato-Ku, Tokyo, Japan, 105-0021. Contact: Hitoshi Funashashi - Tel: (81) 03-3575-5321, Fax: (81) 03-3575-5277. Develops prospective subfranchisors and provides a full range of business development services. We also host and organize a yearly franchise conference in Tokyo. Established: 1960.

REES POLLOCK

7 Pilgrim Street, London, England, EC4V 6DR. - Tel: 071 329 6404. Chartered accountants: advice on UK tax and accounting, franchising in the UK and master licenses, and general business advice. Established: 1990.

ROUSSETY & CO

1957 Malvern Road, East Malvern, Victoria, Australia, 3145. Contact: Maurice Roussety, CEO - Tel: (613) 9885-5588, Fax: (613) 9885-6598, E-Mail: atulloch@roussety.com.au, Web Site: www.roussety.com.au. Accounting and consulting firm specializing in the franchising sector.

ROYAL BANK OF SCOTLAND

42 St. Andrew Square, Edinburgh, UK, EH39 4QX. Contact: G.W. Rose, Head of Franchising - Tel: (44) 0 131 5232178, Fax: (44) 0 131 5561817. UK business bank, franchising and licensing.

SWEDISH FRANCHISE ASSOCIATION

P.O. Box 5512, S 114 85 Stockholm, Stockholm, Sweden, 10329. Contact: Stig H. Sohlberg, CEO - Tel: (46) 87627685, Fax: (46) 86626696. The only trade association for franchising. Established: 1972.

SYNCON GMBH

Syncon Franchise - Consultants

Baverhamerstrasse 12/1st floor, Salzburg, Austria, 5020. Contact: Waltraud Frauenhuber, Managing Director - Tel: (0043) 662-8742 45 0, Fax: (0043) 662-87 42 45 5, E-Mail: office@syncon.at, Web Site: www.syncom.at. International franchise consultants. Established: 1972.

THOMAS EGGAR & CHURCH ADAMS SOLICITORS

Chatham Court, Lesbourne Road, Reigate, Surrey, RH2 7FN. Contact: Michael Crooks - Tel: 01737 240111, Fax: 01737 8319 609. Legal services. Offices also located at Chichester Tel: 01243 486111, Horsham Tel: 01403 214500, London Tel: 0171 2420 841, and Worthing Tel: 01903 234411.

TORMO & ASOCIADOS

Cardenal Marcelo Spinola, 42, Madrid, Spain, 28016. Contact: Eduardo A. Tormo, General Dir. - Tel: (91) 302-7140, Fax: (91) 766-3589. Tormo & Asociados is a franchise consulting firm. Leader in the Spanish market. This company provides services to the franchisors, franchisees and has several franchise publications and seminars. We have 12 offices in Spain and 1 in Portugal. Established: 1991.

WILKINSON & GRIST

6/F Prince's Building, Chater Rd., Central, Hong Kong. Contact: Ms. Ella Cheong, Sr. Partner - Tel: (852) 2524-6011, Fax: (852) 2877-1295, E-Mail: partners@wilgrist.com, Web Site: www.wilgrist.com. All aspects of intellectual property including prosecution, litigation, licensing, franchising and technology transfer for patents, designs, copyrights, trademarks, trade secrets and confidential information. Established: 1860.

ZALDIVAR, MANOVIL, RAGAZZI & ASSOC.

Viamonte 494 - 5 Piso, Buenos Aires, Argentina, 1053. - Tel: (54-1) 312-8454/56, Fax: (54-1) 313-9509. Legal consultants in franchising, national and international.

GENERAL

5 A SEC

Nuevo En Seco, S.A.

Lopez Se Hoyos 370, Madrid, Spain, 28043.Contact: Marco Antonio Garcia-Baile, General Manager - Tel: (91) 388-7744, Fax: (91) 388-7196, E-Mail: nes@5asec.es, Web Site: www.5asec.es. 1 hour trade cleanings franchiseur. Established: 1968 - Franchising Since: 1993 - No. of Units: Company Owned: 15 - Franchsied: 77 - Franchise Fee: 2.850.000 pts - Royalty: 2% turnover - Total Inv: 22-24 millions pts - Financing: Yes.

ACCASTILLAGE DIFFUSION

Intermer S.A.

Zi du Bois de Leuze, BP 41, Saint-Martin de Crau, France, BP41-13552. Contact: Jean Marc Bailly, Chairman - Tel: (33) 4 47 90 0110, Fax: (33) 4 47 90 01 12, E-Mail: intermer@infonie.fr, Web Site: www.accastippage-diffusion.com. Purchasing center and group management. All equipment for nautical leisure, mainly sailing. Includes electronics. Established: 1977 - Franchising Since: 1975 - No. of Units: Franchised: 41 - Franchise Fee: 35,000 F - Royalty: 1% net turnover, 1.5% adv. - Total Inv: 700,000 F.

ALEXANDER/ATHENA LANGUAGE INSTITUTE, ALS
Alexander Internationl
27 Aetorahis St., Thessaloniki, Greece, 54640. Contact: Ms Kate Angeletou, Manager - Tel: (+30)3210-827106, Fax: (+30) 2310 819424, E-Mail: interalex@hol.gr, Web Site: www.als-alexander.org. Small to medium sized language teaching centers/schools. Internationally since 1994. Established: 1966 - Franchising Since: 1970 - No. of Units: Company Owned: 96 - Franchised: 21 - Franchise Fee: US $4,000-$10,000 Euros - Royalty: 5%-15% - Total Inv: $10,000-$200,000 Euros (incl. franchise fee + start-up expenses) - Financing: Yes.

ALPHAGRAPHICS
Alphagraphics UK Ltd.
Thornburgh Rd., Scarborough, Yorkshire, UK, YO11 3UY. Contact: Malcom Eccleston, Managing Director - Tel: (01723) 502222, Toll Free: (0800) 257424, Fax: (01723) 502368, E-Mail: m.eccleston@ alphagraphic.co.uk. Worldwide leader in print and print related services, offering a broad range of design, copy and print products letting our customers easily and effectivley communicate in any publishing medium - any where in the world, anytime. Established:1987 - Franchising Since: 1988 - No. of Units: Franchised: 20 - Franchise Fee: £ 24,000 - Royalty:10% ,7% , 5% reduces with sales level - Total Inv: £150,000 - Financing: Yes through banks.

BIN MASTERS
MDRC Franchising Ltd
Suite 1, Elm House Shackleford Road, Elstead, Surrey, England, GU8 6LB. Contact: Andrew Quail - Tel: (01252) 703 429, Web Site: www.binmasters.co.uk. On-site van-based repair of industrial, commercial and municipal waste containers, including wheeled bins, skips, recycling centers, and rollonoffs. Established: 1990 - Franchising Since: 2002 - No. of Units: Company Owned: 2 - Franchised: 11 - Franchise Fee: £10,500 plus VAT - Royalty: 17.5%.

BOOKENDS™ (NZ) LTD.
Level five, 137 Hereford Street, Christchurch, New Zealand, 8001. Contact: Glori Moyle, Executive Director - Tel: (0064) 3.374-9533, Fax: (0064) 3.374-9522. Bookends™ NZ Ltd. is a specialist educational book, readers and all other printed material to primary and secondary schools throughout New Zealand via a network of franchisees. This is an assured and predictable (government financed) market which is growing strongly in line with the country's population growth. Established: 1988 - Franchising Since: 1991 - No. of Units: Company Owned: 7 - Franchised: 16 - Franchise Fee: Varies between $NZ 25,000-$NZ 35,000 + standard Licence Fee $NZ 5000 (CPI adjustment) + 21/2% GP - Royalty: Not applicable - Total Inv: Varies average investment $NZK purchase plus Licence Fee plus Working Capital of say $15 NZK - Financing: Possible.

BUILDING ENGENHARIA
Rua Recife, 51, Curitiba, Parana, Brazil, 80035-110. Contact: Evilasio, Director - Tel: (041) 252-0726. Structural designs based on system totally informatized with data input extremely easy. Formworks and other details are automated outputs from the data input. Real estate products and services. Established: 1985 - Franchising Since: 1991 - No. of Units: Company Owned: 1 - Franchised: 74 - Franchise Fee: $1,000 - Royalty: 10% over the projects price - Total Inv: Approx. $10,000.

CARD CONNECTION
Card Connection Ltd.
Park House, South St., Farnham, Surrey, England, GU9 7QQ. Contact: Philip McNamara, Franchise Marketing Manager - Tel: (01252) 733177, Fax: (01252) 735611, E-Mail:ho@card-connection.co.uk. Card connection is a franchised greeting card distribution, with over 10,000 outlets nationwide stocking its existing and vibrant product ranges. These high quality designs are distributed through a network of franchisees who operate their own exclusive area. Established: 1992 - Franchising Since: 1992 - No. of Units: Franchised: 80 - Franchise Fee: STG ú 11,650- Royalty: None - Total Inv: STG ú 19,650 (incl. STG ú 8,000 work. cap.) - Financing: Yes.

CCR CAR COMPONENTS RECYCLING GMBH
CCR Components Recycling GMBH
Rosenheimer Str. 139, Munich, Germany, 81671. Contact: Achim Winter, General Manager - Tel: 89/49 00 49 80, Fax: 89/49 00 49 83, Web Site: www.ccr.de. Systematic full-service disposal all kinds of waste - 1 partner. Europewide recycling-logistics. Established: 1991 - Franchising Since: 1993 - No. of Units: Franchised: 50 - Franchise Fee: Approx. 60.000.00-120.000.00 DM - Royalty: 5% on turnover - Total Inv: 80.000.00 DM for trucks; 100.000.00 DM storage - Financing: Advise available.

CENTURY 21 UK LTD.
Brosman House, Darks Lane, Potters Bar, Herts., England, EN6 1BW. Contact: Tanis Baker, Mng. Dir. - Tel: 01707-646465. Real estate franchise. Established: 1971 - Franchising Since: 1971 - No. of Units: Franchised: 40 - Franchise Fee: £10,000 - Royalty: 6% on turnover, 2% ad. fund - Financing: Yes.

CHOICES
Choices MSA Ltd
6 High St., Crawley, West Sussex, England, RH101Bj. Contact: Simon Shinerock, Mgn. Dir. - Tel: (01293) 565644, Fax: (01293)560680, E-Mail: choices@choices.co.uk. Choices the multi service agency is a multi discipline estate agency. Future franchise expansion will be via Interlet-UK a home based lettings network using the WWW as a virtual shop window. Established: 1989 - Franchising Since: 1991 - No. of Units: Company Owned: 2 - Franchised: 2 - Franchise Fee: £2,750 - Royalty: 6% of turnover - Total Inv: £5,000-£10,000 - Financing: Yes.

CINDERELLA DESIGNER GOWNS
Cinderella Designer Gowns Ltd.
Lochrin House, Coatbank St., Coatbridge, Strathclyde, U.K. ML5 3SS. Contact: Jill Greenhalgh, Mng. Dir. - Tel: (0236) 40957. Home run second income, ladies dress hire, ball gowns and cocktail dresses. Established: 1987 - Franchising Since: 1989 - No. of Units: Company Owned: 1 - Franchised: 8 - Total Inv: £10,000.

CINDERELLA HOME SERVICES
323 Kirkdale, Sydenham,London, England, SE23 2RT. Contact: Mrs E. A. Rowland, Dir. Employment agency dealing with placing nannies, domestic cleaners and offering a membership service for babysitting and all temporary childcare and household services. Established: 1982 - Franchising Since: 1990 - No. of Units: Company Owned: 1 - Franchised: 2 - Franchise Fee: £5,750 - Royalty: 7% annual sales - Total Inv: £7,614 - Financing: Yes.

CLIMAT DE FRANCE
B.P. 93, Avenue des Andes, 91943 Les Ulis Cedex, France. Contact: Christian Henneman, Intern. Dev. Mgr. - Tel: 16 (1) 69 28 58 60. French hotel chain. (2 stars chain). Established: 1980 - Franchising Since: 1980 - No. of Units: Company Owned: 20 - Franchised: 140 - Franchise Fee: FF 3,500 per room and FF 50,000 for restaurant - Royalty: 4% C.A. H.T. - Total Inv: FF 12,000,000-15,000,000 TTC - Financing: FF 2-3,000,000.

CLOTHES AID
Unit C, Leory House, 436-438 Essex Road, London, UK, N1 3QP. - Tel: 020 7226 4607, Fax: 0207 704 0737, E-Mail: sam@clothesaid.co.uk, Web Site: www.clothesaid.co.uk. Clothes Aid is a unique franchise that carries out door-to-door collections on behalf of Great Ormond Street Hospital Children's Charity. Franchisees arrange the distribution of charity bags and the subsequent collection of clothing from households in their franchise area. Franchise Fee: £2,950 - Total Inv: £10,000.

COLNEIS GREETING CARDS
Colneis Marketing Ltd.
York House, 2-4 York Road, Felixstowe, Suffolk, UK, 1P11 7QQ. Contact: John Botting, Director - Tel: (01394) 271668, Fax: (01394) 275 114. Greeting card service, sale or return to retail outlet. Established: 1994 - Franchising Since: 1995 - No. of Units: Franchised: 27 - Franchise Fee: Variable £300-£600 - Royalty: None - Total Inv: £9,000-£15,000.

COMPLETE WEED CONTROL
Complete Weed Control Ltd.
7 Astley House, Cromwell Bus. Pk., Banbury Rd., Chipping Norton, Oxfordshire, England, OX7 5SR. Contact: Roger Turner, Mng. Dir. - Tel: (01608) 644044, Fax: (01608) 644722. Amenity and industrial weed control specialists. Established: 1972 - Franchising Since: 1982 - No. of Units: Franchised: 24 - Franchise Fee: £10,000 + ƒ5,500 start up costs - Royalty: 10% on turn over - Financing: 70% according to status

COUNTRYWIDE GARDEN MAINTENANCE SERVICES
TeeJay Court, Aldeley Road, Wilmslow, Cheshire, England, SK9 1NT. Contact: Simon Stott, Dir. - Tel: (01625) 529 000, Fax: (01625) 527 000, E-Mail: simonstott@dial.pipex.com. Franchise operation providing landscape maintenance services on a yearly contract basis to commercial and domestic customers, supported by a strong corporate identity, direct mail, telesales, and advertising. Master licenses are available. Established: 1984 - Franchising Since: 1986 - No. of Units: Company Owned: 1- Franchised: 50 - Royalty: 8%, 2% mktg levy (based on total turnover) - Financing: Yes.

CRESTAR LEARNING CENTRE
39-9 The Boulevard, Mid-Valley City, Kuala Lumpur, Federal, 5 9200. Contact: Arthur NG, Regional General Manager - Tel: 603-22-878-323, Fax: 603-22-878-332, E-Mail: arthurng@crestar.com.ny. Pre-school education and child enrichment programs. Pre-school teacher training. Established: 1978 - No. of Units: Company Owned: 2 - Franchised: 20 - Franchise Fee: $20,000 US - Royalty: 8% on revenue - Total Inv: $45,000-$50,000US - Finanicng: Negotiable.

CRYSTAL GALLERIES LTD.
Rombalds, Rombalds Lane Benrhydding, Ilkley, Yorks, U.K. Contact: Dorothy Bailey, Dir. - Tel: 0943-600344. Personalized engraving process. Established: 1983 - No. of Units: 1 - Approx. Inv: £2,500 - Royalty: 5% - Financing: None.

CULLIGAN INTERNATIONAL COMPANY
Unit 3, Bleinheim Rd., Cressex Ind. Estate, High Wycombe, Bucks, England, HP12 3RD. Contact: R. W. Fitzwilliam, Sales Mgr. - Tel: 0494-36484. Service and operation of your own water treatment company. Established: 1936 - Franchising Since: 1937 - No. of Units: Company Owned: 30 - Franchised: Over 1,000 worldwide - Approx. Inv: £2,500.

DECORATING DEN (UK)
Decor Systems (SW) Ltd.
Bowditch Membury, Axminster, Devon, U.K., EX137TY. - Tel: 404 881789, Fax: 404 881786. Mobile interior decorating business. Established: UK 1989 - Franchising Since: 1970 USA - No. of Units: Company Owned: 3 - Franchised: 30 - Franchise Fee: £10,900-£13,900 - Royalty: 11%-7%, 2% adv. - Financing: Yes, UK Banks.

DENTALKIT SRL
I Neeozi Del Sorriso
Via Del Madonnone 19, Firenze, Italia, 50136. Contact: Vito Rescio, Director Franchising - Tel: (055) 669 - 081. Prodotti per la bellezza del sorriso. Established: 1986 - Franchising Since: 1987 - No. of Units: Company Owned: 1 - Franchise Fee: 36 - Royalty: SI - Total Inv: 150.000.000 lire - Financing: SI.

DIDACTICA (INTERNATIONAL) AG
Sagereistrasse 20, Glattbugg, Zurich, CH, 8152. Contact: H. Dunner, President - Tel: +41(0)1 822 02 44, Fax: +41(0)1 811 02 13. Language school with super learning. Established: 1984 - Franchising Since: 1986 - No. of Units: Company Owned: 6 - Franchised: 30 - Franchise Fee: CHF15,000 - Total Inv: CHF100,000 - Financing: CHF100,000-130,000.

DIFUSAO DE EDUCACAO E CULTURA S/A
Yazigi International
Av. 9 de Julho, 3166, Sao Paulo, Sao Paulo, Brazil, 01406-000. Contact: Claudia Bueno, Mgr., Fran. Dept. - Tel: (011) 884.9600. Yazigi is a large Brazilian language teaching instruction, which was the pioneer to organize a franchise system in Brazil (1963). Today Yazigi teaches languages to approximately 70,000 students yearly in its 170 franchised schools. Established:1950 - Franchising Since:1963 - No. of Units: Company Owned: 3 - Franchised:167 - Franchise Fee: $5,000 (US) - Total Inv: $40,000 (US) incl. fran. fee and installation of the school.

DIRECT ENGLISH
Pearson Education
Pearson Education, Edinburgh Gate, Harlow, Essex, UK, CM20 2JE. Contact: Charlotte Pritchard, Marketing Manager - Tel: (001) 44-1279-62 3898, Fax: (001) 44-1279-62 3350, E-Mail: charlotte.pritchard@personed.ema.com, Web Site: www.directe nglish.com. Self-study English language training. Established: 1724 - Franchising Since: 1997 - No. of Units: Company Owned: 8 - Franchised: 3 - Franchise Fee: $60,000 - Total Inv: $200,000-$250,000 - Financing: Some.

DOR-2-DOR
Zone Marketing (UK) Ltd.
Clare Lodge, 41 Holly Bush Lane, Harpenden, Herts., England, AL5 4AY. Contact: Fran. Dir. - Tel: 44 1582 460977, Fax: 44 1582 462727. Leaflet distribution to residential households. Comprehensive package includes manuals, sales support, free phone sales enquiry line, hotline telephone support and backup. Established:1987 - Franchising Since: 1995 - No. of Units: Company Owned: 1 - Franchised: 50 - Franchise Fee: None - Royalty: £55 per month or 5% of sales, whichever greater.

DUDS 'N SUDS
Duds 'n Suds UK Ltd.
141 Strand Rd., Derry, Northern Ireland, BT48 7RB. - Tel: 01504 262615. Duds 'n Suds laundromats feature, in addition to modern washers and dryers, a big screen TV, an attended snack bar, plenty of comfortable seating, games and more. Duds 'n Suds UK Ltd. is the franchisor of the Duds 'n Suds laundry system for the UK and Ireland. Established: 1991 - Franchising Since: 1992 - No. of Units: Company Owned: 1 - Franchised: 6 - Franchise Fee: £15,000 - Royalty: 5% franchise, 2% adv. - Total Inv: £95,000: £35,000 personal investment - Financing: Yes.

DUSKIN CO., LTD.
Sekaicho Building, 6-24 Nakatsu, 1-Chome Kita-ku, Osaka, 531 Japan. Contact: Eiichi Tominaga, Mgr. Int'l Div. - Tel: (06) 372-8771. Manufacturing, selling and renting of dust control and household products. Fast food and seafood chain. Established: 1963 - Franchising Since: 1963 - No. of Units: Company Owned: 136 - Franchised: 5,000 - Franchise Fee: Varies - Royalty: Varies.

DUTY DRIVER LTD.
42 Station Rd., Twyford, Berks, England, RG10 9N. - Tel: (0734) 320200. Executive agency for part and full time chauffeurs. Established: 1985 - Franchising Since: 1988 - No. of Units: Company Owned: 3 - Franchised: 5 - Royalty: 21% of turnover, marketing & factoring - Total Inv: £15,000: first 2 yrs. adv. & set up - Financing: Yes.

DYNO LOCKS
Dyno-Rod Developments Ltd.
143 Maple Rd., Surbiton, Surrey, England, KT6 4BJ. Contact: Graham Grant, Business Manager - Tel: 081-481 2200, Fax: 081-481 2288. Emergency door/lock opening service. Lock fitting and repair. Mobile service, 24 hours a day, 365 days a year. Established: 1986 - Franchising Since: 1988 - No. of Units: Franchised: 60 - Franchise Fee: £10,000 - Royalty: A.O.R. - Total Inv: £25,000 - Financing: Up to 70% can be financed.

ELMS, THE
Pynnacles Close, Stanmore, Middlesex, HA7 4AF. Contact: Mrs. Barbara Moss, Director - Tel: (0181) 954 8787, Fax: (0181) 954-4020, E-Mail: the.elms@virgin.net, Web Site: www.express-sport.com/homepages/ elms/index.html. Run soccer 5-A-side leagues foe men. Soccer schools for children. Established: 1992 - Franchising Since: 1996 - No. of Units: Company Owned: S-A-Side =34, Schools = 20 - Franchised: S.A. Side =12, Schools =7 - Franchise Fee: S-A-Side = £5,000 + VAT, ƒ4,700 + vat - Total Inv: £7,500 (S-A-Side), ƒ4,750 (Schools) - Financing: Royal bank of Scotland.

FISK SCHOOLS LIMITED
Av. Lins de Vasconcelos, 2594, Sao Paulo, S.P., Brazil, 04112-001. Contact: Bruno Caravati, V.P. - Tel: (55) 011 573 7000, Fax: (55) 11 549-2144. English course as a second language. Group and individual classes. English for all ages. Courses basic through advanced in three years maximum. 35 years of experience. Established: 1958 - Franchising Since: 1960 - No. of Units: Company Owned: 31 - Franchised: 450.

FITMAN, S.A
M.R.W.
Grau Via 163-167 Pol. Iud. Grau Via Sud, Hospitalet, Barcolous Spain, 08908. Contact: Ana Barahona, Director of Franchise - Tel: (34) 93 260 98 00, 900 300 400, Fax: (34) 93 260 9801, E-Mail: mrw@mrw.es, Web Site: www.mrw.es. Transport - courier. Established: 1977 - Franchising Since: 1985 - No. of Units: Franchised: 525 - Franchise Fee: Variable segou zous geogrcfica - Royalty: Porceutsye por uidad de veutc - Total Inv: 3 will. pts - Financing: No.

FLOWER BARROW COMPANY, THE
3 Orchard Crt., Heron Rd., Sowton, Exeter, Devon, U.K., EX2 7LL. Contact: Mrs. S. Taylor, Partner - Tel: (0392) 444788. Manufacturer of dried flower arrangements to sell through franchises. Established: 1985 - Franchising Since: 1990 - No. of Units: Company Owned: 7 - Franchised: 2 - Total Inv: £8,000: barrow & display-£2,000; Stock-£3,000; stationery-£500; set-up-£1,500; training course-£1,000 - Financing: National Westminster Bank, Lloyds Bank.

FORMATIVE FUN
Formative Fun Ltd.
The Old School, Gundry Lane, Bridport, Dorset, U.K., DT6 6JY. Contact: Jane Warren, Mng. Dir. - Tel: (44) 01297 489880, Fax: (44) 01297 489017. The sale of quality educational games, software toys and activity books in an advisory capacity to parents, schools and pre-school groups through a retail advice centre. Established: 1989 - Franchising Since: 1991 - No. of Units: Company Owned: 2 - Franchised: 8 - Franchise Fee: £10,000 - Royalty: 10%, 2% adv. - Total Inv: £10,000 fee + £20-40,000 capital - Financing: Yes.

GB BRICOCENTRE ET GARDEN CENTER
GB-Inno-BM S.A.
20 Ave. des Olympiades, 1140 Bruxelles, Brabant, Belgium. Contact: Mr. Willocq. Do-it-yourself garden. Established: 1973 - Franchising Since: 1978 - No. of Units: Company Owned: 57 - Franchised: 23 - Franchise Fee: 300,000 FB - Total Inv: 16,000,000 FB - Royalty: 6.6% du C.A. TVAC - Financing: 3,500,000 FB.

GIGANTAGRAM
Sunset House, 178B West Malvern Rd., Malvern, Worcs., U.K., WR14 4AZ. Contact: K. Buchmann, M.D. - Tel: (0684) 562661, Fax: (0684) 893271. A business from your own home producing banners, signs and gigantagrams. Established: 1985 - Franchising Since: 1986 - No. of Units: Company Owned: 1 - Franchised: 41 - Franchise Fee: £2,900 - Royalty: £50 per month - Total Inv: £4,950: Fee: £2,900+£2,050.

GOLD VAULT LTD., THE
26 Shetty Park Rd., Shetty Swansea, England. Contact: S. A. Ramsey-Williams, Dir. - Tel: 0792-469639. Dental suppliers. Established: 1985 - Franchising Since: 1986 - No. of Units: Company Owned: 1 - Franchised: 1 - Approx. Inv: £5,000 - Financing: Possible.

GREENALLS INN PARTNERSHIP
Greenalls Ave., P.O. Box #2, Warrington, Cheshire, U.K., WA46RH. Contact: Dennis Whiteley, Bus. Dev. Executive - Tel: 0925-51234. Public house retailing. Established: 1762 - No. of Units: Company Owned: 500 - Franchised: 750 - Royalty: 1% of turnover - Total Inv: £15,000-£20,000 - Financing: Yes.

HELEN O'GRADY CHILDREN'S DRAMA ACADEMY
Helen O'Grady International Pty. Ltd.
5/82 Reserve St., Wembley, Perth, W.A., Australia, 6014. Contact: Steve Griffiths, Mng. Dir. - Tel: (618) 93837800, Fax: (618) 93837810, Web Site: www.helenogrady.com.au. The Helen O'Grady Children's Drama Academy holds after school classes for children in over 600 locations throughout the U.K., Australia, New Zealand, South Africa, Canada, Malaysia and Singapore. Will now consider expressions of interest from suitable organizations for the master licence of U.S.A. and other countries. A unique program aimed at developing confidence, self-esteem and communication skills. Established: 1979 - Franchising Since: 1989 - No. of Units: Company Owned: 1 - Franchised: 75 - Franchise Fee: $35,000 - Royalty: 10% of gross fees - Total Inv: Fran. fee $35,000, set-up costs $5,000 - Financing: Yes.

HOUSE OF COLOUR LTD.
28 The Avenue, Watford, Herts., England, WD1 3NS. Contact: Fran. Dir. - Tel: 01923 211188. Colour analysts and image consultants. Established: 1986 - Franchising Since: 1986 - No. of Units: Company Owned: 1 - Franchised: 80 - Franchise Fee: £5,000 + V.A.T. - Total Inv: £7,500 + V.A.T.

HYDE-BARKER TRAVEL
Market St., Mansfield, Notts., England, NG18 1SR. Contact: M. A. Hyde-Barker, Mng. Dir. - Tel: 0623-31121. Travel agencies. Established: 1948 - Franchising Since: 1985 - No. of Units: 1 - Approx. Inv: £1,500 - Royalty: 1% plus 4% adv. - Financing: No.

IMAGINE TRANSFERS
Broomhills, Braintree, Essex, England, CM7 2RW. Contact: Elaine Janssen, Mng. Dir. - Tel: 01376-320354. Heat transfers and fusion presses for printing T-shirts. Established: 1993 - Franchising Since: 1993 - No. of Units: Company Owned: 7 - Franchised: 100+ - Franchise Fee: £5,000 - Total Inv: £5,000 - Financing: No.

INFOPOINT
Infopoint Ltd.
8 Kings Meadow, Ferry Hinksey Road, Oxford, England, OX9 7PP. Contact: Philip Flookm, M.D. Network of vending machines on outskirts of towns selling town centre maps. Established: 1985 - Franchising Since: 1987 - No. of Units: Company Owned: 10 - Franchised: 6 - Royalty: 2.5% - Total Inv: Min. £2,250 - Financing: Yes.

INTACAB LTD.
West Mayne, Basildon, Essex, England, SS15 6RW. Contact: Mel Lilley, Fran. Dir. - Tel: (0268) 415891. Taxi and private hire service based on the operating methods of the Yellow Cab Company of Chicago. Franchisee benefits from unique computer control and monitoring systems. Established: 1975 - Franchising Since: 1982 - No. of Units: Company Owned: 1 - Franchised: 10 - Franchise Fee: £6,000 - Total Inv: £40,000 min. - Royalty: 7.5% - Financing: 50%.

JARDILAND
Tripode
26 rue de la Maison Rouge Lognes, Marne La Vallee Cedex 2, 77323, France. Contact: Daniel Metivet, Pres. Dir. General - Tel: (1) 60.05.81.63. Telex: 691 169F. Garden centers. Established: 1973 - Franchising Since: 1982 - No. of Units: Company Owned: 76 - Franchised: 46 - Royalty: 1.60% - Total Inv: 5,000,000 FF.

JIM'S MOVING
Horwath Franchising Ltd.
25 New Street Square, London, EC4A 3LN. - Tel: (020) 7917 9824, Fax: (020) 7917 2839, E-Mail: franchising.uk@horwath.com, Web Site: www.jims.net. Largest lawn mowing and garden services. Established: 1982 - Franchising Since: 1989 - No. of Units: Franchised: 2,000 - Franchise Fee: ƒ50,000, including equipment and working capital.

JO JINGLES
Myrtle House, Street Village, NR. Amersham, Buds, HP7 0PX. - Tel: 014947 7 19360, Fax: 01494 7 19361, Web Site: www.jojingles.co.uk. Music class experience with the education slant. Use music and movement, singing, nursery rhymes to entertain and educate children 6 months - 7 years. Established: 1989 - No. of Units: Comnpany Owned: 1 - Franchised: 64 - Franchise Fee: £1,000 - Total Inv: £7,000.

JUST WILLS
Just Wills PLC
Kingsway House 123-125 Goldsworth Road, Woking, Surrey, GU21 1Lr. Contact: Justian de Frias, Chairman & Mng. Dir. - Tel: (01483)720 222, Fax: (01483) 720224. A home visit last will and testament business. A work from home white collar franchise opportunity with positive cash flow and no bad debts, staff or stock. Seven out of ten people die without writing a will giving a huge untapped market. Established: 1989 - Franchising Since: 1992 - No. of Units: Franchised: 137 - Franchise Fee: £15,000 - Royalty: £9.50 - Total Inv: £15,000 - Financing: No.

KANJUKA CO, LTD
Toshiba Osaka Bldg, 2 12 4 Chome Honmachi, Cyuoh-Ku, Osaka, Japan, 541-0053. Contact: Rikishi Katsumoto, Marketing Manager - Tel: (81) 6-6241-8123, Fax: (81) 6-6241-0125, E-Mail: info@mail.kan juku.co.jp, Web Site: www.kanjuku.co.jp. Educational institutions for

students (Juku). Established: 1974 - Franchising Since: 1976 - No. of Units: Company Owned: 2 - Franchised: 1012 - Franchise Fee: 6,000,000 yen (start-up) - Total Inv: 8,000,000 yen - Financing: Yes.

LASER SHOTS
Zone Lase Intl Corp.
Paraguay 515, 5P, Buenos Aires, Argentina, 1057. - Tel: 54 - 1-314-8080, Fax: 54-1-314-4770. We are the master frasnchisors for Latin America for Zone Laser Games, the most advanced Laser Games in the industry. Established: 1993 - Franchising Since: 1995 - No. of Units: Company Owned: 2 - Franchised: 10 - Franchise Fee: Depends on territory - Royalty: 10% - Total Inv: $100,000 US-$500,000 US.

LE CLUB FRANCAIS
Language Clubs (Int.) Ltd.
18/19 High St., Twyford, Hampshire, England, SO21 1RF. Contact: John Ellis, Dir. - Tel: (44) 962-714036. Fun language clubs for children between 3 & 11 years old. Courses available in French, Spanish & German. Established: 1988 - Franchising Since: 1990 - No. of Units: Franchised: 300 U.K. - Franchise Fee: $3,000 - Royalty: 10% - Total Inv: $3,000 - Financing: No.

LIFE TIME TROPHIES
Life Time Sporting Products & Services
397 Dorset Rd, Boronia, Australia. Contact: John Young, Mgr. Dir. Trophies and badges, direct importing, manufacturing plant (wood). Screen printing - Giftware - Plastics. Established: 1980 - Franchising Since: 1984 - No. of Units: Franchised: 12 - Franchise Fee: $20,000 - Royalty: 2.5% gross receipts - Total Inv: $50,000/display, machinery, etc. $30,000 + fran. fee - Financing: No.

M & B MARQUEES
M & B Marquees Ltd.
Premier House Tennyson Drive, Pitsea,Basildon, Essex, U.K., SS13 3BT. Contact: John D. Mansfield, Mng. Dir. - Tel: 01268-558002, Fax: (01268) 552783. Offer a marquee hire service plus a full range of accessories and supporting services. Distinctively designed marquees can be erected quickly on all surfaces. Franchisees are given full training and a defined area. Established: 1976 - Franchising Since: 1985- No. of Units: Company Owned: 1 - Franchised: 35 - Franchise Fee: Dependant on state/territory - Royalty: 9% of turnover + from year two 1% of nat'l adv. - Total Inv: From £50,000 - Financing: Available subject to status.

MASTERSHARP
P.A. Research Ltd.
28 Glen Rd., Boscombe, Bournemouth, Dorset, England, BH5 1H5. Contact: P. Addison, M.D. - Tel: 202-396002, Fax: 202-300111. Mobile tool renovation/sharpening/sales. Established: 1988 - Franchising Since: 1989 - No. of Units: Company Owned: 1 - Franchised: 25 - Franchise Fee: £4,000 - Royalty: £750 per year - Total Inv: £10,500 - Financing: Yes.

MED-PED S.A.
Plaza Med-Ped, Palma Nova, Mallorca, Spain. Contact: Cecil Brown, Fran. Dir. - Tel: (3471) 68 16 32. Moped and scooter rentals to tourists in sunny Mediterranean tourist resorts. Established: 1976 - Franchising Since: 1980 - No. of Units: Company Owned: 4 - Franchised: 6 - Franchise Fee: $12,000 US - Total Inv: $75,000 US - Royalty: 6% gross monthly sales - Financing: No.

MERCERIE PLUS
Mercatique et Distribution
58110 Brinay, Brinay, France. Contact: Michel Rady, Chairman - Tel: 86.84.91.00. Sew Product-Button; embroidery. Established: 1977 - Franchising Since: 1980 - No. of Units: Franchised: 46 - Franchise Fee: 20,000 FF - Total Inv: 300,000 FF.

METRO ROD SERVICES
Metro House, Churchill Way, Macclesfield, Cheshire, England, SK11 6AY. Contact: Alun Mowe, Academy Business Dev. Manager - Tel: (+44) 01625 434444, Fax: (+44) 01625 616687. Drain and pipe cleaning including, high pressure water jetting, cctv, electro mechanical and pipe lining. Established: 1983 - Franchising Since: 1983 - No. of Units: Company Owned: 3 - Franchised: 40 - Franchise Fee: ƒ22,500 - Royalty: 22.5% - Total Inv: ƒ60,000 - Financing: From major high street banks.

MEXICAN CONTACT, THE
R.I.A.M. International
Jupiter St., #41, Cot. Tecamachalco, Mexico City, D.F., Mexico, 53950. - Tel: Fax: 2-51-28-35. Mexican business directories, English/Spanish publications, literature and information about producers and manufacturers of products and services, from various regions of Mexico. Public and private sources. For retailers, distributors, importers and exporters. Representation and agents. Established: 1990 - Franchising Since: 1991 - Franchise Fee: US $350 - Total Inv: Variable - Financing: None.

MILLEBOLLE SRL
Via Speranza 3/A. San Lazzaro Di Savena, (BO), Italia, 40068. - Tel: (051)627-0612. Laundromat - self service brand "Onda Blu". Established: 1992 - Franchising Since: 1993 - No. of Units: Company Owned: 1 - Franchised: 42 - Franchise Fee:£5.000.000-£40.000.000 - Royalty: £500.000-£600.000 - Total Inv:£80.000.000-£200.000.000 - Financing: Yes.

MOBIL' AFFICHE INTERNATIONAL
18 Quai CDT Malbert, Brest-France, 29200. - Tel: (33) 2 98 46 67 50, Fax: (33) 2 98 46 38 12. Selective scrolling display system mounted on truck, bus or billboard. Our patented system allows advertising to move in the heart of town. Posters can be displayed on an original medium awarded silver medal at Geneva, International Inventions Exhibition '97. Established: 1993 - Franchising Since: 1994 - No. of Units: Company Owned: 1 - Franchised: 55 - Franchise Fee: AOR - Royalty: AOR - Total Inv: AOR - Financing: No.

MONSIEUR BRICOLAGE
A.N.P.E.
2 et 4 rue Pierre et Marie Curie, Ingre, France, 45 140. Magasin de bricolage et de decoration. Partnership. Established: 1965 - Franchising Since: 1980 - No. of Units: Company Owned: 1 - Franchised: 230.

MORTAR MASON WALL POINTING
Westleton, Saxmundham, Suffolk, England, 1P17 3BS. Contact: R.J. Hadfield, Director - Tel: (072) 873-608. The mechanical repointing of masonry walls, the mortar being injected into the joint through a nozzle from a ground level pumping unit. Established: 1989 - Franchising Since: 1991 - No. of Units: Company Owned: 1 - Franchised: 1 - Franchise Fee: £8,000 - Royalty: 7.5%, 2.5% adv. - Total Inv: Fran. fee plus equip. £6,000, work cap. £6,000, deposit on van £3,000.

MOSTYNS
Avon Works, Bridge St., Christchurch, Dorset, England, BH2 1DY. Contact: Fran. Dir. Custom-made soft furnishing concept. Developed over the last 40 yrs. All fabrics are exclusive, representing the latest styles at realistic prices. Established: 1950 - Franchising Since: 1965 - No. of Units: Company Owned: 120 - Franchised: 10 - Franchise Fee: £6,000 - Total Inv: Upwards from £20,000 (negotiable) - Financing: No.

MOY
Mexel-Moy
Av. 8 de Julio No. 3030, Lomas de Polanco, Guadalajaro, Jalisco, Mexico, 44960. Contact: Elias Liberas, V.P. Franchise Development - Tel: (523) 663-77-77, Fax: (523) 663-80-62. Family entertainment centers equipped with electronic games. Established: 1989 - Franchising Since: 1991 - No. of Units: Company Owned: 14 - Franchised: 85 - Franchise Fee: N/A - Royalty: N/A - Total Inv: Set up cost is $300,000 LE.

MR. LIFT LTD.
The Lifthouse, Gloucester Rd., Almondsbury, Bristol, Avon, U.K., BS12 4HY. Contact: Rupert Crook, Fran. Dev. Mgr. - Tel: (0454) 618181. Sales, hire and service of new and used fork lift trucks from a modern industrial unit on an industrial estate. Established: 1975 - Franchising Since: 1985 - No. of Units: Company Owned: 3 - Franchised: 3 - Franchise Fee: £7,500 - Total Inv: £75,000 - Royalty: 5% mng. serv. fee, 2.5% adv. - Financing: Up to 2/3 from major UK clearing banks.

NATURAL WAY, THE
The Natural Way Franchising
Dartmouth House. Westlands, Newcastle Under Lyme, Staforrshire, England, ST5 3PA. Contact: Mr. P, Bell-Langford, Director - Tel: (01782) 711122/766766, Fax: (01782) 719019.Individual weight loss

company providing a personal and confidential service based on a one to one consultancy. No drugs involved. All natural foods. Established: 1987 - Franchising Since: 1993 - No. of Units: Company Owned: 22 - Franchised: 32 outlets - Franchise Fee: Nil (free franchise) - Royalty: No royalty - Total Inv: Working capital £.

NIIT LTD
8 Balaji Estae Sudershan Munjal Marg, Kalkaji, New Delhi, India, 110019. Contact: Pradeep Narayanan, General Manager - Tel: (91) 11-6203-238, Fax: (91) 11-6203-299, E-Mail: pna@niitdel.niit.co.in, Web Site: www.niit.com. Education and training in technology, sales and marketing management. Established: 1982 - Franchising Since: 1987 - No. of Units: Company Owned: 70 - Franchised: 450 - Franchise Fee: $300,000-$350,000 - Total Inv: $300,000-$350,000.

NISBETS CHEFSHOP
Nisbets
Kelso House, Waterloo St., Old Market, Bristol, Avon, England, BS2 0PH. Contact: Andrew Nisbet, Mng. Dir. - Tel: (0272) 555843. Supplies equipment, utensils and clothing to college students about to embark on training to be chefs, at the catering colleges around the country, through mobile showrooms. Established: 1983 - Franchising Since: 1993 - No. of Units: Company Owned: 4 - Franchised: 4 - Franchise Fee: £5,500 - Royalty: 10% - Total Inv: £9,870 - Financing: Up to two thirds from High St. banks.

ONSITE TRAINING
Grove House, Great North Rd., Little Paxton, Cambs., U.K., PE19 4EL. Contact: Margaret James, Admin. Mgr. - Computer training. Established: 1985 - Franchising Since: 1989 - No. of Units: Company Owned: 1 - Franchised: 6 - Franchise Fee: £12,000 at present - Royalty: 12.5% - Total Inv: Approx. £25,000 - Financing: Banking approval.

OSCAR PET FOODS
Bannister Mall Mill Mighar Waston, Preston, Lanes, UK, PR5 4DB. Contact: Mgr. Director/ Franchise Mgr. - Tel: (44) 01 772- 62 8822, Fax: (44) 01 772 628528. Mobile home delivery of pet food coupled with pet care service. Direct from Oscar factory to the franchisee. Established: 1990 - Franchising Since: 1993 - No. of Units: Franchised: 110 - Franchise Fee: £5000 - Royalty: 6% - Total Inv: From £5,000-£20,000 - Financing: From all major banks at 70%.

PALS4PETS
2 Croft Close London, NW7 4QL. - Tel: (020) 8201 1606, Web Site: www.pal4pets.com. If you love aniamls and love interagtinbg with people then give us a call. Franchise Fee: £7,000+ Vat.

PANIC LINK P/C
Control Sortation Centre, Melbourne Rd., Lount, Leics., U.K., LE6 5RS. Contact: Heather Wilkinson, Nat. Fran. Mgr. - Tel: 0530 411111. Nationwide parcel delivery and collection service, on a franchised basis. Established: 1987 - Franchising Since: 1988 - No. of Units: Franchised: 95 - Franchise Fee: $10,000 - $20,000 - Royalty: Ongoing fees directly linked to turnover of franchise - Total Inv: Franchise fee, working capital of $5,000-$10,000 - Financing: Through major clearing banks.

PIRTEK
Pirtek (UK) Ltd.
35 Acton Park Estate, The Vale Acton, London, W3, England. Contact: Forbes Petrie, M.D. - Tel: (081) 749-8444. Hydraulic hose supply and replacement via depots and mobile workshops. A 24 hr, 7 days a week service. Established: 1988 - Franchising Since: 1989 - No. of Units: Franchised: 59 - Franchise Fee: £12,500 - Total Inv: £160,000: £70,000 cash, £90,000 financed - Financing: Through main banks.

PIRTEK FLUID SYSTEMS, PTY. LTD.
1/163 Prospect Hwy., Sydney, N.S.W., Australia, 2147. - Tel: (02) 838 7888. Established:1980 - Franchising Since: 1985 - No. of Units: Company Owned: 2 - Franchised: 48 - Franchise Fee: $20,000 - Royalty: 1.5% mgmt., .75% adv. - Total Inv: $260,000-$800,000 - Financing: No.

PIXI DESIGNS
Pixi Designs Wedding Stationery
Brinkwater House Dyke Road, Galway City, Ireland. Contact: Mary or David - Tel: 00 353 86 8346428, Fax: 00 353 86 58346428, E-Mail: pixi.designs@ireland.com, Web Site: www.artpixi.com. Pixi Designs wedding stationery can be your home based business producing quality

product from our designs, to our method/formula, utilizing our website, etc. Get the designs, the know how and the legal right to use our images, by signing up for this franchise today. Established: 2000 - Franchising Since: 2002 - No. of Units: Company Owned: 1 - Franchise Fee: $6,500 - Total Inv: $12,000.

PREMAMAN
Premaman SA
Chaussee de Haecht 1475, Brussels, 1130.Contact: Pierre Dooms, Export Director - Tel: +32-2-240-66-00, Fax: +32-2-248-18-29, E-Mail: secrexport@premaman.be, Web Site: www.premaman.com. Clothing and accessories for babies, junior and mother-to-be. Established: 1953 - No. of Units: Company Owned: 65 - Franchised: 211 - Franchise Fee: $20,000 - Royalty: Outside Europe: None - Total Inv: $100,000 - Financing: 50%.

PRETTY RENOVATION CENTER
Zunftweg 6-8, Burgdorf, FRG, D-31303. Contact: General Manager - Tel: (0049) 5085 224, Fax: (0049) 5085 226. Renovation of all kinds of doors and door frames, kitchens and all other kinds of furniture and stairs. Special systems for all surfaces. Established: 1966 - Franchising Since: 1966 - No. of Units: Company Owned: 1 - Franchised: 220 - Franchise Fee: Starting at DM 9.500 -, depending on system - Royalty: 3% - Total Inv: Starting at DM 24.000, depending on system. Financing: Up to 50% of total investment.

PROFIKIDS COMPUTERSCHULE FUER KINDER
Karlstroße 1/ Unter den Linden, Reutlingen. 72764. Contact: Dr. Ulrich Kramer, Man. Dir. - Tel: (49) 7121-3844-0, Fax: (49) 7121-3844-45, E-Mail:profikids@aol.com, Web Site: www.profikids.com. Computer school for children, students, adults and business. Established: 1994 - Franchising Since: 1995 - No. of Units: Company Owned: 1 - Franchised: 27 - Franchise Fee: DM 25,000 - Royalty: 8% - Total Inv: Approx. DM 70-100,000 - Financing: Bank.

RAPEL RADIO ALARM SYSTEMS (ADMAX) LTD.
39 Church St., Weybridge, Surrey, England, KT13 8DG. Contact: M.A. Webb, Mng. Dir. - Tel: 0932-56526. Radio alarm systems that are flexible, reliable, cost effective and easy to install. Established: 1979 - Franchising Since: 1980 - No. of Units: Company Owned: 1 - Franchised: 12 - Approx. Inv: £160,000.

RECOGNITION EXPRESS
Recognition Express Ltd.
P.O. Box 7, Rugby Rd., Hinckley, Leicestershire, England, LE10 2NE. - Tel: 01455 238133. Manufacture and sale of personalized lapel badges, interior and exterior signs and vehicle livery, on a business to business basis. Established: 1979 - Franchising Since: 1980 - No. of Units: Company Owned: 1 - Franchised: 26 - Franchise Fee: £8,000 - Royalty: 10% of gross mthly. sales - Total Inv: £35,000 (£22,000 equip.) - Financing: Royal Bank of Scotland 70% & leasing (equip.).

REFACE-A-DOOR
Hilmar House, 5 Girton St., Manchester, England, M7 9UR. - Tel: (061) 839-1189. Kitchen and bedroom door panels made to measure to fit and reface existing doors. Rigid panels including wood finishes. Established: 1989 - Franchising Since: 1989 - No. of Units: Franchised: 20 - Franchise Fee: £2,950 - Financing: Yes.

REMAX
Remax Espana
C/ Estudio 29, Madrid, Madrid, 28023. Contact: Terry Gibbons, Director Franchise Sales - Tel: (91) 357-1244, Fax: (91) 357-1329, Web Site: www.Remax.com. International franchisor of real estate offices, offering management training and sales training. (residential and commercial). Established: 1973 - Franchising Since: 1994 - No. of Units: Franchised 3,000 US, Spain 75 - Franchise Fee: 3,000,000 pts, approx $20,000. US - Royalty: 6% + 2% publicity fund - Total Inv: 3+3 (approx) pts $20,000- franchise $10,000-$20,000 start up - Financing: Yes.

ROMAN SPA HYDROMASSAGE
Roman Spa Health & Leisure Products Ltd.
3 Britannia Blgd., Merchant Rd. Hotwells, Bristol, Avon, England, BS8 4QD. Contact: M.J. Fedeczvo, Chairman/Dir. - Tel: (0272) 250120. Direct sales of a unique portable hydromassage system complete with accessories and herbal bath additives. Established: 1986 - Franchising

Since: 1988 - No. of Units: Company Owned: 2 - Franchised: 6 - Franchise Fee: £6,500 - Total Inv: £14,500 + V.A.T. - Financing: Up to 100% depending on status.

S.A. HEYTENS DECOR
Avenue Lavoisier 9, Wavre, Belgium, B7300. Contact: Mr. Y. Neyrinck, Expansion Manager - Tel: (321) 70-235-777, Fax: (321)70-24-23-96. Home decorating, wallpaper, furnishing, fabrics, paints, vinyl floor coverings, fitted carpets, carpets and linen. Established: 1975 - No. of Units: Company Owned: 65.

SCENIC BLUE
The Plant Centre
Brogdale Road, Faversham, Kent, ME13 8X2. - Tel: 01795 533 266, Fax: 01795 591 059, Web Site: www.scenicblue.co.uk. We offer two unique franchise opportunities in landscape garden construction and turf sales. Established: 1992 - Franchising Since: 2000 - No. of Units: Franchised: 30 - Franchise Fee: £15,000+ vat - Total Inv: £20,000+ Vat.

SECURITAL
Group 4 Securital
Farncombe House, Broadway, Worcs., England, WR12 7RJ. - Tel: (0684) 295250. Residential and small business premises alarm market. Established: 1982 - Franchising Since: 1982 - No. of Units: Company Owned: 1 - Franchised: 13 - Approx. Inv: £6,500+l - Royalty: 6% - Financing: Partial.

SELECTAMARK SECURITY SYSTEMS PLC
1 Locks Court, 429 Crofton Rd., Locksbottom, Kent, England, BR6 8NL. - Tel: (44) 01689-860757, Fax: (44) 01689-860693, E-Mail: sales@selectamark.demon.co.uk, Web Site: www.selectamark.co.uk. Permanent, visual security marketing, world distributors of electric transponder identification bank alarm systems. Established: 1985 - Distributing Since: 1996 - No. of Units: Company Owned: 2 - Franchised: 23 - Franchise Fee: US $10,000 - Royalty: 2.5 localised advertising; 1.5 international advertising - Total Inv: US $10,000 - Financing: Yes, 50% deposit, balance over 3 years at 4% interest.

SIGN EXPRESS
Techsign Franchising Participacoes Ltda.
Calcada Das Rosas 43, Barveri, Sao Paulo, Brazil, 06453-000. Contact: Luiz Zaidan, V.P. - Tel: (55 11)7295-8070, Fax: (55 11) 729-8070, E-Mail: signexpress@world.com.br, Web site:www.signexpress.com.br. Sign makers franchise (master franchisee for Brazil). Established: 1991 - Franchising Since: 1992 - No. of Units: Company Owned: 1 - Franchised: 22 - Franchise Fee: $20,000 - Royalty: 5% - Total Inv: $100,000 - Financing: No.

SKILL ALIANCA INGLESA
Skill Alianca Inglesa S/C Ltda.
Av. Indianopolis, 3356, Sao Paulo, SP, Brazil, 04062-003. - Tel: 011 581-09-22. English as a foreign language franchise schools. Established: 1973 - Franchising Since: 1985 - No. of Units: Company Owned: 3 - Franchised: 146 - Franchise Fee: US $3,500 (minor cities) and US $6,500 (major cities) - Royalty: None - Total Inv: US $20,000 - Financing: No.

SOLMANIA
Sonnen-Land, S.A.
Valencia, 384 Pral, Barcelona, Spain, 08013. Contact: Felix Rabassa, Franchise Director - Tel: (34) 3 4577979, Fax: (34) 3 2073303, E-Mail: sonnen-land ncsa.es. Manning centers. Established: 1972 - Franchising Since: 1996 - No. of Units: Company Owned: 9 - Franchised: 25 - Franchise Fee: 1,000.000 - pias ($6.700) - Royalty: 5% - Total Inv: 30,000,000 pias ($200,000) - Financing: Yes.

SOMERFORD CLAIMS PLC.
Somerford Hall, Somerford, Stafford, England, ST19 9DQ. Contact: Bernard Sullman, Fran. Dir. - Tel: 0902 850721. Uninsured loss recovery. Loss of earnings for the taxi industry when a taxi is involved in a non-fault accident. Established: 1987 - Franchising Since: 1989 - No. of Units: Company Owned: 1 - Franchised: 23 - Franchise Fee: £7,500 - Royalty: Percentage of total L.O.E. - Total Inv: Computer equip. £3,000 - Financing: Depending on area.

SOVEREIGN SERVICES
39 Osborne Rd., Eastbourne, E, Sussex, England. - Tel: 0293-547932. Private ambulance service. Established: 1978 - Franchising Since: 1982 - No. of Units: 13 - Approx. Inv: £12,500 - Royalty: 10%, £1,200 adv. - Financing: Bank facility.

SPACEAGE PLASTICS
Spaceage Plastics Ltd.
Spaceage House, 85 Ringwood Rd., Parkstone, Poole, Dorset, England, BH14 0RH. - Tel: 0202-732053. Distributors of rigid and foam plastic building profiles, solid and structured polycarbonate sheets, glazing bars, aerated pvc sheet, rigid pvc sheet, thermoformed pvc door panels. Established: 1982 - Franchising Since: 1990 - No. of Units: Company Owned: 4 - Franchised: 1 - Franchise Fee: £6,000 - Royalty: 5% sales, 1% adv. - Total Inv: £50,000 stock above £6,000 - Financing: Barclays Bank, Plc.

SPICE - THE ADVENTURE GROUP
Spice UK Ltd.
18 Henrietta St., Old Trafford, Manchester, England, M16 9GA. - Tel: 061 872 2213. Adventure sports and social group members pay an annual subscription for monthly newsletter packed full of events, local, national and international. Consultancy available for independent operators. Established: 1980 - Franchising Since: 1986 - No. of Units: Company Owned: 1 - Franchised: 9 - Franchise Fee: £10,000 - Financing: Yes.

SPORTSMANIA
6 Acorn Way, Oak Tree Business Park, Mansfield, NG18 3HD. Contact: Fran. Dir. - Tel: 01623 428197. Discount branded sportswear and footware. We only trade Saturday and Sundays, all prices excluding VAT. Established: 1995 - Franchising Since: 1997 - No. of Units: Company Owned: 4 - Franchised: 3 - Franchise Fee: £10,000 - Royalty: 5% on sales - Total Inv: £20,000 fixtures and fittings/£100 stock/ $40,000 cash reserve - Financing: £50,000 cash, £120,000 can be financed.

STAGECOACH THEATRE ARTS
The Courthouse, Elm Grove, Walton-On-Thames, Surrey, UK, KT12 1LH. Contact: Gary Wolff, Fran. Mgr. - Tel: (44) 01932254 333, Toll Free: 0321 878243 UK only, Fax: (44) 01932222 894, E-Mail: stagecoach@dial.pipex.com, Web Site: www.stagecoach.co.uk. Part-time theatre schools for children ages 6 -16. They receive 1 hour of dance, drama and singing once a week. Established: 1988 - Franchising Since: 1994 - No. of Units: Company Owned: 32 - Franchised: 174 - Franchise Fee: £9,500 - Royalty: 12.5%, 2.5 P.R.fees - Total Inv: £14,000 - Financing: Yes.

STONEASE PAVING PATTERN IMPRINTED CONCRETE LTD.
71 Chapel Rd., Tiptree, Nr. Colchester, Essex, England, 105 ORD. - Tel: (0621) 816083. Concerned with selling and maintaining franchises in pattern imprinted concrete. Established: 1988 - Franchising Since: 1988 - No. of Units: Company Owned: 1 - Franchised: 10 - Franchise Fee: £9,000 + VAT - Royalty: £1 per sq. meter concrete layed - Financing: Have loan companies interested in assisting.

SYMPATHY
Franchise Brokers Espana S.l.
P. Victor Vines, 11, Alicante, Spain, 03016. Contact: Florentino Heras, Manager - Tel: (96) 592.96.20, Fax: (96) 512.20.14, E-Mail: info@sympathy.es, Web Site: www.sympathy.es. Introduction services franchise offering a large array of services. Winner of The Best Business Concept prize. Established: 1990 - Franchising Since: 1993 - No. of Units: Company Owned: 3 - Franchised: 25 - Franchise Fee: $10.000 - Royalty: $300.00 month - Total Inv: $20,000 - Financing : Yes.

THE ANIMAL SITTER *
The Animal Sitter
3 Heol Barru Energlyn Caerphilly, CF832LX. Contact: Alyson Hayes - Tel: 02920865551, E-Mail: theanimalsitter@aol.com, Web Site: www.theanimalsitter.co.uk. The practical alternative to kennels and catteries. Pet sitting/dog walking and pet transportation. Franchise Fee: $6,780 - Royalty: 7% - Total Inv: $6,780 - Financing: No.

THE GLOBAL TRAVEL GROUP
Glendale House, Glendale Business Park, Sandycroft, Nr chester, CH5 2DL. - Tel: 0870 7365736, Fax: 0870 7353736, E-Mail: enquiries@globaltravelgroup.com, Web Site: www.globaltravelgroup.com. Global offers you the chance to start your very own fully bonded travel business from home, office or retail base. Established: 1992 - Investment Required: £16,000 + VAT.

THE LITTLE SKOOL-HOUSE
The Little Skool-House International Pte Ltd
Blk 70 Geylang Bahru #02-2719, Singapore, 330070. Contact: Ms Jessica Wang - Tel: (65) 6391 9244, Fax: (65) 6293 3460, E-Mail: info@littleskoolhouse.com, Web Site: www.littleskoolhouse.com. The Little Skool-House is a premium preschool provider which offers a comprehensive franchise package and professional expertise to assist local and regional partners to embark on a challenging and rewarding business in quality early childhood care and education. Established: 1994 - Franchising Since: 1994 - No. of Units: Company Owned: 2 - Franchised: 4 - Franchsie Fee: $60,000 - Royalty: 5% - Total Inv: $200,000-$300,000.

THE PERCY INSTITUTE OF INTERNATIONAL PROTOCOL
LST Protocol International Pte Ltd
30 Raffles Place, #23-00 Caltex House, 048622. Contact: Ms Shee Suh Yng - Tel: (65) 6233 6832, Fax: (65) 6233 6857, E-Mail: percetiq@percyinstitute.com, Web Site: www.thepercyinstitute.com. We are an etiquette and protocol consultancy working with multinationals, schools, organizations and individuals to develop the interpersonal skills critical to success. Established: 1992 - Franchising Since: 2002 - No. of Units: Company Owned: 1 - Franchised: 0 - Franchise Fee: Contact for details.

TIGHTS MACHINE, THE
Tight Fit Ltd.
P.O. Box 48, Bury St. Edmunds, Suffolk, England, IP286PQ. Contact: T.D. Elliot, Dir. - Tel: (0044) 0 1284811737, Fax: (0044) 0 1284811737, E-Mail: tightfit@dial.pipex.com. Vending machines for the sale of hosiery, hygiene products, breath freshners etc and the stock to go in them. Established: 1988 - Franchising Since: 1989 - No. of Units: Company Owned: 1 - Franchised: 12 - Total Inv: From £1,000 for machines and stock.

TINTORERIAS RAPIDAS PRESSTO
Cor Sec S.L.
C/Fuencarrai 123, 5, Madrid, Spain, 28010. - Tel: (34) 1 448 58 61, Fax: (34) 1 593 05 95. One hour dry clean with top quality. Established: 1994 - Franchising Since: 1995 - No. of Units: Company Owned: 22 - Franchised: 110 - Franchise Fee: US $10,500 - Royalty: US$210/Month - Total Inv: US $120,000.

TIOLI CALLIGRAPHICS LTD.
2 Royal Bldg., The Parade, Liskeard, Cornwall, England, PL14 6AF. - Tel: 0579-44029. Custom glass engraving while-you-wait. Established: 1981 - Franchising Since: 1985 - No. of Units: Company Owned: 5 - Franchised: 1 - Approx. Inv: £10,000 minimum - Royalty: 10% - Financing: No.

TOTALINE
Springer Carrier S/A
Av. Indianópolis 2840, Sao Paulo, SP, 04062-003. Contact: Franchise Department - Tel: (011) 55 85 21 99, Fax: (011) 50 71 01 43. Sale of equipment and parts for air conditioning and refrigeration. Established: 1993 - Franchising Since: 1996 - No. of Units: Company Owned: 7 - Franchised: 4 - Franchise Fee: $15,000 - Royalty: 4% - Total Inv: $250,000 - Financing: No.

TRAVEL BAZAAR, THE
Dooley Travel Group PLC
221 Westbourne Park Rd., London, U.K, W11 1EA. Contact: Riaz Dooley, Mng. Dir. - Tel: (071) 221-6095/1729, Fax: 229-3595. Air ticket brokers/seat sale specialist on discounted air fares worldwide. Package holidays/special interest tours/conferences. Hotel booking agents/theater and sporting events bookings. Established: 1979 - Franchising Since: 1981 - No. of Units: Company Owned: 5 - Franchised: 59 - Franchise Fee: £1500 - Royalty: None, once training provided, with

all the knowhow and contacts, they are fully responsible to run their business - Total Inv: £2000-£6000 - Financing: Yes, secured against assets and personal guarantees.

TROPHY UK
Riverside House, St. Simon St., Salford, Manchester, England, M3 7ET. - Tel: 01144 61 839 5737. Mobile pet food franchise. Professional door-to-door pet food service throughout the UK with an enormous market. Trophy offers its customers a variety of tinned dog and cat food, complete food in a variety of protein levels, brawn, biscuits. Established: 1992 - Franchising Since: 1992 - No. of Units: Franchised: 300+ - Franchise Fee: £6,995 plus VAT - Royalty: £25 per week plus VAT first year, £15 per week plus VAT thereafter - Financing: Advice and assistance available to home-owners.

TUMBLE TOTS
Tumble Tots (UK) Ltd.
Blue Bird Park, Bromsgrove Rd., Hunnington, Halesowen, West Midlands, B62 0TT. Contact: UK FranchiseSales Manager - Tel: (0121) 585-7003, Fax: (0121) 585-6891, E-Mail: tumbletots_uk@btinternet.com, Web Site: www.tumbletots.com. Active physical play program for children from 6 months, which helps to develop their physical and social skills. There are 5 different age groups and children attend a weekly 45 - minute session. Franchises operate a mobile business within a geographical area. Established: 1979 - Franchising Since: 1984 - No. of Units: Company Owned: 1 - Franchised: 85 - Franchise Fee: £3,600-£5,800 (the license fee for 2 years) - Royalty: N/A, an annual license fee is charged - Total Inv: £13,000-£15,500 (excludes working capital and vehical) - Financing: From major high street banks who are familiar with Tumble Tots Operations.

UTICOLOR
Uticolor (Great Britain) Ltd.
30-32 Chase Rd., London, England, NW10 6QN. - Tel: 081 965 6869. Leather and vinyl repair, reconditioning and renovation service. Established: 1974 - Franchising Since: 1977 - No. of Units: Company Owned: 1 - Franchised: 24 - Franchise Fee: £10,000-£12,000 - Royalty: 10%-7% - Total Inv: £10,000-£12,000 - Financing: Yes.

VAL-U-PAK
Zone Marketing (UK) Ltd.
Clarke Lodge, 41 Holly Bush Lane, Harpenden, Herts., England, AL5 4AY. Contact: Jeff Frankling, Fran. Dir. - Tel: 44 1582 460977, Fax: 44 1582 462727. Packs of discount vouchers promoting local shops and businesses distributed to local residential households. Established: 1987 - Franchising Since: 1989 - No. of Units: Company Owned: 1 - Franchised: 4 - Royalty: £55 per month or 5% of sales, whichever greater - Financing: Package now being relaunched with no up front franchise fee.

VERLAG DEUTSCHER STADTPLANE GMBH
Gustener Straße 1818, Titz -Ameln, Germany, 52445. Contact: Mr. Karl-Heinz Rolka, Mgr. - Tel: 0 2463-6772, Fax: 0 2463-6777. Distribution of maps and guides in over 400 cities worldwide. Special editions for various targeted groups, guest guides, guides for building and construction, guides for cultural events, automobile guides and cartographic present items. Established: 1973 - Franchising Since: 1975 - No. of Units: Company Owned: 12 - Franchised: 172 - Franchise Fee: DM 50.000.00-120.000.00 - Royalty: 3% - Total Inv: DM 60.000.000 - DM 140.000.00 - Financing: Eventually.

VIDEO VAN
Video Van Franchising
Office Ste. 4, Saunderton Carriage Site, Wycombe Rd., Saunderton, Buckinghamshire, UK, HP14 4HX. Contact: Doug Greaves, Partner - Tel: 01494 562468. Door to door video film delivery service to a regular customer base. Established: 1985 - Franchising Since: 1991 - No. of Units: Company Owned: 2 - Franchised: 18 - Franchise Fee: £4,995 - Total Inv: £4,995 - Financing: No.

WALL STREET INSTITUTE DE MEXICO
Ibsen 43 8th, Mexico, D.F., 11550. Contact: Development Manager - Tel: (525) 280 - 1225 or 281 - 3940, Fax: (525) 281-3747, E-Mail: 12bieg2@andromed2.tectel.com.mx. W.S.I. is the english school with the most technologically advanced system of learning that makes one of a kind. The number of centers have grown to more than 220 in the

international market. Established: 1995 - Franchising Since: 1996 - No. of Units: Company Owned: 1 - Franchised: 12 - Franchise Fee: $50,000 US - Royalty: 7% - Total Inv: $160,000 US - Financing: Yes.

WASTE WHACKER LTD.
Holbrook, Ipswich, Suffolk, England, IP9 1PT. - Tel: 0473-328272. Design, production and marketing of waste disposal equipment. Established: 1982 - Franchising Since: 1982 - No. of Units: Company Owned: 1 - Franchised: 5 - Approx. Inv: £670 min.

HEALTH AND BEAUTY AIDS AND SERVICES

'2FT ORTHOTICS'
'2ft Orthotics Int'l Pte Ltd'
15-02 Far East Shopping Ctr. 545 Orchard Rd., Singapore, 238882. Contact: Craig Wight - Tel: (65) 6735-6547, Fax: (65) 6737-9501, E-Mail: Admin@2ft.com, Web Site: www.2ft.com/franchise.htm. Provider of solutions for adults and children with common foot related problems. Main service/product is custom fitted 'arch supports' or 'orthotics' that are designed to correct 10 common foot problems. Complete marketing, management, operations formula; all training provided, medical background not required; computerized foot analysis equipment; mobile orthotic lab to increase sales & awareness; all cash, high returns, financial freedom, almost no competition. Established: 1976 - Franchising Since: 1996 - No. of Units: Company Owned: 2 - Franchised: 2 - Total Inv: USD $95,000.00.

APOTIK MEDICINE SHOPPE
Pharma Care Medicine Shoppe
JL. Gading Kirana Timur, Blok A 13/33, Jakarta, Indonesia, 14240. Contact: Karimah Muhammad, Operations Manager - Tel: (021)451 6169, Fax: (021) 451 5281. Medicine Shoppe franchise - providing management and technical support for licensees in retail medicine shoppe pharmacies in Indonesia. Established: 1995 - Franchising Since: 1996 - No. of Units: Franchised: 3 - Franchise Fee: $10,000 US Royalty: 5% (Gross Sales) - Total Inv: $540,000 US - Financing: No.

ASSOCIATION FOR APPLIED HYPNOSIS, THE
33 Abbey Park Rd., Grimsby, South Humbs., England, DN32 0HS. Contact: Franchise Director. Persons with acceptable medical-psychology qualifications trained to use specially developed, complimentary natural therapy techniques for the purpose of relieving and resolving a variety of stress related psychosomatic, psychoneurotic, habit and other problems. Supervised Practices. Established: 1980 - Franchise Fee: $6,000 (includes training and subsequent supervision) - Royalty: $1,500 p.a. (includes membership fees) - Total Inv: Normal office costs; travelling and accommodation costs extra.

BEKA COIFFEUR'S
Beka International
Rua Oscar Freire 565, Sao Paulo, SP, Brazil, 01426-001. Contact: Metairon, Dir. - Tel: (011) 881-0355. Hair's beauty cosmetic franchise hairdressers, make up, esthetic. Established: 1967 - Franchising Since: 1991 - No. of Units: Company Owned: 1 - Franchised: 4 - Franchise Fee: US$5,000 - Royalty: 5% F.B. - Total Inv: US$120,000 - Financing: 50%.

BODY & FACE PLACE, THE
12 Glenthrone Mews, 115 Glenthrone Rd., London, England, W6 0LJ. Contact: Don Kennedy/ Tim MacAndrews, Directors. Natural beauty retailers and manufacturers. Established: 1986 - Franchising Since: 1986 - No. of Units: 5 - Franchised: 71 - Franchise Fee: Approx £70,000 - Royalty: 4% mgmt. fee - Financing: Bank loan.

BODY REFORM, UK LTD
46 Vale Business Park, Cowbridge Wales, U.K., CF71 7PF. Contact: D. Bushell, Mktg. Dir. - Tel: 01446-771483, Fax: 01446-771385, E-Mail: sales@body-reform.com.uk. Natural cruelty free toiletries and cosmetics manufactured at above address marketed through corporate style detail outlets - Body Reform Shops. Master licenses available internationally. Established: 1985 - Franchising Since: 1990 - No. of Units: Company Owned: 3 - Franchised: 60 - Total Inv: £40,000-£100,000 sterling.

BODY SHOP, THE
Body Shop International, Plc.,
Watersmead Bus. Park, Littlehampton, W. Sussex, England, BN17 6L7. Contact: Peter Tyson, Gen. Mgr., New Markets - Tel: 44 1243 731 500. Retailing of skin and hair care products and colour cosmetics with a philosophy that is committed to environmental change. Established: 1976 - Franchising Since: 1977 - No. of Units: Company Owned: 216 - Franchised: 1040 - Franchise Fee: Varies - Royalty: Varies - Total Inv: Varies - Financing: Varies.

COMMUNITY CARELINE SERVICES
Community Careline Services Ltd.
2nd floor, Sandringham House, Christopher St., Salford, England, M5 4PT. - Tel: 0161 877 4477, Fax: 0161 877 6700. Home support services for the elderly and those with disabilities. A service established as an alternative to residential care. Established: 1990 - Franchising Since: 1993 - No. of Units: Company Owned: 2 - Franchised: 240 - Franchise Fee: £20,000 + VAT - Royalty: 6% turnover - Total Inv: £35,000 + VAT £20,000 f.f., £15,000 working cap. - Financing: Partial.

CROWN OPTICAL CENTRE
Crown Eyeglass Plc.
Blakewater Rd., Glenfield Park, Blackburn, England, BB1 5QH. Contact: Ms. D. Singer, Fran. Dir. - Tel: 0254 51535. Manufacturers, distributors and retailers via franchised outlets of prescription glasses and ready made reading glasses. Established: 1984 - Franchising Since: 1984 - No. of Units: Company Owned: 4 - Franchised: 54 - Franchise Fee: £40,000 - Royalty: Nil - Total Inv: £40,000 - Financing: By arrangement.

DOLLOND & AITCHISON
Dollond & Aitchison Group, Plc.
1323 Coventry Rd., Yardley, Birmingham, England, B23 8LP. Contact: John Humphreys / Mary Bishop, Dev. Dir. / Dev. Dir. - Tel: 021-706-6133, Night Line: 021-697-2402. Opticians. Established: 1750 - Franchising Since: 1988 - No. of Units: Company Owned: 378 - Franchised: 71 - Franchise Fee: £3,000-£6,000 - Royalty: 7.5% - Total Inv: Min. £10,000 - Financing: Banks.

FAMILY CARE MEDICAL SYSTEMS
Franquiciadora Del Norte S.A. DE CV Periferico De La Juventud #8719, Chihuahua, Chile, 31125. Contact: Gustavo Navejas, General Director - Tel: (52) 14 251779, Fax: (52) 14 251812. Primary care health centers (lab, x-ray, minor surgery pharmacy, consultation). Established: 1994 - Franchising Since: 1996 - No. of Units: Company Owned: 1 - Franchised: 4 - Franchise Fee: $40,000 US - Royalty: 5.5% plus 1.5% adv. - Total Inv: $300,000 US.

FARMAROSA
Contifarma, S.L.
Avd. Atenas, 75 Zocorozas local 54, Las Rozas, Madrid, 28230. Contact: Jose A. Bodega, Director Comercial - Tel: 916.317.916, Fax:916 319 907, E-Mail: farma@irinfo.es, Web Site: www.irinfo.es/farmarosa. Oficinas De Parafarmacia. Venta De Products Para La salvo. Established: 1994 - Franchising Since: 1995 - No. of Units: Company Owned: 1 - Franchised: 43 - Franchise Fee: 2,650.000 PTS. - Royalty: 3% - Total Inv: 7,000.000 pts - Financing: BBV.

FIRST IMPRESSIONS
The Coach House, Ramsey Manor, 37 High St., Burwell, Cambridge, England, CB5 0HD. - Tel: 01638 741166, Fax: 01638 742253, E-Mail: pl@firstimpressions.demon.co.uk. Colour and image consulting, personal and corporate. Established: 1987 - Franchising Since: 1987 - No. of Units: Company Owned: 1 - Franchised: 150 - Franchise Fee: £2,950.

FRANCESCO GROUP
Francesco Group Holdings Ltd.
Woodings Yard, Bailey St., Stafford, Staffordshire, U.K., ST17 4BG. Contact: Frank Dellicompagni, Director - Tel: (01785) 247175, Fax: (01785) 257127, E-Mail: headoffice@francescogroup.co.uk, Web Site: www.francescogroup.co.uk. A large chain of hairdressing salons based within the midlands, who look towards quality hairdressing and styling. The future through the progressive philosophy. Established: 1967 - Franchising Since: 1983 - No. of Units: Company Owned: 5 - Franchised: 17 - Franchise Fee: None - Royalty: 10% net sales - Total Inv: £30,000, working capital ƒ10,000 - Financing: Yes.

FRESH SHOPS COSMETICS
Nectar Cosmetics Espana, S.L.
Camino de Hormiqueras, #124, Madrid, Madrid, 28031. Contact: Rito Naranso/Enrique Revuelta, Managing Directors - Tel: (00) 34-91-380-2767, Fax: (00) 34-91-380 3450. Close your eyes, breathe in and relax as mother nature does the rest. Use the "mood enhancing" qualities of our products with their medicinal values of essential oils to alter or strengthten your moods and emotion. It couldn't be easier. Established: 1998 - Franchising Since: 1998 - No. of Units: Company Owned: 2 - Franchised: 3 - Franchise Fee: 1.000.0000 ptas - Total Inv: 4-5.000.000ptas - Financing: Yes.

HOMEOPATIA DR. WALDEMIRO PEREIRA
Homeopatia Waldemira Pereria Lab. Indl. F. Ltda
Av. Mal. Floriano Peixoto, 7709, Curitiba, Parana, Brazil, 81.650-000. Contact: Pereira/Waldemiro, Director - Tel: (041) 276-9622. Farmaceutical industries homeopatic Brazilian natural products - franchising to drug stores. Established: 1933 - Franchising Since: 1991 - No. of Units: Company Owned: 6 - Franchised: 3 - Franchise Fee: US$3,500 - Royalty: 5% - Total Inv: US$25,000 - Financing: No.

J.T. LAZARTIGUE (UK) LTD.
20 James St., London, England, W1M 5HN. Contact: G. Makhoul, Dir. - Tel: (071) 629-6487. Diagnostic and advisory hair centre. Also, market and sell own brand of hair products and cosmetics. Established: 1975 - Franchising Since: 1975 - No. of Units: Company Owned: 22 - Franchised: 120 - Royalty: 7% of turnover, 5% adv. - Total Inv: £60,000 - Financing: No.

JACQUES JANINE
Jacques & Jeanie Adm. e Part. S/A
Rua Augusta, 2763 - conjunto 21,Sao Paulo, SP, Brazil, 01413-100. Contact: Nelson Chemin, Franchising Director - Tel: (5511) 883-7088, Fax: (5511) 853-8911, E-Mail: janine@dialdata.com.br. Jacques Janine company, specializing in beauty care, develops a professional and efficient work in service of beauty, in the fields of hair, facial and corporal esthetics, make up, manicure, pedicure, etc. using what is most advanced in equipments, products and specialized staff. Established: 1957 - Franchising Since: 1990 - No. of Units: Company Owned: 7 - Franchised: 31 - Franchise Fee: R$15,000 - Royalty: 5% - Total Inv: R$300,000.

L'ACQUA DI FIORI
Sofcon Ltda
Rua Rio de Janerio, 600/15, Andar, Belo Horizonte, MG, 30.160-041. - Tel: 005531- 212-5599, Fax: 005531-212-7848. Stores of fine perfumes and cosmetics supplied from industry of companies group. Established: 1980 - Franchising Since: 1983 - No. of Units: Company Owned: 6 - Franchised: 734 - Royalty: Included in the price of the products - Total Inv: US $30.000 unit (rent/location not included).

LADY OF AMERICA
P.O. Box 181, Leatherhead, Surrey, KT22 7FA. - Tel: 01372 279 791, Fax: 01372 279 794, E-Mail: info@ladyofamerica.co.uk, Web Site: www.ladyofamerica.com. Health club since 1984 with over 240 clubs and over one million members worldwide. Franchise Fee: £27,000 - Finanicng: Funding up to 70% available from the high street banks.

NATIONAL SLIMMING CENTRES
National Slimming Centres
3, Trinity House, 161, Old Christchurch Rd., Bournemouth, Dorset, England, BH1 1JW. Contact: Mr. S. Hass, Joint Man. Director - Tel: (01202) 555233, (0800) 065-5959, Fax: (01202) 290835, E-Mail: info@slimmingcentres.co.uk, Web Site: www.slimmingcentres.co.uk. Medically supervised weight loss programme + collagen replacement therapy + schlerotherapy and general medical treatments. Established: 1982 - Franchising Since: 1987 - No. of Units: Company Owned: 23 - Franchised: 11 - Franchise Fee: £7,500 - Royalty: 10% of gross takings - Total Inv: £25,000-£30,000 approx - Financing: No.

NECTAR BEAUTY SHOPS
The Nectar Group
1 Meadowbank Road, Carrickfergus, Co Antrim, 3738 8XX. Contact: Mr. W. B. Waring, Sales Director - Tel: 01960 351580, Fax: 01960 351740, E-Mail: info@nectar.eunet.co.uk, Web Site: www.nectar-cosmetics.com. Retailing over 250 body care products. Established: 1981 - Franchising Since: 1984 - No. of Units: Company Owned: 6 - Franchised: 280 - Franchise Fee: UK single outlet £10,000 Overseas by agreement - Royalty: None - Total Inv: Fran. fee £10,000 (UK) stock £15,000 shoplifting £25,000 approx.

NECTAR, LAS TIENDAS DE COSMETICA NATURAL
Nectar Cosmetics Espana, S.L.
Camino de Hormiqueras, #124, Madrid, Madrid, 28031. Contact: Rito Naranjo/Enrique Revelto, Managing Directors - Tel: (+00) 34-91-380 2767, Fax: (+00) 34-91-380 3450. Over 300, 100/100 natural cosmetic products for the carefulness of the body, the high lighting of the beauty and to preserve the skin youth like, 85 shops working successfully. Rentability, dynamic business. Established: 1990 - Franchising Since: 1990 - No. of Units: Company Owned: 2 - Franchised: 83 - Franchise Fee: 2.000.000 ptas - Total Inv: 6-7.000.000Ptas - Financing: Yes.

OPTIMAX LASER EYE CLINICS
128 Finchley Road, London, UK, NW3 5HT. Contact: Franchise Director - Tel: (44) 171 794 2108, Fax: (44) 171 431 7159. World's largest laser eye clinic operator. Offers PRK treatment for correction of short-sight and astigmatism. Established: 1992 - Franchising Since: 1995 - No. of Units: Company Owned: 7 clinics - Franchised: 10 - Franchise Fee: $1,000,000 US.

SIMONE MAHLER
Laboratoires Simone Mahler
106 Quai Des Chartrons, Bordeaux, Gironde, France, 33082. Contact: C.B. Ginebre, President - Tel: (33) 5 52 19 01 19, (0800) 85 78 78, Fax: (33) 5 56 50 01 79, E-Mail: simone-mahler@simone-mahler.fr. High value products and services to beauty salons. Client management with tailor-made techniques (beauty prescription, skin check up). Very relaible treatments and products with high % of natural actives. Training to products, services , selling and management Established: 1946 - Franchising Since: 1972 - No. of Units: Company Owned: 15 - Franchised: 50 - Franchise Fee: 50,000 usd - Royalty: 3% - Total Inv: 80,000-120,000 usd - Financing: 3rd party (80%).

SOUNTEX HEARING SYSTEMS PTE LTD
28 Ayer Rajah Crescent #02-01, Singapore, 139959. Contact: Kieran McCarry, GM - Tel: (65) 773-8085, Fax: (65) 773-8095, E-Mail: kerensa.ang@sni.siemens.com.sg, Web Site: www.sountex.com.sg. Sountex is a full business format franchise that retails the latest in Siemens hearing aid technology. Sountex provides its franchisees with comprehensive and continued training along with total a support system designed to help their business succeed. Established: 1997 - Franchising Since: 1997 - No. of Units: Franchised: 10 - Franchise Fee: Depends on territory - Royalty: Varies.

THE CAPELLI SALON *
Park House South Street, Farnham, Surrey, GU9 7QQ. - Tel: 01252 892 350, Fax: 01252 892 351, Web Site: www.capellisp.com. Supply product to 100's of salons. Established: 2002 - Franchising Since: 2003 - No. of Units: Company Owned: 1 - Franchise Fee: £9,500 + Vat.

TRIMLINE HEALTH & FITNESS CENTRES
Kreativ Properties Ltd.
6 Burwell Close, Healey, Rochdale, Lanchester, England, 0L12 6DQ. - Tel: (0706) 33797. Health and fitness centres. Established: 1976 - Franchising Since: 1989 - No. of Units: Franchised: 4 - Franchise Fee: £5,000 - Royalty: 8% per annum - Total Inv: £80,000 new site basic scheme + initial fee - Financing: Yes, existing clubs on some occasions can be acquired at less the cost.

PHOTO, PRINTING AND ART

4 INGLETES
Los Cuatro Ingletes S.A.
C/CID n, 2 A Apdo Correos, 14.770, Madrid, Spain, 28080. Contact: Carmen Peralta, Fran. Dept. - Tel: (34-1) 5769345, Fax: (34-1) 4354879, E-Mail: pea@sei.es. Framing stores. Between a traditional framing shop and art gallery. Exclusive products, all styles, impeccable service. Established: 1983 - Franchising Since: 1984 - No. of Units: Company

Owned: 11 - Franchised: 32 - Franchise Fee: $11,000 US - Royalty: 5% - Total Inv: $41,000 US - Financing: We require, also contacts for master franchising.

CHROMA COPY
42-44 Broadwick St., London, England, W1V 3DF. Contact: Franchise Director - Tel: (01) 734-0744/5. Printing and copying services. Established: 1979 - No. of Units: 25+.

HIGH LEVEL PHOTOGRAPHY
Mount Pleasant, Elm Corner Ockham, Guildford, Surrey, U.K., GU23 6PX. Contact: John Power, Bus. Dev. Mgr. Elevated video and photographic services. Established: 1983 - Franchising Since: 1989 - No. of Units: Company Owned: 3 - Franchised: 1.

KALL-KWIK PRINTING
Kall Kwik Printing, (UK) Ltd.
106 Pembroke Rd, Ruiscip, Middlesex, Ruislip, Middlesex, England, HA4 8NW. Contact: Franchising Mgr. - Tel: 01895 87200, 0500 872060, Fax: 01895 872110, E-Mail: franchise.sales@kallkwik.co.uk. Print, copy, design centres, provide services to businesses in the local vicinity. Established: 1978 - Franchising Since: 1979 - No. of Units: Franchised: 184 - Franchise Fee: £4,500 - Royalty: 10% - Total Inv: £132,000 - Financing: Yes.

PDC COPYPRINT
PDC International PLC
1 Church Lane, East Grinstead, West Sussex, U.K., RH19 3AZ. Contact: Stephen W. Ricketts, Managing Director - Tel: (01342) 315321, Fax: (01342) 327117, E-Mail: intl@pdccopyprint.com. High street business printing, design and copying service. Established: 1967 - Franchising Since: 1981 - No. of Units:Franchised: 35 - Franchise Fee: £7,500 - Royalty:10% reducing to 5% - Total Inv: £111,000 including £31,000 working cap. - Financing: 70%.

PIP PRINTING
Printnet Ltd.
15 Newman St., London, England, W1P 3HD. Contact: Mr. C. Bowman, Chairman - Tel: 071-636 2571. Printing of business and personal stationery - letterheads, visiting cards, leaflets, forms, invoices - copying, colour copying and printing - artwork anddesign. Established: 1993 - Franchising Since: 1993 - No. of Units: Franchised: 17.

PRINTDESIGNS
Chester Rd., Kelsall, Tarperley, Cheshire, U.K., CLO6 0RJ. Contact: C. David Gattie, M.D. - Tel: 0829-52095. Graphic design, artwork, typesetting, and printing. Established: 1978 - Franchising Since: 1989 - No. of Units: Company Owned: 2 - Franchised: 2 - Franchise Fee: £6,000 - Royalty: 6%, 4% adv. levy - Total Inv: Initially £60,000 - phased inv. - Financing: Yes.

PT BEKAINDO SEJAHTERA
Jl. Cideng Barat 12 BB, Jakarta, Indonesia, 10150. Contact: Ms. Irene Jong, General Mgr. - Tel: (021) 6348634, Fax: (021) 6348631. Glamour and fashion photography. Established: 1992 - No. of Units: Company Owned: 6 - Franchise Fee: $75,000 US, Royalty: 5% from gross sales - Total Inv: $200,000 US includes franchise fee - Financing: No.

SHOP PHOTO VIDEO
16 Rue au Pain, Versailles, France, 78000. Contact: Mr. Ferrero, Dir - Tel: 1-39-50-02-36. Photographic, movie and video material. Established: 1962 - Franchising Since: 1966 - No. of Units: Company Owned: 4 - Franchised: 45 - Royalty: 1%.

SIR SPEEDY INDONESIA
Jl. Kerajinan no. 13A, Jakarta, Indonesia, 11140. Contact: Director - Tel: (6221) 628 0613.600 7479. 629 6721, Fax: (6221) 628-0612, E-Mail: speedy@centrin.net.id. Printing, copying, digital network. Established: 1968 - Franchising Since: 1968 - No. of Units: Franchised: 1,500 - Franchise Fee: 20.000.000 - Royalty: 5% - Total Inv: US $100,000.

SNAP PRINTING
Snap Franchising Ltd.
383 Scarborough Beach Road, Osborne Park, WA, Australia, 6017. Contact: Tim Hantke, C.E.O. - Tel: (61) 8 9 443-4666, Fax: (61) 8 9 443-7333, E-Mail: thantke@snapprinting.com, Web Site: www.snap print.com.au. Franchising quick printing. Established: 1967 - Franchising

Since: 1979 - No. of Units: Company Owned: 1 - Franchised: 140 - Franchise Fee: Aus$42,000 - Royalty: 6% x sales yr. 1, 8% thereafter - Total Inv: From Aus$1500,000 - Financing: From banks.

SNAPPY SNAPS
11/12 Glenthorne, London, U.K., W6 0LJ. Contact: Hugh Jones, Recruitment Manager - Tel: (0181) 741-7474, Fax: (0181) 748-3849, E-Mail: info@snappysnaps.co.uk, Web Site: www.snappysnaps.co.uk. A professional one stop photographic retailer, offering the very latest in photo developing from traditional 35 mm to aps and digital services. Established: 1983 - Franchising Since: 1987 - No. of Units: Franchised: 70 - Franchise Fee: £12,500 - Royalty: 6% - Total Inv: £130,000 - Financing: Yes, min. input £25,000.

RETAIL

ACTUA-SA
16 Cite Joly, 75011, Paris, France. Contact: Daniel Dorra - Tel: (1) 48.05.23.16. Furniture, sofa and gift stores. Established: 1974 - Franchising Since: 1976 - No. of Units: Company Owned: 5 - Franchised: 30 - Franchise Fee: 40,000 FHT, Total Inv: 300,000-800,000 - Royalty: 5% - Financing: 50%.

AIRCOAST
Air Motion Enterprise
112, JIn Rahmat, Bata Pahat, Johor, 83000. Contact: Terrance, CEO - Tel: 60 197 572 560, Fax: 60 743 125 60, E-Mail: info@aircoast.com, Web Site: www.eonenet.com/members/aircoast. Manufacturers a line of unique detachable roller skates sneakers. Established: 2000 - Franchising Since: 2001 - No. of Units: Company Owned: 10 - Franchised: 23 - Total Inv: $500. US.

APOLLO BLINDS
Apollo Window Blinds Ltd.
Cold Heseldone Ind. Est, Murton, Seaham, Co. Durham, SR78ST. Contact: Graham Mylchreest, General Mgr. - Tel: (0191) 513-0061, Fax: (0191) 513-0516. Retailing of all types of window covering products, including vertical, venetian, roller, pleated, Austrian, festoons and roman blinds, plus curtains, tracks and poles. Established: 1970 - Franchising Since: 1972 - No. of Units: Company Owned: 1 - Franchised: 60 - Franchise Fee: £9999 - Royalty: TBA - Total Inv: £25000 - Financing: Yes up to 70%.

APPLEWOODS
Applewoods International Ltd
Clevedon Gate, Hither Green, Clevedon, U.K, BS21 6XT. Contact: Nick Fisher, Manager of Public Relations - Tel: (+44) 1275 345600, Fax: (+44) 1275 343112, E-Mail: info@applewoods.com, Web Site: www.applewoods.com. Manufacturers and distributors of Applewoods Body care and home fragrance products to Applewoods and other stores in over 20 countries world wide. Professional training and on-going support for all franchisees is provided. Established: 1978 - Franchising Since: 1992 - No. of Units: Franchised: On application - Total Inv: On application - Financing: No.

BABYBOTTE BEVERLY
Bidegain SA
Avenue Montardon, Pau, 64000 Cedex, France. Contact: Jean-Jacques Schott - Tel: (59) 32-01-25. Children's shoes. Established: 1980 - Franchising Since: 1982 - No. of Units: Company Owned: 4 - Franchised: l5 - Approx. Inv: 700,000 FF - Royalty: 2%.

BIZARRE
Bizarre Ind. Com. Roupas Ltda.
Estrada do Campo Limpo, 3464, Sao Paulo, SP, Brazil, 05744.000. Contact: Rufino M. Bizarre, Director Commercial - Tel: (055) 011 5511 6162, Fax: (055)011 5511 5650. Bizarre is a youth teenage wear company. Products, pants jeans, t-shirts, jackets, shirts, dresses and etc. It's a casual clothing company. Established: 1980 - Franchising Since: 1990 - No. of Units: Company Owned: 7 - Franchised: 5 - Franchise Fee: US $15,000 - Royalty: 2% - Total Inv: US $60,000.

BLAZES FIREPLACE AND HEATING CENTRES
Blazes Fireplace Centres (Franchising) Ltd.
Signature House, 21 Parker St, Burnley,Lancs, BB11 1AP. - Tel: (+44) 01282 831176, Fax: (+44) 01282 424411. Little competition in this growth market. We bring a living room setting into our showrroms and offer a "one stop" inclusive service. the demand for living flame fires is still grwoing at a rapid rate. Established: 1990 - No. of Units: Franchised: 50 - Franchise Fee: £8,000 - Total Inv: £42,000.

BOB'S TILE CENTERS
Unit 48, Shand Kydd Ind. Estate, Somerford Rd., Christchurch, Dorset, England. Contact: L.Platt, Dir. - Tel: 0202-474222. Retail tiles and ancillary lines. Established: 1970 - Franchising Since: 1983 - No. of Units: Company Owned: 15 - Franchised: 2 - Total Inv: £15,000 - Royalty: 10%.

BRICO
New G.I.B., S.A
Chee De Charleroi 239, (1060) Brussels, Belgium. Contact: H. J. Ruys, Dev. Mgr. - Tel: (02) 536 57 71. One stop shopping D.I.Y. centers for home improvement, home beautification and gardening with specialized assortments and customer services. Established: 1973 - Franchising Since: 1978 - No. of Units: Company Owned: 47 - Franchised: 61 - Franchise Fee: 450,000 BF - Royalty: 6.60% on turnover - Financing: 5,000,000 BF.

C' ART SRL
14 Via Buonarroti, Rome, Italy, 00185. Contact: Mr. Diveroli, President - Tel: (06)487-3670. Stationery and gifts. Established: 1900 - Franchising Since: 1985 - No. of Units: Company Owned: 8 - Franchised: 54 - Franchise Fee: None - Royalty: 2% - Total Inv: 80,000,000 Lire.

CALZEDONIA SPA
Via Salieri N. 30, Vallese Di Oppeano, Verona, Italia, 37050. Contact: Francesca Trentini, Sviluppo Franchising - Tel: (045) 6984 111. A new way of selling hosiery, body stockings, swimsuits, children's and men's socks. Established: 1986 - Franchising Since: 1987 - No. of Units: Company Owned: 42 - Franchised: 449 - Franchise Fee £10,000,000 - Royalty: No - Total Inv: £120,000,000-£130,000,000 - Financing: No.

CAROLL
Caroll International
30 Rue de Calebrai, Paris, France, 75019. Contact: Henri Foare, Directeur Commercial - Tel: (33-1) 53 26 53 26, Fax: (33-1) 53 26 53 00. Women's apparel. Caroll stores sell goods belonging to Caroll International, and get a commission on the basis of the turnover. Deliveries of new styles every week. Target: active women aged 30-40 looking for the best value of their money and style. Established: 1963 - Franchising Since: 1980 - No. of Units: Company Owned: 100 - Franchised: 90 - Franchise Fee: FF 50,000 - Total Inv: FF 400,000/80 sq. meters.

CASH CONVERTERS
15-17 Gentlemens Field Westmill Rd, Ware, Herts., England, SG12 0EF. Contact: Marie Hare, Mng. Dir. - Tel: 0920 485696. Pawnbrokers/retailers of high quality secondhand goods in an upmarket high profile, sophisticated environment. Established: 1991 - Franchising Since: 1992 - No. of Units: Company Owned: 3 - Franchised: 28 - Franchise Fee: £25,000 - Royalty: Fixed fee £250/wk. - Total Inv: £80,000 - Financing: Partial.

CASH CONVERTERS
Cash Converters Spain S.L
Bravo Murilo, 243, Madrid, 28020. Contact: Gustrvo Romero, Franchise Manager - Tel: (91) 571-0915, Fax: (91) 579-7131, E-Mail: casthconverters@und.servicom.es, Web Site: www.cash-converters.com.au. Buy-sell second hand products. Established: 1996 - Franchising Since: 1997 - No. of Units: Company Owned: 3 - Franchised: 27 - Franchise Fee: $41,000 (us) - Royalty: 2.7% (us) per month - Total Inv: $300.000-$350.000 (us).

CASH GENERATOR
Caroline House, 115-125 Bradshawgate, Bolton, UK, BL2 1BJ. Contact: Brian Lewis - Tel: 01 204 371871, Fax: 01 204 371900, E-Mail: info@cashgenerator.co.ik, Web Site: www.cashgenerator.net. We buy and sell brand new and pre-used goods. Average store turnover £1.59m - Investment opportunities from £15k plus borrowings.

CATIMINI
94 Rue Choletaise, BP 67, Saint Macaire-en-Mauges, France, 49450. Contact: Catherine Rochais, Fran. Dir. - Tel: 41.55.33.55. Children's clothing and accessories (0-l2 yrs). Established: 1972 - Franchising Since: 1982 - No. of Units: Company Owned: 22 - Franchised: 45 - Franchise Fee: 65,000 F - Total Inv: 550,000 F - Royalty: 3% C.A. H.T. (1.5% for training, 1.5% for adv.) - Financing: 50% of total inv.

CENOURA
Velouma, S.A.
Rua Junqueira - Baixo -Apartado 2- Vilar do Paraiso, Valadares-Poto, Portugal, 4408. Contact: Jose Valdemar Carvalho, Franchising Department - Tel: (351) (02) 711-2880, Fax: (02) 712-7613. Babies wear (0-1 yr); childrens wear (2-16 yrs) and maternity wear. Established: 1972 - Franchising Since: 1984 - No. of Units: Company Owned: 15 - Franchised: 23 - Franchise Fee: PTE 1.500.00$00 - Royalty: 2% upon buyings - Total Inv: PTE 13.000.000 (ruffly).

CHRISTIAENSEN
GB-Immo-BM B.P. 999, 1000 Bruxelles,Brabant,Belgium. Contact: Foret Marcel - Tel: (02) 582-29-17. Toys and games. Established: 1982 - No. of Units: Company Owned: 73 - Franchised: 62 - Franchise Fee: $200,000.

CINERENT BENELUX
Schiestraat 38, Noordwijk, Zuid, The Netherlands, 2201AS. - Tel: (01719) 56222. Rent videos. Established: 1987 - Franchising Since: 1987 - No. of Units: Company Owned: 2 - Franchised: 80 - Franchise Fee: 3%.

CLARKS SHOP, THE
C&J Clark Ltd.
40 High St., Somerset, England, BA16 0YA. - Tel: 01458-43131. Retailing of branded footwear for men, women, and children. Established: 1825 - Franchising Since: 1984 - No. of Units: Company Owned: 400+ - Franchised: 125 - Franchise Fee: £7,500 - Royalty: Management services charge approx. 1% of turnover - Total Inv: Fixtures-fittings £45,000; stock £45,000; w.cap./fees £20,000 - Financing: Yes, guaranteed loan scheme through major bank. U.K. availability only at present.

COLCCI
Colcci Ind. e Com. do Vestuario Ltda.
Av. Otto Renaux, 377, Brusque, SC, Brasil, 88350-000. Contact: Supervisor - Tel: (0055) 47 351-3399, Fax: 47 355-0668. Manufacturer and commercialization of "Fashion & Sportswear" clothing (also accessories) for both sexes on the adult and childish segments. Established: 1986 - Franchising Since: 1989 - No. of Units: Company Owned: 4 - Franchised: 206 - Franchise Fee: R$20,000 - Total Inv: R$70,000 (fran. fee plus R$20,000 standard furniture, R$30,000 initial clothing stock) - Financing: No.

COLLECTION 5
Mercatigue et Distribution
58110, Brinay, France. Contact: Michel Rady - Tel: 16 (86) 84 91 00. Haberdasher's shop. Established: 1970 - Franchising Since: 1975 - No. of Units: Company Owned: 20 - Franchised: 30 - Approx. Inv: 250,000 FF.

COMPUTER KINETICS
P & G Enterprises Ltd.
15 Warwich Dr., Greenham, Newbury, England, RG14 7TT. - Tel: 0823-358611. Specializes in F.M.S. electronics. Established: 1983 - No. of Units: 1 - Approx. Inv: £13,500 - Royalty: 10% - Financing: To suitable locations.

CORRE CORRE
Corre Corre S.A.
Travesia Industrial N 87, Barcelona, Spain, 08907. Contact: Franchise & Marketing Director - Tel: (34) 3 263 30 90, Fax: (34) 333 66 074. Corre Corre is the Spanish leader in the sports retailing market, with about 100 stores in Spain. The product lines commercialized are: sport shoes, sportswear and all kinds of complements from leading brands. Established: 1985 - Franchising Since: 1989 - No. of Units: Company Owned: 55 - Franchised: 33 - Franchise Fee: 2,500,000 ESP - Royalty:

132,000 ESP / monthly - Total Inv: 15,000,000 ESP - Financing: We can provide special credit lines with financial corporations operating under lower market conditions.

DEVLYN OPTICALS
Optics Devlyn SA de Cv
M. de Cervantes Saavedra #25, Mexico City, DF, 11520.Contact: Franchise Director - Tel: (525) 2624100, Fax: (525) 2500560, E-Mail: devlyn@mail.infolatina.com.mx, Web Site: www.devlyn.com.mx. Retail sales of optical products and services. Established: 1936 - Franchising Since: 1991 - No. of Units: Company Owned: 280 - Franchised: 100 - Franchise Fee: $10,000 US - Royalty: 7% royalty + 5% publicity - Total Inv: $100,000 US.

DISMARINA
Cia - Vidraria Santa Marina
DPD, Ave. Santa Marina U 482, Sao Paulo, SP, Brazil, 05036-903. Contact: Franchise & Commercial Mgr. - Tel: 55 11 874 79 54. Wholesale/distribution of warehouse products in retail shops. Technology is informatics/force sale administration/logistic. Established: 1987 - Franchising Since: 1987 - No. of Units: Franchised: 90 - Royalty: 10% - Total Inv: $10,000 US - Financing: None.

DOGSBODY & CAT TAILS
17 High St., Staple Hill, Bristol, England, BS16 5HA. - Tel: 0272 560672. High Street retail and/or pet grooming stores. Retail stores sell wide range of pet accessories and pet foods - leading brands and own brand natural foods. Our products are tested on humans for animals. Established: 1989 - Franchising Since: 1993 - No. of Units: Company Owned: 3 - Franchised: 1 - Franchise Fee: £10,000 + VAT - Royalty: 10% from gross sales (6% mgmt. fee, 2% local adv., 2% nat'l. adv.) - Total Inv: From £25,000-£35,000, incl. fran. fee, stock, shopfitting, signage, etc. - Financing: Subject to status, 50% banks.

DORBER COLLECTION, THE
110 Saltergate, Chesterfield, Derbyshire, England, S4J 1NE. - Tel: 1246 551755. Greeting cards and add-on products supplied to retailers on sale or return. Full training, extensive product range, good returns. Established: 1990 - Franchising Since: 1994 - No. of Units: Company Owned: 1 - Franchised: 5 - Franchise Fee: £1,650 - Royalty: None - Total Inv: £8,500 - Financing: No.

DURHAM PINE
137 High St. W., Gateshead, England, NE8 1EJ. - Tel: (0191) 4771402, Fax: (0191) 4775418. Retailers of pine furniture. Established: 1986 - Franchising Since: 1991 - No. of Units: Company Owned: 11 - Franchise Fee: £6,750 - Royalty: 5% of gross sales - Total Inv: £42,000 - Financing: Yes.

DYMOCKS BOOKSTORES
6th Floor, 428 George Street, Sydney, Australia, 2000. Contact: Mr. P. Allen, Franchise Development Manager - Tel: (02) 9224-0411, Fax: (02) 9224 9401, E-Mail: petera@dymocks.com.au, Web Site: www.dymocks.com.au. Retail bookselling based on the traditional style book store, providing an extensive book range, excellent customer service and value for money in a comfortable retail enviroment. Established: 1879 - Franchising Since: 1986 - No. of Units: Company Owned: 6 - Franchised: 89 - Franchise Fee: From $37,500 - Royalty: 6% of turn over - Total Inv: Varies on store size from $450,000.

ELIO CECCHINI L'ART DE LA FROMAGERIE
57 bd de Souville, Carpentras, Vaucluse, France, 84200. Contact: Picter Cecchini - Tel: 1690 63 28 20. Retail cheese shop. Established: 1981 - Franchising Since: 1982 - No. of Units: Company Owned: 7 - Franchised: 4 - Franchise Fee: 50,000 FF - Total Inv: 200,000-400,000 F H.T. - Royalty: 2-1.5%.

FLOOR COVERINGS INTERNATIONAL (UK) LTD.
High Quality House, Sandbeck Way, Wetherby, W.Yorkshire, LS22 7DN. Contact: Director - Tel: 01937-588456, Toll Free: 0800-228877, Fax: 01937-588178, E-Mail: sales@floorcoverings.co.uk. Retailers of floor coverings including carpet, ceramics, hardwood, laminates, vinyls via a mobile showroom direct to consumers homes. Approximately 20% of business to builders, hotels, clubs and restaurants. Established: 1995 - Franchising Since: 1995 - No. of Units: Franchised: 185 - Franchise

Fee: 3 packages, £9,950-£14,950, £17,950 plus VAT - Royalty: 5% of retail sales value, 2% adv. contribution - Total Inv: Franchise fee plus a minimum of £6,000 - Financing: Via all major banks.

FOCUS MICROSYSTEMS
Sherlock House, Bayswater Farm Rd., Headington, Oxford, U.K., OX3 8BX. Contact: Mr. Duncan Samuel, Man. Dir. - Tel: (01865) 766 241, Fax: (01865) 750 937. Focus are a computer systems house providing full systems for specialist market sectors. Complete with their own software team. Established: 1981 - Franchising Since: 1993 - No. of Units: Company Owned: 1 - Franchised: 1 - Franchise Fee: £15,000 - Royalty: 10% of turnover - Total Inv: £15,000 - Financing: Yes.

GENEVIEVE LETHU
BP 22-5 Passage du Cotre-Le Gabut, F17002 La Rochelle, France. - Tel: 46.68.40.00. Franchising Since: 1972 - No. of Units: Company Owned: 5 - Franchised: 60 - Franchise Fee: 70,000 FF HT - Royalty: 5% Ht du CA HT.

GRANNY MAY'S MANAGEMENT
25-27 Waterloo St., Surry Hills, N.S.W., Australia, 2010. - Tel: (02) 9 281-7978, Fax: (02) 9 281-9539. Retail sales of cards, gifts, licensed merchandise, stationery, wrapping paper, novelties, partyware, apparel, prints, posters, and all goods sold as per the Granny May's concept or included in any Granny May's catalogue. Established: 1980 - Franchising Since: 1983 - No. of Units: Company Owned: 10 - Franchised: 74 - Franchise Fee: $30,000-$50,000 - Royalty: 5% - Total Inv: $200,000-$250,000 approx. - Financing: Franchisees directed to various banks.

HAMILTONS
Hamiltons Confectioners Ltd.
Stanton Court, Stanton, Nr. Broadway, Worcs., England, WR12 7NE. Contact: Andrew Campbell, Chairman/Mgr. Dir. - Tel: (01386) 882287, Fax: (01386) 882287, E-Mail: 101711.2342@compuserve.com. Old fashioned sweet shops specializing in sweets and hand made chocolates. Established: 1986 - Franchising Since: 1993 - No. of Units: Company Owned: 2 - Franchised: 4 - Franchise Fee: £5,000 - Royalty: Through purchase of goods - Total Inv: £40,000 - Financing: No.

HARRIET WEBSTER'S TRADITIONAL TOFFEE & FUDGE
Harriet Webster's Ltd.
Unit 8, Moor Lane Trading Est., Sherburn In Elmet, Leeds, England, LS25 6ES. Contact: T. Webster, Mng. Dir. - Tel: 01977-681141, Fax: 01977-683768. Retail of traditional English toffee and fudge sold from victorian style handlers located in prime positions. Established: 1991 - Franchising Since: 1992 - No. of Units: Company Owned: 1 - Franchised: 140 - Total Inv: From £5,000 work, includes equipment and stock, training - Financing: 50%.

HOUSE OF SOMETHING DIFFERENT
12/16 Church Hill, Loughton, England. Contact: Fran. Dir. - Tel: 01-502-2286 or 01-502-0215. Fireplaces and grates. Also gas, coal and electric fires. Established: 1980 - Franchising Since: 1984 - No. of Units: Company Owned: 5 - Franchised: 3 - Approx. Inv: £40,000 - Royalty: 2.5% plus 2% adv. - Financing: Yes.

HUGO BOSS
Hugo Boss Moda Ltda.
Av. Reboucas, 3995, Sao Paulo, Brazil, 05401. Contact: Willy H. Herrmann, General Mgr. - Tel: (011) 210-3200. Men's fashion. Established: 1988 - Franchising Since: 1988 - No. of Units: Franchised: 40 - Royalty: 21% - Total Inv: US $500,000 - Financing: No.

IN TOTO KITCHENS
Wakefield Rd., Gildersome, Morley, N. Leeds, England, LS27 7JZ. Contact: Fran. Oper. Mgr. - Tel: 0532-524131. Retailing fitted kitchens. Established: 1980 - Franchising Since: 1980 - No. of Units: Company Owned: 1 - Franchised: 32 - Franchise Fee: £5,000 - Total Inv: Approx. £35,000 - Financing: Subject to status.

INFINITIF
26, rue du Caire, 75 002 Paris, France. - Tel: 43-39-97-03. Ladies ready to wear garments. Established: 1970 - Franchising Since: 1970 - No. of Units: Company Owned: 19 - Franchised: 16 - Franchise Fee: 50.000 F - Royalty: 2% of sales - Total Inv: 8,000 F - Financing: No.

INSPORT
Sportsforum UK, Ltd.
Hemel Hempstead Ski Centre, St. Albans Hill, Hemel Hempstead, Herts., U.K., HP3 9NH. Contact: Alan Deeprose, Fran. Dir. - Tel: (0442) 241321. General sports retailing of equipment and clothing. Established: 1974 - Franchising Since: 1988 - No. of Units: Franchised: 7 - Franchise Fee: £6,000 - Royalty: 8% of turnover - Total Inv: £60,000 (£20,000 cap. required) - Financing: No.

JACADI
Rue DiDerot 26, Nanterre, France, 92028. Contact: International Director - Tel: (33) 1 41 91 91 91, Fax: (33) 1 41 91 90 56. Children wear. Established: 1980 - Franchising Since: 1982 - No. of Units: Company Owned: 20 - Franchised: 380 - Franchise Fee: $20,000 US - Royalty: 4% of retail turnover - Total Inv: $200,000 US.

JULIO
Grupo Julio S. A . de CV
Calz. de Tlalpan 509 1ER Piso Col. Alamos, Mexico, DF, Mexico, 03400. - Tel: (525) 5 38 40 08, (525) 5 38 42 91, Fax: (525) 5 38 23 23. Women apparel and accessories stores. Established: 1975 - Franchising Since: 1992 - No. of Units: Company Owned: 23 - Franchised: 18 - Total Inv: US $60,000 approx. store set up, US $50,000 inven. - Financing: No.

K.A.S.
2405, Brasilio Itibere, Curitiba, PR, Brazil, 80.230-050. - Tel: 55.41.3220661, Fax: 55.41.2232590. Fitness and dance wear. Established: 1981 - Franchising Since: 1991 - No. of Units: Company Owned: 8 - Franchised: 4 - Franchise Fee: US $10,000 - Royalty: 10% - Total Inv: US $50,000 - Financing: No.

KLEINS
Kleins Franchising Pty. Ltd.
1 Abbotts Rd., Dandenong, Victoria, Australia, 3175. - Tel: (03) 9706 4966. Fashion accessory retailer specializing in fashion jewellery. Established: 1982 - Franchising Since: 1990 - No. of Units: Company Owned: 45 - Franchised: 150 - Franchise Fee: On application - Royalty: 15%, 5% adv. - Total Inv: Dependant on site - Financing: On application.

LEADERS HEALTH FOOD STORES
105 London Rd., Brighton, Sussex, England, BN1 4JG. Contact: Fran. Dir. - Tel: (0273) 695001. Health food stores. Established: 1955 - Franchising Since: 1983 - No. of Units: Company Owned: 32 - Franchised: 4 - Franchise Fee: £4,000 - Total Inv: £20,000-£40,000 including stock - Royalty: 4% net.

LPC - LIVROS PERSONALIZADOS PARA CRIANCAS
J.E.J. Editora E. Comercio Ltda.
Rua Tatui, No. 94, Sao Paulo, SP, Brazil, 01409-010. Contact: Judy Schechtmann, Pres. - Tel: (011) 883-1582, Fax: (011) 883-1582. Personalized childrens books - with a computer and a laser printer we personalize the book with the name of the children in 5 minutes. Established: 1991 - Franchising Since: 1991 - No. of Units: Franchised: 25 - Franchise Fee: US $4,000 - Royalty: None - Total Inv: US $8,000.

MEGA SPORTS
Tradentrance Ltd.
Bankfield Business Park, Quebec Street, Bolton, BL3 5JN. - Tel: 0845 130 4704, Fax: 01204 373516, E-Mail: mail@megasports.uk.com, Web Site: www.megasports.uk.com. Discount warehouses offer clearance ranges of top brand and quality footwear and designer clothing. Franchise Fee: £40,000-£60,000 - Total Inv: £170,000.

MIDLAND WATERLIFE FRANCHISING
154 High St., Bromsgrove, Worcestershire, England, BG1 8AR. - Tel: 0527-70676. Retail aquatic outlets located in garden centers and other selected outlets. Established: 1983 - Franchising Since: 1983 - No. of Units: Company Owned: 3 - Franchised: 10 - Franchise Fee: £4,000 - Royalty: 2% adv. on net sales - Total Inv: Fixture & fittings £20,000-£25,000, stock £20,000 - Financing : Yes, help to finance.

MOVING STORE
D'ieteren Sport
Parc Industriel de La Vallee du Hain, Wauthier Braine, Belgium, 1461. Contact: Marc Bauduin, Fran. Mgr. - Tel: (2) 367 1417, Fax: (2) 367 1450. Sales of bicycles and accessories. Established: 1995 - Franchising

Since: 1995 - No. of Units: Company Owned: 1 - Franchised: 8 - Franchise Fee: 300.000 Bef - Royalty: 3.5% fee plus 3% advertising - Total Inv: +6000.000 Bef - Financing: 1.500.000 Bef.

MPC, MOBILE PHONE CENTRE
80 Baxter Avenue, Southend-On-Sea, Essex, England, SS2 6HZ. Contact: Tim Stone, Bus. Dev. Director - Tel: (01702) 226666, Fax: (01702) 226678, E-Mail: mpc.co.uk. Mobile phone retailer. Established: 1984 - Franchising Since: 1991 - No. of Units: Company Owned: 1 - Franchised: 51 - Franchise Fee: $7,000 - Royalty: Nil - Total Inv: $35,000 ($7,000 fee, $10,000 working capital, remainder initial costs) - Financing: Yes.

NATALY'S
18 Avenue du General Gallieni, Nanterre, France, 92007. Contact: Miss Clair, Exp. Man. - Tel: 47.25.24.74. Offer a wide range of products (furniture, clothes, toys) for children from 0 to 6 and the pregnant women through a channel of similar shops decorated to create a special Nataly's concept. Established: 1953 - Franchising Since: 1960 - No. of Units: Company Owned: 185 - Franchised: 165 - Total Inv: Min. cash requirement.

NATIONAL SCHOOLWEAR CENTRES
Highcliffe House, 411-413 Station Road, Highcliffe - Dorset, U.K., BH23 5EN. Contact: John Lee - Tel: 01425 610700, 01425 270541. We offer a very different and unique franchise. We specialise in retailing of general schoolwear and uniforms. Full training provided.

NEVADA BOB'S
Nevada Bob UK Ltd.
The Rotunda, Broadgate Circle, London, England, EC2M 2BNS. Contact: Philip Smith, Fran. Dir. - Tel: 0171 628 4999, Fax: 0171 628-7999, E-Mail: mitch@nevadabob.co.uk. The chain of professional golf stores, retailing all major brands and offering a vast selection of different products with professional advice offered. Established: 1990 - Franchising Since: 1990 - No. of Units: Company Owned: 4 - Franchised: 40 - Franchise Fee: £47,500 - Royalty: 3% of turnover - Total Inv: £160,000(£47,500 franchise fee / £55,000 shopfitting/rest working capital acess - Financing: Contacts with banks.

OXIGENIO
Oxigenio Ind. Do Vest. Ltda
Rua Prof. Stroele, No 99, Petropolis, RJ, Brazil, 25680-170. Contact: (55) 242 43 3376. Clothing and accessories for teenager, young people and children. More than 800 types of products. T-shirts, shorts, backpacks, wallets, tennis shoes, hats, jeans, bikinis, handbags, others. Established: 1964 - Franchising Since: 1988 - No. of Units: Company Owned: 4 - Franchised: 11 - Franchise Fee US $10,000 - Royalty: None - Total Inv: US $50,000 - Financing: Yes.

PEARLE OPTICIENS
Pearle B.V
Amersfoortstraat 84 A, Soesterberg, Netherlands, 3769 A. Contact: Ger M. Schilder, Dir. of Franchise - Tel: (033)469-7200, Fax: (033)461-6641. Optical retail company. Established: 1959 - Franchising Since: 1982 - No. of Units: Company Owned: 49 - Franchised: 81 - Franchise Fee: DFL 20,000 - Royalty: 8.5% of net sales - Total Inv: Approx. DFL 375,000 (include leasehold, Imp, fixt and furn, equip, inventory, EDP store system etc.) - Financing: Base financing structure with ABN AMRO Bank and INQ Bank.

PERSONALIZED BOOK COMPANY
Best Books
2 The Grove, Mount Street, Diss, Norfolk, U.K., IP22 3QQ. Contact: Jane Hutton-Williams, Owner - Tel: (00) 44-1379-641444, Fax: (00) 44-1379-641444, E-Mail: sales@bestbook.co_uk, Web Site: www.bestbook.com.uk. Personalized books and gifts using our software, books and gifts can be generated in a few minutes. Established: 1989 - Franchising Since: 1995 - No. of Units: Company Owned: 1 - Franchised: 180 - Franchise Fee: From £1,295 - Total Inv: £1,295 plus computer and laser printer.

PHYTÁ COSMÉTICOS
Pie Comércio De Cosméticos Ltda.
Rua Leopol do Couto de Magalhães Junior, 146-10, São Paulo, SP, 04542-000. Contact: Damian Waldman, President - Tel: (011) 866-1406, Fax: (011)7295.6450. Chain of cosmetic/perfumery shops offering leading international perfumes, treatment and make up brands, besides highly trained product orientation and clinic. Established: 1992 - Franchising Since: 1993 - No. of Units: Company Owned: 3 - Franchised: 10 - Franchise Fee: US$12.000.00 - Royalty: 4% of gross sales - Total Inv: US$170.000.00 - Financing: No.

PINE STORE, THE
Pine Plus Ltd.
Unit 1, Brockhampton Lane, Havant, Hants, England, PO9 1LU. Contact: Robin Sutherland, Mng. Dir. - Tel: (0705) 498018. Pine furniture specialists. Established: 1982 - Franchising Since: 1994 - No. of Units: Company Owned: 10 - Franchised: 4 - Franchise Fee: £12,500 - Royalty: 5% of sales - Total Inv: Up to £70,000 dependent on location (£40,000 stock) - Financing: Yes.

PRIMETIME VIDEO LTD.
Primetime Video Group Ltd.
Trafalga House, 5/7 High Lane, Chorlton, Manchester, England, M21 1DJ. - Tel: 061-860-4853. Home entertainment centers, hiring, renting and selling videos, games, books, computers, confectionery. Established: 1982 - Franchising Since: 1991 - No. of Units: Company Owned: 36 - Franchised: 1 - Franchise Fee: £50,000 - £150,000 - Royalty: £10,000 legal fees & contract cost - Total Inv: £10,000 royalty, £30,000 + stock, £10,000 lease, £20,000 fittings - Financing: Yes.

ROSE BENEDETTI
Rose Benedetti Modas Ltda.
R. Padre Joao Manoel, 1055, Sao Paulo, Brazil, 01411. - Tel: (011) 881 1744, Fax: 282 8005. Creates, produces and sells costume jewelry such as earrings, necklaces, rings, belts and bracelets. Known and admired by Brazilian men and women as a role model of success. Established: 1973 - Franchising Since: 1985 - No. of Units: Company Owned: 6 - Franchised: 5 - Franchise Fee: $30,000 - Royalty: 3%,5% adv. - Total Inv: $95,000.

RUSPA - LEATHER GOODS DIV.
Via C. Colombo, 2, Robassomero (TO), Italy, 10070. - Tel: (011) 9241066. Producer of leather goods. Worldwide license for Giueiaro Design, Pininearina, Vinci brands. Established: 1948 - Franchising Since: 1993 - No. of Units: Company Owned: 1 - Franchised: 20 - Franchise Fee: US $100,000 - Royalty: 2% - Total Inv: US $60,000 per single shop - Financing: No.

RYMAN
Swallowfield Way, Hayes, Mddx., England, UB3 1DQ. - Tel: 081-569-3000. Retail stationers. Established: 1893 - Franchising Since: 1986 - No. of Units: Company Owned: 87 - Franchised: 24 - Franchise Fee: £10,000 - Total Inv: £100,000 - Financing: No.

SEVENOAKS SOUND & VISION
Sevenoaks Hifi & Video
109-113 London Rd., Sevenoaks, Kent, TN13 1BH. Contact: Malcolm Blockley, Franchise Director - Tel: 01732 455 911, Fax: 01732 460 230. Retailers of specialist hifi, video home cinema. Established: 1972 - Franchising Since: 1992 - No. of Units: Company Owned: 14 - Franchised: 20 - Franchise Fee: £10,000 - Royalty: 5%, 2% advertising - Total Inv: £75,000 (£40,000 stock, £20,000 shop fitting, £10,000 license, £5,000 legal) - Financing: Yes 2/3rds.

SLIDEROBES WARDROBES
61 Boucher Crescent, Boucher Road, Belfast, BT126HU. Contact: Alan Brown - Tel: (02890 681 034. Sliding door fitted wardrobes provides a stylish and functional solution to customers pressing need for storage space. Established: 1983 - Franchising Since: 1999 - Franchise Fee: £25,000 - Royalty: 9.5% - Total Inv: £82,000.

SNAP-ON-TOOLS LTD.
Dunham House, 85-99 Cross St., Sale, Cheshire, England, M33 1FU. - Tel: (061) 969-0126. Mobile sales of tools and equipment. Established: 1926 - Franchising Since: 1966 - No. of Units: 280 - Approx. Inv: £5,000.

SPAR CONVENIENCE STORES
332 Clepington Rd., Dundee, Tayside, DD3 8SJ. Contact: Mr. Jim Carroll, Franchise Mgr. - Tel: 0382 818771. Retail convenience stores trading seven days a week, from 7am-10pm, selling alcohol, fresh foods, confectionery, soft drinks and groceries. Established: 1922 - Franchising Since: 1988 - No. of Units: Franchised: 21 - Franchise Fee: £2,000-£5,000 + stock (approx. £20,000) - Royalty: 1.5% of gross weekly turnover - Total Inv: £25,000-£30,000 - Financing: Yes.

STAR BOOKSTORE
Sien-I Trading(S) Pte Ltd
Blk 824 Tampines St. 81 #01-34, Singapore, 520824. Contact: Alex Chen - Tel: (+65) 678 76560, Fax: (+65) 678 75856, E-Mail: alexto@singnet.com.sg, Web Site: www.star-bookstore.com. Star Bookstore is a book rental business. Besides being an established brand name, our franchise package comes complete with book rental software, a membership pre-payment system using stored-value cards, and expertise on how to make your Star Bookstore a success. Established: 1980 - Franchising Since: 1998 - No. of Units: Company Owned: 1 - Franchised: 1 - Total Inv: SGD90,000 (600sqf).

STRAP-ON WRISTWEAR
1 Sharman Ave. St. Annes-on-Sea, Lancs., England, FY8 3AR. - Tel: (0253) 726186. The sale and repair of watches and accessories such as batteries, straps, bracelets, etc. Sites are provided in major hypemarkets and shopping centres. Established: 1969 - Franchising Since: 1991 - No. of Units: Company Owned: 3 - Franchise Fee: £5,000 - Royalty: None - Total Inv: £15,000 - Financing: £10,000.

TALASSIO
Angmering House, Sea Lane, Angmering on Sea, W. Sussex, England, BN16 1NB. - Tel: (0903) 782121. Retail sales and hire of ladies, gentlemen and children's wedding attire. Established: 1981 - Franchising Since: 1989 - No. of Units: Company Owned: 3 - Franchised: 6 - Franchise Fee: On application - Financing: Yes, full support 5 year forecast.

TOK & STOK
Estok Com. E. Representacoes Ltda.
Av.Tucunare, 500, Tambore, Barueri, Spain, 06460-020. - Tel: (011)7296-8600, Fax: (011)7269-8589. Furniture, tableware, eating utensils, pots and pans, bowls, glasses, cork, ivory, shell, amber and plastic goods for retailing trade. Established: 1977 - Franchising Since: 1990 - No. of Units: Company Owned: 12 - Franchised: 1 - Franchise Fee: US $250,000 - Royalty: 5% - Total Inv: $250,0000-$500,000 - Financing: No.

TRIPODE JARDILAND
26 eur de la Maison Rouge, Lognes, 77323 Marne la Vallee Cedex 2, France. - Tel: 60 05 81 63. Telex: 691 169. Franchise garden centers. Established: 1973 - Franchising Since: 1982 - No. of Units: Company Owned: 73 - Franchised: 41 - Royalty: 1.60% du CA - Total Inv: 4 Million FF.

TWIST
35 Kensington Church St., London, England, W8 4LL. - Tel: 071 938 3806. Innovative own label ladies fashion outlets. Complete clothing system which appeals to wide age/socio-economic groups due to its easy styles and simple styles. Perfect for 90's women. Established: 1987 - Franchising Since: 1988 - No. of Units: Company Owned: 6 - Franchised: 1 - Franchise Fee: £10,000 - Total Inv: £40,000 - Financing: No.

VIDEOLAND
Videoland Nederland B.V.
Schiestraat 38, Noordwijk, Zuid, The Netherlands, 2200 AB. - Tel: (1719) 56222. Rental of videos. Established: 1984 - Franchising Since: 1984 - No. of Units: Company Owned: 5 - Franchised: 150 - Franchise Fee: 5% turnover - Royalty: Hfl. 5.000,00 - Total Inv: Hfl. 250,000 - Financing: No.

LATE ENTRIES

ATLANTIC WINDSHIELD REPAIR *
107 C David Green Rd., Birmingham, AL, 35244. - Tel: (877) 230-4487, Fax: (702) 995-2724, Web Site: www.atlanticwindshieldrepair.com. Windshield repair. Established: 1997 - Franchising Since: 2004 - No. of Units: Company Owned: 2 - Franchised: 8 - Franchise Fee: $19,000 - Royalty" 6% - Total Inv: $25,000-$45,000

BOGART GOLF *
P.O. Box 16506, Fernandina, FL, 32035. - Tel: (904) 227-1581, Fax: (904) 227-1581, Web Site: www.bogartgolf.com. Video golf instruction & development. Established: 2004 - Franchising Since: 2004 - No. of Units: Company Owned: 3 - Franchise Fee: $30,000.

BUTTERCUP BAKE SHOP *
866 United Nations Plaza Suite 440, New York, NY, 10017. - Tel: (212) 350-9940, E-Mail: franchise@buttercupbakeshop.com, Web Site: www.buttercupbakeshop.com. Delicious cakes, cookies, muffins and more. Established: 1999 - Franchising Since: 2004 - No. of Units: Company Owned: 1 - Franchised: 2 - Franchise Fee: $30,000 - Royalty: 5% - Total Inv: $269,500-$395,000 - Financing: No.

CHANTICLEAR PIZZA *
7362 University Ave, NE, Suite 310, Fridley, MN, 55432. - Tel: (768) 862-2230, Fax: (768) 862-7977, Web Site: www.chanticlearpizza.com. Pizza restaurant offering delivery. Established: 1964 - Franchising Since: 2003 - No. of Units: Company Owned: 2 - Franchised: 14 - Franchise Fee: $20,000 - Royalty: 4% - Total Inv: $152,500-$208,500.

COSI, INC *
1751 Lake Cook Road, Deerfield, IL, 60015. - Tel: (847) 444-3200, Fax: (847) 597-8884, Web Site: www.getcosi.com. Premium restaurant that offers flavourful food and beverages. Established: 1996 - Franchising Since: 2004 - No. of Units: Company Owned: 97 - Franchise Fee: $40,000 - Royalty: 5% - Total Inv: $762,600-$899,800 - Financing: No.

CRABBY BILLS *
14237 Feather Sound Drive, Clear Water, FL, 33762. Contact: Greg Pawers - Tel: (727) 432-7430, Fax: (727) 593-5997, Web Site: www.crabbybills.com. Seafood restaurant. Established: 1983 - Franchising Since: 2004 - No. of Units: Company Owned: 8 - Franchised: 1.

DENTAL PEOPLE *
8400 Normandale Lake Blvd, #920, Bloomington, MN, 55437. - Tel: (866) 921-4995, Fax: (952) 921-4996, Web Site: www.dentalpeopleusa.com. Staffing services for dental pracxtices. Established: 2000 - Franchising Since: 2004 - No. of Units: Company Owned: 1 - Franchise Fee: $30,000 - Royalty: 5% - Total Inv: $60,000-$100,000.

DREAMLAND BAR-B-QUE *
2090 Columbiana Rd, Suite 4300, Vestavia Hills, AL, 35216. - Tel: (205) 822-9800, Fax: (205) 822-8866, E-Mail: fransales@dreamlandbbq.com, Web Site: www.dreamlandbbq.com. Serving Dreamland BBQ ribs. Established: 1958 - Franchising Since: 2003 - No. of Units: Company Owned: 2 - Franchised: 6 - Total Inv: $605,000-$1136,000.

DUKE SANDWICH *
1001 Poinsett Highway, Greenville, SC, 29609. Contact: Andrew Smart - Tel: (864) 232-4640, fax: (864) 232-1001, Web Site: www.dukesandwich.com. Serving nutritious and delicious lunches for under $5.00. Established: 1917 - Franchising Since: 2004.

EARL OF SANDWICH *
7598 West Sandlake Rd, Orlando, FL, 32819. Contact: Lynette McKee - Tel: (407) 992-2989, Fax: (407) 992-2987, E-Mail: lynette@earlofsandwichusa.com, Web Site: www.earlofsandwichusa.com. Serving signature hot hand carved roast beef sandwiches, wraps, fresh fruit smoothies and more. Established: 2004 - Franchising Since: 2004 - No. of Units: Company Owned: 1 - Total Inv: $179,200-$368,000.

GRINS 2 GO, INC. *
9404 Genessee Ave, Suite 100, La Jolla, CA, 92037. Contact: Harish Babla - Tel: (858) 558-4948, Fax: (858) 558-4947, E-Mail: hbabla@grins2go.com, Web Site: www.grins2go.com. Photography. Established: 2004 - Franchising Since: 2004 - Franchise Fee: $17,500-$25,000 - Royalty: 7% - Total Inv: $82,000-$267,000.

OBERWEIS FRANCHISE SYSTEMS *
951 Ice Cream Drive, Sweet One, North Aurora, IL, 60542. Contact: Robert Stidham - Tel: (630) 801-6100, Fax: (630) 897-0562, Web Site: www.oberweisdairy.com. Old fashioned ice cream store. Established: 1927 - Franchising Since: 2004 - No. of Units: Company Owned: 32 - Franchise Fee: $24,000-$30,000 - Royalty: Varies - Total Inv: $497,250-$756,000 - Financing: No.

PARABLE FRANCHISING LLC *
3563 Empleo Street, San Luis Obispo, CA, 93401. - Tel: (805) 543-2644, Fax: (805) 543-2136. Christian retail book store. Established: 1981 - Franchising Since: 2004.

STAR LADY FITNESS *
608 Georgia Dr, Bethel, OH, 45106. Contact: Gary - Tel: (513) 734-3378, Web Site: www.starladyfitness.com. Women's only circuit training fitness center. Established: 2003 - Franchising Since: 2004 - No. of Units: Company Owned: 6 - Franchised: 1 - Franchise Fee: $25,000 - Royalty: Varies - Total Inv: $40,000.

TRULY FRAMELESS *
7414 S.W. 48th Street, Miami, FL, 33156. - Tel: (305) 284-8621, Fax: (305) 667-3355, Web Site: www.trulyframeless.com. Frameless shower enclosures. Established: 2002 - Franchising Since: 2004 - No. of Units: Company Owned: 2 - Franchise Fee: $30,000 - Royalty: 7% - Total Inv: $40,800.

WILD WING CAFE *
202 Coleman Blvd, Mt. Pleasant, SC, 29464. - Tel: (843) 216-7601, Fax: (843) 216-7602, Web Site: www.wildwingcafe.com. Hot wings, cold beer & good times. Franchise Fee: $30,000 - Royalty: 2% - Total Inv: $275,000-$500,000.

INDEX

I

M